Sapling Plus

Pre-class Tutorials

Introduce new topics in a more manageable, less intimidating way, to help students better retain what they've learned for class time.

Everything You Need in a Single Learning Path

SaplingPlus is the first system to support students and instructors at every step, from the first point of contact with new content to demonstrating mastery of concepts and skills. It is simply the best support for Principles of Economics.

Classroom Activities

Foster student curiosity and understanding through "clicker" questions (via iClicker Campus) and curated active learning activities.

Test Bank

Multiple-choice and short-answer questions to help instructors assess students' comprehension, interpretation, and ability to synthesize.

Developing Understanding

LearningCurve Quizzes identify knowledge gaps and then nudge each student to fill those gaps through an enhanced eBook, videos, and interactives.

Assessment

Homework Assignments—with an intuitive approach to graphing—offer multi-part questions and targeted feedback.

For more information on SaplingPlus, visit www.macmillanlearning.com.

Enhance your experience of the text with these engaging videos from Marginal Revolution University...

How Does the Invisible Hand Deliver Roses?

MODERN PRINCIPLES OF ECONOMICS

MODERN PRINCIPLES OF ECONOMICS

Fourth Edition

Tyler Cowen
George Mason University

Alex Tabarrok
George Mason University

worth publishers
Macmillan Learning
New York

Vice President, Social Sciences: Charles Linsmeier
Vice President, Content Management: Catherine Woods
Director of Content and Assessment: Shani Fisher
Program Manager: Thomas Digiano
Development Editors: Bruce Kaplan and Andrew Sylvester
Director of Media Editorial, Social Sciences: Noel Hohnstine
Media Editor: Lindsay Neff
Assistant Editor: Courtney Lindwall
Marketing Manager: Andrew Zierman
Marketing Assistant: Chelsea Simens
Media Project Manager: Andrew Vaccaro
Assessment Manager: Kristyn Brown
Assessment Editor: Joshua Hill
Director of Content Management Enhancement: Tracey Kuehn
Managing Editor: Lisa Kinne
Director of Design, Content Management: Diana Blume
Senior Design Manager: Blake Logan
Senior Content Project Manager: Edgar Doolan
Senior Photo Editor: Robin Fadool
Senior Workflow Supervisor: Paul Rohloff
Composition: Lumina Datamatics, Inc.
Printing and Binding: LSC Communications
Cover Image and Title Image: Hand holding globe: dem10/E+/Getty Images; Globe: Leonello
    Calvetti/Science Photo Library/Getty Images

Library of Congress Control Number: 2017959199

ISBN-13: 978-1-319-09872-8
ISBN-10: 1-319-09872-X

WORTH PUBLISHERS

One New York Plaza
Suite 4500
New York, NY 10004-1562
www.macmillanlearning.com

Economics is the study of how to get the most out of life.

Tyler and Alex

ABOUT THE AUTHORS

Tyler Cowen (left, in North Korea) is Holbert C. Harris Professor of Economics at George Mason University. His latest book is *The Complacent Class*. With Alex Tabarrok, he writes an economics blog at MarginalRevolution.com. He has published in the *American Economic Review, Journal of Political Economy,* and many other economics journals. He also writes regularly for the popular press, including *Bloomberg,* the *Washington Post, Forbes,* the *Wilson Quarterly, Money Magazine,* and many other outlets.

Alex Tabarrok (right, in South Korea) is Bartley J. Madden Chair in Economics at the Mercatus Center at George Mason University. His latest book is *Launching the Innovation Renaissance*. His research looks at bounty hunters, judicial incentives and elections, crime control, patent reform, methods to increase the supply of human organs for transplant, and the regulation of pharmaceuticals. He is the editor of the books *Entrepreneurial Economics: Bright Ideas from the Dismal Science* and *The Voluntary City: Choice, Community, and Civil Society,* among others. His papers have appeared in the *Journal of Law and Economics, Public Choice, Economic Inquiry,* the *Journal of Health Economics,* the *Journal of Theoretical Politics,* the *American Law and Economics Review,* and many others. Popular articles have appeared in the *New York Times,* the *Wall Street Journal, Forbes,* and many other magazines and newspapers.

BRIEF CONTENTS

Part 5: Decision Making for Businesses, Investors, and Consumers

Part 6: Economic Growth

Part 7: Business Fluctuations

Part 8: Macroeconomic Policy and Institutions

Part 9: International Economics

CONTENTS

Part I: Supply and Demand

Part 2: The Price System

Part 4: Government

Part 6: Economic Growth

Part 7: Business Fluctuations

Part 8: Macroeconomic Policy and Institutions

PREFACE: TO THE INSTRUCTOR

> The prisoners were dying of scurvy, typhoid fever, and smallpox, but nothing was killing them more than bad incentives.

That is the opening from Chapter 1 of *Modern Principles*, and only an economist could write such a sentence. Only an economist could see that incentives are operating just about everywhere, shaping every aspect of our lives, whether it be how good a job you get, how much wealth an economy produces, and, yes, how a jail is run and how well the prisoners are treated. We are excited about this universal and powerful applicability of economics, and we have written this book to get you excited too.

In the first three editions, we wanted to accomplish several things. We wanted to show the power of economics for understanding our world. We wanted to create a book full of vivid writing and powerful stories. We wanted to present modern economics, not the musty doctrines or repetitive examples of a generation ago. We wanted to show—again and again—that incentives matter, whether discussing the tragedy of the commons, political economy, or what economics has to say about wise investing. Most generally, we wanted to make the invisible hand visible, namely to show that there is a hidden order behind the world that can be illuminated by economics.

Guiding Principles and Innovations: In a Nutshell

Modern Principles offers the following features and benefits:

1. We teach the economic way of thinking.

2. Less is more. This is a textbook of *principles*, not a survey or an encyclopedia. We use fewer yet more consistent and more comprehensive models.

3. No tools without applications. Real-world vivid applications are used to develop theory. Applications are not pushed aside into distracting boxes that students do not read.

4. Today's students live in a globalized economy. Events in China, India, Europe, and the Middle East affect their lives. *Modern Principles* features international examples and applications throughout, rather than just segregating all of the international topics in a single chapter.

5. *Modern Principles* has a more intuitive development of markets and their interconnectedness than does any other textbook. More than any other textbook, we teach students how the *price system* works.

6. *Modern Principles* helps students to see the invisible hand. We offer an intuitive proof of several "invisible hand theorems." For example, we show that through the operation of incentives and the price system, well functioning markets will minimize the aggregate sum of the costs of production even though no one intends this result. Local knowledge creates a global benefit.

7. We offer an entire chapter (Chapter 22) on incentives and how they apply to business decisions, sports, and incentive design. When, for instance, should you reward your employees with a tournament form of compensation, and when a straight salary? Most texts are oddly silent on such practical issues, but it is precisely such issues that interest many students and show them the relevance of the economic way of thinking. We also offer an entire chapter on network goods, including the value of Facebook, the tech sector, and how markets for music work.

8. We offer an entire chapter (Chapter 23) on the stock market, a topic of concern to many students. We teach the basic trade-off between risk and return and explain why it is a good idea to diversify investments. We also explain the microeconomics of bubbles.

9. Other textbooks do not offer a balanced treatment of real business cycle theory and New Keynesian theory, instead favoring one theory and relegating the other to a few pages that are poorly integrated with the overall macro model. In contrast, we believe that adequately explaining business fluctuations, unemployment, and both the potential and limits of monetary and fiscal policy requires a balanced but unified treatment that draws on ideas from both models.

10. Why are some nations rich and other nations poor? *Modern Principles* has more material on development and growth than any other principles textbook.

11. *Modern Principles* offers the most intuitive development of the Solow model of growth in any textbook, starting with Chapter 28 and continuing in the Chapter 33 appendix.

12. Financial panics and asset bubbles are covered—a topic of great interest in today's environment! In fact, we included substantial material on banking panics, bubbles, wealth shocks, and the importance of financial intermediation in the very first draft of Modern Principles. Our book incorporates these topics from the ground floor rather than squeezing the material into boxes or appended paragraphs. There are separate and comprehensive chapters on financial intermediation (Chapter 29) and on the stock market (Chapter 23). We also cover the financial crisis that began in 2007 ... and the subsequent recession and attempts at recovery.

13. *Modern Principles* explains how fiscal and monetary policy work differently, depending on whether the shock hitting the economy is a real shock or a nominal shock.

14. We look closely at unemployment, its nature and causes, including the unusually long duration of unemployment experienced in the United States after the financial crisis. We also look at labor force participation rates in the United States over time and around the world. Why have women increased their labor force participation and why are only one-third of Belgian men aged 55–64 in the labor force?

15. Our game theory chapters (Chapters 15 and 16) are especially geared toward modern real-world choices and problems. Naturally, we cover cartel behavior. We also cover network externalities extensively. In many high-tech and online markets, the value of a good depends on how many other people are using the same good. Students are very familiar with examples such as Facebook and they want to know how the principles of economics apply to these contemporary goods. We even challenge students by showing how the principles

of network externalities apply to cultural goods and even to the songs they listen to!

16. A modern text needs to place economics in context. We have a whole chapter on normative judgments (Chapter 21). It covers the assumptions behind cost-benefit analysis, the idea of a Pareto improvement, and the ethical judgments that have been used to praise or condemn economic reasoning. Rightly or wrongly, commentators often mix economic and moral judgments and we teach students to recognize which is which. We stress to the student that economics cannot answer normative issues but the student should be aware of what those normative issues are.

Make the Invisible Hand Visible

One of the most remarkable discoveries of economic science is that under the right conditions the pursuit of self-interest can promote the social good. Nobel laureate Vernon Smith put it this way:

> At the heart of economics is a scientific mystery . . . a scientific mystery as deep, fundamental and inspiring as that of the expanding universe or the forces that bind matter. . . . How is order produced from freedom of choice?

We want students to be inspired by this mystery and by how economists have begun to solve it. Thus, we will explain how markets generate cooperation from people across the world, how prices act as signals and coordinate appropriate responses to changes in economic conditions, and how profit maximization leads to the minimization of industry costs (even though no one intends such an end).

We strive to make the invisible hand visible, and we do so with the core idea of supply and demand as the organizing principle of economics. Thus, we start with supply and demand, including producer and consumer surplus and the two ways of reading the curves, and then we build equilibrium in its own chapter, then elasticity, then taxes and subsidies, then the price system, then price ceilings and floors, then international trade, and then externalities. All of this material is based on supply and demand so that students are continually gaining experience using the same tools to solve more and deeper problems as they proceed. The interaction of supply and demand generates market prices and quantities, which in turn lies behind the spread of information from one part of a market economy to another. Thus, we show how the invisible hand works through the *price system*.

In Chapter 7 we show how the invisible hand links romantic American teenagers with Kenyan flower growers, Dutch clocks, British airplanes, Colombian coffee, and Finnish cell phones. We also show how prices signal information and how markets help to solve the *great economic problem* of arranging our limited resources to satisfy as many of our wants as possible.

The focus on the invisible hand, or *the price system*, continues in Chapter 8. As in other texts, we show how a price ceiling causes a shortage. But a shortage in one market can spill over into other markets (e.g., shortages of oil in the 1970s meant that oil rigs off the coast of California could not get enough oil to operate). In addition, a price ceiling reduces the incentive to move resources from low-value uses to high-value uses, so in the 1970s we saw long lines for gasoline in some states yet *at the same time* gas was plentiful in other states just a few hours away. Price ceilings, therefore, cause a misallocation of resources across markets as well as a shortage within a particular market. We think of Chapters 7 and 8 as a package: Chapter 7 illustrates the price system when it is working and Chapter 8 illustrates what happens when the price system is impeded.

Students who catch even a glimpse of the invisible hand learn something of great importance. Civilization is possible only because under some conditions the pursuit of self-interest promotes the public good.

In discussing the invisible hand, we bring more Hayekian economics into the classroom without proselytizing for Hayekian politics. That is, we want to show how prices communicate information and coordinate action while still recognizing that markets do not always communicate the right information. Thus, our chapters on the price system are rounded out with what we think is an equally interesting and compelling chapter on externalities. The subtitle of Chapter 10, "When the Price Is Not Right," harkens directly back to Chapter 7. By giving examples where the price signal is right and examples where the price signal is wrong, we convey a sophisticated understanding of the role of prices.

Demonstrate the Power of Incentives

Our second goal in writing *Modern Principles of Economics* is to show—again and again—that incentives matter. In fact, incentives are the theme throughout *Modern Principles*, whether discussing the supply of oil, the effects of price controls, or the gains from international trade. In Chapter 22, Managing Incentives, we explain topics such as the trade-offs between fixed salaries and piece rates, when tournaments work well, and how best to incentivize executives. This chapter can be read profitably by anyone with an interest in *incentive design*—by managers, teachers, even parents! Chapter 22 will be of special interest to business and MBA students (and professors).

Present Modern Models and Vivid Applications

"Modern" is our third goal in writing *Modern Principles*. For example, Chapter 14 focuses entirely on price discrimination. We cover not just traditional models but also tying and bundling. Students today are familiar with tied goods like cell phones and minutes, or printers and ink, as well as with bundles like Microsoft Office. A modern economics textbook should help students *understand their world*.

Throughout the text, we cover business issues as diverse as why businesses cluster and how network externalities push businesses to compete "for the market" rather than "in the market," to how successful cartels such as the NBA deal with the incentive to cheat, to how businesses actually go about price discriminating. Our chapter on incentives, already mentioned, is critical for managers in a variety of fields.

We also present a modern perspective on the costs and benefits of market power. A significant amount of market power today is tied to innovation, patents, and high fixed costs. Understanding the trade-offs involved with pricing AIDS drugs at marginal cost, for example, is critically important to understanding pharmaceutical policy. Similar issues arise with music, movies, software, chip design, and universities. Our material on monopoly and innovation is consistent with and provides a foundation for modern theories of economic growth.

What's New in the Fourth Edition?

We have updated coverage and applications throughout the text, and, to reflect changes in the world since the publication of the third edition and to include topics and examples that will be most relevant to students today, we have also added two key features to the text: **Ask FRED exercises** and **Marginal Revolution University videos.** These features help clarify concepts, enliven the text, and engage the student in an active learning environment filled with real, practical data and applications.

The hallmark of the fourth edition of *Modern Principles of Economics* is the unique partnership between Worth Economics and Marginal Revolution University (MRU). Founded by Tyler Cowen and Alex Tabarrok as an instructional extension of their world-renowned Marginal Revolution blog, MRU features perhaps the most extensive series of economics education videos available. More than 150 of these videos have been deeply integrated into the pedagogy of *Modern Principles*, extending the authors' perspectives into the online learning space, and providing valuable tools for both instructors and students throughout the learning path.

This unprecedented system consists of three types of video that can be utilized in conjunction with the text material and with online assessment in a variety of ways:

1. **Engagement Videos** (18): Providing a succinct (5–7 minutes) overview of topics within the chapter, the authors themselves show just how economics impacts the daily lives of students.

   - Since they are intended to be viewed in conjunction with material in the text, Engagement Videos are specifically listed as part of the outline at the opening of each chapter.
   - Students can watch these videos within the e-Book itself or access them via QR codes within the print version of the text.
   - Best assigned prior to class to help introduce new topics, each engagement video features a short, auto-graded quiz to help students recall the information for class time. These videos work especially well for pre-class preparation when paired with FlipItEcon tutorials.

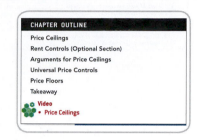

CHAPTER OUTLINE

Price Ceilings
Rent Controls (Optional Section)
Arguments for Price Ceilings
Universal Price Controls
Price Floors
Takeaway
Video
• Price Ceilings

interactive activity

AUGUST 1971:

RICHARD NIXON

Price Ceilings

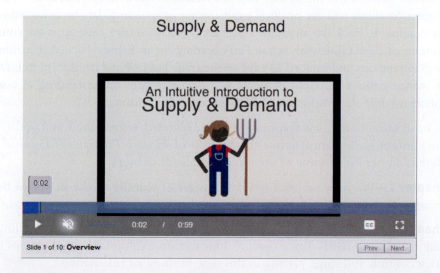

Supply & Demand

An Intuitive Introduction to
Supply & Demand

0:02

0:02 / 0:59

Slide 1 of 10: Overview   Prev   Next

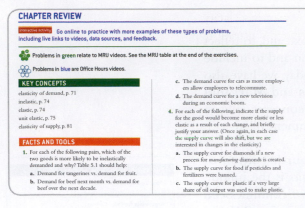

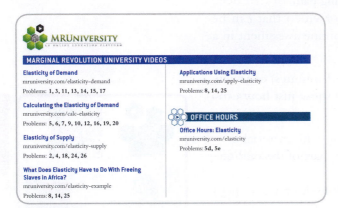

2. Lecture Videos (146): Designed to complement coverage in the text, these videos are slightly longer (7–10 minutes) than engagement videos, and feature straightforward exposition of topics by the authors.

- Lecture Videos can be used as a remediation tool for students, helping fill knowledge gaps that may persist after class time and/or reading the book. End-of-chapter problems marked in green relate directly to both Engagement and Lecture videos and can aid in identifying knowledge gaps.

- Within SaplingPlus, green end-of-chapter problems feature targeted feedback that links to the relevant Lecture Video or Engagement Video.
- Lecture Videos are also ideal for online or distance learning courses. Instructors can assign these videos, along with the accompanying auto-graded quiz, to cover material in greater depth or explore topics outside of those covered during "class time."

3. Office Hours Videos (5): The direct result of feedback from both instructors and students since the launch of MRU, Office Hours videos feature a staff economist working through some of the more intricate problems and models found in the book—another great remediation tool that can make for more efficient student/instructor interactions.

- Within SaplingPlus, blue end-of-chapter problems feature targeted feedback that links to the relevant Office Hours Video.

At the conclusion of the end-of-chapter problems, you will find a complete list of the MRU videos for that chapter. Each video listing contains a shortened URL to that video (live links within either LaunchPad or SaplingPlus), as well an inventory of the end-of-chapter problems that pertain to that particular video.

The **Ask FRED** exercises require students to use the Federal Reserve Economic Database to build and manipulate data sets related to the concepts discussed in the chapter. Students will get practical experience manipulating data by being asked, for example, to track the impact of a sales tax on tobacco sales, tease apart the components of Real GDP, analyze the Fed's holdings of mortgage-backed securities, or graph exports and imports to explore the trade balance and its relation to GDP. In working these problems, students will gain a greater understanding of core concepts while also working with an impressive data resource.

In addition to the new features, we have expanded, restructured, and updated the content presentation across this edition of *Modern Principles of Economics.* Here is a brief list of some of the more significant changes:

Chapter 1: We have added a new discussion of scarcity as the driver of the great economic problem.

Chapter 8: We have added a new section in our discussion of Price Ceilings that asks: Does UBER Price Gouge? This section explores the implications of price controls and surge pricing in this new business of ridesharing.

Chapter 11: This chapter has been reorganized to give the reader more clarity on the general principles of maximizing profits before exploring the question: What Quantity to Produce?

Chapter 13: The section on Economies of Scale and the Regulation of Monopoly has been revised and recast as Sources of Market Power, with a leaner presentation and a new discussion of antitrust law and merger policy.

Chapter 17: The presentation of Product Differentiation has been expanded to include new material on ease of purchase.

Chapter 18: The discussion of Preference-Based Discrimination has been expanded.

Chapter 26: The discussion of net exports has been expanded to help students understand the difference between an identity and an economic approach. A new discussion, on the Health of Nations, has been added to our discussion of the Problems with GDP as a Measure of Output and Welfare.

Chapter 29: An expanded discussion of fire sales and fire storms has been added to the presentation of the shadow banking system.

Chapter 34: The Federal Reserve has completely changed its operating procedure and we reflect and discuss these changes, especially Payment of Interest on Reserves. The section Federal Reserve and Systemic Risk has been reorganized and renamed The Federal Reserve Is the Lender of Last Resort and reorganized; the discussion of the monetary policy of the Fed in response to the financial crisis of 2008 has been expanded and updated.

Chapter 36: The discussion of Social Security has been expanded, and the discussions of tax and spending policies have been updated.

Chapter 37: The presentation of Fiscal Policy has been reorganized, and the discussion of the multiplier effect has been greatly expanded to more thoroughly explain the factors that affect the size of the multiplier.

Alternative Paths Through the Book

Modern Principles of Economics has been written with trade-offs in mind and it's easy to pick and choose from among the chapters when time constrains. We offer a few quick suggestions. Chapter 7 is fun to teach but more difficult to test than some of the other chapters. But don't worry, you will find plenty of testable material in other chapters, and for your best students the introduction to the price system in Chapters 7 and 8 will be an eye-opener!

We spend more time on price controls than do other books because we don't confine ourselves to the usual shortage diagram. We illustrate the general equilibrium effects of price controls. We have also included a section of advanced material on the losses from random allocation that may be skipped in larger classes or if time constrains.

We have greatly simplified the presentation on cost curves and removed most of production theory, so do take the time to cover monopoly and the chapter on price discrimination. Students love the material on price discrimination because once they understand the concepts, they see the applications all around them. Chapter 16, Competing for Monopoly: The Economics of

Network Goods, is a very appealing chapter for students, and we recommend it for its applications, but if you don't have time, it can be skipped.

Asteroid deflection and the decline of the tuna fisheries are a must, so do cover Chapter 19 on public goods and the tragedy of the commons. Once again, students appreciate the focus on important, real-world applications of the economic way of thinking.

Chapters 20 and 21 on political economy and ethics are optional. If you can teach only one chapter, we think Chapter 20 on political economy has crucial material for avoiding the nirvana fallacy: We should always compare real-world markets with real-world governments when doing political economy. Chapter 21 on ethics works very well in smaller classes with lots of student interaction—we think it important that the philosophy professors are not the ones who get the only say on questions of ethics!

Chapter 22, Managing Incentives, is fun to teach but it goes beyond the core and can be skipped. We believe this chapter will be especially appropriate for management, MBA, and pre-law students.

We encourage everyone to teach Chapter 23 on stock markets, time permitting.

Chapter 25, Consumer Choice, is for those instructors who wish to cover indifference curves in considerable detail.

Instructors could cover only a portion of the Solow model in Chapter 28. We sometimes do this in our larger classes so this will be a good choice for many. The chapter has been written so that the most intuitive and important aspects of the model are covered in the beginning, more difficult and detailed material in the middle may be skipped, and then important material on growth and ideas is covered toward the end of the chapter. The material in the middle may be skipped without loss of continuity. Instructors with smaller and more advanced classes can easily cover the full chapter. The instructor's guide offers excellent tips from John Dawson for covering this material.

One important point: It is **not** at all necessary to teach the Solow model to cover our chapters on business fluctuations. The supply side is dealt with by using a long-run aggregate supply curve, which is explained in those chapters without relying on the Solow model.

We have divided the chapters on macroeconomic policy and institutions so that an instructor can cover monetary policy without covering the details of the Federal Reserve system and open market operations, and one can cover fiscal policy without covering the details of the federal budget: taxes and spending. The details are important and these chapters place monetary and fiscal policy within an institutional context, so we do not necessarily recommend this limited approach, but when time is limited, more options are better than fewer.

Finally, one could skip international finance. To us, international economics means primarily that economics can help us to understand the world, not just one country and not just one time. As a result, we have included many international examples throughout *Modern Principles*. If time constrains, the details of tariffs, exchange rates, and trade deficits may be left to another course. Alas, we live in a finite world.

Most of all, we hope that *Modern Principles* helps you, the teacher, to have fun! We love economics and we have fun teaching economics. We have written this text for people not afraid to say the same. Don't hesitate to e-mail us with your questions, thoughts, and experiences, or just to say hello!

Acknowledgments

We are most grateful to the following reviewers, both users and nonusers, for their careful chapter reviews used in the development of the fourth edition of *Modern Principles*.

Lian An
University of North Florida

Oz Aydemir
Broome Community College

Justin Barnette
Kent State University

Jodi Beggs
Northeastern University

Douglas Bice
Middle Georgia State University—Macon

James Bolchalk
Kent State University—Geauga Campus

Karla Borja
University of Tampa

Carter Braxton
University of Minnesota—Twin Cities

Paul Byrne
Washburn University

Anoshua Chaudhuri
San Francisco State University

Susan Christoffersen
Philadelphia University

Gregory Colson
The University of Georgia

Manabendra Dasgupta
University of Alabama at Birmingham

John Deskins
West Virginia University

Eva Dziadula
University of Notre Dame

Carlos Elias
Radford University

Mallika Garg
University of Louisville

Pedro Gete
Georgetown University

Bob Gillette
University of Kentucky

Christian Glupker
Grand Valley State University

Alan Grant
Baker University

Jeremy Groves
Northern Illinois University

Mike Hammock
Middle Tennessee State University

Andrew Hanssen
Clemson University

Darcy Hartman
Ohio State University

Joshua Hill
Montana State University, Billings

Paul Holmes
Ashland University

Andres Jauregui
Columbus State University

Lillian Kamal
University of Hartford

Jongsung Kim
Bryant University

Mikhail Kouliavstev
Stephen F. Austin State University

Robert Krol
California State University, Northridge

Jim Lee
Texas A&M at Corpus Christi

Susane Leguizamon
Western Kentucky University

Melody Lo
The University of Texas at San Antonio (UTSA)

John Mbaku
Weber State University

Neil Meredith
West Texas A&M University

Karl A. Mitchell
Queens College, The City University of New York

Chuck Moul
Miami University (Ohio)

Eric Parsons
University of Missouri

Antonio Rodriguez
Texas A&M International University

Duane Rosa
West Texas A&M University

Paul Roscelli
Canada College

Kyle Ross
Kansas State University

Jason C. Rudbeck
The University of Georgia

Scott Sandok
Hennepin Technical College

Nori Sasaki
McHenry County College

Kurt Von Seekamm
Salem State University

Angela Seidel
Saint Francis University

James Self
Indiana University

Daniel M. Settlage
The University of Arkansas—Fort Smith

Senad Sinanovic
Clemson University

Jennifer Sobotka
Radford University

Timothy Terrell
Wofford College

Kawin Thamtanajit
University of Delaware

Edward Timmons
Saint Francis University

Randall Waldron
John Brown University

Ashlie Warnick
Carroll Community College

Tara Westerhold
Western Illinois University

And we would also like to acknowledge again the contributions of the following reviewers whose comments and suggestions helped to shape the first three editions of this text.

Rashid Al-Hmoud
Texas Tech University

Michael Applegate
Oklahoma State University

J. J. Arias
Georgia College and State University

Scott Baier
Clemson University

Jim Barbour
Elon University

David Beckworth
Texas State University

Robert Beekman
University of Tampa

Ryan Bosworth
North Carolina State University

Jennifer Brown
Eastern Connecticut State University

Douglas Campbell
University of Memphis

Randall Campbell
Mississippi University

Michael Carew
Baruch College

Shawn Carter
Jacksonville State University

Suparna Chakraborty
Baruch College and Graduate Center, The City University of New York

Philip Coelho
Ball State University

Jim Couch
North Alabama University

Scott Cunningham
University of Georgia

Amlan Datta
Texas Tech University

John Dawson
Appalachian State University

Timothy M. Diette
Washington and Lee University

Ann Eike
University of Kentucky

Harold Elder
University of Alabama

Tisha Emerson
Baylor University

Molly Espey
Clemson University

Patricia Euzent
University of Central Florida

William Feipel
Illinois Central University

Paul Fisher
Henry Ford College

Amanda S. Freeman
Kansas State University

Gary Galles
Pepperdine University

Neil Garston
California State University, Los Angeles

Bill Gibson
The University of Vermont

David Gillette
Truman State University

Lynn G. Gillette
Sierra Nevada College

Gerhard Glomm
Indiana University

Stephan F. Gohmann
University of Louisville

Michael Gootzeit
University of Memphis

Carole Green
University of South Florida

Paul Grimes
Mississippi State University

Philip J. Grossman
St. Cloud State University

Darrin Gulla
University of Kentucky

Kyle Hampton
The Ohio State University

Joe Haslag
University of Missouri—Columbia

Sarah Helms
University of Alabama—Birmingham

Matthew Henry
University of Georgia

Bradley Hobbs
Florida Gulf Coast University

John Hsu
Contra Costa College

Jeffrey Hummel
San Jose State University

Sarah Jackson
Indiana University of Pennsylvania

Dennis Jansen
Texas A&M University

Bruce Johnson
Centre College

Veronica Kalich
Baldwin Wallace College

Lillian Kamal
University of Hartford

John Keating
University of Kansas

Logan Kelly
Bryant University

Brian Kench
University of Tampa

Kate Krause
University of New Mexico

David Kreutzer
James Madison University

Robert Krol
California State University, Northridge

Daniel Kuo
Orange Coast College

Gary Lape
Liberty University

Rodolfo Ledesma
Marian College

Jim Lee
Texas A&M University—Corpus Christi

Daniel Lin
American University

Solina Lindahl
California State Polytechnic University

Edward Lopez
San Jose State University

Hari Luitel
St. Cloud State University

Michael Mace
Sierra College

Douglas Mackenzie
State University of New York—Plattsburgh

Michael Makowsky
Towson University

John Marcis
Coastal Carolina University

Catherina Matraves
Michigan State University

Norman Maynard
The University of Oklahoma

Meghan Millea
Mississippi State University

Stephen Miller
University of Nevada, Las Vegas

Ida Mirzaie
The Ohio State University

David (Mitch) Mitchell
South Alabama University

Ranganath Murthy
Bucknell University

Todd Myers
Grossmont College

Andre Neveu
Skidmore College

Joan Nix
Queens College, The City University of New York

Lydia Ortega
San Jose State University

Alexandre Padilla
Metropolitan State College of Denver

Zuohong Pan
Western Connecticut State University

Biru Paksha Paul
State University of New York—Cortland

John Perry
Centre College

Steven Peterson
The University of Idaho

Gina C. Pieters
University of Minnesota

Dennis Placone
Clemson University

Jennifer M. Platania
Elon University

Brennan Platt
Brigham Young University

William Polley
Western Illinois University

Benjamin Powell
Suffolk University

Margaret Ray
University of Mary Washington

Dan Rickman
Oklahoma State University

Fred Ruppel
Eastern Kentucky University

Mikael Sandberg
University of Florida

Jeff Sarbaum
University of North Carolina at Greensboro

Michael Scott
University of Oklahoma

James Self
Indiana University

David Shideler
Murray State University

Mark Showalter
Brigham Young University

Randy Simmons
Utah State University

Martin Spechler
Indiana University—Purdue University, Indianapolis

David Spencer
Brigham Young University

Richard Stahl
Louisiana State University

Dean Stansel
Florida Gulf Coast University

Liliana V. Stern
Auburn University

Kay Strong
Bowling Green State University—Firelands

Jim Swofford
University of South Alabama

Sandra Trejos
Clarion University of Pennsylvania

Marie Truesdell
Marian College

Norman T. Van Cott
Ball State University

Kristin A. Van Gaasbeck
California State University—Sacramento

Michael Visser
Sonoma State University

Yoav Wachsman
Coastal Carolina University

Doug Walker
Georgia College and State University

Christopher Waller
Notre Dame University

Tyler Watts
Ball State University

Robert Whaples
Wake Forest University

Mark Wheeler
Western Michigan University

Jonathan Wight
University of Richmond

Steven Yamarik
California State University, Long Beach

We would like to thank the following instructors who have aided us in the preparation and extensive review of the ancillary package. This list of contributors and reviewers is comprehensive of those who have contributed across editions at this time and will continue to grow as new resources are developed.

Tori Knight
Carson-Newman University

Paul Fisher
Henry Ford Community College

Alanna Holowinsky
Red River College

John Dawson
Appalachian State University

Anne Walker
Boise State University

Jeremy Groves
Northern Illinois University

Kevin Beckwith
Salem State University

Angela Seidel
Saint Francis University

Ashlie Warnick
Northern Virginia Community College

Heather Leau
Vanderbilt University

Thomas Dunn

Jim Swofford
University of South Alabama

Benjamin Powell
Suffolk University

Solina Lindahl
California Polytechnic State University

Michael Applegate
Oklahoma State University

David Gillette
Truman State University

David Youngberg
George Mason University

Eli Dourado
George Mason University

Garett Jones
George Mason University

Jennifer Platania
University of West Florida

David Kalist
Shippensburg University of Pennsylvania

Mark Wheeler
Western Michigan University

Bhavneet Walia
Western Illinois University

Sheng Yang
Black Hills State University

Lillian Kamal
University of Hartford

James Self
Indiana University

Kyle Hampton
University of Alaska, Anchorage

Kenneth Slaysman
York College of Pennsylvania

Irina Pritchett
North Carolina State University

James Watson
University of Colorado—Boulder

Pat Euzent
University of Central Florida

Brett Block
University of Colorado—Boulder

Douglas Campbell
University of Memphis

Ryan Oprea
University of California, Santa Cruz

Margaret Aproberts-Warren
University of California, Santa Cruz

Tyler Watts
Ball State University

We were fortunate to have eagle-eyed readers of the proofs of the book during the production process: Paul Fisher, Henry Ford College, Daniel Lin, American University, and Mark Brady, San Jose State University. Paul Fisher also contributed numerous new problems and solutions. Our student Sarah Oh provided invaluable help in updating figures and tables. The Mercatus Center supplied an essential work environment. Teresa Hartnett has done a great job as our agent.

Most of all we are grateful to the team at Worth. The idea for this book was conceived by Paul Shensa, who has seen it through with wise advice from day one. Bruce Kaplan, our original development editor, is the George Martin of book production; he has done a tremendous amount of nitty-gritty work on the manuscript to make every note just right and he has offered excellent counsel throughout. We are very fortunate that Bruce has been succeeded by Andrew Sylvester, who has brought fresh eyes to the project and has pushed us to keep improving and innovating. Thanks as well to Tom Digiano, Program Manager for Economics, and Assistant Editor Courtney Lindwall, whose hard work throughout helped to keep things moving smoothly.

We are fortunate to have had such a talented production and design group for our book. Paul Rohloff and Edgar Doolan coordinated the entire production process with the help of Lisa Kinne. Diana Blume created the beautiful interior design and the cover, along with Blake Logan. Robin Fadool went beyond the call of duty in tracking down sometimes obscure photos. It has been a delight to work with all of them.

Lindsay Neff put together the media team and ably brought the supplements and media package to market.

Andrew Zierman stands out in the marketing of this book. He has been energetic and relentless.

Most of all, we want to thank our families for their support and understanding. Tyler wishes to offer his personal thanks to Natasha and Yana. It is Alex's great fortune to be able to thank Monique, Connor, and Maxwell and his parents for years of support and encouragement.

Tyler Cowen
Alex Tabarrok

MODERN PRINCIPLES OF ECONOMICS

1

The Big Ideas

The prisoners were dying of scurvy, typhoid fever, and smallpox, but nothing was killing them more than bad incentives. In 1787, the British government had hired sea captains to ship convicted felons to Australia. Conditions on board the ships were monstrous; some even said the conditions were worse than on slave ships. On one voyage, more than one-third of the men died and the rest arrived beaten, starved, and sick. A first mate remarked cruelly of the convicts, "Let them die and be damned, the owners have [already] been paid for their passage."[1]

The British public had no love for the convicts, but it wasn't prepared to give them a death sentence either. Newspapers editorialized in favor of better conditions, clergy appealed to the captains' sense of humanity, and legislators passed regulations requiring better food and water, light and air, and proper medical care. Yet the death rate remained shockingly high. Nothing appeared to be working until an economist suggested something new. Can you guess what the economist suggested?

Instead of paying the captains for each prisoner placed on board ship in Great Britain, the economist suggested paying for each prisoner that walked off the ship in Australia. In 1793, the new system was implemented and immediately the survival rate shot up to 99%. One astute observer explained what had happened: "Economy beat sentiment and benevolence."[2]

The story of the convict ships illustrates the first big lesson that runs throughout this book and throughout economics: *incentives matter.*

By **incentives**, we mean rewards and penalties that motivate behavior. Let's take a closer look at incentives and some of the other big ideas in economics. On first reading, some of these ideas may seem surprising or difficult to understand. Don't worry: we will be explaining everything in more detail.

We see the following list as the most important and fundamental contributions of economics to human understanding; we call these contributions *Big Ideas.* Some economists might arrange this list in a different manner or order, but these are generally accepted principles among good economists everywhere.

Incentives are rewards and penalties that motivate behavior.

1

Meet Your Authors

Big Idea One: Incentives Matter

When the captains were paid for every prisoner that they took on board, they had little incentive to treat the prisoners well. In fact, the incentives were to treat the prisoners badly. Instead of feeding the prisoners, for example, some of the captains hoarded the prisoners' food, selling it in Australia for a tidy profit.

When the captains were paid for prisoners who survived the journey, however, their incentives changed. Whereas before, the captains had benefited from a prisoner's death, now the incentive system "secured to every poor man who died at least one sincere mourner."[3] The sincere mourner? The captain, who was at least sincere about mourning the money he would have earned had the poor man survived.

Incentives are everywhere. In the United States, we take it for granted that when we go to the supermarket, the shelves will be stocked with kiwi fruit from New Zealand, rice from India, and wine from Chile. Every day we rely on the work of millions of other people to provide us with food, clothing, and shelter. Why do so many people work for our benefit? In his 1776 classic, *The Wealth of Nations*, Adam Smith explained:

> It is not from the benevolence of the butcher, the brewer, or the baker, that we expect our dinner, but from their regard to their own interest.

Do economists think that everyone is self-interested all the time? Of course not. We love our spouses and children just like everyone else! But economists do think that people respond in predictable ways to incentives of all kinds. Fame, power, reputation, sex, and love are all important incentives. Economists even think that benevolence responds to incentives. It's not surprising to an economist, for example, that charities publicize the names of their donors. Some people do give anonymously, but how many buildings on your campus are named Anonymous Hall?

Big Idea Two: Good Institutions Align Self-Interest with the Social Interest

The story of the convict ships hints at a second lesson that runs throughout this book: When self-interest aligns with the broader public interest, we get good outcomes, but when self-interest and the social interest are at odds, we get bad outcomes, sometimes even cruel and inhumane outcomes. Paying the ship captains for every prisoner who walked off the ship was a good payment system because it created incentives for the ship captains to do the right thing, not just for themselves but also for the prisoners and for the government that was paying them.

It's a remarkable finding of economics that under the right conditions markets align self-interest with the social interest. You can see what we mean by thinking back to the supermarket example. The supermarket is stocked with products from around the world because markets channel and coordinate the self-interest of millions of people to achieve a social good. The farmer who awoke at 5 AM to tend his crops, the trucker who delivered the goods to the market, the entrepreneur who risked his or her capital to build the supermarket—all of these people acted in their own interest, but in so doing, they also acted in your interest.

In a striking metaphor, Adam Smith said that when markets work well, those who pursue their own interest end up promoting the social interest, as if led to do so by an "invisible hand." The idea that the pursuit of self-interest can be in the social interest—that at least sometimes, "greed is good"—was one of the most surprising discoveries of economic science, and after several hundred years this insight is still not always appreciated. Throughout this book, we emphasize ways in which individuals acting in their self-interest produce outcomes that were not part of their intention or design, but that nevertheless have desirable properties.

Not from benevolence but from self-interest

Markets, however, do not always align self-interest with the social interest. Sometimes the invisible hand is absent, not just invisible. Market incentives, for example, can be too strong. A firm that doesn't pay for the pollution that it emits into the air has too great an incentive to emit pollution. Fishermen sometimes have too strong an incentive to catch fish, thereby driving the stock of fish into collapse. In other cases, market incentives are too weak. Did you get your flu shot this year? The flu shot prevents you from getting the flu (usually) but it also reduces the chances that other people will get the flu. When deciding whether to get a flu shot, did you take into account the social interest or just your self-interest?

When markets don't properly align self-interest with the social interest, another important lesson of economics is that government can sometimes improve the situation by changing incentives with taxes, subsidies, or other regulations.

Big Idea Three: Trade-offs Are Everywhere

Vioxx users were outraged when in September 2004 Merck withdrew the arthritis drug from the market after a study showed that it could cause strokes and heart attacks. Vioxx had been on the market for five years and had been used by millions of people. Patients were angry at Merck and at the Food and Drug Administration (FDA). How could the FDA, which is charged with ensuring that new pharmaceuticals are safe and effective, have let Vioxx onto the market? Many people demanded more testing and safer pharmaceuticals. Economists worried that approved pharmaceuticals could become too safe.

Too safe! Is it possible to be too safe?! Yes, because trade-offs are everywhere. Researching, developing, and testing a new drug cost time and resources. On average, it takes about 12 years and $1 billion to bring a new drug to market. More testing means that approved drugs will have fewer side effects, but there are two important trade-offs: *drug lag* and *drug loss*.

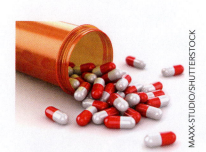

Are pharmaceuticals too safe?

Testing takes time so more testing means that good drugs are delayed, just like bad drugs. On average, new drugs work better than old drugs. So the longer it takes to bring new drugs to market, the more people are harmed who could have benefited if the new drugs had been approved earlier.[4] You can die because an unsafe drug is approved—you can also die because a safe drug has *not yet* been approved. This is *drug lag*.

Testing not only takes time, it is costly. The greater the costs of testing, the fewer new drugs there will be. The costs of testing are a hurdle that each potential drug must leap if it is to be developed. Higher costs mean a higher hurdle, fewer new drugs, and fewer lives saved. You can die because an unsafe drug is approved—you can also die because a safe drug is *never* developed. This is *drug loss*.

Thus, society faces a trade-off. More testing means the drugs that are (eventually) approved will be safer but it also means more drug lag and drug loss. When thinking about FDA policy, we need to look at both sides of the trade-off if we are to choose wisely.

> A resource is **scarce** when there isn't enough to satisfy all of our wants.

The inevitability of trade-offs is the consequence of a big fact about the world, **scarcity**. We face trade-offs because we don't have enough resources to satisfy all of our wants—more of this means less of that. The **great economic problem** is how to arrange our scarce resources to satisfy as many of our wants as possible. So how do we solve this problem? One goal of this textbook is to explain the role of markets and prices in solving the great economic problem.

> The **great economic problem** is how to arrange our scarce resources to satisfy as many of our wants as possible.

Trade-offs are closely related to another important idea in economics, opportunity cost.

Opportunity Cost

> The **opportunity cost** of a choice is the value of the opportunities lost.

Every choice involves something gained and something lost. The **opportunity cost** of a choice is the value of the opportunities lost. Consider the choice to attend college. What is the cost of attending college? At first, you might calculate the cost by adding together the price of tuition, books, and room and board—that might be $22,000 or more a year. But that's not the opportunity cost of attending college. What opportunities are you losing when you attend college?

The main opportunity lost when you attend college is (probably) the opportunity to have a full-time job. Most of you reading this book could easily get a job earning $25,000 a year or maybe quite a bit more (Bill Gates was a college dropout). If you spend four years in college, that's $100,000 that you are giving up to get an education. The opportunity cost of college is probably higher than you thought. Perhaps you ought to ask more questions in class to get your money's worth! (But go back to the list of items we totaled earlier—tuition, books, and room and board—one of these items should *not* count as part of the opportunity cost of college. Which one? Answer: Room and board is not a cost of college if you would have to pay for it whether you go to college or not.)

The concept of opportunity cost is important for two reasons. First, if you don't understand the opportunities you are losing when you make a choice, you won't recognize the real trade-offs that you face. Recognizing trade-offs is the first step in making wise choices. Second, most of the time people do respond to changes in opportunity costs—*even when money costs have not changed*—so if you want to understand behavior, you need to understand opportunity cost.

What would you predict, for example, would happen to college enrollment during a recession? The price of tuition, books, and room and board doesn't fall during a recession but the opportunity cost of attending college does fall. Why? During a recession, the unemployment rate increases so it's harder to get a high-paying job. That means you lose less by attending college when the unemployment rate is high. We therefore predict that college enrollments increase when the unemployment rate increases; in opportunity costs terms, it is cheaper to go to college. In 2009, as the unemployment rate soared, the college enrollment rate hit 70.1%, the highest rate ever.

Big Idea Four: Thinking on the Margin

Robert is cruising down Interstate 80 toward Des Moines, Iowa. Robert wants to get to his destination quickly and safely and he doesn't want to get a speeding ticket. The speed limit is 70 mph but he figures the risk of a ticket is low if he travels just a little bit faster, so Robert sets the cruise control to 72 mph. The road is straight and flat, and after 20 minutes he hasn't seen another car, so he thumbs it up a few clicks to 75. As he approaches Des Moines, Robert spots a police cruiser and thumbs it down to 70. After Des Moines it's nothing but quiet cornfields once again, so he thumbs it up to 72. Crossing the state line into Nebraska, Robert notices that the speed limit is 75, so he thumbs it up to 77 before thumbing it down again as he approaches Omaha.

Thinking on the margin A little bit faster? Or a little bit slower?

Robert and his thumb illustrate what economists mean by thinking on the margin. As Robert drives, he constantly weighs benefits and costs and makes a decision: a little bit faster or a little bit slower?

Thinking on the margin is just making choices by thinking in terms of marginal benefits and marginal costs, the benefits and costs of a little bit more (or a little bit less). Most of our decisions in life involve a little bit more of something or a little bit less, and it turns out that thinking on the margin is also useful for understanding how consumers and producers make decisions. Should the consumer buy a few more apples or a few less? Should the oil well produce a few more barrels of oil or a few less?

In this book, you will find lots of talk about marginal choices, which includes marginal cost (the additional cost from producing a little bit more), marginal revenue (the additional revenue from producing a little bit more), and marginal tax rates (the tax rate on an additional dollar of income). This point about margins is really just a way of restating the importance of trade-offs. If you wish to understand human behavior, look at the trade-offs that people face. Those trade-offs usually involve choices about a little bit more or a little bit less.

The importance of thinking on the margin did not become commonplace in economics until 1871, when marginal thinking was simultaneously described by three economists: William Stanley Jevons, Carl Menger, and Leon Walras. Economists refer to the "marginal revolution" to explain this transformation in economic thought.

Big Idea Five: The Power of Trade

When Alex and Shruti trade, both of them are made better off. (Alex does regret buying a certain polka-dot sweater so take this as a general principle, not a mathematical certainty.) The principle is simple but important because exchange makes Alex and Shruti better off whether Alex and Shruti live in the same country and share the same language and religion or they live worlds apart geographically and culturally. The benefits of trade, however, go beyond those of exchange. The real power of trade is the power to increase production through specialization.

Few of us could survive if we had to produce our own food, clothing, and shelter (let alone our own cell phones and jet aircraft). Self-sufficiency is death. We survive and prosper only because specialization increases productivity. With specialization, the auto mechanic learns more about cars and the thoracic surgeon learns more about hearts than either could if each one of them needed to repair both cars and hearts. Through the division of knowledge, the sum total of knowledge increases and in this way so does productivity.

Trade also allows us to take advantage of economies of scale, the reduction in costs created when goods are mass-produced. No farmer could ever afford a combine harvester if he was growing wheat only for himself, but when a farmer grows wheat for thousands, a combine harvester reduces the cost of bread for all.

Martha Stewart may be the world's best ironer but she once sheepishly admitted that she doesn't always do her own ironing. Why not? Everyone can benefit from trade, even those who are not especially productive. The reason is that especially productive people can't do everything! Martha Stewart may be able to iron a blouse better than anyone else in the world, but she still hires people to do her ironing because for her an hour of ironing comes at the price of an hour spent running her business. Given the choice of spending an hour ironing or running her business, Martha Stewart is better off running her business. In other words, Martha Stewart's *opportunity cost* of ironing is very high.

The theory of comparative advantage says that when people or nations specialize in goods in which they have a low opportunity cost, they can trade to mutual advantage. Thus, Martha Stewart can benefit by buying ironing services even from people who are not as good at ironing as she is. Notice that the better Martha Stewart gets at running her business, the greater her cost of ironing. So when Martha becomes more productive, this increases her demand to trade. In a similar way, the greater the productivity of American business in producing jet aircraft or designing high-technology devices, the greater will be our demand to trade for textiles or steel.

Big Idea Six: The Importance of Wealth and Economic Growth

Every year, several hundred million people contract malaria. In mild cases, malaria causes fever, chills, and nausea. In severe cases, malaria can cause kidney failure, coma, brain damage and, for about a million people a year—mostly children—death. Today, we think of malaria as a "tropical" disease but malaria was once common in the United States. George Washington caught malaria, as did James Monroe, Andrew Jackson, Abraham Lincoln, Ulysses S. Grant, and James A. Garfield. Malaria was present in America until the late 1940s, when the last cases were wiped out by better drainage, removal of mosquito breeding sites, and the spraying of insecticides. The lesson? Wealth—the ability to pay for the prevention of malaria—ended the disease in the United States. And wealth comes from economic growth. So the incidence of malaria is not just about geography; it's also about economics.

Malaria is far from the only problem that diminishes with wealth and economic growth. In the United States, one of the world's richest countries, 993 out of every 1,000 children born survive to the age of 5. In Liberia, one of the world's poorest countries, only about 765 children survive to age 5 (i.e., 235 of every 1,000 children die before seeing their fifth birthday). Overall, it's the wealthiest countries that have the highest rates of infant survival.

Indeed, if you look at most of the things that people care about, they are much easier to come by in wealthier economies. Wealth brings us flush toilets, antibiotics, higher education, the ability to choose the career we want, fun vacations, and, of course, a greater ability to protect our families against catastrophes. Wealth also brings women's rights and political liberty, at least in most (but not all) countries. Wealthier economies lead to richer and more fulfilled, even happier lives, as seen in Figure 1.1. In short, *wealth matters, and understanding economic growth is one of the most important tasks of economics.*

FIGURE 1.1

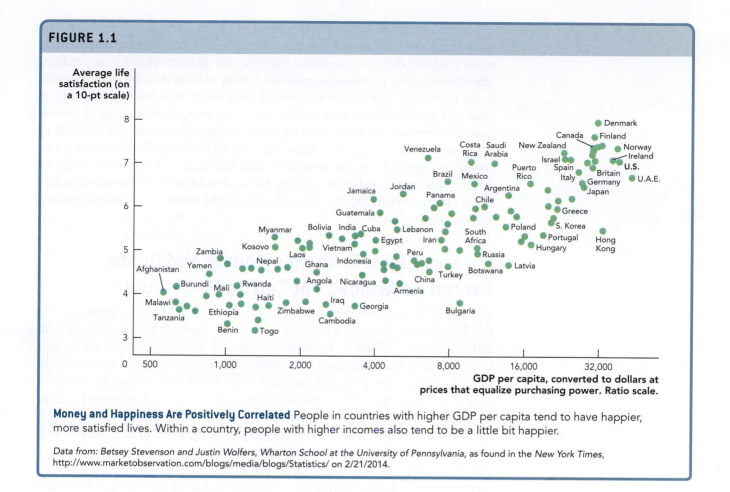

Money and Happiness Are Positively Correlated People in countries with higher GDP per capita tend to have happier, more satisfied lives. Within a country, people with higher incomes also tend to be a little bit happier.

Data from: Betsey Stevenson and Justin Wolfers, Wharton School at the University of Pennsylvania, as found in the New York Times, http://www.marketobservation.com/blogs/media/blogs/Statistics/ on 2/21/2014.

Big Idea Seven: Institutions Matter

If wealth is so important, what makes a country rich? The most proximate cause is that wealthy countries have lots of physical and human capital per worker and they produce things in a relatively efficient manner, using the latest technological knowledge. But why do some countries have more physical and human capital and why is it organized well using the latest technological knowledge? In a word, incentives, which of course brings us back to Big Idea One.

Entrepreneurs, investors, and savers need incentives to save and invest in physical capital, human capital, innovation, and efficient organization. Among the most powerful institutions for supporting good incentives are property rights, political stability, honest government, a dependable legal system, and competitive and open markets.

Consider South and North Korea. South Korea has a per capita income more than 10 times greater than its immediate neighbor, North Korea. South Korea is a modern, developed economy but in North Korea people still starve or can go for months without eating meat. And yet both countries were equally poor in 1950 and, of course, the two countries share the same language and cultural and historical background. What differs is their economic systems and the incentives at work.

Macroeconomists are especially interested in the incentives to produce new ideas. If the world never had any new ideas, the standard of living would eventually stagnate. But entrepreneurs draw on new ideas to create new products like iPhones, new pharmaceuticals, self-driving cars, and many other innovations. Just about any device you use in daily life is based on a multitude of ideas and discoveries, the lifeblood of economic growth. New ideas, of course, require incentives and that means an active scientific community and the freedom and incentive to put new ideas into action. Ideas also have peculiar properties. One apple feeds one person but one idea can feed the world. Ideas, in other words, aren't used up when they are used and that has tremendous implications for understanding the benefits of trade, the future of economic growth, and many other topics.

Big Idea Eight: Economic Booms and Busts Cannot Be Avoided but Can Be Moderated

We have seen that growth matters and that the right institutions foster growth. But no economy grows at a constant pace. Economies advance and recede, rise and fall, boom and bust. In a recession, wages fall and many people are thrown into miserable unemployment. Unfortunately, we cannot avoid all recessions. Booms and busts are part of the normal response of an economy to changing economic conditions. When the weather is bad in India, for example, crops fail and the economy grows more slowly or perhaps it grows not at all. The weather doesn't much affect the economy in the United States, but the U.S. economy is buffeted by other unavoidable shocks.

Although some booms and busts are part of the normal response of an economy to changing economic conditions, not all booms and busts are normal. The Great Depression (1929–1940) was not normal, but rather it was the most catastrophic economic event in the history of the United States. National output plummeted by 30 percent, unemployment rates exceeded 20 percent, and the stock market lost more than two-thirds of its value. Almost overnight the United States went from confidence to desperation. The Great Depression, however, didn't have to happen. Most economists today believe that if the government, especially the U.S. Federal Reserve, had acted more quickly and more appropriately, the Great Depression would have been shorter and less deep. At the time, however, the tools at the government's disposal—monetary and fiscal policy—were not well understood.

Today, the tools of monetary and fiscal policy are much better understood. When used appropriately, these tools can reduce swings in unemployment and GDP. Unemployment insurance can also reduce some of the misery that accompanies a recession. The tools of monetary and fiscal policy, however, are not all-powerful. At one time it was thought that these tools could end all recessions, but we know now that this is not the case. Furthermore, when used poorly, monetary and fiscal policy can make recessions worse and the economy more volatile.

A significant task of macroeconomic theory is to understand both the promise and the limits of monetary and fiscal policy in smoothing out the normal booms and busts of the macroeconomy.

Big Idea Nine: Inflation Is Caused by Increases in the Supply of Money

Yes, economic policy can be useful but sometimes policy goes awry, for instance, when **inflation** gets out of hand. Inflation, one of the most common problems in macroeconomics, refers to an increase in the general level of prices. Inflation makes people feel poorer but, perhaps more important, rising and especially volatile prices make it harder for people to figure out the real values of goods, services, and investments. For these and other reasons, most people (and economists) dislike inflation.

But where does inflation come from? The answer is simple: Inflation is caused by a sustained increase in the supply of money. When people have more money, they spend it, and without an increase in the supply of goods, prices must rise. As Nobel laureate Milton Friedman once wrote: "Inflation is always and everywhere a monetary phenomenon."

The United States, like other advanced economies, has a central bank; in the United States that bank is called the Federal Reserve. The Federal Reserve has the power and the responsibility to regulate the supply of money in the American economy. This power can be used for good, such as when the Federal Reserve holds off or minimizes a recession. But the power also can be used for great harm if the Federal Reserve encourages too much growth in the supply of money. The result will be inflation and economic disruption.

In Zimbabwe, the government ran the printing presses at full speed for many years. By the end of 2007, prices were rising at an astonishing rate of 150,000 percent per year. The United States has never had a problem of this scope or anything close to it but inflation remains a common concern.

Amazingly, the inflation rate in Zimbabwe kept rising. In January of 2008, the government had to issue a 10-million-dollar bank note (worth about 4 U.S. dollars), and a year later they announced a 20-*trillion*-dollar note that bought about what 10 million dollars had a year earlier. In early 2009, the inflation rate leaped to billions of percent per month! Finally, in April of 2009 the government stopped issuing the Zimbabwean dollar altogether and permitted trade using foreign currencies such as the South African rand and U.S. dollar.

Inflation is an increase in the general level of prices.

AP PHOTO

A billionaire in Zimbabwe

Big Idea Ten: Central Banking Is a Hard Job

The Federal Reserve ("the Fed"), is often called on to combat recessions. But this is not always easy to do. Typically, there is a lag—often of many months—between when the Fed makes a decision and when the effects of that decision on the economy are known. In the meantime, economic conditions have changed so you should think of the Fed as shooting at a moving target. No one can foresee the future perfectly and so the Fed's decisions are not always the right ones.

As mentioned, too much money in the economy means that inflation will result. But not enough money in the economy is bad as well and can lead to a recession or a slowing of economic growth. These ideas are an important and extensive topic in macroeconomics, but the key problem is that a low or falling money supply forces people to cut their prices and wages and this adjustment doesn't always go smoothly.

The Fed is always trying to get it "just right," but some of the time it fails. Sometimes the failure is a mistake the Fed could have avoided, but other times it simply isn't possible to always make the right guess about where the world is headed. Thus, in some situations the Fed must accept a certain amount of either inflation or unemployment. Central banking relies on economic tools, but in the final analysis it is as much an art as a science.

Most economists think that the Fed does more good than harm. But if you are going to understand the Fed, you have to think of it as a highly fallible institution that faces a very difficult job.

The Biggest Idea of All: Economics Is Fun

When you put all these ideas and others together, you see that economics is both exciting and important. Economics teaches us how to make the world a better place. It's about the difference between wealth and poverty, work and unemployment, happiness and misery. Economics increases your understanding of the past, present, and future.

As you will see, the basic principles of economics hold everywhere, whether it is in a rice paddy in Vietnam or a stock market in São Paulo, Brazil. No matter what the topic, the principles of economics apply to all countries, not just to your own. Moreover, in today's globalized world, events in China and India influence the economy in the United States, and vice versa. For this reason, you will find that our book is truly international and full of examples and applications from Algeria to Zimbabwe.

But economics is also linked to everyday life. Economics can help you think about your quest for a job, how to manage your personal finances, and how to deal with debt, inflation, a recession, or a bursting stock market bubble. In short, economics is about understanding your world.

We are excited about economics and we hope that you will be too. Perhaps some of you will even become economics majors. If you are thinking about majoring, you might want to know that a bachelor's degree in economics is one of the best-paying degrees, with starting salaries just behind chemical and nuclear engineering. That reflects the value of an economics degree and the world's recognition of that value. But if your passion lies elsewhere, that's okay too; a course in the principles of economics will take you a long way toward understanding your world. With a good course, a good professor, and a good textbook, you'll never look at the world the same way again. So just remember: *See the Invisible Hand. Understand Your World.*

CHAPTER REVIEW

interactive activity   Go online to practice with more examples of these types of problems, including live links to videos, data sources, and feedback.

   Problems in green relate to MRU videos. See the MRU table at the end of the exercises.

KEY CONCEPTS

incentives, p. 1

scarcity, p. 4

great economic problem, p. 4

opportunity cost, p. 4

inflation, p. 9

FACTS AND TOOLS

1. A headline[5] in the *New York Times* read: "Study Finds Enrollment Is Up at Colleges Despite Recession." How would you rewrite this headline now that you understand the idea of opportunity cost?

2. When bad weather in India destroys the crop, does this sound like a fall in the total "supply" of crops or a fall in people's "demand" for crops? Keep your answer in mind as you learn about economic booms and busts later on.

3. How much did national output fall during the Great Depression? According to the chapter, which government agency might have helped to avoid much of the Great Depression had it acted more quickly and appropriately?

4. The chapter lists four things that entrepreneurs save and invest in. Which of the four are actual objects, and which are more intangible, like concepts or ideas or plans? Feel free to use Wikipedia or some other reference source to get definitions of unfamiliar terms.

5. Who has a better incentive to work long hours in a laboratory researching new cures for diseases: a scientist who earns a percentage of the profits from any new medicine she might invent, or a scientist who will get a handshake and a thank you note from her boss if she invents a new medicine?

6. In the discussion of Big Idea Five, the chapter says that "self-sufficiency is death" because most of us would not be able to produce for ourselves the food and shelter that we need to survive. In addition to *death*, however, one could also say that self-sufficiency is *boredom* or *ignorance*. How

does specialization and trade help you to avoid boredom and ignorance?

THINKING AND PROBLEM SOLVING

7. In recent years, Zimbabwe has had hyperinflation, with prices tripling (or more!) every month. According to what you learned in this chapter, what do you think the government can do to end this hyperinflation?

8. Some people worry that machines will take jobs away from people, making people permanently unemployed. Only 150 years ago in the United States, most people were farmers. Now, machines do almost all of the farm work and fewer than 2% of Americans are farmers, yet that 2% produces enough food to feed the entire country while still exporting food overseas.

   a. What happened to all of those people who used to work on farms? Do you think most adult males in the United States are unemployed nowadays, now that farm work is gone?

   b. Some people say that it's okay for machines to take jobs because we'll get jobs fixing the machines. Just from looking around, do you think that most working Americans are earning a living by fixing farm equipment? If not, what do you think most working people are doing instead? (We'll give a full answer later in this book.)

9. Let's connect Big Ideas Six and Nine: Do you think that people in poor countries are poor because they don't have enough money? In other words, could a country get richer by printing more pieces of paper called "money" and handing those out to its citizens?

10. Nobel Prize winner Milton Friedman said that a bad central banker is like a "fool in the shower." In a shower, of course, when you turn the faucet, water won't show up in the showerhead for a few seconds. So if a "fool in the shower" is always making big changes in the temperature based on how the water feels *right now*, the water is likely to swing back and forth between too

hot and too cold. How does this apply to central banking?

11. According to the United Nations, there were roughly 300 million humans on the planet a thousand years ago. Essentially all of them were poor by modern standards: They lacked antibiotics, almost all lacked indoor plumbing, and none traveled faster than a horse or a river could carry them. Today, between 1 and 3 billion humans are poor out of about 7 billion total humans. So, over the last thousand years, what has happened to the *fraction* of humans who are poor: Did it rise, fall, or stay about the same? What happened to the total *number* of people living in deep poverty: Rise, fall, or no change?

CHALLENGES

12. We claim that part of the reason the Great Depression was so destructive is because economists didn't understand how to use government policy very well in the 1930s. In your opinion, do you think that economists during the Great Depression would have agreed? In other words, if you had asked them why the Depression was so bad, would they have said, "Because the government ignored our wise advice," or would they have said, "Because we don't have any good ideas about how to fix this"? What does your answer tell you about the confidence of economists and other experts?

13. Some problems that economists try to solve are easy *as economic problems* but hard *as political problems*. Medical doctors face similar kinds of situations: Preventing most deaths from obesity or lung cancer is easy *as a medical problem* (eat less, exercise more, don't smoke) but hard *as a self-control problem*. With this in mind, how is ending hyperinflation like losing 100 pounds?

14. As Nobel Prize winner and *New York Times* columnist Paul Krugman has noted, the field of economics is a lot like the field of medicine: They are fields where knowledge is limited (both are new as real scientific disciplines) and where many cures are quite painful (opportunity cost), but where regular people care deeply about the issues. What are some other ways that economics and medicine are alike?

15. Economics is sometimes called "the dismal science." Of the big ideas in this chapter, which sound dismal—like bad news?

MARGINAL REVOLUTION UNIVERSITY VIDEOS

Meet Your Authors

www.mruniversity.com/intro-econ

Zimbabwe and Hyperinflation

mruniversity.com/hyperinflation

Problems: **7**

The Power of Trade and Comparative Advantage

haos, conflict, and war may dominate the news, but it's heartening to know that there is also an astounding amount of world *cooperation*. The next time you are in your local supermarket, stop and consider how many people cooperated to bring the fruits of the world to your table: kiwis from New Zealand, dried apricots from Turkey, dates from Egypt, mangoes from Mexico, bananas from Guatemala. How is it that farmers in New Zealand wake up at 5 AM to work hard tending their fields so that you, on the other side of the world, may enjoy a kiwi with your fruit salad?

This chapter is about a central feature of our world, trade. It's about how you eat reasonably well every day yet have little knowledge of farming, it's about how you cooperate with people whom you will never meet, and it's about how civilization is made possible.

We will focus on three of the benefits of trade:

1. Trade makes people better off when preferences differ.
2. Trade increases productivity through specialization and the division of knowledge.
3. Trade increases productivity through comparative advantage.

Trade and Preferences

In September 1995, Pierre Omidyar, a 28-year-old computer programmer, finished the code for what would soon become eBay. Searching around for a test item, Omidyar grabbed a broken laser pointer and posted it for sale with a starting price of $1. The laser pointer sold for $14.83. Astonished, Omidyar contacted the winning bidder to make sure he understood that the laser pointer was broken. "Oh yes," the bidder replied, "I am a collector of broken laser pointers." At that instant, Omidyar knew eBay was going to be a huge success. Within just a few years, he would become one of the richest men in the United States.

eBay profits by making buyers and sellers happy.

Today, eBay operates in more than 30 countries and earns billions of dollars in revenue. eBay's revenues, however, are a small share of the total value that is created for the hundreds of millions of buyers and sellers who trade everything on eBay from children's toys to the original Hollywood sign. Trade creates value by moving goods from people who value them less to people who value them more. Sam, for example, was going to trash the old Fisher Price garage that his kids no longer play with. Instead, Sam sells it on eBay to Jen who pays $65.50. What had been worth nothing is now worth at least $65.50. Value has been created. Trade makes Sam better off, Jen better off, and it makes eBay, the market maker who brought Sam and Jen together, better off. Trade makes people with different preferences better off.

Specialization, Productivity, and the Division of Knowledge

Simple trades of the kind found on eBay create value, but the true power of trade is discovered only when people take the next step, specialization. In a world without trade, no one can afford to specialize. People will specialize in the production of a single good only when they are confident that they will be able to trade that good for the many other goods that they want and need. Thus, as trade develops, so does specialization, and specialization turns out to vastly increase productivity.

How long could you survive if you had to grow your own food? Probably not very long. Yet most of us can earn enough money in a single day spent doing something other than farming to buy more food than we could grow in a year. Why can we get so much more food through trade than through personal production? The reason is that specialization greatly increases productivity. Farmers, for example, have two immense advantages in producing food compared to economics professors or students: Because they specialize, they know more about farming than other people, and because they sell large quantities, they can afford to buy large-scale farming machines. What is true for farming is true for just about every field of production—specialization increases productivity. Without specialization and trade, we would each have to produce our own food as well as other goods, and the result would be mass starvation and the collapse of civilization.

Contra episode 56, even Spock's brain could not come close to running a modern economy; the work needed to do that would have to be spread across millions of brains. For this reason, some economists consider "Spock's Brain" to be the worst Star Trek episode ever.

The human brain is limited and there is much to know. Thus, it makes sense to divide knowledge across many brains and then trade. In a primitive agricultural economy in which each person or household farms for themselves, each person has about the same knowledge as the person next door. In this case, the combined knowledge of a society of 1 million people barely exceeds that of a single person.[1] A society run with the knowledge of one brain is a poor and miserable society.

In a modern economy, many millions of times more knowledge is used than could exist in a single brain. In the United States, for example, we don't just have doctors—we have neurologists, cardiologists, gastroenterologists, gynecologists, and urologists, to name just a few of the many specializations in medicine. Knowledge increases productivity so specialization increases total output. All of this knowledge is possible, however, only because each person can specialize in the production of one good and then trade for all other desired goods. Without trade, specialization is impossible.

The extent of specialization in a modern economy explains why no one knows the full details of how even the simplest product is produced. A Valentine's Day rose may have been grown in Kenya, flown to Amsterdam on a refrigerated airplane, and trucked to Topeka by drivers staying awake with Colombian coffee. Each person in this process knows only a small part of the whole, but with trade and market coordination, they each do their part and the rose is delivered without anyone needing to understand the whole process.

The extent of specialization in modern society is remarkable. We have already mentioned the many specializations in medicine. We also have dog walkers, closet organizers, and manicurists. It's common to dismiss the latter jobs as frivolous, but trade connects all markets. It's the dog walkers, closet organizers, and manicurists who give the otolaryngologists—specialists in the nose, ear, and throat—the time they need to perfect their skills.

The division of knowledge increases with specialization and trade. Economic growth in the modern era is primarily due to the creation of new knowledge. Thus, one of the most momentous turning points in the division of knowledge happens when trade is extensive enough to support large numbers of scientists, engineers, and entrepreneurs, all of whom specialize in producing new knowledge.

Every increase in world trade is an opportunity to increase the division of knowledge and extend the power of the human mind. During the Communist era, for example, China was like an island cut off from the world economy: 1 billion people who neither traded many goods nor many ideas with the rest of the world. The fall of the Berlin Wall and the opening to the world economy of China, Russia, Eastern Europe, and other nations greatly adds to the productive stock of scientists and engineers and is one of the most promising signs for the future of the world. Billions of minds have been added to the division of knowledge and cooperation around the world has been extended further than ever before.

Consider the many ideas and innovations that make life better, from antibiotics, to high-yield, disease-resistant wheat, to the semiconductor. Insofar as those goods have originated in one place and then been spread around the world, improving the lives of millions or billions, it is because of trade.

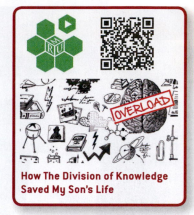

How The Division of Knowledge Saved My Son's Life

Reducing trade barriers, Berlin 1989

STRINGER/REUTERS/NEWSCOM

Comparative Advantage

A third reason to trade is to take advantage of differences. Brazil, for example, has a climate ideally suited to growing sugar cane, China has an abundance of low-skill workers, and the United States has one of the best educated workforces in the world. Taking advantage of these differences suggests that world production can be maximized when Brazil produces

Comparative advantage: It's a good thing. Martha Stewart may be the world's best ironer but she has admitted that she doesn't always do her own ironing. That's smart! Every hour Martha spends ironing is an hour less she has to run her billion-dollar business. The cost of ironing is too high for Martha Stewart, even if she is the world's best. Martha can be most productive if she does what she does *most* best.

Absolute advantage is the ability to produce the same good using fewer inputs than another producer.

A **production possibilities frontier** shows all the combinations of goods that a country can produce given its productivity and supply of inputs.

sugar, China assembles iPads, and the United States devotes its efforts to designing the next generation of electronic devices.

Taking advantage of differences is even more powerful than it looks. We say that a country has an **absolute advantage** in production if it can produce the same good using fewer inputs than another country. But to benefit from trade, a country need not have an absolute advantage. For example, even if the United States did have the world's best climate for growing sugar, it might still make sense for Brazil to grow sugar and for the United States to design iPads, if the United States had a bigger advantage in designing iPads than it did in growing sugar.

Here's another example of what economists call comparative advantage. Martha Stewart doesn't do her own ironing. Why not? Martha Stewart may, in fact, be the world's best ironer but she is also good at running her business. If Martha spent more time ironing and less time running her business, her blouses might be pressed more precisely but that would be a small gain compared with the loss from having someone else run her business. It's better for Martha if she specializes in running her business and then trades some of her income for other goods, such as ironing services, and of course many other goods and services as well.

The Production Possibility Frontier

The idea of comparative advantage is subtle but important. In order to give a precise definition, let's explore comparative advantage using a simple model. Suppose that there are just two goods, computers and shirts, and one input, labor. Assume that in Mexico, it takes 12 units of labor to make one computer and 2 units of labor to produce one shirt, and suppose that Mexico has 24 units of labor. Mexico, therefore, can produce 2 computers and 0 shirts or 0 computers and 12 shirts, or they can have any combination of computers and shirts along the line in the left panel of Figure 2.1 labeled Mexico's PPF. Mexico's PPF, short for Mexico's **production possibilities frontier**, shows all the combinations of computers and shirts that Mexico can produce given its productivity and supply of inputs. Mexico cannot produce outside of its PPF.

Similarly, assume that there are 24 units of labor in the United States but that in the United States it takes 1 unit of labor to produce either good. The United States therefore can produce 24 computers and 0 shirts, or 0 computers and 24 shirts, or any combination along the U.S. PPF shown in the right panel of Figure 2.1.

A PPF illustrates trade-offs. If Mexico wants to produce more shirts, it must produce fewer computers, and vice versa: It moves along its PPF. That's just another way of restating the fundamental principles of scarcity and opportunity cost.

Opportunity Costs and Comparative Advantage

In fact, there is a close connection between opportunity costs and the PPF. Looking first at the U.S. PPF in the right panel of Figure 2.1, notice that the slope, the rise over the run, is $-24/24 = -1$. In other words, for every

FIGURE 2.1

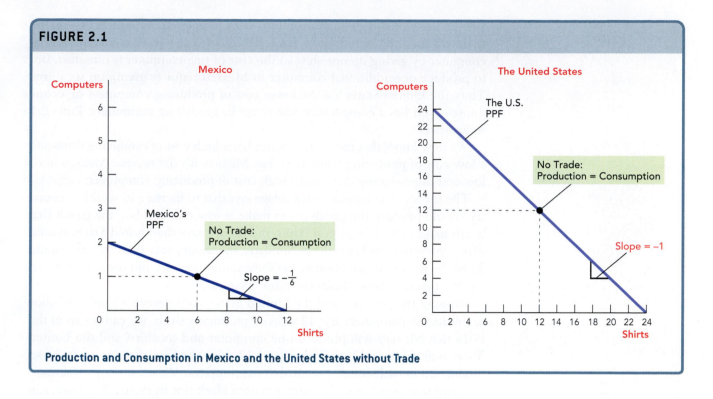

Production and Consumption in Mexico and the United States without Trade

additional shirt the United States produces, it must produce one fewer computer. One shirt has an opportunity cost of one computer and vice versa.

Now consider Mexico's PPF. The rise over the run is $-2/12 = -1/6$. In other words, for every additional shirt that Mexico produces, it must produce 1/6th less of a computer. Once again, the slope of the PPF tells us the opportunity cost. In Mexico, 1 shirt costs 1/6th of a computer, or 1 computer costs 6 shirts. We summarize the opportunity costs in Table 2.1.

Now here is the key. The (opportunity) cost of a shirt in the United States is one computer but the (opportunity) cost of a shirt in Mexico is just one-sixth of a computer. Thus, even though Mexico is less productive than the United States, Mexico has a lower cost of producing shirts! Since Mexico has the lower opportunity cost of producing shirts, we say that Mexico has a **comparative advantage** in producing shirts.

A country has a **comparative advantage** in producing goods for which it has the lower opportunity cost.

TABLE 2.1 OPPORTUNITY COSTS

Country	Opportunity Cost of 1 Computer	Opportunity Cost of 1 Shirt	
Mexico	6 shirts	1/6 of a computer	Mexico is the ←low-cost producer of shirts.
United States	1 shirt	1 computer	

The United States is the low-cost producer of computers.

Now let's look at the opportunity cost of producing computers. Again, the trade-off for the United States is easy to see: It can produce one additional computer by giving up one shirt so the cost of one computer is one shirt. But to produce one additional computer in Mexico requires giving up six shirts! Thus, the United States has the lower cost of producing computers or, economists say, it has a comparative advantage in producing computers. Table 2.1 summarizes.

We now know that the United States has a high cost of producing shirts and a low cost of producing computers. For Mexico, it's the reverse: Mexico has a low cost of producing shirts and a high cost of producing computers.

The theory of comparative advantage says that to increase its wealth, a country should produce the goods it can make at low cost and buy the goods that it can make only at high cost. Thus, the theory says the United States should make computers and buy shirts. Similarly, the theory says that Mexico should make shirts and buy computers. Let's use some numbers and some pictures to see whether the theory holds up in our example.

Suppose that Mexico and the United States each devote 12 units of labor to producing computers and 12 units to producing shirts. We can see from the PPFs that Mexico will produce one computer and six shirts and the United States will produce 12 computers and 12 shirts. At first, there is no trade, so production in each country is equal to consumption. We show the production–consumption point of each country with a black dot in Figure 2.1. Now, can Mexico and the United States make themselves better off through trade? Yes.

Imagine that Mexico moves 12 units of its labor out of computer production and into shirt production. Thus, Mexico specializes completely by allocating all 24 units of its labor to shirt production, thereby producing 12 shirts. Similarly, suppose that the United States moves 2 units of its labor out of shirt production and into computers—thus producing 14 computers and 10 shirts. Production in Mexico and the United States is now shown by the green points in Figure 2.2.

So, to finish the story, can you now see a way in which both Mexico and the United States can be made better off? Sure! Imagine that the United States trades one computer to Mexico in return for three shirts. Mexico is now able to consume one computer and nine shirts (three more shirts than before trade), while the United States is able to consume 13 computers (one more than before trade) and 13 shirts (one more than before trade).

Amazingly, both Mexico and the United States can now consume outside of their PPFs. In other words, before trade, Mexico could not have consumed one computer and nine shirts because this was outside their PPF. Similarly, before trade, the United States could not have consumed 13 computers and 13 shirts. But with trade, countries are able to increase their consumption beyond the range that was possible without trade.

Thus, when each country produces according to its comparative advantage and then trades, total production and consumption increase. Importantly, both Mexico and the United States gain from trade even though the United States is more productive than Mexico at producing *both* computers and shirts.

The theory of comparative advantage not only explains trade patterns it also tells us something remarkable: A country (or a person) will *always* be the low-cost seller of some good. The reason is clear: The greater the advantage a country has in producing A, the greater the cost to it of producing B. If you are a great pianist, the cost to you of doing anything else is very high. Thus, the

FIGURE 2.2

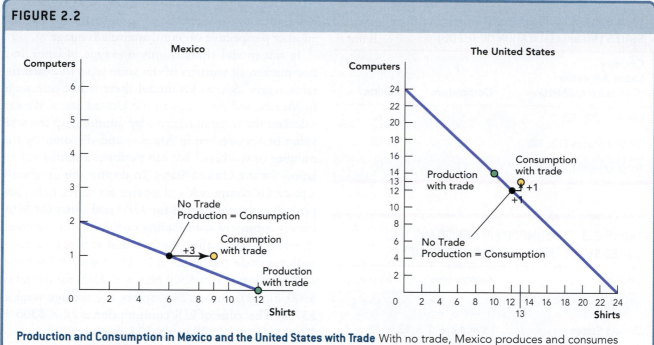

Production and Consumption in Mexico and the United States with Trade With no trade, Mexico produces and consumes one computer and six shirts and the United States produces and consumes 12 computers and 12 shirts. With specialization, Mexico produces zero computers and 12 shirts and the United States produces 14 computers and 10 shirts. By trading three shirts for one computer, Mexico increases its consumption (compared to the no-trade situation) by three shirts and the United States increases its consumption by one computer and one shirt.

greater your advantages in being a pianist, the greater the incentive you have to trade with other people for other goods. It's the same way for countries. The more productive the United States is at producing computers, the greater its demand will be to trade for shirts. Thus, countries with high productivity can always benefit by trading with lower-productivity countries, and countries with lower productivity need never fear that higher-productivity countries will outcompete them in the production of all goods.

When people fear that a country can be outcompeted in everything, they are making a common mistake, namely confusing absolute advantage with comparative advantage. A producer has an absolute advantage over another producer if it can produce more output from the same input. But what makes trade profitable is differences in comparative advantage, and a country will always have some comparative advantage.

Thus, everyone can benefit from trade. From the world's greatest genius down to the person of below-average ability, no individuals or countries are so productive or so unproductive that they cannot benefit from inclusion in the worldwide division of labor. The theory of comparative advantage tells us something vital about world trade and about world peace. Trade unites humanity.

Comparative Advantage and Wages

Comparative advantage is a difficult story to grasp. Most of the world hasn't got it yet so don't be too surprised if it takes you some time as well. You may at first be bothered by the fact that we did not explicitly discuss wages. Won't a country like the United States be uncompetitive in trade with low-wage countries like Mexico?

TABLE 2.2 CONSUMPTION IN MEXICO AND THE UNITED STATES (NO SPECIALIZATION OR TRADE)

Country Labor Allocation (Computers, Shirts)	Computers	Shirts
Mexico (12, 12)	1	6
United States (12, 12)	12	12
Total consumption	13	18

TABLE 2.3 CONSUMPTION IN MEXICO AND THE UNITED STATES (SPECIALIZATION AND TRADE)

Country	Computers	Shirts
Mexico	1	9 = 6 + 3
United States	13 = 12 + 1	13 = 12 + 1
Total consumption	14	22

In fact, wages are in our model, we just need to bring them to the surface. Doing so will provide another perspective on comparative advantage.

In our model, there is only one type of labor. In a free market, all workers of the same type will earn the same wage.* So, in this model there is just one wage in Mexico and one wage in the United States. We can calculate the wage in Mexico by summing up the total value of *consumption* in Mexico and dividing by the number of workers.† We can perform a similar calculation for the United States. To do this, we need only a price for computers and a price for shirts. Let's suppose that computers sell for $300 and shirts for $100 (this is consistent with trading one computer for three shirts as we did earlier). Let's look first at the situation with no trade (see Table 2.2). The value of Mexican consumption is $1 \times \$300$ plus $6 \times \$100$ for a total of $900. Since there are 24 workers, the average wage is $37.50. The value of U.S. consumption is $12 \times \$300 + 12 \times \$100 = \$4,800$ so the U.S. wage is $200.

Now consider the situation with trade (see Table 2.3). The value of Mexican consumption is now $1 \times \$300 + 9 \times \$100 = \$1,200$ for a wage of $50, while the U.S. wage is now $216.67 (check it!). Wages in both countries have gone up, just as expected.

But notice that the wage in Mexico is lower than the wage in the United States, both before and after trade. The reason is that the productivity of labor is lower in Mexico. Ultimately, it's the productivity of labor that determines the wage rate. Specialization and trade let workers make the most of what they have—it raises wages as high as possible given productivity—but trade does not directly increase productivity.‡ Trade makes both Einstein and his less clever accountant better off, but it doesn't make the accountant a skilled scientist like Einstein.

In summary, workers in the United States often fear trade because they think that they cannot compete with low-wage workers in other countries. Meanwhile, workers in low-wage countries fear trade because they think that they cannot compete with high-productivity countries like the United States! But differences in wages reflect differences in productivity. High-productivity countries have high wages; low-productivity countries have low wages. Trade means that workers in both countries can raise their wages to the highest levels allowed by their respective productivities.

---

* In a free market, the same good will tend to sell for the same price everywhere. Imagine that the wages in computer manufacturing exceed the wages in shirt manufacturing. Everyone wants a higher wage, so workers in the shirt industry will try to move to the computer industry. As the supply of workers in computer manufacturing increases, however, wages in the computer sector will fall. And, as the supply of workers in shirt manufacturing decreases, wages in that sector will increase. Only when workers of the same type are paid the same wage is there no incentive for workers to move.
† We calculate the value of consumption because at the end of the day workers care about what they consume, not what they produce.
‡ Trade can increase productivity by improving the division of knowledge and by diffusing information about advanced production techniques. These advantages of trade are important but the logic of comparative advantage does not require an increase in productivity.

Adam Smith on Trade

Notice that we have so far talked about trade without distinguishing it much from "international trade." Adam Smith had an elegant summary connecting the argument for trade to that for international trade:

> It is the maxim of every prudent master of a family never to attempt to make at home what it will cost him more to make than to buy. The tailor does not attempt to make his own shoes, but buys them of the shoemaker. The shoemaker does not attempt to make his own clothes, but employs a tailor. What is prudence in the conduct of every private family can scarce be folly in that of a great kingdom. If a foreign country can supply us with a commodity cheaper than we ourselves can make it, better buy it of them with some part of the produce of our own industry employed in a way in which we have some advantage.[2]

Trade and Globalization

Does everyone always benefit from increased trade? No. In our simple model, workers within a country can easily switch between the shirt and computer sectors. In the real world, workers in the sector with increased demand (computers in the United States, shirts in Mexico) will see their wages rise while workers in the sector with decreased demand (shirts in the United States, computers in Mexico) will see their wages fall. Workers in sectors with falling wages will move to sectors with rising wages until wages in the sectors equalize, but the transition isn't always easy or quick. We will take another look at the gains and losses from trade in Chapter 9. Overall, however, greater trade increases total wealth. That typically brings benefits to a great many people in all parts of the trading world. We can see this theme throughout history.

Decreases in transportation costs, integration of world markets, and increased speed of communication have made the world a smaller place. But globalization is not new; rather, it has been a theme in human history since at least the Roman Empire, which knit together different parts of the world in a common economic and political area. When these trade networks later fell apart, the subsequent era was named "The Dark Ages."

Later, the European Renaissance arose from revitalized trade routes, the rebirth of commercially based cities, and the spread of science from China, India, and the Middle East. Periods of increased trade and the spread of ideas have been among the best for human progress. As economist Donald Boudreaux puts it: "Globalization is the advance of human cooperation across national boundaries."[3]

Takeaway

Simple trade makes people better off when preferences differ, but the true power of trade occurs when trade leads to specialization. Specialization creates enormous increases in productivity. Without trade, the knowledge used by an entire economy is approximately equal to the knowledge used by one brain. With specialization and trade, the total sum of knowledge used in an economy increases tremendously and far exceeds that of any one brain.

BETTMANN/GETTY IMAGES

Adam Smith (1723–1790), author of *The Wealth of Nations* and one of the greatest economists of all time. When Smith could not finish teaching one semester, he told his students he would refund their tuition. When the students refused the refund saying they had learned so much already, Smith wept. We, however, will not refund the purchase price of this book even if you read only half of it. We are not as good economists as was Adam Smith.

CHECK YOURSELF

- What does specialization do to productivity? Why?
- How does trade let us benefit from the advantages of specialization?
- Usain Bolt is the world's fastest human. Usain could probably mow his lawn very quickly, much more quickly and at least as well as Harry, who mows lawns for a living. Why would Usain Bolt pay Harry to mow his lawn rather than do it himself?

International trade is trade across political borders. The theory of comparative advantage explains how a country, just like a person, can increase its standard of living by specializing in what it can make at low (opportunity) cost and trading for what it can make only at high cost. When we apply the logic of opportunity cost to trade, we discover that everyone has a comparative advantage in something, so everyone can benefit from inclusion in the world market.

CHAPTER REVIEW

interactive activity   Go online to practice with more examples of these types of problems, including live links to videos, data sources, and feedback.

 Problems in green relate to MRU videos. See the MRU table at the end of the exercises.

KEY CONCEPTS

absolute advantage, p. 16

production possibilities frontier, p. 16

comparative advantage, p. 17

FACTS AND TOOLS

1. Use the idea of the "division of knowledge" to answer the following questions:

    a. Which country has more knowledge: Utopia, where in the words of Karl Marx, each person knows just enough about hunting, fishing, and cattle raising to "hunt in the morning, fish in the afternoon, [and] rear cattle in the evening," or Drudgia, where one-third of the population learns only about hunting, one-third only about fishing, and one-third only about cattle raising?

    b. Which planet has more knowledge: Xeroxia, each of whose 1 million inhabitants knows the same list of 1 million facts, or Differentia, whose 1 million inhabitants each know a different set of 1 million facts? How many facts are known in Xeroxia? How many facts are known in Differentia?

2. In *The Wealth of Nations*, Adam Smith said that one reason specialization makes someone more productive is because "a man commonly saunters a little in turning his hand from one sort of employment to another." How can you use this observation to improve your pattern of studying for your four or five college courses this semester?

3. Opportunity cost is one of the tougher ideas in economics. Let's make it easier by starting with some simple examples. In the following examples, find the opportunity cost: Your answer should be a *rate*, as in "1.5 widgets per year" or "6 lectures per month." Ignoring Adam Smith's insight from the previous question, assume that these relationships are simple linear ones, so that if you put in twice the time, you get twice the output, and half the time yields half the output.

    a. Erin has a choice between two activities: She can repair one transmission per hour or she can repair two fuel injectors per hour. What is the opportunity cost of repairing one transmission?

    b. Katie works at a customer service center and every hour she has a choice between two activities: answering 200 telephone calls per hour or responding to 400 emails per hour. What is the opportunity cost of responding to 400 phone calls?

    c. Deirdre has a choice between writing one more book this year or five more articles this year. What is the opportunity cost of writing half a book this year, in terms of articles?

4. a. American workers are commonly paid much more than Chinese workers. *True or false:* This is largely because American workers are typically more productive than Chinese workers.

    b. Julia Child, an American chef (and World War II spy) who reintroduced French cooking to Americans in the 1960s, was paid much more than most American chefs. *True or false:* This was largely because Julia Child was much more productive than most American chefs.

5. According to the *Wall Street Journal* (August 30, 2007, "In the Balance"), it takes about 30 hours to assemble a vehicle in the United States. Let's use that fact plus a few invented numbers to sum up the global division of labor in auto manufacturing. In international economics, "North"

is shorthand for the high-tech developed countries of East Asia, North America, and Western Europe, while "South" is shorthand for the rest of the world. Let's use that shorthand here.

a. Consider the following productivity table: Which region has an absolute advantage at making high-quality cars? Low-quality cars?

	Number of Hours to Make One High-Quality Car	Number of Hours to Make One Low-Quality Car
North	30	20
South	60	30

b. Using the information in the productivity table, estimate the opportunity cost of making high- or low-quality cars in the North and in the South. Which region has a comparative advantage (i.e., lowest opportunity cost) for manufacturing high-quality cars? For low-quality cars?

	Opportunity Cost of Making One High-Quality Car	Opportunity Cost of Making One Low-Quality Car
North	___ low-quality cars	___ high-quality cars
South	___ low-quality cars	___ high-quality cars

c. One million hours of labor are available for making cars in the North, and another 1 million hours of labor are available for making cars in the South. In a no-trade world, let's assume that two-thirds of the auto industry labor in each region is used to make high-quality cars and one-third is used to make low-quality cars. Solve for how many of each kind of car will be produced in the North and South, and add up to determine the total global output of each type of car. (Why will both kinds of cars be made? Because the low-quality cars will be less expensive.)

	Output of High-Quality Cars	Output of Low-Quality Cars
North		
South		
Global output		

d. Now allow specialization. If each region completely specializes in the type of car in which it holds the comparative advantage, what will the global output of high-quality cars be? Of low-quality cars? In the following table, report your answers. Is global output in each kind of car higher than before? (We'll solve a problem with the final step of trade in the Thinking and Problem Solving section.)

	Output of High-Quality Cars	Output of Low-Quality Cars
North		
South		
Global output		

6. It has been reported that John Lennon was once asked whether Ringo was the best drummer in the world, and he quipped, "He's not even the best drummer in the Beatles!" (Paul also drummed on some of the White Album.) Assuming that this story is true and that Lennon was correct, explain, using economics, why it could still make sense to have Ringo on drums.

THINKING AND PROBLEM SOLVING

7. Fit each of the following examples into one of these reasons for trade:

I. *Division of knowledge*

II. *Comparative advantage*

a. Two recently abandoned cats, Bingo and Tuppy, need to quickly learn how to catch mice in order to survive. If they also remain well groomed, they stand a better chance of surviving: Good grooming reduces the risk of disease and parasites. Each cat could go it alone, focusing almost exclusively on learning to catch mice. The alternative would be for Bingo to specialize in learning how to groom well and for Tuppy to specialize in learning how to catch mice well.

b. Supreme Court Chief Justice John Roberts hires attorneys who are less skilled than himself to do his taxes and routine legal work.

8. Nobel laureate Paul Samuelson said that comparative advantage is one of the few ideas in economics that is both "true and not

obvious." Since it's not obvious, we should practice with it a bit. In each of the cases, who has the absolute advantage at each task, and who has the comparative advantage?

a. In 30 minutes, Kana can either make miso soup or she can clean the kitchen. In 15 minutes, Mitchell can make miso soup; it takes Mitchell an hour to clean the kitchen.

b. In one hour, Ethan can bake 20 cookies or lay the drywall for two rooms. In one hour, Sienna can bake 100 cookies or lay the drywall for three rooms.

c. Kara can build two glass sculptures per day or she can design two full-page newspaper advertisements per day. Sara can build one glass sculpture per day or design four full-page newspaper ads per day.

d. Data can write 12 excellent poems per day or solve 100 difficult physics problems per day. Riker can write one excellent poem per day or solve 0.5 difficult physics problems per day.

9. The federal education reform law known as No Child Left Behind requires every state to create standardized tests that measure whether students have mastered key subjects. Since the same test is given to all students in the same grade in the state, this encourages all schools within a state to cover the same material. According to the division of knowledge model, what are the costs of this approach?

10. In this chapter, we've often emphasized how specialization and exchange can create more *output*. But sometimes the output from voluntary exchange is difficult to measure and doesn't show up in GDP statistics. In each of the following cases, explain how the two parties involved might be able to make themselves *both* better off just by making a voluntary exchange.

a. Alan received two copies of *Gears of War* as birthday gifts. Burton received two copies of *Halo* as birthday gifts.

b. Jeb has a free subscription to *Field and Stream* but isn't interested in hunting. George has a free subscription to the *Miami Herald* but isn't all that interested in Florida news.

c. Pat has a lot of love to give, but it is worthless unless received by another. Terry is in the same sad situation.

11. Many people talk about manufacturing jobs leaving the United States and going to other places, like China. Why isn't it possible for all jobs to leave the United States and go overseas (as some people fear)?

12. Suppose the following table shows the number of labor hours needed to produce airplanes and automobiles in the United States and South Korea, but one of the numbers is unknown.

	Number of Hours to Produce One Airplane	Number of Hours to Produce One Auto
South Korea	2,000	?
United States	800	5

a. Without knowing the number of labor hours required to produce an auto in South Korea, you can't figure out which country has the comparative advantage in which good. Can you give an example of a number for the empty cell of the table that would give the United States the comparative advantage in the production of airplanes? What about South Korea?

b. Who has the absolute advantage in the production of airplanes? What about autos?

c. What exact number would you have to place in the empty cell of the table for it to be impossible that trade between the United States and South Korea could benefit both nations?

13. In the chapter, you saw how to create a production possibilities frontier for the United States and Mexico. Let's take a look at how to combine these PPFs to make one PPF for the U.S.–Mexico trade alliance. You'll use the same set of axes that was used in the chapter: computers on the vertical axis and shirts on the horizontal axis. Refer to Figure 2.1 and Table 2.1 as needed.

a. First, you need to plot the endpoints of the PPF by figuring out the maximum numbers of computers and shirts. If both the United States and Mexico produced only computers, how many would they produce? What if they only produced shirts? Plot these two points and label them as *A* (all computers) and *Z* (all shirts). The PPF for the U.S.–Mexico trade alliance is going to look a little different from the PPFs for the individual countries, so we don't want to simply connect the two points with a straight line. We need to figure out the rate at which the U.S.–Mexico trade alliance gives up computers to get shirts (or vice versa).

b. Starting at point *A*, if citizens of the United States or Mexico decided they wanted more shirts, where would those shirts be produced? Why? What do you think the PPF should look like as the U.S.–Mexico trade alliance initially moves away from point *A*?

c. Starting at point *Z*, if citizens of the United States or Mexico decided they wanted more computers, where would those computers be produced? Why? What do you think the PPF should look like as the U.S.–Mexico trade alliance initially moves away from point *Z*?

d. Plot the point at which each country is completely specializing in the good for which it has the comparative advantage. Label this point *B*. Connect points *A*, *B*, and *Z*. This is the PPF for the U.S.–Mexico trade alliance. Can you describe how this PPF is a combination of the two nations' separate PPFs?

e. Suppose now that a third nation, Haiti, enters the trade alliance. In Haiti, the opportunity cost of a computer is 12 shirts, and Haiti has the labor necessary to produce 1 computer (or 12 shirts). Can you draw a new PPF for the U.S.–Mexico–Haiti trade alliance?

f. Okay, what will happen to the PPF as more and more countries join the trade alliance? What would it look like with an infinite number of countries?

CHALLENGES

14. In the computers and shirts example from the chapter, the United States traded one computer to Mexico in exchange for three shirts. This is not just an arbitrary ratio of shirts to computers, however. Let's explore the *terms of trade* a little bit more.

a. Why is trading away a computer for three shirts a good trade for the United States? Why is it also a good deal for Mexico?

b. What if, instead, the agreed-upon terms of trade were one computer for eight shirts. Would this trade still benefit both the United States and Mexico?

c. What is the maximum (and minimum) number of shirts that a computer can trade for if the United States and Mexico are both to benefit from the trade?

15. Go to *www.Ted.com* and search for Thomas Thwaites's talk, "How I Built a Toaster—from Scratch." How much money and time do you think Thwaites spent building his toaster? How long do you think it would have taken Thwaites to earn enough money in, say, a minimum wage job to buy a toaster? Comment on the division of labor and the importance of specialization in increasing productivity.

WORK IT OUT

For interactive, step-by-step help in solving the following problem, go online.

Here's another specialization and exchange problem. This problem is wholly made-up, so that you won't be able to use your intuition about the names of countries or the products to figure out the answer.

a. Consider the following productivity table: Which country has an absolute advantage at making rotids? At making taurons?

	Number of Hours to Make One Rotid	Number of Hours to Make One Tauron
Mandovia	50	100
Ducennia	150	200

b. Using the information in the productivity table, estimate the opportunity cost of making rotids and taurons in Mandovia and Ducennia. Which country has a comparative advantage at manufacturing rotids? At making taurons?

	Opportunity Cost of Making One Rotid	Opportunity Cost of Making One Tauron
Mandovia	___ taurons	___ rotids
Ducennia	___ taurons	___ rotids

c. One billion hours of labor are available for making products in Mandovia, and 2 billion hours of labor are available for making products in Ducennia. In a no-trade world, let's assume that half the labor in each country gets used to make each product. (In a semester-long international trade course, you'd build a bigger model that would determine just how the workers are divided up according to the forces of supply and demand.) Fill in the table.

	Output of Rotids	Output of Taurons
Mandovia		
Ducennia		
Total output		

d. Now allow specialization. If each country completely specializes in the product in which it holds the comparative advantage, what will the total output of rotids be? Of taurons? Is the total output of each product higher than before?

	Output of Rotids	Output of Taurons
Mandovia		
Ducennia		
Total output		

e. Finally, let's open up trade. Trade has to make both sides better off (or at least no worse off), and in this problem as in most negotiations, there's more than one price that can do so (just think about haggling over the price of a car or a house). Let's pick out a

case that makes one side better off and leaves the other side just as well off as in a no-trade world. The price both sides agree to is three rotids for two taurons. Ship 5 million taurons in one direction, and 7.5 million rotids in the other direction (you'll have to figure out on your own which way the trade flows). In the following table, calculate the amount that each country gets to consume. Which country is better off under this set of prices? Which one is exactly as well off as before?

	Consumption of Rotids	Consumption of Taurons
Mandovia		
Ducennia		
Total consumption		

f. This time, the trade negotiations turn out differently: It's two rotids for one tauron. Have the correct country ship 10 million rotids, have the other send 5 million taurons, and fill out the table. One way to make sure you haven't made a mistake is to make sure that "total consumption" is equal to "total output" from part d: We can't create rotids and taurons out of thin air! Are both countries better off than if there were no trade? Which country likes this trade deal better than the deal from part e?

	Consumption of Rotids	Consumption of Taurons
Mandovia		
Ducennia		
Total consumption		

MARGINAL REVOLUTION UNIVERSITY VIDEOS

The Big Ideas of Trade

mruniversity.com/trade-ideas

Problems: **2, 6, 7, 9, 10**

Comparative Advantage

mruniversity.com/comp-advantage

Problems: **1, 2, 7, 9, 10**

Another Look at Comparative Advantage

mruniversity.com/comp-advantage-2

Problems: **1–6, 7, 8, 10, 12**

Comparative Advantage Homework

mruniversity.com/comp-advantage-hw

Problems: **5, 9, 10, 14**

How the Division of Knowledge Saved My Son's Life

mruniversity.com/division-labor

3

Supply and Demand

The world runs on oil. Every day about 82 *million* barrels of "black gold" flow from the earth and the sea to fuel the world's demand. Changes in the demand for and supply of oil can plunge one economy into recession while igniting a boom in another. In capitals from Washington to Riyadh, politicians carefully monitor the price of oil and so do ordinary consumers. Gasoline is made from oil so when world events like war in the Middle East disrupt the oil supply, prices at the corner gas station rise. The oil market is arguably the single most important market in the world.

The most important tools in economics are supply, demand, and the idea of equilibrium. Even if you understand little else, you may rightly claim yourself economically literate if you understand these tools. Fail to understand these tools and you will understand little else. In this chapter, we use the supply and demand for oil to explain the concepts of supply and demand. In the next chapter, we use supply, demand, and the idea of equilibrium to explain how prices are determined. So pay attention: This chapter and the next one are important. Really important.

The Demand Curve for Oil

How much oil would be demanded if the price of oil were $5 per barrel? What quantity would be demanded if the price were $20? What quantity would be demanded if the price were $55? A demand curve answers these questions. A **demand curve** is a function that shows the quantity demanded at different prices.

In Figure 3.1 on the next page, we show a hypothetical demand curve for oil and a table illustrating how a demand curve can be constructed from information on prices and quantities demanded. The demand curve tells us, for example, that at a price of $55 per barrel buyers are willing and able to buy 5 million barrels of oil a day or, more simply, at a price of $55 the **quantity demanded** is 5 million barrels a day (MBD).

Demand curves can be read in two ways. Read "horizontally," we can see from Figure 3.2 that at a price of $20 per barrel demanders are willing and able to buy 25 million barrels of oil per day. Read "vertically," we can see that the maximum price that demanders are willing to pay for 25 million barrels of oil a day is $20 per barrel. Thus, demand curves tell us the quantity demanded at

A **demand curve** is a function that shows the quantity demanded at different prices.

The **quantity demanded** is the quantity that buyers are willing and able to buy at a particular price.

29

FIGURE 3.1

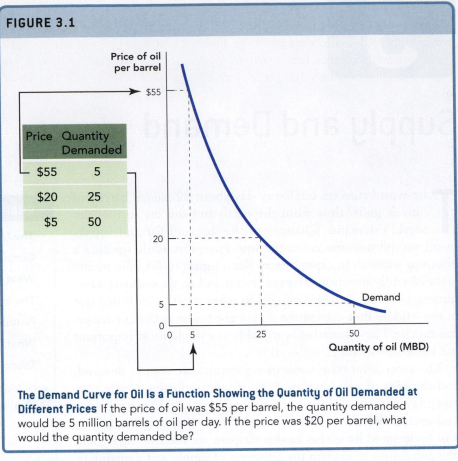

Price	Quantity Demanded
$55	5
$20	25
$5	50

The Demand Curve for Oil Is a Function Showing the Quantity of Oil Demanded at Different Prices If the price of oil was $55 per barrel, the quantity demanded would be 5 million barrels of oil per day. If the price was $20 per barrel, what would the quantity demanded be?

any price or the maximum willingness to pay (per unit) for any quantity. Some applications are easier to understand with one reading than with the other so you should be familiar with both.

Ok, a demand curve is a function that shows the quantity that demanders are willing to buy at different prices. But what does the demand curve *mean*? And why is the demand curve negatively sloped; that is, why is a greater quantity of oil demanded when the price is low?

FIGURE 3.2

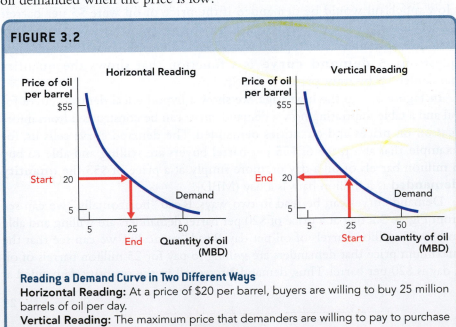

Reading a Demand Curve in Two Different Ways
Horizontal Reading: At a price of $20 per barrel, buyers are willing to buy 25 million barrels of oil per day.
Vertical Reading: The maximum price that demanders are willing to pay to purchase 25 million barrels of oil per day is $20 per barrel.

Oil has many uses. A barrel of oil contains 42 gallons, and a little over half of that is used to produce gasoline (19.5 gallons) and jet fuel (4 gallons). The remaining 18.5 gallons are used for heating and energy generation and to make products such as lubricants, kerosene, asphalt, plastics, tires, and even rubber duckies (which are actually made not from rubber but from vinyl plastic).

Oil, *however, is not equally valuable in all of its uses*. Oil is more valuable for producing gasoline and jet fuel than it is for producing heating or rubber duckies. Oil is very valuable for transportation because in that use oil has few substitutes. There is no reasonable substitute for oil as jet fuel, for example, and although some hybrids like the Prius are moderately successful, pure electric cars like the Tesla remain costly. There are more substitutes for oil in heating and energy generation. In these fields, oil competes directly or indirectly against natural gas, coal, and electricity. Within each of these fields there are also more and less valuable uses. It's more valuable, for example, to raise the temperature in your house on a winter's day from 40 degrees to 65 degrees than it is to raise the temperature from 65 degrees to 70 degrees. Vinyl has high value as wire wrapping because it is fire-retardant, but we can probably substitute wooden toy boats for rubber duckies.

The fact that oil is not equally valuable in all of its uses explains why the demand curve for oil has a negative slope. When the price of oil is high, consumers will choose to use oil *only* in its most valuable uses (e.g., gasoline and jet fuel). As the price of oil falls, consumers will choose to also use oil in its less and less valued uses (heating and rubber duckies). Thus, a demand curve summarizes how millions of consumers choose to use oil given their preferences and the possibilities for substitution. Figure 3.3 illustrates these ideas with a demand curve for oil.

In summary, a demand curve is a function that shows the quantity that demanders are willing and able to buy at different prices. The lower the

interactive activity

Why Does the Demand Curve Slope Down and Why Is This Important?

FIGURE 3.3

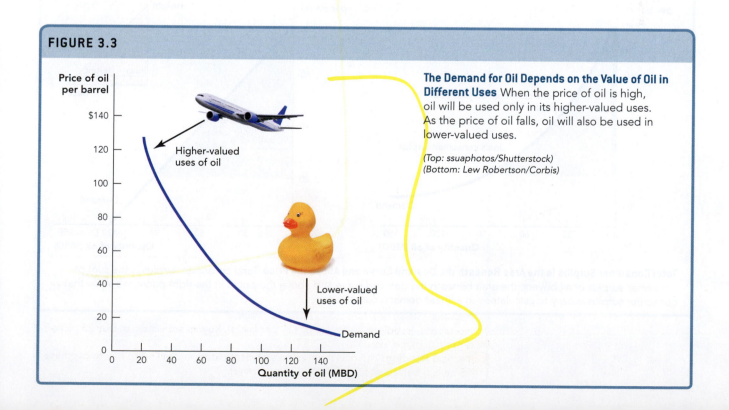

Higher-valued uses of oil

Lower-valued uses of oil

Demand

Price of oil per barrel

Quantity of oil (MBD)

The Demand for Oil Depends on the Value of Oil in Different Uses When the price of oil is high, oil will be used only in its higher-valued uses. As the price of oil falls, oil will also be used in lower-valued uses.

(Top: ssuaphotos/Shutterstock)
(Bottom: Lew Robertson/Corbis)

price, the greater the quantity demanded—this is often called the "law of demand."

Consumer Surplus

If a consumer, say, the president of the United States, is willing to pay $80 per barrel to fuel his jet plane but the price of oil is only $20 per barrel, then the president earns a consumer surplus of $60 per barrel. If Joe is willing to pay $25 and the price of oil is $20 per barrel, then Joe earns a consumer surplus of $5 per barrel. For most of the products that you buy, you would probably be willing to pay more than the price, if you had to. The difference between what you are willing to pay and what you must pay (the price) is consumer surplus. Put differently, consumer surplus is the consumer's gain from exchange. **Consumer surplus** is the consumer's gain from exchange. Adding up consumer surplus for each consumer and for each unit, we can find **total consumer surplus**. On a graph, *total consumer surplus is the shaded area beneath the demand curve and above the price* (see Figure 3.4).

It's often convenient to approximate demand and supply curves with straight lines—this makes it easy to calculate areas like consumer surplus. The right panel of Figure 3.4 simplifies the left panel. Now we can calculate consumer surplus using a little high school geometry. Recall that the area of a triangle is $\frac{\text{Base} \times \text{Height}}{2}$. The base of the consumer surplus triangle is 90 million barrels and the height is $60 = \$80 - \$20$, so consumer surplus equals \$2,700 million ($\frac{1}{2} \times$ 90 million $\times$ \$60).

> **Consumer surplus** is the consumer's gain from exchange, or the difference between the maximum price a consumer is willing to pay for a certain quantity and the market price.
>
> **Total consumer surplus** is measured by the area beneath the demand curve and above the price.

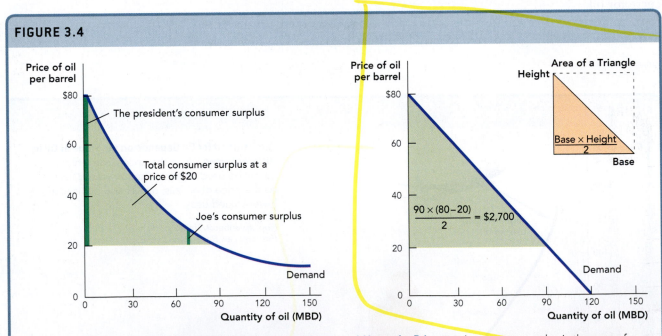

FIGURE 3.4

Total Consumer Surplus Is the Area Beneath the Demand Curve and Above the Price Total consumer surplus is the sum of consumer surplus of all buyers, the area beneath the demand curve and above the price. In the right panel, we show that consumer surplus is easy to calculate with a linear demand curve.

What Shifts the Demand Curve?

The demand curve for oil tells us the quantity of oil that people are willing to buy at a given price. Assume, for example, that at a price of $25 per barrel, the world demand for oil is 70 million barrels per day. An increase in demand means that at a price of $25, the quantity demanded increases to, say, 80 million barrels per day. Or, equivalently, it means that the maximum willingness to pay for 70 million barrels increases to say $50 per barrel. The left panel of Figure 3.5 shows an increase in demand. *An increase in demand shifts the demand curve outward, up and to the right.*

The right panel of Figure 3.5 shows a decrease in demand. *A decrease in demand shifts the demand curve inward, down and to the left.*

What kinds of things will increase or decrease demand? Unfortunately for economics students, a lot of things! Here is a list of some important demand shifters:

Important Demand Shifters

- Income
- Population
- Price of substitutes
- Price of complements
- Expectations
- Tastes

If you must, memorize the list. But keep in mind the question, "What would make people willing to buy a greater quantity at the same price?" Or equivalently, "What would make people willing to pay more for the same quantity?" With these questions in mind, you should always be able to come up with a fairly good list on your own.

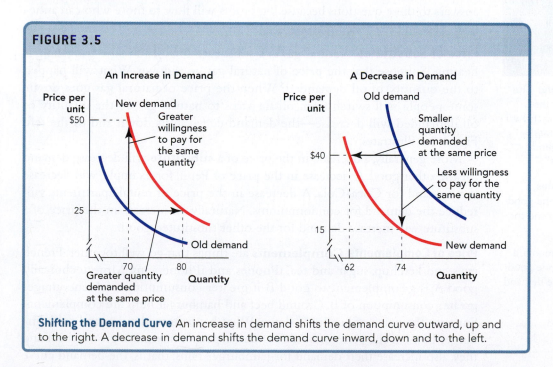

FIGURE 3.5

An Increase in Demand

A Decrease in Demand

Shifting the Demand Curve An increase in demand shifts the demand curve outward, up and to the right. A decrease in demand shifts the demand curve inward, down and to the left.

A **normal good** is a good for which demand increases when income increases.

An **inferior good** is a good for which demand decreases when income increases.

MARK HAMILTON/FLIRT/CORBIS/GLOW IMAGES

Demographics and demand The number of old people in the United States is increasing. How will this increase in the elderly population shift the demand curve for different goods?

If two goods are **substitutes**, a decrease in the price of one good leads to a decrease in demand for the other good.

If two goods are **complements**, a decrease in the price of one good leads to an increase in the demand for the other good.

Here are some examples of demand shifters in action.

Income When people get richer, they buy more stuff. In the United States, people buy bigger cars when their income increases and big cars increase the demand for oil. When income increases in China or India, many people buy their first car and that too increases the demand for oil. Thus, an increase in income will increase the demand for oil exactly as shown in the left panel of Figure 3.5.

When an *increase* in income *increases* the demand for a good, we say the good is a **normal good**. Most goods are normal; for example, cars, electronics, and restaurant meals are normal goods. Can you think of some goods for which an increase in income will *decrease* the demand? When we were young economics students, we didn't have a lot of money to go to expensive restaurants. For 50 cents and some boiling water, however, we could get a nice bowl of instant Ramen noodles. Ah, good times. When our income increased, however, our demand for Ramen noodles decreased—we don't buy Ramen noodles anymore! A good like Ramen noodles for which an *increase* in income *decreases* the demand is called an **inferior good**. What goods are you consuming now that you probably wouldn't consume if you were rich? Economic growth is rapidly increasing the incomes of millions of poor people in China and India. What goods do poor people consume in these countries today that they will consume less of 20 years from now?

Population More people, more demand. That's simple enough. Things get more interesting when some subpopulations increase more than others. The United States, for example, is aging. Today the 65-year-old and older crowd makes up about 14.5 percent of the population. By 2030, 19.4 percent of the population will be 65 years or older. In fact, demographers estimate that by 2030, 18.2 million people in the United States will be over 85 years of age![1] What sorts of goods and services will increase in demand with this increase in population? Which will decrease in demand? Entrepreneurs want to know the answers to these questions because big profits will flow to those who can anticipate new and expanded markets.

Price of Substitutes Natural gas is a substitute for oil in some uses such as heating. Suppose that the price of natural gas goes down. What will happen to the quantity of oil demanded? When the price of natural gas goes down, some people will switch from oil furnaces to natural gas, so the quantity of oil demanded will decrease—the demand curve shifts down and to the left. Figure 3.6 illustrates.

More generally, a decrease in the price of a **substitute** will decrease demand for the other good. A decrease in the price of Pepsi, for example, will decrease the demand for Coca-Cola. A decrease in the price of rental apartments will reduce the demand for condominiums. Naturally, an increase in the price of a substitute will increase demand for the other substituted good.

Price of Complements **Complements** are things that go well together: French fries and ketchup, sugar and tea, iPhones and iPhone apps. More technically, good A is a complement to good B if greater consumption of A encourages greater consumption of B. Ground beef and hamburger buns are complements. Suppose the price of beef goes down. What happens to the demand for hamburger buns? If the price of beef goes down, people buy more ground beef and they also increase their demand for hamburger buns; that is, the demand curve for hamburger buns shifts up and to the right. A supermarket having a sale on ground beef, for example, will also want to stock up on hamburger buns.

FIGURE 3.6

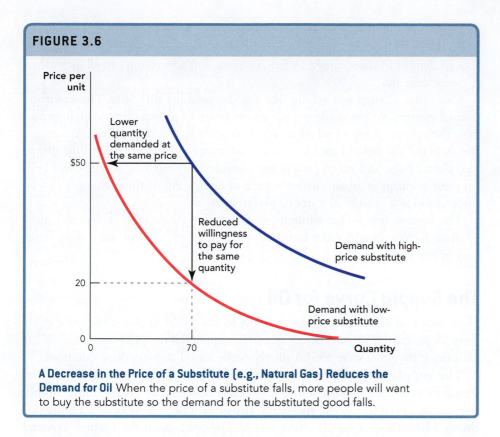

A Decrease in the Price of a Substitute (e.g., Natural Gas) Reduces the Demand for Oil When the price of a substitute falls, more people will want to buy the substitute so the demand for the substituted good falls.

A decrease in the price of a complement increases the demand for the complementary good. An increase in the price of a complement decreases the demand for the complementary good. It sounds complicated, so just remember that ground beef and hamburger buns are complements and you should be able to work out the relationship.

Expectations In July 2007, a construction worker in the oil fields of southern Nigeria was kidnapped. On hearing the news, oil prices around the world jumped to record high levels.[2] Was a single construction worker so critical to the world supply of oil? No. What spooked the world's oil markets was the fear that the kidnapping was the beginning of large-scale disruption in the Niger Delta, Nigeria's main oil-producing region and the base for many antigovernment rebels. Fear of future disruptions increased the demand for oil as businesses and governments worked to increase their emergency stockpiles. In other words, *the expectation of a reduction in the future oil supply increased the demand for oil today.*

You have probably responded to expectations about future events in a similar way. When the weather forecaster predicts a big storm, many people rush to the stores to stock up on storm supplies. In the week before Hurricane Sandy hit New Jersey, for example, sales of flashlights and batteries skyrocketed.

Expectations are powerful—they can be as powerful in affecting demand (and supply) as events themselves.

Tastes In the 1990s, doctors warned that too much fat could lead to heart attacks and demand for beef decreased. The 2001 publication of *Dr. Atkins' New Diet Revolution*, a book promising weight loss on a high-protein, low-carb diet, increased the demand for beef. Steakhouses like Outback Steakhouse and the Brazilian-inspired Fogo De Chão started to appear everywhere.

LeBron James's three NBA championships, four Most Valuable Player awards, and two Olympic gold medals have made him one of the most sought after

CHECK YOURSELF

■ Economic growth in India is raising the income of Indian workers. What do you predict will happen to the demand for automobiles? What about the demand for charcoal bricks for home heating?

■ As the price of oil rises, what do you predict will happen to the demand for mopeds?

The **supply curve** is a function that shows the quantity supplied at different prices.

The **quantity supplied** is the amount of a good that sellers are willing and able to sell at a particular price.

athletes in the world for product endorsements. Nike pays LeBron millions of dollars. Why? Because LeBron's endorsement increases the demand for Nike shoes. Changes in tastes caused by fads, fashions, and advertising can all increase or decrease demand.

Can tastes change something like the demand for oil? Sure. The environmental movement has made people more aware of global climate change and how the consumption of oil adds carbon dioxide to the atmosphere. As a result, the demand for hybrid cars has increased, more people are recycling things like plastic bags, and more people are considering installing solar power cells on their rooftops as an alternative source of energy. All of these changes can be understood as a change in tastes or preferences.

The bottom line is that while many factors can shape market demand, most of these factors should make intuitive sense. After all, you are, on a daily basis, part of market demand.

The Supply Curve for Oil

How much oil would oil producers supply to the world market if the price of oil were $5 per barrel? What quantity would be supplied if the price were $20? What quantity if the price were $55? A supply curve for oil answers these questions.

The **supply curve** for oil is a function showing the quantity of oil that suppliers would be willing and able to sell at different prices, or, more simply, the supply curve shows the **quantity supplied** at different prices. Figure 3.7 shows a hypothetical supply curve for oil. The price is on the vertical axis and the quantity of oil is on the horizontal axis. The table beside the graph shows

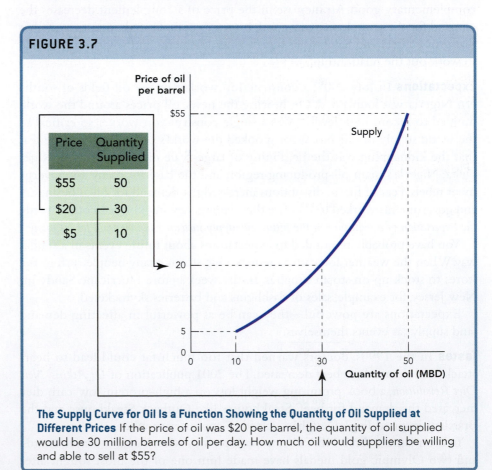

FIGURE 3.7

Price	Quantity Supplied
$55	50
$20	30
$5	10

The Supply Curve for Oil Is a Function Showing the Quantity of Oil Supplied at Different Prices If the price of oil was $20 per barrel, the quantity of oil supplied would be 30 million barrels of oil per day. How much oil would suppliers be willing and able to sell at $55?

how a supply curve can be constructed from a table of prices and quantities supplied.

The supply curve tells us, for example, that at a price of $20 the quantity supplied is 30 million barrels of oil a day.

As with demand curves, supply curves can be read in two ways. Read "horizontally," Figure 3.8 shows that at a price of $20 per barrel suppliers are willing to sell 30 million barrels of oil per day. Read "vertically," the supply curve tells us that to produce 30 million barrels of oil a day, suppliers must be paid at least $20 per barrel. Thus, the supply curve tells us the maximum quantity that suppliers will supply at different prices or the minimum price at which suppliers will sell different quantities. The two ways of reading a supply curve are equivalent, but some applications are easier to understand with one reading and some with the other so you should be familiar with both.

Our hypothetical supply curve is not realistic because we just made up the numbers. But now that we know the technical meaning of a supply curve—*a function that shows the quantity that suppliers would be willing and able to sell at different prices*—we can easily explain its economic meaning.

Saudi Arabia, the world's largest oil producer, produces about 10 million barrels of oil per day. Surprisingly, the United States is not far behind, producing nearly 9 million barrels per day. But there is one big difference between Saudi oil and U.S. oil: U.S. oil costs much more to produce. The United States has been producing major quantities of oil since 1901 when, after drilling to a depth of 1,020 feet, mud started to bubble out of an oil well dug in Spindletop, Texas. Minutes later the drill bit exploded into the air and a fountain of oil leapt 150 feet into the sky. It took nine days to cap the well, and in the process a million barrels of oil were spilt. No one had ever seen so much oil. Within months the price of oil dropped from $2 per barrel to just 3 cents per barrel.[3]

It's safe to say that the United States will never see another gusher like Spindletop. Today the typical new well in the United States is drilled to a depth of more than 1 mile. Instead of gushing, most of the wells must be pumped or flooded with water to push the oil to the surface.[4] All this makes oil production

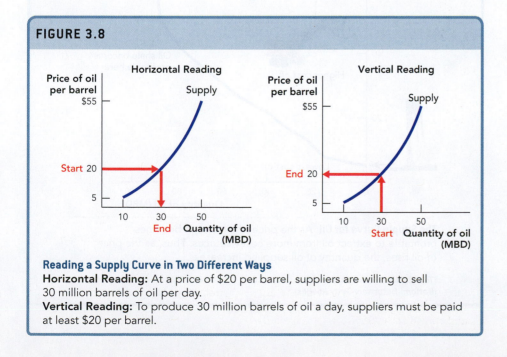

FIGURE 3.8

Reading a Supply Curve in Two Different Ways
Horizontal Reading: At a price of $20 per barrel, suppliers are willing to sell 30 million barrels of oil per day.
Vertical Reading: To produce 30 million barrels of oil a day, suppliers must be paid at least $20 per barrel.

Why Do (most) Supply Curves Slope Up and Why Is This Important?

in the United States much more expensive than it used to be and much more expensive than in Saudi Arabia, where oil is more plentiful than anywhere else in the world.

In Saudi Arabia, lifting a barrel of oil to the surface costs about $2. Costs in Iran and Iraq are only slightly higher. Nigerian and Russian oil can be extracted at a cost of around $5 and $7 per barrel, respectively. Alaskan oil costs around $10 to extract. Oil from Britain's North Sea costs about $12 to extract. There is more oil in Canada's tar sands than in all of Iran, but it costs about $22.50 per barrel to get the oil out of the sand.[5] In the continental United States, one of the oldest and most developed oil regions in the world, lifting costs are about $27.50. At a price of $40 per barrel, it becomes profitable to "sweat" oil out of Oklahoma oil shale.

Putting all of this together, we can construct a simple supply curve for oil. At a price of $2 per barrel, the only oil that would be profitable to produce would be oil from the lowest-cost wells in places like Saudi Arabia. As the price of oil rises, oil from Iran and Iraq become profitable. When the price reaches $5, Nigerian and then Russian producers begin to just break even. As the price rises yet further toward $10, Alaskan oil starts to break even and then become profitable. North Sea, Canadian, and then Texan oil fields come online and increase production as the price rises further. At higher prices, it becomes profitable to extract oil using even more exotic technologies or deeper wells in more inhospitable parts of the world. Figure 3.9 illustrates.

FIGURE 3.9

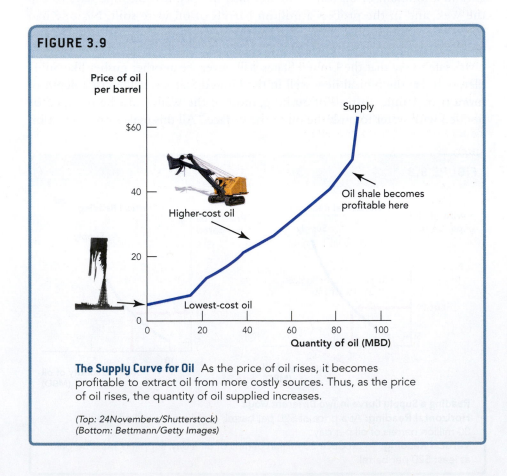

The Supply Curve for Oil As the price of oil rises, it becomes profitable to extract oil from more costly sources. Thus, as the price of oil rises, the quantity of oil supplied increases.

(Top: 24Novembers/Shutterstock)
(Bottom: Bettmann/Getty Images)

What's important to understand about Figure 3.9 is that as the price of oil rises, it becomes profitable to produce oil using methods and in regions of the world with higher costs of production. The higher the price of oil, the deeper the wells.

In summary, a supply curve is a function that shows the quantity that suppliers would be willing and able to sell at different prices. The higher the price, the greater the quantity supplied—this is often called the "law of supply."

Producer Surplus

Figure 3.9 suggests two other concepts of importance. If the price of oil is $40 per barrel and Saudi Arabia can produce oil at $2 per barrel, then we say that Saudi Arabia earns a **producer surplus** of $38 per barrel. Similarly, if the price of oil is $40 per barrel and Nigeria can produce at $5 a barrel, Nigeria earns a producer surplus of $35 per barrel. More generally, the difference between the lowest price that a producer is willing to sell a good for and the actual price is the producer's surplus, the producer's gain from exchange. Adding the producer surplus for each producer for each unit, we can find total producer surplus. Fortunately, this is easy to do on a diagram. *Total producer surplus is the area above the supply curve and below the price* (see Figure 3.10).

Consumer surplus measures the consumer's benefit from trade, and producer surplus measures the producer's benefit from trade. If we add the two surpluses together, we get a measure of the total gains from trade, to market participants. All else equal, more benefits are better so throughout this text, we will be using consumer plus producer surplus as a measure of welfare to compare different institutions and policies such as markets, monopolies, price controls, quotas, taxes and subsidies. Which of these institutions maximizes total benefits and under what conditions? Of course, sometimes not all else is equal, and in Chapter 10 on externalities and in Chapter 21 on ethics, we will be looking at situations where it's important to add to our measure of benefits (and costs) to take into account the effect of trade on bystanders and on broader social interests.

> **Producer surplus** is the producer's gain from exchange, or the difference between the market price and the minimum price at which a producer would be willing to sell a particular quantity.

> **Total producer surplus** is measured by the area above the supply curve and below the price.

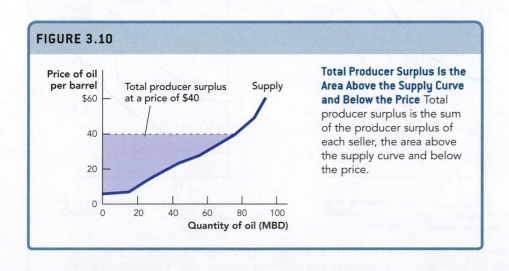

FIGURE 3.10

Total Producer Surplus Is the Area Above the Supply Curve and Below the Price Total producer surplus is the sum of the producer surplus of each seller, the area above the supply curve and below the price.

What Shifts the Supply Curve?

The second important concept suggested by Figure 3.9 is the connection between the supply curve and costs. What happens to the supply curve when the cost of producing oil falls? Suppose, for example, that a technological innovation in oil drilling such as sidewise drilling allows more oil to be produced at the same cost. What happens to the supply curve? The supply curve tells us how much suppliers are willing to sell at a particular price. The new technology makes some oil fields profitable that were previously unprofitable, so *at any price* suppliers are now willing to supply a greater quantity. Equivalently, the new technology lowers costs, so suppliers will be willing to sell any given quantity at a lower price. Either way, economists say that a decrease in costs increases supply. In terms of the diagram, *a decrease in costs means that the supply curve shifts down and to the right,* which the left panel of Figure 3.11 illustrates. Of course, *higher costs mean that the supply curve shifts in the opposite direction, up and to the left* as illustrated in the right panel of Figure 3.11.

Once you know that a decrease in costs shifts the supply curve down and to the right and an increase in costs shifts the supply curve up and to the left, then you really know everything there is to know about supply shifts. It can take a little practice, however, to identify the many factors that can change costs. Here are some important supply shifters:

Important Supply Shifters

- Technological innovations and changes in the price of inputs
- Taxes and subsidies
- Expectations
- Entry or exit of producers
- Changes in opportunity costs

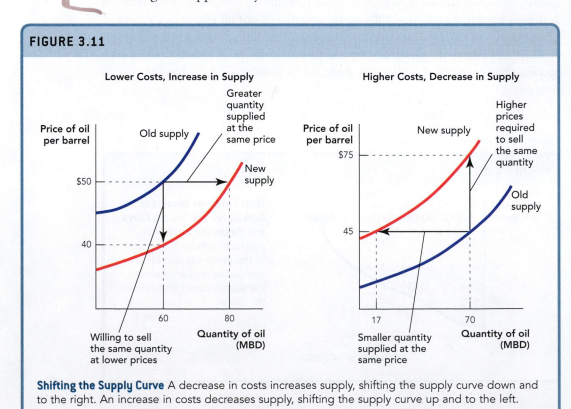

FIGURE 3.11

Lower Costs, Increase in Supply

Higher Costs, Decrease in Supply

Shifting the Supply Curve A decrease in costs increases supply, shifting the supply curve down and to the right. An increase in costs decreases supply, shifting the supply curve up and to the left.

It can also help in analyzing supply shifters to know that sometimes it's easier to think of cost changes as shifting the supply curve right or left, and other
times it's a little easier to think of cost changes as shifting the supply curve up
or down. These two methods of thinking about supply shifts are equivalent
and correspond to the two methods of reading a supply curve, the horizontal
and vertical readings, respectively. We will give examples of each method as we
examine some cost shifters in action.

Technological Innovations and Changes in the Price of Inputs We have already
given an example of how improvements in technology can reduce costs, thus
increasing supply. A reduction in input prices also reduces costs and thus has a
similar effect. A fall in the wages of oil rig workers, for example, will reduce the
cost of producing oil, shifting the supply curve down and to the right as in the
left panel of Figure 3.11. Alternatively, an increase in the wages of oil rig workers will increase the cost of producing oil, shifting the supply curve up and to
the left as in the right panel of Figure 3.11.

Taxes and Subsidies We can get some practice using up or down shifts to analyze a cost change by examining the effect of a $10 oil tax on the supply curve
for oil. As far as firms are concerned, a tax on output is the same as an increase
in costs. If the government taxes oil producers $10 per barrel, this is exactly the
same to producers as an increase in their costs of production of $10 per barrel.

In Figure 3.12, notice that before the tax, firms require $40 per barrel to sell
60 million barrels of oil per day (point *a*). How much will firms require to sell
the same quantity of oil when there is a tax of $10 per barrel? Correct, $50.
What firms care about is the take-home price. If firms require $40 per barrel to
sell 60 million barrels of oil, that's what they require regardless of the tax. When
the government takes $10 per barrel, firms must charge $50 to keep their take-
home price at $40. Thus, in Figure 3.12, notice that the $10 tax shifts the supply curve up by exactly $10 at *every point* along the curve.

It's important to avoid one possible confusion. All we have said so far is that a
$10 tax shifts the supply curve for oil up by $10. We haven't said anything about
the effect of a tax on the *price* of oil—that's because we have not yet analyzed
how market prices are formed. We are saving that topic for Chapter 4.

FIGURE 3.12

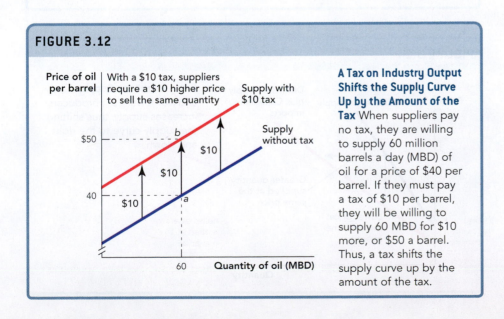

A Tax on Industry Output
Shifts the Supply Curve
Up by the Amount of the
Tax When suppliers pay
no tax, they are willing
to supply 60 million
barrels a day (MBD) of
oil for a price of $40 per
barrel. If they must pay
a tax of $10 per barrel,
they will be willing to
supply 60 MBD for $10
more, or $50 a barrel.
Thus, a tax shifts the
supply curve up by the
amount of the tax.

How does a subsidy, a tax-benefit, or write-off shift the supply curve? We will save that analysis for the end-of-chapter problems but here's a hint: A subsidy is the same as a negative or "reverse" tax.

Expectations Suppliers who expect that prices will increase in the future have an incentive to sell less today so that they can store goods for future sale. Thus, the expectation of a future price increase shifts today's supply curve to the left as illustrated in Figure 3.13. The shifting of supply in response to price expectations is the essence of *speculation*, the attempt to profit from future price changes.

Entry or Exit of Producers When the United States signed the North American Free Trade Agreement (NAFTA), reducing barriers to trade among the United States, Mexico, and Canada, Canadian producers of lumber entered the U.S. market and increased the supply of lumber. We can most easily think about this as a shift to the right of the supply curve.

In Figure 3.14, the domestic supply curve is the supply curve for lumber before NAFTA. The curve labeled domestic supply plus Canadian imports is the supply curve for lumber after NAFTA allowed Canadian firms to sell in the United States with fewer restrictions. The entry of more firms meant

FIGURE 3.13

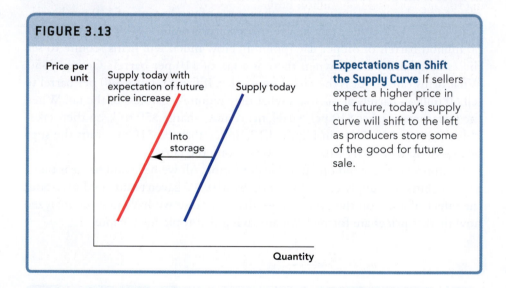

Expectations Can Shift the Supply Curve If sellers expect a higher price in the future, today's supply curve will shift to the left as producers store some of the good for future sale.

FIGURE 3.14

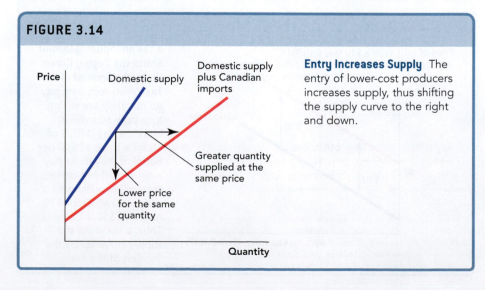

Entry Increases Supply The entry of lower-cost producers increases supply, thus shifting the supply curve to the right and down.

that at any price a greater quantity of lumber was available; that is, the supply curve shifted to the right.*

In a later chapter, we discuss the effects of foreign trade at greater length.

Changes in Opportunity Costs The last important supply shifter, changes in opportunity costs, is the trickiest to understand. Recall from Chapter 1 that when the unemployment rates increase, more people tend to go to college. If you can't get a job, you aren't giving up many good opportunities by going to college. Thus, when the unemployment rate increases, the (opportunity) cost of college falls and so more people attend college. Notice that to understand how people behave, you must understand their opportunity costs.

Now suppose that a farmer is currently growing soybeans but that his land could also be used to grow wheat. If the price of *wheat* increases, then the farmer's opportunity cost of growing soybeans increases and the farmer will want to shift land from soybean production into the more profitable alternative of wheat production. As land is taken out of soybean production, the supply curve for soybeans shifts up and to the left.

In Figure 3.15, notice that before the increase in the price of wheat, farmers would be willing to supply 2,800 million bushels of soybeans at a price of $5 per bushel (point *a*). But when the price of wheat increases, farmers are willing to supply only 2,000 million bushels of soybeans at a price of $5 per bushel because an alternative use of the land (growing wheat) is now more valuable. Equivalently, before the increase in the price of wheat, farmers were willing to sell 2,800 million bushels of soybeans for $5 per bushel, but after their opportunity costs increase, farmers require $7 per bushel to sell the same quantity (point *c*).

FIGURE 3.15

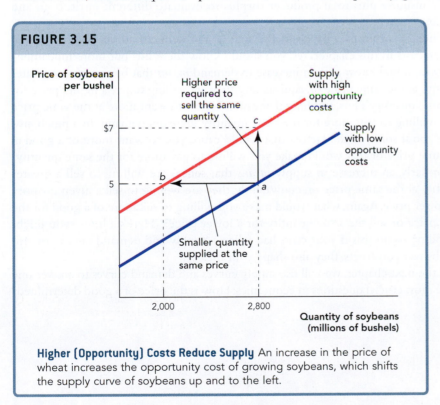

Higher (Opportunity) Costs Reduce Supply An increase in the price of wheat increases the opportunity cost of growing soybeans, which shifts the supply curve of soybeans up and to the left.

---

* It is equally correct to think of new entrants as shifting the supply curve down. Remember, it's ultimately costs that shift supply, and what increases supply is entry of *lower-cost* producers. Industry costs fell when Canadian producers entered the market because many Canadian producers had lower costs than some U.S. producers. As lower-cost Canadian producers entered the industry, higher-cost U.S. producers exited the industry, and industry costs decreased, thus shifting the supply curve down.

CHECK YOURSELF

■ Technological innovations in chip making have driven down the costs of producing computers. What happens to the supply curve for computers? Why?

■ The U.S. government subsidizes making ethanol as a fuel made from corn. What effect does the subsidy have on the supply curve for ethanol?

Similarly, a decrease in opportunity costs shifts the supply curve down and to the right. If the price of wheat falls, for example, the opportunity cost of growing soybeans falls and the supply curve for soybeans will shift down and to the right. It's just another example of a running theme throughout this chapter, namely that both supply and demand respond to incentives.

Takeaway

In this chapter, we have presented the fundamentals of the demand curve and the supply curve. The next chapter and much of the rest of this book build on these fundamentals. We thus give you fair warning. If you do not understand this chapter and the next, you will be lost!

A key point to know is that a demand curve is a function showing the quantity demanded at different prices. In other words, a demand curve shows how customers respond to higher prices by buying less and to lower prices by buying more. Another key point is that, similarly, a supply curve is a function showing the quantity supplied at different prices. In other words, a supply curve shows how producers respond to higher prices by producing more and to lower prices by producing less.

The difference between the maximum price a consumer is willing to pay for a product and the market price is the consumer's gain from exchange or consumer surplus. The difference between the market price and the minimum price at which a producer is willing to sell a product is the producer's gain from exchange or producer surplus. You should be able to identify total consumer and producer surplus, the total gain from exchange, on a diagram. In future chapters, we will be using total consumer plus total producer surplus to evaluate different institutions and policies.

When it comes to what shifts the supply and demand curves, we have listed some factors in this chapter. Yes, you should know these lists but more fundamentally you should know that an increase in demand *means* that buyers want a greater quantity at the same price or, equivalently, they are willing to pay a higher price for the same quantity. Thus, anything that causes buyers to want more at the same price or be willing to pay more for the same quantity increases demand. In a pinch, just think about some of the factors that would cause you to want more of a good at the same price or that would make you willing to pay more for the same quantity.

Similarly, an increase in supply *means* that sellers are willing to sell a greater quantity at the same price or, equivalently, they are willing to sell a given quantity at a lower price. Again, what would make you willing to sell more of a good for the same price or sell the same quantity for a lower price? (Here's a hint—you might be willing to do this if your costs had fallen.) Supply and demand curves are not just abstract constructs, they also shape your life.

In the next chapter, we will use supply curves and demand curves to answer one of the most crucial questions in economics: How is the price of a good determined?

CHAPTER REVIEW

 interactive activity Go online to practice with more examples of these types of problems, including live links to videos, data sources, and feedback.

Problems in **green** relate to MRU videos. See the MRU table at the end of the exercises.

KEY CONCEPTS

demand curve, p. 29

quantity demanded, p. 29

consumer surplus, p. 32

total consumer surplus, p. 32

normal good, p. 34

inferior good, p. 34

substitutes, p. 34

complements, p. 34

supply curve, p. 36

quantity supplied, p. 36

producer surplus, p. 39

total producer surplus, p. 39

FACTS AND TOOLS

1. When the price of a good increases, the quantity demanded _____. When the price of a good decreases, the quantity demanded _____.

2. When will people search harder for substitutes for oil: When the price of oil is high or when the price of oil is low?

3. Your roommate just bought a Nike+ Sportwatch for $160. She would have been willing to pay $250 for a device that could improve her morning runs by measuring the speed, distance, and duration of the runs, and calculating the calories she burns. How much consumer surplus does your roommate enjoy from the Nike+ Sportwatch?

4. What are three things that you'll buy less of once you graduate from college and get a good job? What kinds of goods are these called?

5. When the price of Apple MacBooks goes down, what probably happens to the demand for laptops featuring Microsoft Windows?

6. a. When the price of olive oil goes up, what probably happens to the demand for corn oil?

   b. When the price of petroleum goes up, what probably happens to the demand for natural gas? To the demand for coal? To the demand for solar power?

7. a. If everyone thinks that the price of tomatoes will go up next week, what is likely to happen to demand for tomatoes today?

   b. If everyone thinks that the price of gasoline will go up next week, what is likely to happen to the demand for gasoline today? (*Note:* Is this change in demand caused by consumers or by gas station owners?)

8. Along a supply curve, if the price of oil falls, what will happen to the quantity of oil supplied? Why?

9. If the price of cars falls, are carmakers likely to make more or fewer cars, according to the supply curve? (Notice that the "person on the street" often thinks the opposite is true!)

10. When is a pharmaceutical business more likely to hire highly educated, cutting-edge workers and use new, experimental research methods: When the business expects the price of its new drug to be low or when it expects the price to be high?

11. Imagine that a technological innovation reduces the costs of producing high-quality steel. What happens to the supply curve for steel?

12. When oil companies expect the price of oil to be higher next year, what happens to the supply of oil today?

13. Do taxes usually increase the supply of a good or reduce the supply?

THINKING AND PROBLEM SOLVING

14. Consider the following supply curve for oil. Note that MBD stands for "millions of barrels per day," the usual way people talk about the supply of oil:

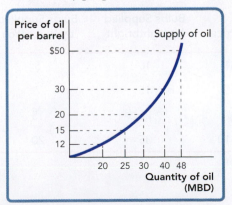

a. Based on this supply curve, fill in the table:

Price	Quantity Supplied
$12	
	40

b. If the price for a barrel of oil was $15, how much oil would oil suppliers be willing to supply?

c. What is the lowest price at which suppliers of oil would be willing to supply 20 MBD?

15. From the following table of prices per 100 pencils and quantities supplied (in hundreds of pencils), draw the supply curve for pencils:

Price	Quantity Supplied
$5	20
$15	40
$25	50
$35	55

16. Suppose LightBright and Bulbs4You were the only two suppliers of lightbulbs in Springfield. Draw the supply curve for the lightbulb industry in Springfield from the following table for the two companies. To create this "lightbulb industry supply curve," note that you'll add up the *total* number of bulbs that the industry will supply at a price of $1 (15 bulbs), and then do the same for the prices of $5, $7, and $10.

Price	Bulbs Supplied by Lightbright	Bulbs Supplied by Bulbs4You
$1	10	5
$5	15	7
$7	25	15
$10	35	20

17. Using the following diagram, identify and calculate total producer surplus if the price of oil is $50 per barrel. Recall that for a triangle, Area = $(1/2) \times$ Base $\times$ Height. (You never thought you'd use that equation unless you became an engineer, did you?)

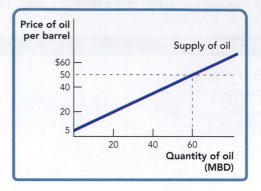

18. In Sucrosia, the supply curve for sugar is as follows:

Price (per 100-pound bag)	Quantity
$30	10,000
$50	15,000
$70	20,000

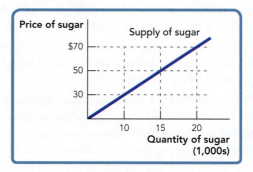

Under pressure from nutrition activists, the government decides to tax sugar producers with a $5 tax per 100-pound bag. Using the figure above, draw the new supply curve. After the tax is enacted, what price will bring forth quantities of 10,000? 15,000? 20,000? Give your answers in the table:

Price (per 100-pound bag)	Quantity
	10,000
	15,000
	20,000

19. Consider the farmers talked about in the chapter who have land that is suitable for growing both wheat and soybeans. Suppose all farmers are currently farming wheat but the price of soybeans rises dramatically.

   a. Does the opportunity cost of producing wheat rise or fall?

   b. Does this shift the supply curve for wheat (as in one of the panels of Figure 3.11), or is it a movement along a fixed supply curve?

   What direction is this shift or movement? Illustrate your answer in the following figure:

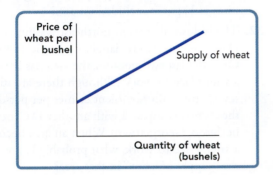

20. Consider the following demand curve for oil:

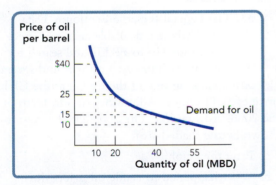

   a. Using this demand curve, fill in the following table:

Price	Quantity Demanded
	55
$25	

   b. If the price was $10, how much oil would be demanded?

   c. What is the maximum price (per barrel) that demanders will pay for 20 million barrels of oil?

21. From the following chart, draw the demand curve for pencils (in hundreds):

Price	Quantity Demanded (100s)
$5	60
$15	45
$25	35
$35	20

22. If the price of glass dramatically increases, what are we likely to see a lot less of: glass windows or glass bottles? Why?

23. Let's think about the demand for LED TVs.

   a. If the price for a 60-inch LED TV is $800, and Newhart would be willing to pay $3,000, what is Newhart's consumer surplus?

   b. Consider the following figure for the total demand for LED TVs. At $800 per TV, 1,200 TVs were demanded. What would be the total consumer surplus? Calculate the total, and identify it on the diagram.

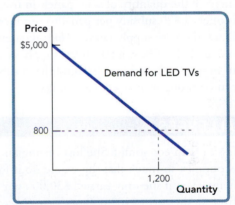

   c. Where is Newhart in the figure?

24. If income increases and the demand for good X shifts as shown in the figure, then is good X a normal or inferior good? Give an example of a good like good X.

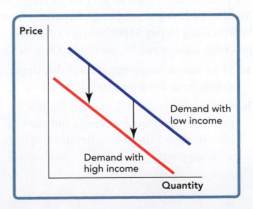

25. Assume that butter and margarine are substitutes. What will happen to the demand curve for butter if the price of margarine increases? Why?

26. Cars and gasoline are complements. What will happen to the demand curve for gasoline if the price of cars decreases? Why? (*Hint:* What happens to the quantity demanded of cars?)

27. Suppose that the supply curve for solar panels is as shown in the diagram:

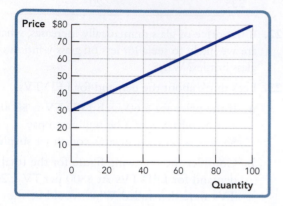

The government decides that it would like to increase the quantity of solar panels in use, so it offers a $20 subsidy per panel to producers. Draw the new supply curve. (*Hint:* Remember our analysis of how a tax affects supply, as shown in Figure 3.12, and bear in mind that a subsidy can be thought of as a "negative tax.")

CHALLENGES

28. Jessica is an economist. She loves being an economist so much that she would do it for a living even if she only earned $30,000 per year. Instead, she earns $103,000 per year. (*Note:* This is the average salary of new economists with a PhD degree.) How much producer surplus does Jessica enjoy?

29. The economist Bryan Caplan recently found a pair of $10 arch supports that saved him from the pain of major foot surgery. As he stated on his blog (econlog.econlib.org), he would have been willing to pay $100,000 to fix his foot problem, but instead he paid only a few dollars.

  a. How much consumer surplus did Bryan enjoy from this purchase?

  b. If the sales tax was 5 percent on this product, how much revenue did the government raise when Bryan bought his arch supports?

  c. If the government could have taxed Bryan based on his *willingness to pay* rather than on how much he *actually* paid, how much sales tax would Bryan have had to pay?

30. For most young people, working full-time and going to school are substitutes: You tend to do one or the other. When it's tough to find a job, does that raise the opportunity cost of going to college or does it lower it? When it's tough to find a job, does the demand for college rise or fall?

31. What should happen to the "demand for speed" (measured by the average speed on highways) once airbags are included on cars?

32. The industrial areas in northeast Washington, D.C., were relatively dangerous in the 1980s. Over the last two decades, the area has become a safer place to work (although there are still several times more violent crimes per person in these areas compared with another D.C. neighborhood, Georgetown). When an area becomes a safer place to work, what probably happens to the "supply of labor" in that area?

Ask FRED

interactive activity

33. The Federal Reserve Economic Data (FRED) database is available at https://fred.stlouisfed.org/. Go to FRED and search for data on crude oil prices. You will find several series; click on one of them such as the Global price of WTI Crude. Adjust the dates to focus in on the 2006–2010 period. The 2008–2009 recessions is shown by the shaded area.

  a. Print the graph.

  b. What happened to crude oil prices during the recession, especially as the recession continued?

  c. Do you think the change in price was driven more by a shift to demand or to supply? Using the lists of important demand and supply shifters from Chapter 3, what was the major factor shifting demand or supply?

  d. Draw a demand and supply curve diagram. Label the initial price the "pre-recession price." Show the new demand or supply curve. Label the new price the "recession price."

  e. FRED has several series for the oil price. Why doesn't it matter which one we use?

WORK IT OUT

For interactive, step-by-step help in solving the following problem, go online.

The supply curve for rice is as follows:

Price (per 100-pound bag)	Quantity
$40	10,000
$60	15,000
$80	20,000

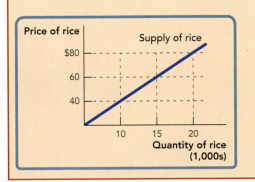

Price of rice

Supply of rice

$80
60
40

10 15 20

Quantity of rice (1,000s)

Under pressure from nutrition activists, the government decides to tax rice producers with a $5 tax per 100-pound bag. Using the preceding figure, draw the new supply curve. After the tax is enacted, what price will bring forth quantities of 10,000? 15,000? 20,000? Give your answers in the table:

Price (per 100-pound bag)	Quantity
	10,000
	15,000
	20,000

MRUNIVERSITY
AN ONLINE EDUCATION PLATFORM

MARGINAL REVOLUTION UNIVERSITY VIDEOS

Why Does the Demand Curve Slope Down and Why Is This Important?

mruniversity.com/demand

Problems: **1**

Why Do (most) Supply Curves Slope Up and Why Is This Important?

mruniversity.com/supply

Problems: **1–5, 14–18**

A Deeper Look at the Demand Curve

mruniversity.com/deeper-look-demand

Problems: **20, 21, 23**

The Demand Curve Shifts

mruniversity.com/demand-shifts

Problems: **2–7, 10, 20–26, 28–30**

A Deeper Look at the Supply Curve

mruniversity.com/deeper-look-supply

Problems: **14–17**

The Supply Curve Shifts

mruniversity.com/supply-shifts

Problems: **11, 13, 18, 19, 31, 32**

Equilibrium

How Supply and Demand Determine Prices

I n Chapter 3, we introduced the supply curve and the demand curve. In that chapter, we wrote things like "if the price is $20 per barrel, the quantity supplied will be 50 million barrels per day (MBD)" and "if the price is $50, the quantity demanded will be 120 MBD." But how is price determined?

We are now ready for the big event: equilibrium. Figure 4.1 puts the supply curve and demand curve for oil together in one diagram. Notice the one point where the curves meet. The price at the meeting point is called the equilibrium price and the quantity at the meeting point is called the equilibrium quantity.

The equilibrium price is $30 and the equilibrium quantity is 65 MBD. What do we mean by equilibrium? We say that $30 and 65 are the equilibrium price and quantity because at any other price and quantity, economic forces are put in play that push prices and quantities toward these values. The equilibrium price and quantity are the only price and quantity that in a free market are stable. The sketch at right gives an intuitive feel for what we mean by equilibrium—the force of gravity pulls the ball down the side of the bowl until it comes to a state of rest. We will now explain the economic forces that push and pull prices toward their equilibrium values.

Thinking About Equilibrium

Equilibrium and the Adjustment Process

Imagine that demand and supply were as in Figure 4.1 on the next page, but the price was above the equilibrium price of $30, say at $50—we would then have the situation depicted in the left panel of Figure 4.2 on page 53.

At a price of $50, suppliers want to supply 100, but at that price the quantity demanded by buyers is just 32, which creates an excess supply, or

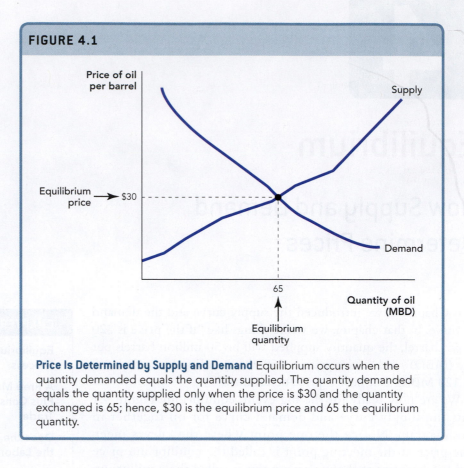

FIGURE 4.1

Price of oil per barrel

Supply

Equilibrium price → $30

Demand

65

Quantity of oil (MBD)

Equilibrium quantity

Price Is Determined by Supply and Demand Equilibrium occurs when the quantity demanded equals the quantity supplied. The quantity demanded equals the quantity supplied only when the price is $30 and the quantity exchanged is 65; hence, $30 is the equilibrium price and 65 the equilibrium quantity.

A **surplus** is a situation in which the quantity supplied is greater than the quantity demanded.

A **shortage** is a situation in which the quantity demanded is greater than the quantity supplied.

The **equilibrium price** is the price at which the quantity demanded is equal to the quantity supplied.

surplus, of 68. What will suppliers do if they cannot sell all of their output at a price of $50? Hold a sale! Each seller will reason that by pricing just a little bit below his or her competitors, he or she will be able to sell much more. *Competition will push prices down whenever there is a surplus.* As competition pushes prices down, the quantity demanded will increase and the quantity supplied will decrease. Only at a price of $30 will equilibrium be restored because only at that price does the quantity demanded (65) equal the quantity supplied (65).

What if price is below the equilibrium price? The right panel of Figure 4.2 shows that at a price of $15 demanders want 95 but suppliers are only willing to sell 24, which creates an excess demand, or **shortage**, of 71. What will sellers do if they discover that at a price of $15, they can easily sell all of their output and still have buyers asking for more? Raise prices! Buyers also have an incentive to offer higher prices when there is a shortage because when they can't buy as much as they want at the going price, they will try to outbid other buyers by offering sellers a higher price. *Competition will push prices up whenever there is a shortage.* As prices are pushed up, the quantity supplied increases and the quantity demanded decreases until at a price of $30 there is no longer an incentive for prices to rise and equilibrium is restored.

If competition pushes the price down whenever it is above the **equilibrium price** and it pushes the price up whenever it is below the equilibrium price, what happens at the equilibrium price? *The equilibrium price is stable because at the equilibrium price the quantity demanded is exactly equal to the quantity supplied.* Because every buyer can buy as much as he or she wants at the equilibrium price, buyers don't have an incentive to push prices up. Since every seller can

FIGURE 4.2

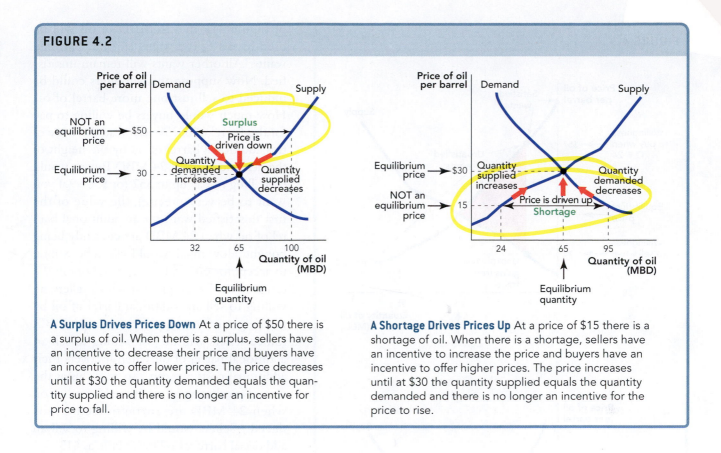

A Surplus Drives Prices Down At a price of $50 there is a surplus of oil. When there is a surplus, sellers have an incentive to decrease their price and buyers have an incentive to offer lower prices. The price decreases until at $30 the quantity demanded equals the quantity supplied and there is no longer an incentive for price to fall.

A Shortage Drives Prices Up At a price of $15 there is a shortage of oil. When there is a shortage, sellers have an incentive to increase the price and buyers have an incentive to offer higher prices. The price increases until at $30 the quantity supplied equals the quantity demanded and there is no longer an incentive for the price to rise.

sell as much as he or she wants at the equilibrium price, sellers don't have an incentive to push prices down. Of course, buyers would like lower prices, but any buyer who offers sellers a lower price will be scorned. Similarly, sellers would like higher prices, but any seller who tries to raise his or her asking price will quickly lose customers.

Who Competes with Whom?

Sellers want higher prices and buyers want lower prices so the person in the street often thinks that sellers compete *against* buyers.

But economists understand that regardless of what sellers want, what they do when they compete is lower prices. *Sellers compete with other sellers.* Similarly, buyers may want lower prices but what they do when they compete is raise prices. *Buyers compete with other buyers.*

If the price of a good that you want is high, should you blame the seller? Not if the market is competitive. Instead, you should "blame" other buyers for outbidding you.

A Free Market Maximizes Producer Plus Consumer Surplus (the Gains from Trade)

Figure 4.3 provides another perspective on the market equilibrium. Consider panel A. At a price of $15 suppliers will voluntarily produce 24 MBD. But notice that this is only enough oil to satisfy some of the buyers' wants. Which ones? The buyers will allocate what oil they have to their highest-valued wants. In panel A of Figure 4.3, the 24 MBD of oil will be used to satisfy the wants labeled "Satisfied wants." All other wants will remain unsatisfied. Now suppose that suppliers could be induced to sell just one more barrel of oil. How much would buyers be willing to pay for this barrel of oil? We can read the value of this additional barrel of oil by the height of the demand curve at 24 MBD. Buyers would be willing to pay up to $57 (or $56.99 if you want to be very precise), the value of the first unsatisfied want for an additional barrel of oil when 24 MBD are currently being bought. How much would sellers be willing to accept for one additional barrel of oil? We can read the lowest price at which sellers are willing to sell an additional barrel of oil by the height of the supply curve at 24 MBD. (Since sellers will be just willing to sell an additional barrel of oil when it covers their additional costs, we can also read this as the cost of producing an additional barrel of oil when 24 MBD are currently being produced.) Sellers would be willing to sell an additional barrel of oil for as little as $15.

Buyers are willing to pay $57 for an additional barrel of oil, and sellers are willing to sell an additional barrel for as little as $15. Trade at any price between $57 and $15 can make both buyers and sellers better off. There are potential gains from trade so long as buyers are willing to pay more than sellers are willing to accept. Now notice that *there are unexploited gains from trade at any quantity less than the* **equilibrium quantity**. Economists believe that in a free market unexploited gains from trade won't last for long. We expect, therefore, that in a free market the quantity bought and sold will increase until the equilibrium quantity of 65 is reached.

We have shown that gains from trade push the quantity toward the equilibrium quantity. What about a push for trade coming from the other direction? In a free market, why won't the quantity bought and sold *exceed* the equilibrium quantity?

Now consider panel B of Figure 4.3. Suppose that for some reason suppliers produce a quantity of 95 MBD. At a quantity

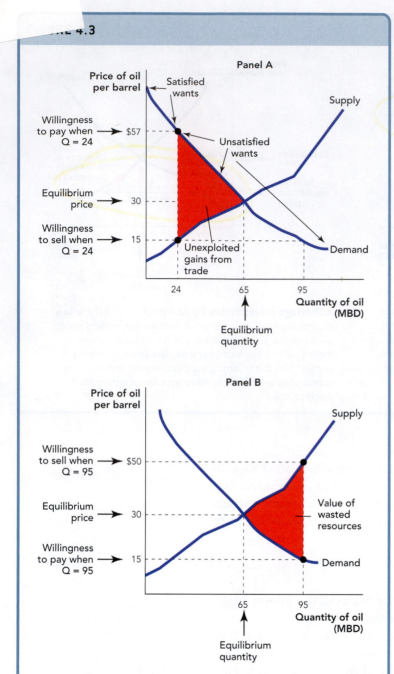

FIGURE 4.3

At the Equilibrium Quantity There Are No Unexploited Gains from Trade or Any Wasteful Trades

Panel A: Unexploited gains from trade exist when quantity is below the equilibrium quantity. Buyers are willing to pay $57 for the 24th unit and sellers are willing to sell the 24th unit for $15, so not trading the 24th unit leaves $42 in unexploited gain from trade. Only at the equilibrium quantity are there no unexploited gains from trade.

Panel B: Resources are wasted at quantities greater than the equilibrium quantity. Sellers are willing to sell the 95th unit for $50, but buyers are willing to pay only $15 so selling the 95th unit wastes $35 in resources. Only at the equilibrium quantity are there no wasted resources.

of 95, it costs suppliers $50 to produce the last barrel of oil (say, by squeezing it out of the Athabasca tar sands). How much is that barrel of oil worth to buyers? Again, we can read this from the height of the demand curve at 95 MBD. It's only $15 (they get a few extra rubber duckies). So if quantity supplied exceeds the equilibrium quantity, it costs the sellers more to produce a barrel of oil than that barrel of oil is worth to buyers.

In a free market, suppliers won't spend $50 to produce something they can sell for at most $15—that's a recipe for bankruptcy.* We expect, therefore, that in a free market, the quantity bought and sold will decrease until the equilibrium quantity of 65 MBD is reached.

Suppliers won't try to drive themselves into bankruptcy, but if they did, would this be a good thing? Even at the equilibrium quantity, buyers have unsatisfied wants. Wouldn't it be a good idea to satisfy even more wants? No. The reason is that resources are wasted if the quantity exceeds the equilibrium quantity.

Imagine once again that suppliers were producing 95 units and thus were producing many barrels of oil whose cost exceeded their worth. This would be a loss not just to the suppliers but also to society. Producing oil takes resources—labor, trucks, pipes, and so forth. Those resources, or the value of those resources, could be used to produce something people really are willing to pay for—economics textbooks, for example, or iPads. If we waste resources producing barrels of oil for $50 that are worth only $15, we have fewer resources to produce goods that cost only $32 but that people value at $75. We have only a limited number of resources and getting the most out of those resources means producing neither too little of a good (as in panel A of Figure 4.3) nor too much of a good (as in panel B). Markets can help us to achieve this goal.

Figure 4.3 shows why in a free market there tends not to be unexploited gains from trade—at least not for long—or wasteful trades. Put these two things together and we have a remarkable result. *A free market maximizes the gains from trade.* The gains from trade can be broken down into producer surplus and consumer surplus, so we can also say that *a free market maximizes producer plus consumer surplus.*

Figure 4.4 illustrates how the gains from trade—producer plus consumer surplus—are maximized at the equilibrium price and quantity. Maximizing the gains from trade, however, requires more than just producing at the equilibrium price and quantity. In addition, goods must be produced at the lowest possible cost and they must be used to satisfy the highest value demands. In Figure 4.4, for example, notice that every seller has lower costs than every nonseller. Also, every buyer has a higher willingness to pay for the good than every nonbuyer.

Imagine if this claim were not true; suppose, for example, that Joe is willing to pay $50 for the good and there are two sellers: Alice with costs of $40 and Barbara with costs of $20. It's possible that Joe and Alice could make a deal, splitting the gains from trade of $10. But this trade would not maximize the gains from trade because if Joe and Barbara trade, the gains from trade are much higher, $30. Over time, both Joe and Barbara will figure this out, so in equilibrium, we expect

The **equilibrium quantity** is the quantity at which the quantity demanded is equal to the quantity supplied.

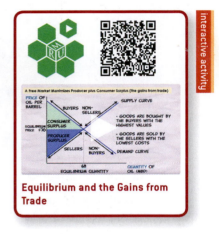

Equilibrium and the Gains from Trade

---

* Can you think of when suppliers might do this? What about if they were being subsidized by the government? In that case, the buyers might value the good less than the cost to sellers, but so long as the government makes up the difference, the sellers will be happy to sell a large quantity. See Chapter 6 for more on subsidies.

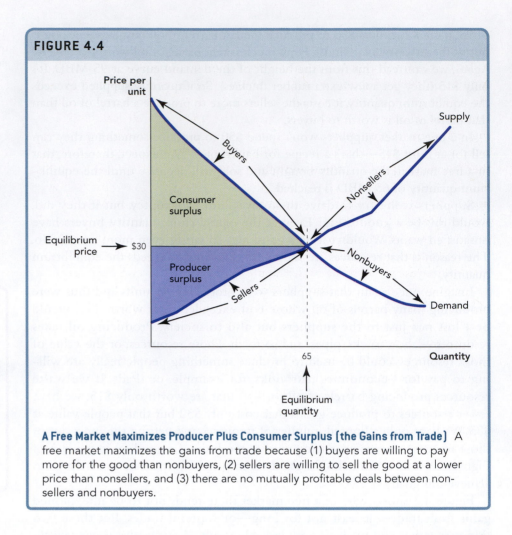

FIGURE 4.4

Price per unit

Supply

Buyers

Consumer surplus

Nonsellers

Equilibrium price → $30

Producer surplus

Nonbuyers

Sellers

Demand

65 Quantity

Equilibrium quantity

A Free Market Maximizes Producer Plus Consumer Surplus (the Gains from Trade) A free market maximizes the gains from trade because (1) buyers are willing to pay more for the good than nonbuyers, (2) sellers are willing to sell the good at a lower price than nonsellers, and (3) there are no mutually profitable deals between nonsellers and nonbuyers.

CHECK YOURSELF

■ As the price of cars goes up, which marketplace wants will be the first to stop being satisfied? Give an example.

■ In the late 1990s, telecommunication firms laid a greater quantity of fiber-optic cable than the market equilibrium quantity (as proved by later events). Describe the nature of the losses from too much investment in fiber-optic cable. What market incentives exist to avoid these losses?

■ Suppose that Kiran values a good at $50. Store A is willing to sell the good for $45, and store B is willing to sell the same good for $35. In a free market, what will be the total consumer surplus? Now suppose that store B is prevented from selling. What happens to the total consumer surplus?

Joe to trade with Barbara, not Alice. Thus, when we say that a free market maximizes the gains from trade, we mean three closely related things:

1. The supply of goods is bought by the buyers with the highest willingness to pay.

2. The supply of goods is sold by the sellers with the lowest costs.

3. Between buyers and sellers, there are no unexploited gains from trade and no wasteful trades.

Together, these three conditions imply that the gains from trade are maximized.

One of the remarkable lessons of economics is that under the right conditions, the pursuit of self-interest leads not to chaos but to a beneficial order. The maximization of consumer plus producer surplus in markets populated solely by self-interested individuals is one application of this central idea.

Does the Model Work? Evidence from the Laboratory

It's easy to see the equilibrium price and quantity when we draw textbook supply and demand curves, but in a real market the demanders and sellers do not know the true curves. Moreover, the conditions required to maximize the gains from trade are quite sophisticated. So how do we know whether the model really works?

In 1956, Vernon Smith launched a revolution in economics by testing the supply and demand model in the lab. Smith's early experiments were simple. He took a group of undergraduate students and broke them into two groups, buyers and sellers. Buyers were given a card that indicated their maximum willingness to pay. Sellers were given a card that indicated their cost, the minimum price at which they would be willing to sell. The buyers and sellers were then instructed to call out bids and offers ("I will sell for $3.00" or "I will pay $1.50"). Each student could earn a profit by the difference between their willingness to pay or sell and the contract price. For example, if you were a buyer and your card said $3.00 and you were able to make a deal with a seller to buy for $2.00, then you would have made a $1.00 profit.

The students knew only their own willingness to pay or to sell, but Vernon Smith knew the actual shape of the supply and demand curves. Smith knew the curves because he knew exactly what cards he had handed out. Data from one of Smith's first experiments are shown in Figure 4.5. Smith handed out 11 cards to sellers and 11 to buyers. The lowest-cost seller had costs of 75 cents, the next lowest-cost seller had costs of $1.00. Thus, at any price below 75 cents the quantity supplied on the market supply curve was zero; between 75 cents and $1, the quantity supplied was 1 unit; between $1.00 and $1.25, the next highest cost, 2 units; and so forth. Looking at the figure can you see how many units demanders were willing to buy at a price of $2.65? At a price of $2.65, the quantity demanded is 3 units. (To test yourself, identify, by their willingness to pay, exactly which three buyers are willing to buy at a price of $2.65.)

Smith knew from the graph that the equilibrium price and quantity as predicted by the supply and demand model were $2.00 and 6 units, respectively.

FIGURE 4.5

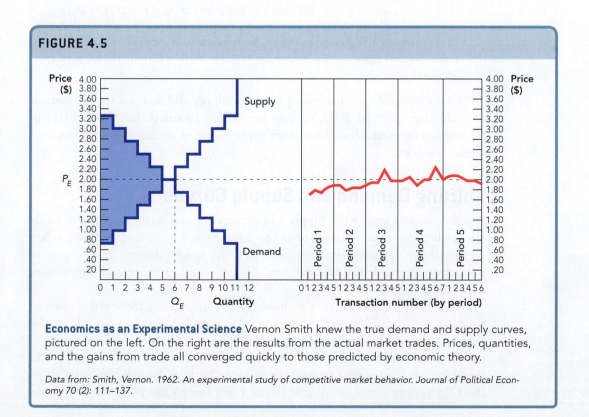

Economics as an Experimental Science Vernon Smith knew the true demand and supply curves, pictured on the left. On the right are the results from the actual market trades. Prices, quantities, and the gains from trade all converged quickly to those predicted by economic theory.

Data from: Smith, Vernon. 1962. An experimental study of competitive market behavior. Journal of Political Economy 70 (2): 111–137.

J. SCOTT APPLEWHITE/AP PHOTO

The idea of economics as an experimental science came to Vernon Smith in a fit of insomnia in 1956. Nearly 50 years later, Smith was awarded the 2002 Nobel Prize in Economics.

But what would happen in the real world? Smith ran his experiment for 5 periods, each period about 5 minutes long. The right side of the figure shows the price for each completed trade in each period. The prices quickly converged toward the expected equilibrium price and quantity so that in the last period the average price was $2.03 and the quantity exchanged was 6 units.

Smith's market converged rapidly to the equilibrium price and quantity exactly as predicted by the supply and demand model. But recall that the model also predicts that a free market will maximize the gains from trade. Remember our conditions for efficiency, which in this context are that the supply of goods must be bought by the demanders with the highest willingness to pay, the supply of goods must be sold by the suppliers with the lowest costs, and the quantity traded should be equal to 6 units, neither more nor less.

So what happened in Smith's test of the market model? In the final period, 6 units were bought and sold and the buyers had the six highest valuations and the sellers the six lowest costs—exactly as predicted by the supply and demand model. Producer plus consumer surplus or total surplus was maximized. In fact, in the entire experiment only once was a seller with a cost greater than equilibrium price able to sell and only once was a buyer with a willingness to pay less than the equilibrium price able to buy—so total surplus was very close to being maximized throughout the experiment.

Vernon Smith began his experiments thinking that they would prove the supply and demand model was wrong. Decades later he wrote:

> I am still recovering from the shock of the experimental results. The outcome was unbelievably consistent with competitive price theory. . . . But the results *can't* be believed, I thought. It must be an accident, so I must take another class and do a new experiment with different supply and demand schedules.[1]

Many thousands of experiments later, the supply and demand model remains of enduring value. In 2002, Vernon Smith was awarded the Nobel Prize in Economics for establishing laboratory experiments as an important tool in economic science.

Shifting Demand and Supply Curves

Another way of testing the supply and demand model is to examine the model's predictions about what happens to equilibrium price and quantity when the supply or demand curves shift. Even if the model doesn't give us precise predictions (outside the lab), we can still ask whether the model helps us to understand the world.

Imagine, for example, that technological innovations reduce the costs of producing a good. As we know from Chapter 3, a fall in costs shifts the supply curve down and to the right as shown in Figure 4.6. The result of lower costs is a lower price and an increase in quantity. Begin at the Old Equilibrium Price and Quantity at point *a*. Now a decrease in costs shifts the Old Supply curve down and to the right out to the New Supply curve.

FIGURE 4.6

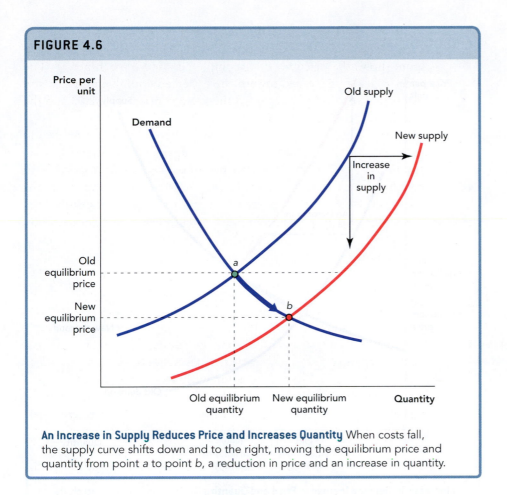

An Increase in Supply Reduces Price and Increases Quantity When costs fall, the supply curve shifts down and to the right, moving the equilibrium price and quantity from point *a* to point *b*, a reduction in price and an increase in quantity.

Notice at the Old Equilibrium Price there is now a surplus—in other words, now that their costs have fallen, suppliers are willing to sell more at the old price than demanders are willing to buy. The excess supply, however, is temporary. Competition between sellers pushes prices down, and as prices fall, the quantity demanded increases. Prices fall and quantity demanded increases until the New Equilibrium Price and Quantity are established at point *b*. At the new equilibrium, the quantity demanded equals the quantity supplied.

We can see this process at work throughout the economy. As technological innovations reduce the price of computer chips, for example, prices fall and the quantity of chips—used in everything from computers to cell phones to toys—increases.

What about a decrease in supply? A decrease in supply will raise the market price and reduce the market quantity, exactly the opposite effects to an increase in supply. But don't take our word for it. Draw the diagram. The key to learning demand and supply is not to try to memorize everything that can happen. Instead, focus on learning how to use the tools. If you know how to use the tools, then simply by drawing a few pictures, you can deduce what happens to price and quantity for any configuration of demand and supply and for any set of shifts.

Figure 4.7 shows the same process for an increase in demand. Begin with the Old Equilibrium Price and Quantity at point *a*. Now suppose that demand

FIGURE 4.7

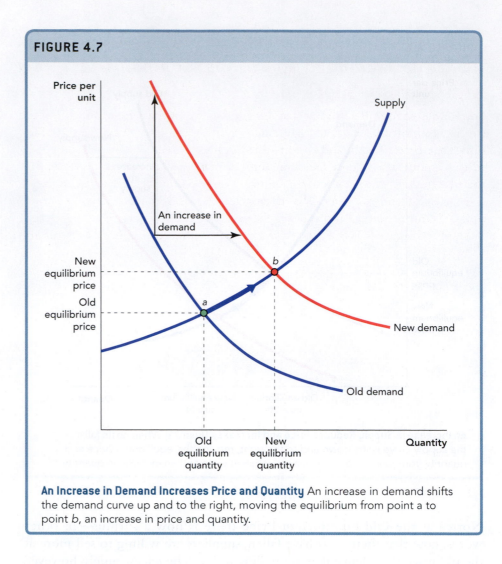

An Increase in Demand Increases Price and Quantity An increase in demand shifts the demand curve up and to the right, moving the equilibrium from point *a* to point *b*, an increase in price and quantity.

CHECK YOURSELF

- Flooding in Iowa destroys some of the corn and soybean crop. What will happen to the price and quantity for each of these crops?
- Resveratrol, which is found in the plant Japanese knotweed (and is also a component of red wine), has recently been shown to increase life expectancy in worms and fish. What are your predictions about the price and quantity of Japanese knotweed grown?
- Draw a graph showing the supply and demand for hybrid cars before and after an increase in the price of gasoline. What do you predict will happen to the price of hybrids as the price of gasoline rises?

increases to New Demand. As a result, the price and quantity are driven up to the New Equilibrium Price and Quantity at point *b*. Notice this time we omitted discussion of the temporary transition. So here's a good test of your knowledge. Can you explain *why* the price and quantity demanded increased with an increase in demand? (*Hint:* What happens at the Old Equilibrium Price after Demand has increased to New Demand?)

Of course, if we can analyze an increase in demand, then a decrease in demand is just the opposite: A decrease in demand will tend to decrease price and quantity. Once again, draw the diagram!

Do you recall the list of demand and supply shifters that we presented in Chapter 3? We can now put all that knowledge to good use. With demand, supply, and the idea of equilibrium, we have powerful tools for analyzing how changes in income, population, expectations, technologies, input prices, taxes and subsidies, alternative uses of industry inputs, and other factors will change market prices and quantities. In fact, with our tools of demand, supply, and equilibrium, we can analyze and understand *any* change in *any* competitive market.

Terminology: Demand Compared with Quantity Demanded and Supply Compared with Quantity Supplied

Sometimes economists use very similar words for quite different things. (We're sorry but unfortunately it's too late to change terms.) In particular, there is a big difference between demand and quantity demanded. For example, an increase in the quantity demanded is a movement *along* a fixed demand curve. An increase in demand is a *shift* of the entire demand curve (up and to the right).

Don't worry: You are *already* familiar with these differences; we just need to point them out to you and explain the associated differences in terminology. Panel A of Figure 4.8 is a repeat of Figure 4.6, showing that an increase in

FIGURE 4.8

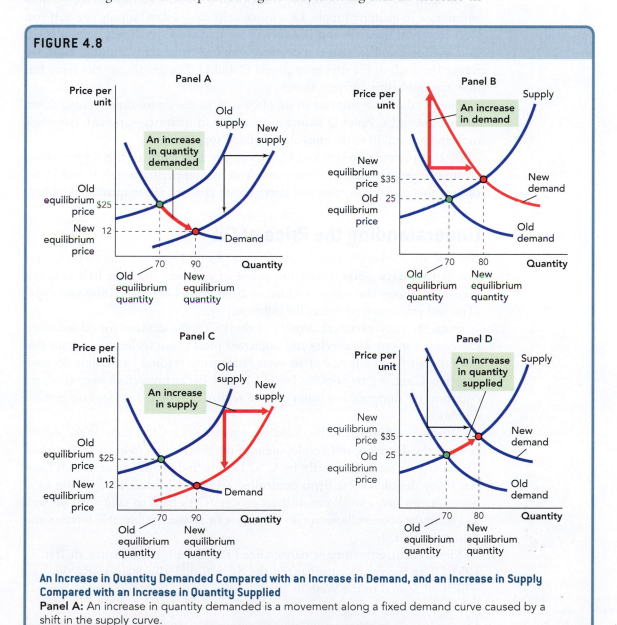

An Increase in Quantity Demanded Compared with an Increase in Demand, and an Increase in Supply Compared with an Increase in Quantity Supplied

Panel A: An increase in quantity demanded is a movement along a fixed demand curve caused by a shift in the supply curve.

Panel B: An increase in demand is a shift in the demand curve up and to the right.

Panel C: An increase in supply is a shift in the supply curve down and to the right.

Panel D: An increase in quantity supplied is a movement along a fixed supply curve caused by a shift in the demand curve.

supply reduces the equilibrium price and increases the equilibrium quantity. But now we emphasize something a little different—the increase in supply pushes the price down, thereby causing an increase in the *quantity demanded* from 70 units to 90 units. Notice that the increase in the quantity demanded is a movement along the demand curve. In panel A, the demand has not changed, only the quantity demanded. Notice also that changes in the quantity demanded are always caused by changes in supply. In other words, *shifts* in the supply curve cause movements *along* the demand curve.

Panel B is a repeat of Figure 4.7 and it shows an *increase in demand*. Notice that an increase in demand is a shift in the entire demand curve up and to the right. Indeed, we can also think about an increase in demand as the creation of a new demand curve, appropriately labeled New Demand.

Similarly, an increase in supply is a *shift* of the entire supply curve, whereas an increase in quantity supplied is a movement *along* a fixed supply curve. If you look closely at panels A and B, you will see that we have already shown you a shift in supply and a change in quantity supplied! But to make things clear, we repeat the analysis for supply in panels C and D: The graphs are the same but now we emphasize different things.

Panel C shows an increase in supply, a shift in the entire supply curve down and to the right. Panel D shows an increase in quantity supplied, namely a movement from 70 to 80 units along a fixed supply curve.

By comparing panels A and C, we can see that shifts in the supply curve create changes in quantity demanded. And by comparing panels B and D, we can see that shifts in the demand curve create changes in the quantity supplied.

Understanding the Price of Oil

We can use the supply and demand model to understand some of the major events that have determined the price of oil over the past half century. Figure 4.9 shows the *real price* of oil in 2016 dollars between 1960 and 2016. (The real price corrects prices for inflation.)

From the early twentieth century to the 1970s, the demand for oil increased steadily, but major discoveries and improved production techniques meant that the supply of oil increased at an even faster pace, leading to modest declines in price. Contrary to popular belief, slightly declining prices over time are common for minerals and other natural resources supplied under competitive conditions.

Although the streets of Baghdad were paved with tar as early as the eighth century, the discovery and development of the modern oil industry in the Middle East were made primarily by U.S., Dutch, and British firms much later. For many decades, these firms controlled oil in the Middle East, giving local governments just a small cut of their proceeds. It's hard to take your oil well and leave the country, however, so the major firms were vulnerable to taxes and nationalization.

The Iranian government nationalized the British oil industry in Iran in 1951.* The Egyptians nationalized the Suez Canal, the main route through which oil flowed to the West, in 1956, leading to the Suez Crisis—a brief war

---

* The nationalization was reversed in 1953 when the government of Mohammad Mosaddeq was toppled by a CIA-backed coup that brought the king, Mohammad Reza Pahlavi, back to power. The coup would have repercussions a quarter century later with the coming of the Iranian Revolution, when the American-backed government was overthrown by Islamic radicals.

FIGURE 4.9

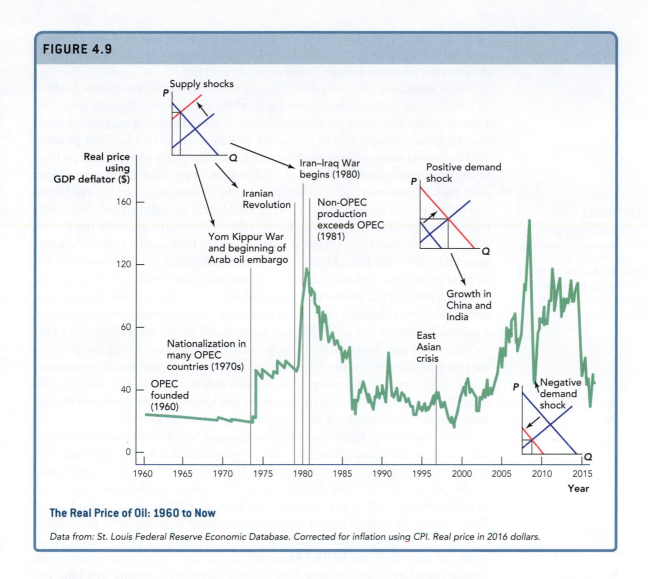

The Real Price of Oil: 1960 to Now

Data from: St. Louis Federal Reserve Economic Database. Corrected for inflation using CPI. Real price in 2016 dollars.

that pitted Egypt against an alliance of the United Kingdom, France, and Israel. Further nationalizations and increased government control of the oil industry occurred throughout the 1960s and early 1970s.

OPEC, the Organization of the Petroleum Exporting Countries, was formed in 1960.* Initially, OPEC restricted itself to bargaining with the foreign nationals for a larger share of their oil revenues. By the early 1970s, however, further nationalizations in the OPEC countries made it possible for OPEC countries to act together to reduce supply and raise prices.

A triggering event for OPEC was the Yom Kippur War. Egypt and Syria attacked Israel in 1973 in an effort to regain the Sinai Peninsula and the Golan Heights, which Israel had captured in 1967. In an effort to punish Western countries that had supported Israel, a number of Arab exporting nations cut oil production. Supply had been increasing by about 7.5 percent per year in the previous decade, but between 1973 and 1974 production was dead flat.

---

* OPEC was founded by Iran, Iraq, Kuwait, Saudi Arabia, and Venezuela, later joined by Qatar (1961), Indonesia (1962–2009, 2016), Libya (1962), the United Arab Emirates (1967), Algeria (1969), Nigeria (1971), Ecuador (1973–1992), Gabon (1975–1994), and Angola (2007). Ecuador rejoined OPEC in 2007 and Gabon rejoined in 2016.

►►SEARCH ENGINE

Statistics on world energy prices, consumption, production, reserves, and other areas can be found at the **BP Statistical Review of World Energy**. The **Energy Information Administration** focuses on the United States.

Prices tripled in just one year. The large increase in price from a small decline in supply (relative to what it would have been without the cut in production) demonstrated how much the world depended on oil.

Prices stabilized, albeit at a much higher level, after 1974, but political unrest in Iran in 1978, followed by revolution in 1979, cut Iranian oil production. This time the reduction in supply was accidental rather than deliberate, but the result was the same—sharply higher prices. When Iraq attacked Iran in 1980, production in both countries diminished yet again, pushing prices to their highest level in the twentieth century—$75.31 in 2005 dollars. Prices might have been driven even higher if demand had not been reduced by a recession in the United States.

Higher prices attract entry. In 1972, the United Kingdom produced 2,000 barrels of oil per day. By 1978, with the opening of the North Sea wells, the United Kingdom was producing 1 million barrels per day. In the same period, Norway increased production from 33,000 to 287,000 barrels per day and Mexico doubled its production from 506,000 barrels per day to just over 1 million barrels per day. By 1982, non-OPEC production exceeded OPEC production for the first time since OPEC was founded. Iranian production also began to recover, increasing by 1 million barrels per day in 1982. Prices began to fall during the 1980s and 1990s.

Prices can also fluctuate with shifts in demand. A sharp fall in the price of oil came in 2009 when the United States and many of the major economies in the world were in the trough of a deep recession. Incomes fell, reducing the demand for oil and reducing the price. As the United States slowly recovered, however, the demand for oil increased, driving up the price.

The economies of China and India have surged in the early twenty-first century to the point where millions of people are for the first time in the history of their country able to afford an automobile. In 1949, the Communists confiscated all the private cars in China. As late as 2000, there were just 6 million cars in all of China, but by 2010 more vehicles were bought in China than in the United States, almost 18 million in that one year alone. Total highway miles quadrupled between 2000 and 2010.[2] This increased demand for oil pushed prices up to levels not seen since the 1970s.* Moreover, unlike temporary events such as the Iranian Revolution and the Iran–Iraq War, the increase in demand in China and in other newly developing nations will not reverse soon. In the United States, there's nearly one car for every two people. China has a population of 1.3 billion people, so there is plenty of room for growth in the number of cars and thus the demand for oil. On the other hand, new discoveries and techniques such as fracking are increasing the supply of oil. Electric cars may also reduce the demand for oil. As you can see from the graph, oil prices are difficult to predict; the reason is that the social, technological and geo-political factors that shift the demand and supply curves are difficult to predict. Nevertheless, demand and supply analysis is extremely useful in understanding how shifts in these factors influence the price of oil.

Takeaway

Now that you have finished reading this chapter, you should read it again. Really. Understanding supply and demand is critical to understanding economics, and in this chapter we have covered the most important aspects of the supply and demand

CHECK **YOURSELF**

■ In Figure 4.9, you will notice a jump in oil prices around 1991. What happened in this year to increase price? Was it a supply shock or a demand shock?

■ In Figure 4.9, during what period would you include a small figure for positive supply shocks (increases in supply)? Explain the causes behind the positive supply shocks and the effect of these shocks on the price of oil.

---

* Improved technology is continually lowering the cost of discovering and producing oil (shifting the supply curve down and to the right), so what has happened in recent years is not simply an increase in demand but an increase in demand that has outstripped the increase in supply.

model, namely how supply and demand together determine equilibrium price and quantity. You should understand, among other ideas, the following:

1. Market competition brings about an equilibrium in which the quantity supplied is equal to the quantity demanded.

2. Only one price/quantity combination is a market equilibrium and you should be able to identify this equilibrium in a diagram.

3. You should understand and be able to explain the incentives that enforce the market equilibrium. What happens when the price is above the equilibrium price? Why? What happens when the price is below the equilibrium price? Why?

4. The sum of consumer and producer surplus (the gains from trade) is maximized at the equilibrium price and quantity, and no other price/quantity combination maximizes consumer plus producer surplus.

5. You should know from Chapter 3 the major factors that shift demand and supply curves and from this chapter be able to explain and predict the effect of any such shift on the equilibrium price and quantity.

6. A "change in demand [the demand curve]" is not the same thing as "a change in quantity demanded"; a "change in supply [the supply curve]" is not the same thing as "a change in quantity supplied."

Most important, you should be able to work with supply and demand to answer questions about the world.

CHAPTER REVIEW

`interactive activity` **Go online to practice with more examples of these types of problems, including live links to videos, data sources, and feedback.**

 Problems in green relate to MRU videos. See the MRU table at the end of the exercises.

KEY CONCEPTS

surplus, p. 52

shortage, p. 52

equilibrium price, p. 52

equilibrium quantity, p. 54

FACTS AND TOOLS

1. If the price in a market is above the equilibrium price, does this create a surplus or a shortage?

2. When the price is above the equilibrium price, does greed (in other words, self-interest) tend to push the price down or up?

3. Jon is on eBay, bidding for a first edition of the influential Frank Miller graphic novel *Batman: The Dark Knight Returns*. In this market, who is Jon competing with: the seller of the graphic novel or the other bidders?

4. Now, Jon is in Japan, trying to get a job as a full-time translator; he wants to translate English TV shows into Japanese and vice versa. He notices that the wage for translators is very low. Who is the "competition" pushing the wage down: Does the competition come from businesses who hire the translators or from the other translators?

5. Jules wants to purchase a Royale with cheese from Vincent. Vincent is willing to offer this tasty burger for $3. The most Jules is willing to pay for the tasty burger is $8 (after all, his girlfriend is a vegetarian, so he doesn't get many opportunities for tasty burgers).

   a. How large are the potential gains from trade if Jules and Vincent agree to make this trade? In other words, what is the sum of producer and consumer surplus if the trade happens?

b. If the trade takes place at $4, how much producer surplus goes to Vincent? How much consumer surplus goes to Jules?

c. If the trade takes place at $7, how much producer surplus goes to Vincent? How much consumer surplus goes to Jules?

6. What happened in Vernon Smith's lab? Choose the right answer:

a. The price and quantity were close to equilibrium but gains from trade were far from the maximum.

b. The price and quantity were far from equilibrium and gains from trade were far from the maximum.

c. The price and quantity were far from equilibrium but gains from trade were close to the maximum.

d. The price and quantity were close to equilibrium and gains from trade were close to the maximum.

7. When supply falls, what happens to quantity demanded in equilibrium? (This should get you to notice that both suppliers and demanders change their behavior when one curve shifts.)

8. a. When demand increases, what happens to price and quantity in equilibrium?

b. When supply increases, what happens to price and quantity in equilibrium?

c. When supply decreases, what happens to price and quantity in equilibrium?

d. When demand decreases, what happens to price and quantity in equilibrium?

9. a. When demand increases, what happens to price and quantity in equilibrium?

b. When supply increases, what happens to price and quantity in equilibrium?

c. When supply decreases, what happens to price and quantity in equilibrium?

d. When demand decreases, what happens to price and quantity in equilibrium?

No, this is not a mistake. Yes, it is that important.

10. What's the best way to think about the rise in oil prices in the 1970s, when wars and oil embargoes wracked the Middle East? Was it a rise in demand, a fall in demand, a rise in supply, or a fall in supply?

11. What's the best way to think about the rise in oil prices in the last 10 years, as China and India have become richer: Was it a rise in demand, a fall in demand, a rise in supply, or a fall in supply?

THINKING AND PROBLEM SOLVING

12. Suppose the market for batteries looks as follows:

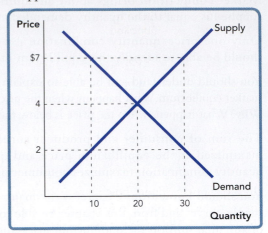

What are the equilibrium price and quantity?

13. Consider the following supply and demand tables for bread. Draw the supply and demand curves for this market. What are the equilibrium price and quantity?

Price of One Loaf	Quantity Supplied	Quantity Demanded
$0.50	10	75
$1	20	55
$2	35	35
$3	50	25
$5	60	10

14. If the price of a one-bedroom apartment in Washington, D.C., is currently $1,000 per month, but the supply and demand curves look as follows, then is there a shortage or surplus of apartments? What would we expect to happen to prices? Why?

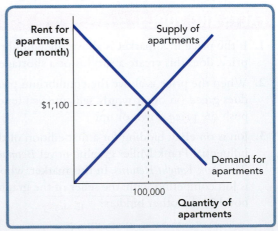

15. Determine the equilibrium quantity and price without drawing a graph.

Price of Good X	Quantity Supplied	Quantity Demanded
$22	100	225
$25	115	200
$30	130	175
$32	150	150
$40	170	110

16. In the following figure, how many pounds of sugar are sellers willing to sell at a price of $20? How much is demanded at this price? What is the buyer's willingness to pay when the quantity is 20 pounds? Is this combination of $20 per pound and a quantity of 20 pounds an equilibrium? If not, identify the unexploited gains from trade.

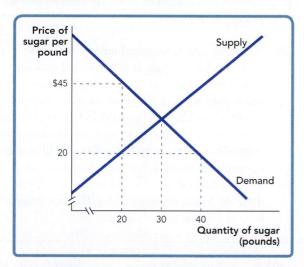

17. The market for marbles is represented in the graph. What is the total producer surplus? The total consumer surplus? What are the total gains from trade?

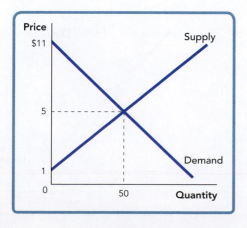

18. Suppose you decided to follow in Vernon Smith's footsteps and conducted your own experiment with your friends. You give out 10 cards: 5 cards to buyers with the figures for willingness to pay of $1, $2, $3, $4, and $5, and 5 cards to sellers with the amounts for costs of $1, $2, $3, $4, and $5. The rules are the same as Vernon Smith implemented.

   a. Draw the supply and demand curves for this market. At a price of $3.50, how many units are demanded? And supplied?

   b. Assuming the market works as predicted, and the market moves to equilibrium, will the buyer who values the good at $1 be able to purchase? Why or why not?

19. If the price of margarine decreases, what happens to the demand for butter? What happens to the equilibrium quantity and price for butter? What would happen if butter and margarine were not substitutes? Use a supply and demand diagram to support your answer.

20. The market for sugar is diagrammed:

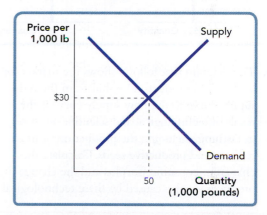

   a. What would happen to the equilibrium quantity and price if the wages of sugar cane harvesters increased?

   b. What if a new study was published that emphasized the negative health effects of consuming sugar?

21. If a snowstorm was forecast for the next day, what would happen to the demand for snow shovels? Is this a change in quantity demanded or a change in demand? This shift in the demand curve would affect the price; would this cause a change in quantity supplied or a change in supply?

22. In recent years, the Paleo diet, which emphasizes eating more meat and fewer grains, has become very popular. What do you suppose that has done to the price and quantity of bread? Use supply and demand analysis to support your answer.

23. In recent years, there have been news reports that toys made in China are unsafe. When those news reports show up on CNN and Fox News, what probably happens to the demand for toys made in China? What probably happens to the equilibrium price and quantity of toys made in China? Are Chinese toymakers probably better or worse off when such news comes out?

24. Here's a quick problem to test whether you really understand what producer surplus and consumer surplus mean, rather than just relying on the geometry of demand and supply. For each of the two diagrams that follow, calculate producer surplus, consumer surplus, and total surplus. Assume the curves are perfectly vertical and perfectly horizontal.

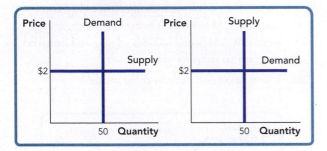

25. The diagram that follows shows the market for agricultural products. The shift from the old supply curve to the new supply curve is the result of technological and scientific advances in farming, including the production of more resilient and productive seeds. Calculate the change in consumer surplus and the change in producer surplus caused by these technological advances. Are buyers better or worse off as a result of these advancements? What about sellers? (Note that you cannot calculate consumer surplus directly with the information given in the diagram, but you don't need that information to calculate the *change* in consumer surplus.)

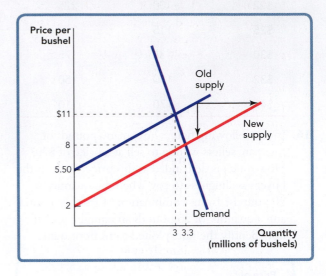

26. Now that you've mastered interpreting shifts in demand and supply, it's time to add another wrinkle: simultaneous shifts in both demand and supply. Most of the time, when we explore simultaneous shifts of demand and supply, we can determine the impact on either equilibrium price *or* equilibrium quantity, but not both. Fill in the missing cells in the following table to see why. Because two curves can shift in two directions, there are four cases to consider. The first column is done for you as an example.

	Case 1	Case 2	Case 3	Case 4
Change in demand	Increase	Increase	Decrease	Decrease
How demand change affects price	↑			
How demand change affects quantity	↑			
Change in supply	Increase	Decrease	Increase	Decrease
How supply change affects price	↓			
How supply change affects quantity	↑			
Combined effect of demand and supply on price	?			
Combined effect of demand and supply on quantity	↑			

27. In the last problem, you saw how simultaneous shifts in demand and supply can leave us with uncertainty about the impact on price or on quantity. An increase in both demand and supply will increase equilibrium quantity but have an ambiguous effect on equilibrium price. However, if we knew that there was a *significant* increase in demand and only a *small* increase in supply, we could conclude that the price would probably rise overall, albeit not by as much as would have been the case if supply had not increased slightly.

In each of the following examples, there are a *major* event and a *minor* event. Determine whether each change relates to demand or to supply, and then figure out the impact on price and quantity; be sure to say something about the relative magnitudes of the price and quantity changes.

a. *Market:* Rock salt

Major event: A bitterly cold and unusually snowy winter season has significantly depleted the amount of available rock salt.

Minor event: There is another snowstorm, and roads and sidewalks need to be salted.

b. *Market:* Smartphones

Major event: The proliferation of fast, reliable, affordable (or free) wi-fi and cellular signals increases the usability of smartphones.

Minor event: The production of smartphones is marked by modest technological advances.

c. *Market:* Canned tomatoes

Major event: A large canned tomato manufacturer begins to use cheap imported tomatoes from Mexico rather than domestic tomatoes.

Minor event: This causes a public relations fiasco, resulting in an organized effort to boycott canned tomatoes.

CHALLENGES

28. For many years, it was illegal to color margarine yellow (margarine is naturally white). In some states, margarine manufacturers were even required to color margarine pink! Who do you think supported these laws? Why? (*Hint:* Your analysis in question 8 from the previous section is relevant!)

29. Think about two products: "safe cars" (a heavy car such as a BMW 530xi with infrared night vision, four-wheel antilock brakes, and electronic stability control) and "dangerous cars" (a lightweight car such as _____ [name removed for legal reasons, but you can fill in as you wish]).

a. Are these two products substitutes or complements?

b. If new research makes it easier to produce safe cars, what happens to the supply of safe cars? What will happen to the equilibrium price of safe cars?

c. Now that the price of safe cars has changed, how does this impact the demand for dangerous cars?

d. Now let's tie all these links into one simple sentence:

In a free market, as engineers and scientists discover new ways to make cars safer, the number of dangerous cars sold will tend to

_____.

30. Many clothing stores often have clearance sales at the end of each season. Using the tools you learned in this chapter, can you think of an explanation why?

31. a. If oil executives read in the newspaper that massive new oil supplies have been discovered under the Pacific Ocean but will likely only be useful in 10 years, what is likely to happen to the supply of oil *today*? What is the likely equilibrium impact on the price and quantity of oil *today*?

b. If oil executives read in the newspaper that new solar-power technologies have been discovered but will likely only become useful in 10 years, what is likely to happen to the supply of oil *today*? What is the likely equilibrium impact on the price and quantity of oil *today*?

c. What's the short version of these scenarios? Fill in the blank: If we learn *today* about promising *future* energy sources, today's price of energy will _____ and today's quantity of energy will _____.

32. Economists often say that prices are a "rationing mechanism." If the supply of a good falls, how do prices "ration" these now-scarce goods in a competitive market?

33. When the crime rate falls in the area around a factory, what probably happens to wages at that factory?

34. Let's take the idea from the previous question and use it to explain why businesses sometimes try to make their employees happy. If a business can make a job seem fun (by offering inexpensive pizza lunches) or at least safe (by nagging the city government to put police patrols around the factory), what probably happens to the supply of labor? What happens to the equilibrium wage if a factory or office or laboratory becomes a great place where people "really want to work"? How does this explain why the hourly wage for the median radio or television announcer is only $14.88 per hour, lower than almost any other job in the entertainment or broadcasting industry?

interactive activity

WORK IT OUT

For interactive, step-by-step help in solving the following problem, go online.

Consider the following supply and demand tables for milk. Draw the supply and demand curves for this market. What are the equilibrium price and quantity?

Price of One Gallon	Quantity Supplied	Quantity Demanded
$1	20	150
$2	40	110
$4	70	70
$6	100	50
$10	120	20

MARGINAL REVOLUTION VIDEOS AND PROBLEMS

The Equilibrium Price

mruniversity.com/equilibrium

Problems: **1, 7, 8, 30**

Equilibrium and the Gains from Trade

mruniversity.com/explore-equilibrium

Problems: **1–5, 12–17, 24**

Does the Equilibrium Model Work?

mruniversity.com/equilibrium-model

Problems: **6–11, 18–23, 25, 28–29**

Supply and Demand Terminology

mruniversity.com/basic-terminology

Problems: **25–27, 30, 32**

5

Elasticity and Its Applications

In the fall of 2000, Harvard sophomore Jay Williams flew to the Sudan where a terrible civil war had resulted in many thousands of deaths. Women and children captured in raids by warring tribes were being enslaved and held for ransom. Working with Christian Solidarity International, Williams was able to pay for the release of 4,000 people. But did Williams do the right thing? It's a serious question and one that is surprisingly complex, both morally and economically. By paying for the release of slaves, could Williams have encouraged more people to be enslaved? If so, by how much? Slavery is an abomination. Because of the terrible effects of slavery, careful thought about the best way to deal with the problem is essential. Perhaps surprisingly, the economic concept of elasticity can help to identify the most effective policies to end slavery.

In this chapter, we develop the tools of demand and supply elasticity. To be honest, at first these tools will seem dry and technical. Stick with us, however, and you will see how the concept of elasticity is useful for dealing with important questions such as how best to help people held as slaves for ransom, why the war on drugs can generate violence, why gun buyback programs are unlikely to work, and how to evaluate proposals to increase drilling in the Arctic National Wildlife Refuge (ANWR).

In Chapter 4, we discussed how to shift the supply and demand curves to produce *qualitative* predictions about changes in prices and quantities. Estimating elasticities of demand and supply is the first step in *quantifying* how changes in demand and supply will affect prices and quantities.

The Elasticity of Demand

When the price of a good increases, individuals and businesses will buy less. But how much less? A lot or a little? The **elasticity of demand** measures how responsive the quantity demanded is to a change in price—the more responsive quantity demanded is to a change in the price, the more elastic is the demand curve. Let's start by comparing two different demand curves.

CHAPTER OUTLINE

The Elasticity of Demand

Applications of Demand Elasticity

The Elasticity of Supply

Applications of Supply Elasticity

Using Elasticities for Quick Predictions (Optional)

Takeaway

Appendix: Other Types of Elasticities

 Videos
- **What Does Elasticity Have to do with Freeing Slaves in Africa?**
- **Office Hours: Elasticity**

The **elasticity of demand** measures how responsive the quantity demanded is to a change in price; more responsive equals more elastic.

71

In Figure 5.1, when the price increases from $40 to $50, the quantity demanded decreases from 100 to 20 along demand curve E but only from 100 to 95 along demand curve I—thus, demand curve E is more elastic than demand curve I.

Elasticity is not the same thing as slope, but they are related and for our purposes you won't make any mistakes if you follow the elasticity rule:

> *Elasticity rule:* If two linear demand (or supply) curves run through a common point, then at any given quantity the curve that is flatter is more elastic.

Determinants of the Elasticity of Demand

Of the two curves in Figure 5.1, which do you think would best represent the demand curve for oil?

There are few substitutes for oil in its major use, transportation, so when the price increases by a lot, the quantity demanded falls by only a little. Thus, the demand curve for oil is not very elastic and would be best represented by demand curve I.

The fundamental determinant of the elasticity of demand is how easy it is to substitute one good for another. The fewer substitutes for a good, the less elastic the demand. The more substitutes for a good, the more elastic the demand.

When the price of oil goes up, people grumble but few stop using cars, at least not right away. But what happens to the elasticity of the demand for oil over time? The demand for oil tends to become more elastic over time because the more time people have to adjust to a price change, the better they can substitute one good for another. In other words, there are more

FIGURE 5.1

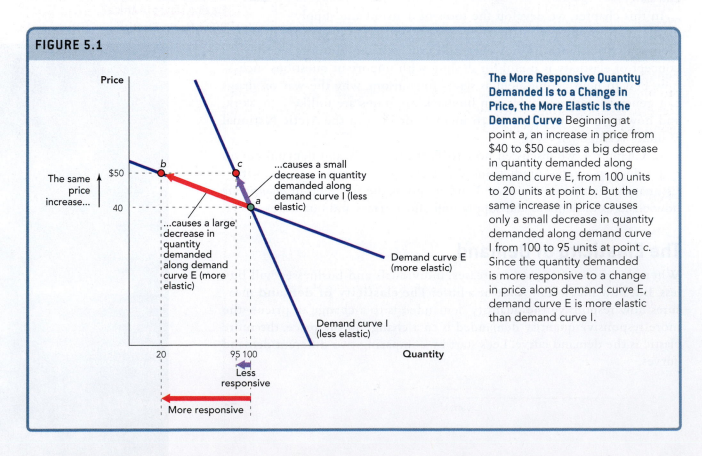

The More Responsive Quantity Demanded Is to a Change in Price, the More Elastic Is the Demand Curve Beginning at point *a*, an increase in price from $40 to $50 causes a big decrease in quantity demanded along demand curve E, from 100 units to 20 units at point *b*. But the same increase in price causes only a small decrease in quantity demanded along demand curve I from 100 to 95 units at point *c*. Since the quantity demanded is more responsive to a change in price along demand curve E, demand curve E is more elastic than demand curve I.

substitutes for oil in the long run than in the short run. Since the OPEC oil price increases in the 1970s (see Figure 4.9 in Chapter 4), the U.S. economy has slowly substituted away from oil by moving toward other sources of energy such as coal, nuclear, and hydroelectric. It took many years, but today the U.S. economy uses about half the amount of oil per dollar of GDP than it did in the 1970s.[1]

In the long run, there are even substitutes for oil in transportation. One reason that mopeds are more popular and SUVs less popular in Europe than in the United States is that taxes make the price of gasoline much higher in Europe than in the United States. Europeans have adjusted by buying more mopeds and smaller cars and driving fewer miles—Americans would do the same if the price of gasoline were expected to increase permanently.

If the price of oil increases by a significant amount for a long period, then even the organization of cities will change as people move from suburbia toward apartments and townhouses located closer to work. It may seem odd to think of moving closer to work as a "substitute for oil," but people adjust to price increases in many ways and economists think of all these adjustments as involving substitutes. If the price of cigarettes goes up and people decide to satisfy their oral cravings by chewing carrots, then carrots are a substitute for cigarettes.

In short, the more time people have to adjust to a change in price, the more elastic the demand curve will be.

Let's compare the demand for Orange Crush, a particular brand of orange soda, with the demand for orange soda. There are many good substitutes for Orange Crush, including Orangina, Fanta, and Slice (Wikipedia lists 36 types of orange soda). As a result, the demand for Orange Crush is very elastic because even a small increase in the price of Orange Crush will result in a large decrease in the quantity demanded as people switch to the substitutes. The demand curve for orange soda, however, is less elastic because there are fewer substitutes for orange soda than there are for Orange Crush and the substitutes such as root beer or cola are not as good. We illustrate this in Figure 5.2. The general point is that the demand for a specific brand of a product is more elastic than the demand for a product category. We will come back to this point when we look in more depth at competition and monopoly in Chapters 12 and 13.

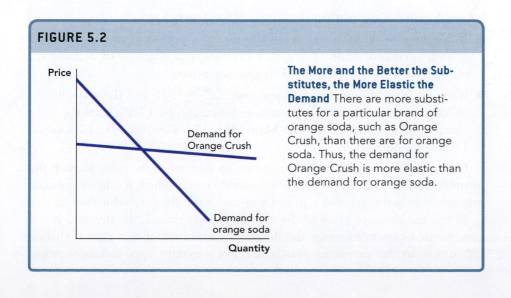

FIGURE 5.2

Price

Demand for Orange Crush

Demand for orange soda

Quantity

The More and the Better the Substitutes, the More Elastic the Demand There are more substitutes for a particular brand of orange soda, such as Orange Crush, than there are for orange soda. Thus, the demand for Orange Crush is more elastic than the demand for orange soda.

What counts as a good substitute depends on a buyer's preferences, as well as on objective properties of the good. If the price of Coca-Cola increases at the supermarket, many people will buy Pepsi but others will keep on buying Coca-Cola because for them Pepsi is *not* a good substitute. So, some people have a more elastic demand for Coca-Cola, while other people have a less elastic demand. A closely related idea is that demand is less elastic for goods that people consider to be "necessities" and is more elastic for goods that are considered "luxuries." Of course, for some people their morning coffee at Starbucks *is* a necessity and for others it's a luxury. Let's summarize by saying that the demand for necessities—however a person defines that term—tends to be less elastic and the demand for luxuries tends to be more elastic.

The higher a person's income, the less concerned they are likely to be with the price of an item; thus, higher income makes demand less elastic. In 2008, the price of wheat tripled, and many people all around the world bought less bread. But neither of the authors of this book cut back much on his consumption of bread. The price of bread is too small a portion of our budgets to worry very much about its price, so our consumption of bread is not very elastic. On the other hand, when the price of housing increases, we buy smaller houses just like everyone else. Thus, the larger the share of a person's budget devoted to a good, the more elastic his or her demand for that good is likely to be.

We summarize the determinants of the elasticity of demand in Table 5.1.

TABLE 5.1 SOME FACTORS DETERMINING THE ELASTICITY OF DEMAND

Less Elastic	More Elastic
Fewer substitutes	More substitutes
Short run (less time)	Long run (more time)
Categories of product	Specific brands
Necessities	Luxuries
Small part of budget	Large part of budget

Calculating the Elasticity of Demand

The elasticity of demand has a precise definition with important properties. The elasticity of demand is the percentage change in the quantity demanded divided by the percentage change in price.

$$\text{Elasticity of demand} = E_d = \frac{\text{Percentage change in quantity demanded}}{\text{Percentage change in price}}$$

$$= \frac{\%\Delta Q_{\text{Demanded}}}{\%\Delta \text{Price}}$$

where Δ (delta) is the mathematical symbol for "change in."

- If the price of oil increases by 10% and over a period of several years the quantity demanded falls by 5%, then the long-run elasticity of demand for oil is $-5\%/10\% = -0.5$, or 0.5 in absolute terms.

- If the price of Minute Maid orange juice falls by 10% and the quantity of Minute Maid orange juice demanded increases by 17.5%, then the elasticity of demand for Minute Maid OJ is $17.5\%/-10\% = -1.75$, or 1.75 in absolute terms.[2]

Elasticities of demand are always negative because when the price goes up, the quantity demanded always goes down (and vice versa), which is why economists sometimes drop the negative sign and work with the absolute value instead.

When the absolute value of the elasticity is less than 1, the demand is not very elastic or economists say the demand is **inelastic**; if it is greater than 1, economists say that demand is **elastic**; and if it is exactly equal to 1, economists

The **elasticity of demand** is a measure of how responsive the quantity demanded is to a change in price. It is computed by

$$E_d = \frac{\%\Delta Q_{\text{Demanded}}}{\%\Delta \text{Price}}$$

$|E_d| > 1 = $ *Elastic*
$|E_d| < 1 = $ *Inelastic*
$|E_d| = 1 = $ *Unit elastic*

say that demand is **unit elastic**. So in our calculations, oil has inelastic demand and Minute Maid orange juice has elastic demand.

Using the Midpoint Method to Calculate the Elasticity of Demand To calculate an elasticity, you need to know how to calculate the percentage change in quantity and the percentage change in price. That is a bit trickier than it sounds. To see why, let's suppose that you observe the price and quantity pairs shown in the table on the next page (careful readers will note that these points correspond to points *a* and *b* along demand curve E in Figure 5.1).

If you think of moving from point *a* to point *b* (let's call this moving from "before" to "after"), then the quantity demanded falls from 100 to 20 so the change in quantity demanded is −80. What is the percentage change in quantity demanded?

If the beginning quantity, Q_{Before}, is 100 and the ending quantity, Q_{After}, is 20, it seems natural to calculate the percentage change in quantity like this:

	Price	Quantity Demanded
Point *a*	$40	100
Point *b*	$50	20

$$\frac{\Delta Q}{Q} = \frac{Q_{After} - Q_{Before}}{Q_{Before}} = \frac{20 - 100}{100} = \frac{-80}{100} = -0.8 = -80\%$$

But now think of moving from point *b* to point *a*. In this case, quantity demanded increases from 20 to 100 and it now seems natural to calculate the percentage change in quantity like this:

$$\frac{\Delta Q}{Q} = \frac{Q_{After} - Q_{Before}}{Q_{Before}} = \frac{100 - 20}{20} = \frac{80}{20} = 4 = 400\%$$

In the first case, we are thinking of a percentage decrease in quantity and in the second of a percentage increase in quantity so it's easy to see why one number is negative and the other positive. But why are the numbers so different when we are calculating exactly the same change?

The different values occur because the base of the calculation changes. If you are driving 100 mph and decrease speed to 20 mph, it's natural to say that your speed went down by 80% because you calculate using a base of 100. But if you are driving 20 mph and you increase speed to 100 mph, it's natural to say that you increased your speed by 400% since you now use 20 as the base. Economists would like to calculate the same number for elasticity whether the quantity (or speed) decreases from 100 to 20 or increases from 20 to 100.

To avoid problems with the choice of base, economists calculate the percentage change in quantity by dividing the change in quantity by the *average or midpoint quantity*—the base is thus the same whether you think about quantity as increasing or decreasing.

Here is the formula:

$$\textbf{Elasticity of demand} = E_d = \frac{\%\Delta Q_{Demanded}}{\%\Delta \textbf{Price}}$$

$$= \frac{\dfrac{\textbf{Change in quantity demanded}}{\textbf{Average quantity}}}{\dfrac{\textbf{Change in price}}{\textbf{Average price}}} = \frac{\dfrac{Q_{After} - Q_{Before}}{(Q_{After} + Q_{Before})/2}}{\dfrac{P_{After} - P_{Before}}{(P_{After} + P_{Before})/2}}$$

In this case, we calculate the percentage change in quantity demanded as $\frac{-80}{(100+20)/2} \times 100 = -133.3\%$ and we also use the midpoint formula for the percentage change in price, which is $\frac{50-40}{(50+40)/2} \times 100 = 22.2\%$. With these two numbers, we can now calculate the elasticity of demand over this portion of the demand curve:

$$E_d = \frac{-133.3\%}{22.2\%} = -6$$

Notice absolute value of the elasticity, 6, is greater than 1, so the demand is elastic over this range.

It's most important that you understand the concept of elasticity. To calculate an elasticity, don't worry too much; just remember where the formula is located and plug in the numbers.

Total Revenues and the Elasticity of Demand

A firm's revenues are equal to price per unit times quantity sold.

Revenue = Price × Quantity, or R = P × Q

Elasticity measures how much Q goes down when P goes up, so you might suspect that there is a relationship between elasticity and revenue. Indeed, the relationship is remarkably useful: If the demand curve is inelastic, then revenues go up when the price goes up. If the demand curve is elastic, then revenues go down when the price goes up.

Let's give some intuition for this result. Imagine that the demand curve is inelastic, thus not responsive to price. This means that when P goes up by a lot, Q goes down by a little, like this

$\uparrow$

$P \times Q$

$\downarrow$

So when the demand curve is inelastic, what will happen to revenues? If P goes up by a lot and Q goes down by a little, then revenues will go up.

$\uparrow$ $\uparrow$

$R = P \times Q$

$\downarrow$

Thus, when the demand curve is inelastic, revenues go up when the price goes up and, of course, revenues will go down when the price goes down.

We can also show the relationship in a diagram. Figure 5.3 shows an inelastic demand curve on the left and an elastic demand curve on the right.[*] Revenue is $P \times Q$, so revenue is equal to the area of a rectangle with height equal to price and width equal to the quantity; for example, when the price is $40 and the quantity is 100, revenues are $4,000, or the area of the blue rectangle (note that the blue and green rectangles overlap).

In both diagrams, the blue rectangles show revenue at a price of $40 and the green rectangles show revenues at the higher price of $50. Compare the size of the blue and green rectangles when the demand curve is inelastic (on the left) and when the demand curve is elastic (on the right). What do you see? When the demand curve is inelastic, an increase in price increases revenues (the green

---

[*] These curves are the same curves as in Figure 5.1, so they run through a common point, and thus we can apply our elasticity rule, which tells us that at any given quantity the flatter curve is more elastic than the steeper curve.

FIGURE 5.3

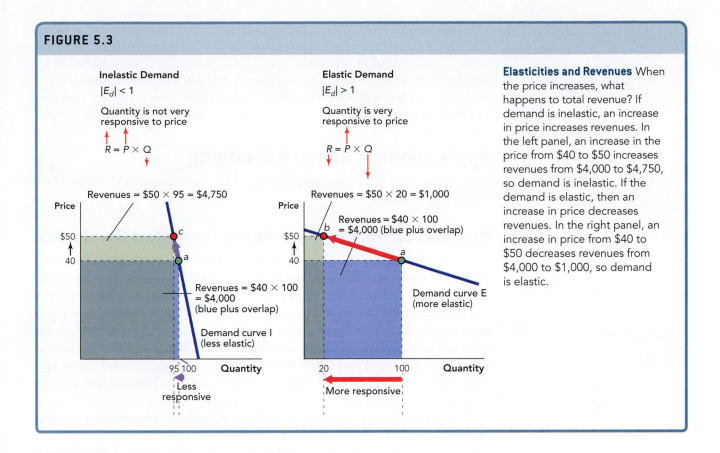

Inelastic Demand

$|E_d| < 1$

Quantity is not very responsive to price

$R = P \times Q$

Revenues = $50 \times 95 = $4,750

Price

$50

40

c

a

Revenues = $40 \times 100 = $4,000 (blue plus overlap)

Demand curve I (less elastic)

95 100   **Quantity**

Less responsive

Elastic Demand

$|E_d| > 1$

Quantity is very responsive to price

$R = P \times Q$

Revenues = $50 \times 20 = $1,000

Price

$50

40

b

Revenues = $40 \times 100 = $4,000 (blue plus overlap)

a

Demand curve E (more elastic)

20   100   **Quantity**

More responsive

Elasticities and Revenues When the price increases, what happens to total revenue? If demand is inelastic, an increase in price increases revenues. In the left panel, an increase in the price from $40 to $50 increases revenues from $4,000 to $4,750, so demand is inelastic. If the demand is elastic, then an increase in price decreases revenues. In the right panel, an increase in price from $40 to $50 decreases revenues from $4,000 to $1,000, so demand is elastic.

rectangle is bigger than the blue rectangle), but when the demand curve is elastic, an increase in price decreases revenues (the green rectangle is smaller than the blue rectangle).

Of course, the relationships hold in reverse as well. If the demand curve is inelastic, a price decrease causes a decrease in revenues, and if the demand curve is elastic, a price decrease causes an increase in revenues.

Can you guess what happens to revenues when price increases or decreases and the demand curve is unit elastic? Right, nothing! When the demand curve is unit elastic, a change in price is exactly matched by an equal and opposite percentage change in quantity so revenues stay the same. Unit elasticity is the dividing point between elastic and inelastic curves.

You should be able to use all of these relationships on an exam. Table 5.2 summarizes what we have covered so far.

TABLE 5.2 ELASTICITY AND REVENUE

Absolute Value of Elasticity	Name	How Revenue Changes with Price
$|E_d| < 1$	Inelastic	Price and revenue move together.
$|E_d| > 1$	Elastic	Price and revenue move in opposite directions.
$|E_d| = 1$	Unit elastic	When price changes, revenue stays the same.

If you must, memorize the table. At least one of your textbook authors, however, can never remember the relationship between elasticity and total revenue. So, instead of memorizing the relationship, he always derives it by drawing little diagrams like those in Figure 5.3. If you can easily duplicate these diagrams, you too will always be able to answer questions involving elasticity and total revenue.

Applications of Demand Elasticity

Let's put to work what you have learned so far about demand elasticity. Here are two applications.

How American Farmers Have Worked Themselves Out of a Job

Using the same inputs of land, labor, and capital, American farmers can produce more than twice as much food today as they could in 1950—that's an amazing increase in productivity. The increase in productivity means that Americans can produce more food per person today than in 1950. But how much more food can Americans eat? Although it doesn't always seem this way, Americans want to consume only so much more food even if the price falls by a lot. So what type of demand curve does this suggest? An inelastic demand curve; and remember, when the demand curve is inelastic, a fall in price means a fall in revenues.

The left panel of Figure 5.4 shows how American farmers have worked themselves out of a job. Increases in farming productivity have reduced cost, shifting the supply curve down and reducing the price of food. But because the demand curve for food is inelastic, the quantity of food demanded has increased by a smaller percentage than the price has fallen. As a result, farming revenues have declined. Notice that in the left panel of Figure 5.4, the blue rectangle (farm revenues today) is smaller than the green rectangle (revenues in 1950)—just as we showed in Figure 5.3.

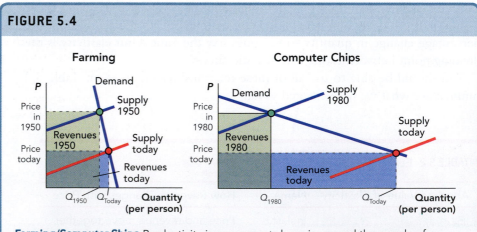

FIGURE 5.4

Farming/Computer Chips Productivity improvements have increased the supply of food and the supply of computer chips, thus reducing the prices of these goods. The demand for food, however, is inelastic, while the demand for computer chips is elastic. As a result, the decrease in the price of food has driven down farm revenues, while the decrease in the price of computer chips has driven up computer chip revenues.

Increases in productivity, however, do not always mean that revenue falls. In the last several decades, productivity has increased in computer chips even faster than in farming. But as the price of computer chips has fallen, the quantity of computer chips demanded has increased even more. Computer chips are now not just in computers but in phones, televisions, automobiles, and toys. As a result, revenues for the computer chip industry have increased and made computing a larger share of the American economy. What type of demand curve does this suggest? An elastic demand curve. The right panel in Figure 5.4 illustrates how an increase in productivity in computing has shifted the supply curve down and reduced prices, but the quantity of computer chips demanded has increased by an even greater percentage than the price has fallen. As a result, computer chip revenues have increased.

The lesson is that whether a demand curve is elastic or inelastic has a tremendous influence on how an industry evolves over time. If you want to be in on a growing industry, it helps to know the elasticity of demand.

Why the War on Drugs Is Hard to Win

It's hard to defeat an enemy that grows stronger the more you strike against him or her. (See the movies *Rocky I, II, III, IV, V, Rocky Balboa,* and *Creed.*) The war on drugs is like that. We illustrate with a simple model.

The U.S. government spends over \$40 billion a year arresting over 1.5 million people and deterring the supply of drugs with police, prisons, and border patrols.[*] This, in turn, increases the cost of smuggling and dealing drugs. (The war on drugs also increases the costs of buying drugs. We could include this factor in our model, but to keep the model simple, we will focus on increases in the costs of supplying drugs.) When costs go up, suppliers require a higher price to supply any given quantity so the supply curve shifts up—in Figure 5.5 from "Supply with no prohibition" to "Supply with prohibition."[†]

FIGURE 5.5

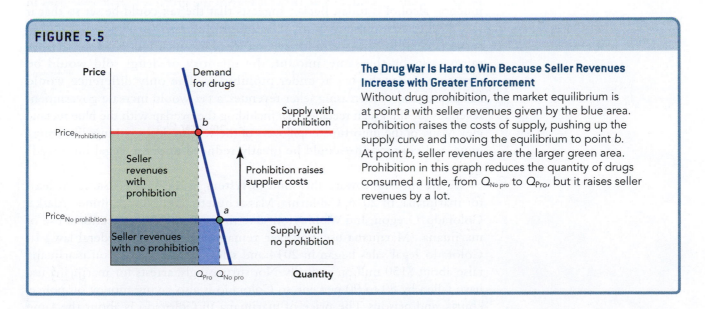

The Drug War Is Hard to Win Because Seller Revenues Increase with Greater Enforcement
Without drug prohibition, the market equilibrium is at point *a* with seller revenues given by the blue area. Prohibition raises the costs of supply, pushing up the supply curve and moving the equilibrium to point *b*. At point *b*, seller revenues are the larger green area. Prohibition in this graph reduces the quantity of drugs consumed a little, from $Q_{No\,pro}$ to Q_{Pro}, but it raises seller revenues by a lot.

[*] See Miron, Jeffrey A. 2004. *Drug War Crimes: The Consequences of Prohibition* (Oakland, CA: Independent Institute) and Kleiman, Mark, Jonathan P. Caulkins, and Angela Hawken. 2011. *Drugs and Drug Policy: What Everyone Needs to Know* (New York: Oxford University Press) for two good analyses of the war on drugs from an economic perspective.
[†] Note that we have assumed that the supply of drugs is perfectly horizontal, which is plausible for an agricultural product whose production can be expanded or contracted very easily without an increase in costs. We discuss the elasticity of supply at greater length in the next section.

In many states personal marijuana use is now legal and the government, rather than criminals, is profiting from marijuana sales.

The most important assumption in Figure 5.5 is that the demand curve is inelastic. It's hard to get good data on how the quantity of drugs demanded varies with the price, but most studies suggest that the demand for illegal drugs is quite inelastic, approximately 0.5. Inelastic demand is also plausible from what we know intuitively about how much people are willing to pay for drugs even when the price rises. Economists have much better data on the elasticity of demand for cigarettes, which one can think of as the elasticity of demand for the drug nicotine and it too is about 0.5.[3]

What happens to seller revenues when the demand curve is inelastic and the price rises? (Review Figure 5.3 if you don't know immediately.) When the demand curve is inelastic, an increase in price increases seller revenues. In Figure 5.5, the blue rectangle is seller revenues at the no prohibition price; the much larger green rectangle is seller revenues with prohibition. Prohibition increases the cost of selling drugs, which raises the price, but at a higher price, revenues from drug selling are greater even if the quantity sold is somewhat smaller.

The more effective prohibition is at raising costs, the greater are drug industry revenues. So, more effective prohibition means that drug sellers have more money to buy guns, pay bribes, fund the dealers, and even research and develop new technologies in drug delivery (like crack cocaine). It's hard to beat an enemy that gets stronger the more you strike against him or her.

The war on drugs is difficult to win, but that doesn't necessarily mean that it's not worth fighting. Nobel Prize-winning economist Gary S. Becker, however, suggests a change in tactics. Suppose drugs were legal but taxed, much as alcohol is today. Becker suggests that the tax could be set so that it raised seller costs exactly as much as did prohibition (in Figure 5.5 simply relabel "Supply with prohibition" as "Supply with tax"). Since the tax raises costs by the same amount, the quantity of drugs sold would be the same under the tax as under prohibition. The only difference would be that instead of increasing seller revenues, a tax would increase government revenues (by the green rectangle *not* including the overlap with the blue rectangle). Many of the unfortunate spillovers of the war on drugs—things like gangs, guns, and corruption—could be greatly reduced under a "legal but taxed" system.[*]

We are moving toward this kind of system in the United States, at least for marijuana. In 2016, California, Massachusetts, and Nevada joined Alaska, Colorado, Oregon, and Washington state in legalizing the recreational use of marijuana. (Marijuana use, however, remains illegal under Federal law.) In Colorado, legal sales began in 2014 and sales and other taxes on marijuana raise about $150 million annually. Not surprisingly, arrests for marijuana use have fallen by 80 to 90 percent, so Colorado is also saving money on police, courts, and prisons. The price of marijuana in Colorado is about the same or a bit higher than in states where marijuana is illegal but the quality and

* On the benefits of a tax system for currently illegal drugs, see Becker, Gary S., Kevin M. Murphy, and Michael Grossman. 2006. The market for illegal goods: The case of drugs. *Journal of Political Economy* 114(1): 38–60.

variety of marijuana and methods of delivery (e.g., edibles) has increased tremendously. One worry is that as with alcohol, a minority of consumers account for a majority of use. In Colorado, for example, daily users account for 69% of total marijuana consumption so serious problems can develop in a minority even when the majority of people enjoy casual use.[4] Outright prohibition of marijuana appears to be ending but much work remains to be done on precisely how marijuana and other drugs will be taxed and regulated.

Let's turn now to the elasticity of supply.

The Elasticity of Supply

When the price of a good like oil increases, suppliers will increase the quantity supplied, but by how much? Will the quantity supplied increase by a lot or by a little? The **elasticity of supply** measures how responsive the quantity supplied is to a change in price. To see the intuition, let's take a look at Figure 5.6, which shows two different supply curves.

In Figure 5.6, when the price increases from $40 to $50, the quantity supplied increases from 80 to 85 along supply curve I but by the much larger amount from 80 to 170 along supply curve E. Since the quantity supplied is more responsive to a change in price, supply curve E is more elastic than supply curve I.

CHECK YOURSELF

- Which is more elastic, the demand for computers or the demand for Dell computers?
- The elasticity of demand for eggs has been estimated to be 0.1. If the price of eggs increases by 10%, what will happen to the total revenue of egg producers or in other words the total spending on eggs? Will it go up or down?
- If a fashionable clothing store raises its prices by 25%, what does that suggest about the store's estimate of the elasticity of demand for its products?

The **elasticity of supply** measures how responsive the quantity supplied is to a change in price.

FIGURE 5.6

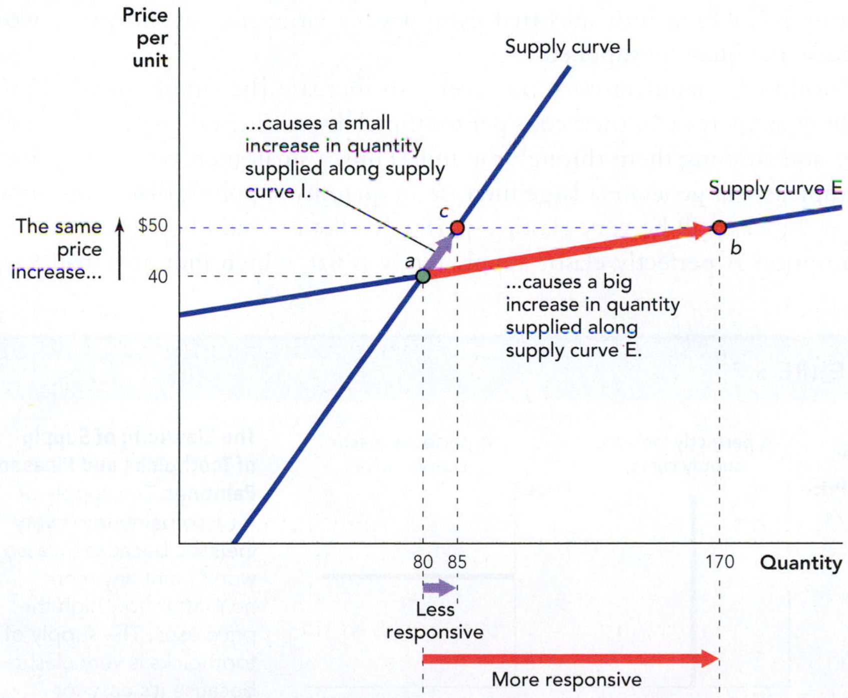

The More Responsive Quantity Supplied Is to a Change in Price, the More Elastic the Supply Curve Beginning at point *a*, an increase in price from $40 to $50 causes a small increase in quantity supplied along supply curve I, from 80 to 85 units (at point *c*). But the same increase in price causes a big increase in quantity supplied along supply curve E, from 80 to 170 units (at point *b*). Since the quantity supplied is more responsive to a change in price, supply curve E is more elastic than supply curve I.

Determinants of the Elasticity of Supply

Which supply curve, supply curve I or supply curve E, do you think would better represent the supply curve for oil? Even large increases in the price of oil will not increase the quantity of oil supplied by very much because it's not easy to quickly increase the production of oil. Producing more oil requires time and a significant increase in the costs of exploration and drilling. Thus, the supply curve for oil is not very elastic (we could also say inelastic) and would be better represented by supply curve I.

The fundamental determinant of the elasticity of supply is how quickly per-unit costs increase with an increase in production. If increased production requires much higher per-unit costs, then supply will be less elastic—or inelastic. If production can increase without much increasing per-unit costs, then supply will be elastic.

It's usually difficult to increase the supply of raw materials like oil, coal, and gold without increasing costs—remember from Chapter 3 that the higher the price, the deeper the mine—so the supply of raw materials is often inelastic. The supply of manufactured goods is usually more elastic since production can often be increased at similar costs per unit by building more factories. To fully understand the elasticity of supply, let's consider two goods that represent polar cases of the elasticity of supply: Picasso paintings and toothpicks.

Picasso won't be painting any more canvases no matter how high the price of his paintings rises so the supply of Picasso paintings is not at all elastic—perfectly inelastic would be a good working assumption.* A perfectly inelastic supply curve is a vertical line. We show an example in the left panel of Figure 5.7, which indicates that even a very large increase in price won't increase the quantity supplied.

Toothpick manufacturers, however, can increase the supply of toothpicks without an increase in their costs per toothpick by cutting down just a few more trees and running them through the mill. Thus, a small increase in the price of toothpicks will generate a large increase in quantity supplied; that is, the supply of toothpicks will be very elastic—perfectly elastic would be a good working assumption. A perfectly elastic supply curve is flat, which indicates that even a

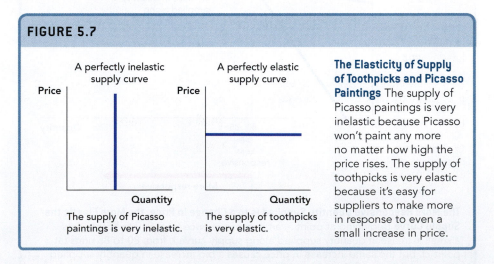

FIGURE 5.7

The Elasticity of Supply of Toothpicks and Picasso Paintings The supply of Picasso paintings is very inelastic because Picasso won't paint any more no matter how high the price rises. The supply of toothpicks is very elastic because it's easy for suppliers to make more in response to even a small increase in price.

* Why isn't the supply of Picasso paintings perfectly inelastic for certain? The supply of newly created Picasso paintings is perfectly inelastic, but with a higher price more people will be induced to sell their Picasso paintings, so the market supply of Picasso paintings will be very inelastic but not necessarily perfectly inelastic.

tiny increase in price increases the quantity supplied by a very large amount. We show a perfectly elastic supply curve in the right panel of Figure 5.7.

It's easy to expand the supply of toothpicks because even if the toothpick industry doubles in size, the increases in the demand for wood will be negligible, so the toothpick industry can expand without pushing up the price of its primary input, wood. But if the housing industry were to double in size, the demand for wood would increase dramatically, and since it takes time to plant and harvest new trees, the price of wood and thus the price of houses would increase in the short run. More generally, supply is more elastic when the industry can be expanded without causing a big increase in the demand for that industry's inputs.

A closely related point is that the local supply of a good is much more elastic than the global supply. The supply of oil to the world is inelastic because world production won't increase without a significant increase in the cost of production per barrel. But imagine that more people move to Austin, Texas, increasing the demand for oil in that city. It's very easy to ship more oil to Austin from other parts of the United States so the supply of oil to Austin is well approximated by a perfectly elastic supply curve.

As with demand, supply tends to be more elastic in the long run than in the short run because in the long run, suppliers have more time to adjust. Suppliers can respond to an increase in the price of bicycles fairly quickly by running currently existing factories at higher capacity. Given more time, however, suppliers can increase output at lower cost by building new factories.

For some goods, it's almost impossible to increase output much in the short run. The best Scotch whisky, for example, is aged in oak barrels for 10, 20, or even 30 years. If the price of such high-quality Scotch whisky increases today, it will be at least 10 years before supply can increase.

We summarize the primary factors that determine the elasticity of supply in Table 5.3.

Pablo Picasso 1881–1973

GJO MILI/GETTY IMAGES

TABLE 5.3 PRIMARY FACTORS DETERMINING THE ELASTICITY OF SUPPLY	
Less Elastic	More Elastic
Difficult to increase production at constant unit cost (e.g., some raw materials)	Easy to increase production at constant unit cost (e.g., some manufactured goods)
Large share of market for inputs	Small share of market for inputs
Global supply	Local supply
Short run	Long run

Calculating the Elasticity of Supply

The elasticity of supply also has a precise definition. The **elasticity of supply** is the percentage change in the quantity supplied divided by the percentage change in price.

The **elasticity of supply** is a measure of how responsive the quantity supplied is to a change in price. It is computed by

$$E_s = \frac{\%\Delta Q_{\text{Supplied}}}{\%\Delta \text{Price}}$$

Examples:

- If the price of cocoa rises by 10% and the quantity supplied increases by 3%, then the elasticity of supply for cocoa is $\frac{3\%}{10\%} = \mathbf{0.3}$.
- If the price of coffee falls by 10% and the quantity supplied of coffee falls by 1.5%, then the elasticity of supply for coffee is $\frac{-1.5\%}{-10\%} = \mathbf{0.15}$.[5]

Using the Midpoint Method to Calculate the Elasticity of Supply As with demand elasticities, it's important to calculate percent changes for supply elasticities using the midpoint method. Here is the midpoint formula for the elasticity of supply.

$$\text{Elasticity of supply} = E_s = \frac{\%\Delta Q_{\text{Supplied}}}{\%\Delta \text{Price}}$$

$$= \frac{\dfrac{\text{Change in quantity supplied}}{\text{Average quantity}}}{\dfrac{\text{Change in price}}{\text{Average price}}} = \frac{\dfrac{Q_{\text{After}} - Q_{\text{Before}}}{(Q_{\text{After}} + Q_{\text{Before}})/2}}{\dfrac{P_{\text{After}} - P_{\text{Before}}}{(P_{\text{After}} + P_{\text{Before}})/2}}$$

Applications of Supply Elasticity

Let's examine two important issues in public policy, gun buybacks and slave redemption. In both cases, understanding the elasticity of supply is critical if we are to evaluate these policies wisely.

Gun Buyback Programs

"Guns for groceries" is how the Los Angeles Police Department advertises their annual gun buyback program. A handgun will get you a $100 gift card good for groceries at a local store, and an assault weapon is worth a $200 gift card. The guns can be turned in "no questions asked." You don't even have to go to the police station; the LAPD set up a drive-through at a local shopping mall. One Christmas, the program was so popular that it created traffic congestion and long lines. Gun buybacks have been held in recent years in Baltimore, Santa Fe, Camden, NJ, and many other cities across the nation. But do the programs work?

The theory of gun buybacks is that gun buybacks (1) reduce the number of guns in circulation and (2) reductions in the number of guns in circulation reduces crime. It's not obvious that point (2) is true—guns are used for self-defense as well as for crime so fewer guns could mean more crime. But we don't have to decide that controversial question here because simple economic theory suggests that point (1) is false—gun buybacks in a city like Los Angeles are unlikely to reduce the number of guns in circulation. Let's see why.

We can analyze the effect of this program with a few questions. What kinds of guns are most likely to be sold at the gun buyback, high-quality or low-quality guns? And, what is the elasticity of supply of such guns to a city like Los Angeles?

The best gun to sell at a buyback is one that you can't sell anywhere else, so buybacks attract low-quality guns. In one Seattle buyback, 17% of the guns turned in didn't even fire.[6]

Only in America: A drive-through gun buyback program.

Now here is the key question: What is the elasticity of supply of low-quality guns to a city like Los Angeles? Recall from Table 5.3 that local supply curves are typically more elastic than global or national supply curves. It's estimated that there are 200 to 300 million guns in the United States so there are plenty of low-quality guns—so many that the supply of such guns to Los Angeles will be very elastic—elastic enough to make perfectly elastic a good working assumption.

Now that we know that the supply of low-quality guns to Los Angeles is very elastic, let's draw the diagram and analyze the policy. In Figure 5.8, we draw a perfectly elastic supply curve. With no buyback, the price of a low-quality, used gun is $84 and 1,000 guns are traded in Los Angeles. The gun buyback program increases the demand for used guns, shifting the demand curve outward, and the increase in demand pushes up the quantity of guns supplied in Los Angeles to 6,000 units. But the supply is so elastic that the price of guns doesn't increase, so even though the police buy 5,000 guns, the quantity of guns traded on the streets stays at 1,000. In other words, there is no net change in the number of guns on the streets of Los Angeles.

If this seems difficult to believe, imagine that instead of guns, the Los Angeles police decided to buy back shoes. Remember, the idea of a gun buyback is to reduce the number of guns in Los Angeles. Now, do you think that a shoe buyback would reduce the number of shoes in Los Angeles? Of course not. What will happen? People will sell their old shoes, the ones they don't wear anymore. Some enterprising individuals might even buy old shoes from thrift shops and sell those to the police. (In one Oakland gun buyback, some enterprising gun dealers from Reno, Nevada, drove to Oakland and sold the police more than 50 low-quality guns.[7]) The shoe buyback is unlikely to cause people to go shoeless, and for the same reasons a gun buyback is unlikely to cause people to go gunless.

The key point is that if the police can't drive up the price of guns, then they can't reduce the quantity of guns demanded on the streets. And the price of guns is determined not in Los Angeles, but in the national market for guns where millions of guns are bought and sold; thus a police buyback of a few thousand guns is too small to influence the price.

FIGURE 5.8

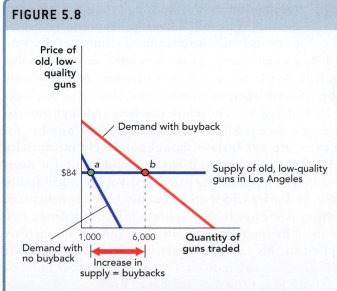

Elasticity and Gun Buybacks In the initial equilibrium at point *a*, 1,000 low-quality guns are traded. When police buy guns, the demand for guns increases, but since the supply of guns to a local region is very elastic, the street price of guns does not increase. As a result, the police can buy as many guns as they want, but there is no decrease in the number of guns on the street.

It's even possible that gun buybacks will *increase* the number of guns in circulation. Suppose that gun buybacks become a common and permanent feature of the market for guns. Before the gun buyback, a purchaser of a new gun expects that it will eventually wear out or otherwise fall in value until it becomes worthless. But when gun buybacks are common, someone buying a gun knows that if it stops working, he can always sell it to the government. A buyback makes new guns more valuable; now they come with an insurance policy protecting against declines in value, which increases the demand for new guns.[8] You have probably experienced the same effect—students are more willing to buy an expensive textbook if they know they can easily sell it at the end of the semester (but do keep *this* book forever!).

Given the economic analysis, it's not surprising that studies of gun buybacks have shown them to be ineffective at reducing crime.[9]

The Economics of Slave Redemption

Let's return to our opening example. Recall that Harvard sophomore Jay Williams flew to the Sudan in fall 2000 to buy the freedom of people who had been enslaved. Working with Christian Solidarity International, Williams was able to buy and free 4,000 people. Donations came from all over the United States, including a fourth-grade class in Denver.[10]

MICHAEL DWYER/AP PHOTO

Jay Williams (right) in the Sudan

The policy of slave redemption has been controversial. Some groups such as Christian Freedom International, equally as humanitarian as Christian Solidarity International, have argued that slave redemption can make a bad situation even worse. Perhaps surprisingly, at the heart of the controversy is the concept of the elasticity of supply. If groups who pay to free people from slavery increase the demand for slaves, what effect will this have on the price of slaves and on the incentives of those who traffic in people?

In Figure 5.9, we show the best case for slave redemption, when the supply curve is perfectly inelastic (vertical). When the supply curve is perfectly inelastic, there is a fixed number of slaves no matter what the price. As a result, every person ransomed and freed is one less person held in captivity. People like Jay Williams may have been implicitly assuming a fixed number of slaves when they flew to the Sudan.

Let's take a closer look at Figure 5.9. Before the slave redemption program begins, the price of a slave is $15, at the time a realistic number for slaves in Sudan, and there are 1,000 slaves bought and held in captivity every year (point *a*). With the redemption program, the demand for slaves increases (shifts outward), which pushes the price of slaves up to $50 (point *b*). Now here is the key: At a price of $50, the quantity of slaves demanded by potential slave owners decreases to 200 (point *c*). The remaining 800 slaves are bought and freed by the redeemers. Because there is no increase in the quantity supplied in this case, every slave purchased means one

FIGURE 5.9

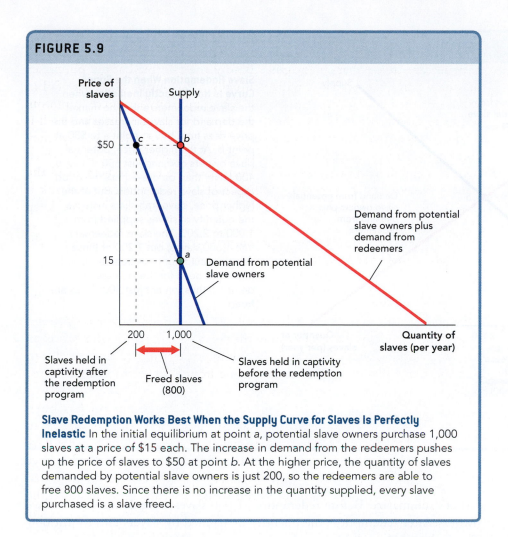

Slave Redemption Works Best When the Supply Curve for Slaves Is Perfectly Inelastic In the initial equilibrium at point *a*, potential slave owners purchase 1,000 slaves at a price of $15 each. The increase in demand from the redeemers pushes up the price of slaves to $50 at point *b*. At the higher price, the quantity of slaves demanded by potential slave owners is just 200, so the redeemers are able to free 800 slaves. Since there is no increase in the quantity supplied, every slave purchased is a slave freed.

less person held in slavery. Note that slave redemption works by driving up the price of slaves so high that potential owners cannot afford to buy slaves. In other words, to work well, slave redeemers must outbid potential slave owners.

Unfortunately, the supply of slaves is unlikely to be perfectly inelastic. We return to one of the primary lessons of this book, incentives. When people enter the market to buy back slaves and increase the price of slaves, they increase the incentive to capture more slaves.

Figure 5.10 analyzes the more realistic case—when the supply curve is not perfectly inelastic. In the initial equilibrium, the price of slaves is $15 and potential owners buy 1,000 slaves (point *a*). When the redeemers enter the market, the demand for slaves increases and the price increases from $15 to $30 (point *b*). The price of slaves does not increase as much as when the supply curve was perfectly inelastic because some of the increased demand for slaves is met by a greater quantity supplied. At a price of $30, the quantity of slaves demanded by potential owners falls from 1,000 to 600 (point *c*), but notice also that the total number of people captured by traffickers increases by 1,200 to 2,200 (point *b*). Of these 2,200, 1,600 are freed by the redeemers, leaving 600 held in captivity.

FIGURE 5.10

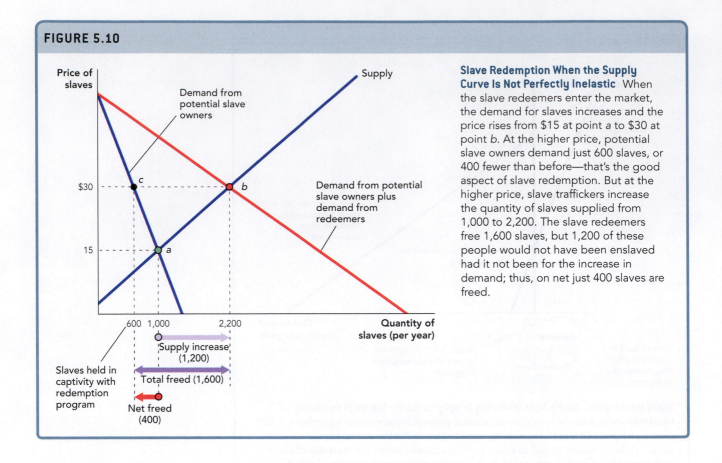

Slave Redemption When the Supply Curve Is Not Perfectly Inelastic When the slave redeemers enter the market, the demand for slaves increases and the price rises from $15 at point *a* to $30 at point *b*. At the higher price, potential slave owners demand just 600 slaves, or 400 fewer than before—that's the good aspect of slave redemption. But at the higher price, slave traffickers increase the quantity of slaves supplied from 1,000 to 2,200. The slave redeemers free 1,600 slaves, but 1,200 of these people would not have been enslaved had it not been for the increase in demand; thus, on net just 400 slaves are freed.

Let's summarize: Before redemption, 1,000 slaves were demanded by slave owners. After redemption, the quantity demanded by slavers falls to just 600. This is the good result of the redemption program. But due to the higher price of slaves, slave traffickers increase the quantity of slaves from 1,000 to 2,200. The redeemers free 1,600 of these 2,200 slaves, but 1,200 of these would not have been enslaved had it not been for the increase in demand. Thus, on net, the slave redeemers free just 400 slaves.

The key point is this: The additional demand for slaves from those who wish to free slaves pushes up the price of slaves, which reduces the quantity demanded—that's good. But the higher price also pushes up the quantity supplied—that's bad.

Thus, slavery redemption programs create a true dilemma. The groups that buy freedom can reduce the number of slaves held in captivity, but only at the price of increasing the number of people who are enslaved for at least some time. An economist can point to this dilemma, but economics does not offer a solution (and unfortunately neither does anyone else).

Is there any evidence on the effect of slave redemption programs? Remember that one sign of whether the redemption program is working is how much the program increases the price of slaves. Higher prices mean that the redeemers are outbidding potential slave traffickers. Data on slave prices in the Sudan are unreliable, but the fragmentary data that do exist are not encouraging. Although the redemption program initially appeared to raise prices, prices soon began to fall.[11] Recall that supply tends to be more elastic in the long run—thus, the data on prices are consistent with a supply curve that became more elastic over time. Since redemption programs are less effective when the elasticity of supply is greater, the data on prices suggest that the program became less effective over time.

Finally, let us note some further complications. Slavery in the Sudan was part of a larger civil war (1983–2005)—the government in Khartoum permitted and even encouraged slave traffickers who attacked the government's enemies. When redeemers bought slaves, therefore, they may also have been helping to fund shock troops in a civil war. Guns bought with money received from selling slaves could be used to kill as well as to enslave. Even if we concluded that slave redemption was on average good for the slaves, it might not have been good once we account for all of the *external effects* of enriching slave raiders. (We explain the idea of external effects at greater length in Chapter 10.)

Ultimately, the only way to truly end slavery is to raise the punishment for buying, selling or owning slaves to so high a level that there is no longer a market for slaves. Slave raiding in the Sudan ended with the end of the civil war and the signing of a peace agreement in 2005. An unknown number of people, however, may still be held in captivity.*

What Does Elasticity Have to do with Freeing Slaves in Africa?

Using Elasticities for Quick Predictions (Optional)

Economists are often asked to predict how shifts in demand and supply will change market prices. Two simple price-change formulas make it possible to make quick predictions for price changes using elasticities.[12]

- Percent change in price from a shift in demand $= \dfrac{\text{Percent change in demand}}{|E_d| + E_s}$

- Percent change in price from a shift in supply $= -\dfrac{\text{Percent change in supply}}{|E_d| + E_s}$

These formulas are approximations that work well when the percent change in demand or supply is small, say, 10% or less.[13] Let's apply the formula to an interesting problem.

How Much Would the Price of Oil Fall If the Arctic National Wildlife Refuge Were Opened Up for Drilling?

The Arctic National Wildlife Refuge (ANWR) is the largest of Alaska's 16 national wildlife refuges. It is believed to contain significant deposits of petroleum. Former President George W. Bush argued in favor of drilling in ANWR.

> Increasing our domestic energy supply will help lower gasoline prices and utility bills. We can and should produce more crude oil here at home in environmentally responsible ways. The most promising site for oil in America is a 2,000 acre site in the Arctic National Wildlife Refuge, and thanks to technology, we can reach this energy with little impact on the land or wildlife.[14]

Some environmentalists disagree about whether the oil can be produced in environmentally responsible ways. We will leave that debate to others. What

CHECK YOURSELF

- A computer manufacturer makes an experimental computer chip that critics praise, leading to a huge increase in the demand for the chip. How elastic is supply in the short run? What about the long run?

- Will the same increase in the demand for housing increase prices more in Manhattan or in Des Moines, Iowa?

---

* For more on the difficult ethics and economics of slave redemption, see the essays in Appiah, Kwame Anthony, and Martin Bunzl. 2007. *Buying Freedom: The Ethics and Economics of Slave Redemption* (Princeton, NJ: Princeton University Press). See especially Chapter 1, "Some Simple Analytics of Slave Redemption," by Dean S. Karlan and Alan B. Krueger, for the incisive economic analysis that we have drawn on.

At what price should we drill for oil in ANWR?

do economists say about the former president's assertion that "Increasing our domestic energy supply will help lower gasoline prices and utility bills"? An increase in supply will lower prices, but by how much?

The Department of Energy's Energy Information Service (EIS) predicts that production from ANWR will average about 800,000 barrels per day, or a little bit less than 1% of worldwide oil production. Let's be generous and suppose that ANWR increases world supply by 1%. Since the elasticity of demand for oil is about −0.5 and in the long run the best estimate of the elasticity of supply is about 0.3, using our price formula, we have

$$\textbf{Percent change in price of oil from a 1\%}$$
$$\textbf{increase in supply} = -\frac{1\%}{0.5 + 0.3}$$
$$= -1.25\%$$

A 1.25% fall in price won't seem like very much when you are gassing up at the pump, but don't forget that *every user of oil in the world* will benefit from the fall in price—so a fall of 1.25% is nothing to sneeze at.

So should we drill for oil in ANWR or not? The answer will depend on the value of conservation, the costs of drilling for oil (including the costs of a potential oil spill such as occured in the Gulf of Mexico), and the price and quantity of oil that can be recovered. Not an easy calculation!

Takeaway

The elasticity of demand measures how responsive the quantity demanded is to a change in price—the more responsive, the more elastic the demand. Similarly, the elasticity of supply measures how responsive the quantity supplied is to a change in price—the more responsive, the more elastic the supply.

In Chapter 4, we learned how to shift the supply and demand curves to produce *qualitative* predictions about changes in prices and quantities. Estimating elasticities of demand and supply is the first step in *quantifying* how changes in demand and supply will affect prices and quantities. You should know how to calculate elasticities of demand and supply using data on prices and quantities.

The elasticity of demand tells you how revenues respond to changes in price along a demand curve. If the $|E_d| < 1$, then price and revenue move together, and if $|E_d| > 1$, then price and revenue move in opposite directions. We used these relationships to explain why decreases in the price of food have made farming a smaller share of the economy, but decreases in the price of computer chips have made computing a larger share of the economy. We also used the same relationship to explain why the war on drugs can strengthen the very people it is trying to weaken.

You don't need to do statistical studies of demand and supply to get useful information about elasticities. Once you understand the concept, a little common sense will tell you that the supply curve for low-quality guns in Los Angeles is very elastic. And, if you can reason that the supply of low-quality guns to Los Angeles is very elastic, a little economics will tell you that gun buyback programs are a waste of taxpayer dollars. Similar reasoning suggests how slave redemption programs might harm more people than they benefit.

Elasticity is a bit dry but it's a very useful concept, and it will appear again when we come to discuss taxes in Chapter 6 and monopoly in Chapter 13.

CHAPTER REVIEW

interactive activity   Go online to practice with more examples of these types of problems, including live links to videos, data sources, and feedback.

 Problems in green relate to MRU videos. See the MRU table at the end of the exercises.

 Problems in blue are Office Hours videos.

KEY CONCEPTS

elasticity of demand, p. 71

inelastic, p. 74

elastic, p. 74

unit elastic, p. 75

elasticity of supply, p. 81

FACTS AND TOOLS

1. For each of the following pairs, which of the two goods is more likely to be inelastically demanded and why? Table 5.1 should help:

   a. Demand for tangerines vs. demand for fruit.

   b. Demand for beef next month vs. demand for beef over the next decade.

   c. Demand for Exxon gasoline at the corner of 7th and Grand vs. demand for gasoline in the entire city.

   d. Demand for insulin vs. demand for vitamins

2. For each of the following pairs, which of the two goods is more likely to be elastically supplied? Table 5.3 should help:

   a. Supply of apples over the next growing season vs. supply of apples over the next decade.

   b. Supply of construction workers in Binghamton, New York, vs. supply of construction workers in New York State.

   c. Supply of breakfast cereal vs. supply of food

   d. Supply of gold vs. supply of computers

3. Indicate whether the demand for the good would become more elastic or less elastic after each of the following changes. (Note that in each of these cases, the demand curve may also shift inward or outward, but in this question we are interested in whether the demand becomes more or less elastic.) Briefly justify your answer.

   a. The demand curve for soap after wide understanding that bacteria and other organisms cause and spread disease.

   b. The demand curve for coal after the invention of nuclear power plants.

   c. The demand curve for cars as more employers allow employees to telecommute.

   d. The demand curve for a new television during an economic boom.

4. For each of the following, indicate if the supply for the good would become more elastic or less elastic as a result of each change, and briefly justify your answer. (Once again, in each case the supply curve will also shift, but we are interested in changes in the elasticity.)

   a. The supply curve for diamonds if a new process for *manufacturing* diamonds is created.

   b. The supply curve for food if pesticides and fertilizers were banned.

   c. The supply curve for plastic if a very large share of oil output was used to make plastic.

   d. The supply curve for nurses after several years of increasing wages in nursing.

5. Let's work out a few examples to get a sense of what elasticity of demand means in practice. Remember that in all of these cases, we're moving along a fixed demand curve—so think of supply increasing or decreasing, while the demand curve is staying in the same place.

   a. If the elasticity of demand for college textbooks is −0.1 and the price of textbooks increases by 20%, how much will the quantity demanded change, and in what direction?

   b. In your answer to part a, was your answer in percentages or in total number of textbooks?

   c. If the elasticity of demand for spring break packages to Cancun is −5, and if you notice that this year in Cancun the quantity of packages demanded increased by 10%, then what happened to the price of Cancun vacation packages?

   d. In your college town, real estate developers are building thousands of new student-friendly apartments close to campus. If you want to pay the lowest rent possible, should you hope that demand for apartments is relatively elastic or relatively inelastic?

e. In your college town, the local government decrees that thousands of apartments close to campus are uninhabitable and must be torn down next semester. If you want to pay the lowest rent possible, should you hope that demand for apartments is relatively elastic or relatively inelastic?

f. If the elasticity of demand for ballpoint pens with blue ink is −20, and the price of ball-point pens with blue ink rises by 1%, what happens to the quantity demanded?

g. What's an obvious substitute for ballpoint pens with blue ink? (This obvious substitute explains why the demand is so elastic.)

6. It's an important tradition in the Santos family that they eat the same meal at their favorite restaurant every Sunday. By contrast, the Chen family spends exactly $50 for their Sunday meal at whatever restaurant sounds best.

a. Which family has a more elastic demand for restaurant food?

b. Which family has a unit elastic demand for restaurant food? (*Hint:* How would each family respond to an increase in food prices?)

7. The U.S. Department of Agriculture (USDA) has been concerned that Americans aren't eating enough fruits and vegetables, and they've considered coupons and other subsidies to encourage people—especially lower-income people—to eat these healthier foods. Of course, if people's demand for fruits and vegetables is perfectly inelastic, then there's no point in giving out coupons (thought question: why?). If instead the demand is only somewhat elastic, there may be better ways to spend taxpayer dollars.

This is clearly a situation where you'd want to know the elasticity of fruit and vegetable demand: If people respond a lot to small changes in price, then government-funded fruit and vegetable coupons *could* make poorer Americans a lot healthier, which *might* save taxpayers money *if* they don't have to pay for expensive medical treatments for unhealthy eaters. There are a lot of links in this chain of reasoning—all of which are covered in more advanced economics courses—but the first link is whether people actually have elastic demand for fruits and vegetables. The USDA's Economic Research Service employs economists to answer these sorts of questions, and a recent report contained the following estimated elasticities (*Source:* Diansheng

Dong and Biing-Hwan Lin. 2009. Fruit and vegetable consumption by low-income Americans: Would a price reduction make a difference? *Economic Research Report* 70, USDA).

Fruit	Elasticity of Demand
Apple	−0.16
Banana	−0.42
Grapefruit	−1.02
Grapes	−0.91
Orange	−1.14

a. Based on these demand elasticity estimates, which fruit is most inelastically demanded? Which is most elastically demanded?

b. For which of these fruits would a 10% drop in price cause an increase in total revenue from the sale of that fruit?

c. If the government could offer "10% off" coupons for only three of these fruits, and it wanted to have the biggest possible effect on quantity demanded, which three fruits should get the coupons?

d. Overall, the authors found that for the average fruit, the elasticity of demand was about −0.5. Is the demand for fruit elastic or inelastic?

8. On average, old cars pollute more than newer cars. Therefore, every few years, a politician proposes a cash for clunkers program: The government offers to buy up and destroy old, high-polluting cars. If a cash for clunkers program buys 1,000 old, high-polluting cars, is this the same as saying that there are 1,000 fewer old, high-polluting cars on the road? Why or why not?

9. As we noted in the chapter, many economists have estimated the short-run and long-run elasticities of oil demand. Let's see if a rise in the price of oil hurts oil revenues in the long run. One economist found that in the United States, the long-run elasticity of oil demand is −0.5.

a. If the price of oil rises by 10%, how much will the quantity of oil demanded fall: by 5%, by 0.5%, by 2%, or by 20%?

b. Does a 10% rise in oil prices increase or decrease total revenues to the oil producers?

c. Some policymakers and environmental scientists would like to see the United States cut back on its use of oil in the long run. We can use this elasticity estimate to get a rough measure of how high the price of oil would have to permanently rise in order to get people to make big cuts in oil consumption. How much would the price of oil have to permanently rise in order to cut oil consumption by 50%?

d. France has the largest long-run elasticity of oil demand (−0.6) of any of the large, rich countries, according to Cooper's estimates. Does this mean that France is better at responding to long-run price changes than other rich countries, or does it mean France is worse at responding?

10. Guess whether the demand for cigarettes is elastic or inelastic. Explain your reasoning.

THINKING AND PROBLEM SOLVING

11. Suppose that 200,000 Uber trips are taken every day in New York City and suppose that the elasticity of demand for an Uber trip is −0.5. If the price increased by 10% how many Uber trips would be taken in a day?

12. A movie theatre owner runs an experiment. She decreases prices 2% and discovers that ticket sales increase by 5%. Also, she increases prices by 1% and discovers that sales decrease by 2%. What should the owner do to maximize revenue?

13. In Figure 5.1 we showed two demand curves. On the demand curve labeled E for more elastic, the quantity demanded was 100 at a price of $40 and 20 at a price of $50. For the demand curve labeled I for less elastic or inelastic, the quantity demanded was 100 at a price of $40 and 95 at a price of $50. Using the mid-point formula, calculate the elasticity of demand for these two curves and check that they were labeled correctly.

14. During the Middle Ages, the African city of Taghaza quarried salt in 200-pound blocks to be sent to the salt market in Timbuktu, in present-day Mali. Travelers report that Taghazans used salt instead of wood to construct buildings.

Compared with other towns without big salt mines, was the demand for *wood* more elastic or less elastic in Taghaza? How do you know?

15. Suppose that drug addicts pay for their addiction by stealing: So the higher the total revenue of the illegal drug industry, the higher the amount of theft. If a government crackdown on drug suppliers leads to a higher price of drugs, what will happen to the amount of stealing if the demand for drugs is elastic? What if the demand for drugs is inelastic?

16. Henry Ford famously mass-produced cars at the beginning of the twentieth century, starting Ford Motor Company. He made millions because mass production made cars cheap to make, and he passed some of the savings to the consumer in the form of a low price. Cars became a common sight in the United States thereafter. Keeping total revenue and its relationship with price in mind, do you expect the demand for cars to be elastic or inelastic given the story of Henry Ford?

17. In Chapter 10, you'll see that we purchased permits to pollute the air with sulfur dioxide (SO_2). We didn't use the permits: Instead, we threw them out. In other words, we bought permits for the same reason the government buys guns in gun buyback programs—to prevent what we bought from being used. As we discussed in the chapter, gun buyback programs have failed. So why is our plan to buy permits more likely to get SO_2 out of the air than the government's plan to get guns off the street?

18. How might elasticities help to explain why people on vacation tend to spend more for food and necessities than the local population?

19. In the short run, the price elasticity of the demand and supply of electricity can be very low.

a. How might revenue for the electricity industry change if one power plant were shut down for maintenance, reducing supply?

b. If one power company owned many power plants, would it have a short-term incentive to keep all of its plants running, or could it have a short-term incentive to shut down a power plant now and then?

20. Immigration is a fact of life in the United States. This will lead to a big boost in the labor supply. What field would you rather be in: a field where the demand for your kind of labor is elastic or a field where the demand for your kind of labor is inelastic?

21. In the world of fashion, the power to imitate a trendy look is the power to make money. Stores such as H&M and Forever 21 focus on imitating fashions wherever possible: As soon as they see that a new look is coming along, something people are willing to pay a high price for, they start cranking out that look. Do these imitation-centered stores make the supply of clothing more elastic or less elastic? How can you tell?

22. The relationship between elasticity of demand and total revenue can be a helpful shortcut, particularly if your professor likes to give multiple-choice exams. For each of the following examples, calculate how much money each consumer spends at the low price and at the high price, and decide whether the right answer for a question asking for the price elasticity of demand on a multiple-choice exam would be

(a) -2.33, (b) -1.17, (c) -1.00, or (d) -0.56. Remember, if the consumer spends more money at the lower price, demand must be elastic. (*Warning:* Two of these will require a bit of guesstimation.)

   a. When the price of a movie ticket rises from $6 to $8 for senior citizens, Gary (a senior citizen) decides to go to the movies every other day (15 times per month) instead of every day (30 times per month).

   b. When the price of a large specialty coffee drink rises from $3 to $4, Martha reduces her weekly consumption from 7 to 5.

   c. When $P_X = \$10.00$, $Q_X^D = 30$. When $P_X = \$7.50$, $Q_X^D = 40$.

23. Let's practice the midpoint formula. Calculate the elasticity of demand for each of the goods or services in the table that follows.

Good or Service	Beginning Price	Beginning Quantity	Ending Price	Ending Quantity	Elasticity
Daily movie ticket sales in Denver, Colorado	$6	50,000	$10	40,000	
Weekly milk sales at Loma Vista Elementary School	$1	1,000	$1.50	800	
Weekly round-trip ticket sales, New York to San Francisco	$500	10,000	$1,000	9,000	
Annual student enrollments, Upper Tennessee State University	$6,000	40,000	$9,000	39,000	

CHALLENGES

24. In this chapter, we've emphasized that the elasticity of supply is higher in the long run than in the short run. In a lot of cases, this is surely true: If you see that jobs pay more in the next state over, you won't move there the next week but you might move there next year. But sometimes the short-run elasticity will be *higher* than the long-run elasticity.

   Austan Goolsbee found an interesting example of this when he looked at the elasticity of income of highly paid executives with respect to taxes. In 1993, then President Bill Clinton passed a law raising income taxes. This tax hike was fully expected: He campaigned on it in 1992.

   a. What do you expect happened to executive income in the first year of the tax increases? What about in subsequent years? (*Source:* Goolsbee, Austan. 2000. What happens when you tax the rich? Evidence from executive compensation. *Journal of Political Economy* 108(2): 352–378. For a book on the topic written by a leading economist, see Joel Slemrod (Ed.), 2000. *Does Atlas Shrug?* [Cambridge, MA: Harvard University Press].)

   (*Hint:* Top executives have a lot of power over when they get paid for their work: They can ask for bonuses a bit earlier, or they can cash out their stock options a bit earlier. Literally, this isn't their "labor supply"; it's more like their "income supply.")

b. Goolsbee estimated that the short-run elasticity of "income supply" for these executives was 1.4, while the long-run elasticity of "income supply" was 0.1. (*Note:* Goolsbee used a variety of statistical methods to look for these elasticities, and all came to roughly the same result.) If taxes pushed down their take-home income by 10%, how much would this cut the amount of income supplied in the short run? In the long run?

c. You are a newspaper reporter. Your editor tells you to write a short feature story with this title: "Goolsbee's research proves that tax hikes make the rich work less." Make your case in one sentence.

d. You are a newspaper reporter. Your editor tells you to write a short feature story with this title: "Goolsbee's research proves that tax hikes have little effect on work by the wealthy." Make your case in one sentence.

e. Which story is more truthful?

25. We saw that a gun buyback program was unlikely to work in Los Angeles. If the entire United States ran a gun buyback program, would that be better at eliminating guns or worse? Why? What about if the gun buyback was also accompanied by a law making (at least some) guns illegal?

26. Using the data from the ANWR example, what will be the percentage increase in quantity supplied if ANWR raises supply by 1%? No, this isn't a trick question, and the formula is already there in the chapter. Why isn't this number just 1%?

Ask FRED

interactive activity

27. Using the FRED economic database (https://fred.stlouisfed.org/), let's compare expenditures on cell phones with the price of phones. Unfortunately, as is often the case, it's difficult to find the exact data we want, but if you search for "real expenditures telephone," you will find a series of expenditure on telephone and facsimile equipment (faxes—maybe you have heard of them?). Then click Edit Graph and Add Line. When you search for "expenditures telephone price," you should find a price series (make sure it says price index) for telephones and facsimile equipment. To make comparisons easier, change the units to Index and set the index equal to 100 around 2001 for both series. Print the graph.

a. Between 2001 and 2015, what happened to expenditures? Prices?

b. Is the demand for telephones elastic or inelastic?

WORK IT OUT

interactive activity

For interactive, step-by-step help in solving the following problem, go online.

Figure 5.3 and Table 5.2 both set out some important but tedious rules. Let's practice them, since they are quite likely to be on an exam. For each of the following cases, state whether the demand curve is relatively steep or flat and whether a *fall* in price will raise total revenue or lower it. In this case, note that we present the elasticity in terms of its absolute value.

a. Elasticity of demand = 0.7

b. Elasticity of demand = 3.0

c. Elasticity of demand = 20.0

d. Elasticity of demand = 1.05

e. Elasticity of demand = 0.95

MARGINAL REVOLUTION UNIVERSITY VIDEOS

Elasticity of Demand
mruniversity.com/elasticity-demand

Problems: **1, 3, 11, 13, 14, 15, 17**

Calculating the Elasticity of Demand
mruniversity.com/calc-elasticity

Problems: **5, 6, 7, 9, 10, 12, 16, 19, 20**

Elasticity of Supply
mruniversity.com/elasticity-supply

Problems: **2, 4, 18, 24, 26**

What Does Elasticity Have to Do With Freeing Slaves in Africa?
mruniversity.com/elasticity-example

Problems: **8, 14, 25**

Applications Using Elasticity
mruniversity.com/apply-elasticity

Problems: **8, 14, 25**

OFFICE HOURS

Office Hours: Elasticity
mruniversity.com/elasticity

Problems: **5d, 5e**

CHAPTER 5 APPENDIX

Other Types of Elasticities

Economists often compute elasticities any time one variable is related to another variable. Klick and Tabarrok, for example, find that a 50% increase in the number of police on the streets reduces automobile theft and theft from automobiles by 43%, so the elasticity of auto crime with respect to police is $-43\%/50\% = -0.86$. Gruber, who studies church attendance, finds an interesting relationship: The more people give to their church, the less likely they are to attend! In other words, people regard money and time as substitutes and those who give more of one are likely to give less of the other. Gruber calculates that a 10% increase in giving leads to an 11% decline in attendance or an elasticity of attendance with respect to giving of $-11\%/10\% = -1.1$.[15]

Thus, any time there is a relationship between two variables A and B, you can always express the relationship in terms of an elasticity. Two other frequently used elasticities in economics are the cross-price elasticity of demand and the income elasticity of demand.

The Cross-Price Elasticity of Demand

The cross-price elasticity of demand measures how responsive the quantity demanded of good A is to the price of good B.

$$\frac{\text{Percentage change in quantity demanded of good } A}{\text{Percentage change in price of good } B} = \frac{\%\Delta Q_{\text{Demanded},A}}{\%\Delta P_{\text{Price},B}}$$

Given data on the quantity demanded of good A at two different prices of good B, the cross-price elasticity can be calculated using the following formula:

$$= \frac{\dfrac{\text{Change in quantity demanded } A}{\text{Average quantity } A}}{\dfrac{\text{Change in price } B}{\text{Average price } B}} = \frac{\dfrac{Q_{\text{After},A} - Q_{\text{Before},A}}{(Q_{\text{After},A} + Q_{\text{Before},A})/2}}{\dfrac{P_{\text{After},B} - P_{\text{Before},B}}{(P_{\text{After},B} + P_{\text{Before},B})/2}}$$

The cross-price elasticity of demand is closely related to the idea of substitutes and complements. If the cross-price elasticity is positive, an increase in the price of good B increases the quantity of good A demanded so the two goods are substitutes. If the cross-price elasticity is negative, an increase in the price of good B decreases the quantity of good A demanded so the two goods are complements.

- If the cross-price elasticity > 0, then goods A and B are substitutes.
- If the cross-price elasticity < 0, then goods A and B are complements.

The Income Elasticity of Demand

The income elasticity of demand measures how responsive the quantity demanded of a good is with respect to changes in income.

$$\text{Income elasticity of demand} = \frac{\text{Percentage change in quantity demanded}}{\text{Percentage change in income}}$$

$$= \frac{\%\Delta Q_{\text{Demanded}}}{\%\Delta_{\text{Income}}}$$

As usual, given data on the quantity demanded at two different income levels, the income elasticity of demand can be calculated as

$$= \frac{\dfrac{\textbf{Change in quantity demanded}}{\textbf{Average quantity}}}{\dfrac{\textbf{Change in income}}{\textbf{Average income}}} = \frac{\dfrac{Q_{After} - Q_{Before}}{(Q_{After} + Q_{Before})/2}}{\dfrac{I_{After} - I_{Before}}{(I_{After} + I_{Before})/2}}$$

The income elasticity of demand can be used to distinguish normal from inferior goods. Recall from Chapter 3 that when an *increase* in income *increases* the demand for a good, we say the good is a *normal good*. And a good like Ramen noodles, for which an *increase* in income *decreases* the demand, is called an *inferior good*.

■ If the income elasticity of demand > 0, then the good is a normal good.

■ If the income elasticity of demand < 0, then the good is an inferior good.

Sometimes economists also distinguish normal from "luxury" goods, defined as one where, say, a 10% increase in income causes more than a 10% increase in the quantity of the good demanded. Thus,

■ If the income elasticity of demand > 1, then the good is a luxury good.

Ask FRED

interactive activity

Using the FRED economic database (https://fred.stlouisfed.org/), let's compare people's purchases of groceries with their purchases of electronics and appliances. At FRED, search for "retail trade grocery," then click on Edit Graph and Add Line; search for "retail trade electronics." Both series should be in millions of dollars, but since grocery stores sell much more than electronics stores, the scales make it difficult to see the changes. Switch units to Index and then set the index equal to 100 in December of 2007, the beginning of the 2007–2009 recession. Do this for both series. Print the graph.

a. What happened to food sales over the 2007–2009 recession? What about sales of electronics?

b. What does your answer to part (a) suggest about the income elasticity of food and electronics?

c. The data includes electronics and appliance stores. Why might appliance purchases be especially income elastic compared to food, at least over the short run?

6

Taxes and Subsidies

Billionaire hedge fund manager David Tepper paid so much in state income taxes that when he moved from New Jersey to Florida, the state of New Jersey had to scramble to adjust its budget calculations. Tepper may have moved for the better weather, but by moving he also saved hundreds of millions of dollars since Florida does not have a personal income tax. Tepper, who is in his early 60s, may also have been thinking about the future. If Tepper dies as a resident of Florida instead of New Jersey, his heirs stand to inherit billions more because, unlike New Jersey, Florida has no state estate tax. (Unless he moves abroad, however, Tepper will still have to pay the Federal estate tax.) It's not just billionaires who pay attention to estate taxes, however. There is a small but noticeable trend for elderly wealthy people to move from high estate-tax states to low estate-tax states.[1] Elderly wealthy people can reduce their estate tax by changing *where* they die. Could they also change the estate tax by changing *when* they die?

In fact, two economists, Joshua Gans and Andrew Leigh, found that in Australia a potential $10,000 reduction in the estate tax prompted people to postpone death by about a week! If that sounds incredible, it may help to know that there is also a small but noticeable trend for people to live until after their birthdays or other major events. New York hospitals, for example, reported fewer deaths than usual in the last week of 1999—the last week of the twentieth century—and more deaths than usual in the first week of the twenty-first century. If death can be postponed for major events, then why not postpone death to save on taxes? Or if that fails, don't call the coroner until the lower tax rate is in effect.

If all this seems a bit macabre, don't worry—not only can deaths be postponed for tax reasons, births can also be advanced. Parents get a tax deduction for dependents like children, and so long as the child is born before the clock strikes midnight on December 31, the family gets the deduction for the entire year. Thus, compared with a child born in early January, a child born in late December can save parents thousands of dollars. Journalist David Leonhardt wrote about this incentive in the *New York Times*:

> Unless you're a cynic, or an economist, I realize you might have trouble believing that the intricacies of the nation's tax code would impinge on something as sacred as the birth of a child. But it appears that you would be wrong.

Not only are more children born in late December than in early January, but also the extra births appear to be clustered among those who have the most to gain from a tax deduction, exactly as a cynic or an economist would predict. Leonhardt coined the term "national birth day" to indicate the day of the year on which the largest number of births occurs. For a long time, "national birth day" was around mid-September (probably because it was cold and dark the previous December!). But amazingly, as induced labor, Caesarian sections, and taxes have all increased, the day of the year on which the largest number of births occur has now moved to late December![2]

In this chapter, we examine taxes and also subsidies, which are payments from the government for production. The analysis will draw on our understanding of demand and supply and also on our understanding of elasticity from the last chapter.

Commodity Taxes

Commodity taxes are taxes on goods. Well-known commodity taxes include those on fuel, liquor, and cigarettes, although in the United States most commodities are taxed in one way or another. We will emphasize the following truths about commodity taxation:

1. Who ultimately pays the tax does *not* depend on who writes the check to the government.

2. Who ultimately pays the tax *does* depend on the relative elasticities of demand and supply.

3. Commodity taxation raises revenue and creates deadweight loss (i.e., reduces the gains from trade).

Who Ultimately Pays the Tax Does Not Depend on Who Writes the Check

Imagine that the government is considering a tax on apples. The government can collect the tax in either of two ways (assume that each method is equally costly to implement). The government can tax apple sellers $1 for every basket supplied, or they can tax apple buyers $1 for every basket of apples bought. Which tax scheme is better for apple buyers?

Surprisingly, the answer is that the tax has exactly the same effects whether it is "paid" for by sellers or "paid" for by buyers. Who ultimately pays a tax is determined not by the laws of Congress but by the laws of supply and demand.

Let's consider the effect of a $1 tax on apple sellers, which we analyze beginning with panel A of Figure 6.1. As discussed in Chapter 3, as far as sellers are concerned, a tax is the same as an increase in costs. Thus, if with no tax, sellers require a minimum of $1 per basket to sell 250 baskets of apples, then with a $1 tax they will require $2 per basket to sell the same quantity—$1 for their regular costs and $1 for their tax cost. Similarly, if with no tax, sellers require a minimum of $3 per basket to sell 1,250 baskets, then with a $1 tax they will require $4 per basket. Following through on this logic, we see that a $1 tax shifts the supply curve up at every quantity by exactly $1.

Panel B of Figure 6.1 adds a demand curve to show the effect of the tax on the market for apples. With no tax, the equilibrium is at point *a* with a price of $2 per basket and a quantity of 700. If apple sellers must pay a $1 tax for every basket supplied, the supply curve shifts up by $1 and the new equilibrium is at point *b* with a higher price of $2.65 and a smaller quantity consumed of 500.

Students are sometimes surprised that a $1 tax does not necessarily raise the price by $1. To see why, imagine that the price did rise by $1. In that case, the price would rise to $3 at point *c*. But is point *c* an equilibrium?

No. Point *c* is not an equilibrium because at point *c*, the quantity supplied is greater than the quantity demanded. In other words, apple sellers in this market find that if they try to pass all of the tax onto apple buyers by raising the price to $3 per basket, there are not enough buyers to purchase 700 baskets, so sellers have excess supply. What incentives does this create? As they compete to obtain buyers, sellers must bid the price down. As the price falls, sellers supply fewer apples until the new equilibrium is reached at point *b*.

With the tax, buyers pay $2.65 per basket and sellers receive $1.65 per basket ($2.65 minus the $1 tax they must send to the government). Notice that the difference between the price that buyers pay and the price that sellers receive is equal to the tax. In fact, so long as the tax doesn't drive the industry out of existence, it will always be the case that

The tax = Price paid by buyers − Price received by sellers

What happens if instead of taxing sellers, the government taxes buyers? We illustrate beginning with panel A of Figure 6.2. Imagine that before the tax buyers were willing to pay up to $4 per basket to purchase 100 baskets. If buyers must pay a $1 tax *on top of the price*, what is the most that they will now be willing to pay? Correct, $3. That is, if the buyers value the apples at $4 per basket but they must pay a tax of $1 to the government, then the most the buyers will be willing to pay the apple suppliers is $3 per basket (since the total price including the tax will now be $4). Similarly, if before the tax buyers were willing to pay up to $2 per basket to purchase 700 baskets, then after the $1 tax

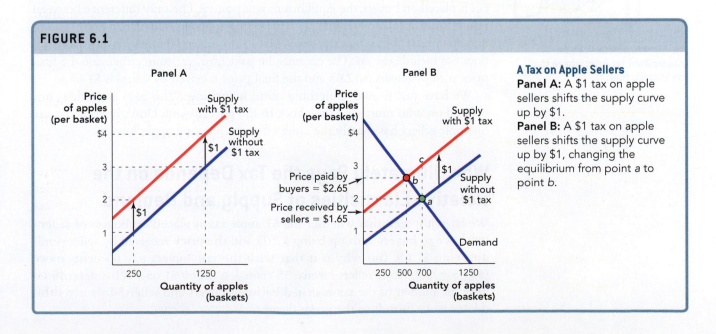

FIGURE 6.1

Panel A

Panel B

A Tax on Apple Sellers
Panel A: A $1 tax on apple sellers shifts the supply curve up by $1.
Panel B: A $1 tax on apple sellers shifts the supply curve up by $1, changing the equilibrium from point *a* to point *b*.

FIGURE 6.2

Panel A

Price of apples (per basket)

$4

3

2

1

Demand with $1 tax

Demand without $1 tax

$1

$1

100   700   1250

Quantity of apples (baskets)

Panel B

Price of apples (per basket)

$4

3

2

1

Demand with $1 tax

Supply with $1 tax

Price paid by buyers = $2.65

Price received by sellers = $1.65

b

a

d

Supply without $1 tax

Demand without $1 tax

250 500 700   1250

Quantity of apples (baskets)

A Tax on Apple Buyers
Panel A: A $1 tax on apple buyers shifts the demand curve down by $1.
Panel B: A $1 tax on apple buyers shifts the demand curve down by $1, changing the equilibrium from point *a* to point *d*.

The burden of a tax can be transmitted far from where the tax initially hits.

they will be willing to pay to the sellers at most $1 per basket for the same quantity. Following through on this logic, we see that a tax of $1 on buyers shifts the demand curve down at every quantity by $1.

Panel B shows the market for apples. With no tax, the equilibrium is at point *a* with a price of $2 and a quantity of 700. With the $1 tax on apple buyers, the demand curve shifts down by $1 and the new equilibrium is at point *d* with a price of $1.65 and a quantity of 500.

Notice that with the tax, apple buyers pay a total price of $2.65 ($1.65 in market price plus $1 tax) and apple sellers receive $1.65. In other words, the price buyers pay, the price sellers receive, and the quantity traded (500 baskets) are identical to what they were when the tax was placed on apple sellers.

We can see what is going on by showing in panel B of Figure 6.2 a dotted supply curve, the supply curve *if* there were a $1 tax on sellers (exactly as in Figure 6.1). If the $1 tax is placed on sellers, the equilibrium is at point *b*. If the tax is placed on buyers, the equilibrium is at point *d*. The only difference between points *b* and *d* is that when the tax is placed on suppliers, the market price ($2.65) *includes* the tax, but when the tax is placed on buyers, the market price ($1.65) does not include the tax. The tax must be paid, however, so in either case the final price paid by buyers is $2.65 and the final price received by sellers is $1.65.

We have just shown something quite surprising. Who pays a tax does not depend on who must send the check to the government. Don't be fooled; a tax on apple sellers has exactly the same effects as a tax on apple buyers.

Who Ultimately Pays the Tax Depends on the Relative Elasticities of Supply and Demand

We have just seen that whether the $1 apple tax is placed on buyers or sellers, the price to buyers ends up being $2.65 and the price received by sellers ends up being $1.65. But why is it that with the tax, buyers pay 65 cents more ($2.65 − $2), while sellers receive 35 cents less ($2 − $1.65)? What determines how the burden of the tax is shared between buyers and sellers? To answer this question, we introduce the *wedge shortcut*.

The Wedge Shortcut

The most important effect of a tax is to drive a tax wedge between the price paid by buyers and the price received by sellers. Recall that

The tax = Price paid by buyers − Price received by sellers

If we focus on the wedge aspect of a tax, we can simplify our tax analysis. In Figure 6.3, instead of shifting curves, we start with a tax of $1 and we "push" this vertical "tax wedge" into the diagram until the top of the wedge just touches the demand curve and the bottom of the wedge just touches the supply curve. The top of the wedge at point *b* gives us the price paid by the buyers ($2.65), the bottom of the wedge at point *d* gives us the price received by sellers ($1.65), and the quantity at which the wedge "sticks" is 500 baskets, exactly as before.

Using the wedge shortcut, we show that whether buyers or sellers pay a tax is determined by the relative elasticities of demand and supply. Recall from Chapter 5 that the elasticity of demand measures how responsive the quantity demanded is to a change in price and the elasticity of supply measures how responsive the quantity supplied is to a change in price. We show that *when demand is more elastic than supply, demanders pay less of the tax than sellers. When supply is more elastic than demand, suppliers pay less of the tax than buyers.*

In panel A of Figure 6.4, we draw a demand curve that is more elastic than the supply curve. So who will pay most of the tax? Sellers. To see why sellers will pay most of the tax, push the tax wedge into the diagram. Notice that at the quantity that the tax wedge sticks, the price paid by buyers is only a small amount above the price with no tax. The price received by sellers, however, falls well below the price with no tax. Thus, when demand is more elastic than supply, buyers pay less of the tax than sellers.

FIGURE 6.3

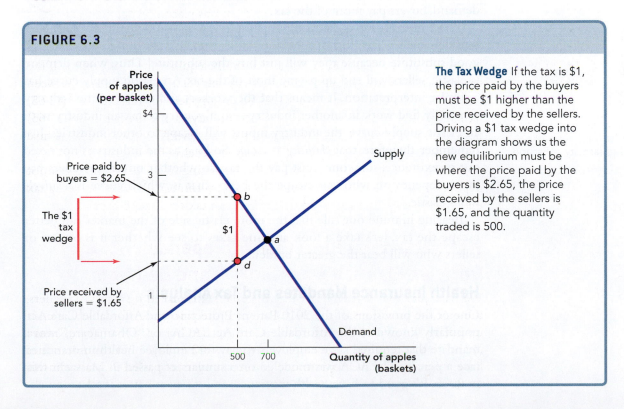

The Tax Wedge If the tax is $1, the price paid by the buyers must be $1 higher than the price received by the sellers. Driving a $1 tax wedge into the diagram shows us the new equilibrium must be where the price paid by the buyers is $2.65, the price received by the sellers is $1.65, and the quantity traded is 500.

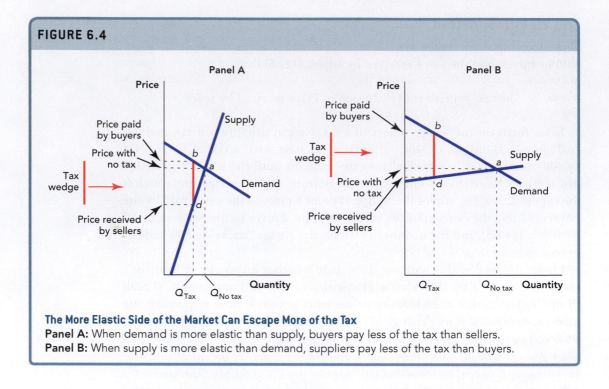

FIGURE 6.4

Panel A

Panel B

The More Elastic Side of the Market Can Escape More of the Tax
Panel A: When demand is more elastic than supply, buyers pay less of the tax than sellers.
Panel B: When supply is more elastic than demand, suppliers pay less of the tax than buyers.

In panel B of Figure 6.4, we draw a supply curve that is more elastic than the demand curve. So who will pay most of the tax? Buyers. To see why buyers will pay most of the tax, take the tax wedge and push it into the diagram. At the point that the wedge "sticks," notice that the price paid by buyers has risen far above the price with no tax. The price received by sellers, however, has fallen only just below the price with no tax. Thus, when supply is more elastic than demand, buyers pay more of the tax.

The intuition for these results is simple. An elastic demand curve means that demanders have lots of substitutes and you can't tax someone who has a good substitute because they will just buy the substitute! Thus, when demand is elastic, sellers will end up paying most of the tax. An elastic supply curve has a similar interpretation. It means that the workers and capital in the industry can easily find work in another industry—so if you try to tax an industry with an elastic supply curve, the industry inputs will escape to other industries. Just remember, therefore, that *elasticity = escape*. So long as the industry is not taxed out of existence, someone must pay the tax, so whether buyers or sellers pay more depends on who can escape the best—that is, which curve is *relatively* more elastic.

Bearing in mind our rule that the more elastic side of the market can better escape the tax, let's take a look at some taxes to see whether it is buyers or sellers who will bear the greater burden.

Elasticity = Escape

Health Insurance Mandates and Tax Analysis

One of the provisions of the 2010 Patient Protection and Affordable Care Act, popularly known as the Affordable Care Act (ACA) or "Obamacare," was a mandate that required large employers to pay for employee health insurance or face a penalty. The ACA was modeled on a similar act passed in Massachusetts in 2006. It's good to have health insurance, and it's even better if someone else is paying for it. But who really pays? The ACA and Massachusetts laws required that firms buy health insurance for every full-time worker hired so we can think of these mandates as a tax on labor. Who pays the tax? As we now know, who pays more of the tax depends on whether supply or demand is more elastic. So consider, is it easier for firms to escape the tax by not employing or for workers to escape the tax by not working?

Can firms escape the tax? Yes, in a lot of ways. If the tax on labor gets too high, firms can substitute capital (machines) for labor, they can move overseas, or they can close up shop altogether. Can workers escape the tax? It's not so easy. Most workers would continue to work even if their wages were lower because the costs of leaving the labor force are high. Thus, for most workers, the elasticity of labor supply is low (this is especially true for working-age men; men nearing retirement and married women tend to have higher elasticities of labor supply). The demand for labor, therefore, is likely to be more elastic than the supply of labor. Remember that when demand is more elastic than supply, then sellers (i.e., workers = sellers of labor) will pay most of the tax in the form of lower wages. This is the situation depicted in panel A of Figure 6.4. We are now many years into the ACA and it is still a hot-button issue in politics that is undergoing change. Nevertheless, are there any succinct conclusions regarding the tax burden of the act? Yes.

Studies of the Massachusetts mandate estimate that the wages of workers who gained health insurance because of the law fell by about the same amount as the cost of the coverage to firms.[3] In other words, most of the burden of the law fell on workers through lower wages, exactly as our model predicts. Broadly speaking the same thing is true of the ACA. In addition to an employer mandate, the national ACA also involves an individual mandate, taxpayer-funded subsidies for purchase of health insurance by low-income individuals, and an expansion in taxpayer-funded Medicaid. Thus the burden of the entire Act is complicated. The Congressional Budget Office, however, estimates that when employers add insurance coverage because of the law, "workers' wages will adjust by roughly the employers' cost of providing that coverage."[4]

Just because workers bear the costs of a law requiring firms to purchase health insurance, doesn't mean that the law is a bad idea. It's quite reasonable to want everyone in society to have health insurance and requiring employers to purchase health insurance is one way, albeit not necessarily the best way, to move toward this goal. What is important is that citizens not be fooled into thinking that the law is a free lunch at the expense of their employer. Tax analysis is useful because it helps us to see the true benefits and costs of economic policy and thus to choose wisely.

Who Pays the Cigarette Tax?

States tax cigarettes at very different rates. New Jersey, for example, taxes cigarettes at $2.70 per pack while South Carolina taxes cigarettes at just 57 cents per pack (2016 rates). Who ultimately pays the cigarette tax? Buyers or sellers? As usual, who pays depends on the relative elasticities of demand and supply.

As you might expect, given the addictive nature of nicotine, smokers have an inelastic demand for cigarettes, around −0.5. What

ENVISION/GETTY IMAGES

What a drag it is being taxed Heavy taxes encourage smokers to smoke fewer cigarettes, but they also encourage smokers to choose cigarettes with higher nicotine levels. High cigarette taxes have also been shown to increase smoking intensity—when taxes are high, smokers inhale more deeply and they smoke down to the butt.

about suppliers? Before you answer, remember that we are analyzing *state* cigarette taxes so the relevant question is how easily can a cigarette manufacturer escape a state tax?

A manufacturer can easily escape a state tax by selling elsewhere. In fact, because it's so easy for a cigarette manufacturer to ship its product around the country, the elasticity of supply to any one state is very large, which means that buyers will bear almost all of the tax—as illustrated in panel B of Figure 6.4.

If the price paid by buyers increases by almost the amount of the tax, then the price received by sellers must be almost the same in all states regardless of the tax. To see why this makes sense, imagine what would happen if manufacturers earned less money per pack selling cigarettes in a high-tax state like New Jersey than in a low-tax state like South Carolina. If this happened, manufacturers would ship fewer cigarettes to New Jersey and more to South Carolina, and this would continue until the after-tax price was the same in both states.

We can easily test this theory. A pack of cigarettes sold for about $5.85 in South Carolina and $8.20 in New Jersey (2016), so the price to buyers was 40% higher in New Jersey. But the after-tax price received by sellers was about the same, $5.28 in South Carolina ($5.85–$.57) versus $5.50 in New Jersey ($8.20–$2.70). (The small differences can probably be accounted for by other costs of doing business that differ between New Jersey and South Carolina.)

By the way, one argument for high cigarette taxes is that the government should discourage smoking. State taxes, however, are a bad method of discouraging smoking in the United States. A New Jersey tax will discourage smoking by residents of New Jersey but, as we have seen, to escape the New Jersey tax, cigarette manufacturers will ship more cigarettes to other states, which pushes cigarette prices down in those states, thereby increasing the quantity demanded. A New Jersey tax, therefore, will decrease smoking in New Jersey but this will be partially offset by increased smoking in other states. It's more difficult for cigarette manufacturers to escape federal taxes than state taxes so if the goal is to reduce national consumption, a federal tax is superior to a state tax.

A Commodity Tax Raises Revenue and Reduces the Gains from Trade (Creates a Deadweight Loss)

A tax generates revenues for the government but also reduces the gains from trade. In the left panel of Figure 6.5, we show the apple market with no tax; the equilibrium price is $2 and the equilibrium quantity is 700. Consumer surplus is shown in green and producer surplus is shown in blue. As emphasized in Chapter 4, in a free market trade occurs whenever the buyer's willingness to pay exceeds the supplier's willingness to sell (i.e., whenever the demand curve lies above the supply curve). A free market maximizes the gains from trade, the sum of consumer and producer surplus.

In the right panel, we show the same market with a $1 tax (this is identical to Figure 6.3 only this time we have labeled some of the areas). The tax is $1 per basket and 500 baskets are traded, so tax revenues are shown by the purple rectangle and are equal to $500 = $1 × 500.

The tax decreases consumer and producer surplus, as you can see by comparing the green and blue areas in the left and right panels. *Some* of the consumer and producer surplus is transferred to the government in the form of

interactive activity

Understanding Tax Revenue and Deadweight Loss

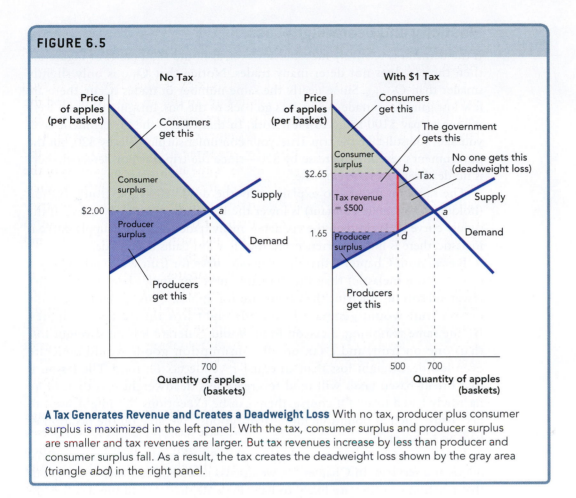

FIGURE 6.5

A Tax Generates Revenue and Creates a Deadweight Loss With no tax, producer plus consumer surplus is maximized in the left panel. With the tax, consumer surplus and producer surplus are smaller and tax revenues are larger. But tax revenues increase by less than producer and consumer surplus fall. As a result, the tax creates the deadweight loss shown by the gray area (triangle *abd*) in the right panel.

tax revenues, but notice that consumer and producer surplus together decrease by more than government revenue increases—the difference is the gray triangle (*abd*) labeled "deadweight loss." A **deadweight loss** is the reduction in total surplus caused by a market distortion or inefficiency. In this case the deadweight loss is caused by the tax.

To understand why a tax creates a deadweight loss, let's take a simple case. Imagine that you are willing to pay $50 for a bus ride to New York City when the price of a ticket is $40. Thus, you take the trip and earn $10 in consumer surplus ($50 − $40). Now suppose the government imposes a $20 tax, which increases the price of the ticket to $60. Do you take the trip? No, since the price of the ticket now exceeds your willingness to pay, you do not go to New York City. Thus, you lose $10 in consumer surplus. Does the government gain any tax revenue? No. Your loss of $10 is not compensated for by any increase in government revenue and thus is a deadweight loss. In short, the deadweight loss of a tax is the lost gains from the trips (trades) that do not occur because of the tax.

A key factor determining deadweight loss is the elasticities of supply and demand. Figure 6.6, for example, shows that the deadweight loss from taxation is larger the more elastic the demand curve. To understand why, remember that deadweight loss is the lost gains from trade. If the demand curve is relatively elastic, as in the left panel of Figure 6.6, then the tax deters a lot of trades, Q_{Tax} is much less than $Q_{No\ tax}$, so the lost gains from trade are large. It's just like the bus story—if the demand curve is elastic, then the tax means many lost bus trips.

A **deadweight loss** is the reduction in total surplus caused by a market distortion or inefficiency.

Elasticity and Deadweight Loss

If the demand is relatively inelastic, however, as in the right panel of Figure 6.6 then the tax does not deter many trades. Notice that Q_{Tax} is only slightly smaller than $Q_{No\ tax}$. Since nearly the same number of trades occur, there are few lost gains from trade. Again, let's go back to the bus. Imagine that you were willing to pay $100 to go to New York. In that case, if the government taxes you $20, you still take the trip. True, your consumer surplus falls by $20, but the government's revenues increase by $20—since the trip was not deterred, there is no deadweight loss in this case.

The same intuition also explains why the deadweight loss from taxation (holding tax revenue constant) is lower the less elastic the supply curve. If the supply curve is elastic, then the tax deters many trades, but if the supply curve is inelastic, there is little deterrence and thus few lost gains from trade.

Recall from Chapter 5 that the demand curve for fruit will tend to be less elastic (more inelastic) than the demand curve for apples because there are fewer substitutes for fruit than there are for apples. Thus, an equal-revenue tax on fruit would generate less deadweight loss than a tax on apples. By the same reasoning, a tax on food would generate less deadweight loss than one on fruit, and a tax on all consumption goods would generate even less deadweight loss than an equal-revenue tax on food. The lesson is that broad-based taxes will tend to create less deadweight loss than more narrowly based taxes. Of course, there can be exceptions. We might want to tax "bads," such as pollution, more than "goods." We take up the taxation of bads in Chapter 10.

Even though taxes create a deadweight loss, they also pay for beneficial goods and services. In Chapter 19, we discuss in more detail when the goods that taxation provides are likely to have benefits that exceed the deadweight loss caused by taxation.

FIGURE 6.6

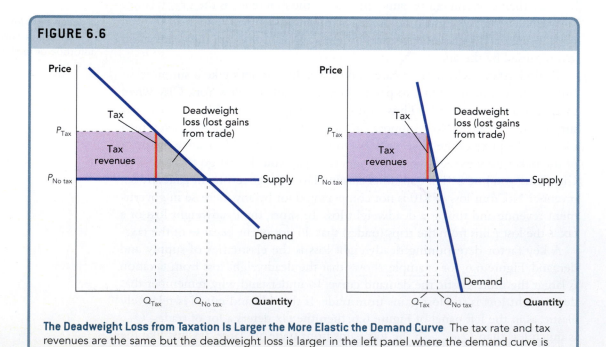

The Deadweight Loss from Taxation Is Larger the More Elastic the Demand Curve The tax rate and tax revenues are the same but the deadweight loss is larger in the left panel where the demand curve is more elastic.

Subsidies

A subsidy is a reverse tax: Instead of taking money away from consumers (or producers), the government gives money to consumers (or producers). The close connection between subsidies and taxes means that their effects are analogous. We emphasize the following facts about commodity subsidies:

1. Who gets the subsidy does *not* depend on who gets the check from the government.

2. Who benefits from a subsidy *does* depend on the relative elasticities of demand and supply.

3. Subsidies must be paid for by taxpayers and they create inefficient *increases* in trade (deadweight loss).

With a tax, the price paid by the buyers exceeds the price received by sellers. A subsidy reverses this relationship so the price received by sellers exceeds the price paid by buyers, the difference being the amount of the subsidy. In other words:

> The subsidy = Price received by sellers − Price paid by buyers

We can analyze subsidies using the same wedge shortcut as before, except now we push the wedge from the right side of the diagram toward the left side. In Figure 6.7 on the next page, we show that with a $1 subsidy, sellers of apples will receive $2.40 per basket, but buyers will pay only $1.40, the difference of $1 being the subsidy amount.

FIGURE 6.7

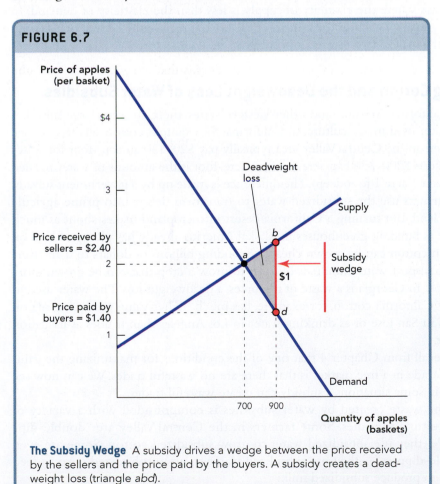

The Subsidy Wedge A subsidy drives a wedge between the price received by the sellers and the price paid by the buyers. A subsidy creates a deadweight loss (triangle *abd*).

A subsidy means that the sellers are receiving more than buyers are paying, so who is making up the difference? Taxpayers. The cost to taxpayers is the amount of the subsidy times the number of units subsidized. In Figure 6.7: $1 × 900 or $900.

Just like a tax, a subsidy also creates a deadweight loss. A tax creates a deadweight loss because with the tax, some beneficial trades fail to occur. A subsidy creates a deadweight loss for the reverse reason: With the subsidy, some nonbeneficial trades do occur. In Figure 6.7, notice that for the baskets between 700 and 900, the supply curve lies above the demand curve (i.e., line segment *ab* lies above line segment *ad*). The height of the supply curve tells us the cost of producing these baskets. The height of the demand curve tells us the value of these baskets to buyers. Producing baskets for which the cost exceeds the value creates waste, a deadweight loss measured by the triangle *abd*. In other words, the resources used to produce those extra baskets have an opportunity cost, and they could produce more value in some other part of the economy.

As with taxes, the wedge analysis shows that it doesn't make a difference whether buyers are subsidized $1 for every unit bought or sellers are subsidized $1 for every unit sold.

Similarly, we showed that who bears the burden of a tax depends on the relative elasticities of supply and demand. Exactly the same forces determine who gets the benefit of a subsidy. The rule is simple: Whoever bears the burden of a tax receives the benefit of a subsidy. Figure 6.8 illustrates the intuition for the case where the elasticity of supply is less than the elasticity of demand. In this case, suppliers bear the burden of the tax but receive the benefit of a subsidy.

Let's analyze two examples of subsidies in action.

King Cotton and the Deadweight Loss of Water Subsidies

In California, Arizona, and other western states, there are very large subsidies to water used in agriculture. In California, for example, cotton, alfalfa, and rice farmers in the Central Valley area typically pay $20–$30 an acre-foot for water that costs $200–$500 an acre-foot (an acre-foot is the amount of water needed to cover 1 acre 1 foot deep). The difference is made up by a government subsidy.

Farmers use the subsidized water to transform desert into prime agricultural land. But turning a California desert into cropland makes about as much sense as building greenhouses in Alaska! America already has plenty of land on which cotton can be grown cheaply. Spending billions of dollars to dam rivers and transport water hundreds of miles to grow a crop that can be grown more cheaply in Georgia is a waste of resources, a deadweight loss. The water used to grow California cotton, for example, has much higher value producing silicon chips in San Jose or as drinking water in Los Angeles than it does as irrigation water.

Recall from Chapter 4 that one of the conditions for maximizing the gains from trade in a free market is that there are no wasteful trades. We can now see how in some situations a subsidy can create wasteful trades.

The waste created by water subsidies is compounded with a variety of agricultural subsidies. Some farmers in the Central Valley are "double-dippers"—they use subsidized water to grow subsidized cotton. Some are even "triple-dippers"—they use subsidized water to grow subsidized corn to feed cows to produce subsidized milk!

FIGURE 6.8

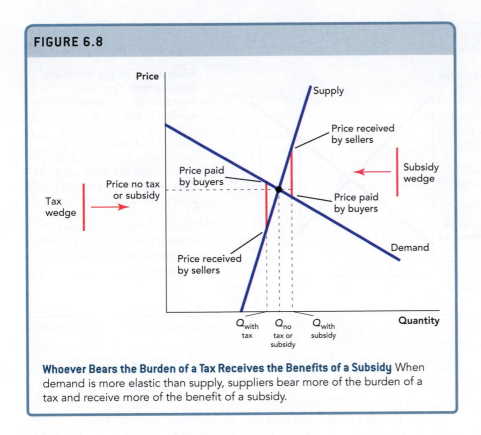

Whoever Bears the Burden of a Tax Receives the Benefits of a Subsidy When demand is more elastic than supply, suppliers bear more of the burden of a tax and receive more of the benefit of a subsidy.

Who benefits from the water subsidy? Is it California cotton suppliers or cotton buyers? Remember that suppliers receive more of the benefit of a subsidy than buyers when the elasticity of demand is greater than the elasticity of supply (as in Figure 6.8). Can you explain why the elasticity of demand for California cotton is much greater than the elasticity of supply? The elasticity of demand for *California* cotton is very high since cotton grown elsewhere is almost a perfect substitute. In other words, the price of cotton is determined on the world market for cotton, and California production is too small to have much of an influence on the world price. It's not surprising, therefore, that it's not cotton consumers who lobby for water subsidies but the farmers in California's Central Valley. Central Valley California farmers are politically powerful and they have been subsidized since 1902!

Wage Subsidies

It's difficult to see why California cotton should be subsidized when cotton from Georgia (or India, China, or Pakistan) is just as good, but subsidies are not always bad for social welfare. Just as a tax might be beneficial if it reduced smoking, a subsidy might be beneficial if it increased something of special importance (see Chapter 10 for more on when taxes and subsidies might be beneficial). Nobel Prize winner Edmund Phelps, for example, is a strong advocate of using wage subsidies to increase the employment of low-wage workers.

In Phelps's plan, firms would be subsidized for every low-wage worker that they hire. A subsidy makes hiring a low-wage worker even cheaper, thus increasing the demand for labor. In Figure 6.9, a wage subsidy increases the wage received by workers and decreases the wage paid by firms so employment increases from Q_m to Q_s.

FIGURE 6.9

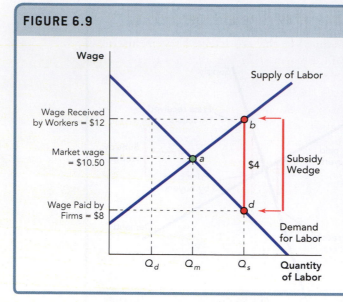

A Subsidy to Wages Increases Employment The free market wage for low-skill workers is $10.50. A subsidy to firms that hire low-wage workers increases the wage received by workers to $12 and reduces the wage paid by firms to $8. As a result, employment increases from Q_m to Q_s. The cost of the subsidy to the government is the subsidy amount, $4, times the number of workers employed, Q_s.

Wage subsidies can be costly. The cost of the subsidy is the subsidy amount ($4 in Figure 6.9) times the number of workers who are hired under this program (Q_s in Figure 6.9). Wage subsidies, however, could have offsetting benefits to taxpayers, making their total cost less than it first appears. Phelps argues, for example, that if wages and employment among low-skilled workers were higher, welfare payments would be lower. He also suggests that encouraging work among those with the least skills would reduce crime, drug dependency, and the culture of so-called rational defeatism that keeps many people in poverty.

The United States does have one program that is similar to a wage subsidy. It's called the Earned Income Tax Credit (EITC). The EITC is a cash subsidy to the earnings of low-income workers. The main difference between the EITC and a Phelps wage subsidy is that Phelps would like to subsidize all low-wage workers. The EITC, however, is targeted at families with children—the subsidy is much smaller for workers without children. The EITC has been successful at increasing employment among single mothers but it doesn't do much for single men.

In his book *Rewarding Work*, Phelps argues that wage subsidies are a better way to help low-skill workers than the minimum wage. We will return to this question in Chapter 8 when we take up price ceilings and price floors.

Takeaway

We used supply and demand to explain the effects of taxes and subsidies. Using the wedge shortcut, you should be able to show that taxes decrease the quantity traded, subsidies increase the quantity traded, and both taxes and subsidies create a deadweight loss. We showed that, surprisingly, the burden of a tax and the benefit of a subsidy do not depend on who sends or receives the government check. Instead, who bears the burden of a tax and who receives the benefit of a subsidy depend on the relative elasticities of supply and demand. In particular, if you remember that *elasticity = escape*, then you will know that the side of the market (buyers or sellers) with the more elastic curve will escape more of the tax.

CHECK YOURSELF

■ To promote energy independence, the U.S. government provides a subsidy to corn growers if they convert the corn to ethanol, a fuel used in some cars. Because of this subsidy, what happens to the quantity supplied of ethanol, and what happens to the price received by corn growers and the price paid by ethanol buyers?

■ The U.S. government subsidizes college education in the form of Pell grants and lower-cost government Stafford loans. How do these subsidies affect the price of college education? Which is relatively more elastic: supply or demand? Who benefits the most from these subsidies: suppliers (colleges) or demanders of education (students)?

We also showed that elasticities of demand and supply determine the dead-weight loss of a tax. The more elastic either the demand or the supply curve is, the more a tax deters trade, and the more trades that are deterred, the greater the dead-weight loss (for a given amount of tax revenue). As a result, it is better to tax goods with inelastic demands. Equal-revenue taxes on broad-based goods (for example, food) tend to have lower deadweight loss than taxes on narrowly based goods (for example, apples) because broad-based goods have more inelastic demands.

The tools of supply and demand are very powerful. In this chapter, we have shown how we can use these tools to understand taxes and subsidies

CHAPTER REVIEW

 interactive activity Go online to practice with more examples of these types of problems, including live links to videos, data sources, and feedback.

Problems in **green** relate to MRU videos. See the MRU table at the end of the exercises.

KEY CONCEPTS

deadweight loss, p. 107

FACTS AND TOOLS

1. As we saw in Chapter 4, economists' idea of equilibrium borrows a lot from physics. Let's push the physics metaphors a bit further. Here, we focus just on the supply side. For each set of words in brackets, circle the correct choice:

   a. When the government subsidizes an activity, resources such as labor, machines, and bank lending will tend to gravitate [toward/away from] the activity that is subsidized and will tend to gravitate [toward/away from] activity that is not subsidized.

   b. When the government taxes an activity, resources such as labor, machines, and bank lending will tend to gravitate [toward/away from] the activity that is taxed and will tend to gravitate [toward/away from] activity that is not taxed.

2. Junk food has often been criticized for being unhealthy and too cheap, enticing the poor to adopt unhealthy lifestyles. Suppose that the state of Oklakansas imposes a tax on junk food.

   a. What needs to be true for the tax to actually deter people from eating junk food: Should junk food demand be elastic or should it be inelastic?

   b. If the Oklakansas government wants to strongly discourage people from eating junk food, when will it need to set a higher tax rate: When junk food demand is elastic or when it is inelastic?

   c. But hold on a moment: The supply side matters as well. If junk food supply is highly elastic—perhaps because it's not that hard to start selling salads with low-fat dressing instead of mayonnaise- and cheese-laden burgers—does that mean that a junk food tax will have a bigger effect than if supply were inelastic? Or is it the other way around?

   d. Let's combine these stories now. If a government is hoping that a small tax can actually discourage a lot of junk food purchases, it should hope for:

   I. Elastic supply and inelastic demand

   II. Elastic supply and elastic demand

   III. Inelastic supply and elastic demand

   IV. Inelastic supply and inelastic demand

3. As we saw in the chapter, a lot turns on elasticity. Decades ago, Washington, D.C., a fairly small city, wanted to raise more revenue by increasing the gas tax. Washington, D.C., shares borders with Maryland and Virginia, and it's very easy to cross the borders between D.C. and one or both states without even really noticing: The suburbs just blend together.

a. How elastic is the demand for gasoline *sold at stations within D.C.*? In other words, if the price of gas in D.C. rises, but the price in Maryland and Virginia stays the same, will gasoline sales at D.C. stations fall a little, or will they fall a lot?

b. Take your answer to part a into account when answering this question. So, when Washington, D.C., increased its gasoline tax, how much revenue did it raise: Did it raise a little bit of revenue, or did it raise a lot of revenue?

c. How would your answer to part b change if D.C., Maryland, and Virginia all agreed to raise their gas tax simultaneously? These states have heavily populated borders with each other, but they don't have any heavily populated borders with other states.

4. In Figure 6.5, what is the total revenue raised by the tax, in dollars? What is the deadweight loss from the tax, in dollars? (*Note:* You've seen the formula for the latter before. We'll let you look around a little for this one.)

5. a. Once again: Why does the text say that *elasticity = escape*? (This is worth remembering: Elasticity is one of the toughest ideas for most economics students.)

b. Which two groups of workers did we say have a relatively high elasticity of labor supply? Keep this in mind as politicians debate raising or lowering taxes on different types of workers: These two groups are the ones most likely to make big changes in their behavior.

6. Suppose that Maria is willing to pay $40 for a haircut, and her stylist Juan is willing to accept as little as $25 for a haircut.

a. What possible prices for the haircut would be beneficial to both Maria and Juan? How much total surplus (that is, the sum of consumer and producer surplus) would be generated by this haircut?

b. If the state where Maria and Juan live instituted a tax on services that included a $5 per haircut tax on stylists and barbers, what happens to the range of haircut prices that benefit both Maria and Juan? Will the haircut still happen? Will this tax alter the total economic benefit of this haircut?

c. What if instead the tax was $20?

THINKING AND PROBLEM SOLVING

7. Some people with diabetes absolutely need to take insulin on a regular basis to survive. Pharmaceutical companies that make insulin could find a lot of other ways to make some money.

a. If the U.S. government imposes a tax on insulin producers of $10 per cubic centimeter of insulin, payable every month to the U.S. Treasury, who will bear most of the burden of the tax: insulin producers or people with diabetes? Or can't you tell from the information given?

b. Suppose instead that because of government corruption, the insulin manufacturers convince the U.S. government to pay the insulin makers $10 per cubic centimeter of insulin, payable every month *from* the U.S. Treasury. Who will get more of the benefit of this subsidy: insulin producers or people with diabetes? Or can't you tell from the information given?

8. Let's see if we can formulate any real laws about the economics of taxation. Which of the following *must* be true, as long as supply and demand curves have their normal shape (i.e., they aren't perfectly vertical or horizontal, and demand curves have a negative slope while supply curves have a positive slope). More than one may be true.

If there is a tax:

a. The equilibrium quantity must fall, and the price that buyers pay must rise.

b. The equilibrium quantity must rise, and the price that sellers pay must rise.

c. The equilibrium quantity must fall, and the price that sellers receive must fall.

d. The equilibrium quantity must rise, and the price that buyers receive must fall.

(*Note:* The correct answer[s] to this question was [were] actually controversial until Nobel laureate Paul Samuelson created a simple mathematical proof in his legendary graduate textbook, *Foundations of Economic Analysis*.)

9. Using the following diagram, use the wedge shortcut to answer these questions:

a. If a tax of $2 were imposed, what price would buyers pay and what price would suppliers receive? How much revenue would be raised by the tax? How much deadweight loss would be created by the tax?

b. If a subsidy of $5 were imposed, what price would buyers pay and what price would suppliers receive? How much would the subsidy cost the government? How much deadweight loss would be created by the subsidy?

10. When government is trying to raise tax revenue, it sometimes attempts to target higher-income people because they are in a better position to bear the burden of a tax. However, it can be very difficult to earn tax revenue from wealthy people.

a. Consider the progressive nature of the U.S. federal income tax system: It's designed so that higher incomes are taxed at higher tax rates. Thinking about the elasticity of labor supply, why might it be more difficult to collect tax revenue from a wealthy individual than from a poor person, all else equal?

b. Another way governments have tried to collect taxes from the wealthy is through the use of luxury taxes, which are exactly what they sound like: taxes on goods that are considered luxuries, like jewelry or expensive cars and real estate. What is true about the demand for luxuries? Consider jewelry. Is a luxury tax more likely to hurt the buyers of jewelry or the sellers of jewelry?

c. The chapter began by discussing another tax that targets wealthy individuals: the estate tax. Comment on the effectiveness of this tax (in terms of government revenue), considering the demand of wealthy individuals for leaving an inheritance.

11. As we learned in Chapter 4, the competitive market equilibrium maximizes gains from trade. Taxes and subsidies, by altering the market outcome, reduce the gains from trade. Does this happen primarily because of the impact of taxes and subsidies on *prices* or the impact of taxes and subsidies on *quantities*?

12. Consider the following diagram of a tax. The triangular area representing deadweight loss is highlighted, and its dimensions are labeled "Base" and "Height" (recall that the formula for the area of a triangle is $\frac{1}{2} \times$ Base $\times$ Height).

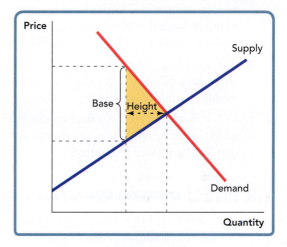

a. In order to calculate the deadweight loss of a tax, you don't need the entire demand and supply diagram; you just need to know two numbers, the *base* and *height* of the deadweight loss triangle. What is the real-life meaning of the base? What about the height?

b. Can you turn your answers to part a into general rules about the deadweight loss associated with taxes? Try phrasing it like this but replacing the part in brackets: "The larger the [base or height], the more deadweight loss is generated by a given tax."

c. Holding the base constant, the height and thus the deadweight loss would get larger if the demand curve or the supply curve were more _____.

d. Without having a diagram as a reference, can you answer the preceding questions for a subsidy?

13. Suppose your state government has decided to tax doughnuts. Currently, in your state, 300,000 doughnuts are sold every day. Three possible taxes are being considered by lawmakers: a 20-cent per doughnut tax, which would decrease doughnut sales by 50,000 per day; a 25-cent per doughnut tax, which would decrease doughnut sales by 100,000 per day; and a 50-cent per doughnut tax, which would decrease doughnut sales by 150,000 doughnuts per day.

    a. Calculate the amount of tax revenue generated by each tax and the deadweight loss caused by each tax.

    b. If the goal of your state government is simply to raise the most tax revenue, which tax is preferable?

    c. If the goal of your state government is to raise tax revenue in the most efficient manner (with the least deadweight loss per dollar of revenue), which tax is preferable?

    d. What other goal might your state government have when creating this kind of tax besides raising tax revenue?

14. How is it that a tax creates a deadweight loss by *decreasing* quantity, but a subsidy creates a deadweight loss by *increasing* quantity?

Ask FRED

15. Go to the FRED Economic Database (https://fred.stlouisfed.org/) and find tobacco taxes in Texas. In what year (1991–2016) would you guess Texas raised the sales tax on tobacco?

CHALLENGES

16. Let's apply the economics of taxation to romantic relationships.

    a. What does it mean to have an inelastic demand for your boyfriend or girlfriend? How about an elastic demand?

    b. Sometimes relationships have taxes. Suppose that you and your boyfriend or girlfriend live one hour apart. Using the tools developed in the chapter, how can you predict which one of you will do most of the driving? That is, which one of you will bear the majority of the relationship tax?

17. a. In the opening scene of the classic Eddie Murphy comedy *Beverly Hills Cop*, Axel Foley, a Detroit police officer, is stopping a cigarette smuggling ring. Of course, smugglers don't pay the tax when the cigarettes cross state lines. Which way do you suspect the smugglers were moving the cigarettes, based on economic theory? From the high-tax North to the low-cost South, or vice versa?

    b. In our discussion of taxation, we've acted as if it were effortless to pass and enforce tax laws. But of course, law enforcement officials, including the Internal Revenue Service, put a lot of effort into enforcing tax laws. Let's think for a moment about what kind of taxes are easiest to collect, just based on the basic ideas we've covered. Who will make the most effort to escape a tax: the party who is elastic or the party who is inelastic? (*Hint:* It doesn't matter whether we're talking about suppliers or demanders.)

    (*Note:* Public administration researchers know the most about this topic. Carolyn Webber and Aaron Wildavsky's surprisingly enjoyable classic, *A History of Taxation and Expenditure in the Western World*, sets out just how difficult it's been for most Western governments to collect taxes.)

18. Let's get some practice with the "wedge trick," and use it to learn about the relationship between subsidies and lobbying. The U.S. government has many subsidies for alternative energy development: Some are just called subsidies; some are called tax breaks instead. Either way, they work just like the subsidies we studied in this chapter. We'll look at the market for windmills.

    a. In the two figures, one is a case where the sellers of windmills have an elastic supply and the buyers of windmills (local power companies) have inelastic demand. In the other case, the reverse is true. Which is which?

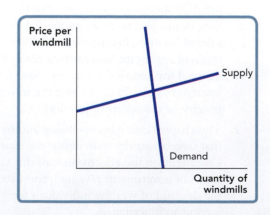

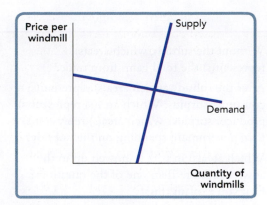

b. In which case will a subsidy cut the price paid by the buyers the most: When demand is elastic or when it is inelastic? (It'll be easiest if you use the wedge trick.) Is this the first or second graph?

c. In which case will a subsidy increase the price received by the sellers more: When supply is elastic or when it is inelastic? Again, which graph is this?

d. Now look at how producer surplus and consumer surplus change in these two cases. To see this, remember that producer surplus is the area *above* the supply curve and below the price, and consumer surplus is the area *below* the demand curve and above the price. So in the first graph, who gets the lion's share of any subsidy-driven extra surplus: suppliers or demanders? Is that the inelastic group or the elastic group? In other words, whose surplus triangle gets bigger faster as the quantity increases? (You might try shading in these triangles just to be sure.)

e. Now it's time for the second graph. Again, who gets the lion's share of any subsidy-driven extra surplus: suppliers or demanders? Is that the inelastic group or the elastic group?

f. There's going to be a pattern here in parts d and e: The more [elastic or inelastic?] side of the market gets more of the extra surplus from the subsidy.

g. When Congress gives subsidies for the alternative energy market, it is hoping that a small subsidy can get a big increase in output: In other words, they are hoping that the equilibrium quantity will be *elastic*. At the same time, the groups most likely to lobby Congress for a big alternative energy subsidy are going to be the groups that get the most extra surplus from any subsidy. After all, if the subsidy doesn't give them much surplus, they're not likely to ask Congress for it.

So here's the big question: Will the groups that are most likely to *lobby* for a subsidy be the same groups that are most likely to *respond to* the subsidy? (*Note:* This is a general lesson about the incentives for lobbying: It's not just a story about the alternative energy industry.)

19. As you learned in the chapter, the elasticities of demand and supply are crucial in determining how the burden of a tax (or the benefit of a subsidy) is divided between buyers and sellers. Under what conditions for supply or demand would a seller actually be able to avoid bearing any of the burden of a tax? Under what conditions would a subsidy benefit only the sellers of a good?

20. In the chapter, most of the taxes we discussed were equal to a certain dollar amount per unit. In this case, a tax on sellers results in a parallel upward shift of the supply curve; a tax on buyers results in a parallel downward shift of the demand curve. In reality, however, many taxes are expressed as a percentage. Graphically, how would you show a 100% tax on the sellers of a good? How would you show a 100% tax on the buyers of a good? One of the results of this chapter is that it doesn't matter on whom the tax is levied; the result is the same. Show graphically that this also applies to *percentage* taxes.

WORK IT OUT

For interactive, step-by-step help in solving this problem, go online.

Consider the following supply and demand diagram. In this market, the government subsidizes the production of this good, and the subsidy wedge is indicated.

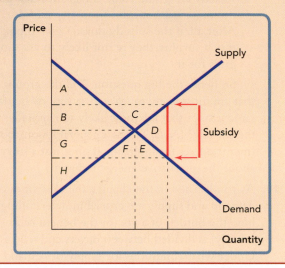

a. Without the subsidy, which area(s) represent(s) the total gains from trade?

b. After the subsidy, which area(s) represent(s) consumer surplus? Which area(s) represent(s) producer surplus? Which area(s) represent(s) total government spending on this subsidy?

c. Which area(s) in part b showed up in the answer to more than one of the questions? Can you explain this?

MARGINAL REVOLUTION UNIVERSITY VIDEOS

Commodity Taxes
mruniversity.com/commodity-taxes

Problems: **1, 2, 16, 20**

Who Pays the Tax?
mruniversity.com/who-pays-tax

Problems: **1, 2, 5, 7–10, 13, 16–20**

Understanding Tax Revenue and Deadweight Loss
mruniversity.com/tax-revenue

Problems: **3, 4, 6, 10–14, 19**

Subsidies
mruniversity.com/subsidies

Problems: **1, 11, 18**

Wage Subsidies
mruniversity.com/wage-subsidies

Problems: **5**

7

The Price System: Signals, Speculation, and Prediction

A price is a signal wrapped up in an incentive. That may sound a little abstract, but it's one of the most fundamental insights in economics. Prices convey important information and they create an incentive to respond to that information in socially useful ways. In this chapter, you'll see how one market influences another and then how an entire series of markets in a global economy fit together. Prices are the key force integrating markets and motivating entrepreneurs. We will have plenty of examples in this chapter, but keep your eye on the primary theme: The price system creates rich connections between markets and enables societies to mobilize vast amounts of knowledge toward common ends, yet without a central planner.

Markets Link the World

Let's take a closer look at the story of just one product. It's Valentine's Day. You have just given your boyfriend or girlfriend a beautiful, single-stemmed rose, one of 180 million that will be sold today.[1] Where did the rose come from and how did it get into your hands?

Chances are good that your rose was grown in Kenya in the Lake Naivasha area to the northwest of Nairobi.[2] Over 50,000 tons of roses are grown in Kenya every year, almost all for export. The Kenyan women who do most of the fieldwork know very little about the strange Western celebration of love called Saint Valentine's Day, but they don't have to. What they do know is that they get paid more when the roses are debudded so that they bloom just in time for delivery on February 14.

No one wants to give (or receive) a wilted rose, so everyone involved in the rose business has an incentive to move quickly. In a matter of hours after picking, the roses travel in cooled trucks from the field to the airport in Nairobi, where they are loaded onto refrigerated aircraft. Within a day, the flowers are in Aalsmeer, Holland.

Aalsmeer is the home of the world's largest flower market. On a typical working day, 20 million flowers are flown into this tiny

interactive activity

How Does the Invisible Hand Deliver Roses?

The Aalsmeer flower auction in action

Dutch town. The flowers are paraded in lots before large clocks, clocks that measure not time but prices. Beginning with a high price, the clocks quickly tick downward until a bidder stamps a button indicating that he or she is willing to buy at that price. By the end of the day, 20 million flowers have been sold, and they are once again packed onto cooled airplanes to be flown to the world's buyers in London, Paris, New York, and Topeka. From Kenya to your girlfriend's or boyfriend's hand in 72 hours.[3]

The worldwide market links romantic American teenagers with Kenyan flower growers, Dutch clocks, British airplanes, Colombian coffee (to keep the pilots awake), Finnish cell phones, and much, much more. To bring just one product to your table requires the cooperative effort of millions.

Moreover, this immense cooperation is voluntary and undirected. Each of millions of people acting in his or her own self-interest play a role, but no one knows the full story of how a Kenyan rose becomes a gift of love in Topeka because the full story is too complex. Nevertheless, every Valentine's Day you can count on the fact that your local florist will have roses for sale.

The market is the original Web, and it's more dense, interconnected, and alive with intelligence than its computer analog.

Markets Link to One Another

In Chapters 3 and 4, we showed how the supply and demand for oil determine the price of oil. Now we return to oil but this time as an example of how shifts in supply and demand in one market ripple across the worldwide market, changing distant people and products in ways that no one can foresee.

The Kenyan flower industry was one unforeseen consequence of changes in the market for oil. Prior to the 1970s, roses were grown in American greenhouses. Higher prices for oil raised heating costs so much that it became cheaper to grow roses in warm countries and ship them to cold countries.[*] If roses had been heavier, the higher costs of transportation might have outweighed the lower costs of heating, but even with higher fuel costs, transportation costs in the modern world have been falling.

It's not obvious that the right way to respond to an increased scarcity of oil is to move flower production from California to Kenya. No one planned such a response in advance. Instead, creative entrepreneurs responded to the increase in the price of oil in ways that no one predicted or planned. Entrepreneurs are constantly on the lookout for ways to lower costs, and their cost-cutting measures link markets that at first seem like they are a world away.

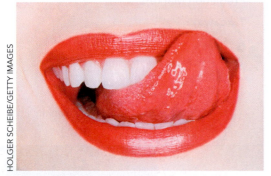

HOLGER SCHEIBE/GETTY IMAGES

The world is linked in fascinating ways. In Peru, workers roam the hillsides collecting millions of female cochineal bugs from their cactus pad nests. After dunking in hot water, drying and grinding, the bugs make an excellent red dye. The dye is used to color many products including yogurt (look for carmine in the ingredients), red Smarties, and even lipstick!

From Oil to Candy Bars and Brick Driveways

How does the price of oil affect the price of candy bars? One way is obvious: Higher energy costs increase the cost of producing most products, including

---

[*] The shift of flower production from America to Kenya and other equatorial countries like Colombia and Ecuador in the 1980s is part of a trend. Two decades earlier, declines in transportation costs and relative increases in the relative costs of heating, land, and labor moved flower production from New York and Pennsylvania to Florida and California. On the evolution of the cut flower industry, see Mendez, Jose A. 1991. *The Development of the Colombian Cut Flower Industry*. The World Bank. WPS 660.

candy bars. But the market also links oil and candy bars in more subtle ways. For instance, ethanol is the active ingredient in alcoholic beverages, but it's also a good fuel that can be made from a variety of crops like corn or sugar cane. Brazil is the largest producer and consumer of fuel ethanol in the world, so much so that it has managed to reduce its gasoline consumption by 40% by adopting flexible fuel vehicles that can run on ethanol, gasoline, or any combination of the two.[4] Brazil is also the largest producer of sugar in the world.

Surprised? Corn and oil are substitutes.

MARTIN SHIELDS/ALAMY

Can you see the connection between the price of oil and the price of candy bars now? As the price of oil has increased, the Brazilians have shifted sugar cane from sugar production to ethanol production, thereby holding down fuel costs but increasing the price of sugar.[5]

What about brick driveways? A 42-gallon barrel of crude oil is refined into approximately 19.5 gallons of gasoline, 9.7 gallons of fuel oil, 4 gallons of jet fuel, 1.4 gallons of asphalt, and a number of other products.[6] To some extent, these divisions are fixed. (Asphalt is what you get after you separate out the other products.) But oil refiners do have some flexibility, and when the price of gasoline is relatively high, it pays for them to pull every last drop of gasoline out of a barrel of crude, leaving less crude to make the remaining products. A higher price of gasoline, therefore, means a reduced supply of asphalt. A reduced supply of asphalt pushes up the price of asphalt. When the price of oil rose to $70 a barrel in 2006, for example, the price of using asphalt to pave an average-sized driveway rose by $300.[7] Seeing the higher price, homeowners turned to substitutes such as concrete, cobblestones, and brick.

Solving the Great Economic Problem

Markets around the world are linked to one another. A change in supply or demand in one market can influence markets for entirely different products thousands of miles away. But what does all this linking accomplish? The **great economic problem** is to arrange our scarce resources to satisfy as many of our wants as possible. Let's imagine that war in the Middle East reduces the supply of oil. We must economize on oil. But how? It would be foolish to reduce oil equally in all uses—oil is more valuable in some uses than in others. We want to shift oil out of low-valued uses, where we can do without or where good substitutes for oil exist, so that we can keep supplying oil for high-valued uses, where oil has few good substitutes.

One way to make this shift would be for a central planner to issue orders. The central planner would order so much oil to be used in the steel industry, so much for heating, and so much for Sunday driving. But how would the central planner know the value of oil in each of its millions of uses? No one knows for certain all the uses of oil, let alone which uses of oil are high-valued uses and which are low-valued uses. Is the oil used to produce steel more valuable than the oil used to produce vegetables? Even if steel is worth more than vegetables, the answer isn't obvious because electricity might be a good substitute for oil in producing steel but not for producing vegetables. To estimate the value of oil in different uses, therefore, the central planner would have to

The **great economic problem** is to arrange our scarce resources to satisfy as many of our wants as possible.

A Price Is a Signal Wrapped Up in an Incentive

Opportunity cost. The true cost of a motorcycle is not its money price but rather a lawnmower. The true cost is the opportunity cost—what the resources that went into the motorcycle could have produced had the motorcycle not been built.

It is part of the marvel of a free market that, under the right conditions, the money price of the motorcycle exactly represents the value of the resources that went into producing the motorcycle, namely the value those resources would have had in their next highest-valued use.

gather information about all the uses of oil and all of the substitutes for oil in each use (and all of the substitutes for the substitutes!). Using this information, the central planner would then have to somehow compute the optimal allocation of oil and then send out thousands of orders directing oil to its many uses in the economy.

The task of central planning is impossibly complex and we haven't yet discussed incentives. Why would anyone have an incentive to send truthful information to the central planner? Each user of oil would surely announce that their use is the high-valued use for which no substitute is possible. And what incentive would the central planner have to actually direct oil to its high-value uses?

The U.S. government briefly tried to centrally plan the allocation of oil during the 1973–1974 oil crisis. President Nixon even went so far as to forbid gas stations from opening on Sundays in an attempt to reduce Sunday driving! We describe the consequences of this approach to the oil crisis at greater length in the next chapter. The Soviet Union and China went much further than the United States and tried to centrally plan entire economies. Central planning on a large scale, however, failed and has now been abandoned throughout virtually all the world (Cuba and North Korea, both very poor countries, are the exceptions).

The central planning approach failed because of problems of *information* and *incentives*. We need a better approach.

Users of oil have a lot of information about the value of oil in their own uses, much more information than could ever be communicated to a central planner. We need to take advantage of this information without attempting to communicate it to a central bureaucracy. Ideally, each user of oil would compare the value of oil in their use with the value of oil in alternative uses, and each user of oil would have an incentive to give up the oil if it has a lower value in their use than in alternative uses. This is exactly what the price system accomplishes.

Let's go back to the person thinking about whether to pave the driveway with asphalt or brick. This person knows the value of a paved driveway but doesn't know what uses the asphalt has elsewhere in the economy. He or she does know the price of asphalt, and *in a free market, the price of asphalt is equal to the value of the asphalt in its next highest-value use*. Take a look at Figure 7.1, which is just the now-familiar supply and demand diagram. Remember that the value of a good in its various uses is given by the height of the demand curve. Notice that the equilibrium price splits the uses of the good into two—above the equilibrium price are the high-value, satisfied demands; below the price are the low-value, unsatisfied demands. Now what is the value of the highest-value demand that is not satisfied? It's just equal to the market price (or if you like, "just below" the market price). In other words, if one more barrel of oil became available, the highest-value use of that barrel would be to satisfy the first presently unsatisfied demand. The market price tells us the value of the good in its next highest-valued use.

When a consumer compares the price of asphalt to the value of asphalt for paving his driveway, he is comparing *the value of asphalt on his driveway to its opportunity cost*. And remember, because markets are linked, the price of asphalt is linked to the price of oil, and the price of oil is linked to the demand for automobiles in China and the supply of ethanol and the price

FIGURE 7.1

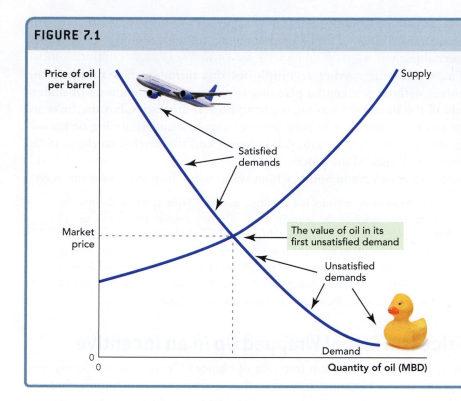

The Market Price and Opportunity Cost The market price splits the uses of oil into two. Above the price are the uses of oil whose value is greater than the price; in a free market, these demands will be satisfied. Below the price are the uses of oil whose value is less than the price; in a free market, these are the unsatisfied demands. Notice that the value of oil in the first unsatisfied demand is just slightly below the market price.

(Top: ssuaphotos/Shutterstock)
(Bottom: Lew Robertson/Corbis)

of sugar. . . . So when the consumer compares the value of asphalt in paving his driveway to the price of asphalt, he may be comparing the value of asphalt in paving his driveway to the value of 500 gallons of gasoline used by a motorist in Brazil. Or, in other words, when you decide whether to drive to school or take the bus, you are deciding whether your use of oil is more valuable than the billions of other uses of oil in the world that are presently unsatisfied!

The market solves the information problem by collapsing all the relevant information in the world about the uses of oil into a single number, the price. As Nobel laureate Friedrich Hayek wrote:[*]

> The most significant fact about this system is the economy of knowledge with which it operates . . . by a kind of symbol [the price], only the most essential information is passed on and passed on only to those concerned. . . . The marvel is that in a case like that of a scarcity of one raw material, without an order being issued, without more than perhaps a handful of people knowing the cause, tens of thousands of people whose identity could not be ascertained by months of investigation, are made to use the material or its products more sparingly; i.e., they move in the right direction.

In addition to solving the information problem, the price system also solves the incentive problem. It's in a consumer's interest to pay attention to prices! When the price of an oil product like asphalt

Friedrich A. Hayek (1899–1992) explained the marvel of the price system.

HULTON ARCHIVE/GETTY IMAGES

[*] Hayek's classic paper, "The Use of Knowledge in Society," is deep but easy to read. You can find it online by searching for "Hayek use of knowledge in society." The original citation is Hayek, Friedrich A., 1945. The use of knowledge in society. *American Economic Review* 35(4): 519–530.

increases, consumers have an incentive to turn to substitutes like bricks and, in so doing, they free up oil to be used elsewhere in the economy where it is of higher value.

The worldwide market accomplishes this immense task of allocating resources without any central planning or control. No one knows or understands all the links between oil, sugar, and brick driveways, but the links are there and the market works even without anyone's understanding or knowledge. Amazed by what he saw, Adam Smith said the market works as if "an invisible hand" guided the process.

Nobel laureate Vernon Smith, whom we met in Chapter 4, put it this way:

> At the heart of economics is a scientific mystery: How is it that the pricing system accomplishes the world's work without anyone being in charge? Like language, no one invented it. None of us could have invented it, and its operation depends in no way on anyone's comprehension or understanding of it. . . . The pricing system—How is order produced from freedom of choice?—is a scientific mystery as deep, fundamental and inspiring as that of the expanding universe or the forces that bind matter.[8]

A Price Is a Signal Wrapped Up in an Incentive

How is order produced from freedom of choice? That is a scientific mystery, and prices are the biggest clue to the solution. Prices do much more than tell people how much they must shell out for a burger and fries. Prices are incentives, prices are signals, prices are predictions. To understand the market, you need to better understand prices.

When the price of oil rises, all users of oil are encouraged to economize—perhaps by simply using less but also by thinking about substitutes: everything from electric cars to moving flower cultivation overseas. An increase in the price of oil is also a signal to suppliers to invest more in exploration, to look for alternatives like ethanol, and to increase recycling. Do you know the most recycled product in America? It's asphalt.[9]

Politicians and consumers sometime fail to understand the signaling role of prices. After a hurricane, the prices of ice, generators, and chainsaws often skyrocket. Consumers complain of price gouging, and politicians call for price controls. That's understandable, because it can seem doubly harsh to be hit by a hurricane *and* high prices. But the price system is just doing its job. A skyrocketing price is like a flare being shot into the night sky that shouts—bring ice here! A price control eliminates the signal to bring ice into the devastated area as quickly as possible.

The high price of ice in a hurricane-devastated area signals a profit opportunity for ice suppliers. Buy ice where the price is low and deliver it to where the price is high. As the supply of ice in the hurricane-devastated area increases, the price will fall. More generally, price signals and the accompanying profits and losses tell entrepreneurs what areas of the economy consumers want expanded and what areas they want contracted. If consumers want more computers, prices and profits in the computer industry will increase and the industry will expand.

Losses may be an even more important signal than profits. Entrepreneurs who fail to compete with lower costs and better products

A skyrocketing price is a signal to bring resources here!

take losses and their businesses contract or even go bankrupt. Bankruptcy is bad for a business but can be good for capitalism. Ever heard of Smith Corona, Polaroid, Pan Am, or Hechingers? At one point, each of these companies led its industry, but today all are either bankrupt or much smaller than at their peak. In a free market, no firm is so powerful that it does not daily face the market test. As a result, *in a successful economy there will be many unsuccessful firms.*

Speculation

Suppose that you expect that a war in the Middle East is likely next year and that, if it should occur, the supply of oil will decrease, thereby pushing up the price of oil. How could you profit from your expectation? The way to make money is to buy low and sell high, so you should buy oil today when the price is low, hold the oil in storage, and then sell it next year after war breaks out, when the price is higher. Figure 7.2 on the next page shows this process, which is called **speculation**. We have used vertical supply curves, meaning that the amount of oil is fixed, to simplify the diagram.

The top panel shows what happens without speculation. Production today is high and today's price is low (point *a*). Future production, however, will be disrupted by the war, pushing up the future price (point *b*). Notice that without speculation, the war disrupts the oil market and prices jump from point *a* to point *b*.

The bottom panel shows what happens with speculation. Speculators buy oil today and they put it into storage—this reduces the quantity available for consumption today and pushes up today's price (point *c*). Next year, however, when the war occurs, production is low but consumption is higher than it would have been without speculation and prices are lower because the speculators sell oil from their inventories (point *d*). Notice that with speculation, preparations are made for any disruption in oil production and oil prices are smoothed.

Speculators raise prices today but lower prices in the future. As a result, speculators have an image problem: the media often report when speculators raise prices but rarely do they report when speculators lower prices. Overall, however, society is better off from speculation because speculators move oil from when it has low value (today) and move it to when it has high value (the future). When producers put oil in storage, society doesn't get to consume that oil so some wants become unsatisfied—the loss in value from these unsatisfied wants is measured by the blue area in the (bottom) left panel of Figure 7.2 (once again, the value of the good in its various uses is measured by the height of the demand curve). But when the speculators sell that oil in the future, consumption increases—more wants are satisfied—and the value of this increase in consumption is measured by the much larger blue area in the right panel. Thus, when speculators are right, they move oil from today, where it has low value, to the future, where the value of oil is much higher—in the process making society better off.

Speculators, of course, don't always guess correctly. But speculators put their money where their mouth is. They have strong incentives to be as accurate as possible because when they are wrong, they lose money—a lot of money. Bad speculators soon find themselves out of a job. Anyone who is able to be a speculator for a long time is either very, very lucky or just very good. So, on net, speculators tend to make prices more informative, even though in particular instances many speculators are wrong.

CHECK YOURSELF

- Imagine that whenever the supply of oil rose or fell, the government sent text messages to every user of oil asking them to use more or less oil as the case warranted. Suppose that the messaging system worked very well. Is such a messaging system likely to allocate resources as well as prices? Why or why not? What is the difference between the message system and the price system?
- Firms in the old Soviet Union never went bankrupt. How do you think this influenced the rate of innovation and economic growth?

Speculation is the attempt to profit from future price changes.

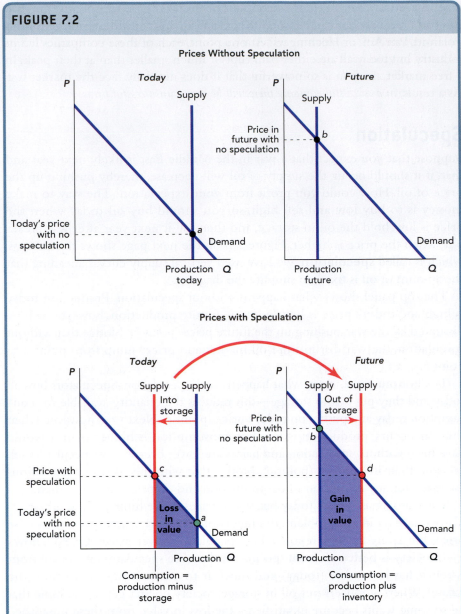

FIGURE 7.2

Prices Without Speculation

Today

Future

Prices with Speculation

Speculation Tends to Smooth Prices over Time and Increase Welfare The top panel shows the price of oil, oil consumption, and oil production in an economy without speculation. In the panel on the left, Today, the equilibrium is at point *a*, the price is low, and oil consumption and production are high. In the panel on the right, Future, the price of oil is high because the disruption has reduced the production of oil. Since no oil was stored from the previous period, the consumption of oil is also reduced.

The bottom panel shows what happens with speculation. In the left panel, oil speculators buy oil and put it into storage, pushing up the price of oil and reducing consumption today—thus, the equilibrium shifts from point *a* to point *c*. In the future when the price of oil is high (at point *b*), speculators sell their oil from storage. The oil flowing out of storage pushes the price down and allows people to consume more oil even though production is low.

The value of oil to consumers (in blue) falls today when oil is put into storage, but rises by an even larger amount in the future when oil is in short supply and speculators move their stocks out of storage.

A careful observer of Middle East politics might have very good information about the probability of war in the Middle East but have no easy way to store oil. Fortunately, the market provides a way to speculate in oil without building oil tanks in your backyard.

A speculator can buy oil **futures**. Oil futures are contracts to buy or sell a given quantity of oil at a specified price with delivery set at a specified time and place in the future. On the New York Mercantile Exchange (NYMEX), you can buy futures for light, sweet crude oil to be delivered in Cushing, Oklahoma, at 30, 36, 48, 72, or 84 months in the future at a price agreed on today. What makes futures contracts important is that despite specifying delivery and acceptance in Cushing, almost all futures contracts actually settle in cash.

Let's see how this works. Suppose Tyler believes that the price of oil will be higher in the future than what other people are expecting. Tyler buys an oil contract that gives him the right to 1,000 barrels of oil to be delivered (in Cushing) 30 months in the future. Tyler agrees that on delivery he will pay the seller, Alex, $50 per barrel or $50,000. Similarly, Alex has agreed to deliver 1,000 barrels of oil in Cushing in 30 months. Thirty months from now, Tyler's expectation is proven correct—the actual or "spot" price of oil is $82. If Tyler went to Cushing, he could physically accept the oil from Alex, give him $50,000 and then turn around and sell the oil to someone else for $82 per barrel for a profit of $32 per barrel or $32,000. Instead of doing that, however, Tyler and Alex could agree to *cash settlement*. Alex has agreed to give Tyler 1,000 barrels of oil, which are currently worth $82,000, for a price of $50,000. Instead of giving Tyler the oil, suppose that Alex gives Tyler the cash difference, $32,000, and they call it even. The advantage of cash settlement is that Tyler and Alex can both speculate on the price of oil without ever accepting or delivering oil. Moreover, neither Tyler nor Alex ever have to go to Cushing, which is sadly lacking in good ethnic restaurants.*

Futures markets are used not only for speculation but also for reducing risk. An airline that wants to know in advance what its fuel costs are going to be next year can lock in the price by buying oil on the futures market. Instead of buying futures, farmers can sell futures. A soybean farmer plants the crop today but does not harvest it until next year when the soybean price could be quite different from today's spot price. To avoid the price risk, the farmer can sell futures, that is, agree to sell so many soybeans at harvest time at a price agreed on today. Futures markets are also common in currencies. Suppose that Ford expects to sell 1,000 cars in Germany for 25,000 euros each. At the end of the year, how many dollars will Ford make? Ford doesn't know because the euro/dollar exchange rate can fluctuate. By selling euro futures, Ford can lock in the exchange rate.

Futures are standardized contracts to buy or sell specified quantities of a commodity or financial instrument at a specified price with delivery set at a specified time in the future.

DOUGLAS PULSIPHER/ACCLAIM IMAGES

Markets see the future with futures markets.

CHECK YOURESELF

■ Speculation occurs in stocks as well as commodities. In 2008, Lehman Brothers, a Wall Street investment banking firm, complained that speculators were driving the price of its stock lower and lower. During this time, Lehman continued to give rosy forecasts. Later in 2008, Lehman Brothers went bankrupt. Why was the forecast of the speculators more informative on net than the statements being issued from Lehman?

---

* Technically, this describes a forward contract. The difference between forward and futures contracts is not important for making the point that cash settlement allows anyone to speculate in oil even if he or she neither wants nor has any oil to trade.

 The technical difference between futures and forwards is that in a futures contract the buyer and the seller do not contract directly but rather each works through a middleman, the New York Mercantile Exchange (NYMEX). NYMEX guarantees that neither the buyer nor the seller will cheat on the deal. NYMEX does this by *marking the contract to market* on a daily basis, which means that there is a small cash settlement every day until the final day. For example, if the day after Tyler and Alex signed the contract the spot price moved to $51, then Alex would have to pay some extra money to NYMEX. If the day after the contract was signed, the spot price moved to $49, then Tyler would have to pay some extra money to NYMEX. NYMEX holds onto the money, keeping a running tab, until the final day when it releases the total to the party with the net gain. In this way, NYMEX's losses are limited even if one party refuses to honor the deal.

Signal Watching

Speculators who think that a war in the Middle East is likely will buy oil futures, pushing up the futures price (the price agreed on today for delivery in the future). If the futures price is much higher than the spot or current price, that is a sign that smart people with their own money on the line think that supply disruptions may soon occur. Futures prices for oil, currencies, and many commodities can be found in a newspaper or online, so anyone who wants to forecast events in the Middle East can benefit from reading price signals.

Futures prices can be extraordinarily informative about future events. The major factor determining the price of orange juice futures, for example, is the weather. If bad weather is expected to cause a frost destroying many oranges, the price of OJ futures will be high. If good weather and a bumper crop are expected, the price will be low. The economist Richard Roll found that the futures price for OJ was so sensitive to the weather that it could be used to improve the predictions of the National Weather Service![10]

It's not hard to see the future if you know where to look. In December 1991, the United Nations and the Worldwatch Institute warned that wheat would be very scarce in the coming year. Economist Paul Heyne looked in the newspaper and found that on that day the price of wheat was $4.05 a bushel. But the futures price for the following December was $3.51. Speculators, unlike the Worldwatch Institute, were not forecasting increased scarcity. In whose forecast would you put more confidence: that of the Worldwatch Institute or that of wheat speculators? Why?*

The futures price of oil can be used to predict war in the Middle East, but that is a side benefit of the futures market and not its purpose. Factors other than war (e.g., the decisions of OPEC, oil discoveries, and the demand for oil) also affect oil futures, so the futures price of oil is a *noisy signal* of war in the Middle East. A phone line with static—that's a noisy signal. Electrical engineers work to increase the signal-to-noise ratio on cell phones. More recently, economic engineers have begun to design markets to increase the signal-to-noise ratio of prices.

Prediction Markets

A **prediction market** is a speculative market designed so that prices can be interpreted as probabilities and used to make predictions.

If markets are good at predicting the future even though they evolved to do something else, imagine how useful they might be if they were designed to predict. Beginning in the late 1980s, economic engineers began to design **prediction markets**, speculative markets designed so that prices can be interpreted as probabilities and used to make predictions.[11]

The best known prediction market is the Iowa Electronic Markets. The Iowa market lets traders use real money to buy and sell "shares" of political candidates. During the 2016 election, for example, traders on the Iowa Electronic Markets could buy shares in Donald Trump and Hillary Clinton. A share in Hillary Clinton, for example, would pay $1 if Hillary Clinton won the election and nothing otherwise. Suppose that the market price of a Clinton share is 75 cents. What does this market price suggest about the probability of Hillary Clinton winning the election?

---

* By the way, Heyne's forecast was correct—wheat was not especially scarce in 1992. Did you put your confidence in the right place?

To answer this question, think about each share as a bit like a lottery ticket. The ticket pays $1 if Clinton wins and nothing if she loses. How much would you be willing to pay for this lottery ticket if Clinton has a 20% chance of winning? How much would you be willing to pay for this lottery ticket if Clinton has a 75% chance of winning? If Clinton has a 20% chance of winning, then a lottery ticket that pays $1 if she wins, and nothing otherwise, is worth about 20 cents on average (0.2 × $1). If Clinton has a 75% chance of winning, then the lottery ticket is worth about 75 cents (0.75 × $1). Thus, working backward, if we see that people are willing to pay 75 cents for a Clinton lottery ticket, we can infer that they think that Clinton has about a 75% probability of winning the election. In this way, we can use market prices to predict elections!

On November 1, a week before the election on November 8, the polls were predicting a Clinton victory, as were the Iowa markets. Statistician Nate Silver's model, which was based on national and state polls, gave Trump a 29% chance of winning. The prediction markets suggested a Trump victory was more likely, 40%, but still less likely than a Clinton victory. In fact, Donald Trump won the election in what to most people was a surprise. The markets appeared to be a bit better than the polls but were the markets still wrong? Not necessarily. Events with a 40% chance are predicted to happen 40% of the time! To evaluate the markets, we have to examine many predictions. In fact, in more than 20 years of predicting U.S. and foreign elections, primaries and other political events, the Iowa political markets have proven to be more accurate on average than polls. Uncertainty will always be with us and social scientists have to remain humble about our ability to predict the future. But markets are a good way of aggregating information and prediction markets have performed well relative to other methods of predicting the future.

The Hollywood Stock Exchange (http://www.HSX.com) is also proving that the innovative use of markets can be profitable. The Hollywood Exchange lets traders buy and sell shares and options in movies, music, and Oscar contenders. Trading on the Hollywood Exchange is conducted in make-believe "Hollywood Dollars," but the goal of the HSX—which is owned by a subsidiary of the Wall Street firm Cantor Fitzgerald—is profit. Some 800,000 people trading on HSX for fun have proven that HSX prices are reliable predictors of future film profits. Figure 7.3 graphs market predictions of opening revenues on the x-axis against actual opening revenues on the vertical axis. If all predictions were perfect, then predicted revenues would be exactly equal to actual revenues and all the observations would lie on the 45-degree red line. No one can predict the future perfectly, of course. Movies above the red line did better than predicted and movies below the red line did worse than predicted. The market predicted that *The Adventures of Pluto Nash*, a 2002 movie starring Eddie Murphy, would take in opening weekend revenues of over $10 million. In fact, *The Adventures* was the biggest financial bomb of all time with costs of $100 million and revenues of $4.41 million, just over half of that generated on the opening weekend before word of mouth sent it straight to the reject pile. *The Fast and the Furious*, however, was an unexpected hit, earning opening revenues of $41.6 million

On November 1, 2016, a share that paid $1 if Donald Trump won the U.S. presidential election was selling for 40 cents and a share that paid $1 if Hillary Clinton won the U.S. presidential election was selling for 60 cents. What was the market predicting?

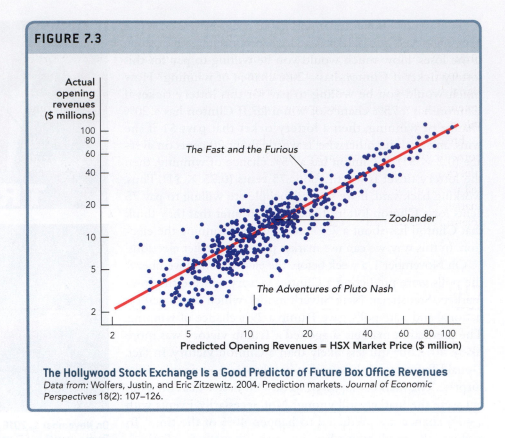

FIGURE 7.3

Actual opening revenues ($ millions)

The Fast and the Furious

Zoolander

The Adventures of Pluto Nash

Predicted Opening Revenues = HSX Market Price ($ million)

The Hollywood Stock Exchange Is a Good Predictor of Future Box Office Revenues
Data from: Wolfers, Justin, and Eric Zitzewitz. 2004. Prediction markets. *Journal of Economic Perspectives* 18(2): 107–126.

when less than half that amount, just $19.6 million, had been predicted. You know which movie resulted in lots and lots of sequels.

Although market predictions are sometimes a little high and sometimes a little low, they are centered on the 45-degree line, which means that they are correct on average. The market, for example, predicted that *Zoolander* would have opening revenues of $15.03 million and actual revenues were $15.7 million. Perhaps the biggest sign of the accuracy of the HSX market is that HSX sells its data to Hollywood studios eager to improve their predictions about future blockbusters.

The use of prediction markets is expanding rapidly, but what's important for our purposes is that prediction markets help to illustrate how *all* markets work. Market prices are signals that convey valuable information. Buyers and sellers have an incentive to pay attention to and respond to prices and in so doing they direct resources to their highest-value uses. That means everyone can make the most out of limited resources.

Takeaway

No market is an island. Markets are linked geographically, through time and across different goods. The price of gasoline at your local gasoline station is linked to the market for oil in China. The price of oil today is linked to the expectations about the market for oil in the future and, through investment, to the market for oil in the past. Markets in one good are linked to markets in other goods. The supply and demand of flowers, asphalt, and candy bars are all linked through the worldwide market.

The worldwide market is neither designed nor, because it is so complex, is it ever completely understood. The market acts like a giant computer to arrange our limited resources to satisfy as many of our wants as possible. Prices are the heart of the market process. A price is a signal wrapped up in an incentive because prices signal the value of resources to consumers, suppliers, and entrepreneurs, and they incentivize everyone to take appropriate actions to respond to scarcity and changing circumstances.

Free market prices work as signals because through buying and selling, prices come to reflect important pieces of information. The futures price of oil, for example, can signal war in the Middle East and the futures price of orange juice can tell us about the weather in Florida. Market prices can be so informative that new markets (prediction markets) are being created to help businesses, governments, and scientists predict future events.

CHAPTER REVIEW

interactive activity   Go online to practice with more examples of these types of problems, including live links to videos, data sources, and feedback.

  Problems in **green** relate to MRU videos. See the MRU table at the end of the exercises.

KEY CONCEPTS

the great economic problem, p. 121

speculation, p. 125

futures, p. 127

prediction market, p. 128

FACTS AND TOOLS

1. **a.** Suppose you'd like to do five different things, each of which requires exactly one orange. Complete the following table, ranking your highest-valued orange-related activity (1) to your lowest-valued activity (5).

Activity	Rank of Preference
Give a friend the orange.	
Throw the orange at a person you don't like.	
Eat the orange.	
Squeeze the orange to drink the juice.	
Use the orange as decorative fruit.	

   b. Suppose the price per orange is high enough that you buy only four. What activity do you not do?

   c. How low would the price of oranges have to fall for you to purchase five oranges? What does the price at which you would just purchase the fifth orange tell us about the value you receive from the fifth-ranked activity?

2. The supply and demand for copper change constantly. New sources are discovered, mines collapse, workers go on strike, products that use it wane in and out of popularity, weather affects shipping conditions, and so on.

   a. Suppose you learned that growing political instability in Chile (the largest producer of copper) will greatly reduce the productivity of its mines in two years. Ignoring all other factors, which curve (demand or supply) will shift which way in the market for copper two years from now?

   b. Will the price rise or fall as a result of this curve shift?

   c. Given your answer in part b, would a reasonable person buy copper to store for later? Why or why not? Ignore storage costs.

d. As a result of many people imitating your choice in part c, what happens to the current price of copper?

e. Does the action in parts c and d encourage people to use more copper today or less copper today?

3. In this chapter, we noted that successful economies are more likely to have many failing firms. If a nation's government instead made it impossible for inefficient firms to fail by giving them loans, cash grants, and other bailouts to stay in business, why is that nation likely to be poor? (*Hint:* Steven Davis and John Haltiwanger. 1999. "Gross Job Flows." In *Handbook of Labor Economics* [Amsterdam: North-Holland] found that in the United States, 60% of the increase in U.S. manufacturing efficiency was caused by people moving from weak firms to strong firms.)

4. For you, personally, what is your opportunity cost of doing this homework?

5. Suppose you are bidding on a used car and someone else bids above the highest amount that you are willing to pay. What can you say for sure about that person's monetary value of the good compared to yours?

6. Sometimes speculators get it wrong. In the months before the Persian Gulf War, speculators drove up the price of oil: The average price in October 1990 was $36 per barrel, more than double its price in 1988. Oil speculators, like many people around the world, expected the Gulf War to last for months, disrupting the oil supply throughout the Gulf region. Thus, speculators either bought oil on the open market (almost always at the high speculative price) or they already owned oil and just kept it in storage. Either way, their plan was the same: to sell it in the future, when prices might even be higher.

As it turned out, the war was swift: After one month of massive aerial bombardment of Iraqi troops and a 100-hour ground war, then President George H. W. Bush declared a cessation of hostilities. Despite the fact that Saddam Hussein set fire to many of Kuwait's oil fields, the price of oil plummeted to about $20 per barrel, a price at which it remained for years.

a. Is buying oil for $36 a barrel and selling it for $20 per barrel a good business plan? How much profit did speculators earn, or how much money did they lose, on each barrel?

b. Why did the speculators follow this plan?

c. When the speculators sold their stored oil in the months after the war, did this massive resale tend to increase the price of oil or decrease it?

d. Do you think that many consumers complained about speculators or even realized that speculators were influencing the price of oil in spring 1991?

7. You manage a department store in Florida, and one winter day you read in the newspaper that orange juice futures have fallen dramatically in price. Should your store stock up on more sweaters than usual, or should your store stock up on more Bermuda shorts?

8. Take a look at Figure 7.3. If investors in the Hollywood Stock Exchange were too optimistic on average, would the dots tend to cluster above the red diagonal line or below it? How can you tell?

9. Let's see if the forces of the market can be as efficient as a benevolent dictator. Since laptop computers are increasingly easy to build and since they allow people to use their computers wherever they like, an all-wise benevolent dictator would probably decree that most people buy laptops rather than desktop computers. This is especially true now that laptops are about as powerful as most desktops. In answering questions a–c, answer in words as well as by shifting the appropriate curves in the following figures.

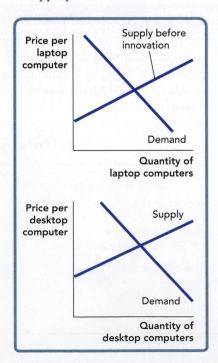

a. Since it's become much easier to build better laptops in recent years, laptop supply has increased. What does this do to the price of laptops?

b. Laptops and desktops are substitutes. Now that the price of laptops has changed, what does this do to the demand for desktop computers?

c. And how does that affect the quantity supplied of desktop computers?

d. Now let's look at the final result: Once it became easier to build good laptops, did "invisible hand" forces push more of society's resources into making laptops and push resources away from making desktops? (*Note:* Laptop sales first outnumbered desktop sales in 2008.)

THINKING AND PROBLEM SOLVING

10. Andy enters into a futures contract, allowing him to sell 5,000 troy ounces of gold at $1,000 per ounce in 36 months. After that time passes, the market price of gold is $950 per troy ounce. How much does Andy make or lose?

11. Circa 1200 BCE, a decreasing supply of tin due to wars and the breakdown of trade led to a drastic increase in the price of bronze in the Middle East and Greece (tin being necessary for its production). It is around this time that blacksmiths developed iron- and steel-making techniques (as substitutes for bronze).

a. How is the increasing price of bronze a signal?

b. How is the increasing price an incentive?

c. How do your answers in parts a and b help explain why iron and steel became more common around the same time as the increase in price?

d. After the development of iron, did the supply or demand for bronze shift? Which way did it shift? Why?

12. In 1980, University of Maryland economist Julian Simon bet Stanford entomologist Paul Ehrlich that the price of any five metals of Ehrlich's choosing would fall over 10 years. Ehrlich believed that resources would become scarcer over time as the population grew, while Simon believed that people would find good substitutes, just as earlier people developed iron

as a substitute for scarce bronze. The price of all five metals that Ehrlich chose (nickel, tin, tungsten, chromium, and copper) fell over the next 10 years and Simon won the bet. Ehrlich, an honorable man, sent a check in the appropriate amount to Simon.

a. What does the falling price tell us about the relative scarcity of these metals?

b. What *could have* shifted to push these prices down: demand or supply? And would demand have increased or decreased? And supply?

13. In this chapter, we explored how prices tie all goods together. To illustrate this idea, suppose new farming techniques drastically increased the productivity of growing wheat.

a. Given this change, how would the price of wheat change?

b. Given your answer in part a, how would the price of cookbooks specializing in recipes using wheat flour change?

c. Given your answer in part b, how would the price of paper change?

d. Given your answer in part c, how would the price of pencils change? (*Hint:* Are paper and pencils substitutes or complements?)

e. Given your answer in part d, how would the quantity of graphite (used in pencils) consumed change?

14. The law of one price states that if it's easy to move a good from one place to another, the price of identical goods will be the same because traders will buy low in one region and sell high in another. How is our story about the effect of speculators similar to the lesson about the law of one price?

15. Let's build on this chapter's example of asphalt. Suppose a new invention comes along that makes it easier and much less expensive to recycle clothing: Perhaps a new device about the size of a washing machine can bleach, reweave, and redye cotton fabric to closely imitate any cotton item you see in a fashion magazine. Head into the laundry room, drop in a batch of old clothes, scan in a couple of pages from *Vogue*, and come back in an hour.

a. If you think of the "market for clothing" as "the market for new clothing," does this shift the demand or the supply curve, and in which direction?

b. If you think of the "market for clothing" as "the market for clothing, whether it's new or used," does this shift the demand or the supply curve, and in which direction?

c. What will this do to the price of new, unrecycled clothing?

d. After this invention, will society's scarce productive resources (machines, workers, retail space) flow *toward* the "new clothing" sector or away from it?

(*Note:* This question might sound fanciful but three-dimensional printers, which can create plastic or plaster prototypes of small items such as toys, cups, etc., have fallen dramatically in price. Every day, you're getting just a little bit closer to having your own personal *Star Trek* replicator.)

16. Robin is planning to ask Peggy to the Homecoming dance. Before he asks her, he wants to know what are the chances that she'll say yes. Robin is a scientist so he considers two paths to estimate the probability that Peggy will say yes.

I. Ask 10 of his friends, "Do you think she'll really say yes?"

II. Tell another 10 of his friends, "I'm starting a betting market. I'll pay $10 if she says yes, $0 if she says no. I'm offering this bet only once, to the highest bidder. Start bidding against each other for a chance at $10!"

a. According to the evidence in this chapter, one of these methods will work better. Which one, and why?

b. If the highest bid from Group II is $1 (along with a few lower bids of $0.75, $0.50, and zero), then roughly what's the chance that Peggy will say yes to Robin?

c. If the highest bid from Group II quickly shoots up to about $9, then what's the chance that Peggy will say yes to Robin?

17. A classic essay about how markets link to each other is entitled "I, Pencil," written by Leonard E. Read (his real name). It is available for free online at the *Library of Economics and Liberty*. As you might suspect, it is written from the point of view of a pencil. One line is particularly famous: "No single person on the face of this earth knows how to make me."

Based on what you've learned in this chapter about how markets link the world, how is this true?

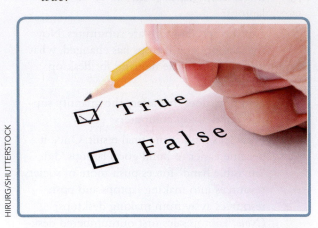

HIRURG/SHUTTERSTOCK

CHALLENGES

18. In *The Fatal Conceit*, economist Friedrich A. Hayek, arguing against central planning, wrote: "The curious task of economics is to demonstrate to men how little they really know about what they imagine they can design." In other words, people generally assume that they can plan out the best procedure for producing a good (such as the Valentine's Day rose mentioned at the beginning of the chapter), but as we learned, that's not true. What are some of the different roles that the price system plays in creating this order? (*Hint:* Key words are "links," "signals," and "incentives.")

19. One question that economics students often ask is, "In a market with a lot of buyers and sellers, who sets the price of the good?" There are two possible correct answers to this question: "Everyone" and "No one." Choose one of the two as your answer, and explain in one or two sentences why you are correct.

20. This chapter emphasized the ability of an orderly system to emerge without someone explicitly designing the entire system. How does the evolution of language illustrate a type of spontaneous order?

21. Are you in favor of "price gouging" during natural disasters? Why or why not?

22. What is the opportunity cost of the economics profession?

WORK IT OUT

interactive activity

For interactive, step-by-step help in solving this problem, go online.

Two major-party presidential candidates are running against each other in the 2020 election. The Democratic Party candidate promises more money for corn-based ethanol research, and the Republican Party candidate promises more money for defense contractors. In the weeks before the election, defense stocks take a nosedive.

a. Who is probably going to win the election: the pro-ethanol candidate or the pro-defense spending candidate?

b. We talked about how price signals are sometimes noisy. Think of two or three other markets you might want to look at to see if your answer to part a is correct.

MRUNIVERSITY
AN ONLINE EDUCATION PLATFORM

MARGINAL REVOLUTION UNIVERSITY VIDEOS

How Does the Invisible Hand Deliver Roses?
mruniversity.com/rose
Problems: **2, 17, 18**

A Price Is a Signal Wrapped up in an Incentive
mruniversity.com/price-signals
Problems: **2, 11, 12, 18, 20, 21**

Markets Link the World
mruniversity.com/markets
Problems: **13**

The Great Economic Problem
mruniversity.com/econ-problem
Problems: **1**

Information and Incentives
mruniversity.com/info-incentives
Problems: **1, 4, 5, 9, 11, 12, 18, 21**

Speculation
mruniversity.com/speculation
Problems: **2, 4–7, 15**

Prediction Markets
mruniversity.com/prediction-markets
Problems: **8, 10, 12, 14, 16, 22**

8

Price Ceilings and Floors

On a quiet Sunday in August of 1971, President Richard Nixon shocked the nation by freezing all prices and wages in the United States. It was now illegal to raise prices—even if both buyers and sellers voluntarily agreed to the change. Nixon's order, one of the most significant peacetime interventions into the U.S. economy ever to occur, applied to almost all goods, and even though it was supposed to be in effect for only 90 days, it would have lasting effects for more than a decade.

In Chapter 7, we explained how a price is "a signal wrapped up in an incentive"; that is, we explained how prices signal information and create incentives to economize and seek out substitutes. We also explained how markets are linked geographically, across different products, and through time. In this chapter, we show how price controls—laws making it illegal for prices to move above a maximum price (price ceilings) or below a minimum price (price floors)—interfere with all of these processes. We begin by explaining how a price control affects a single market, and then we turn to how price controls delink some markets and link others in ways that are counterproductive.

Price Ceilings

Nixon's price controls didn't have much effect immediately because prices were frozen near market levels. But the economy is in constant flux and market prices soon shifted. At the time of the freeze, prices were rising because of inflation, so the typical situation came to resemble that in Figure 8.1, with the controlled price below the uncontrolled or market equilibrium price.

When the maximum price that can be legally charged is below the market price, we say that there is a **price ceiling**. Economists call it a price ceiling because prices cannot legally go higher than the ceiling. Price ceilings create five important effects:

1. Shortages
2. Reductions in product quality
3. Wasteful lines and other search costs
4. A loss of gains from trade
5. A misallocation of resources

A **price ceiling** is a maximum price allowed by law.

137

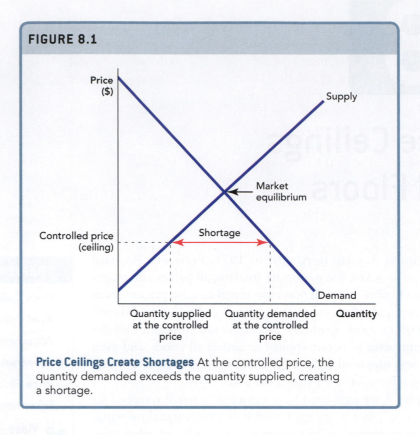

FIGURE 8.1

Price
($)

Supply

Market
equilibrium

Controlled price
(ceiling)

Shortage

Demand

Quantity supplied
at the controlled
price

Quantity demanded
at the controlled
price

Quantity

Price Ceilings Create Shortages At the controlled price, the
quantity demanded exceeds the quantity supplied, creating
a shortage.

A shortage of vinyl in 1973 forced Capitol
Records to melt down slow sellers so they
could keep pressing Beatles' albums.

Shortages

When prices are held below the market price, the quantity demanded exceeds the quantity supplied. Economists call this a shortage. Figure 8.1 shows that the shortage is measured by the difference
between the quantity demanded at the controlled price and the
quantity supplied at the controlled price. Notice also that the lower
the controlled price is relative to the market equilibrium price, the
larger the shortage.

In some sectors of the economy, shortages appeared soon after
prices were controlled in 1971. Increased demand in the construction
industry, for example, meant that price controls hit that sector especially hard. Ordinarily, increased demand for steel bars, for example,
would increase the price of steel bars, encouraging more production.
But with a price ceiling in place, demanders could not signal their
need to suppliers nor could they provide suppliers with an incentive
to produce more. As a result, shortages of steel bars, lumber, toilets
(for new homes), and other construction inputs were common. By
1973, there were shortages of wool, copper, aluminum, vinyl, denim, paper,
plastic bottles, and more.

Reductions in Quality

At the controlled price, demanders find that there is a shortage of goods—
they cannot buy as much of the good as they would like. Equivalently, at the
controlled price, sellers find that there is an excess of demand or, in other
words, *sellers have more customers than they have goods*. Ordinarily, this would be

an opportunity to profit by raising prices, but when prices are controlled, sellers can't raise prices without violating the law. Is there another way that sellers can increase profits? Yes. It's much easier to evade the law by cutting quality than by raising price, so when prices are held below market levels, quality declines.

Thus, even when shortages were not apparent, quality was reduced. Books were printed on lower-quality paper, $2'' \times 4''$ lumber shrank to $1\frac{5}{8}'' \times 3\frac{5}{8}''$, and new automobiles were painted with fewer coats of paint. To help deal with the shortage of paper, some newspapers even switched to a smaller font size.[1]

Another way quality can fall is with reductions in service. Ordinarily, sellers have an incentive to please their customers, but when prices are held below market levels, sellers have more customers than they need *or want*. Customers without potential for profit are just a pain so when prices cannot rise, we can expect service quality to fall. The full-service gasoline station, for example, disappeared with price controls in 1973, and instead of staying open for 24 hours, gasoline stations would close whenever the owner wanted a lunch break.

Wasteful Lines and Other Search Costs

The most serious shortage during the 1970s was for oil. The OPEC embargo in 1973 and the reduction in supply caused by the Iranian Revolution in 1979 increased the world price of oil, as we saw in Chapter 4. In the United States, however, price controls on domestically produced oil had not been lifted and the United States thus faced intense shortages of oil and the classic sign of a shortage, lines.

Figure 8.2 on the next page focuses on the third consequence of controlling prices below market prices: wasteful lines.

At the controlled price of $1, sellers supply Q_s units of the good. How much are demanders willing to pay (per unit) for these Q_s units? Recall that the demand curve shows the willingness to pay, so follow a line from Q_s up to the demand curve to find that demanders are willing to pay $3 per unit for Q_s units. The price controls, however, make it illegal for demanders to offer sellers a price of $3, but there are other ways of paying for gas.

Knowing that there is a shortage, some buyers might bribe station owners (or attendants) to fill up their tanks. Suppose that the average tank holds 20 gallons. Buyers would then be willing to pay $60 for a fill-up, the legal price of $20 plus a $40 under-the-table bribe. Thus, if bribes are common, the total price of gasoline—the legal price plus the bribe price—will rise to $3 per gallon ($60/20 gallons).

Corruption and bribes can be common, especially when price controls are long-lasting, but they were not a major problem during the gasoline shortages of the 1970s. Nevertheless, the total price of gasoline did rise well above the controlled price. Instead of competing by paying bribes, buyers competed by their willingness to wait in line. Remember that at the controlled price the quantity of gasoline demanded is greater than the quantity supplied, so some buyers are going to be disappointed—they are going to get less gasoline than they want and some buyers may get no gasoline at all. Buyers will compete to avoid being left with nothing. Let's assume that all gasoline station owners refuse bribes. Unfortunately, honesty does not eliminate the shortage.

TETRA IMAGES/CORBIS

The Great Matzo Ball Debate In 1972, AFL-CIO boss George Meany complained that the number of matzo balls in his favorite soup had sunk from four to three, in effect raising the price.

C. Jackson Grayson, chairman of the U.S. Price Commission, was worried about the bad publicity, so on *Face the Nation* he triumphantly held aloft a can of Mrs. Adler's soup claiming that his staff had opened many cans and concluded there were still four balls per can.

Whoever was right about the soup, Meany was certainly the better economist: Price ceilings reduce quality.

Price Ceilings

interactive activity

FIGURE 8.2

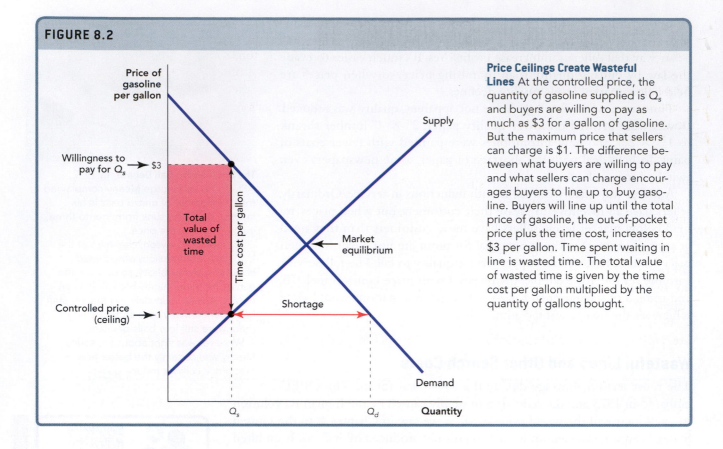

Price Ceilings Create Wasteful Lines At the controlled price, the quantity of gasoline supplied is Q_s and buyers are willing to pay as much as $3 for a gallon of gasoline. But the maximum price that sellers can charge is $1. The difference between what buyers are willing to pay and what sellers can charge encourages buyers to line up to buy gasoline. Buyers will line up until the total price of gasoline, the out-of-pocket price plus the time cost, increases to $3 per gallon. Time spent waiting in line is wasted time. The total value of wasted time is given by the time cost per gallon multiplied by the quantity of gallons bought.

A first-come/first-served system is honest, but buyers who get to the gasoline station early will get the gas, leaving the latecomers with nothing. In this situation, how long will the lineups get?

Suppose that buyers value their time at $10 an hour and, as before, the average fuel tank holds 20 gallons. Eager to obtain gas during the shortage, a buyer arrives at the station early, perhaps even before it opens, and must wait in line for an hour before he is served. His total price of gas is $30: $1 per gallon for 20 gallons in out-of-pocket cost plus $10 in time cost. Since the total value of the gas is $60, that's still a good deal. But if it's a good deal for him, it's probably a good deal for other buyers, too, so the next time he wants to fill up, he is likely to discover that others have preceded him and now he has to wait longer. How much longer? Following the logic to its conclusion, we can see that the line will lengthen until the total cost for 20 gallons of gasoline is $60: $20 in cash paid to the station owner plus $40 in time costs (4 hours worth of waiting). The price per gallon, therefore, rises to $3 ($60/20 gallons)—exactly as occurred with bribes!

Price controls do not eliminate competition. They merely change the form of competition. Is there a difference between paying in bribes and paying in time? Yes. Paying in time is much more wasteful. When a buyer bribes a gasoline station owner $40, at least the gasoline station owner gets the bribe. But when a buyer spends $40 worth of time or four hours waiting in line,

When the quantity demanded exceeds the quantity supplied, someone is going to be disappointed.

the gasoline station owner doesn't get to add four hours to his life. The bribe is transferred from the buyer to the seller, but the time spent waiting in line is simply lost. Figure 8.2 shows that when the quantity supplied is Q_s, the total price of gasoline will tend to rise to $3: a $1 money price plus a time-price of $2 per gallon. The total amount of waste from waiting in line is given by the shaded area, the per gallon time price ($2) multiplied by the number of gallons bought (Q_s).*

Lost Gains from Trade (Deadweight Loss)

Price controls also reduce the gains from trade. In Figure 8.3, at the quantity supplied Q_s, how much would demanders pay for one *additional* gallon of gasoline? The willingness to pay for a gallon of gas at Q_s is $3, so demanders would be willing to pay just a little bit less, say, $2.95, for an additional gallon. How much would suppliers require to sell an additional gallon? Supplier cost is read off the supply curve, so reading up from the quantity Q_s to the supply curve, we find that the willingness to sell at Q_s is $1; suppliers would be willing to supply an additional unit for just a little bit more, say, $1.05.

Demanders are willing to pay $2.95 for an additional gallon of gas, suppliers are willing to sell an additional gallon for $1.05, and so there is $1.90 of

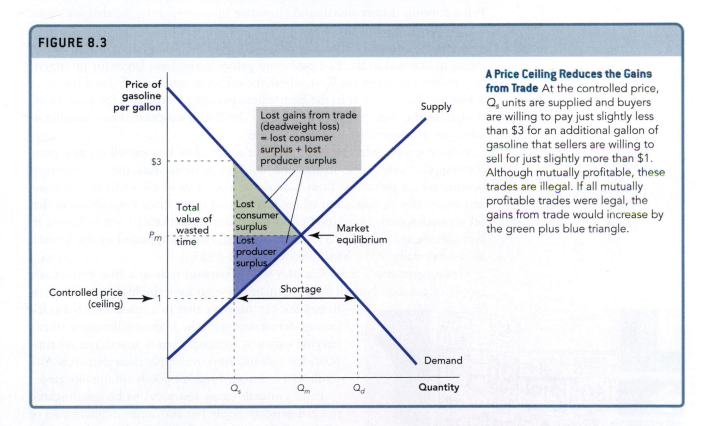

FIGURE 8.3

A Price Ceiling Reduces the Gains from Trade At the controlled price, Q_s units are supplied and buyers are willing to pay just slightly less than $3 for an additional gallon of gasoline that sellers are willing to sell for just slightly more than $1. Although mutually profitable, these trades are illegal. If all mutually profitable trades were legal, the gains from trade would increase by the green plus blue triangle.

* We need to qualify this slightly. If *every* buyer has a time value of $10 per hour, then the total time wasted will be the area as shaded in the diagram. If some buyers have a time value lower than $10, say, $5 per hour, they will wait in line for four hours, paying $20 in out-of-pocket costs but only $20 in time costs. If these buyers value the gasoline as highly as does the marginal buyer, at $60 for 20 gallons, they will earn what economists call a "rent" of $20; thus, not all of the rectangle would be wasted. Regardless of whether all of the rectangle or just some of the rectangle is wasted, it's important to see that (1) price ceilings generate shortages and lineups, (2) the lineups mean that the total price of the controlled good is higher than the controlled price (and perhaps even higher than the uncontrolled price), and (3) the time spent waiting in line is wasted.

potential gains from trade to split between them. But it's illegal for suppliers to sell gasoline at any price higher than $1. Buyers and sellers want to trade, but they are prevented from doing so by the threat of jail. If the price ceiling were lifted and trade were allowed, the quantity traded would expand from Q_s to Q_m and buyers would be better off by the green triangle labeled "Lost consumer surplus," while sellers would be better off by the blue triangle labeled "Lost producer surplus." But with a price ceiling in place, the quantity supplied is Q_s and together the lost consumer and producer surplus are lost gains from trade (economists also call this a **deadweight loss**).

Recall from Chapter 4 that we said that in a free market the quantity of goods sold maximizes the sum of consumer and producer surplus. We can now see that in a market with a price ceiling, the sum of consumer and producer surplus is not maximized because the price control prevents mutually profitable gains from trade from being exploited.

In addition to these losses, price controls cause a misallocation of scarce resources; let's see how that works in more detail.

> A **deadweight loss** is the reduction in total surplus caused by a market distortion or inefficiency.

Misallocation of Resources

In Chapter 7, we explained how a price is a signal wrapped up in an incentive. Price controls distort signals and eliminate incentives. Imagine that it's sunny on the West Coast of the United States, but on the East Coast a cold winter increases the demand for heating oil. In a market without price controls, the increase in demand in the East pushes up prices in the East. Eager for profit, entrepreneurs buy oil in the West, where the oil is not much needed and the price is low, and they move it to the East, where people are cold and the price of oil is high. In this way, the price increase in the East is moderated and supplies of oil move to where they are needed most.

Now consider what happens when it is illegal to buy or sell oil at a price above a price ceiling. No matter how cold it gets in the East, the demanders of heating oil are prevented from bidding up the price of oil, so there's *no signal* and *no incentive* to ship oil to where it is needed most. Price controls mean that oil is misallocated. Swimming pools in California are heated, while homes in New Jersey are cold. In fact, this was exactly what happened in the United States, especially in the harsh winter of 1972–1973.

Once again recall from Chapter 4 that we said that in a free market the supply of goods is bought by the demanders who have the highest willingness to pay. We can now see that in a market with a price ceiling, demanders with the highest willingness to pay have no easy way to signal their demands nor do suppliers have an incentive to supply their demands. As a result, in a controlled market goods are misallocated.

Price controls cause resources to be misallocated not just geographically, but also across different uses of oil. Recall from Chapter 3 that the demand curve for oil shows the uses of oil from the highest-valued to the lowest-valued uses. In case you forgot, Figure 8.4 shows the key idea: High-valued uses are at the top of the curve and low-valued uses at the bottom. Without market prices, however, we have no guarantee that oil will flow to its highest-valued uses. As we have just

Distorted signals cause resources to be misallocated.

seen, in a situation with price controls, it's possible to have plenty of oil to heat swimming pools in California (hello, rubber ducky!) and not enough oil for heating cold homes in New Jersey. Similarly, in 1974 *Business Week* reported, "While drivers wait in three-hour lines in one state, consumers in other states are breezing in and out of gas stations."[2]

Figure 8.5 illustrates the problem more generally. As we know, at the controlled price, the quantity demanded Q_d exceeds the quantity supplied Q_s and there is a shortage. Ideally, we would like to allocate the quantity of oil supplied Q_s, to its highest-valued uses; these are illustrated at the top of the demand curve by the thick line. But the potential consumers of the oil with the highest-valued uses are legally prevented from signaling their high value by offering to pay oil suppliers more than the controlled price. Oil suppliers, therefore, have no incentive to supply oil to just the highest-valued uses. Instead, oil suppliers will give the oil to any user who is willing to pay the controlled price—but most of these users of oil have

FIGURE 8.4

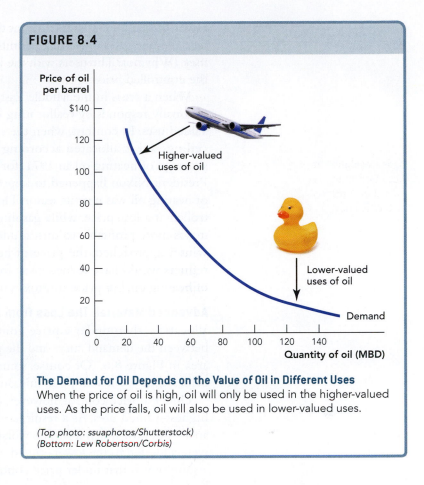

The Demand for Oil Depends on the Value of Oil in Different Uses
When the price of oil is high, oil will only be used in the higher-valued uses. As the price falls, oil will also be used in lower-valued uses.

(Top photo: ssuaphotos/Shutterstock)
(Bottom: Lew Robertson/Corbis)

FIGURE 8.5

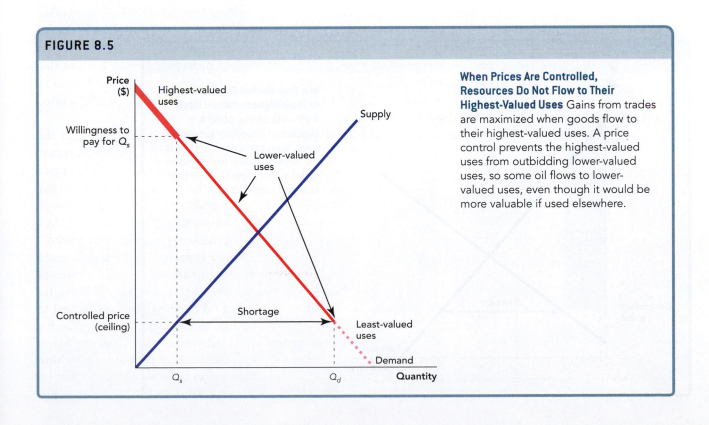

When Prices Are Controlled, Resources Do Not Flow to Their Highest-Valued Uses Gains from trades are maximized when goods flow to their highest-valued uses. A price control prevents the highest-valued uses from outbidding lower-valued uses, so some oil flows to lower-valued uses, even though it would be more valuable if used elsewhere.

lower-valued uses. Like the lines at the gas station, it's first-come/first-served. In fact, the only uses of oil that definitely will not be satisfied are the least-valued uses. (Why not? The users with the least-valued uses are not even willing to pay the controlled price.)

When a crisis in the Middle East reduces the supply of oil, the price system rationally responds by reallocating oil from lower-valued uses to the highest-valued uses. In contrast, when the supply of oil is reduced and there are price ceilings, oil is allocated according to random and often trivial factors. The shortage of heating oil in 1971, for example, was exacerbated by the fact that President Nixon happened to impose price controls in *August* when the price of heating oil was near its seasonal low.[3] Since the price of heating oil was controlled at a low price, while gasoline was controlled at a slightly higher price, it was more profitable to turn crude oil into gasoline than into heating oil. As winter approached, the price of heating oil would normally have risen and refiners would have turned away from gasoline production to the production of heating oil, but price controls removed the incentive to respond rationally.

Advanced Material: The Loss from Random Allocation If there were no misallocation, then under a price control, consumer surplus would be the area between the demand curve and the price up to the quantity supplied, the green area in Figure 8.6. (Of course, some of this surplus will likely be eaten up by bribes, time spent waiting in line, and so forth as explained earlier.)

Under a price control, however, the good is not necessarily allocated to the highest-valued uses. As a result, consumer surplus will be less than the green area—but how much less? The worst-case scenario would occur if all the goods were allocated to the lower-valued uses, but that seems unlikely. A more realistic assumption is that under price controls, goods are allocated randomly so that a high-valued use is as likely as a low-valued use to be satisfied.

FIGURE 8.6

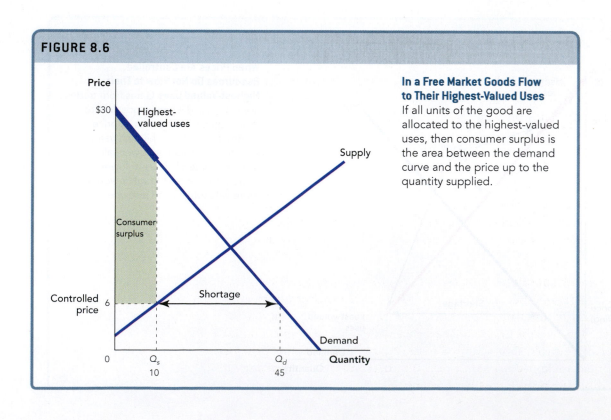

In a Free Market Goods Flow to Their Highest-Valued Uses
If all units of the good are allocated to the highest-valued uses, then consumer surplus is the area between the demand curve and the price up to the quantity supplied.

FIGURE 8.7

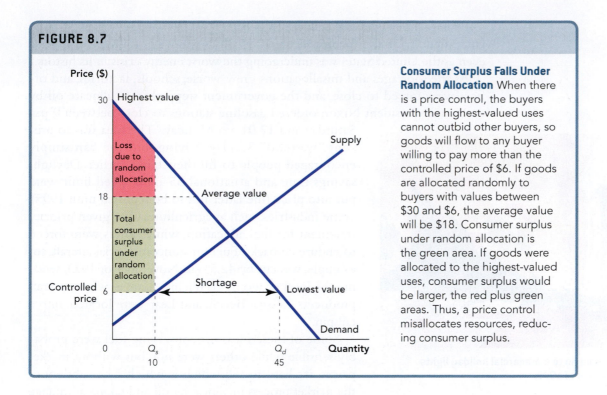

Consumer Surplus Falls Under Random Allocation When there is a price control, the buyers with the highest-valued uses cannot outbid other buyers, so goods will flow to any buyer willing to pay more than the controlled price of $6. If goods are allocated randomly to buyers with values between $30 and $6, the average value will be $18. Consumer surplus under random allocation is the green area. If goods were allocated to the highest-valued uses, consumer surplus would be larger, the red plus green areas. Thus, a price control misallocates resources, reducing consumer surplus.

In Figure 8.7 we show two uses. The highest-valued use has a value of $30 and the lowest-valued use has a value of $6. Now imagine that one unit of the good is allocated randomly between these two uses. Thus, with a probability of $\frac{1}{2}$, it will be allocated to the use with a value of 30, and with a probability of $\frac{1}{2}$, it will be allocated to the use with a value of 6. On average, how much value will this unit create? The average value will be

$$\text{Average value} = \frac{1}{2} \times \$30 + \frac{1}{2} \times \$6 = \$18$$

Extending this logic, it can be shown that if every use between the highest-valued use and the lowest-valued use is *equally* likely to be satisfied, then the average value is $18. Thus on average, a randomly allocated unit of the good will create a value of $18. If there are, say, 10 units allocated, then the total value of those units will be 10 × $18 = $180. Since the average value is $18 and the controlled price is $6, consumer surplus is the green area in Figure 8.7 labeled total consumer surplus under random allocation. But notice that the green area in Figure 8.7, consumer surplus under random allocation, is much less than the green area in Figure 8.6, consumer surplus under allocation to the highest-valued uses. The difference is the red area in Figure 8.7, the loss due to random allocation.

Misallocation and Production Chaos Shortages in one market create breakdowns and shortages in other markets, so the chaos of price controls expands even into markets without price controls. In ordinary times, we take it for granted that products will be available when we want them, but in an economy with many price controls, shortages of key inputs can appear at any time. In 1973, for example, million-dollar construction projects were delayed because a few thousand dollars worth of steel bar was unavailable.[4]

Perhaps the height of misallocation occurred when shortages of steel drilling equipment made it difficult to expand oil production; this mistake took place even as the United States was undergoing the worst energy crisis in its history.[5]

As the shortages and misallocations grew worse, schools, factories, and offices were forced to close, and the government stepped in to allocate oil by command. President Nixon ordered gasoline stations to close between 9 pm Saturday and 12:01 am Monday.[6] The idea was to prevent "wasteful" Sunday driving, but the ban simply encouraged people to fill their tanks earlier. Daylight savings time and a national 55-mph speed limit were put into place (the latter not to be repealed until 1995). Some industries, such as agriculture, were given priority treatment for fuel allocation, while others were forced to endure cutbacks. Fuel for noncommercial aircraft, for example, was cut by 42.5% in November of 1973, sending the local economy of Wichita, Kansas, where aircraft producers Cessna, Beech, and Lear were located, into a tailspin.[7]

Some of these ideas for conserving fuel were probably sensible while others were not, but without market prices, it's hard to tell which is which. The subtlety of the market process in allocating oil and taking advantage of links between markets is difficult, even impossible, to duplicate. C. Jackson Grayson was chairman of President Nixon's Price Commission, but after seeing how controls worked in practice, he said:

> Our economic understanding and models are simply not powerful enough to handle such a large and complex economic system better than the marketplace.[8]

THE EVERETT COLLECTION

President Nixon said no to commercial holiday lights during the Christmas of 1973.

The End of Price Ceilings

Price controls for most goods were lifted by April 1974, but controls on oil remained in place. Over the next seven years, controls on oil would be eased but at the price of substantial increases in complexity and bureaucracy. In September 1973, for example, price controls were lifted on new oil. "New oil" was defined as oil produced on a particular property in excess of the amount that had been produced in 1972. Decontrol of new oil was a good idea because it increased the incentive to develop new deposits. The two-tier system, however, also created wasteful gaming as firms shut down some oil wells only to drill "new" wells right next door.[9] The battle between entrepreneurs and regulators was met with increasingly complex rules. Thus, the two-tier program was extended to three tiers, then five, then eight, then eleven.

Price controls on oil ended as abruptly as they had begun when on the morning of January 20, 1981, Ronald Reagan was inaugurated as president, and before lunch with Congress, he performed his first act as president—eliminating all controls on oil and gasoline. As expected, the price of oil in the United States rose a little but the shortage ended overnight. Within a year, prices began to fall as supply increased and within a few years they were well below the levels of 1979. Fluctuations in the price of oil have continued to occur, of course, but since the ending of controls, there has been no shortage of oil in the United States.

Does UBER Price Gouge?

Price controls continue to play a role in markets today, and again the common theme is that price controls reduce the gains from trade and lead to a misallocation of resources.

Consider the ride-sharing service Uber, which you may have used. Uber is an app on your smart phone that brings together demanders and suppliers of car rides. Instead of calling a taxi, you put in a request on Uber and are quoted a price. If you accept, someone will come and pick you up in their personal vehicle.

Uber, in setting the price for each ride, considers local information about supply and demand. If a big concert has just ended or if it's raining, then demand may be especially high and Uber will often charge a higher price—called the surge price. Because Uber drivers get a share of the price, higher prices incentivize drivers to drive where and when demand has increased—where the big concert is getting out or when it's raining, for example. After a spike in demand following an Ariana Grande concert at Madison Square Garden, for example, Uber prices surged and the number of Uber drivers in that area increased by more than 75%.[10] Similarly, when it's raining in New York City, it's been estimated that the number of Uber rides goes up by about 25%. In contrast, taxis, which are fixed in number and do not have surge pricing, increase their number of rides by only 4% when it's raining.[11]

The higher price also reduces the number of people who want a ride. The higher the price, the more likely you will just walk, take your bike, or go an hour later when overall demand is lower. You could even try another ride-sharing service or call a cab. A recent study estimated that if the Uber price goes up by 10%, the quantity demanded falls by about 5.1%, for an implied price elasticity of −0.51 (i.e., −5.1/10%).[12] The net result of Uber adjusting prices is that the quantity supplied and the quantity demanded are equalized. Even in busy times, anyone can get a ride fairly quickly so long as they are willing to pay the price.

Not everyone, however, likes surge pricing. In New York City, a 2015 bill promised to outlaw surge pricing, on the grounds that it is unfair, especially to the poor who cannot afford to pay the higher surge price. If passed, as has already happened in New Delhi, India, such a law would lead to shortages. Precisely when users need rides the most, the price would be kept low by the law, and the quantity demanded would exceed the quantity supplied, as in Figure 8.1. The shortage would mean a long wait before you can get a ride, especially if it's raining.

By the way, the same study showed that if consumers spend a dollar on Uber, they receive about an extra $1.60 in consumer surplus, and that is with surge pricing. Indeed, that is in part *because* surge pricing allocates rides to the high demanders. A price control would mean that the people with the highest demand for a ride would no longer have a way to signal that demand and rides would be allocated randomly instead of to those who value them the most. The net result would be a loss due to misallocation, as was shown in Figure 8.7.

The older, traditional system of hailing cabs in the street also had price controls, although not in such a visible manner. When the cab picks you up, by law the cabbie typically has to charge you the regular price, even if it is raining or a

Uber drivers work more when it's raining.

OLIVIER LABAN-MATTEI/AFP/GETTY IMAGES

cab is hard to come by. In Manhattan, sometimes it is very difficult to find a cab at rush hour and these hidden price controls are one of the reasons why (the supply of taxis is also limited by law). In the late 1980s in Tokyo when asset prices were booming, cab seekers would bid extra for cab rides. For instance, if it were raining, an eager cab–seeker might hold up two fingers when trying to hail the cab. That is a sign the rider is willing to pay twice the normal fare, and of course cabs are more likely to stop for such high bidders. Holding up three fingers would signal a willingness to triple the price. That was an earlier form of surge pricing, just with a more primitive technology, and it evolved spontaneously through market competition for taxis.

Rent Controls (Optional Section)

A **rent control** is a price ceiling on rental housing, such as apartments, so everything we have learned about price ceilings also applies to rent controls. Rent controls create shortages, reduce quality, create wasteful lines and increase the costs of search, cause a loss of gains from trade, and misallocate resources.

Shortages

Rent controls usually begin with a "rent freeze," which prohibits landlords from raising rents. Since rent controls are often put into place when rents are rising, the situation quickly comes to look like Figure 8.8, with the controlled rent below the market equilibrium rent.

Apartments are long-lasting goods that cannot be moved, so when rent controls are first imposed, owners of apartment buildings have few alternatives but to absorb the lower price. In other words, the short–run supply curve for apartments is inelastic. Thus, Figure 8.8 shows that even though the rent freeze may

A **rent control** is a price ceiling on rental housing.

FIGURE 8.8

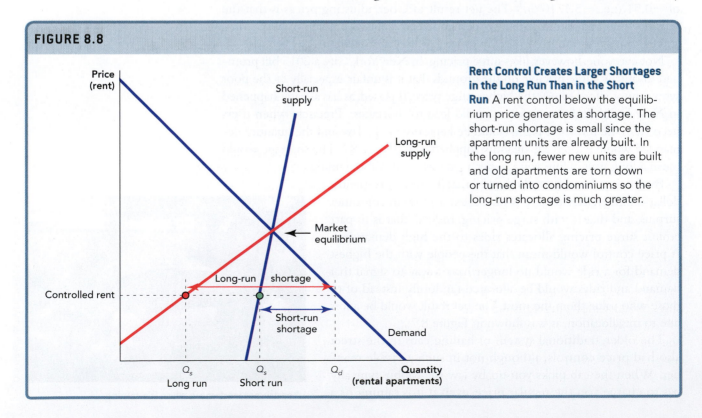

Rent Control Creates Larger Shortages in the Long Run Than in the Short Run A rent control below the equilibrium price generates a shortage. The short-run shortage is small since the apartment units are already built. In the long run, fewer new units are built and old apartments are torn down or turned into condominiums so the long-run shortage is much greater.

result in rents well below the market equi-librium level, there is only a small reduction in the quantity supplied in the short run.

In the long run, however, fewer new apartment units are built and older units are turned into condominiums or torn down to make way for parking garages or other higher-paying ventures. Thus, the long-run supply curve is much more elastic than the short-run supply curve, and the shortage grows over time from the short-run short-age to the long-run shortage.

Although old apartment buildings can't disappear overnight, future apartment buildings can. Developers look for profits over a 30-year or longer time frame, so even a modest rent control can sharply reduce the value of new apartment construction. Developers who fear that rent controls are likely will immediately end their plans to build. In the early 1970s, for example, rent control was debated in Ontario, Canada, and put into place in 1975. In the five years before controls were put into place, devel-opers built an average of 27,999 new apart-

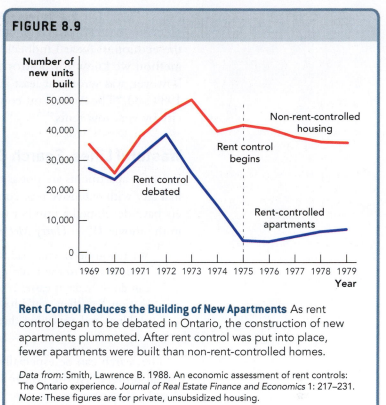

FIGURE 8.9

Rent Control Reduces the Building of New Apartments As rent control began to be debated in Ontario, the construction of new apartments plummeted. After rent control was put into place, fewer apartments were built than non-rent-controlled homes.

Data from: Smith, Lawrence B. 1988. An economic assessment of rent controls: The Ontario experience. *Journal of Real Estate Finance and Economics* 1: 217–231. *Note:* These figures are for private, unsubsidized housing.

ments per year. In the five years after controls were put into place, developers built only 5,512 apartments per year. Figure 8.9 graphs the number of new apartment starts and the number of new house starts per year from 1969 to 1979. The sharp drop in new apartment construction in the years when rent controls first started to be debated is obvious. But perhaps the drop was due to other factors like the state of the economy. To test for this possibility, we also graph the number of new houses that were built annually during this time. The demand for houses and the demand for apartments respond similarly to the economy, but price controls on houses were never debated or imposed. We can see from Figure 8.9 that prior to 1972 the number of new apartment starts was similar to the number of new house starts. But when rent control became a possibility, apartment construction fell but the construction of houses did not. Thus, it's likely that rent control and not the general state of the economy (which would also have affected house starts) was responsible for the sharp drop in the number of new apartments built.

Reductions in Product Quality

Rent controls also reduce housing quality, especially the quality of low-end apartments. When the price of apartments is forced down, owners attempt to stave off losses by cutting their costs. With rent controls, for example, own-ers mow the lawns less often, replace lightbulbs more slowly, and don't fix the elevators so quickly. When the controls are strong, cheap but serviceable apartment buildings turn into slums and then slums turn into abandoned and hollowed-out apartment blocks. In Manhattan, for example, 18% of the rent-controlled housing is "dilapidated or deteriorating," a much higher percentage than in the uncontrolled sector.[13] Rent controls in European countries have tended to be more restrictive than in the United States, leading the economist Assar Lindbeck to remark, "Rent control is the most effective method we know for destroying a city, except for bombing it."[14] Lindbeck, however, was wrong, at least according to Vietnam's foreign minister who in 1989 said, "The Americans couldn't destroy Hanoi, but we have destroyed our city by very low rents."[15]

Wasteful Lines, Search Costs, and Lost Gains from Trade

Lines for apartments are not as obvious as for gasoline, but finding an apartment in a city with extensive rent controls usually involves a costly search. New Yorkers have developed a number of tricks to help them, as Billy Crystal explained in the movie *When Harry Met Sally*:

> What you do is, you read the obituary column. Yeah, you find out who died, and go to the building and then you tip the doorman. What they can do to make it easier is to combine the obituaries with the real estate section. Say, then you'd have "Mr. Klein died today leaving a wife, two children, and a spacious three-bedroom apartment with a wood-burning fireplace."

The search can be especially costly for people who landlords think are not "ideal renters." At the controlled price, landlords have more customers than they have apartments, so they can pick and choose among prospective renters. Landlords prefer to rent to people who are seen as being more likely to pay the rent on time and not cause trouble for other tenants, for example, older, richer couples without children or dogs. Landlords might also discriminate on racial or other grounds. Indeed, a landlord who doesn't like your looks can turn you down and immediately rent to the next person in line. Landlords can discriminate even if there are no rent controls, but without rent controls, the vacancy rate will be higher because the quantity of apartments will be larger and turnover will be more common, so landlords who turn down prospective renters will lose money as they wait for their ideal renter. Rent controls reduce the price of discrimination, so remember the law of demand: When the price of discrimination falls, the quantity of discrimination demanded will increase.

Bribing the landlord or apartment manager to get a rent-controlled apartment is also common. Bribes are illegal but they can be disguised. An apartment might rent for $500 a month but come with $5,000 worth of "furniture." Renters refer to these kinds of tie-in sales as paying "key money," as in the rent is $500 a month but the key costs extra. Nora Ephron, the screenwriter for *When Harry Met Sally*, lived for many years in a five-bedroom luxury apartment that thanks to rent control cost her just $1,500 a month. She did, however, have to pay $24,000 in key money to get the previous renter to move out!

JG PHOTOGRAPHY/ALAMY

A rent-controlled apartment—furnished.

The analysis of lost gains from trade from rent controls is exactly the same as we showed in Figure 8.3 for price controls on gasoline. At the quantity supplied under rent control, demanders are willing to pay more for an apartment than sellers would require to rent the apartment. If buyers and sellers were free to trade, they could both be better off, but under rent control, these mutually profitable trades are illegal and the benefits do not occur.

Misallocation of Resources

As with gasoline, apartments under rent control are allocated haphazardly—some people with a high willingness to pay can't buy as much housing as they want, even as others with a low willingness to pay consume more housing than they would purchase at the market rate. The classic example is the older couple who stay in their large rent-controlled apartment even after their children have moved out. It's a great deal for the older couple, but not so good for the young couple with children who as a result are stuck in a cramped apartment with nowhere to go.

Economists can estimate the amount of misallocation by comparing the types of apartments that renters choose in cities like New York, which has had rent controls since they were imposed as a "temporary" measure in World War II, with the types of apartments that people choose in cities like Chicago, which has a free market in rental housing. In one recent study of this kind, Edward Glaeser and Erzo Luttmer found that as many as 21% of the renters in New York City live in an apartment that has more or fewer rooms than they would choose if they lived in a city without rent controls.[16] This misallocation of resources creates significant waste and hardship.

Rent Regulation

In the 1990s, many American cities with rent control changed policy and began to eliminate or ease rent controls. Some economists refer to these new policies not as rent control but as "rent regulation." A typical rent regulation limits price increases without limiting prices. Price increases, for example, might be limited to, say, 10% per year. Thus, rent regulations can protect tenants from sharp increases in rent, while still allowing prices to rise or fall over several years in response to market forces. Rent regulation laws usually also allow landlords to pass along cost increases so the incentive to cut back on maintenance is reduced. Economists are almost universally opposed to rent controls but some economists think that moderate rent regulation could have some benefits.[17]

Arguments for Price Ceilings

Without price controls on oil in 1973, some people might not have been able to afford to heat their homes. Without rent controls, some people may not be able to afford appropriate housing. It's not obvious that the poor are better off with shortages than with high prices. Nevertheless, *if* price controls were the *only* way to help the poor, then this would be an argument in favor of price controls.

Price controls, however, are never the only way to help the poor and they are rarely the best way. If affordable housing is a concern, for example, then a better policy than rent controls is for the government to provide housing vouchers. Housing vouchers, which are used extensively in the United States, give qualifying consumers a voucher worth, say, $500 a month that can be applied to any unit of housing.[18] Unlike rent controls, which create shortages, vouchers *increase* the supply of housing. Vouchers can also be targeted to consumers who need them, whereas rent controls in New York City have subsidized millionaires.

There are a few other sound arguments for price controls. The best case for price controls is to discipline monopolies. Alas, this explanation does not fit price controls on gasoline, apartments, bread, or almost all of the goods that price controls are routinely placed on. We will look at this special case more extensively in Chapter 13.

One of the primary reasons for price controls may be that the public, unlike economists, does not see the consequences of price controls. People who have not been trained in economics rarely connect lineups with price controls. During the gasoline shortages of the 1970s, probably not one American in ten understood the connection between the controls and the shortage—most consumers blamed big oil companies and rich Arab sheiks.

Universal Price Controls

We have seen that price controls in the United States caused shortages, lineups, delays, quality reductions, misallocations, bureaucracy, and corruption. And the U.S. experience with extensive price controls was short, just a few months for most goods, and a few years for oil and a handful of other goods. What would happen if price controls on all goods remained in place for a lengthy period of time? An economy with permanent, universal price controls is in essence a "command economy," much as existed in the Communist countries prior to the fall of the Berlin Wall. In *The Russians*, Hedrick Smith described what it was like for consumers living in the Soviet Union in 1976[19]

In the former Soviet Union, never-ending shortages meant that lining up for hours to get bread, shoes, or other goods was normal.

The list of scarce items is practically endless. They are not permanently out of stock, but their appearance is unpredictable. . . . Leningrad can be overstocked with cross-country skis and yet go several months without soap for washing dishes. In the Armenian capital of Yerevan, I found an ample supply of accordions but local people complained that they had gone for weeks without ordinary kitchen spoons or tea samovars. I knew a Moscow family that spent a frantic month hunting for a child's potty while radios were a glut on the market. . . .

The accepted norm is that the Soviet woman daily spends two hours in line, seven days a week. . . . I have known of people who stood in line 90 minutes to buy four pineapples . . . three and a half hours to buy three large heads of cabbage only to find the cabbages were gone as they approached the front of the line, 18 hours to sign up to purchase a rug at some later date, all through a freezing December night to register on a list for buying a car, and then waiting 18 months for actual delivery, and terribly lucky at that.

The never-ending shortage of goods in the former Soviet Union suggests another reason why price controls are not eliminated even when doing so would make most people better off. Shortages were beneficial to the very same party elite who controlled prices. With all goods in permanent shortage, how did anyone in the Soviet Union obtain goods? By using *blat*. *Blat* is a Russian word meaning one has connections that can be used to get favors. As Hedrick Smith put it:

> In an economy of chronic shortages and carefully parceled-out privileges, blat is an essential lubricant of life. The more rank and power one has, the more blat one normally has . . . each has access to things or services that are hard to get and that other people want or need.

Consider the manager of a small factory that produces radios. Music may be the food that feeds people's souls but the manager would also like some beef. Shortages mean that the manager's salary is almost useless in helping him to obtain beef but what does he have of value? He has access to radios. If the manager can find a worker in a beef factory who loves music, he will have *blat*, a connection and something to trade. Even if he can't find someone with the exact opposite wants as he has, access to radios gives the manager power because people will want to do favors for him. But notice that the manager of the radio factory has *blat* only because of a shortage of radios. If radios were easily available at the market price, then the manager's access would no longer be of special value. The manager of the radio factory wants low prices because then he can legally buy radios at the official price and use them to obtain goods that he wants. Ironically, the managers and producers of beef, purses, and televisions all want shortages of their own good even though all would benefit if the shortages of all goods were eliminated.

Blat is a Russian word but it's a worldwide phenomena. Even in the United States, where by world standards corruption is low, *blat* happens. During the 1973–1974 oil crisis, for example, when the Federal Energy Office controlled the allocation of oil, it quickly became obvious that the way to get more oil was to use *blat*. Firms began to hire former politicians and bureaucrats who used their connections to help the firms get more oil. Today, the *blat* economy is much larger—about half of all federal politicians who leave office for the private sector become lobbyists.

Price Floors

When governments control prices, it is usually with a price ceiling designed to keep prices below market levels, but occasionally the government intervenes to keep prices above market levels. Can you think of an example? Here's a hint. Buyers usually outnumber sellers, so it's probably no accident that governments intervene to keep prices below market levels more often than they intervene to keep prices above market levels. The most common example of a price being controlled above market levels is the exception that proves the rule because it involves a good for which sellers outnumber buyers. Here's another hint. You own this good.

The good is labor, and the most common example of a price that is controlled above the market level is the minimum wage.

CHECK YOURSELF

■ In the 1984 movie *Moscow on the Hudson*, a Soviet musician defects to the United States. Living in New York, he cannot believe the availability of goods and finds that he cannot break away from previous Soviet habits. In one memorable scene, he buys packages and packages of toilet paper. Why? Using the concepts from this chapter, explain why hoarding occurs under price controls and why it is wasteful.

■ Shortages in the former Soviet Union were very common, but why were there also surpluses of some goods at some times?

A **price floor** is a minimum price allowed by law.

When the minimum price that can be legally charged is above the market price, we say that there is a **price floor**. Economists call it a price floor because prices cannot legally go below the floor. Price floors create four important effects:

1. Surpluses
2. Lost gains from trade (deadweight loss)
3. Wasteful increases in quality
4. A misallocation of resources

Surpluses

Figure 8.10 graphs the demand and supply of labor and shows how a price held above the market price creates a surplus, a situation in which the quantity of labor supplied exceeds the quantity demanded. We have a special word for a surplus of labor: unemployment.

The idea that a minimum wage creates unemployment should not be surprising. If the minimum wage did not create unemployment, the solution to poverty would be easy—raise minimum wages to $10, $20, or even $100 an hour! But at a high enough wage, none of us would be worth employing.

Can a more moderate minimum wage also create unemployment? Yes. A minimum wage of $7.25 an hour, the federal minimum in 2017, won't affect most workers who, because of their productivity, already earn more than $7.25 an hour. In the United States, for example, more than 95% of all workers paid by the hour already earn more than the minimum wage. A minimum wage, however, will decrease employment among low-skilled workers. The more employers have to pay for low-skilled workers, the fewer low-skilled workers they will hire.

Young people, for example, often lack substantial skills and are more likely to be made unemployed by the minimum wage. About a quarter of all workers

FIGURE 8.10

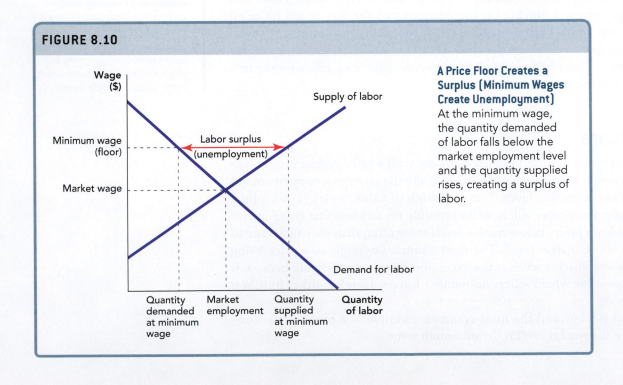

A Price Floor Creates a Surplus (Minimum Wages Create Unemployment)
At the minimum wage, the quantity demanded of labor falls below the market employment level and the quantity supplied rises, creating a surplus of labor.

earning the minimum wage are teenagers (ages 16–19) and about half are less than 25 years of age.[20] Studies of the minimum wage verify that the unemployment effect is concentrated among teenagers.[21]

In addition to creating surpluses, a price floor, just like a price ceiling, reduces the gains from trade.

Lost Gains from Trade (Deadweight Loss)

Notice in Figure 8.11 that at the minimum wage employers are willing to hire Q_d workers. Employers would hire more workers if they could offer lower wages and, importantly, workers would be willing to work at lower wages if they were allowed to do so. If employers and workers could bargain freely, the wage would fall and the quantity of labor traded would increase to the level of market employment. Notice that at the market employment level, the gains from trade increase by the green and blue triangles. The green triangle is the increase in consumer surplus (remember that in this example it is the employers who are the consumers of labor) and the blue triangle is the increase in producer (worker) surplus. Since the minimum wage prevents employment from reaching the market employment level, there is a loss of consumer and producer surplus.

Although the minimum wage creates some unemployment and reduces the gains from trade, the influence of the minimum wage in the American economy is very small. Even for the young, the minimum wage is not very important because although most workers earning the minimum wage are young, most young workers earn more than the minimum wage. As noted, a majority of workers earning the minimum wage are younger than 25 years old but 88% of workers younger than 25 earn more than the minimum wage.[22]

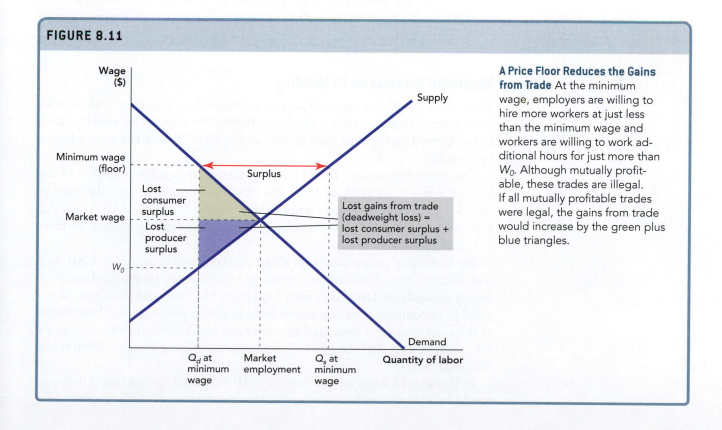

FIGURE 8.11

A Price Floor Reduces the Gains from Trade At the minimum wage, employers are willing to hire more workers at just less than the minimum wage and workers are willing to work additional hours for just more than W_0. Although mutually profitable, these trades are illegal. If all mutually profitable trades were legal, the gains from trade would increase by the green plus blue triangles.

Should the minimum wage be called the "Robot Employment Act"?

These facts may surprise you. The minimum wage is hotly debated in the United States. Democrats often argue that the minimum wage must be raised to help working families. Republicans respond that a higher minimum wage will create unemployment and raise prices as firms pass on higher costs to customers. Neither position is realistic. At best, the minimum wage will raise the wages of some teenagers and young workers whose wages would increase anyway as they improve their education and become more skilled. At worst, the minimum wage will raise the price of a hamburger and create unemployment among teenagers, many of whom will simply choose to stay in school longer (not necessarily a bad thing). The minimum wage debate is more about rhetoric than reality.

Even though small increases in the U.S. minimum wage won't change much, large increases would cause serious unemployment.

Keep in mind that there are substitutes for minimum wage workers. Higher minimum wages, for example, increase the incentive to move production to other cities, states, or countries where wages are lower. The United States imports lots of fruits and vegetables because it is cheaper to produce these abroad and ship them to the United States than it is to produce them here. Many minimum wage jobs are service jobs that cannot be moved abroad but firms can substitute capital—in the form of machines—for labor. If the minimum wage were to increase substantially, we might even see robots flipping burgers.

To explain the other important effects of price floors—wasteful increases in quality and a misallocation of resources—we turn from minimum wages to airline regulation.

Wasteful Increases in Quality

Many years ago, flying on an airplane was pleasurable; seats were wide, service was attentive, flights weren't packed, and the food was good. So airplane travel in the United States must have gotten worse, right? No, it has gotten better. Let's explain.

The Civil Aeronautics Board (CAB) extensively regulated airlines in the United States from 1938 to 1978. No firm could enter or exit the market, change prices, or alter routes without permission from the CAB. The CAB kept prices well above market levels, sometimes even denying requests by firms to lower prices!

We know that prices were kept above market levels because the CAB only had the right to control airlines operating *between* states. In-state airlines were largely unregulated. Using data from large states like Texas and California, it was possible to compare prices on unregulated flights to prices on regulated flights of the same distance. Prices on flights between San Francisco and Los Angeles, for example, were half the price of similar-length flights between Boston and Washington, D.C.

In Figure 8.12, firms are earning the CAB-regulated fare on flights that they would be willing to sell at the much lower price labeled "Willingness to sell."

FIGURE 8.12

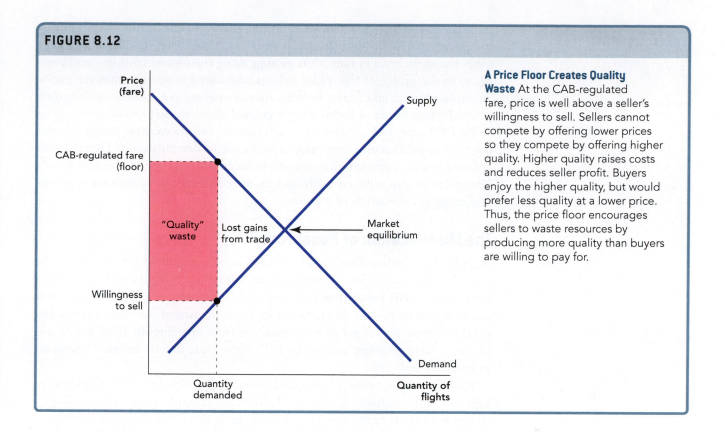

A Price Floor Creates Quality Waste At the CAB-regulated fare, price is well above a seller's willingness to sell. Sellers cannot compete by offering lower prices so they compete by offering higher quality. Higher quality raises costs and reduces seller profit. Buyers enjoy the higher quality, but would prefer less quality at a lower price. Thus, the price floor encourages sellers to waste resources by producing more quality than buyers are willing to pay for.

Initially, therefore, regulation was a great deal for the airlines, who took home the red area as producer surplus.

A price floor means that prices are held *above* market levels, so firms want more customers. The price floor, however, makes it illegal to compete for more customers by lowering prices. So how do firms compete when they cannot lower prices? Price floors cause firms to compete by offering customers higher quality.

When airlines were regulated, for example, they competed by offering their customers bone china, fancy meals, wide seats, and frequent flights. Sounds good, right? Yes, but don't forget that the increase in quality came at a price. Would you rather have a fine meal on your flight to Paris or a modest meal and more money to spend at a real Parisian restaurant?

If consumers were willing to pay for fine meals on an airplane, airlines would offer that service. But if you have flown recently, you know that consumers would rather have a lower price. An increase in quality that consumers are not willing to pay for is a wasteful increase in quality. Thus, as firms competed by offering higher quality, the initial producer surplus was wasted away in frills that consumers liked but would not be willing to pay for—hence, the red area in Figure 8.12 is labeled "'Quality' waste."

Airline costs increased over time for another reason. The producer surplus initially earned by the airlines was a tempting target for unions who threatened

Despite being more efficient than its rivals, airline regulation prevented Southwest from entering the national market until deregulation in 1978. Today, Southwest Airlines is one of the largest airlines in the world.

to strike unless they got their share of the proceeds. The airlines didn't put up too much of a fight because, when their costs rose, they could apply to the CAB for an increase in fares, thus passing along the higher costs to consumers. Many of the problems that older airlines have faced in recent times are due to generous pension and health benefits they are paying out, benefits which were granted when prices of flights were regulated above market levels.

By 1978, costs had increased so much that the airlines were no longer benefiting from regulation and were willing to accede to deregulation.[23] Deregulation lowered prices, increased quantity, and reduced wasteful quality competition.[24] Deregulation also reduced waste and increased efficiency in another way—by improving the allocation of resources.

The Misallocation of Resources

Regulation of airline fares could not have been maintained for 40 years if the CAB had not also regulated entry. Firms wanted to enter the airline industry because the CAB kept prices high, but the CAB knew that if entry occurred, prices would be pushed down. So under the influence of the older airlines, the CAB routinely prevented new competitors from entering. In 1938, for example, there were 16 major airlines; by 1974, there were just 10 despite 79 requests to enter the industry.

Restrictions on entry misallocated resources because low-cost airlines were kept out of the industry. Southwest Airlines, for example, began as a Texas-only airline because it could not get a license from the CAB to operate between states. (Lawsuits from competitors also nearly prevented Southwest from operating in Texas.) Southwest was able to enter the national market only after deregulation in 1978.

The entry of Southwest was not just a case of increasing supply. One of the virtues of the market process is that it is open to new ideas, innovations, and experiments. Southwest, for example, pioneered consistent use of the same aircraft to lower maintenance costs, greater use of smaller airports like Chicago's Midway, and long-term hedging of fuel costs. Southwest's innovations have made it one of the most profitable and largest airlines in the United States. Southwest's innovations have spread, in turn, to other firms such as JetBlue Airways, easyJet (Europe), and WestJet (Canada). Regulation of entry didn't just increase prices; it increased costs and reduced innovation. Deregulation improved the allocation of resources by allowing low-cost, innovative firms to expand nationally. Deregulation is the major reason why, today, flying is an ordinary event for most American families, rather than the province of the wealthy.

Takeaway

Price ceilings have several important effects: They create shortages, reductions in quality, wasteful lines and other search costs, a loss of gains from trade, and a misallocation of resources.

After reading this chapter, you should be able to explain all of these effects to your uncle. Also, to do well on the exam, you should be able to draw a diagram showing the price ceiling and correctly labeling the shortage. On the same diagram, can you locate the wasteful losses from waiting in line and the lost gains from trade? Review Figures 8.2 and 8.3 if you are having trouble with these questions. You should also understand why a price ceiling reduces product quality and how

CHECK YOURSELF

■ The European Union guarantees its farmers that the price of butter will stay above a floor. The floor price is often above the market equilibrium price. What do you think has been the result of this?

■ The United States has set a price floor for milk above the equilibrium price. Has this led to shortages or surpluses? How do you think the U.S. government has dealt with this? (*Hint:* Remember the cartons of milk you had in elementary school and high school? What was their price?)

price ceilings misallocate resources, not just in the market with the price ceiling but potentially throughout the economy.

Price floors create surpluses, a loss of gains from trade, wasteful increases in quality, and a misallocation of resources.

After reading this chapter, you should be able to explain all of these effects to your aunt. Can you show, using the tools of supply and demand, why a price floor creates a surplus, a deadweight loss, and a wasteful increase in quality? You should be able to label these areas on a diagram. You should also be able to explain how price floors cause resources to be misallocated.

CHAPTER REVIEW

interactive activity   Go online to practice with more examples of these types of problems, including live links to videos, data sources, and feedback.

 Problems in **green** relate to MRU videos. See the MRU table at the end of the exercises.

KEY CONCEPTS

price ceiling, p. 137
deadweight loss, p. 142
rent control, p. 148
price floor, p. 154

FACTS AND TOOLS

1. How does a free market eliminate a shortage?

2. When a price ceiling is in place keeping the price below the market price, what's larger: quantity demanded or quantity supplied? How does this explain the long lines and wasteful searches we see in price-controlled markets?

3. Suppose that the quantity demanded and quantity supplied in the market for milk is as follows:

Price per Gallon	Quantity Demanded	Quantity Supplied
$5	1,000	5,000
$4	2,000	4,500
$3	3,500	3,500
$2	4,100	2,000
$1	6,000	1,000

a. What is the equilibrium price and quantity of milk?

b. If the government places a price ceiling of $2 on milk, will there be a shortage or surplus of milk? How large will it be? How many gallons of milk will be sold?

4. If a government decides to make health insurance affordable by requiring all health insurance companies to cut their prices by 30%, what will probably happen to the number of people covered by health insurance?

5. The Canadian government has wage controls for medical doctors. To keep things simple, let's assume that they set one wage for all doctors: $100,000 per year. It takes about 6 years to become a general practitioner or a pediatrician, but it takes about 8 or 9 years to become a specialist like a gynecologist, surgeon, or ophthalmologist. What kind of doctor would you want to become under this system? (*Note:* The actual Canadian system does allow specialists to earn a bit more than general practitioners, but the difference isn't big enough to matter.)

6. Between 2000 and 2008, the price of oil increased from $30 per barrel to $140 per barrel, and the price of gasoline in the United States rose from about $1.50 per gallon to more than $4.00 per gallon. Unlike in the 1970s when oil prices spiked, there were no long lines outside gas stations. Why?

7. Price controls distribute resources in many un-intended ways. In the following cases, who will probably spend more time waiting in line to get scarce, price-controlled goods? Choose one from each pair:

   a. Working people or retired people?

   b. Lawyers who charge $800 per hour or fast-food employees who earn $8 per hour?

   c. People with desk jobs or people who can disappear for a couple of hours during the day?

8. In the chapter, we discussed how price ceilings can put goods in the wrong *place*, as when too little heating oil wound up in New Jersey during a harsh winter in the 1970s. Price controls can also put goods in the wrong *time* as well. If there are price controls on gasoline, can you think of some periods during which the shortage will get worse? (*Hint:* Gas prices typically rise during the busy Memorial Day and Labor Day weekends.)

9. a. Consider Figure 8.8. In a price-controlled market like this one, when will consumer surplus be larger: in the short run or in the long run?

   b. In this market, supply is more elastic, more flexible, in the long run. In other words, in the longer term, landlords and homebuilders can find something else to do for a living. In light of this and in light of the geometry of producer surplus in this figure, do rent controls hurt landlords and homebuilders more in the short run or in the long run?

10. Business leaders often say that there is a "short-age" of skilled workers, and so they argue that immigrants need to be brought in to do these jobs. For example, an AP article was entitled "New York farmers fear a shortage of skilled workers," and went on to point out that a special U.S. visa program, the H-2A program, "allows employers to hire foreign workers temporarily if they show that they were not able to find U.S. workers for the jobs." (*Source:* Thompson, Carolyn. May 13, 2008. N.Y. farmers fear a shortage of skilled workers. *Associated Press.*)

    a. How do unregulated markets cure a "labor shortage" when there are no immigrants to boost the labor supply?

    b. Why are businesses reluctant to let unregulated markets cure the shortage?

11. a. If the government forced all bread manufacturers to sell their products at a "fair price" that was half the current, free-market price, what would happen to the quantity supplied of bread?

    b. To keep it simple, assume that people must wait in line to get bread at the controlled price. Would consumer surplus rise, fall, or can't you tell with the information given?

    c. With these price controls on bread, would you expect bread *quality* to rise or fall?

12. A review of the jargon: Is the minimum wage a "price ceiling" or a "price floor"? What about rent control?

13. How do U.S. business owners change their behavior when the minimum wage rises? How does this impact teenagers?

14. The basic idea of deadweight loss is that a willing buyer and a willing seller can't find a way to make an exchange. In the case of the minimum wage law, the reason they can't make an exchange is because it's illegal for the buyer (the firm) to hire the seller (the worker) at any wage below the legal minimum. But how can this really be a "loss" from the worker's point of view? It's obvious why business owners would love to hire workers for less than the minimum wage, but if all companies obey the minimum wage law, why are some workers still willing to work for less than that?

Ask FRED

Interactive activity

15. Go the FRED economic database (https://fred.stlouisfed.org/) and search for "percent hourly paid minimum wage."

    a. In 2015, what percent of hourly workers were paid the minimum wage or less?

    b. Hourly wage workers are about three-fifths of total workers (the remainder work on salary). Almost all salaried workers earn above the minimum wage. So what percent of all workers earn the minimum wage or less?

THINKING AND PROBLEM SOLVING

16. In rich countries, governments almost always set the fares for taxi rides. The prices for taxi rides are the same in safe neighborhoods and in dangerous neighborhoods. Where is it easier to find a cab? Why? If these taxi price controls were ended, what would probably happen to the price and quantity of cab rides in dangerous neighborhoods? (Aside: How do you think ride-sharing apps like Uber and Lyft have affected this problem?)

17. When the United States had price controls on oil and gasoline, some parts of the United States had a lot of heating oil, while other states had long lines. As in the chapter, let's assume that winter oil demand is higher in New Jersey than in California. If there had been no price controls, what would have happened to the prices of heating oil in New Jersey and in California and how would "greedy businesspeople" have responded to these price differences?

18. On January 31, 1990, the first McDonald's opened in Moscow, capital of the then Soviet Union. Economists often described the Soviet Union as a "permanent shortage economy," where the government kept prices permanently low in order to appear "fair."

    "An American journalist on the scene reported the customers seemed most amazed at the 'simple sight of polite shop workers . . . in this nation of commercial boorishness.'"

    a. Why were most Soviet shop workers "boorish" when the McDonald's workers in Moscow were "polite"?

    b. What does your answer to the previous question tell you about the power of economic incentives to change human behavior? In other words, how entrenched is "culture"?

19. Let's count the value of lost gains from trade in a regulated market. The government decides it wants to make basic bicycles more affordable, so it passes a law requiring that all one-speed bicycles sell for $30, well below the market price. Use the following data to calculate the lost gains from trade, just as in Figure 8.3. Supply and demand are straight lines.

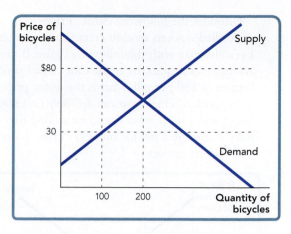

a. What is the total value of wasted time in the price-controlled market?

b. What is the value of the lost gains from trade?

c. Note that we haven't given you the original market price of simple bicycles—why don't you need to know it? (*Hint:* The answer is a mix of geometry and economics.)

20. During a crisis such as Hurricane Sandy, governments often make it illegal to raise the price of emergency items like flashlights and bottled water. In practice, this means that these items get sold on a first-come/first-served basis.

    a. If a person has a flashlight that she values at $5, but its price on the black market is $40, what gains from trade are lost if the government shuts down the black market?

    b. Why might a person want to sell a flashlight for $40 during an emergency?

    c. Why might a person be willing to pay $40 for a flashlight during an emergency?

    d. When will entrepreneurs be more likely to fill up their pickup trucks with flashlights and drive into a disaster area: when they can sell their flashlights for $5 each or when they can sell them for $40 each?

21. A "black market" is a place where people make illegal trades in goods and services. For instance, during the Soviet era, it was common for American tourists to take a few extra pairs of Levi's jeans when visiting the Soviet Union: They would sell the extra pairs at high prices on the illegal black market.

Consider the following claim: "Price-controlled markets tend to create black markets." Let's illustrate with the following figure. If there is a price ceiling in the market for cancer medication of $50 per pill, what is the *widest* price range within which you can *definitely* find both a buyer and a seller who would be willing to illegally exchange a pill for money? (There is only one correct answer.)

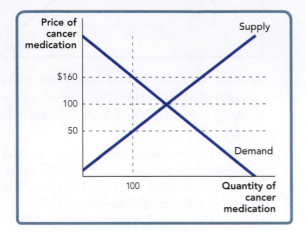

22. So, knowing what you know now about price controls, are you in favor of setting a $2 per gallon price ceiling on gasoline? Create a pro–price control and an anti–price control answer.

23. a. As we noted, Assar Lindbeck once said that short of aerial bombardment, rent control is the best way to destroy a city. What do you think Lindbeck might mean by this?

   b. How does paying "key money" to a landlord reduce the severity of Lindbeck's "bombardment"?

24. In the town of Freedonia, the government declares that all street parking must be free: There can be no parking meters. In an almost identical town of Meterville, parking costs $5 per hour (or $1.25 per 15 minutes).

   a. Where will it be easier to find parking: in Freedonia or Meterville?

   b. One town will tend to attract shoppers who hate driving around looking for parking. Which one?

   c. Why will the town from part b also attract shoppers with higher incomes?

25. In the late 1990s, the town of Santa Monica, California, made it illegal for banks to charge people ATM fees. As you probably know, it's almost always free to use your own bank's ATMs, but there's usually a fee charged when you use

another bank's ATM. (*Source:* The war on ATM fees, *Time*, November 29, 1999.) As soon as Santa Monica passed this law, Bank of America stopped allowing customers from other banks to use their ATMs: In bank jargon, B of A banned "out-of-network" ATM usage.

In fact, this ban lasted for only a few days, after which a judge allowed banks to continue to charge fees while awaiting a full court hearing on the issue. Eventually, the court declared the fee ban illegal under federal law. But let's imagine the effect of a full ban on out-of-network fees.

a. In the figure, indicate the new price per out-of-network ATM transaction after the fee ban. Also clearly label the shortage.

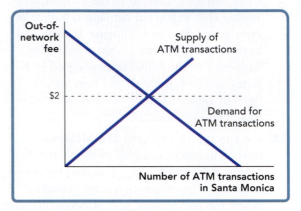

b. Calculate the exact amount of producer and consumer surplus in the out-of-network ATM market in Santa Monica after the ban. How large is producer surplus? How large is consumer surplus?

26. Consider Figure 8.9. Your classmate looks at that chart and says, "Apartment construction slowed down years before rent control was passed, and after rent control was passed, more apartments were built. Rent control didn't cut the number of new apartments, it raised it. This proves that rent control works." What is wrong with this argument?

27. Rent control creates a shortage of housing, which makes it hard to find a place to live. In a price-controlled market, people have to waste a lot of time trying to find these scarce, artificially cheap products. Yet Congressman Charles B. Rangel, the chairman of the powerful House Ways and Means Committee, lived in *four* rent-stabilized apartments in Harlem. Why are powerful individuals often able to "find" price-controlled goods much more often than the nonpowerful? What does this tell us about the political side effects of price controls?

(*Source:* Republicans question Rangel's tax break support, the *New York Times,* November 25, 2008.)

28. In the 1970s, AirCal and Pacific Southwest Airlines flew only within California. As we mentioned, the federal price floors didn't apply to flights within just one state. A major route for these airlines was flying from San Francisco to Los Angeles, a distance of 350 miles. This is about the same distance as from Chicago, Illinois, to Cleveland, Ohio. Do you think AirCal flights had nicer meals than flights from Chicago to Cleveland? Why or why not?

29. President Jimmy Carter didn't just deregulate airline prices. He also deregulated much of the trucking industry as well. Trucks carry almost all of the consumer goods that you purchase, so almost every time you purchase something, you're paying money to a trucking company.

    a. Based on what happened in the airline industry after prices were deregulated, what do you think happened in the trucking industry after deregulation? You can find some answers here: http://www.econlib.org/Library/Enc1/TruckingDeregulation.html. For another look that is critical of trucking deregulation, but comes to basically the same answers, see Michael Belzer, 2000. *Sweatshops on Wheels: Winners and Losers in Trucking Deregulation.* Thousand Oaks, CA: SAGE.

    b. Who do you think asked Congress and the president to keep price floors for trucking: consumer groups, retail shops like Walmart, or the trucking companies?

30. Suppose you're doing some history research on shoe production in ancient Rome, during the reign of the famous Emperor Diocletian. Your documents tell you how many shoes were produced each year in the Roman Empire, but they don't tell you the price of shoes. You find a document stating that in the year 301, Emperor Diocletian issued an "edict on prices," but you don't know whether he imposed price *ceilings* or price *floors*—your Latin is a little rusty. However, you can clearly tell from the documents that the number of shoes actually exchanged in markets fell dramatically, and that both potential shoe sellers and potential shoe buyers were unhappy with the edict. With the information given, can you tell whether Diocletian imposed a ceiling or a floor? If so, which is it? (Yes, there really was an edict of Diocletian, and Wikipedia has excellent coverage of ancient Roman history.)

Emperor Diocletian issued an Edict on Maximum Prices in the year 301 in an effort to control inflation. As usual, the edict created shortages, disruptions in trade, and a black market. *Copia et demanda legi parendum.*

31. In the market depicted in the figure, there is either a price ceiling or a price floor—surprisingly, it doesn't matter which one it is: Whether it's an $80 price floor or a $30 price ceiling, the chart looks the same.

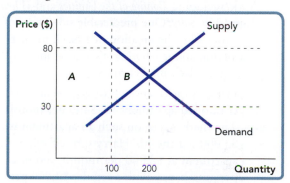

    In the chart, there's a rectangle and a triangle. One represents the value lost from the "deals that don't get made" and one represents the value lost from "the deals that do get made." Which is which?

32. We noted that in the 1970s price floors on airline tickets caused wasteful increases in the quality of airline trips. Does the minimum wage cause wasteful increases in the quality of workers? If so, how? In other words, how are minimum-wage workers like airplane trips?

33. The city of Mumbai in India imposed rent controls on apartments in 1947. Despite inflation and changes in land value, allowable rents have hardly increased since that time! Use what you know about rent controls to speculate about the quality of rent-controlled buildings in Mumbai.

CHALLENGES

34. If a government decided to impose price controls on gasoline, what could it do to avoid the time wasted waiting in lines? There is surely more than one solution to this problem.

BETTMANN/GETTY IMAGES

35. In New York City, some apartments are under strict rent control, while others are not. This is a theme in many novels and movies about New York, including *Bonfire of the Vanities* and *When Harry Met Sally*. One predictable side effect of rent control is the creation of a black market. Let's think about whether it's a good idea to allow this black market to exist.

a. Harry is lucky enough to get a rent-controlled apartment for $300 per month. The market rent on such an apartment is $3,000 per month. Harry himself values the apartment at $2,000 per month, and he'd be quite happy with a regular $2,000 per month New York apartment. If he stays in the apartment, how much consumer surplus does he enjoy?

b. If he illegally subleases his apartment to Sally on the black market for $2,500 per month and instead rents a $2,000 apartment, is he better off or worse off than if he obeyed the law?

36. Let's measure consumer surplus if the government imposes price controls and goods ended up being randomly allocated among those consumers willing to pay the controlled price. If the demand and supply curves are as in the figure, then:

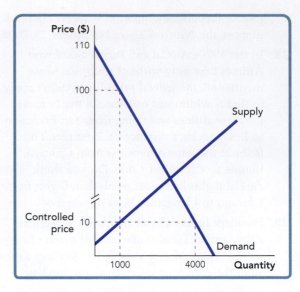

a. What is consumer surplus under the price control?

b. What would consumer surplus be if the quantity supplied were 1,000 but the goods were allocated to the highest-value users?

37. Antibiotics are often given to people with colds (even though they are not useful for that purpose), but they are also used to treat life-threatening infections. If there was a price control on antibiotics, what do you think would happen to the allocation of antibiotics across these two uses?

38. In a command economy such as the old Soviet Union, there were no prices for almost all goods. Instead, goods were allocated by a "central planner." Suppose that a good like oil becomes more scarce. What problems would a central planner face in reallocating oil to maximize consumer plus producer surplus?

39. Labor unions are some of the strongest proponents of the minimum wage. Yet in 2008, the median full-time union member earned $886 per week, an average of over $22 per hour (http://www.bls.gov/news.release/union2.nr0.htm). Therefore, a rise in the minimum wage doesn't directly raise the wage of many union workers. So why do unions support minimum wage laws? Surely, there's more than one reason why this is so, but let's see if economic theory can shed some light on the subject.

a. Skilled and unskilled labor are substitutes: For example, imagine that you can hire four low-skilled workers to move dirt with shovels at $5 an hour, or you can hire one skilled worker at $24 an hour to move the same amount of dirt with a skid loader. Using the tools developed in Chapter 3, what will happen to the demand for skilled labor if the price of unskilled labor increases to $6.50 per hour?

b. If the minimum wage rises, will that increase or decrease the demand for the average union worker's labor? Why?

c. Now, let's put the pieces together: Why might high-wage labor unions support an increase in the minimum wage?

40. In our Uber example, we said that after a spike in demand around Madison Square Garden, the number of Uber rides increased by more than 75% in the surrounding area, but when it starts to rain, Uber rides increase by the still substantial but lesser amount of 25%. Can you suggest one reason why the supply response is different in the two situations? (*Hint:* Think about elasticities of supply.)

WORK IT OUT

interactive activity

For interactive, step-by-step help in solving this problem, go online.

Suppose that the market for coats can be described as follows:

Price	Quantity Demanded (millions)	Quantity Supplied (millions)
$120	16	20
$100	18	18
$80	20	16
$60	22	14

a. What are the equilibrium price and quantity of coats?

b. Suppose the government sets a price ceiling of $80. Will there be a shortage, and if so, how large will it be?

c. Given that the government sets a price ceiling of $80, how much will demanders be willing to pay per unit of the good (i.e., what is the true price)? Suppose that people line up to get this good and that they value their time at $10 an hour. For how long will people wait in line to obtain a coat?

MARGINAL REVOLUTION UNIVERSITY VIDEOS

Price Ceilings: The US Economy Flounders in the 1970s

mruniversity.com/price-ceilings

Problems: **1–3, 8–10, 28, 34, 38**

Price Ceilings: Shortages and Quality Reduction

mruniversity.com/shortages-and-quality

Problems: **2–4, 9, 11, 16**

Price Ceilings: Lines and Search Costs

mruniversity.com/lines-search-costs

Problems: **5–7, 19**

Price Ceilings: Deadweight Loss

mruniversity.com/deadweight-loss

Problems: **14, 31**

Price Ceilings: Misallocation of Resources

mruniversity.com/resources

Problems: **1, 8, 10, 20, 21**

Price Ceilings: Rent Controls

mruniversity.com/rent-controls

Problems: **9, 12, 23, 25–28, 35–37**

Price Floors: The Minimum Wage

mruniversity.com/min-wage

Problems: **12, 13, 32, 39**

Price Floors: Airline Fares

mruniversity.com/airlines

Problems: **16–18, 28, 29**

Why Do Governments Enact Price Controls?

mruniversity.com/price-controls

Problems: **22, 34**

Price Controls and Communism

mruniversity.com/controls-and-communism

Problems: **38**

9

International Trade

E conomics textbooks should never have chapters on "international trade." The word "international" suggests that international trade is a special type of trade requiring new principles and arguments. When Casey and Frank trade, Casey and Frank are made better off. When Casey and Francisco trade, Casey and Francisco are made better off. The politics are different but the economics don't change much if Frank lives in El Paso and Francisco lives in Ciudad Juarez. International trade is trade.

In Chapter 2, we discussed the "big picture" view of trade and why trade is generally beneficial. To recap:

1. Trade makes people better off when preferences differ.

2. Trade increases productivity through specialization and the division of knowledge.

3. Trade increases productivity through comparative advantage.

All of these reasons hold for trade between nations as well as trade within nations. What is different in this chapter is that we will focus our analysis on a single market. Using the tools of supply and demand, we will discuss the prices at which trade occurs and how trade in a single market affects consumers and producers in that market. We will also show how to analyze restrictions on trade, such as tariffs and quotas. We close by evaluating some of the arguments, both economic and political, against international trade.

Analyzing Trade with Supply and Demand

Let's look at trade—and trade restrictions—using tools that you are already familiar with: demand and supply.

Figure 9.1 shows a domestic demand curve and a domestic supply curve for semiconductors. If there were no international trade, the equilibrium would be, as usual, at $P^{\text{No trade}}$, $Q^{\text{No trade}}$. Suppose, however, that this good can also be bought in the world market at the world price. To simplify, we will assume that the U.S. market is small relative to the world market, so U.S. demanders can buy as many semiconductors as they want without pushing up the world price. In terms of our diagram, the world supply curve is flat (perfectly elastic) at the world price.

Given that U.S. consumers can buy as many semiconductors as they want at the world price, how many will they buy? As usual, we read the quantity demanded off the domestic demand curve so at the world price, U.S. consumers will demand $Q_d^{\text{Free trade}}$ semiconductors. How many semiconductors

FIGURE 9.1

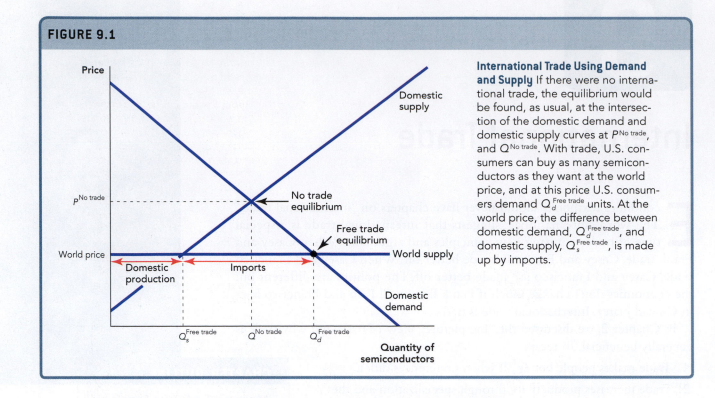

International Trade Using Demand and Supply If there were no international trade, the equilibrium would be found, as usual, at the intersection of the domestic demand and domestic supply curves at $P^{\text{No trade}}$, and $Q^{\text{No trade}}$. With trade, U.S. consumers can buy as many semiconductors as they want at the world price, and at this price U.S. consumers demand $Q_d^{\text{Free trade}}$ units. At the world price, the difference between domestic demand, $Q_d^{\text{Free trade}}$, and domestic supply, $Q_s^{\text{Free trade}}$, is made up by imports.

will be supplied by *domestic* suppliers? As usual, we read the quantity supplied off the domestic supply curve so domestic suppliers will supply $Q_s^{\text{Free trade}}$ units. Notice that $Q_d^{\text{Free trade}} > Q_s^{\text{Free trade}}$, so where does the difference come from? From imports. In other words, with international trade, domestic consumption is $Q_d^{\text{Free trade}}$ units; $Q_s^{\text{Free trade}}$ of these units are produced domestically and the remainder, $Q_d^{\text{Free trade}} - Q_s^{\text{Free trade}}$, are imported.

Analyzing Tariffs with Demand and Supply

Many countries, including the United States, restrict international trade with tariffs, quotas, or other regulations that burden foreign producers but not domestic producers—this is called **protectionism**. A **tariff** is simply a tax on imports. A **trade quota** is a restriction on the quantity of foreign goods that can be imported: Imports greater than the quota amount are forbidden or heavily taxed.

Figure 9.2 shows how to analyze a tariff. The figure looks imposing but it's really the same as Figure 9.1 except that now we analyze domestic consumption, production, and imports before and after the tariff. Before the tariff, the situation is exactly as in Figure 9.1: $Q_d^{\text{Free trade}}$ units are demanded, $Q_s^{\text{Free trade}}$ units are supplied by domestic producers, and imports are $Q_d^{\text{Free trade}} - Q_s^{\text{Free trade}}$.

The tariff is a tax on imports so—just as you learned in Chapter 3—the tariff (tax) shifts the world supply curve up by the amount of the tariff. For example, if the world price of semiconductors is $2 per unit and a new tariff of $1 per semiconductor is imposed, then the world supply curve shifts up to $3 per unit.

At the new, higher price of semiconductors, two things happen. First, there is an increase in the domestic production of semiconductors as domestic suppliers respond to the higher price by increasing production. In the diagram, domestic

Protectionism is the economic policy of restraining trade through quotas, tariffs, or other regulations that burden foreign producers but not domestic producers.

A **tariff** is a tax on imports.

A **trade quota** is a restriction on the quantity of goods that can be imported: Imports greater than the quota amount are forbidden or heavily taxed.

FIGURE 9.2

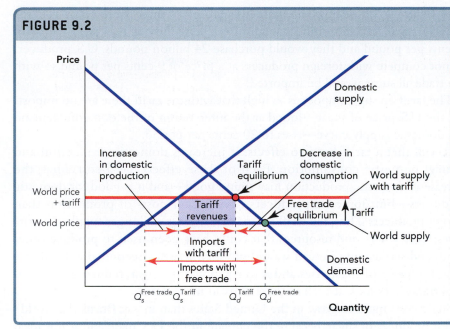

International Trade Using Demand and Supply: Tariffs A tariff shifts the world supply curve up by the amount of the tariff, thus raising the world price. In response to the higher price, consumers reduce their purchases from $Q_d^{\text{Free trade}}$ to Q_d^{Tariff} and domestic suppliers increase their production from $Q_s^{\text{Free trade}}$ to Q_s^{Tariff}. Since domestic consumption decreases and domestic production increases, the quantity of imports falls from $Q_d^{\text{Free trade}} - Q_s^{\text{Free trade}}$ to $Q_d^{\text{Tariff}} - Q_s^{\text{Tariff}}$.
The government collects revenues from the tariff equal to the tariff × the quantity of imports, which is shown as the blue area.

production increases from $Q_s^{\text{Free trade}}$ to Q_s^{Tariff}. Second, there is a decrease in domestic consumption from $Q_d^{\text{Free trade}}$ to Q_d^{Tariff} as domestic consumers respond to the higher price by buying fewer semiconductors. Since the quantity produced by domestic suppliers rises and the quantity demanded by domestic consumers falls, the quantity of imports falls. Specifically, imports fall from $Q_d^{\text{Free trade}} - Q_s^{\text{Free trade}}$ to the smaller amount $Q_d^{\text{Tariff}} - Q_s^{\text{Tariff}}$.

Figure 9.2 illustrates one more important idea. A tariff is a tax on imports so tariffs raise tax revenue for the government. The revenue raised by a tariff is the tariff amount times the quantity of imports (the quantity taxed). Thus, in Figure 9.2 the tariff revenue is given by the blue area.

The Costs of Protectionism

Now that we know that a tariff on an imported good will increase domestic production and decrease domestic consumption, we can analyze in more detail the costs of protectionism. The U.S. government, for example, greatly restricts the amount of sugar that can be imported into the United States. As a result, U.S. consumers typically pay 50% to 100% more for sugar than the world price, depending on the year. So, let's look in more detail at the costs of sugar protectionism.

To simplify our analysis, we make two assumptions. First, we assume that the tariff is so high that it completely eliminates all sugar imports. Although a small amount of sugar is allowed into the United States at a low tariff rate, anything above this small amount is taxed so heavily that no further imports occur. Our assumption that the tariff eliminates all sugar imports is not a bad approximation to what actually happens. Second, we assume that if we had complete free trade, all sugar would be imported. This is also a reasonable assumption because, as we will explain shortly, sugar can be produced elsewhere at much lower cost than in the United States. Making these two assumptions will focus attention on the key ideas. See Challenge question 15 at the end of the chapter for a more detailed analysis.

Analyzing Trade and the Welfare Cost of Tariffs

interactive activity

▶▶**SEARCH ENGINE**

Information on sugar and the U.S. sugar tariff can be found at the *USDA Economic Research Service, Sugar Briefing Room.*

In Figure 9.3, we show the market for sugar. If there were complete free trade in sugar, U.S. consumers would be able to buy at the world price of 9 cents per pound and they would purchase 24 billion pounds. U.S. producers cannot compete with foreign producers at a price of 9 cents per pound so with free trade all sugar would be imported.

The tariff on sugar imports is so high that with the tariff there are no imports and the U.S. price of sugar—found at the intersection of the domestic demand and domestic supply curve—rises to 20 cents per pound.

Recall that a tariff has two effects: It increases domestic production and reduces domestic consumption. Each of these effects has a cost. First, the increase in domestic production may sound good—and it is good for domestic producers—but domestic producers have higher costs of production than foreign producers. Thus, the tariff means that sugar is no longer supplied by the lowest-cost sellers, and resources that could have been used to produce other goods and services are instead wasted producing sugar. Second, due to higher costs, the price of sugar rises and fewer people buy sugar, reducing the gains from trade. Let's look at each of these costs in more detail.

Sugar costs more to grow in the United States than in, say, Brazil, the world's largest producer of sugar, because the climate in the U.S. mainland is not ideal for sugar growing and because land and labor in Florida, where a lot of U.S.

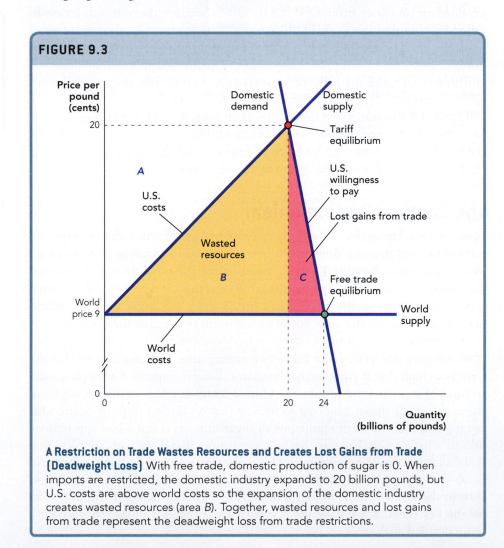

FIGURE 9.3

A Restriction on Trade Wastes Resources and Creates Lost Gains from Trade (Deadweight Loss) With free trade, domestic production of sugar is 0. When imports are restricted, the domestic industry expands to 20 billion pounds, but U.S. costs are above world costs so the expansion of the domestic industry creates wasted resources (area *B*). Together, wasted resources and lost gains from trade represent the deadweight loss from trade restrictions.

sugar is grown, have many alternative uses that are high in value. Sugar farmers in Florida, for example, have to douse their land with expensive fertilizers to increase production—in the process creating environmental damage in the Florida Everglades.[1] The excess resources—the fertilizer, land, and labor—that go into producing U.S. sugar could have been used to produce other goods like oranges and theme parks for which the United States and Florida are better suited.

Recall from Chapter 3 that the supply curve tells us the cost of production so at the equilibrium price the cost of producing an additional pound of sugar in the United States is exactly 20 cents. In other words, in the United States it takes 20 cents worth of resources like land and labor to produce one additional pound of sugar. That same pound of sugar could be bought in the world market for just 9 cents so the tariff causes 11 cents worth of resources to be wasted in producing that last pound of sugar.

The total value of wasted resources is shown in Figure 9.3 by the yellow area labeled "Wasted resources"; that area represents the difference between what it costs to produce 20 billion pounds of sugar in the United States and what it would cost to buy the same amount from abroad. We can calculate the total value of wasted resources using our formula for the area of a triangle.

The height of the yellow triangle is $20 - 9$ or 11 cents per pound, the base is 20 billion pounds, so the area is 110 billion cents, or $1.1 billion. The sugar tariff wastes $1.1 billion worth of resources.

Notice that if the sugar tariff were eliminated, the price of sugar in the United States would fall to the world price of 9 cents per pound and U.S. production would drop from 20 billion pounds to 0 pounds. It's important to see that the reduction in U.S. production is a *benefit* of eliminating the tariff because it frees up resources that can be used to produce other goods and services.

There is another cost to the tariff. Remember from Chapter 3 that the demand curve tells us the value of goods to the demanders, so at the equilibrium price demanders are willing to pay up to 20 cents for a pound of sugar. World suppliers, however, are willing to sell sugar at 9 cents per pound. U.S. consumers and world suppliers could make mutually profitable gains from trade, but they are prevented from doing so by the threat of punishment. The value of the lost gains from trade is given by the pink area (area C). Again, we can calculate this area using our formula for the area of a triangle ($[20 - 9]$ cents per pound $\times$ 4 billion pounds divided by 2) = 22 billion cents or $0.22 billion.

Thus, the total cost of the sugar tariff to U.S. citizens is $1.1 billion of wasted resources plus $0.22 billion of lost gains from trade for a total loss of $1.32 billion.

Do you remember from Chapter 4 the three conditions that explain why a free market is efficient? Here they are again:

1. The supply of goods is bought by the buyers with the highest willingness to pay.

2. The supply of goods is sold by the sellers with the lowest costs.

3. Between buyers and sellers, there are no unexploited gains from trade or any wasteful trades.

A tariff or quota that restricts consumers from trading with foreign producers means that the market is not free, so we should expect some of the conditions in our list to be violated. In this case, conditions 2 and 3 are violated. A tariff reduces efficiency because the supply of goods is no longer sold by the sellers

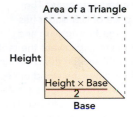

Area of a Triangle

Height

$\dfrac{\text{Height} \times \text{Base}}{2}$

Base

How to smuggle sugar The high price of U.S. sugar has encouraged smuggling and attempts to circumvent the tariff. In the 1980s when the U.S. price was four times the world price, Canadian entrepreneurs created super-high-sugar iced tea. The "tea" was shipped into the United States and then sifted for the sugar, which was resold. To combat this entrepreneurship, the U.S. government created even more tariffs for sugar-containing products like iced tea, cake mixes, and cocoa.

Data from: Economic Report of the President 1986, Chapter 4.

with the lowest costs, and with a tariff, there are unexploited gains from trade between buyers and sellers.

Some of these benefits of trade may sound fairly abstract, but for a lot of people, they are a matter of life and death. If Brazilian sugar cane farmers could sell more of their products to U.S. consumers, many more of the farmers could afford to eat better or to improve their housing with proper water and sewage. But don't think the United States is the only party at fault here. The Brazilian government places a lot of tariffs on foodstuffs from the United States and for many Brazilians, including the very poor, this makes food more expensive. The end result is that U.S. consumers pay a high price for sugar and poor Brazilians have less to eat and less money to spend when they need to take their kids to the doctor.

Winners and Losers from Trade

We can arrive at this same total loss in another revealing way. The sugar tariff raises the price of sugar to U.S. consumers, which reduces consumer surplus. Recall from Chapter 3 that consumer surplus is the area underneath the demand curve and above the price. Thus, consumer surplus with the tariff is the area above the price of 20 cents and below the demand curve (not all of which is shown in Figure 9.3). As the price falls from 20 cents to 9 cents, consumer surplus increases by area $A + B + C$, which has a value (check it!) of $2.42 billion. Or, put differently, the tariff costs consumers $2.42 billion in lost consumer surplus.

The tariff increases price, which increases producer surplus, the area above the supply curve and below the price. Thus, the tariff increases U.S. producer surplus by area A, which has a value of $1.10 billion.

Notice that U.S. consumers lose more than twice as much from the tariff as U.S. producers gain. The total loss to U.S. citizens is the $2.42 billion loss to consumers minus the $1.10 billion gain to producers, for a total loss of $1.32 billion a year, *exactly as we found before*.

Our two methods of analyzing the cost of the sugar tariff are equivalent, but they emphasize different things. The first method calculates social loss directly and emphasizes where the loss comes from: wasted resources and lost gains from trade. The second method focuses on *who* gains and *who* loses. Domestic producers gain but U.S. consumers lose even more.

Why does the government support the U.S. sugar tariff when U.S. consumers lose much more than U.S. producers gain? One clue is that the costs of the sugar tariff are spread over millions of consumers so the costs per consumer are small. The benefits of the tariff, however, flow to a small number of producers, each of whom benefits by millions of dollars. As a result, the producers support and lobby for the tariff much more actively than consumers oppose the tariff. It's often been said that the rational rule of politics is to spread costs and concentrate benefits.

The politics of lobbying point our attention to yet another cost of protectionism. When a country erects a lot of tariffs against foreign competition, the producers in that country will spend a lot of their time, energy, and money lobbying the government for protection. Those same resources could be spent on production and innovation, not lobbying. Protectionism tends to create a society that pits one interest group against the other and seeds social discord.

Free trade, in contrast, creates incentives for people to cooperate toward common and profitable ends.

Arguments Against International Trade

It would take several books to analyze all the arguments against international trade. We will take a closer look at some of the most common arguments:

- Trade reduces the number of jobs in the United States.
- It's wrong to trade with countries that use child labor.
- We need to keep certain industries at home for reasons of national security.
- We need to keep certain "key" industries at home because of beneficial spillovers onto other sectors of the economy.
- We can increase U.S. well-being with strategic trade protectionism.

Trade and Jobs

When the United States reduces tariffs and imports more shirts from Mexico, the U.S. shirt industry will contract. As a result, many people associate free trade with lost jobs. As economists, however, we want to trace the impact of lower tariffs beyond the most immediate and visible effects. So let's trace what happens when a tariff is lowered, paying particular attention to the effect on jobs.

When the price of shirts falls, U.S. consumers have more money in their pockets that they can use to buy other goods. The increased consumer spending on Scotch tape, bean bag chairs, x-ray tests, and thousands of other goods leads to increased jobs in these industries. These jobs gains may be more difficult to see than the job losses in the U.S. shirt industry but they are no less real. But what about the money that is now going to Mexican shirt producers instead of to U.S. shirt producers? Isn't it better to "Buy American" and keep this money at home?

When Mexican producers sell shirts in the United States, they are paid in dollars. But what do Mexicans want dollars for? Ultimately, everyone sells to buy. Mexican producers might use their dollars to buy U.S. goods. In this case, the increased U.S. spending on imports of Mexican shirts leads directly to increased Mexican spending on U.S. goods (i.e., U.S. exports).

But what happens if the Mexican shirt producers want to buy Mexican goods or European goods rather than U.S. goods? To buy Mexican or European goods, the Mexican shirt producers will need pesos or euros. Fortunately, they can trade their dollars for pesos or euros on the foreign exchange market. Suppose the Mexicans trade their dollars to someone in Germany who in return gives them euros. Why would a German want to trade euros for dollars? Remember that people sell to buy. Thus, Germans want dollars so that they can buy U.S. goods or U.S. assets. So once again, the increased spending on Mexican shirt imports leads to an increase in U.S. exports (in this case, to Germany) and thus an increase in jobs in U.S. exporting industries.

Our thought experiment reveals an important truth: *We pay for our imports with exports.* Think about it this way: Why would anyone sell us goods if not to get goods in return? Thus, trade does not eliminate jobs—it moves jobs from import-competing industries to export industries. And remember: Although

CHECK YOURSELF

- Who benefits from a tariff? Who loses?
- Why does trade protectionism lead to wasted resources?
- If there are winners and losers from trade restrictions, why do we hear more often from the people who gain from trade restrictions than from the people who lose?
- Identify the deadweight loss area in Figure 9.3 and describe in words what is lost.

Thomas Edison Destroyer of jobs or benefactor of humanity? Yes.

trade does not change the number of jobs, it does raise wages, as we demonstrated in Chapter 2 on comparative advantage.

If we import more, we must (eventually) export more but we don't necessarily import and export the same types of goods. That can have implications for how the benefits of international trade are distributed. Let's go back to the idea of comparative advantage. Compared to the rest of the world the United States has a lot of highly educated, skilled workers, so the United States is likely to have a comparative advantage in producing complex goods like aircraft, construction machinery, and specialized computer chips. Other countries, such as China, have an abundance of unskilled workers, so China has a comparative advantage in producing less complex goods like clothing, footwear, and simpler manufactured goods. Increased trade with a country like China, therefore, tends to shift U.S. production from unskilled to skilled products, from shirt production to aircraft production. That's good for workers in the aircraft industry and for consumers of shirts but not so good for workers in the U.S. shirt industry who may not be able to adjust easily. Between 1996 and 2006, imports from China increased by a factor of six from about $50 billion per year to $300 billion per year, a large change in a short period of time. This increase in trade was disruptive to U.S. industries that suddenly found themselves competing with Chinese rivals.

Changing jobs can be traumatic, but in a dynamic and growing economy, job loss and job gain are two sides of the same coin. It's difficult to have one without the other. All change generates losers and winners. Thomas Edison destroyed the whale oil industry with his invention of the electric lightbulb in 1879. That was bad for whalers but good for people who like to read at night (and very good for the whales). Compact discs destroyed jobs in the vinyl record industry and then MP3s destroyed jobs in the CD industry. Music lovers, however, gained access to tens of millions of songs on services like Spotify at a price less than the cost of a dozen Beatles CDs in 2001. Every change produces winners and losers but over time job creation has outpaced job destruction. The result has been a tremendous increase in the standard of living.

Job destruction is ultimately a healthy part of any growing economy, but that doesn't mean we have to ignore the costs of transitioning from one job to another. Unemployment insurance, savings, and a strong education system can help workers respond to shocks. Trade restrictions, however, are not a good way to respond to shocks. Trade restrictions save *visible* jobs, but they destroy jobs that are just as real but harder to see.

Child Labor

Is child labor a reason to restrict trade? In part, this is a question of ethics on which reasonable people can disagree, but our belief, for which we will give reasons, is that the answer is no.

In 1992, labor activists discovered that Walmart was selling clothing that had been made in Bangladesh by subcontractors who had employed some child workers. Senator Tom Harkin angrily introduced a bill in Congress to prohibit firms from importing any products made by children under the age of 15. Harkin's bill didn't pass, but in a panic the garment industry in Bangladesh dismissed 30,000 to 50,000 child workers. A success? Before we decide, we need to think about what happened to the children who were thrown out of work. Where did these children go? To the playground? To school? To a better job? No. Thrown out of the garment factories, the children went to work elsewhere, many at jobs like prostitution with worse conditions and lower pay.[2]

The pin factory Lewis Hine photograph of bowling alley boys in New Haven, CT. Circa 1910.

About 14% of all children aged 5–14 around the world work for a significant number of hours each week. The vast majority of these children work in agriculture, often alongside their parents, and not in export industries. Restrictions on trade, therefore, cannot directly reduce the number of child workers, and by making a poor country poorer, trade restrictions may increase the number of child workers. In fact, studies have shown that more openness to trade increases income and reduces child labor.[3]

Child labor is more common in poor countries and it was common in nineteenth-century Great Britain and the United States when people were much poorer than today. Child labor declined in the developed world as people got richer.

The forces that reduced child labor in the developed world are also at work in the developing world. The vertical axis of Figure 9.4 shows the percentage of children ages 10–14 who are laboring in 132 countries across the world. Real GDP per capita is shown on the horizontal axis. The sizes of the circles are

FIGURE 9.4

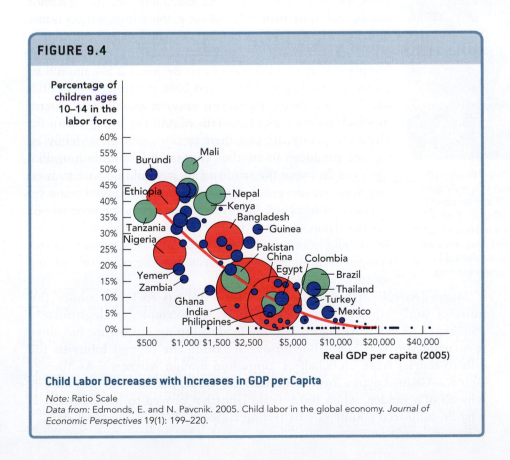

Percentage of children ages 10–14 in the labor force

Real GDP per capita (2005)

Child Labor Decreases with Increases in GDP per Capita

Note: Ratio Scale
Data from: Edmonds, E. and N. Pavcnik. 2005. Child labor in the global economy. *Journal of Economic Perspectives* 19(1): 199–220.

proportionate to the total number of child laborers, so although the percentage of child laborers is much higher in Burundi (48.5%) than in India (12%), there are many more child laborers in India. The lesson of Figure 9.4 is that economic growth reduces child labor.

The real cause of child labor is poverty, not trade. Thus, to reduce child labor, we should focus on reducing poverty rather than on reducing trade; putting up trade barriers is likely to be ineffective or even counterproductive.

Governments and nonprofits from the developed world can help developing countries reduce child labor by helping them to improve the quality of schooling and to lower the opportunity cost of education. In Bangladesh, at about the same time that child workers were being thrown out of work by the Harkin bill, the government introduced the Food for Education program. The program provides a free monthly stipend of rice or wheat to poor families who have at least one child attending school that month. The program has been very successful at encouraging school attendance. Even more important, increased education of children today means richer parents tomorrow—parents who will no longer feel crushed by the forces of poverty, or in other words parents who will have enough wealth to feed their children *and* send them to school.[4]

Trade and National Security

If a good is vital for national security but domestic producers have higher costs than foreign producers, it can make sense for the government to tax imports or subsidize the production of the domestic industry. It may make sense, for example, to support a domestic vaccine industry. In 1918, more than a quarter of the U.S. population got sick with the flu and more than 500,000 died, sometimes within hours of being infected. The young were especially hard-hit and, as a result, life expectancy in the United States dropped by 10 years. No place in the world was safe, as between 2.5% and 5% of the entire world population died from the flu between 1918 and 1920. Producing flu vaccine requires an elaborate process in which robots inject hundreds of millions of eggs with flu viruses. In an ordinary year, there are few problems with buying vaccine produced in another country, but if something like the 1918 flu swept the world again, it would be wise to have significant vaccine production capacity in the United States.[5]

Vital for national security? In 1954 the U.S. government declared that mohair, the fleece of the Angora goat, was vital for national security (it can be used to make military uniforms). For nearly 40 years mohair producers received millions of dollars in annual payments. Finally, after much ridicule, the program was eliminated in 1993 . . . only to be reestablished in 2002. Hard to believe? Yes, but we aren't kidding.

NORMAN EGGERT/ALAMY

Don't be surprised, however, if every domestic producer in trouble claims that their product is vital for national security. Everything from beeswax to mohair, not to mention steel and computer chips, has been protected in the name of national security.

More generally, it's common for protectionists to lobby under the guise of some other motive. Many people, for example, are legitimately concerned about working conditions in developing countries, but does it surprise you that U.S. labor unions are often the biggest lobbyists for bills to restrict trade on behalf of "oppressed foreign workers"? As Youssef Boutros-Ghali, Egypt's former minister for trade, put it, "The question is why all of a sudden, when third world labor has proved to be competitive, why do industrial countries start feeling concerned about our workers? . . . It is suspicious."[6]

Key Industries

Another argument that in principle could be true is the "it's better to produce computer chips than potato chips" argument. The idea is that the production of computer chips is a key industry because it generates spillovers, benefits that go beyond the computer chips themselves (see Chapter 10 for more on spillovers). Protectionism isn't the best policy in this case (in theory, a subsidy would work better), but if a subsidy isn't possible, then protectionism might be a second-best policy with some net benefits.

The words "in principle" and "might" are well chosen. The "computer chips are better than potato chips" argument can't be faulted on logic alone, but it's not very compelling. To address this particular example, most computer chips today are cheap, mass-manufactured commodities. The United States rightly doesn't specialize in this type of manufacturing and is better off for it, even though this used to be a common argument for protectionism against foreign computer chips.

Second, it is difficult to know which industries are the ones with the really important spillovers. In the late 1980s, many pundits argued that HDTV would be a technology driver for many related industries. Japan and the European Union subsidized their producers to the tune of billions of dollars. The United States lagged behind. In the end, however, Japan and the EU chose an analog technology that is now considered obsolete and HDTV has yet to produce significant benefits for the broader economy, even if it does give you a really nice picture at home.

Amazon: Superproductivity Innovations in retailing and warehousing may not seem like a key technology but the retail sector is one of the largest sectors in any developed economy. Innovations in warehouse logistics, wireless identification and package tracking, and database integration have made firms like Amazon and Walmart leaders in their field and have significantly contributed to economy-wide increases in productivity.[7]

Strategic Trade Protectionism

In some cases, it's possible for a country to use tariffs and quotas to grab a larger share of the gains from trade than would be possible with pure free trade. The idea is for the government to help domestic firms to act like a cartel when they sell to international buyers. Oddly, the way to do this is to limit or tax exports. A tax or limit on exports reduces exports but can drive up the price enough so that net revenues increase. Of course, this can only work if international buyers have few substitutes for the domestic good. Could this work in practice? Yes, in many ways OPEC is a possible example. OPEC limits exports, and because the demand for oil is inelastic, this increases oil revenues.

Oil is a special good, however, because it is found in large quantities in just a few places in the world. The United States would have a much harder time using strategic trade protectionism because there are more substitutes for U.S.-produced goods. The U.S. economy, or any advanced economy, would also have another problem. Oil is Saudi Arabia's only significant export so when that nation raises the price of oil, the rest of the world can't threaten to retaliate by putting tariffs on Saudi Arabia's other exports. But if the United States were to try to grab a larger share of the gains from trade, in, say, computers, other countries could respond with tariffs on our grain exports. A trade war could easily make both countries worse off. Trying to divide the pie in your favor usually makes the pie smaller.

CHECK YOURSELF

- Over the past 30 years, most U.S. garment manufacturing has moved overseas, to places such as India and China, where wages are lower. The result of this shift has been a sizable drop in the number of garment workers in the United States. While bad for these workers, why has this trend been a net benefit for the United States?

- What would happen if the U.S. government decided that computer chip manufacturing was a strategic national industry and provided monetary grants to Silicon Valley companies? Trace the effects of this policy on Silicon Valley companies, foreign competitors, and the cost and benefit to U.S. taxpayers and consumers.

Takeaway

We have shown in this chapter how to use demand and supply curves to analyze trade and the costs of trade protectionism.

Restrictions on trade waste resources by transferring production from low-cost foreign producers to high-cost domestic producers. Restrictions on trade also prevent domestic consumers from exploiting gains from trade with foreign producers, creating deadweight losses. Domestic producers can benefit from trade restrictions, but domestic consumers lose more than the producers gain. Trade restrictions sometimes persist because the benefits from restrictions are often concentrated on small groups who lobby for protection, while the costs of restrictions are spread over millions of consumers and can be small for each individual.

We have set out various common arguments for restricting trade. Some of these arguments are valid, but they are usually of limited applicability

CHAPTER REVIEW

interactive activity Go online to practice with more examples of these types of problems, including live links to videos, data sources, and feedback.

 Problems in green relate to MRU videos. See the MRU table at the end of the exercises.

 Problems in blue are Office Hours videos.

KEY CONCEPTS

protectionism, p. 168

tariff, p. 168

trade quota, p. 168

FACTS AND TOOLS

1. The Japanese people currently pay about four times the world price for rice. If Japan removed its trade barriers so that Japanese consumers could buy rice at the world price, who would be better off and who would be worse off: Japanese consumers or Japanese rice farmers? If we added all the gains and losses to the Japanese, would there be a net gain or net loss? Who would make a greater effort lobbying, for or against, this reduction in trade barriers: Japanese consumers or Japanese rice farmers?

2. The supply curve for rice in Japan slopes upward, just like any normal supply curve. If Japan eliminated its trade barriers to rice, what would happen to the number of workers employed in the rice-producing industry in Japan: Would it rise or fall? What would these workers probably do over the next year or so? Will they ever work again?

3. In Figure 9.3, consider triangles B and C. One of these could be labeled "Workers and machines who could be better used in another

sector of the economy," while the other could be labeled "Consumers who have to pay more than necessary for their product." Which is which?

4. In his book *The Choice,* economist Russ Roberts asks how voters would feel about a machine that could convert wheat into automobiles.

   a. Do you think that voters would complain that this machine should be banned, since it would destroy jobs in the auto industry?

   b. Would this machine, *in fact,* destroy jobs in the auto industry? If so, would roughly the same number of jobs eventually be created in other industries?

   c. Here is Roberts's punch line: If voters were told that the wonder machine was in fact just a cargo ship that exported wheat and imported autos from a foreign country, how would voters' attitudes toward this machine change?

5. Spend some time driving in Detroit, Michigan—the Motor City—and you're sure to see bumper stickers with messages like "Buy American" or "Out of a job yet? Keep buying foreign!" or "Hungry? Eat your foreign car!" Explain these bumper stickers in light of what you've learned in this chapter. Who is hurt by imported automobiles? Who benefits?

6. This chapter pointed out that trade restrictions on sugar cause U.S. consumers to pay more than

twice the going world price for sugar. However, you are very unlikely to ever encounter bumper stickers that say things like "Out of money yet? Keep taxing foreign sugar!" or "Hungry? It's probably because domestic sugar is so expensive!" Why do you think it is that these bumper stickers are not popular?

7. Of the three conditions that explain why a free market is efficient (from Chapter 4), which condition or conditions cease to hold in the case of a tariff on imported goods? Which condition or conditions continue to hold even in the case of a tariff on imports?

THINKING AND PROBLEM SOLVING

8. **a.** Just to review: Back in Chapter 8, we illustrated price ceilings with a horizontal line below the equilibrium price. Did price ceilings create surpluses or shortages?

   b. The horizontal line in Figure 9.1 doesn't represent a surplus or a shortage. What does it represent?

   c. Figure 9.1 considers the case of a country that can buy as many semiconductors as it wants at the same world price. Why do people in this country only buy $Q_d^{\text{Free trade}}$ units? Why don't they buy more of this inexpensive product?

9. Figure 9.1 looks at a case in which the world price is below the domestic no-trade price. Let's look at the case in which the world price is *above* the domestic no-trade price. We'll work with the market for airplanes shown in the following figure.

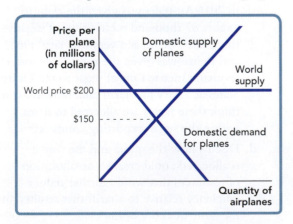

   a. In the figure, use the Quantity axis to label $Q_s^{\text{Free trade}}$ and $Q_d^{\text{Free trade}}$. This is somewhat similar to Figure 9.1.

   b. What would you call the gap between $Q_s^{\text{Free trade}}$ and $Q_d^{\text{Free trade}}$?

   c. Also following Figure 9.1, label "Domestic consumption" and "Domestic production."

   d. Will domestic airplane buyers—airlines and delivery companies like FedEx—have to pay a higher or a lower price under free trade compared with the no-trade alternative? Will domestic airplane buyers purchase a higher or a lower quantity of planes if there's free trade in planes?

   e. Based on your answer to part d, would you expect domestic airplane demanders to support free trade in planes or oppose it?

10. In the text, we discuss sugar farmers in Florida who use unusually large amounts of fertilizer to produce their crops; they do so because their land isn't all that great for sugar production. If we translate this into the language of the supply curve, would these Florida sugar farms be those on the lower-left part of a supply curve or those along the upper right of the supply curve? Why?

11. Many people will tell you that, whenever possible, you should always buy U.S.-made goods. Some will go further and tell you to spend your money on goods produced in your own state whenever possible. (Just do a simple Google search for "Buy [any state]" and you'll find a Web site encouraging this kind of thinking.) The idea is that if you spend money in your state, you help the economy of *your* state, rather than the economy of some other state. By the same logic, shouldn't one buy only goods produced in one's own city? Or on one's own street? Where does this thinking lead to? And how does it relate to Big Idea Five from Chapter 1?

12. Some people argue for protectionism by pointing out that other countries with whom we trade engage in "unfair trade practices," and that we should retaliate with our own protectionist measures. One such policy is the policy of some countries to subsidize exporting industries. India, for example, subsidizes its steel industry. Obviously, U.S. steel producers are hurt by this policy and would like to restrict imported steel from India. Is this a good reason to place tariffs on Indian steel? Why or why not?

13. In March 2002, then President George W. Bush put a tariff on imported steel as a means of protecting the domestic steel industry. In February, before the tariff went into effect, the U.S. produced 7.4 million metric tons of crude steel and imported about 2.8 million metric tons

of steel products at an average price of $363 per metric ton. Two months later, after the tariff was in effect, U.S. production increased to 7.9 million metric tons. The volume of imported steel fell to about 1.7 million metric tons, but the price of the imported steel rose to about $448 per metric ton. The following supply and demand diagram shows this situation (along with an estimated no-trade domestic equilibrium at a price of $625 per metric ton and a quantity of 8.9 million metric tons).

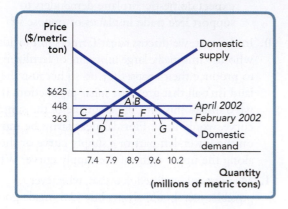

Determine which areas on the graph represent each of the following:

a. The increase in producer surplus gained by U.S. steel producers as a result of the tariff

b. The loss in consumer surplus suffered by U.S. steel consumers as a result of the tariff

c. The revenue earned by the government because of the tariff

d. The wasted resources and lost gains from trade (deadweight loss) created by the tariff

14. For each of the four parts of question 13, calculate the *values* of these areas in dollars. How much of the deadweight loss is due to the overproduction of steel by higher-cost U.S. steel producers, and how much is due to the underconsumption of steel by U.S. steel consumers?

CHALLENGES

15. In the chapter, we focused on a sugar tariff that eliminated all imports. Let's now take a look at the case where the sugar tariff eliminates some but not all imports. We will also examine the closely related case of a quota on sugar imports. The figure shows a tariff on sugar that raises the U.S. price to 20 cents per pound but at that price some sugar is imported even after the tariff.

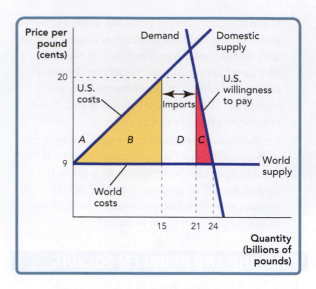

a. Label the free trade equilibrium, the tariff equilibrium, wasted resources, lost gains from trade, and tariff revenues.

b. Now imagine that instead of a tariff, the U.S. government uses a quota that forbids imports of sugar greater than 6 billion pounds. (Equivalently, imagine a tariff that is zero on the first 6 billion pounds of imports but then jumps to a prohibitive level after that quantity of imports—this is closer to how the system works in practice.) Under the quota system what does area *D* represent? Would importers of sugar prefer a tariff or a quota?

c. The sugar quota is allocated to importing countries based on imports from these countries between 1975 and 1981 (with some subsequent adjustments). For example, in 2016 Australia was given the right to export 87 thousand metric tons of sugar to the United States at a very low tariff rate, and Belize was given the right to export 11.5 thousand metric tons of sugar to the United States at a very low tariff rate. How do you think these rights are allocated to firms within the sugar-exporting countries?

d. Discuss how the quota and the way it is allocated could create a misallocation of resources that would further reduce efficiency relative to a tariff that resulted in the same quantity of imports.

16. In a 2005 *Washington Post* article ("The Road to Riches Is Called K Street"), Jeffrey Birnbaum noted that there were 35,000 registered lobbyists in Washington, D.C., people whose primary job is asking the federal government for something.

A lobbyist who comes with long experience as an aide to a powerful politician will earn at least $200,000 per year. Many lobbyists (not all) are attempting to restrict trade to turn consumer surplus into producer surplus.

a. Let's focus just on the lobbyists who are restricting trade. If the United States were to amend the Constitution to permanently ban all tariffs and trade restrictions, these lobbyists would lose their jobs, and they'd have to leave Washington to get "real jobs." Would this job change raise U.S. productivity or lower it?

b. Would most of these lobbyists likely earn more after the amendment was enacted or less?

c. How can you reconcile your answers to parts a and b?

17. One of the assumptions made in the chapter was that the U.S. market for sugar was small relative to the overall world market for sugar, so that when the United States entered the world market for sugar, and U.S. buyers began to buy imported sugar, the price did not change. If we relax this assumption, how do you think that would affect Figure 9.1? How would the outcome differ from the outcome under the assumption of the relatively small market?

18. The following tables show the domestic supply and demand schedules for bushels of flaxseed (used as an edible oil and a nutrition supplement) in the United States and Kazakhstan, with prices measured in U.S. dollars and quantities measured in millions of bushels.

a. In which country is flaxseed cheaper to produce? In which country do the consumers of flaxseed value it more?

b. Complete the bottom table by describing each nation's willingness to import or export flaxseed at each price. One row has been done for you as an example.

c. If the United States and Kazakhstan entered into free trade with only one another, what would be the price of flaxseed, and what quantity of flaxseed would be traded?

d. For each of the following four constituent groups, determine whether free trade between the United States and Kazakhstan

	Price	$2	$4	$6	$8	$10	$12	$14	$16	$18	$20
U.S.	Q_D	12	11	10	9	8	7	6	5	4	3
	Q_S	0	1	2	3	4	5	6	7	8	9

	Price	$2	$4	$6	$8	$10	$12	$14	$16	$18	$20
Kz	Q_D	5.5	5	4.5	4	3.5	3	2.5	2	1.5	1
	Q_S	1.5	3	4.5	6	7.5	9	10.5	12	13.5	15

At a price of . . .	the United States would be willing to . . .	and Kazakhstan would be willing to . . .
$2	import 12 million bushels	import 4 million bushels
$4		
$6		
$8		
$10		
$12		
$14		
$16		
$18		
$20		

would help or harm the members of that group. Calculate the change in consumer or producer surplus in each country as necessary to support your claim.

  i. The buyers of flaxseed in Kazakhstan

  ii. The sellers of flaxseed in Kazakhstan

  iii. The buyers of flaxseed in the United States

  iv. The sellers of flaxseed in the United States

e. Suppose the sellers of flaxseed in the importing country successfully lobby for protection in the form of a $4 tariff per bushel of flaxseed. Describe the impact of this tariff on flaxseed trade and on the consumer and producer surpluses you calculated in part d. How much deadweight loss does this tariff generate?

WORK IT OUT

For interactive, step-by-step help in solving this problem, go online.

According to Chinese government statistics, China imported over 1 million cars in 2012. Let's see what would happen to consumer and producer surplus if China were to ban car imports. To keep things simple, let's assume that if car imports were banned, the equilibrium price of cars (holding quality constant!) would rise by $5,000.

a. In the figure, shade the area that represents the total gains when car imports are allowed into China.

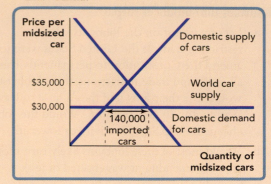

b. Once China bans the import of cars, what is the dollar value of the lost gains from trade? (*Hint:* The chapter provides the formula.)

c. If car imports are banned, Chinese car producers will be better off and Chinese car consumers will be worse off. A polygon in the figure shows the surplus that will shift from consumers to producers. Write the word "Transfer" in this polygon. (*Hint:* It's not the area you calculated in part b.)

d. If quality *weren't* held constant, what would you expect to happen to the additional Chinese cars produced after the import ban? Would they be as good as the ones that used to be imported? (*Hint:* Which types of cars do you think that China imports? Low-quality or high-quality? Why?)

MRUNIVERSITY
AN ONLINE EDUCATION PLATFORM

MARGINAL REVOLUTION UNIVERSITY VIDEOS

Tariffs and Protectionism

mruniversity.com/tariffs

Problems: **1–3, 7–10, 13, 14**

Arguments Against International Trade

mruniversity.com/arguments-trade

Problems: **2, 5, 6, 12**

OFFICE HOURS

Office Hours: Trade

mruniversity.com/trade

Problems: **14**

10

Externalities: When the Price Is Not Right

On a sunny day in June 1924, a young man developed a blister on his toe after playing a game of tennis. A week later, he was dead from a bacterial infection. The young man had been given the best medical care possible: He was the son of the president of the United States. President Coolidge wept when he learned that all the "power and the glory of the presidency" could not prevent the death of his son from a simple blister.

The president's son, Calvin Jr., was probably killed by a bacterium called *Staphylococcus aureus* or *staph* for short. Penicillin could easily have cured him, but penicillin was not discovered until 1928. When penicillin and other antibiotics became widely available in the 1940s, they were hailed as miracle drugs. Dying from a blister became a thing of the past—until recently.

Staph has evolved. Today it is resistant to penicillin and some "superbug" strains are resistant to almost all antibiotics. The Centers for Disease Control estimate that at least 11,000 people in the United States are killed every year from staph infections that are resistant to antibiotics. *Staphylococcus aureus* is now spreading around the globe.

Antibiotic resistance is a product of evolution. Any population of bacteria includes some bacteria with unusual traits, such as the ability to resist an antibiotic's attack. When a person takes an antibiotic, the drug kills the defenseless bacteria, leaving the unusually strong bacteria behind. Without competition for resources, these stronger bacteria multiply. When the same antibiotic is applied again and again, the stronger bacteria get even stronger until after many generations of bacteria, the antibiotic loses its power to perform miracles.

Evolution is a powerful force so it was inevitable that staph would grow resistant to penicillin eventually, but staph has grown more resistant more quickly than was necessary. The problem is that antibiotics are overused.

Antibiotic users get all the benefits of antibiotics but they do not bear all of the costs. The person who demands an antibiotic must pay a **private cost** for the antibiotic, the market price. But because bacteria spread widely, each use of an antibiotic creates a small increase in bacterial resistance, which raises the probability that other people could die from a simple infection. For example, when a teenager takes tetracycline for acne, there is an increase in antibiotic-resistant bacteria on the skin of *other* members of his or her family. Antimicrobial

A **private cost** is a cost paid by the consumer or the producer.

183

detergents that are washed down the sink enter into the environment where they increase the proportion of resistant bacteria for us all. Almost half of all antibiotics are used on farm animals, not to treat disease but primarily because they accelerate growth (the FDA has recently begun to phase out some antibiotic use in animals to help prevent resistance). Bacteria that develop resistance on the farm travel onto and into human beings, where they may cause incurable infections.

In a sense, each use of antibiotics pollutes the environment with more resistant and stronger bacteria. Thus, each use of antibiotics creates an **external cost,** a cost that is paid not by the consumers or producers of antibiotics but by bystanders to the transaction. The **social cost** of antibiotic use is the cost to everyone: the private cost plus the external cost.

Since the external cost is not paid by consumers or producers, it is not built into the price of antibiotics. So when patients or farmers choose whether to use more antibiotics, they compare their private benefits with the market price, but they ignore the external costs just as a factory will ignore the cost of the pollution that it emits into the atmosphere (assuming there are no regulations forbidding this). Since antibiotic users ignore some relevant costs of their actions, antibiotics are overused. Alternatively stated, since the price of antibiotics does not include all the costs of using antibiotics, the price sends an imperfect signal—the price is too low and so antibiotics are overused. Thus, the problem of antibiotic resistance is about evolution *and* economics. Evolution drives antibiotic resistance, but the process is happening much faster than we would like because antibiotic users do not take into account the external costs of their choices.

External Costs, External Benefits, and Efficiency

This chapter is about products, like antibiotics, for which some of the costs or benefits of the product fall on bystanders. These costs or benefits are called external costs or external benefits or, for short, **externalities.** (External costs are sometimes also called negative externalities, and external benefits are sometimes also called positive externalities.) When externalities are significant, markets work less well and government action can increase social surplus.

In Chapter 4, we showed that a market equilibrium maximizes consumer plus producer surplus (the gains from trade). But maximizing consumer plus producer surplus isn't so great if bystanders are harmed in the process. Everyone counts, not just the consumers and producers of a particular product. So, when we evaluate how well a market with externalities is working, we want to look at **social surplus,** namely consumer surplus plus producer surplus plus everyone else's surplus.

To show why a market with externalities *does not* maximize *social surplus,* it's useful to briefly review why a market equilibrium *does* maximize *consumer plus producer surplus* (see also Chapter 4). The key is to remember that you can read the value of the *n*th unit of a good from the height of the demand curve and the cost of the *n*th unit of a good from the height of the supply curve. For example, imagine that buyers and sellers are currently exchanging 99 units of a good. What is the value to buyers and the costs to sellers of one additional unit, the 100th unit? In Figure 10.1, you can read the value to buyers from the height of the demand curve at the 100th unit, namely $22. You can read

An **external cost** is a cost paid by people other than the consumer or the producer trading in the market.

The **social cost** is the cost to everyone: the private cost plus the external cost.

Externalities are external costs or external benefits, that is, costs or benefits, respectively, that fall on bystanders.

Social surplus is consumer surplus plus producer surplus plus everyone else's surplus.

the cost to sellers from the height of the supply curve at the 100th unit, namely $10. Since the value of the 100th unit exceeds the additional cost of the 100th unit, there is an incentive to trade, namely an opportunity to increase consumer and producer surplus. Following this logic, trade is mutually profitable up until the 210th unit is sold. The value to buyers of the 210th unit is $13 and the cost to sellers of producing that additional unit is $13 so at this point there are no further incentives to trade. If any fewer units were traded, gains from trade would be left on the table. If any more units were traded, the cost of those units would exceed their value. Thus, gains from trade are maximized at the market equilibrium of 210 units.

Let's call the price and quantity that maximize social surplus the **efficient equilibrium.** If there are no significant externalities, the market equilibrium is also the efficient equilibrium (because if there are no significant external costs or benefits, maximizing producer plus consumer surplus is the same as maximizing everyone's surplus). But if there are significant externalities, the market equilibrium is no longer the efficient equilibrium, as we will now show.

External Costs

Panel A of Figure 10.2 on the next page shows the market equilibrium for antibiotics. As usual, the market equilibrium maximizes consumer plus producer surplus. But now the use of antibiotics creates an external cost, a cost to people who are neither buying nor selling antibiotics. At the market equilibrium, the price of a round of antibiotics—such as your doctor would prescribe to cure an infection—is $5 and we will assume that the external cost of antibiotic use is $7, a number that is consistent with one study of the matter.[1] The private cost plus the external cost is the social cost of antibiotic use.

In Panel B of Figure 10.2, we add the external cost to the supply curve to show the social cost curve. Because the social cost curve takes into account *all* of the costs of antibiotic use, we use the social cost curve to figure out the **efficient quantity,** the quantity that maximizes social surplus. The efficient quantity $Q_{Efficient}$ is found where the demand curve intersects the social cost curve.

To see exactly why the market equilibrium is *not* efficient, let's consider the value to buyers and the social costs of the Q_{Market} unit of the good. The height of the demand curve at the Q_{Market} unit (the black arrow labeled "Private value") tells us that this unit has a private value of $5. The height of the social cost curve at Q_{Market} (the green arrow labeled "Social cost") tells us that this unit has a social cost of $12. Thus, producing this unit creates a social loss or deadweight loss of $7. Following this logic, you can see that reducing output increases social surplus so long as the social cost of an additional prescription of antibiotics exceeds the buyer value, that is, so long as the social cost curve lies above the demand curve. Thus, to maximize social surplus, output should be reduced to $Q_{Efficient}$, the point at which the social cost curve intersects the demand curve and where the social costs of an additional unit just equal the value.

FIGURE 10.1

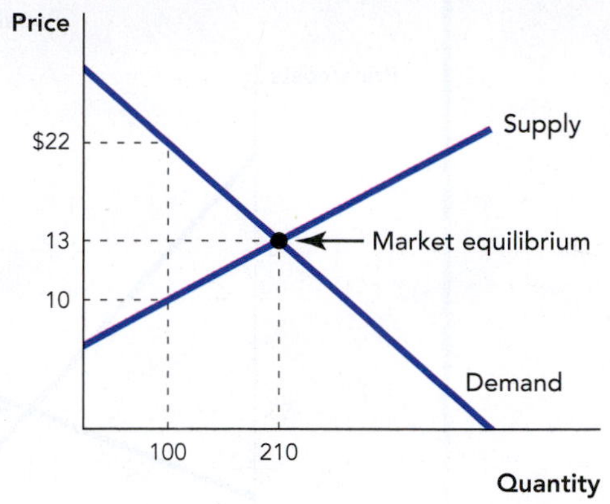

Reviewing Gains from Trade The value of the 100th unit to buyers is $22. The cost of the 100th unit to sellers is $10. At the 100th unit, there is a $12 gain from exchange. Gains from trade are maximized when a total of 210 units are exchanged. Notice that the value of the 210th unit is just equal to the cost of the 210th unit.

The **efficient equilibrium** is the price and quantity that maximize social surplus.

The **efficient quantity** is the quantity that maximizes social surplus.

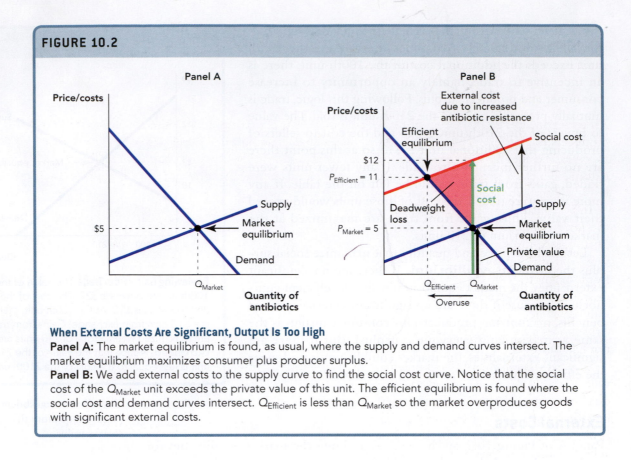

FIGURE 10.2

Panel A

Panel B

When External Costs Are Significant, Output Is Too High
Panel A: The market equilibrium is found, as usual, where the supply and demand curves intersect. The market equilibrium maximizes consumer plus producer surplus.
Panel B: We add external costs to the supply curve to find the social cost curve. Notice that the social cost of the Q_{Market} unit exceeds the private value of this unit. The efficient equilibrium is found where the social cost and demand curves intersect. $Q_{Efficient}$ is less than Q_{Market} so the market overproduces goods with significant external costs.

A final way of illustrating the overuse of antibiotics is to notice that *if the users did bear all the costs of antibiotic use, that is, if the private cost included the $7 external cost, then the supply curve would shift upward and would be the same as the social cost curve.* The market equilibrium would then be the same as the efficient equilibrium, that is, buyers would purchase $Q_{Efficient}$ units. But for determining efficient quantities, who bears the costs is irrelevant—*costs are costs regardless of who bears them.* Thus, $Q_{Efficient}$ is the efficient quantity when antibiotic users pay all of the costs *and* when they pay only some of the costs— the only difference is that when other people bear some of the costs, antibiotic users purchase more antibiotics, so $Q_{Market} > Q_{Efficient}$.

The last way of explaining why antibiotics are overused suggests one potential solution to the problem of external costs. If antibiotic users had to pay a tax just equal to the external costs, $7, they would demand only the amount $Q_{Efficient}$. Remember from Chapter 6 that we can analyze a tax by shifting the supply curve up by the amount of the tax. Thus, in Figure 10.2, notice that a tax set equal to the level of the external cost would shift the supply curve up so that it exactly overlays the social cost curve. The market quantity would then fall from Q_{Market} to $Q_{Efficient}$. Thus, a tax set equal to the external cost would once again mean that the market equilibrium was the efficient equilibrium!

A tax on an ordinary good increases deadweight loss, as discussed in Chapter 6, but a tax on a good with an external cost reduces deadweight loss and raises revenue. For these reasons, there is a strong argument for taxing goods with external costs. Such taxes are often called **Pigouvian taxes,** after the economist Arthur C. Pigou (1877–1959) who first focused attention on

A **Pigouvian tax** is a tax on a good with external costs.

externalities and how they might be corrected with taxes. We will return to look at solutions to external cost problems in more detail after we have examined a parallel issue, external benefits.

External Benefits

An **external benefit** is a benefit to people other than the consumers or the producers trading in the market. Consider, for example, another medical good, vaccines. Vaccines benefit the person who is vaccinated but they also create an external benefit for other people because people who have been vaccinated are less likely to harbor and spread disease-causing viruses.*

In a typical year, for example, some 36,000 Americans die from the flu, a contagious respiratory disease caused by influenza viruses. Fortunately, millions of Americans get a yearly vaccination—a "flu shot"—that is usually effective at preventing the flu. Flu viruses spread from person to person when someone who *already has the flu* coughs or sneezes. As a result, when one person gets a flu shot, the expected number of people who get the flu falls by more than one. So getting a flu shot is a real public service. Get a flu shot. The life you save may not be your own.

So what's the problem? The problem is not the millions of Americans who get a flu shot—it's the even larger number of Americans who don't get one. When an individual compares the private costs and benefits of getting a flu shot, it may be quite sensible not to get one. It takes time to get a shot, it costs money, and often a slight fever and ache are associated with the vaccine itself. The problem is that the person getting the shot bears all these costs but doesn't receive all the benefits. As a result, fewer people get flu shots than is efficient.

In Figure 10.3 on the next page, for example, we show the demand and supply of vaccines. Demanders compare their private value of vaccines with their private costs and purchase Q_{Market} units at the price P_{Market}. Vaccination, however, reduces the probability that a disease spreads so there are external benefits from vaccination. The social value curve counts *all* the benefits of vaccine use, the private value plus the external benefits, so the efficient quantity is found where the social value curve intersects the supply curve.

To see exactly why the market equilibrium is not efficient, consider in Figure 10.3 the private and social value of the Q_{Market} unit of vaccination. This unit has a private cost of $20 (the black arrow labeled "Private cost"), but it has a social value of $40 (the green arrow labeled "Social value"). Thus, consuming more units would increase social surplus. Following this logic, you can see that increasing output increases social surplus so long as the social value of an additional flu shot exceeds the private cost, that is, so long as the social value curve is above the supply curve. Thus, to maximize social surplus, output should increase to $Q_{Efficient}$, the unit for which social value just equals the costs of production.

A final way of illustrating the underuse of vaccines is to notice that *if* people who got a flu shot did receive all the benefits of vaccination, then their demand curve would shift upward by $20 and would be the same as the social

An **external benefit** is a benefit received by people other than the consumers or producers trading in the market.

A private cost and a social benefit

COMMERCIAL EYE/GETTY IMAGES

---

* An antibiotic could also have an external benefit in the case of infections that can be easily transmitted. Not all infections are easily transmitted, however, and the external costs due to antibiotic resistance appear to be much larger than any external benefits.

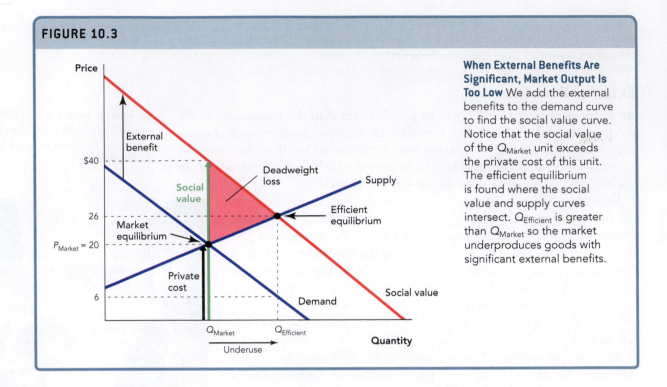

FIGURE 10.3

When External Benefits Are Significant, Market Output Is Too Low We add the external benefits to the demand curve to find the social value curve. Notice that the social value of the Q_{Market} unit exceeds the private cost of this unit. The efficient equilibrium is found where the social value and supply curves intersect. $Q_{Efficient}$ is greater than Q_{Market} so the market underproduces goods with significant external benefits.

A **Pigouvian subsidy** is a subsidy on a good with external benefits.

value curve. The market equilibrium would then be the same as the efficient equilibrium, that is, buyers would purchase $Q_{Efficient}$ units. But for determining efficiency, *who* receives the benefits is irrelevant—benefits are benefits regardless of who receives them. Thus, $Q_{Efficient}$ is the efficient quantity when vaccine users receive all of the benefits of vaccination *and* when they receive only some of the benefits—the only difference is that when other people receive some of the benefits, fewer people purchase flu shots, so $Q_{Market} < Q_{Efficient}$.

The last way of thinking about the problem of external benefits also suggests one potential solution. If every time someone was vaccinated, they were given a subsidy of $20, the monetary equivalent of the external benefit, they would demand the amount $Q_{Efficient}$. Recall from Chapter 6 that we can analyze a subsidy by shifting up the demand curve by the amount of the subsidy. Thus, in Figure 10.3, notice that a subsidy set equal to the level of the external benefit would shift the demand curve up and increase the market quantity from Q_{Market} to $Q_{Efficient}$. In other words, if set correctly, a subsidy will make the market equilibrium equal to the efficient equilibrium. In addition, unlike in Chapter 6 where we looked at subsidies on ordinary goods, a subsidy on a good with an external benefit will reduce deadweight loss, thereby increasing social surplus.

A subsidy on a good with an external benefit is often called a **Pigouvian subsidy,** again after Pigou, who first discussed these issues. Another way of thinking about Pigouvian taxes and subsidies is to recall from Chapter 7 that market prices are signals. But when there are external costs or benefits, the market price sends the wrong signal. If there are external costs, the market price is too low, thus resulting in overconsumption. A Pigouvian tax increases the price so that the after-tax price sends the correct signal. Similarly, if there are external benefits, the market price is too high, thus resulting in underconsumption. A Pigouvian subsidy reduces the price so that the after-subsidy price sends the correct signal.

Let's look in more detail at how to solve problems caused by external costs or benefits. We will discuss private solutions to problems created by externalities and three types of solutions involving government: taxes and subsidies (which we have mentioned already), command and control, and tradable permits.

Private Solutions to Externality Problems

In a classic paper on externalities, the Nobel Prize–winning economist James Meade wrote that the market for honey was inefficient. As they make honey, bees pollinate fruits and vegetables, which is an important benefit to farmers. Since pollination is an external benefit of honey production, Meade argued there was too little honey being made.

Meade was right about the bees, but wrong about the market for honey. Bee pollination is a thriving business for which beekeepers are paid. In fact, in the United States, beekeepers manage around half a billion bees that they truck around the country to rent out to farmers. Since farmers pay beekeepers to pollinate their crops, the "external benefit" becomes **internalized**—the beekeepers earn money from the pollination of fruits and vegetables and so expand production toward the efficient quantity, the quantity that takes into account the benefits of bees for honey production and for fruit and vegetable production.[2]

The lesson of the bees is that our earlier story was a bit too pessimistic. The market equilibrium can be efficient even when there are externalities, *if* there is systematic trading in those externalities. To see which externalities the market can handle, let's take a closer look at why the market for pollination works reasonably well.

The market for pollination works because transaction costs are low and property rights are clearly defined. **Transaction costs** are all the costs necessary to reach an agreement. The costs of identifying and bringing buyers and sellers together, bargaining, and drawing up a contract are all transaction costs. Transaction costs are low for beekeepers and farmers because farms are large and bees don't fly that far. So when a beekeeper places bees in the center of a large farm, the beekeeper and the farmer know that the bees will pollinate the crops owned by the farmer who is paying and not pollinate some other farmer's crops. As a result, the externality from bees is limited to one farmer at a time and can be internalized with one transaction.

Property rights over farms and bees are also clearly defined. Everyone knows that the beekeeper has the right to the benefits created by bee pollination, so if the farmer wants bees to pollinate his crops, he must pay the beekeeper. This works for beekeepers and farmers, but as you will see, property rights in other externalities are not as clearly defined and this makes transactions more difficult; you might say that unclear property rights are a type of transaction cost, since they make it harder to trade.

It's not so difficult for beekeepers to trade with farmers, but how many transactions would it take to internalize the external benefit created when someone has a flu shot? When one person is vaccinated, thousands of other people benefit by a small amount, especially if the vaccinated person spends a lot of time in airports. When Alex has the flu and coughs while boarding a plane, he could spread the flu virus to dozens of other people, each of whom

Internalizing an externality means adjusting incentives so that decision makers take into account all the benefits and costs of their actions, private and social.

Transaction costs are all the costs necessary to reach an agreement.

Bees create external beenefits.

ISTOCK/GETTY IMAGES

could in turn pass it on to many others. If Alex receives a flu shot, all these people are better off. In theory, if each of these people paid Alex a small amount for getting a flu shot, Alex would be more likely to get a flu shot. But the transaction costs of arranging a deal like this are enormous—simply to identify the beneficiaries is difficult and getting thousands of them to send a check to Alex is next to impossible (trust us, we have tried!).

What about property rights? We assumed that other people might be willing to pay Alex to get a flu shot because the flu shot creates an external benefit. But when Alex spreads the flu, he imposes an external cost on other people. Maybe Alex should have to pay other people when he doesn't get a flu shot! Even when other transaction costs are low, if property rights are not well defined—who should have to pay whom—it will be difficult to solve externality problems with bargaining.

Ronald Coase, another Nobel Prize winner, summarized the situations in which markets alone can solve the externality problems in what has come to be called the **Coase theorem.** The Coase theorem says that if transaction costs are low and property rights are clearly defined, then private bargains will ensure that the market equilibrium is efficient even when there are externalities. In other words, in these cases trading makes sure that just the right amount of the externality is produced. If there were either too little or too much of the externality, trading would push the quantity to the optimum level.

Recall that in a free market, the quantity of goods sold maximizes the sum of consumer and producer surplus. If the conditions of the Coase theorem are met, we can replace this with the even stronger conclusion that in a free market, the quantity of goods sold will maximize social surplus, the sum of consumer, producer, and everyone else's surplus.

But the conditions of the Coase theorem are often *unlikely* to be met. Transaction costs for many externalities are high and property rights are often not clearly defined. Thus, markets alone will *not* solve all externality problems.

The importance of the Coase theorem lies not in suggesting that markets alone might solve externality problems, but in suggesting a solution—the creation of new markets. If property rights can be clearly defined and transaction costs reduced, then a market for externalities might develop. If such a market does develop, we know from the Coase theorem that it will have all the efficiency properties of ordinary markets.

Government can play a role in defining property rights and reducing transaction costs. In fact, governments have helped to create working markets in many externalities, verifying the insights of the Coase theorem. Next, we discuss one of these new markets, a market in the right to emit pollution.

Government Solutions to Externality Problems

We have already discussed one kind of government solution to externality problems, namely taxes and subsidies. Two other solutions are also common: command and control and tradable allowances for the activity in question. We will look at both of these solutions in the context of another externality, acid rain, and we will also offer some comparisons with taxes and subsidies.

Acid rain damages forests and lakes, it corrodes metal and stone, and in the form of particulates, it creates haze and increases lung diseases such as asthma and bronchitis. Acid rain is caused when sulfur dioxide (SO_2) and

The **Coase theorem** posits that if transaction costs are low and property rights are clearly defined, private bargains will ensure that the market equilibrium is efficient even when there are externalities.

nitrogen oxides (NO_x) are released into the atmosphere. A majority of SO_2 and a significant fraction of NO_x are created in the process of generating electricity from coal. Let's look at how the government has reduced the external cost of acid rain.

Command and Control

When external costs are significant, we know that $Q_{Market} > Q_{Efficient}$, so the most obvious (but not necessarily the best) method to reduce the external cost of electricity generation is for the government to order firms to use (or make) less electricity. This is called a command and control method. Command and control methods are not always efficient. The government, for example, issued a command and control regulation that required manufacturers to make clothes washers that use less electricity. *Consumer Reports* reviewed the clothes washers produced under this new standard and the reviewers were not happy with the results:[3]

> Not so long ago you could count on most washers to get your clothes very clean. Not anymore. Our latest tests found huge performance differences among machines. Some left our stain-soaked swatches nearly as dirty as they were before washing. For best results, you'll have to spend $900 or more.

> What happened? As of January [2007], the U.S. Department of Energy has required washers to use 21 percent less energy, a goal we wholeheartedly support. But our tests have found that traditional top-loaders, those with the familiar center-post agitators, are having a tough time wringing out those savings without sacrificing cleaning ability, the main reason you buy a washer.

The problem with command and control is that there are typically many methods to achieve a goal and the government may not have enough information to choose the least costly method. Let's suppose, for example, that the Department of Energy's regulation on clothes washers reduces electricity consumption by 1% (this number is too large but it will do for our purposes). Now let's compare command and control with a tax on electricity consumption that causes people to reduce their electricity consumption by *exactly the same amount*, 1%.[4] Faced with an increase in price, how would people choose to reduce their electricity consumption?

If the price of electricity increased, some people would choose to cut back on electricity by turning their lights off more often or by switching to lower-consumption LED bulbs. Other people would respond by turning down the heat or the air conditioning, or by buying a cover for their pool, or by installing insulation in their attic. The ways in which people would reduce electricity consumption are as different as the people themselves. But notice that probably very few people would respond to an increase in the price of electricity by spending a *lot* more on a clothes washer that saves electricity or by buying a clothes washer that saves electricity but doesn't clean very well. Thus, the government's method of reducing electricity consumption is not the lowest-cost method.

A tax on electricity can reduce the consumption of electricity by exactly the same amount as a regulation on clothes washers but a tax will cost less. The tax costs less because a tax gives people the flexibility to reduce consumption in the way that is least costly to them. Recall from Chapter 7 that prices are signals. A tax on electricity sends a signal to every user of electricity that says "Economize!" But the tax leaves it to each person to use his or her local knowledge and unique preferences to choose the least costly method of economizing.

It's better to reduce electricity consumption with a tax than with a regulation on clothes washers, but we can do even better. After all, we don't really want to reduce *electricity*—we want to reduce *pollutants* like SO_2 and NO_x. It's true that pollutants are a by-product of electricity generation but there are many ways of reducing SO_2 and NO_x other than by producing less electricity. Thus, taxing the pollutants directly is a better way of creating incentives to reduce pollution than is taxing electricity. Taxing the pollutants directly gives firms the maximum flexibility to adopt the least costly methods of reducing pollution. Remember it's the pollutants that are creating the external cost so taxing the pollutants sends the right signal.

Command and control is not always a bad idea. The advantage of using incentives like taxes to control an externality is flexibility. The government corrects the price with a tax or subsidy so the price sends the right signal and people adapt using their own information and preferences (with all the benefits of the price system that we described in Chapters 4 and 7). But flexibility is not always desirable. Consider, for example, one of the great triumphs of humanity—the eradication of smallpox. Smallpox killed 300–500 million people in the twentieth century alone. As late as 1967, 2 million people died and millions more were scarred and blinded from smallpox, but in that year the World Health Organization (WHO) launched a program of mass vaccination, intensive surveillance, and immediate quarantine. The WHO program relied on command and control because so long as *any* reservoir of smallpox remained anywhere on the planet, the virus could reemerge and spread worldwide. To be successful, the WHO could not rely on taxes because it needed everyone to follow its policies—flexibility was not desirable. Fortunately, the WHO program was successful and by 1978 smallpox was extinct—the first and so far the only human infectious disease to be stopped dead in its tracks.[*]

The bottom line is that command and control can be useful if the best approach to a problem is well known and if success requires very strong compliance. If it's important to control the externality at the least possible cost and if the government doesn't have full information, then more flexible approaches such as taxes and subsidies are preferable.

Tradable Allowances

Another type of command and control program is to require that firms reduce pollutants by a specific quantity. In the 1970s, for example, the government limited SO_2 from all generators of electricity to a maximum rate. The problem with this approach is that because of differences in location, fuel, and technology, it's much cheaper to reduce emissions of SO_2 from some firms than from others. By treating all firms the same, the government reduced flexibility and increased the cost of eliminating a given amount of pollution.

A simple example illustrates the problem with quantity restrictions and a potential solution. Suppose that there are two firms. We begin with a command

---

[*] Command and control continues to be used today in handling other infectious diseases. Before registering for classes, for example, school-age children and college and university students must show that they have had their MMR vaccine (preventing measles, mumps, rubella).

and control regulation that limits each firm to 100 tons of SO_2 emissions in a year. Now imagine that reducing pollution at High-Cost Industries is expensive, so High could save $1,100 if it were allowed to produce 101 tons of SO_2 instead of being limited to 100 tons. Low-Cost Industries can control its pollution quite cheaply, so if Low reduces its pollution level even further to 99 tons, its costs increase by only $200.

Now imagine that the CEOs of High and Low approach the head of the Environmental Protection Agency with a proposal. The CEOs suggest that High be allowed to increase its pollution level by 1 ton to 101 tons. High will also pay $500 to Low. In return, Low will cut its pollution level by 1 ton to 99 tons. It's clear why High and Low want the deal—it's profitable. High cuts its pollution control costs by $1,100 for which it pays $500 for a net increase in profit of $600. Low increases its pollution control costs by $200, but it receives a $500 payment for a net increase in profit of $300. But should the EPA accept this deal?

Yes, if the EPA cares about social surplus, it should accept the deal. Notice that pollution stays exactly the same, 200 units, so the deal does not harm the environment. The deal, however, does increase profits by $900 ($600 to High and $300 to Low). Should the EPA care about firm profits? Maybe not directly, but notice why profits increase in this example. Profits increase because the costs of reducing pollution fall. By trading, the firms reduce the cost of eliminating the last unit of pollution from $1,100 to just $200—a $900 fall in costs and that represents an increase in resources available to society.

So, let's ask our question in a different way. Should the EPA care about decreasing the costs of reducing pollution? Of course the answer is yes. If we can reduce the same amount of pollution at lower cost, that means more resources are available for other goods. And the lower the costs of eliminating pollution, the more pollution it makes sense to eliminate.

What we have shown is that trading pollution allowances is like a new technology that reduces pollution at lower cost. The EPA should always be in favor of new technologies to reduce pollution and so it should also be in favor of trades in the right to pollute.

Tradable Allowances in Practice A formal version of the tradable allowances system that we have just described was created by the Clean Air Act of 1990. Under this reform, the EPA distributes pollution allowances to generators of electricity, and each allowance gives the owner the right to emit 1 ton of SO_2. Firms may trade allowances as they see fit and they have organized sophisticated markets in tradable allowances. Firms can even bank allowances for future use. The EPA monitors each firm's emissions of SO_2, and it also tracks how many allowances each firm owns so no firm can emit more pollution than it has allowances for. Congress sets the total number of allowances.

The EPA's tradable allowances program has been very successful, as SO_2 emissions have been reduced, air quality has improved, and illness has been reduced.[5] Remarkably, as shown in Figure 10.4, electricity generation has increased even as SO_2 emissions have decreased.

Should We Trade the Right to Pollute?

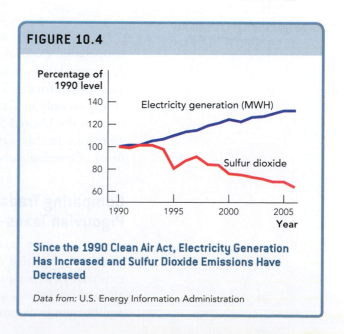

FIGURE 10.4

Percentage of 1990 level

Electricity generation (MWH)

Sulfur dioxide

Since the 1990 Clean Air Act, Electricity Generation Has Increased and Sulfur Dioxide Emissions Have Decreased

Data from: U.S. Energy Information Administration

The EPA's system of tradable allowances is a successful application of the Coase theorem. Recall that the Coase theorem says that markets can internalize externalities when transaction costs are low and property rights are clearly defined. The Clean Air Act of 1990 clearly defined rights to emit SO_2, and the EPA has reduced transaction costs by distributing the allowances, monitoring emissions, and creating a database that tracks ownership. Trading in markets has then allocated the allowances among firms in the way that minimizes the costs of reducing pollution.

One of the most interesting aspects of the market in rights to emit sulfur dioxide is that anyone can participate in this market, not just generators of electricity. We bought the rights to emit 30 pounds of SO_2. We don't intend to emit any pollutants; rather, we bought the rights and ripped them up in order to create more clean air. Environmentalists and industry often oppose one another, but when markets in externalities are created, environmentalists can buy pollutants and industry is happy to sell—as always, trade makes both parties better off.

An important result of the SO_2 trading program is that firms that generate electricity from relatively clean sources such as solar power can make money by selling their pollution allowances. In contrast, firms that generate electricity from relatively dirty sources must buy allowances. In essence, clean energy is subsidized and dirty energy is taxed—thus, a program of tradable allowances correctly reflects the fact that clean energy has lower social costs than dirty energy.

The success of the acid rain program in reducing SO_2 emissions at low cost and concern over global climate change motivated President Barack Obama to propose a tradable allowances plan for carbon dioxide, a greenhouse gas that contributes to global warming. Tradable allowances in carbon dioxide would change the economics of all energy, not just electricity, and would create incentives for firms to move toward nuclear, solar, and biomass fuels that contribute less to global warming. Since global warming is a worldwide problem, tradable allowances ideally would be distributed and bought and sold on a worldwide basis. As of yet, however, not enough cooperation exists in the world community to establish such a system. Smaller programs, however, have been created around the world including in Europe and in California. The California Cap and Trade program limits carbon emissions only in California but it lets California firms buy permits from any firm in the United States that can prove that it has limited its own carbon emissions. In this way, the California program reduces the cost to California firms of limiting carbon emissions to the lowest possible U.S. cost.

The Clean Air Conservancy
has permanently retired 30
pounds of Sulfur Dioxide
emissions allowances on behalf of

**Alex Tabarrok
and
Tyler Cowen**

RETIRED NOVEMBER 2007

30
Pounds

THINK.BREATHE.LIVE.

ALEX TABARROK

We bought the right to pollute.

Comparing Tradable Allowances and Pigouvian Taxes—Advanced Material

There is a close relationship between using Pigouvian taxes and tradable allowances to solve externality problems. A tax set equal to the level of the external cost is equivalent to tradable allowances, where the number of allowances is set equal to the efficient quantity. To achieve the efficient equilibrium in Figure 10.5, for example, the government can either use taxes

FIGURE 10.5

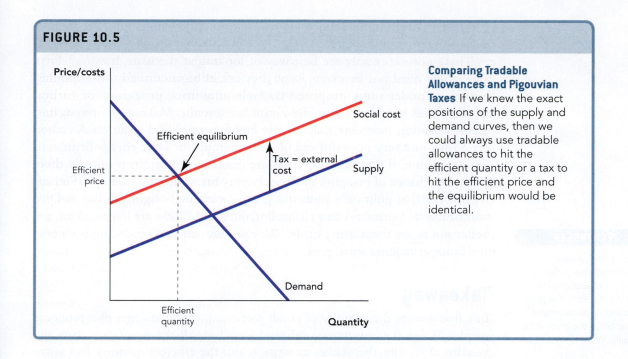

Comparing Tradable Allowances and Pigouvian Taxes If we knew the exact positions of the supply and demand curves, then we could always use tradable allowances to hit the efficient quantity or a tax to hit the efficient price and the equilibrium would be identical.

to raise the price to the efficient price or it can use allowances to reduce the quantity to the efficient quantity. The equilibrium is identical no matter which method is used.

Differences between Pigouvian taxes and tradable allowances do occur when there is uncertainty. Imagine, for example, that we know any quantity above a certain threshold level of SO_2 will acidify thousands of lakes and thus cause an environmental disaster. Any level below the threshold, however, will be acceptable or at least tolerable. In this case, tradable allowances are best because we can set the allowance below the threshold level and be certain that we will avoid disaster. If we set a tax, however, and we don't know the exact position of the supply curve, then we could easily set the tax too low, leading to SO_2 emissions above the threshold level. A fixed quantity, even if tradable, is like a command and control regulation, and just as in our discussion of eliminating smallpox, the best argument for command and control is when flexibility is not a virtue.

On the other hand, sometimes we know a lot about the cost that a unit of SO_2 creates, but we aren't sure about the efficient quantity of pollution because demand and supply are changing. If the supply curve in Figure 10.5 were to shift down, for example, if the cost of producing electricity falls, the efficient quantity will increase. With a Pigouvian tax, the adjustment to the new equilibrium occurs automatically, but with allowances we could be stuck with a quantity of allowances that is much lower than the new efficient quantity. In this case, a Pigouvian tax is best because it can more easily adjust to changes in demand and supply.

The second difference between taxes and pollution allowances is not economic but political. With a tax, firms must pay the government for each ton of pollutant that they emit. With pollution allowances, firms must either use the pollution allowances that they are given or, if they want to emit more, they must buy allowances from other firms. Either way, firms that are given allowances in the initial allocation get a big benefit compared with having to pay taxes. Thus, some people say that pollution allowances equal corrective taxes plus corporate welfare.

That's not necessarily the best way of looking at the issue, however. First, allowances need not be given away; they could be auctioned to the highest bidder, as under some proposed tradable allowance programs for carbon dioxide—this would also raise significant tax revenue. Making progress against global warming, moreover, may require building a political coalition. A carbon tax pushes one very powerful and interested group, the large energy firms, into the opposition. If tradable allowances are instead given to firms initially, there is a better chance of bringing the large energy firms into the coalition. Perhaps it's not fair that politically powerful groups must be bought off, but as Otto von Bismarck, Germany's first chancellor, once said, "Laws are like sausages, it is better not to see them being made." We can only add that producing both laws and sausages requires some pork.

Takeaway

In a free market, the quantity of goods sold maximizes consumer plus producer surplus. When the consumers and producers bear all the significant costs and benefits of trading, the market quantity is also the efficient quantity. But when there are external costs or benefits, the market quantity is not the efficient quantity. If it doesn't bear all the costs of pollution, an electricity generator will emit too much pollution. If a person doesn't receive all the benefits of a flu shot, he or she will choose too few flu shots.

There are three types of government solutions to externality problems: taxes and subsidies, command and control, and tradable allowances. Market prices do not correctly signal true costs and benefits when there are significant external costs or benefits. Taxes and subsidies can adjust prices so that they do send the correct signals. When external costs are significant, the market price is too low, so an optimal tax raises the price. When external benefits are significant, the market price is too high, so an optimal subsidy lowers the price.

Command and control solutions can work but are often high-cost because they are inflexible and do not take advantage of differences in the costs and benefits of eliminating and producing the externality.

The Coase theorem explains that the ultimate source of the externality problem is too few markets. If property rights can be clearly defined and transaction costs reduced, then markets in the externality will solve the problem and will do so at the lowest cost. In recent years, successful markets have been created in the right to emit sulfur dioxide, and new markets are being used to reduce the gases that contribute to global warming.

CHECK YOURSELF

■ Government sets a total quantity of tradable pollution allowances and auctions them off. After the auction, the price for an individual allowance is high. Over time, the price falls dramatically. What does this tell you?

■ The local government has decided to set and apportion tradable allowances for pollution in your neighborhood. Name three groups that would press for a large total quantity of allowances. Name three groups that would press for a smaller total quantity of allowances. Considering these groups, how likely is it that government would set a total quantity of allowances that would achieve an efficient equilibrium?

CHAPTER REVIEW

interactive activity Go online to practice with more examples of these types of problems, including live links to videos, data sources, and feedback.

 Problems in green relate to MRU videos. See the MRU table at the end of the exercises.

KEY CONCEPTS

private cost, p. 183

external cost, p. 184

social cost, p. 184

externalities, p. 184

social surplus, p. 184

efficient equilibrium, p. 185

efficient quantity, p. 185

Pigouvian tax, p. 186

external benefit, p. 187

Pigouvian subsidy, p. 188

internalizing an externality, p. 189

transaction costs, p. 189

Coase theorem, p. 190

FACTS AND TOOLS

1. Let's sort the following eight items into private costs, external costs, private benefits, or external benefits. There's only one correct answer for each of questions a–h.

   a. The price you pay for an iTunes download

   b. The benefit your neighbor receives from hearing you play your pleasant music

   c. The annoyance of your neighbor because she doesn't like your achingly conventional music

   d. The pleasure you receive from listening to your iTunes download

   e. The price you pay for a security system for your home

   f. The safety you enjoy as a result of having the security system

   g. The crime that is more likely to occur to your neighbor once a criminal sees a "Protected by alarm" sticker on your window

   h. The extra safety your neighbor might experience because criminals tend to stay away from neighborhoods that have a lot of burglar alarms

2. If the students at your school started saying "thank you" to friends who got flu shots, would this tend to reduce the undersupply of people who get flu shots? Why or why not?

3. a. Consider a factory, located in the middle of nowhere, producing a nasty smell. As long as no one is around to experience the unpleasant odor, are any externalities produced?

   b. Suppose that a family moves in next door to the smelly factory. Do we now have an externalities problem? If so, who is causing it: the factory by producing the smell, the family by moving in next door, or both?

   c. Suppose that the family clearly possesses the right to a pleasant-smelling environment. Does this mean that the factory will be required to stop producing the bad smell? What could happen instead? There are many right answers. (*Hint:* Think about the Coase theorem. Actually, it's *always* a good idea to think about the Coase theorem, whether the topic is smelly factories, labor–management disputes, international peace negotiations, or divorce settlements.)

4. Considering what we've learned about externalities, should human-caused global warming be *completely* stopped? Explain, using the language of social benefits and social costs.

5. In the following cases, the markets are in equilibrium, but there are externalities. In each case, determine whether there is an external benefit or cost and estimate its size. Finally, decide between a tax or a subsidy as a simple way to compensate for the externality. Fill out the table that follows with your answers.

   a. In the market for automobiles, the private benefit of one more small SUV is $20,000 and the social cost of one more small SUV is $30,000.

   b. In the market for fashionable clothes, the marginal social benefit of one more dress per person is $100, and the marginal private benefit is $500. Bonus: Can you tell an externality story that makes sense of these numbers?

Case	External Cost or Benefit?	Size of External Benefit (or Cost If Negative)	Tax It or Subsidize It?
a. SUVs			
b. Fashionable clothes			
c. Ideas			

c. In the market for really good ideas, ideas that will dramatically change the world for the better, the private benefit of one more really good idea (from speaker's fees, book sales, patents, etc.) is $1 million. The marginal social benefit is $1 billion.

6. In which cases are the Coase theorem's assumptions likely to be true? In other words, when will the parties be likely to strike an efficient bargain? How do you know?

a. My neighbor wants me to cut down an ugly shrub in my front yard. The ugly shrub, of course, imposes an external cost on him and on his property value.

b. My neighbors all would love for me to get that broken-down Willys Jeep off my front lawn. It's been years now, after all. And would it be too much for me to paint the house and fill up that 6-foot deep ditch in the front yard? The whole neighborhood is annoyed.

c. A coal-fired electricity plant dumps its leftover hot water into the nearby lake, killing the naturally occurring fish. Thousands of homes line the banks of the lake.

d. A coal-fired electricity plant dumps its leftover hot water into the nearby river, killing the naturally occurring fish downstream. There is one large fishery 1 mile downstream affected by this. After that, the water cools enough so it's not a problem.

7. With electricity, we saw that it was important to tax the pollutant rather than the final product itself. In the following cases, will the proposed taxes actually hit at the source of the external cost, or will it only land an inefficient glancing blow? What kind of tax might be better?

a. Gas-guzzling cars create more pollution, so the government should tax big SUVs at a higher rate.

b. All-night liquor stores seem to generate unruly behavior in nearby neighborhoods, so owners of all-night liquor stores should pay higher property taxes.

c. Bell-bottom jeans insist on coming back every few years, and their ugliness creates external costs for all who see them. Therefore, bell-bottom jeans should be taxed heavily.

d. American parents are worried about their children hearing too much profanity on television. Congress decides to tax TV shows based on the number of profane words used on the shows.

8. When the government expands the number of pollution allowances, does that increase the cost of polluting or cut it? What about when the number of pollution allowances is cut back?

9. Maxicon is opening a new coal-fired power plant, but the government wants to keep pollution down.

a. Based on what we've seen in this chapter, which is a more efficient way to reduce pollution: commanding Maxicon to use one particular air-scrubbing technology that will reduce pollution by 25% or commanding Maxicon to reduce pollution by 25%?

b. If a corrupt government just grants Maxicon all of the (tradable) pollution permits in the entire nation (even though there are many energy companies), does this guarantee that Maxicon will engage in an enormous amount of pollution? Why or why not?

THINKING AND PROBLEM SOLVING

10. When someone is sick, the patient's decision to take an antibiotic imposes costs on others—it helps bacteria evolve resistance faster. But it also gives free benefits to others: It may slow down the spread of infectious disease the same way that vaccinations do. Thus, antibiotics can create external *costs* as well as external *benefits*. In theory, these could cancel each other out, so that just the right amount of antibiotics is being used. But economists think that, on balance, there is overuse of antibiotics, not underuse. Why? (*Hint:* Think on the margin!)

11. A flu shot typically costs about $25–$50 but some firms offer their employees free flu shots. Why might a firm prefer to offer its employees free flu shots if the alternative is an equally costly wage increase?

12. "The environment is priceless." What evidence do you have that this statement is incorrect?

13. Cultural influences often create externalities, for good and ill. A happy movie might make people smile more, which improves the lives of people who don't see the movie. A fashion trend for tight-fitting clothing might hurt the body image of people who think they won't look good in the trendy clothing.

    Let's consider the market for one cultural good that unrealistically raises expectations about the opposite sex: the romance novel. In romance novels, men are dangerous yet safe, they are wealthy yet never at work, they ride high-speed motorcycles yet never get in terrible accidents, they look fantastic even though they never waste endless hours at the gym, and so on. (Of course, advertising that focuses on sexy female models may also unrealistically raise expectations about the opposite sex so feel free to change our example as you see best.)

    a. Consider the following market. Romance novels impose an external cost on men, who have to try to live up to these unrealistic expectations. Illustrate the effect of this external cost in the figure.

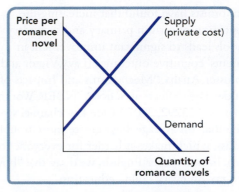

b. Illustrate in the figure the deadweight loss from the externality, before a tax or other solution is imposed.

c. If the government decides to compensate for the externality by imposing a tax on romance novels, should the tax be high enough to stop everyone from reading the novels? Why or why not?

d. Show graphically how big the tax should be per novel.

e. As long as the government spends the money efficiently, does it matter what the government spends the money from the "romance novel tax" on? In other words, could the government just use the money to pay for necessary roads and bridges, or does it need to spend the money to fix the harmful social effects of romance novels?

14. Green Pastures Apartments wants to build a playground to increase demand for its larger-sized apartments but is worried that it will be overcrowded with tenants from the Still Waters Mobile Estates and Twin Pines Townhomes developments nearby.

    a. What type of externality is the playground: external cost or external benefit?

    b. What type of compromise might Green Pastures be able to make with Still Waters and Twin Pines so that all three developments will benefit from the playground? More than one answer is possible, but give just one based on reasoning from this chapter.

15. In Chapter 6, we said that taxes create deadweight losses. When we tax goods with external costs, should we worry about deadweight losses? Why or why not?

16. Economists have found that increasing the proportion of girls in primary and secondary schools leads to significant improvement in students' cognitive outcomes (Lavy, Victor and Schlosser, Analia. "Mechanisms and Impacts of Gender Peer Effects at School." NBER Working Paper No. 13292, 2007.) One key channel seems to be that, on average, boys create more trouble in class, which makes it harder for everyone to learn. In newspaper English, we'd say that "boys are a tax on every child's education."

   a. Using the tools of this chapter, do girls in a classroom provide external costs or benefits? What about boys?

   b. Just based on this study, if you are a parent of a boy, would you rather your son be in a class with mostly boys or mostly girls? What if you are the parent of a girl?

   c. Who should be taxed in this situation? Can you see any problems implementing this tax?

17. In the example of honeybees, we said that the farmers pay the beekeepers for pollination services. But why don't the beekeepers pay the fruit farmers? After all, the beekeepers need the fruit farmers to make honey, so why does the payment go one way and not the other? (*Hint:* What if the honey produced by some fruits and vegetables such as almonds is bitter?)

18. A government is deciding between command and control solutions versus tax and subsidy solutions to solve an externality problem. In each case, explain why you think one is better, using arguments from the chapter.

   a. Suppose that whales are threatened with extinction because a large number of people like to eat whale meat. Governments are torn between banning all whaling except for certain religious ceremonies and heavily taxing all whale meat. Assume that only a few countries in the world consume whale meat, and that they have fairly efficient governments.

   b. Fires create external costs because they spread from one building to another. Should governments encourage subsidies to install sprinklers or should they just mandate that everyone have sprinklers?

   c. Pets who procreate can create external costs due to problems with stray animals. Strays are extremely common on the streets of poor countries. Sterilization can solve the problem, but is a tax/subsidy or command and control a better method to encourage sterilization? Does the best solution depend on the sex of the animal?

CHALLENGES

19. Before Coase presented his theorem, economists who wanted economic efficiency argued that people should be responsible for the damage they do—they should pay for the social costs of their actions. This advice fits nicely with notions of personal responsibility. Explain how the Coase theorem refutes this older argument.

20. A government is torn between selling annual pollution allowances and setting an annual pollution tax. Unlike in the messy real world, this government is quite certain that it can achieve the same price and quantity either way. It wants to choose the method that will pull in more government tax revenue. Is selling allowances better for revenues or is setting a pollution tax better, or will both raise exactly the same amount of revenue? (*Hint:* Recall that tax revenue is a rectangle. Compare the size of the tax rectangle in Figure 10.5 with the most someone will pay for the right to pollute at the efficient level.)

21. Palm Springs, California, was once the playground of the rich and famous—for example, the town has a Frank Sinatra Drive, a Bob Hope Drive, and a Bing Crosby Drive. The city once had a law against building any structure that could cast a shadow on anyone else's property between 9 am and 3 pm (*Source:* Armen Alchian and William Allen. 1964. *University Economics*, Belmont, CA: Wadsworth). What are some alternatives to this command and control solution? Are they any better than this approach?

22. At indoor shopping malls, who makes sure that no business plays music too loud, that no store is closed too often, and that the common areas aren't polluted with garbage? What incentive does this party have to prevent these externalities? Does your answer help explain why parents are quite happy to let their preteen and teen children stroll the malls?

WORK IT OUT

For interactive, step-by-step help in solving this problem, go online.

A local town is under pressure from voters to close a polluting factory. The head of the homeowner's organization argues that the pollution is a menace, and if the full external costs of the pollution were included, the factory would be unprofitable. The homeowners calculate that the pollution generates an external cost of $3,000,000 per year in medical bills and $1,000,000 per year in suppressed property values (the difference in home prices with and without the pollution). The factory, on its books, makes a profit of $5,000,000 per year.

a. What is the external cost of the pollution?

b. If the factory is forced to consider the total social costs of pollution, would it be profitable?

c. How much could the town tax the factory before profits became zero?

d. What does the Coase theorem suggest about negotiations between the town and the factory?

MARGINAL REVOLUTION UNIVERSITY VIDEOS

An Introduction to Externalities

mruniversity.com/externalities

Problems: **1, 10, 11, 13–16**

External Benefits

mruniversity.com/external-benefits

Problems: **2, 5, 14–16**

Command and Control Solutions

mruniversity.com/command-control

Problems: **4, 12, 18, 21**

The Coase Theorem

mruniversity.com/coase

Problems: **3, 6, 7, 17, 19**

Should We Trade the Right to Pollute?

mruniversity.com/pollution-permits

Problems: **8, 20, 22**

A Deeper Look at Tradeable Allowances

mruniversity.com/tradeable-allowances

Problems: **9**

11

Costs and Profit Maximization Under Competition

Drive through the Texas countryside and standing alone in a field of wheat, you will often see a nodding donkey. In Texas, a nodding donkey isn't an animal but an oil pump. Most oil comes from giant oil fields, but in the United States there are over 400,000 "stripper oil wells," oil wells that produce 10 barrels or less per day. That's not much per well, but it adds up to nearly a million barrels of oil a day or about 19% of all U.S. production.[1]

Imagine that you are the owner of a stripper oil well and that you want to maximize your profit. Three questions present themselves:

■ What price to set?

■ What quantity to produce?

■ When to enter and exit the industry?

These three questions are basic to any firm. In this chapter, we will be looking at how to answer these questions in a competitive industry. In later chapters, we will look at these questions for a monopolist.

What Price to Set?

The first of these questions—what price should a firm set?—is the easiest to answer because under some conditions, the firm doesn't set prices; it simply accepts the price that is given by the market. So, let's start with the pricing decision.

If the price of oil is $50 per barrel, will you be able to sell your oil for $100 a barrel? Of course not. Oil is pretty much the same wherever it is found in the world (this is not quite true but it's close enough for our purposes), so even your mother probably won't pay much extra just because it's *your* oil. Thus, you can't charge appreciably more than $50 a barrel. What about charging a lower price? You could charge less but why would you? The world market for oil is so large that you can easily sell all that you can produce at the market price. Thus, your pricing decision is easy; you can't sell *any* oil at a price above the market

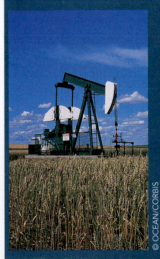

A nodding donkey

© OCEAN/CORBIS

203

price and you can sell *all* your oil at the market price. Thus to maximize profit, you sell at the market price.

To better understand this result, let's recall an insight about the elasticity of demand from Chapter 5: The more and the better the substitutes, the more elastic the demand. With more than 400,000 oil wells in the United States alone, the substitutes for oil from your well are so plentiful that a useful approximation is to think of the demand for your oil as perfectly elastic (flat) at the world price. In Figure 11.1, we compare the world market for oil on the left with the demand for *your* oil on the right.

The price of oil is determined in the world market, where approximately 82 million barrels are bought and sold every day. Your stripper well, however, can at best produce a tiny fraction of world demand, perhaps 10 barrels of oil per day. As a result, the world price of oil won't change by a noticeable amount whether you produce 2, 7, or 10 barrels of oil a day.* This is why in the right panel of Figure 11.1, we draw the demand curve for your oil as flat at the market price—whether you choose to sell 2, 7, or 10 barrels, the price is the same: $50 per barrel. As a result, we say that the competitive firm is a price taker.

Your job as an entrepreneur is greatly simplified if you don't have to decide on the price, and so is our job as economists trying to understand firm behavior. Thus, in this chapter, we are going to simplify by assuming that the demand for a firm's product is perfectly elastic at the market price.

A stripper well doesn't have much influence on the price of oil because there's nothing special about oil from a particular producer, and there are many

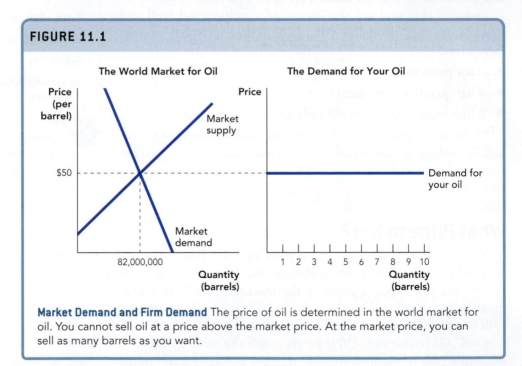

FIGURE 11.1

The World Market for Oil

The Demand for Your Oil

Market Demand and Firm Demand The price of oil is determined in the world market for oil. You cannot sell oil at a price above the market price. At the market price, you can sell as many barrels as you want.

---

* How much is not a noticeable amount? Recall from Chapter 5 that the elasticity of demand is $E_D = \dfrac{\%\Delta Q}{\%\Delta P}$ or, rearranging, $\%\Delta P = \dfrac{\%\Delta Q}{E_D}$. Suppose that the elasticity of demand for oil is 0.5. This means that a 10% increase in the quantity of oil will reduce price by $20\% = \dfrac{10\%}{0.5}$. An increase in the supply of oil of 10 barrels a day is a percentage increase of $\dfrac{10}{82,000,00} \times 100 = 0.000012195122\%$, so price falls by $\dfrac{0.000012195122}{0.5} = 0.0000243902439\%$. At a price of $50 per barrel, this means that an increase in 10 barrels of oil would reduce price to 49.9999987, that is, it would not be noticeable.

buyers and sellers of oil, each small relative to the total market. Generalizing, a perfectly elastic demand curve for firm output is a reasonable approximation when the product being sold is similar across different firms and there are many buyers and sellers, each small relative to the total market. The markets for gold, wheat, paper, steel, lumber, cotton, sugar, vinyl, milk, trucking, glass, Internet domain name registration, and many other goods and services satisfy these conditions.

In addition, don't forget another lesson from Chapter 5: Demand curves are more elastic in the long run. We define the **long run** as the time after all exit and entry has occurred, and the **short run** as the period before exit and entry can occur. Imagine that you are the owner of the only grocery store in a small town. Can you raise prices to exorbitant levels, reasoning that everyone needs food and you are the only seller? In the short run, you probably could. But if you raise prices too high, other sellers will set up shop and your business will be wiped out. Thus, even when there aren't many sellers, there are sometimes many *potential sellers* so a perfectly elastic demand curve can be a reasonable assumption even in a market with a few firms, at least in the long run.

> The **long run** is the time after all exit or entry has occurred.
>
> The **short run** is the period before exit or entry can occur.

Summarizing, economists say that an industry is competitive (or sometimes "perfectly competitive") when firms don't have much influence over the price of their product. This is a reasonable assumption under at least the following conditions:

- The product being sold is similar across sellers.
- There are many buyers and sellers, each small relative to the total market.

  and/or

- There are many potential sellers.

When *do* firms have a lot of influence on the price of their product? Briefly, for purposes of comparison, a firm selling a product for which there are neither many other sellers nor potential sellers has considerable freedom to choose its price. We will analyze how firms choose price and output under these conditions in Chapters 13 through 17.

A competitive firm will sell its output at the market price, but what quantity will it choose to produce?

Maximizing Profits

Before showing how to find the profit maximizing quantity for a competitive firm, let's look at some general principles. Maximizing profits requires knowing what to ignore and what to consider.

Ignore Sunk Costs and Ignore Fixed Costs in the Short Run

Here's a general principle of rational choice: *Ignore what you can't change.* Focus on what you can change. Suppose you pay $15 for a ticket to the movies and the movie is awful. Should you walk out? The price you paid for the ticket is a sunk cost. Your money is gone; you can't get a refund so ignore what you paid for the ticket. Focus on what you can change. Walk out!

Ignoring **sunk cost** can be psychologically difficult. No one likes to admit that they made a mistake. Nevertheless, throwing good money (or time) after bad only makes things worse. By the way, Tyler, at least, practices what he preaches and walks out of movies all the time. Alex finds this harder to do, but he knows he's usually wrong when he continues to watch the movie.

> A **sunk cost** is a cost that cannot be recovered.

CHECK YOURSELF

- In a competitive market, what happens when a firm prices its product above the market price? Below the market price?
- What kind of demand elasticity curve does the competitive firm face?
- How can a firm that produces oil face a very elastic demand curve when the demand for oil is inelastic?

Here's a business example. Suppose that you spend $5,000 to drill your oil well. What influence should that cost have on what quantity you produce? Answer: None. The cost to drill the well is a sunk cost (literally in this case). A sunk cost is a nonrecoverable cost, a cost that you cannot change. Since you can't change a sunk cost it should be ignored.

Here's a trickier example. Suppose that you rent the land on which your oil well sits. One day the landlord tells you that your rent has doubled. Do you change the quantity that you produce? Answer: No. It's tempting to think that since the rent has increased you should produce more. But the rent is the same whether you produce more or less. Since your choice to produce more or less can't change the rent, you should ignore the rent *when deciding what quantity to produce*. Ignore what you can't change.

Why is this example tricky? It's tricky because you can't change the rent by changing how much you produce, but you *can* change the rent by exiting the industry. You are not obligated to pay rent forever. If you exit the industry, your rent will fall. So our principle tells us that we should ignore the rent when choosing what quantity to produce but not when choosing whether or not to exit. More generally, **fixed costs** can't be changed in the short run and so should be ignored for short-run decisions like what quantity to produce, but, fixed costs can be changed in the long run so they should be focused on for long-run decisions like entry or exit.

What makes fixed costs different from sunk costs is that sunk costs are *never* relevant because they cannot be changed by *any* choice. Fixed costs can't be changed by short-run choices but they can be changed by long-run choices and so should be ignored in the former case and focused on in the latter case.

Don't Ignore Opportunity Costs

Maximizing profit requires taking into account *explicit costs* and also *implicit costs*, the costs of foregone alternatives. Imagine that Lian runs a flower shop. Each month she spends $10,000 buying flowers from a wholesaler. The cost of flowers is an **explicit cost** of running her shop, like the rent and electricity that she pays out of pocket by writing a check. But these are not her only costs. If Lian weren't selling flowers, let's suppose that she could be working as a patent attorney earning $7,000 a month. Lian is giving up something of value when she works as a florist, namely the opportunity to earn $7,000 a month, which is also a cost of running a flower shop, even though she is not writing anybody a check. It is an **implicit cost**. When deciding whether she would rather be a florist or a patent attorney, for example, Lian needs to take into account *all* her costs, including opportunity costs.

Accountants typically don't take into account all opportunity costs so **accounting profits** are usually more than **economic profits**. Why is the distinction between accounting and economic profit important? Answer: Because firms want to maximize economic profit, not accounting profit.

Suppose, for example, that you inherit a bookshop, including the building where the shop is located so you pay no rent. Each month the bookshop makes enough to pay the employees; in some months it makes a little bit more so your accounting profits are positive. Is your economic profit positive? Probably not. If you closed the bookshop and rented the building to another firm, your profit might be considerably higher. So when calculating your economic profit, you should include the opportunity cost of renting the building to another firm. The easiest way to do this is to pretend that your bookshop has to pay the

A fixed cost does not vary with the quantity produced

An explicit cost is a cost that requires a money outlay.

An implicit cost is a cost that does not require an outlay of money.

Accounting profit is total revenue minus explicit costs.

Economic profit is total revenue minus total costs, including implicit opportunity costs.

market rate for rent, even if you are paying it to yourself. If your bookshop isn't profitable when it has to pay rent then you should probably sell the bookshop and go into business as a landlord instead.

Calculating economic profit is important for entrepreneurs, who must always think about the future. Is this the best use of our firm's assets? What am I giving up by following this strategy? Could these assets be used to make more profit if I used them in another way?

What Quantity to Produce?

Now that we know what to ignore and what to consider, let's return to the question of what quantity to produce in order to maximize profit. Profit is total revenue minus total cost, so the owner wants to maximize the difference between total revenue and total costs.

Profit = π = Total Revenue − Total Cost

Total revenue is pretty easy to understand. **Total revenues** are simply price times quantity: $(P \times Q)$. If the price of oil is $50 per barrel, then total revenues are $50 per day if 1 barrel is produced per day, $100 if 2 barrels are produced, $150 if 3 barrels are produced, and so forth.

Total cost is simply the cost of producing a given quantity of output. Let's break total cost into two components, fixed costs and variable costs.

Total revenue is price times quantity sold: $TR = P \times Q$

Total costs the costs of producing a given quantity of output.

Total Cost (*TC*) = Fixed Costs (*FC*) + Variable Costs (*VC*)

(Since sunk costs are irrelevant for all choices, we do not include any sunk costs.) Fixed costs are costs, such as rent, that do not vary with output. **Variable costs** are costs that do vary with output. Pumping more oil will require more electricity and maintenance costs for the pump, for example, and also more transportation costs to deliver the oil, so these are all part of variable cost.

The table in Figure 11.2 shows total revenues (*TR*) and total costs (*TC*) for a typical stripper oil well. Profit is the difference between total revenue and total cost, and it is shown in the fourth column. Thus, to find the maximum profit, one method is to look for the quantity that maximizes $TR - TC$. Using the table in Figure 11.2, we can see that the profit-maximizing quantity is 8 barrels of oil per day.

It is helpful, especially in order to create graphs, to use a second method to find the quantity that maximizes profit. Instead of looking at total revenue and total cost, we can compare the increase in revenue from selling an additional barrel of oil, called **marginal revenue**, with the increase in cost from selling an additional barrel, called **marginal cost**. To maximize profit, we will show that the owner wants to keep producing oil so long as Marginal revenue > Marginal cost, which means that the last drop of oil that the firm produces should be the one where Marginal revenue = Marginal cost. Let's step through this argument.

Marginal revenue is the change in total revenue from selling an additional barrel of oil. Suppose that the price of a barrel of oil is $50. Then what is marginal revenue? If the owner sells an additional barrel of oil, his revenues increase by $50, so marginal revenue is just equal to $50, the price. That was easy, because we assumed that the price of oil doesn't change as the firm sells more barrels. In other words we used our assumption that a stripper oil well is in a competitive industry and thus faces a perfectly elastic demand curve at the market price. Thus, we have a simple rule: for a firm in a competitive industry, $MR = P$.

Variable costs are costs that do vary with output.

How Does a Competitive Firm Maximize Profit?

Marginal revenue, *MR*, is the change in total revenue from selling an additional unit.
$$MR = \frac{\Delta TR}{\Delta Q}$$
For a firm in a competitive industry, $MR = $ Price.

Marginal cost, *MC*, is the change in total cost from producing an additional unit.

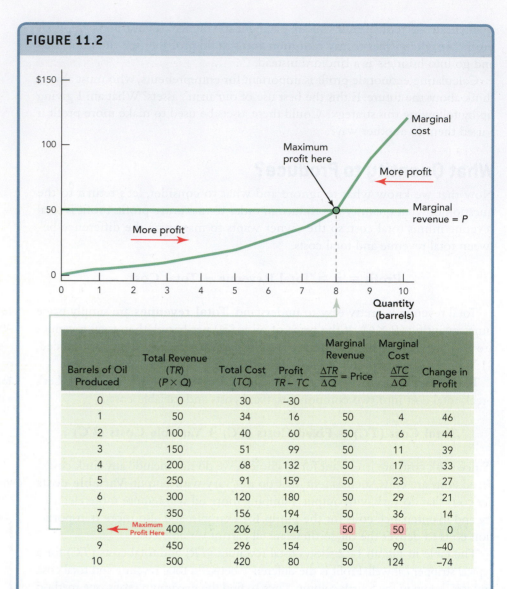

FIGURE 11.2

Barrels of Oil Produced	Total Revenue (TR) (P × Q)	Total Cost (TC)	Profit TR − TC	Marginal Revenue $\frac{\Delta TR}{\Delta Q}$ = Price	Marginal Cost $\frac{\Delta TC}{\Delta Q}$	Change in Profit
0	0	30	−30			
1	50	34	16	50	4	46
2	100	40	60	50	6	44
3	150	51	99	50	11	39
4	200	68	132	50	17	33
5	250	91	159	50	23	27
6	300	120	180	50	29	21
7	350	156	194	50	36	14
8	400	206	194	50	50	0
9	450	296	154	50	90	−40
10	500	420	80	50	124	−74

Maximum Profit Here (at row 8)

Profit Is Maximized by Producing until *MR* = *MC* To maximize profit, a firm compares the revenue from selling an additional unit, marginal revenue (for a firm in a competitive industry, this is equal to the price) to the costs of selling an additional unit, marginal cost. Profit increases from an additional sale whenever *MR* > *MC* so profit is maximized by producing up until the point where *MR* = *MC*.

Marginal cost is the change in total cost from producing an additional barrel of oil. The owner of a small oil well has some choice about whether to produce a little bit more or a little bit less. The owner, for example, can increase the pump rate and produce more oil per day but only by spending more on electricity, on maintenance, and on more frequent pickup and shipping of the oil. The extra costs that come with a little additional production are called marginal costs. Notice, for example, that if the well produces 2 barrels of oil per day, Total cost = 40, and if the well produces 3 barrels per day, then Total cost = 51. Thus, producing the third barrel of oil increases costs by $11, i.e., the marginal cost of the third barrel of oil is $11.

At some point, marginal costs must increase because you can only get so much blood out of a stone and only so much oil out of rock. The well, for example, cannot be pumped more than 24 hours a day. As the well reaches capacity, the marginal cost of an additional barrel approaches infinity!

We can now use the data in Figure 11.2 to find the profit-maximizing quantity using our second method. The owner should keep producing additional barrels so long as the revenue from producing an additional barrel exceeds the cost of producing an additional barrel. The first barrel of oil that the firm produces adds $50 to revenue and $4 to costs, so $MR > MC$, and by producing that barrel the firm can add $46 to profit. On the second barrel the marginal revenue is $50 and the marginal cost is $6 so producing that barrel adds $44 to profit. Following through on this logic, we can see that each additional barrel of oil adds to profit up until the eighth barrel. If the firm produces the ninth barrel of oil, however, it adds $50 to revenue but $90 to costs, so the firm will not want to produce the ninth barrel. The profit-maximizing quantity is thus 8 barrels of oil. Notice that the profit-maximizing quantity is where $MR = MC$, and since $MR = P$ for a competitive firm, we can also say that the profit-maximizing quantity for a competitive firm is where $P = MC$.

Students are often confused by why economists say that the profit-maximizing output is 8 barrels instead of 7 barrels. Why produce the eighth barrel, where $P = MC$, and thus there is no addition to profit? Consider the graph above the table in Figure 11.2. Notice that wherever $P > MC$, producing additional barrels means more profit, and wherever $MC > P$, producing fewer barrels means more profit. Now think about producing oil not in barrels but in drops. Then the graph says that at 7.9999 barrels you still want to add a drop or two but at 8.0001 barrels you want to take away a drop or two. The reason we say profit is maximized where $P = MC$ is that $P = MC$ is the "just right" point between too little and too much.

As the price changes, so does the profit-maximizing quantity. When the price is $50, the profit-maximizing quantity is 8. If the price of oil rises to $100 per barrel, then the firm will expand production. But by how much? The firm will expand until it is once again maximizing profit when $P = MC$. In Figure 11.3 we show how the firm expands production along its MC curve as the price of oil increases from $50 to $100 per barrel.

> To maximize profit a firm in a competitive industry increases output until $P = MC$.

FIGURE 11.3

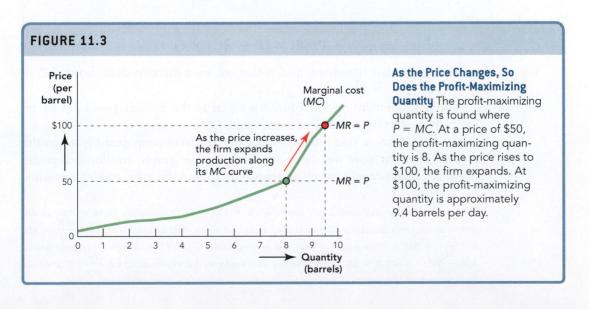

As the Price Changes, So Does the Profit-Maximizing Quantity The profit-maximizing quantity is found where $P = MC$. At a price of $50, the profit-maximizing quantity is 8. As the price rises to $100, the firm expands. At $100, the profit-maximizing quantity is approximately 9.4 barrels per day.

The **average cost** of production is the cost per unit, that is, the total cost of producing Q units divided by Q:

$$AC = \frac{TC}{Q}$$

We have now answered our second question: To maximize profit, the firm should produce the quantity such that $MR = MC$, which for a firm in a competitive industry means produce up until $P = MC$.

By the way, remember that we said that fixed costs should be ignored when deciding how much to produce? Since fixed costs don't change when we increase output, they don't influence marginal costs—thus our profit-maximizing condition, choose the quantity such that $P = MC$, means that fixed costs are irrelevant—our $P = MC$ condition will give us the same profit maximizing quantity whether fixed costs are high or low.[*]

Even though the firm's fixed costs are irrelevant for determining the profit-maximizing quantity, we know that they are relevant for the choice to exit or not. To understand that choice we will now introduce the average cost curve.

Profits and the Average Cost Curve

We have shown that the firm maximizes profits by producing the quantity such that $P = MC$, but a firm can maximize profits and still have low profits or even losses. Just because the firm is doing the best it can doesn't mean that it is doing very well. We would like, therefore, to be able to show profits in a diagram. To do this, we need to introduce the average cost curve.

The **average cost** of production is simply the cost per barrel, that is, the average cost of producing Q barrels of oil is the total cost of producing Q barrels divided by Q: $AC = \frac{TC}{Q}$. For example, in Figure 11.4, we can read from the table within it that the total cost of producing 6 barrels of oil per day is $120; thus, the cost per barrel is $120/6 = $20. Figure 11.4 computes average cost (in the last column) and graphs the average cost curve alongside the price and marginal cost curves.

With a little bit of work, we can now show profit on our graph. Recall that

Profit = Total revenue − Total cost = TR − TC

so we can also write

$$\textbf{Profit} = \left(\frac{\textbf{TR}}{\textbf{Q}} - \frac{\textbf{TC}}{\textbf{Q}}\right) \times \textbf{Q}$$

or

$$\textbf{Profit} = (\textbf{P} - \textbf{AC}) \times \textbf{Q}$$

(To get to the last statement, notice that we used the two definitions, $TR = P \times Q$ and $AC = \frac{TC}{Q}$.)

The last statement says that profit is equal to the average profit per barrel $(P - AC)$ times the number of barrels sold, Q.

We already know that 8 barrels is the profit-maximizing quantity when the price is $50, but now we can show profit on our graph. To illustrate profit, begin at a quantity of 8 barrels and move up to find the price of $50 at point *a*.

[*]If you know calculus, this result is very easy to see: $\pi = TR - TC$. To maximize profit, we take the derivative of the profit function with respect to quantity and set the total equal to zero. Since $\frac{\partial TR}{\partial Q} = MR$ and $\frac{\partial TC}{\partial Q} = MC$ we immediately have our general condition for any firm to maximize profit, $MR - MC = 0$ or $MR = MC$. Notice also that since fixed costs don't vary with Q that $\frac{\partial FC}{\partial Q} = 0$, so fixed costs don't influence marginal cost and thus have no effect on the profit-maximizing quantity.

FIGURE 11.4

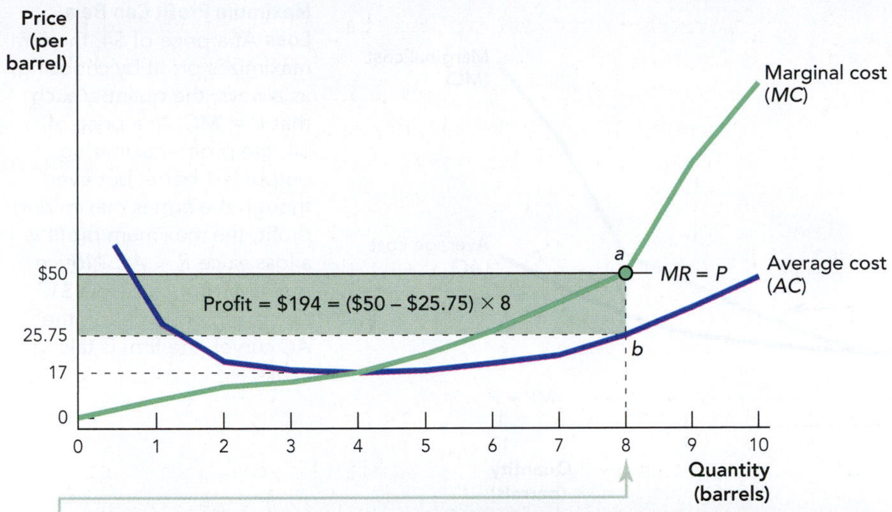

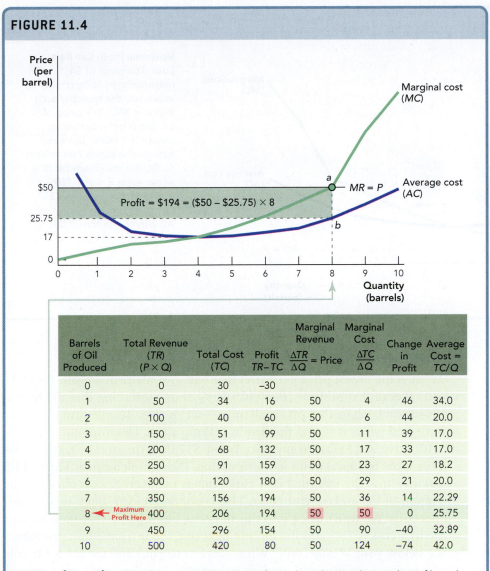

Barrels of Oil Produced	Total Revenue (TR) (P × Q)	Total Cost (TC)	Profit TR–TC	Marginal Revenue $\frac{\Delta TR}{\Delta Q}$ = Price	Marginal Cost $\frac{\Delta TC}{\Delta Q}$	Change in Profit	Average Cost = TC/Q
0	0	30	–30				
1	50	34	16	50	4	46	34.0
2	100	40	60	50	6	44	20.0
3	150	51	99	50	11	39	17.0
4	200	68	132	50	17	33	17.0
5	250	91	159	50	23	27	18.2
6	300	120	180	50	29	21	20.0
7	350	156	194	50	36	14	22.29
8 ← Maximum Profit Here	400	206	194	50	50	0	25.75
9	450	296	154	50	90	–40	32.89
10	500	420	80	50	124	–74	42.0

Profit = (P – AC) × Q Profit is (P – AC) × Q, profit per barrel times the number of barrels produced. When the price is $50 and 8 barrels of oil are produced, profit is shown on the graph as the shaded area. Notice that the price is the height of point *a*, *AC* is the height of point *b*, so that the area (*a* – *b*) × Q is equal to profit or $194 = ($50 – $25.75) × 8.

Now reading down from point *a*, find the average cost from the *AC* curve at point *b*, which is $25.75. (You can also check this by examining the table below the diagram for the *AC* of producing 8 barrels.) The average profit per barrel, $P - AC$, is ($50 – $25.75) or $24.25 per barrel. Finally, since production is 8 barrels, the total profit is $(P - AC) \times Q$ or $24.25 × 8 = $194 per day, the shaded area in the diagram.

As we said earlier, just because a firm is maximizing profits doesn't mean that it is making profits. If the price of oil were to drop to $4 per barrel, what happens? The best the firm could do is produce at $P = MC$. Looking at the *MC* column in the table, $MC =$ $4 at 1 barrel of oil produced. So at a price of $4, the firm produces 1 barrel of oil. But at this price, the firm is taking a loss because $P < AC$. Figure 11.5 illustrates.

FIGURE 11.5

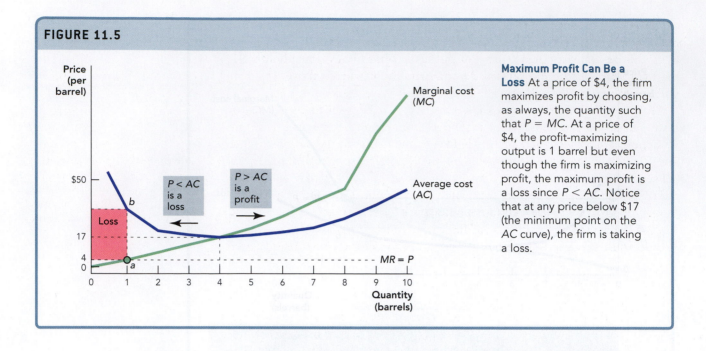

Maximum Profit Can Be a Loss At a price of $4, the firm maximizes profit by choosing, as always, the quantity such that $P = MC$. At a price of $4, the profit-maximizing output is 1 barrel but even though the firm is maximizing profit, the maximum profit is a loss since $P < AC$. Notice that at any price below $17 (the minimum point on the AC curve), the firm is taking a loss.

What is the lowest price per barrel that will give the firm a profit (not take a loss)? Recall that profit is $(P - AC) \times Q$, thus—assuming that the firm is profit-maximizing so $P = MC$ at all times—when $P > AC$, the firm is making a profit, and when $P < AC$, the firm is making a loss. The minimum point of the AC curve is at $17, so at any price below $17 the firm must be taking a loss.

One more technical point is worth noting. Take a look again at Figure 11.5 and notice that the marginal cost curve meets the average cost curve at the minimum of the average cost curve. This is not an accident but a mathematical necessity. We won't delve into this in detail, but suppose that your average grade in a class is 75% and that on the next test, the marginal test, you earn a grade below your average, 60%. What happens to your average grade? It falls. So whenever your marginal grade is below your average grade, your average falls. Now suppose that your average grade is 75% and on the next test, the marginal test, you earn a grade above your average, 80%. What happens to your average? It rises. So whenever your marginal grade is above your average grade, your average rises. What is true for your average and marginal grade is equally true for average and marginal cost. So think about what must happen around the point at which the MC and AC curves meet. When marginal cost is just below average cost, the average cost curve is falling, and when marginal cost is just above average cost, the average cost curve is rising, so AC and MC must meet at the minimum of the AC curve. Thus, on an exam be sure to draw the MC curve rising through the minimum point of the AC curve.

We are now ready to turn to our third question, when should the firm enter or exit the industry?

Entry, Exit, and Shutdown Decisions

Firms seek profits so in the long run firms will enter an industry when $P > AC$ and exit an industry when $P < AC$. Notice that at the intermediate point, when $P = AC$, profits are zero and there is neither entry nor exit.

CHECK YOURSELF

- Use average costs to define profit for the competitive firm.
- Using average cost, describe all the prices at which the firm would make a profit and all the prices at which the firm would make a loss.

In Figure 11.5, we can see that at a price of $4, the firm is taking losses. Thus, in the long run, this firm will exit the industry. In fact, at any price below $17, the firm will be making a loss at any output level. Thus at any price below $17, the firm will exit the industry in the long run. At any price above $17, firms will be making profits and other firms will enter the industry.

Only when $P = AC$, in this case when $P = \$17$, will firms be making zero profits, and there will be no incentive to either enter or exit the industry. Students often wonder why firms would remain in an industry when profits are zero. The problem is the language of economics. By **zero profits**, economists mean what everyone else means by *normal profits*. Remember that average cost includes wages and payments to capital, so even when the firm earns "zero profits," labor and capital are being paid enough to keep them in the industry. Thus, when we say that a firm is earning zero profits, we mean that the price of output is just enough to pay labor and capital their ordinary opportunity costs.

Zero profits, or **normal profits,** occur when $P = AC$. At this price the firm is covering all of its costs, including enough to pay labor and capital their ordinary opportunity costs.

The Short-Run Shutdown Decision

If $P < AC$, the firm is making a loss so it wants to exit the industry but exit typically cannot occur immediately. Remember our stripper oil well and how it rents the land from which it pumps the oil? We said the rent was $30 per day but that doesn't mean the firm can stop paying rent immediately. Rent contracts, for example, often require that the renter give 30 days' notice. So suppose that the firm gives notice to the landowner that in 30 days it will exit and stop paying rent. What does the firm do for the next 30 days? Should it shut down and produce nothing or should it continue to produce something even though it is taking a loss?

If the well shuts down immediately, the firm will lose $30 per day for 30 days. On the other hand, if the price of oil is, say, $11 and if the firm produces 3 barrels of oil (the profit-maximizing amount when $P = \$11$; see the table in Figure 11.4), then the firm will have daily revenues of $33 and daily costs of $51 ($30 rent plus $21 in variable cost; see table in Figure 11.4) for a total daily loss of $18 ($33 − $51). A daily loss of $18 isn't good—that is why the firm wants to exit—but it's better than a daily loss of $30. In other words, by not shutting down, the firm is able to cover all of its variable costs and *some* of its fixed costs (the rent), and that is better than producing nothing and paying the rent.

As usual in economics we can also show this insight with another curve! The firm is taking a loss when:

$$TR < TC$$

Recall that when we divide both sides of this equation by Q, we get our condition for long-run exit, $P < AC$. To understand the firm's optimal short-run shutdown decision we are going to do something very similar. Total cost can be broken down into fixed costs and variable costs.

$$TC = FC + VC$$

But in the short run the firm has no choice about its fixed costs; it has to pay the fixed costs no matter how much output the firm produces. Since choice doesn't influence the fixed costs, the fixed costs should not influence choice. In the short run, the fixed costs are an expense but not an economic

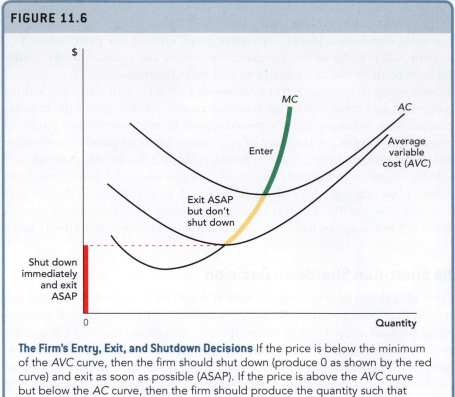

FIGURE 11.6

The Firm's Entry, Exit, and Shutdown Decisions If the price is below the minimum of the AVC curve, then the firm should shut down (produce 0 as shown by the red curve) and exit as soon as possible (ASAP). If the price is above the AVC curve but below the AC curve, then the firm should produce the quantity such that P = MC (along the yellow curve) but exit ASAP. If the price is at or above the AC curve, the firm should remain within the industry producing where P = MC or enter if it is not already in the industry.

(opportunity) cost so they should be ignored. Thus, the firm should shut down immediately only if $TR < VC$, or dividing both sides by Q as before, the firm should shut down immediately only if

$$P < \frac{VC}{Q} = AVC$$

We call $\frac{VC}{Q}$ the average variable cost curve, or AVC, and give an example in Figure 11.6 on the next page. The AVC curve has a very similar shape to the AC curve and it gets closer and closer to the AC curve as Q increases. (Why? This is a good question to test your knowledge—see Thinking and Problem Solving problem 24 at the end of this chapter.)

We can summarize, therefore, all of the firm's entry, exit, and shutdown decisions in Figure 11.6. If the price is so low that the firm can't even cover its average variable cost, then the firm should shut down immediately and exit as soon as possible. If the price is high enough to cover the average variable cost but not all of the fixed costs (i.e., above AVC but below AC), then the firm should minimize its losses by producing the quantity such that $P = MC$ (along the yellow curve) but exit as soon as possible. If the price is high enough to cover the firm's average costs (at or above the AC curve), then the firm should remain in the industry or enter if it is not already in the industry and, of course, produce where $P = MC$.

By the way, the shutdown rule—shut down if you cannot cover your variable costs—can be applied in instances even when long-run exit is not at issue. Seasonal businesses, such as seaside hotels in the northeast of the United States, make their money during the busy season. What about in the winter when few people want to go to the beach? Do they stay open or close for a few months? It depends on whether these hotels can cover their variable costs in the slow season and contribute something to the paying of their fixed costs. This explains why it can sometimes make sense to run a hotel even when it is mostly empty.

Entry, Exit, and Industry Supply Curves

Now that we have examined the output and entry and exit decisions for firms in a competitive market, we can derive the industry supply curve, which you have been working with since Chapter 3. Supply curves can slope upward, be flat, or in rare circumstance even slope downward. We will show that the slope of the supply curve can be explained by how costs change as industry output increases or decreases.

In an **increasing cost industry**, costs increase with greater industry output and this generates an upward-sloping supply curve. In a **constant cost industry**, costs do not change with changes in industry output and this generates a flat supply curve. In a **decreasing cost industry**, costs decrease with greater industry output and this generates a downward-sloping supply curve. Decreasing cost industries are rare.

Let's start with increasing cost industries.

Increasing Cost Industries

In an increasing cost industry, costs rise as industry output increases. The oil industry is an increasing cost industry because greater quantities of oil can be produced only by using more expensive methods such as drilling deeper, drilling in more inhospitable spots, or extracting the oil from tar sands.

To illustrate, let's focus on just two firms. Firm 1 is the firm that we examined earlier. Its oil is located near the surface, so its average costs are low and it enters the industry when the price of oil rises to just $17. Firm 2's oil, however, is located deeper than Firm 1's, and so Firm 2's fixed costs of drilling are higher and its average cost curve is higher than that of Firm 1's. As a result, Firm 2 will not enter the industry until the price of oil reaches $29. We can now build the industry supply curve.

At any price below $17, what is the quantity supplied? Zero. At a price less than $17, the firm is losing money so no firm enters the industry, and the industry supply curve, indicated in the rightmost panel of Figure 11.7 by the red line, shows a quantity supplied of zero. When the price of oil hits $17, Firm 1 enters the industry at its profit-maximizing quantity of 4 barrels and thus industry supply at a price of $17 jumps to 4 barrels. As the price rises, Firm 1 expands along its MC curve and so does industry supply. When the price hits $29, Firm 2 enters the industry with its profit-maximizing quantity of 5 barrels of oil. To find the quantity supplied by the industry, we sum the quantity supplied by each firm in the industry. At a price of $29, Firm 1 supplies 6 barrels of oil

Increasing cost industry is an industry in which industry costs increase with greater output; shown with an upward-sloped supply curve.

Constant cost industry is an industry in which industry costs do not change with greater output; shown with a flat supply curve.

Decreasing cost industry is an industry in which industry costs decrease with an increase in output; shown with a downward-sloped supply curve.

FIGURE 11.7

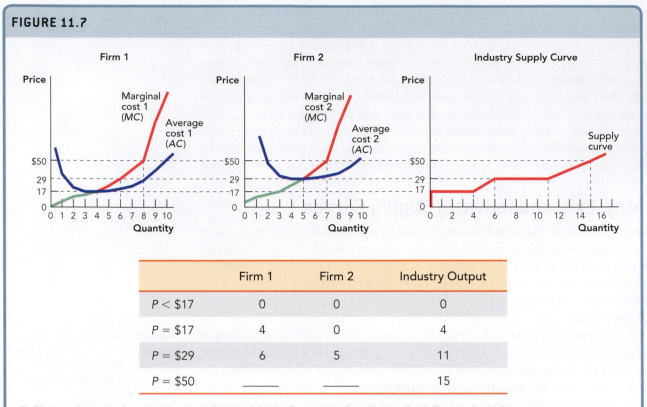

	Firm 1	Firm 2	Industry Output
$P < \$17$	0	0	0
$P = \$17$	4	0	4
$P = \$29$	6	5	11
$P = \$50$	_____	_____	15

To Find the Quantity Supplied by the Industry, Add the Quantities Supplied by Each Firm in the Industry At any price below $17, profits for both Firm 1 and Firm 2 are negative, so industry output is 0. At a price of $17, Firm 1 enters the industry with a profit-maximizing quantity of 4 barrels, so industry output jumps to 4 barrels. As price rises further, Firm 1 expands along its MC curve. At a price of $29, Firm 2 enters the industry with a profit-maximizing quantity of 5 barrels, so total industry output is 11 barrels (6 from Firm 1 and 5 from Firm 2). As price rises further, both firms expand along their marginal cost curve. At any price, industry output is the sum of each firm's output. At a price of $50, what quantity does Firm 1 produce? What quantity does Firm 2 produce? Fill in the blanks in the table and check that the production from Firm 1 and Firm 2 add up to industry output.

and Firm 2 supplies 5 barrels of oil, so industry supply is 11 barrels of oil. As the price rises further, both firms now expand along their respective MC curves. Once again, industry supply at any price is found by adding up the quantity supplied by each firm at that price. Thus at a price of $50, Firm 1 produces 8 barrels of oil and Firm 2 produces 7 barrels of oil, so industry supply at a price of $50 is 15 barrels of oil.

Our explanation of the supply curve is simply a more detailed version of the account in Chapter 3. At a low price, the only oil that is profitable to exploit is the oil that can be recovered at low cost from places like Saudi Arabia. As the price of oil rises, it becomes profitable to supply oil from the North Sea, the Athabasca tar sands, and other higher-cost sources. The analysis in Chapter 3 focused on how a higher price encourages entry from higher-cost producers. This chapter adds to the entry story the idea that as the price increases, each firm expands output by moving along its marginal cost curve.

More generally, any industry that buys a large fraction of the output of an increasing cost industry will also be an increasing cost industry. The gasoline industry, for example, is an increasing cost industry because greater demand for gas will push up the price of oil, which in turn increases the price of gas. The electricity industry is an increasing cost industry because greater demand for electricity pushes up the price of coal, and coal is an increasing cost industry for the same reasons as oil.

Constant Cost Industries

Consider the industry of domain name registrars. Web pages on the Internet have a conventional name, called a domain name, such as that for the National Bureau of Economic Research, which has the domain name NBER.org. But the conventional names are just masks for more difficult-to-remember numbers called IP (Internet Protocol) addresses. When you type www.NBER.org into a browser, the browser sends a message to the Domain Name System (DNS), which looks up and returns the corresponding IP address, in this case http://66.251.72.129/. The IP address tells your browser where to find the information that is posted by the NBER. So, in order to work, every domain name must be registered with the DNS and assigned an IP address. Domain name registrars are firms that manage and register domain names.

The domain name registration industry has two important characteristics. First, domain name registration satisfies all of the conditions for a competitive industry.

■ The product being sold is similar across sellers.

■ There are many buyers and sellers, each small relative to the total market.

■ There are many potential sellers.

As far as the user is concerned, there is little difference between registering with GoDaddy.com or BigRock.in, so the product is similar across sellers. There are many buyers and many sellers. There are hundreds of registrars in the United States alone. Indeed, GoDaddy.com is based in the United States and BigRock.in is based in India; thus, there is *worldwide* trade in domain name registration. Furthermore, not only are there many competitors in the industry, but just about anyone in the world can become an accredited registrar with an investment of a few thousand dollars, so there are many potential competitors.

The second important characteristic of the domain name industry is that the major input for domain name registration is a bank of computers, but all the computers of all the domain name registrars in all the world don't add up to much compared with the world supply of computers. The domain name industry, therefore, can expand without pushing up the prices of its major inputs and thus without raising its own costs. An industry that can expand or contract without changing the prices of its inputs is called a constant cost industry.

These two characteristics, free entry and the fact that the industry demands only a small share of its major inputs, produce the following properties: (1) The price for domain name registration is quickly driven down to the average cost of managing and assigning a domain name, so profits are quickly driven to normal levels; and (2) because average costs don't change much when the industry expands or contracts, the price of domain name registration doesn't change much when the industry expands or contracts so the long-run supply curve is very elastic (flat).

Let's examine these characteristics in turn. One of the largest registrars is GoDaddy.com, which charges $8.99 to register a domain name for one year. What would happen if it raised its price to $14.95 a year? GoDaddy would quickly lose a significant fraction of its business. New customers would choose other firms, and since domains must be renewed every few years, old customers would soon also switch. As a result of this competition, GoDaddy and every other firm in the industry price their services at near average cost and earn a zero or normal profit.

Now consider what happens when the demand for domain names increases. In 2005, there were more than 60 million domain names. Just one year later, there were more than 100 million domain names. If the demand for oil nearly doubled, the price of oil would rise dramatically, but despite nearly doubling in size, the price of registering a domain name did not increase. When an increase in demand hits a constant cost industry, the price rises in the short run as each firm moves up its MC curve. But the expansion of old firms and the entry of new firms quickly push the price back down to average cost.

Figure 11.8 on the next page illustrates how a constant cost industry responds to an increase in demand. The figure looks imposing, but if we consider it in steps, the logic of the story will be clear. In the top panel, we have the initial equilibrium. On the left-hand side of the panel, we illustrate the industry. The market price is P_{lr} ($8.99 in the case of domain name registration), the market quantity is Q_{lr}, and the quantity demanded is exactly equal to the quantity supplied so the industry is in equilibrium. On the right-hand side of the panel, we have a typical firm in the industry. The firm is profit-maximizing because $P = MC$ and it is making a zero or normal profit because $P = AC$. Note that the industry output is Q_{lr} but the firm output is q_{lr}, which indicates that each firm in the industry produces only a small share of total industry output.

In the middle panel on the left, we illustrate an increase in demand from Old demand to New demand. In the short run, the increase in demand increases price to P_{sr}, $9.99, where New demand and Short-run supply meet. The industry quantity increases to Q_{sr}. Where does the increase in quantity come from? It comes from many firms in the industry, each of which produces a little bit more by increasing production along its MC curve. In the middle panel on the right, we show that the typical firm in the industry expands to q_{sr}, and since the price is above average cost, the firm earns profits as illustrated by the shaded area $(P - AC) \times q_{sr}$.

Before turning to the bottom panel, let's remember that the short run is the period before entry (or exit) occurs. In the middle panel, we are illustrating the *first* response to an increase in demand, which is that the price rises and every firm in the industry responds by increasing production along its marginal cost curve. (Indeed, the short-run supply curve is simply the sum of the MC curves for each firm in the industry.)

The increase in price generates above-normal profits for each firm in the industry. Notice that above-normal profits attract new investment and entry. Entry is the *second* response to the increase in demand. In some industries, like the domain name registration industry, entry might take a matter of a few months or even as little as a few weeks, while in other industries it could take several years before significant entry occurs.

When entry does occur, the short-run supply curve shifts to the right, and as it does, the price falls and profits are reduced. Entry doesn't stop until profits return to normal levels so entry continues until price is pushed down to AC. In the long run, after all entry and exit have occurred, profits have returned to normal.

Since the prices of the industry inputs don't change when the industry expands, the AC curve of each firm in the industry doesn't change, so in

FIGURE 11.8

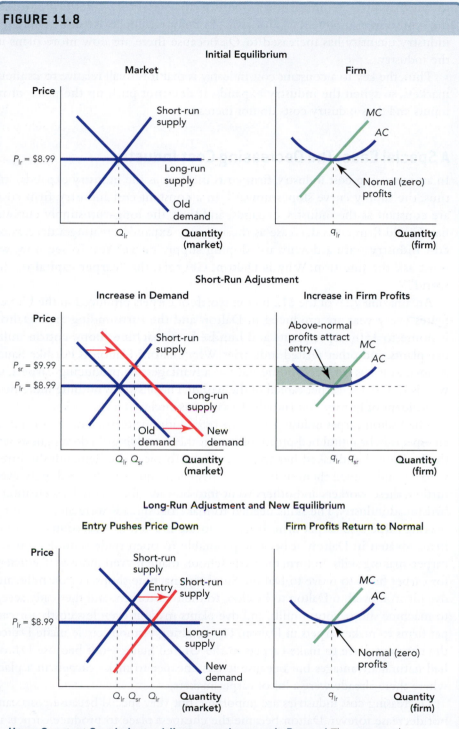

How a Constant Cost Industry Adjusts to an Increase in Demand The top panel
shows the initial industry and firm equilibrium. The market price for domain name
registration is $8.99 and each firm is making a normal profit. In the middle panel,
the demand for registration increases, which pushes up the market price to $9.99. In
the short run, each firm in the industry expands along its *MC* curve and thus market
quantity increases to Q_{sr}. Each firm earns above-normal profits. In the bottom panel,
the above-normal profits attract entry. As more firms enter the industry, the short-run
supply curve shifts to the right and as it does price falls. Firms continue to enter and
the price continues to fall until price returns to $8.99. At that price, firms are once
again earning normal (zero) profits, since $P = AC$.

the new industry, equilibrium price is again equal to P_{lr}, \$8.99. Although the typical firm produces q_{lr}, just as it did before the increase in demand, the industry quantity has increased to Q_{lr} because there are now more firms in the industry.

Thus, the key to a constant cost industry is that it is small relative to its input markets, so when the industry expands, it does not push up the price of its inputs and thus industry costs do not increase.

A Special Case: The Decreasing Cost Industry

In an increasing cost industry, firm costs increase as the industry expands, and thus, the supply curve slopes upward. In a constant cost industry, firm costs are constant as the industry expands, and thus, the long-run supply curve is flat. Could firm costs decrease as the industry expands, creating a decreasing cost industry with a downward-sloping supply curve? Yes. To see how, we must ask the question: Why is Dalton, Georgia, the "carpet capital of the world"?

An amazing 72% of the \$12 billion worth of carpets produced in the United States every year are produced in Dalton and the surrounding area. Dalton is home to 150 carpet plants and hundreds of machine shops, cotton mills, dye plants, and other related industries. Why Dalton? Dalton is not like Saudi Arabia, as it has no outstanding natural advantages for producing carpets, so why is Dalton the carpet capital of the world? The answer is nothing more than an accident of history that launched a virtuous circle.

The Dalton carpet industry began in 1895 with one teenage girl who crafted an especially beautiful bedspread for her brother's wedding. Wedding guests saw the bedspread and asked her to make more. To meet the demand, she hired workers and trained them in her innovative techniques. As demand grew even further, these workers and others went into business for themselves, creating a bedspread industry. The skills needed to make bedspreads were also useful for making carpets, so carpet firms began to locate in Dalton. With so many carpet firms located in Dalton, it became profitable to open trade schools to teach carpet-making skills. In turn, the trade schools made it even more cost-efficient for carpet firms to move to Dalton. Similarly, machine shops, cotton mills, and dye plants moved to Dalton to be close to their customers, and the ready access to machine shops, cotton mills, and dye plants made it even less costly for carpet firms to make carpets in Dalton. The resulting virtuous circle made Dalton the cheapest place to make carpets in the United States—not because Dalton had natural advantages but because it was cheaper to make carpets in a place where there already were a lot of carpet makers.

Decreasing cost industries are important, but very special because costs cannot decrease forever. Dalton became the cheapest place to produce carpets in the United States many years ago and that is unlikely to change any time soon. But if the demand for carpets were to increase today, the cost of making carpets in Dalton would increase, not fall further. The cost of making carpets in Dalton fell when the local industry expanded from 1 to 50 firms, but they didn't fall by nearly as much when the industry expanded from 50 to 100 firms.

Economists use the idea of a decreasing cost industry to explain the history of industry clusters: not just carpets in Dalton, Georgia, but computer technology in Silicon Valley, movie production in Hollywood, and flower distribution in Aalsmeer, Holland. Once the cluster is established, however, constant or increasing costs are the norm. If the demand for carpet were to increase today, for example, the price of carpets would rise, not fall.

Industry Supply Curves: Summary

In an increasing cost industry, costs increase with industry output and the supply curve slopes upward. If the industry is small relative to its input markets so the industry can expand without pushing up its costs, the supply curve will be flat; we call this a constant cost industry. Industry supply curves can even slope downward but this is rare and temporary, although the idea of a decreasing cost industry is important for explaining the existence of industry clusters. Figure 11.9 illustrates the three possibilities.

Takeaway

We have now answered the three questions with which we opened the chapter. What price to set? Answer: A firm in a competitive industry sets its price at the market price. What quantity to produce? Answer: To maximize profit, a competitive firm should produce the quantity that makes $P = MC$. When to exit and enter an industry? Answer: In the short run, the firm should shut down only if price is less than average variable cost. In the long run, the firm should enter if $P > AC$ and exit if $P < AC$.

A competitive industry is one where the product being sold is similar across sellers; there are many buyers and sellers, each small relative to the total market; and/or there are many potential sellers.

We have also shown how profit maximization and entry and exit decisions are the foundation of supply curves. In an increasing cost industry, costs rise as more firms enter so supply curves are upward sloping. In a constant cost industry, costs remain the same as firms enter so the long-run supply curve is flat. And in the rare case of a decreasing cost industry, costs fall as firms enter so supply curves are downward sloping.

FIGURE 11.9

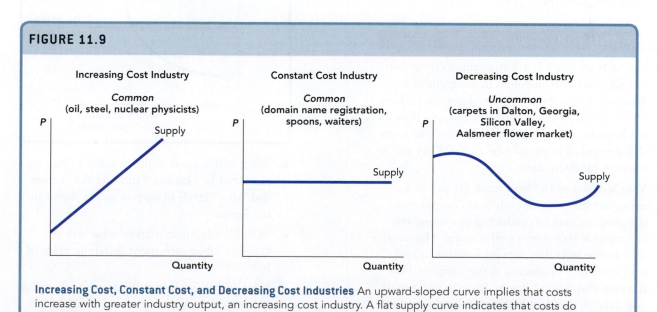

Increasing Cost, Constant Cost, and Decreasing Cost Industries An upward-sloped curve implies that costs increase with greater industry output, an increasing cost industry. A flat supply curve indicates that costs do not change with industry output, a constant cost industry. A downward-sloping curve implies that costs fall with greater industry output, a decreasing cost industry.

CHAPTER REVIEW

 interactive activity   Go online to practice with more examples of these types of problems, including live links to videos, data sources, and feedback.

Problems in green relate to MRU videos. See the MRU table at the end of the exercises.

KEY CONCEPTS

long run, p. 205

short run, p. 205

sunk cost, p. 205

fixed cost, p. 206

explicit cost, p. 206

implicit cost, p. 206

accounting profit, p. 206

economic profit, p. 206

total revenue, p. 207

total cost, p. 207

variable costs, p. 207

marginal revenue, *MR*, p. 207

marginal cost, *MC*, p. 207

average cost, p. 210

zero (normal) profits, p. 213

increasing cost industry, p. 215

constant cost industry, p. 215

decreasing cost industry, p. 215

FACTS AND TOOLS

1. You've been hired as a management consultant to four different companies in competitive industries. They're each trying to figure out if they should produce a little more output or a little bit less in order to maximize their profits. The firms all have typical marginal cost curves: They rise as the firm produces more.

   Your staff did all the hard work for you of figuring out the price of each firm's output and the marginal cost of producing one more unit of output *at their current level of output*. However, they forgot to collect data on how much each firm is actually producing at the moment. Fortunately, that doesn't matter. In your final report, you need to decide which firms should produce more output, which should produce less, and which are producing just the right amount:

   a. WaffleCo, maker of generic-brand frozen waffles. Price = $4 per box, marginal cost = $2 per box.

   b. Rio Blanco, producer of copper. Price = $32 per ounce, marginal cost = $45 per ounce.

   c. GoDaddy.com, domain name registry. Price = $5 per Web site, marginal cost = $2 per Web site.

   d. Luke's Lawn Service. Price = $80 per month, marginal cost = $120 per month.

2. In the competitive electrical motor industry, the workers at Galt Inc. threaten to go on strike. To avoid the strike, Galt Inc. agrees to pay its workers more. At all other factories, the wage remains the same.

   a. What does this do to the marginal cost curve at Galt Inc.? Does it rise, does it fall, or is there no change? Illustrate your answer in the figure.

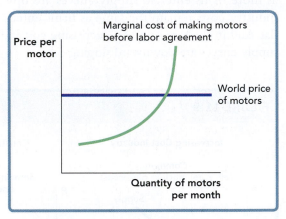

   b. What will happen to the number of motors produced by Galt Inc.? Indicate the "before" and "after" levels of output on the *x*-axis in the figure.

   c. In this competitive market, what will the Galt Inc. labor agreement do to the price of motors?

   d. Surely, more workers will *want* to work at Galt Inc. now that it pays higher wages. Will more workers *actually* work at Galt Inc. after the labor agreement is struck? Why or why not?

3. In Figure 11.8, you saw what happens in the long run when demand rises in a constant cost industry. Let's see what happens when demand falls in such an industry: For instance, think about the market for gasoline or pizza in a small city after the city's biggest textile mill shuts down. In the following figure, indicate the price and quantity of output at three points in time:

   I. In the long run, before demand falls

   II. In the short run, after demand falls

   III. In the long run, after demand falls

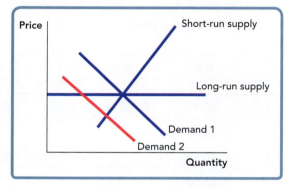

Also, answer the following questions about the market's response to this fall in demand.

   a. When will the marginal cost of production be lowest: At stage I, II, or III?

   b. When firms cut prices, they often do so in dramatic ways. During which stage will the local pizza shops begin making "Buy one, get one free" offers? During which stage will the local gas station be more likely to offer "Free car wash with fill-up?"

   c. When is $P > AC$? $P < AC$? $P = AC$?

   d. Restating the previous question: When are profits positive? Negative? Zero?

   e. Roughly speaking, will the long-run response mostly involve firms leaving the industry, or will it mostly involve individual firms shrinking? The Firm column of Figure 11.8 should help you with the answer.

4. We mentioned that carpet manufacturing looks like a decreasing cost industry. In American homes, carpets are much less popular than they were in the 1960s and 1970s, when "wall-to-wall carpeting" was fashionable in homes. Suppose that carpeting became even less popular than it is today: What would this fall in demand probably do to the price of carpet in the long run?

5. Replacement parts for classic cars are expensive, even though these parts aren't any more complicated than parts for new cars.

   a. What kind of industry is the market for old car parts: an increasing cost industry, a constant cost industry, or a decreasing cost industry? How can you tell?

   b. If people began recycling old cars more in the United States—repairing them rather than sending them off to junkyards—would the cost of spare parts probably rise or probably fall in the long run? Why do you think so?

6. Arguing about economics late one night in your dorm room, your friend says, "In a free market economy, if people are willing to pay a lot for something, then businesses will charge a lot for it." One way to translate your friend's words into a model is to think of a product with highly inelastic demand: items like life-saving drugs or basic food items. Let's consider a market where costs are roughly constant: perhaps they rise a little or fall a little as the market grows, but not by much.

   a. In the long run, is your friend right?

   b. In the long run, what has the biggest effect on the price of a good that people really want: the location of the average cost curve or the location of the demand curve?

7. **a.** In the highly competitive TV manufacturing industry, a new innovation makes it possible to cut the average cost of a 50-inch LCD TV from $1,000 to $600. Most TV manufacturers quickly adopt this new innovation, earning massive short-run profits. In the long run, what will the price of a 50-inch LCD TV be?

   b. In the highly competitive flash drive industry, a new innovation makes it possible to cut the average cost of an 64-gigabyte flash drive, small enough to fit in your pocket, from $5 to $4. In the long run, what will the price of an 64-gigabyte flash drive be?

   c. Assume that the markets in parts a and b are both constant cost industries. If demand rises massively for these two goods, why won't the price of these goods rise in the long run?

   d. In constant cost industries, does demand have any effect on price in the long run?

e. When average cost falls in *any* competitive industry, regardless of cost structure, who gets 100% of the benefits of cost cutting in the long run: consumers or producers?

8. On January 27, 2011, the price of Ford Motor Company stock hit an almost 10-year high at $18.79 per share. (Two years prior, in January 2009, Ford stock was trading for about a *tenth* of that price.)

a. Suppose that on January 27, 2011, you owned 10,000 shares of Ford stock (a small fraction of the almost 3.8 billion shares). Suppose you offered to sell your stock for $18.85 per share, just slightly above the market price. Would you have been successful?

b. What if, on January 27, 2011, you wanted to sell your 10,000 shares of Ford stock but you reduced your asking price to $18.75 per share? Would you have found a lot of willing buyers?

c. What do your answers for parts a and b tell you about the demand curve that you, as an individual seller of Ford stock, face?

9. In November 2010 Netflix announced a new lower price for streaming video direct to home televisions. At the time, Netflix had no serious competitors—Netflix's share of the digital download market was more than 60% (the second firm's was only 8%). Just three months later, Amazon announced that it was entering the market for streaming video. How are these two announcements related?

10. The chapter pointed out that whenever money is used to purchase capital, interest costs are incurred. Sometimes those costs are explicit—like when Alex borrowed the money from the bank—and sometimes those costs are implicit—like when Tyler had to forgo the interest he could have earned had he left his funds in a savings account. If an economist and accountant calculated Alex and Tyler's costs, for whom would they have identical numbers and for whom would the numbers differ?

THINKING AND PROBLEM SOLVING

11. Suppose Sam sells apples, picked from his apple tree, in a competitive market. Assume all apples are equal in quality, but grow at different heights on the tree. Sam, being fearful of heights, demands greater compensation the higher he goes: So for him, the cost of grabbing an apple rises higher and higher, the higher he must climb, as shown in the Total Cost column in the following table. The market price of an apple is $0.50.

a. What is Sam's marginal revenue for selling apples?

b. Which apples does Sam pick first? Those on the low branches or high branches? Why?

c. Does this suggest that the marginal cost of apples is increasing, decreasing, or staying the same as the quantity of apples picked increases? Why?

d. Complete the table.

Apples	Total Cost	Marginal Cost	Marginal Revenue	Change in Profit
1	$0.10	$0.10	$0.50	$0.40
2	$0.22			
3	$0.50			
4	$1.00			
5	$1.73			
6	$2.78			

e. How many apples does Sam pick?

12. How long is the "long run?" It will vary from industry to industry. How long would you estimate the long run is in the following industries?

a. The market for pretzels and soda sold from street carts in the Wall Street financial district in New York

b. The market for meals at newly trendy Korean porridge restaurants

c. The market for electrical engineers

d. After 2012, the market for movies that are suspiciously similar to *The Hunger Games*

13. In this chapter, we discussed the story of Dalton, Georgia, and its role as the carpet capital of the world. A similar story can be used to explain why some 60% of the motels in the United States are owned by people of Indian origin or why, as of 1995, 80% of doughnut shops in California were owned by Cambodian immigrants. Let's look at the latter case. In the 1970s, Cambodian immigrant

Ted Ngoy began working at a doughnut shop. He then opened his own store (and later, stores).*

Ngoy was drawn to the doughnut industry because it required little English, startup capital, or special skills. Speaking the same language as your workers, however, helps a lot.

a. As other Cambodian refugees came to Los Angeles fleeing the tyrannical rule of the Khmer Rouge, which group—the refugees or existing residents—was Ngoy more likely to hire from? Why?

b. Did this make it more or less likely that other Cambodian refugees would open doughnut shops? Why?

c. As more refugees came in, did this encourage a virtuous cycle of Cambodian-owned doughnut shops? Why?

d. At this point in the story, what sort of cost industry (constant, increasing, or decreasing) would you consider doughnut shops owned by Cambodians to be? Why?

e. Why did this cycle not continue forever? What kind of cost structure are Californian doughnut shops probably in now?

14. Ralph opened a small shop selling bags of trail mix. The price of the mix is $5, and the market for trail mix is very competitive. Ralph's cost curves are shown in the figure below.

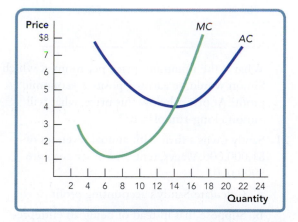

a. At what quantity will Ralph produce? Why?

b. When the price is $5, shade the area of profit or loss in the graph provided and calculate Ralph's profit or loss (round up).

c. If all other sellers of trail mix have the same marginal and average costs as Ralph, should

he expect more or fewer competitors in the future? In the long run, will the price of trail mix rise or fall? How do you know? What will the price of trail mix be in the long run?

15. In the competitive children's pajama industry, a new government safety regulation raises the average cost of children's pajamas by $2 per pair.

a. If this is a constant cost industry, then in the long run, what exactly happens to the price of children's pajamas?

b. If this is an increasing cost industry, will the long-run price of pajamas rise by more than $2 or less? (*Hint:* The long-run supply curve will be shaped just like an ordinary supply curve from the first few chapters. If you treat this like a $2 tax per pair, you'll get the right answer.)

c. If this is an increasing cost industry, how much will this new safety regulation change the average pajama maker's profits in the long run?

d. Given your answer to part c, why do businesses in competitive industries often oppose costly new regulations?

16. In the ancient Western world, incense was one of the first commodities transported long distances. It grew only in the south of the Arabian Peninsula (modern-day Yemen, known then as Arabia Felix) and was transported by camel to Alexandria and the Mediterranean civilizations, notably the Roman Republic. As the republic expanded into a richer and larger empire, the demand for incense grew and planters in Arabia added a second and then a third annual crop (though this incense was not as high in quality). Cultivation also crossed to the Horn of Africa (modern-day Oman) even though such fields were farther away from Rome.[2]

a. How does the lower quality of the additional annual crops illustrate incense as an increasing cost industry? (*Hint:* Think in terms of an amount of good crop produced per unit of currency.)

b. How does the added distance of incense grown in the Horn of Africa illustrate incense as an increasing cost industry?

c. It's more costly to grow incense in Eastern Africa than in Arabia Felix. Which region would you expect to see more incense grown in?

---

* Not only are 60% of the small motels and hotels in the United States owned by East Indians, nearly a third of these owners have the surname Patel; see http://news.bbc.co.uk/2/hi/south_asia/3177054.stm. The story of Cambodian doughnut shops in Los Angeles is from Postrel, Virginia. 1999. *The Future and Its Enemies.* New York: Touchstone, pp. 49–50.

17. You run a small firm. Two management consultants are offering you advice. The first says that your firm is losing money on every unit that you produce. To reduce your losses, the consultant recommends that you cut back production. The second consultant says that if your firm sells another unit, the price will more than cover your increase in costs. In order to reduce losses, the second consultant recommends that you should increase production.

    a. As an economist, can you explain why both facts that the consultants rely on could be true?

    b. Which consultant is offering the correct advice?

18. Paulette, Camille, and Hortense each own wineries in France. They produce inexpensive, mass-market wines. Over the last few years, such wines sold for 7 euros per bottle; but with a global recession, the price has fallen to 5 euros per bottle. Given the information below, let's find out which of these three winemakers (if any) should shut down temporarily until times get better. *Remember:* Whether or not they shut down, they still have to keep paying fixed costs for at least some time (that's what makes them "fixed").

To keep things simple, let's assume that each winemaker has calculated the optimal quantity to produce if they decide to stay in business; your job is simply to figure out if she should produce that amount or just shut down.

Annual Income Statement When Price = 5 euros				
Winemaker	Fixed Costs	Variable Costs	Recession Revenues	Profits
Paulette	50,000	80,000	120,000	
Camille	100,000	40,000	70,000	
Hortense	200,000	250,000	200,000	

    a. First, calculate each winemaker's profit.

    b. Which of these women, if any, earned a profit?

    c. Who should stay in business in the short run? Who should shut down?

    d. Fill in the blank: Even if profit is negative, if revenues are _____ variable costs, then it's best to stay open in the short run.

    e. For which of these wineries, if any, is $P > AC$? You don't need to calculate any new numbers to answer this.

19. Let's explore the relationship between marginal and average a little more. Suppose your grade in your economics class is composed of 10 quizzes of equal weight. You start off the semester well, then your grades start to slip a little, but then you get back into the swing of things, your grades pick up, and you finish off the semester with a bang. Your 10 quiz grades, in order, are: 82, 74, 68, 72, 77, 83, 86, 88, 90, and 100. Graph your *marginal* grades, along with your *average* grade, after each quiz. What do you notice about the relationship between *marginal* and *averages*? Your grades start improving with your fourth quiz grade; does your average also start increasing with your fourth quiz grade? Why or why not?

20. Given the cost function in the following table for Simon, a housepainter in a competitive local market, answer the questions that follow. (You may want to calculate average cost.)

Number of Rooms Painted per Week	Total Cost
0	$100
1	$120
2	$125
3	$145
4	$200
5	$300
6	$460

What is the minimum price per room at which Simon would be earning positive economic profit? At prices below this price, what will Simon's long-run plan be?

21. Sandy owns a firm with annual revenues of $1,000,000. Wages, rent, and other costs are $900,000.

    a. Calculate Sandy's accounting profit.

    b. Suppose that instead of being an entrepreneur, Sandy could get a job with one of the following annual salaries (i) $50,000; (ii) $100,000; or (iii) $250,000. Assume that a job would be as satisfying to Sandy as being an entrepreneur. Calculate Sandy's economic profit under each of these scenarios.

22. You and your roommate are up one night studying microeconomics, and your roommate looks puzzled. You ask what is wrong, and you get this response: "The book says that in the short run fixed costs are an *expense* but not a *cost*—but that doesn't make any sense. How can something be an expense but not a cost?" How do you respond?

23. Use the variable cost information in the following table to calculate average variable cost and average cost (assume fixed cost is $350), and then use this data to answer the questions that follow. One of them might not have an answer.

Q	FC	VC	AVC	AC
10	$350	$100		
20	$350	$180		
30	$350	$240		
40	$350	$300		
50	$350	$450		
60	$350	$630		
70	$350	$840		

a. Give an example of a price at which this firm would want to produce and sell output in *both* the short run *and* the long run.

b. Give an example of a price at which this firm would want to produce and sell output in *neither* the short run *nor* the long run.

c. Give an example of a price at which this firm would want to produce and sell output in the long run but *not* in the short run.

d. Give an example of a price at which this firm would want to produce and sell output in the short run but *not* in the long run.

24. Look carefully at Figure 11.6. What is represented by the space in between the average cost (*AC*) and average variable cost (*AVC*) curves? Why do they get closer together as quantity increases? Will they ever meet?

CHALLENGES

25. The demand for most metals tends to increase over time. Moreover, as we discussed in this chapter and also in Chapter 5, these types of natural resource industries tend to be increasing cost industries. And yet the price of metals compared with other goods has tended to fall slowly over time (albeit with many spikes in between). The following figure, for example, shows an index of prices for aluminum, copper, lead, silver, tin, and zinc from 1900 to 2003 (adjusted for inflation). The trend is downward. Why do you think this is the case?

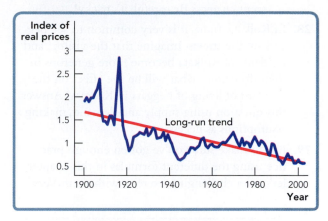

26. Frequent moviegoers often note that movies are rarely based on original ideas. Most of them are based on a television series, a video game, or, most commonly, a book. Why? To help you answer this question, start with the following.

a. Does a movie or a book have a higher fixed cost of production?

b. In 2005, American studios released 563 movies and American publishers produced 176,000 new titles. How does your answer in part a explain such a wide difference? Which is riskier: publishing a book or producing a movie?

c. How does the difference in fixed costs and risk of failure explain why so many movies are based on successful books? As a result, where do you expect to see more innovative plots, dialogues, and characters: in novels or movies?

27. a. In the nineteenth century, economist Alfred Marshall wrote about decreasing cost industries, writing in his *Principles of Economics* (available free online) that "when an industry has thus chosen a locality for itself . . . .[t]he mysteries of the trade become no mysteries; but are as it were in the air." In Chapter 10, we had a concept for benefits that are not internal to a firm but are "as it were in the air." What specific concept from Chapter 10 is at work in a business cluster?

b. In the twenty-first century, economist Michael Porter of the Harvard Business School writes about decreasing cost industries, as well: He calls them "business clusters." Porter's work has been very influential among city and town governments that argue that carefully targeted tax breaks and subsidies can attract investment and create a business cluster in their town, which will subsequently reap the benefits of decreasing costs. Is this argument correct? Be careful, it's tricky!

28. In Kolkata, India, it is very common to see beggars on the streets. Imagine that the visitors and residents of Kolkata become more generous in their donations; what will be the effect on the standard of living of beggars in Kolkata? Answer this question using supply and demand, making assumptions as necessary.

29. Just to make sure you've gotten enough practice using the different formulas in this chapter, let's try a challenging exercise with them. Very little information is given in the following table, but surprisingly, there's enough information for you to fill in all of the missing values—if you remember all of the relationships and can think of creative ways to use them.

30. The theologian Reinhold Niebuhr wrote the famous Serenity Prayer which says:

> God, grant me the serenity to accept the things I cannot change,
>
> Courage to change the things I can,
>
> And wisdom to know the difference.

At the risk of ruining a lovely prayer, how would you interpret this in economic terms?

Quantity	Total Costs	Fixed Costs	Variable Cost	Average Cost	Marginal Cost	Total Revenue	Profit
0				—	—		−80
10					$4		
20	$200						
30			$240			$450	
40							
50				$13.60	$20		

WORK IT OUT

For interactive, step-by-step help in solving this problem, go online.

Suppose Margie decides to lease a photocopier and open up a black-and-white photocopying service in her dorm room for use by faculty and students. Her total cost, as a function of the number of copies she produces per month, is given in the table:

Number of Photocopies per Month	Total Costs	Fixed Costs	Variable Cost	Total Revenue	Profit
0	$100				
1,000	$110				
2,000	$125				
3,000	$145				
4,000	$175				
5,000	$215				
6,000	$285				

a. Fill in the missing numbers in the table, assuming that Margie can charge 6 cents per black-and-white copy.

b. How many copies per month should Margie sell?

c. If the lease rate on the copier were to increase by $50 per month, how would that impact Margie's profit-maximizing level of output? How would this $50 increase in the lease rate affect Margie's profit? What will she do when it is time to renew her lease?

MARGINAL REVOLUTION UNIVERSITY VIDEOS

Introduction to the Competitive Firm

mruniversity.com/competitive-firm

Problems: **8**

How Does a Competitive Firm Maximize Profits?

mruniversity.com/max-profit

Problems: **1, 10, 11, 17, 18, 21**

Maximizing Profit and the Average Cost Curve

mruniversity.com/average-cost-curve

Problems: **2, 3, 19, 20, 22–24, 26, 29**

Entry, Exit, and Supply Curves: Increasing Costs

mruniversity.com/increasing-cost

Problems: **5, 12, 16**

Entry, Exist, and Supply Curves: Constant Costs

mruniversity.com/constant-cost

Problems: **6, 12, 14, 15, 28**

Entry, Exit, and Supply Curves: Decreasing Costs

mruniversity.com/decreasing-cost

Problems: **4, 7, 9, 12, 13, 25, 27**

CHAPTER 11 APPENDIX

Using Excel to Graph Cost Curves

We can use a spreadsheet such as Excel to take some of the drudgery out of graphing and calculating things like marginal revenue and marginal cost. In Figure A11.1, we show some of the data from the chapter on revenues and costs for the oil well. Notice that in cell B5 we show the Excel formula "=$A$2*A5", which takes the price from cell A2 and multiplies it by the quantity in cell A5 to produce total revenue. We then copy and paste this formula into the remainder of the column. We use the $ sign in $A$2 to tell Excel not to adjust the cell reference when we copy and paste (A5 doesn't have dollar signs so it is automatically adjusted to A6, A7, etc. when we copy and paste).

FIGURE A11.1

	B5	▼	f_x =$A$2*A5	
	A	B	C	D
1	Price			
2	50			
3				
4	Barrels of Oil Produced	Total Revenue (P * Q)	Total Cost	
5	0	0	30	
6	1	50	34	
7	2	100	40	
8	3	150	51	
9	4	200	68	
10	5	250	91	
11	6	300	120	
12	7	350	156	
13	8	400	206	
14	9	450	296	
15	10	500	420	
16				

With total revenue and total cost input, it's easy to create the other data that we need. Profit is just total revenue minus total cost, which in Figure A11.2 we show in column D. Marginal revenue and marginal cost are defined as $MR = \frac{\Delta TR}{\Delta Q}$ and $MC = \frac{\Delta TC}{\Delta Q}$. We show in cell F4 how to implement these formulas in Excel. The formula "= (C4 − C3)/(A4 − A3)" takes the cost of producing 2 barrels of oil from cell C4 and subtracts the cost of producing 1 barrel of oil from C3; we then divide by the increase in the number of barrels as we move from producing 1 to 2 barrels. In this case, $MC = (40 − 34)/(2 − 1) = 6$. The formula for MR is entered into Excel in a similar manner.

FIGURE A11.2

F4	▼		f_x =(C4-C3)/(A4-A3)				
	A	B	C	D	E	F	G
1	Barrels of Oil Produced	Total Revenue (P * Q)	Total Cost	Profit	Marginal Revenue (Price)	Marginal Cost	
2	0	0	30	-30			
3	1	50	34	16	50	4	
4	2	100	40	60	50	6	
5	3	150	51	99	50	11	
6	4	200	68	132	50	17	
7	5	250	91	159	50	23	
8	6	300	120	180	50	29	
9	7	350	156	194	50	36	
10	8	400	206	194	50	50	
11	9	450	296	154	50	90	
12	10	500	420	80	50	124	
13							
14							

Average cost is $AC = TC/Q$ and we show this calculation in Figure A11.3.

FIGURE A11.3

G13	▼		f_x =C13/A13				
	A	B	C	D	E	F	G
1	Price						
2	50						
3							
4	Barrels of Oil Produced	Total Revenue (P * Q)	Total Cost	Profit	Marginal Revenue (Price)	Marginal Cost	Average Cost
5	0	0	30	-30			
6	1	50	34	16	50	4	34
7	2	100	40	60	50	6	20
8	3	150	51	99	50	11	17
9	4	200	68	132	50	17	17
10	5	250	91	159	50	23	18.2
11	6	300	120	180	50	29	20
12	7	350	156	194	50	36	22.28571
13	8	400	206	194	50	50	25.75
14	9	450	296	154	50	90	32.88889
15	10	500	420	80	50	124	42
16							

It's now easy to graph *MR, MC,* and *AC.* By highlighting the Marginal Revenue, Marginal Cost, and Average Cost columns, including the labels, and clicking Insert and then Line Chart, we can produce a graph similar to that shown in Figure A11.4 (to get the exact graph, you must also tell Excel to use the barrel numbers in Column 1 on the *x*-axis—you can do this by clicking on the graph, clicking Select Data, and then Edit, Horizontal [Category] Axis Labels).

Remember that the profit-maximizing quantity is found where $MR = MC$. You can check this by looking at the table. You can see what happens to the profit-maximizing quantity when price changes simply by changing the price in cell A2; the graph will change automatically.

FIGURE A11.4

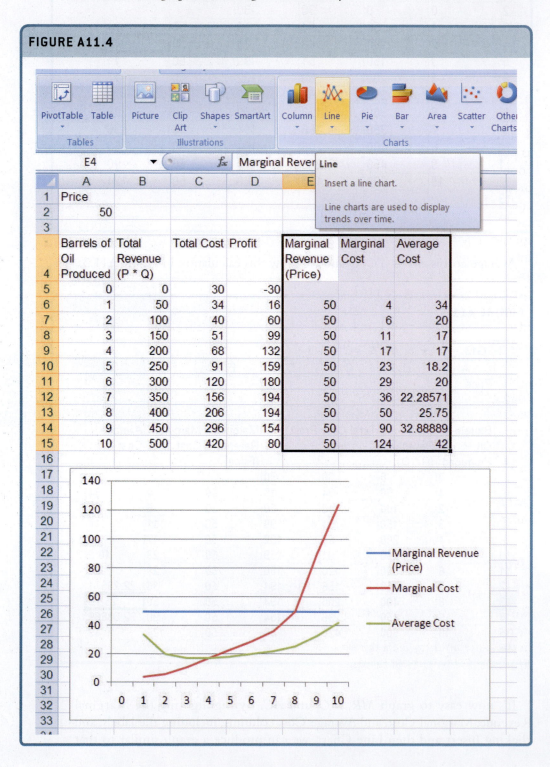

12

Competition and the Invisible Hand

I n Chapter 7, we explained how the price system—the signaling and incentive system—solves the great economic problem of arranging our limited resources to satisfy as many of our wants as possible. We showed how markets connect the world in a great cooperative endeavor, and how price signals and the accompanying profits and losses create incentives for entrepreneurs to direct labor and capital to their highest value uses. Chapter 7 was a "big picture" view of markets. In Chapter 11, we took a closer look at firms and showed that to maximize profit, a firm wants to (1) produce the quantity such that $P = MC$, (2) enter industries where $P > AC$, and (3) exit industries where $P < AC$. In this chapter, we connect these two perspectives on markets.

We also return in this chapter to the invisible hand. Recall Big Idea Two from Chapter 1, namely the metaphor of the invisible hand. With the right institutions, individuals acting in their self-interest can generate outcomes that are neither part of their intention nor design but that nevertheless have desirable properties. In this chapter, we show exactly this: How the conditions for profit maximization under competition lead entrepreneurs to produce outcomes that they neither intend nor design but that nevertheless have desirable properties.

In particular, we show that the $P = MC$ condition for profit maximization in a competitive market balances production across firms in an industry in just the way that minimizes the total industry costs of production. Second, we show that the entry ($P > AC$) and exit ($P < AC$) signals balance production across different industries in just the way that maximizes the total value of production.

Invisible Hand Property 1: The Minimization of Total Industry Costs of Production

We know from the previous chapter that a firm in a competitive industry increases output until $P = MC$. What's even more important is that every firm in the same industry faces the *same* price. Thus, in a competitive market with N firms, the following will be true:

$$P = MC_1 = MC_2 = \ldots = MC_N$$

FIGURE 12.1

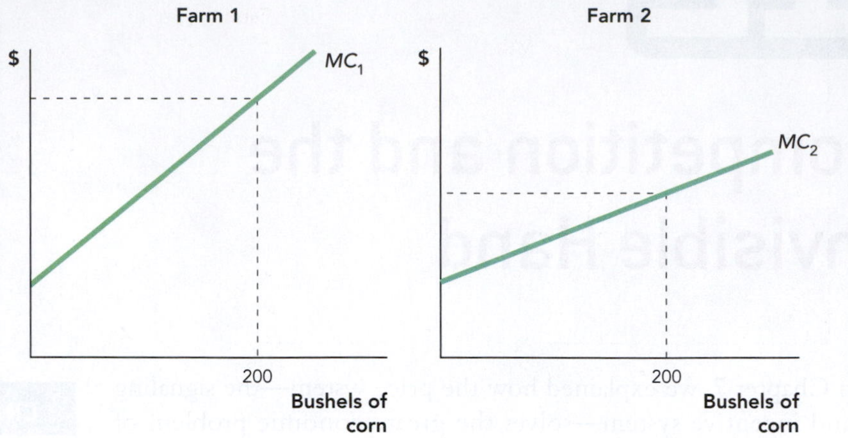

Marginal Cost of Producing 200 Bushels of Corn on Farm 1 and Farm 2 Farm 2 has a lower marginal cost of producing corn than Farm 1. So should we use Farm 2 only?

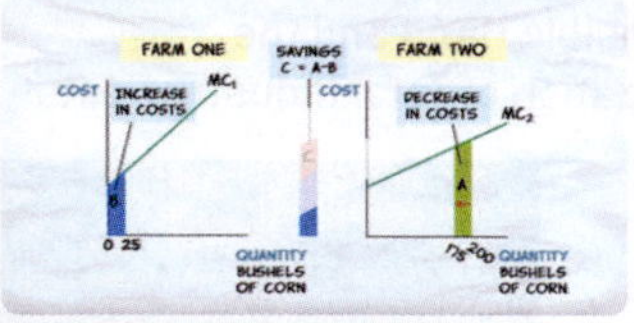

The Invisible Hand and the Minimization of Total Industry Costs

where MC_1 is the marginal cost of firm 1, MC_2 is the marginal cost of firm 2, and so forth. To understand the importance of this condition, let's briefly consider a seemingly different problem. Suppose that you own two farms on which to grow corn. Farm 1 is in a hilly region that is costly to seed and plow. Farm 2 is on land ideal for growing corn. The marginal cost of growing corn on each of these farms is illustrated in Figure 12.1.

Let's say that you would like to grow 200 bushels. It might seem that the lowest-cost way to produce 200 bushels is to produce all 200 bushels on Farm 2. After all, the marginal costs of production on Farm 2 are lower than on Farm 1 for any level of output.

Assume that you did produce all 200 bushels on Farm 2 and no bushels on Farm 1. Can you see a way of lowering your total costs of production?

Let's think in marginal terms. Instead of producing all 200 bushels on Farm 2, what would happen to your total costs of production if you produced, say, 197 bushels on Farm 2 and 3 bushels on Farm 1? Notice from Figure 12.2 that when you produce less on Farm 2, your costs of production decrease by the shaded area labeled *A*—this is the marginal cost of producing those last few bushels on Farm 2. By instead producing those bushels on Farm 1, your costs increase by area *B*, the marginal cost of production on Farm 1. But area *B* is less than area *A*, so by switching some production from Farm 2 to Farm 1, your total costs of producing 200 bushels of corn goes down.

How far can you extend this logic? Clearly, you should continue producing fewer bushels on Farm 2 and more on Farm 1 if the marginal costs of production on Farm 2 exceed those on Farm 1; that is, produce less on Farm 2 and more on Farm 1 if $MC_2 > MC_1$. By the same logic, you should switch production from Farm 1 to Farm 2 if $MC_1 > MC_2$. Put these two statements together and it follows that the way to minimize the total costs of production is to produce just so much on each farm so that the marginal costs of production are equalized, $MC_1 = MC_2$. In the bottom panel of Figure 12.2, we show that

FIGURE 12.2

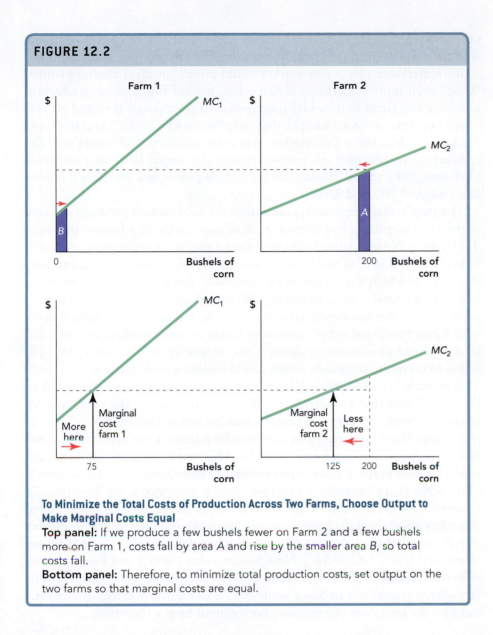

To Minimize the Total Costs of Production Across Two Farms, Choose Output to Make Marginal Costs Equal

Top panel: If we produce a few bushels fewer on Farm 2 and a few bushels more on Farm 1, costs fall by area *A* and rise by the smaller area *B*, so total costs fall.

Bottom panel: Therefore, to minimize total production costs, set output on the two farms so that marginal costs are equal.

the cost-minimizing way to produce 200 bushels of corn is to produce 75 bushels on Farm 1 and 125 bushels on Farm 2.

Now comes the really important part. If you own both farms, you can act as a "central planner" and allocate production across the two farms so that the marginal costs of production are equal and thus the total costs of production are minimized. But now suppose that Farm 1 is in North Carolina and Farm 2 is in Iowa, and let's say Farm 1 is owned by Sandy and Farm 2 by Pat. Let's further suppose that Sandy and Pat will live their entire lives without ever meeting. Is there any way to organize production so that the output is split in exactly the way that you would split it if you owned both farms? Yes, there is.

Sandy and Pat sell their corn in the same market so each of them sees the same price of corn. How will Sandy maximize profits? How will Pat maximize profits? To maximize profits, Sandy will set $P = MC_1$ and Pat will set $P = MC_2$, but this means that $MC_1 = MC_2$! But we know that if $P = MC_1 = MC_2$, then the total costs of production are minimized. Amazingly, in pursuit of their own profit, Sandy and Pat will allocate output across their two farms in exactly the way that a central planner would to minimize the total costs of production!

It's remarkable that a free market could mimic an ideal central planner. What's even more remarkable is that a free market can allocate production across the two farms to minimize total costs even when an ideal central planner could not! Imagine, for example, that only Sandy knows MC_1 and that only Pat knows MC_2. For a free market, this is no problem, and Sandy and Pat, each acting in their own self-interest, choose the output levels that minimize total costs. But a central planner cannot allocate production correctly if it lacks knowledge of MC_1 and MC_2.

The insight that a free market minimizes the total costs of production is one of the most surprising and deepest in all of economics. In a famous phrase in *The Wealth of Nations*, Adam Smith described a similar situation saying that each individual "in this, as in many other cases, [is] led by an invisible hand to promote an end which was no part of his intention." Sandy and Pat don't intend to minimize the total costs of producing 200 bushels of corn; they intend only to make a profit. But this beneficial outcome is the result of their action. Indeed, until Adam Smith and other economists began to study markets, not only did no one intend to minimize industry costs, no one even *knew* that individuals acting to maximize their own profits would minimize industry costs.

Friedrich Hayek, a Nobel Prize–winning economist we discussed in Chapter 7, said that properties like the minimization of the total costs of production were "products of human action but not of human design."

Invisible Hand Property 1 says that even though no actor in a market economy intends to do so, in a free market $P = MC_1 = MC_2 = \ldots = MC_N$ and, as a result, the total industry costs of production are minimized.

Invisible Hand Property 1 provides another perspective on free trade. In Chapter 9, we explained how free trade increased wealth by letting the United States buy goods from the lowest-cost producers. We can now see this in another way. Remember that costs are minimized when $MC_1 = MC_2$ so costs are *not* minimized when $MC_1 \neq MC_2$. Now imagine that Farm 1 and Farm 2 are in different countries with no free trade between them. Sandy and Pat, therefore, face *different* prices for corn. Since Sandy and Pat face different prices, $MC_1 \neq MC_2$ and thus the total costs of producing corn cannot be at a minimum.

CHECK YOURSELF

- If the MC of production on Sandy's farm is higher than on Pat's farm, how should production be rearranged to minimize the total costs of production?

Invisible Hand Property 2: The Balance of Industries

Invisible Hand Property 1 tells us that in a competitive industry, the total industry costs of production are minimized. But we could minimize the total costs of producing corn and still have too much or too little corn. It's good to know that if 20 or 200 million bushels of corn are produced, we get those bushels at the lowest cost, but how many bushels is the right amount? It's the second invisible hand property that ensures the right amount of corn is produced.

Consider two industries, the car industry and the computer industry. Both industries use labor and capital to produce goods. Labor and capital, however, are limited. Recall from Chapter 7 that the great economic problem is to arrange our limited resources to satisfy as many of our wants as possible. So how do we allocate our limited labor and capital across the computer and car industry to satisfy as many of our wants as possible?

Profit in the computer industry is total revenue minus total cost. Total revenue measures the value of the output of the computer industry, the computers. Total cost measures the value of the inputs to the computer industry, the labor and capital. High profits, therefore, mean that outputs of high value are being created from inputs of low value. Profit is a signal that our limited labor and capital are being used productively in satisfying our wants.

Now suppose that the computer industry is more profitable than the car industry—then a unit of labor and capital in the computer industry is creating more value than in the car industry. What we would like, therefore, is for labor and capital to move from the car industry to the computer industry. Or, in other words, to use our limited resources most effectively, we would like resources to flow from low-profit industries to high-profit industries.

Of course, moving labor and capital from low-profit to high-profit industries is exactly what entrepreneurs would like to do! Recall that our condition to enter an industry is $P > AC$, but as we showed in Chapter 11, that's equivalent to $TR > TC$ (divide both sides of $TR > TC$ by Q). So, in a competitive market, the incentives that entrepreneurs have to seek profit and avoid losses align with the social incentive to move labor and capital out of low-value industries and into high-value industries.

Notice that profits encourage entry, but what happens to price and profits when firms enter an industry? As firms enter, supply increases and the price declines, which reduces profits. Losses encourage exit, but what happens to price and profits when firms exit an industry? As firms exit, supply decreases and the price increases, which increases profit (reduces losses). Thus, there is a tendency for the profit rate in all competitive industries to go to zero (normal profits). Since the profit rate tends to the same level in the car and the computer and all other industries, the marginal value of resources in all industries is the same. That's just another way of saying that the total value of production is maximized because if the profit rate in one industry were greater than in another, total value would increase if resources were to move from the less profitable to the more profitable industry.

Invisible Hand Property 1 showed how self-interest worked to minimize the total costs of, say, corn production. Invisible Hand Property 2 shows how the self-interest of entrepreneurs causes them to enter and exit the car, computer, corn, apple, and other industries in such a way that the total value of all production is maximized. An implication of Invisible Hand Property 2 is that the profit rate in all competitive industries tends toward the same level.

The Invisible Hand

Creative Destruction

Although the profit rate in all competitive industries tends toward the same level, that's just a tendency. Change is constant—tastes change, technologies change, and, in their pursuit of profit, entrepreneurs are always trying to discover new and better products and processes—so some profitable industries are always popping up and some unprofitable industries, as well. So, although the great economic problem is never solved completely, in a dynamic economy, resources are always moving toward an increase in the value of production. In a dynamic economy, entrepreneurs listen to price signals and they move capital and labor from unprofitable industries to profitable industries.

Profits pop up all the time, but in a dynamic economy, the entry of new firms quickly whacks them down again.

CAMERON QUINN

According to the **elimination principle,** above-normal profits are eliminated by entry and below-normal profits are eliminated by exit.

These dynamics illustrate a general feature of competitive markets that we call the **elimination principle:** *Above-normal profits are eliminated by entry and below-normal profits are eliminated by exit.*

The elimination principle says that above-normal profits are temporary. Great ideas are soon adopted by others; they diffuse throughout the economy and become commonplace—and no one profits from the commonplace. Since no one profits from the commonplace, *to earn above-normal profits an entrepreneur must innovate.*

The economist Joseph Schumpeter was eloquent on this point. In textbooks, he said, competition is about pushing price down to average cost:

> [But] in capitalist reality as distinguished from its textbook picture, it is not that kind of competition which counts but the competition from the new commodity, the new technology, the new source of supply, the new type of organization . . . competition which commands a decisive cost or quality advantage and which strikes not at the margins of the profits and the outputs of the existing firms but at their foundations and their very lives. . . .

This process of Creative Destruction is the essential fact about capitalism.[1]

Thus, the elimination principle serves as both a warning and an opportunity to entrepreneurs. Stand still and fall behind. Leap ahead and profits may follow. In a dynamic economy, there is a constant dance between elimination and innovation. Above-normal profits are constantly being eliminated by competition, and new sources of profit are constantly being created through innovation.

The Invisible Hand Works with Competitive Markets

We have shown in this chapter that competitive markets have some desirable "invisible hand" properties, but don't forget that the invisible hand works only in certain circumstances. For the competitive process to work, for example, it's important that prices accurately signal costs and benefits. But we already know from Chapter 10 on externalities that prices do not always accurately signal costs and benefits. We can now see from another perspective why this is a problem. If prices don't accurately signal costs and benefits, then Invisible Hand Property 2 won't work perfectly and there will not be an ideal balance between industries. We will get too few resources in some industries and too many resources in other industries.

Similarly, if markets are not competitive, then the invisible hand doesn't work as well. We will be taking up the problem of monopoly in Chapter 13 and oligopoly (a few firms but not many) in Chapter 15, but we can point to the basic issue here. Monopolists and oligopolists earn above-normal profits. We know that if an industry earns above-normal profits, we would like resources to move to that industry, but without the pressure of the competitive process, not enough resources will move and profits will not be eliminated. We can see right away, therefore, that output will be too low in a monopoly or in an oligopoly.

We will also be showing in Chapter 19, Public Goods and the Tragedy of the Commons, that for some types of goods, self-interest either doesn't align with the social interest or sometimes it may align in the wrong direction. All this remind us of the basic point: Good institutions align self-interest with the social interest, but good institutions are sometimes hard to find or create.

CHECK YOURSELF

- In Chapter 7, we saw how prices are signals. In competitive markets, how are profits signals?
- In a competitive market, how does a firm make profits if it has no control over price?

Joseph Schumpeter (1883–1950) In his youth, Schumpeter said he wanted to be "the greatest lover in Vienna, the best horseman in Europe, and the greatest economist in the world." He later claimed to have achieved two of the three, adding that he and horses just didn't get along.

Takeaway

Invisible Hand Property 1 says that by producing where $P = MC$, the self-interested, profit-seeking behavior of entrepreneurs results in the minimization of the total industry costs of production even though no entrepreneur intends this result. Invisible Hand Property 2 says that entry and exit decisions not only work to eliminate profits, they work to ensure that labor and capital move across industries to optimally balance production so that the greatest use is made of our limited resources.

The elimination principle tells us that above-normal profits are eliminated by entry and below-normal profits are eliminated by exit. Perhaps even more importantly, the elimination principle tells us that to earn above-normal profits, a firm must innovate.

Competitive markets do a good job of aligning self-interest with the social interest, but not all markets are competitive.

CHAPTER REVIEW

interactive activity   Go online to practice with more examples of these types of problems, including live links to videos, data sources, and feedback.

 Problems in **green** relate to MRU videos. See the MRU table at the end of the exercises.

KEY CONCEPTS

elimination principle, p. 238

FACTS AND TOOLS

1. Entrepreneurs shift capital and labor across industries in pursuit of profit. Let's look at this a little more closely. Suppose there are two industries: a high-profit industry, Industry H, and a low-profit industry, Industry L. Answer the following questions about these two industries.

   a. If the two industries have similar costs, then what must be true about prices in the two industries?

   b. What does your answer to part a imply about the value of the output in the two industries?

   c. If labor and capital are moved from Industry L to Industry H, what is given up? What is gained?

   d. Suppose instead that the prices in the two industries were identical. In this case, what must be true about the costs in the two industries?

   e. What does your answer to part d imply about the amounts of capital and labor required to produce one unit of output in each industry?

   f. If labor and capital are moved from Industry L to Industry H, are more units of output lost in Industry L or gained in Industry H?

2. Suppose that two industries, the pizza industry and the calzone industry, are equally risky, but rates of return on capital investments are only 5% in the pizza industry and 8% in the calzone industry.

   Which way will capital flow—from the pizza industry to the calzone industry, or from the calzone industry to the pizza industry?

3. We've claimed that the efficient way to spread out work across firms in the same industry is to set the marginal cost of production to be the same across firms. Let's see if this works in an example.

   Consider a competitive market for rolled steel (measured by the ton) with just two firms: SmallCo and BigCo. If we wanted to be more realistic, we could say there were 100 firms like SmallCo and 100 firms like BigCo, but that would just make the math harder without generating any insight. The two firms have marginal cost schedules like this:

| | Marginal Cost | |
Q	SmallCo	BigCo
1	$10	$10
2	$20	$10
3	$30	$10
4	$40	$10
5	$50	$20
6	$60	$30
7	$70	$40
8	$80	$50

a. We'll ignore the fixed costs of starting up the firms just to make things a little simpler. What is the total cost at each firm of producing each level of output? Fill in the table.

| | Total Cost | |
Q	SmallCo	BigCo
1	$10	$10
2	$30	$20
3	$60	
4		
5		
6		
7		
8		

b. What's the cheapest way to make 11 tons of steel? 5 tons?

c. What would the price have to be in this competitive market for these two firms to produce a total of 11 tons of steel? 5 tons?

d. Suppose that a government agency looked at BigCo and SmallCo's cost curves. Which firm looks like the low-cost producer to a

government agency? Would it be a good idea, an efficient policy, for the government to shut down the high-cost producer? In other words, could a government intervention do better than the invisible hand in this case?

e. Let's make part d more concrete: What would the total cost be if BigCo were the only firm in the market, and it had to produce 7 tons of rolled steel? What would marginal and total costs be if SmallCo and BigCo let the invisible hand divvy up the work between them?

4. Let's review the basic mechanism of the elimination principle.

a. When demand rises in Industry X, what happens to profits? Do they rise, fall, or remain unchanged?

b. When that happens, do firms, workers, and capital tend to enter Industry X, or do they tend to leave?

c. Does this tend to increase short-run supply in Industry X or reduce it?

d. In the long run, after this rise in demand, what will profits typically be in Industry X?

THINKING AND PROBLEM SOLVING

5. The elimination principle discussed in this chapter tells us what we can expect in the long run from perfectly competitive markets: zero (normal) profits across industries. If this were the case, and this fate were unavoidable, going into business would seem to be a fairly dismal choice, given that the end result of normal profits is known right out of the gate. Despite this, we constantly see entrepreneurs working hard to earn profits. Is this a waste of time, given what we know about the elimination principle? Is the fate of zero profit unavoidable? What would Joseph Schumpeter say about all of this?

6. How can the market mechanism guarantee that the marginal cost of production will be the same across all firms if those firms have different owners, are in different locations, and have unique cost functions known only to the firms themselves? Why don't these different firms need to have one shared owner or one shared manager to coordinate this "equal marginal cost" condition?

7. We've seen already from this chapter that dividing up output over multiple producers—even when one has higher costs than the other—can lead to lower industry costs, so long as output is divided up such that $MC_1 = MC_2 = MC_N$. You've already done some practice in Facts and Tools question 3 with cost functions presented as tables. Let's try to see how this works graphically.

Take a look at the following two marginal cost functions:

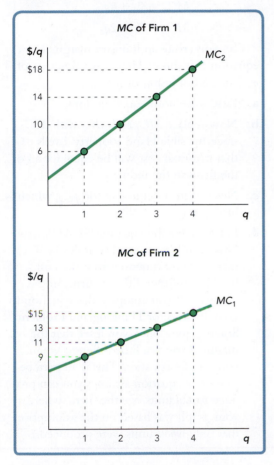

Quantity	Industry-Wide MC
1	$6
2	$9
3	
4	
5	
6	
7	
8	

Based on the graphs of these two marginal cost functions, fill in the table, for industry-wide marginal cost, assuming that production is divided up among the two firms according to Invisible Hand Property 1. Then, create a graph of the industry marginal cost curve. To help you get started, take a look at the table and answer the following questions. Which firm produces the first unit of industry output? Which firm produces the second unit of industry output? Why?

8. In the process of creative destruction, what gets destroyed?

Firms

Workers

Machines

Buildings

Business plans

Valuable relationships

Or some combination of these? The chapter itself contains quite a few ideas about how to answer this question, but you'll have to think hard about the "opportunity cost" for each item on the list.

9. Every year, American television introduces many new shows, only about one-third of which survive past their first season.[2] The few shows that last, however, prove to be very profitable.

a. How does creative destruction explain why studios bother to make new shows if most of them will fail?

b. In the Summer of 2002, *American Idol* premiered on television and became immensely popular. How did FOX and other networks respond to this surprise hit?

c. What happened over the next several years to profits from *American Idol*? You don't need to check FOX's financial statements to get the answer; use the elimination principle!

10. Let's suppose that the demand for allergists increases in California. How does the invisible hand respond to this demand? There is more than one correct answer to this question: Try to come up with two or three.

CHALLENGES

11. Let's take a look at Invisible Hand Property 2 in action using a mathematical example. Suppose an industry is characterized by the equations in the following table. (We're going to assume that all individual firms are identical to make this problem a little simpler.)

Demand	$Q_D = 100 - 2P$
Individual firm's supply	$q_S = 0.5 + 0.1P$
Market supply with n firms	$Q_S = n \times q_S$ $= 0.5n + 0.1nP$
Individual firm's average cost	$AC = 5q_S - 5 + (24.2/q_S)$

a. Suppose 24 firms are in this industry. What is the equation for market supply? What are the equilibrium price and quantity (this can be found by setting $Q_D = Q_S$)? How much profit is each firm earning? According to the elimination principle, what should occur in this industry over time?

b. Suppose 35 firms are in this industry. Answer the same questions from part a.

c. The elimination principle says that profits will be eliminated in the long run, which means that $AC = P$. Using that fact, figure out how many firms will be in this industry in the long run (solve for n).

interactive activity

WORK IT OUT

For interactive, step-by-step help in solving this problem, go online.

Now let's take a look at the equations for the marginal cost functions that are graphed in Thinking and Problem Solving question 7, and see if we can combine them into one equation for industry-wide marginal cost. This is what the two equations for the graphs in the question look like:

$$MC_1 = 2 + 4q_1$$
$$MC_2 = 7 + 2q_2$$

Can you create an industry marginal cost equation that shows MC_{Total} as a function of q_{Total} instead of just q_1 or q_2?

a. First, solve both equations for q.

b. Now, replace MC_1 and MC_2 with MC_{Total}, since Invisible Hand Property 1 tells us that marginal cost will be equal for all of the firms in the industry.

c. Next, write an equation for q_{Total}, which is just $q_1 + q_2$.

d. Finally, solve the equation for MC_{Total}. Now you have created an industry marginal cost function from the cost functions of two different firms in the industry. (If you compare this equation to your answers for Thinking and Problem Solving question 7, you'll see that the marginal cost is a little different when you use the equation. This is, in part, because this equation assumes you can produce *partial* units at either firm, whereas your graph was based on the assumption that only *whole* units were produced.)

MRUNIVERSITY
AN ONLINE EDUCATION PLATFORM

MARGINAL REVOLUTION UNIVERSITY VIDEOS

The Invisible Hand and the Minimization of Total Industry Costs

mruniversity.com/cost-production

Problems: **1–3, 6, 7, 10**

The Balance of Industries and Creative Destruction

mruniversity.com/creative-destruction

Problems: **4, 5, 8, 9, 11**

13

Monopoly

On June 5, 1981, the Centers for Disease Control and Prevention reported that a strange outbreak of pneumonia was killing young, healthy, homosexual men in Los Angeles. Alarm spread as similar reports streamed in from San Francisco, New York, and Boston. What had at first looked like a disease peculiar to homosexual men turned out to be a worldwide killer caused by HIV (the human immunodeficiency virus). Since 1981, AIDS (acquired immune deficiency syndrome) has killed more than 36 million people.

There is no known cure for AIDS, but progress has been made in treating the disease. In the United States, deaths from AIDS dropped by approximately 50% between 1995 and 1997. The major cause of the falling death rate was the development of new drugs called combination antiretrovirals, such as Combivir.[1] The drugs work, however, only if one can afford to take them, and they are expensive. A single pill of Combivir costs about $12.50—at two per day, every day, that's nearly $10,000 per year.[2] If you have the money, $10,000 a year is a small price to pay for life, but there are 35 million people worldwide living with HIV and most of them don't have $10,000.[3]

If HIV drugs were expensive because production costs were high, economists would have little to say about drug pricing. But it costs about 50 cents to produce a pill of Combivir—thus, the price of one pill is about 25 times higher than the cost.[4] In earlier chapters, we emphasized how competitive markets drive the price of a good down to marginal cost. Why hasn't that process worked here? There are three reasons why HIV drugs are priced well above cost.

1. Market power
2. The "you can't take it with you" effect
3. The "other people's money" effect

The primary reason that AIDS drugs are priced well above cost is monopoly or market power, the subject of this chapter. The "you can't take it with you" and "other people's money" effects, which we will also discuss in this chapter, make market power especially strong in the pricing of pharmaceuticals.

Market Power

GlaxoSmithKline (GSK), the world's largest producer of AIDS drugs, owns the patent on Combivir. A patent is a government grant that gives the owner the exclusive rights to make, use, or sell the patented product. GlaxoSmithKline, for

The cause of AIDS, the human immunodeficiency virus (HIV)

INGRAM PUBLISHING/VETTA/GETTY IMAGES

example, is the only legal seller of Combivir. Even though the formula to manufacture it is well-known and easily duplicated, competitors who try to make Combivir or its equivalent will be jailed, at least in the United States and other countries where the patent is enforced.

Market power is the power to raise price above marginal cost without fear that other firms will enter the market.

A monopoly is a firm with market power.

GSK's patent on Combivir gives GSK **market power**, the power to raise price above marginal cost without fear that other competitors will enter the market. A **monopoly** is simply a firm with market power.

India does not recognize the Combivir patent, so in that country competition prevails and an equivalent drug sells for just 50 cents per pill.[5] Thus, economics correctly predicts that competition will drive price down to marginal cost; it's just that GSK's patent prevents competition from operating.

Patents are not the only source of market power. Government regulations other than patents, as well as economies of scale, exclusive access to an important input, and technological innovation can all create firms with market power. We discuss the sources of market power and appropriate responses at greater length later on in this chapter. For now, we want to ask how a firm will use its market power to maximize profit.

How a Firm Uses Market Power to Maximize Profit

We know that a firm with market power will price above cost—but how much above cost? Even a firm with no competitors faces a demand curve, so as it raises its price, it will sell fewer units. Higher prices, therefore, are not always better for a seller—raise the price too much and profits will fall. Lower the price and profits can increase. What is the profit-maximizing price?

Marginal revenue, *MR*, is the change in total revenue from selling an additional unit.

Marginal cost, *MC*, is the change in total cost from producing an additional unit.

To maximize profit, a firm increases output until $MR = MC$.

To maximize profit, a firm should produce until the revenue from an additional sale is equal to the cost of an additional sale. This is the same condition that we discovered in Chapter 11: Produce until **marginal revenue** equals **marginal cost** ($MR = MC$). In Chapter 11, however, calculating marginal revenue was easy because even if a small oil well increases production significantly, the effect on the world price of oil is so small it can be ignored. For a small firm, therefore, the revenue from the sale of an additional unit is the market price ($MR =$ Price). But when a firm's output of a product is large relative to the entire market's output of that product (or very close substitutes), a significant increase in the firm's output will cause the market price of that product to fall. When GSK produces and sells more Combivir, for example, it pushes the price of Combivir down. Thus, for a firm that produces a large share of the market's total output of a product, the revenue from the sale of an additional unit is less than the current market price ($MR <$ Price). In our chapter on Costs and Profit Maximization Under Competition, we said that the competitive firm was a price taker. In contrast, a firm with monopoly power is a price maker; when this firm changes the quantity it produces, it also changes the price at which it can sell.

To understand how a firm with market power will choose what quantity to produce and thus the price at which it sells its product, we need to calculate marginal revenue for a firm that is large enough to influence the price of its product.

We show how to calculate marginal revenue in the table in the left panel of Figure 13.1. Suppose that at a price of $16 the quantity demanded is 2 units, so that total revenue is $32 (2 × $16). If the monopolist reduces the price to $14, it can sell 3 units for a total revenue of $42 (3 × $14). Marginal revenue, the change in revenue from selling an additional unit, is therefore $10 ($42 − $32). Thus, we can always calculate *MR* by looking at the change in total revenue when production changes by one unit.

The right panel of Figure 13.1 shows another way of thinking about marginal revenue. When the monopolist lowers its price from $16 to $14, it makes one additional sale, which increases revenues by the price of one unit, $14—the green area. But to make that additional sale, the monopolist had to lower its price by $2, so it loses $2 on *each* of the two units that it was selling at the higher price for a revenue loss of $4—the red area. Marginal revenue is the revenue gain (green, $14) plus the revenue loss (red, −$4) or $10 (green striped area). Notice that *MR* ($10) is less than price ($14)—once again, this is because to sell more units, the monopolist must lower the price so there is a loss of revenue on sales the firm would have made at the higher price.

Now that you understand the idea of marginal revenue, here's a shortcut for finding it. If the demand curve is a straight line, then the marginal revenue curve is a straight line that begins at the same point on the vertical axis as the demand curve but with twice the slope.[6] Figure 13.2 shows three demand curves and their associated marginal revenue curves. Notice that if the demand curve cuts the horizontal axis at, say, *Z*, then the marginal revenue curve will always cut the horizontal axis at half that amount, *Z*/2.

FIGURE 13.1

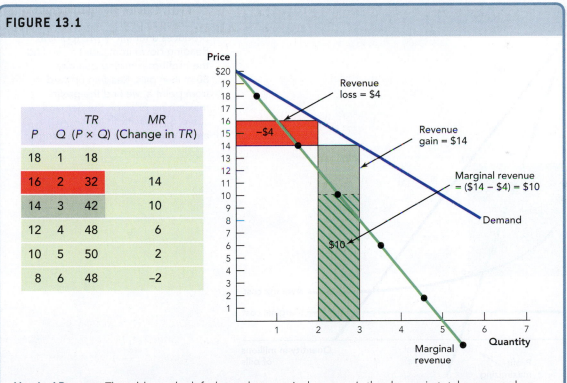

Marginal Revenue The table on the left shows that marginal revenue is the change in total revenue when quantity sold increases by 1 unit. When the quantity sold increases from 2 units to 3 units, for example, total revenue increases from $32 to $42 so marginal revenue, the change in total revenue, is $10.

The figure on the right shows how we can break down the change in total revenue into two parts. When the firm lowers the price from $16 to $14, it sells one more unit and so there is a gain in revenue of $14, the price of that unit, but since to sell that additional unit the firm had to lower the price, it loses $2 on each of its two previous sales so there is a revenue loss of $4. Thus, marginal revenue is the revenue gain on new sales plus the revenue loss on previous sales.

FIGURE 13.2

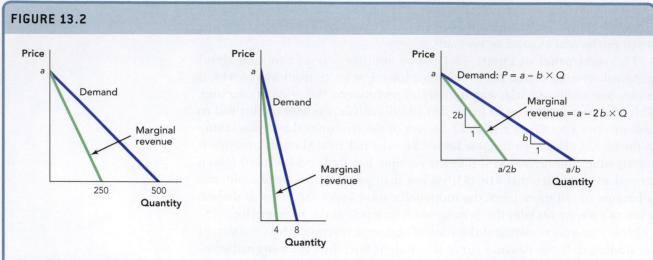

The *MR* Shortcut When the demand curve is a straight line, the marginal revenue curve begins at the same point on the vertical axis as the demand curve and has twice the slope.

FIGURE 13.3

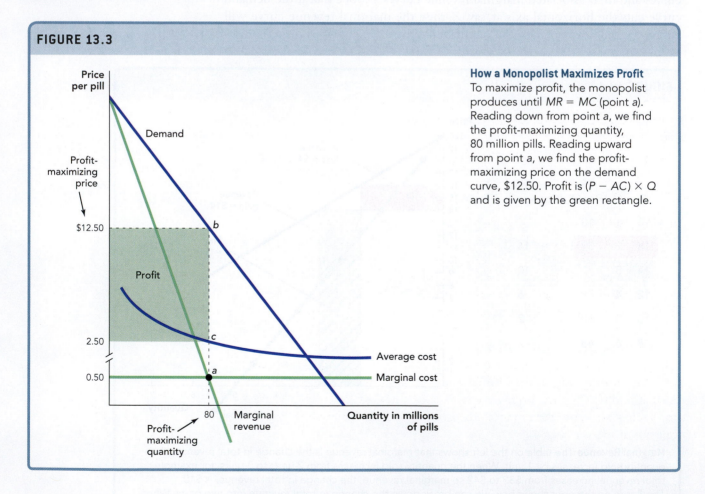

How a Monopolist Maximizes Profit
To maximize profit, the monopolist produces until *MR* = *MC* (point a). Reading down from point a, we find the profit-maximizing quantity, 80 million pills. Reading upward from point a, we find the profit-maximizing price on the demand curve, $12.50. Profit is (P − AC) × Q and is given by the green rectangle.

Figure 13.3 sketches the demand, marginal revenue, marginal cost, and average cost curve for a firm with market power, like GlaxoSmithKline. GSK maximizes profit by producing the quantity where *MR* = *MC*. In Figure 13.3, this is at point *a*, a quantity of 80 million units. What is the maximum price at which the monopolist can sell 80 million units? To find the maximum that consumers will pay for 80 million units, remember that we read up from the quantity supplied of 80 million units to the *demand curve* at point *b*. Consumers are willing to pay as much as $12.50 per pill when the quantity supplied is 80 million pills, so the profit-maximizing price is $12.50.

We can also use Figure 13.3 to illustrate the monopolist's profit. Remember from Chapter 11 that profit can be calculated as $(P - AC) \times Q$. At a quantity of 80 million units, the price is $12.50 (point *b*), the average cost (AC) is $2.50 (point *c*), and thus profit is $(\$12.50 - \$2.50) \times 80$ million units or $800 million, as illustrated by the green rectangle. (By the way, the fixed costs of producing a new pharmaceutical are very large so the minimum point of the AC curve occurs far to the right of the diagram.) Recall that a competitive firm earns zero or normal profits but a monopolist uses its market power to earn positive or *above-normal* profits.

The Elasticity of Demand and the Monopoly Markup

Market power for pharmaceuticals can be especially powerful because of the two other effects we mentioned earlier: the "you can't take it with you" effect and the "other people's money" effect. If you are dying of disease, what better use of your money do you have than spending it on medicine that might prolong your life? If you can't take it with you, then you may as well spend your money trying to stick around a bit longer. Consumers with serious diseases, therefore, are *relatively insensitive to the price of life-saving pharmaceuticals*.

Moreover, if you are willing to spend *your* money on pharmaceuticals, how do you feel about spending *other people's money*? Most patients in the United States have access to public or private health insurance, so pharmaceuticals and other medical treatments are often paid by someone other than the patient. Thus, both the "you can't take it with you" and the "other people's money" effects make consumers with serious diseases relatively insensitive to the price of life-saving pharmaceuticals—that is, they will continue to buy in large quantities even when the price increases.

If GlaxoSmithKline knows that consumers will continue to buy Combivir even when it increases the price, how do you think it will respond? Yes, it will increase the price! When consumers are relatively insensitive to the price, what sort of demand curve do we say consumers have? An inelastic demand curve. The "you can't take it with you" effect and the "other people's money" effect make the demand curve more *inelastic*. Thus, we say that the more inelastic the demand curve, the more a monopolist will raise its price above marginal cost.

Is it ethically wrong for GSK to raise its price above marginal cost? Perhaps, but keep in mind that in the United States, it costs nearly a billion dollars to research and develop the average new drug. Once we better understand how monopolies price, we will return to the question of what, if anything, should be done about market power.

Figure 13.4 illustrates that the more inelastic the demand curve, the more a monopolist will raise its price above marginal cost. On the left side of the figure, the monopolist faces a relatively elastic demand curve, and on the right side a relatively inelastic demand curve. As usual, the monopolist maximizes profit by choosing the quantity at which $MR = MC$ and the highest price that consumers will pay for that quantity. Notice that even though the marginal cost curve is identical in the two panels, the markup of price over marginal cost is much higher when the demand curve is relatively inelastic.

Monopoly Markup

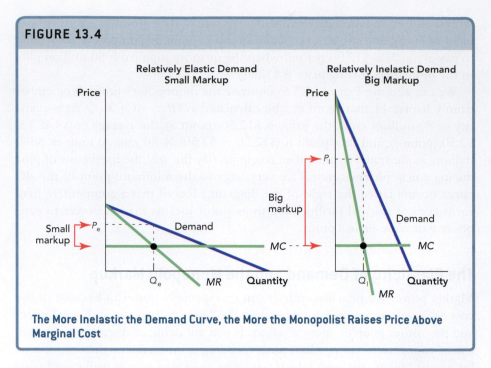

FIGURE 13.4

The More Inelastic the Demand Curve, the More the Monopolist Raises Price Above Marginal Cost

Remember from Chapter 5 that the fewer substitutes that exist for a good, the more inelastic the demand curve. With that in mind, consider the following puzzle. In February of 2014, American Airlines was selling a flight from Washington, D.C., to Dallas for $772. On the same day, it was selling a flight from Washington to San Francisco for $322. That's a little puzzling. You would expect the shorter flight to have lower costs, and Washington is much closer to Dallas than to San Francisco. The puzzle, however, is even deeper. The flight from Washington to San Francisco stopped in Dallas. In fact, the Washington-to-Dallas leg of the journey was on exactly the same flight![7]

Thus, a traveler going from Washington to Dallas was being charged nearly $450 *more* than a traveler going from Washington to Dallas and then on to San Francisco even though both were flying to Dallas on the same plane. Why?

Here's a hint. Each of the major airlines flies most of its cross-country traffic into a hub, an airport that serves as a busy "node" in an airline's network of flights, and most hubs are located near the center of the country. Delta's hub, for example, is in Atlanta. So if you fly cross-country on Delta, you will probably travel through Atlanta. United's hub is in Chicago and American Airlines has its hub in Dallas. Have you solved the puzzle yet?

Of the flights into the Dallas-Fort Worth airport, 84% are on American Airlines, so if you want to fly from Washington to Dallas at a convenient time, you have few choices of airline. But if you want to fly from Washington to San Francisco, you have many choices. In addition to flying on American Airlines, you can fly Delta, United, or Jet Blue. Since travelers flying from Washington to Dallas have few substitutes, their demand curve is inelastic, like the demand curve in the right panel of Figure 13.4. Since travelers flying from Washington to San Francisco have many substitutes, their demand curve is more elastic, like the one in the left panel of Figure 13.4. As a result, travelers flying from Washington to Dallas (inelastic demand) are charged more than those flying from Washington to San Francisco (elastic demand).

You are probably asking yourself why someone wanting to go from Washington to Dallas doesn't book the cheaper flight to San Francisco and then exit in Dallas?

In fact, clever people try to game the system all the time—but don't try to do this with a round-trip ticket or the airline will cancel your return flight. As a matter of contract, most airlines prohibit this and similar practices—their profit is at stake!

The Costs of Monopoly: Deadweight Loss

What's wrong with monopoly? The question may seem absurd—isn't it the high prices? Not so fast. The high price is bad for consumers, but it's good for the monopolist. And what's so special about consumers? Monopolists are people, too. So if we want to discover whether monopoly is good or bad, we need to count the gains to the monopolist equally with the losses to consumers. It turns out, however, that the monopolist gains less from monopoly pricing than the consumer loses. So monopolies are bad—they are bad because, compared with competition, monopolies reduce *total surplus*, the total gains from trade (consumer surplus plus producer surplus).

In Figure 13.5 on the next page, we compare total surplus under competition with total surplus under monopoly. In the left panel, the competitive equilibrium price and quantity are P_c and Q_c. We also label Q_c the optimal quantity because it is the quantity that maximizes total surplus (recall from Chapter 4 that a competitive market maximizes total surplus). For simplicity, we assume a constant cost industry so the supply curve is flat ($MC = AC$) and producer surplus is zero. Total surplus is thus the same as consumer surplus and is shown by the blue triangle.

The right panel shows how a monopolist with the same costs would behave. Setting $MR = MC$, the monopolist produces Q_m, which is much less than Q_c, and prices at P_m. Consumer surplus is now the much smaller blue triangle. Now here is the key point: *Some* of the consumer surplus has been transferred to the monopolist as profit, the green area. But some of the consumer surplus is not transferred; it goes to neither the consumers nor the monopolist; it goes to no one and is lost. We call the lost consumer surplus *deadweight loss*.

To better understand deadweight loss, remember that the height of the demand curve tells you how much consumers are willing to pay for the good, and the height

CHECK YOURSELF

- As a firm with market power moves down the demand curve to sell more units, what happens to the price it can charge on all units?
- What type of demand curve does a firm with market power prefer to face for its products: relatively elastic or inelastic? Why?

FIGURE 13.5

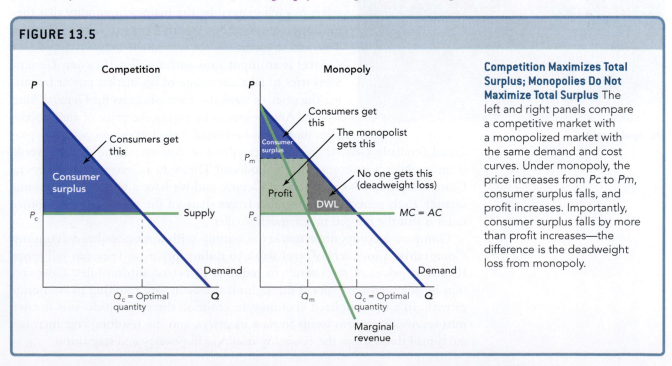

Competition Maximizes Total Surplus; Monopolies Do Not Maximize Total Surplus The left and right panels compare a competitive market with a monopolized market with the same demand and cost curves. Under monopoly, the price increases from P_c to P_m, consumer surplus falls, and profit increases. Importantly, consumer surplus falls by more than profit increases—the difference is the deadweight loss from monopoly.

of the marginal cost curve tells you the cost of producing the good. Now notice that in between the amount that the monopolist produces, Q_m, and the amount that would be produced under competition, Q_c, the demand curve is above the marginal cost curve. In other words, consumers value the units between Q_m and Q_c more than their cost; so if these units were produced, total surplus would increase. But the monopolist does not produce these units. Why not? Because to sell these units, the monopolist would have to lower its price; and if it did so, the increase in revenue would not cover the increase in costs, that is, MR would be less than MC, so the monopolist's profit would decrease.

Let's look at deadweight loss in practice. GlaxoSmithKline prices Combivir at $12.50 a pill, the profit-maximizing price. There are plenty of consumers who can't pay $12.50 a pill but would gladly pay more than the marginal cost of 50 cents a pill. Deadweight loss is the value of the Combivir sales that do not occur because the monopoly price is above the competitive price.

The Costs of Monopoly: Corruption and Inefficiency

Sadly, around the world today, many monopolies are government-created and born of corruption. Indonesian President Suharto (in office from 1967 to 1998), for example, gave the lucrative clove monopoly to his playboy son, Tommy Suharto. Cloves may sound inconsequential, but they are a key ingredient in Indonesian cigarettes, and the monopoly funneled hundreds of millions of dollars to Tommy. A lot of rich playboys buy Lamborghinis—Tommy bought the entire company.

Monopolies are especially harmful when the goods that are monopolized are used to produce other goods. In Algeria, for example, a dozen or so army generals each control a key good. Indeed, the public ironically refers to each general by the major commodity that they monopolize—General Steel, General Wheat, General Tire, and so forth.

Steel is an input into automobiles, so when General Steel tries to take advantage of his market power by raising the price of steel, this increases costs for General Auto. General Auto responds by raising the price of automobiles even more than he would if steel were competitively produced. Similarly, General Steel raises the price of steel even more than he would if automobiles were competitively produced. Throw in a General Tire, a General Computer, and, let's say, a General Electric and we have a recipe for economic disaster. Each general tries to grab a larger share of the pie, but the combined result is that the pie gets much, much smaller.

Compare a competitive market economy with a monopolized economy: Competitive producers of steel work to reduce prices so they can sell more. Reduced prices of steel result in reduced prices of automobiles. Cost savings in one sector are spread throughout the economy, resulting in economic growth. In a monopolized economy, in contrast, the entire process is thrown into reverse. Each firm wants to raise its prices, and the resulting cost increases are spread throughout the economy, resulting in poverty and stagnation.

PETER HARHOLDT/SUPERSTOCK

Monopoly profit

One of the great lessons of economics is to show that good institutions channel self-interest toward social prosperity, whereas poor institutions channel self-interest toward social destruction. Business leaders in the United States are no less self-interested than generals in Algeria. So why are the former a mostly positive force, while the latter are a mostly negative force? It's because competitive markets channel the self-interest of business leaders toward social prosperity, whereas the political structure of Algeria channels self-interest toward social destruction.

The Benefits of Monopoly: Incentives for Research and Development

GlaxoSmithKline prices its AIDS drugs above marginal cost. If GSK didn't have a monopoly, competition would push prices down, more people could afford to buy Combivir, and total surplus would increase (i.e., deadweight loss would decline). So isn't the solution to the monopoly problem obvious? Open up the industry to competition by refusing to enforce the firm's patent or force GlaxoSmithKline to lower its price.

In fact, many countries pursue one or the other of these policies. India, for example, has traditionally not offered strong patent protection, and Canada controls pharmaceutical prices. India's and Canada's policies have successfully kept pharmaceutical prices low in those countries. Many people argue that the United States should also control pharmaceutical prices. Unfortunately, the story is not so simple. We need to revisit our question, what's wrong with monopoly?

In the United States, researching, developing, and successfully testing the average new drug cost nearly $1 billion.[8] Firms must be compensated for these expenses if people expect them to invest in the discovery process. But if competition pushes the price of a pill down to the marginal cost, nothing will be left over for the cost of invention. And he who has no hope of reaping will not sow.

Patents are one way of rewarding research and development. Look again at Figure 13.3, which shows the green rectangle of monopoly profit. It's precisely the expectation (and hope) of enjoying that monopoly profit that encourages firms to research and develop new drugs.

If pharmaceutical patents are not enforced, the number of new drugs will decrease. India is poor and Canada is small, so neither contributes much to the global profit of pharmaceutical firms. But if the United States were to limit pharmaceutical patents significantly or to control pharmaceutical prices, the number of new drugs would decrease significantly.[9] But new drugs save lives. As noted in the introduction, antiretrovirals like Combivir were the major cause of the 50% decrease in AIDS deaths in the United States in the mid-1990s. We should be careful that in pushing prices closer to marginal cost, we do not lose the new drug entirely.

In evaluating pharmaceutical patents, you should keep in mind that patents don't last forever. A patent lasts for at most 20 years, and by the time a new drug is FDA-approved, its effective life is typically only 12–14 years. Once the drug goes off patent, generic equivalents appear quickly and the deadweight loss is eliminated as price falls.

Pharmaceuticals are not the only goods with high development costs and low marginal costs. Information goods of all kinds often have the same cost structure. Video games like Halo, Madden NFL, and The Sims have typical development costs of $7 million to $10 million; Grand Theft Auto IV cost

RANDY M URY/AGE FOTOSTOCK

Thomas Edison spent years experimenting with thousands of materials before he discovered that carbonized bamboo filament would make a long-lasting lightbulb. If anyone could have capitalized on his idea, Edison would not have been able to profit from his laborious research and development and perhaps he would not have done the necessary research in the first place.

Profit fuels the fire of invention.

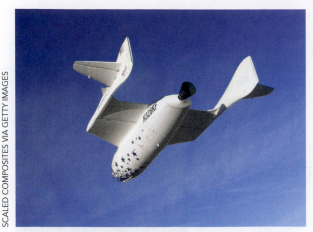

SCALED COMPOSITES VIA GETTY IMAGES

Eyes on the prize Prizes are another way of rewarding research and development without creating monopolies. SpaceShipOne, pictured here, won the $10 million Ansari X Prize for being the first privately developed manned rocket capable of reaching space and returning in a short time. Netflix, the DVD distribution firm, offered and paid a $1 million prize for improvements to its movie recommendation system. The Department of Defense has sponsored prizes for driverless vehicles and Congress established the L-Prize for advances in lightbulb technology.

interactive activity

Patents, Prizes, and Subsidies

CHECK YOURSELF

■ Name some firms with market power that plausibly encourage innovation. Name some firms with market power that do not seem to encourage innovation.

■ If we rewarded innovation with prizes instead of patents, how large do you think the prize should be for a new cancer drug?

more than $100 million to develop. Once the code has been written, however, the marginal cost of distributing on the Internet is close to zero. Prices, typically $40–$60, are therefore well above marginal costs. Since prices exceed marginal costs, there is a deadweight loss, which in theory could be reduced by a price control. Reducing prices, however, would reduce the incentive to research and develop new games. What would you rather have: Pong at $2, or, for $50 a game, a constant stream of new and better games?

Video games may seem trivial, but the trade-off between lower prices today at the expense of fewer new ideas in the future is a central one in modern economies. In fact, modern theories of economic growth emphasize that monopoly—*when it increases innovation*—may increase economic growth.

Nobel prize–winning economic historian Douglass North argues that economic growth was slow and sporadic until laws, including patent laws, were created to protect innovation:

[T]hroughout man's past he has continually developed new techniques, but the pace has been slow and intermittent. The primary reason has been that the incentives for developing new techniques have occurred only sporadically. Typically, innovations could be copied at no cost by others and without any reward to the inventor or innovator. The failure to develop systematic property rights in innovation up until fairly modern times was a major source of the slow pace of technological change.[10]

Patent Buyouts—A Potential Solution?

Is there a way to eliminate the deadweight loss without reducing the incentive to innovate? Economist Michael Kremer has offered one speculative idea.[11] Take a look again at Figure 13.3. The green profit rectangle is the value of the patent to the patent owner, $800 million. Suppose that the government were to offer to buy the rights to the patent at, say, $850 million? The monopolist would be eager to sell at this price. What would the government do with the patent? Rip it up! If the government ripped up the patent, competitors would enter the field, drive the price down to the marginal cost of production, and eliminate the deadweight loss. In other words, Combivir would fall from $12.50 a pill to 50 cents a pill, and more of the world's poor could afford to be treated for AIDS.

The great virtue of Kremer's proposal is that it reduces the price of new drugs without reducing the incentive to develop more new drugs. Indeed, by offering more than the potential profit, the government could even increase the incentive to innovate! As usual, however, there is no such thing as a free lunch. To buy the patent, the government must raise taxes, and we know from Chapter 6 that taxes, just like monopolies, create deadweight losses. Also determining the right price to buy the patent is not easy and some people worry that corruption could be a problem.

Kremer's idea has never been tried on a widespread basis, but despite these problems, economists are becoming increasingly interested in patent buyouts and the closely related idea of prizes as a way to encourage innovation without creating too much deadweight loss.

Sources of Market Power

Patents and government regulation are not the only source of market power. Monopolies may be created by economies of scale, significant barrier to entry, network effects or innovation. Let's give some examples of each case.

Economies of scale are the advantages of large-scale production that reduce average cost as quantity increases. Toyota's factory in Kentucky, for example, produces 500,000 cars a year. Toyota's costs would be much higher if it produced 500 cars in 1000 factories. By concentrating production, Toyota can invest in specialized equipment, such as robots, that lower their costs. If economies of scale are large relative to the size of the market, then *one* large firm can produce at lower cost than many small firms. When a single firm can supply the entire market at lower cost than two or more firms, we say that the industry is a **natural monopoly**.

A subway is a natural monopoly because one subway system could serve the entire market at a lower cost than two systems. Why build two parallel subway tunnels when one is enough? Utilities such as water, natural gas, and cable television are typically natural monopolies because in each case it's much cheaper to run one pipe or cable than to run multiple pipes or cables to the same set of homes. Auto firms are not natural monopolies because the size of the market is larger than are the economies of scale so no single firm dominates the market. Economies of scale, however, do explain why there are a dozen or so major auto manufacturers rather than hundreds. See Chapter 15 for more on oligopolies, industries with a small number of firms.

In Figure 13.5, we compared competitive firms with an *equal cost* monopoly and showed that total surplus was higher under competition. The comparison between competitive firms and natural monopoly is more difficult. Even though natural monopolies produce less than the optimal quantity, competitive firms would also produce less than the optimal quantity because they could not take advantage of economies of scale.

If the economies of scale are large enough, it's even possible for price to be lower under a natural monopoly than it would be under competition. Figure 13.6 shows just such a situation. Notice that the average cost curve for the monopoly is so far below the average cost curves of the competitive firms that the monopoly price is below the competitive price. It's possible, for example, for every home to produce its own electric power with a small generator or solar panel, but the costs of producing electricity in this way would typically be higher than buying electricity produced from a dam, even if the dam charged the monopoly price.

More generally, however, when economies of scale are important we have a trade-off—costs are lower with one or a handful of firms but market power and prices are greater. We will later discuss that trade-off after discussing other causes of monopoly power.

Barriers to entry can also generate monopoly power. One firm, for example, might own an input that is difficult to duplicate. Oil is found in large quantities in only a few places in the world, so a single firm in the right place can monopolize a significant share of the total supply. Saudi Arabia is one of those places, so it has some market power in the oil market. Its market power is enhanced when, instead of competing with other suppliers, it joins with them to form a cartel, a group of firms that acts in concert to maximize total profits. We analyze cartels at greater length in Chapter 15.

Barriers to entry can also be more subtle. Remember the TI-84 Plus graphing calculator that you probably used in high school? The TI-84 hasn't changed

Economies of scale are the advantages of large-scale production that reduces average cost as quantity increases.

A **natural monopoly** is said to exist when a single firm can supply the entire market at a lower cost than two or more firms.

Barriers to entry are factors that increase the cost to new firms of entering an industry.

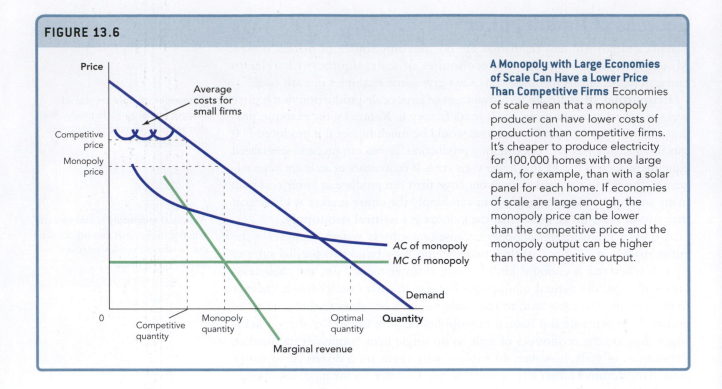

FIGURE 13.6

A Monopoly with Large Economies of Scale Can Have a Lower Price Than Competitive Firms Economies of scale mean that a monopoly producer can have lower costs of production than competitive firms. It's cheaper to produce electricity for 100,000 homes with one large dam, for example, than with a solar panel for each home. If economies of scale are large enough, the monopoly price can be lower than the competitive price and the monopoly output can be higher than the competitive output.

much in over a dozen years; it still has a tiny black and white screen and just 24k of memory. Yet, despite being less powerful and more expensive than other graphing calculators, more TI-84s are sold than any other graphing calculator. Why? Texas Instruments (TI), the maker of the TI-84 Plus, spent a lot of time and effort training high-school teachers to use their calculator and many math textbooks even include exact instructions for solving problems using the TI-84. So teachers assign the TI-84 for their classes. And since the parents, not the teachers, are paying, the teachers don't care much about the price. As a result, the graphing calculator division of Texas Instruments is very profitable. Market entry will eventually break down TI's barrier to entry but sometimes small advantages can mean big profits.

Brands and trademarks can also give a firm market power because the prestige of owning the real thing cannot be easily duplicated. Timex watches tell the time as well as a Rolex, but only the Rolex signals wealth and status.

Network effects are another source of monopoly power. Because everyone wants to be on the site that their friends use, there is a tendency for people to gravitate toward the same site. Thus, Facebook does not have many direct competitors. Similarly, there are only a handful of credit card companies (MasterCard, Visa, American Express). Customers want to have a card that is widely accepted and firms want to accept cards that are widely used, so there is a tendency to gravitate toward one or a handful of credit card companies. We take up the economics of network goods in Chapter 16.

Copyrights are another kind of barrier to entry. Does the picture on the next page look a little familiar? It's the cover from a Russian series of books about Tanya Grotter, an orphan with magical powers, a strange mark on her face, and an evil nemesis called Chuma-del-Tort. The Tanya Grotter series sold well

A Calculating Monopoly

in Russia but is not available in English because J. K. Rowling and the other copyright holders to the Harry Potter series successfully sued for copyright infringement. In the information age, copyrights are becoming an important source of monopoly power.

Finally, monopolies may also arise when a firm innovates, producing a product that no other firm can immediately duplicate. In recent years, Apple has sold about 40% of all smartphones in the United States, even though Apple has many competitors. Why? People simply like iPhones. Apple's high market share, however, isn't guaranteed and has come under increasing threat as other firms improve their products. As with patent monopolies, monopolies produced by innovation involve a trade-off: iPhones are priced higher than they would be if Apple had better competitors, but Apple would have less incentive to innovate if it didn't expect to earn some monopoly profits.

Table 13.1 summarizes common sources of market power.

Tanya Grotter and the Copyright Infringement Lawsuit

TABLE 13.1 SOME SOURCES OF MARKET POWER

Sources of Market Power	Example
Patents	GSK's patent on Combivir
Laws preventing entry of competitors	Indonesian clove monopoly, Algerian wheat monopoly, U.S. Postal Service
Economies of scale	Subways, cable TV, electricity transmission, major highways
Hard-to-duplicate inputs	Oil, diamonds, Rolex watches
Innovation	Apple's iPhone, Wolfram's Mathematica software, eBay
Copyright	Novels, movies, musical compositions, computer software
Network effects	Facebook, eBay, credit cards

Regulating Monopoly

The government has many tools to regulate monopolies. We will examine price controls, government ownership, and antitrust law.

Price Controls

In Chapter 8, we showed that a price control set below the market price would create a shortage. But surprisingly, when the market price is set by a monopolist, a price control can increase output. Let's see how.

If there is no regulation, then the monopolist in Figure 13.7 will choose the usual monopoly price and quantity: P_m, Q_m. But suppose that the government imposes a price control at level P_R. To avoid a loss, the monopolist must charge a price greater than or equal to average cost. But at the price P_R, the only quantity that lets the monopolist avoid a loss is Q_R. Thus, if the government sets $P_R = AC$ at point a, where the AC curve intersects the demand curve, the

FIGURE 13.7

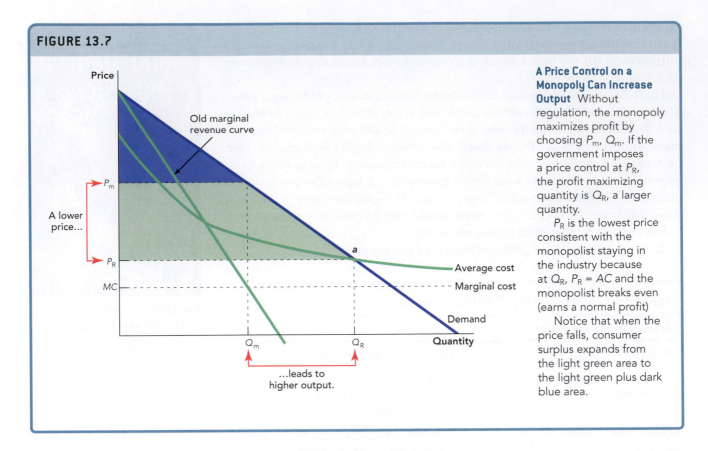

A Price Control on a Monopoly Can Increase Output Without regulation, the monopoly maximizes profit by choosing P_m, Q_m. If the government imposes a price control at P_R, the profit maximizing quantity is Q_R, a larger quantity.

P_R is the lowest price consistent with the monopolist staying in the industry because at Q_R, $P_R = AC$ and the monopolist breaks even (earns a normal profit)

Notice that when the price falls, consumer surplus expands from the light green area to the light green plus dark blue area.

monopolist chooses Q_R and just breaks even. Most importantly, notice that when the government lowers the price from P_m to P_R, output increases from Q_m to Q_R and consumer surplus increases from the light green area to the light green plus dark blue area.

Reducing monopoly prices to the level of average cost seems like a promising policy, but there are problems. When a monopolist's profits are regulated, it doesn't have much incentive to increase quality with innovative new products or to lower costs. Recall our discussion of pharmaceuticals. A price control on pharmaceutical monopolies could lower prices and increase the output of *currently existing drugs*. But reduced profits mean a reduced incentive to invest in research and development, and *that* would result in fewer new drugs. Over time, the net result could be great harm to patients. A price control is equivalent, in this context, to reducing the power of patents and, as we discussed earlier, this could end up harming patients through reduced innovation.

Let's also examine cable TV and electricity regulation before turning to another way to regulate monopolies, merger policy.

I Want My MTV Cable TV is a natural monopoly—at least it was in its early years, before satellite and Internet TV—and it has long been regulated in the United States. Regulating retail subscription rates for cable TV seemed to keep prices low early on, when there were basically only three channels, ABC, CBS, and NBC. Beginning in the 1970s, however, new technology made it possible for cable operators to offer 10, 20, or even 30 channels. But if subscription rates were fixed at the low levels, thereby limiting profit rates, the cable operators would have little incentive to add channels. Recognizing this, Congress lifted caps on pay TV rates in 1979 and on all cable television in 1984. (Cable TV remains largely unregulated today, although there was some further regulation and deregulation in 1992 and 1996, respectively.)

Quality comes at a price

Deregulation of cable TV rates led to higher prices, just as the theory of natural monopoly predicts, but something else happened—the number of television stations and the quality of programming increased dramatically. And, contrary to natural monopoly theory, consumers seemed to appreciate the new channels more than they disliked the higher prices: Even as prices rose, more people signed up for cable television.

Although there were just a few new and excellent shows at first, the number of quality productions has continued to grow. When the only way to pay for TV was advertising, it paid a producer to appeal to mass taste—the more eyes the better, it was believed, even if the eyes were a little bored. First with cable and subscription television and now with services like Netflix and Hulu, it can pay to produce shows that appeal to a smaller number of people, so long as enough of them are willing to pay the subscription fee to support the show. As a result, writers and directors are given much more room to experiment, and they have come up with outstanding entries in crime drama (*The Sopranos*), fantasy (*Game of Thrones*), historical drama (*Boardwalk*), and science fiction (*Westworld*), among others.

The bottom line is that despite increases in prices and in part *because of* the increase in prices, the deregulation of cable TV appears to have created a much more dynamic and exciting market in entertainment. Deregulation of electricity, on the other hand, has proved shocking.

Government Ownership

Electric Shock Government ownership is another potential solution to the natural monopoly problem. In the United States, there are some 3,000 electric utilities, and two-thirds of them are government-owned (the remainder are heavily regulated). Government ownership of utilities began early in the twentieth century when municipalities began owning local distribution companies. In the 1930s, the federal government became a major generator of electricity when it constructed the then largest man-made structures ever built, the Hoover Dam in 1936 and the even larger Grand Coulee Dam in 1941.

The system of government ownership and regulation of electricity worked reasonably well for several decades in providing the United States with cheap power. Without the discipline of competition or a profit motive, however, there is a tendency for a government-run or government-regulated monopoly to become inefficient. Why reduce costs when costs can be passed on to customers? As the price of power in the 1960s and 1970s increased, multibillion-dollar cost overruns for the construction of nuclear power plants drew attention to industry inefficiencies.

Historically, a single firm handled the generation, long-distance transmission, and local distribution of electricity. In the 1970s, however, new technologies reduced the average cost of generating electricity at small scales (in Figure 13.6 you can think of the curves labeled "Average costs for small firms" as moving down). Although the transmission and distribution of electricity remained natural monopolies, the new technologies meant that the generation of electricity was no longer a natural monopoly. Economists began to argue that unbundling generation from transmission and distribution could open up electricity generation to competitive forces, thereby reducing costs.

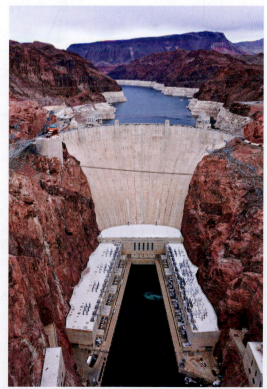

The Hoover Dam The natural monopoly that lights Las Vegas.

ANDREW ZARIVNY/SHUTTERSTOCK

California's Perfect Storm Hoping to benefit from lower costs and greater innovation, California deregulated wholesale electricity prices in 1998. All appeared well in the first two years after deregulation. Then in 2000, a hot summer and an earlier dry winter (low snowfall meant low lake levels and less opportunity for hydroelectric power) led to massive increases in the price of electricity. For example, in April of that year electricity was selling for $26 per megawatt hour (MWh), but by December prices had reached $317 per MWh. For brief periods it had even been as high as $3,900 per MWh. Worse yet, when not enough power was available to meet the demand, blackouts threw more than 1 million Californians off the grid and into the dark.

Mother Nature was not the only one to blame for California's troubles, however. The combination of increased demand, reduced supply, and a poorly designed deregulation plan had created the perfect opportunity for electricity generators to exploit market power. When the demand for electricity is well below capacity, each generator has very little market power. If a few generators had shut down in 1999, for example, the effect on the price would have been minimal because the power from those generators could easily have been replaced with imports or power from other generators. In 1999, then, each generator faced an elastic demand curve. In 2000, however, every generator was critical because nearly every generator needed to be up and running just to keep up with demand. Electricity is an unusual commodity because it is expensive to store; and, if demand and supply are ever out of equilibrium, the result can be catastrophic blackouts. Thus, when demand is near capacity, a small decline in supply leads to much higher prices as utilities desperately try to buy enough power to keep the electric grid up and running. Thus, in early 2000, the demand curve facing each generator was becoming very inelastic. And what happens to the incentive to increase price when demand becomes inelastic? Do you remember the lesson of Figure 13.4, also pictured at left in Figure 13.8?

In the summer and winter of 2000, demand was near capacity and *every* generator was facing an inelastic demand curve. A firm that owned only one generator couldn't do much to exploit its market power: If it shut down, the price of electricity would rise but the firm wouldn't have any power to sell! Because many firms owned more than one generator, however, a terrible incentive was created in 2000. A firm with four generators could shut down one generator, say, for "maintenance and repair," and the price of electricity would rise by so much that the firm could make more money selling the power produced by its three operating generators than it could if it ran all four! Suspiciously, far more generators were taken off-line for "maintenance and repair" in 2000 and early 2001 than in 1999.[12]

California was not the only state to restructure its electricity market in the late 1990s. Texas and Pennsylvania had opened up generation to competition and both have seen modestly lower electricity prices. Restructuring has also occurred in Great Britain, New Zealand, Canada, and elsewhere, but California's experience has demonstrated that unbundling generation from transmission and distribution, which remain natural monopolies, is tricky

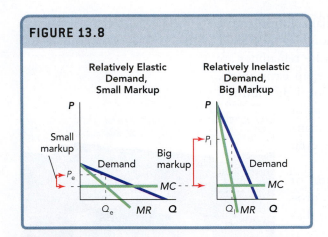

FIGURE 13.8

Relatively Elastic Demand, Small Markup

Relatively Inelastic Demand, Big Markup

CHECK YOURSELF

■ Telephone service used to be a natural monopoly. Why? Is it a natural monopoly today? Discuss how technology can change what is and isn't a natural monopoly.

Antitrust Law and Merger Policy

Two of the most important U.S. **antitrust laws** are the Sherman Act, passed in 1890, and the Clayton Act, passed in 1914. (The word "trust" can be thought of as another term for monopoly, so the antitrust laws are antimonopoly laws.) Together, these two acts give the federal government legal authority to prosecute monopolies or firms' attempts to monopolize. For example, the government can break up a monopoly, prohibit a merger, and prevent various acts that might reduce competition, such as collusion, predatory pricing (pricing below cost to drive a competitor out of business), and exclusive dealing (requiring that a buyer deal with only one seller).

It's important to understand that most of these acts are not illegal in every circumstance. It's not illegal to be a monopolist, for example; it's only illegal to become a monopoly using illegal means. Mergers can be legal, even if they reduce competition. Predatory pricing is always illegal—if proven, but it is difficult to prove. It is not obvious, for example, how to define "below cost" (marginal cost? average cost?); moreover, however defined, pricing below cost can be legal if it's not intended to drive a competitor out of business (think, for example, of sharp discounts on clothing that is no longer in fashion). What all of this means is that the government cannot simply declare that an action is illegal—it must prove it in a court of law. The government wins some antitrust cases and it loses others. In 1984, for example, the government was allowed to break AT&T into eight smaller companies, but in 2001 the courts ruled against breaking Microsoft into two companies, as the government had wanted.

Let's now take a closer look at mergers. In a dynamic, capitalist economy, firms grow, shrink, split, and merge all the time. Prices, technology, and market conditions are constantly changing, and firms must adjust to remain competitive. A firm that sells accounting services on the East Coast, for example, may merge with a firm that sells accounting services on the West Coast; this creates a national firm that can better serve both markets. Or a firm that sells fishing rods may merge with a firm that sells outdoor clothing. Together, the two firms can reduce costs and better serve both markets. When two small firms merge, there is little chance that they will gain market power and be able to significantly raise prices. But, when two large firms merge, there is a potential trade-off between increased market power (and thus higher prices) and lower costs.

When a merger is likely to increase market power but also to increase efficiency, the antitrust authorities must try to balance higher prices with lower costs. In 2015, for example, Staples, the office supply store, offered to buy one of its rivals, Office Depot. The two companies argued that competition from Costco, Amazon, and Walmart had cut into their traditional market and made it difficult for both firms to survive. By merging, the companies hoped to close some stores that were too close to one another and reduce their input costs by buying even more paper and pens in bulk. The firms argued that their costs would fall but competition would still be fierce because of all the other firms in the industry. The government, however, disagreed and argued that the merger would increase market power and increase prices by too much to be justified. A federal judge agreed with the government and blocked the merger.

Was the judge correct? It's hard to know for certain. If Staples and Office Depot slowly close some stores over the next few years, then we will have fewer firms, as the antitrust authorities feared, but without the cost savings that

The **antitrust laws** give the federal government legal authority to prosecute monopolies or attempts to monopolize

might have come with a merger. On the other hand, if both firms continue to compete vigorously, then the government's position is more likely to be vindicated.

Antitrust law is a very contested area of law and it is not uncommon to find economists testifying on both sides of an antitrust trial. Merger or no merger, therefore, the economists usually end up profiting from hefty consulting fees—another reason why it's good to be an economist.

Takeaway

After reading this chapter, you should be able to find marginal revenue given either a demand curve or a table of prices and quantities (as in Figure 13.1). Given a demand and marginal cost curve, you should be able to find and label the monopoly price, the monopoly quantity, and deadweight loss. With the addition of an average cost curve, you should be able to find and label monopoly profit. You should also be able to demonstrate why the markup of price over marginal cost is larger the more inelastic the demand—this relationship will also be useful in the next chapter.

What makes monopoly theory interesting and a subject of debate among economists is that it's not always obvious whether monopolies are good or bad. Instead, we are faced with a series of trade-offs. Patent monopolies, such as the one on Combivir, create a trade-off between deadweight loss and innovation. The monopolist prices its product above marginal cost, but without the prospect of monopoly profits, there might be no product at all.

Natural monopolies also involve trade-offs, this time between deadweight loss and economies of scale. Deadweight loss means that monopoly is not optimal, but when economies of scale are large, competitive outcomes aren't optimal either. Regulating monopoly seems to offer an escape from this trade-off, but as we saw in our analysis of cable TV and electricity regulation, the practice of regulation is much more complicated than the theory. Cable TV regulation kept prices low but it kept quality low as well. Overall, deregulation of cable television rates worked surprisingly well, at least according to the consumers who flocked to cable even as rates rose. In contrast, electricity deregulation left California at the mercy of firms wielding market power.

Antitrust laws like the Sherman Act and the Clayton Act give the U.S. government the legal authority to prosecute monopolies or attempts to monopolize. Mergers between large firms are often challenged by the government, and they typically create a difficult trade-off between increases in market power and reductions in cost.

Economists don't always agree on the best way to navigate the trade-offs between market power, innovation, and efficiency. Many monopolies, however, perhaps most on a world scale, are "unnatural"—they neither support innovation nor efficiency. They are instead created to transfer wealth to politically powerful elites. For these monopolies, economics does offer guidance—open the field to competition! Alas, economics offers less clear guidance about how to convince the elites to follow the advice of economists.

CHAPTER REVIEW

 interactive activity Go online to practice with more examples of these types of problems, including live links to videos, data sources, and feedback.

Problems in **green** relate to MRU videos. See the MRU table at the end of the exercises.

KEY CONCEPTS

market power, p. 244

monopoly, p. 244

marginal revenue, *MR,* p. 244

marginal cost, *MC,* p. 244

barriers to entry, p. 253

economies of scale, p. 253

natural monopoly, p. 253

antitrust laws, p. 259

FACTS AND TOOLS

1. In the following diagram, label the marginal revenue curve, the profit-maximizing price, the profit-maximizing quantity, the profit, and the deadweight loss.

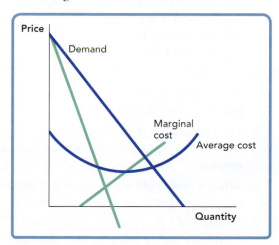

2. **a.** Consider a market like the one illustrated in Figure 13.5, where all firms have the same average cost curve. If a competitive firm in this market tried to set a price above the minimum point on its average cost curve, how many units would it sell?

   b. If a monopoly did the same thing, raising its price above average cost, what would happen to the number of units it sells: Does it rise, fall, or remain unchanged?

c. What accounts for the difference between your answers to parts a and b?

3. **a.** In the textbook *The Applied Theory of Price,* D. N. McCloskey refers to the equation $MR = MC$ as the rule of rational life. Who follows this rule: monopolies, competitive firms, or both?

   b. Rapido, the shoe company, is so popular that it has monopoly power. It's selling 20 million shoes per year, and it's highly profitable. The marginal cost of making extra shoes is quite low, and it doesn't change much if the company produces more shoes. Rapido's marketing experts tell the CEO of Rapido that if it *decreased* prices by 20%, it would sell so many more shoes that profits would rise. If the expert is correct, at its current output, is $MC > MR$, is $MC = MR$, or is $MR > MC$?

   c. If Rapido's CEO follows the expert's advice, what will this do to marginal revenue: Will it rise, fall, or be unchanged? Will Rapido's total revenue rise, fall, or be unchanged?

   d. Apollo, another highly profitable shoe company, also has market power. It's selling 15 million shoes per year, and it faces marginal costs quite similar to Rapido's. Apollo's marketing experts conclude that if the company *increased* prices by 20%, profits would rise. For Apollo, is $MC > MR$, is $MC = MR$, or is $MR > MC$?

4. **a.** When selling e-books, music on iTunes, and downloadable software, the marginal cost of producing and selling one more unit of output is essentially zero: $MC = 0$. Let's think about a monopoly in this kind of market. If the monopolist is doing its best to maximize profits, what will marginal revenue equal at a firm like this?

   b. All firms are trying to maximize their profits ($TR - TC$). The rule from part a tells us that in the special case in which marginal cost is zero, "profit maximization" is equivalent to which of the following statements?

"Maximize total revenue."

"Minimize total cost."

"Minimize average cost."

"Maximize average revenue."

5. **a.** What's the rule: Monopolists charge a higher markup when demand is highly elastic or when it's highly inelastic?

  b. What's the rule: Monopolists charge a higher markup when customers have many good substitutes or when they have few good substitutes?

  c. For the following pairs of goods, which producer is more likely to charge a bigger markup? Why?

   i. Someone selling new trendy shoes, or someone selling ordinary tennis shoes?

   ii. A movie theater selling popcorn or a New York City street vendor selling popcorn?

   iii. A pharmaceutical company selling a new powerful antibiotic or a firm selling a new powerful cure for dandruff?

6. In 1996, the X Prize Foundation created what became known as the Ansari X Prize—a $10 million prize for the first nongovernment group to send a reusable manned spacecraft into space twice within two weeks. In 2004, it was won by the Tier One project, financed by Microsoft cofounder Paul Allen.

  a. An answer you can find on the Internet: How high did *SpaceShipOne* fly when it won the Ansari X Prize?

  b. How much did it cost to develop *SpaceShipOne*? Was the $10 million prize enough to cover the costs? Why do you think Microsoft cofounder Paul Allen invested so much money to win the prize? Do Allen's motivations show up in our monopoly model?

7. Which of the following is true when a monopoly is producing the profit-maximizing quantity of output? More than one may be true.

  Marginal revenue = Average cost

  Total cost = Total revenue

  Price = Marginal cost

  Marginal revenue = Marginal cost

8. **a.** Consider a typical monopoly firm like that in Figure 13.3. If a monopolist finds a way to cut marginal costs, what will happen: Will it pass along some of the savings to the consumer in the form of lower prices, will it paradoxically raise prices to take advantage of these fatter profit margins, or will it keep the price steady?

  b. Is this what happens when marginal costs fall in a competitive industry, or do competitive markets and monopolies respond differently to a fall in costs?

9. **a.** Where will profits be higher: when demand for a patented drug is highly inelastic or when demand for a patented drug is highly elastic? (Figure 13.4 may be helpful.)

  b. Which of those two drugs is more likely to be "important?" Why?

  c. Now, consider the lure of profits: If a pharmaceutical company is trying to decide what kind of drugs to research, will it be lured toward inventing drugs with few good substitutes or drugs with many good substitutes?

  d. Is your answer to part c similar to what an all-wise, benevolent government agency would do, or is it roughly the opposite of what an all-wise, benevolent government agency would do?

10. True or False?

  a. When a monopoly is maximizing its profits, price is greater than marginal cost.

  b. For a monopoly producing a certain amount of output, price is less than marginal revenue.

  c. When a monopoly is maximizing its profits, marginal revenue equals marginal cost.

  d. Ironically, if a government regulator sets a fixed price for a monopoly *lower* than the unregulated price, it is typically *raising* the marginal revenue of selling more output.

  e. In the United States, government regulation of cable TV cut down the price of premium channels to average cost.

  f. When consumers have many options, monopoly markup is lower.

  g. A patent is a government-created monopoly.

THINKING AND PROBLEM SOLVING

11. In addition to the clove monopoly discussed in this chapter, Tommy Suharto, the son of Indonesian President Suharto (in office from 1967 to 1998), owned a media conglomerate, Bimantara Citra. In their entertaining book, *Economic Gangsters* (Princeton University Press, 2008), economists Raymond Fisman and Edward Miguel compared the stock price of Bimantara Citra with that of other firms on Indonesia's stock exchange around July 4, 1996, when the government announced that President Suharto was traveling to Germany for a health checkup. What do you think happened to the price of Bimantara Citra shares relative to other shares on the Indonesian stock exchange? Why? What does this tell us about corruption and monopoly power in Indonesia?

12. a. Sometimes, our discussion of marginal cost and marginal revenue unintentionally hides the real issue: the entrepreneur's quest to maximize total profits. Here is information on a firm:

Demand: $P = 50 - Q$ Fixed cost $= 100$
Marginal cost $= 10$

Using this information, calculate total profit for each of the values in the following table, and then plot total profit in the figure. Clearly label the amount of maximum profit and the quantity that produces this level of profit.

Quantity	Total Revenue	Total Cost	Total Profit
18			
19			
20			
21			
22			
23			

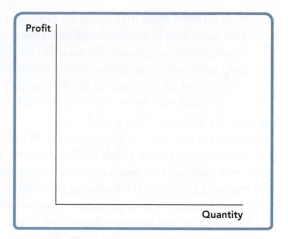

b. If the fixed cost increased from 100 to 200, would that change the shape of this curve at all? Also, would it shift the location of the curve to the left or right? Up or down? How does this explain why you can ignore fixed costs most of the time when thinking about a monopoly's decision-making process?

13. When a sports team hires an expensive new player or builds a new stadium, you often hear claims that ticket prices have to rise to cover the new, higher cost. Let's see what monopoly theory says about that. It's safe to treat these new expenses as fixed costs: something that doesn't change if the number of customers rises or falls. You have to pay Miguel Cabrera the same salary whether people show up or not; you have to make the interest payments on the new Comerica Park whether the seats are filled or not. Treat the local sports team as a monopoly in this question, and to keep it simple, let's assume there is only one ticket price.

a. As long as the sports team is profitable, will a mere rise in fixed costs raise the equilibrium ticket price, lower the equilibrium ticket price, or have no effect whatsoever on the equilibrium ticket price? Why?

b. In fact, it seems common in real life for ticket prices to rise after a team raises its fixed costs by building a fancy new stadium or hiring a superstar player: In recent years, it's happened in St. Louis's and San Diego's baseball stadiums. What's probably shifting to make this happen? Name *both* curves, and state the direction of the shift.

c. So, do sports teams spend a lot of money on superstars so that they can pass along the costs to the fans? Why *do* they spend a lot on super-stars, according to monopoly theory? (*Note:* Books like *Moneyball* and *The Baseball Economist* apply economic models to the national pastime, and it's common for sports managers to have solid training in economic methods.)

14. Earlier we mentioned the special case of a monopoly where $MC = 0$. Let's find the firm's best choice when more goods can be produced at no extra cost. Since so much e-commerce is close to this model—where the fixed cost of inventing the product and satisfying government regulators is the only cost that matters—the $MC = 0$ case will be more important in the future than it was in the past. In each case, be sure to see whether profits are positive! If the "optimal" level of profit is negative, then the monopoly should never start up in the first place; that's the only way it can avoid paying the fixed cost.

    a. $P = 100 - Q$ Fixed cost $= 1,000$

    b. $P = 2,000 - Q$ Fixed cost $= 900,000$
    (Driving the point home from part a.)

    c. $P = 120 - 12Q$ Fixed cost $= 1,000$

15. a. Just based on self-interest, who is more likely to support strong patents on pharmaceuticals: young people or old people? Why?

    b. Who is more likely to support strong patent and copyright protection on video games: people who really like old-fashioned videogames or people who want to play the best, most advanced video games?

    c. How are parts a and b really the same question?

16. Common sense might say that a monopolist would produce more output than a competitive industry facing the same marginal costs. After all, if you're making a profit, you want to sell as much as you can, don't you? What's wrong with this line of reasoning? Why do monopolistic industries sell less than competitive industries?

17. In the early part of the twentieth century, it was cheaper to travel by rail from New York to San Francisco than it was to travel from New York to Denver, even though the train to San Francisco would stop in Denver on the way.

    a. Denver is a city in the mountains. Suggest alternate ways to get there from New York without taking the train.

    b. San Francisco is a city on the Pacific Ocean. Suggest alternate ways to get there from New York without taking the train.

    c. Why was San Francisco cheaper?

    d. How is this story similar to the one told in this chapter about prices for flights from Washington, D.C., to either Dallas or San Francisco?

18. This chapter told the story of how the 2000 California energy shortage was aggravated by price deregulation.

    a. Suppose you are an entrepreneur who is interested in building a power plant to take advantage of the high prices for energy. Seeing rising energy costs, would price deregulation make it more or less likely you would build a new power plant? Why?

    b. It's very difficult to build and operate a new power plant, largely because new plants have to comply with a long list of environmental and safety regulations. Compared with a world with fewer such regulations, how do these rules change the average cost of building and operating a power plant? Why?

    c. Do these regulations make it more or less likely that you will build a new power plant? Why?

    d. Do these regulations increase or decrease the market power of power plants that already exist?

19. The lure of spices during the medieval period wasn't driven merely by the desire to improve the taste of food (Europe produced saffron, thyme, bay leaves, oregano, and other spices for that). The lure of nutmeg, mace, and cloves came from their mystique. Spices became a symbol of prestige (just as Louis Vuitton and Ferrari are today). Most Europeans didn't even know that they grew in the tiny chain of islands that is called the Spice Islands today.

    a. Suppose you grow much of the spices in the Spice Islands. Knowing that few people could compete with you, how would you adjust your production to maximize your profits?

    b. Suppose you heard rumors that the Europeans to whom you often sell are also becoming fascinated by the mechanical clock, a new invention that was spreading across Europe as a new novelty and as yet another symbol of prestige. How would this change your optimal production? Why?

    c. Once Europeans made contact with the Americas, a new, high-status novelty arose:

chocolate. Was this good news or bad news for you, the monopolist in the Spice Islands?

20. China developed gunpowder, paper, the compass, water-driven spinning machines, and many other inventions long before its European counterparts. Yet the Chinese did not adopt cannons, industrialization, and many other applications until *after* the West did.

   a. Suppose you are an inventor in ancient China and suddenly realize that the fireworks used for celebration could be enlarged into a functioning weapon. It would take time and money to develop, but you could easily sell the cutting-edge result to the government. If there is a strong patent system, would you put a big investment into developing this technology? Why or why not?

   b. Suppose there were no patent system, but you could still sell your inventions to the government. Compared with a world with a good patent law, would you be more inclined, less inclined, or about equally inclined to invest in technological development? Why?

CHALLENGES

21. a. For the following three cases, calculate

   i. The marginal revenue curve

   ii. The level of output where $MR = MC$ (i.e., set the equation from item i equal to marginal cost and solve for Q)

   iii. The profit-maximizing price (i.e., plug your answer from equation ii into the demand curve)

   iv. Total revenue and total cost at this level of output (something you learned in Chapter 11)

   v. What entrepreneurs really care about—total profit

   Case A: Demand: $P = 50 - Q$
   Fixed cost = 100   Marginal cost = 10

   Case B: Demand: $P = 100 - 2Q$
   Fixed cost = 100   Marginal cost = 10

   Case C: Demand: $P = 100 - 2Q$
   Fixed cost = 100   Marginal cost = 20

   b. What's the markup in each case? Measure it two ways: first in dollars, as price minus marginal cost, and then as a percentage markup ($[100 \times (P - MC)/MC$, reported as a percent]).

   c. If you solved part b correctly, you found that when costs rose from case B to case C, the monopolist's optimal price increased. Why didn't the monopolist charge that same higher price when costs were lower? After all, it's a monopolist, so it can charge what price they want. Explain in language that your grandmother could understand.

22. In Challenges question 21, what was the deadweight loss of monopoly in each of the three cases? (*Hint:* Where does the marginal cost curve cross the demand curve? The same place it does under competition.) Is this number measured in dollars, in units of the good, or in some other way?

23. a. In 2006, Medicare Part D was created to subsidize spending on prescription drugs. What effect would you expect this expansion to have on pharmaceutical prices? What principle in the chapter would explain this result?

   b. Given your answer in part a, what effect on pharmaceutical research and development would you predict?

   c. Whatever answer you gave in part a, can you think of an argument for the opposite prediction? (*Hint:* In writing the Part D law, Congress said that subsidized drug plans must cover all pharmaceuticals in some "protected" classes, such as AIDS drugs, but that in other areas subsidized plans could pick and choose which drugs to offer. Understanding this difference may lead to different predictions.)

24. In 1983, Congress passed the Orphan Drug Act, which gave firms that developed pharmaceuticals to treat rare diseases (diseases with U.S. patient populations of 200,000 people or fewer) the exclusive rights to sell their pharmaceutical for seven years, basically an extended patent life. In other words, the act gave greater market power to pharmaceutical firms who developed drugs for rare diseases. Perhaps surprisingly, a patient organization, the National Organization for Rare Disorders (NORD), lobbied for the act. Why would a patient group lobby for an act that would increase the price of pharmaceuticals to its members? Why do you think the act was specifically for rare diseases?

25. For Kremer's patent buyout proposal (mentioned in the chapter) to work, the government needs to pay a price that's high enough to encourage pharmaceutical companies to develop new drugs. How can the government find out the right price? Through an auction, of course. In Kremer's plan, it works roughly like this: The government announces that it will hold an auction the next time that a company invents a powerful anti–AIDS drug. Once the drug has been invented and thoroughly tested, the government holds the auction. Many firms compete in the auction—just like on eBay—and the highest bid wins. Now comes the twist: After the auction ends, a government employee rolls a six-sided die. If it comes up "1," then the highest bidder gets the patent, it pays off the inventor, and it's free to charge the monopoly price. If the die comes up "2" through "6," then the government pays the inventor whatever the highest bid was, and then it tears up the patent. The auction had to be held to figure out how much to pay, but most of the time it's the government that does the paying. Similarly, most of the time, citizens get to pay marginal cost for the drug, but one-sixth of all new drugs will still charge the monopoly price.

a. In your opinion, would taxpayers be willing to pay for this?

b. Using Figure 13.5 to guide your answer, what polygon(s) would these firms' bid be equal to?

c. If the government wins the die roll, what net benefits do consumers get, using Figure 13.5's polygons as your answer? (Be sure to subtract the cost of the auction!)

26. a. Let's imagine that the firm with cost curves illustrated in the left panel of the following figure is a large cable TV provider. Assuming that the firm is free to maximize profit, label the profit-maximizing price, quantity, and the firm's profit.

b. Now assume that the firm is regulated and that the regulator sets the price so that the firm earns a normal (zero) profit. What price does the regulator set and what quantity does the firm sell? (Label this price and quantity on the diagram.)

c. Which price and quantity pair do consumers prefer, that in part a or in part b? Do consumers benefit from price regulation?

d. Imagine that the cable TV provider can invest in fiber optic cable (high-definition), better programming, movie downloading, or some other service that increases the demand for the product, as shown in the right panel. If the firm were regulated as in part b, do you think it would be more or less likely to make these investments?

e. Given your answer in part d, revisit the question of price regulation and make an argument that price regulation could harm consumers once you take into account dynamic factors. Would this argument apply to all consumers or just some? If so, which ones?

WORK IT OUT

For interactive, step-by-step help in solving this problem, go online.

Earlier we mentioned the special case of a monopoly in which $MC = 0$. Let's find the firm's best choice when more goods can be produced at no extra cost. Since so much e-commerce is close to this model—where the fixed cost of inventing the product and satisfying government regulators is the only cost that matters—the $MC = 0$ case will be more important in the future than it was in the past. In each case, be sure to see whether profits are positive! If the "optimal" level of profit is negative, then the monopoly should never start up in the first place; that's the only way it can avoid paying the fixed cost.

a. $P = 200 - Q$ Fixed cost $= 1,000$

b. $P = 4,000 - Q$ Fixed cost $= 900,000$
(Driving the point home from part a.)

c. $P = 120 - 12Q$ Fixed cost $= 1,000$

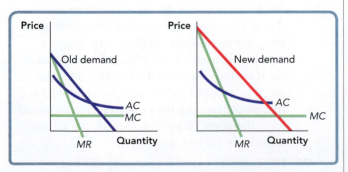

MARGINAL REVOLUTION UNIVERSITY VIDEOS

Maximizing Profit under Monopoly

mruniversity.com/monopoly-profit

Problems: **1–4, 7, 8, 10, 12, 14–16, 18, 19, 21, 26**

The Monopoly Markup

mruniversity.com/monopoly-markup

Problems: **46, 11, 20, 22–25**

The Costs and Benefits of Monopoly

mruniversity.com/costs-benefits-monopoly

Problems: **6, 11, 20, 22–25**

Patents, Prizes, and Subsidies

mruniversity.com/patents

Problems: **6, 15, 20, 23–25**

14

Price Discrimination and Pricing Strategy

After months of investigation, police from Interpol swooped down on an international drug syndicate operating out of Antwerp, Belgium. The syndicate had been smuggling drugs from Kenya, Uganda, and Tanzania into the port of Antwerp for distribution throughout Europe. Smuggling had netted the syndicate millions of dollars in profit. The drug being smuggled? Heroin? Cocaine? No, something more valuable, Combivir. Why was Combivir, the anti-AIDS drug we introduced in Chapter 13, being illegally smuggled from Africa to Europe when Combivir was manufactured in Europe and could be bought there legally?[1]

The answer is that Combivir was priced at $12.50 per pill in Europe and, much closer to cost, about 50 cents per pill in Africa. Smugglers who bought Combivir in Africa and sold it in Europe could make approximately $12 per pill, and they were smuggling millions of pills. But this raises another question. Why was GlaxoSmithKline (GSK) selling Combivir at a much lower price in Africa than in Europe? Remember from Chapter 13 that GSK owns the patent on Combivir and thus has some market power over pricing. In part, GSK reduced the price of Combivir in Africa for humanitarian reasons, but lowering prices in poor countries can also increase profit. In this chapter, we explain how a firm with market power can use **price discrimination**—selling the same product at different prices to different customers—to increase profit.

CHAPTER OUTLINE

Price Discrimination

Price Discrimination Is Common

Is Price Discrimination Bad?

Tying and Bundling

Takeaway

Appendix: Solving Price Discrimination Problems with Excel (Advanced Section)

Video
- Should Cable Companies Be Required to Sell by the Channel?

Price discrimination is selling the same product at different prices to different customers.

Price Discrimination

Figure 14.1 shows how price discrimination can increase profit. In the left panel we show the market for Combivir in Europe and in the right panel the market in Africa. The demand curve in Africa is much lower and more elastic (price sensitive) than in Europe because, on average, Africans are poorer than Europeans.

Now let's suppose for the moment that Europe is the only market. What price should GSK set? We know from Chapter 13 that the profit-maximizing quantity is found where marginal revenue equals marginal cost. From $MR = MC$ in the left panel, we find that the profit-maximizing quantity is Q_{Europe}. The profit-maximizing price is the highest price that consumers will pay to purchase Q_{Europe} units, which we label P_{Europe}. Profit is given by the green area labeled $Profit_{Europe}$.

269

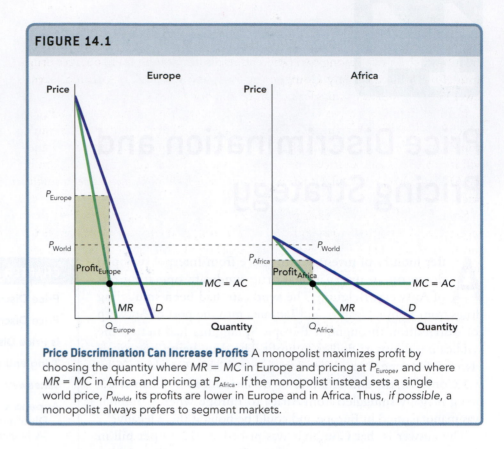

FIGURE 14.1

Price Discrimination Can Increase Profits A monopolist maximizes profit by choosing the quantity where $MR = MC$ in Europe and pricing at P_{Europe}, and where $MR = MC$ in Africa and pricing at P_{Africa}. If the monopolist instead sets a single world price, P_{World}, its profits are lower in Europe and in Africa. Thus, *if possible*, a monopolist always prefers to segment markets.

Similarly, if Africa were the only market, GSK would choose the profit-maximizing quantity Q_{Africa} and the profit-maximizing price P_{Africa}, which would generate profit in the amount $Profit_{Africa}$.

But what price should GSK set if it wants to have a single "world price" for both Europe and Africa? If GSK wants a single world price, it should lower the price in Europe and raise the price in Africa, setting a price somewhere between P_{Europe} and P_{Africa}, say, at P_{World}. (In a more advanced class, we would solve for the exact profit-maximizing world price, but that level of detail is not necessary here.)

But remember that P_{Europe} is the profit-maximizing price in Europe and P_{Africa} is the profit-maximizing price in Africa, so by lowering the price in Europe, GSK must be reducing profit in Europe. Similarly, by raising the price in Africa, GSK must be reducing profit in Africa. Thus, profit at the single price P_{World} must be less than when GSK sets two different prices earning the combined profit: $Profit_{Europe} + Profit_{Africa}$.

We have now arrived at the first principle of price discrimination: *(1a) If the demand curves are different, it is more profitable to set different prices in different markets than a single price that covers all markets.*

We also know from Chapter 13 and from Figure 14.1 how a monopolist should set prices. Recall that the more inelastic the demand curve, the higher the profit-maximizing price. In this case, the demand for Combivir is more inelastic (less sensitive to price) in the European market than in the African market, so the price is higher in Europe. This really isn't an independent principle; it's an implication of profit maximization, as we showed in Chapter 13. But it's a useful reminder, so we will add to our first principle: *(1b) To maximize profit, the monopolist should set a higher price in markets with more inelastic demand.*

The first principle of price discrimination tells us that GSK wants to set a higher price for Combivir in Europe than in Africa. But we also know from the introduction that setting two different prices for Combivir encourages drug smuggling. Smugglers buy Combivir at P_{Africa} and sell at P_{Europe}, which leaves fewer sales for GSK. A smuggler's profit comes out of GSK's pocket.

If smuggling is extensive, GSK will end up selling most of its output at P_{Africa}, which is less profitable than if GSK set a single world price. Thus, if GSK can't stop the drug smugglers, it will abandon its attempt at price discrimination and will instead set a single price—perhaps a single world price such as P_{World} or, if the African market is small, GSK may abandon Africa altogether and set a single price of P_{Europe}.

Smuggling is a special example of a more general (and legal) process that economists call **arbitrage**—buying low in one market and selling high in another market. Thus, we arrive at the second principle of price discrimination: *(2) Arbitrage makes it difficult for a firm to set different prices in different markets, thereby reducing the profit from price discrimination.*

We summarize the principles of price discrimination.

> **Arbitrage** is taking advantage of price differences for the same good in different markets by buying low in one market and selling high in another market.

The Principles of Price Discrimination

1a. If the demand curves are different, it is more profitable to set different prices in different markets than a single price that covers all markets.

1b. To maximize profit, the firm should set a higher price in markets with more inelastic demand.

2. Arbitrage makes it difficult for a firm to set different prices in different markets, thereby reducing the profit from price discrimination.

The first principle tells us that a firm *wants* to set different prices in different markets. The second principle tells us that a firm may not be *able* to set different prices in different markets. To succeed at price discrimination, the monopolist must prevent arbitrage.

Preventing Arbitrage

If it wants to profit from price discrimination, GSK must prevent the Combivir that it sends to Africa from being resold in Europe. GSK has a number of tools to discourage smuggling. GSK, for example, sends red Combivir pills to Africa and sells white Combivir in Europe. If GSK detectives find red Combivir in Europe, they know that a GSK distributor has broken its agreement. Using special bar codes on each package, GSK can then track the smuggled pills back to the distributor who was supposed to distribute them in Africa. Interpol is called in to make arrests.

Markets can differ in more ways than geographically. Rohm and Haas is a producer of plastics. One of its plastics, methyl methacrylate (MM), was used in industry and also in dentistry as a material for dentures. MM had lots of substitutes as an industrial plastic but few as a denture material, so Rohm and Haas sold MM for industrial uses at 85 cents per pound and sold a slightly different version designed for dentures at $22 per pound. At these prices,

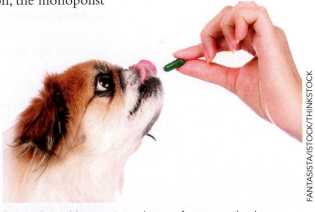

Preventing arbitrage Animals are often prescribed exactly the same pharmaceuticals as humans. The pharmaceutical firms know that people won't pay as much to save Oscar (elastic demand) as to save Uncle Oscar (inelastic demand) so they set low prices for the veterinary market and high prices for the human market even when the same drug is being sold. Arbitrage is sometimes reduced by making the animal product in inconvenient dosages or forms (do you really want an injectable or suppository designed for a horse?). Most fundamentally, vets cannot legally write prescriptions for humans so the pharmaceutical firms are able to set different prices in the two markets without fear of much arbitrage.

it wasn't long before enterprising individuals started buying industrial MM and converting it to denture MM. Just like GSK, Rohm and Haas needed a way to prevent arbitrage between the two markets.

One bold thinker came up with what Rohm and Haas internal documents called "a very fine method of controlling the bootleg situation." The innovator suggested that Rohm and Haas should mix industrial MM with arsenic. This wouldn't reduce the value of MM in industry, but it would surely deter people from making it into dentures! Rohm and Haas's legal department rejected this plan, but the company came up with an idea nearly as good: They planted a *rumor* that industrial MM was mixed with arsenic![2]

Although Rohm and Haas never implemented the poisoning idea, the U.S. government has. The government taxes alcohol but subsidizes ethanol fuel. To prevent arbitrage, that is, to prevent entrepreneurs from buying ethanol fuel and converting it to drinkable alcohol, the government requires that ethanol fuel be poisoned!

It's easier to prevent arbitrage of some products than of others. A masseuse, for example, may easily set different prices for different customers because it's difficult for a customer who buys a massage at the low price to resell it to another customer at the higher price. Services, in general, are difficult to arbitrage.

Price Discrimination Is Common

Once you know the signs, price discrimination is easy to see. Movie theaters, for example, often charge less for seniors than for younger adults. Is this because theater owners have a special respect for the elderly? Probably not. More likely it's that theater owners realize that young people have a more inelastic demand for movies than seniors. Thus, theater owners charge a high price to young people and a low price to seniors. It would probably be even more profitable if theater owners could charge people who are on a date more than married people (no one likes to look cheap on a date). But it's easy for theater owners to judge age and not so easy for them to figure out who is on a date and who is married.

Students don't always pay higher prices, however. Stata is a well-known statistical software package. It costs a business $1,295 to buy Stata, but registered students pay only $145. Thus, it's not about age—the young sometimes pay more and sometimes pay less—it's about how age correlates with what businesses really care about, which is how much the customer is willing to pay.

Here's another example. Airlines know that businesspeople are typically less sensitive to the price of an airline ticket than are vacationers (i.e., businesspeople have more inelastic demand curves). An airline would like, therefore, to set a high price for businesspeople and a low price for vacationers, as illustrated in Figure 14.2.

But airlines can't very well say to their customers, "Are you flying on business? Okay, the price is $600. Going on a vacation? The price is $200." So how can airlines segment the market?

Airlines set different prices according to characteristics that are correlated with the willingness to pay. Vacationers, for example, can easily plan their trips weeks or months in advance. Businesspeople, however, may discover that they need to fly tomorrow. Thus, if a customer wants to fly to Tampa, Florida, in two weeks' time he or she is probably a vacationer and the airline will charge that person a low price, but if the customer wants to fly tomorrow, the price will be

FIGURE 14.2

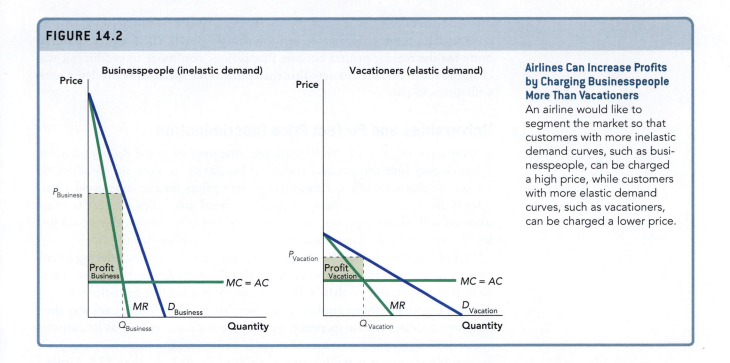

Businesspeople (inelastic demand)

Price

$P_{Business}$

Profit
Business

$MC = AC$

MR $D_{Business}$

$Q_{Business}$ Quantity

Vacationers (elastic demand)

Price

$P_{Vacation}$

Profit
Vacation

$MC = AC$

MR $D_{Vacation}$

$Q_{Vacation}$ Quantity

Airlines Can Increase Profits by Charging Businesspeople More Than Vacationers
An airline would like to segment the market so that customers with more inelastic demand curves, such as businesspeople, can be charged a high price, while customers with more elastic demand curves, such as vacationers, can be charged a lower price.

higher. On the day these words were written, U.S. Airways was charging $113 to fly from Washington, D.C., to Tampa with two weeks' notice but more than three times as much, $395, to fly tomorrow. Except for the dates, the flights were identical. Figure 14.3 illustrates how one airline charged many different prices for the same flight.

Similarly, publishers know that hard-core fans are willing to pay a high price for the latest Harry Potter book, while others will buy only if the price is low. Publishers would like to charge the hard-core fans a high price and the less devoted a low price. How can they do this? One way is to start with a high price and then lower it once the hard-core fans have bought their fill. Thus, when *Harry Potter and the Half-Blood Prince* hit the shelves, it retailed at $34.99 in hardback, but when the paperback was released about a year later, it sold for just $9.99. Does it cost more to produce a hardback? Yes, but not much more, maybe a dollar or two. The hard-core fans pay a higher price not because costs are higher, but because the publisher knows that they are willing to pay a higher price.

A more subtle form of price discrimination occurs when firms offer different versions of a product for the purpose of segmenting customers into different markets. IBM, for example, offered one of its laser printers in two models: the regular version and the Series E (E for economy). The regular version printed at 10 pages per minute, the Series E printed at 5 pages per minute. The regular version was much more expensive than the Series E. What's surprising is that the Series E cost more to produce. In fact, the only

FIGURE 14.3

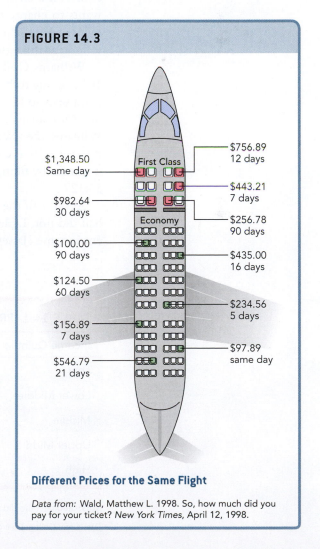

$1,348.50
Same day

$982.64
30 days

$100.00
90 days

$124.50
60 days

$156.89
7 days

$546.79
21 days

First Class

Economy

$756.89
12 days

$443.21
7 days

$256.78
90 days

$435.00
16 days

$234.56
5 days

$97.89
same day

Different Prices for the Same Flight

Data from: Wald, Matthew L. 1998. So, how much did you pay for your ticket? *New York Times*, April 12, 1998.

difference between the regular and the Series E was that the Series E printer contained an extra chip that slowed the printer down! IBM wasn't charging more for the regular printer because that printer cost more to produce; it was charging more because it knew that the demand for speed was correlated with willingness to pay.

Universities and Perfect Price Discrimination

Universities are one of the biggest practitioners of price discrimination, although they hide this practice under the blanket of "student aid." Student aid is a way of charging different students different prices for the same good. Consider Williams College, a small, prestigious liberal arts college. In 2016, some students at Williams paid the sticker price of $64,090, while others paid just $3,127 for exactly the same education. Why the big difference in price?

Part of the story is that Williams College was doing good by offering financial aid to students from poorer families. But Williams College was also doing well. To see why, notice that Williams College is a lot like an airline. If U.S. Airways is going to fly an airplane from New York to Los Angeles anyway, then U.S. Airways can increase its profits by filling extra seats so long as its customers are willing to pay the marginal costs of flying (say, the extra fuel costs). Of course, if a customer is willing to pay $800 to fly to L.A., then U.S. Airways wants to charge that customer $800 and not less. But if the marginal cost of flying is $100, then U.S. Airways can increase its profits by filling an empty seat so long as the customer is willing to pay at least $101.

Williams College is a lot like an airline because if Ancient Greek History 101 is going to be taught anyway, then Williams can increase its profits by filling extra seats so long as its students are willing to pay the marginal costs of teaching. Of course, if a student is willing to pay $64,090 for a year of education at Williams, then Williams wants to charge that student $64,090 and not less. But if the marginal costs of teaching are $3,127 a year, then Williams can increase its profits by filling an empty seat so long as the student is willing to pay at least $3,127.

About half the students at Williams paid the full sticker price of $64,090, but half did not. Table 14.1 shows the average price paid by students in five different income classes, low to high, after taking into account "financial aid."

TABLE 14.1 PRICE DISCRIMINATION AT WILLIAMS COLLEGE, 2016

Income Quintile	Family Income	Average Net Price
Low	$0–$30,000	$3,127
Lower Middle	$30,001–$48,000	$4,971
Middle	$48,001–$75,000	$7,419
Upper Middle	$75,001–$110,000	$16,899
High	$110,001+	$38,936

Note: Students who did not apply for financial aid, about half the student body, paid $64,090.

Data from: CollegeCalc.org, using data from the United States Department of Education.

The difference in price is extreme. Even the airlines, masters of price discrimination, can rarely charge some customers 20 times what they charge other customers. Williams has a big advantage over the airlines, however. Williams has an extraordinary amount of information about its customers.

To receive financial aid, Williams demands that students and their parents submit their tax returns to Williams. Williams, therefore, has very detailed information about the income of its customers, and it uses that information to set many different prices. Table 14.1 shows *average* prices within each income class, but, in fact, Williams divided prices even more finely, setting a different price, for example, to a student with family income of $30,000 than one with family income of $35,000. In theory, Williams could offer a different price to each one of its students, charging each student his or her maximum willingness to pay. This is what economists call **perfect price discrimination**.

Figure 14.4 shows how perfect price discrimination works in a market like education, where each customer buys one unit of the good. Alex values education the highest, Tyler the second highest, Robin the third highest, all the way down to Bryan who thinks that education has very little value. A firm that has a lot of information about Alex, Tyler, Robin, and Bryan can set four different prices, charging each of them their maximum willingness to pay (or, if you like, a penny less than their maximum willingness to pay). Thus, Alex is charged the most and Bryan the least.

Since a perfectly price-discriminating (PPD) monopolist charges each consumer his or her maximum willingness to pay, consumers end up with zero

Under **perfect price discrimination (PPD)**, each customer is charged his or her maximum willingness to pay.

FIGURE 14.4

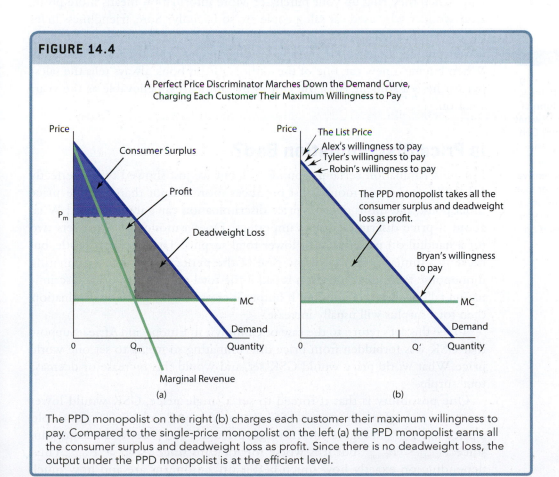

A Perfect Price Discriminator Marches Down the Demand Curve, Charging Each Customer Their Maximum Willingness to Pay

The PPD monopolist on the right (b) charges each customer their maximum willingness to pay. Compared to the single-price monopolist on the left (a) the PPD monopolist earns all the consumer surplus and deadweight loss as profit. Since there is no deadweight loss, the output under the PPD monopolist is at the efficient level.

consumer surplus. All of the gains from trade go to the monopolist. This is bad for consumers but does have a beneficial side effect: Since the PPD monopolist gets all the gains from trade, the PPD monopolist has an incentive to maximize the gains from trade, and maximizing the gains from trade means no dead-weight loss.

In Chapter 13, we showed that a single-price monopoly creates a dead-weight loss, but this is not true for a perfectly price-discriminating monopoly. In Figure 14.4, notice that whenever a consumer's willingness to pay is higher than marginal cost, then that consumer is sold a unit of the good—but this means that the PPD monopoly produces the efficient quantity! In fact, the perfectly price-discriminating monopolist produces until $P = MC$ (i.e., $Q^{\star}$ units), exactly as does a competitive firm!

Another way of seeing why the perfectly price-discriminating monopolist produces the efficient quantity is to remember that all firms want to produce until $MR = MC$. For a competitive firm, $MR = P$, so the competitive firm produces until $P = MC$. For a single-price monopolist, $MR < P$, so the single-price monopolist produces less than the competitive firm. But what is MR for a PPD monopolist? It's P and thus the PPD monopolist also sets $P = MC$. Can you explain why as a PPD monopolist moves down the demand curve selling to additional customers, its MR is always equal to price?

Detailed information about its customers helps Williams College set each student's price close to that student's maximum willingness to pay, thus maximizing Williams's revenue. Ever wonder why many retailers ask for your zip code when they ring up your purchase? More information means more profit. Ever wonder why used car salespeople are so friendly? Sure, friendliness helps to sell cars, but what you think of as friendly talk is really a clever strategy to learn as much about you as possible so the salesperson can price accordingly. When buying a new car, one of the authors of this book always tells the salesperson he is a student. Alas, the ruse is becoming less believable as the years wear on.

Is Price Discrimination Bad?

Price discrimination certainly sounds bad, but we just showed that a perfectly price-discriminating monopolist produces more output than a single-price monopolist, and this is good so price discrimination can't always be bad. What about if price discrimination is imperfect? Does a monopolist that sets two (or a handful of) prices raise or lower total surplus? The answer is subtle, but there is a similar intuition to the case of the perfectly price-discriminating monopolist. Price discrimination is bad if the total output with price discrimination falls or stays the same, but if output increases under price discrimination, then total surplus will usually increase.

To see this, let's return to the case of Combivir in Europe and Africa. Suppose that GSK was forbidden from price discriminating so it had to set one world price. What world price would GSK set, and would this increase or decrease total surplus?

One possibility is that if forced to set a single price, GSK would lower the price enough so that some Africans could buy Combivir—for example, a price like P_{World} in Figure 14.1. A single price of P_{World} is better for Europeans since $P_{\text{World}} < P_{\text{Europe}}$, but it is worse for Africans since $P_{\text{World}} > P_{\text{Africa}}$. Thus, depending on exactly how much better off Europeans are and how much

CHECK YOURSELF

- Is the early bird special (eating dinner at a restaurant before 6:00 pm or 6:30 pm) a form of price discrimination? If so, what are the market segments? Can you think of another explanation for this type of pricing?

- Why is it much more expensive to see a movie in a theater than to wait a few months and see it at home on demand? Can you give an explanation based on price discrimination?

worse off Africans are at P_{World}, price discrimination could be better or worse than single pricing.

How likely is it, however, that GSK would lower the price to P_{World}? Two-thirds of the 630 million people living in Africa live on less than a dollar a day. Thus, even when GSK sells Combivir at close to its cost of 50 cents a pill, most Africans with AIDS cannot afford Combivir. GSK, therefore, cannot make up for a low price by selling large volumes of Combivir to Africans. Thus, if GSK cannot set two different prices, it will probably abandon the African market altogether and sell to the world at P_{Europe}. At P_{Europe}, only Europeans can afford to buy Combivir.

At the single price of P_{Europe}, are Europeans better off than with price discrimination? No, the price to Europeans hasn't changed and thus the quantity of Combivir consumed by Europeans is the same under both pricing systems. What about Africans? At the single price of P_{Europe}, Africans pay more for Combivir than with price discrimination and they consume less. Thus, in the most plausible case, forcing GSK to set a single price doesn't help Europeans but does hurt Africans. Alternatively stated, price discrimination in this case increases total surplus because price discrimination increases output—with price discrimination, Europeans consume as much Combivir as with a single price, but Africans increase their consumption from what it would be with a high single price.

Why Misery Loves Company and How Price Discrimination Helps to Cover Fixed Costs

In industries with high fixed costs, price discrimination has another benefit. To explain why, we ask a strange question. Imagine that there are two diseases that if left untreated are equally deadly. One of the diseases is rare, the other is common. If you had to choose, would you rather be afflicted with the rare disease or the common disease? Take a moment to think about this question because there is a definite answer.

It's much better to have the common disease because there are more drugs to treat common diseases than to treat rare diseases, and more drugs means greater life expectancy. Patients diagnosed with a rare disease are 45% more likely to die before the age of 55 than patients diagnosed with a more common disease.*

The reason there are more drugs to treat common diseases is the market is larger. Simply put, it costs about the same to develop a drug for a rare or a common disease but the revenues are much greater for a drug that treats a common disease. Thus, the larger the market, the more profitable it is to develop a drug for that market.

The fact that profits increase with market size explains why price discrimination can benefit *Europeans*, as well as Africans. We have already shown that Africans benefit from price discrimination because of lower prices. Europeans benefit because price discrimination increases the profit from producing pharmaceuticals, and more profit means more research and development, more new drugs, and greater life expectancy.

---

* "Rare" is defined as a disease in the bottom quarter of incidence in the United States in 1998; "common" is defined as a disease in the top quarter of incidence. See Lichtenberg, Frank R., and Waldfogel, Joel, June 2003, *Does Misery Love Company? Evidence from Pharmaceutical Markets Before and After the Orphan Drug Act*. NBER Working Paper No. W9750. Available at http://www.ssrn.com/abstract=414248.

Pharmaceuticals are not the only industry with high fixed costs—airlines, chemicals, universities, software, and movies all have a similar cost structure. Low prices for vacationers, for example, can benefit business travelers because the extra profit that airlines earn from selling to vacationers encourages airlines to offer more flights to more places at more times. The synthetic fabric Kevlar is five times stronger by weight than steel and is used to make bulletproof vests as well as auto tires. As a bulletproof vest, Kevlar has few substitutes, but as tire belting, it has many. As a result, DuPont charges more for Kevlar used in vests than for Kevlar used in belting. If DuPont had to charge the same price in all markets, Kevlar might not be used for belting at all, and Du Pont would have lower profits and less incentive to innovate.

Tying and Bundling

Everyone knows that airlines charge different prices to different customers for the same flight. Senior citizen and student discounts are obvious. Universities advertise their scholarship policies—even if they don't always advertise that this is a way of increasing profit! But other types of price discrimination are more subtle and difficult to see. Let's take a look at tying and bundling, two types of price discrimination that are hidden to the untrained observer.

Tying

Why are printers so cheap and ink so expensive? As we write this chapter, one remarkable Hewlett-Packard (HP) photo printer/scanner/copier sells for just $69. A full set of color ink cartridges, however, will set you back $44. At that price, it almost pays to buy a new printer (which comes with a cartridge) every time you run out of ink! Clearly, HP is pricing its printers low and making its profit from selling ink. HP is not alone in pursuing this strategy. Xbox game consoles are priced below cost, and Xbox games are priced above cost. Cell phones are priced below cost and phone calls are priced above cost. Why?

Think of HP as selling not printers and ink, but the package good, "ability to print color photos." HP wants to charge a high price to consumers with a high willingness to pay and a low price to consumers with a low willingness to pay. Consumers with a high willingness to pay for the "ability to print color photos" probably want to print a lot of color photos. Consumers with a low willingness to pay probably want to print only the occasional color photo. By charging a high price for ink, HP is charging high-willingness-to-pay consumers a high price. Yet, because the price of printers is low, consumers who have only a low willingness to pay are charged a low price.

HP's pricing scheme is especially brilliant because the price is so flexible. Instead of two prices, there are many: one for a consumer who prints 10 photos a month, another for a consumer who prints 15 photos a month, and yet another for a consumer who prints 100 photos a month.

For HP's scheme to work, it's critical that no one else but HP be allowed to sell ink for HP printers—HP must *tie* its printers to HP ink cartridges, which is why this form of price discrimination is called **tying**. If competitors could easily enter the market for ink, the price of ink would fall to marginal cost and HP's pricing scheme would fall apart. HP manages to keep competitors out of the market for ink in a clever way—the HP ink cartridge contains not just ink, but also a crucial and patented component of the printer head. Since other

Tying occurs when to use one good, the consumer must use a second good that is sold (only) by the same firm. A firm can price-discriminate by tying two goods and carefully setting their prices.

firms are forbidden by law from manufacturing the printer head, and since the head and the ink must be packaged together, HP manages to keep competitors out of the market for ink. Well, almost. There is an active market in *refilling* HP printer heads, which is much cheaper than buying them new.

HP's strategy illustrates both the benefits and costs of price discrimination. Price discrimination, as usual, may increase output by lowering the price to users who only want to print the occasional photo. Price discrimination also spreads the fixed costs of research and development—which are extensive for color photo printers—over more users, thus encouraging more innovation. But putting printer heads in the ink cartridge rather than in the printer probably raises the total cost of printing. Although there are some advantages to disposable printer heads, HP is spending the extra money not to benefit consumers but to keep competitors out of the ink business. Since the extra costs of production don't benefit consumers, they are a cost of price discrimination.

By the way, in addition to price discrimination, HP is probably also taking advantage of a bit of consumer irrationality. When comparing printers, consumers *should* look at the total price, printer plus ink, over the entire lifetime of the printer. But it takes some work to estimate the total price, and consumers who are shortsighted may focus on amazingly cheap printers rather than astonishingly expensive ink.

Bundling

Goods are **bundled** when they must be bought in a package. Nike doesn't sell right and left shoes individually; Nike sells shoes only in a right-and-left bundle.* Toyota doesn't sell engines, steering columns, and wheels. It sells a bundle called a car. As the examples suggest, most bundling is easily explained as a way to reduce costs. But why does Microsoft sell Word, Excel, Outlook, Access, and PowerPoint in a bundle called Microsoft Office?

Unlike buying a car piece by piece, it would not be difficult for consumers to buy the Office products individually and assemble them as they wanted. Almost every car buyer wants an engine and four wheels, but not every Office buyer wants Microsoft Access. So why does Microsoft bundle? Note that Microsoft does sell most Office products individually, but the sum of the individual prices far exceeds the price of the bundle, so most consumers buy Office.

Bundling is a type of price discrimination. Suppose that we have two consumers, Amanda and Yvonne, whose maximum willingness to pay for Word and Excel is as given in Table 14.2.

Microsoft can sell each product individually or it can sell Word and Excel together as a bundle. Let's calculate profit for each possibility. To make our lives simple, we will assume that the marginal costs of production are zero (which is approximately true—it costs very little to download Word).

If Microsoft sets prices individually, there are two sensible choices for the price of Word: $40 or $100. If Microsoft sets a price of $40 for Word, both Amanda and Yvonne will buy, and profit will be $80. If Microsoft sets a price of $100, Amanda alone will buy but profit will be higher, $100. Similarly, Microsoft can sensibly sell Excel for $20 or $90. Profit is higher at

Bundling is requiring that products be bought together in a bundle or package.

TABLE 14.2 MAXIMUM WILLINGNESS TO PAY FOR WORD AND EXCEL

	Amanda	Yvonne
Word	$100	$40
Excel	$20	$90

---

* The difference between tying and bundling is that bundled goods are sold one to one. Every right shoe comes with a left shoe. Tied goods are sold one to many. Every HP printer is tied to a variable number of ink cartridges, depending on consumer demand.

TABLE 14.3 MAXIMUM WILLINGNESS TO PAY FOR OFFICE

	Amanda	Yvonne
Word	$100	$40
Excel	$20	$90
Office = Word + Excel	$120	$130

a price of $90 because 2 × $20 = $40 < $90. If Microsoft sets prices individually, therefore, it will charge $100 for Word and $90 for Excel for a total profit of $190 = $100 + $90.

Now consider bundling Word and Excel and selling them as Office. What price to set? To calculate this, we need to know the maximum amount that Amanda and Yvonne will pay for Word plus Excel. We calculate this in Table 14.3.

Amanda is willing to pay up to $120 for the Office bundle and Yvonne is willing to pay up to $130. What is the profit-maximizing price for the Office bundle? Microsoft will set the bundle price at $120 and sell two Office bundles for a total profit of $240. What has happened to Microsoft's profit compared with when it set prices individually? When Microsoft priced Word and Excel individually, its profit was just $190. When Microsoft sells Word and Excel in a bundle called Office, its profits increase by $50, or 26%. Why?

Notice that in this example bundling is equivalent to a sophisticated scheme of (almost) perfect price discrimination. At a bundle price of $120, we can think of Amanda as being charged $100 for Word and $20 for Excel, and Yvonne as being charged $40 for Word and $80 for Excel. But in order to implement this price discrimination scheme directly, Microsoft would have to know a lot about Amanda's and Yvonne's willingness to pay for Word and Excel and Microsoft would have to prevent Yvonne from buying Word at $40 and reselling it to Amanda (and similarly keep Amanda from reselling Excel to Yvonne). When Microsoft bundles, however, it's easier to price-discriminate because although Amanda and Yvonne place very different values on Word and Excel, they have similar values for Office. Microsoft, therefore, knows more about the demand for Office than about the demand for Word or Excel, and the more Microsoft knows about demand, the easier it is for Microsoft to price-discriminate.

As with other forms of price discrimination, bundling can increase efficiency, especially when fixed costs are high and marginal costs are low. In our example, when Microsoft set prices individually, only Amanda bought Word and only Yvonne bought Excel. This is inefficient because Amanda values Excel at $20 and the costs of providing Excel is zero (and similarly for Yvonne and Word). When Microsoft bundles, Amanda and Yvonne buy both Word and Excel, which increases total surplus.

Total surplus without bundling is $190. What is total surplus with bundling? It's $250. Check that you understand where this number came from.

Furthermore, the costs of producing software are primarily the fixed costs of research and development. Bundling means that these fixed costs are spread across more consumers, which raises the incentive to innovate.

Bundling and Cable TV

Bundling is quite common. LexisNexis sells online access to a bundle of thousands of newspapers, journals, and references. Disneyland bundles many attractions and sells them for a single entrance fee. The buffet at China Garden is a bundle of food. Bundling, however, can be controversial. Cable TV operators sell television channels in a bundle. Recently, this practice has come under attack, with many politicians arguing for "à la carte" pricing, that is, pricing

Should Cable Companies Be Required to Sell by the Channel?

by the channel. Critics of bundling complain that consumers should not be forced to pay for channels that they don't watch. The claim seems sensible at first, but does it add up? Would the critics also say that the buffet at China Garden forces consumers of kung pao chicken to pay for unwanted egg foo young?

Bundle pricing makes sense for cable operators because customers have a high willingness to pay for some channels and a low willingness to pay for other channels, but the high- and low-value channels differ by customer. The demand for the bundle, however, is more similar across customers. Since it costs the cable company very little to offer every channel to every customer, bundling can increase profit and efficiency. The idea is exactly the same as we showed with the Microsoft Office example. In Table 14.3, change Word to the Food Network and Excel to Lifetime (and see also end-of-chapter Challenges question 21).

As usual, bundling is most likely to be beneficial in a high-fixed-cost, low-marginal-cost industry. Cable TV is a high-fixed cost, low-marginal cost industry. Over the last decade, for example, one cable operator, Comcast, spent $40 billion laying new cable. Once the cable is laid, the marginal cost of carrying another channel is low, especially with high bandwidth fiber optic cable. In cases like this, bundling doesn't cost the firm very much (and may even be cheaper than individual pricing), and by increasing profit, it increases the incentive to spend resources on the fixed costs of development.

Takeaway

Price discrimination—selling the same good to different customers at different prices—is a common feature of many markets. The most obvious form of price discrimination is when a firm sets different prices in different markets—as, for example, when GSK sells Combivir for a high price in Europe and a low price in Africa. Firms also price goods based on characteristics that are correlated with willingness to pay so student and senior discounts are a form of price discrimination, as are the different prices that airlines set for the same flight depending on how far in advance the flight is booked.

Price discrimination isn't always easy. To price-discriminate, the firm must prevent consumers who are charged a low price from reselling to consumers who would be charged a high price, that is, prevent arbitrage. Price discrimination also requires that the firm know a lot about its customers. The more the firm knows, the better it can price-discriminate. If the firm knew exactly how much each of its customers valued its product and it could prevent arbitrage, the firm could charge each customer that customer's maximum willingness to pay—this is called perfect price discrimination. Universities come closest to practicing perfect price discrimination because to provide scholarships, the university can demand a lot of information about the income of its students and their families and it's hard to resell an education.

Tying and bundling are less obvious forms of price discrimination. By setting a low price for printers and a high price for ink, HP is setting different prices for the "ability to print color photos"—a low price for those who print only occasionally and a high price for those who print often. Cell phones are priced below cost and cell phone calls are priced above cost for the same reason.

Bundling goods in a package can also be a form of price discrimination. When consumers place very different values on package components but similar values on the package, bundling can increase profits.

MODERN PRINCIPLES OF
ECONOMICS

fourth edition

See the invisible hand. Understand your world.

Tyler Cowen | Alex Tabarrok

Textbooks are bundles of chapters.

CHECK YOURSELF

- If cell phone companies were not allowed to tie cell phones with service plans, what do you predict would happen to the price of cell phones and what do you predict would happen to the price of cell phone calls?
- When is bundling likely to increase total surplus?

Firms want to price-discriminate because price discrimination increases profits. Price discrimination may also increase total surplus. Price discrimination is most likely to increase total surplus when it increases output and when there are large fixed costs of development. Price discrimination for pharmaceuticals, for example, lowers the price for consumers in poor countries (thus, increasing output) and, by increasing profits, price discrimination increases the incentive to research and develop new drugs.

CHAPTER REVIEW

interactive activity   Go online to practice with more examples of these types of problems, including live links to videos, data sources, and feedback.

 Problems in green relate to MRU videos. See the MRU table at the end of the exercises.

KEY CONCEPTS

price discrimination, p. 269

arbitrage, p. 271

perfect price discrimination, p. 275

tying, p. 278

bundling, p. 279

FACTS AND TOOLS

1. True or false? A business that price-discriminates will generally charge some customers more than marginal cost, and it will generally charge other customers less than marginal cost.

2. Two customers, Fred and Lamont, walk into Grady's Used Pickups. Who probably has a more inelastic demand for one of Grady's pickups: people like Lamont, who are good at shopping around, or people like Fred, who know what they like and just buy it?

3. Who probably has more elastic demand for a Hertz rental car: someone who reserves a car online weeks before a trip, or someone who walks up to a Hertz counter after he walks off an airplane following a 4-hour flight? Who probably gets charged more?

4. When arbitrage is easy in a market of would-be price discriminators, who is more likely to get priced out of the market: those with elastic demand or those with inelastic demand?

5. There are people who absolutely must have the latest fashions. Can you classify them as probably having elastic or inelastic demand?

6. Why would a firm hand out coupons for its products rather than just lowering the price? (*Hint:* At your school, what kind of students use coupons to buy their pizza? What kind of students *never* use coupons to buy their pizza?)

7. Where will you see more price discrimination: in monopoly-type markets with just a few firms or in competitive markets with many firms? Why?

8. When will a monopoly create more output: when it is allowed to and can perfectly price-discriminate or when the government bans price discrimination?

9. Some razors, like Gillette's Fusion and Venus razors, have disposable heads. The razor comes with an initial pack with a razor handle plus three or four heads; after that, you need to buy refills separately.

   a. Where do you think Gillette gets more revenue: by selling the initial pack or by selling the refills?

   b. The next time you buy a new razor, are you going to spend more time looking at the price of the razor or at the price of the refills?

THINKING AND PROBLEM SOLVING

10. Subway, the fast-food chain, sells foot-long sandwiches for $5 each. However, Subway still sells 6-inch sandwiches for considerably more than $2.50 each, that is, at a higher price per inch of sub.

a. Can you think of a way that in theory you could make money from Subway's pricing practices? Would this method work in practice? What does this tell you about the limits of arbitrage?

b. In many of our price discrimination examples, we think that businesses try to break customers into two groups: more price-sensitive and less price-sensitive. What kinds of Subway customers fit into the first group? Into the second?

Busy lawyers with 20-minute lunches

College students

Health-conscious soccer moms

Long-haul truck drivers

11. A dry cleaner has a sign in its window: "Free Internet Coupons." The dry cleaner lists its Web site, and indeed there are good discounts available with the coupons. Most customers don't use the coupons.

a. What probably would be the main difference between customers who use the coupons and those who don't?

b. Some people might think "The dry cleaner offers the coupons to get people in the door to try the place out, but then the customers will pay the normal high price afterward." But the coupons are always there, so even repeat customers can keep using the coupons. Is this a mistake on the business owner's part? (*Hint:* Think about marginal cost.)

12. **a.** When will a firm find it easier to price-discriminate: before the existence of eBay or afterward?

b. Which of the two "principles of price discrimination" does this invoke?

13. As we saw in this chapter, drug companies often charge much more for the same drug in the United States than in other countries. Congress often considers passing laws to make it *easier* to import drugs from these low-price countries (it also considers passing laws to make it illegal to import these drugs, but that's another story).

If one of these laws passes, and it becomes effortless to buy AIDS drugs from Africa or antibiotics from Latin America—drugs that are made by the same companies and have essentially the same quality controls as the drugs here in the United States—how will drug companies change the prices they charge in Latin America and Africa? Why?

14. Some people think that *businesses* create monopolies by destroying their competition, and there is certainly some truth to that. But as we learned from Obi-Wan Kenobi, "[Y]ou will find that many of the truths we cling to depend greatly on our own point of view." For instance, some people (Convenience Shoppers) love shopping at one particular store and will switch stores only when a product is outrageously expensive, while other people (Bargain Shoppers) will gladly spend hours looking through newspaper advertisements searching for the best deal.

a. When both kinds of people, the Convenience Shoppers and the Bargain Shoppers, are shopping at the same Walmart, who is more likely to stick to their prearranged shopping list, and who is more likely to splurge on a little something?

b. Which group does Walmart have monopoly power over? Which group does Walmart have no monopoly power over?

c. Does this mean that the same shop can simultaneously be a "monopolist" to some customers and a "competitive firm" to other customers? Why or why not?

d. Does this mean that Darth Vader really *did* kill Anakin Skywalker?

15. Where are you more likely to see businesses "bundling" a lot of goods into one package: in industries with high fixed costs and low marginal costs (like computer games or moviemaking), or in industries with low fixed costs and high marginal costs (like doctor visits, where the doctor's time is expensive)?

16. Isn't it surprising that movies, with tickets that cost around $10, often use vastly more economic resources than stage plays, where tickets can easily cost $100?

Compare, for example, a live stage performance of Shakespeare's *Hamlet* with a movie of *Hamlet*.

a. In which field is the marginal cost of one more showing lower: on stage or on screen?

b. "Bundling" in a movie or stage performance might show up in the form of adding special effects, expensive actors, or fancy costumes: Some customers might not be too interested in an Elizabethan revenge drama, but they show up to see Liam Neeson waving an authentic medieval dagger. Is it better to think of these extra expenses as "fixed costs" or "marginal costs"?

c. In which setting will it be easier for a business to cover its total costs: in a "bundled" stage production or in a "bundled" movie production?

17. When is a pharmaceutical company more likely to spend $100 million to research a new drug: when it knows it will be able to charge different prices in different countries or when it knows that it will be required to charge the same price in different countries? Why?

18. True or false? A price-discriminating business will sometimes be willing to spend money to make a product worse.

19. Let's calculate the profit from price discrimination. The average daily demand for dinners at Paradise Grille, an upscale casual restaurant, is as follows:

Demand for dinners by senior citizens:

$P = 50 - 0.5Q$ $MR = 50 - Q$

Demand for dinners by others:

$P = 100 - Q$ $MR = 100 - 2Q$

Marginal cost = 10 in both cases

a. What is the profit-maximizing price for each group?

b. Translate this into real-world jargon: If you owned this restaurant, what "senior citizen discount" would you offer, in percent?

c. Ignoring fixed costs, how much profit would Paradise Grille make if it did this?

d. If it became illegal to discriminate on the basis of age, you would face only one demand curve. Adding up these two demand curves turns out to yield

$$P = 67 - \left(\frac{1}{3}\right)Q \quad MR = 67 - \left(\frac{2}{3}\right)Q$$

What are the optimal price and quantity in this unified market? Are the total meals sold in this discrimination-free market higher or lower than in part a?

e. What is the profit in this discrimination-free market?

20. At the Kennedy Center for the Performing Arts in Washington, D.C., if you make a $120 donation per year, you are allowed to go to a small room before the concert and drink free coffee and eat free cookies. If you make a donation of $1,200 per year, you are allowed to go to a *different* small room before the concert and drink the *same* free coffee and eat the *same* free cookies. There are always a lot of people in both rooms before the concert. Why doesn't everybody just pay the $120 instead of the higher price?

CHALLENGES

21. In the following table, we consider how Alex, Tyler, and Monique would fare under à la carte pricing and under bundling for cable TV when there are two channels: Lifetime and the Food Network.

Alex and Tyler like to watch *Project Runway* so they each place a higher value on Lifetime than on the Food Network. Monique is practicing to be an Iron Chef in her second life so she places a higher value on the Food Network than on Lifetime.

Maximum Willingness to Pay for Cable TV			
	Alex	Tyler	Monique
Lifetime	10	15	3
The Food Network	7	4	9
The Bundle	15	19	12

a. If the channels are priced individually, the most profitable prices for the cable operator turn out to be 10 for Lifetime and 7 for the Food Network. At these prices, who buys what channel and how much profit is there?

b. Let's just check to see if these prices really are profit-maximizing. What would profit be if the cable company raised Lifetime to a price of 11 and Food Network to a price of 8?

c. At the profit-maximizing prices, how much total consumer surplus would there be for the three of them? (Recall that consumer surplus is just each customer's willingness to pay minus the amount each person actually paid.)

d. Now consider what happens under bundling: Customers get a take-it-or-leave-it offer of both channels or nothing at all. The profit-maximizing bundle price turns out to be 12, and at that price, Alex, Tyler, and Monique all subscribe. How much consumer surplus is there at this price? How much profit? And, most important, what would profit equal if the cable company raised the price to 13 instead?

22. Consider the following seating arrangement for a concert hall:

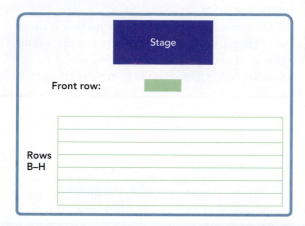

The front row seats only two people. Rows B–H, about 50 feet back from the front row, seat 20 people per row.

a. Would these front-row seats sell for more or for less than the front-row seats at a typical concert hall? Why?

b. Why don't we see concert halls set up like this?

23. a. In competitive markets in the long run, if there are two kinds of steaks, "regular" and "high-quality Angus beef," and the regular beef sells at a lower price, is this an example of price discrimination?

b. How is this different from the HP printer story in this chapter?

24. Amanda and Yvonne are thinking of going out to the movies. Amanda likes action flicks more, but Yvonne likes a little bit of romance. Warner Bros. is trying to decide what kind of movies to make this year. Should it make one movie for release this summer, an action flick with a romantic subplot, or should it make two movies for release this summer: an action flick and a romantic drama?

Here's the two friends' willingness to pay for the separate kinds of movies. As you can see, both Amanda and Yvonne are annoyed by the idea of a hybrid movie: Each would rather see her favorite kind of movie.

Maximum Willingness to Pay for a Movie Ticket		
	Amanda	Yvonne
Pure action	$10	$2
Pure romance	$2	$10
Action + romance	$9	$9

Now, let's look at this from Warner Bros.' point of view. You're the midlevel executive who has to decide which project to green light. Your marketing people have figured out that there are 5 million people like Amanda and 5 million people like Yvonne in the United States, and they'll only see one film per summer. To make things simple, assume that the marginal cost of showing the movie one more time is zero, and that ticket prices are fixed at $8.

a. If the cost of producing any of the three films is $30 million, what should the studio do: make the two films or just the one hybrid film? Of course, the right way to find the answer is to figure out which choice would generate the most profit for Warner Bros.

b. Of course, the hybrid might cost a bit more to make. What if the hybrid costs $40 million to make, the pure action flick $30 million, and the romance a mere $15 million? What's the best choice now: one hybrid or two pure films?

c. Let's see how much prices would have to change for the answer to this question to change. Holding all else equal, how low would the cost of the pure romance film have to fall before the two-movie deal would get the green light?

d. (Hard) There's an underlying principle here: The "unbundled" two-movie deal won't get the green light unless its total cost is less than what? The answer is not a number—it's an idea. Is this likely to happen in the real world? Why or why not?

25. Think about the kind of 40-year-old who pulls out a faded, obviously expired student ID to get a discount ticket at a movie theater: What can you predict about his or her willingness to pay for a full-price movie? Is the movie theater making a mistake when it lets him or her pay the student price?

26. We mentioned that airlines charge much more for flights booked at the last minute than for flights booked well in advance, even for exactly the same flight. This is because people who tend to book at the last minute tend to have inelastic demand. Think of other characteristics that airlines use to vary their pricing: Do you think these characteristics are correlated with business travel or any other sort of inelastic demand? (If you don't fly too often, just ask someone who does: "What's the key to getting the lowest possible airfare?")

27. Apple's iTunes music service sells music by the song. Other services, such as Spotify and Pandora, sell subscriptions to a library of music. Using the material in this chapter, which type of service do you think is most likely to succeed in the marketplace and why?

interactive activity

WORK IT OUT

For interactive, step-by-step help in solving the following problem, go online.

If Congress passed a privacy law making it illegal for colleges to ask for parents' tax returns, would that tend to help students from high-income families or students from low-income families?

MRUNIVERSITY
AN ONLINE EDUCATION PLATFORM

MARGINAL REVOLUTION UNIVERSITY VIDEOS

Introduction to Price Discrimination

mruniversity.com/price-discrimination

Problems: **1–3, 5–7, 10, 12–14, 20, 26**

The Social Welfare of Price Discrimination

mruniversity.com/price-discrimination-society

Problems: **4, 8, 11, 18, 19, 25**

Tying

mruniversity.com/tying

Problems: **9, 23**

Should Cable Companies Be Required to Sell by the Channel?

mruniversity.com/bundling

Problems: **15–17, 21, 22, 24**

CHAPTER 14 APPENDIX

Solving Price Discrimination Problems with Excel (Advanced Section)

Excel's Solver tool can be used to solve difficult price discrimination problems. Imagine that there are two groups of customers with the following demand curves:

$$Q_1^D = 330 - 2 \times P_1$$
$$Q_2^D = 510 - 4 \times P_2$$

where Q_1^D is the quantity demanded by Group 1 when it faces price P_1 and Q_2^D is the quantity demanded by Group 2 when it faces price P_2. We could think of these markets as Europe and Africa or as business travelers and vacationers, similar to the way we did in the text. The monopolist has the following costs:

$$\text{Costs} = 1,000 + Q^2$$

where Q is the quantity produced by the monopolist.

   The monopolist's goal is simple: It wants to choose prices P_1 and P_2 in order to maximize its profits. We will assume that the two markets are distinct, so arbitrage is not possible. Although the goal is simple, the solution is difficult. In fact, this problem is considerably more difficult than any of the problems we dealt with in the text. In the text, we assumed that marginal cost was constant (a flat MC curve). Assuming constant marginal costs simplified the problem because it meant that when the monopolist produced more in Market 1, the costs of producing another unit in Market 2 didn't change. In our problem here, marginal cost is increasing—which means that when the monopolist produces more in Market 1, its cost of producing an additional unit in Market 2 also increases. In an intermediate or graduate economics class, you would use calculus to solve a problem like this.

   In the real world, business managers and entrepreneurs must solve problems like this every day and they don't all know calculus, so we will show you how to solve the problem using Excel. First, let's write down what we know. In Figure A14.1, we highlight the equation for Q_1^D, which we enter as "=330−2*B2". We put the price for Group 1 in cell B2. We want to find the profit-maximizing price for Group 1 but we don't know what it is, so for now we just put a zero in cell B2. The equation and price for Group 2 are entered similarly.

FIGURE A14.1

B3		f_x =330-2*B2	
	A	B	C
1		Group 1	Group 2
2	Price	$0.00	$0.00
3	Quantity Demanded	330.00	510.00
4			

Now we enter the formula for the monopolist's cost. The total quantity produced by the monopolist is simply the quantity produced for Group 1 plus the quantity produced for Group 2. Thus, we can rewrite the monopolist's costs as

$$\text{Costs} = 1{,}000 + (Q_1^D + Q_2^D)^2$$

In Figure A14.2, we have entered the monopolist's costs in cell B5 as "=1000+(B3+C3)^2".

FIGURE A14.2

	B5		f_x =1000+(B3+C3)^2	
	A	B	C	
1		Group 1	Group 2	
2	Price	$0.00	$0.00	
3	Quantity Demanded	330.00	510.00	
4				
5	Monopoly Cost	$706,600.00		
6				

It is important to see that what matters here is the formula for costs; the number in the picture, $706,600.00, is simply the monopolist's costs if the monopolist set P_1 and P_2 at zero and produced everything its customers demanded at those prices!

Finally, we enter the formula for profits, as shown in Figure A14.3.

FIGURE A14.3

	B6		f_x =B2*B3+C2*C3-B5	
	A	B	C	
1		Group 1	Group 2	
2	Price	$0.00	$0.00	
3	Quantity Demanded	330.00	510.00	
4				
5	Monopoly Cost	$706,600.00		
6	Monopoly Profit	-$706,600.00		
7				

Profits are revenues minus costs so we enter into Excel "=B2*B3+ C2*C3−B5", which is price times the quantity demanded for Group 1 plus price times quantity demanded for Group 2 minus total costs. Excel now has enough information to solve this problem. In Excel 2011, the Solver function is found under the Data tab (but you may first have to add-in the Solver application—see Excel help for instructions on how to do this). Clicking on the Solver button produces Figure A14.4.

FIGURE A14.4

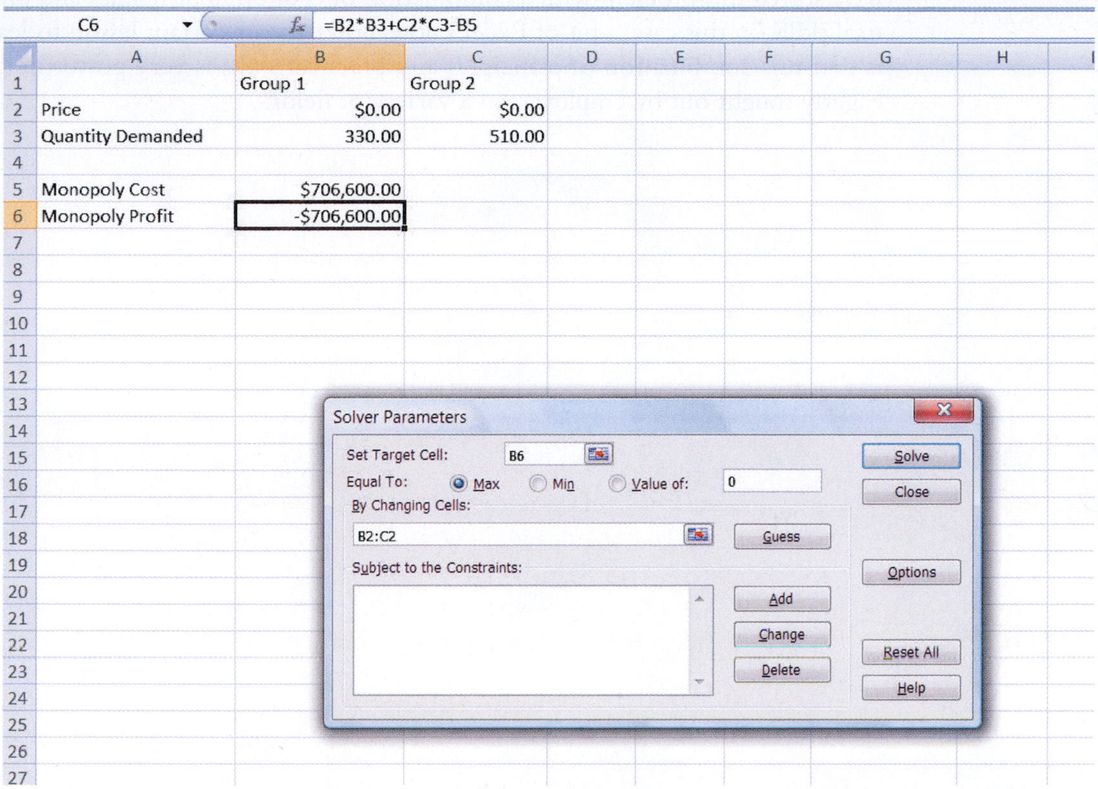

	C6	▼		f_x	=B2*B3+C2*C3-B5					
	A	B	C	D	E	F	G	H	
1		Group 1	Group 2						
2	Price	$0.00	$0.00						
3	Quantity Demanded	330.00	510.00						
4									
5	Monopoly Cost	$706,600.00							
6	Monopoly Profit	-$706,600.00							

Solver Parameters

Set Target Cell: B6

Equal To: ⦿ Max ○ Min ○ Value of: 0

By Changing Cells: B2:C2

Subject to the Constraints:

[Solve] [Close] [Guess] [Options] [Add] [Change] [Delete] [Reset All] [Help]

Our target is profits so in the Solver box next to "Set Target Cell", we enter B6. We want a maximum of profits, so make sure the "Equal to" button is filled in on Max. Finally, we are going to maximize profits by changing prices, so in the box for "By Changing Cells", we enter "B2:C2". Now we click Solve and Excel finds the answer shown in Figure A14.5.

FIGURE A14.5

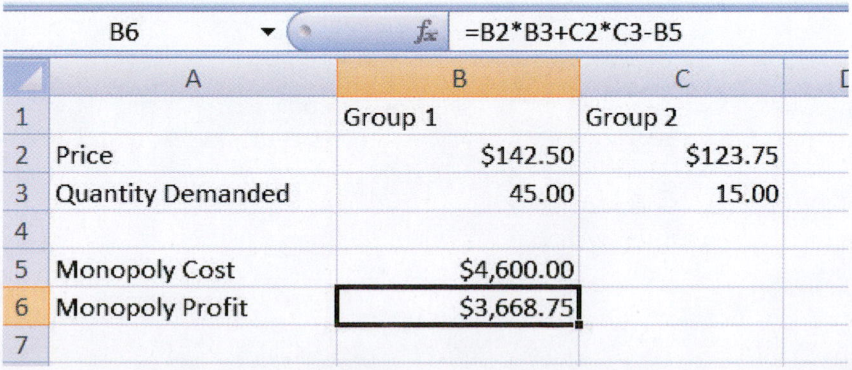

	B6	▼	f_x	=B2*B3+C2*C3-B5	
	A	B	C	D
1		Group 1	Group 2	
2	Price	$142.50	$123.75	
3	Quantity Demanded	45.00	15.00	
4				
5	Monopoly Cost	$4,600.00		
6	Monopoly Profit	$3,668.75		
7				

Excel tells us that the profit-maximizing prices are $142.50 for Group 1 and $123.75 for Group 2. At these prices, Group 1 customers buy 45 units, Group 2 customers buy 15 units, and monopoly profits are $3,668.75.

Once you understand the basic ideas, it's easy to make these models even more realistic by adding bells and whistles such as more groups. Notice that we have solved this problem with a combination of economic principles and practical skills (in this case, a bit of Excel know-how). An important lesson to learn is that this combination of principles and practical skills is very powerful and eagerly sought out by employers in a variety of fields.

15

Oligopoly and Game Theory

As oil prices neared a historic high in July 1979, President Jimmy Carter spoke to the nation. Quoting a concerned American, Carter said, "Our neck is stretched over the fence and OPEC has a knife." What is OPEC and what power did OPEC have to control the price of oil?

OPEC, which is short for the Organization of the Petroleum Exporting Countries, is a **cartel**, a group of suppliers who try to act together to reduce supply, raise prices, and increase profits. In other words, a cartel is a group of suppliers who try to act as if they were a monopolist.

We analyzed monopoly in Chapter 13 so we have a good understanding of what cartels are *trying* to achieve, but the question we address in this chapter is, when will cartels be *able* to achieve their goals? As we will see, it's not easy for a group of firms to act as if they were a monopolist. But even when a group of firms is not able to coordinate or collude to act like a monopolist, prices are likely to be higher in an industry with a small number of firms than in a highly competitive market. We call an industry that is dominated by a small number of firms an **oligopoly**. Thus, we begin our chapter by discussing cartels, an oligopoly that acts like a monopolist, and then move to a more general discussion of oligopoly.

In this chapter, we also introduce a new tool: game theory. Game theory is the study of **strategic decision making**. An example illustrates what we mean. In Las Vegas, craps players make decisions, but poker players make strategic decisions. Craps is a dice game and deciding when and how much to bet can be complicated, but the outcome depends only on the dice and the bet and not on how other people bet. In contrast, poker is a game of strategy because a good poker player must forecast the decisions of other players, knowing that they in turn are trying to forecast his or her decisions. Game theory is used to model decisions in situations in which the players interact.

Although we introduced game theory with an example from poker, a game in the usual sense of the word, game theory is used to study decision making in any situation that is interactive in a significant way. Game theory has also been used to study war, romance, business decisions of all kinds, evolution, voting, and many other situations involving interaction.

In this chapter, we use game theory to look at the economics of oligopoly.

A **cartel** is a group of suppliers who try to act *as if* they were a monopoly.

An **oligopoly** is a market that is dominated by a small number of firms.

Strategic decision making is decision making in situations that are interactive.

Cartels

Figure 15.1 shows the price for a barrel of oil from 1960 to 2016. We will focus in this chapter on the dramatic increase in the price of oil in the early 1970s and on the almost equally dramatic fall in the early 1980s. Between 1970 and 1974, the price of oil shot up from $7 per barrel to almost $38 a barrel. What happened? The answer is simple: Led by Saudi Arabia, a cartel of oil-exporting countries cut back on their production of oil.*

The left panel of Figure 15.2 shows a competitive market in a constant-cost industry so the supply curve is flat (the constant-cost assumption makes the analysis simpler but is not necessary); remember that in a competitive market each supplier earns zero economic profit. The right panel shows the *same market* but now run *as if* it were controlled by a monopolist; profits, shown in green, are maximized. A cartel is not a monopolist, but if all the firms in a market could be convinced to cut supply so that total supply fell from Q_c to Q_m, then

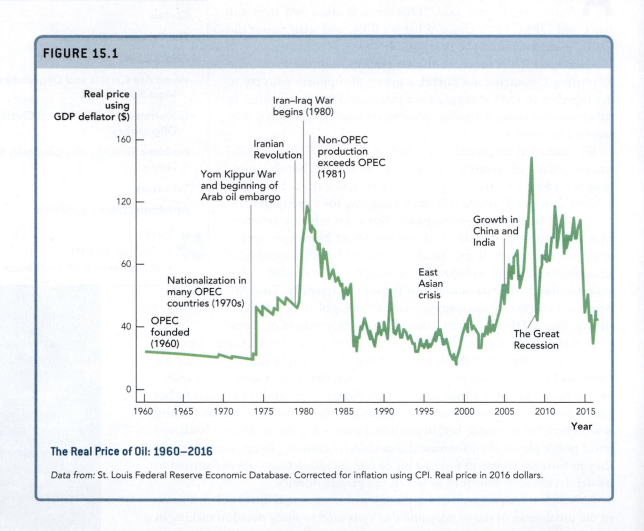

FIGURE 15.1

The Real Price of Oil: 1960–2016

Data from: St. Louis Federal Reserve Economic Database. Corrected for inflation using CPI. Real price in 2016 dollars.

---

* OPEC began in 1960 with five founding members—Iran, Iraq, Kuwait, Saudi Arabia, and Venezuela—and was initially not very powerful. But as more countries joined and nationalized their oil fields, it grew in power. The original five were joined by Qatar (1961), Indonesia (1962–2009, 2016), Libya (1962), United Arab Emirates (1967), Algeria (1969), Nigeria (1971), Ecuador (1973–1992, 2007–), Gabon (1975–1995, 2016–), and Angola (2007).

FIGURE 15.2

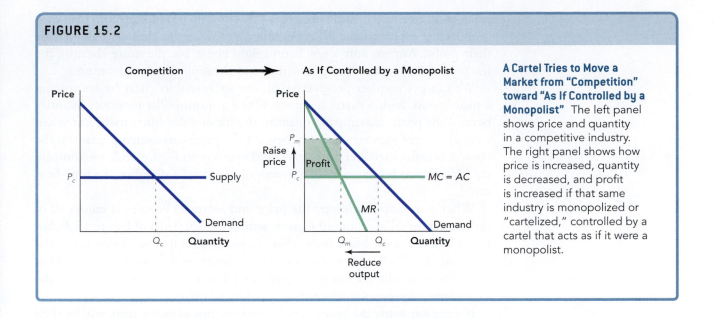

A Cartel Tries to Move a Market from "Competition" toward "As If Controlled by a Monopolist" The left panel shows price and quantity in a competitive industry. The right panel shows how price is increased, quantity is decreased, and profit is increased if that same industry is monopolized or "cartelized," controlled by a cartel that acts as if it were a monopolist.

each firm could share in the "monopoly" profits. Thus, a cartel is an organization of suppliers who try to move the market from the left panel of Figure 15.2 to the right panel, that is, from "Competition" toward "As If Controlled by a Monopolist."

Very few cartels can move an industry from competition to pure monopoly, but Figure 15.2 shows the basic tendency of cartels to reduce output and raise price.

It might seem from this short look at OPEC that cartels are all-powerful. But in reality few cartels—unless they have strong government support—have much control over market price for very long. A cartel is a deal in which businesspeople promise: "I will raise my price and cut back my production if you promise to do the same." But will the promise be kept?

Cartels tend to collapse and lose their power for three reasons:

1. Cheating by the cartel members
2. New entrants and demand response
3. Government prosecution and regulation

OPEC, although a relatively successful cartel by historical standards, could not keep the price of oil high for very long. By 1986, the price of oil had plummeted from its previous heights of $75 per barrel to around $20 per barrel and sometimes falling as low as $10 per barrel. OPEC nations were unhappy, but there was little they could do to keep oil prices high.

How did this happen? To understand, let's turn to the first reason why cartels collapse, namely cheating by the cartel members.

The Incentive to Cheat

If a cartel succeeds, cartel members earn high profits on each barrel of oil that comes out of the ground, but this same desire for profit makes the cartel fall apart. Members will cheat on the cartel agreement. That is, they will promise to reduce production, but when everyone else reduces production and the price of oil rises, some cartel members will cheat by producing more than they promised. If everyone else is keeping their promises, the cheaters will increase their profits. At first, only a few firms might cheat, but the more cheaters, the less profitable it is to reduce production and cheating will soon increase.

We can get another perspective on the incentive to cheat by comparing a monopolist with a cartel member. When a monopolist increases quantity beyond the profit-maximizing quantity, the monopolist hurts itself. But when a cartel cheater increases quantity beyond the profit-maximizing quantity, the cheater benefits itself and hurts *other cartel members*. In Figure 15.3, we compare the incentive to lower price for a monopolist and for a member of a four-firm cartel.

When a monopolist lowers the price and increases its sales, it enjoys all of the gains from selling more (the green area in the left panel of Figure 15.3), but it also bears all of the losses from selling its previous output at a lower price (the red area). But if a four-firm cartel member cheats on the cartel, it enjoys all of the gains from selling more (the green area), but it bears only a quarter of the losses from a lower price (the red area in the right panel).

If a cheater hurts the other cartel members, not so many tears will be shed by the cheater. This is especially true for the OPEC cartel. Iran and Iraq, for example, fought a major war from 1980 to 1988, with more than 800,000 people killed. The war saw the use of poison gas, chemical weapons, and child soldiers as advance scouts to trigger land mines. While this war was going on, Iran

FIGURE 15.3

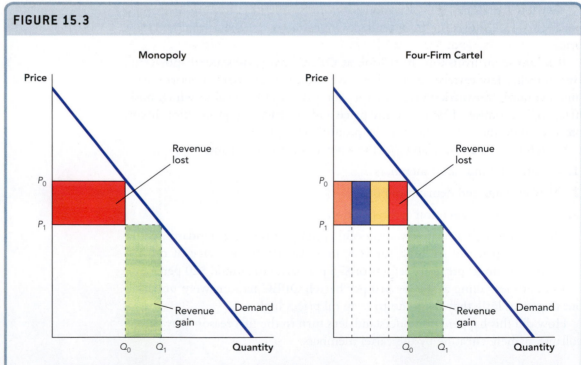

The Incentive to Cheat When a monopolist increases quantity from Q_0 to Q_1 it gets all of the revenues from the new sales (the green area) but it also bears all of the losses from the lower price on old sales (the red area). The red plus green area is equal to marginal revenue (see Chapter 11).

When a single firm in a four-firm cartel increases quantity from Q_0 to Q_1 it gets all of the revenues from the new sales (the green area), but the fall in price is spread across all firms in the industry in proportion to their sales, so the cartel member loses only the much smaller red area. The cartel member, therefore, has a much larger incentive to increase output than does the monopolist.

and Iraq were both in OPEC. Each nation, in effect, was promising it would not undercut the other when it came to selling more oil at a lower price. Do you really think they felt obliged to keep their word?

And so have most cartels ended. The more successful the cartel is in raising member profits, the greater the incentive to cheat. And once a cartel falls apart, it is difficult to put it back together again. Everyone correctly expects cheating to be the norm.

No One Wins the Cheating Game

It's useful to show the incentive to cheat in another way, using what is called a payoff table. With more than two firms, the payoff table would be quite complicated and hard to draw in two dimensions, but the same logic of cheating applies if there are just two firms. So imagine that the oil market is dominated by two large firms, Saudi Arabia and Russia.

Saudi Arabia has two choices, or strategies, Cooperate (by cutting back production) or Cheat. These strategies are shown in Figure 15.4 by the rows of the payoff table. Russia also has the same two strategies, shown as the columns of the payoff table.

The two numbers in each box of the table are the payoffs to the players; the first number is the payoff to Saudi Arabia, the second to Russia. For instance, if both Saudi Arabia and Russia choose to cooperate by cutting back production, the payoff is $400 (million per day) to Saudi Arabia and $400 (million per day) to Russia. If Saudi Arabia cheats and Russia cooperates, then the payoff to Saudi Arabia is $500 and the payoff to Russia is $200.

I promise never to cheat on you. Venezuelan President Hugo Chavez (left) hugs Saudi Crown Prince Abdullah bin Abdul Aziz Al Saud during an OPEC summit in 2000.

Now let's see what the "players" will do in this "game." Consider the incentives faced by Saudi Arabia. If Russia cooperates, then Saudi Arabia can choose Cooperate and receive a payoff of $400 or choose Cheat and receive a payoff of $500. Since $500 is more than $400, Saudi Arabia's best strategy *if Russia cooperates* is to cheat.

FIGURE 15.4

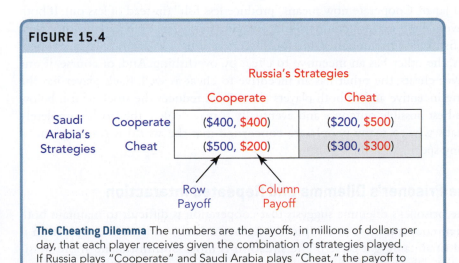

The Cheating Dilemma The numbers are the payoffs, in millions of dollars per day, that each player receives given the combination of strategies played. If Russia plays "Cooperate" and Saudi Arabia plays "Cheat," the payoff to Saudi Arabia is $500 and the payoff to Russia is $200. In this game, Cheat is a better strategy for each player no matter what the other player's strategy. Thus, the equilibrium of this game (shaded) is (Cheat, Cheat).

A **dominant strategy** is a strategy that has a higher payoff than any other strategy no matter what the other player does.

What is Saudi Arabia's best strategy if Russia cheats? If Russia cheats, Saudi Arabia can cooperate and earn a payoff of $200 or Saudi Arabia can cheat and earn a payoff of $300. Cheat is again the more profitable strategy. A strategy that has a higher payoff than any other strategy, no matter what the other player does, is called a **dominant strategy**. In this setup, cheating is a dominant strategy for Saudi Arabia.

Cheating is also a dominant strategy for Russia. If Saudi Arabia cooperates, Russia earns $500 by choosing Cheat and $400 by choosing Cooperate. If Saudi Arabia cheats, Russia earns $300 by choosing Cheat and $200 by choosing Cooperate. Thus, both Saudi Arabia and Russia will cheat and we shade (Cheat, Cheat) to show that this is the equilibrium outcome of the game.

The logic is compelling but also surprising. When Saudi Arabia and Russia each follow their individually sensible strategy of Cheat, each receives a payoff of $300. If Saudi Arabia and Russia instead both chose to cooperate, a strategy that is not individually sensible, they will receive a higher payoff of $400. Thus, when Saudi Arabia acts in its interest and Russia acts in its interest, the result is an outcome that is in the interest of neither. That is a dilemma well verified by both theory and evidence.

The Prisoner's Dilemma

The **prisoner's dilemma** is the negative counterpart to the invisible hand.

The analysis we have just given of cartel cheating is one version of a very famous game called the **prisoner's dilemma**. The prisoner's dilemma describes situations where the pursuit of self-interest leads to a group or social outcome that is in the interest of no one. The prisoner's dilemma is the negative counterpart to the invisible hand. The pursuit of self-interest can, with the right rules, lead to the social interest—that's the invisible hand. The pursuit of self-interest can also lead, with the wrong rules, to an outcome that no one intends and no one wants.

To give another example of this phenomenon, the world's stock of fish is rapidly being depleted. To understand why, replace Saudi Arabia and Russia in Figure 15.4 with two large fishing firms or countries, say the United States and Japan. Cooperate now means "produce less fish" (instead of less oil). If both players choose Cooperate, fishing revenue can be maximized and the stock of fish will be maintained for future generations. But if one player cooperates, the other has an incentive to cheat by overfishing. And, of course, if one player cheats, the other has an incentive to cheat as well. Each player has the same incentive and so both players cheat. That reduces the stock of fish below the best possible outcome and eventually it may deplete the stock completely. That's why so many people are concerned that the world is running out of many species of fish.

The Prisoner's Dilemma and Repeated Interaction

The prisoner's dilemma suggests that cooperation is difficult to maintain both when cooperation is good (preventing overfishing) and when cooperation is bad (maintaining a cartel). The situation is more optimistic and more pessimistic with repeated interactions! If the same players engage with one another repeatedly, they are more likely to cooperate than if they meet and play the prisoner's dilemma just once. The political scientist Elinor Ostrom, who was awarded the Nobel Prize in economics in 2009, has shown, for example, that

CHECK YOURSELF

- When Great Britain discovered large oil deposits in the North Sea, why didn't it immediately join OPEC?
- What is the surprising conclusion of the prisoner's dilemma?

fishermen do not invariably overfish common fishing grounds. In small communities with repeated interaction, people generally find rules or norms, such as limits on how much it is okay to take, that lead to greater cooperation, and that limit the prisoner's dilemmas. We will have more to say about overfishing in Chapter 19.

For the same reasons, however, cheating does not always break down cartels when a small number of players interact repeatedly. The asphalt industry, for example, is notorious for cartel-like behavior (asphalt is the tar-like material used for paving roads). Thousands of firms produce asphalt so you might think that cartels wouldn't work. The problem is that asphalt is costly to transport and it has to be kept hot, so a firm can't deliver asphalt at a reasonable price anywhere more than an hour or so away from its place of production. In rural regions, that limits the number of bidders on a road contract to just a handful of firms.

When only a handful of firms can realistically bid on a road contract, it becomes profitable to collude. For instance, the firms could secretly agree to all submit high bids, while agreeing that on each bid cycle one firm will be the "low" bidder, and then rotating the identity of this firm over time so that each firm shares in the profits. In the 1980s, the government prosecuted over 600 bid-rigging cases in the asphalt industry. What's most interesting, however, is that there is evidence that the cartels did not disappear, even after this prosecution.

Government prosecution eliminated explicit agreements to rig bids but it didn't solve the underlying problem. In many parts of the country, there are still only a handful of firms that can realistically bid on a contract. Moreover, the same firms face each other repeatedly and each firm understands that if they bid aggressively on every contract, then no one will ever profit very much. In this situation, strategies often evolve that can duplicate collusive outcomes even without explicit agreement. If Firm A bids low today, for example, Firm B can punish them by bidding low on the next contract. But if Firm A cooperates by submitting a high bid today, then Firm B can cooperate by submitting a high bid tomorrow. This strategy—do whatever your partner did the last period—is called "tit for tat" and it can be very effective at developing **tacit collusion**, collusion without explicit agreement or communication.

Another strategy is for firms to tacitly agree on territories—"I won't underbid you in this area if you don't underbid me in this other area." Between 2005 and 2007, for example, over one thousand road contracts were put up for bid by the Kentucky government and a stunning 63% had only one bidder! Moreover, two clever economists, David Barrus and Frank Scott, discovered that the pattern of bids wasn't random.[1] Remember that asphalt firms have to deliver their product within about an hour of production. What Barrus and Scott discovered is that the firms weren't bidding for every potential contract within their one-hour radius. Instead, the firms more often made bids just within the county in which the firm had its production plant. A firm might bid on a contract 40 miles away in the same county, for example, but not bid on a contract just 10 miles away but in another county. Even though county lines are irrelevant to the economics of asphalt production, they had become a focal point for firms to tacitly collude.

Most importantly, notice that it's much harder to prosecute collusion when the colluding firms never meet or discuss an agreement and the only signal of collusion is not bidding!

Tacit collusion occurs when firms limit competition with one another but they do so without explicit agreement or communication.

The Prisoner's Dilemma Has Many Applications

The prisoner's dilemma has a remarkable number of applications throughout economics and the social sciences and even in biology, computer science, and philosophy. We show a few examples in Figure 15.5.

FIGURE 15.5

FLOWGRAPH/GETTY IMAGES

The Arms Race Few people wanted to develop the hydrogen bomb but no one wanted the other side to develop it first so we ended up in a very dangerous world.

MARIOGUTI/GETTY IMAGES

There Is Trouble with the Trees Each tree grows tall to try to grab up all the light. But when all the trees do, none gain an advantage and all expend resources in fruitless competition.

FRANZ PFLUEGL/SHUTTERSTOCK

Standing Room Only At the concert everyone stands to get a better view but no one gets it (unless you have a very good friend).

RODNEY TURNER KRT/NEWSCOM

Battle of the Brands Coke and Pepsi have spent billions trying to convince buyers that their brand is better. The war has been profitable . . . for the advertising agencies.

Oligopolies

Cartels are difficult to form and maintain, but an oligopoly that fails to form a cartel is still very likely to maintain prices above competitive levels. In Figure 15.3, we showed how a cartel member has an incentive to cheat on the agreement by lowering price and producing more than the assigned quota. Exactly the same diagram shows why the price in an oligopoly is likely to be below the monopoly price. A firm in an oligopoly that produces more and cuts price earns all the gains for itself, but bears only a fraction of the costs. Thus, prices in an oligopoly are likely to be below monopoly levels, but how will prices in an oligopoly compare with competitive levels?

In Figure 15.6, we show how an oligopolist has an incentive to raise prices above competitive levels. Imagine first that the oligopolistic market is producing at competitive levels. Recall from Chapter 11 that this means the price is equal to marginal cost and no firm is making an above-normal profit. In Figure 15.6, the competitive price and quantity are P_0 ($= MC$) and Q_0. Now suppose that one firm in, say, a four-firm oligopoly were to cut output by $Q_0 - Q_1$, thus raising the price to P_1. At P_1, every firm in the industry is making a profit since $P_1 > MC$. In particular, even the firm that cut its output increased its profits since before it was making zero profits and now it is making positive profits, as shown by the green area.

In a competitive industry, no firm is able to influence the price, so a competitive firm has no incentive to reduce output. In an oligopoly, each firm is large relative to the total size of the market. Thus, a firm in an oligopoly has some influence over the price and therefore has an incentive to reduce output and increase price from the competitive level.

Figures 15.3 and 15.6 tell us that price in an oligopoly is likely to be below monopoly levels but above competitive levels. Moreover, we can also see that the more firms in the oligopoly, the greater the incentive to cut price from monopoly levels and the smaller the incentive to increase price above competitive levels. Thus, we can also predict that the more firms in an industry, the closer price will be to competitive levels.

Can we be more precise about pricing in an oligopolistic market? Economists have developed many models of oligopolistic pricing. Famous models in this literature include those by Bertrand, Cournot and Nash, and Stackelberg.

FIGURE 15.6

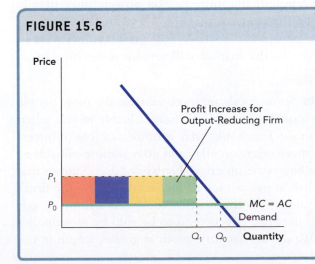

The Incentive to Raise Price Above Competitive Levels in an Oligopoly The competitive equilibrium is shown at P_0, Q_0. In the competitive equilibrium no firm makes an above-normal profit since $P = MC$. Even though no firm makes an above-normal profit, a competitive firm has no control over the price and thus cannot increase its profits by reducing output. But a firm in a four-firm oligopoly who reduces quantity by the amount $Q_0 - Q_1$ increases the market price to P_1 which is greater than MC. The increase in price increases the profits of the firm that cuts output (the green area), as well as increasing the profits of the other firms in the industry.

Barriers to entry are factors that increase the cost to new firms of entering an industry.

Each of these models has its uses, but it's difficult to say that one model is best for all purposes. A lot depends on factors specific to the industry; the right model for the auto industry might not be the right model for the soft-drink industry or the aircraft industry. The field of industrial organization has a lot more to say about the specifics of oligopoly.

When Are Cartels and Oligopolies Most Successful?

As with monopolies, cartels and oligopolies tend to be most successful when there are significant **barriers to entry,** that is, factors that increase the cost to new firms of entering an industry. Table 15.1 lists some important barriers to entry.

Control over a Key Resource or Input Oil and diamonds are two goods in which cartels have been partially successful because these natural resources are found in only a few places in the world (but see the sidebar on diamonds!). As a result, it's possible for a few firms or countries to control a significant share of the world's output. Similarly, Indonesia and Grenada, taken together, control 98% of the world's supply of nutmeg, a hard-to-replace spice used in many baking recipes. The nutmeg cartel has had some success. Copper, however, is a natural resource that is distributed more widely. The copper cartel (International Council of Copper Exporting Countries) controls no more than one-third of the world's copper reserves and as a result has not been able to raise prices in any significant manner. There are also good substitutes for copper in most uses, including plastic, aluminum, and recycled copper. The copper case is more typical than diamonds or oil.

TABLE 15.1 SOME BARRIERS TO ENTRY
Control over a key resource or input
Economies of scale
Network effects
Government barriers

Economies of Scale The advantages of large-scale production mean that it is much cheaper for five car manufactures to make 3 million cars each than for 500 manufacturers to make 30,000 cars each. When economies of scale are important, bigger means cheaper. Bigger firms, however, also means fewer firms, each with potentially more market power. Since people want cheaper cars more than they want extreme variety, it is never going to be optimal to have 500 car manufacturers in the United States so the market will remain something of an oligopoly.

Network Effects Some goods are more valuable the more people use them. Facebook, for example, is more valuable to you when your friends also use Facebook. eBay is more valuable to buyers when there are more sellers on eBay, and eBay is more valuable to sellers the more buyers are on eBay. "Network effects" means that firms can snowball in size as each new customer makes the firm's product more valuable to the next customer. As a result, goods with significant network effects tend to be sold by monopolies or oligopolies. We discuss network goods at greater length in the next chapter.

MACIEJ FROLOW/GETTY IMAGES

Is the diamond cartel forever? Diamonds are found in only a few places in the world. As a result, for decades the DeBeers cartel has been able to keep prices high. This diamond however, was not mined—it was *printed*. Human-made diamonds are as beautiful as natural diamonds—even an expert jeweler cannot tell them apart. Human-made diamonds could break the DeBeers cartel.

Government Barriers Governments sometimes try to combat monopolies and oligopolies with antitrust law. At other times, governments create barriers to entry with licenses or other regulations that limit entry. Let's take a closer look at both situations

Government Policy Toward Cartels and Oligopolies

Most cartels have been illegal in the United States since the Sherman Antitrust Act of 1890. ("Trust" is simply an old word for monopoly. The antitrust laws give the government the power to prohibit or regulate business practices that may be anticompetitive.) In the early 1990s, for example, four firms controlled 95% of the world market for lysine, an amino acid used to promote growth in pigs, chickens, and cattle. The firms—Archer Daniels Midland (USA), Ajinomoto (Japan), Kyowa Hakko Kogyo (Japan), and Sewon America Inc. (South Korea)—held secret meetings around the world at which they agreed to act in unison to reduce quantity and raise prices.

What the conspirators didn't know was that one of them was a mole. A high-ranking executive at ADM informed the FBI of the cartel. Working with FBI equipment, the mole videotaped meetings at which the conspirators discussed how to split the market and keep prices high.

With the evidence in hand, the FBI and the Department of Justice put the conspirators on trial. Three executives of Archer Daniels Midland, including the vice president, Michael D. Andreas, were fined and imprisoned. One of the Japanese executives was also sentenced to prison, but he fled the country and is currently a fugitive from U.S. law.

More generally, the antitrust laws in the United States and similar laws in Europe can be used to block mergers or even to break up very large firms. In the 1970s, for example, AT&T was the sole provider of telephone service throughout the United States. That particular monopoly was legally sanctioned but in due time the government changed its mind, and in 1974 the antitrust division of the Department of Justice sued AT&T. The lawsuit led to the breakup of AT&T into eight independent companies in 1984. The breakup of AT&T increased the number of new entrants into the industry, providing a spur to companies such as Sprint and MCI. The Department of Justice continues to regulate the phone industry. In 2011, for example, the division blocked a proposed merger between AT&T and T-Mobile out of fear that such a merger would diminish competitive pressure.

Watch the FBI's secret video of the lysine cartel meeting to fix prices.

UNITED STATES DEPARTMENT OF JUSTICE ANTITRUST DIVISION

interactive activity

Government-Supported Cartels

Governments don't always prosecute cartels or break down barriers to entry. In fact, sometimes governments reduce competition and create barriers to entry. OPEC, for example, is a cartel of oil exporting *governments*. In fact, most successful cartels operate with clear legal and governmental backing. Governments are the ultimate cartel enforcers because they can throw cheaters in jail. In the United States, government-controlled milk cartels combine with subsidies and quotas to raise the price of milk. This cartel is extremely stable. Any seller who breaks it is fined or sent to jail. In the past, the U.S. government has supported cartels in coal mining, agriculture, medicine, and other areas; some but not all of these restrictions have been lifted.

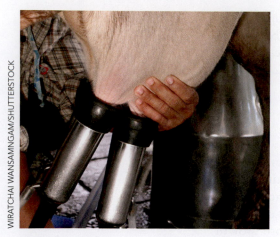

Who is being milked? The government-enforced milk cartel increases the price of milk.

Government-enforced monopolies and cartels are a serious problem facing poor nations today. They plague Mexico, Russia, Indonesia, most of the poor nations in Africa, and many other locales.

A government-supported cartel usually means higher prices, lower-quality service, and less innovation. People with new ideas find it harder or impossible to enter the market. Furthermore, people spend their energies trying to get monopoly or cartel privileges from governments, rather than innovating or finding new ways to service consumers. Governments become more corrupt. For these reasons, most economists generally oppose government-enforced cartels. Those cartels are put in place to serve special interests—usually the politically connected cartel members—rather than consumers or the general citizenry.

Business Strategy and Changing the Game

The prisoner's dilemma game suggests that collusion is difficult (although as we also saw there are more possibilities for collusion/cooperation with repeated interactions). Every firm wants market power, however, so what can firms do? One possibility is to change the game! Let's take a look at two strategies that on the surface seem competitive and proconsumer but that may also have hidden and less beneficial consequences: price match guarantees and loyalty programs such as frequent flyer points.

The Danger of Price Matching Guarantees

What's not to like when a firm guarantees that it will match the price of any competitor and even pay the consumer 10% of the difference? Isn't this a great example of competition at its finest? Not so fast. To evaluate the effects of these policies, we need some game theory.

Suppose that Lowe's and Home Depot are locked into a price war over refrigerator sales. Each firm could set a high price of $1,000 or a low price of $800. Let's also assume that costs are zero (this is convenient but doesn't affect the results) and that there are 1,000 consumers. If both firms set a high price, each gets 500 consumers and makes a profit of $500,000 ($1,000 × 500). If one firm sets a low price ($800) while the other firm continues to set a high price, then the low-price firm gets all the customers (1,000) and makes more money, $800,000. If both firms set a low price, then they again split the market and each makes $400,000. The payoffs are shown in Figure 15.7.

Notice that this is just another version of the prisoner's dilemma. No matter what strategy Lowe's chooses, it's best for Home Depot to choose Low Price, and no matter what strategy Home Depot chooses, it's best for Lowe's to choose Low Price. Thus each firm chooses its dominant strategy and the equilibrium outcome is Low Price, Low Price.

But now let's imagine that each firm offers to match any competitor's price plus give the consumer 10% of the difference. Assume, for example, that Home Depot posts a price of $800. Which firm gets the sales? If Home Depot posts a price of $800 but Lowe's guarantees to match the price and give the consumer

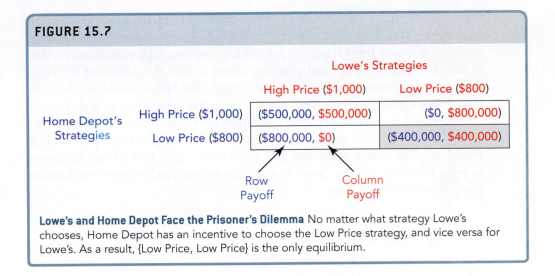

FIGURE 15.7

Lowe's Strategies

		High Price ($1,000)	Low Price ($800)
Home Depot's Strategies	High Price ($1,000)	($500,000, $500,000)	($0, $800,000)
	Low Price ($800)	($800,000, $0)	($400,000, $400,000)

Row Payoff   Column Payoff

Lowe's and Home Depot Face the Prisoner's Dilemma No matter what strategy Lowe's chooses, Home Depot has an incentive to choose the Low Price strategy, and vice versa for Lowe's. As a result, {Low Price, Low Price} is the only equilibrium.

10% of the difference, then a consumer can, in effect, buy the refrigerator from Lowe's for $780 ($800 minus 10% of the $200 difference in posted price). By lowering its price, Home Depot ensures that Lowe's sells all the refrigerators and makes $780,000 in profit. Notice that it's Lowe's, the firm with the *high posted price*, that makes the profits! Similarly, if Lowe's posts a Low Price while Home Depot posts a High Price, Home Depot gets all the sales and the profits! Cutting prices no longer looks like a good idea. As before, if both firms choose High Price, they split the market and make $500,000 each, and if both choose Low Price, they make $400,000 each. The new payoffs are shown in Figure 15.8.

The price match guarantee changes the payoffs and that changes the game. In the new game, the dominant strategy is to choose High Price. Once again, let's look at Lowe's incentives. If Home Depot chooses High Price, then Lowe's earns $500,000 by choosing High Price and only $0 by choosing Low Price. If Home Depot chooses Low Price, then Lowe's earns $780,000 by choosing High Price and only $400,000 by choosing Low Price. Thus, whatever choice

FIGURE 15.8

Lowe's Strategies

		High Price ($1,000)	Low Price ($800)
Home Depot's Strategies	High Price ($1,000)	($500,000, $500,000)	($780,000, $0)
	Low Price ($800)	($0, $780,000)	($400,000, $400,000)

The Price Match Game Each firm promises to match any competitor's posted price and give customers 10% of the difference in posted prices. If Home Depot posts a Low Price of $800 and Lowe's posts a High Price of $1,000, then customers are better off buying from Lowe's because Lowe's matches Home Depot's posted price and gives customers 10% of the difference. Thus, when Home Depot lowers its price, Lowe's will get all of the customers and the profits! Similarly, if Lowe's lowers its price and Home Depot does not, Home Depot gets all the profits. In this game, posting a High Price is always more profitable than posting a Low Price! Thus, High Price is a dominant strategy and the equilibrium is {High Price, High Price}.

Home Depot makes, it's better for Lowe's to choose High Price! Once again what makes this work is that when Lowe's chooses to post a Low Price, consumers run to buy from Home Depot, which, despite a high posted price, offers to match the Lowe's price and give consumers 10% of the difference in prices. The game is symmetric so for the same reasons that Lowe's has an incentive to choose High Price, Home Depot also has an incentive to choose High Price.

Amazingly, a price match guarantee that looks proconsumer changes the equilibrium strategies from {Low Price, Low Price} to {High Price, High Price}. A price match guarantee and a promise to pay 10% of the difference in price turns out to be a clever strategy that reduces the incentive of firms to compete with lower prices!

The High Price of Loyalty

In addition to price guarantees, businesses can also reduce their incentives to lower prices by using loyalty plans. A customer loyalty plan gives regular customers special treatment or a better price. The best-known customer loyalty plans are probably frequent flyer miles on airlines, but you will find customer loyalty plans at Barnes & Noble, at Starbucks, and at your local Giant and Safeway supermarkets.

Let's take a look at frequent flyer plans. If you join a frequent flyer plan, you get points every time you fly, points that can be used to get a free ticket to Hawaii or Paris once you have accumulated enough. Alex and Tyler are both members of the United frequent flyer plan because United has the most flights out of Washington, D.C., our usual takeoff point. Now when we book travel we are slightly more likely to book a United flight so that we can accumulate points toward a free trip. So what's not to like?

The trick is this: Suppose United, Delta, and the other major airlines all offer frequent flyer plans. Loyal customers of each of these companies feel good that they are getting points toward a free trip, but once customers are loyal—that is, once they are a bit locked in—the different airlines don't have to compete with each other quite as much. United realizes that if it raises its prices a little, its customers will remain loyal, and if it lowers its prices a little, the customers of the other airlines will also remain loyal! Thus, United has more incentive to raise its prices and less incentive to lower its prices. Loyalty increases monopoly power, and each airline, facing a more inelastic demand curve, will raise prices. See Figure 15.9. As a result, the net effect of more points is higher prices! A cynic might say that exploitation is the price of loyalty.

When you get your free flight to Hawaii, you feel like a winner, but the reality is that you are being conned just a little. It does you no good, however, to stay out of the plans and refuse to use the points. If you refuse to join the loyalty plan, you lose the points. Furthermore, your refusal won't increase competition in the airline market enough to get airlines to lower their prices across the board. Customers are better off refusing to join the loyalty plan only if all or most of them refuse, in which case each airline will face a

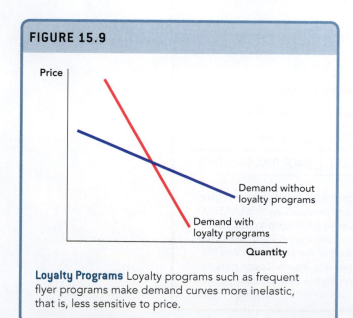

FIGURE 15.9

Loyalty Programs Loyalty programs such as frequent flyer programs make demand curves more inelastic, that is, less sensitive to price.

more elastic demand curve and prices will fall for everyone. Loyalty plans put customers in a type of prisoner's dilemma—it's good for a single customer to join the loyalty plan, but if all the customers join, the result is bad for them as a whole. As you know from the analysis of the prisoner's dilemma, it's going to be difficult to organize a mass boycott of loyalty plans.

By the way, limiting competitive pressure is not the only motivation for customer loyalty plans like frequent flyer programs. Frequent flyer programs also are a form of price discrimination (Chapter 14), as perhaps only the more budget-conscious travelers take the trouble to sign up for miles and cash them in, sometimes altering their flight plans to save the money. Over time, the budget-conscious travelers, who redeem their miles conscientiously and thus get some free flights, pay lower average prices for flying than do the non-budget-conscious travelers. Frequent flyer programs also encourage business travelers to sometimes take the more expensive flight; the traveler will get miles on the preferred airline but the employer will pay the higher price; the airline is indirectly "bribing" the employee to take advantage of the employer. Finally, firms may deliberately let employees keep their frequent flyer miles, even if it means paying for higher ticket prices come reimbursement time. It's one way of rewarding employees while skirting taxes (legally) because the use of frequent flyer miles is not considered taxable income or a reward. If you really value the extra flights, you can save up to 40% in value by avoiding the taxation of ordinary monetary income and by taking your marginal compensation in the form of miles. Frequent flyer miles are a good example of how, if you look closely, you will see economics everywhere.

Other Ways of Changing the Game

Firms want market power and sometimes that can be at the expense of consumers, but keep in mind that the pursuit of market power can often lead to the social good! One reason that firms innovate, for example, is that by doing so they can produce a good with fewer substitutes. Fewer substitutes means a more inelastic demand curve and that means that firm can charge a higher price and earn a higher profit (all else being equal). Similarly, firms also try to reduce the number of substitutes for their product by differentiating their product with different styles or varieties. Apple, Samsung, and Microsoft all produce cell phones but by differentiating the features, looks, and capabilities, they compete with one another less than if the phones were more similar.

Innovation and product differentiation, however, are usually good things so the pursuit of market power is part of what makes for a competitive, dynamic economy. Less competition is good for firms but at the same time we want firms to have an incentive to innovate. The market is not just a process for reducing price to marginal cost—it's also a discovery process, a way of figuring out what products and features consumers really want. We will discuss product differentiation and competing for market (monopoly) power at greater length in Chapters 16 and 17.

Takeaway

An oligopoly is a market dominated by a small number of firms. A cartel is an oligopoly that is able to maximize its joint profits by limiting competition and producing the monopoly quantity.

The OPEC cartel remains important but its influence on the price of oil has diminished due to cheating, new entrants, and substitute products. Most market cartels are not stable either. Either businesses cheat on the cartel agreement or new competitors enter the market. Governments break up some cartels, but they also enforce many others. When you observe a harmful cartel, you should ask whether some governmental rule or regulation might be at fault.

Oligopolies form when there are significant barriers to entry, such as control of a key resource or input, economies of scale, network effects, or government barriers. Although firms in an oligopoly are unlikely to be able to produce the joint profit-maximizing quantity, neither are they likely to produce as much as in a highly competitive market. Prices in an oligopoly, therefore, tend to be below monopoly prices but above competitive prices.

Game theory is the study of strategic interaction. A dominant strategy is a strategy that has a higher payoff no matter what the other player(s) do.

The prisoner's dilemma game explains why cheating is common in cartels and more generally how individual interest can make cooperation difficult even when cooperation is better for everyone in the group than noncooperation. Firms use a variety of strategies to reduce competitive pressures. An analysis of price matching guarantees and customer loyalty programs shows that they can reduce competition and raise prices. Innovation and product differentiation can also reduce competitive pressures but at the same time are part of a dynamic economy that discovers valuable new goods and services.

CHAPTER REVIEW

interactive activity Go online to practice with more examples of these types of problems, including live links to videos, data sources, and feedback.

KEY CONCEPTS

cartel, p. 291

oligopoly, p. 291

strategic decision making, p. 291

dominant strategy, p. 296

prisoner's dilemma, p. 296

tacit collusion, p. 297

barriers to entry, p. 300

Nash equilibrium, p. 313

FACTS AND TOOLS

1. Let's start off by working out a few examples to illustrate the lure of the cartel. To keep it simple on the supply side, we'll assume that fixed costs are zero so marginal cost equals average cost. We'll compare the competitive outcome ($P = MC$) to what you'd get if the firms all agreed to act "as if"

they were a monopoly. In all cases, we'll use terms from the following diagram:

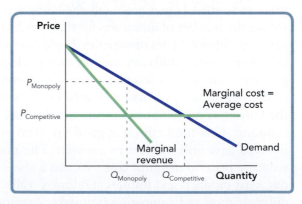

a. First, let's see where the profits are. Comparing this figure with Figure 15.2, shade the rectangle that corresponds to monopoly profit.

b. What is the formula for this rectangle in terms of price, cost, and quantity?

c. Let's look at the market for one kind of apple: Gala. Assume that there are 300 producers of Gala apples and that $MC = AC = \$0.40$ per pound. In a competitive market, price will be driven down to marginal cost. Let's assume that when $P = MC$, each apple grower produces 2 million pounds of apples for a total market production of 600 million pounds. Now imagine that the apple growers form a cartel and each agrees to cut production to 1 million pounds, which drives the price up to $\$0.70$ per pound. Calculate profit per pound and total industry profit if the apple growers behave "as if" they were a monopoly and are able to produce according to the following table:

$P_{Monopoly}$	$Q_{Monopoly}$
$0.70/lb	300 million lb
Profit per pound$_{Monopoly}$	Total industry Profit$_{Monopoly}$
_____	_____

d. If a single apple grower broke from the cartel and produced an extra million pounds of apples, how much additional profit (approximately) would this apple grower make?

2. Take a look at the reasons presented in the chapter for why cartels collapse. For each of the following pairs, choose the case in which the cartel is more likely to stick together.

a. An industry where it's easy for new firms to enter vs. an industry where the same firms stick around for decades.

b. When the government makes it legal for all the firms to agree on prices vs. when the government makes it illegal for all firms in an industry to agree on prices. (*Note:* The Sherman Antitrust Act made the latter generally illegal in 1890, but President Franklin Roosevelt's National Industrial Recovery Act temporarily legalized price-setting cartels during the Great Depression.)

c. Cartels in which all the industry leaders went to the same schools and live in the same neighborhood vs. cartels where the industry leaders don't really know or trust each other. (*Hint:* As Adam Smith said in *The Wealth of Nations,* "People of the same trade seldom meet together, even for merriment and diversion, but the conversation ends in a conspiracy against the public, or in some contrivance to raise prices.")

d. An industry in which it's easy for a firm to sell a little extra product without anyone knowing (e.g., music downloads) vs. an industry where all sales are public and visible (e.g., concert tickets).

3. The prisoner's dilemma game is one of the most important models in all of social science: Most games of trust can be thought of as some kind of prisoner's dilemma. Here's the classic game: Two men rob a bank and are quickly arrested. The police do not have an airtight case; they have just enough evidence to put each man in prison for one year, a slap on the wrist for a serious crime.

If the police had more evidence, they could put the men away for longer. To get more evidence, they put the men in separate interrogation rooms and offer each man the same deal: If you testify against your accomplice, we will drop all the charges against you (and convict the other guy of the full penalty of 10 years of prison time). Of course, if both prisoners take the deal, the police will have enough evidence to put both prisoners away and they will each get 6 years. And, as noted, if neither testifies, both will get just 1 year of prison time. What's the best thing for each man to do?

In each cell in the following table, the first number is the number of years Butch will spend in prison, and the second is the number that Sundance will spend in prison given the strategies chosen by Butch and Sundance. If years in prison are minuses, then we can write up the problem like this:

		Sundance	
		Keep quiet	Testify
Butch	Keep quiet	$(-1, -1)$	$(-10, 0)$
	Testify	$(0, -10)$	$(-6, -6)$

a. If Sundance keeps quiet, what's the best choice (highest payoff) for Butch: keep quiet or testify?

b. If Sundance chooses testify, what's the best choice for Butch: keep quiet or testify?

c. What's the best choice for Butch? What's the best choice for Sundance?

d. Using the definition in this chapter, does Butch have a "dominant strategy"? If so, what is it?

e. What is your prediction about what will happen?

f. How does this help explain why the police never put two suspects in the same interrogation room? (Note the similarity between this question and the earlier Adam Smith quote.)

4. Your professor probably grades on a curve, implicitly if not explicitly. This means that you and your classmates could each agree to study half as much, and you would all earn the same grade you would have earned without the agreement. What do you think would happen if you tried to enact this agreement? Why? Which model in this chapter is most similar to this conspiracy?

5. In many college towns, rumors abound that the gas stations in town collude to keep prices high. If this were true, where would you expect this conspiracy against the public to work best? Why?

a. In towns with dozens of gas stations or in towns with fewer than 10?

b. In towns where the city council has many environmental and zoning regulations, making it difficult to open a new gas station, or in towns where there is a lot of open land for development?

c. In towns where all the gas stations are about equally busy or in towns where half the gas stations are always busy and half tend to be empty?

6. Suppose you have a suit that needs altering, and you take it to three different tailors in the same mall to get an estimate of the cost of the alterations. All three tailors give you the exact same estimate of $25. What are two different explanations for the similarity of the price quotes? (*Hint:* One is consistent with competition and one is not.)

THINKING AND PROBLEM SOLVING

7. Usually, we think of cheating as a bad thing. But in this chapter, cheating turns out to be a very good thing in some important cases.

a. Who gets the benefit when a cartel collapses through cheating: consumers or producers?

b. Does this benefit usually show up in a lower price, a higher quantity, or both?

c. Does cheating increase consumer surplus, producer surplus, or both?

d. So, is cheating good for the cheaters or good for other people?

8. Firms in a cartel each have an incentive individually to lower the prices they charge.

a. Suppose there was a government regulation that set minimum prices. Would this regulation tend to strengthen cartels, weaken them, or have no effect?

b. Another way that one firm can cheat on a cartel is to offer a higher-quality product to consumers. Suppose there was a government regulation that standardized the quality of a good. Would this regulation tend to strengthen cartels, weaken them, or have no effect?

9. In the late fifteenth century, Europe consumed about 2 million pounds of pepper per year. At this time, Venice (ruled by a small, tightly knit group of merchants) was the major player in the pepper trade. But after Portuguese explorer Vasco da Gama blazed a path around Africa into the Indian Ocean in 1498, Venice found itself competing with Portugal's trade route. By the mid-sixteenth century, Europeans consumed 6 to 7 million pounds per year, much of it through Lisbon. After da Gama's success, the price of pepper fell.

a. During the fifteenth century, was it likely that a cartel was restricting pepper imports? Why or why not?

b. If the price of pepper before 1498 had been lower, would da Gama have been more willing or less willing to sail around South Africa's Cape of Good Hope? Why?

c. What happened in 1498 that turned a successful cartel into a less successful cartel?

d. The ruling merchants of Venice had no political power in other parts of Europe. Why is that important in understanding how European pepper consumption more than tripled in just over half a century?

10. In 1890, Senator Sherman (of the Sherman Antitrust Act mentioned earlier) pushed through the legislation that bears his name, which gave the government significant power to "bust up" cartels, presumably in order to increase output. More than a century later, economist Thomas J. DiLorenzo examined the industries commonly

accused of being cartels and found those industries increased output by an average of 175% from 1880 to 1890—seven times the growth rate of the economy at the time.

Suppose the industries were conspiring. Indeed, let's suppose that these cartels grew ever stronger in the decade before the Sherman Act became law. If that were true, would we expect output in these industries to grow by so much? In other words, is DiLorenzo's evidence consistent with the standard story of the Sherman Antitrust Act?

11. In 2005, economist Thomas Schelling won the Nobel Prize in economics, in part for his development of the concept of the "focal point" in game theory. Focal points are a way to solve a coordination game. If two people both benefit by choosing the same option but cannot communicate, they will choose the most obvious option, called the focal point. Of course, what's obvious will vary from culture to culture: whether to wear business attire or just shorts and a T-shirt, whether to use Apple or Microsoft products, whether to arrive at meetings on time or late. In all these cases, having a group agree on one focal point is more important than which particular focal point you all agree on. Therefore, people will look for cultural clues so that they can find the focal point. (*Note:* Schelling wrote two highly readable books that won him the Nobel Prize: *Micromotives and Macrobehavior* and *The Strategy of Conflict.*)

   a. Suppose you are playing a game in which you and another player have to choose one of three boxes. You can't communicate with the other player until the game is over. One box is blue and the other two are red. If the two of you choose the same box, you win $50, otherwise, you get nothing. Which box do you choose: the blue box or one of the red boxes? Why?

   b. Suppose that you and another player have to write down on a slip of paper *any* price in dollars and cents between $90.01 and $109.83. If you both write down the same price, you'll each win that amount of money. If your numbers don't match, you get nothing. Again, you can't communicate with the other player until the game is over. What number will both of you probably choose?

   c. Many "slippery slope" arguments are really stories about focal points. In the United States during debates over banning guns or restricting speech, people will argue that *any*

limitation follows a "slippery slope." What do they mean by that? (*Hint:* Attorneys often worry about "gray areas" and they prefer "bright line tests.")

   d. Schelling used the idea of the focal point to explain implicit agreements on the limits to war. Poison gas, for example, was not used in World War II and the agreement was largely implicit. Since focal points have to be obvious, explain why there was no implicit agreement that "some" poison gas would be allowed, but "a lot" of poison gas would not be allowed.

12. Suppose the five landscapers in your neighborhood form a cartel and decide to restrict output to 16 lawns each per week (for a total of 80 lawns in the entire market) to keep prices high. The weekly demand curve for lawn-mowing services is shown in the following chart. Assume that the marginal cost of mowing a lawn is a constant $10 per lawn.

The Market for Lawn-Mowing Services

   a. What is the market price under the cartel's arrangement? How much profit is each landscaper earning per week under this arrangement?

   b. Suppose one untrustworthy landscaper decides to cheat and increase her own output by an additional 10 lawns. For this landscaper, what is the total increase in revenue from such behavior? What is the marginal revenue per lawn from cheating? Which is higher: the marginal revenue from the extra lawns or the marginal cost?

   c. Is it a good idea for the untrustworthy landscaper to cheat? What considerations, other than weekly profit, might enter into the landscaper's decision about whether to cheat?

13. Looking for dominant strategies is a great way to find an equilibrium in many games. However, there are also a lot of games in which this won't work because not all players have dominant strategies. If one player has a dominant strategy but the other doesn't, game theorists remove the first player's dominated strategies (the strategies that are always worse than some other strategy) and then continue to work toward solving the game with what's left. Let's take a look at an example of this. Consider the following payoff table, where the outcomes are written in the form {A's payoff, B's payoff}. Each player has four choices, which might make this game seem intimidating, but it's not.

		B's Strategies		
	Red	Blue	Green	Yellow
Red	(1, 3)	(2, 7)	(3, 5)	(4, 6)
Blue	(2, 2)	(3, 2)	(6, 3)	(4, 4)
Green	(3, 2)	(6, 1)	(1, 3)	(3, 2)
Yellow	(4, 0)	(4, 0)	(5, 0)	(5, 1)

A's strategies (rows: Red, Blue, Green, Yellow)

Start off by trying to figure out whether any player has a strategy that is never best, and then eliminate it. The first one is done for you; no matter what move A makes, B's best response is never to play Red. Since B will never play Red, we don't even have to consider that as part of the game. Next, figure out if there's a move A will never make, then B, and so on. What is the equilibrium?

		B's Strategies		
	~~Red~~	Blue	Green	Yellow
Red	~~(1, 3)~~	(2, 7)	(3, 5)	(4, 6)
Blue	~~(2, 2)~~	(3, 2)	(6, 3)	(4, 4)
Green	~~(3, 2)~~	(6, 1)	(1, 3)	(3, 2)
Yellow	~~(4, 0)~~	(4, 0)	(5, 0)	(5, 1)

A's strategies (rows: Red, Blue, Green, Yellow)

CHALLENGES

14. The French economist Antoine Cournot developed an interesting model of competition in an oligopoly that now bears his name. In a Cournot oligopoly, all of the firms know that the total output from all firms will determine the price (based on the downward-sloping market demand curve), but they make independent and simultaneous decisions about how much output to produce. Cournot developed this model after observing how a spring water duopoly (two firms) behaved. So let's look at a duopoly example.

For each firm to decide how much to produce, it must make a guess about how much the other firm is going to produce. Also, the firms basically assume that once the other firm has decided how much to produce, it can't really change its decision.

Here's an example. Suppose the market demand curve for gallons of fresh spring water looks like the one in the next table and, to keep things simple, the marginal cost of spring water is zero. If Firm X believes that Firm Y is going to produce 100 gallons of spring water, for example, then Firm X knows that if it produces 0 gallons, the price will be $2.75; if it produces 100 gallons, the price will be $2.50, and so on. Basically, Firm X will face its own demand curve where all of the quantities are lower by 100.

Market Demand	
Price	Quantity Demanded (gal)
$3.00	0
$2.75	100
$2.50	200
$2.25	300
$2.00	400
$1.75	500
$1.50	600
$1.25	700
$1.00	800
$0.75	900
$0.50	1,000

Based on this demand schedule, calculate the demand schedule that Firm X would face if it suspected Firm Y was going to produce 0, 200, 400, or 600 gallons of spring water. Then, figure out the profit-maximizing amount of spring water for Firm X to produce in response. Fill in the table.

If Firm Y produces . . .	. . . then Firm X should produce . . .
0 gal	
200 gal	
400 gal	
600 gal	

What you have just constructed is what economists would call Firm X's *reaction function*. Even though Firm X thought about the different choices Firm Y could make, Firm Y is not actually going to choose just any random level of output. In fact, Firm Y has its own reaction function, where it considers how best to respond to what it thinks Firm X is doing. Because both firms have the same zero marginal cost, the two reaction functions are symmetrical. (Thus, Firm Y's reaction function looks the same, only with "X" and "Y" switched.)

Graph the two reaction functions. Do you notice any points that stand out? Describe why this point represents an equilibrium for both firms.

15. The following diagram shows the monthly demand for hot dogs in a large city. The marginal cost (and average cost) is a constant $2 per hot dog.

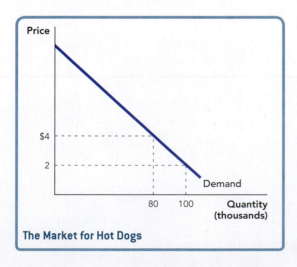

The Market for Hot Dogs

a. If the market for hot dogs is perfectly competitive, how many hot dogs will be sold per month, and at what price? Suppose there are 100 identical firms in this perfectly competitive market. How many hot dogs is each firm selling, and what are the profits for each firm?

b. Suppose the market was almost perfectly competitive, so that each firm has *some* very limited ability to change the price. What would happen if one of the firms in this market reduced its output by one half, and no other firm changed its output? What would happen to the price of a hot dog? How much profit would the firm earn as a result?

c. Discuss the ability of one firm to reduce output and raise the market price if the market for hot dogs was instead an oligopoly made up of four firms, each initially producing 25,000 hot dogs per month. If only one firm reduced its output by half, what would happen to the price of a hot dog? How much profit could this firm potentially earn?

d. Compare your answers for parts b and c. What does this tell you about the ability to earn profits in perfect competition vs. oligopoly?

16. In our chapter on *Competition and the Invisible Hand*, we quoted the Austrian economist, Joseph Schumpeter, who said that in textbooks the most important fact about competition is that competition pushes price down to marginal cost. However, Schumpeter goes on to say:

.… in capitalist reality as distinguished from its textbook picture, it is not this competition which counts but the competition from the new commodity, the new technology, the new source of supply, the new type of organization…competition which commands a decisive cost or quality advantage and which strikes not at the margins of the profits and the outputs of the existing firms but at their foundations and their very lives. This kind of competition is more effective than the other as a bombardment is in comparison with forcing a door, and so much more important that it becomes a matter of comparative indifference whether competition in the ordinary sense functions more or less promptly...

ULLSTEIN BILD/GETTY IMAGES

Joseph Schumpeter (1883–1950) wrote that what was most important in a capitalist economy were the gales of "creative destruction."

a. Relate Schumpeter's statement to the models of monopoly and oligopoly discussed in this and earlier chapters. In what ways are these market forms inefficient? In what ways might they be efficient or beneficial?

b. The terms *static efficiency* and *dynamic efficiency* are sometimes used in economics. Is there a trade-off between the two types of efficiency? How might we evaluate this trade-off?

WORK IT OUT

interactive activity

For interactive, step-by-step help in solving this problem, go online.

Consider the following demand schedule for Rainbow Looms. Assume that the marginal cost of producing a Rainbow Loom is a constant $2.50.

Price ($/Rainbow Loom)	Quantity Demanded (Rainbow Loom)
$17.50	0
$15.00	12
$12.50	24
$10.00	36
$7.50	48
$5.00	60

a. How many Rainbow Looms would be produced under a Rainbow Loom monopoly?

b. If instead of a monopoly, a two–firm cartel controlled the Rainbow Loom market, how many packs of Rainbow Looms would each firm want to produce in order to maximize industry profits?

c. Determine whether it would be possible for one of the two firms in the cartel to earn higher profits by producing more than the industry profit-maximizing quantity you calculated in part b.

CHAPTER 15 APPENDIX

Nash Equilibrium

The games examples in this chapter can be solved by looking for a dominant strategy, a strategy that is best regardless of what the other player does. Even in simple games, however, there often isn't a dominant strategy. Consider a simple game called the Left, Right game. Olaf and Frida must decide whether to drive their cars on the left side of the road or on the right. The payoff for each combination of choices is illustrated in the payoff matrix in Figure A15-1.

The key point, of course, is that Olaf and Frida have positive payoffs when they both choose Left or when they both choose Right, but it's a disaster when Olaf chooses Left and Frida chooses Right or vice versa. When Olaf and Frida both choose Left, the payoffs are 2,2, and when Olaf and Frida both choose Right, the payoffs are 5,5. But when Olaf and Frida choose different strategies, either {Left, Right} or {Right, Left}, they end up crashing their cars and the payoffs are −10,−10. So what is the equilibrium to this game?

Unlike in the prisoner's dilemma, there is no dominant strategy in this game, no strategy that is best for each player regardless of what the other player does. We can still look for equilibria, however, by drawing on the ideas of John Nash. Nash, who was awarded a Nobel Prize for his contributions to game theory and whose life was featured in the movie *A Beautiful Mind*, defined an equilibrium as a situation in which no player has an incentive to change strategy unilaterally. That is now called a **Nash equilibrium**.

In the Left, Right game, there are two Nash equilibria. Let's start by examining the paired strategies {Left, Left}. Is this a Nash equilibrium? If Frida chooses Left, does Olaf have an incentive to change strategy? No. Olaf earns 2 by choosing Left and −10 by switching to Right, so if Frida chooses Left, then Olaf does not have an incentive to change strategy. If Olaf chooses

Office Hours: Nash Equilibrium

A **Nash equilibrium** is a situation such that no player has an incentive to change strategy unilaterally.

FIGURE A15.1

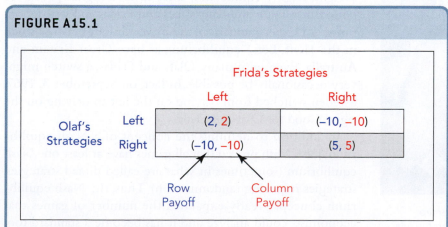

The Left, Right Game Driving on either the left or the right is okay so long as everyone makes the same choice. There are two Nash equilibria in this game: {Left, Left} or {Right, Right}.

Left, does Frida have an incentive to change strategy? No. Frida earns 2 by choosing Left and −10 by choosing Right, so if Olaf chooses Left, Frida does not have an incentive to switch. Since neither player has an incentive to unilaterally change strategy, {Left, Left} is a Nash equilibrium. By similar reasoning, you should be able to show that {Right, Right} is also a Nash equilibrium.

Is {Right, Left} a Nash equilibrium? If Frida chooses Left, does Olaf have an incentive to change strategy? Yes. Olaf earns −10 by choosing Right and 2 by switching to Left, so if Frida chooses Left then Olaf would have an incentive to change strategy to Left. Since at least one of the parties has an incentive to change strategy, {Right, Left} cannot be a Nash equilibrium (in fact, Olaf and Frida both have an incentive to change but we need show only that one of them has an incentive to change to show that a situation is not a Nash equilibrium). By similar reasoning you should be able to show that {Left, Right} is also not a Nash equilibrium.

If a player can increase his or her payoff by changing strategy, they probably will change it. So game theory predicts that the outcome of a game will be a Nash equilibrium. If there is more than one equilibrium, however, game theory alone doesn't tell us which equilibrium will be the outcome. In the Left, Right game, {Left, Left} is a Nash equilibrium and so is {Right, Right}, and indeed when we look around the world we see people in some countries driving on the right and in other countries such as Great Britain and Australia driving on the left. Why the difference? Probably nothing more than accidents of history or other random factors.

According to the payoff matrix, Olaf and Frida earn 2,2 in the {Left, Left} equilibrium and 5,5 in the {Right, Right} equilibrium. In our world, it is in fact better to drive on the right since more countries drive on the right and more cars are built for driving on the right. If Olaf and Frida were the only two players and if they played this game repeatedly (say they had to choose Right or Left every day), then it would be a good bet that they would eventually end up at the {Right, Right} equilibrium since it has a higher payoff for both. But if there are many Olafs and Fridas and less opportunity for experimentation, the players might become stuck in the {Left, Left} equilibrium, as have Great Britain and Australia. Even with many Olafs and Fridas, a switch might very occasionally be possible. In fact, on September 3, 1967, Sweden switched from driving on the left to driving on the right! Good for Olaf and Frida.

In addition to defining the concept of a Nash equilibrium, John Nash proved that all games have at least one Nash equilibrium (sometimes in what are called mixed strategies, strategies requiring randomization). Thus, the Nash equilibrium concept greatly expanded the number of games that economists could analyze and it has become a standard tool in economics.

Coordination On September 3, 1967, the entire country of Sweden switched from driving on the left to driving on the right!

Chapter 15 Appendix Questions

 Problems in blue are Office Hours videos.

1. Cat and mouse is a simple game in which each player can choose either Right or Left. If the cat and mouse both choose Right or both choose Left, however, that is very bad for the mouse but good for the cat. If the cat and mouse choose different strategies that is good for the mouse but not good for the cat.

   Can you find a Nash equilibrium in this game?

2. Bob and Al are prestigious rival magicians who have developed a new trick that is very popular. If both magicians perform five times a week, each will earn a profit of $6,000. If one magician does a single show while the other does five shows, the former gets a profit of $1,000 and the latter gets a profit of $15,000. If both magicians perform only one show a week, each will earn $10,000.

   a. Use this information to complete the table. (*Hint:* It'll look a lot like Figure 15.4.)

   Al

		1 Show	5 Shows
Bob	1 Show	,	,
	5 Shows	,	,

   b. Suppose Al does one show. What is Bob's preferred strategy?

   c. Suppose Al does five shows. What is Bob's preferred strategy?

   d. What is Bob's dominant strategy?

   e. Suppose Bob does one show. What is Al's preferred strategy?

   f. Suppose Bob does five shows. What is Al's preferred strategy?

   g. What is Al's dominant strategy?

   h. What is the Nash equilibrium?

   i. Magicians are famously hesitant to reveal the secrets behind their magic, even to other magicians. Based on what you've learned in this question, why do they act like this? Is letting other magicians in on your secrets an optimal strategy?

3. Imagine that two players are competing over a valuable resource. Each player has two options. He or she can either be aggressive and demand the entire resource, or the player can offer to split the resource equally. The literature uses the word "Hawk" to describe the aggressive behavior and the word "Dove" to describe the sharing behavior. If two Hawks meet, then both will demand the resource, neither will give in, and there will be a fight. If a Hawk meets a Dove, the Hawk will take the resource and the Dove will get nothing. If two Doves meet, the resource will be shared equally.

   Assume that the value of the resource is 60, the cost of losing a fight is 100, and if two Hawks fight, each of them has a 50% chance of losing.

   Here's the payoff matrix:

		B's Strategies	
		Hawk	Dove
A's Strategies	Hawk	,	,
	Dove	,	,

   a. Oops! The payoffs are missing. You'll have to fill them in. Remember, if there's a fight, there is a 50% chance of winning 60 but also a 50% of losing the fight, which has a payoff -100. What's the expected outcome? If both animals choose Dove, assume that they peacefully split the resource. If one is a Hawk and the other is the Dove, the Hawk gets the resource, and the Dove receives nothing . . .

   b. Explain why {Hawk-Dove} and {Dove-Hawk} are both Nash equilibriums.

   c. The Hawk-Dove game is often used to discuss international relations. Can you explain why a country might like to be perceived as a Hawk? What are the dangers of being a Hawk? What are the dangers of being a Dove?

   d. Biologists also use game theory to understand animal behavior, but they interpret the strategies a little differently. Instead of allowing an animal to choose a strategy, they assume that x percent of animals in a population will always play Hawk and $100 - x$ percent of animals in a population will always play Dove, and they also assume that animals will meet randomly.

Biologists argue that if Hawk has an expected higher payoff than Dove, then Hawks will outcompete Doves so that over time, evolution will increase the percentage of animals playing Hawk. Similarly, if Dove has a higher payoff, then over time, evolution will increase the percentage of animals playing Dove.

Can you find a strategy that is *evolutionarily stable*; that is, can you find a strategy where the percentages of animals playing Hawk and Dove are stable over time?

Here are two hints: Let x be the percentage of animals playing Hawk. If 0% of animals play Hawk ($x = 0\%$) and thus all play Dove, is that evolutionarily stable? If all animals play Hawk ($x = 100\%$), is that evolutionarily stable?

MARGINAL REVOLUTION UNIVERSITY VIDEOS

Nash Equilibrium

mruniversity.com/nash

Problems: 2

16

Competing for Monopoly: The Economics of Network Goods

As of 2017, there were two billion active users on Facebook. Why post your profile on Facebook? It's simple: Facebook is where everyone else posts a profile or goes to view profiles. If you are a teenager, unless you want to be a hermit, it is better to belong to the same network as your friends. Similarly, Match.com, the largest Internet dating service, claims to have over 20 million users.[1] If you are looking to date or marry, Match.com has the largest selection of potential partners and so you are most likely to use it.

Some markets involve building or coordinating a network, and those markets usually have some special properties. We wrote this book in Microsoft Word and not in some other software package. Why? It's not that we firmly believe that Word is superior to other programs. In fact, we've hardly tried most of the other programs. Instead, we knew that both of us had a copy of Word and we were both familiar with writing in Word. Even more important, we knew that our editor and publisher could work with Word files. Notice that we chose to use Word even though there are other software packages such as OpenOffice that are *free*.

In each of these examples, the value of the good depends on how many other people use the good. Facebook, Match.com, and Microsoft Word are all more valuable to one consumer when other consumers also use these goods. Thus, a **network good** is a good whose value to one consumer increases the more that other consumers use the good.

These examples hint at some of the interesting features of network goods that we will be exploring in this chapter. When networks are important, we typically see the following:

A **network good** is a good whose value to one consumer increases the more that other consumers use the good.

Features of Markets for Network Goods

1. Network goods are usually sold by monopolies or oligopolies.
2. When networks are important, the "best" product may not always win.
3. Competition in the market for network goods is "for the market" instead of "in the market."

By the way, did you notice the tension between features 1 and 3? Network goods are often sold by monopolies or oligopolies (feature 1), but competition *for* these markets can be intense (feature 3). In fact, the tension between these features of network-good markets has led to a debate about when the antitrust laws should be applied to network markets and when potential competition alone is enough to discipline monopolies. We will be looking at this debate at greater length in this chapter. Let's look at each of these features in turn.

Network Goods Are Usually Sold by Monopolies or Oligopolies

Microsoft is one of the most profitable corporations on earth. Most of its profit comes from selling its operating system and software at prices above marginal cost. Microsoft can price above marginal cost not because its products are necessarily the best in some absolute sense but because most people want to use the same software as most other people. Microsoft products are, in most cases, the most likely to be compatible with other products and other readers, writers, and publishers.

The power of coordination in "Office-like" software is so strong that Microsoft can sell Office for hundreds of dollars even though there are *free* alternatives such as OpenOffice, Think Free Office, and Google Docs, all of which are roughly similar in quality to Office. But don't make the mistake of thinking that if one of these products became the dominant standard, we would all enjoy free software. The only reason these products are given away for free is that the owners hope to become the dominant standard so that they can charge a high price!

Sometimes the pressures for coordination are strong, but other factors mean that more than one firm can compete in the market. eBay is the market leader in online auctions and it uses its market power to charge higher prices than would occur in a standard competitive market. But a handful of other firms in the industry offer slightly different features. Craigslist, for example, is able to compete with eBay because it offers buyers and sellers a way to buy and sell locally, which is especially useful for products that are expensive to ship. As we saw in the previous chapter, a market dominated by a small number of firms is called an oligopoly.

The market for Internet dating is an oligopoly simply because most people want to join large networks with many other people. But it's not a monopoly because OKCupid and eHarmony compete with the market leader Match.com by offering different matching algorithms. In addition, there are competing niche services, such as JDate.com (for those looking for a Jewish partner), but notice that JDate dominates its competitors within that niche.

The "Best" Product May Not Always Win

In markets with network goods, it's possible for the market to "lock in" to the "wrong" product or network. We can illustrate using a coordination game as shown in Figure 16.1, similar in structure to the prisoner's dilemma we showed in the previous chapter. Alex and Tyler are choosing whether to use software from Apple or Microsoft to write their textbook. Alex's choices or strategies are the rows, Tyler's are the columns. What Alex and Tyler most want to avoid is making different choices. If Alex chooses Microsoft and Tyler chooses Apple, it will be difficult for them to work together so their payoffs will be low, just (3,3). And the same thing is true if Alex chooses Apple and Tyler chooses Microsoft. Alex and Tyler receive the highest payoffs if both are using the same software. So, if Alex chooses Apple, it will make sense for Tyler to choose Apple, and vice versa. In other words, if Alex and Tyler both choose Apple, then neither will have an incentive to change his strategy.

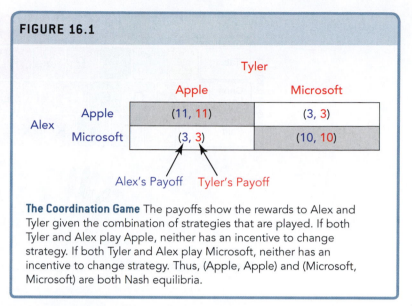

FIGURE 16.1

The Coordination Game The payoffs show the rewards to Alex and Tyler given the combination of strategies that are played. If both Tyler and Alex play Apple, neither has an incentive to change strategy. If both Tyler and Alex play Microsoft, neither has an incentive to change strategy. Thus, (Apple, Apple) and (Microsoft, Microsoft) are both Nash equilibria.

More formally, economists say a situation is an equilibrium if no player in the game has an incentive to change his or her strategy unilaterally. This is also called a **Nash equilibrium** after John Nash, the mathematician. The outcome (Apple, Apple) is an equilibrium because neither Alex nor Tyler has an incentive to change his strategy unilaterally, that is, given that Tyler chooses Apple, Alex wants to choose Apple and vice versa.

But notice that (Apple, Apple) is not the only equilibrium in this **coordination game**. If Alex chooses Microsoft, then Tyler will also want to choose Microsoft, and vice versa. Thus, (Microsoft, Microsoft) is also an equilibrium strategy. The payoffs to the (Microsoft, Microsoft) equilibrium are slightly lower than the payoffs to the (Apple, Apple) equilibrium. Nevertheless, (Microsoft, Microsoft) is still an equilibrium because if Alex and Tyler do choose Microsoft, neither will have an incentive to switch. So which equilibrium, (Apple, Apple) or (Microsoft, Microsoft), will Alex and Tyler end up at?

If Alex and Tyler really are the only players in this game, they could probably talk to each other and coordinate on the best equilibrium, which is (Apple, Apple). But in reality the coordination game is between Alex, Tyler, and many other people. Coordinating on the best equilibrium is not so easy when many people are involved and when they do not all agree about whether Apple really is better than Microsoft. So what will determine the final equilibrium? The classic answer is "accidents of history."

It's an accident of history that computer keyboards are laid out according to the QWERTY design (so named for the keys on the top left side). But is QWERTY the best possible layout for keyboards? According to some studies, a different layout of the keys called the Dvorak design allows for faster and easier typing. So why is the QWERTY design dominant? QWERTY came first, and once people learned to type on a QWERTY keyboard, typewriter manufacturers had an incentive to sell QWERTY typewriters. And, of course, once most manufacturers were selling QWERTY typewriters, it made sense to learn how to type on the QWERTY keyboard. Thus, the QWERTY design became "locked in." If you're wondering, QWERTY is the only way that your authors know how to type.

A **Nash equilibrium** is a situation in which no player has an incentive to change strategy unilaterally.

A **coordination game** is one in which the players are better off if they choose the same strategies than if they choose different strategies, and there is more than one strategy on which to potentially coordinate.

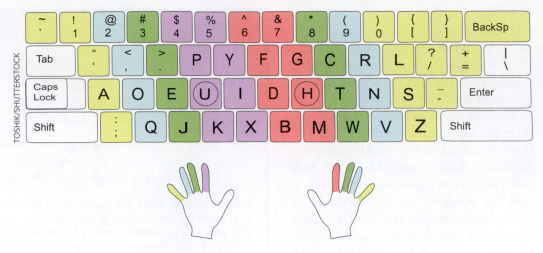

TOSHIK/SHUTTERSTOCK

The Dvorak keyboard Would you type faster?

The QWERTY story needs to be taken with a grain of salt, however. The first study showing that the Dvorak layout was better than QWERTY was a 1944 study by the U.S. Navy. But who authored the 1944 study? None other than Lieutenant-Commander August Dvorak. Any guesses as to who created the Dvorak keyboard? Later studies have failed to show big advantages to either keyboard. Thus, it makes sense that few people bother to learn Dvorak even though it's now easy to reprogram a computer keyboard according to any design.*

Competition Is "For the Market" Instead of "In the Market"

Network goods are usually sold by monopolies or oligopolies, but what makes these markets different from standard monopolies and oligopolies is the ease and speed by which the monopoly can change hands. Currently, Facebook is the dominant social network today but less than five years ago, it was not clear whether MySpace, Friendster, or Facebook would become Number 1. Facebook eventually pulled away from the pack, as it offered a cleaner page, more and better apps, and better ability to tag and track your friends.[2]

Google looks dominant in search, but Microsoft is betting that Bing will grab some market share. Facebook is growing, but Google+ is a potential threat. Maybe today's dominant firm will be dethroned, maybe not, but it's a mistake to think that a large market share, taken alone, implies that competition is absent. Competition for the market can dethrone market leaders very quickly.

Since Facebook and other network firms could be dethroned by a new entrant, these firms must make choices in light of *potential* competition. Markets in which potential competition disciplines firms are called "contestable."

A market is **contestable** if a competitor could credibly enter and take away business from the incumbent. Contestability does not require that such entry actually occurs, only that it can potentially occur.

A market is **contestable** if despite few firms the threat of potential competition is enough to make the market behave competitively.

*The QWERTY story was made prominent by David, Paul A. 1985. Clio and the economics of QWERTY. *American Economic Review* 75: 332–337 and is criticized in Liebowitz, Stan J., and Stephen E. Margolis. 1990. The fable of the keys. *Journal of Law & Economics* 33(1): 1–25.

Contestability disciplines an incumbent firm even if the incumbent has a large market share because the mere threat of entry acts as a competitive force. For instance, fear of potential competitors motivates Facebook to keep its prices low (free!) and to keep advertising relatively unobtrusive. To the extent a market, even a network market, is contestable, it is hard for everyone to get locked into the wrong network, as explained previously.

Limiting Contestability with Switching Costs

Facebook, of course, doesn't want its market to be contested. They remember what happened to Friendster, even if no one else does. So, incumbent firms often try to limit the contestability of the markets they operate in. Facebook, for instance, encourages its users to load as many photos onto the site as possible. The company doesn't charge you for adding more photos, even though the viewing of those photos increases their server costs. Why does Facebook allow so many free photos? In part, they want to attract more users, but it's not just that. Facebook knows that if you load a lot of your photos onto their site, it will be more costly for you to switch to another networking site.

If a new social networking site came along that was 3% better than Facebook, but all your photos were loaded onto your Facebook profile, would you switch? Maybe not. If you haven't kept copies of all those old photos, in a neat and organized way, you are especially unlikely to switch (recall that we gave some other examples of how firms increase switching costs to increase market power in Chapter 15).

Here's another example. Apple has pursued a similar strategy of increasing switching costs with its iPhone, but they have gone further to make the export of content difficult. It is easy to download music, videos, TV shows, and other forms of media content onto your iPhone. That makes more people want to buy an iPhone, which can serve as a traveling movie theater, museum, and music hall, all in one. Yet once all that material is on your iPhone, it is difficult to export it to other systems. You can't easily send it from your iPhone to your television or to your personal computer or to your Blackberry, even though technologically such transfers should be quite easy, if only the operating system would allow them. Apple wants to increase the costs of your switching to a competitor's product line.

Antitrust and Network Goods

In 2000, the Department of Justice brought a lawsuit against Microsoft, on the grounds that the company tried to monopolize operating systems and use its operating system to promote its other products. Windows, for example, was packaged with Internet Explorer, and this helped Internet Explorer replace Netscape as the leading market browser. In 1996, Netscape held 80% of the browser market according to some estimates, but by 2002, Internet Explorer had taken almost all of Netscape's market share.[3]

To be sure, it seems that Microsoft was guilty of "intent to monopolize," as defined by the antitrust laws. It is less clear that Microsoft's behavior made consumers worse off. Netscape's open-source spinoff, Firefox, is widely available today, as is Google's browser, Chrome; Apple's browser, Safari; and many others. Thus, there is considerable competition in this market. Switching to another browser is easy, but many of us don't bother because the quality of all browsers

CHECK YOURSELF

- You change your cell phone provider and get a new cell phone. Why can't you easily move your address list from your old cell phone to your new cell phone?
- Just about everyone uses Google for online searches, so how can we say that Google is in a contestable market?

is high. More generally, during the 1990s, consumers benefited as Microsoft prices fell and the software added many new features.

The dilemma facing the antitrust authorities is that we know the market for network goods will be dominated by a handful of firms. Thus, the question is not monopoly versus competition (in the sense of competition from many firms in the market), but rather it is one monopoly versus another. It's not obvious that consumers are better off when Netscape has a market share of 80% than when Internet Explorer has a market share of 80%. What is important is that competition *for the market* is not impeded. Regulators claim that Microsoft did impede competition for the market by giving away Internet Explorer for free in a bundle with Windows. Maybe, but that is a tough claim to either prove or refute.

Microsoft settled with the government in 2001. The agreement was that the company would give its competitors the knowledge and technologies to produce software that would interact seamlessly with Windows.

Music Is a Network Good

Finally, network products aren't found just in high tech. Most people want to listen to popular music, so music is a network good. If you listen to music that is popular, you can swap songs with your friends, go to concerts together, and talk about the same people. Thus, popular music is a more valuable good; namely, it offers more benefits to the listener than does obscure music.

In fact, an ingenious experiment by Duncan J. Watts, a sociologist at Columbia University, demonstrated that tastes in music have a strong social component.[4] Watts asked thousands of people to listen to and rate some bands that they had never heard of. If they liked a song, participants could download it for free. The trick was that some of the participants saw only the names of the songs and bands, but others also saw how many times the songs had previously been downloaded by other participants. If tastes in music are independent of what other people are listening to, knowing how many people had previously downloaded a song should be irrelevant. You should just download the songs you like, right?

But Watts discovered that the more downloads a song had, the more people wanted to download the song! So if a few early participants happened to like and download a song, that song got even more downloads. As a result, when participants saw previous downloads, accidents of history turned some songs and bands into big hits, while others languished. Even more surprisingly, when Watts ran his experiment again and again, the songs that turned into hits were different every time!

So what does this mean? Well, look at two of the principles we outlined for network industries, namely that the best product may not always win and that *potential* competition is often important. You'll find both of those phenomena in music markets. Some bands catch a lucky break and become popular fairly quickly. That popularity feeds on itself so a small head start is turned into a big market advantage even if the band is not necessarily the "best." Was Britney Spears ever that good an entertainer? At the same time there are lots of different entertainers and potential entertainers that compete to be seen as the market leader. Stars can rise or fall quickly depending on public perceptions of popularity. As with other network goods, at any one point in time a handful of entertainers dominate the airwaves and make the most revenues. But a large market share today is no guarantee of popularity in the future, so older stars fear being dethroned by hot, young new stars.

Takeaway

Network goods exist when many different users wish to share the same system or product; Microsoft Word and Facebook are examples. In these cases, we usually find monopolies or oligopolies because of the advantages offered when many customers can share a common system. Sometimes a firm may achieve market power by selling or creating a network good. Once such networks take off, they become large very rapidly and tend to be sold by one or only a handful of major firms. Since networks often grow rapidly and offer significant revenue potential, many entrepreneurs will try to set the standard for the network.

Sometimes customers will end up "locked in" to the wrong network, or at least users will disagree as to whether the better network has won out. There is a coordination problem involved in switching from one network to another, since virtually everyone must make a coordinated change. The end result is that often not everyone is happy with the dominant network.

Still, network markets often are highly competitive, as different firms compete to be the dominant player. This competition induces them to upgrade their products, make them more convenient, and introduce innovations. It is common that a new market leader will leapfrog the old leader and replace it. The more contestable the market, the greater the incentive for product improvement and the less likely that customers will be locked into the wrong network. Businesses often take actions to deliberately increase switching costs.

CHAPTER REVIEW

interactive activity Go online to practice with more examples of these types of problems, including live links to videos, data sources, and feedback.

KEY CONCEPTS

network good, p. 317
Nash equilibrium, p. 319
coordination game, p. 319
contestable markets, p. 320

FACTS AND TOOLS

1. Antitrust laws make certain "anticompetitive" practices illegal because these practices raise prices and reduce output, which reduces the total amount of consumer surplus. Explain why antitrust action may not be helpful or necessary in markets that are:

   a. Characterized by network goods

   b. Highly contestable

2. Explain the difference between competition "in the market" and competition "for the market." What impact does each kind of competition have on prices and output in a market? Is one better than the other? How does the distinction make the application of antitrust laws more complicated?

3. LinkedIn is an online professional networking site, much like Facebook or MySpace, except that it's for connecting with classmates and colleagues to create networks that may be helpful in, among other things, finding job opportunities. The site boasts approximately half a billion members and claims to be the "world's largest professional network on the Internet." What made LinkedIn the largest professional network site? Since it is already the largest, does that mean LinkedIn will always be the largest? Why or why not?

4. For each of the following pairs, determine which business is more likely to operate in a contestable market, and explain why.

    a. The only clothing store in a small town vs. the only natural gas provider in a small town

    b. The only clothing store in a small town vs. the only cable TV provider in a small town (What recent technologies make part b different from part a?)

    c. De Beers diamond mining vs. H&R Block tax preparation services

5. In the following three games, is each a coordination game or a prisoner's dilemma? The best way to check is to see if there is exactly one Nash equilibrium; another way is to see if there is a dominant strategy for each player. To keep it a little challenging, we won't give the actions obvious labels that might give away the answer. Higher numbers are always better:

    a.

		Player B	
		Left	Right
Player A	Up	(3, 3)	(5, 5)
	Down	(5, 5)	(1, 1)

    b.

		Player B	
		Left	Right
Player A	Up	(100, 100)	(600, 50)
	Down	(50, 600)	(500, 500)

    c.

		Player B	
		Left	Right
Player A	Up	(8, 6)	(7, 5)
	Down	(3, 0)	(9, 9)

6. The mantra of Amazon.com CEO Jeff Bezos is "Get big fast." As we saw in Chapter 13 on monopoly, one reason to "get big fast" is because in some industries the firm's average cost will plummet as the firm expands—so size helps on the supply side. In this chapter, network effects illustrated how size helps on the demand side. With this in mind, explain the following real-world drives to get big fast: Do you think it's mostly about increasing returns or mostly about network effects? Explain why:

    a. Second Life, an online virtual world, lets people use many of its features for free. To use the best features, you have to pay.

    b. Likewise, Match.com, the online dating site, lets people post profiles, look at other people's profiles, and even get mail from other members for free. To send an e-mail to a member, you have to pay.

    c. Adobe Acrobat Reader is free, but the software to create sophisticated Adobe documents is not.

    d. King Gillette (real name) gave away his first disposable razor blades in 1885. They came free with the purchase of a box of Cuban cigars.

    e. Amazon.com itself.

THINKING AND PROBLEM SOLVING

7. If you get a crack in your windshield, you can take your car to an auto glass repair shop where they will gladly try to repair your windshield, so you can avoid having to replace it. They guarantee their work, too; if the repair is not successful, they will allow you to apply the money you already paid for the unsuccessful repair toward the purchase of a new windshield. Sounds terrific, but how does this strategy relate to the material in the chapter? If all auto glass repair shops employ this strategy, what impact do you think this has on the price of a new windshield?

8. Every so often, rumors float around Facebook claiming that the social networking site is going to begin charging its users a small monthly fee. So far, those rumors have always turned out to be false.

    a. Do you use Facebook? If so, how much would you be willing to pay per month for access to Facebook? (If you don't use Facebook—as unlikely as that is nowadays—how much do you imagine the typical user would be willing to pay to use it?)

    b. Besides the price itself, what else would determine whether it was worth it to you to pay for Facebook? Is your response independent of others' responses?

c. Do you think Facebook ever will charge users a fee? What are some reasons Facebook might do this? What are some arguments against this idea?

9. Deciding which side of the road to drive on is a kind of coordination game. In some countries, people drive on the right side of the road, and in other countries (notably the United Kingdom and some of its former colonies), they drive on the left. These customs developed hundreds of years ago. If there were a single world standard, car companies could save some money by not having to produce both left and right types, and cars would be a little bit cheaper. Why do you think it is that these customs persist? In other words, what keeps the world "locked in" to two separate kinds of cars?

10. Consider the shipping container (the large box that stacks on cargo ships and attaches to trucks). If all containers are the same size and design, then the container can pass seamlessly between ships, trains, trucks, and cranes along the way. Today, the standard dimensions are 8 feet wide, 8.5 feet tall, and 40 feet long. (The recent book *The Box* tells the surprisingly gripping tale of how this size came to be the standard, and how it has cut the cost of shipping worldwide.) Let's see how this standard dimension illustrates the meaning of "Nash equilibrium."

a. Suppose an inventor created a new shipping container that was slightly cheaper to make, as well as stronger, but it *had* to be 41 feet long. Keeping the idea of standardization in mind, would this inventor be successful? Why or why not?

b. Suppose a container manufacturer reduced the strength of the end walls of his containers (saving him $100 per container made). Although this makes no difference to containers on a ship, containers on a train are at risk as the container bumps against the flatcar when the train hits the brakes. Who would tend to oppose these weaker, cheaper containers: the company whose products are stored in the container, the train companies who transport the goods, or both?

c. Why does Federal Express, the overnight delivery company, require everyone to use FedEx packaging for most shipments?

11. It's more efficient to go shopping when everyone else is shopping: This is one explanation for the rise of Christmas as a shopping season. Even many people who don't celebrate Christmas do a lot of shopping and gift giving during this season. At the other extreme, a "dead mall" is one of the dreariest sights of modern consumer capitalism. Let's see how a pleasant shopping experience is a network good.

ATLANTIDE PHOTOTRAVEL/GETTY IMAGES

Facebook for those without computers

a. Part of the pleasure of walking through a mall is the pleasure of seeing and being seen. When will you see more people at the mall: in the months before Christmas or at other times? So if you like seeing people, when will *you* tend to go to the mall? (This is an example of the "multiplier effects" so common in economics.)

b. When you were in high school (or perhaps middle school), you may have spent time hanging out at a mall. How was the mall like Facebook, MySpace, or other social networking Web sites?

c. Malls will spend more money on decorations and entertainment when they can spread this cost over a large number of consumers. Again, when will you expect to see more of these extra expenses: in the months before Christmas or at other times?

d. If Christmas is so great for malls, why don't they have Christmas every month, spending money on decorations and singers all the time? Of course, they *try* to do this with Easter and back-to-school and Valentine's Day, and so forth, but why do these attempts fail so miserably compared with the big success of Christmas? Answer in the language of network goods. (*Hint:* Once there's a big chunk of the population committed to using Facebook, what's the benefit to setting up another pseudo-Facebook?)

12. Suppose a friend is taking an economics course at another college or university and his professor uses a different textbook. Your friend, after learning about monopolies and the lost gains from trade that result from monopolies, becomes very agitated about firms with market power, and he makes this statement: "It should be strictly forbidden for any company, in any market, to have more than 50% market share—market power like this always leads to higher prices, deadweight loss and inefficiency!" After you calm him down, how would you respond to this statement? Is your friend right?

CHALLENGES

13. Why doesn't everyone just switch to one language?

14. Nobel Laureate Paul Krugman once asked, "Who would enter a demolition derby without the incentive of a prize?" (Source: Krugman, Paul. 1998. Soft microeconomics: The squishy case against you-know-who. *Slate*. www.slate .com/id/1933/. Posted April 24, 1998.)

    a. The "demolition derby" he was talking about was the battle over Internet browsers: Many enter the battle, but only one (or two) survive. But let's take his story literally: If there were two cars in a demolition derby, and each car costs $20,000 to build, and one car will be totally destroyed, how big will the prize probably have to be to get two people to enter if there's a 50–50 chance of losing all your investment?

Netscape?

    b. What if we want a really good demolition derby: one where 10 of these cars compete but only one survives. About how big will the prize have to be now?

    c. Let's draw the lesson for network goods: Since competition in network good markets is competition "for the market," then it's like winning a prize in a demolition derby. If there's a fixed price of starting up a new social networking Web site (you need so many computers, so many nerds, so many advertisers), then when would you see a lot of firms competing for the prize: when the prize is large or when the prize is small? Thus, if we want a lot of competition *for the market,* do we necessarily want to restrict the profits of the winner?

15. The market for college textbooks is an interesting one. One thing that makes it unique is that the person who chooses the textbook (the professor) is not the person who purchases the textbook (the student). Therefore, much of a textbook publishing company's marketing is geared toward college professors. Most publishers of economics textbooks have developed (or have partnered with other companies to provide) online homework-management systems. This textbook has one, as you may already know if your professor is using it. Explain how a homework-management system might benefit a professor. What impact might a homework-management system have on switching costs?

WORK IT OUT

For interactive, step-by-step help in solving this problem, go online

interactive activity

Prisoner's dilemmas are common in real life, but not all real-life games are as dismal as the prisoner's dilemma. One game, known as "stag hunt," describes situations where cooperation is possible but fragile. The philosopher Jean-Jacques Rousseau described the game. He said that a lot of social situations are like going hunting with a friend: If you both agree to hunt for a large male deer (a stag), then you each have to hold your positions near each end of a valley so that the animal can't escape. If you both hold to your positions, then you will almost surely get your kill.

MINDY SCHAUER/PRESS/COSTA MESA/USA/NEWSCOM

If one hunter wanders off to hunt the easier-to-find rabbit, however, then the stag will almost surely get away. Rabbit hunting works fine as a solo sport, but to catch a deer, you need a team effort. This is the usual way of writing the game:

	Hume	
	Hunt Stag	Hunt Rabbit
Hunt Stag	(5, 5)	(0, 3)
Hunt Rabbit	(3, 0)	(3, 3)

(Rousseau labels the rows: Hunt Stag, Hunt Rabbit)

a. If Rousseau is quite sure that Hume will hunt stag, will he also hunt stag?

b. If Rousseau is quite sure that Hume will hunt rabbit, will Rousseau still hunt stag?

c. There are two Nash equilibria here: What are they? (Check by looking in each box and asking, "Would one player unilaterally change his choice between rabbit and stag?" If so, this isn't an equilibrium.)

d. Of these two equilibria, economists call one the "payoff-dominant equilibrium" and the other the "risk-dominant equilibrium." You can figure out which is which by the process of elimination. What do you think is the biggest risk that might push someone to choose the "risk-dominant equilibrium"?

e. Is this a coordination game or is there a dominant strategy?

f. In the coordination games we looked at in previous questions, if you failed to coordinate, things turned out badly. Is that the case here?

g. Anytime someone says, "I'll do it as long as I'm not the only one," they're probably describing a stag hunt. Wearing a cocktail dress to a dinner party, making a solid team effort, keeping your lawn mowed—all might be examples of stag hunts. In a stag hunt, if you think the other players are nice, then you'll want to be nice yourself. But if you suspect they're not nice, you'll probably just be a "rugged individualist" and go hunt the rabbit on your own. With this in mind, think of two more examples of stag hunt situations on your own.

(For an excellent, somewhat technical treatment of how people might agree to hunt stag across many areas of life, see Skyrms, Brian. 2004. *The Stag Hunt and the Evolution of Social Structure*. Cambridge, UK: Cambridge University Press. Skyrms is a philosopher who uses the tools of game theory to investigate important social questions.)

17

Monopolistic Competition and Advertising

Y ou can find a mystery at Amazon.com. In fact, you can find 2,530 mysteries, including novels by Janet Evanovich, Stephen King, and James Patterson. What we have in mind, however, is a different but closely related economic puzzle or mystery.

In some ways, the market for books appears to be very competitive. There are lots of choices and very few barriers to entry. Authors today, for example, don't even need access to an expensive printing press because they can "print" their books electronically and sell them on Amazon alongside books from established publishers like HarperCollins. Yet even though the market appears competitive, prices are above marginal cost. It doesn't cost $18 to print the latest Stephen King novel, even including delivery, and it certainly doesn't cost $14.99 to deliver the book electronically to a Kindle or iPad. Why are prices higher than marginal cost in a market with lots of choices and few barriers to entry?

In other ways, however, the market for books looks like a monopoly. Anyone can sell mysteries but only Stephen King can sell Stephen King novels. In fact, copyright law makes it a crime for anyone else to sell a Stephen King novel until 70 years after his death! Thus, there is a significant barrier to entry for selling Stephen King novels. True, it is legal to write and sell mysteries in the *style* of Stephen King but many readers find that Stephen King substitutes are just not as horrifying as the real thing. As a result, Stephen King faces a downward-sloping demand curve and he is not forced to price at marginal cost.

In this chapter, we will be looking at a type of market structure that combines some features of competitive markets with some features of monopoly, namely **monopolistic competition**. Monopolistic competition describes a market with the following features:

- *Many sellers:* There are lots of firms in the market and lots of potential firms.

- *Free entry:* Firms can enter or exit the market without restriction. As a result, firms will enter when $P > AC$ and exit when $P < AC$ so, just as with competitive markets, in the long run profits are driven to zero (normal) with $P = AC$.

- *Product differentiation:* Each firm produces a product that is somewhat different from its competitors. Thus, each firm faces a downward-sloped demand curve.

Monopolistic competition is a market with a large number of firms selling similar but not identical products.

329

Perfectly competitive markets also feature many sellers and free entry so what makes monopolistic competition different is the final feature, product differentiation. Recall our example of a perfectly competitive market, the market for oil. If you owned a small oil well, you would face a perfectly elastic demand curve because one seller's oil is pretty much the same as another seller's oil. As we said in Chapter 11, even your mother probably wouldn't pay extra for *your* oil.

But instead of owning a small oil well, suppose you owned a small restaurant. There are many sellers in the restaurant business and there is free entry, but the food in your restaurant will probably be a little bit different from the food in other restaurants. Indeed, some of your customers might be willing to pay a bit extra to eat in your restaurant compared to the next best substitute. As a small restaurant owner, if you raise your prices a little, you will lose some but not all of your customers, and if you lower prices a little, you will sell more but you won't suddenly find yourself with lines out the door. In other words, unlike the owner of a small oil well, as a small restaurant owner, you would face a downward-sloping demand curve.

Sources of Product Differentiation

Products can be differentiated along any dimension that people care about, such as taste, style, features, or location.

Taste is one obvious source of product differentiation. McDonald's, Burger King, and Wendy's all sell hamburgers but most people have a favorite among the three. Coca-Cola, Pepsi, and RC all produce cola but if Coca-Cola raised its prices by 5 cents it wouldn't lose all of its customers. Style is also a source of product differentiation. Levi's, 7 For All Mankind, and American Eagle all produce denim jeans but some people do not regard these products as close substitutes. Apple, Motorola, and Samsung all produce cell phones with different styles and also a range of slightly different features, and most people are not indifferent to all the choices. Even when consumers are indifferent about the brand, such as Shell vs. Chevron gasoline, they might prefer one gasoline station simply because it is closer or more convenient.

Products can also be differentiated by location or by ease of purchase. The milk at 7-Eleven, for example, is the same milk as at your local grocery store but usually it's a bit more expensive. Why? Although the milk is identical, it can be more convenient to buy it at 7-Eleven (hence the name "convenience store"), especially if you are already buying gas. The different location and the bundling of milk and gas make milk at 7-Eleven a slightly different product from milk at the grocery store, so prices can be slightly different.

Ease of purchase can also make a surprisingly big difference in how willing people are to buy. Your authors buy a lot of books, but we don't always search to find the lowest price. Instead, we are more likely to find something on Amazon and hit "Buy now with 1-Click." We could save some money by searching Barnes & Noble, Walmart, and other stores but we are willing to pay a little bit extra for the convenience. Amazon's Dash buttons take this one step further. Once you set up the Wi-Fi button, you don't even have to be on the Web. One press and the product will be delivered to your door, albeit at a slightly higher price than you would pay elsewhere.

You might also have noticed one other feature about differentiated products—they are often highly advertised. Firms want consumers to perceive

Amazon's Dash button means that you will never run out of Pop-tarts, even if you pay a bit extra for the convenience.

their products as different and better because that increases their market power. Advertising, therefore, isn't just about informing consumers about price and availability. It can also be used to increase perceptions of product differentiation. We will say much more about advertising later in this chapter.

The Monopolistic Competition Model

Monopolistic competition takes the standard model of monopoly but allows for the free entry of competing business firms. To see how this works, let's imagine the economic situation for the very first Chinese restaurant in our town of Fairfax, Virginia. In the short run, the first Chinese restaurant would use its market power to make profits, much like a monopoly. Unlike a monopoly, however, those profits would attract more entrants.

As more restaurants open, the demand curve facing the former monopolist shifts down and to the left, as some of the previous customers start patronizing other restaurants. In Figure 17.1 we show this process.

We begin on the left when the first Chinese restaurant in Fairfax has a monopoly. As you know, a monopoly maximizes profit by producing the quantity such that $MR = MC$. Profit is given by $(P - AC) \times Q$ and is shown by the green rectangle. All of this is exactly the same as for monopoly discussed in Chapter 13. The difference comes in the long run. No barriers to entry prevent an entrepreneur from starting a new Chinese restaurant in Fairfax so monopoly profits attract entry. Entry reduces the demand for the original restaurant. The firm continues to make profits so long as price is greater than average cost, $P > AC$, but that means entry occurs so long as $P > AC$.

FIGURE 17.1

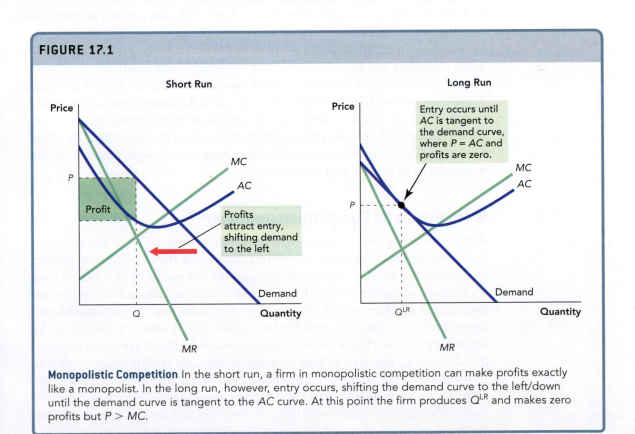

Monopolistic Competition In the short run, a firm in monopolistic competition can make profits exactly like a monopolist. In the long run, however, entry occurs, shifting the demand curve to the left/down until the demand curve is tangent to the AC curve. At this point the firm produces Q^{LR} and makes zero profits but $P > MC$.

The end result is that the demand curve is driven to the left and down until it becomes tangent to (just touching) the average cost (AC) curve. At this point, $P = AC$ and each firm in the industry is earning zero economic profits.

It's the entry of competing business firms that drives the move from the left side of Figure 17.1 to the right side. Indeed, Yahoo lists 346 restaurants in or near Fairfax as serving some form of Chinese food.

Although producers under monopolistic competition don't earn above-normal profits, they still are charging prices above marginal cost, $P > MC$, as you can see in the right panel of Figure 17.1. When $P > MC$, output is not at the efficient level. Remember that the price P measures the value to consumers of one additional meal, and the MC curve at Q^{LR} tells us the cost of producing one additional meal. Thus, when $P > MC$, the value of an additional meal exceeds the cost of an additional meal and social surplus would be higher if the firm produced more. Production under monopolistic competition, just as with monopoly, is not perfectly efficient.

A monopolistic competitive firm is able to charge $P > MC$ because its product is slightly different from the product of other firms. Your authors have a favorite Chinese restaurant in Fairfax—China Star. It's where we take visitors to the university for lunch. The food there is spicier and the menu has some tasty dishes, such as scallion fried fish, that you can't find elsewhere. Call us fussy if you like, but such features are specific examples of what is called product differentiation. Since there are no perfect substitutes for China Star, it can price its scallion fried fish above marginal cost and yet not lose us as customers. Product differentiation also means that under monopolistic competition, a firm does not produce at the minimum of its AC curve. To see this in a picture, Figure 17.2 compares long-run output under monopolistic competition (on the left) with that under competition (on the right).

A competitive firm, sometimes also called a perfectly competitive firm, produces a product like oil that has perfect substitutes. As a result, the firm can't control the price of its product, and just to earn zero profits, it must produce at the output level that minimizes average costs. A monopolistic competitive firm produces a slightly different product than its competitors, and so it can reduce output and raise the price without losing all of its customers. But when a monopolistic competitive firm reduces output, it no longer produces at the minimum of its average cost curve.

Is Monopolistic Competition Inefficient?

Although monopolistic competitive firms don't produce at the minimum of their average cost curves, an offsetting advantage is the possibility of greater dynamism and product variety. If a restaurant comes up with a new recipe, for example, or some new and interesting décor, the demand curve for that restaurant's product will shift up and to the right and that restaurant will enjoy higher profits. Or consider the market for books introduced at the beginning of the chapter. Books are priced at higher than marginal cost but there is a continual stream of authors who are trying to innovate and become the next Stephen King or J. K. Rowling. Although monopolistic competitive industries feature some market power, usually in the longer run, consumers are better off from the new products and the better matching of products to tastes.

FIGURE 17.2

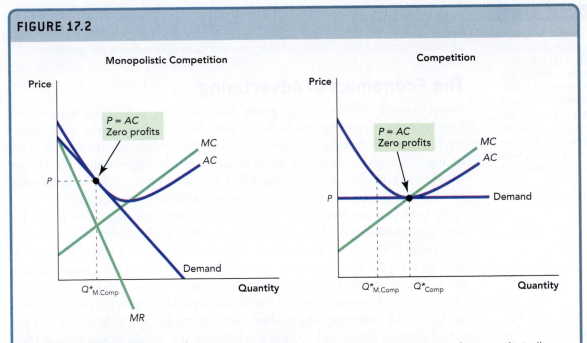

Comparing Monopolistic Competition and Competition In the long run, competitive and monopolistically competitive firms produce where $P = AC$ and earn zero profits. Each firm in monopolistic competition offers a slightly different product and so each firm faces a downward-sloping demand curve. As a result, firms under monopolistic competition charge prices above marginal cost, they produce a smaller quantity compared with competitive firms, and Q^* is not at minimum average cost. In the case of competitive firms, each firm produces exactly the same product so there are perfect substitutes for each firm's products. As a result, the demand curve is perfectly elastic, production quantity is higher than under monopolistic competition, and output is at the point that minimizes average costs.

Note that for comparison we show the monopolistic competition output level, $Q^*_{M.Comp}$, and the competitive output level, Q^*_{Comp}, in the right panel.

We can see both the benefits and the costs of monopolistic competition in the market for drinking water. Water is simple: It's uniform, and it's often available for free. So who would imagine that you could sell water by the bottle for billions of dollars? And yet bottled water products like Dasani, Fiji, and Voss sell over $100 billion worth worldwide. The fact that there are many producers of bottled water means that the average costs of production is not minimized— bottled water would be cheaper if we could consolidate production in just a few firms, each of which would produce more. (And it would be even cheaper if we just used tap water.) On the other hand, many people do have a favorite brand of water so the product variety and experimentation of the industry does create value. Yes, sometimes we think this is a bit absurd—we have seen people buy bottled water at a restaurant instead of tap water even when the bottled water comes from exactly the same source! On the other hand, mineral water, sparkling water, and flavored waters, not to mention soft drinks, coffee, and tea (all mostly water), are different and it's hard to say how different is different enough to justify the extra costs.

Keep in mind also that the market is a discovery process. Consumers may not even know that they want a product until entrepreneurs test the market and make new discoveries. Who knew that consumers would love milk shakes blended with coffee? Starbucks, however, has made millions selling Frappuccinos.

As inefficiencies go, the fact that average cost is not minimized under monopolistic competition is typically considered fairly minor, but it is one way of understanding how monopolistic competition differs from competition.

The Economics of Advertising

Firms that sell undifferentiated goods don't advertise very much because any benefits from advertising would flow mostly to other firms in the same industry. If a carrot farmer, for example, advertised how delicious carrots were, most of any additional sales would go to other carrot farmers—unless the farmer could somehow convince consumers that her carrots were different and better. Firms will only pay for advertising if they sell a differentiated good.

Perhaps you are wondering about some counterexamples. You may have seen advertisements for Milk ("Got Milk?"), Pork ("The Other White Meat"), or Cotton ("The Fabric of our Lives"). Each of these goods is undifferentiated so who is paying for the commercials? These examples are the exceptions that prove the rule because the advertising campaigns for these products are funded through special programs run by the Agricultural Marketing Service, a division of the U.S. Department of Agriculture. Since firms in these industries won't pay for advertising themselves (even if the industry as a whole would benefit from the advertising—an example of a prisoner's dilemma), the government requires that any firm in the industry pay a special tax earmarked for advertising. The industry as a whole benefits from the advertising, although individual farmers sometimes gripe about the special taxes.

Monopolies are also less likely to advertise since they aren't worried about a competitor gaining market share. The U.S. Postal Service (USPS), for example, doesn't advertise first-class mail very much since no other firm is allowed to compete in that market. The USPS, however, does advertise its parcel delivery services, since it competes in that market with FedEx and UPS.

Firms with differentiated products are the most likely to advertise because (1) unlike carrot farmers, they can advertise their specific product rather than the industry category and (2) they want more customers since $P > MC$ (unlike in a perfectly competitive industry). But why does advertising increase sales?

Informative Advertising

One reason that advertising increases sales is that it informs consumers about price, quality, and availability. Supermarkets, for example, send out newspaper supplements boasting of low prices for hamburger, apples, and milk. Price advertising is part of the competitive process, and there is good evidence for how advertising lowers prices and improves consumer welfare. In some states, for example, it used to be illegal for optometrists to advertise prices for eyeglasses; this restriction allowed economists to test the effect of advertising on prices. Would the states with advertising restrictions have lower prices for eyeglasses, on the theory that optometrists would save money if they didn't advertise and would pass on these lower costs to consumers? Or would states with restrictions on advertising have higher prices, on the theory that without advertising there would be less competition? The states that allowed price advertising for eyeglasses had systematically lower eyeglass prices; in other words, advertising improves the competitive process. The same pattern—lower prices where advertising is allowed—has been true for prescription drugs, retail gasoline prices, eye exams, and legal services.[1]

Other times, advertising promotes messages of quality, thereby informing consumers and also giving suppliers a better incentive to meet quality standards. Once it was discovered that high-fiber cereals may help prevent cancer, and such advertising was allowed by law, companies had (1) a greater incentive to produce and advertise high-fiber cereals and (2) consumers became better informed about the benefits of high-fiber cereals and they ate more of the healthier cereals.[2] These two processes were mutually reinforcing.

Advertising as Signaling

Sometimes advertising doesn't appear to be about price, quality, or availability but the ad itself could be informative. If a new product debuts with a lot of accompanying advertising, consumers might infer that the seller expects the product to make a big splash, as with the iPad ads in Germany. The biggest piece of information is the ad itself. Apple was trying to get German consumers to think, either explicitly or implicitly, "If they're spending so much advertising on this new product, they must expect it to have a long and profitable life. There really is something to this iPad after all." That makes potential customers more interested in buying or at least sampling the product. Similarly, if a new movie or musical release is accompanied by a lot of ads, consumers will rationally infer that the producers expect the new product to hit it big; for a while, it seemed that *Jurassic World* commercials were everywhere. It might seem that the advertising creates the demand, but we also have to take into account that the firms who believe that their products are likely to be hits are the ones who have the biggest incentive to advertise.

Advertising Changes Our Tastes

It's obvious that a lot of advertising is simply about trying to change our minds and not about information at all. You can watch a Coca-Cola ad on YouTube that has no words, catchy music, lots of beautiful images, including tumbling snowmen, no information about price, a cool dude pulling a Coke out of a vending machine, and at the end you see on the screen the simple words, "The Coke side of life."[3] Coke ads have been, well, vague for many years. Previous slogans include "The pause that refreshes," "Thirst knows no season," "Things go better with Coke," and "The real thing."[4] It's not so well-known that Coca-Cola publicized the idea, through its ads, of Santa as an old man in a red suit, but that shows how central Coke ads have been to our national consciousness.[5] It's not obvious how these messages have anything to do with informing buyers about Coca-Cola, if only because just about everyone already has heard of Coke. Worldwide, for all brands, Coca-Cola spends several billion dollars a year on advertising. Through advertising, Coca-Cola is trying to make the demand for Coca-Cola more inelastic. By persuading us that Pepsi is *not* a close substitute, Coca-Cola reduces the elasticity of demand and nudges the market in the direction of monopoly.

Yet, is persuasion through advertising always such a bad thing? Persuasion can give us tastes that appear silly or unjustified to outside observers, such as when we believe that drinking a particular beer will make us more suave or more attractive to potential dates. Nonetheless, persuasion also can deepen our enjoyments and our memories.

Is Advertising Good?

interactive activity

Can you tell the difference?

How about now?

COSTI IOSIF/SHUTTERSTOCK

COSTI IOSIF/SHUTTERSTOCK

Here's an example of how advertising gives us richer memories. In a blind taste test performed by researchers, the subjects reported roughly equal preferences for Coke and Pepsi. As part of the same test, the subjects were given one cup labeled as "Coke" and another cup, also containing Coke, but unlabeled. The subjects reported greater enjoyment from drinking the labeled cup, and brain scans showed that they were activating the memory regions of their brain when they offered these reports. The researchers suspected that the subjects were associating Coke with fond images from ads or from earlier moments in their lives. It was not possible to replicate the same effect of "enhanced enjoyment from memory" when labeled and unlabeled Pepsi were put in the cups and sampled by subjects. In other words, the very act of thinking about the Coke brand has resonance with a lot of customers.[6]

It's possible to read this story in two differing ways. Are the people who enjoy the Coke being "manipulated" or "tricked" by the advertisers? (If so, do your friends ever manipulate or trick you in the same way? Do you ever manipulate or trick them?) Or do the Coke ads mean many of us enjoy the Coca-Cola product more? Do the ads themselves enhance consumer welfare by turning a sweet, fizzy drink into something more? It's common that people bring their value judgments to bear on advertising, as some will condemn and others will praise persuasive ads; economic science itself does not give us a means of deciding which ads are good and which are bad, all things considered. What we do know is that persuasive advertising can create some market power by brand differentiation, but at the same time advertising also helps people enjoy a lot of products.

Advertising Lowers the Price of Many Products

Advertising, whether informative or persuasive, also helps finance many useful goods and services. Why is Google available on the Web for free? Because the company earns income by selling click-through ads and thus doesn't need to charge users of a Web search. In fact, Google has an incentive to provide search services for free in order to maximize the number of people who will see the ads that it sells. Facebook, Instagram, and Twitter are all free to consumers because of advertising. Advertising also makes newspapers, magazines, and cable TV much cheaper than otherwise would be the case. For instance, a typical newspaper earns more from its ads than from its subscriptions revenue. In this sense, you, as a reader benefit from ads even if you don't care about the advertised products. Not everyone enjoys every ad but advertising is an important part of what makes business work—at the most fundamental level, advertising is about bringing businesses and customers together.

Takeaway

A monopolistically competitive industry features many sellers, free entry, and differentiated products.

Since products are differentiated, each firm retains a downward-sloped demand curve and P remains above MC. Free entry, however, means that in the long run price is driven down until $P = AC$ and each firm earns a zero economic profit. Monopolistically competitive industries have lots of variety but products are not produced at minimum average cost.

CHECK YOURSELF

- Wood is used to build houses. All houses have windows. Why do we see advertisements for different window makers but not for different producers of wood?

- Which category of advertising described in this chapter best explains a product endorsed by a famous athlete? Why? What if the product has nothing to do with sports, such as antifreeze or autos?

Advertising can be informative as in advertising about price, quality, and availability. Advertising can also increase perceptions of product differentiation, which allows firms to increase prices. Put differently, advertising can add to consumers' understanding and enjoyment of a product by changing what the product means to them.

CHAPTER REVIEW

 interactive activity Go online to practice with more examples of these types of problems, including live links to videos, data sources, and feedback.

Problems in green relate to MRU videos. See the MRU table at the end of the exercises.

KEY CONCEPTS

monopolistic competition, p. 329

FACTS AND TOOLS

1. Though its name can sometimes cause confusion for students, the market structure we call "monopolistic competition" is so named because it has some features of monopoly and some features of competition.

   a. In what ways is a monopolistically competitive market like a monopoly? In what ways is it like competition?

   b. Which of the outcomes of monopolistically competitive markets is a direct result of its monopoly-like features? Which outcome is a result of its competitive features? Can you summarize these results, so that they can be applied to product markets in general?

2. In a city like New York, the market for stand-up comedians is likely to be monopolistically competitive. Explain why this is so. If the market is monopolistically competitive, then what can be said about prices, output, and profits in this market?

3. Fill in the blanks with "=," "<," or ">" as appropriate to describe the long-run outcome in a monopolistically competitive market.

   a. MC ___ AC

   b. P ___ AC

   c. MR ___ MC

   d. P ___ MC

4. For each of the following items, describe how the market that these sellers participate in resembles monopolistic competition. For bonus points (if your professor agrees), describe briefly the strategies that sellers in the market use in order to differentiate their products.

   a. New car dealerships

   b. Real estate agents

   c. Landscapers

THINKING AND PROBLEM SOLVING

5. As you read in the chapter, the requirements for an industry to be considered monopolistically competitive are that there are many firms and those firms are producing unique, or differentiated, products. One industry in which we find differentiated products is the recording industry. Not only are there many genres of music (iTunes lists almost 50), but within each genre there are countless artists as well.

   Over the past few decades, technology has reduced the fixed costs of recording and the marginal costs of distributing music. In 1979, for example, the average studio bill for an album was more than $30,000 ($170,000 in today's dollars). Nowadays, with digital recording technology, an artist or band can record an entire album for a few thousand dollars and the album can be distributed at low cost as MP3s on the Internet, with no record store involved.

   a. What do you expect to happen to the music industry because of the evolution of much cheaper recording technology? What do you expect to happen to the number of recording artists?

b. Suppose there are initially only two recording artists in all of the record industry: the Decemberists (an indie rock band) and Yo-Yo Ma (a famous cellist). How many MP3s will they each be able to sell? Who would buy MP3s from the Decemberists? What about from Yo-Yo Ma? Will anybody buy MP3s from both?

c. Now suppose that another artist joins the industry: Isobel Campbell (an indie rock cellist!). What will happen to the demand curves for MP3s that the Decemberists and Yo-Yo Ma face? Will they keep all of their fans? Will they keep *any* of their fans? What do you think will happen to the total number of MP3s sold in the industry?

d. Generally speaking, as technology makes it cheaper and cheaper to produce MP3s, and as more and more bands join the music industry, what will happen to the total number of MP3s downloaded by music fans? What will happen to the MP3s sold by each individual band? What will happen to the profits of each band?

6. In a famous article on advertising,[7] Gary Becker and Kevin Murphy wrote about advertisements that run during television programs: "One can say either that advertising pays for the programming—the usual interpretation—or that programming compensates for the advertising, which is our preferred interpretation." Viewing ads during a television program (or hearing them during a radio broadcast) makes consumers worse off, so they must be compensated (with programming) for having experienced the ads. On the other hand, print ads in newspapers and magazines can be avoided by consumers, so these ads must make consumers better off; otherwise, no one would ever read them. Use this theory to answer the following questions:

a. Think about the different types of advertisements discussed in the chapter (informative, signaling, part of the product). Which type is more likely to appear on TV? Which type is more likely to appear in a newspaper or magazine? Often you'll see television commercials, especially for pharmaceuticals, that say: "See our ad in *such-and-such* magazine." What does this say about the difference between television and print ads?

b. Becker and Murphy wrote their article before TiVo and other DVR systems became popular. Nowadays, ads on television are avoidable (to a degree), just like ads in a newspaper. What impact do you think this new technology has on the types of ads you see on TV?

Can you see the influence of the DVR in this picture?

7. Why do you think chain restaurants like Chili's, Applebee's, and TGI Fridays are always changing their menus—introducing new appetizers, new entrees, and new cocktails? Are they all just trying to find the perfect menu, or is there something else going on?

8. Wrigley's spends around $30 million per year on intense, over-the-top commercials that claim to showcase what it feels like to chew 5® Gum—Wrigley's second most popular gum brand. Despite claiming, in a tongue-in-cheek way, to provide information about the gum to viewers, it is obvious that very little information is embedded in the high-concept, visually stimulating commercials. So what is the point of the advertising? How would an economist view this type of advertising? How do you view it? Would it be better to have a perfectly competitive market in gum?

9. Many restaurants are not 100% full all day long, especially in the late morning and during the afternoon. Economists call this "excess capacity" and it is a characteristic result of monopolistic competition. What would restaurants have to do in order to be closer to 100% full all of the time? Why won't they do this?

WORK IT OUT

For interactive, step-by-step help in solving this problem, go online.

Let's compare monopolistic competition with perfect competition.

a. Do competitive firms make profits in the short run? How about in the long run?

b. Do monopolistically competitive firms make profits in the short run? How about in the long run?

c. Is there a difference in profits between competition and monopolistic competition? If so, what accounts for it?

d. Examine Figure 17.2. In the figure, what are the differences between monopolistic competition and competition?

e. In Figure 17.2, one specific point represents the price we pay for product differentiation. What is it?

MARGINAL REVOLUTION VIDEOS AND PROBLEMS

Is Advertising Good?

mruniversity.com/econ-advertising

Problems: **6, 8**

18

Labor Markets

A janitor in the United States earns about $12 an hour; a typical janitor in India earns less than $1 an hour. Why is there such a difference? Why does one person earn so much more than the other? After all, janitors in both countries do many of the same things: they clean windows and floors, scrub toilets, remove trash, and so forth.

If you think the differences in wages have to do with supply and demand, you are on the right track.

Wages are determined in the market for labor just like other prices are determined.

In this chapter, we look more deeply at the factors underlying the demand for labor and the supply of labor. A deeper understanding explains how wages are determined at a fundamental level, why most Americans earn so much by global standards, why education raises wages, whether and how much labor unions help workers, and how discrimination still shapes labor markets today.

The Demand for Labor and the Marginal Product of Labor

A firm is willing to hire a worker when the worker increases the firm's revenues more than the firm's costs. Economists call the increase in revenue created by hiring an additional worker the **marginal product of labor (MPL).** The increase in costs created by hiring an additional worker is, for a competitive firm, simply the worker's wage (including the cost of other compensation like health benefits). Thus, we can say that a firm is willing to hire a worker when the marginal product of labor is greater than the wage.

When the Cleveland Cavaliers signed (in fact, re-signed) star player LeBron James in 2014, they went from having the second-worst record in the NBA to two straight appearances in the NBA Finals, including a championship in 2016. Not only did the Cavaliers win more games when they hired LeBron, their attendance increased and they sold more merchandise. In the long run, the value of their TV contract was higher too. When the Cavaliers hired LeBron, their revenues increased by a lot. That's why the Cavaliers were willing to pay him $100 million over three years. LeBron's salary may seem high but so was LeBron's marginal product.

McDonald's considers marginal product when the company hires people to keep its restaurants clean and in good running order. No one wants to eat in a

The **marginal product of labor (MPL)** is the increase in a firm's revenues created by hiring an additional laborer.

restaurant that looks unclean, so a cleaner restaurant increases profit. But how clean is clean enough? At some point, cleanliness costs more than it's worth. Thus, to maximize profit, *McDonald's will hire janitors so long as the increase in revenue from hiring an additional janitor exceeds the janitor's wage.*

To make that more concrete, let's consider the marginal product of labor as we vary the number of janitors, as in Table 18.1.

You'll notice a few things about these numbers. First, the marginal product of labor generally declines as more labor is hired. If there is one janitor, he or she will focus on the most important tasks so the marginal product of labor is high. As McDonald's adds janitors, each subsequent janitor is assigned to a less important task so the marginal product of labor falls.

We can see from Table 18.1 that if McDonald's hires three janitors, then the marginal product of labor (per hour) is $24. If McDonald's hires four janitors, the marginal product of labor is $20, and so forth. But how many janitors will McDonald's hire? That depends on the wage.

If a janitor's wage is above $35 an hour, then McDonald's will hire zero janitors. If the wage falls to, say, $32 an hour, McDonald's will compare the additional revenues from hiring a janitor (the MPL), $35 an hour, to the cost of hiring the janitor, $32 an hour. Since the MPL is greater than the wage W, McDonald's will make the hire. If the wage falls to $28, McDonald's will hire a second janitor. If the wage falls to $22, McDonald's will hire a third janitor and so forth.

Notice that when the wage falls, McDonald's hires more janitors and assigns them to less important tasks, so as the wage falls, so does the MPL. The wage and the marginal product of labor will always be very close together since McDonald's will keep hiring workers so long as the MPL is greater than W.

If we know the marginal product of labor, we can derive the demand curve for labor. In Figure 18.1, for example, we show McDonald's demand curve for janitors. From the figure and from Table 18.1, you can see that if the wage is $10, then McDonald's will hire seven janitors.

Of course, we still have not explained what determines the wage. To do that, we need to remember that many firms demand janitors, so the wage of janitors

TABLE 18.1 THE MARGINAL PRODUCT OF LABOR

Number of Janitors	Task	Marginal Product of Labor (MPL per hour)
One	Clean restrooms, once a day.	$35
Two	Empty trash.	$30
Three	Clean restrooms, second time in a day.	$24
Four	Wash floors.	$20
Five	Pick up outside trash.	$16
Six	Clean restrooms, third time in a day.	$12
Seven	Clean windows.	$11
Eight	Remove gum from the bottom of tables.	$8

FIGURE 18.1

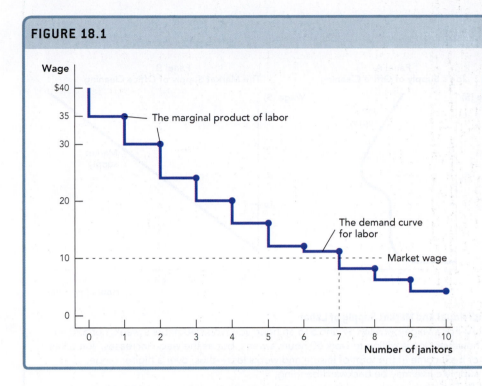

The Marginal Product of Labor Determines a Firm's Demand Curve for Labor The marginal product of the first janitor is $35. If the wage is above $35, McDonald's will hire no janitors. If the wage falls to just below $35, McDonald's will find it profitable to hire one janitor. The marginal product of the second janitor is $30. If the wage falls below $30, McDonald's will hire its second janitor. If the wage falls below $24, McDonald's will find it profitable to add a third janitor and so forth.

will be determined by the *market* demand and supply of janitors. But don't worry, the market demand for janitors is very similar to McDonald's demand for janitors. At a high wage, only some firms (and some individual consumers, such as the very wealthy) will demand janitors. As the wage falls, more and more firms will demand janitors and each firm will demand more janitors, as we saw with McDonald's. Thus, the market demand for cleaners is downward-sloping, as usual.

Supply of Labor

The market supply curve for labor will be upward-sloping, again as usual. In other words, high wages encourage a greater supply of labor. That's intuitive but we do have to take into account one complication. An *individual's* labor supply curve need not slope upward throughout its range. When Bruce Springsteen was paid $100 a night, he toured constantly just to pay the rent. Now that he is paid hundreds of thousands of dollars a night, Springsteen tours less often. If his wage is already high, even Joe the janitor might decide that he would prefer spending more time with his family to working more hours at an even higher wage rate.

Figure 18.2 illustrates. In panel A, if the wage is between $7 and $16 an hour, Joe works 40 hours a week, so over this range Joe's supply curve for labor is vertical. If the wage rises to $20 an hour, Joe is willing to work overtime and he puts in 50 hours a week (a positively sloped labor supply curve). At $20 an hour, Joe is making a comfortable income—enough so that if his wage rises even further, Joe would prefer to work fewer hours and instead enjoy the money he is making by taking more leisure time. Thus, it is quite plausible that as the wage rises to $28 an hour, Joe asks his bosses for less overtime (a negatively sloped, or backward-bending, labor supply curve).

CHECK YOURSELF

- Why does the marginal product of labor fall as more workers are hired?

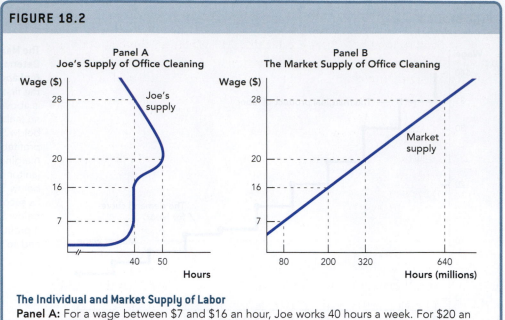

FIGURE 18.2

Panel A
Joe's Supply of Office Cleaning

Panel B
The Market Supply of Office Cleaning

The Individual and Market Supply of Labor

Panel A: For a wage between $7 and $16 an hour, Joe works 40 hours a week. For $20 an hour, however, Joe is willing to work 50 hours a week; but as the wage increases, Joe takes more of his income in the form of leisure and works less—thus, over a higher range, Joe's labor supply curve may be backward-bending.

Panel B: The labor supply curve for the market is positively sloped throughout because even if Joe works less as the wage rises (over some range), many other workers enter the office cleaning industry as the wage rises.

Although Joe's supply curve for labor could have a zero, positive, or even negative slope, the market supply curve for labor is very likely to be positively sloped. Why? Let's go back to when Joe was earning $7 an hour and putting in 40 hours a week. When the wage rises to $16 an hour, Joe doesn't work more hours; but, at a higher wage, Mary, who was working in the restaurant business, is likely to switch to office cleaning. Thus, in panel B, we show the market supply of janitors. When the wage increases, the market supply increases for two reasons: first, some workers—although not all—are likely to work more as the wage increases. Second, and more important, when the wages of janitors increase, that attracts workers from other industries. Together, these two factors mean that even if some individuals supply less labor at a higher wage, a higher wage increases the quantity of labor supplied overall.

Thus, an upward-sloping *market* supply curve is the normal situation.

We can now put together the supply and demand for janitors in the usual fashion to represent the market for janitors.

In the United States, there are about 4.2 million janitors, each working about 40 hours a week (168 million hours a week in total) and earning an average wage of $10 an hour. Thus, the market for janitors can be represented in Figure 18.3. As usual, the price (wage) is found at the intersection of the demand for janitors and the supply of janitors.

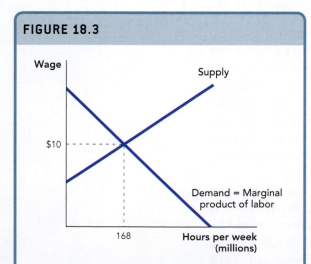

FIGURE 18.3

Market Demand for Janitors The price of labor (wage) is determined in the market for labor. In this case, the wage of janitors is determined by the demand and supply of janitors.

By the way, recall that we said earlier that the wage and the marginal product of labor will always be very close together. That is because a firm will keep hiring workers so long as MPL is greater than W. When we think about many firms and many workers, it often simplifies things to say that the MPL = W. Thus, we know that in the United States, the marginal product of a janitor is about $10 an hour.

Labor Market Issues

Now that we know the basic principles underlying the demand and supply of labor, let's turn to some specific questions and issues that our principles can help us to understand.

CHECK YOURSELF

■ Why might an individual's supply of labor curve be backward-bending? Explain.

Why Do Janitors in the United States Earn More Than Janitors in India Even When They Do the Same Job?

The short answer for why janitors in the United States earn more than janitors in India—even though janitors in India work as hard or harder—is that janitors in the United States have a higher marginal product. Janitors in the United States have a higher marginal product for two reasons, demand and supply. The demand or willingness to pay for janitors in the United States is higher than in India not because U.S. janitors clean more offices per hour but because the price that people are prepared to pay for a clean office is higher in the United States. Janitors in the United States work for productive firms like McDonald's or in office buildings producing valuable products and that raises the demand for their cleaning work.

To put it in a single sentence, the U.S. janitor gets the benefit of productivity in many other sectors of the U.S. economy. A typical janitor in India might earn less than $1,000 per year. That same worker, if he wins the green card lottery and comes to the United States, might instead earn over $20,000 in a similar job or even up to $30,000, depending on location and hours. It's not that he has suddenly learned new cleaning techniques but rather that he is working in a more productive economy.

Let's look a little more closely at the differences between the typical U.S. and Indian office building. The U.S. office building has more and better equipment such as more and better printers, copiers, and computers. Overall, there is more capital invested in the U.S. workplace, and that makes the U.S. office building more productive. That building also has a better marketing department, longer global reach for its sales force, and greater investment in building up the brand name of the product. Most importantly, the U.S. office is producing a more valuable product.

Since it's more valuable to keep a productive workplace clean than to keep a less productive workplace clean, the wages of U.S. janitors are higher than those in India.

There is no doubt that you are a very productive person—perhaps you know how to use a computer, have some artistic talents, and write well. Now look around the world—how much would these skills earn you in another country? Your skills are yours alone, but your wage is determined not by your skills alone but by the productivity of the entire economy.

The second reason that janitors in the United States have a higher marginal product than janitors in India is that the supply of janitors in the United States is lower than in India.

Figure 18.4 shows the two reasons why the wages of janitors are lower in India than in the United States. First, the demand for janitors is higher in the United States because U.S. firms are more productive than firms in India overall.

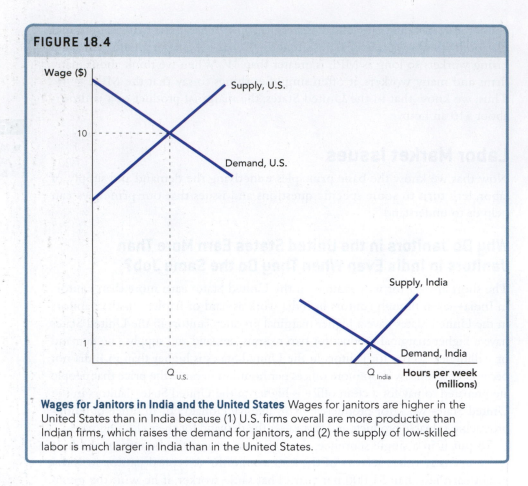

FIGURE 18.4

Wages for Janitors in India and the United States Wages for janitors are higher in the United States than in India because (1) U.S. firms overall are more productive than Indian firms, which raises the demand for janitors, and (2) the supply of low-skilled labor is much larger in India than in the United States.

Human capital is tools of the mind, the stuff in people's heads that makes them productive.

Second, the supply of low-skilled labor in India is higher than it is in the United States. Of course, India has more workers than the United States, but what's more important than India's total population is that India has a great many low-skilled workers who eagerly compete for the job of janitor. A much greater proportion of Indians than Americans, for example, would consider a cleaning job in a modern office building to be a very attractive job. Since many Indians compete for the job of janitor, the wages of janitors are pushed down.

Human Capital

Americans are fortunate to work in a productive economy. But high wages are not just the result of fortunes of birth. Wages within America differ greatly from worker to worker so let's look at some of the reasons why.

Some workers have higher wages than others because they have more human capital. Physical capital is tools like computers, bulldozers, and 3D printers. **Human capital** is tools of the mind, the stuff in people's heads that makes them productive. Human capital is not something we are born with—it is produced by investing time and other resources in education, training, and experience.

Of course, investing in human capital usually costs money; it costs not just what a doctor spends on medical school tuition but what he or she could have earned during those eight years in medical school, namely opportunity cost. But, in general, investments in human capital bring a good return in the United States. In recent years, college graduates have made almost twice as much as high school graduates.

Panel A of Figure 18.5 shows annual wages by education level. Clearly more education, on average, brings a higher wage.

FIGURE 18.5

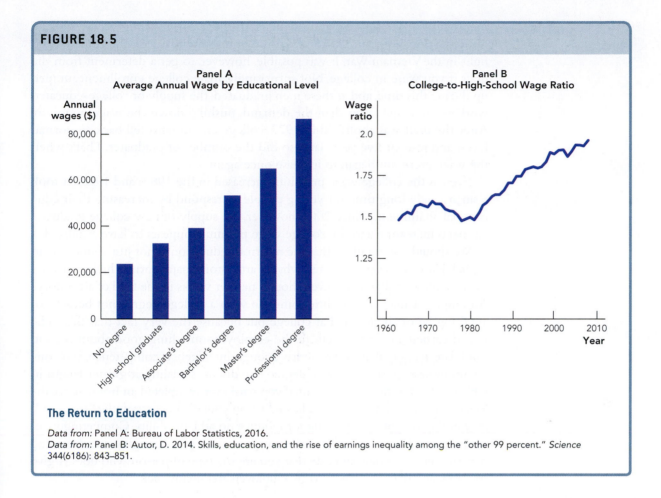

Panel A
Average Annual Wage by Educational Level

Panel B
College-to-High-School Wage Ratio

The Return to Education

Data from: Panel A: Bureau of Labor Statistics, 2016.
Data from: Panel B: Autor, D. 2014. Skills, education, and the rise of earnings inequality among the "other 99 percent." *Science* 344(6186): 843–851.

Panel B shows that the return to a college education has been rising over time. College pays off more now than ever before. The line is the ratio of the wages of college graduates to that of high school graduates, or the "college wage premium." From the 1960s to the 1980s, wages for people with a college degree were approximately 1.5 times higher than the wages of a high school graduate. Today, however, wages for people with a college degree are almost double the wages of a high school graduate, in part because wages for those with college degrees have been going up and also in part because wages for those with just a high school degree have been going down in inflation-adjusted terms.

Why has the return to human capital increased so dramatically? Demand and supply. Today's labor market is demanding and rewarding workers who have numeracy, communication skills, creativity, and technical knowledge. Many of these skills are taught or demonstrated by having a college education. At the same time, the demand for less-skilled labor has been decreasing, in part due to changes in technology such as automation, and in part due to increased trade with countries like China with a large supply of low-skilled labor. The net effect has been an increase in the college wage premium.

The supply of educated labor also matters. Although more workers are college-educated today than ever before, the increase in college-educated workers was faster in the 1960s and 1970s than it was in the 1980s and 1990s. As a result, the college wage premium increased more rapidly in the 1980s and 1990s than in previous decades. By the way, did you notice the fall in the wage premium between 1971 and 1981? The best explanation for this appears to be

Econ Duel: Is Education Signaling or Skill Building?

men who were trying to avoid the draft! In the late 1960s and early 1970s, the United States government forced some young men to join the military and fight in the Vietnam War. It was possible, however, to get a deferment from the draft if you were in college. Not surprisingly, male college enrollment jumped up during this time, and as these men graduated, the supply of college-educated workers increased faster than the demand, pushing down the wage premium. After the draft was abolished in 1973, college enrollments fell back to normal levels and four or five years later so did the number of graduates. That's when the wage premium began to increase once again.

Even as the college wage premium increased in the 1980s and 1990s, it took a surprisingly long time for young people to respond by increasing their educational attainment. Since 2004, however, the supply of new college graduates has been increasing and the college wage premium appears to have stabilized.

We should also mention that the return to education is not just about human capital. Have you ever wondered why an art history major earns a higher income than a high school graduate even though neither works in the field of art history? An employer may want to hire someone with a college degree not because of anything he or she learned at college but because the very fact that this individual earned a degree signals to the employer something good about the job candidate, namely that he or she has enough intelligence, competence, and conscientiousness to earn a college degree (we discuss signaling at greater length in Chapter 24). For the same reasons, if you have ever completed an Ironman triathlon, you might want to subtly indicate that on your résumé (say, under "Interests") even if the job you are applying for requires no athletic ability. Competing in an Ironman triathlon doesn't increase your productivity at managing an advertising department, but it does indicate that you are the type of person who doesn't give up easily and that is a characteristic employers frequently seek.

Compensating Differentials

The supply of labor depends on the real wage, but the real wage of a job includes not just the monetary pay but also how much fun the job is. Some people work for nice bosses; others work for tyrants. Some jobs are dangerous; others are very safe. Some jobs are interesting; others are a bore.

Right now being a fisherman is the most dangerous job in the United States, more dangerous than being a police officer or a firefighter. There are a lot of accidents out on the water. Most of all, a lot of people just slip and fall overboard. Being a truck driver is dangerous, too, mostly because of road accidents. That's why those professions earn relatively high wages, especially given that they do not demand a college degree.[1]

It's simple supply and demand. The danger of a dangerous job reduces the supply of labor, pushing the supply curve for labor to the left and up, as shown in Figure 18.6.

FIGURE 18.6

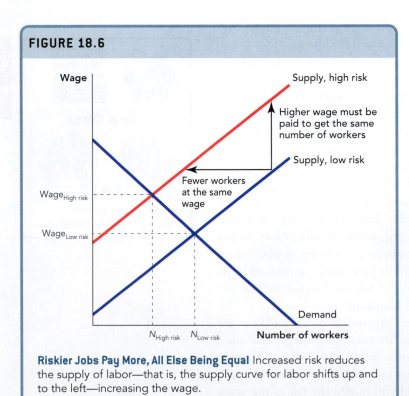

Riskier Jobs Pay More, All Else Being Equal Increased risk reduces the supply of labor—that is, the supply curve for labor shifts up and to the left—increasing the wage.

The resulting wage is higher than it otherwise would be, and that is what economists call a compensating differential. It is called a **compensating differential** because a difference in wages compensates for the difference in working conditions.

A **compensating differential** is a difference in wages that offsets differences in working conditions.

There's a lesson here. People talk all the time about wanting interesting, fun, and rewarding jobs but *beware*: being an accountant might be boring, but all else being equal, that's a sign of higher wages. Being a musician is fun but most musicians don't make a lot of money. The higher wage of accountants compensates for the lack of fun or, equivalently, the greater fun of being an artist compensates for the lack of money.

To see this in more detail, consider the following principle: *Similar jobs must have similar compensation packages.* Imagine that being an accountant or a musician requires similar amounts of skill, education, training, and so forth. Now what would happen if musicians were paid higher wages than accountants? Higher wages *and* more fun can't be beat so the supply of musicians will increase and the supply of accountants will decrease. But the increased supply of musicians will drive down the wages of musicians and the decreased supply of accountants will drive up the wages of accountants. In fact, musician wages will fall and accountant wages will rise until a typical young person deciding on a career will be more or less indifferent: Higher wages and less fun equal lower wages and more fun. Figure 18.7 illustrates the main idea.

Every job has a different combination of wages, benefits, fun, risk, and other conditions. Some workers will choose jobs with less risk but lower wages, while others will prefer jobs with more risk but higher wages. In fact, workers who choose the less risky jobs are "buying" safety with a reduction in their wages. Now consider who is more likely to buy safety, a rich worker or a poor worker?

The rich buy more safety for the same reason they buy more BMWs—buying safety is one of the things that money is good for! We've already noted that

The Tradeoff Between Fun and Wages

FIGURE 18.7

Similar Jobs

Wage | Fun

Accounting

Fun | Wage

Music

Wages Adjust Until Similar Jobs Have Similar Compensation Packages

being a fisherman is a dangerous job. It should come as no surprise that many of these fishermen are recent immigrants to the United States. But it's not the immigrants from wealthy Sweden who take the fishing jobs. Instead, it's poor immigrants from Honduras who concentrate in the fishing trade. These poorer immigrants need the money the most and are less willing to buy safety by taking jobs with lower wages.

The same reasoning explains why jobs in the United States are much safer than similar jobs in poorer countries. Workers in the United States use their wealth to buy more smoke detectors, fire extinguishers, and airbags on their cars and they also "buy" more job safety. Thus, one of the most important reasons why job safety increases over time is economic growth.

In other words, workers become less willing to accept risk as economic growth makes them wealthier. You might take a dangerous job if you need the money to feed your family, but not if you need the money to feed your family at The French Laundry, one of the best and most expensive restaurants in the United States.

Government regulation has improved the quality of American jobs, as well (see below), but increasing wealth and the profit incentive are the main drivers behind this process. Are you surprised that the pursuit of profit leads to *greater* job safety? Remember that firms must pay workers to take on higher risks, the compensating differentials we talked about earlier. But the process works the other way just as well—when firms make jobs safer, they can pay lower wages, thus increasing their profits.

Take a job like coal mining. An American coal miner will earn between $50,000 and $80,000 annually—let's say for purposes of argument, $70,000.[2] If that sounds like a pretty good wage to you, it is because coal mining is not especially fun. But how much would wages have to be if coal mining in the United States were as dangerous as in China, where the mortality rate per ton of coal is 100 times higher? Coal miners might demand $100,000 to take on the extra risk. That's an extra $30,000 per coal miner per year that firms would have to pay because of riskier working conditions. If the mining company can make the mines safer for less than that, obviously their incentive is to invest in safety.

Economists have estimated how much more firms must pay American workers to take on risk and the numbers are very large, by one estimate $245 billion in recent years. In comparison, OSHA (the Occupational Safety and Health Administration), which oversees workplace safety, levies fines every year of about $150 million. These numbers imply that fear of government fines is not that big a cost, compared with having to pay higher wages for riskier jobs. In other words, market competition—employers luring laborers by offering better packages of wages and working conditions—is the major factor in making jobs safer.

Coal mining is a tough job anywhere, but in China the death rate per ton of coal is more than 100 times higher than in the United States.

So, as workers become wealthier and less willing to take on risk, firms have greater incentives to increase job safety—which explains why jobs are safer today than they were in the past and why jobs are safer in wealthier countries than in poorer countries.

The pursuit of profit, however, doesn't always lead to greater safety, which is why government regulation also has a role to play. Compensating differentials give firms an incentive to increase safety only if workers *know* that a job is risky. If workers don't know about or underestimate risk, they won't demand higher wages. A government agency like OSHA can help to ensure that firms do not hide job risks. Even more important, in the United States, firms are required to buy workers' compensation insurance—which pays workers for on-the-job injuries. Crucially, the premiums that firms must pay to buy this insurance are *experienced-based*, which means that the more injuries a firm has, the more it must pay for insurance. Thus, workers' compensation programs give firms an incentive to reduce risk so they can save money on insurance. Since the insurance premiums a firm must pay are based on actual injuries, this incentive works even when workers do not know or underestimate risk.

Do Unions Raise Wages?

It is commonly suggested that unions are a fundamental reason why wages are so high in some countries and so low in other countries. Yet the evidence does not bear out this view. The more unionized countries do not obviously have higher levels of wages. For instance, the United States and Switzerland have much lower levels of unionization (11% and 18%, respectively, in recent years) than does most of Western Europe, where unionization rates can run between 30% and 80%. Yet the United States and Switzerland have equally high or higher wage levels.

It is true that wages in unionized jobs tend to be higher than in nonunionized jobs for similar workers. Studies that compare the wages of unionized electricians to the wages of nonunionized electricians, for example, typically find that unionized electricians have wages about 10% to 15% higher than nonunionized electricians. But this doesn't mean that unions could raise wages in all jobs because the primary method that unions use to raise wages is to reduce industry employment.[3]

If you are wondering how unions raise wages and reduce employment, it is easy to see on a supply and demand graph. By restricting their membership and threatening to strike unless employers hire union labor, unions reduce the supply of labor to an industry. The reduction in labor supply shifts the supply curve for labor to the left and up, as shown in Figure 18.8. Notice that the reduction in the supply of labor increases wages but reduces employment from $N_{\text{Without union}}$ to $N_{\text{With union}}$.

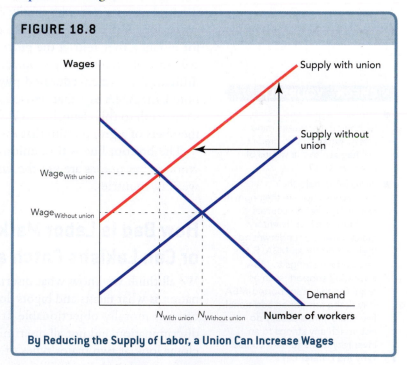

FIGURE 18.8

By Reducing the Supply of Labor, a Union Can Increase Wages

Unions can be beneficial in ensuring that employees are treated fairly and by improving labor/management relations, but the main reason that unions raise wages is through restricting the supply of labor. In this respect, a union is quite similar to a cartel, like those we discussed in Chapter 15. The OPEC oil cartel raises the price of oil by restricting the supply of oil and unions raise the wages of labor by restricting the supply of labor.

Unions also can lower wages, although this effect is more difficult to see. First, consider what happens to the workers who are not hired in the unionized industry—these workers must seek employment in other industries, which increases the supply of labor to those other industries and drives wages down. Second, unions sometimes bring strikes and work stoppages, which can slow down an entire economy. For instance, the British economy was highly unionized from 1970 to 1982; this coincided with Britain's period of long economic decline relative to other nations.[4] In 1970, dockworkers were on strike for so long that it shut down almost all of Britain's main ports. Coal miners went on strike in 1972, which led to a shortage of electricity. A three-day workweek was implemented for a short time to save power. In 1974, the miners went on strike again and a shortened workweek was implemented again. Ten years later, the British experienced another strike that lasted for almost one year. Prime Minister Margaret Thatcher limited the government-supplied privileges of the British unions during the 1980s. Since that time, Britain has grown rapidly and by the 1990s was a wealthier country than the more unionized France or Germany.

When people think of unions, the longshoreman's union or a union of electricians often comes to mind, but it's important to remember that doctors, lawyers, dentists, accountants, and other professionals have their own type of union, called a professional association. The American Medical Association (AMA), for example, works to restrict the supply of physicians for the same reason that an electrician's union works to reduce the supply of electricians. It's very difficult to get into a medical school, for example. The AMA says that restricting the supply of physicians is necessary to maintain high standards. Maybe that is true, but restricting the supply of physicians also maintains high wages. The AMA lobbies for laws that make competing against physicians more difficult; for instance, they restrict the procedures that can be legally performed by nurse practitioners, midwives, chiropractors, and pharmacists, and they make it more difficult for foreign-educated physicians to practice in the United States. As noted, the AMA says that restrictions are necessary to maintain quality; there is some truth to this claim, but, as always, you should be somewhat skeptical when members of a group claim that their high wages are good for you!

The bottom line is this: unions can raise the wages of particular classes of workers, but unions are not the fundamental reason why wages are high in the wealthy countries.

How Bad Is Labor Market Discrimination, or Can Lakisha Catch a Break?

We all think we know what discrimination is. Discrimination is *bad*. Discrimination is what racists and bigots do. And, yes, that is partly right: Discrimination often is morally objectionable. It's also true that there are different types of discrimination and not all discrimination is motivated by prejudice. Let's take a closer look at two major types of discrimination, statistical discrimination and preference-based discrimination.

Statistical Discrimination

Let's say you are walking down a dark alley, late at night, in the warehouse district of your city. Suddenly, you hear footsteps behind you. You turn around and you see an old lady walking her dachshund. Do you breathe a sigh of

CHECK YOURSELF

■ Suppose a new and cheap technology increases mine safety. What do you predict will happen to the wages of mine workers?

■ Firms often help their employees improve their human capital by offering courses on things such as inventory management or underwriting their tuition for an MBA. Firms often attach strings to MBA education support, such as requiring that a supported-MBA stay at the firm for an additional five years. Firms usually do not attach any strings to an inventory management course. Why the difference?

relief? Probably. Would you breathe the same sigh of relief if you saw an angry young man in a dark leather jacket, muttering to himself? What if he was holding a knife? What if he was walking with his two-year-old daughter in a baby stroller?

One way of reading this story is to claim that you are discriminating against young men, relative to old ladies, or relative to young men with baby girls at their side. Another way of describing this story is that you are using information rationally. A mugger is far more likely to be an angry young man in a leather jacket than an old lady walking her dachshund. Maybe both descriptions capture some aspect of the reality, but suddenly discrimination isn't so simple a concept anymore.

Statistical discrimination is using information about group averages to make conclusions about individuals. Not every young man in a leather jacket walking the warehouse district late at night is a mugger and not every young man with a baby girl at his side is safe, but that's the way to bet. Although statistical discrimination is a useful shorthand for making some decisions, it also causes people to make many errors. They refuse to deal with some people they really ought to. They may refuse to hire some people who deserve the job. We gave one example of this earlier—employers may not look carefully at workers without college degrees, even though some of these workers are just as intelligent and industrious as those with college degrees. It is called statistical discrimination because, in essence, the employer is treating the worker as an abstract statistic. Even though statistical discrimination is not motivated by malice, its long-run consequences can be harmful to the penalized groups.

Over time, markets tend to develop more subtle and more finely grained ways of judging people and judging job candidates. An employer can give prospective employees multiple interviews and psychological tests, Google previous histories or writings, look up people on Facebook, ask for more references, and so on, all to get an accurate picture of the person. Eventually, these practices break down the crudest methods of statistical discrimination but, of course, some statistical discrimination always remains.

Statistical discrimination tends to be most persistent when people meet in purely casual settings with no repeat interactions, such as in a dark alley late at night. It is profit-seeking employers, who make money from finding and keeping the best workers, who have the greatest incentive to overcome unfairness.

> **Statistical discrimination** is using information about group averages to make conclusions about individuals.

How many times a day do you discriminate?

TIMOTHY TADDER/GETTY IMAGES

Preference-Based Discrimination

A second kind of discrimination—preference-based discrimination—is based on a plain, flat-out dislike of some group of people, such as a race, religion, or gender. We're going to lay out three different kinds of preference-based discrimination: discrimination by employers, discrimination by customers, and discrimination by employees. The first of these is easiest for a market economy to overcome while the last is the most difficult to solve.

Discrimination by Employers When most people think of discrimination, they think of an employer with bigoted tastes. Some employers just don't want to hire people of a particular race, ethnicity, religion, or gender. If this discrimination is widespread, the wages of people who are discriminated against will fall since the demand for their labor falls. But fortunately, this kind of discrimination, if taken alone, tends to break down for two reasons: Employer discrimination is expensive to the employer and it leaves the bigot open to being outcompeted.

Imagine, for example, that black workers are widely discriminated against and thus that their wages are lower than those of white workers. Say that a firm can hire white workers for $10 an hour or equally productive black workers for $8 an hour. Imagine that the firm needs 100 workers. If it hires black workers instead of white workers, the firm can increase its profits by $2 per hour per worker. Thus, by hiring black workers, the firm can increase its profits by $1,600 per day ($2 saving per hour for 100 workers for 8 hours a day), $8,000 per week (5 days a week), or $400,000 in a year (50 working weeks). Even a prejudiced employer will likely think twice about discriminating when it costs $400,000 a year just to indulge the prejudice.

In fact, the profit-hungry firm could earn *more than* $400,000 by hiring black workers because it could also take advantage of its lower costs to reduce prices and thus sell more output. So, profit-hungry firms benefit discriminated-against workers in two ways. First, they increase the demand for discriminated-against workers, thereby increasing their wages. Second, those firms tend to drive firms that irrationally discriminate out of business.

The logic of profit-maximization implies that employer discrimination is costly, especially in the long run, not that it never happens. Consider, for example, two studies of the job market for low-wage labor in New York City. In 2004, researchers sent paired individuals to apply for jobs—the pairs had equivalent résumés and similar demographics but one person in the pair was black and the other was white. The black applicants received significantly fewer callbacks than the equivalent white applicants. Six years later, the same researchers went back to their data and found that many of the firms that they had studied had gone out of business. But remarkably, 36% of the firms that had discriminated had gone out of business, but only 17% of the nondiscriminating firms had failed. Whether the discriminators failed because they discriminated or because the discriminating firms were simply less well run is unclear, but in either case the market tended to reward the firms that hired rationally and without prejudice. Bigotry is bad for business.*

In 1947, Brooklyn Dodgers General Manager Branch Rickey hired Jackie Robinson to be the first black player in modern major league baseball. Robinson already had extensive experience in what were then called the "Negro leagues," and he proved to be an immediate star. Robinson won the Rookie of the Year award and then in his third season he won the MVP award. The second black player in major league baseball Larry Doby, proved to be a star for the Cleveland Indians. The baseball teams that moved first to hire black players had a competitive advantage and eventually all teams had to follow, whether or not they were run by bigots.

Of course, that story is about baseball, but it applies to the broader world of business, as well. If employer-driven discrimination is depressing the wages of a group of people, you can make money by hiring them.

MLB PHOTOS/GETTY IMAGES

Jackie Robinson, the first African-American to play in modern Major League Baseball Robinson faced great discrimination but he was a profitable hire for the Brooklyn Dodgers.

---

* The two studies are: Pager, Devah, Bruce Western, and Bart Bonikowski. 2009. "Discrimination in a low-wage labor market: A field experiment." *American Sociological Review* 74 (5): 777–799; and Pager, Devah. 2016. "Are firms that discriminate more likely to go out of business?" *Sociological Science* 3: 849–859.

If the pursuit of profit raises wages so that all workers earn their marginal product, why do women earn less than men? It's often said, for example, that women earn about 80 cents per the dollar earned by men. The trouble with this widely reported statistic, however, is that it compares the wages of all women with those of all men—the statistic does not mean that a woman with the same qualifications earns less than a man for doing the same job.

One factor lowering wages for women as a group is that women tend to have less job experience than men of the same age because they sometimes leave the job force, typically to take care of children. In fact, if we compare the wages of single men and single women, single women earn just as much as single men. Married women without children also earn about as much as married men without children.

Men may have specialized in higher-paying fields and they also take more dangerous jobs. Remember those coal miners we discussed earlier with an average wage of $70,000? Most of them are men, perhaps because women prefer jobs with lower wages but less risk.

Over time, women have moved toward higher-paying sectors (more lawyers and economists, for instance) and there has been a long decline in the birth rate. Since women are having fewer children and they are having their children at later ages, that is helping women earn higher wages.

Nevertheless, some discrimination against women may yet remain, but it is probably more subtle than employer discrimination. We need to look at the roles of customers and employees to better understand other forms of discrimination.

Discrimination by Customers When the customers drive discrimination, owners are not always so keen to hire undervalued, victimized workers. If employing underpaid black workers upsets the customers, it's not a surefire way for an employer to earn more money.

Let's revisit the story of Jackie Robinson and Branch Rickey. You might wonder why Branch Rickey hired Robinson in 1947 but not 1946. It's not that one day Branch Rickey stopped being prejudiced against African Americans; he may not have been prejudiced in the first place. Rather, in 1947, Rickey sensed that his ticket-buying customers were ready for the idea of watching a black man play baseball in a Brooklyn Dodgers uniform. The lesson is that sometimes discrimination comes from the customers of a business, not always from the owners or managers.

Or let's consider a lunch counter or hamburger joint in the Deep South in 1957, before the civil rights movement had much influence. Part of the problem was that state laws did not allow mixed-race establishments. But part of the problem came from customers, as well. At that time, many white customers didn't like the idea of eating a hamburger while sitting next to a black person. These white customers demanded separate facilities, so usually there were separate lunch counters and separate restaurants for white and black people in many parts of the United States. The entrepreneur running the lunch counter may or may not have been racist, but in any case the preferences of his customers encouraged him to discriminate and to keep out black patrons.

Don't make the mistake of thinking customer-based discrimination has vanished from modern America. It's usually done in a more subtle manner, but many country clubs, restaurants, and other businesses try to encourage "the right kind of customers." They're not always concerned about race per se, but often they seek customers who dress a certain way, have the right kind of jobs, come from the right part of town, and so on. The result is sometimes de facto segregation, even though the restaurant or country club owner is simply responding to the preferences of his consumers for a particular cultural style or "feel."

By the way, the decline of employer-based discrimination, through market forces, also tends to weaken customer-based discrimination. Marketplace transactions bring different groups into regular contact with each other. Many white people who started listening to black music on the jukebox in the 1950s, or who saw Jackie Robinson play baseball, started asking themselves what was so wrong with integrated lunch counters. Discrimination is also weakened by economic growth more generally. For instance, declining costs of production make it possible for businesses to take more chances. If a small town has only two lunch counters, maybe neither will take a chance with integration. If the town grows and also the costs of starting a new business fall, suddenly there are seven lunch counters. Maybe one will experiment with integration. In the long run, no successful market economy has succeeded in maintaining widespread formal segregation.

Discrimination by Employees Customers and employers aren't the only possible sources of discrimination. Sometimes workers don't want to mix with people from different groups. In India, many workers don't want to work alongside Dalits, workers from a low caste who are considered impure. In the United States, some firefighters—rightly or wrongly—don't want women to have equal status in the firehouse. Similarly, some men in the armed forces don't think that women or gay men should serve in combat and some men are looked on with suspicion if they want to work at a day care center.

The profit incentive doesn't necessarily break down discrimination of this kind. An employer in India who hires Dalits, for example, may find that he has to pay other workers a higher wage to compensate them for the negative of working with Dalits. As a result, it's cheaper to discriminate than to hire everyone equally. Similarly, if you hire a woman into an all-male firehouse that doesn't want women, morale may fall and some men may leave for other jobs. As a result, employers are less likely to hire a person, even a productive person, from the victimized group.

Of course, an employer might hire only Dalits, or if women are not welcome in firehouses, an employer may set up an entirely new firehouse, one equipped with women and nonprejudiced men, but starting from scratch in this fashion isn't always so easy to do.

Discrimination of this kind can be self-reinforcing and difficult to identify. If it's unpleasant for women to work in firehouses, then many women who want to be firefighters won't want to work in firehouses. Few women are hired but employers might say that's because few women are applying. Maybe it won't look like discrimination at all, but discrimination will still be a force at work.

Discrimination by Government

So far we've been talking about discrimination in markets but it's important to remember that governments discriminate, too. Government is sometimes part of the problem rather than part of the solution. We've already mentioned that prosegregation policies in the American South, before the civil rights movement, often came from governments. Governments required separate hospitals for black and white patients, separate public and private schools, separate churches, separate cemeteries, separate public restrooms, and separate restaurants, hotels, and train service. Before prosegregation laws were passed after the Civil War, many parts of the South were moving (albeit sometimes hesitantly) toward more integration.

Government discrimination didn't just occur in the U.S. South. The Federal government also routinely discriminated against African-Americans. The Federal Housing Administration (FHA), for example, was set up during the Great Depression to insure home mortgages thereby encouraging more mortgage lending. But, until 1968, the FHA restricted its subsidies to all-white neighborhoods and refused to insure loans to blacks or even to whites in integrated neighborhoods. This practice of "redlining" made it more difficult and expensive for blacks to obtain mortgages and it encouraged segregated neighborhoods.

The best known example of widespread government segregation was the apartheid system of South Africa, which was enforced from 1948 until the early 1990s. ("Apartheid" is a word in the Afrikaaner language that translates literally as "apartness.") Under this arrangement, black people had to live in special areas and could not compete with white workers for many jobs. But this highly unjust situation was enforced by government laws, and enacted by white minority governments (black citizens also couldn't vote). Once those laws were removed, black people moved into many jobs and received higher wages. Many forms of implicit segregation continue in South Africa, but some of the most egregious examples of discrimination have fallen away. Many employers are happy to hire the most productive workers they can find, regardless of the skin color or ethnic background of those workers.

Why Discrimination Isn't Always Easy to Identify

Two economists had a neat idea. They sent around two sets of identical résumés. On one set of résumés, the names were quite traditional and did not identify the background of the person applying. An applicant named "John Smith," for instance, could be either white or black. The second set of résumés had more unusual names on them—names like "Lakisha Washington" or "Jamal Jones." As you may know, those are names closely associated with African Americans. Names can tell you a lot about who a person is. In recent years, more than 40% of the black girls born in California were given names that, in those same years, not one of the roughly 100,000 white newly born California girls was given.*

The result was striking: the resumes with the black names received many fewer interview requests. The job applicants with the "whiter" names received 50% more calls.

But that is not the end of the story. Steven Levitt (of *Freakonomics* fame) and Roland Fryer (a Harvard professor and an African American) set out to test how much African American names really mattered in the long run for earnings. It seems that having a "black name" does not appear to hurt a person's chances in life, once the neighborhood that person comes from is controlled for. In other words, the number of interviews a person gets at first may not matter so much in the long run. Levitt and Fryer consider two possibilities. It may be that the so-called black names get fewer interviews, but they end up with jobs of equal quality. Alternatively, people with African American–sounding names may have fewer chances in white communities but greater chances in black communities; the two tendencies might balance each other out.

One point to note is that in the résumé experiment, by far the most common outcome of submitting a résumé, for both the white and black candidates and regardless of name, was not receiving any interview requests at all.

---

* That is from Bertrand, Marianne, and Sendhil Mullainathan. 2004. "Are Emily and Greg more employable than Lakisha and Jamal? A field experiment on labor market discrimination." *The American Economic Review* 94(4): 991–1013. For the earnings study, see Fryer Jr., Roland G., and Steven D. Levitt. 2002. "The causes and consequences of distinctively black names." *Quarterly Journal of Economics* 119(3): 767–805.

The lesson is that just about everyone can expect a lot of rejection before they find the job that is right for them.

Did you know that good-looking people earn more, even if they have the same job credentials? That's right, good-looking people earn about 5% more. Tall people earn more, too, again if they are compared with shorter people with the same paper credentials. Under one account, an extra inch in height translates into a 1.8% increase in wages.*

But these studies also show just how difficult it is to identify true discrimination. For instance, maybe tall people are paid more because they are more self-confident and not because anyone discriminates against shorter people. One study found that what best predicts wages, in this context, is *the height a man had at the time of high school* and not the height he ends up with as an adult. So if you were a tall person in high school, maybe that built up your self-confidence and makes you a better leader today, even if you stopped growing while your friends kept on getting taller.[†]

One question is why employers might prefer to hire tall people and to pay them more. One possibility is simply that the employer has an unreasonable preference against shorter people. Another possibility is that the employer is subconsciously tricked into thinking the taller leader is better, without ever realizing it. Yet another option is that the taller leader really is better (for the firm) because subordinates are more likely to pay that person respect. Again, we don't know the right answer, and this illustrates just how difficult it is to estimate the scope of labor market discrimination.

In many cases, market forces have succeeded in making some discrimination go away, or at least markets have minimized some of the bad effects of discrimination. But few people doubt that discrimination remains a feature of our world today.

GARY SALTER/CORBIS/GLOW IMAGES

Did the man on the left get the better deal?

CHECK YOURSELF

■ From a profit-making perspective, why is employer discrimination just plain dumb?

■ Of the three types of discrimination—employer, customer, employee—which has been affected most by market economies? Which has been affected least? Why?

Takeaway

It is no accident that workers in some countries earn much more than workers in other countries. Workers in wealthy, high-wage countries work with more physical capital, they have more education and training (human capital), and they work in a more efficient and flexible setting. Those are the fundamental reasons why wages are high.

The theory of compensating differentials explains why fun jobs pay less and dangerous jobs pay more. As wealth increases, workers become more willing to give up money for safety and so job safety increases over time and is higher in wealthier countries than in poorer countries.

Unions can raise some workers' wages, often at the expense of other workers, but unions are not a fundamental reason why wages are high in wealthy countries.

At least two kinds of discrimination occur in labor markets, statistical discrimination and preference-based discrimination. Markets tend to break down discrimination over time, because profit-seeking employers are looking to hire the most productive workers. Nonetheless, this force is imperfect and some discrimination persists.

---

* For a survey of this literature, see Engemann, Kristie M., and Michael T. Owyang. April, 2005. "So much for that merit raise: The link between wages and appearance." *The Regional Economist.* http://www.stlouisfed.org/publications/re/2005/b/pdf/appearance.pdf
† Persico, Nicola, Andrew Postlewaite, and Dan Silverman. 2004. "The effect of adolescent experience on labor market outcomes: The case of height." *Journal of Political Economy*, 112(5): 1019–1053.

CHAPTER REVIEW

 interactive activity Go online to practice with more examples of these types of problems, including live links to videos, data sources, and feedback.

Problems in green relate to MRU videos. See the MRU table at the end of the exercises.

KEY CONCEPTS

marginal product of labor (MPL), p. 341

human capital, p. 346

compensating differential, p. 349

statistical discrimination, p. 353

FACTS AND TOOLS

1. In Chapter 3, we listed six important demand shifters. Since the demand for labor is like the demand for any other good, those same factors apply here. Let's look at factors that might shift the demand for janitors at the McDonald's we discussed. For each of the following cases, state whether labor demand will rise or fall, and also state which of the six factors seems to be causing the shift in demand.

   a. A new junior high school opens up across the street from the McDonald's.

   b. Customers become much more concerned about clean restaurants: They'll walk out if there's dirt on the floor.

   c. As robots like the Roomba vacuum cleaner become cheaper, the McDonald's buys some robots to do half of the janitors' work.

2. Now let's do the same with shifts in Joe's labor supply from Figure 18.2. We listed five important supply shifters in Chapter 3. For each example, state whether you think Joe's labor supply will tend to increase or decrease as a result of the change, and state which of the five factors seem to cause the supply shift.

   a. The government raises Joe's income tax rate, so now he pays 20% of his wages to the government instead of the old 10%.

   b. The price of comfortable work shoes falls dramatically. Now, his feet won't ache nearly as much after a full day of work.

   c. While in Las Vegas for the weekend, Joe wins a $1 million jackpot.

3. Let's apply the idea of compensating differentials to janitorial jobs. Suppose there are two quite similar restaurants in the same town, OrangeBee's and the City Inn. Both have the same demand for janitorial labor. But all the janitors in town know that it's much more fun to work at City Inn.

   a. Which restaurant will pay a higher wage for janitors? Why?

   b. Which restaurant will hire more jani-tors? Why?

4. According to the theory of compensating differentials, which low-skilled jobs in the United States will tend to pay the most:

   a. The safe jobs or the dangerous jobs?

   b. The fun jobs or the boring jobs?

   c. The dead-end jobs or the first-rung-on-the-ladder jobs?

5. As mentioned, OSHA fines companies for unsafe workplaces. At the same time, the labor market also "fines" companies that give their workers dangerous jobs. The fines of the marketplace are larger than the U.S. government's fines by about what factor: a factor of 10, of 100, of 1,000, or of 10,000?

6. The director of human resources at ToyCo is hiring new engineers. She's got a stack of 250 applications, and she's going to do a little research. She sits down and does a little cyber-snooping on all 250, and she finds the following:

   i. Of the 150 who have Facebook pages, 50 are holding a bottle of beer in their profile photo, and 100 aren't.

   ii. Of the 100 who have their own Web sites, 20 have more than two typos.

   iii. Of the 150 who have Facebook pages, 25 have at least two friends who have apparently spent time in prison, according to a quick check of public records.

   a. Each of these are cases of sending bad signals. In each case, describe what you think these might be signals of.

b. In each case, is the bad signal 100% correct? For example, is every applicant with three or four typos on their personal Web site worse than every applicant with an error-free page?

c. In each case, is the bad signal probably better or probably worse than having no signal at all? In other words, should the bad signal get at least a little bit of weight in the balance if the HR director's only goal is to hire the best workers?

7. It is commonly said that women earn 80 cents for every dollar that a man earns, even when doing the same job. Let's assume this is literally true in order to see how an entrepreneur would respond to this fact.

a. Netrovia, a battery manufacturer, has an all-male workforce. It pays $10 million per year in salary to these men, and has annual profits of $1 million. You've just been hired as an outside consultant to help Netrovia raise its profits. Your advice is to fire all the men and replace them with women. If Netrovia followed your advice, what would Netrovia's salary costs fall to? How much would this decision raise Netrovia's profits?

b. After your success at Netrovia, you start getting a lot more consulting jobs. You give the same advice to all the companies looking to boost profits: Fire your men and hire an all-female workforce for 20% less. What will this do to the demand for female labor? And what will this tend to do to women's wages?

8. Michael Lynn, a social psychologist in Cornell's School of Hotel Administration, has spent years studying tipping (his homepage has well tested advice on how to increase your tips). He finds that men tip more when they have a female server, while women tend to tip more when they have a male server. This sounds a lot like discrimination by customers.

a. If this is a fact, who will tend to apply for jobs waiting tables at truck stops: mostly men or mostly women?

b. If this is a fact, who will tend to apply for jobs waiting tables at steakhouses: mostly men or mostly women?

c. If this is a fact, who will tend to apply for jobs waiting tables at vegetarian restaurants: mostly men or mostly women?

d. In these three cases, does your experience match up with what this simple theory

predicts? If there's a contradiction, what do you think the simple model is missing?

9. True or false?

a. The marginal product of labor is the amount of extra profit that a firm will earn if it hires one more worker.

b. The benefit of having a college education has increased since the 1960s.

c. The wage gap between high school graduates and high school dropouts is insignificant.

d. By definition, a labor supply curve cannot have a negative slope.

e. Compensating differentials is a government program that pays injured workers.

f. The main reason that an immigrant earns more when he moves from Algeria to France is because the French have strong labor unions.

g. If customers are racist and sexist, then self-interest will tend to push entrepreneurs to engage in racist and sexist hiring.

h. If some employers are bigots but others are not, the bigoted employers will be able to hire good workers for less money and will tend to drive the fair-minded employers out of business.

THINKING AND PROBLEM SOLVING

10. Construction jobs in New Chongqing pay $20 per hour. The job isn't that safe: a lot of sharp objects, a lot of ways to fall off a building. The city council of New Chongqing decides to set some job safety regulations for the construction industry. Let's assume that the government enforces these new regulations effectively and fairly, so that half as many workers get hurt on the job. Let's also assume that the city council makes the taxpayers pay the cost of making these jobs safer, so there's no noticeable shift in the labor demand curve.

a. After these new job safety regulations come into effect, will workers be more willing to take these jobs than before or less willing than before?

b. Is that like a rise in the supply of labor or like a fall in the supply of labor?

c. Let's put it all together: What will these job safety regulations do to the wage for construction jobs in New Chongqing?

d. What principle from this chapter does this illustrate?

e. In the United States, OSHA doesn't make taxpayers pay the cost of making jobs safer. Instead, OSHA requires employers to spend the money themselves to make their firm's jobs safer. Thus, OSHA requirements work like a tax on labor demand. What would this probably do to the demand curve for construction labor: Would it increase or decrease construction labor demand?

11. One way to think about wages for different jobs is to see it as another application of the law of one price. We came across this law when we discussed speculation in Chapter 7, and it came up again when we discussed international trade in Chapter 9. The basic idea is that the supply of workers will keep adjusting until jobs that need the same kinds of workers earn the same wage. If *similar* workers earned *different* wages, then the workers in the low-paid jobs would reduce their labor supply, and the workers in the high-paid jobs would face more competition from those low-paid workers.

Let's look at 100 computer programmers who are trying to decide whether to work for one of two companies: Robotron or Korrexia. To keep things simple, assume that both companies are equally fun to work for, so you don't need to worry about compensating differentials here. The marginal product of labor (per additional hour of work) is in the following table:

Number of Programmers per Firm	Robotron's MPL ($)	Korrexia's MPL ($)
10	200	110
20	150	80
30	120	60
40	110	50
50	80	40
60	60	20
70	50	10
80	40	0
90	20	0
100	10	0

a. These two firms are the whole market for programmer labor. In the next table, estimate the programmer demand curve by adding up the quantity of programmers demanded at each wage. For example, at a wage of $80 per hour, Robotron would hire 50 workers (since the first 50 workers have an MPL ≥ 80) and Korrexia 20, so the total demand is 70 workers.

Wage ($)	Number of Programmers Demanded
200	10
150	
120	
110	
80	50 + 20 = 70
60	
50	
40	
20	
10	

b. The programmers in this town are going to work at one of these two places for sure: Their labor supply is vertical, or in other words, perfectly inelastic, with supply = 100. So, what will the equilibrium wage be? Just as in Figure 18.1, the numbers may not work out exactly—so use your judgment to come up with a good answer.

c. Now, head back to the first table: About how many programmers will work at Robotron and how many at Korrexia? Again, use your judgment to come up with a good answer.

d. Suppose 50 more programmers come to town. What will the wage be now? And how many will work at each firm?

12. We've seen what happens when job safety regulations are imposed. Now let's see what happens when they're taken away.

a. If a radical free-market, antiregulation government comes to power in the land of Pelerania, and it begins dismantling job safety regulations, what will this tend to do to the supply of labor for dangerous jobs in Pelerania: Will it increase or decrease?

b. Will that push wages in dangerous jobs up or down?

c. What will this do to the supply of labor in safer jobs? And to the number of people working in safer jobs?

d. Overall, will employers have to pay for their decision to offer dangerous jobs, or will they have a free lunch handed to them by the new government?

13. As we saw, unions can raise wages in a sector of the economy by restricting the number of workers in that sector. Let's see what tends to happen to the workers who don't get jobs in those favored unionized sectors. We'll recycle the computer programmer data to illustrate:

Number of Programmers per Firm	Robotron's MPL ($)	Korrexia's MPL ($)
10	200	110
20	150	80
30	120	60
40	110	50
50	80	40
60	60	20
70	50	10
80	40	0
90	20	0
100	10	0

a. As before, there are 100 workers. In 2084, after decades of complaining about low wages, the programmers at Robotron have a secret-ballot vote and form a union. Their new union bargains for a wage of $80 per hour, and the newly unionized programmers are very excited. How many workers will Robotron hire at the new, higher wage?

b. How many Robotron workers just got laid off? Compare your answer to part a against the answer to question 11c to find out.

c. A natural choice for the other programmers is to look for work at Korrexia: As before, the remaining workers have perfectly inelastic labor supply, so all 100 workers are going to work at one of the two firms. What's the wage for the nonunion Korrexia workers? How many programmers work for Korrexia?

d. You might think that one solution is to unionize both firms and lift wages for all the programmers. If the unions negotiate a high-wage contract and unionized wages rise to $110 at both firms, how many of the 100 workers will have jobs?

14. Suppose that we tax CEO salaries very highly, as some are proposing in the United States. What is your prediction about CEO perks such as jets and in-house chefs?

15. **a.** The average person doesn't like working the night shift. According to the theory of compensating differentials, are night-shift wages probably higher or lower than day-shift wages?

b. Most companies do their high-skilled work during the day shift: The big meetings, the major deliveries, the crucial repair work—all get done during the day. As a result, firms prefer to hire workers with more human capital during day-shift work, and they prefer to hire less-skilled workers at night. According to the theory of human capital, are night-shift wages probably higher or lower than day-shift wages?

c. Just based on these two theories, will night-shift work pay more than day-shift work on average, will it pay less on average, or can't you tell with the information given?

d. Economist Peter Kostiuk, in a 1990 article in the *Journal of Political Economy*, wanted to see whether the theory of compensating differentials was true for U.S. workers. He had information on the wages, education backgrounds, and work experience of U.S. workers, and he knew whether they worked the day shift or the night shift. On average, those who worked the night shift actually earned about 4% *less* than workers on the day shift. Is this probably because of compensating differentials, or is it probably because of human capital differences?

e. Kostiuk then used statistical techniques to simulate how much a typical low-skilled worker would earn if he were switched from the day shift to the night shift. The answer? The low-skilled worker would earn 44% *more* money, on average. Is this 44% wage increase caused by lower supply of night-shift labor, or is it caused by a higher demand for night-shift labor?

16. True or false? Morticians are paid lower wages than other workers because very few people want to work with dead bodies.

17. One way that Jim Crow segregation laws operated was by providing worse government schools for black students. This widened the human capital gap between black workers and white workers (this human capital gap has narrowed dramatically since the successes of the 1960s Civil Rights Movement). Would this form of government segregation tend to increase statistical discrimination on the basis of race or lower it? How can you tell?

18. In the United States, it's legal to work for free: We call this an "unpaid internship."

    a. Why will college students take these zero-wage jobs when they could get a minimum wage job instead?

    b. Which idea in this chapter does this sound like?

    c. Just for thought: Why do you think federal law allows people to work for free, but not for $1 per hour? Is it just an oversight on the part of government, or do you think there's some grand design at work?

CHALLENGES

19. In the decades after the Civil War, most streetcar companies in the South discriminated against one class of citizens: smokers. Customers who wanted to smoke had to ride in the back of the car. Around 1900, many governments in the South passed laws mandating segregation by race instead. As Jennifer Roback documented in the *Journal of Economic History* in 1986, many streetcar operators protested against this new form of segregation. Assuming that these entrepreneurs were driven by self-interest alone rather than a desire for equality, why would they do that?

20. We mentioned that "a [college] degree signals... something good about the job candidate, namely that they have enough intelligence, competence, and conscientiousness to earn a college degree." This view, put forward by Nobel laureate Michael Spence, is unsurprisingly known as the signaling theory of education. Taken to the extreme, signaling theorists say that you suffer through college not because you get valuable job skills, but only because it's a good way to prove that you were *already* smart and capable before you started college.

    a. Suppose you want to prove this theory wrong: You want to show that college courses really do make you a better worker, just like the human capital theorists say. How would you go about proving that? Remember, just showing that college graduates earn more isn't evidence!

    b. If that's too difficult, at least explain why the following plausible-sounding tests of human capital vs. signaling aren't very good tests at all:

    i. Looking at wages of people with degrees compared with people without degrees

    ii. Comparing wages for people whose parents can afford college with wages for people whose parents can't afford college

21. In a market economy, firms with more workers can make and sell more output—that goes without saying. The marginal product of labor tells you how much extra revenue each extra worker generates. Economists tend to use one particular equation to sum up the link between workers, revenue, and the marginal product of labor: We call it the production function. Let's practice with it just a little here.

    a. At Dunder Mifflin, the hourly revenue production function works like this:

$$\text{Revenue} = 100 \times \sqrt{\text{(Number of semiskilled workers)}}$$

    This is a way of saying that in order to sell product, you actually need workers to do work. Use this formula to fill out the "Total Revenue" column in the next table.

Number of Workers	Total Revenue ($)	Marginal Product of Labor ($)
0	0	N/A
1	100	100
2	141	41
3		
4		
5		

b. As we mentioned in the chapter, the marginal product of labor is the extra revenue that's generated by each extra worker. It's the change in revenue from adding one more worker. Fill out that column, as well.

c. If the market wage for semiskilled workers is $25 per hour, how many workers should Dunder Mifflin hire?

22. In Chapter 8, we analyzed a minimum wage in the usual way, as a price floor, and we showed that a minimum wage creates unemployment. Now suppose that firms must pay the minimum wage but they can adjust the working conditions, such as increasing the pace of work, reducing lunch breaks, cutting back on employee discounts, and so forth. Will the minimum wage create (as much) unemployment if firms adjust in this way? (*Hint:* Think of the balance in Figure 18.7.)

Ask FRED

23. Using the FRED Economic database (https://fred.stlouisfed.org/), find the median weekly earnings of high school graduates (no college) who are 25 years of age or over. Click Edit Graph then Add Line, and add the median weekly earnings of people with a bachelor's degree or higher who are 25 years of age or older.

a. In the first quarter of 2016, what were the weekly earnings of high school graduates without a college degree? What were the weekly earnings of college graduates?

b. What accounts for the different weekly earnings?

WORK IT OUT

For interactive, step-by-step help in solving this problem, go online.

One way to think about wages for different jobs is to see it as another application of the law of one price. We came across this law when we discussed speculation in Chapter 7, and it came up again when we discussed international trade

in Chapter 9. The basic idea is that the supply of workers will keep adjusting until jobs that need the same kinds of workers earn the same wage. If *similar* workers earned *different* wages, then the workers in the low-paid jobs would reduce their labor supply, and the workers in the high-paid jobs would face more competition from those low-paid workers.

Let's look at 100 computer programmers who are trying to decide whether to work for one of two companies: Robotron or Korrexia. To keep things simple, assume that both companies are equally fun to work for, so you don't need to worry about compensating differentials here. The marginal product of labor (per additional hour of work) is in the following table:

Number of Programmers per Firm	Robotron's MPL ($)	Korrexia's MPL ($)
10	100	55
20	75	40
30	60	30
40	55	25
50	40	20
60	30	10
70	25	5
80	20	0
90	10	0
100	5	0

a. These two firms are the whole market for programmer labor. In the next table, estimate the programmer demand curve by adding up the quantity of programmers demanded at each wage. For example, at a wage of $40 per hour, Robotron would hire 50 workers (since the first 50 workers have a MPL ≥ 40) and Korrexia 20, so the total demand is 70 workers.

Wage ($)	Number of Programmers Demanded
100	10
75	
60	
55	
40	50 + 20 = 70
30	
25	
20	
10	
5	

b. The programmers in this town are going to work at one of these two places for sure: Their labor supply is vertical, or in other words, perfectly inelastic, with supply = 100. So, what will the equilibrium wage be? Just as in Figure 18.1, the numbers may not work out exactly—so use your judgment to come up with a good answer.

c. Now, head back to the first table: About how many programmers will work at Robotron and how many at Korrexia? Again, use your judgment to come up with a good answer.

d. Suppose 50 more programmers come to town. What will the wage be now? And how many will work at each firm?

MRUNIVERSITY
AN ONLINE EDUCATION PLATFORM

MARGINAL REVOLUTION UNIVERSITY VIDEOS

The Marginal Product of Labor
mruniversity.com/marginal-product-labor
Problems: **9, 11, 13, 21**

Human Capital and Signaling
mruniversity.com/signaling-human-capital
Problems: **6, 17, 18, 20**

The Tradeoff Between Fun and Wages: No Such Thing as a Free Lunch
mruniversity.com/tradeoff
Problems: **3, 5, 7, 8, 12, 16, 22**

Compensating Differentials
mruniversity.com/comp-differentials
Problems: **4, 9, 10, 14, 15**

Do Unions Raise Wages?
mruniversity.com/unions
Problems: **13**

19

Public Goods and the Tragedy of the Commons

Armageddon almost happened on September 29, 2004. We aren't talking about the final battle described in the Bible, but what happened in *Armageddon* the movie. In *Armageddon*, an asteroid is discovered to be on a collision course with Earth and NASA recruits a group of roughneck oil drillers to rocket into space, deflect the asteroid, and save civilization. *Armageddon* the movie is a bit absurd, but it got a few things right. Even an asteroid the size of an apartment building would hit Earth with the force of a 4-megaton nuclear bomb. On September 29, 2004, an asteroid called Toutatis, 2.9 *miles* long by 1.5 *miles* wide, narrowly missed Earth. If Toutatis had hit, it would have meant the end of civilization.

The probability of death by asteroid is remarkably high—by some calculations about the same as death by passenger aircraft crash. How can this be? Although the probability of an asteroid hitting Earth is very small, a lot of people would be killed if one did hit, so the probability of death by asteroid is much larger than most people imagine. It doesn't happen very often but watch out when it does.*

Let's assume that we have convinced you that the danger from an asteroid collision is real and thus that asteroid deflection would be a valuable good to have. Markets provide us with all kinds of valuable goods like food, clothing, and cell phones, but you can't buy asteroid deflection in the market. Even if everyone were to become convinced of the benefits of asteroid deflection, you probably will *never* be able to buy asteroid deflection in the market. To see why, we need to take a closer look at some of the common properties of ordinary goods and some of the special properties of asteroid deflection.

When you spend $100 on a new pair of jeans, you get the exclusive use of a new pair of jeans. If you don't spend $100 on a new pair of jeans, you are excluded from using the jeans. In other words, the $100 makes a big difference in whether or not you get the jeans. That's obvious.

Public Goods and Asteroid Defense

interactive activity

---

* Everyone dies from something. In the United States, the probability of death by car crash is about 1 in 100 and the probability of death by commercial airplane crash is about 1 in 20,000. Chapman and Morrison (1994) estimate that the probability of death by asteroid collision is also about 1 in 20,000. See Chapman, Clark and David Morrison. 1994. Impacts on the earth by asteroids and comets: Assessing the hazard. *Nature* 367: 33–40.

Now consider paying $100 toward asteroid deflection. What do you get for your $100? There are really only two situations to consider: Either enough other people pay for asteroid deflection so that the asteroid will be deflected even without your $100 or so few other people pay that the asteroid will not be deflected even with your $100.* Either way, your $100 makes no appreciable difference in the amount of asteroid deflection that you will receive. In other words, you get the same amount of asteroid deflection whether you pay or don't pay.

Since your $100 doesn't get you more asteroid deflection but it does get you a new pair of jeans, most people will buy the jeans rather than the asteroid deflection. As a result, we see a lot of firms selling jeans and none selling asteroid deflection. That's a problem because asteroids are a threat to everyone on the planet.

Jeans are an example of a private good. Asteroid deflection is an example of what economists call a public good, a good that markets are unlikely to produce in efficient quantities. Let's look more closely at these terms and the differences between jeans and asteroid deflection.

Four Types of Goods

Jeans are different from asteroid deflection for two reasons. First, as we said, people are willing to pay for jeans because paying makes the difference between getting the jeans or not—nonpayers can be cheaply excluded or prevented from consuming jeans. But people aren't willing to pay for asteroid deflection because paying makes no appreciable difference in how much asteroid deflection they consume—nonpayers cannot be excluded from consuming the benefits of asteroid deflection. When a person can easily be prevented from using a good, economists say the good is excludable. When a person cannot be easily prevented from using a good, economists say the good is **nonexcludable**. Jeans are excludable; asteroid deflection is nonexcludable.

> A good is **nonexcludable** if people who don't pay cannot be easily prevented from using the good.

The second reason why asteroid deflection is different from jeans is that when one person is wearing a pair of jeans, it's not easy for a second person to wear the same jeans. But two people can enjoy the benefits of the same asteroid deflection. In fact, billions of people can enjoy the benefits of the same asteroid deflection. But don't try fitting a billion people into the same pair of jeans!

When one person's use of a good reduces the ability of another person to use the same good, economists say the good is rival. When one person's use of a good does not reduce the ability of another person to use the same good, economists say the good is **nonrival**. Jeans are rival; asteroid deflection is nonrival.

> A good is **nonrival** if one person's use of the good does not reduce the ability of another person to use the same good.

These two factors, whether a good is excludable or nonexcludable and whether it is rival or nonrival, can be used to divide goods into four types, as in Table 19.1. We have already given an example of a private good, a good that is excludable and rival. Jeans are a private good; hamburgers and contact lenses are other familiar examples. We have also given one example of a public good, a good that is nonexcludable and nonrival. Asteroid deflection is nonexcludable and nonrival. National defense is another example. Let's take a closer look at the differences between private and public goods and then we will examine the other two categories of goods, club goods and common resources.

---

* The probability that your $100 makes the difference between a successful asteroid deflection and an unsuccessful asteroid deflection is so small that we can ignore it.

TABLE 19.1 FOUR TYPES OF GOODS

	Excludable	Nonexcludable
Rival	**Private Goods** Jeans Hamburgers Contact lenses	**Common Resources** Tuna in the ocean The environment Public roads
Nonrival	**Club Goods** Cable TV Wi-Fi Digital music	**Public Goods** Asteroid deflection National defense Mosquito control

Private Goods and Public Goods

Private goods are excludable and rival. Since private goods are excludable, they can be provided by markets—someone who doesn't pay, doesn't get; so there is an incentive to pay for and thus to produce these goods. Furthermore, since the goods are rival, excludability doesn't result in inefficiency—in a competitive market the only people who will be excluded from consuming a private good are the people who are not willing to pay what it costs to produce the good, and that's efficient.

Public goods are nonexcludable and nonrival. Since public goods are nonexcludable, it's difficult to get people to pay for them voluntarily. Markets, therefore, will tend to underprovide public goods.

Public goods are also nonrival, which means that one person's use doesn't reduce the ability of another person to use the good. As a result, 7 billion people can be protected from an asteroid strike for the same cost as protecting 1 million people. Since public goods are nonrival, the losses from the failure to provide these goods can be especially large.

Let's look at another public good, mosquito control. Mosquitoes are annoying insects. With the spread of the West Nile virus in the United States, they are also dangerous. Mosquitoes can be killed by spraying, but spraying just one house won't do much good for its owners because mosquitoes from other areas will quickly repopulate any small region, so you have to spray a city or neighborhood. But who will pay to spray a city or neighborhood? If some people do pay, then many others are likely to **free ride,** sit back and enjoy the benefits without contributing to their share of the costs. Fewer mosquitoes mean fewer mosquitoes for everyone, not just those who pay for mosquito control. If a lot of people free ride, then mosquito control will be underprovided by the market even though it is a valuable good.

The benefits of public goods provide an argument for taxation and government provision. By taxing everyone and producing the public good, government can make people better off. Many cities and counties, for example, pay for mosquito control from government tax revenues. National defense is another example of a public good that would be difficult to provide voluntarily but is provided by government.

Private goods are excludable and rival.

Public goods are nonexcludable and nonrival.

A **free rider** enjoys the benefits of a public good without paying a share of the costs.

The English philosopher Thomas Hobbes (1588–1679) explained under what conditions individuals might voluntarily give up their rights.

I authorise and give up my right of governing myself to this man, or to this assembly of men, on this condition; that thou give up, thy right to him, and authorise all his actions in like manner.

— *Leviathan*, Chapter 17

A **forced rider** is someone who pays a share of the costs of a public good but who does not enjoy the benefits.

It may seem paradoxical that people can be made better off by requiring them to do something that they would not choose to do voluntarily, but the paradox can be resolved. Imagine that there are a million people, all of whom want national defense, but none of whom chooses to voluntarily contribute to national defense because of the incentive to free ride. Now imagine that this group is offered the following plan: "The government will tax each of you and use the proceeds to pay for national defense but only if you all agree to the plan." It's quite possible that even though none contribute voluntarily, all will agree to be taxed, *so long as everyone else is also taxed*.

Of course, just because everyone *can* be made better off by taxation does not mean that everyone *will* be made better off. Some people want more national defense, some people want less, pacifists want none. So, taxation means that some people will be turned into **forced riders,** people who must contribute to the public good even though their benefits from the public good are low or even negative.

What quantity of the public good should the government produce? In principle, the government should produce the amount that maximizes consumer plus producer surplus or the total benefits of the public good minus the total costs. But, in practice, figuring this out is very difficult. The total benefit of a public good, for example, is the sum of the benefits to each individual. But some individuals value the public good more than others and there is no easy way to find out exactly how much each person values the good.

We showed in Chapter 4 that (under certain conditions) a market automatically produces the quantity of a good that maximizes consumer plus producer surplus. We now know that one of the required conditions is that the good be a private good, a good that is rival and excludable. Unfortunately, no one has yet discovered a workable process that, as if guided by an "invisible hand," produces optimal amounts of public goods.

Voting and other democratic procedures can help to produce information about the demand for public goods, but these processes are unlikely to work as well at providing the optimal amounts of public goods as do markets at providing the optimal amounts of private goods (see Chapter 20 for more). Thus, we have more confidence that the optimal amount of toothpaste is purchased every year ($2.3 billion worth in recent years) than the optimal amount of defense spending ($660 billion) or the optimal amount of asteroid deflection (close to $0). In some cases, we could get too much of the public good with many people being forced riders, and in other cases, we could get too little of the public good. Nevertheless, since markets are challenged to provide public goods, we are probably fortunate that government can provide public goods even if the method is imperfect.

One final point about public goods: A public good is *not* defined as a good produced in the public sector. If the government started to produce jeans, for example, that does not make jeans a public good. The government does produce mail delivery even though mail delivery is not a public good. Similarly, asteroid deflection is a public good even though, as of yet, the government does not produce very much asteroid deflection.

Club Goods

Club goods are goods that are excludable but nonrival. A television show like *Game of Thrones*, for example, is excludable—you must buy HBO to watch the show, at least in its first run—but it's also nonrival because when one person watches, this does not reduce the ability of another person to watch. Clearly, markets can provide goods that are excludable but nonrival, but they do so at the price of some efficiency. HBO prohibits some people from watching *Game of Thrones*, for example, even though they would be willing to pay the cost (close to zero for an additional viewer) but not the price (say, $15.99 a month).

In practice, the inefficiency from the underprovision of most nonrival private goods like television, music, and software is not that big a deal. The fixed costs of producing these goods must be paid somehow and we do not want to lose the diversity, creativity, and responsiveness provided by markets.

Entrepreneurs are constantly looking for ways to turn nonexcludable, nonrival goods such as television into club goods (nonrival but excludable), such as cable television, so that they can be provided at a profit. Furthermore, entrepreneurs can sometimes find clever ways of profiting from nonrival goods *even without relying on exclusion.*

The Peculiar Case of Advertising

Radio and broadcast television are peculiar goods because although they are public goods, nonrival *and* nonexcludable, they are provided in large quantities by markets. How is this possible? When radio first appeared, no one could figure out how to make a profit from it and most people thought that government provision would be necessary if people were to benefit from this amazing discovery. After much experimentation, however, entrepreneurs did discover how to give radio away for free (the efficient solution) and yet still make a profit—they discovered advertising. Advertisers pay for the costs of programming that is then given away for free.

Advertising, of course, is not a perfect solution to the problem of nonexcludability and nonrivalry, but for radio and broadcast television, it has worked fairly well. Advertising works so well that some nonrival goods are provided without exclusion even when exclusion would be cheap. Google, for example, spends billions of dollars indexing the Web and developing search algorithms and then it offers its product to anyone in the world for free. Google could exclude people who don't pay for its service, but Google has discovered that selling advertising while providing its services for free is more profitable.

Finally, Wi-Fi is an interesting example of a nonrival but potentially excludable public good because it is currently provided in just about every possible manner. Wi-Fi is sold by private firms like Sprint who exclude non-payers by requiring security codes. Other firms offer Wi-Fi for free but only if you watch advertising. Cafés such as Panera Bread offer free Wi-Fi to help attract

CHECK YOURSELF

- What happens if government provides more of a public good than is efficient? Who is hurt? Who benefits? Use national defense as an example.

Club goods are goods that are excludable but nonrival.

Common resources are goods that are nonexcludable but rival.

The **tragedy of the commons** is the tendency of any resource that is unowned and hence nonexcludable to be overused and undermaintained.

customers. Wi-Fi is also given away by people who choose not to close their access points. In Houston, the government taxes citizens to pay for the network and then offers free access. Each of these methods has its advantages and disadvantages.

Common Resources and the Tragedy of the Commons

Common resources are goods that are nonexcludable but rival. An example is tuna in the ocean. Until they are caught, the tuna are unowned—hence nonexcludable—and it's difficult to prevent anyone from fishing for tuna. But tuna are not public goods since when one person catches and consumes a tuna, that leaves fewer tuna for other people. The result of nonexcludability and rivalry is often the **tragedy of the commons,** overexploitation and undermaintenance of the common resource. As a result of the tragedy of the commons, tuna are being driven toward extinction.

Since 1960, the tuna catch has decreased by 75% (see Figure 19.1). The southern bluefin is highly prized as sushi and demand has increased as sushi has become more trendy. The increase in demand and the decrease in the catch have driven up prices so much that a single choice tuna can now fetch $50,000 or more at the Tokyo fish market. As a result of the high price, corporations hunt tuna across the oceans in fast ships using satellites, sophisticated radar, and onboard helicopters. The sad truth is that so many fish are caught, various types of sushi may soon become a thing of the past.

Tuna aren't the only fish headed toward extinction. A 2006 paper in *Science* estimated that if the long-term trend continues, *all* of the world's major seafood stocks will collapse by 2048. Already nearly 30% of seafood species have

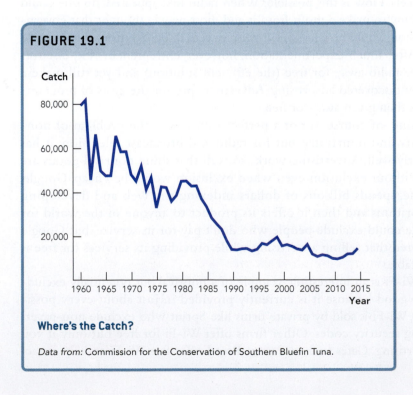

FIGURE 19.1

Catch

Where's the Catch?

Data from: Commission for the Conservation of Southern Bluefin Tuna.

collapsed (defined as a decline in the catch of 90%). As seafood species decline so do all the species that depend on them in the food chain. Overfishing is draining the oceans of fish.

Overfishing, however, is not primarily caused by increased demand. People like to eat chickens even more than they like to eat tuna but chickens are not going extinct. Why not? The difference is that chickens are owned and tuna, "chickens of the sea," are unowned.

To see why ownership means that chickens are plentiful and tuna are scarce, let's take a closer look at the incentives of fishermen and chicken ranchers.

Everyone, including the fishermen whose livelihoods depend on tuna, knows that tuna are being fished to extinction. So, you might think that the logical thing for a tuna fisherman to do is to fish less. But that's not correct. If Haru, a Japanese tuna fisherman, fishes less, will there be more tuna for him to catch in the future? No; if Haru fishes less, that just leaves more tuna for other fishermen to catch—fishing less doesn't help Haru because he doesn't own the tuna until it's in the hold of his ship. Since Haru doesn't own the tuna in the ocean, he has no way of securing the fruits of his restraint.

Compare the incentives facing Haru with those facing Frank Perdue, the legendary chicken entrepreneur. Will Frank Perdue ever let his chickens go extinct? Of course not. Perdue makes money from his chickens, so to maximize profits, he will keep his stock of chickens healthy and growing. If Perdue "overfishes" his chickens, he pays the price. If Perdue exercises restraint and grows his flock, he gets the benefit. In short, Frank Perdue will never kill the chicken that lays his golden eggs.

The problem of overfishing is one example of the *tragedy of the commons*, the tendency for any resource that is unowned to be overused and undermaintained. The theory goes back at least to Aristotle who in criticizing Plato's idea of raising children in common said, "that which is common to the greatest number has the least care bestowed upon it."[1]

Do you live with other students? Take a look at your kitchen—that's the tragedy of the commons. Other examples of the tragedy of the commons include the slaughter of the open-range buffalo during the nineteenth century, deforestation in the African Sahel region, and the hunting of elephants to near extinction.

The tragedy of the commons applies especially strongly to resources like fish, forests, and agricultural land because these resources must be carefully maintained to remain useful. But when resources are unowned, the users do not have strong incentives to invest in maintenance because maintenance mostly creates an external benefit, not a private benefit. In other words, the fisherman who throws the small fish back mostly increases other people's future catch, not his own. The tragedy of the commons is thus a type of externality problem like those we examined in Chapter 10.

We typically call something a *tragedy* of the commons when the lack of maintenance is so severe that exploitation

The difference is ownership.
Chickens (owned, not endangered)

SCOTT STULBERG/GETTY IMAGES

"Chickens of the Sea" (unowned, endangered)

BRIAN SKERRY/NATIONAL GEOGRAPHIC GETTY IMAGES

The tragedy of the commons

PATRIK GIARDINO/GETTY IMAGES

is pushed beyond the point where the resource reproduces itself. To maintain a healthy stock of fish, for example, the yearly catch of fish must be no more than the yearly increase in fish population. If a population of 100 fish grows by 10% every year, then fishermen can catch 10 fish *forever*. But if the fishermen catch just one more fish, 11 fish per year, the stock of fish will be extinct in just 26 years. (See the chapter appendix for a proof.) So, the fishermen who overfish are not just driving the fish into extinction, they are driving *their own way of life* into extinction—that's a tragedy.

Happy Solutions to the Tragedy of the Commons

The tragedy of the commons can sometimes by averted in small groups. Elinor Ostrom, the first woman to win a Nobel Prize in economics, found that all over the world, small villages and tribes have avoided the tragedy of overfishing a lake or overgrazing a pasture through the enforcement of norms. A tribe member who takes too many fish from the common lake will be shunned, like someone who litters in a public park. A tribe member who exercises restraint and throws the small fish back will be respected. Tragedy of the commons problems, however, are more difficult to solve when a lot of unrelated people have access to the common good.

Command and control and, more recently, tradable allowances have been used to solve tragedy of the commons problems, just as they have been used to solve other externality problems, as discussed in Chapter 10. When fishing stocks have neared depletion, for example, governments have tried command and control solutions like limiting the number of fishing boats. To protect their salmon fishery, British Columbia limited the number of boats in 1968. Unfortunately, the scheme did not work well because the fishermen installed more powerful engines and better electronics for finding fish—this is often called "capital stuffing" because the fishermen stuffed their boats with expensive capital so those boats could be more effective. As a result of capital stuffing, the value of the typical fishing boat tripled in just 10 years; not surprisingly, the salmon fishery continued to decline. Similar problems have occurred when governments have restricted the number of days that fishing is allowed.

New Zealand pioneered an alternative approach in 1986 with individual transferable quotas (ITQs). ITQs are similar to the pollution allowances that we looked at in Chapter 10; the owner of an ITQ has the right to catch a certain share of the total allowable catch of fish. The total allowable catch is set by the government. If the fishing stock increases then the government can increase the total allowable catch which means that each fisherman can catch more.[2] ITQs can be bought and sold and the government does not restrict the types of boats or equipment that the fishermen use so resources are not wasted by capital stuffing.

The ITQ system has been very successful. Figure 19.2 shows that after the ITQ system was put into place, the fish catch in New Zealand increased—in other words, preventing the fishermen from overfishing *increased* the amount of fish that they caught! This may seem paradoxical but it's just a reminder of why the tragedy of the commons is a tragedy—when each fisherman chooses to fish rather than show restraint, the net result is less fish for everyone.[*] The same

Elinor Ostrom Ostrom's detailed investigation of forests, fisheries, oil fields, grazing lands, and other commons around the world showed that sometimes tragedy can be avoided. She was awarded the Nobel Prize in Economics in 2009.

---

*Thus, the tragedy of the commons can also be understood as a prisoner's dilemma, which we introduced in Chapter 15.

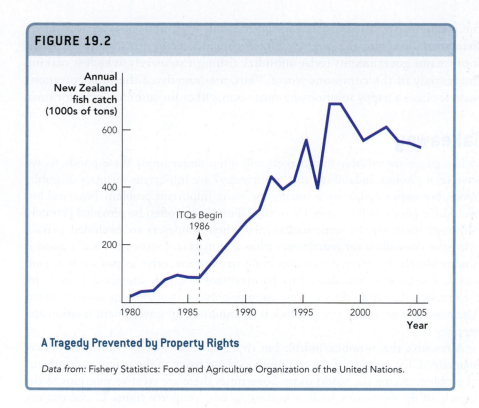

FIGURE 19.2

Annual New Zealand fish catch (1000s of tons)

ITQs Begin 1986

A Tragedy Prevented by Property Rights

Data from: Fishery Statistics: Food and Agriculture Organization of the United Nations.

How to Save a Dying Ocean

logic works in reverse—when each fisherman shows restraint the net result is a growing fish population, a higher total allowable catch and more fish for everyone.

New Zealand was able to create an ITQ system and rescue its fishery because most of the New Zealand fish live and spawn within 200 miles of New Zealand's shore—the economic zone that international law assigns exclusively to New Zealand. Thus, the New Zealand government was able to create property rights and exclude anyone who didn't have the right to fish (i.e., an ITQ) from catching fish within its waters. Property rights in other common resources such as African elephants have also been created and have resulted in substantial improvements.

Unfortunately, it's not easy to create property rights in all common resources. Southern bluefin tuna, for example, migrate throughout the Pacific, and some have been tagged and tracked across thousands of miles of ocean. So any solution to the tragedy of the tuna commons will require a multicountry agreement. That's not impossible. In the 1970s, scientists discovered that certain chemicals commonly used in aerosols could disrupt the ozone layer, which protects the earth from UV-B radiation. Protecting the ozone layer is a public good since it is nonexcludable and nonrival. Fortunately, an international treaty called the Montreal Protocol has been signed by 195 of the 196 United Nations member states and it restricts the use of chemicals that damage the ozone layer. The treaty is widely regarded as the most successful environmental treaty since emissions of ozone-depleting chemicals have declined and the ozone layer has begun to recover.[3]

Similarly, if there were world agreement, technology could be used to tag tuna and create property rights, but as we know from our discussion of the Coase theorem in Chapter 10, the more parties required to make an agreement, the greater the transactions costs and the less likely a solution. Moreover, rather than working to create property rights or restrict fishing to sustainable levels, most major governments today subsidize fishing extensively, which is making the tragedy of the commons worse. Thus, the tragedy of the tuna commons may not have a happy solution any time soon, either for sushi lovers or for tuna.

Takeaway

Public goods are valuable but markets will often undersupply these goods. As we have seen, "nonexcludability" and "nonrivalry" are important qualities of public goods, but nonexcludability is usually the more important problem. Nonrival but excludable goods such as cable TV or digital music can often be provided privately. Although there may be some inefficiency when nonpayers are excluded, private provision does allow for entrepreneurship and market discovery. When a good is nonexcludable, however, demanders don't have an incentive to pay for the good and, as a result, suppliers don't have an incentive to supply the good. That's why, for instance, the world doesn't have enough protection against an asteroid strike. The benefit of providing public goods is an argument for government taxation and supply.

A resource that is nonexcludable but rival will tend to be overused and undermaintained. The tragedy of the commons explains many of the major environmental problems facing the world today. Sometimes there are creative solutions to the tragedy of the commons, such as instituting new property rights. Unfortunately, creating property rights is not automatic and may require extensive understanding of economic principles and agreement among many of the world's governments.

In short, many of the world's problems arise when property rights to goods are either not possible, not protected, or not easily implemented.

CHAPTER REVIEW

interactive activity Go online to practice with more examples of these types of problems, including live links to videos, data sources, and feedback.

 Problems in **green** relate to MRU videos. See the MRU table at the end of the exercises.

KEY CONCEPTS

nonexcludable, p. 368

nonrival, p. 368

private good, p. 369

public good, p. 369

free rider, p. 369

forced rider, p. 370

club goods, p. 371

common resources, p. 372

tragedy of the commons, p. 372

FACTS AND TOOLS

1. Take a look at the following list of goods and services:

Apples

Open-heart surgery

Cable television

Farm-raised salmon

Yosemite National Park

Central Park, New York City

The Chinese language

The idea of calculus

a. Is each item on the list excludable or non-excludable? Sometimes the border is a little fuzzy, but justify your answer if you think there's any ambiguity.

b. Rival or nonrival?

c. Based on your answers to parts a and b, sort each good or service into one of the four categories from Table 19.1.

d. How do you exclude people from a park?

2. Which of the following are free riders, which are forced riders, and which are just people paying for public goods?

a. In Britain, Alistair pays a tax to support the British Broadcasting Corporation. He doesn't own a radio or TV.

b. Monica pays her local property taxes and state income taxes. Police patrol her neighborhood regularly.

c. Richard, a young boy in 1940s Los Angeles, jumps on board the streetcar without paying.

d. In the United States, Sara pays taxes to fund children's immunizations. She lives out in the forest, has no family, and rarely sees other people.

e. In Japan, Dave, a tourist from the United States, enjoys the public parks.

3. **a.** Is education—a college course, for instance—excludable?

b. Is education a rival good? That is, if your class has more students, do you get a worse education on average? Do students (and parents) typically prefer smaller class sizes? Do professors typically prefer smaller classes? Does it usually cost more for a school to educate more students?

c. According to the standard economists' definition of a public good—the definition we use in this chapter—is education a public good?

d. Into which of the four categories from Table 19.1 does education seem to fit best?

4. Emeril says, "In my economics class, I learned that the only way to fund public goods was to have the government tax citizens to pay for those goods. Is that what you learned?"

Rachel responds, "Actually, in my class, we used *Modern Principles*, and we learned that there are other ways to fund public goods, like _____." Complete Rachel's statement.

5. The Patagonian toothfish is a large, ugly fish that can weigh 200 pounds. In the 1990s, it became very popular under its new name, the Chilean sea bass. Soon, it almost became extinct.

a. Why was the Chilean sea bass almost driven to extinction?

b. Some top chefs boycotted the Chilean sea bass in the hope of increasing the stock. Why was this unsuccessful?

c. Australia now enforces limits on the catch. Why would this tend to be more successful than the boycott?

6. **a.** The nation of Alphaville has been hunting its deer population to extinction. The government decrees strict limits on the number of hunters, and on the number of rounds of ammunition that each hunter can take into the hunt. Hunters, like fishermen, are a creative lot: What will "capital stuffing" look like in this case?

b. What would an individual transferable quotas (ITQ) system look like in this case?

c. Do real governments use quotas like this to control deer populations? If you don't know the answer, just ask your classmates: There's probably a hunter or two in your course.

7. This chapter noted that chickens and the "chicken of the sea" (tuna) are fundamentally different in terms of population though they are both food. Indeed, chickens are eaten far more than tuna, and chickens are abundant compared with their ocean-living cousins.

a. What difference between these two species does this chapter identify as the explanation for this seemingly strange puzzle?

b. As population and prosperity have increased, the demand for chicken has increased. What happens to the price of chickens as a result? Why?

c. Because of the rules humans have concerning chickens, what happens to the number of people raising chickens as a result of the price change? Why? What happens to the number of chickens? Why?

d. What happens to the price of tuna as population and prosperity increase? Why?

e. Because of the rules humans have concerning tuna, what happens to the number of people harvesting tuna as a result of the price change? Why?

8. **a.** Why did the fish catch *increase* in New Zealand after the amount that each fisherman could catch was *limited* by a quota?

b. Given your answer to part a, would an individual fisherman in New Zealand want to catch more fish than he's allowed, if he knew no one would ever catch him?

c. So given your answer to part b, does the New Zealand system depend on government enforcement to work, or will individual fishermen agree out of self-interest to abide by the ITQ?

THINKING AND PROBLEM SOLVING

9. In 2008, Jean Nouvel won the Pritzker Architecture Prize (the highest prize in architecture). One of his most notable works is the Torre Agbar (pictured), a breakthrough skyscraper that lights up each night thanks to more than 4,000 LED devices—a pricey but purely cosmetic feature.

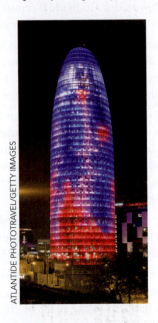

ATLANTIDE PHOTOTRAVEL/GETTY IMAGES

a. Many people enjoy looking at the Torre Agbar. Just considering that enjoyment, how would you classify the Torre Agbar: rival or nonrival? Why?

b. The Torre Agbar is the third-tallest building in Barcelona. For the purposes of enjoying its illuminated façade, would you classify the building as an excludable or nonexcludable good? Why?

c. Based on your answers, is the LED façade a public good?

d. Companies often hire architects like Nouvel to create beautiful buildings that are expensive to design, build, and maintain, yet they cannot charge people to look at them. This chapter offered one possible explanation for this puzzle. What's the explanation and how does it help justify the construction of a widely enjoyed building? (*Hint:* The building is the headquarters for Grupo Agbar, a company dedicated to the distribution and treatment of water in countries all over the world. For most of you, this is the first time you've heard of this company.)

10. **a.** "A public good is just a good that provides large external benefits." Discuss.

b. "A tragedy of the commons occurs when using a good causes massive external costs." Discuss. In parts a and b, compare the definitions from Chapter 10 with those from this chapter.

11. **a.** Has the rise of the Internet and file sharing turned media such as movies and music into public goods? Why?

b. Taking your answer in part a into account, would government taxation and funding of music improve social welfare? In your answer, at least *mention* some of the practical difficulties of doing this.

12. We mentioned that the tragedy of the commons is a form of prisoner's dilemma, something we saw back in Chapter 15. As is so often the case in economics, the same model can apply to many different settings. Let's recycle Facts and Tools question 5b from Chapter 16 just to emphasize the point:

		Player B	
		Left	Right
Player A	Up	(100, 100)	(600, 50)
	Down	(50, 600)	(500, 500)

a. We have given you very generic strategies: up, down, left, and right. Relabel the matrix so the game applies to fishermen and the tragedy of the commons.

b. Which set of strategies would give the fishermen the highest joint payoff?

c. Which set of actions would be equivalent to the following choice: "One fisherman decided not to conserve and instead to catch more than his fair share." (There are two correct answers here.)

   d. Which set of actions is the one and only Nash equilibrium? How would you describe it in terms of these two fishermen?

13. As already mentioned, the line between "public good" and "private good" is genuinely blurry. Electronic tolls on roadways are making excludability a little bit easier every year. In your view, should we continue to think of roads as public goods? (To be more accurate, we really should say, "Should we continue to think of *travel* on uncongested roads as public goods?")

14. The massive stone faces that pepper Easter Island puzzled people for centuries. What happened to the civilization that erected these faces? A clue is that the island currently has no trees. Trees would have been necessary to make the boats to bring the stones to the island and to then roll those stones into place. Archeological digs have discovered the island *did* have trees very long ago, but it's believed that the natives used up all the trees until they had no choice but to leave. Can you think of an explanation for why people would behave in this way? The following questions may suggest an answer.

JAMES L. AMOS/GETTY IMAGES

   a. Who bore the cost of planting new trees? Who benefited from planting new trees?

   b. As the population of the island grew, what happened to the number of trees? Why?

   c. Biologist Jared Diamond, writing on the subject of trees in Easter Island, asked, "What were they thinking when they cut down the last palm tree?"[4] What do you think the person who cut down that last palm tree was thinking, if he acted like a person facing a tragedy of the commons?

15. Economists typically remind people to weigh the costs of an action against the benefits of that action. Let's invent some examples where it's just too expensive or too risky to solve the very real problems discussed in this chapter.

   a. It's possible that it would just cost too much to defend the earth from asteroids, where the best option, all things considered, is just to hope for the best. Invent an extreme example where this is the case—your example might take place in a world with different technology, different type of government, and so forth.

   b. What about saving the tuna? Invent an example where the best option is to just let the fishermen do what they want, even if tuna go extinct.

CHALLENGES

16. a. Two girls are sharing a cold chocolate milk, as in the picture. How long do you think it will take them to drink all the milk? How long would it take if each girl had her own glass and half the milk? Can you see a problem when the girls drink from a common glass?

SEAN JUSTICE/CORBIS

   b. What is going on in this picture of an East Texas oil field in 1919? Can you see the problem?

BYGONE COLLECTION/ALAMY

c. Why did we put these two questions together? (*Hint:* A speech from the movie *There Will Be Blood* gets at the same question—it's based on a 1924 speech by U.S. Senator Albert Fall of New Mexico.)

17. Some media companies (especially in music and movie industries) run ads claiming that downloading or copying media is the same thing as stealing a DVD from a store. Let's see if this is the case.

   a. Is a DVD a nonrival good? Why or why not?

   b. Suppose someone stole a DVD from a retail outlet. Regardless of how that person values the DVD, does the movie company lose any revenue as a result of the theft? Why or why not?

   c. Suppose someone illegally downloaded a movie instead of purchasing it. Also suppose that person placed a high value on the movie (he or she valued it more than the price required to purchase it legally). Does the movie company lose any revenue as a result of the theft? Why or why not?

   d. Suppose someone illegally downloaded a movie instead of purchasing it. Also suppose that person placed a low value on the movie (he or she valued it less than the price required to purchase it legally). Does the movie company lose any revenue as a result of the theft? Why or why not?

   e. How is illegally downloading media like retail theft and how is it not?

18. The economic theory of public goods makes a very clear prediction: If the benefits of some action go to strangers, not to yourself, then you won't do that action. Economists have run dozens of experiments testing out this prediction. (You can find a readable article by Nobel laureate Elinor Ostrom summarizing the results in the summer 2000 issue of the *Journal of Economic Perspectives*.)

   A typical "public goods game" is quite simple: Everyone in the experiment is given, say, $5 each, theirs to take home if they like. They're told that if they donate money to the common pool, all the money in the pool will then be doubled. The money in the pool will then be divided equally among all players, whether they contributed to the pool or not. That's the whole game. Let's see what a purely self-interested person would do in this setting. (*Hint:* A public goods game is just like a prisoner's dilemma, only with more people.)

   a. If 10 people are playing the game, and they all chip in their $5 to the pool, how much will be in the pool *after* it doubles?

   b. So how much money does each person get to take home if everyone puts the money into the pool?

   c. Now, suppose that you are one of the players, and you've seen that all nine other players have put in all their money. If you keep your $5, and the pool money gets divided up equally among all 10 of you, how much will you have in total?

   d. So are you better or worse off if you keep your money?

   e. What if none of the nine had put money into the pot: If you were the only one to put your money in, how much would you have afterward? Is this better or worse than if you'd just kept the money yourself?

   f. So if you were a purely self-interested individual, what's the best thing to do regardless of what the other players are doing: Put all the money in, put some of it in, or put none of it in? (Answer in percent.) Do the benefits of donating go to you or to other people?

   g. If people just cared about "the group," they'd surely donate 100%. In part f, you just said what a purely self-interested person would do. In the dozens of studies that Ostrom summarizes, people give an average of 30% to the common pool. So, are the people in these studies closer to the pure self-interest model from part f, or are they closer to the pure altruist model of human behavior?

19. Canada's Labrador Peninsula (which includes modern-day Newfoundland and most of modern-day Quebec) was once home to an indigenous group, the Montagnes, who, in contrast to their counterparts in the American Southwest, established property rights over land. This institutional change was a direct result of the increase in the fur trade after European traders arrived.[5]

   a. Before European traders came, the amount of land in the Labrador Peninsula far exceeded the indigenous people's needs.

Hunting animals specifically for fur was not yet widely practiced. What can you conclude about the relative scarcity of land or animals? Why?

b. Before the European arrival, land was commonly held. Given your answer in part a, did the tragedy of the commons play out for the indigenous Montagnes? (Remember, air is also commonly held.)

c. Once the European traders came, the demand for fur increased. Do you expect the tragedy of the commons to play out under these circumstances? Why or why not?

d. The Montagnes established property rights over the fur trade, allocating families' hunting territory. This led to rules ranging from when an animal is accidentally killed in a neighbor's territory to laws governing inheritance. Why did the Montagnes create property rights only after the European traders came?

20. It's one of the ironies of American history that when the pilgrims first arrived at Plymouth Rock, they promptly set about creating a communal society in which all shared equally in the produce of their land. As a result, the pilgrims were soon starving to death.

Fortunately, "after much debate of things," Governor William Bradford ended the corn commons, decreeing that each family should keep the corn that it produced. In one of the most insightful statements of political economy ever written, Bradford described the results of the new and old systems.

[Ending the corn commons] had very good success, for it made all hands very industrious, so as much more corn was planted than otherwise would have been by any means the Governor or any other could use, and saved him a great deal of trouble, and gave far better content. The women now went willingly into the field, and took their little ones with them to set corn; which before would allege weakness and inability; whom to have compelled would have been thought great tyranny and oppression.

The experience that was had in this common course and condition, tried sundry years and that amongst godly and sober men, may well evince the vanity of that conceit of Plato's and other ancients applauded by some of later times; that the taking away of property and bringing in community into a commonwealth would make them happy and flourishing; as if they were wiser than God. For this community (so far as it was) was found to breed much confusion and discontent and retard much employment that would have been to their benefit and comfort. For the young men, that were most able and fit for labour and service, did repine that they should spend their time and strength to work for other men's wives and children without any recompense. The strong, or man of parts, had no more in division of victuals and clothes than he that was weak and not able to do a quarter the other could; this was thought injustice. The aged and graver men to be ranked and equalized in labours and victuals, clothes, etc., with the meaner and younger sort, thought it some indignity and disrespect unto them. And for men's wives to be commanded to do service for other men, as dressing their meat, washing their clothes, etc., they deemed it a kind of slavery, neither could many husbands well brook it. Upon the point all being to have alike, and all to do alike, they thought themselves in the like condition, and one as good as another; and so, if it did not cut off those relations that God hath set amongst men, yet it did at least much diminish and take off the mutual respects that should be preserved amongst them. And would have been worse if they had been men of another condition. Let none object this is men's corruption, and nothing to the course itself. I answer, seeing all men have this corruption in them, God in His wisdom saw another course fitter for them.

(*Source*: Bradford, William. *Of Plymouth Plantation, 1620–1647*. Edited by Samuel Eliot Morison. New York: Modern Library, 1967.)

a. Imagine yourself a pilgrim under the communal (commons) system. If you worked hard all day in the fields, would that increase your share of the food by a lot or a little? Describe the incentive to work under the communal system.

b. Under this system, what type of good was the pilgrim's harvest?

c. According to Bradford, the communal system "retard[ed] much employment that would have been to their benefit and comfort." Why would the communal system reduce something that would have been to the pilgrim's benefit? How would you describe this using the tools of economics?

d. According to Bradford, what happened to the amount of food produced and the amount of labor after the communal system was abolished and workers got to keep a larger share of what they produced?

e. Read Bradford's statement carefully. What other effects did the communal system create? (Note that economists typically ignore these kinds of effects.)

interactive activity

WORK IT OUT

For interactive, step-by-step help in solving this problem, go online.

a. American bison once freely roamed the Great Plains. In the 1820s, there were some 30 million bison in the United States but a survey in 1889 counted just 1,091. Why were the bison driven to near extinction? How were the bison like tuna?

b. At some restaurants and grocery stores, you can buy bison burgers, made from farm-raised bison. Is this good news or bad news if we want more bison around?

MRUNIVERSITY
AN ONLINE EDUCATION PLATFORM

MARGINAL REVOLUTION UNIVERSITY VIDEOS

Public Goods and Asteroid Defense

mruniversity.com/public-goods

Problems: **3**

A Deeper Look at Public Goods

mruniversity.com/public-goods-2

Problems: **1–3, 9, 10, 13**

Club Goods

mruniversity.com/club-goods

Problems: **4, 11**

The Tragedy of the Commons

mruniversity.com/tragedy-commons

Problems: **5–8, 10, 12, 14–16, 18–20**

CHAPTER 19 APPENDIX

The Tragedy of the Commons: How Fast?

We can use a simple spreadsheet to see how quickly common resources can become tragically overexploited and ruined. Suppose that we start with a stock of 100. This could be 100 million fish or 100 thousand elephants, or 100 units of agricultural quality or other common resource. Let's suppose that this resource grows or reproduces itself by 10% every year. We can then set up our spreadsheet as shown in Figure A19.1. The key cell is Cell B3, which contains the formula $=B2*(1+\$C\$2)-\$D\$2$. This formula takes the stock of fish in the previous year from cell B2, multiplies it by 1 plus the growth rate in Cell C2 (using the dollar signs to make sure that this cell reference stays the same when we copy it elsewhere), and then subtracts the annual catch or usage in Cell D2 (which we initially set at 10) to get the stock in this year.

FIGURE A19.1

	B3			f_x	=B2*(1+$C$2)-$D$2	
	A	B	C		D	E
1	Year	Stock	Natural Growth Rate		Annual Catch	
2	1	100		0.10	10	
3	2	100				
4	3	100				
5	4	100				
6	5	100				
7	6	100				
8	⋮	⋮				
9						
10						

We now copy and paste Cell B3 into Cells B4 onward. It's fairly obvious that if a stock of 100 fish grows by 10% every year, then a catch of 10 is sustainable forever and this is what our spreadsheet indicates.

What is more surprising is how quickly an increase in the catch can drive a stock to extinction. If we change the annual catch in Cell D2 to 11, for example, we get the result in Figure A19.2.

FIGURE A19.2

	A	B	C	D
1	Year	Stock	Natural Growth Rate	Annual Catch
2	1	100	0.10	11
3	2	99		
4	3	97.9		
5	4	96.69		
6	5	95.359		
7	6	93.8949		
8	7	92.28439		
9	8	90.51283		
10	9	88.56411		
11	10	86.42052		
12	11	84.06258		
13	12	81.46883		
14	13	78.61572		
15	14	75.47729		
16	15	72.02502		
17	16	68.22752		
18	17	64.05027		
19	18	59.4553		
20	19	54.40083		
21	20	48.84091		
22	21	42.725		
23	22	35.9975		
24	23	28.59725		
25	24	20.45698		
26	25	11.50267		
27	26	1.652941		
28	27	-9.18177		
29				

Notice that the decline starts slowly, but by year 27 the stock of fish has gone negative; that is, the fish are extinct. You can experiment with different assumptions about growth rates and catches to see how long stocks can be sustained under different scenarios.

20

Political Economy and Public Choice

I f you have read this far, you may now be asking, "What's wrong with the world?" Economists tend to favor free and competitive markets and to be skeptical about policies like price controls, tariffs, command and control regulation, and high inflation rates. Yet around the world, markets are often suppressed, monopolies are supported, and harmful policies, such as those just listed, are quite common. Why do the arguments of economists fall on deaf ears?

One possible answer is that politicians are right to reject mainstream economics. As we explore in Chapter 21, some people do argue that mainstream economics ignores important ethical values. Or perhaps mainstream economics is simply wrong about economics. Of course, that is not our view, so you will have to seek other books to judge that question for yourself. A third answer to what's wrong with the world and the one we will explore in this chapter is . . . can you guess? Bad incentives.

A good incentive system aligns self-interest with the social interest. In Chapters 7 and 10, we explored the conditions under which markets do and do not align self-interest with the social interest. It's now time to turn to government. The critical question is this: When does the self-interest of politicians and voters align with the social interest and when do these interests collide? This question is at the heart of political economy, or **public choice**, which is the study of political behavior using the tools of economics.

We will begin this chapter looking at some of the major institutions and incentives that govern the behavior of voters and politicians in a democracy. As we will see, democracies have many problems, including voter ignorance, control of politics by special interests, and political business cycles. Yet, to quote Winston Churchill, "No one pretends that democracy is perfect or all-wise. Indeed, it has been said that democracy is the worst form of government except all those other forms that have been tried from time to time."[1] Thus, in the latter half of the chapter, we look at nondemocracies and some of the reasons why nondemocracies have typically failed to produce either wealth or political or economic liberty for their citizens.

Let's begin with voters and the question: "Do voters have an incentive to be well informed about politics?"

Public choice is the study of political behavior using the tools of economics.

385

Voters and the Incentive to Be Ignorant

Knowledge is a good thing, but sometimes the price of knowledge is too high. Imagine that your professor changed the grading scheme. Instead of awarding grades based on individual performance, your professor averages test scores and assigns the same grade to everyone. Will you study more or less under this new grading scheme? We think that most people would study less because studying now has a lower payoff. Let's say that before the change an extra few hours of studying would raise your grade by 10 points. What is the payoff to studying under the new system? Imagine that there are 100 people in your class. The same hours of studying will now raise your grade by just 10/100 or 0.1 points.* Studying doesn't pay under the second system because your grade is mostly determined by what other people do, not by what you do.

Now let's apply the same idea to politics. When you choose a politician, does studying their record have a high payoff? No. Studying position papers, examining voting histories, and listening to political speeches is sometimes entertaining, but it doesn't offer much concrete return. Even when studying changes your vote, your vote is very unlikely to change the outcome of the election. Studying politics doesn't pay because the outcome of any election is mostly determined by what other people do, not by what you do.

Rational ignorance occurs when the benefits of being informed are less than the costs of becoming informed.

Economists say that voters are **rationally ignorant** about politics because the incentives to be informed are low.

It's not hard to find evidence that Americans are uninformed about politics. Consider the following questions. Who is the speaker of the U.S. House of Representatives? Who sings "Single Ladies (Put a Ring on It)"? Be honest. Which question was it easier for you to answer? And which question is more important? (At the time of writing, Paul Ryan is speaker of the House. "Single Ladies" is a Beyoncé hit.)

Not knowing who the speaker of the House is might not be critical, but Americans are equally uninformed or worse—misinformed—about important political questions. For example, in one survey Americans were asked to name the two largest sources of government spending out of the following six choices.

- Welfare
- Interest on the federal debt
- Defense
- Foreign aid
- Social Security
- Health care

Amazingly, 41% named foreign aid as one of the two biggest programs. But foreign aid is by far the smallest program of the six listed. Do you know the correct answers? The two biggest programs are defense and Social Security. Americans were not even close to the correct answers; for instance, the second most popular choice was welfare, which, though a large program, is still much smaller than defense and Social Security.[2]

---

* It's possible that some people could study more under the new system. Under the old system, studying only raises an individual's grade, but under the new system, it raises everyone's grades! Thus, if there are some super-altruistic students, they might study more under the new system. We have not met many such students. Have you?

Similarly, by their own admission, most Americans know "not much" or "nothing" about important pieces of legislation such as the USA Patriot Act. Most Americans cannot estimate the inflation rate or the unemployment rate to within five percentage points. Hundreds of surveys over many decades have shown that most Americans know little about political matters. Of course, we'd all like to change that—we are glad you are reading this book!—but in the meantime it is simply a fact. And it appears to be a fact that is not easily changed.

Why Rational Ignorance Matters

Ignorance about political matters is important for at least three reasons. First, if voters don't know what the USA Patriot Act says or what the unemployment rate is, then it's difficult to make informed choices. Moreover, voters who think that the unemployment rate is much higher than it actually is are likely to make quite different choices than if they knew the true rate. The difficulty is compounded if voters don't know the positions that politicians take on the issues, and it is worse yet if voters don't know much about possible solutions to problems such as unemployment. Voters are supposed to be the drivers in a democracy, but if the drivers don't know where they are or how to get to where they want to go, they are unlikely to ever arrive at their desired destination.

Second, voters who are rationally ignorant will often make decisions on the basis of low-quality, unreliable, or potentially biased information. Not everyone has read a good principles of economics textbook and those who haven't are likely to vote in ways that are quite different from someone who is better informed.* It's not really surprising, for example, that better-looking politicians get more votes even if good looks have nothing to do with policy. Once again, we should not expect too much in the way of wise government policy when voters are rationally ignorant.

The third reason that rational ignorance matters is that not everyone is rationally ignorant. Let's look at this in more detail.

Special Interests and the Incentive to Be Informed

Let's return to the sugar quota discussed in Chapter 9. As you may recall, the government restricts how much sugar can be imported into the United States. As a result, the U.S. price of sugar is about double the world price. American consumers of candy, soda, and other sweet goods pay more for these goods than they would if the quota was lifted. Why does the government harm sugar consumers, many of whom are voters?

Although sugar consumers are harmed by the quota, few of them even know of the quota's existence. That's rational because even though the quota costs consumers more than a billion dollars, the costs are diffused over millions of consumers, costing each person about $5 or $6 per year. Even if sugar consumers did know about the quota, they probably wouldn't spend much

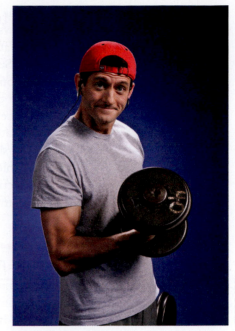

Rational ignorance Do you recognize this man?

GREGG SEGAL

CHECK YOURSELF

- Would you expect more rational ignorance about national issues among national voters or about local issues among local voters? Make an argument for both possibilities.

* For a superb treatment of this issue, see Caplan, Bryan. 2007. *The Myth of the Rational Voter: Why Democracies Choose Bad Policies*. Princeton, NJ: Princeton University Press.

time or effort to oppose it. Will you? After all, just writing a letter to your local newspaper opposing the quota might cost $5 or $6 in time and trouble, and what's the probability that your letter will change the policy?

Sugar consumers, therefore, won't do much to oppose the quota but what about U.S. sugar producers? U.S. sugar producers benefit enormously from the quota. As we saw in Chapter 9, if the quota were lifted, most sugar producers in Florida would be outcompeted by producers in Brazil where better weather makes sugar cheaper to produce. But with the quota, U.S. producers are shielded from competition and sugar farming in Florida becomes very profitable. Moreover, although there are millions of sugar consumers, sugar production is concentrated among a handful of producers. Each producer benefits from the quota by millions of dollars.

Sugar producers, unlike sugar consumers, have a lot of money at stake so they have a strong incentive to be *rationally informed*. The sugar producers know when the sugar quota comes up for a vote, they know who is pictured on the previous page, they know who is on the House and Senate agricultural committees that largely decide on the quota, they know which politicians are running for reelection and in need of campaign funds, and they act accordingly. Table 20.1, for example, lists the members of the Senate Agricultural Committee in 2008 and the amount of money from 2006 to 2008 that they received from the American Crystal Sugar Political Action Committee (PAC), an industry lobby group in favor of the sugar quota.

As you can see, 13 of the 21 senators on the Agricultural Committee (perhaps not coincidentally just over a majority!) received money from the American Crystal Sugar PAC. Many senators on the committee *also* received money from the American Sugar Cane League, the Florida Sugar Cane League, the American Sugarbeet Growers Association, and the U.S. Beet Sugar Association! Nor is that the end of the story. The owners and executives of the major players in the sugar industry also donate campaign funds as individuals. The "sugar barons" José and Alfonso Fanjul, for example, head Florida Crystals Corporation, which is one of the country's largest sugar cane growers. The Fanjuls donate money to the Florida Sugar Cane League and give money to politicians in their own names. Interestingly, José directs most of his support to Republicans, while his brother Alfonso supports Democrats. Do

TABLE 20.1 SPECIAL INTERESTS ARE RATIONALLY INFORMED

Senators on the Agriculture Committee, 2008	Donations from the American Crystal Sugar PAC (2006–2008)
Tom Harkin, D-IA	$15,000
Sherrod Brown, D-OH	$15,000
Saxby Chambliss R-GA	$10,000
Mitch McConnell, R-KY	$10,000
Robert Casey, Jr., D-PA	$10,000
E. Benjamin Nelson, D-NE	$8,000
Amy Klobuchar, D-MN	$7,000
Patrick J. Leahy, D-VT	$6,000
Max Baucus, D-MT	$6,000
Pat Roberts, R-KS	$3,000
Kent Conrad, D-ND	$2,000
Ken Salazar, D-CO	$2,000
Debbie Stabenow, D-MI	$1,000
Richard G. Lugar, R-IN	$0
Thad Cochran, R-MS	$0
Blanche Lincoln, D-AR	$0
Lindsey Graham, R-SC	$0
Norm Coleman, R-MN	$0
Mike Crapo, R-ID	$0
John Thune, R-SD	$0
Charles Grassley, R-IA	$0

Data from: Federal Election Commission data compiled by OpenSecrets.org.

you think there is a difference of political opinion between the two brothers? Or can you think of another explanation for their pattern of donations? Other Fanjul family members, including brothers, wives, daughters, sons, and even sisters-in-law, are also active political contributors.

A Formula for Political Success: Diffuse Costs, Concentrate Benefits

The politics behind the sugar quota illustrate a formula for political success: Diffuse costs and concentrate benefits. The costs of the sugar quota are diffused over millions of consumers, so no consumer has much of an incentive to oppose the quota. But the benefits of the quota are concentrated on a handful of producers; they have strong incentives to support the quota. So, the sugar quota is a winning policy for politicians. The people who are harmed are rationally ignorant and have little incentive to oppose the policy, while the people who benefit are rationally informed and have strong incentives to support the policy. Thus, we can see one reason why the self-interest of politicians does not always align with the social interest.

The formula for political success works for many types of public policies, not just trade quotas and tariffs. Agricultural subsidies and price supports, for example fit the diffused costs and concentrated benefits story. It's interesting that the political power of farmers has *increased* as the share of farmers in the population has *decreased*. The reason? When farmers decline in population, the benefits of, for example, a price support become more concentrated (on farmers) and the costs become more diffused (on nonfarmers).

The benefits of many government projects such as roads, bridges, dams, and parks are concentrated on local residents and producers, while the costs of these projects can be diffused over all federal taxpayers. As a result, politicians have an incentive to lobby for these projects even when the benefits are smaller than the costs.

Consider the infamous "Bridge to Nowhere," a proposed bridge in Alaska that would connect the town of Ketchikan (population 8,900) with its airport on Gravina Island (population 50) at a cost to federal taxpayers of $320 million. At present, a ferry service runs to the island but some people in the town complain that it costs too much ($6 per car). If the town's residents had to pay the $320 million cost of the bridge themselves—that's $35,754 each!—do you think they would want the bridge? Of course not, but the residents will be happy to have the bridge if most of the costs are paid by other taxpayers.

As far as the residents of Ketchikan are concerned, the costs of the bridge are *external costs*. Recall from Chapter 10 that when the costs of a good are paid for by other people—rather than the consumers or producers of the good—we get an inefficiently large quantity of the good. In Chapter 10, we gave the example of a firm that pollutes—since the firm doesn't pay all the costs of its production, it produces too much. The same thing is true here, except the external cost is created by government. When government makes it possible to push the costs of a good onto other people—to *externalize the cost*—we get too much of the good. In this case, we get too many bridges to nowhere.

The formula for political success works for tax credits and deductions, as well as for spending. The federal tax code, including various regulations and rulings, is more than 60,000 pages long and it grows every year as politicians add special interest provisions. Tax breaks for various manufacturing industries, for example, have long been common, but in 2004, the term "manufacturing" was significantly expanded so that oil and gas drilling as well as mining and timber could be included as manufacturing industries. The new tax breaks were worth some $76 billion to the firms involved. One last-minute provision even defined "coffee roasting" as a form of manufacturing. That provision was worth a lot of *bucks* to one famous corporation.

Every year Congress inserts many thousands of special spending projects, exemptions, regulations, and tax breaks into major bills. A multibillion-dollar lobbying industry works the system on behalf of their clients, and it is not unusual for those lobbies, in essence, to propose and even write up the details of the forthcoming legislation. Many lobbyists are former politicians who find that lobbying their friends can be very profitable.

When benefits are concentrated and costs are diffuse, resources can be wasted on projects with low benefits and high costs. Consider a special interest group representing 1% of society that proposes a simple policy which benefits the special interest by $100 and costs society $100. Thus, the policy benefits the special interest by $100 and it costs the *special interest* just $1 (if you are wondering where that came from, $1 is 1% of the total cost to society). The special interest group will certainly lobby for a policy like this.

But now imagine that the policy benefits the special interest by $100 but costs society twice as much, $200. The policy is very bad for society, but it's still good for the special interest, which gets a benefit of $100 at a cost (to the lobby) of only $2 ($2 is 1% of the total social costs of $200). Indeed, a special interest representing 1% of the population will benefit from any policy that transfers $100 in its favor, even if the costs to society are nearly 100 times as much!

If each policy, taken on its own, wastes a few million or billion dollars worth of resources, the country will be much poorer. A country with many inefficient policies will have less wealth and slower economic growth. No society can get rich by passing policies with benefits that are less than costs.

In extreme situations, an economy can falter or even collapse when fighting over the division of the pie becomes more profitable than making the pie grow larger. The fall of the Roman Empire, for instance, was caused in part by bad political institutions. As the Roman Empire grew, courting politicians in Rome became a more secure path to riches than starting a new business. Toward the end of the empire, the emperors taxed peasant farmers heavily. Rather than spending the money on roads or valuable infrastructure, the activities that had made Rome powerful and rich, tax revenues were used to pay off privileged insiders and to placate the public in the city of Rome with "bread and circuses." When the empire finally collapsed in 476 CE, the tax collector was a hated figure and the government enjoyed little respect.[3]

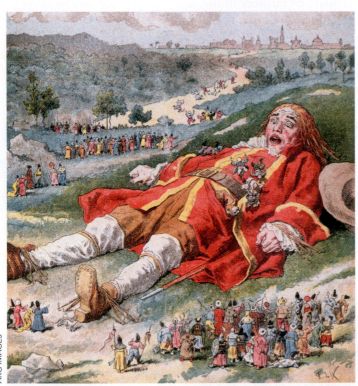

AKG IMAGES

Many small distortions can tie a giant down.

Voter Myopia and Political Business Cycles

We turn now from the microeconomics of political economy to an application in macroeconomics. Rational ignorance and another factor, voter myopia, can encourage politicians to boost the economy before an election to increase their chances of reelection.

Presidential elections appear to be fought on many fronts. Candidates battle over education, war, health care, the environment, and the economy. Pundits scrutinize the daily chronicle of events to divine how the candidates advance and retreat in public opinion. Personalities and "leadership" loom large and are reckoned to swing voters one way or another. When the battle is done, historians mark one personality and set of issues as having won the day and as reflecting the "will of the voters."

But economists and political scientists have been surprised to discover that a simpler logic underlies this apparent chaos of seemingly unique and momentous events. Over the past 100 years, the American voter has voted for the party of the incumbent when the economy is doing well and voted against the incumbent when the economy is doing poorly. Voters are so responsive to economic conditions that the winner of a presidential election can be predicted with considerable accuracy, even if one knows nothing about the personalities, issues, or events that seem, on the surface, to matter so much.

The green line in Figure 20.1 shows, for each presidential election since 1948, the share of the two-party vote won by the party of the incumbent (that is, a share greater than 50% usually means the presidency stayed with the incumbent party and a share less than 50% usually means the presidency switched party). The blue line is the share of the two-party vote predicted by just three variables: growth in personal disposable income (per capita) in the year of the election, the inflation rate in the year of the election, and a simple measure of how long the incumbent party has been in power. Notice that these three variables alone give us great power to predict election results.

More specifically, the incumbent party wins elections when personal disposable income is growing, when the inflation rate in the election year is low, and

CHECK YOURSELF

- President Ronald Reagan set up a commission to examine government spending and cut waste. It had some limited success. If special interest spending is such a problem, why don't we set up another federal commission to examine government waste? Who would push for such a commission? Who would resist it? What will be its prospects for success?

- A local library expanded into a new building to establish a local history collection. The state senator found some state money and had that contributed to the library. Who benefits from this? Who ultimately pays for it?

FIGURE 20.1

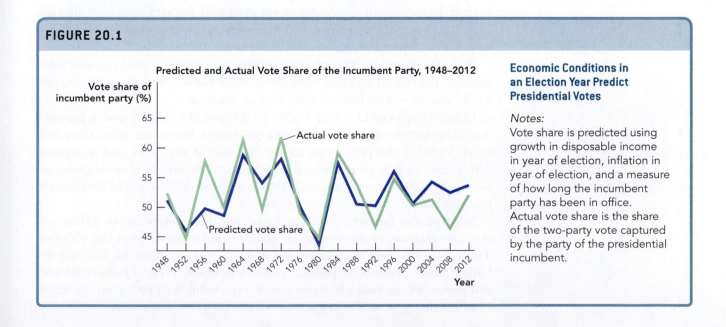

Predicted and Actual Vote Share of the Incumbent Party, 1948–2012

Economic Conditions in an Election Year Predict Presidential Votes

Notes:
Vote share is predicted using growth in disposable income in year of election, inflation in year of election, and a measure of how long the incumbent party has been in office. Actual vote share is the share of the two-party vote captured by the party of the presidential incumbent.

when the incumbent party has not been in power for too many terms in a row. Personal disposable income is the amount of income a person has after taxes. It includes income from wages, dividends, and interest but also income from welfare payments, unemployment insurance, and Social Security payments. The inflation rate is the general increase in prices. The last variable, a measure of how long the incumbent party has been in power, reduces a party's vote share. Voters seem to get tired or disillusioned with a party the longer it has been in power, so there is a natural tendency for the presidency to switch parties even if all else remains the same.

Figure 20.1 tells us that voters are responsive to economic conditions, but more deeply it tells us that voters are surprisingly responsive to economic *conditions in the year of an election*. Voters are myopic—they don't look at economic conditions over a president's entire term. Instead, they focus on what is close at hand, namely economic conditions in the year of an election. Politicians who want to be reelected, therefore, are wise to do whatever they can to increase personal disposable income and reduce inflation in the year of an election even if this means decreases in income and increases in inflation at other times. Is there evidence that politicians behave in this way? Yes.

One of the most brazen examples comes from President Richard Nixon. Just two weeks before the 1972 election, he sent a letter to more than 24 million recipients of Social Security benefits. President Nixon's letter read:

Higher Social Security Payments

Your social security payment has been increased by 20 percent, starting with this month's check, by a new statute enacted by Congress and signed into law by President Richard Nixon on July 1, 1972.

The President also signed into law a provision that will allow your social security benefits to increase automatically if the cost of living goes up. Automatic benefit increases will be added to your check in future years according to the conditions set out in the law.

Of course, higher Social Security payments must be funded with higher taxes, but Nixon timed things so that the increase in payments started in October but the increase in taxes didn't begin until January, that is, not until after the election! Nixon was thus able to shift benefits and costs so that the benefits hit before the election and the costs hit after the election.

To be fair, President Nixon's policies were not unique or even unusual. Government benefits of all kinds typically increase before an election while taxes hardly ever do—taxes increase only after an election!

Using 60 years of U.S. data, Figure 20.2 shows the growth rate in personal disposable income in each quarter of a president's 16-quarter term. Growth is much higher in the year before an election than at any other time in a president's term. In fact, in an election year personal disposable income grows on average by 3.01% compared with 1.79% in a nonelection year. The difference is probably not due to chance.

Inflation also follows a cyclical pattern, but since voters dislike inflation, it tends to decrease in the year of an election and increase after the election. These patterns have been observed in many other countries, not just the United States. We also see political patterns at lower levels of politics. Mayors and governors, for example, try to increase the number of police on the streets in an election year, so that crime will fall and people will feel safer.

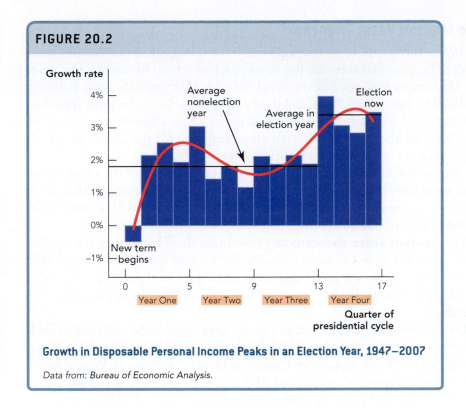

FIGURE 20.2

Growth in Disposable Personal Income Peaks in an Election Year, 1947–2007

Data from: Bureau of Economic Analysis.

There are a limited number of things that a president can do to influence the economy, so presidents do not always succeed in increasing income during an election year. Presidents can influence transfers and taxes much more readily than they can influence pure economic growth. This is one reason why cyclical patterns are more difficult to see in GDP statistics than they are in personal disposable income.

Two Cheers for Democracy

You might be wondering by now: Why isn't everything from the federal government handed out to special interest groups and why aren't politicians always reelected? Do the voters ever get their way? In fact, voters in a democracy can be very powerful. If you want to think about when voters matter most and when lobbies and special interests matter most, turn to the idea of incentives.

When a policy is specialized in its impact, difficult to understand, and affects a small part of the economy, it is likely that lobbies and special interests get their way. Let's say the question is whether the depreciation deduction in the investment tax credit should be accelerated or decelerated. Even though this issue is important to many powerful corporations, you can expect that most voters have never heard of the issue and that it will be settled behind closed doors by a relatively small number of people.

But when a policy is highly visible, appears often in the news and on social media, and has a major effect on the lives of millions of Americans, the voters are likely to have an opinion. The point isn't that voter opinions are always well informed or rational, but that voters do care about some of the biggest issues such as Social Security, Medicare, and taxes and when they do care, politicians have an incentive to serve them. But how exactly does voter opinion translate into policy? After all, opinions are divided, so which voters will get their way in a democracy?

CHECK YOURSELF

■ If voters are myopic, will politicians prefer a policy with small gains now and big costs later, or a policy with small costs now but big gains later?

The Median Voter Theorem

To answer this question, we develop a model of voting called the "median voter model." Imagine that there are five voters, each of whom has an opinion about the ideal amount of spending on Social Security. Max wants the least spending, followed by Sofia, Inez, Peter, and finally Alex, who wants the most spending. In Figure 20.3, we plot each voter's ideal policy along a line from least to most spending. We also assume that each voter will vote for the candidate whose policy position is closest to his or her ideal point.

The median voter is defined as the voter such that half of the other voters want more spending and half want less spending. In this case, the median voter is Inez, since compared with Inez, half of the voters (Paul and Alex) want more spending and half the voters (Max and Sofia) want less spending.

> The **median voter theorem** says that when voters vote for the policy that is closest to their ideal point on a line, then the ideal point of the median voter will beat any other policy in a majority rule election.

The **median voter theorem** says that under these conditions, the median voter rules! Or to put it more formally, the median voter theorem says that when voters vote for the policy that is closest to their ideal point on a line, then the ideal point of the median voter will beat any other policy in a majority rule election.

Let's see why this is true and, as a result, how democracy will tend to push politicians toward the ideal point of the median voter. First, consider any two policies such as those adopted by Candidate D and Candidate R. Which policy will win in a majority rule election? Max and Sofia will vote for Candidate D since D's policy is closer to their ideal point than R's policy. But Inez, Peter, and Alex will vote for Candidate R. By majority rule, Candidate R will win the election. Notice that, of the two policies offered, the policy closest to that of the median voter's ideal policy won the election.

Most politicians don't like to lose. So in the next election Candidate D may shift her position, becoming Candidate D′. By exactly the same reasoning as before, Candidate D′ will now win the election. If we repeat this process, the

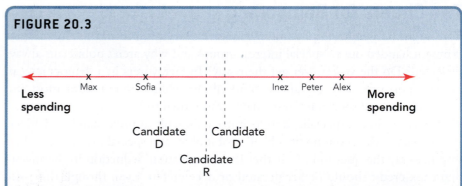

FIGURE 20.3

The Median Voter Theorem Each voter has an ideal policy, marked by an x, on the less-to-more spending line. Voters will vote for the candidate whose policy is closest to their ideal. The median voter is the voter such that half of the other voters want more spending and half of the other voters want less spending—Inez is the median voter. Under majority rule, the ideal policy of the median voter will beat any other policy. Consider any two candidate policies, such as those of Candidate D and Candidate R. Candidate D will receive two votes (Max and Sofia) and Candidate R will receive three votes (Inez, Peter, and Alex). But Candidate R's position can be beaten by a policy even closer to the ideal policy of the median voter, such as that of Candidate D′. Over time, competition pushes both candidates toward the ideal policy of the median voter, which is the only policy that cannot be beaten.

only policy that is not a *sure loser* is the ideal point of the median voter (Inez). As Candidates D and R converge on the ideal point of the median voter, there will be little difference between them and each will have a 50% chance of winning the election.[*]

The median voter theorem can be interpreted quite generally. Instead of thinking about less spending and more spending on Social Security, for example, we can interpret the line as the standard political spectrum of left to right. In this case, the median voter theorem can be interpreted as a theory of democracy in a country such as the United States where there are just two major parties.

The median voter theorem tells us that in a democracy, what counts are noses—the number of voters—and not their positions per se. Imagine, for example, that Max decided he wanted even less spending or that Alex decided he wanted even more spending. Would the political outcome change? No. According to the median voter theorem, the median voter rules, and if the median voter doesn't change, then neither does policy. Thus, under the conditions given by the median voter theorem, democracy does not seek out consensus or compromise or a policy that maximizes voter preferences, on average—it seeks out a policy that cannot be beaten in a majority rule election.

The median voter theorem does not always apply. The most important assumption we made was that voters will vote for the policy that is closest to their ideal point. That's not necessarily true. If no candidate offers a policy close to Max's ideal point, he may refuse to vote for anyone, not even the candidate whose policy is (slightly) closer to his own ideal. In this case, a candidate who moves too far away from the voters on her wing may lose votes even if her position moves closer to that of the median voter. As a result, this type of voter behavior means that candidates do not necessarily converge on the ideal point of the median voter.

We have also assumed that there is just one major dimension over which voting takes place. That's not necessarily true either. Suppose that voters care about two issues, such as taxes and war, and assume that we cannot force both issues into a left–right spectrum (so knowing a person's views about taxes doesn't necessarily predict much about his or her views about war). With two voting dimensions, it's very likely that there is *no* policy that beats every other policy in a majority rule contest, so politics may never converge on a stable policy.

To understand why a winning policy sometimes doesn't exist, consider an analogy from sports. Imagine holding a series of (hypothetical) boxing matches to figure out who is the greatest heavyweight boxer of all time. Suppose that Muhammad Ali beats Lennox Lewis and Lewis beats Mike Tyson but Tyson beats Muhammad Ali. So who is the greatest of all time? The question may have no answer if there is more than one dimension to boxing skill, so Ali has the skills needed to beat Lewis and Lewis has the skills needed to beat Tyson, but Tyson has the skills to beat Ali. In a similar way, when there is more than one dimension to politics, no policy may exist that beats every other policy. In terms of politics, the result may be that every vote or election brings a new winner, or alternatively, constitutions and procedural restrictions may slow down the rate of political change. The U.S. Constitution, for example, requires

[*] In terms of the game theory discussed in Chapters 15 and 16, the ideal policy of the median voter is the only policy that cannot be beaten by another policy and thus the only Nash equilibrium of a two-candidate game is for both candidates to choose this policy.

that new legislation must pass two houses of Congress and evade the president's veto, which is more difficult than passing a simple majority rule vote.

As a predictive theory of politics, the median voter theorem is applicable in some but not all circumstances. The theorem, however, does remind us that politicians have substantial incentives to listen to voters on issues that the voters care about. This is a powerful feature of democracy, although of course the quality of the democracy you get will depend on the wisdom of the voters behind it.

Democracy and Nondemocracy

Our picture of democracy so far has been a little disillusioning, at least compared with what you might have learned in high school civics. Yet when we look around the world, democracies tend to be the wealthiest countries, and despite the power of special interests, they also tend to be the countries with the best record of supporting markets, property rights, the rule of law, fair government, and other institutions that support economic growth.

Figure 20.4 graphs an index meant to capture good economic policy, called the economic freedom index (with higher numbers indicating greater economic freedom), on the horizontal axis against a measure of the standard of living on the vertical axis (gross national income per capita in 2007). The figure shows two things. First, there is a strong correlation between economic freedom and a higher standard of living. Second, the countries that are most democratic (full democracies are shown in red) are among the wealthiest countries in the world and the countries with the most economic freedom. The only interesting exceptions to this rule are Singapore and Hong Kong; both score very highly on economic freedom and the standard of living but are not quite full democracies.

Notice, however, that in part there is an association between democracy and the standard of living because greater wealth creates a greater demand for democracy. When citizens have satisfied their basic needs for food, shelter, and security, they demand more cerebral goods, such as the right to participate in the political process. This is exactly what happened in South Korea and Taiwan,

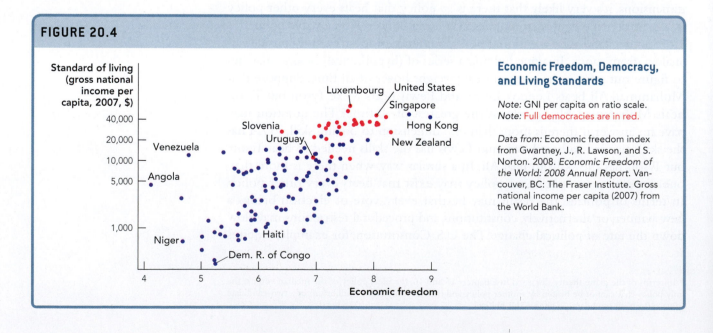

FIGURE 20.4

Economic Freedom, Democracy, and Living Standards

Note: GNI per capita on ratio scale.
Note: Full democracies are in red.

Data from: Economic freedom index from Gwartney, J., R. Lawson, and S. Norton. 2008. *Economic Freedom of the World: 2008 Annual Report.* Vancouver, BC: The Fraser Institute. Gross national income per capita (2007) from the World Bank.

two countries that became more democratic as they grew wealthier. Many people think that China may become a more democratic country as it grows wealthier; we will see. But it's not just that wealth brings democracy. Democracy also seems to bring wealth and favorable institutions. Democracies must be doing something right. We therefore need to examine some of the benefits of democratic decision making.

We've already discussed rational ignorance under democracy, but keep in mind that public ignorance is often worse in nondemocracies.[4] In many quasi democracies and in nondemocracies, the public is not well informed because the media are controlled or censored by the government.

In Africa, for example, most countries have traditionally banned private television stations. In fact as of 2000, 71% of African countries had a state monopoly on television broadcasting. Most African governments also control the largest newspapers in the country. Government ownership and control of the media are also common in most Middle Eastern countries and, of course, the former Communist countries controlled the media extensively.

Control of the media has exactly the effects that we would expect from our study of rational ignorance in democracies—it enables special interests to control the government for their own ends. Greater government ownership of the press, for example, is associated with lower levels of political rights and civil liberties, worse regulation (more policies like price controls that economists think are ineffective and wasteful), higher levels of corruption, and a greater risk of property confiscation. The authors of an important study of media ownership conclude that "government ownership of the press restricts information flows to the public, which reduces the quality of the government."[5]

Citizens in democracies may be "rationally ignorant," but on the whole they are much better informed about their governments than citizens in quasi democracies and nondemocracies. Moreover, in a democracy, citizens can use their knowledge to influence public policy at low cost by voting. In a democracy, knowledge is power. In nondemocracies, knowledge alone is not enough because intimidation and government violence create steep barriers to political participation. Many people just give up or become cynical. Other citizens in nondemocracies fall prey to propaganda and come to accept the regime's portrait of itself as a great friend of the people.

The importance of knowledge and the power to vote for bringing about better outcomes is illustrated by the shocking history of mass starvation.

Democracy and Famine

At first glance, the cause of famine seems obvious—a lack of food. Yet the obvious explanation is wrong or at least drastically incomplete. Mass starvations have occurred during times of plenty, and even when lack of food is a contributing factor, it is rarely the determining factor of whether mass starvation occurs.

Many of the famines in recent world history have been intentional. When Stalin came to power in 1924, for example, he saw the Ukrainians, particularly the relatively wealthy independent farmers known as kulaks, to be a threat. Stalin collectivized the farms and expropriated the land of the kulaks, turning them out of their homes and sending hundreds of thousands to gulag prisons in Siberia.

Agricultural productivity in Ukraine plummeted under forced collectivization and people began to starve. Nevertheless, Stalin continued to ship food

Democracy and Famines

out of Ukraine. Peasants who tried to escape starving regions were arrested or turned back at the border by Stalin's secret police. Desperate Ukrainians ate dogs, cats, and even tree bark. Millions died.[6]

The starvation of Ukraine was intentional and it's clear that it would not have happened in a democracy. Stalin did not need the votes of the Ukrainians and thus they had little power to influence policy. Democratically elected politicians will not ignore the votes of millions of people.

Even unintentional mass starvations can be avoided in democracies. The 1974 famine in Bangladesh was not on the scale of that in Ukraine, but still 26,000 to 100,000 people died of mass starvation. It was probably the first televised starvation, and it illustrates some important themes in the relationship between economics and politics.

Floods destroyed much of the rice crop of 1974 at the same time as world rice prices were increasing for other reasons. The flood meant that there was no work for landless rural laborers who in ordinary years would have been employed harvesting the rice.

The lower income from work and the higher rice prices, taken together, led to starvations. Yet in 1974, Bangladesh in the aggregate did not lack for food. In fact, food per capita in 1974 was at an all-time high, as shown in Figure 20.5.

Mass starvation occurred not because of a lack of food per se, but because a poor group of laborers lacked both economic and political power. Lack of economic power meant they could not purchase food. Lack of political power meant that the elites then running Bangladesh were not compelled to avert the famine. Bangladesh continued to pursue bad economic policies; for instance, government regulations made it very difficult to purchase foreign exchange so it wasn't easy for capitalists to import rice from nearby Thailand or India. In fact, rice was even being smuggled out of Bangladesh and into India to avoid price controls and other regulations.

Amartya Sen, the Nobel Prize–winning economist and philosopher, has argued that whether a country is rich or poor, "no famine has taken place in the history of the world in a functioning democracy." The precise claim can be disputed depending on how one defines "functioning democracy" but the lesson Sen draws is correct:

> Perhaps the most important reform that can contribute to the elimination of famines, in Africa as well as in Asia, is the enhancement of democratic practice, unfettered newspapers and—more generally—adversarial politics.[7]

Economists Timothy Besley and Robin Burgess have tested Sen's theory of democracy, newspapers, and famine relief in India.[8] India is a federal democracy with 16 major states. The states vary considerably in their susceptibility to food crises, newspaper circulation, education, political competition, and other factors.

Besley and Burgess ask whether state governments are more responsive to food crises when there is more political competition and more newspapers. Note that both of these factors are important. Newspapers won't work without political competition and

FIGURE 20.5

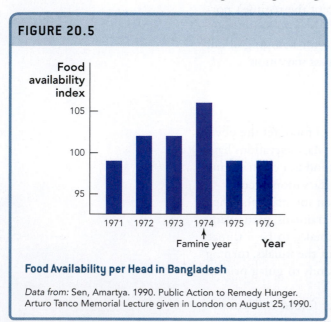

Food Availability per Head in Bangladesh

Data from: Sen, Amartya. 1990. Public Action to Remedy Hunger. Arturo Tanco Memorial Lecture given in London on August 25, 1990.

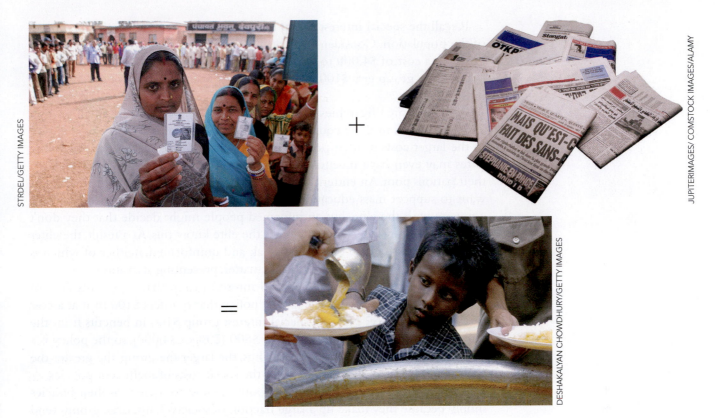

Democracy, newspapers, and famine relief

political competition won't work without newspapers. Knowledge and power together make the difference.

Besley and Burgess find that greater political competition is associated with higher levels of public food distribution. Public food distribution is especially responsive in election and preelection years. In addition, as Sen's theory predicts, government is more responsive to a crisis in food availability when newspaper circulation is higher. That is, when food production falls or flood damage occurs, governments increase food distribution and calamity relief more in states where newspaper circulation is higher. Newspapers and free media inform the public and spur politicians to action.

Democracy and Growth

Democracies have a good record of not killing their own citizens or letting them starve to death. Not killing your own citizens or letting them starve may seem like rather a low standard, but many governments have failed to meet this standard so we count this accomplishment as a serious one favoring democracies. Democracies also have a relatively good record of supporting markets, property rights, the rule of law, fair government, and other institutions that promote economic growth, as shown in Figure 20.4.

One reason for the good record of democracies on economic growth may be that the *only* way the public as a whole can become rich is by supporting efficient policies that generate economic growth. In contrast, small (nondemocratic) elites can become rich by dividing the pie in their favor even if it means making the pie smaller.

Recall the special interest group that we discussed earlier that made up 1% of the population. Consider a policy that transfers $100 to the special interest group at a cost of $4,000 to society. Will the group lobby for the policy? Yes, because the group gets $100 in benefits but it bears only $40 of the costs (1% of $4,000).

By definition, oligarchies or quasi democracies are ruled by small groups. Thus, the rulers in these countries don't have much incentive to pay attention to the larger costs of their policies as borne by the broader public. The ruling elites may even have incentives to promote and maintain policies that keep their nations poor. An entrenched, nondemocratic elite, for example, might not want to support mass education. Not only would a more educated populace compete with the elite, but an informed people might decide that they don't need the elite any more and, of course, the elite know this. As a result, the elites will often want to keep the masses weak and uninformed, neither of which is good for economic growth or, for that matter, preventing starvation.

But now let's think about a special interest group that represents 20% of society. Will this special interest favor a policy that transfers $100 to it at a cost of $4,000 to society? No. The special interest group $100 in benefits from the transfer but its share of the costs is now $800 (20% of $4,000), so the policy is a net loser even for the special interest. Thus, the larger the group, the greater the group's incentives to take into account the social costs of inefficient policies.

Large groups are more concerned about the cost to society of their policies simply because they make up a large fraction of society. Thus, large groups tend to favor more efficient policies. In addition, the more numerous the group in charge, the less lucrative transfers are as a way to get rich. A small group has a big incentive to take $1 from 300 million people and transfer it to themselves. But a group of 100 million that takes $1 from each of the remaining 200 million gets only $2 per person. Even if you took one hundred times as much, $100, from each of the 200 million people and gave it to the 100 million, that's only $200 each. Pretty small pickings. It's usually better for a large group to focus on policies that increase the total size of the pie.

In other words, the greater the share of the population that is brought into power, the more likely that policies will offer something for virtually everybody, and not just riches for a small elite.

The tendency for larger groups to favor economic growth is no guarantee of perfect or ideal policies, of course. As we have seen, rational ignorance can cause trouble. But on the big questions, a democratic leader simply will not want to let things become too bad. That's a big reason why democracies tend to be pretty good—although not perfect—for economic growth.

Takeaway

Incentives matter, so a good institution aligns self-interest with the social interest. Does democracy align self-interest with the social interest? Sometimes. On the negative side, voters in a democracy have too little incentive to be informed about political matters. Voters are rationally ignorant because the benefits of being informed are small—if you are informed, you are more likely to choose wisely at the polls, but your vote doesn't appreciably increase the probability that society will choose wisely, so why bother to be informed? Being informed creates an external benefit because your informed vote benefits everyone, but we know from Chapter 10 that goods with external benefits are underprovided.

CHECK YOURSELF

■ The free flow of ideas helps markets to function. How does the free flow of ideas help democracies to function?

Rational ignorance means that special interests can dominate parts of the political process. By concentrating benefits and diffusing costs, politicians can often build political support for themselves even when their policies generate more costs than benefits.

Incumbent politicians can use their control of the government to increase the probability that they will be reelected. Politicians typically increase spending before an election and increase taxes only after the election. Voters pay attention to current economic conditions even when the prosperity is temporarily and artificially enhanced at the expense of future economic conditions.

Our study of political economy can usefully be considered a study of government failure that complements the theory of market failure presented in Chapter 10 on externalities and Chapter 13 on monopoly. When markets fail to align self-interest with the social interest, we get market failure. When the institutions of government fail to align self-interest with the social interest, we get government failure. No institutions are perfect and trade-offs are everywhere—this is a key lesson when thinking about markets and government.

A close look at democracy can be disillusioning, but the record of democracies on some of the big issues is quite good. It's hard for politicians in a democracy to ignore the major interests of voters. And if things do go wrong, voters in a democracy can always "throw the bums out" and start again with new ideas. Partially as a result, democracies have a good record on averting mass famines, maintaining civil liberties like free speech, and supporting economic growth. Most of all, democracies tend not to kill their own citizens, who after all are potential voters.

CHAPTER REVIEW

interactive activity **Go online to practice with more examples of these types of problems, including live links to videos, data sources, and feedback.**

 Problems in green relate to MRU videos. See the MRU table at the end of the exercises.

KEY CONCEPTS

public choice, p. 385

rational ignorance, p. 386

median voter theorem, p. 394

FACTS AND TOOLS

1. Which of the following is the smallest fraction of the U.S. federal budget? Which are the two largest categories of federal spending?

    Welfare

    Interest on the federal debt

    Defense

    Foreign aid

    Social Security

    Health care

2. **a.** How many famines have occurred in functioning democracies?

    b. What percentage of famines occurred in countries without functioning democracies?

3. Around 138 million voters participated in the 2016 U.S. presidential election. Imagine that you are deciding whether to vote in the next presidential election. What do you think is the probability that your vote will determine the outcome of the election? Is it greater than 1%, between 1% and 0.1%, between 0.1% and 0.01%, or less than 0.01% (i.e., less than 1 in 10,000)?

4. If a particular government policy—like a decision to go to war or to raise taxes—works only when citizens are informed, is that an argument for that policy or against that policy?

5. True or false?

   a. During Bangladesh's worst famine, average food per person was much lower than usual.

   b. Democracies are less likely to kill their own citizens than other kinds of governments.

   c. Surprisingly, newspapers aren't that important for informing voters about hungry citizens.

   d. Compared with a dictatorship or oligarchy, democracies have a stronger incentive to make the economic pie bigger.

   e. Compared with most other countries, full democracies tend to put a lot of restrictions on markets and property rights.

   f. When it comes to disposable income, American presidents seem to prefer "making a good first impression" rather than "going out with a bang."

   g. When the government owns most of the TV and radio stations, it's motivated to serve the public interest, so voters tend to get better, less biased information.

6. The median voter theorem is sometimes called the "pivotal voter theorem." This is actually a fairly good way to think of the theorem. Why?

7. Perhaps it was in elementary school that you first realized that if everyone in the world gave you a penny, you'd become fantastically rich. This insight is at the core of modern politics. Sort the following government policies into "concentrated benefits" and "diffuse benefits."

   a. Social Security

   b. Tax cuts for families

   c. Social Security Disability Insurance for the severely disabled

   d. National Park Service spending for remote trails

   e. National Park Service spending on the National Mall in Washington, D.C.

   f. Tax cuts for people making more than $250,000 per year

   g. Sugar quotas

THINKING AND PROBLEM SOLVING

8. David Mayhew's classic book *Congress: The Electoral Connection* argued that members of Congress face strong incentives to put most of their efforts into highly visible activities like foreign travel and ribbon-cutting ceremonies, instead of actually running the government. How does the rational ignorance of *voters* explain why *politicians* put so much effort into these highly visible activities?

9. An initiative on Arizona's 2006 ballot would have handed out a $1 million lottery prize every election: The only way to enter the lottery would be to vote in a primary or general election. How do you think a lottery like this would influence voter ignorance?

10. We mentioned that voters are myopic, mostly paying attention to how the economy is doing in the few months before a presidential election. If they want to be rational, what should they do instead? In particular, should they pay attention to all four years of the economy, just the first year, just the last two years, or some other combination?

11. In his book *The Myth of the Rational Voter*, our GMU colleague Bryan Caplan argues that not only can voters be rationally ignorant, they can even be rationally irrational. People in general seem to *enjoy* believing in some types of false ideas. If this is true, then they won't challenge their own beliefs unless the cost of holding these beliefs is high. Instead, they'll enjoy their delusion.

    Let's consider two examples:

    a. John has watched a lot of Bruce Lee movies and likes to think that he is a champion of the martial arts who can whip any other man in a fight. One night, John is in a bar and he gets into a dispute with another man. Will John act on his beliefs and act aggressively, or do you think he is more likely to rationally calculate the probability of injury and seek to avoid confrontation?

    b. John has watched a lot of war movies and likes to think that his country is a champion of the military arts that can whip any other country in a fight. John's country gets into a dispute with another country. John and everyone else in his country go to the polls to vote on war. Will John act on his beliefs and vote for aggression, or do you think he is more likely to rationally calculate the probability of defeat and seek to avoid confrontation?

12. In the television show *Scrubs*, the main character J. D. is a competent and knowledgeable doctor.

He also has very little information outside of the field of medicine, admitting he doesn't know the difference between a senator and a representative and believes New Zealand is near "Old Zealand."

a. Suppose J. D. spends some time learning some of these common facts. What benefits would he receive as a result? (Assume there are no benefits for the sake of knowledge itself.)

b. Suppose instead J. D. spends that time learning how to diagnose a rare disease that has a slight possibility of showing up in one of his patients. What benefits would he receive as a result? (Again, assume there are no benefits for the sake of knowledge itself.)

c. Make an *economic* argument that even given your answer to part b, voters have too little incentive to be informed about political matters.

13. Driving along America's interstates, you'll notice that few rest areas have commercial businesses. Vending machines are the only reliable source of food or drink, much to the annoyance of the weary traveler looking for a hot meal. Thank the National Association of Truck Stop Operators (NATSO), who consistently lobby the U.S. government to deny commercialization. They argue:

> Interchange businesses cannot compete with commercialized rest areas, which are conveniently located on the highway right-of-way . . . Rest area commercialization results in an unfair competitive environment for privately-operated interchange businesses and will ultimately destroy a successful economic business model that has proven beneficial for both consumers and businesses.[9]

The sorrow of a land without burgers

a. How does NATSO make travel more expensive for consumers?

b. Do you think most Americans have heard of NATSO and the legislation to commercialize rest stops? How does your answer illustrate rational ignorance? Do you think that the owners of interchange businesses (i.e., restaurants, gas stations, and other businesses located near but not on highways) have heard of NATSO?

c. Why does NATSO often succeed in its lobbying efforts despite your answer to part a? (*Hint:* What is the concentrated benefit in this story? What is the diffused cost?)

14. The following figure shows the political leanings of 101 voters. Voters will vote for the candidate who is closest to them on the spectrum, as in the typical median voter story. Again as usual, politicians compete against each other, entering the "political market" just as freely as firms enter the economic market back in Chapter 11.

a. Which group of voters will get their exact wish: the group on the left, the center-left, the center-right, or the right?

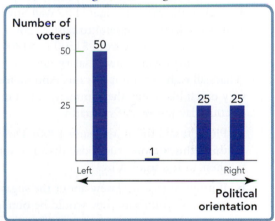

b. Now, four years later, it's time for a new election. Suppose that in the meantime, the two right-leaning groups of voters have merged: The 25 center-right voters move to the far right, forming a far-right coalition. In the new election, whose position will win now?

c. As you've just seen, there's a "pivotal voter" in this model. Who is it?

15. Let's rewrite a sentence from the chapter concerning the Roman Empire: "As the American Empire grew, courting politicians in Washington became a more secure path to riches than starting a new business." Does this seem true today? If it started happening, how would you be able

to tell? In your answer, put some emphasis on market signals that could point in favor of or against the "decadent empire" theory. (*Hint:* By some measures, Moscow has the highest real estate prices in the world, and it's probably not due to low housing supply.)

CHALLENGES

16. Is rational ignorance the whole explanation for why voters allow programs like the sugar quota to persist? Perhaps not. In the early 1900s, the government of New York City was controlled by a Democratic Party organization known as Tammany Hall. In a delightful essay entitled "Honest Graft and Dishonest Graft" by George Plunkitt, one of the most successful politicians from the Tammany machine, he argued that voters actually approve of these kinds of government-granted favors. (The essay and the entire book, *Plunkitt of Tammany Hall: A Series of Very Plain Talks on Very Practical Politics*, are available for free online.)

    For example, Plunkitt said that ordinary voters like it when government workers get paid more than the market wage: "The Wall Street banker thinks it is shameful to raise a [government] clerk's salary from $1500 to $1800, but every man who draws a salary himself says, 'That's all right. I wish it was me.' And he feels very much like votin' the Tammany ticket on election day, just out of sympathy."

    a. Plunkitt said this in the early 1900s. Do you think this is more true today than it was back then, or less true? Why?

    b. If more Americans knew about the sugar quota, do you think they would be outraged? Or would they approve, saying, "That's all right, I wish it was me"? Why?

    c. Overall, do you think that real-world voters prefer a party that gives special favors to narrow groups, even if those voters aren't in the favored group? Why?

17. a. When a drought hits a country, and a famine is possible, what probably falls more: the demand for food or the demand for haircuts? Why?

    b. Who probably suffers more from a deep drought: people who own farms or people who own barbershops? (*Note:* The answer is on page 164 of economist Amartya summary of his life's work, *Development as Freedom, 1999.*)

    c. Sen emphasizes that "lack of buying power" is more important during a famine than "lack of food." How does Sen's barber story illustrate this?

18. Political scientist Jeffrey Friedman and law professor Ilya Somin say that since voters are largely ignorant, that is an argument for keeping government simple. Government, they say, should stick to a few basic tasks. That way, rationally ignorant voters can keep track of their government by simply catching a few bits of the news between reruns of *Modern Family*.

    a. What might such a government look like? In particular, what policies and programs are too complicated for today's voters to easily monitor? Just consider the U.S. federal government in your answer.

    b. Which current government programs and policies are fairly easy for modern voters to monitor? What programs do you think that you and your family have a good handle on?

    c. Can you think of easy replacements for the too complex programs in part a? For instance, cutting one check per farmer and posting the amount on a Web site might be easier to monitor than the hundreds of farm subsidies and low-interest farm loans that exist today.

19. We mentioned that the median voter theorem doesn't always work, and sometimes a winning policy doesn't exist. This fact has driven economists and political scientists to write thousands of papers and books, both proving that fact and trying to find good workarounds. The most famous theoretical example of how voting doesn't work is the Condorcet paradox. The Marquis de Condorcet, a French nobleman in the 1700s, wondered what would happen if three voters had the preferences like the ones in the following table. Three friends are holding a vote to see which French economist they should read in their study group. Here are their preferences:

	Jean	Marie	Claude
1st choice	Walras	Bastiat	Say
2nd choice	Bastiat	Say	Walras
3rd choice	Say	Walras	Bastiat

a. They vote by majority rule. If the vote is Walras vs. Say, who will win? Say vs. Bastiat? Bastiat v. Walras?

b. They decide to vote in a single-elimination tournament: Two votes and the winner of the first round proceeds on to the final round. This is the way many sporting events and legislatures work. Now, suppose that Jean is in charge of deciding in which order to hold the votes. He wants to make sure that his favorite, Walras, wins the final vote. How should he stack the order of voting to make sure Walras wins?

c. Now, suppose that Claude is in charge instead: How would Claude stack the votes?

d. And Marie? Comment on the importance of being the agenda setter.

(In case you think these examples are unusual, they're not. Any kind of voting that involves dividing a fixed number of dollars can easily wind up the same way—check for yourself! Condorcet himself experienced another form of democratic failure: He died in prison, a victim of the French Revolution that he supported.)

20. In the previous question, you showed that sometimes there may be no policy that beats every other policy in a majority rule election and, as a result, the agenda can determine the outcome. In the previous question, all of the policy choices on the agenda were as good as any other, but this is not always the case. Imagine that three voters, L, M, and R, are choosing among seven candidates. The preferences of the voters are given in the following table. Voter M, for example, likes Grumpy the best and Doc the least.

Preferences for President of Voters L, M, R			
	Voter L	Voter M	Voter R
1st Choice	Happy	Grumpy	Dopey
2nd Choice	Sneezy	Dopey	Happy
3rd Choice	Grumpy	Happy	Sleepy
4th Choice	Dopey	Bashful	Sneezy
5th Choice	Doc	Sleepy	Grumpy
6th Choice	Bashful	Sneezy	Doc
7th Choice	Sleepy	Doc	Bashful

a. Imagine that we vote according to a given agenda starting with Happy vs. Dopey. Who wins? We will help you with this one. Voter L ranks Happy above Dopey, so voter L will vote for Happy. Voter M prefers Dopey to Happy, so voter M will vote for Dopey. Voter R ranks Dopey above Happy so voter R will vote for Dopey. So _____ wins.

b. Now take the winner from part a and match him against Grumpy. Who wins?

c. Now take the winner from part b and match him against Sneezy. Who wins?

d. Now take the winner from part c and match him against Sleepy. Who wins?

e. Now take the winner from part d and match him against Bashful. Who wins?

f. Finally, take the winner from part e and match him against Doc. Who wins?

g. We have now run through the entire agenda so the winner from part f is the final winner. Here is the point. Look carefully at the preferences of the three voters. Compare the preferences of each voter for Happy (or Grumpy or Dopey) with the final winner. Fill in the blank: Majority rule has led to an outcome that _____ voter regards as worse than some other possible outcome. The answer to this question should shock you.

(This question is drawn from the classic and highly recommended introduction to game theory, *Thinking Strategically* by Avinash K. Dixit and Barry J. Nalebuff [New York: W. W. Norton, 1993].)

21. In the 1998 Minnesota gubernatorial election, there were three main candidates: Norm Coleman (the Republican), Jesse "The Body" Ventura (an Independent), and Hubert Humphrey III (the Democrat). Although we can't know for certain, the voters probably ranked the candidates in a way similar to that found in the following table. The table tells us, for example, that 35% of the voters ranked Coleman first, Humphrey second, and Ventura third; and 20% of the voters ranked Ventura first, Coleman second, and Humphrey third; and so forth.

Minnesota Gubernatorial Election, 1998			
Rank	35%	28%	20%	17%
1	Coleman	Humphrey	Ventura	Ventura
2	Humphrey	Coleman	Coleman	Humphrey
3	Ventura	Ventura	Humphrey	Coleman

a. Suppose the election is by plurality rule, which means that the candidate with the most first-place votes wins the election. Who wins in this case?

b. In Challenges question 19, you were introduced to the Marquis de Condorcet. Today, voting theorists call a candidate a Condorcet *winner* if he or she can beat every other candidate in a series of 1:1 or *"face-off"* elections. Question 19 showed you that in some cases, there is no Condorcet winner. What about in the Minnesota gubernatorial election of 1998?

c. A Condorcet winner beats every other candidate in a face-off. A Condorcet loser loses to every other candidate in a face-off. Was there a Condorcet loser in the 1998 Minnesota gubernatorial election (given the preferences we have estimated)?

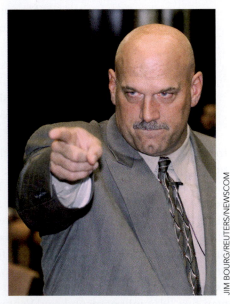

Jesse "The Body" Ventura
Who are you calling a loser?

JIM BOURG/REUTERS/NEWSCOM

interactive activity

WORK IT OUT

For interactive, step-by-step help in solving this problem, go online.

Let's walk through the median voter theorem in a little more detail. Consider a town with three voters, Enrique, Nandini, and Torsten. The big issue in the upcoming election is how high the sales tax rate should be. As you'll learn in macroeconomics (and in real life), on average, a government that wants to do more spending has to bring in more taxes, so "higher permanent taxes" is the same as "higher government spending." Enrique wants low taxes and small government, Nandini is in the middle, and Torsten wants the biggest town government of the three. Each one is a stubborn person, and his or her favorite position—what economic theorists call the "ideal point"—never changes in this problem. Their preferences can be summed up like this, with the x denoting each person's favorite tax rate:

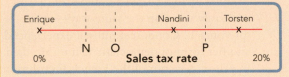

a. Suppose there are two politicians running for office, N and O. Who will vote for N? Who will vote for O? Which candidate will win the election?

b. O drops out of the campaign after the local paper reports that he hasn't paid his sales taxes in years. P enters the race, pushing for higher taxes, so it's N vs. P. Voters prefer the candidate who is closest to them, as in the text. Who will vote for N? Who will vote for P? Who will win? Who will lose?

c. In part b, you decided who was heading for a loss. You get a job as the campaign manager for this candidate just a month before election day. You advise her to retool her campaign and come up with a new position on the sales tax. Of course, in politics as in life, there's more than one way to win, so give your boss a choice: Provide her with two different positions on the sales tax, both of which would beat the would-be winner from part b. She'll make the final pick herself.

d. Are the two options you recommended in part c closer to the median voter's preferred option than the loser's old position, or are they further away? So in this case, is the median voter theorem roughly true or roughly false?

MARGINAL REVOLUTION UNIVERSITY VIDEOS

Democracy and Famines

mruniversity.com/seniii-democracy-and-famines

Problems: **2, 5**

21

Economics, Ethics, and Public Policy

Is it okay to export pollution from rich to poor countries? Larry Summers said not only that it was, but also that exporting pollution should be encouraged. Summers, if you don't already recognize the name, is one of the best economists of his generation, and a former president of Harvard, secretary of the Treasury, and lead advisor to President Obama. In a memo to some of his colleagues when he was chief economist at the World Bank, Summers wrote:

> Just between you and me, shouldn't the World Bank be encouraging *more* migration of the dirty industries to the LDCs [Less Developed Countries]? . . .
>
> The measurements of the costs of health impairing pollution depend on the foregone earnings from increased morbidity and mortality. From this point of view a given amount of health impairing pollution should be done in the country with the lowest cost, which will be the country with the lowest wages. I think the economic logic behind dumping a load of toxic waste in the lowest wage country is impeccable and we should face up to that.*

Unfortunately for Summers, his memo didn't remain "just between you and me." When it was leaked to the press, there was a firestorm of controversy, not just against Summers but against economics and the type of "impeccable" economic reasoning that Summers found convincing.

If you found Larry Summers's memo disturbing, what about some of the ideas of Nobel prize–winning economist Gary Becker? Becker said that we should legalize the trade in human kidneys. In fact, in a survey, Robert Whaples found that 70% of the economists he surveyed (128 members of the American Economic Association) agreed or strongly agreed with this idea.[1] Right now more than 100,000 Americans are waiting for kidney transplants. Many of them will die; others will undergo painful and exhausting dialysis for three days a week, four hours a day. The hospital waiting lists run for five years or more to get a kidney from a willing donor. In case you didn't know, the law won't allow kidneys to be bought and sold, so at a price of zero we have a severe kidney shortage (see Chapter 8 for a discussion of how price controls work).

*The Summers memo can be widely found online.

409

Becker said that to alleviate the shortage, we should allow people to sell their kidneys (you only need one of the two you have). Many citizens of poorer countries would be willing to sell their kidneys for a few thousand dollars or less; in fact, some of these people are selling their kidneys on the black market right now.

Thus, we have two outstanding economists, one of whom said we should export pollution *to* poor countries, while the other said we should import kidneys *from* poor countries. No doubt, these two economists would probably also agree with each other!

Economists sometimes draw a distinction between positive economics and normative economics. **Positive economics** is about describing, explaining, or predicting economic events. For instance, if a quota restricts imports of sugar, the price of sugar will increase and people will buy less sugar. That's true whether or not we think that sugar is good for people. **Normative economics** is about making recommendations on what economic policy should be. Is a sugar quota a good policy? That depends on what we think is good and who we think counts most when we measure benefits and costs.

> **Positive economics** is describing, explaining, or predicting economic events.
>
> **Normative economics** is recommendations or arguments about what economic policy should be.

Not all of this chapter is economics—much of it touches on ethics and morals—but it is still important material for understanding economics as a broader approach to the world. First, economics has limitations and you need to know what they are. It helps to know which ethical values are left out of economic theory. Second, sometimes you will hear bad or misleading arguments against economics, and you need to know those, too, and where they fall short.

We warn you, however, that in this chapter our primary goal is to raise questions rather than provide answers. And we try not to present our own normative claims. Instead, we consider the normative claims made by other people, especially critics of economics, and how they intersect with the positive economics that you have learned already.

The Case for Exporting Pollution and Importing Kidneys

The case for exporting pollution and importing kidneys is actually a familiar one: trade makes people better off. One person wants the kidney more than the money; the other wants the money more than the kidney. Both people can be made better off by trade.

Similarly, it's not surprising that the rich are willing to pay the poor to take some of their pollution. On the margin, the rich value health more than money and the poor value money more than health, so both can be made better off by trade.

What's wrong with these trades? Plenty, according to many people who argue that economic reasoning ignores important values. Economists, it has been said, know the price of everything and the value of nothing.

Some of the objections to standard economic reasoning that we will examine are:

1. The problem of exploitation.
2. Meddlesome preferences.
3. Fair and equal treatment.
4. Cultural goods and paternalism.

5. Poverty, inequality, and the distribution of income.

6. Who counts? Should some count for more?

Let's consider each in turn. You can think of these as the major reasons why not everyone thinks that voluntary exchanges are, in every case, a good idea.

Exploitation

Is the seller of a kidney being exploited? To focus on the difficult issues, let's assume that the seller is of good mind and fully informed about all the risks of donating a kidney. Even in this situation, many people argue that someone selling a kidney is being exploited. Dr. Francis Delmonico, a transplant surgeon and prominent opponent of kidney sales, argues that "payments eventually result in the exploitation of the individual. It's the poor person who sells."[2]

Delmonico is correct that a poor person is more likely to sell a kidney than a rich person. But does this mean that the poor person who sells a kidney is being exploited? Let's consider three cases.

- Case 1: Alex buys a kidney from Ajay.
- Case 2: Alex pays Ajay to clean his house.
- Case 3: George Mason University pays Alex to grade exams.

In all three cases, the seller would not sell if he were wealthier. So are the sellers (Ajay in the first two cases and Alex in the third) being exploited? We may feel that there is something different about selling a kidney, but it's difficult to see the dividing line that separates exploitation from exchange. Many people in rich and poor countries alike take jobs that involve significant risks. The yearly mortality rate for commercial fishermen in Alaska, for example, is seven times higher than the mortality rate for donating a kidney—so why is donating a kidney different from fishing in Alaska?[3]

One response is that for a poor person the money is exploitative because the circumstances of poor people give them little choice but to sell things they would rather keep. But consider which of the three following cases is most exploitative:

- Case 1: Someone asks you to donate a kidney but offers you nothing in return.
- Case 2: Someone offers you $5,000 to donate a kidney.
- Case 3: Someone offers you $500,000 to donate a kidney.

Few people would say that case 1 involves exploitation. But what about case 2 and case 3? If case 2 is exploitative, then case 3 must be even more exploitative—after all, the temptation to sell is many times greater. In fact, many more people, including a great many people in rich countries, would accept an offer of $500,000 to sell one of their kidneys. But it seems odd to say that case 3 is the *most* exploitative case. The usual story is that buyers exploit sellers by offering them too little, not too much! But if bigger offers are less exploitive, then case 2 can't be exploitative either because case 2 is case 1 plus some money and how can offering someone more be a way to exploit them?

If someone offered *you* $500,000 to sell your kidney, would you feel exploited? Probably not. After all, you could always say no. But if case 3 doesn't exploit you, it's hard to see how case 2 exploits Ajay. Maybe Ajay needs the money more than you but imagine, for example, that 10% of the people

Kidneys for Sale?

in India would accept $5,000 for a kidney and 12% of people in the United States would accept $500,000 for a kidney. Does this make the larger offer more exploitive?

Keep in mind that everyone agrees that abject poverty is itself a problem. Overall, it would be better if people had access to clean water, good health care, and more wealth. The issue is whether it's wrong to offer to buy things from the poor just because they are poor. We will be returning to the issue of poverty and the distribution of income later in the chapter.

One more point: we assumed for the sake of argument that the seller of the kidney was of good mind and understood all the risks. One possible response is to say that no one ever understands the risks well enough to make trades like this. If that is the case, however, then we ought to ban gifts of kidneys as well as sales. In fact, thousands of people voluntarily give one of their kidneys away every year and we generally regard such people as heroes. But we don't allow anyone to buy or sell a kidney, despite the fact that doing so could save many thousands of lives.

Meddlesome Preferences

Even if exploitation isn't an issue, many people have a gut feeling that trading kidneys for money is just wrong. How much should this gut feeling count when thinking about justice?

Consider this: is it okay to eat a horse? Not in California. Millions of Californians voted for a law that says, "No restaurant, cafe, or other public eating place may offer horsemeat for human consumption." The market in horsemeat is open, however, in Europe and Japan where you'll find horse on the menu at many restaurants. In Japan, it's even common to find raw horsemeat for, the sale as a kind of sushi. But in the United States, the National Horse Protection League doesn't want anyone eating horses—especially foreigners—so it took out full-page ads in the *New York Times* to lobby for a ban on the export of horses to save them from a "brutal fate designed to feed foreign coffers."

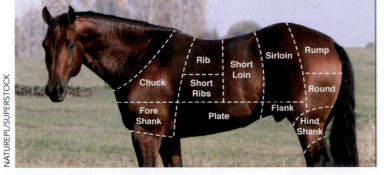

NATUREPL/SUPERSTOCK

Horse, it's what's for dinner.

In America the horse is, so to speak, a sacred cow (unlike in India where the cow is a sacred cow). So should horsemeat be banned? And if horsemeat is banned because people don't like the idea of someone eating horses, should kidney sales be banned because some people don't like the idea of someone trading kidneys? And what about homosexuality, interracial dating, or various religious practices that do not meet with anything close to universal approval? Often these practices offend someone, so how much should these meddlesome preferences count?

Preferences about what other people do, even when those other people don't interfere in any direct way with what you do, are sometimes called meddlesome preferences. It's often difficult to resolve meddlesome preferences with other values that are considered important, such as liberty, rights, or religious freedom. We—Alex and Tyler—don't usually put much normative weight on meddlesome preferences (we think that "live and let live" should be more popular), but that's one of our value judgments, not anything intrinsic to being economists.

Fair and Equal Treatment

The notion of fair and equal treatment also can run up against the value of trade and efficiency. Consider some of the programs to make mass transit accessible to disabled passengers. In New York City, it has long been the case that buses are capable of accepting passengers in wheelchairs. In essence, the bus "kneels down" until the wheelchair can board and then the bus elevates again.

Equipping buses in this fashion was very costly. A study commissioned by Ed Koch, the mayor of New York City at the time of bus conversion, estimated that it would have been cheaper for each wheelchair user or severely handicapped person to take a taxi than refit all buses. Not only would it have cost less, but it would have been more convenient, as well. But would that have been the right thing to do? On one side of the equation stands the virtue of efficiency. Taxpayers would have saved money and disabled people, if they took taxis, would have had easier and more luxurious transport options. But defenders of the bus investments claimed that the principle of "equal treatment" was more important than buying each disabled person free taxi trips for life. Even if the taxpayers and disabled people both agreed that taxis were preferable, the critics were saying that more is involved in mass transit than getting a person from place A to place B. Mass transit was, in part, about the sacred value of equal treatment and not making people feel different or disadvantaged.

Economics does not make distinctions between the sacred and the profane, but these issues underlie many arguments about public policy. When thinking about trade-offs, we need to be aware of the resulting tensions and subtleties, many of which are ethical in nature.

Cultural Goods and Paternalism

A closely related issue is whether governments should support some goods even when the public isn't willing to pay for them. The French government, for example, spends 1.5% of French GDP a year subsidizing culture and related "higher values."[4] The implicit judgment is that culture is "more valuable" than what people will otherwise spend their money on, and that government is a better judge of "what is best" than are private individuals, at least for these particular sums of money.

The French also place a minimum quota on how many French-language movies must be shown on TV, specifically 40% of the total. For a while, there was even a French ministry of rock 'n' roll, to support the production of French-language popular music. The government tried to give the French people French rock 'n' roll instead of the American and British rock music that the French people were buying. Supporters of the policy say that subsidizing French culture is valuable in its own right, and that the aesthetic judgments of the marketplace should not be the final ones.

The pragmatic criticism of French policy argues that these subsidy schemes tend to be counterproductive and wasteful. Maybe French movies would be more successful if they had to appeal to French consumers rather than to the French bureaucrats who hand out the subsidies. The more philosophical criticism is

The French government sees a dark side to American culture, but when it premiered in Paris, the French public made the opening day revenues of *Spiderman 3* the highest in French history.

EVERETT COLLECTION, INC

that people should be allowed to spend their money as they choose. In the latter view, freely chosen values have a moral worth of their own that is to be respected.

Of course, it is not just the French who give special support to some cultures and not others. The American government exempts the Amish, a small religious community living predominantly in Ohio, Pennsylvania, and Indiana, from many forms of taxation and compulsory education. America's approximately 300 Indian reservations have a special legal status, in part because the U.S. government takes special care to preserve those cultures. The U.S. federal government also spends money supporting the arts (though the American government spends less than does the French government), in part, because some people want to encourage a higher quality of art than they think will arise through the marketplace and voluntary charity. In fiscal 2016, the U.S. budget for the National Endowment for the Arts was just under $148 million.

Poverty, Inequality, and the Distribution of Income

Perhaps the problem with kidney sales and exporting pollution to poor countries is not trade per se, but the poverty and inequality that make the trade happen. We might accept that when a poor person sells a kidney to a rich person, both are made better off, but still rue the fact that the poor person is poor. In earlier chapters, we emphasized that under certain conditions, markets maximize consumer plus producer surplus—that is an important virtue—but as the kidney example illustrates, in addition to efficiency, we may also have concerns about justice or equity. With a different distribution of income, the demand and supply curves would shift and the poor might not want to sell their kidneys at a price that the rich could afford—that too would be efficient and it might also be more just.

But what is a just distribution of income? How much is owed to the poor? How much is owed to the rich? Questions like these are at the heart of many debates about foreign aid, trade, taxation, health care, and immigration, to name just a few controversial areas.

Many economists have turned to moral philosophy to seek support for their normative policy judgments, and three views have proven especially influential: John Rawls's maximin principle, utilitarianism, and Robert Nozick's entitlement theory of justice. These three views have very different implications for how we, as citizens, should judge the distribution of income and the status of voluntary marketplace transactions.

Rawls's Maximin Principle

Rawls's maximin principle says that justice requires maximizing the benefits going to society's most disadvantaged group.

John Rawls's *A Theory of Justice*, published in 1971, argued that questions of income and wealth distribution are keys for evaluating social policy. Rawls, a Harvard philosopher, laid out the **maximin principle**, namely that a government should (without violating people's basic rights) maximize the benefits going to society's most disadvantaged group. The notion of "maximizing the minimum" led to the phrase "maximin." For Rawls, doing well by the worst-off group is more important than improving the lot of better-off groups. Rawls deliberately rejects the economist's idea of trade-offs, instead concluding that the worst-off group should be the clear first priority.

Rawls's argument for making the worst-off the first priority is that if no one knew what position they held in society, that is, if people were behind a "veil of ignorance," then they would want a rule that maximized the position of the worst-off, just in case they turned out to be the worst-off! In economic terms, Rawls believed that people were extremely risk-averse.

To see how maximin works in practice, consider a simple example with three people, Red, Blue, and Green.

Now let's compare Society A where Red, Blue, and Green have equal incomes of 100 to Society B where the respective incomes are 150, 100, and 50. Rawls's maximin principle implies that Society A is better or more just than Society B because the worst-off person in Society B, Green, has more income in Society A. Notice that the only difference between Society A and B is that income is more equally distributed in A than in B; average income is identical so it doesn't seem unreasonable to prefer Society A to Society B.

Society	Red	Blue	Green	Average Income
A	100	100	100	100
B	150	100	50	100
C	600	600	99	433
D	1096	102	101	433

But now let's compare Society A with Society C. In Society C, Red and Blue are much better off than in Society A and Green is slightly worse off. Notice that average income in Society C is more than four times as high as in Society A. Which society would you rank as the better society? Which society does maximin rank more highly? The maximin principle says that Society A is better than Society C because the worst-off person in Society C, Green, is better off in Society A. The maximin principle says that the extra income of Red and Blue counts for nothing; only the income of the least well-off person counts.

It's sometimes said that the maximin principle favors societies with more equal division of incomes but that is not necessarily true. Let's compare Society A with Society D. Even though income is perfectly egalitarian in Society A, the maximin principle says that Society D is better because, once again, the income of the least well-off person is higher. The maximin principle even prefers Society D to Society C, even though Society C has a more equal division of the same average income.

The maximin principle is influential among philosophers but less so among economists who, as you know, tend to think in terms of trade-offs between values. A little bit less income for the worst-off might be acceptable if it comes with a big enough gain to others. Lower average income might be acceptable if income is a little bit more equally divided, and so forth.

Utilitarianism

Under **utilitarianism**, we try to implement the outcome that brings the greatest sum of utility or "happiness" to society. The best known utilitarian philosopher today is Peter Singer, whom you also may know as an advocate of animal rights.

When it comes to redistribution, a utilitarian approach tries to determine which people have the greatest need for some additional income. For instance, an extra dollar for a poor person may go toward a doctor's visit, but an extra dollar for a rich person may just go toward buying an extra silk tie. The poor person probably gets greater happiness from the extra dollar. The utilitarian is likely to suggest that some amount of money be redistributed from rich people

Utilitarianism is the idea that the best society maximizes the sum of utility.

toward poor people. Unlike Rawls, however, utilitarians are not always trying to make the poorest people as well off as possible. Utilitarians advocate redistributing income only up to the point where the marginal change in utility created from the redistribution is positive. They try to maximize the total sum of utility, not the utility of the worst-off person. So, in principle, utilitarianism (unlike maximin) allows the poor to undergo some extra suffering, provided that suffering is outweighed by enough gains elsewhere in the economy.

What might limit the amount of wealth a utilitarian would redistribute from rich to poor? Incentives! Taking money away from richer people decreases their incentive to earn, so more redistribution could reduce overall wealth by enough to reduce total utility. A utilitarian recipe therefore might involve only a modest amount of redistribution, especially if people are very responsive to incentives. Utilitarianism will also take into account the incentive effects of redistribution on the poor. Giving dollars to poor people is not always the best way to improve their welfare. As Milton Friedman once said, if you pay people to be poor, you're going to have a lot of poor people.

Notice that the usual assumption in economics is that a dollar is a dollar no matter who gets the dollar, so utilitarianism needs to make assumptions that extend beyond those of economic theory. Economic theory does not assume that a dollar is worth more to a poor person than to a rich person and standard economic tools don't give us any easy way to measure happiness or utility. In fact, many economists believe that comparing the happiness of two people is not very scientific. We might think that the poor person gets more happiness than the rich person from an extra dollar of wealth, but perhaps the poor person is a monk who neither needs nor wants money, while the rich person really does desire another silk tie. Maybe the rich person is rich precisely because he loves money and worked very hard to get it. We aren't saying that this is the case; we are only pointing out that there is no natural unit of measurement of utility, and human beings have very different preferences.

Most economists do believe in a safety net and a welfare state to take care of the poor people in a wealthy society. But this belief doesn't have to be rooted in any very strict comparison of utilities between rich people and poor people. Economists frequently portray the social safety net as a way of obtaining insurance against bankruptcy, major health-care problems, and other bad outcomes. If you think that insurance has value, and that private markets might not provide this insurance on their own (see Chapter 24 for a discussion), that provides some case for a social safety net. Utilitarians go further, however, and try to offer very specific recipes for just how much money should be transferred from the rich to the poor.

WALT DISNEY PICTURES/PHOTOFEST

Uncle Scrooge has a high and very slowly diminishing marginal utility of wealth. Uncle Scrooge loves wealth so much that a consistent utilitarian would endorse increasing total utility by taking a dollar from a poor duck like Donald and giving it to rich Uncle Scrooge. Are you a consistent utilitarian? Or an inconsistent utilitarian?

Robert Nozick's Entitlement Theory

Whether we accept Rawls's maximin principle or prefer utilitarianism or choose almost any other theory of justice, one thing is clear. There is no guarantee that the distribution of income generated by market forces will be anything like what these theories describe as the just distribution. Most theories of justice, therefore, will call for some amount of taxation and redistribution, using the force of government. One of the few exceptions is Robert

Nozick's entitlement theory of justice, which is also known as a libertarian theory of justice.

Robert Nozick, another Harvard philosopher, laid out a moral system very different from that of Rawls. Nozick was far more sympathetic to the market economy than was Rawls, and he outlined a defense of the market in a 1974 book called *Anarchy, State, and Utopia*. Nozick argued that the pattern of the distribution of income was irrelevant. What mattered was whether income differences were *justly acquired* and thus Nozick focused on the process by which income is distributed.

Nozick argued that if John wishes to trade with Mary, that decision should be up to John and Mary alone, provided they do not infringe on the rights of others. In the words of Nozick, all capitalist acts between consenting adults should be allowed. Nozick admitted and indeed emphasized that such trades, performed on a cumulative basis, would result in different and indeed unequal outcomes and opportunities for people, but he saw nothing wrong with those inequalities. Nozick went further and positively endorsed those inequalities that resulted from freely chosen market transactions, devoid of coercive force or fraud.

Nozick offered a classic rebuttal to Rawlsian and other theories of justice. Nozick said let's imagine that one day we create a world in which the distribution of wealth is exactly as described by some theory of justice. Let's say the distribution of wealth is exactly like that described by *your* theory of justice. Now, Nozick said, imagine someone like J. K. Rowling, the author of the Harry Potter book series (Nozick actually used the example of Wilt Chamberlain, the basketball star of the 1960s and 1970s).

Rowling, let us say, writes another Harry Potter book and she offers to sell a copy to anyone who is willing to buy. Of course, many people are very willing to buy Rowling's book, and so person by person money is transferred from book buyers to Rowling. Rowling becomes very rich, so at the end of the day, the distribution of wealth will be very different than at the beginning of the day, when by assumption all was just. Yet how can the new distribution of wealth, the one with a very rich J. K. Rowling, be unjust? No one's rights were violated in the process and indeed everyone, including both the fans and Rowling, was made better off every time Rowling sold a book. All that has happened has been voluntary, peaceful trade. A just and rightful trade, Nozick's theory would imply. So why should any outsider disapprove of the resulting pattern of wealth?

Note that this example is not fanciful: When she wrote her first book, J. K. Rowling was an unemployed single mother living on welfare. Yet Rowling became the first author ever to become a billionaire solely through her written works and today her income is thousands of times higher than that of her average fan.

Nozick's example is a direct criticism of the view that equality of outcome is important. Nozick argues that what we should care about is the justness of the process that leads to differences in wealth—theft is bad and should be condemned and rectified, but voluntary, peaceful trade should not be condemned even when it leads to large differences in wealth.

In the libertarian account, what is just is to respect an individual's rights. One way to think of libertarian rights is that they are "side constraints" on possible government actions. The libertarian view corresponds to some common intuitions. For instance, as discussed, many people in the world need kidneys;

Nozick's entitlement theory of justice says that the distribution of income in a society is just if property is justly acquired and voluntarily exchanged.

otherwise, they will die or require dialysis. You have two good kidneys and need only one to live. Is it okay to take a kidney from you against your will? Is it okay to draft your kidney for the greater good? Is it okay to redistribute kidneys?

If you believe the answer to that question is no, you have taken one big step toward the libertarian theory of justice. If you want to think about the next step, a libertarian would ask, if it's not okay to draft your kidney, why is it okay to draft your whole body? And if redistributing kidneys is wrong, isn't redistributing income wrong for similar reasons?

Philosophers continue to debate the relevance of the perspectives of Rawls, utilitarianism, and Nozick, among other ideas. One contribution of the economist is simply to insist that people should be more focused on producing rather than redistributing wealth. Moral philosophers sometimes write as if all the goods were just sitting there on the table ready to be divvied up, but economists know this isn't true. Economists usually stress the importance of producing the wealth in the first place.

CHECK YOURSELF

■ The libertarian theory rejects kidney redistribution as unjust. What about the utilitarian theory or Rawl's maximin principle?"

Who Counts? Immigration

When economists evaluate a public policy like trade or immigration, they tend to count the benefits and costs to all individuals equally, regardless of where they live. But this isn't always how politics works. Usually, national governments weigh the welfare of their citizens more heavily—usually much more heavily—than the welfare of foreigners.

Immigration is the most salient current issue where the welfare of citizens is counted much more than the welfare of foreigners. Some people argue that immigration hurts U.S. citizens because low-skilled immigrants reduce the wages of low-skilled Americans. Other people argue that immigrants add to the U.S. economy through their entrepreneurship and their willingness to work at very tough jobs.

On net, careful studies indicate that immigration has some positive and some negative effects, but the U.S. economy is so large that overall immigration is not such a big issue—economists who support and oppose immigration agree on this conclusion. People debate the pluses and minuses of additional immigration, and often this is an emotional issue, but again, no matter what your view, the net cost or benefit is likely small relative to the entire U.S. economy.[5]

So let's assume that immigration is either a small benefit or a small cost to U.S. citizens. Everyone agrees, however, that immigration is a huge benefit to the immigrants. The typical Mexican immigrant today comes from a small village in Chiapas, Guerrero, Oaxaca, or some other very poor part of Mexico. People in those villages usually earn no more than a dollar or two a day. If they come to the United States, they can earn $10 an hour or more. Of course, they send a lot of this money home to their families. Remittances, most of which come from the United States, are Mexico's number one leading "import" industry. Remittances often make the difference between hunger and plenty, or between a collapsing village and a revitalized one. Immigration matters a great deal to the many thousands of Mexicans who cross the border every year and to those who would come if it were easier to do so.

Does his well-being count?

FRED GREAVES/REUTERS/NEWSCOM

So, if the United States is making decisions about its immigration policy, how much should it weigh the benefits accruing to Mexicans from immigration? We're talking not just about the Mexicans who arrive in this country (some of whom may become citizens), but also the Mexicans back home receiving the remittances. Economics tends to be cosmopolitan in its implications since it treats all people equally, no matter where those people live. If the gains to foreigners are counted as much as the gains to nationals, then Mexican immigration into the United States will look especially beneficial. But again, not everyone buys the presumption that the welfare of foreigners should count for as much as the welfare of U.S. citizens. A presidential candidate who held that assumption as a campaign platform would be unlikely to win election.

Foreign aid is another policy issue where we must ask whether our government should be looking after American citizens or people in other countries. In reality, the amount of money the American government spends on foreign aid is very low. The exact sum is difficult to determine, because in the government budget, "foreign aid" and "military assistance" are not completely distinct categories. But, by standard accounts, formal measures of foreign aid amount to less than $30 billion per year, or less than 1% of the federal budget.[6] Of course, simply sending money to other countries does not always make them better off; some foreign aid is captured by corrupt elites or used for bad ends. Still you could say the same about some of the money the U.S. government spends at home! The point is this: It remains within the voters' power to have the federal government spend less money on American citizens and more money on needy people overseas. If you are worried about corruption, why not just drop some dollar bills from a helicopter flying over a poor country?

Whether we should do this will depend, in part, on your views as to "who counts?" and "how much?"

Economic Ethics

When economists recommend ideas like exporting pollution or paying for kidneys, they are often said to be ignoring ethics. Economists sometimes agree, perhaps with a bit of pride! But a closer look shows that this is not true. Even though the predictions of economics are independent of any ethical theory, there are ethical ideas behind normative economic reasoning. An economist who rejects the idea of exploitation in kidney purchases, for example, is treating the seller of kidneys with respect—as a person who is capable of choosing for him- or herself even in difficult circumstances.

Similarly, economists don't second-guess people's preferences very much. If people like wrestling more than opera, then so be it; the economist, acting as an economist, does not regard some preferences as better than others. In normative terms, economists once again tend to respect people's choices.

Respect for people's preferences and choices leads naturally to respect for trade—a key action that people take to make themselves better off. As we saw in Chapter 10 on externalities, economists recognize that trade can sometimes make the people who do not trade worse off. Nonetheless, the basic idea that people can make decisions and know their own preferences leads economists to be very sympathetic to the idea of noncoercive trade.

Economists also tend to treat all market demands equally, no matter which person they come from. Whether you are white or black, male or female, quiet

How the Dismal Science Got Its Name

or talkative, American or Belgian, your consumer and producer surplus count for the same in an economic assessment of a policy choice.

None of this is to say that economists are always right in their ethical assumptions. As we warned you in the beginning, this chapter has more questions than answers. But the ethical views of economists—respect for individual choice and preference, support for voluntary trade, and equality of treatment—are all ethical views with considerable grounding and support in a wide variety of ethical and religious traditions. Perhaps you have heard that Thomas Carlyle, the Victorian-era writer, called economics the "dismal science." What you may not know is that Carlyle was a defender of slavery and when he made that statement he was attacking the ethical views of economics. Economists like John Stuart Mill believed that all people were able to make rational choices; that trade, not coercion, was the best route to wealth; and that everyone should be counted equally, regardless of race. As a result, Mill and the laissez-faire economists of the nineteenth century opposed slavery, believing that everyone was entitled to liberty. It was these ethical views that Carlyle found dismal.[*] We beg to differ.

Takeaway

Economics stresses the core idea of gains from trade. Yet in many circumstances, not everyone approves of gains from trade, mostly for ethical reasons. Not everyone thinks that kidneys should be bought and sold and not everyone thinks that pollution should be exported to poor countries. Intuitions about fairness, equitable treatment, distribution, and other matters often clash with the economic notion of increasing gains from trade.

We respect the distinction between positive economics—predicting what will happen—and normative judgments—what should be done. So we haven't tried to answer these ethical dilemmas or give you our sense of the best possible ethical theory. But we do know that if you want to understand and participate in debates about economic policy in the real world, then you must also have some understanding of different ethical theories and their foundations.

[*] "The Secret History of the Dismal Science" is discussed in an excellent article of that title by David M. Levy and Sandra J. Peart, available online at http://www.econlib.org/library/Columns/LevyPeartdismal.html#.

CHAPTER REVIEW

Go online to practice with more examples of these types of problems, including live links to videos, data sources, and feedback.

KEY CONCEPTS

positive economics, p. 410

normative economics, p. 410

Rawls's maximin principle, p. 414

utilitarianism, p. 415

Nozick's entitlement theory of justice, p. 417

FACTS AND TOOLS

1. a. In this chapter, we never actually defined "exploitation." What is one dictionary definition of the word?

b. Decide whether the six cases of alleged exploitation we discussed earlier in the chapter fit your dictionary's definition. Yes, this will involve quite a bit of personal judgment, as will most of this chapter's questions.

c. In your opinion, does the dictionary definition go too far or not far enough when it comes to labeling some voluntary exchanges as exploitation?

2. Of the three ethical theories we discuss (Rawlsian, utilitarian, and Nozickian), which two are most different from the third? In what way are the two different from the third?

3. One of Nozick's arguments against utilitarianism was the "utility monster": a person who *always* gets enormous happiness from every extra dollar, more happiness than anyone else in society. If such a person existed, the utilitarian solution would be to give all the wealth in society to Nozick's utility monster; any other income distribution would needlessly waste resources. This possibility was appalling to Nozick. Nozick's argument is intentionally extreme, but we can use it as a metaphor to think about the ethics of real-world income redistribution.

a. Do you know any utility monsters in your own life: people who get absurdly large amounts of happiness from buying things, owning things, going places? Perhaps a family member or someone from high school?

b. Do you know any utility misers? That would be people who don't get much pleasure from anything they do or anything they own, even though they probably have enough money to buy what they want.

c. In your view, would it be ethical for the government to distribute income from real-world utility misers to real-world utility monsters? Why or why not?

4. a. Just thinking about yourself, if you did not know in advance whether you were a Red, Blue, or Green person, would you rather live in Society A, B, C, or D, discussed in the Rawls's section of the chapter? Why?

b. Which society would you like least? Why?

5. Rawlsians support government income redistribution to the worst-off members of society. If "society" means the whole world, how much redistribution might be involved? In other words, what fraction of people in the rich countries might have to give most of their income to people in the poorest countries? Keep in mind that the poorest Americans have clean water, guaranteed food stamps, and free health care, while billions of people around the world lack such guarantees.

6. Would a "global utilitarian" (someone who values the utility of everyone in the world equally, without giving more weight to people in their own country) who lives in America want more immigrants from poor countries or more immigrants from rich countries? Why?

THINKING AND PROBLEM SOLVING

7. To a Rawlsian, would the world be better off without the Harry Potter novels and one additional billionaire?

8. Some people say that the right to equal treatment has no price. But it seems that most people don't really believe that: Those are just polite words that we tell one another. Consider the following cases:

a. What if it costs $10 million per kneeling bus?

b. What if it costs $10,000 to hire translators to translate ballots into a rare language spoken by fewer than 10 voters?

c. What if it costs the lives of dozens of police officers to ensure the right of a persecuted minority to vote?

d. At these prices, is the right to equal treatment too expensive for society to buy it? In each case, describe what you think the exact price cutoff should be (in dollars or lives), and briefly explain how you came to that decision. Why not twice the price? Why not half?

9. The line between "having a meddlesome preference" and "recognizing an externality" is not always clear. Both are ways of saying, "What you're doing bothers me." As we used it in this chapter, a "meddlesome preference" is something that reasonable people should just not worry about so much. By contrast, "recognizing an externality" is a way of advancing the subject for public discussion and perhaps even for a vote. In the town you grew up in, which of the following issues were considered things that should be left to individuals and which were things that should be put up for a vote? Is there a good way of distinguishing between the two?

a. The amount of pollution emitted by a local factory

b. How much noise would be allowed after 11 PM

c. Whether siblings should be allowed to marry, even if it is consensual

d. Where liquor stores could be located

e. How people should dress in public

f. How many children someone should have

10. Let's see how a utilitarian dictator would arrange things for Adam, Eve, and Lilith. One heroic assumption that utilitarians make is that you can actually compare happiness and misery across different people: In reality, brain scans are making this easier to do but it's still a lot of guesswork. Let's suppose that this utilitarian dictator has eight apples to distribute: The table shows the utility that each person receives from their first apple (a lot), but extra apples give less extra happiness (apples give "diminishing marginal utility," in economic jargon).

Utility per Apple	Adam	Eve	Lilith
1st	1,000	600	1,200
2nd	140	500	200
3rd	20	400	100
4th	1	300	50

a. So, if the dictator wants to maximize the sum of Adam, Eve, and Lilith's utility, how many apples does each person get?

b. If instead, Lilith received 2,000 units of utility from the first apple, how would this change the optimal utilitarian distribution?

11. **a.** The "trolley problem" is a famous ethical puzzle created by Philippa Foot: You are the conductor of a trolley (or subway or streetcar or train) that is heading out of control down a track. Five innocent people are tied to the track ahead of you: If you run over them, they will surely die. If you push a lever on your trolley, it will shift onto another track, where one unfortunate person is tied up. Either you *let* five people die or you *choose* to kill one person: Those are your only choices. Which will you choose and why? Which ethical view from this chapter best fits your reasoning? (If you Google "trolley problem," you will find many other interesting ethical dilemmas to debate with your friends.)

b. Another ethical dilemma sounds quite different: You are a medical doctor trying to find five organ donors to save the lives of five innocent people. A new patient comes in for a checkup, and you find that this patient has five organs exactly compatible with the five innocent people. Do you kill the one innocent patient to save the lives of five innocents? Suppose you will never get caught: Perhaps you live in a country where people don't care about such things. Is this the same dilemma? Is it the same dilemma from a utilitarian perspective?

12. What do you think best describes the reason that trade in recreational drugs is illegal: fear of exploitation, meddlesome preferences, notions of fairness, paternalism, concerns about equality, or some other factor?

13. Based on the tools from this chapter, how could a person reasonably justify a ban on gambling?

14. Compare a Rawlsian view with a utilitarian view on the question of whether it should be legal to copy movies and music freely.

CHALLENGES

15. Should responsible adults be allowed to sell a kidney? Why or why not? If so, what restrictions would you place on such sales, if any? (For more on this issue, link to the Kidney for Sale video on page 411.)

16. **a.** In your view, when should governments enforce a "live and let live" rule: on issues that matter most to people (e.g., matters of life and death, matters of how much income to give to the government, matters of religion, matters of sexuality) or on the issues that matter least to people (e.g., what flavors of spices are permitted at the dinner table, what kind of clothing is acceptable in public)?

b. Europeans fought a lot of wars in the 1500s over the right to meddlesome preferences. Thinking back on your history courses, what preferences did Europeans want to meddle with?

c. What was the usual argument given in the 1500s for why it was right to meddle with other people's preferences?

17. Philosopher Alastair Norcross poses the following question. Suppose that 1 billion people are suffering from a moderately severe headache that will last a few hours. The only way to alleviate their headache is for one person to die a horrible death. Can the death of this one person ever be justified in a cost-benefit sense?

18. If the rich countries were able to send individual cash payments to people in poor countries, bypassing possibly corrupt governments, would you let rich countries pay people in poor countries to take their high-polluting factories? If so, how high would the annual payment have to be per family? If not, why not?

19. You would probably sacrifice yourself to save all of humanity, but you probably wouldn't sacrifice yourself to save the life of one random stranger. What number is your cutoff: How many lives would you have to save for you to voluntarily face sure death?

20. Some people feel inequality is justified if the people with unequal outcomes accepted risks voluntarily; it was simply the case that some won and some lost. Imagine two people, each spending $10,000 on lottery tickets, but only one of them wins. We end up with one poor person and one multimillionaire.

   Is this inequality better or worse than if one person is born into a rich family and the other is born into a poor family? What exactly is the difference and why?

21. Sometimes poor countries have a lot of people; India has more than 1 billion residents. Indians are relatively poor, and we know that as families become wealthy, they tend to limit their number of children. So, a much wealthier India, over time, would probably have many fewer than 1 billion inhabitants. Would this make for a better India or a worse India? Although each Indian would have much more, there would be fewer Indians. As a result, is there any argument for keeping India poor, so as to have a higher number of people? If not, why not? In general, what can economics tell us about the ideal number of people in a society? Anything at all?

22. Let's say that Tom, who is 25 years old, wants to smoke a cigarette. Consider the following two situations.

   a. Tom is smoking. Suddenly, the government comes along and tells Tom that he cannot do this. The government claims that Tom is inflicting an "external cost" on other human beings. Is this a good policy or bad policy?

   b. Tom is smoking a cigarette at home with no one else around. Suddenly, the government comes along and tells Tom that he cannot do this. The government claims that Tom is inflicting an "external cost" on another human being. Tom asks who this might be? The government says that the 65-year-old Tom will be harmed by the smoking-today-Tom. The government claims that today-Tom isn't doing enough to look out for the well-being of future-Tom. Does this argument make any sense? Is it ethically correct? If so, can and should we trust our government to make these decisions for our future selves?

WORK IT OUT

interactive activity

For interactive, step-by-step help in solving this problem, go online.

Let's see how a utilitarian dictator would arrange things for Charles, Elizabeth, and Mary. One heroic assumption that utilitarians make is that you can actually compare happiness and misery across different people. In reality, brain scans are making this easier to do but it's still a lot of guesswork. Let's suppose that this utilitarian dictator has eight oranges to distribute: The table shows the utility that each person receives from their first orange (a lot), but extra oranges give less extra happiness (oranges give "diminishing marginal utility," in economic jargon).

Utility per Orange	Charles	Elizabeth	Mary
1st	2,000	1,200	2,400
2nd	280	1,000	400
3rd	40	800	200
4th	2	600	100

a. So, if the dictator wants to maximize the sum of Charles's, Elizabeth's, and Mary's utilities, how many oranges does each person get?

b. If instead, Mary received 4,000 units of utility from the first orange, how would this change the optimal utilitarian distribution?

22

Managing Incentives

A good social system aligns self-interest with the social interest. A successful organization aligns self-interest with the organization's interest.

Organizations—businesses, governments, teams—whose interests conflict with the interests of their members don't last very long. It's often not easy, however, to align everyone's incentives. Incentives matter—this is one of the key lessons of this book—but getting the incentives right is not always easy. Managers of businesses and sports teams, voters, politicians, parents, all must think about and choose incentives. This chapter is about getting the incentives right and what happens when we get the incentives wrong.

Lesson One: You Get What You Pay For

Every May, Chicago public school students take a standardized test. Students are used to being tested, graded, and rewarded accordingly, but beginning in May 1996, teachers and principals had a lot more than usual on the line: Schools with low scores would be closed, teachers reassigned, and principals fired. The idea, of course, was to give educators stronger incentives to work harder and better. If grading was good for the students, why not for the teachers?

Stronger incentives do give teachers and principals an incentive to put in extra hours and search for better teaching methods. But how else can teachers raise the grades of their students? Here's a hint: Some students also use this method. That's right—they cheat. Indeed, teachers can cheat a lot better than students because they know which answers are correct! Two economists who understand incentives, Brian Jacob and Steven Levitt (the latter of *Freakonomics* fame), started to look carefully at test data and asked: Would teachers really cheat to raise student grades?[1] Sure enough, Jacob and Levitt found odd patterns in the data—students who got easy answers wrong and difficult answers right, groups of students who had exactly the same right and wrong answers, and students who received high grades during a test year but low grades the year after. Most telling for an economist was that the indicators of cheating were much stronger after the penalty for low-performing schools went into effect than before!

Perhaps you think that teachers' cheating to raise student grades is a good idea! But it wasn't what the proponents of strong incentives for teachers had in mind. Not all teachers cheated, but cheating was surprisingly common. Jacob and Levitt estimated that cheating occurred in at least 4% to 5% of classrooms.

425

Other researchers have found that after the introduction of strong incentives, a lot more students are declared learning disabled.[2] Why? Test scores of students called "learning disabled" are usually not counted when it comes to rewarding teachers and principals.

Does all this mean that strong incentives for teachers are a bad idea? Not necessarily. Students who learn more, earn more. If strong incentives for teachers do increase true scores, even by a small amount, maybe it's a good idea even if some of the better scores are due to cheating.[3]

A similar example of incentives for cheating comes from corporate finance. In the 1980s, chief executive officers (CEOs) were given much stronger incentives to increase their firm's stock price. Instead of being paid a straight salary, they were awarded stock options. These are complicated financial instruments, but what you need to know is that they pay off only if the stock rises above a certain price. As with strong incentives for teaching, strong incentives encouraged CEOs to work harder and smarter. It also encouraged them to cheat by manipulating earnings reports to make their firms appear more profitable than they really were. Enron and the other scandals of the 1990s and first decade of the 2000s were, in part, the result. Were strong incentives worth it? If the shareholders believed that on average the costs of cheating exceeded the benefits of encouraging harder work, they would offer their CEOs fewer options and other strong incentives. But so far most of these incentives have stayed in place, albeit with more monitoring of potentially bad behavior.

Shareholders, however, are not the only ones who can be harmed when a company like Enron or Lehman Brothers collapses, so their choice of CEO incentive scheme may not reflect everyone's interests and may not be best for society as a whole. (Recall our discussion of externalities in Chapter 10.) Incentive schemes, for example, that give executives big bonuses for very good performance but don't penalize them very much for very bad performance can encourage executives to take on too much risk. In part for this reason, investment banks such as Bear Stearns and Lehman Brothers took on lots of risk in mortgage securities, and their collapses helped lead to the financial crisis of 2008. Executive compensation, therefore, has become a subject of political controversy. We will return to executive compensation later on in this chapter.

When designing an incentive scheme, remember this: You get what you pay for. That sounds good but there is a problem. What if what you pay for is not exactly what you want? If you pay for higher test scores, you will get higher test scores. But test scores are an imperfect measure of what you really want— more productive teachers and more knowledgeable students. What you pay for is higher stock prices, but what you really want is a more profitable firm. Usually, stock prices reflect a firm's fundamental value, but even the market can be fooled sometimes!

The closer "what you pay for" is to "what you want," then the more you can rely on strong incentives. Careful design of an incentive scheme can narrow the gap between what you want and what you can pay for. After Jacob and Levitt published their results, the administrators of Chicago Public Schools, to their credit, fired some teachers, and instituted new procedures to make cheating more difficult. After the Enron scandal, investors demanded more independent financial audits. The stronger the incentives, the more it pays to invest in careful measurement and auditing, and vice versa.

If you can't bridge the gap between "what you pay for" and "what you want," then weak incentive schemes can be better than strong incentive schemes.

Prisons for Profit?

Should the management of prisons be contracted out to the private sector? The owners of a private firm have a strong incentive to cut costs and improve productivity because they get to keep the resulting profits. If a public prison cuts costs, there is more money in the public treasury but no one gets to buy a yacht, so the incentive to cut costs is much weaker.

In 1985, Kentucky became the first state to contract out a prison to a for-profit firm. Private prisons in the United States today hold about 128,000 prisoners, about 8% of all prisoners in the country. Should efficient private prisons replace inefficient public prisons? Economists Oliver Hart, Andrei Shleifer, and Robert Vishny (collectively known as HSV) say no. HSV don't question that the profit motive gives private prisons stronger incentives than public prisons to cut costs—HSV say that's the problem! Suppose that we care about costs but we also care about prisoner rehabilitation, civil rights, and low levels of inmate and guard violence. What we pay for is cheap prisons, but what we want is cheap but high-quality prisons. If we can't measure and pay for quality, then strong incentives could encourage cost cutting at the expense of quality.

Prisons for Profit? Private prisons in the United States hold about 8% of all prisoners. England and Wales (11%) and Australia (19%) also use private prisons.

The principle is a general one, a strong incentive scheme that incentivizes the wrong thing can be worse than a weak incentive scheme. One car dealer in California advertises that its sales staff is not paid on commission.[4] Why would a store advertise that its sales staff do not have strong incentives to help you? The answer is clear to anyone who has tried to buy a car. High-pressure dealers who pounce on you the moment you enter the showroom and bombard you with high-pressure sales tactics ("I can get you 15% off the sticker, but you have to act NOW!") may sell cars to first-time buyers, but the strategy is too unpleasant to win many repeat customers. Car dealers who rely on repeat business usually prefer a low-pressure, informative sales staff.

In theory, a car dealer could have strong incentives *and* repeat business by paying its sales staff based on their "nice" sales tactics, but in practice, it's too expensive to monitor how salespeople interact with clients. Cheating by the sales staff would be difficult to detect and thus would be common. Paying the sales staff a salary instead of a commission calms them down a bit. Of course, there is a price to be paid for weak incentives. Imagine that Joe's Honda pays its sales staff on commission, while Pete's Subaru pays its staff a straight salary. Which dealership do you expect to be open late at night and on Sundays?

What about prisons? Are HSV correct that weak-incentive public prisons are better than strong-incentive private prisons? Not necessarily. HSV assume that cutting quality is the way to cut cost. But sometimes higher quality is also a path to lower costs. Low levels of inmate and guard violence, for example, are likely to reduce costs. And respect for prisoner's civil rights? That can save on legal bills. When quality and cost cutting go together, a private firm has a strong incentive to increase quality.

HSV may also underestimate how well quality can be measured. Measuring intensively pays off more when incentives are strong. Unsurprisingly, therefore, private prison companies and government purchasers have made extensive efforts to measure the quality of private prisons.

Finally, don't forget that weak incentives reduce the incentive to cut costs but they don't increase the incentive to produce high quality! Public prisons might use their slack budget constraints to offer high-quality rehabilitation programs, or they might instead offer prison guards above-market wages. Which do you think is more likely?

Nevertheless, whether HSV are right or wrong about private prisons, their argument is clever. The usual argument against government bureaucracy is that without the profit incentive, public bureaucracies won't have an incentive to cut costs. HSV suggest this is exactly why public bureaucracies may sometimes be better than private firms.[5]

Piece Rates vs. Hourly Wages

A majority of workers are paid by the hour but a significant number are paid by the piece. An hourly wage pays workers for their inputs (of time); a **piece rate** pays workers for their output. Agricultural workers, for example, are often paid by the number of pieces of fruit or vegetable that they pick. Garment workers are often paid per item completed. Salespeople are often paid, in part, by the number of sales that they make. When should workers be paid by the hour and when should they be paid by the piece?

Piece rates increase the incentive to work hard and can work well when output is easy to measure so "what you pay for" is close to "what you want." Piece rates are common in agricultural work because it's easy to measure the number of apples picked and this is close to what the employer wants. Even in agricultural work, however, the employer wants not just apples but ripe and unbruised apples so piece rates usually require some form of quality control. Piece rates do not work well when quality is important but quality control is expensive.

In the early days of computing, IBM paid its programmers per line of code. Can you see the problem? When IBM paid by the line, IBM programmers produced lots of code, but in their rush to earn more money, the programmers often wrote low-quality code. IBM's incentive scheme rewarded what was measurable—lines of code—at the expense of what IBM really wanted but what was difficult to measure, high-quality code. IBM quickly stopped paying its workers by the line and switched to hourly wages. Hourly wages reduced the incentive to work hard but also reduced the incentive to rush the work before it was ready.

The advantage of piece rates is that, if used properly, they can greatly increase productivity. The auto-glass installer Safelite Glass Corporation switched from an hourly wage system to a piece rate. Safelite was able to handle the quality control issue by linking every job with a worker so that if a quality problem arose, the worker who was responsible for that windshield installation had to fix it on his or her own time. Productivity quickly improved by an astonishing 44%.[6] About half of the increase in productivity was due to the same workers working harder, including lower absenteeism and fewer sick days, but the other half of the productivity increase was due to another important effect of piece rates. A piece rate system attracts more productive workers.

Consider two firms, one of which pays workers by the piece and the other pays workers by the hour. Now consider two workers, one of whom can install five windshields a day, the other just three. Which worker will be attracted to which firm? The piece rate firm will attract the more productive worker

A **piece rate** is any payment system that pays workers directly for their output.

because piece rates give productive workers a chance to earn more money. The hourly wage plan will attract workers who are relatively less productive or even "lazy."

The differences between workers in productivity can be surprisingly large. One California wine grower switched from paying grape pickers by the hour to paying by the pound. Previously, the firm had paid its workers $6.20 per hour. Under piece rates the average pay was effectively $6.84 per hour, about the same as before, but some workers were making as much as $24.85 an hour.

When some workers are more productive than other workers, piece rates will tend to increase inequality in earnings. Under the hourly wage, every grape picker earned $6.20 an hour. Under the piece rate, some earned $6.84, while others earned $24.85. Information technology is making it easier to measure the output of all kinds of workers, not just grape pickers. As a result, performance pay (piece rates, commissions, bonuses, and other rewards tied directly to output) is becoming more common in the U.S. economy and this is one reason why the inequality of earnings has increased.[7]

The increase in effective pay under piece rates explains why both firms and employees can benefit from piece rates. Under hourly wages, workers don't have an incentive to work harder even when they can do so at low cost. Piece rates benefit productive workers by giving them an opportunity to use their skills to make more money. Piece rates also benefit firms by increasing productivity more than wages.

Even though firms and workers can both benefit from piece rates, piece rates are sometimes not implemented because of distrust. Workers fear that if they respond to a new piece rate plan by increasing productivity (and thus wages), the firm will respond by reducing the piece rate in the next period (e.g., paying less per pound of grapes picked). In the old Soviet Union, factory managers who increased productivity in response to new incentives were often denounced because their increased performance proved that they had previously been lazy! Of course, this greatly reduced the incentive to increase productivity. Similarly, workers won't work harder if they expect that higher productivity will be punished with lower piece rates. Firms that want to introduce piece rates must build trust with their workers.

Lesson Two: Tie Pay to Performance to Reduce Risk

Consider an auto dealer who wants to motivate her sales staff. Let's assume that all the auto dealer cares about is sales, so she is not worried that strong incentives will make her sales staff too pushy. Are strong incentives now the best? Maybe not.

Auto sales depend on more than hard work. Sales also depend on factors the staff has no control over, such as the price and quality of the car, the price of gas, and the state of the economy. If incentives tie earnings directly to sales, the sales staff are going to do great when the economy is booming but poorly when the economy is in a recession.

When sales vary for reasons having little to do with hard work, strong incentives may be more expensive than they are worth. Most people don't like risk. Which would you prefer, $100 for sure or a gamble that pays $200 with probability $\frac{1}{2}$ and $0 with probability $\frac{1}{2}$? Gambling in Las Vegas can be fun but most

CHECK YOURSELF

- Lincoln Electric is a firm famous for using piece rates. Lincoln Electric also has a policy of guaranteed employment. How are these two policies related?

- In the United States, restaurant customers have the option of adding a tip to the restaurant bill. In much of Europe, a "tip" is added on automatically. Where would you expect waiters to be more attentive?

people will prefer $100 for certain over a gamble with the same expected payoff. Similarly, suppose that there are two jobs: job 1 pays $100,000 a year for sure, job 2 pays $200,000 in a good year but $0 in a bad year. Suppose also that good and bad years are equally likely, so, on average, job 2 also pays $100,000 a year. Which job would you prefer? If the wages are the same on average, most people will prefer job 1, the less risky job. How high would the average wage have to be for you to prefer job 2? $110,000, $150,000, $175,000? The precise number is less important than the principle: The riskier payments are to workers, the more a firm must pay on average. Thus, if the sales staff has to bear the risk of a bad economy or a low-quality car, they will demand a big bonus for every sale. But if the sales staff demand a big bonus, what is left over for the owner? If the sales staff is sufficiently afraid to face these risks, the owner and the staff might not be able to agree on a mutually profitable strong incentive plan.*

Weak incentives insulate the sales staff from risk. If the owner is better able than the sales staff to bear the risk of a recession (perhaps because she is wealthier), weak incentives may be mutually profitable. In essence, the owner can sell the staff "recession insurance" by paying them with a fixed or nearly fixed salary. The sales staff "buy" the insurance by accepting smaller bonuses but, of course, their pay is more stable.

Bearing the risk of a recession might be worth it if hard work from the sales force is also the critical factor in sales. But if the state of the economy is a significant determinant of sales, then strong incentives have created risk with very little motivational advantage. Imagine if rewards were based solely on luck—what incentive would there be to exert effort? Similarly, if rewards are mostly based on luck, the incentive to exert effort will be low and many potential employees won't want to face those risks at a price the owner is willing to pay.

Tournament Theory

When sales depend heavily on outside factors such as the state of the economy, tying bonuses directly to sales will reward or penalize agents for outcomes that are often beyond their control—thus, shifting risk to the agent but giving the agent little incentive to exert effort. One way a manager can reduce an agent's risk is to tie rewards more closely to actions that a sales agent does control. A surprising way to do this is to pay bonuses based not on a sales agent's absolute number of sales but on their sales relative to other agents—for example, giving a bonus to the sales agents with the highest, second-highest, and third-highest sales. For obvious reasons, economists call a compensation scheme in which pay is based on relative performance, a **tournament.**

A **tournament** is a compensation scheme in which payment is based on relative performance.

If they are used cleverly, tournaments can tie rewards more closely to actions that an agent controls, thereby improving productivity and pay. To see how a tournament works in the business world, let's start with sports, an area where we are all used to thinking about tournaments.

Imagine a golf game in which players are paid based on the total number of strokes to finish the course (by the nature of golf, fewer strokes mean better play and thus higher payments). If the weather is bad, scores will be high and players won't earn very much even if they work hard. If the weather is good (clear day, no wind), scores will be low and players will earn a lot even if they

*Or worse, the sales staff may be eager to sell cars when the economy is good but may quit the day the economy turns sour.

don't work very hard. Either way, when players are paid based on their absolute scores, random forces—such as the weather—will influence how much the players earn.

Now imagine that players are playing in a tournament with a fixed number of prizes, which of course is usually the case. The fixed number of prizes means that the players are competing *against one another* rather than against some external standard of achievement. Since every player plays with the same weather, the weather no longer influences rewards. Thus, a tournament limits the amount of risk from the external environment. A lot of sporting events, not just golf, are organized in the form of tournaments. Tournaments are also common in the business world.

For instance, paying sales agents based on relative sales will reduce environment risk, risk from external factors that are common to all the agents. When sales agents are paid based on relative sales, factors that the agents do not control such as the state of the economy, the quality of the product, and the price of competing products will no longer influence agent rewards. *Here is the key*: when factors that an agent doesn't control no longer influence rewards, then factors that an agent does control—factors like effort—become more important determinants of rewards. Thus, pay for relative performance such as that used in a tournament can reduce risk and tie rewards more closely to actions that an agent controls. This will mean harder work, less risk, more output, and higher pay.

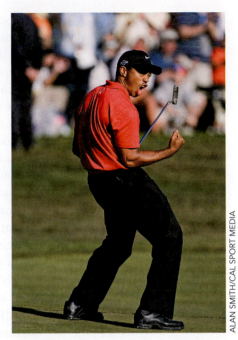

Bonus!

ALAN SMITH/CAL SPORT MEDIA

Improving Executive Compensation with Pay for Relative Performance

A good compensation scheme ties rewards to actions that an agent controls. How would you use the idea of *pay for relative performance* to tie executive pay more closely to actions that executives control?

Today, a large fraction of an executive's pay is tied to the stock price of his or her firm. When the value of the firm rises, executives are often able to cash in stock options at profitable prices. But many factors other than executive effort or ability influence the price of a stock. When the economy does well, for example, the price of most stocks goes up. Similarly, when the price of oil goes up, the stock price of firms in the oil industry tends to go up—and surprisingly, so does the pay of executives in the oil industry, despite the fact that these executives have no control over the price of oil.[8] Of course, when the price of oil falls, these executives are paid less, despite the fact that they may be working as hard as, or harder than, ever. The bottom line is that quite a bit of executive pay appears to be based on luck. But payment based on luck is not a good compensation scheme on either the upside or downside.

Is there a better way to pay executives? Instead of paying based on how well their stock performs, how about paying executives based on how well their stock performs *relative to other firms in the same industry*? If executives were paid based on relative performance, they wouldn't reap big windfall profits when the industry boomed (due to no virtue of their own) but neither would they necessarily be paid less when the industry declined (due to no fault of their own).

Pay for relative performance seems to make a lot of sense but it has not been widely adopted. As a result, some observers suspect that the complicated stock option schemes currently used to reward executives are less about creating incentives than about creative accounting that takes advantage of shareholders who do not closely monitor how much the executives are being paid. Interestingly, firms that have at least one very large shareholder—and thus at least one shareholder with an incentive to monitor the firm closely—do appear to base more executive pay on relative performance.[9]

In recent times, the American economy has experienced another problem with compensating senior managers, especially in banking and finance: Sometimes the incentive is to take too many "long tail" risks, namely risks that rarely go bad, but when they do, they go very, very bad. Let's say a bank manager encourages his staff to make risky mortgage loans that go bad only once every 30 years, but when they do, they endanger the very existence of the bank and perhaps even the banking system. Most of the time the risks pay off, the bank prospers, and the managers get a nice bonus. Sooner or later, however, the mortgages go bad and the bank ends up insolvent or in need of a government bailout. How much do the managers suffer? Usually, they don't have to give back their old bonuses and often the worst thing that happens—if that—is they are fired. In 2008, two investment banks, Bear Stearns and Lehman Brothers, went bankrupt. This wasn't good for their managers, but over the 2000–2008 period, they had already pulled out about $1.4 billion (Bear Stearns) and $1 billion (Lehman Brothers) in cash bonuses and equity sales.[10] Thus, even though these managers took on huge risks, they still profited handsomely. Many of them found other jobs or retired on their previous bonuses, so the penalties to discourage excess risk-taking aren't so strong. Prior to the financial crisis of 2007–2009, the U.S. financial system took too many risks of this nature. It remains to be seen whether better incentives can be designed to overcome this problem.

Environment Risk and Ability Risk

A tournament insulates rewards from *environment risk* due to outside factors that are common to all the players, but it adds another type of risk called *ability risk*. Imagine that you had to compete in a golf game against Tiger Woods. Would you put in more effort if you were paid based on the number of strokes or if you were paid based on who wins the game? The probability that you could beat Tiger Woods at golf is so low that if all you cared about was money, it would make sense to give up right away—why exert effort in a hopeless cause? Of course, for the same reason, Tiger Woods won't need to try very hard either!

Remember, an ideal incentive scheme ties rewards to factors that an agent controls, such as effort. But winning at golf takes more than effort; it also takes ability. As far as a player is concerned, someone else's ability is just like the weather or the state of the economy; it's not under his or her control. A golf tournament between players with highly unequal abilities doesn't tie rewards to effort; it ties rewards to ability and that often causes people to shirk and slack. Thus, tournaments work best when the risk from the outside environment is more important than ability risk.

Tournaments can be structured to reduce ability risk. At a professional golf tournament, for example, players play in rounds with the weakest players being eliminated in early rounds, so when the final and most important round is played, the players have similar abilities. Similarly, tournaments are often split into age classes or experience classes (beginner, intermediate, expert) so that abilities are similar and each player has a strong incentive to work hard. In amateur but serious golf games, when players of different ability compete together, the high-ability players will often be handicapped, which makes competition more intense for all the players. A manager who wants a lot of effort will also structure tournaments so that rewards are closely tied to effort. A manager, for example, might create junior and senior sales positions with tournaments played within each class of employee.

Tournaments in business might seem a bit unusual but they are quite common. About one-third of U.S. corporations evaluate employees based on relative performance.[11] Under the hard-nosed CEO Jeff Bezos, employees at Amazon must compete against one another for a limited number of promotions, and employees ranked in the bottom 10% are often shown the door (a so-called rank-and-yank system). Even when employees are not explicitly rewarded based on relative performance, tournaments are often implicit. Lawyers, for example, compete to earn the prize of becoming a partner. Becoming the president of a corporation is a lot like winning a tournament. Imagine that a corporation has eight vice presidents and one president—the vice presidents compete to become the next president. The fact that moving up the corporate ladder is like competing in a tournament may also shed some light on the large salaries and perks of many corporate presidents. Personal chefs, corporate jets, and lavish parties might be a sign of an abuse of power but the perks of presidency may also motivate the eight vice presidents. In part, the high salaries and perks of corporate presidents are intended as motivation for those beneath them.

Tournaments are wonderful at encouraging competition but sometimes competition can be too fierce. In a tournament, when one player falters, the others gain, so tournaments can discourage cooperation. One corporate vice president might be unwilling to mentor another if she sees a competitor waiting to take away her job. Thus, as usual, compensation schemes must be carefully designed to balance a variety of goals.

Tournaments can encourage too much competition.

DOUG MILLS/AP PHOTO

Tournaments and Grades

Let's apply some of the insights from tournament theory to a competition that you are very familiar with: the competition for grades. Some professors grade on a curve, while others use an absolute scale. When a professor "grades on a curve," there are a fixed number of "prizes"—A's, B's, C's—for each class. The competition for grades becomes a tournament.

The costs and benefits of being graded on a curve are just like the more general analysis of tournaments. Grading on a curve reduces environment risk but increases ability risk. Can you think of some examples of environment risk? Suppose that your professor is hard to understand—perhaps the professor has an accent or teaches the material too quickly or is simply not a good teacher (unlike us!). Fortunately, if the professor grades on a curve, his or her bad performance doesn't mean you have to fail. Bad teaching will reduce how much you learn but bad teaching harms everyone's performance. If the professor grades on a curve, bad teaching need not reduce your grade or reduce your incentive to study.

A bad teacher who grades on an absolute scale, however, is double trouble. First, bad teaching means that you won't learn much. Second, if the grading is on an absolute scale, not learning much means that even if you work hard, you will get a low grade. There isn't much incentive to work hard in that case.

Grading on a curve, however, does have disadvantages—grading on a curve means that you will be competing directly with the other students in the class. If you happen to be in a class with a handful of super-brilliant students, it's like golfing against Tiger Woods (unless *you* are the academic Tiger Woods). Even if you learn a lot and work hard, you won't get a high grade and that reduces your incentive to study.

Grading on a curve, therefore, creates better incentives to study when the big risk is that the professor will be bad (an environment risk), but it reduces the incentive to study when students are of very different abilities (ability risk). Grading on an absolute scale creates better incentives to study when students are of very different abilities (ability risk), but reduces the incentive to study when the big risk is that professors will be bad (environment risk).

What are some other effects of grading on a curve? Remember, tournaments tend to reduce cooperation. If your professor grades on a curve, other students might be less willing to help you with your homework (or you might be less willing to help them!). Study groups will probably be less common. Some students might even try to sabotage other students. Tournaments can also encourage the wrong kinds of cooperation. If a professor grades on a curve, in theory all the students could get together and agree not to study very much. This probably wouldn't happen in a large class, but if two sales agents regularly compete for the "salesperson of the month" award, they could collude to reduce effort and rotate the prize between them.

Here's another problem for you to think about. Suppose that the environment risk is not bad professors but rather difficult material. Imagine, for example, that some classes are more difficult than other classes (quantum physics 101 vs. handball 101). If you really wanted to learn a little about quantum physics, but you were afraid of reducing your GPA, what type of grading system would you prefer? And to ask the classic economist's question: under what conditions? See Thinking and Problem Solving question 14 for further discussion of this question.

Lesson Three: Money Isn't Everything

Incentives are powerful, but not all powerful incentives are for money. If you want to keep meetings short, make everyone stand until the meeting is over. All of a sudden the cost of talking is higher so people have an incentive to talk less.

Other powerful rewards include the feeling of identification and belonging that comes from being part of a team, the joy that comes from a job well done, and the status that comes from success on one's own terms. Intrinsic motivation is when you want to do something simply for feelings of enjoyment and pride. Ideally, firms would like their employees to be motivated by intrinsic rewards like pride in a job well done, as well as extrinsic rewards like money.

A good manager will get workers to enjoy doing what the manager wants. One way of doing this is to encourage workers to identify with the corporation and its goals in the same way that sports fans identify with their team. Many workers, for example, are given shares of stock in the company they work in. Currently, about 20 million American employees own a part of their employers.[12] Since most workers don't have much control over the value of the entire company, this doesn't make sense as a monetary incentive. But workers are more likely to identify with their company if they are also part owners of their company. Workers who identify with their company see corporate success as their success. Sports fans celebrate when their teams win championships even though the fans didn't receive any monetary rewards. In a company with strong worker identification, high profits are a cause for celebration even if the workers don't receive raises. Workers who identify with their company are more likely to see themselves in the same boat as other workers and to think and act more like a team or sometimes even like a family. This is also why many companies run staff retreats or invest in softball teams.

Successful businesses take great care to create the right **corporate culture.** Corporate culture is the shared collection of values and norms that govern how people interact in an organization or firm. Sometimes it is said that corporate culture is "how things get done around here."

The American military is one of the most successful creators of a powerful "corporate culture." In the military, a team member may sacrifice his or her life for the sake of the team. Business corporations can rarely rely on this intensity of identification, but a strong corporate culture can help align incentives. Recall that one of the big problems with monetary incentives is that the firm can't always measure what it wants. A firm that can't measure quality, for example, may be worried about creating strong incentives for quantity. But a firm with workers who value high quality for its own sake can have the best of both worlds—high quality and high quantity. Corporate culture helps firms incentivize what is difficult to measure.

The importance of morale and good relations extends beyond the business corporation. You can see these same principles at work in your everyday life.

Intrinsic and extrinsic motivation can work together but not always. When intrinsic motivation is strong, people are sometimes insulted by offers of money. If you ask a friend to give you a ride to the airport, the friend would probably say yes (well, *some* friends . . . maybe not all friends). Offer your friend $20 for a ride and all of a sudden the friend feels like a taxi driver, not a friend. The friend who might have done it for free will turn down the job for $20. In one advice column, a woman complained that her husband promised to "pay her by the pound" to lose weight (the advice column did not say whether the husband was an economist). This marriage probably was not a happy one, and we should not expect this proposed transaction to succeed.

Similarly, it is not always possible to pay a son or a daughter to do the dirty dishes. Nagging doesn't always work well either but paying money can be worse. When the parents pay money, the daughter feels less familial obligation. Once she says to herself, "Doing the dishes is a job for money," the daughter is no more obligated to do her parent's dishes than she is to get a job at a restaurant to do other people's dishes.

In these cases, payment causes external motivation to replace internal motivation. Yet for some tasks, internal motivation is what gets the job done; payment can be counterproductive.

Note that payment from a restaurant will get the same daughter to show up for work on time. Having her own job—which is a signal of adulthood and independence—is "cool" and makes the daughter feel like a grown-up. Money from parents, which feels like an allowance for tots or like a means of parental control, will not boost the daughter's internal motivation to do the dishes.

Corporate culture is the shared collection of values and norms that govern how people interact in an organization or firm.

The lesson is this: Monetary rewards are most effective when they are supported by intrinsic motivation and measures of social status. Good entrepreneurs understand these connections, and they design their workplaces so that money, intrinsic motivation, and status incentives work together. Money can't buy you love, however, and sometimes love is the incentive that makes family and personal relationships work well. Money can't buy you duty or honor either, so even within firms and other organizations such as the military, monetary incentives must be used with care. Understanding when extrinsic and intrinsic rewards complement one another and when they are at odds is today more of an art than a science. Questions like these are on the cutting edge of social psychology and behavioral economics.

Lesson Four: Nudges Can Work

Incentives, whether intrinsic or extrinsic, are not the only thing that can change behavior. Sometimes small changes in how a choice is presented, or "framed," can matter a great deal. Do you prefer beef that is 80% lean or beef that is 20% fat? Of course, those are just two different ways of presenting the same choice but supermarkets know that advertising 80% lean sells better. And have you noticed that supermarkets place the attractive candy and gossip magazines next to the checkout line rather than beside the dishwasher detergent in Aisle 7? Someone who needs detergent is going to buy detergent regardless of what aisle it's in but most of us feel a bit guilty about candy and gossip. We enjoy these items even if we also think we consume too much of them. Putting the candy and gossip at the checkout turns it into an "impulse buy": Just one moment of weakness and the salesclerk has already rung the item up. And where do supermarkets put the boring but often purchased items like milk? At the back of the store so you have to walk past the cookies and other temptations to get what you want.

Planning where, when, and how choices are made is sometimes called "choice architecture," and in the case of a supermarket the choice architecture is geared toward getting us to spend more. In contrast, some employers now put healthier foods in especially visible spots in their work cafeterias, so as to encourage healthy eating (and lower health insurance costs) among their employees. For much the same reason, one of your authors bought a refrigerator with clear fruit and vegetable drawers placed at eye level.

Cass Sunstein and Richard Thaler, a lawyer and an economist, have written a best-selling book called *Nudge*, which considers a variety of ways that governments and other organizations can use small changes in the choice architecture—what they call "nudges"—to change or improve decisions.

Most people, for example, don't like to deviate too much from the norm, so in some cases just telling people what is normal or average can change their behavior. In San Marcos, California, the local utility company told people whether they were using more or less energy compared to the average in their neighborhood. People who learned that they were using more electricity than average lowered their consumption in future periods even though the price of electricity didn't

change. The change was especially large when people with above-average consumption also received a frowning emoticon on their bill while people with below average consumption earned a smiley face.[13] By the way, good job on studying so hard. ☺

In Chapter 21 on ethics, we discussed how some economists propose to increase the supply of transplant organs by paying donors for their kidneys. Of course, that's a controversial option. A nudge might be less controversial. For instance, in the United States a person must choose to become an organ donor by signing a donor card. In Austria, everyone is automatically considered to be an organ donor unless they have signed a *nondonor* card. Either option is pretty easy but in the United States only 42% of potential donors have signed donor cards while in Austria only 1% have signed nondonor cards. As a result, 99% of Austrians are potential organ donors, more than double the U.S. percentage. Maybe Austrians are just more willing to be organ donors, but Sunstein and Thaler argue that more Americans would be willing donors if the choice to do so was made just a little bit easier.[14]

Inspired by Sunstein and Thaler, the British government has created a Behavioral Insights Team, popularly called the "nudge unit," to try to find small nudges to get people to do things the government wants, such as pay their taxes on time, insulate their attics, sign up for organ donation, and stop smoking during pregnancy.

From these examples, perhaps you can see both the potential of the nudge concept but also why it is not popular with everyone. Sometimes nudging is considered a form of manipulation or a step toward controlling more of our choices. Some individuals object to nudges all the more when they are performed by governments because of the fear that this represents a Big Brother paternalistic relationship. Advocates of nudging techniques stress their non-coercive nature, how they are based on freedom of choice, and the potential for better outcomes.

The general lesson is this. Economists usually think that what matters for choice are preferences and constraints such as prices and income. And, of course, incentives do matter. But other things matter too and sometimes how choices are presented can change which choices are made, even without changing more fundamental factors. Smiley faces won't solve the problem of climate change. For that we probably do need changes in the price of greenhouse gas emissions. But if a nudge can moderately improve outcomes at very low cost, why not nudge?

Takeaway

Incentives are a double-edged sword. When aligned with the social interest, incentives can be powerful forces for good but misaligned incentives can be equally powerful forces for bad. One of the goals of economics is to understand what institutions generate good incentives.

On a less grand level, getting the incentives right is an important goal of managers who want to motivate employees, stockholders who want to motivate managers, parents who want to motivate children, and consumers who want to motivate real estate agents, physicians, or lawyers among many others.

In this chapter, we discussed four lessons to help get the incentives right. Lesson one: You get what you pay for, but what you pay for is not always what you want. Sometimes the gap between what you pay for and what you want arises because

CHECK YOURSELF

- Is Christmas wasteful? Instead of presents, wouldn't it be more efficient to give cash that can be used to buy what the recipient really wants? Why don't we see cash gifts more often?
- Some parents and increasingly some schools are using cash to pay students for good grades. Good idea or not?

the incentive plan is badly designed. More often the gap arises because measuring exactly what you want is difficult, so you must pay for something that is more easily measurable but is not exactly what you want. When the gap between what you pay for and what you want is large, strong incentives can be worse than weak incentives. As it becomes easier to measure things like quality, however, strong incentive plans are becoming more common.

Lesson two: Tying pay to performance reduces risk. Strong incentives put more risk on agents from factors beyond their control, and to bear this risk, the agents will demand greater compensation. Sales agents on commission, for example, bear the risk that the economy goes into a downturn or that the product they sell is of low quality. As a result of this increased financial risk, sales agents on commission must be paid higher average wages than sales agents on salary. A firm must ask whether the strong incentives created by commissions increase sales enough to justify the higher average wages.

A good incentive plan will reduce unnecessary risk by tying rewards to actions that an agent controls and that are effective in increasing output. Different incentive plans like commissions, bonuses, and tournaments impose different types of risks on agents. Which incentive plan is best will depend on which risks are most important.

Lesson three: Money isn't everything. In addition to earning money, workers want to enjoy their work, identify with a team, and be respected. Successful corporations provide these rewards, as well as monetary rewards. Monetary rewards can be paid only for what is measurable, but a successful corporate culture can help firms incentivize what is difficult to measure. Monetary rewards are most effective when they are supported by intrinsic motivation and measures of social status.

Lesson four: Nudges can work. Sometimes small differences in how a choice is presented or framed can make surprisingly large differences in what people choose. Time, effort, and attention are all scarce so if a choice can be presented in a way that is quick, easy, and obvious, people are more likely to make that choice.

Successful leaders will draw on all four lessons of this chapter to design and frame incentives that align the interests of their employees, agents, and followers with their own interests.

CHAPTER REVIEW

interactive activity   Go online to practice with more examples of these types of problems, including live links to videos, data sources, and feedback.

KEY CONCEPTS

piece rate, p. 428

tournament, p. 430

corporate culture, p. 435

FACTS AND TOOLS

1. This chapter had four big lessons. Each of the following situations illustrates one and (we think) only one of those lessons. Which one?

   a. Militaries throughout the world give medals, citations, and other public honors to members of the military who excel in their duties.

b. People tip for good service after their meal is concluded.

c. Real estate agents work on commission, but office managers at a real estate office are paid a straight salary.

d. In Pennsylvania in 2009, two judges received $2.6 million in bribes from a juvenile prison. The more people they sent to jail, the more they received from the prison owners. What tipped off prosecutors was that the judges were sentencing teens to such harsh sentences for relatively minor crimes. One teenager was sent to prison for putting up a Facebook page that said mean things about her school principal; another accidentally bought a stolen bicycle. (Both judges pled guilty.)

e. Studies have shown that when employers initially enroll all workers in a retirement plan, the workers save more than when they must ask to join the retirement plan, even when in both cases workers can quit or join the plan at any time.

2. An American church sends 10 missionaries to Panama for three years to find new converts. Every six months, the missionary with the most new converts gets to be the supervising missionary for the next six months. This basically means that he or she gets to drive a car, while the other nine have to walk or ride bicycles. Clearly, this is a tournament. Now consider the following two cases. For which case will the church's incentive plan work better? (*Hint:* Think about ability risk vs. environment risk.)

Case 1: Missionaries specialize in different regions: Some stay in rich neighborhoods for the whole six months, others stay in poor neighborhoods for the whole six months.

Case 2: Missionaries move from region to region every few weeks, so that all missionaries spend a little time in every kind of Panamanian neighborhood.

3. Clever marketers understand choice architecture. Why are clearance racks in clothing stores usually located in the back of the store rather than in the front?

4. The basketball player Tim Hardaway was once promised a big bonus if he made a lot of assists. Can you think of any problems that such an incentive scheme might cause? Many professional athletes get a bonus if they win a championship. Is this kind of incentive better or worse than a basketball player's bonus for assists? Why?

5. Let's return to Big Idea Four (thinking on the margin) back in Chapter 1. Why are calls to give harsher penalties to drug dealers and kidnappers often met with warnings by economists?

6. Why are salespeople so much more likely than other kinds of workers to be paid on a "piece rate" (i.e., on commission)? What is it about the kind of work they do that makes the high-commission + low-base-salary combination the equilibrium outcome?

7. Unlike in the previous question, sometimes piece rates don't work so well. Why might the following incentive mechanisms turn out to be more trouble than they're worth?

a. An industrial materials company pays welders by the number of welds per hour. Of course, the company pays only for necessary welds.

b. A magazine publisher pays its authors to write "serial novels" one chapter at a time. The authors are paid by the word (common in the nineteenth century and how Dickens and Dostoyevsky made their livings).

8. The typical corporate executive's incentive package offers higher pay when the company's stock does well. One proposal for such executive merit pay is to instead pay executives based on whether their firm's stock price does better or worse than the stock price of the average firm in their own industry. Does this proposal solve an environment risk problem or an ability risk problem? How can you tell?

THINKING AND PROBLEM SOLVING

9. In 1975, economist Sam Peltzman published a study of the effects of recent safety regulations for automobiles. His results were surprising: Increased safety standards for automobiles had no measurable effect on passenger fatalities. Pedestrian fatalities in automobile accidents, however, increased. (This is now known as the Peltzman effect and has been tested repeatedly over the decades.)

a. Why might more *pedestrians* be killed when a car has *more* safety features?

b. Economists have looked for ways out of Peltzman's dilemma. Here's one possible solution: Gordon Tullock, our colleague at George Mason, has argued that cars could have long spikes jutting out of the steering column pointed directly at the driver's heart. Keeping Peltzman's paper and the role of incentives in mind, would you expect this safety mechanism to result in an increase, decrease, or no change in automobile accident fatalities? Why?

c. Would a pedestrian who never drives or rides in cars tend to favor Tullock's solution? Why or why not?

10. One reason it's difficult for a manager to set up good incentives is because it's easy for employees to lie about how they'll respond to incentives. For example, Simple Books pays Mary Sue to proofread chapters of new books. After an author writes a draft of a book, Simple sends chapters out to proofreaders like Mary Sue to make sure that spelling, punctuation, and basic facts are correct.

As you can imagine, some books are easy to proofread (perhaps Westerns and romances), while others are hard to proofread (perhaps engineering textbooks). But what's difficult or easy is often in the eye of the beholder: Simple can't tell which books are particularly easy for Mary Sue to proof, so they have to take her word for it. Let's see how this fact influences the publishing industry.

In the following figure, $Q^\star$ is the number of chapters in the new book *Burned: The Secret History of Toast*. It's a strange mix of chemistry and history, so Simple isn't sure how Mary Sue will feel about proofing it. The marginal cost curve shows Mary Sue's true willingness to work: The more chapters she has to read, the more you have to pay her. If Simple offers to pay her $50 per chapter, as shown, she'll actually finish the job.

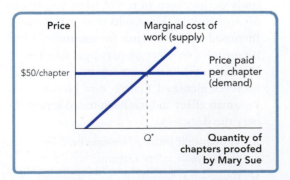

a. If Mary Sue wants to bluff, claiming that the book is actually painful to read, what is that equivalent to?

Supply curve shifting left

Supply curve shifting right

Demand curve shifting down

Demand curve shifting up

Once you decide, make the appropriate shift in the figure.

b. The publisher just *has* to have Mary Sue proof all $Q^\star$ chapters of *Burned*: All its other proofreaders are busy. The publisher will pay what it needs to for her to finish the book. This is the same as another curve shift in a certain direction: Draw in this shift in the figure.

c. What did Mary Sue's complaining do to her price per chapter? What did it do to her workload?

d. (Bonus) You've seen how Mary Sue's bluffing influenced the outcome. What are some things that Simple might do to keep this from happening?

11. Who do you think is in favor of forbidding baseball player contracts from including bonuses based on playing skill? Owners or players? Why?

12. In the short, readable classic *Congress: The Electoral Connection,* David Mayhew uses the basic ideas of incentives and information as a pair of lenses through which to view members of Congress. What he saw was quite simple: The urge for reelection drives everything. Thus, members are driven by self-interest to give the voters in their home district as much as possible. Of course, voters face the same problem in judging members of Congress that any manager faces when evaluating an employee: Some outputs are harder to measure than others, so voters focus on measurable outputs. With that in mind, what will voters be most likely to care about? Choose one from each pair and briefly explain why you made that choice.

a. How many dollars come to the district for new hospitals and highways vs. how many dollars are spent on top-secret military research.

b. How well the member behaved in private meetings with Chinese leaders vs. how the member sounded on *Meet the Press*.

c. How well the member did in reforming the Justice Department vs. how well the member did at the Turkey Toss back in the district last Thanksgiving.

(As you've seen, voters' focus on the visible can easily drive the member's entire career. Mayhew's book was an important early work in "public choice," the use of basic microeconomic ideas like self-interest and strategy to study political behavior. For more on the topic, Kenneth Shepsle and Mark Bonchek's short textbook *Analyzing Politics* is highly recommended. See also Chapter 20 of this textbook.)

13. In the movie business, character actors are typically paid a fixed fee, while movie "stars" are typically paid a share of the box office revenues. Why the difference? Try to give two explanations based on the ideas in this chapter.

14. Let's return to the question we posed in the chapter: Suppose that the big environment risk is not bad professors but rather hard material. Imagine, for example, that some classes are more difficult than other classes (quantum physics 101 vs. handball 101). If you really wanted to learn a little about quantum physics but you were afraid of reducing your GPA, you'd face a tough choice. A curve is better for you than an absolute scale, but even if your professor grades on a curve, you're probably still sitting in a class with other well-trained physics majors. Let's see if we can find a work-around.

a. At your school, are there certain times of the day when the less serious, more fun-loving tend to take their classes? If so, what time is that? If you sign up for a section scheduled then, you might look better on the curve.

b. Some schools offer simplified (we won't say "dumbed down") versions of some hard courses. Does your school offer anything like this? If so, does it allow majors to take the same sections as the nonmajors? How is this sorting related to tournament theory?

c. If you were a professor, which teaching schedule would you rather have: two sections where the majors and nonmajors are mixed together, or one section with the majors and one with the nonmajors?

15. When an accused defendant is brought before a judge to schedule a trial, the judge may release the defendant on his or her "own recognizance"

or the judge may demand that the defendant post bail, an amount of cash that the defendant must give to the court and that will be forfeited if the defendant fails to appear. Many defendants don't have the cash, so they borrow the money from a bail bondsperson. So if the defendant fails to appear, the bail bondsperson is out the money, unless the defendant is recaptured within 90–180 days. To recover their money, a bail bondsperson will hire bail enforcement agents, also known as bounty hunters, to track down the missing defendant. If the bounty hunters don't find the defendant, they don't get paid.

This Dog knows how to hunt.

DAVID HOWELLS/GETTY IMAGES

a. If defendants released on their own recognizance fail to appear, they are pursued by the police, but if they are released on bail borrowed from a bondsperson and they fail to appear, they will be pursued by bounty hunters. Which type of defendant do you think is more likely to fail to appear, and which type is more likely to be recaptured if they do fail to appear? Why?

b. Perhaps surprisingly, bounty hunters tend to be quite courteous and respectful even to defendants who have tried to skip town. Can you think of one reason why?

16. a. Why do so many charitable activities like marathons, walks, and 5K runs give the participants "free" T-shirts, wristbands, hats, bumper stickers, and so forth?

b. Charitable organizations could probably make a lot of money for their cause by selling these items on their Web sites, but you usually have to actually attend the "2018 Cancer Run" to get the "2018 Cancer Run" T-shirt. Why?

17. Waiters and waitresses are generally paid very low hourly wages and receive most of their compensation from customer tips.

    a. As the owner of a restaurant, what do you want from your waitstaff?

    b. Which element of a waiter's or waitress's compensation—the hourly wage or the tips—represents a method of "tying pay to performance"?

    c. Which element of a waiter's or waitress's compensation—the hourly wage or the tips—plays the role of "insurance" that the restaurant owner provides for the waitstaff? Against what are the waiters and waitresses being insured?

    d. Theoretically, a restaurant owner could pay workers a higher wage, raise menu prices, and make the restaurant strictly tip-free. Or, the owner could eliminate the wage, reduce menu prices, and encourage greater tipping by alerting customers to the fact that the waitstaff do not earn an hourly wage. What are the potential pros and cons (from the point of view of the restaurant owner) of each system?

18. In early 2004, Donald Trump took the idea of using a tournament for hiring executives to a whole new level with the premiere of the TV show *The Apprentice*. On the show, a group of contestants compete for a position running one of Trump's many companies for a starting annual salary of $250,000. Generally speaking, on each episode, the contestants are divided up into teams and compete to most successfully complete some business-related task, and a member of the losing team is eliminated.

    a. Contestants for *The Apprentice* are carefully auditioned and screened, to make sure that each contestant has the skills necessary to do well on the show. Why do you think this screening is done? What kind of risk is being eliminated by this audition process? What would happen if there was one contestant who, right from the beginning, demonstrated more potential and greater capabilities than the other contestants?

    b. Though only one contestant will end up with the job at the conclusion of the show, each must try to prove his or her worth to Trump by performing well in the team challenges. What impact do you think the tournament structure of this "ultimate job interview" has on these team challenges?

    c. Some of the challenges can be quite demanding, and the contestants often work very hard. Wouldn't it be easier if they all shirked the challenge rather than working hard? Trump would still (presumably) have to choose one of them as the winner—and chances are it would be the same person whether everybody worked hard or not. Why are the contestants not likely to all agree to stop trying so hard?

19. Suppose a CEO wanted more of her employees to get flu shots. How many of the four big lessons in this chapter can you employ to come up with different solutions? (Don't worry if they're not all feasible or practical—that's the reason there are four big lessons in this chapter, not just one.)

20. A growing anticorruption campaign in India has a clever new tool: a zero-rupee note. The impressive note looks just like a 50-rupee note, but is clearly marked as being worthless and contains anticorruption messages. Indians are encouraged to give these notes to public officials who demand or expect bribes. Over 3 million of the notes have been distributed since 2007. A Twitter user tweeted economist Richard Thaler (of *Nudge* fame) to ask whether this counted as a nudge. What do you think his answer was, and why?

21. Researchers seem to have a lot of fun testing different nudges to see how well they work. In one experiment, they placed mirrors in shopping carts so customers at a grocery store were forced to look at themselves while they shopped. How would you expect this kind of nudge would impact shoppers' behavior? (PS: It worked!)

CHALLENGES

22. Let's tie together this chapter's story on incentives with Chapter 15's story about cartels. Suppose your economics professor grades on a curve: The average score on each test becomes a B–. If all of the students in your class form a conspiracy to cut back on studying, point out how this cartel might break down just like OPEC's cartel breaks down during some decades.

23. What type of systems in the United States help overcome the incentives of physicians to order medically unnecessary tests?

24. In his path-breaking book *Managerial Dilemmas*, political scientist Gary Miller says that a good corporate culture is one that gets workers to work together even when they face prisoner's dilemmas (we discussed the prisoner's dilemma in detail in Chapter 15). In a healthy corporate culture, you feel guilty if you're being lazy while your buddy is working. Let's sum up "guilt" as simply as possible: It's some number "X" that represents how you feel. These figures are adapted from Figure 15.4.

		Stan	
		Work	Shirk
Kyle	Work	(4, 4)	(2, X)
	Shirk	(X, 2)	(3, 3)

a. What does X have to be to keep this from being a prisoner's dilemma? Answer with a range (e.g., greater than 12.5, less than −2).

b. Now, there are two Nash equilibria in this problem. What are they? Using the language of Chapters 15 and 16, what kind of game has this just become?

c. There's an idea buried in the questions from Chapter 16 that will "point" Stan and Kyle toward the best possible outcome. What is it? (Keep in mind that a good corporate culture can help with this part, too.)

25. a. Many HMOs pay their doctors based, in part, on how many patients the doctor sees in a day. What problems does this incentive system create?

b. If HMOs pay their doctors a fixed salary, what problems does this incentive system create?

c. Ideally, we would like to pay doctors based on how long their patients live! What problems exist in implementing this type of system?

26. In most big cities, taxicab fares are fairly standardized, and they are regulated by local governments. For the sake of simplicity, assume that a cab driver works for a licensed taxicab company, and he or she pays a fixed daily fee for the use of the taxi; all fares and tips go to the driver.

a. In Atlanta, Georgia, meter rates are $2.50 for the first 1/8 mile and $0.25 for each additional 1/8 mile. What are the benefits of allowing cab drivers to charge fares based on the number of miles driven? In other words, what good behavior is encouraged—or what bad behavior is discouraged—by this? What are the possible drawbacks?

b. In addition to the meter rates, there is a $21 per hour waiting fee. Why do you think there is a waiting fee? If cab drivers could not charge a waiting fee, how might that change their behavior? What if cab drivers were always just paid an hourly wage of $21 per hour? What would be the benefits and drawbacks of this payment scheme?

c. For some fairly standard trips in Atlanta, there are flat fees. A trip from the airport to anywhere downtown, for example, is always $30 (plus $2 for each additional person). What are the potential benefits and drawbacks of this kind of compensation scheme? Why might a city require this payment scheme for trips from the airport?

d. In the chapter, we talked about the importance of the gap between *what you pay for* and *what you want*. What is it that Atlanta's City Council and taxi customers *want* from the cab drivers in Atlanta? Which basis for cab fares (miles, hours, trips) comes closest to closing the gap between what is *wanted* and what is *paid for*?

WORK IT OUT

For interactive, step-by-step help in solving this problem, go online.

Punishments can be an incentive, not just rewards. Consider an assembly line. Why wouldn't you necessarily want to reward the fastest worker on the assembly line? What other incentive system might work?

23

Stock Markets and Personal Finance

I n 1992, television reporter John Stossel decided to challenge the experts of Wall Street. As a student, Stossel had taken classes from economist Burton Malkiel whose book *A Random Walk Down Wall Street* claimed that the money and fame that went to stock-picking gurus were a sham and a waste. According to Malkiel: "A blindfolded monkey throwing darts at a newspaper's financial pages could select a portfolio that would do just as well as one carefully selected by experts."[1]

Instead of using a monkey, Stossel himself threw darts at a giant wall-sized version of the stock pages of the *Wall Street Journal*. Stossel followed his portfolio for nearly a year and compared the return with the portfolios picked by major Wall Street experts. Stossel's portfolio beat 90% of the experts! Not surprisingly, none of the experts would speak to him on camera about their humiliating loss. The lesson, according to Stossel, is that if you are paying an expert a lot of money to pick your stocks, it is probably you who are the monkey.

In this chapter, we explain why Stossel's amusing experiment is backed up by economic theory and by many careful empirical studies. We will also be giving you some investment advice in this chapter. No, we can't promise you the secret to getting rich. Most of the get-rich-quick schemes sold in books, investment seminars, and newsletters are scams. Economics, however, does provide some important lessons for investing wisely. We can't tell you how to get rich quick, but we can perhaps help you to get richer slowly.

Throughout this chapter, we emphasize a core principle of economics: There's no such thing as a free lunch. That's just another way of saying that you shouldn't expect something for nothing, or that trade-offs are everywhere. Let's see how the principle applies to personal finance.

Passive vs. Active Investing

Many people invest in the stock market through a mutual fund. A mutual fund pools money from many customers and invests the money in many firms, in return, of course, for a management fee. Some of these mutual funds, called "active funds," are run by managers who try to pick stocks—these mutual funds often charge higher than average fees. Other mutual funds are called "passive

445

FIGURE 23.1

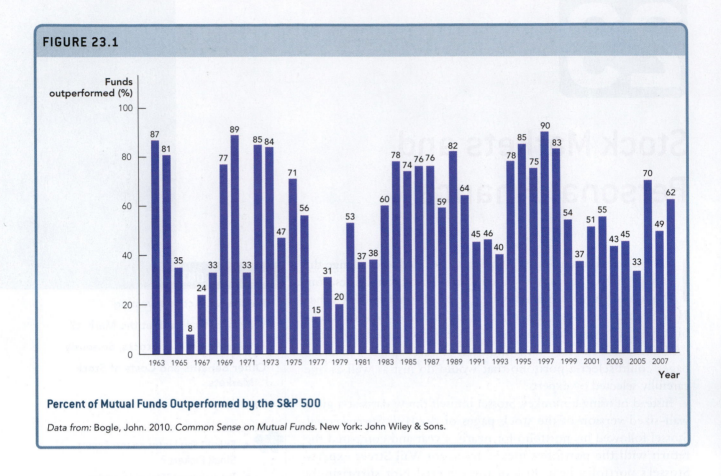

Percent of Mutual Funds Outperformed by the S&P 500

Data from: Bogle, John. 2010. *Common Sense on Mutual Funds.* New York: John Wiley & Sons.

funds" because they simply attempt to mimic a broad stock market index such as Standard and Poor's 500 (S&P 500), a basket of 500 large firms broadly representative of the U.S. economy.

Figure 23.1 shows that in a typical year passive investing in the S&P 500 Index beats about 60% of all mutual funds. In any given year, some mutual funds beat the index, but what is telling is that the funds that beat the index are different nearly every year! In other words, the funds that beat the index in one year probably just got lucky that year. One study that looked over 10 years found that passive investing beat 97.6% of all mutual funds![2] Overall, it is clear that very few mutual fund managers can consistently beat the market averages.

It is possible that a very small number of experts can systematically beat the stock market. Sometimes Warren Buffett, who promotes long-term investing for value, is cited as an example of a person who sees farther than the rest of the market. He started out as a paperboy and worked his way up to a $52 billion fortune by purchasing undervalued stocks.

Some economists even think that Buffett, and a few others like him, just got lucky. If enough people are out there trying to pick stocks, you're going to have a few who get lucky many times in a row. Take a look at Figure 23.2. At the top of the figure, we start out with 1,000 experts, each of whom flips a coin to predict whether the market will go up or down in the following year. After one year, 500 of the experts will turn out to be right. After two years, 250 experts will have been right two years in a row. At the end of five years, just 31 out of 1,000 experts will have been right five years in a row. The experts who get it

FIGURE 23.2

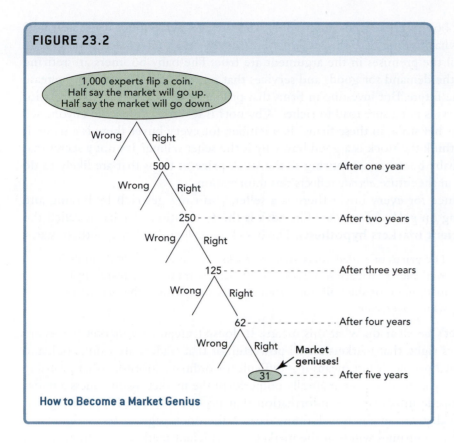

1,000 experts flip a coin.
Half say the market will go up.
Half say the market will go down.

Wrong / Right

500 - After one year

Wrong / Right

250 - - - - - - - - - - - - - - - - - - After two years

Wrong / Right

125 - - - - - - - - - - - - - After three years

Wrong / Right

62 - - - - - - - - - - After four years

Wrong / Right

Market geniuses!

31 - - - - - - - - After five years

How to Become a Market Genius

correct every time will be lauded as geniuses on CNBC and their advice will be eagerly sought. But the reality is that they just got lucky.

Is Buffett skilled or lucky? We're not so sure, but we do know this: Right now there is a small industry of people following the moves of Warren Buffett, trying to guess what he will say and do next. It is harder and harder for Buffett to get a big jump on the rest of the stock market. Even if Buffett could beat the market at first, it is not so clear he can beat the market any longer.

Why Is It Hard to Beat the Market?

These results aren't just an accident. Nor is it a statement about the stupidity of mutual fund managers. We know a few of these managers and most of them are pretty smart. Rather, the difficulty of beating the stock market is a tribute to the power of markets and the ability of market prices to reflect information.

Think about it this way: For every buyer of a stock, there is a seller. The buyer thinks the price is going up, the seller thinks the price is going down. There is a disagreement. On average, who do you think is more likely to be correct, the buyer or the seller? Of course, the answer is neither. But if on average buyers and sellers have about the same amount of information, stock picking can't work very well.

Consider the following bit of pseudo investment advice. The number of senior citizens will double by 2050. So the way to make money is to invest in companies that produce goods and services that senior citizens want, things like assisted living facilities, medical care for the elderly, and retirement homes. The

Should You Listen to the Expert Stock Pickers?

baby boom can be a boom for you, If You Invest Now! Sounds plausible, right? So, what's wrong with this argument?

All the premises in the argument are true: The baby boomers are retiring and the demand for goods and services that senior citizens want will increase in the future. But investing in firms that produce goods and services for senior citizens is not a sure road to riches. Why not? If it were, why would anyone sell his or her stock in these firms? Remember, for every buyer there is a seller. If you think the stock is a good buy, why is the seller selling? It's not a secret that the baby boomers are retiring so the stock price of firms that are likely to do well in the future *already* reflects this information.

Since for every buyer there is a seller, you can't get rich by buying and selling on *public information*. This idea is the foundation of what is called the **efficient markets hypothesis.** The best-known form of this hypothesis states:

The **efficient markets hypothesis** says that the prices of traded assets reflect all publicly available information.

> The prices of traded assets, such as stocks and bonds, reflect all publicly available information. Unless an investor is trading on inside information, he or she will not systematically outperform the market as a whole over time.

Let's be clear on what this means. It doesn't mean that market prices are always right, that markets are all powerful, or that traders are calm, cool, and rational people. It just means it is difficult for ordinary investors (that probably means you, too!) to systematically outperform the market, again, unless a trader has inside information—information that no one else has. It's restating our point that you might as well throw darts at the stock pages as try to figure out which companies will beat the market. The efficient markets hypothesis is just another way of saying there is no such thing as a free lunch.

So if you do have some information that no one else has, can you make money in the stock market? Yes, but you have to act very quickly. Within *minutes* of the news that the Russian nuclear power plant at Chernobyl had melted down, shares in U.S. nuclear power plant companies tumbled, the price of oil jumped, as did the price of potatoes. Why potatoes? Clever traders on Wall Street figured out that the disaster at Chernobyl meant that the Ukrainian potato crop would be contaminated, so they bought American potato futures to profit from the coming rise in prices. The traders who acted quickly made a lot of money, but as they bought and sold, prices changed and signaled to other people that something was going on. Quite quickly, the inside information became public information and the opportunities for profit evaporated.

The only way you can take advantage of information that other people don't have is to start buying or selling large numbers of shares. But once you start the buying or selling, the rest of the market knows something is up. That is why secrets do not last very long in the stock market and that is another reason why it is so hard to beat the market as a whole.

Some people believe that they have found exceptions to the efficient markets hypothesis. For instance, it is commonly believed that you can make more money by buying stocks when prices are low, or by buying right after prices have fallen. That sounds good, doesn't it? Buying at lower prices. It feels like what you do when you go to Walmart. But buying a stock isn't like buying a lawn chair or a banana. The value of a stock is simply what its price will be in future periods of time. The banana, in contrast, you can simply eat for pleasure, no matter what the future price of bananas. Often lower prices mean that

interactive activity

The Efficient Market Hypothesis

prices are going to stay low or fall even more and that means lower returns on owning stocks. Some studies find that you can do slightly better with your investments by buying right after prices have fallen. But do you know what? If you adjust those higher returns to account for the broker commissions that you have to pay for the extra trading, the higher returns pretty much go away.

A field of study known as "technical analysis" looks for deep patterns in stock and asset prices. Maybe you've heard on the financial news that stocks have "broken through a key support point" or "moved into a new trading range." If you dig deeper, you will find a claim that stock prices exhibit predictable mathematical patterns. For instance, if a stock hovers in the range of $100 a share but does not exceed that level, and one day goes over $100, it might be claimed that the stock is now expected to skyrocket to a much higher level. Hardly. One nice thing about studying the stock market is that there is a lot of very good data. One team of economists studied 7,846 different strategies of technical analysis. Their conclusion was that none of them systematically beat the market over time.[3]

For most investors, the efficient markets hypothesis looks like a pretty good description of reality.

How to Really Pick Stocks, Seriously

Ok, you probably can't beat the market without a lot of luck on your side. But we do still have four pieces of important advice. *Very* important advice. If you apply this advice over the course of your life, you will probably save thousands of dollars, and if you become rich, you may save millions of dollars. (Suddenly, this textbook seems like a real bargain!) No, we don't have a get-rich-quick formula for you, but there are a few simple mistakes you can avoid to your benefit and at no real cost, other than a bit of time and attention. Let's go through each piece of advice in turn.

Diversify

The first secret to picking stocks is to pick lots of them! Since picking stocks doesn't work well, the "secret" to wise investing is to invest in a large basket of stocks—to diversify. Diversification lowers the risk of your portfolio, how much your portfolio fluctuates in value over time.

By picking a lot of stocks, you limit your overall exposure to things going wrong in any particular company. When the energy company Enron went bankrupt in 2001, many Enron employees had put most of their life's wealth in . . . can you guess? . . . Enron stock. That's a huge mistake, whether you work at the company or not. If you put all your eggs in one basket, it is a disaster if the handle on that basket breaks. Instead, you should buy many different stocks, in many different sectors of the economy, and, yes, in many countries, too. You'll end up with some Enrons, but you'll also have some big winners, such as Google and Apple. And if Google and Apple have become Enrons and gone under since this book was published, well, that is just further reason why you should diversify!

Modern financial markets have made diversification easy. Mutual funds let you invest in hundreds of stocks with just one purchase. And since stock picking doesn't work well, diversification has no downside—it reduces risk without reducing your expected return.

CHECK YOURSELF

■ Is it better to invest in a mutual fund that has performed well for five years in a row or one that has performed poorly for five years in a row? Use the efficient markets hypothesis to justify your answer.

We are focusing on diversification across stocks but there are all kinds of risks in the world and you should diversify across as many of those risks as possible. U.S. stocks, for example, tend to fluctuate in value along with the growth rate of the U.S. economy. You can reduce this source of risk by including a large number of international firms in your portfolio. Bonds, art, housing, and human capital (your knowledge and skills) all have associated returns and risks, and for a given amount of return, you minimize your risk by diversifying across many assets.

If you accept the efficient markets hypothesis, and you accept the value of diversification, your best trading strategy can be summed up very simply. It is called **buy and hold**. That's right, buy a large bundle of stocks and just hold them. You don't have to do anything more. You will be diversified, you will not be trying to beat the market, and you can live a peaceful, quiet life.

Some of the simplest ways to buy and hold mean that you replicate the well-known stock indexes. Just for your knowledge, here are a few of those indexes:

The *Dow Jones Industrial Average* (or the Dow for short) is the most famous stock price index. The Dow is composed of 30 leading American stocks, each of these counted equally, whether the company is large or small. The Dow is not a very diversified index.

The *Standard and Poor's 500* (S&P 500) is a much broader index of stocks than the Dow; as the name indicates, it consists of the prices of 500 different stocks. Unlike in the Dow, the larger companies receive greater weight in the index than the smaller companies. The S&P 500 is a better indicator of the market as a whole than the Dow.

The *NASDAQ Composite Index* averages the prices of all the companies traded on NASDAQ, or National Association of Securities Dealers Automated Quotations, over 3,000 securities. The NASDAQ index contains more small stocks and high-tech stocks relative to the Dow or the S&P 500.

Notice that diversification changes our understanding of what makes a stock risky, or not risky. You might at first think that a risky stock is one whose price moves up and down a lot. Not exactly. If investors are diversified, and indeed most of them are, their risk depends on how much their portfolio moves up and down, not on how much a single stock moves up and down. A single stock might move up and down all the time but still an overall diversified portfolio won't change in value much if some of your stocks are moving up while others are moving down.

According to finance economists, the riskiest stocks are those that move up and down in harmony with the market. For instance, many real estate stocks are risky because they are highly cyclical. They move up a lot when times are good (and the rest of the market is high) and they move down a lot when times are bad. When a recession comes, a lot of people just can't afford to buy a new house. In contrast, for an example of a relatively safe stock, consider the discount outlet Walmart. When bad times come, yes, Walmart loses some business. But Walmart also gains some business because people who used to shop at Nordstrom now have less money and some of them will now shop at Walmart. In this regard, Walmart is partly protected from business downturns.[4] Many health-care stocks are safe in a similar way. Even if times are bad, you're probably not going to postpone that triple bypass operation; if you do, you won't be around to see when times are good again. In other words, if you care about

To **buy and hold** is to buy stocks and then hold them for the long run, regardless of what prices do in the short run.

Diversify, Diversify, Diversify!

the risk of a stock, don't just look at how the price of that stock moves. Look at how the price varies with the rest of the market. In the language of finance economists or statisticians, the riskiest stocks are those with the highest *covariance* with the market as a whole.

The lesson here is that if you are worried about risk, think about your portfolio as a whole, rather than obsessing over any single stock. Or let's be more specific: If you are going to become an aerospace engineer, don't buy a lot of stock in aerospace companies. The value of your human capital—which is worth a lot—is already tied up in that industry. Don't make your overall portfolio riskier by putting more eggs in that basket. If anything, buy stocks that do well when aerospace does poorly. More generally, finance theorists say that the least risky assets *for you* are assets that are *negatively correlated* with *your portfolio*. What this means is that you should try to buy assets that rise in value when the rest of your portfolio is falling in value. Are you afraid that high energy prices will cripple the prospects for your career? Buy stock in a company that builds roads in Saudi Arabia. If oil prices stay high, the gains of that road-building company will partially offset your other losses. The lesson applies to more than stocks. If you become a dentist, you run the risk that a new technology will eliminate cavities. So try to limit your risk by diversifying your portfolio: Marry an optician or an engineer, not another dentist!

Avoid High Fees

We have some other advice for picking stocks. Avoid investments and mutual funds that have high fees or "loads," as they are sometimes called. It simply isn't worth it.

Let's say for instance that you wish to invest in the S&P 500. Some funds charge management and administrative fees of 0.05% of your investment, but other funds can charge up to ten or twenty times as much for investing in exactly the same basket of stocks.

The funds with the higher fees don't give you much of value in return. The lesson is simple: Don't pay the higher fees!

Often when your broker calls you up to make a stock purchase, that purchase involves a relatively high fee. (Have you ever wondered why the broker is making the call?) Before buying or selling a stock in these circumstances, you should ask what the fee is to make the transaction. Understand the incentives of the person you are dealing with: The greater the number of transactions that the broker can get you to make, the more money the broker usually earns. Might that explain why he or she is telling you to buy or sell? Or maybe this really is a "once in a lifetime opportunity."

Even small fees can add up to large differences in returns over time. Let's say you are investing $10,000 over 30 years. If you invest with a firm that charges 0.10% a year in fees and the stock market gives a real return of 7% a year, then in 30 years you will have earned $74,016. If you invest in a firm that charges 1% a year, then in 30 years you will have about $57,434. The higher fees cost you $16,582 and, as we have shown, you probably got nothing for your extra fees. Small differences in growth or loss rates, when compounded over time, make for a big difference. The same is true for your portfolio.

That brings us to a corollary principle, to which we now turn.

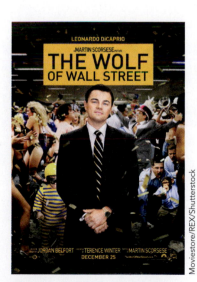

What are the Wolf's incentives? Jordan Belfort, the New York stockbroker whose life was chronicled in Martin Scorsese's movie the *Wolf of Wall Street*, made millions by charging small investors high fees to buy dubious investments.

Moviestore/REX/Shutterstock

Compound Returns Build Wealth

If one investment earns a higher rate of return each year than another investment, in the long run that makes a big difference. Imagine you buy a well-diversified portfolio of stocks and every year you reinvest all of your dividends. A simple approximation, called the rule of 70, explains how long it will take for your investment to double in value given a specified rate of return.

Rule of 70: If the rate of return (annual percent increase in value including dividends) of an investment is x%, then the doubling time is $70/x$ years.

Table 23.1 illustrates the rule of 70 by showing how long it takes for an investment to double in value given different returns. With a return of 1%, an investment will double approximately every 70 years ($70/1 = 70$). If returns increase to 2%, the value of your investment will double every 35 years ($70/2 = 35$). Consider the impact of a 4% return. If this rate of return is sustained, then the value of an investment doubles every 17.5 years ($70/4 = 17.5$). In 70 years, the value doubles 4 times, reaching a level 16 times its starting value!

The rule of 70 is just a mathematical approximation but it bears out the key concept that when compounded, small differences in investment returns can have a large effect. To make this more concrete, if you have a long time horizon, you probably should invest in (diversified) stocks rather than bonds.

TABLE 23.1 YEARS TO DOUBLE USING THE RULE OF 70

Annual Return (%)	Years to Double
0	Never
1	70
2	35
3	23.3
4	17.5

In the long run, stocks offer higher returns than bonds. Since 1802, for example, stocks have had an average real rate of return of about 7% per year, while bonds have paid closer to 2% per year.[5] Using our now familiar rule of 70, we know that money that grows at 7% a year will double in 10 years, but money that grows at 2% a year won't double for 35 years. Alternatively, growing at 7% a year, $10,000 will return $76,122 in 30 years, but if that investment grows at 2% a year, the return over that same period of time will be only $18,113.

Stocks, however, have the potential for greater losses than do bonds because bond holders and other creditors are always paid before shareholders. You are unlikely to lose much money if you buy high-grade corporate or government bonds, but the stock market is highly volatile and it does periodically crash. Nonetheless, in American history, stocks almost always outperform bonds over any 20-year time period you care to examine, including the period of the Great Depression and World War II. Stocks are usually the better long-term investment.

Of course, that doesn't mean that everyone should invest so heavily in stocks. In any particular year, or even over the course of a month, week, or day, stocks can go down in value quite a bit. If you are 80 years old and managing your retirement income, you probably shouldn't in-vest much in stocks. If you have to send your twins to college in two years' time, you might want some safer investments, as well. Nor does the past necessarily predict the future—just because stocks outperformed bonds in the past doesn't mean that will continue to happen. Remember to diversify!

interactive activity

The Rule of 70

The No-Free-Lunch Principle, or No Return Without Risk

The differences between stocks and bonds, as investment vehicles, reflect a more general principle. There is a systematic **trade-off between return and risk**. Figure 23.3, for example, shows the trade-off between return and risk on four asset classes. U.S. T-bills are safe but have low returns. You can get a higher return by buying stock in a group of large firms such as in the S&P 500, but the value of those firms fluctuates a lot more than the value of T-bills, so to get the higher return, you need to bear higher risk.[*]

If you want even more risk than an investment in the stock market, numerous schemes give you a chance of making a killing. The simplest of such strategies is to take all your money, fly to Las Vegas, and bet on "black" for a spin of the roulette wheel. Yes, there is a 47.37% chance that you double your wealth. That's a high return, sort of. Sadly, there is also a 52.63% chance that you will lose everything you have, including your credit rating and the trust of your spouse and children. That's what we call high risk.

Remember this story when you hear about a high-flying "hedge fund" or other fancy investment device. It's easy to generate high returns for a few years by getting lucky and doubling down (betting all your winnings again). Take a look again at Figure 23.3. Higher returns come at the expense of higher risk.

This no-free-lunch principle can help you evaluate some other investments, as well. Let's say you come into a tidy sum of money and you start wondering

> The **risk–return trade-off** means higher returns come at the price of higher risk.

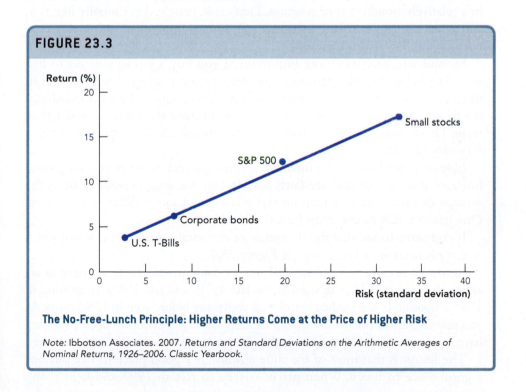

FIGURE 23.3

The No-Free-Lunch Principle: Higher Returns Come at the Price of Higher Risk

Note: Ibbotson Associates. 2007. *Returns and Standard Deviations on the Arithmetic Averages of Nominal Returns, 1926–2006. Classic Yearbook.*

---

[*] We measure risk using the standard deviation of the portfolio return. The standard deviation is a measure of how much the return tends to fluctuate from its average level: thus, the larger the standard deviation, the greater the risk. A rule of thumb is that there is a 68% probability of being within ±1 standard deviation of the mean return. For the S&P 500, for example, the mean return is about 12% and the standard deviation is about 20% so in any given year, there is a 68% probability that the return will be between −8% and 32%. Of course, there is a 32% probability that something else could happen! But beware! The rule of thumb is only an approximation. Risk in the real world can rarely be modeled with perfect mathematical accuracy.

whether you should invest in art. Overall, should you expect art to be a better or inferior financial investment, compared with the market as a whole?

A lot of people—probably most people—buy art because they want to look at it. They enjoy hanging it on their walls. In the language of economics, art yields "a nonmonetary return," which is just our way of saying it is fun to look at. Now suppose that investments in art earned just as high a return as investments in stocks. In that case, art would be fun to have on the wall *and* would be an excellent investment. But wait, that sounds like a free lunch doesn't it? So what does the no-free-lunch principle predict?

We know that the expected returns on different assets, adjusted for risk, should be equal. So if some asset yields a higher "fun" return, those assets should, on average, yield a lower financial return. And that is exactly what we find with art. On average, art underperforms the stock market by a few percentage points a year. You can think of the lower returns as the price of having some beautiful art on your wall. Again, it's the no-free-lunch principle in action.

This kind of analysis applies not just to art but also to real estate. Let's say you want to buy a home. Can you expect superior or inferior financial returns over time? This question is a little trickier than the art question because two different and opposing forces operate. Let's look at each in turn.

First, a home tends to be a risky asset for most purchasers. Let's say you buy a $300,000 home by putting down $200,000 and borrowing the remainder. That home is probably a fairly big chunk of your overall wealth and it puts you in a relatively nondiversified position. That's risk, people don't usually like risk, and as we saw above, riskier assets earn, all other things equal, higher expected returns (the risk-return trade-off).

Second, and probably more important, if you buy a house, you get to live in it. The house, like the painting, provides you with personal services and in this case those services are valuable. Many people enjoy their backyard and the feeling of owning a home and being able to paint the walls any color they want. These nonmonetary returns mean that houses can be expected to pay a relatively low financial return.

Indeed, if we look at the financial returns on real estate over a long time horizon, it turns out they are fairly low. In fact, for long periods of time, the average financial rate of return on real estate is not much different from zero. One lesson is that houses must be lots of fun!

If you want to see that the downside of real estate investments is not just a recent phenomenon, take a look at Figure 23.4.

In the 50 years from 1947 to 1997, real housing prices hardly changed at all, although with some blips upward in the late 1970s and late 1980s. Beginning in 1997, a housing boom pushed prices well above any before seen in U.S. history. As you probably know, prices tumbled dramatically starting in 2006, but since 2011 they have risen and are now once again higher than at any time in the twentieth century.

The lesson is that most of the time a house is a good place to live but not a good place to invest. When prices started to rise in 1997 and kept rising year after year, many people thought that real estate was the investment of the century—"they ain't making any more," people said. But the no-free-lunch principle tells us that precisely because houses are a good place to live, we should not also expect them to be a good investment. All other things equal, fun activities yield lower financial returns than nonfun activities.

When prices rose, some people got lucky and made a killing, but other people tried to do the same and ended up bankrupt. So don't expect to make a

FIGURE 23.4

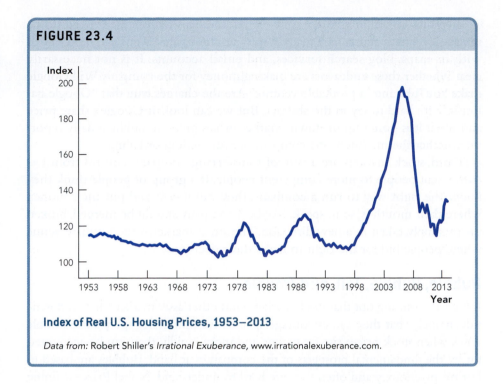

Index of Real U.S. Housing Prices, 1953–2013

Data from: Robert Shiller's *Irrational Exuberance,* www.irrationalexuberance.com.

killing in the real estate market, and remember to diversify! One more point. Are you one of those people who doesn't like to mow the lawn? Do you dread the notion of choosing homeowner's insurance or worrying about when your roof will fall in? The lesson is simple: Don't buy a house, you won't have fun, and the financial returns won't make it worth your while.

Other Benefits and Costs of Stock Markets

Throughout this chapter, we've recommended against gambling with all or most of your money. We've recommended buy and hold, based on a diversified portfolio. But hey, maybe some of you are into gambling. You know what? If you want to take risk for the sake of risk alone, the U.S. stock market offers the best odds in the world, better than Las Vegas and better than your local bookie. People on average make money in the U.S. stock market and that is because the productive capacity of the U.S. economy is expanding through economic growth. There is more profit to go around and that means you have a good chance of making some really lucrative investments.

Stock markets have uses beyond investment. First, new stock and bond issues are important to a company as a means of raising capital for new investment (investment now in the economic sense of increasing the capital stock). Stock markets also reward successful entrepreneurs and thus encourage people to start companies and look around for new ideas. The founders of Google are now very rich and selling company shares to the stock market helped make them so. A well-functioning stock market helps companies such as Google get going or expand.

Second, the stock market gives us a better idea of how well firms are run. The stock price is a signal about the value of the firm. When the stock price is increasing, especially when it is increasing relative to other stocks, this is a signal that the firm is making the right investments for future profits. When the stock is declining, especially when it is declining relative to other stocks, this is

CHECK YOURSELF
- How does investing in stocks of other countries help to diversify your investments?
- Many people dream of owning a football or baseball team. Would you expect the return on these assets to be relatively high or low?

a signal that something has gone wrong and perhaps management needs to be replaced. Some critics allege that Google has dominated Web search but failed with its maps, blog search services, and email accounts. It is not necessarily clear whether these endeavors are making money for the company. Will Google make YouTube into a profitable venture? Are the charges true that "Google has lost it"? It's hard to say in the abstract. But we can look at Google's share price and see if it is going up or down. Market prices give the public a daily report on whether the managers of a company are succeeding or failing.

Third, stock markets are a way of transferring company control from less competent people to more competent people. If a group of people think they know the right way to run a company, they can buy it and put their money where their mouth is, so to speak. Maybe a company should be merged, broken up, or simply taken in a new direction. The stock market is the ultimate venue where people bid for the right to make these decisions.

Bubble, Bubble, Toil, and Trouble

It's worth pointing out that stock markets (and other asset markets) have a downside, namely that they can encourage speculative bubbles. A speculative bubble arises when stock prices rise far higher, and more rapidly, than can be accounted for by the fundamental prospects of the companies at hand. Bubbles are based in human psychology and often they are hard to understand. Nobel Prize–winning economist Vernon Smith, whom you met in Chapter 4, has found that speculative bubbles and crashes occur in experimental markets, even when traders are given enough information to easily calculate an asset's true value.[6] Inexperienced traders are more prone to bubbles, but even experienced traders can fall for bubbles when the trading environment changes. Speculative bubbles and crashes have significant costs, as we will discuss, so economists are trying to better understand bubbles and how market institutions can be designed to help avoid them.

During the dot.com era, circa 2000, many Internet or dot.com stocks had very high prices even though many of these companies had never earned a dime of profit or for that matter any revenue. Many of the tech stocks were listed on the NASDAQ stock exchange. As you can see in Figure 23.5, in the space of five years the NASDAQ Composite Index more than tripled from a monthly average of about 1,200 to over 4,000 before falling back down again. Many people made a lot of money on the ride up and many people—maybe the same people, maybe others—lost a lot of money on the ride down.

If you can spot speculative bubbles on a consistent basis, yes, you can become very wealthy. But, of course, a speculative bubble is usually easier to detect with hindsight than at the time. Apple and Google might have looked like speculative bubbles, too; the only problem is that they never burst. Betting too soon that high prices will end is also one way to go bankrupt.

Speculative bubbles, and their bursting, can hurt an economy. During the rise of the bubble, capital is invested in areas where it is not actually very valuable. A second wave of problems comes when the bubble crashes. Lower stock prices (or lower home prices) mean that people feel poorer and so they will spend less. The collapse of the bubble also means that workers must move from one sector to another, such as from high tech to retailing, or from real estate to export industries. Shifting labor from one sector of an economy to another creates labor adjustment costs.

We saw both of these problems with the dot.com bubble and the real estate bubble leading up to the crash of housing prices in 2007–2008. During

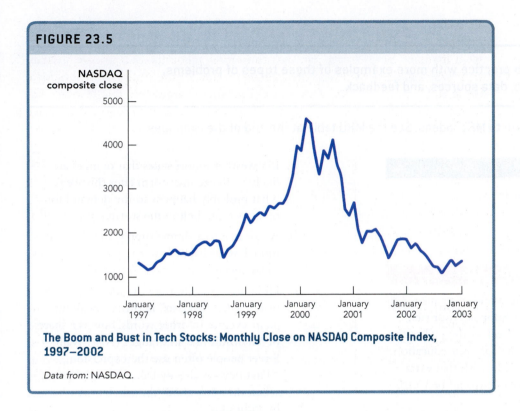

FIGURE 23.5

NASDAQ composite close

5000

4000

3000

2000

1000

January 1997 | January 1998 | January 1999 | January 2000 | January 2001 | January 2002 | January 2003

The Boom and Bust in Tech Stocks: Monthly Close on NASDAQ Composite Index, 1997–2002

Data from: NASDAQ.

the dot.com boom years, for example, we invested too much in stringing fiber-optic cable across the world's oceans—cable that later proved to be unprofitable. Similarly, during the housing boom we invested too much in houses that later were abandoned. In addition, the boom in housing prices led banks to be much too lax about the value of financial assets backed by portfolios of mortgages. When housing prices started to fall and people began to default on their mortgages, the value of these asset-backed securities plummeted and banks found themselves nearing bankruptcy. To stave off bankruptcy, these banks cut back on lending, transmitting problems in the housing markets to the wider economy and helping to generate the lengthy recession beginning in late 2008.

Yes, bubbles can be a problem, but few people doubt that we are better off with active trading in stock and asset markets. One partial solution is to have greater transparency in assessing the value of companies and assets. Economists continue to research asset markets and the possibility of limiting bubbles and subsequent crashes. But, for now, there is no surefire solution for getting rid of asset bubbles.

Takeaway

We have stressed some simple and practical points. It is difficult for an investor to consistently beat the market over long periods. You are well-advised to diversify your investments. Avoid fees and try to generate a high compound return over time. Understand that the promise of higher returns is often accompanied by higher risk.

Viewed as a whole, stock markets and other trading markets give investors a chance to earn money, diversify their holdings, express opinions on the course of the market, and hedge risks. Stock markets also play a role in financing innovative new firms. Stock markets appear to be subject to speculative bubbles, but active stock markets are an important part of a healthy growing economy.

CHECK YOURSELF

■ The Federal Reserve was criticized for not stepping in and bursting the housing bubble, which would have prevented the housing collapse. Do you think this criticism is valid, based on what you read in this section?

CHAPTER REVIEW

interactive activity   Go online to practice with more examples of these types of problems, including live links to videos, data sources, and feedback.

 Problems in green relate to MRU videos. See the MRU table at the end of the exercises.

KEY CONCEPTS

efficient markets hypothesis, p. 448

buy and hold, p. 450

risk–return trade-off, p. 453

FACTS AND TOOLS

1. Before we plunge into the world of finance, let's review the rule of 70. Suppose your rich aunt hands you a $3,000 check at the end of the school year. She tells you it's for your education. But what should you *really* do with that extra money? Let's see how much it would be worth if you saved it for a while.

   a. If you put it in a bank account earning 2% real annual return on average, how many years would it take before it was worth $6,000? Until it was worth $12,000?

   b. If you put it in a Standard and Poor's 500 (S&P 500) mutual fund earning an average 7% real return every year, how many years would it take before it was worth $6,000? Until it was worth $12,000?

   c. Suppose you invest a little less than half your money in the bank and a little more than half in a mutual fund, just to play it somewhat safe, so that you can expect a 5% real return on average. How many years now until you reach $6,000 and $12,000?

2. Let's do something boring just to drive home a point: Count up the number of years in Figure 23.1 in which more than half of the mutual funds managed to beat the S&P 500 index. (Recall that the Standard and Poor's 500 is just a list of 500 large U.S. corporations—it's a list that overlaps a lot with the Fortune 500.) What percentage of the time did the experts actually beat the S&P 500?

3. Consider the supply and demand for oranges. Orange crops can be destroyed by below-freezing temperatures.

   a. If a weather report states that oranges are likely to freeze in a storm later this week, what probably happens to the demand for oranges *today*, before the storm comes?

   b. According to a simple supply and demand model, what happens to the price of oranges today given your answer to part a.

   c. How does this illustrate the idea that stock prices *today* "bake in" information about *future* events? In other words, how is a share of Microsoft like an orange? (*Note:* Wall Street people often use the expression, "That news is already baked into the price," when they talk about the efficient markets hypothesis.)

4. In the United States, high-level corporate officials have to publicly state when they buy or sell a large number of shares in their own company. They have to make these statements a few days after their purchase or sale. What do you think probably happens (choose a, b, c, or d) when newspapers report these true "insider trades"? (*Note:* The right answer according to theory is actually true in practice.)

   a. When insiders sell, prices rise, since investors increase their demand for the company's shares.

   b. When insiders sell, prices fall, since investors increase their demand for the company's shares.

   c. When insiders sell, prices fall, since investors decrease their demand for the company's shares.

   d. When insiders sell, prices rise, since investors decrease their demand for the company's shares.

5. Let's see how fees can hurt your investment strategy. Let's assume that your mutual fund grows at an average rate of 7% per year—before subtracting the fees. Using the rule of 70:

   a. How many years will it take for your money to double if fees are 0.5% per year?

b. How many years will it take for your money to double if fees are 1.5% per year (not uncommon in the mutual fund industry)?

c. How many years to double if fees are 2.5% per year?

6. a. If you talk to a broker selling the high-fee mutual fund, what will he or she probably tell you when you ask them, "Am I getting my money's worth when I pay your high fees?"

b. According to Figure 23.1, is your broker's answer likely to be right most of the time?

THINKING AND PROBLEM SOLVING

7. Your brother calls you on the phone telling you that Google's share price has fallen by about 25% over the past few days. Now you can own one small slice of Google for only $540 a share (the price on the day this question was written). Your brother says he is pretty sure the stock is going to head back up to $700 very soon and you should buy.

Should you believe your brother? (*Hint:* Remember someone is selling shares whenever someone else is buying.)

8. In most of your financial decisions early in life, you'll be a buyer, but let's think about the incentives of people who sell stocks, bonds, bank accounts, and other financial products.

a. Walking in the shopping mall one day, you see a new store: the Dollar Store. Of course, you've seen plenty of dollar stores before, but none like this one: The sign in the window says, "Dollars for sale: Fifty cents each." Why will this store be out of business soon?

b. If business owners are self-interested and fairly rational people, will they ever open up this dollar store in the first place? Why or why not?

c. This dollar store is similar to stories people tell about "cheap stocks" that you might hear of on the news. Fill in the blank with any prices that make sense: "If the shares of this company were really worth _____, no one would really sell it for _____."

9. How is "stock market diversification" like putting money in a bank account?

10. Warren Buffett often says that he doesn't want a lot of diversification in his portfolio. He says

that diversification means buying stocks that go up along with stocks that go down; but he only wants to buy the stocks that go up! From the point of view of the typical investor, what is wrong with this reasoning?

11. There are three stocks available: a solar energy firm, an oil firm, and an airline. You can invest in two. Which two?

Ask FRED

interactive activity

12. How easy is it to spot a bubble? Go to the FRED economic database (https://fred.stlouis-fed.org/) and search for NASDAQ. You should find the NASDAQ Composite Index. Graph it and click Max to show all the data available.

a. What happened to the index between November of 1998 and February of 2000? Then what happened?

b. What happened to the index between October of 2009 and October of 2014? Then what happened?

c. Are you willing to make a bet about the future direction of the NASDAQ?

CHALLENGES

13. What is so bad about bubbles? If the price of Internet stocks or housing rises and then falls, is that such a big problem? After all, some people say, most of the gains going up are "paper gains" and most of the losses going down are "paper losses." Comment on this view.

14. Mr. Wolf calls you with what he says is a tremendous opportunity in the stock market. He has inside knowledge about a pharmaceutical company and he says that the price will go up tomorrow. Of course, you are skeptical and decline his offer. The next day the price does go up. Mr. Wolf calls again and says not to worry, tomorrow the price will go down and that will be a good time to buy. Again, you decline. The next day the price does go down. Mr. Wolf calls you over the next several weeks and every time he calls his predictions about the stock price prove to be amazingly accurate. Finally, he calls to tell you that tomorrow is the big one, the day the price will skyrocket. Mr. Wolf has been accurate many times in a row so you empty your bank account to buy as much stock as possible. The next day the price of the stock goes nowhere. What happened?

WORK IT OUT

For interactive, step-by-step help in solving this problem, go online.

Let's see how fees can hurt your investment strategy. Let's assume that your mutual fund grows at an average rate of 5% per year—before subtracting the fees. Using the rule of 70:

a. How many years will it take for your money to double if fees are 0.5% per year?

b. How many years will it take for your money to double if fees are 1.5% per year (not uncommon in the mutual fund industry)?

c. How many years to double if fees are 2.5% per year?

MARGINAL REVOLUTION VIDEOS AND PROBLEMS

Should You Listen to the Expert Stock Pickers?

mruniversity.com/pick-stocks

Problems: **6**

The Efficient Market Hypothesis

mruniversity.com/beat-market

Problems: **7, 8, 10, 14**

Diversify, Diversify, Diversify!

mruniversity.com/stock-diversify

Problems: **5**

The Rule of 70

mruniversity.com/rule-70

Problems: **1, 5**

24

Asymmetric Information: Moral Hazard and Adverse Selection

Your authors flew to New York for a meeting with Macmillan Education, the publisher of this textbook. We arrived at the airport and jumped in a cab to take us to Madison Avenue (home of many publishers and advertisers, hence the term "Mad Men"). As the car moved through New York, Tyler asked the driver why we weren't taking the usual route. "Traffic," the driver answered. Uh-huh. When we arrived at 41 Madison, the bill was noticeably larger than usual. Had we been taken for a ride? Hard to say, maybe there *was* traffic on Harlem River Drive. We let it go, as Macmillan was paying the bill anyway. (Did the driver also suspect we would be reimbursed?) On the 37th floor, our publisher greeted us: "We need a new chapter for the new edition, something important with real world relevance. What is it going to be?" We answered in unison, "asymmetric information."

Asymmetric information is when one party to an exchange has more or better information than the other party. Taxi drivers often do have better information than their customers about traffic, and so it sometimes makes sense to defer to their judgment about the best route. On the other hand, our driver might have figured that two out-of-towners going to a business meeting might not recognize (or care) that he was jacking up the bill. We can't be sure, and that is why the taxi driver's ploy worked, if indeed it was a ploy.

One clever team of economists decided to test how often taxi drivers use their information advantage for their own gain. The economists arranged for similar people to take a cab ride from an airport to a hotel. Each rider carried a GPS unit to precisely track the time and distance the cab traveled and they left the airport just minutes apart, so traffic conditions were the same. After nearly 350 trips and thousands of miles traveled, the economists found that half the passengers were taken on detours that lengthened the ride by about 10%. OK, but maybe the taxi drivers simply didn't know the shortest route. That's why the most important part of the experiment was that some of the passengers were trained to appear to be from out-of-town while others were trained to appear as locals. The economists found that detouring wasn't random: Passengers who appeared to be from out-of-town were detoured more often. The taxi

Asymmetric information is when one party to an exchange has more or better information than the other party.

461

drivers were taking the longest detours when their information advantage appeared to be the greatest.[1]

Problems of asymmetric information aren't limited to cab rides. In many markets, the seller of a service is also the expert who diagnoses how much service is needed. We rely, for example, on physicians, auto mechanics, and dentists to fix problems and also to tell us what the problem is. If the auto mechanic tells you that you need a Johnson rod, well, maybe you do and maybe you don't—it's hard for a nonexpert to tell. We often buy products or services for which it's difficult to estimate the quality. Is that used car a lemon or a plum? Firms must also estimate the quality of their potential employees and sometimes even of their customers. Out of all these applicants for the job, which one is the best? Out of all these potential buyers of health insurance, which are likely to be healthiest?

The **principal–agent problem**: How can a principal incentivize an agent to work in the principal's interest even when the agent has information that the principal does not?

More generally, economists call these problems **principal–agent problems**. How can a principal incentivize an agent to work in the principal's interest even when the agent has information that the principal does not? The problem applies not just to buyers and sellers but to employers and employees (see more in Chapter 18), to voters and politicians (Chapter 20), and even to dating and the animal kingdom (this chapter!).

Markets work best when traders know exactly what is being traded. When that is the case, markets will attract both buyers and sellers because each side expects trade to be *mutually* profitable. But when one party to a (potential) trade has more or better information than the other party, the less informed party may withdraw from the market and decide that trade is too risky or not in his or her interest. In extreme cases, asymmetric information can mean that markets fail to exist.

In Chapter 10 we saw that markets may not be ideal when there are significant effects on bystanders. In one sense, asymmetric information is a more severe challenge to markets than externalities because problems of asymmetric information mean that markets may not work well even for buyers and sellers! In another way, the problem is less severe. Buyers and sellers don't have an incentive to solve externality problems but buyers and sellers do have an incentive to solve problems of asymmetric information so they can complete mutually profitable trades. As we will see, market institutions, as well as laws and regulations, have evolved to deal with problems of asymmetric information. To understand the solutions, however, we must first understand the problem.

Let's begin with the problem of moral hazard.

Moral Hazard

Parties with better information may be tempted to exploit their information advantage at the expense of their trading partners; this possibility is called **moral hazard**. The taxi driver who takes the long route to jack up the fare, or the auto mechanic or the dentist who recommends unnecessary services—these are all examples of moral hazard.

Moral hazard is when an agent tries to exploit an information advantage in a dishonest or undesirable way.

No one wants to be ripped off but the problem of moral hazard runs deeper than a transfer of wealth from buyer to seller. Let's focus on the example of the mechanic. Suppose the mechanic tells you that you need an engine overhaul when all your car really needs is a minor new part. Overhauling the engine isn't just a ripoff, it's a waste of time and resources—the economy is producing a good that no one actually wants or needs.

A second problem occurs when buyers, knowing that the mechanic might rip them off, decide not to buy any service at all. Frankly, we don't always listen to our dentist, especially when our dentist recommends expensive treatments. Sometimes that is the right thing to do but some services really are needed even when they are expensive. Refusing service means there's no possibility of a rip-off but also no possibility of mutual gain through trade.

The bottom line is that if we lived in a world of symmetric information, sometimes we would get less treatment and sometimes we would get more. Both of these deviations represent a cost of asymmetric information.

For most goods, asymmetric information isn't a big deal. You may not know how the new item on the restaurant menu tastes but you buy it once, and if you like it, you buy it again, and if not, well, the cost of trying and sampling was low. In the case of auto mechanics, dentists, and surgeons—not to mention marriage partners (see later in this chapter!)—the decisions we must make are more expensive, longer-lasting, and more difficult to reverse, so we need to think carefully about asymmetric information.

There are two solutions to asymmetric information and moral hazard problems: either provide more information, thereby reducing the asymmetry, or reduce the incentive for the knowledgeable party to exploit their information advantage. Let's examine each of these solutions.

Overcoming Moral Hazard by Providing More Information

The Internet has played a big role in helping overcome asymmetric information problems by making it easier for buyers to pool their knowledge. On Angie's List, for example, buyers can find reviews of local auto mechanics and plumbers. Yelp provides similar reviews for restaurants. Reviews of sellers on Amazon Marketplace help potential buyers judge which sellers are most likely to deliver on their promises. Reviews have two advantages. First, they make it easier to avoid shady mechanics. Second, they raise the cost to mechanics of exploiting their information advantage.

The shady mechanic always faces a risk: If buyers think that they have been ripped off, they won't return with repeat business. Before the Internet, an upset buyer might have warned away a few friends and family. But with the Internet, an upset buyer can warn the world and that decreases the incentive for sellers to attempt a moral hazard rip-off.

More generally, the Internet has increased the value of having a good reputation. Two economists, Daniel Houser and John Wooders, found that sellers with good reputations on eBay were able to sell their goods for higher prices.[2] The Internet has also increased the cost of having a bad reputation, as students who post compromising pictures on Facebook may discover to their chagrin.

For all of their virtues, however, consumer review sites like Yelp overcome asymmetric information problems only imperfectly. We know some authors who ask their friends to post friendly and presumably nonobjective reviews on Amazon. Some stores have hired fake reviewers to praise their product, or condemn the product of a rival. In response to these problems, Yelp even set up a sting operation to catch fakers. In other words, a new kind of asymmetric information problem is introduced into the market, namely assessing the honesty and accuracy of the reviews themselves.

The general problem is that the more important a rating becomes, the greater the incentive to fake or manipulate that rating. *U.S. News & World Report* reviews and rates U.S. colleges and universities, and these ratings have a big influence on where students want to study. But where does *U.S. News and World Report* get the data to rate universities? Often from the universities themselves! We won't mention names (don't worry, we're sure *your* institution wouldn't do anything wrong), but colleges have engaged in such practices as lying about the class rank and SAT scores of admitted freshmen, lying about student retention rates, lying about fund-raising success, and misrepresenting student–faculty ratios. Other times, the college does not lie but rather manipulates admission practices to achieve higher scores. One university offered financial incentives for *admitted* students to retake the SAT, so that the university could report a higher average SAT score among its students.[3] Other colleges have delayed the admission of students with lower SAT scores so that these lower scores would not be counted when average SAT data were collected.

When we can't rely on seller or buyer reviews, third-party organizations can sometimes be trusted to provide independent advice. The magazine and Web site *Consumer Reports* (*CR*) tests and rates a wide variety of products, from washing machines to cars to computers, not to mention bassinets and blood glucose meters—all to help their subscribers and paid-up users of their Web site make better informed decisions. To demonstrate its credibility, *CR* does all of its own tests (it doesn't rely on what the sellers claim) and it will not accept advertisements or other forms of payment from the companies whose products are being rated.

Organizations like *CR*, however, are probably underprovided relative to their social usefulness. Many forms of information are a *public good*, which means that it is difficult to exclude nonpayers (and also that consumption is nonrival; see Chapter 19). Nonexcludability makes it hard to sell information even when the information is valuable. Let's say, for instance, that an individual can either pay for CR or she can go to Google and try to get that same information for free. Most people opt for the cheaper option, and indeed if you Google "best new cars" you will come across plenty of free information, some of it even drawn from *CR*. Once the underlying research has been produced, it tends to make its way into the world, whether in someone else's article, blog post, or tweet, and Google will bring us much of that information, again for free. The result is that many people **free ride** on all the testing and research that *CR* does to produce its product ratings. Since not everyone who benefits from *CR*'s research pays for it, the market for such information is smaller than ideal.

By the way, did you know that *CR* forbids its ratings from being used in any product advertisements? *CR* argues that this prevents even the hint of impropriety. Notice that this policy also makes it harder to find *CR* ratings, except by buying *Consumer Reports* magazine. Thus, the no-advertising policy also helps *CR* to prevent free riders.

Since buyers are reluctant to pay for information, independent third-party reviewers often aren't as independent as we would like. The bond-rating companies Standard and Poor's and Moody's evaluate the creditworthiness of companies and also of financial securities, including mortgage securities. The rating companies are supposed to help buyers pick safe securities on the basis of objective data. The recent track record of these companies, however, isn't good. Right up until the financial crash of 2007–2008, for example, the credit rating companies were rating many mortgage-backed securities as very safe. A short time later, the largest wave of real estate defaults in the United States since the Great Depression made quite a few of these securities very

A **free rider** consumes but does not pay.

bad investments. If you are wondering who paid for these ratings, it was the firms whose securities were being rated, not potential buyers. If credit rating companies are too critical, they may lose business from their true customers, the finance firms who want favorable reports about the securities that they are selling. Arguably, the rating companies were biased because they were trying to please those who paid them.

The ratings companies would have better incentives if they were paid directly by buyers, but again the buyers won't pay because of free rider problems, as there are many buyers for any potential security but typically only one main issuer. In general, information problems are difficult to solve completely because damping down one problem often inflates another.

Overcoming Moral Hazard by Creating Better Incentives

Better-informed buyers are one solution to asymmetric information problems. A second solution is to give sellers less of an incentive to exploit their information advantage. We have already seen how reputation can make sellers less willing to exploit their information advantage. Splitting the selling of a service from the diagnosis of how much service is needed can also help to reduce moral hazard. Before signing the deed, for example, most house buyers will hire a house inspector, and indeed often a mortgage lender will require this. Since the house inspector is paid by the buyer, the inspector has no incentive to underreport bad news. In addition, it's illegal for house inspectors to profit from any repairs that they recommend, so inspectors also do not have an incentive to overreport bad news.

Similarly, for major medical decisions, it makes sense to seek a second opinion. Not only will you get more information, but if you tell the second doctor that she will not be performing the service regardless, you are likely to get an opinion stripped of moral hazard.

Part of the original Hippocratic Oath, which physicians swear, reads, "Whatever houses I may visit, I will come for the benefit of the sick, remaining free of all intentional injustice [and] of all mischief." The oath and the professional ethics and training that come with it probably do limit moral hazard. But as always, economics is about thinking on the margin, and even physicians appear to make choices that on the margin are shaded to their benefit.

Obstetricians are typically paid more when a baby is delivered via caesarean section, a surgical procedure, than by vaginal delivery. Are you surprised that when the fee for c-sections increases, so does the number of c-sections? Incentives matter. Interestingly, when the patient is herself a physician, and thus better informed than the average patient, we do not see this relationship, and that further indicates the importance of more symmetric information. A further test of the theory of moral hazard as applied to obstetricians comes from HMOs, or health maintenance organizations, which are one form of health care provider. HMOs pay their obstetricians a salary that is *not* dependent on the delivery method. As expected, patients in HMOs have lower c-section rates (relative to similar non–HMO patients). Don't assume, however, that we can remove incentives completely. C-sections are also more common on Fridays, probably because physicians (and some patients!) would like to free up their weekends.[4]

There are even ways to overcome some of the problems with taxi drivers. If you don't trust the standard cabs, try booking a vehicle through Uber or some of the other smart phone apps. You can specify the destination and arrange the fare in advance.

Instead of trying to eliminate a seller's incentives, another method of reducing moral hazard is to better align the buyer's and seller's incentives. How do you know your lawyer is working hard on your case and not being lazy? Without a lot of expert knowledge and monitoring, it's hard to know. To overcome the potential moral hazard problem, plaintiffs often pay their lawyers with a contingent fee—the lawyer is paid, typically a third of any judgment, *only* if the case is won. Real estate agents are also paid only if the house sells but in this case the contingent fee, typically 3% of the price of the house, is much smaller than a lawyer's fee. As a result, real estate agents are more eager to sell houses quickly than are homeowners. If waiting an additional week raises the price by $1,000, that's an extra $970 for the homeowner and only $30 more for the agent. Interestingly, when agents sell their own homes, they use their information advantage and keep their houses on the market about 10 days longer than similar houses sold by owners with agents.[5]

Finally, don't think that moral hazard is limited to markets. Politicians typically have more information than voters and bureaucrats often have more information than politicians. A deep-seated problem of political science is how to incentivize politicians and bureaucrats to act in the public interest and not to use their information advantage for their own interest. Competitive elections, checks and balances, a free and independent press, and other institutions all can be understood as ways to limit moral hazard in politics (we take up more of these issues in Chapter 20).

Let's be honest: Moral hazard is everywhere because self-interest is everywhere (even if you don't think that self-interest is the only motivation). Recall Big Idea Two from Chapter 1: Good Institutions Align Self-Interest with the Social Interest. When it comes to moral hazard, reputation, ratings, and contract design, such as contingent fees, are some of the institutions that align self-interest with the social interest. Most importantly, note that these institutions are continually evolving in response to new challenges.

Let's turn now to another problem of asymmetric information.

Adverse Selection

Groucho Marx, the famous comedian, once said that he didn't want to belong to any club that would have him as a member. Believe it or not, the economist George Akerlof won a Nobel Prize for analyzing when Groucho-type reasoning makes sense and what the consequences are for market equilibrium and efficiency! Groucho was using the fact that a club was offering him membership to infer something about the quality of the club, namely that the club couldn't be very exclusive. Akerlof analyzed the more general situation of **adverse selection**, when an offer conveys negative information about what is being offered.

Adverse selection occurs when an offer conveys negative information about the product being offered.

Quick: Who is most likely to want health insurance? Answer: the sick. That's adverse selection: The offer, in this case the offer to buy health insurance, conveys the negative information that the buyer is likely to have above-average health care costs. Notice that Groucho didn't want to join a club that most wanted him as a member, and insurance companies don't want to sell insurance to the people who most want to buy—this is the basic problem of adverse selection.

Let's give another example that was first analyzed by Akerlof. Suppose that there are two types of used cars: lemons (used cars with a lot of problems) and plums (used cars in excellent mechanical shape). Lemons are worth $8,000; plums are worth $12,000. Suppose also that among the currently owned cars there are equal numbers of lemons and plums. Now, here is the key assumption of asymmetric information: Assume that only sellers know the true quality of their car and that there is no cheap way for buyers to distinguish lemons from plums. The market structure is simple but the assumption of asymmetric information has surprising consequences.

Suppose that you were a buyer in this market. How much would you be willing to pay for a used car? You might reason that since there are equal numbers of lemons and plums, the probability is $\frac{1}{2}$ that you will be purchasing a lemon and $\frac{1}{2}$ that you will be purchasing a plum. Thus, you would be willing to pay the expected or average value, namely $(\frac{1}{2} \times \$8,000) + (\frac{1}{2} \times \$12,000) = \$10,000$.

This reasoning is incomplete. To see why, now put yourself in the shoes of a seller with a plum, a high-quality used car. Buyers are willing to pay only $10,000 for a used car, but your car is worth $12,000. Do you sell? No.

Now put yourself back in the shoes of the buyer and think like Groucho. Even if half of the existing cars are plums, does it make sense to assume that half of the cars *for sale* are plums? No. In fact, no owner of a plum will want to sell, so the mere fact that a car is offered for sale suggests that it's a lemon. How much are you willing to pay for a used car now?

Since buyers know that every used car for sale is a lemon, the most they will be willing to pay for a used car is $8,000.

Notice what is wrong with this outcome. Even if lots of people would like to buy a plum at $12,000 and lots of people would like to sell a plum at $12,000, there is no market for plums. Plums—the high-quality used cars—don't trade. That is a market failure.

We assumed that there were only two types of used cars, but the outcome gets even more disturbing when there are many qualities of used car from low to high. The general logic is that of the vicious circle, or "death spiral." Buyers can't easily tell the quality of a used car so they play the averages. An average price, however, means that the owners of higher-quality autos aren't getting a good price for their cars. The owners of high-quality used cars drop out of the market, thereby reducing the average quality of the cars for sale and, in turn, reducing how much buyers are willing to pay. The process continues until only the worst lemons are for sale.

Of course, in the real world not every used car for sale is a lemon. The reality is that about 35 million used cars (and small trucks) are bought and sold in an average year in the United States, as compared to about 12 million new cars.[6] It hardly seems that the used car market has shut down, nor are used vehicle sales in the United States overwhelmingly dominated by low-quality lemons.

Now that we understand the problem, let's turn to some of the market institutions, laws, and regulations that have evolved to deal with adverse selection.

Asymmetric Information and Used Cars

Type of car	Lemons (low quality)	Plums (high quality)
Value	$8,000	$12,000

In the market for used cars... The lemons are the only used cars that will be bought and sold.

How does the used car market manage to work as well as it does?

First, potential buyers can have an experienced mechanic look over the car. Similarly, used cars are also often accompanied by what are called "CARFAX" reports, which detail the repair history of the car. Both of these techniques help to overcome information asymmetry and increase trade.

Second, millions of used cars today are certified, which means they are bought by a dealer, inspected, repaired and refurbished, and then sold with an extended warranty. The warranty reduces consumer fears about getting a lemon. A warranty also makes the dealer's promise to sell a plum **credible** because if a dealer sells a lemon, the dealer ends up paying. Warranties are best when they are never used! The firm selling the warranty is often the original manufacturer of the car. For example, Mercedes offers warranties for certified preowned Mercedes vehicles. Thus, Mercedes' reputation for high-quality new cars is also on the line when they sell certified preowned cars. That also reassures consumers and communicates the message that the car is really a good one.

Similarly, notice that many used cars are bought and sold between friends and family. If your brother tells you that his car is a plum, you may be more likely to believe him—because he's your brother and also because if the car isn't a plum, you can punish him in ways that you could not punish a stranger! In essence, reputation outside the market for used cars helps to sell used cars.

Third, suppose that some sellers of used cars will sell even when the price is low. Perhaps some owners of used cars simply love that new car smell and want to replace their used car regardless. Other owners have leased their cars and want a new car every two years, or perhaps they simply need the cash. If some used car owners sell even if they have a plum, that action raises the expected value of used cars and makes buyers more willing to buy and (other) sellers more willing to sell. Thus, the presence of some sellers who sell regardless of price keeps the price high enough so that other owners of plums want to sell.

Adverse selection hasn't shut down the market for used cars because market institutions have developed to reduce information asymmetry and its consequences. It's not that everyone has a great experience buying a used car (or a new car, for that matter), but the used car market is an active and well-functioning market that gives many people the chance to buy (or sell) personal transportation at a discounted price.[7] Still, an understanding of the dangers of adverse selection helps us understand how to do a better job buying or selling used cars.

Adverse Selection in Health Insurance

Let's look in more detail at the challenge of selling health insurance. When a health insurance company offers a policy, it worries that perhaps the sickest individuals, or those with the greatest potential future problems, are the ones most likely to buy. After all, a perfectly healthy person doesn't benefit much from the reimbursements offered by health insurance, unless, of course, some sudden accident befalls them. But if only the sick buy insurance, the insurance company has to raise its rates to reflect the higher costs. The higher rates in turn make health insurance an even worse deal for healthy individuals, pushing them out of the market. As rates rise and healthy individuals drop out of the market, the composition of customers becomes even more costly for the

A **credible** promise is one that the promisor has an incentive to keep.

CHECK YOURSELF

■ Go to eBay and search for Picassos. What do you infer about these Picassos?

health insurance company, which in turn pushes rates yet higher. Figure 24.1 illustrates this process, which is sometimes called the "adverse selection death spiral," with some specific numbers and assumptions.

As in the market for used cars, some market features help limit this adverse selection problem:

Inspections or Checkups An insurance company can inspect the health of potential insurance customers to overcome asymmetric information and adjust rates accordingly. If insurance companies can charge people different

FIGURE 24.1

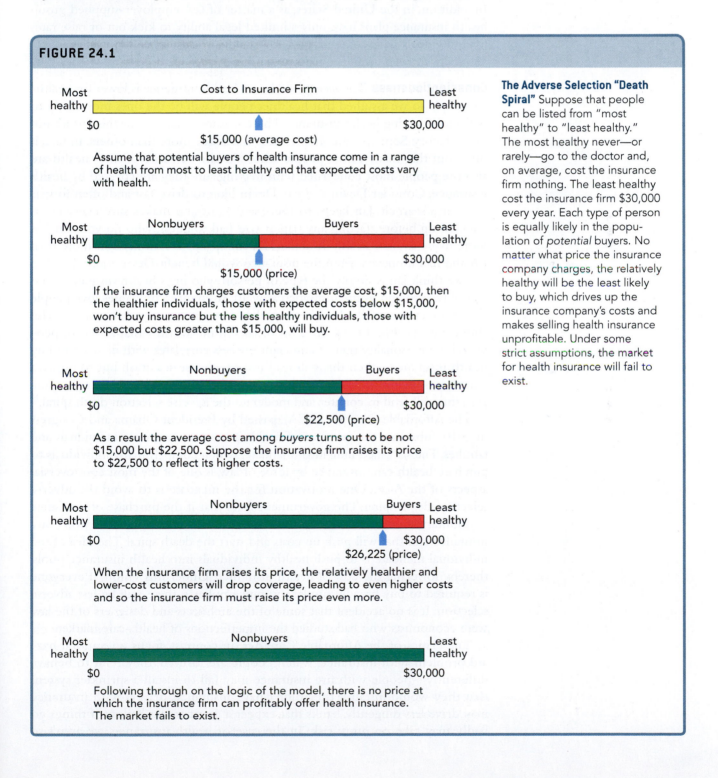

Most healthy   Cost to Insurance Firm   Least healthy

$0 $15,000 (average cost) $30,000

Assume that potential buyers of health insurance come in a range of health from most to least healthy and that expected costs vary with health.

Most healthy   Nonbuyers   Buyers   Least healthy

$0 $15,000 (price) $30,000

If the insurance firm charges customers the average cost, $15,000, then the healthier individuals, those with expected costs below $15,000, won't buy insurance but the less healthy individuals, those with expected costs greater than $15,000, will buy.

Most healthy   Nonbuyers   Buyers   Least healthy

$0 $22,500 (price) $30,000

As a result the average cost among *buyers* turns out to be not $15,000 but $22,500. Suppose the insurance firm raises its price to $22,500 to reflect its higher costs.

Most healthy   Nonbuyers   Buyers   Least healthy

$0 $26,225 (price) $30,000

When the insurance firm raises its price, the relatively healthier and lower-cost customers will drop coverage, leading to even higher costs and so the insurance firm must raise its price even more.

Most healthy   Nonbuyers   Least healthy

$0 $30,000

Following through on the logic of the model, there is no price at which the insurance firm can profitably offer health insurance. The market fails to exist.

The Adverse Selection "Death Spiral" Suppose that people can be listed from "most healthy" to "least healthy." The most healthy never—or rarely—go to the doctor and, on average, cost the insurance firm nothing. The least healthy cost the insurance firm $30,000 every year. Each type of person is equally likely in the population of *potential* buyers. No matter what price the insurance company charges, the relatively healthy will be the least likely to buy, which drives up the insurance company's costs and makes selling health insurance unprofitable. Under some strict assumptions, the market for health insurance will fail to exist.

rates depending on their expected costs, the adverse selection "death spiral" will be avoided.

Group Plans An insurance company can emphasize sales to groups, such as through the workplace, to increase the chances of signing up both healthy and unhealthy customers. In fact, most health insurance in the United States is not bought by individuals but by firms that purchase insurance for their employees as a group. Since healthier individuals typically cannot opt out of their employer's group health insurance plan, this limits adverse selection problems. In addition, in the United States, as a matter of law, employer-supplied group health insurance plans have only a limited legal ability to kick out or raise rates for individuals who come down with financially costly health problems. That also helps to keep insurance markets working.

Conscientiousness The *monetary* value of health insurance is lower for healthier people so we assumed that healthier people will be the ones most likely to opt out of buying health insurance. There is some evidence for this but it's not the full story. Some people simply value insurance more than others. In fact, it turns out that many of the people who take the best care of their health are also the people most concerned with making sure they are covered by health insurance. Consider Devin and Jan. Devin likes to drive fast and often forgets to wear a seatbelt. Jan keeps to the speed limit and makes sure everyone is buckled up before starting any trip. If you had to guess, who do you think is more likely to have health insurance, Devin or Jan? Devin needs it more than Jan and in a monetary sense the insurance would benefit Devin more than Jan, but we think Jan is simply the type of person who buys health insurance (and probably auto and home insurance as well). Insurance companies love people with temperaments like Jan's because they buy insurance and they are careful about their health. If there are a lot of Jans in the world—that is, lots of people whose personality trait of conscientiousness correlates with demand to buy health insurance—then this will lead not to adverse selection but to positive selection (sometimes called "propitious selection"). Even if there are only some Jans, this will tend to counter and moderate the adverse selection death spiral.[8]

The Affordable Care Act (ACA), passed by President Obama and Congress in 2010, subsidizes the purchase of health insurance for poorer individuals and families. The so-called individual mandate, which compels many individuals to purchase health care insurance by force of law, is one of the most controversial aspects of the ACA. One motivation for the mandate is to avoid the adverse selection death spiral. The government fears that if the purchase of insurance is voluntary, then, even with the subsidies, many healthy individuals won't buy insurance and that will push up costs and start the death spiral. The idea of the individual mandate is to push healthy individuals into health insurance pools, thereby lowering the cost of health insurance. Under this vision, if everyone is required to buy broadly similar insurance policies, there will be less adverse selection. It is no accident that some of the architects and designers of the law were economists who had studied the imperfections of health-care markets.

The critics of the Affordable Care Act, in contrast, focus on a moral hazard problem with insurance. When people are insured, they tend to behave differently—people with fire insurance may fail to install a sprinkler system that they would install if they didn't have insurance, drivers with insurance may drive less diligently, banks that expect a government bailout if things go badly may take on more risk. In the case of health insurance, we aren't so

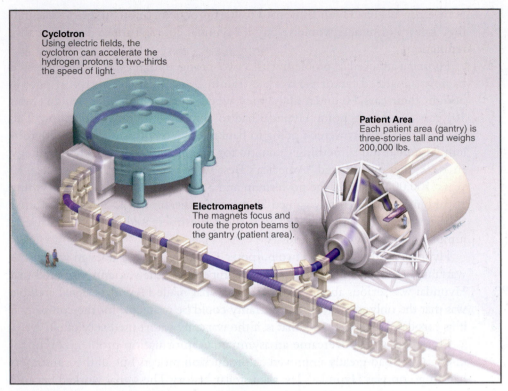

Cyclotron
Using electric fields, the cyclotron can accelerate the hydrogen protons to two-thirds the speed of light.

Patient Area
Each patient area (gantry) is three-stories tall and weighs 200,000 lbs.

Electromagnets
The magnets focus and route the proton beams to the gantry (patient area).

Proton Therapy High-tech science or moral hazard?

much worried about a person taking on more risk but of demanding more services. When patients, doctors, and hospitals know an insurance company is paying the final bill, the patients tend to demand more procedures and treatments. Doctors and hospitals, in turn, supply those procedures and treatments, knowing they will be paid for them, and that is a form of moral hazard at the expense of the insurance companies.

Hospitals around the country, for example, have been building nuclear particle accelerators—which were once used only by physicists looking to understand the universe!—to treat cancer. The accelerators cost hundreds of millions of dollars and involve massive magnets and giant buildings. Unfortunately, there is very little evidence that so-called proton therapy improves health and even less that we need dozens of these facilities in the United States. If patients had to pay for these treatments out of pocket, they would be unlikely to want them but when insurance companies and taxpayers are the ones paying the bills, patients will demand them and hospitals will supply them.

Health care in the United States already consumes about 18% of GDP. Critics of the Affordable Care Act worry that by reducing price signals and market incentives in favor of greater reliance on government guarantees, health-care costs may rise even further, creating longer-run harms.

Signaling as a Response to Asymmetric Information

Hyundai Motor Company was founded in South Korea in 1967 and began selling cars in the United States in 1986. Hyundai cars were inexpensive and sold reasonably well but Hyundai was perceived as a low-quality brand with a poor repair history. Hyundai wanted to start producing more luxurious cars but they knew consumers wouldn't buy if Hyundai couldn't shake its low-quality reputation.

Hyundai attacked its problem with a two-pronged strategy. First, they invested in new, advanced factories, worker training, and quality control. If people bought their cars, Hyundai knew they would last but Hyundai couldn't wait 10 years to prove its point. Hyundai had to get people to buy its cars now if all the new investments weren't going to bankrupt the company. To solve its problem, Hyundai did something dramatic for the second prong of their strategy. In 1998, they introduced "America's Best Warranty" on all their vehicles, 10 years/100,000 miles on the powertrain and 5 years/60,000 miles on everything else. Hyundai immediately gained 28 points in the annual JD Power Customer Satisfaction survey and the next year their sales increased by 82%, the largest jump in the history of the industry.

A signal is an expensive action that is taken to reveal information.

Hyundai's warranty served two purposes. First, if something does go wrong, the warranty has value as insurance. But more importantly, the warranty **signaled** that Hyundai was serious about quality. In fact, what made Hyundai's signal credible was that the only way Hyundai's warranty could be profitable for the company is if its cars didn't break down—that is, if the warranty wasn't used very often!

Hyundai's signal overcame an asymmetric information problem. Hyundai knew that it had greatly improved its production process but all the consumers had to go on was Hyundai's less than stellar history. The signal worked because offering a warranty is cheap for a company that produces high-quality cars but expensive for a company that produces low-quality cars.

Signaling in the Job Market

You are an aspiring software programmer and you see the perfect job being advertised in Silicon Valley at a starting salary of $90,000 a year. Awesome! You really want the job and, remembering your economics lesson that incentives matter, you tell the interviewer that you would be willing to take the job for just $75,000. You are confident that you have underbid the other applicants and so will get the job. You don't get the job. What happened? Your reasoning about the power of underbidding is correct if the interviewer can easily evaluate the quality of all the job candidates. Who wouldn't want high quality at a low price? But evaluating job candidates is notoriously difficult. Some candidates who look good on paper are disasters in practice, and vice versa. The interviewer doesn't know your true quality. As a result, when the interviewer hears your offer to work for much less, the interviewer may infer that you are desperate—a low-quality candidate who can't get a job elsewhere—not someone the company wants to hire. Once again, this is a problem of adverse selection: The interviewer is worried that the people who most want the job are not the people the firm most wants to hire. This is one reason why unemployed people often find it harder to get hired than do similar employed workers looking for a new job.

Offering to work for low pay sends a signal that you might be a low-quality worker. How could you signal a potential employer about your high quality? Here's a hint: You might be signaling right now. We hope that you are learning something from this textbook that will be useful to you in your future career. One theory of education, however, says that education pays not because it offers any practical advice but only because a degree is a signal of IQ and conscientiousness, including grit and determination.

As professional academics, we have in fact noticed that not every degree actually prepares people for the real world. A lot of study seems to consist of relatively academic exercises with few practical applications. Some degrees do pay more, including chemical engineering and economics! But if you graduate with a degree in art or ancient Greek history, don't despair. Most degrees pay even if your eventual job has nothing to do with your degree. Signaling helps explain why. It's easier for someone with a high IQ and good work habits to get a degree—almost any degree—than it is for someone with a low IQ and a lack of determination. Thus, completing a degree signals to employers that you are likely to have the kinds of qualities that employers are willing to pay for.

Consider the following thought experiment. Which do you think would pay more, a diploma from Harvard without a Harvard education or a Harvard education without the diploma? There is some evidence for the former. If education were only about learning and not at all about signaling, you would expect that people who took all the courses except *one* would receive almost as big a boost in their wages as a person who took all the courses and graduated with a diploma. After all, the two individuals have nearly the same education. And yet people with a degree earn much more than people with nearly the same education but without the degree. In the literature, this is called the "sheepskin effect" (degrees were made of sheepskin a long time ago) because it says that the sheepskin you hang on the wall is worth a large fraction of the value of the education.[9] The lesson here is to finish your degree!

Econ Duel: Is Education Signaling or Skill Building?

Signaling in Dating, Marriage, and the Animal Kingdom

Signaling pervades our lives, and it is not restricted to narrowly economic transactions. Criminals, for example, often need to signal to each other their propensities to break the law, yet without incriminating themselves should they be dealing with an undercover police officer. Facial tattoos are one way to do this because the tattoo shows that the person has given up on any chance of achieving a normal, mainstream life. In South African prisons, for instance, such tattoos are a common way for true criminals to identify each other and verify that they really are disreputable lawbreakers. One South African prisoner had the phrase "Spit on my grave" tattooed across his forehead and "I hate you, Mum" imprinted on his left cheek. That's a pretty good sign that person is not looking to go straight or to reform and enter mainstream life.[10]

Employers interview potential employees extensively because it's much cheaper to avoid hiring a bad employee than it is to fire one. It's also much cheaper to avoid marrying a bad partner than it is to divorce one. Thus, you can think of dating as a series of marriage interviews! As with a job interview, marriage interviews contain a lot of signaling.

Recall the aspiring programmer who offers to work for less money. The programmer's offer is rejected because employers fear that someone who is so desperate for work that they offer to work for less is actually worth less. In this respect, getting a job and getting a date are not so different. Dating

RICHARD I'ANSON/GETTY IMAGES

TIINA TUOMAALA/ALAMY

If I weren't such a stud, could I afford this?

experts—not just economists—recommend, for example, that for both men and women, it's important not to look too eager.

Engagement rings are a signal of our commitment to our partners or potential partners but to work they have to be expensive. An expensive ring is a signal because expensive rings are cheaper if you truly expect to remain married! If you think that rings are bought because they are beautiful rather than for signaling, consider the following thought experiment. How long would the tradition of giving a diamond engagement ring last if a new technology made diamonds cheap?

Many women, when they marry, face the choice of whether to take the last name of their husband or perhaps to adopt a joint, hyphenated last name. If the woman takes the last name of her husband, it is a signal that a future divorce will be especially costly to her. She would then either be stuck with the last name of a man she has fallen out of love with, or she would have to change her name once again, which could make it harder to establish or keep a reputation and create costs for her professional life. On the other hand, if a woman keeps her maiden name, she is signaling a strong attachment to building or maintaining a career reputation. Some women try to have it both ways by using two names (one at the workplace, the other at home) or by using hyphenated names, while many other people wonder why this burden of adjustment is distributed so fully on women and not on men.

Signaling even pervades the animal kingdom. Charles Darwin was perplexed by the peacock's tail. Why would a peacock use so many of its resources on a tail that not only didn't help it survive but that actually hindered survival by making it more difficult for the peacock to escape predators? The theory of signaling and sexual selection offers an answer. Since only the healthiest and most robust peacocks can grow large and beautiful tails, the peacock's tail signals to peahens that the peacock is healthy, has good genes, and would make a good partner for procreation.

Is Signaling Good?

Signaling creates benefits by generating information, but in most signaling models there is some inefficiency. It typically takes at least four years to get a degree, and if education doesn't add much to future productivity, then that's four years of effort just to signal IQ and perseverance. Maybe you have fun during the university years but university can't be too much fun or everyone would do it, even those without high IQs and perseverance. Ideally, there might be a cheaper way to communicate this information to potential employers. We see the same issues with diamond rings. If there were a cheaper way to signal commitment, you could get your partner a much cheaper cubic zirconia ring and use the savings to buy a nice Viking refrigerator. Solving these problems isn't easy, however. We are both professors of economics and believe us when we say that we didn't even try to eliminate the costs of signaling with diamond rings.

Finally, note that while signaling eases some problems of asymmetric information, it creates others. In particular, when signaling is rife, some moral hazard problems may become worse. Let's go back to education as a signal of worker productivity. If finishing an education gets you higher wages whether or not you learn anything useful, that sad reality removes some of the pressure on colleges and universities to teach you something useful. Students might prefer to learn something practical rather than just jumping through hoops, but professors will find it easier to teach what interests them and many administrators will tolerate this. After all, conscientious students will still attend and finish college simply to get the higher wages, whether or not they learn very much. We return again to a key theme of this chapter: many asymmetric information problems can be eased or traded in for easier-to-handle information problems, but asymmetric information will continue as a general market phenomenon.

Takeaway

Markets work best when both buyers and sellers know exactly what is being exchanged. When one party to an exchange has more or better information than the other party, we get problems of asymmetric information, such as moral hazard and adverse selection.

Moral hazard is when an agent tries to exploit an information advantage in a dishonest or undesirable way. Not all people try to exploit their information advantage but incentives do matter. When moral hazard is possible, the less informed party may be exploited and resources may be consumed without generating value (the mechanic who replaces the part that doesn't need replacing). Or, fearing moral hazard, parties with less information may simply decide not to trade, thereby reducing the gains from trade.

Adverse selection occurs when an offer conveys negative information about the product being offered. When buyers can't easily evaluate the quality of a good, they may assume that any good offered for sale will be of low quality and they will be willing to pay only accordingly. Sellers, seeing that the price is low, will choose to sell only the low-quality good. Buyers and sellers both get what they paid for (unlike with moral hazard) but both would be better off if they could also buy and sell high-quality goods.

Moral hazard and adverse selection problems challenge markets, but market institutions, laws, and regulations have evolved to deal with these problems. Ratings, reviews, and inspections all work to generate more information and to reduce asymmetry. Reputation and certification, second opinions (separating the provider of information from the provider of the service), and contingent fees all help to align buyer and seller interests. Even when the relevant information cannot be shown directly (only the heart knows its secrets), sometimes it can be signaled by an investment in something else.

The solutions to asymmetric information problems are never without cost and they are rarely perfect or complete. Ratings and reviews can be faked, reputations are sometimes undeserved, contracts rarely fully align incentives, and signals are noisy. Nevertheless, we think that understanding the problems of asymmetric information and their (partial) solutions can help you to understand and navigate your world.

CHAPTER REVIEW

 interactive activity   Go online to practice with more examples of these types of problems, including live links to videos, data sources, and feedback.

Problems in green relate to MRU videos. See the MRU table at the end of the exercises.

KEY CONCEPTS

asymmetric information, p. 461

principal–agent problem, p. 462

moral hazard, p. 462

free rider, p. 464

adverse selection, p. 466

credible, p. 468

signal, p. 472

FACTS AND TOOLS

1. Determine whether the following situations represent problems caused by asymmetric information. If so, determine whether they represent problems of moral hazard or adverse selection.

   a. Unrest in the Middle East causes oil speculators to buy up oil futures, driving gasoline prices higher.

   b. Karol is halfway to work before he realizes that he forgot to lock the back door. Because he has renter's insurance, he decides it is not worth being late just to go home to lock the door.

   c. Joanne applies for a job as a part-time manager at a fast-food restaurant. Her MBA makes her overqualified for the job, yet the position goes to someone else who doesn't have a college degree.

   d. Frances lives in an apartment above a restaurant, and her apartment always smells like burgers and fries. She has tried unsuccessfully to get the restaurant owner to remedy the problem.

   e. The potential costs of long-term care (such as a nursing home stay) can be very high and also very uncertain. Despite this, the private market for long-term care in the United States has remained fairly small.

2. Describe how the following facts represent solutions to problems of asymmetric information.

   a. Auto insurance rates are higher for teenagers than for nonteenagers.

   b. Your car insurance coverage probably includes a deductible—an amount that you have to pay out of pocket before your insurance coverage kicks in.

   c. Many states have laws like Virginia's that give customers the right to keep or inspect parts that are removed by an auto mechanic.

   d. For many couples, weddings are lavish affairs that cost tens of thousands of dollars and are attended by hundreds of guests.

3. George Akerlof's model of the used car market results in a market in which only lemons are sold and there is no market for high-quality used cars. But, in fact, we observe that the used car market is a robust market in which millions of used cars of varying quality are sold. Does that mean Akerlof's model is wrong? Why or why not?

4. In September of 2008, the Federal Reserve announced a "bailout" for AIG, which had gone bankrupt after having its credit rating downgraded in the wake of the financial crisis of 2007–2008. Can you think of an argument against such a bailout that is related to the material in this chapter? Where's the information asymmetry?

5. Explain the difference between moral hazard and adverse selection. In general, which problem is more likely to arise prior to making a transaction, and which problem is more likely to arise after the transaction has been made?

THINKING AND PROBLEM SOLVING

6. Consider the market for medical insurance. What information might buyers in this market have that insurance companies don't have? Here's a harder question: What information might sellers of medical insurance have that buyers don't have?

7. Health economists use the phrase "supplier-induced demand" to describe the ability that physicians have to influence their patients' demand for medical care. One of the reasons that this ability exists is asymmetric information.

   a. What do physicians know more about than patients?

   b. If physicians can influence their patients' demand, then what would prevent them from always providing diagnoses of severe conditions that require expensive (profitable) treatments?

   c. Health economists point out that third-party payment schemes (such as medical insurance that pays your medical bills for you) also contribute to supplier-induced demand. How would third-party payment exacerbate the problems of asymmetric information?

8. Evan Soltas is a popular economics blogger (http://evansoltas.com/) who began capturing the attention of top economics thinkers while still in high school. His understanding of economics and economics issues would have been impressive even for a professional economist with years of training. After graduating from high school, he went off to Princeton to major in economics. Since Evan doesn't have much to learn about economics—at least not much at the undergraduate level—this decision might seem confusing to some people, but you're a gifted economist now too. Explain Evan's decision.

9. Suppose your band is about to take off, so you go out and buy a brand-new Marshall Tube Head and Cabinet amplifier for the list price of about $4,200. But, you band breaks up after you've used it only once. You hang on to it for a year or so in case your drummer and bass player can work out their differences, but it never happens. You finally decide to sell it on Craigslist. Since you know it's been used only once, and it's been properly stored for a year, you reason that it's still worth close to what you paid for it, so you list it for $3,800—almost 10% off of the new price. How is this going to turn out?

10. Kaplan Test Prep offers courses and private tutoring arrangements that prepare students for standardized tests, such as the GRE, GMAT, or LSAT (tests that you may take soon). Kaplan offers students a "Higher Score Guarantee," which essentially promises that your score when you take the test after completing a Kaplan course will be higher than your prior test score (or your "diagnostic" score if it's your first time taking the test). If it's not, you can take the course again or get your money back.

   a. Discuss how this guarantee functions as insurance.

   b. Discuss how this guarantee functions as a signal.

11. Consider the following unusual insurance products. For each one, determine whether you think this insurance product could exist in the marketplace, or whether it would be subject to moral hazard or adverse selection (or both).

   a. GPA insurance for people with 4.0 GPAs after two years of college that pays out if you ever have a semester with a GPA lower than 3.50.

   b. GPA insurance for anyone that pays out if you ever have a semester with a GPA lower than 3.50.

   c. Loneliness insurance that pays out if you reach a certain age and still have not married.

   d. Toe-stubbing insurance that pays out any time you stub your toe.

   e. Insurance that pays out if and only if you get hit and killed by a school bus.

12. When the cause of death is suicide, life insurance policies typically pay out only when the suicide occurred after an exclusionary period has passed, usually around a year after purchasing the life insurance. Why do life insurance companies insist on an exclusionary period? If you compared suicide rates in the year before and the year after the exclusionary period, what do you predict you would find?

13. You are driving on a trip and have two choices on the highway to stop for a snack: a well-known chain or a local restaurant that you have never heard of but that looks okay. What lessons from this chapter might lead you to choose the chain even if you think that their food is just average? Might you choose differently if you had access to the Internet? Might you choose differently if these two choices were in your neighborhood?

CHALLENGES

14. Consider a restaurant that wants to avoid kitchen fires. The restaurant could make many investments both to avoid the fires in the first place and to quickly and safely put them out if they do occur. Suppose that the marginal cost (MC) and marginal benefit (MB) of these investments in fire control technologies is illustrated in the following figure.

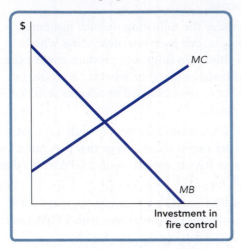

a. If no fire insurance is available, how much investment in fire control would the restaurant purchase?

b. If *full* insurance is available, how much investment in fire control would the restaurant purchase?

c. The moral hazard incentivized by full insurance creates a deadweight loss. Show the deadweight loss in the diagram.

d. Suppose that the insurance policy would only cover 50% of the losses from fire; that is, the restaurant has a 50% copay. How much fire control would the restaurant purchase?

e. Suppose that the insurance policy would cover only 50% of the losses but the insurance company also offered a discount on insurance to restaurants that installed water sprinklers or other fire suppression technologies. How would the curves shift? What quantity of fire investment would be purchased? Comment on the role of copays and discounts.

15. "Black box" insurance is a new type of auto insurance that requires that the buyer install a black box in their car that monitors speed, distance traveled, acceleration, time of day, and other factors. Discuss the effects of this type of insurance on different drivers and their behavior. The terms "adverse selection," "moral hazard," and "signaling" should all be relevant.

16. Home cleaning services and general contractors often advertise that they are bonded. What this means is that the seller of the service has put up money with a third party that is available to the buyer if, for example, the cleaners damage or steal property or if the general contractor fails to complete the project or completes it in a substandard way. Using the concepts of moral hazard and signaling, explain the purpose of bonding. As a bonus, why is bonding used for these services in particular?

17. The following demand and supply diagram represents the market for routine outpatient appointments with a primary care physician. D_1 shows the annual demand for a typical patient when he or she has no insurance and must pay the entire price of the appointment out of pocket. D_2 shows how the typical patient responds to the price when he or she has to pay only 50% out of pocket, with the rest covered by medical insurance.

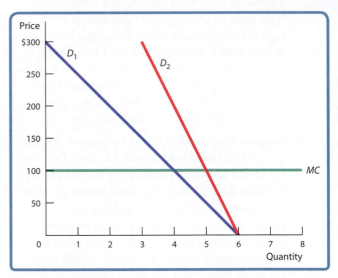

a. Can you explain the shape/position of demand curve D_2?

Suppose the marginal cost of an appointment is $100 and the market is perfectly competitive. Answer all of the following questions twice: once considering a market *without* medical insurance and once considering a market *with* medical insurance.

b. How many physician appointments will the typical patient have each year without and with insurance?

c. How much will the patient pay for physician appointments each year? How much will be paid by the insurance company?

d. What is the total annual value to the patient of the appointments?

e. Comparing your answers to parts c and d, what is the amount of net total surplus generated by the market for these physician appointments?

f. How does this relate to the chapter?

18. Human-made diamonds, which are just as beautiful and essentially indistinguishable from mined diamonds, are becoming much cheaper to produce. Diamond engagement rings, therefore, could soon become much less expensive. Great news for people who plan to get married, right? Or wrong? Explain.

WORK IT OUT

interactive activity

For interactive, step-by-step help in solving this problem, go online.

A private equity firm is considering whether to take over another firm, called the "target." The target has several projects in the pipeline so no one is certain exactly what the target is worth but estimates are that it is worth anywhere between 0 and 100, with each value equally likely. Although the value of the target is uncertain, the private equity firm knows that the target is currently ill managed and that in their hands they could increase the target's value by 50%, that is, multiply the target's value by a factor of 3/2. If the firm is currently worth 60, for example, it would be worth 60 × (3/2) = 90 after new management is installed.

a. Find a mutually profitable price for the acquisition, that is, a price such that, on average or in expectation, the owners of both the target and the private equity firm expect to profit. (*Hint:* It helps to know that, when any outcome between *a* and *b* is equally likely, the expected or average outcome is *a* + (*b* − *a*)/2, as illustrated in the diagram. (FYI, if you have taken statistics, this is a property of the uniform distribution.)

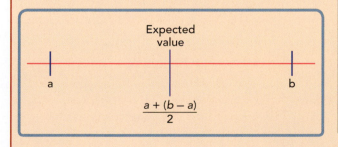

b. Now assume that the current owners of the target know whether the projects in the pipeline are going well or not and so they know the current value of the firm. Only the outsider buyer, the private equity firm, is uncertain about the value of the target, which they continue to estimate is worth between 0 and 100, with each value equally likely. Until the target is bought, information about its true value cannot be credibly communicated to the potential buyer. Naturally, the current owners will sell only if the private equity firm offers them at least as much or more than the current value.

Notice that we have transformed a problem of uncertain but symmetric information into a problem of asymmetric information.

Consider the mutually profitable price that you arrived at in part a. Is the price still mutually profitable? Why or why not? If not, find a new mutually profitable price for the acquisition (if you can). Remember that it is still the case that the firm will be worth 50% more if it is acquired by the buyer.

c. Comment on asymmetric information and trade.

MARGINAL REVOLUTION UNIVERSITY VIDEOS

Asymmetric Information and Used Cars

mruniversity.com/asymmetric-info

Problems: **1–3, 9**

Asymmetric Information in Health Insurance

mruniversity.com/asymmetric-info-health

Problems: **6, 11, 15, 17**

Moral Hazard

mruniversity.com/moral-hazard

Problems: **4, 5, 7, 14, 16**

Solutions to Moral Hazard

mruniversity.com/moral-hazard-solutions

Problems: **12, 13**

Signaling

mruniversity.com/signaling

Problems: **8, 10, 18**

25

Consumer Choice

In this chapter, we take a deeper look at how rational consumers choose. In previous chapters, we analyzed a fairly simple choice. What should a consumer do when the price of a good falls? Buy more! That was easy. In this chapter, we look at more complicated choices such as whether a consumer should shop at Costco. Costco, like Sam's Club or BJ's, offers lower prices, but to shop there, you have to pay a membership fee. How much will consumers be willing to pay to shop at Costco? As you might imagine, this is a key question for Costco managers!

We will also be looking at how much labor a worker should supply in response to a lower wage. In our chapter on labor supply, we pointed out that a worker might respond to a lower wage by working less (called the substitution effect) or the worker might choose to work more to make up for the shortfall in income at the lower wage (the income effect). In this chapter, we introduce two new tools—budget constraints and indifference curves—that will help us understand in greater detail the substitution and income effects, and how consumers and workers choose when faced with complicated decisions.

How to Compare Apples and Oranges

Despite being warned not to, consumers do compare apples and oranges. In fact, consumers have to compare apples, oranges, and every other good if they are to spend their limited budget wisely.

Apples and oranges both produce value or, in economic terms, "utility" for the consumer. We call the increase in utility generated by an additional apple the **marginal utility** of an apple and denote it MU_A. We will assume that marginal utility is diminishing. **Diminishing marginal utility** means that the first apple is great, the second good, the third not bad, and so on. Figure 25.1, for example, shows a marginal utility curve for apples on the left and a marginal utility curve for oranges on the right. In the figure, the marginal utility of the first apple is 70 "utils," the second is 60 utils, the third is 58 utils, and so forth.

But apples and oranges aren't free. There is a price for apples, which we write as P_A, and there is a price for oranges, which we write as P_O. A

Marginal utility is the change in utility from consuming an additional unit.

Diminishing marginal utility means that each additional unit of a good adds less to utility than the previous unit.

FIGURE 25.1

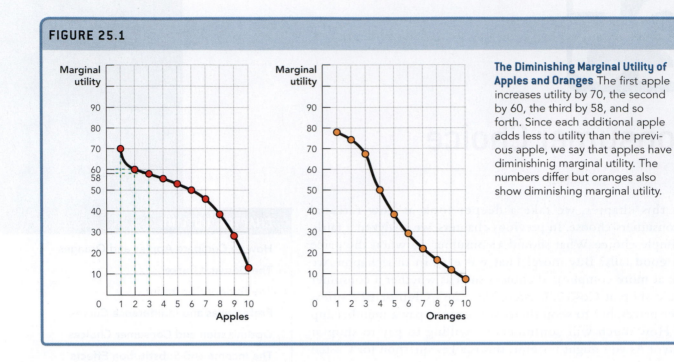

The Diminishing Marginal Utility of Apples and Oranges The first apple increases utility by 70, the second by 60, the third by 58, and so forth. Since each additional apple adds less to utility than the previous apple, we say that apples have diminishinig marginal utility. The numbers differ but oranges also show diminishing marginal utility.

Introduction to Consumer Choice

consumer might love oranges more than any other fruit, but if the price of oranges is high, that consumer may buy apples. The real problem a consumer faces, therefore, is not to choose apples and oranges directly, but to choose how many dollars to spend on apples and how many dollars to spend on oranges. Apples and oranges are two alternative ways of generating utility from dollars. So how should a consumer allocate her dollars between apples and oranges?

As usual, the way to solve this problem is to think on the margin. Each additional dollar allocated to apples generates a certain amount of utility. For example, if the marginal utility of an apple is 70 and the price of apples is $2 per apple, then the marginal utility per dollar spent on apples is 35. More generally, the marginal utility per dollar spent on apples is $\frac{MU_A}{P_A}$. To simplify, if we suppose that $P_A = P_O = \$1$, then we can use the same figure as before, except now the axis is in terms of marginal utilities per dollar.

So which combination of apples and oranges maximizes utility? It's easiest to begin with a bundle that doesn't maximize utility. Once we understand why such a bundle doesn't maximize utility, the solution to the problem will become clear.

Consider Figure 25.2 and suppose that the consumer has $10 in income and she buys 10 oranges and no apples. From the right panel, we can see that the 10th orange is generating 9 utils per dollar. Now consider how much utility would be generated by consuming one dollar less of oranges and one dollar more of apples. From the left panel, we can see that the first dollar spent on apples will generate 70 utils. Thus, by consuming one fewer orange (−9 utils) and one more apple (+70 utils), the consumer can get an increase of 61 utils in total utility.

Keep following this logic. Should the consumer consume 9 oranges and 1 apple? No. Notice that the marginal utility per dollar of the second apple exceeds the marginal utility per dollar of the ninth orange, so the consumer

FIGURE 25.2

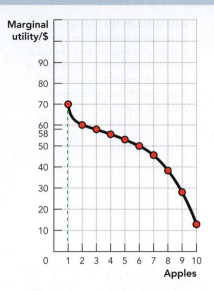

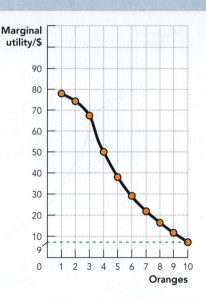

Diminishing Marginal Utility
Imagine that apples and oranges are $1 each. The curves now show the marginal utility per dollar of spending on apples and oranges. Suppose the consumer spends her entire budget of $10 on oranges. The 10th dollar of spending on oranges increases utility by 9. If the consumer spent one dollar less on oranges (−9 utils) and one dollar more on apples (+70 utils), the consumer's total utility would increase by 61.

can increase total utility by shifting another dollar of consumption away from oranges and toward apples.

In other words, if the marginal utility per dollar of apples is higher than the marginal utility per dollar of oranges, then the consumer gets more "bang from a buck" spent on apples than on oranges. Thus, she should buy more apples and fewer oranges:

If $\frac{MU_A}{P_A} > \frac{MU_O}{P_O}$, then buy more apples and fewer oranges.

By exactly the same logic, if the marginal utility of apples were less than that of oranges, then the consumer gets more bang from a buck spent on oranges. Thus, she should buy fewer apples and more oranges, that is,

If $\frac{MU_A}{P_A} < \frac{MU_O}{P_O}$, then buy fewer apples and more oranges.

Putting these two conditions together, we find that there is only one condition when the consumer cannot increase utility by adjusting her spending, that is, only one condition when the consumer is maximizing utility:

If $\frac{MU_A}{P_A} = \frac{MU_O}{P_O}$, then utility is maximized.

Figure 25.3 shows that if one follows this logic, the point of maximum utility for the consumer is to consume 6 apples and 4 oranges.

We have derived our rule for just two goods, but the idea is perfectly general. Thus, to maximize utility, the **optimal consumption rule** says that a consumer should allocate his or her spending so that the marginal utility per dollar is equal for all purchases:

$$\frac{MU_A}{P_A} = \frac{MU_O}{P_O} = \frac{MU_i}{P_i} = \cdots \frac{MU_z}{P_z}$$

Even if you don't consciously think of the "marginal utility per dollar of an apple" as a specific number, the rule tells us that to maximize utility, we should spend our bucks until the bang from a buck is the same for all purchases.

The **optimal consumption rule** says that to maximize utility, a consumer should allocate spending so that the marginal utility per dollar is equal for all purchases.

FIGURE 25.3

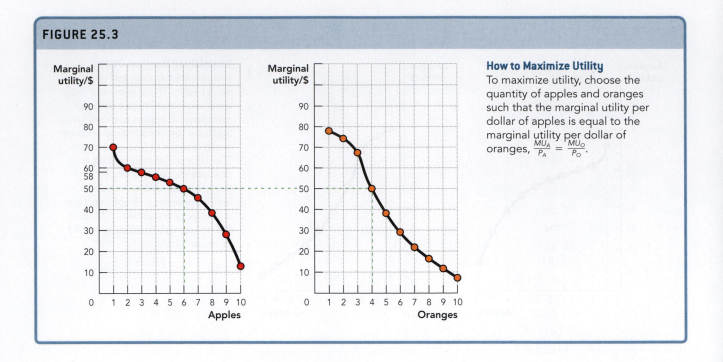

How to Maximize Utility
To maximize utility, choose the quantity of apples and oranges such that the marginal utility per dollar of apples is equal to the marginal utility per dollar of oranges, $\frac{MU_A}{P_A} = \frac{MU_O}{P_O}$.

The Demand Curve

The optimal consumption rule also gives us an informal explanation for why a consumer's demand curve slopes downward. Suppose that the consumer is currently maximizing utility, so the two-goods version of the optimal consumption rule says:

$$\frac{MU_A}{P_A} = \frac{MU_O}{P_O}$$

Now imagine that the price of apples P_A increases. An increase in P_A means that apples now provide less utility per dollar, so we have $\frac{MU_A}{P_A} < \frac{MU_O}{P_O}$. But recall our previous rule:

If $\frac{MU_A}{P_A} < \frac{MU_O}{P_O}$, then buy fewer apples and more oranges.

We can see that an increase in the price of apples leads to the consumer buying fewer apples. The optimal consumption rule therefore gives us a foundation for demand curves based on individual choice.

The optimal consumption rule is an intuitive and useful way of thinking about how consumers choose to allocate their dollars, but we have derived the rule informally and in a form that makes it difficult to make specific predictions. It's not obvious from the optimal consumption rule, for example, how changes in income affect choices. We also showed how an increase in P_A means that a consumer should buy fewer apples and more oranges, but we didn't say much about whether or when the dominant effect is fewer apples and when the dominant effect is more oranges. The theory, as we presented it, also puts this strange idea of "utils" front and center even though no one has ever seen a util. We can fix all of these problems and produce a richer, more complete theory by developing consumer choice theory a bit more formally. Fortunately, the optimal consumption rule will continue to hold true even in our richer model.

The Budget Constraint

Imagine that there are only two goods as before, but just for variety, we will switch to gasoline and pizza. Gasoline is $2 per gallon and pizzas are $10 apiece. Let's suppose that the consumer has $100 of income. Figure 25.4 shows the consumer's **budget constraint**, namely all of the bundles of gasoline and pizza that the consumer can afford given his income and prices. For example, the consumer could buy 50 gallons of gas and 0 pizzas, or 10 pizzas and 0 gallons of gas, or any consumption bundle along the line connecting these two points. The consumer cannot afford bundles that are "outside" the budget constraint. For example, the consumer cannot afford the red bundle of 40 gallons and 6 pizzas. (How much income would the consumer need to afford this bundle?)

In addition to the points along the budget constraint, the consumer can also afford any point that is "inside" the budget constraint, such as the green point of 10 gallons and 4 pizzas. If the consumer bought this bundle of goods, however, he would spend $60 ($2 × 10 + $10 × 4), leaving him with $40 in income. Note, however, that in this model, there are only two goods and no future periods so saving doesn't have any benefits. Thus, a consumer will always want to purchase a consumption bundle that lies on the budget constraint.

The budget constraint depends on the consumer's income and also on the prices of gasoline and pizza. Let's look at income first. Imagine, for example, that the consumer had $140 of income. Now the consumer could purchase any of the consumption bundles shown in Figure 25.5.

> A **budget constraint** shows all the consumption bundles that a consumer can afford given their income and prices.

FIGURE 25.4

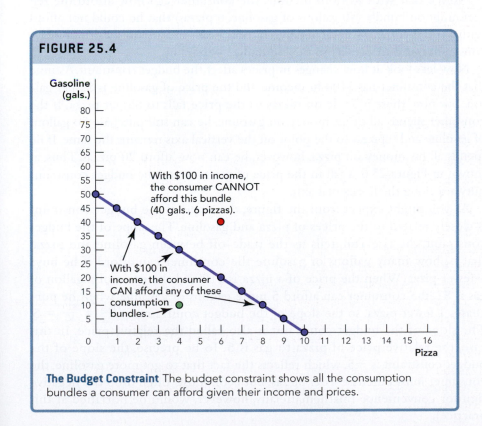

With $100 in income, the consumer CANNOT afford this bundle (40 gals., 6 pizzas).

With $100 in income, the consumer CAN afford any of these consumption bundles.

The Budget Constraint The budget constraint shows all the consumption bundles a consumer can afford given their income and prices.

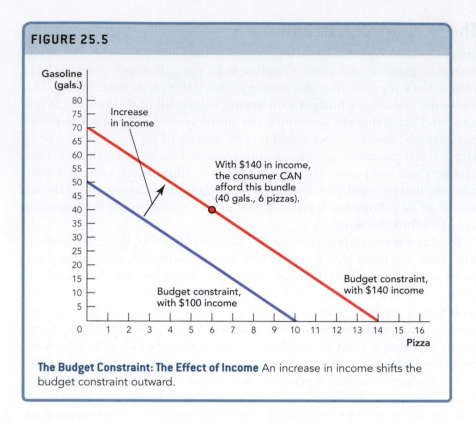

FIGURE 25.5

Increase in income

With $140 in income, the consumer CAN afford this bundle (40 gals., 6 pizzas).

Budget constraint, with $140 income

Budget constraint, with $100 income

The Budget Constraint: The Effect of Income An increase in income shifts the budget constraint outward.

The Budget Constraint

Notice that with $140 in income, the consumer can now afford the red consumption bundle (40 gallons of gasoline, 6 pizzas) that he could not afford with $100 income. More generally, an increase in income pushes the budget constraint outward, parallel to the old budget constraint.

Now let's look at how changes in prices affect the budget constraint. Assume that the consumer has $100 in income and the price of gasoline is $2 per gallon, but now there is a sale on pizzas so the price falls to $5 per pizza. If the consumer spends all of his money on gasoline, he can still purchase 50 gallons of gasoline and 0 pizzas so the point on the vertical axis remains the same. If he spends all his money on pizza, however, he can now afford 20 pizzas. Thus, as shown in Figure 25.6, a fall in the price of pizzas *rotates* the budget constraint outward along the horizontal axis.

As you might expect from the figure, the slope of the budget constraint is closely related to the prices of pizza and gasoline. The slope of the budget constraint, the rise/run, tells us the trade-off between gasoline and pizza, that is, how many gallons of gasoline the consumer can afford if he buys 1 fewer pizza. When the price of a pizza is $10 and the price of a gallon of gas is $2, the consumer can afford 5 more gallons of gasoline when he purchases 1 fewer pizza, so the slope of the budget constraint is $\frac{P_{\text{Pizza}}}{P_{\text{Gas}}} = \frac{\$10}{\$2} = 5$. The slope of the budget constraint is also called the relative price. In this case, the relative price of pizza to gas is 5. To be precise, the slope of the budget constraint is −5, which reflects the fact that to get more gasoline, the consumer must purchase *fewer* pizzas, but economists often drop the negative sign for convenience (mathematicians, however, would be horrified at this practice).

FIGURE 25.6

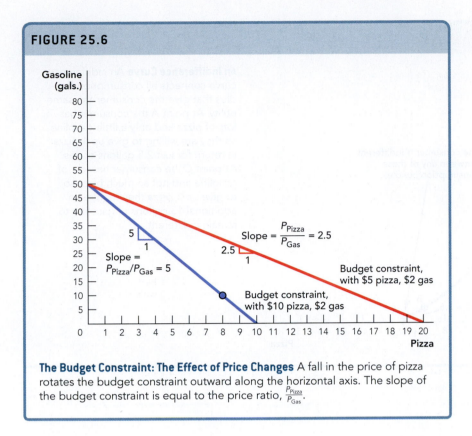

The Budget Constraint: The Effect of Price Changes A fall in the price of pizza rotates the budget constraint outward along the horizontal axis. The slope of the budget constraint is equal to the price ratio, $\frac{P_{Pizza}}{P_{Gas}}$.

When the price of pizza falls to $5 per pizza, the consumer can afford 2.5 additional gallons of gasoline when he purchases 1 fewer pizza, so the slope of the budget constraint falls to $\frac{P_{Pizza}}{P_{Gas}} = \frac{\$5}{\$2} = 2.5$. We can now draw a consumer's budget constraint for any income and set of prices. We know that the consumer will choose a consumption bundle somewhere along the budget constraint, but to say more about the exact consumption bundle, we need to say more about preferences.

Preferences and Indifference Curves

Consider a particular consumption bundle, say, bundle *A* in Figure 25.7. Now let's find all the bundles that the consumer regards as *just as good as* bundle *A*. If bundle *A* is just as good as bundle *B*, we say the consumer is indifferent between bundle *A* and bundle *B*, or equivalently, we say that bundle *A* and bundle *B* give the consumer an equal amount of utility. An indifference curve connects all the bundles that give the consumer an equal amount of utility and so we have drawn an indifference curve in Figure 25.7 showing all the consumption bundles that give an equal amount of utility to bundle *A*.

The indifference curve in Figure 25.7 is curved inward. Let's explain why this is a plausible shape for indifference curves. Notice that bundle *A* has 10 pizzas and 0 gallons of gas—that's an awful lot of pizza and not so much gas, or at least not so much gasoline. Since the consumer has a lot of pizza at bundle *A*, he probably would be willing to give up a pizza to get just a few

FIGURE 25.7

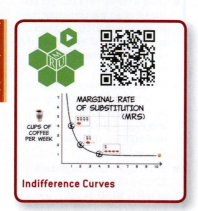

Gasoline (gals.) vs **Pizza**

Points on the indifference curve: D at (2, 75), C at (3, 60), B at (9, 5), A at (10, 5).

Slope = MRS = 15 (at C, with a rise of 15 and run of 1)

The consumer is indifferent between any of these consumption bundles.

An indifference curve connects all the consumption bundles that give the consumer the same utility.

Slope = MRS = 2.5 (at A/B)

An Indifference Curve An indifference curve connects all consumption bundles that give the consumer the same utility. At point *A* the consumer has lots of pizza and only a little gasoline so they are willing to give up 1 pizza in return for just 2.5 gallons of gas. At point *C* the consumer has lots of gasoline and not so much pizza so to give up 1 pizza they require an additional 15 gallons of gasoline to remain indifferent.

The **marginal rate of substitution (MRS)** is the rate at which the consumer is willing to trade one good for another and remain indifferent. The MRS is equal to the slope of the indifference curve at that point.

gallons of gasoline—say, 2.5 gallons for 1 pizza—which would place the consumer at bundle *B*. The number of gallons per pizza that the consumer requires to remain indifferent is called the **marginal rate of substitution (MRS)** and is given by the slope of the indifference curve (noting, once again, that we have dropped the negative sign).

But now consider bundle *C*. At bundle *C*, the consumer has fewer pizzas and more gas than at bundle *A*, so to remain indifferent, the consumer now requires 15 additional gallons of gasoline to give up 1 pizza. As the consumer gives up more pizza and gets more gasoline, pizza becomes more valuable and gasoline less valuable, so the consumer requires more and more gasoline in return for the same number of pizzas. Graphically, what this behavior implies is an indifference curve that is curved inward.

In Figure 25.8, we illustrate a second indifference curve showing all the consumption bundles that have the same utility as consumption bundle *Y*. What is the relationship between the *ABCD* indifference curve and the *XYZ* indifference curve? Compare consumption bundles *C* and *Y*. Consumption bundle *Y* has more gasoline and more pizza than consumption bundle *C*, so we can say for sure that consumption bundle *Y* has higher utility or is more preferred than consumption bundle *C*. But how does consumption bundle *C* compare with consumption bundle *Z* (which has more gasoline but fewer pizzas) or consumption bundle *X* (which has more pizzas but less gasoline)? We know that bundle *Y* is preferred to *C* but we also know that the consumer is indifferent between *X*, *Y*, and *Z*, so it follows that bundles *X* and *Z* are also preferred to bundle *C*. In fact, through a similar argument, we can say that any consumption bundle on *XYZ* is preferred to any consumption bundle on *ABCD*. This means that indifference curves toward the northeast

FIGURE 25.8

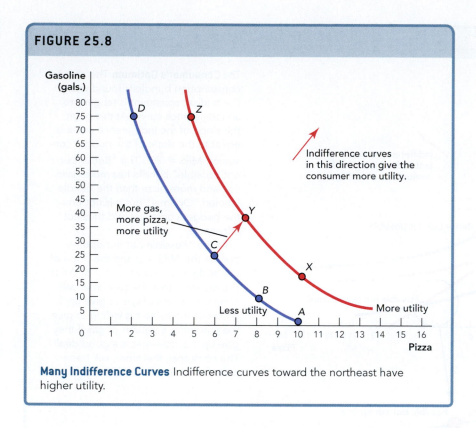

Many Indifference Curves Indifference curves toward the northeast have higher utility.

of the diagram give the consumer more utility, so the consumer wants to be as far to the northeast as possible.

Optimization and Consumer Choices

Now that we understand budget constraints and preferences, we can find the consumer's optimal consumption bundle. We know that the consumer must be on (or inside) the budget constraint and the consumer wants to be on the indifference curve that is the farthest to the northeast. Thus, to find the optimal consumption bundle, we look for the consumption bundle that is on the highest indifference curve but still on the budget constraint. Figure 25.9 on the next page illustrates.

Notice from Figure 25.9 that at the optimal bundle, the slope of the indifference curve is equal to the slope of the budget constraint. This is not an accident but a requirement. To see why, try to "push" an indifference curve as far as you can toward the northeast while still keeping at least one point on the budget constraint. The point of maximum utility is found where the indifference curve has been pushed just far enough to touch the budget constraint at a single point—the optimal point.

More formally, consider the point labeled "Possible but not optimal." This point is on the consumer's budget constraint, which explains why it is possible. Why isn't this point optimal? At "Possible but not optimal," the slope of the indifference curve is 2, which means that the consumer needs just 2 additional gallons of gas to be indifferent to giving up 1 pizza. The slope of the budget constraint is 5, which means that the consumer can get 5 gallons of

CHECK YOURSELF

■ Use an argument similar to the one we used in the last paragraph to show that (1) indifference curves can never cross and (2) indifference curves must have a negative slope.

FIGURE 25.9

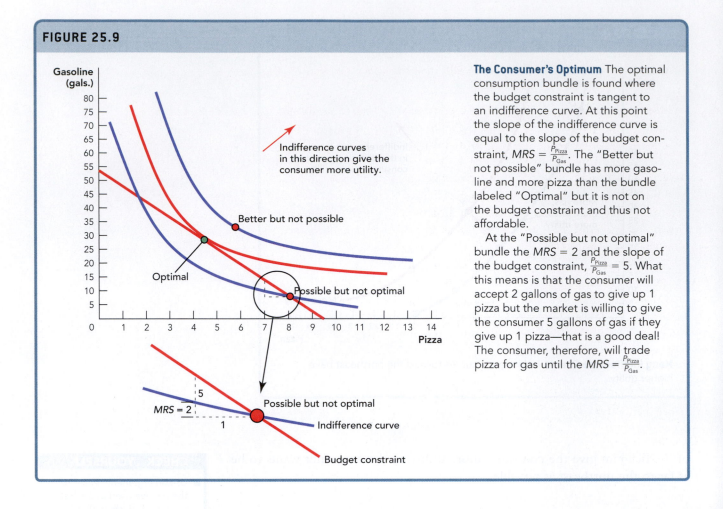

The Consumer's Optimum The optimal consumption bundle is found where the budget constraint is tangent to an indifference curve. At this point the slope of the indifference curve is equal to the slope of the budget constraint, $MRS = \frac{P_{Pizza}}{P_{Gas}}$. The "Better but not possible" bundle has more gasoline and more pizza than the bundle labeled "Optimal" but it is not on the budget constraint and thus not affordable.

At the "Possible but not optimal" bundle the $MRS = 2$ and the slope of the budget constraint, $\frac{P_{Pizza}}{P_{Gas}} = 5$. What this means is that the consumer will accept 2 gallons of gas to give up 1 pizza but the market is willing to give the consumer 5 gallons of gas if they give up 1 pizza—that is a good deal! The consumer, therefore, will trade pizza for gas until the $MRS = \frac{P_{Pizza}}{P_{Gas}}$.

gas if he gives up 1 pizza—that's more gas than he requires to be indifferent! Thus at "Possible but not optimal," the consumer can increase his utility by buying more gas and fewer pizzas and therefore this point cannot be optimal. In fact, what we have just shown is that the consumer can always do better if the slope of the indifference curve is different from the slope of the budget constraint.

Thus, remembering that the slope of the indifference curve is the *MRS* and the slope of the budget constraint is the price ratio, we can write that the optimal consumption bundle is found where

Slope of indifference curve = $MRS = \frac{P_{Pizza}}{P_{Gas}}$ = Slope of budget constraint

Perhaps you are wondering how $MRS = \frac{P_{Pizza}}{P_{Gas}}$ relates to the optimal consumption rule stated earlier:

$$\frac{MU_{Pizza}}{P_{Pizza}} = \frac{MU_{Gas}}{P_{Gas}}$$

or rearranging

$$\frac{MU_{Pizza}}{MU_{Gas}} = \frac{P_{Pizza}}{P_{Gas}}$$

Can you guess what we are going to say next? Correct, it turns out that $MRS = \frac{MU_{\text{Pizza}}}{MU_{\text{Gas}}}$, so fortunately our two conditions for optimal consumption, $\frac{MU_{\text{Pizza}}}{P_{\text{Pizza}}} = \frac{MU_{\text{Gas}}}{P_{\text{Gas}}}$ and $MRS = \frac{P_{\text{Pizza}}}{P_{\text{Gas}}}$, are really just two ways of writing the same thing.*

Now that we know how to find the consumer's optimal consumption bundle, we can show how the optimal bundle changes as income and prices change. Figure 25.10, for example, shows how a consumer responds to a decrease in the price of pizzas from \$10 to \$5. When $P_{\text{Pizza}} = \$10$ and $P_{\text{Gas}} = \$2$, the consumer maximizes utility by choosing 6 pizzas and 20 gallons of gas at the point labeled "Old optimum." As we showed in Figure 25.6, a decrease in the price of pizzas rotates the budget constraint along the horizontal axis. With the new budget constraint, the consumer chooses 9 pizzas and 27.5 gallons of gas at the point labeled "New optimum."

Notice that a fall in the price of pizza increases the number of pizzas purchased, but in this example it also increases the number of gallons of gasoline consumed. At first, this result may seem confusing: Why should a fall in the price of pizza increase the consumption of gasoline? The reason is that a fall in the price of pizza has two effects, the income effect and the substitution effect. Let's now explain these two effects.

FIGURE 25.10

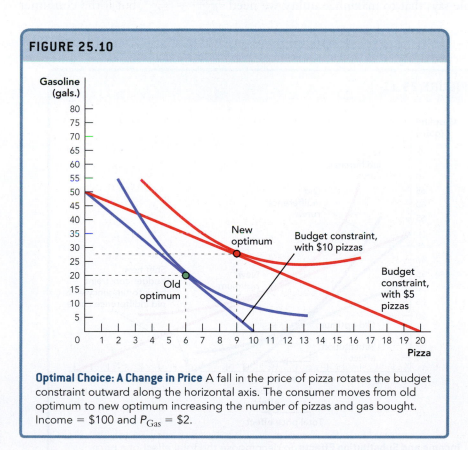

Optimal Choice: A Change in Price A fall in the price of pizza rotates the budget constraint outward along the horizontal axis. The consumer moves from old optimum to new optimum increasing the number of pizzas and gas bought. Income = \$100 and $P_{\text{Gas}} = \$2$.

---

* The proof is slightly involved but not difficult. Suppose that we take away from a consumer a small amount of pizza, Δ_{Pizza}, and we give him in return a small amount of gas, Δ_{Gas}; then the change in total utility, ΔU, from this exchange is $\Delta U = -\Delta_{\text{Pizza}} \times MU_{\text{Pizza}} + \Delta_{\text{Gas}} \times MU_{\text{Gas}}$. Along an indifference curve, total utility is constant, so $\Delta U = 0$ and thus $-\Delta_{\text{Pizza}} \times MU_{\text{Pizza}} + \Delta_{\text{Gas}} \times MU_{\text{Gas}} = 0$. Then rearrange to find $\Delta_{\text{Gas}}/\Delta_{\text{Pizza}} = MU_{\text{Pizza}}/MU_{\text{Gas}}$. But $\Delta_{\text{Gas}}/\Delta_{\text{Pizza}}$ is the MRS, the slope of the indifference curve, so we have shown that $MRS = MU_{\text{Pizza}}/MU_{\text{Gas}}$.

interactive activity

Consumer Optimization

The Income and Substitution Effects

When the price of pizza was $10, the consumer bought 6 pizzas for a total pizza spending of $60. When the price of pizza falls to $5, the consumer can buy 6 pizzas for $30, so the drop in the price of pizza gives the consumer an additional $30 to spend. With greater income, the consumer may choose to spend more money on pizza *and* more money on gas. More generally, a fall in the price of a good means the consumer's income goes further than before, so a fall in price is in some ways similar to an increase in income.

A price change is more than a change in income, however. Imagine that the price of pizza falls from $10 to $5, which, as we said, gives the consumer an extra $30 to spend. Feeling richer, the consumer heads to the market to buy more pizza and gasoline, but on the way a pickpocket takes the extra $30. Without the extra income, should the consumer still change his consumption bundle? Yes. The price of pizza has fallen relative to the price of gas and the consumer should take advantage of this change in relative prices by consuming more pizza. Of course, if the consumer has been pickpocketed on the way to market, the only way he can consume more pizza is by consuming less gasoline. Even so, the consumer will be better off by substituting pizza for gasoline in response to the change in relative prices. Remember, the optimal consumption rule says that to maximize utility, we need $\frac{MU_{Pizza}}{P_{Pizza}} = \frac{MU_{Gas}}{P_{Gas}}$, but if the consumer

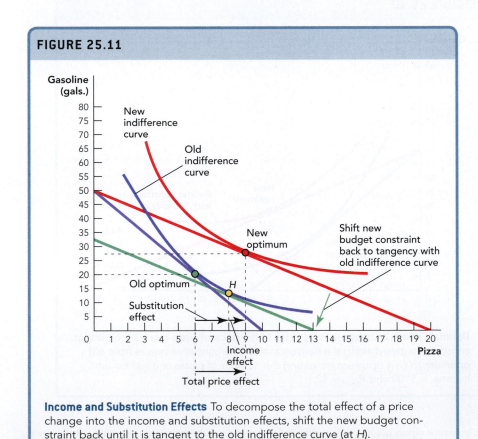

FIGURE 25.11

Income and Substitution Effects To decompose the total effect of a price change into the income and substitution effects, shift the new budget constraint back until it is tangent to the old indifference curve (at *H*).

The substitution effect is given by change in consumption along the old indifference curve from the "Old optimum" to point *H*. The income effect is given by the change in consumption from point *H* to the "New optimum."

was maximizing utility before the price change, then after the P_{Pizza} falls, it must be that $\frac{MU_{\text{Pizza}}}{P_{\text{Pizza}}} > \frac{MU_{\text{Gas}}}{P_{\text{Gas}}}$. This tells us that after P_{Pizza} falls, the consumer should buy more pizza and less gas.

Thus, a change in price causes consumers to change their consumption bundle for two reasons, *the income effect* and the relative price, or *substitution effect*. In Figure 25.11, we show how to decompose the total effect of a price change into the income and substitution effects. The fall in the price of pizza causes the consumer to shift from buying 6 pizzas at the old optimum to buying 9 pizzas at the new optimum. This is the total effect of the price change. To decompose the total effect, we take the new budget constraint, which reflects the new relative prices, and we shift it back toward the origin until it is tangent to the old indifference curve at point H. The shifting back of the budget constraint is like the pickpocket we describe earlier—we reduce the consumer's income until the consumer has the same utility level (is on the same indifference curve) as before the price change.*

We can now define the substitution and income effects more precisely. The **substitution effect** is the change in consumption caused by a change in relative prices holding the consumer's utility level constant. Thus, in Figure 25.11, the substitution effect is the change in consumption from "Old optimum" to point H. The **income effect** is the change in consumption caused by the change in purchasing power from a price change. Thus, in Figure 25.11, the income effect is given by the movement from H to "New optimum."

> The **substitution effect** is the change in consumption caused by a change in relative prices holding the consumer's utility level constant.
> The **income effect** is the change in consumption caused by the change in purchasing power from a price change.

Applications of Income and Substitution Effects

We have now developed the key tools that we need to better understand consumer and worker choice. Let's look at some applications of income and substitution effects.

Losing Your Ticket

Have you ever bought a concert or movie ticket and then lost it? When should you buy another ticket? If you lost your ticket, you probably feel foolish or angry. Many of us react emotionally in a situation like this, and perhaps we decide that fate is against us and that we weren't really meant to see the concert or movie anyway. The better course of action, however, can be determined by some cooler thinking and a little economics.

Let's say you lose a movie ticket on which you spent $10. What is the price if you wish to buy another ticket? It's still $10. You are still comparing the movie against other uses for the $10. In terms of the substitution effect, the price hasn't changed so there should be no change in your assessment. Either the movie is worth giving up $10 worth of other goods or it is not.

What about the income effect? Well, you're out the $10 and thus you are poorer. That's a fairly small negative income effect. If you're really poor, though, it might induce you to make fewer purchases, including movie ticket purchases. But for most people, the income effect should be very small, so small that it can be safely ignored. Thus, if the ticket cost $10, you should buy another ticket.

---

* If you are following very closely, you may notice that our pickpocket leaves the consumer with just enough income to purchase the old bundle at the point labeled "Old optimum" but our graphical pickpocket takes a little bit more. The first version of the income effect is called the *Slutsky income effect*, while the second is called the *Hicks income effect* after its originators. For a small price change, the difference between these two versions of the income effect is slight and can be ignored, which is what we do here.

Alternatively, let's say you lose a Lady Gaga concert ticket, which cost you $200 on StubHub. There is still no change in the price, at least assuming that the price on StubHub hasn't changed, so the logic of substitution still says buy another ticket. But now the negative income effect is larger than in the case of the movie ticket. It shouldn't bother a well-off person, but some of you will feel noticeably poorer and you may wish to reconsider buying another concert ticket for $200.

The motto of the story: If you lose cheap tickets, replace them for sure. If you lose expensive tickets, you need to compare the income effect with the substitution effect. For a sufficiently wealthy person, even the loss of an expensive concert ticket shouldn't create a very big income effect. Poorer people may wish to think twice.

How Much Should Costco Charge for Membership?

Costco, one of the largest retailers in the world, offers low prices on many consumer goods. But to shop at Costco, you have to join the Costco "club" and pay a yearly membership fee. How much should Costco charge for membership?

To answer this question, let's create a budget constraint and indifference curve diagram with income on the vertical axis and goods you can buy at Costco on the horizontal axis. Without Costco membership, the consumer faces the blue budget constraint in Figure 25.12, labeled "Without Costco Membership," and consumes the No Costco bundle. Costco members pay lower prices, so if there were no membership fee, Costco members would face the red budget constraint, labeled "With Costco membership," and consume the "Costco without fee" bundle.

Costco, however, wants to charge as high a membership fee as possible. How much can the retailer charge? The membership fee is equivalent to a decrease in the consumer's income, so another way of asking this question is to ask how much can we decrease the consumer's income and still leave the consumer at least as well-off with Costco membership as without it? If we shift the green budget line, which reflects the lower prices at Costco, back toward the origin, we can shift the line until it is tangent to the old indifference curve at the point labeled "Costco with fee." At "Costco with fee," the consumer is indifferent between joining Costco, paying the fee, and enjoying the lower prices, and not joining Costco, saving on the fee, but paying higher prices. Since income is on the vertical axis, we can easily read the ideal membership fee off the graph.

Costco charges $55 for membership. This may not seem like a lot, but in 2015 membership fees earned Costco revenues of $2.53 billion dollars, which exceeded its profits of $2.38 billion. Costco, therefore, is very concerned with setting the ideal membership fee.

Labor Supply

In Chapter 18, we discussed how a worker's labor supply curve can be backward-bending; that is, a decrease in the wage could cause a worker to work more. At first, this might seem surprising. Why would a worker work more hours when the payoff to working is going down? To see the intuition, imagine a janitor, perhaps an immigrant from a developing country, whose wage falls. The janitor may choose to work more hours in response to the lower wage, because at a lower wage, he needs to work more hours to make enough money to

FIGURE 25.12

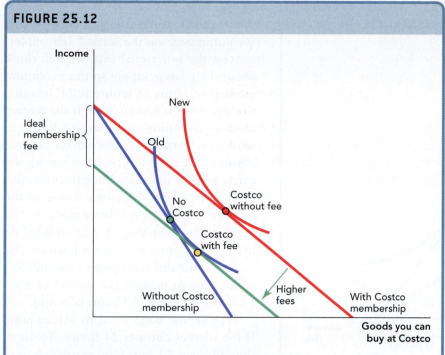

How Much Should Costco Charge for Membership? Without Costco member-ship the price ratio is given by the slope of the "Without Costco membership" budget constraint and the consumer chooses the bundle at "No Costco." If the consumer joins Costco they can buy the goods that Costco sells at lower prices so the budget constraint rotates out. With no membership fee the con-sumer would consume the bundle at "Costco without fee."

Costco would like to charge as high a membership fee as possible. The membership price is a decrease in the consumer's income so we can ask how much income can we take from the consumer and still leave the consumer at least as well-off as without membership?

The ideal membership fee (from Costco's point of view!) is the reduction in income that keeps the consumer on their old indifference curve. With the ideal membership fee the consumer consumes the bundle at "Costco with fee."

put his children through college. Similarly, when the Beatles were young and unknown, they were paid low wages but they played 4 to 5 sets a day, 7 days a week in German strip clubs, just to make ends meet. As their fame grew, so did their wages and the Beatles responded by playing fewer hours. Eventu-ally, they stopped touring altogether, and a few years after that, they split up completely.

More generally, remember that a lower wage has two effects: the substitu-tion effect and the income effect. When the wage decreases, that's the same as a decrease in the price of leisure so the substitution effect says you should "buy" more leisure by working fewer hours. When the wage decreases, however, that also makes you poorer. The income effect says that when your income falls, you should buy fewer (normal) goods including leisure.

Notice that the substitution and income effects work in opposite directions in this case. If the substitution effect dominates, the worker works fewer hours when the wage rate falls. If the income effect dominates, the worker works more hours when the wage rate falls.

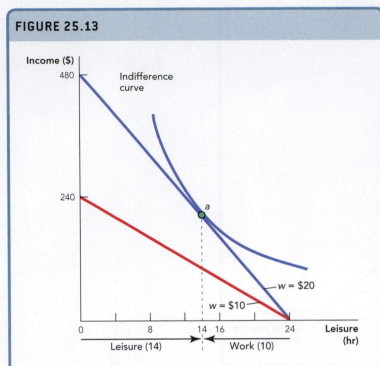

FIGURE 25.13

The Income–Leisure Model of Labor Supply Leisure is measured on the horizontal axis moving toward the right so work hours are measured toward the left. Suppose the wage is $20 an hour. By choosing 24 hours of leisure, the worker earns $0. By choosing 0 hours of leisure (24 hours of work), the worker earns $480. The blue budget constraint thus shows all the income–leisure possibilities open to the worker when the wage is $20 an hour. At the optimal choice the worker chooses 14 hours of leisure (10 hours of work).

The red budget constraint shows all the income–leisure possibilities open to the worker when the wage is $10 an hour.

In Figure 25.13, we explain the basics of the income–leisure model of labor supply. We put income on the vertical axis and leisure on the horizontal axis. We will think about daily labor supply so the maximum number of hours of leisure is 24. Imagine that the wage is $20 an hour. If the worker chooses 24 hours of leisure (0 hours of work), she earns $0. If the worker chooses 0 hours of leisure (24 hours of work), she earns $480 a day. The budget constraint labeled $w = \$20$, therefore, shows all the income–leisure possibilities open to the worker when the wage is $20 an hour. As usual, the optimum is found where the budget constraint is tangent to the indifference curve. At point *a*, the worker chooses 14 hours of leisure (10 hours of work).

Suppose the wage is cut to $10 an hour. If the worker chooses 24 hours of leisure, she still earns $0, but if the worker chooses 0 hours of leisure (24 hours of work), her take-home pay falls to $240. The budget constraint labeled $w = \$10$, therefore, shows all the income–leisure possibilities open to the worker when the wage is $10 an hour. The worker will choose a new point (not shown) on the new budget constraint.

In Figure 25.14, we use this model to show how a decrease in the wage can decrease or increase labor supply. In the top left panel, the worker chooses 14 hours of leisure (10 hours of work) when the wage is $20 an hour. A decrease in the wage causes the worker to increase leisure to 16 hours (8 hours of work). We haven't drawn the substitution and income effects in the diagram (we leave that as an exercise), but since the total effect of the decrease in wages is a decrease in labor supply, we know that in this case the substitution effect dominates. The top right panel translates the same information into a labor supply diagram.

In the bottom left panel, the worker chooses 14 hours of leisure (10 hours of work) when the wage is $20 an hour. A decrease in the wage causes the worker to decrease leisure to 12 hours (12 hours of work). Since the total effect of the decrease in wage is an increase in labor supply, we know that in this case the income effect dominates. The bottom right panel shows that over this wage range, the worker has a backward-bending labor supply curve.

Labor Supply and Welfare Programs

Let's use the income–leisure model to examine the labor supply effects of welfare programs. The traditional model of welfare works like a guaranteed minimum income under which the government subsidizes or "tops up" the income of any worker who earns less than the guaranteed amount. For example,

FIGURE 25.14

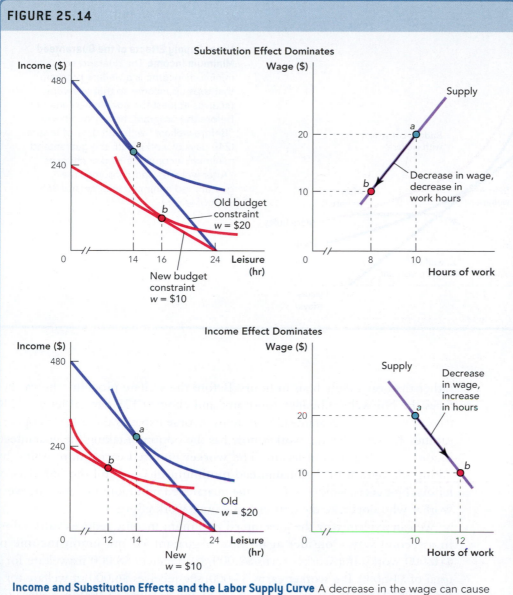

Income and Substitution Effects and the Labor Supply Curve A decrease in the wage can cause a worker to work fewer or more hours depending on the balance of the substitution and income effects. In the top left panel the substitution effect (not shown) dominates, so a decrease in the wage from $20 to $10 increases leisure from 14 hours a day to 16 (i.e., a decrease in work from 10 to 8 hours). The same information is shown in the top right panel but translated into a labor supply diagram. When the substitution effect dominates we get a positively sloped supply curve.

In the bottom left panel a decrease in the wage from $20 to $10 causes the worker to decrease leisure hours from 14 hours a day to 12 (i.e., an increase in work hours from 10 to 12 hours). The same information is translated into a labor supply diagram in the bottom right panel. When the income effect dominates we get a negatively sloped, or "backward-bending," supply curve.

suppose the guaranteed minimum income for an individual is $10,000 a year; in that case, an individual with yearly earnings of $6,000 would receive $4,000 in welfare payments.

The economics of this program are shown in Figure 25.15. We use the same setup as before, only now we measure leisure and work on a yearly basis in days

FIGURE 25.15

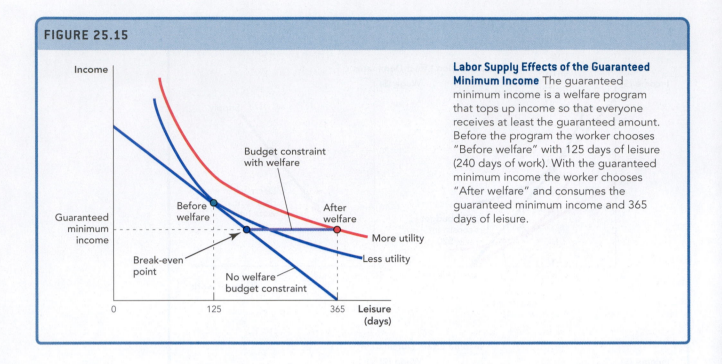

Labor Supply Effects of the Guaranteed Minimum Income The guaranteed minimum income is a welfare program that tops up income so that everyone receives at least the guaranteed amount. Before the program the worker chooses "Before welfare" with 125 days of leisure (240 days of work). With the guaranteed minimum income the worker chooses "After welfare" and consumes the guaranteed minimum income and 365 days of leisure.

rather than on a daily basis in hours. Before the welfare program, the worker faces the No welfare budget constraint and chooses 125 days of leisure (240 days of work.) The guaranteed minimum income expands the worker's opportunities. In particular, the worker now has the option of taking the guaranteed income and 365 days of leisure. The worker pictured earns more utility by taking the option of the guaranteed minimum income and the 365 days of leisure. Not every worker will take the guaranteed minimum income, but every worker who does take the option will reduce work effort.

We can explain why the guaranteed minimum income reduces work effort in a second way. Consider again how a guaranteed minimum income of $10,000 works. If a worker earns $2,000, she receives $8,000 in welfare for a total of $10,000. If a worker earns $4,000, she receives $6,000 in welfare for a total of $10,000. If a worker earns $7,000, she receives $3,000 in welfare for a total of $10,000. Do you see a pattern? Under the guaranteed minimum income, for every $1 in income that the worker earns, the government subtracts $1 in welfare so the worker's take-home pay doesn't change. Thus, under the guaranteed minimum income, a worker faces a 100% tax rate until he is earning more than $10,000 a year (the break-even point). Thus, under a guaranteed minimum income, many workers will choose to work 0 hours. How many hours would you work if you faced a 100% marginal tax rate?

On the one hand, most people feel that a welfare program is necessary to help those in need. On the other, we don't want to discourage work effort. Even a low-paying job, for example, may lead to a higher-paying job in the future. The trade-off between ethics and the disincentive effects of welfare programs have bedeviled policymakers for decades. In fact, economists dating as far back as Adam Smith and John Stuart Mill in the 18th and 19th centuries have worried about this problem.[1]

Several resolutions to this trade-off have been suggested, none of which is perfect. We will mention two briefly. One possibility is to focus on the 100%

tax rate faced by people on welfare. Instead of reducing the welfare payment by $1 for every $1 of earnings, how about reducing payments by, say, $0.50 for every dollar of earnings? This is called a negative income tax (NIT) program. Under a negative income tax, for example, a worker who works 0 hours would receive $10,000 in welfare for a total of $10,000. But a worker who earned $4,000 would receive $8,000 in welfare (not $6,000 as before) for a total of $12,000. In this way, some of the incentives to work are restored for those receiving welfare.

Unfortunately—precisely because the program is more generous—the negative income can encourage more people to reduce labor supply at least somewhat and to take at least some welfare, even if they are able to work. Under the traditional guaranteed income program, for example, a worker who was earning, say, $14,000 a year might refuse the option of $10,000 a year and 365 days of leisure, but under a negative income tax, that same individual might be happy to accept $12,000 a year with 200 days of leisure.

Even though the negative income tax can encourage some people to partially reduce their hours of work, it encourages everyone to have at least some kind of job. If having a job, even a part-time job, is what matters for gaining experience, learning skills, moving up the work ladder, and so forth, then the NIT may work acceptably well.

Another approach is to limit how much welfare a person can accept or put various requirements on welfare recipients. If a person knows in advance that welfare is available only for a limited time, for example, he or she will treat welfare as more of an insurance program to be used only in bad times rather than as a guaranteed minimum income to be used as an alternative to work.

In practice, the United States has pursued both of these approaches to various degrees. The Earned Income Tax Credit (EITC), for example, supplements the wages of low-wage workers. For instance, depending on your income and other factors, if you earn $100 at work, the government tops it off, through the tax system, to make it worth $120. Unlike a negative income tax, the EITC is available only to workers. The EITC, however, helps offset the incentive to quit work, as contained in some of the other welfare programs, and makes the total package more like a negative income tax. From another direction, the Personal Responsibility and Work Opportunity Reconciliation Act (PRWORA) of 1996 put limits on welfare. Under PRWORA, a person can receive only 5 years of welfare benefits over his or her lifetime, and after 2 years on welfare, recipients must work at least 30 hours a week.

Both of these programs appear to have been relatively successful at encouraging welfare recipients to enter the job force. Analyzing the incentive and disincentive effects of welfare programs continues to be an active area of research for economists.

Takeaway

Economists use the language of prices and marginal utilities to analyze consumer decisions and, in general, consumers choose to allocate their dollars so the marginal utility per dollar of all purchases is equalized. To maximize utility, allocate dollars such that

$$\frac{MU_A}{P_A} = \frac{MU_O}{P_O} = \frac{MU_i}{P_i} = \cdots \frac{MU_z}{P_z}$$

This equation may look tough, but it simply reflects what happens when consumers allocate their money wisely.

The budget constraint represents how much money a consumer has to spend and the prices that the consumer faces. If we put together a budget constraint and information about consumer preferences—as expressed in the form of indifference curves—we can solve for a consumer's optimal consumption bundle. This is a standard economic story, namely that preferences and constraints come together to shape an outcome.

The concepts of income and substitution effects, and more generally preferences and constraints, are useful for analyzing many economic problems. This includes how labor supply responds to welfare programs, how much Costco should charge for membership, and whether you should replace a lost concert ticket.

CHAPTER REVIEW

interactive activity Go online to practice with more examples of these types of problems, including live links to videos, data sources, and feedback.

 Problems in **green** relate to MRU videos. See the MRU table at the end of the exercises.

KEY CONCEPTS

marginal utility, p. 481

diminishing marginal utility, p. 481

optimal consumption rule, p. 483

budget constraint, p. 485

marginal rate of substitution (MRS), p. 488

substitution effect, p. 493

income effect, p. 493

FACTS AND TOOLS

1. The table at right shows the marginal utility a consumer receives from the weekly consumption of On-Demand movie rentals and Thai takeout meals. One On-Demand movie rental costs $5, and Thai takeout costs $10 per meal. Suppose this consumer is currently (for some reason) eating Thai takeout 10 times per week and is spending all of her $100 income, so that she has no money left over for movie rentals. Is the consumer maximizing utility?

On-Demand Movies	Marginal Utility	Thai Takeout Meals	Marginal Utility
1	50	1	50
2	30	2	45
3	20	3	40
4	15	4	35
5	10	5	30
6	8	6	25
7	6	7	20
8	4	8	15
9	2	9	10
10	1	10	5

2. Imagine that for the past two years, you've consumed only two goods: lattes and scones. As you're probably aware, prices tend to go up over time. If the price of your latte increased from $2 to $3 over the last two years, and the price of scones increased from $1.50 to $2.25, what impact would this have on your budget

constraint if your $240 weekly take-home pay didn't change at all over the same two-year period? Draw both budget constraints on the same set of axes. What if you were able to negotiate a raise to $360 per week? Draw this final budget constraint on the same set of axes as the first two. How does your final budget constraint compare with your original budget constraint from two years ago?

3. You learned in the chapter that the process of utility maximization involves a comparison of marginal utilities per dollar, which are calculated as marginal utility divided by price. Consider two goods that most people consume at least some of during their lives: apples and cars.

   a. If utility maximization was only about marginal utility (not marginal utility per dollar), which good (apples or cars) would consumers want to consume? Would they ever consume the other good?

   b. If utility maximization was only about price (as opposed to marginal utility divided by price), which good (apples or cars) would consumers want to consume? Would they ever consume the other good?

   c. Given your answers to parts a and b, and given the observation that some people eat apples *and* drive cars, explain why utility maximization involves a comparison of marginal utility *divided* by price, and not just one or the other.

4. Fill in the blanks with either "good X" or "good Y," where good X is measured on the x-axis and good Y is measured on the y-axis.

   a. If the price of _____ is $8 and the price of _____ is $12, then the price ratio (also the slope of the budget constraint) is 1.5.

   b. A price ratio of 1.5 means that the consumer is able to trade 1 unit of _____ for 1.5 units of _____.

   c. If another unit of _____ would give a consumer 20 extra units of utility, and another unit of _____ would give a consumer 10 extra units of utility, then the marginal rate of substitution for this consumer is equal to 2.

   d. A marginal rate of substitution of 2 means that, from the consumer's point of view, 1 more unit of _____ is as good as 2 more units of _____.

   e. If the price ratio is 1.5 and the marginal rate of substitution is 2, then the market values _____ more than the consumer does, and the consumer values _____ more than the market does. In this case, the consumer ought to buy less of _____ and more of _____.

5. Suppose Haya has $120 of income left each week after she pays her bills and puts some money away in a savings account, and she has two ways to spend this extra money: go to the movies, which costs $18 including popcorn and a soda, or go out to a club with several friends, which costs $33 including the cover charge and drinks. Assuming these are her only two choices to spend the extra money, what can you say about the following bundles of going to the movies and clubbing? Which of these could possibly be the utility-maximizing bundle?

   a. 3 movies and 2 nights out at the club

   b. 2 movies and 3 nights out at the club

   c. 2 movies and 2 nights out at the club

6. The utility-maximizing bundle of goods is found at the point of tangency between the budget constraint and an indifference curve. In the following diagram, the utility-maximizing bundle is the one labeled point K. There are two different, but equally important, ways to interpret this point.

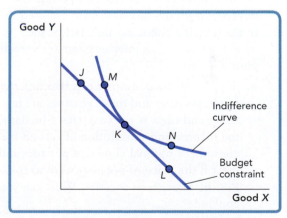

   a. Of the three points on the consumer's budget constraint (J, K, and L), what makes K special?

   b. Of the three points on the consumer's indifference curve (M, K, and N), what makes K special?

7. Is marginal utility always diminishing? Consider playing cards. If playing cards were purchased one at a time, what would be true about the

marginal utility of the 51st playing card compared with the marginal utility of the 52nd playing card? Why do you think it's okay for economists to assume that marginal utility diminishes? How does the concept of marginal utility explain why playing cards are not sold individually, but only as entire 52-card decks?

THINKING AND PROBLEM SOLVING

8. In Major League Baseball, teams in the American League use a designated hitter (DH) to bat in place of the pitcher, while teams in the National League require their pitchers to bat. Sports economists have noted that in the National League, batters are hit by pitches 15% less often than in the American League. Can you use the concepts from this chapter to explain this behavior from the point of view of the pitcher's utility-maximizing decision about whether to throw pitches high and inside (where they are more likely to hit the batter)?

9. Consider Facts and Tools question 2. Explain the income and substitution effects of the price changes on your optimal consumption bundle when the latte and scone prices increased, but your income did not.

10. With inferior goods (like ramen noodles), the income effect works in the opposite direction from the income effect discussed in the text. If a consumer feels richer, she would buy less of an inferior good. If she feels poorer, more.

    a. Suppose that a consumer eats two different foods: potatoes and meat. Potatoes are inferior and meat is a luxury. Describe both the income and substitution effects on the consumer's optimal choice of potatoes and meat if the price of potatoes were to rise. Put the two effects together. What can you conclude?

    b. What if you knew for sure that the substitution effect dominated the income effect? What would happen to the consumer's optimal choices for potatoes and meat?

    c. What if instead you knew that the income effect dominated the substitution effect? What would happen in this case? Why is this result a bit unusual?

11. eMusic is a popular subscription MP3 Web site. For a monthly membership fee, you can download MP3s for a price that's about half of what MP3s cost at iTunes or Amazon. Consider someone with $50 worth of income to spend on entertainment each month and who can choose to buy MP3s or "other stuff"—with a price equal to $1 per unit, so that other stuff is measured in dollars. Create budget constraints for each of the different eMusic membership plans. Prices have been rounded to make things simpler. (To simplify things, we'll assume that the consumer will use his entire eMusic balance each month, even though eMusic members don't have to do this. We'll also just think about MP3 singles, not albums.)

    a. No membership: The consumer has to purchase MP3s from another Web site, at $1 each.

    b. eMusic Basic: For $12/month, the consumer gets 24 MP3 downloads. After that, the consumer would have to buy MP3s at another Web site for $1 each.

    c. eMusic Plus: For $16/month, the consumer gets 34 MP3 downloads. After that, the consumer would have to buy MP3s at another Web site for $1 each.

    d. eMusic Premium: For $21/month, the consumer gets 46 MP3 downloads. After that, the consumer would have to buy MP3s at another Web site for $1 each.

    e. eMusic Fan: For $32/month, the consumer gets 73 MP3 downloads. After that, the consumer would have to buy MP3s at another Web site for $1 each.

    Which plan do you think will be most popular? Which will be the least popular? Although eMusic has hundreds of thousands of members, most people are not members of eMusic. What must be true about their indifference curves? How many MP3s do these people download per month?

12. In this chapter, we focused a lot on budget constraints, but time is an additional constraint that consumers face. Jackson has $40 per week to spend on leisure activities. He likes to bowl and to play racquetball. Bowling costs $4 per game, and a day pass to the racquet club costs $8. Jackson only has 7 hours of leisure time per week, and both bowling and racquetball each take 1 hour per game. Construct Jackson's budget constraint and his time constraint on the

same diagram. Consider each of the consumption bundles that follow that could possibly be Jackson's utility-maximizing bundle. How does each of these bundles relate to Jackson's two constraints?

a. Bowling twice per week and playing racquetball four times per week

b. Bowling four times per week and playing racquetball three times per week

c. Bowling six times per week and playing racquetball once per week

CHALLENGES

13. This chapter argues that the ideal membership fee from Costco's point of view would leave consumers indifferent between shopping at Costco and shopping elsewhere. Do you think most of the shoppers at Costco are indifferent? What prevents Costco from setting its ideal fee?

14. Assume a consumer earns $50 in period 1 and $150 in period 2, and that saving and borrowing are both interest-free. Draw a budget constraint. Now let's see if we can add some more real-life detail.

a. Draw a new budget constraint for the consumer if the period 1 income remains at $50, but the period 2 income falls to $100. Use the ideas of income and substitution effects to describe how this change would affect the optimal choice of the consumer.

b. Now let's add another wrinkle: an interest rate. Assume as before that the consumer earns $50 in period 1 and $150 in period 2. Construct a budget constraint for a consumer that can earn 20% interest by saving money in period 1 for use in period 2, but also has to pay 20% interest to borrow money from period 2 for use in period 1. (These interest rates are high so that the impact is obvious on your graph; the results will still hold—although less dramatically—with lower interest rates.) What is the substitution effect of the addition of the interest rate? The income effect is more complicated, because it depends on the consumer's preferences, which could be revealed by the pre-interest-rate behavior.

c. In February 2017, the average interest rate on money market and savings accounts was 0.26%, but the average rate on a variable-rate credit card was 16.43%. Obviously, the previous assumption that the interest rate is the same for borrowers and savers is not very realistic. Again, using more dramatic interest rates, can you construct a budget constraint for a consumer with the same initial endowment as previously who faces a 1% interest rate for saving and a 50% interest rate for borrowing? What do you notice about this budget constraint?

15. Currently, if you join Disney's movie club, you get 4 DVDs for $1 each, but you have to commit to buying at least 5 more DVDs at $20 each over the next year. Suppose the normal market price of a DVD is $16.

a. Construct two budget constraints: one for a consumer who joins Disney's movie club and another for a consumer who doesn't. Assume that both consumers have $112 worth of income. Place income on the vertical axis just as in Figure 25.12.

b. What kind of consumer is likely to get more utility from joining Disney's movie club? What kind of consumer would not?

c. If Disney's movie club wanted to charge an additional membership fee to generate more revenue, what would be the maximum it could charge for membership?

16. Two special cases might result in indifference curves that look a little different from the ones discussed in the text.

a. If two goods are perfect substitutes, that means the consumer would always be willing to trade one for the other in a certain, fixed proportion. In this case, the MRS would be constant, which means that indifference curves would be straight lines. Suppose a consumer's MRS between two goods X and Y is a constant 2.5, which means that the consumer is always willing to give up 1 unit of good X for 2.5 units of good Y. If the consumer has $180 in income to spend, the price of good X is $20 per unit, and the price of good Y is $10 per unit, what is this consumer's utility-maximizing bundle of X and Y? Answer the question by thinking it through and then show with a diagram (including a budget constraint and an indifference curve) why your answer works.

b. If two goods are perfect complements, indifference curves have a very unusual shape. Let's see if you can reason through this one. Consider left and right shoes. For most people, having left shoes alone (or right shoes alone) does not really provide any utility; rather, people get utility from having a pair of shoes that they can wear. In this case, left and right shoes are perfect 1:1 complements. Can you figure out what indifference curves would look like in such a case? To do this, it might be helpful to think about questions like the following: If someone has 4 right shoes and 4 (matching) left shoes, what's the marginal utility of an extra right shoe? If a consumer had to compare the bundles (4 left shoes, 4 right shoes), (4 left shoes, 5 right shoes), and (7 left shoes, 4 right shoes), how would these bundles rank? Would any of these bundles be better than the others?

interactive activity

WORK IT OUT

For interactive, step-by-step help in solving this problem, go online.

Suppose we wanted to investigate the saving and borrowing behavior of consumers. It's not that difficult to extend our basic model. We can use the same framework as before, but define our two goods as "consumption in period 1" (horizontal axis) and "consumption in period 2" (vertical axis).

a. Construct a budget constraint for a consumer who earns $100 in income in period 1 and $300 of income in period 2. Label this point *E* for the "Endowment" point. Assume that he can choose to save some income in period 1 to be used in period 2, or to borrow some income from period 2 to use in period 1. (Let's imagine the consumer saves the money by putting it in a piggy bank and can borrow money from his parents, who don't charge interest.)

b. For the consumer in the situation just described, do you think he would consume at his endowment point or would he borrow or save?

MARGINAL REVOLUTION UNIVERSITY VIDEOS

Introduction to Consumer Choice
mruniversity.com/consumer

Problems: **1**

The Budget Constraint
mruniversity.com/budget-constraint

Problems: **2, 5**

Indifference Curves
mruniversity.com/optimization

Problems: **4, 6**

Consumer Optimization
mruniversity.com/indifference-curves

Problems: **4, 6, 16**

26

GDP and the Measurement of Progress

A visitor to India is immediately struck by the contrast between extreme poverty and rapid economic growth. Squalor in India is obvious; two-thirds of India's population lives on less than $3 a day. Throughout India, you will see many people living in slums without easy access to steady electricity, clean, piped water, or toilets.

But India's growing wealth is also obvious: Cell phones are everywhere, new stores are opening, access to clean water is increasing, literacy is rising, and people are better fed. In the cities, there are more restaurants, more clothing shops, more factories, and more cars. India today has at least 100 million people at an American or European standard of living—a remarkable increase from just a few decades ago.

As a rough way of summarizing these changes in economic output and the standard of living, economists look to a country's Gross Domestic Product (GDP) and its gross domestic product per capita, two statistics designed to measure the value of economic production.

Figure 26.1 on the next page shows India's real GDP per capita—or GDP per person—between 1970 and 2015. Since a series of liberalization reforms were put in place in the 1990s, India's real GDP per capita has been growing rapidly. In the eleven years between 2003 and 2014, for example, real GDP grew at average rate of 6% per year leading to a doubling of real GDP per capita! As we will discuss, real GDP per capita is a rough measure of a country's standard of living. Thus, in the 11 years preceding 2014, the standard of living in India roughly doubled. That is a notable improvement over India's previous growth performance and it represents the growing wealth of many people in India.

Table 26.1 lists GDP and GDP per capita for the 10 largest economies in 2014 (converted into U.S. dollars using PPP corrections). In the United States, where GDP was $16.49 trillion and the population was 319 million, GDP per capita was $51,622. Although China is the world's largest economy with a 2014 GDP of $17.15 trillion, it has a population of 1.4 billion people, so per capita GDP is only $12,523, a little bit less than Brazil ($15,101) and a little bit more than Indonesia ($10,010). Similarly, India has the third largest economy but, after China, it has the world's second largest population, so GDP per capita in India is only $5,534.

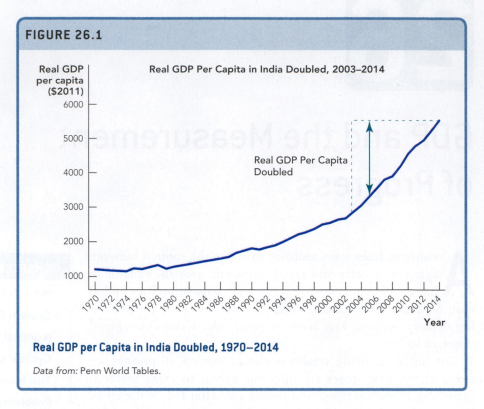

FIGURE 26.1

Real GDP Per Capita in India Doubled, 2003–2014

Real GDP per Capita in India Doubled, 1970–2014

Data from: Penn World Tables.

Okay, we can see that GDP per capita gives us a rough guide to a country's standard of living, but what is GDP actually measuring? In this chapter, we will explain:

- What the GDP statistic means and how it is measured
- The difference between the level of GDP and the growth rate of GDP
- The difference between nominal GDP and real GDP

TABLE 26.1 THE 10 LARGEST COUNTRIES RANKED BY GDP (2014)

	GDP (billions of U.S. dollars)	GDP per Capita (U.S. dollars)	Population (millions)
China	$17,150	$12,523	1,369
United States	$16,490	$51,622	319
India	$7,168	$5,534	1,295
Japan	$4,596	$36,249	127
Germany	$3,554	$44,067	81
Russia	$3,493	$24,353	143
Brazil	$3,112	$15,101	206
Indonesia	$2,547	$10,010	254
France	$2,417	$36,566	66
United Kingdom	$2,350	$36,530	64

Data from: Penn World Table 9.0 (2011 dollars, Real GDP at Constant National Prices, Population)

- How growth in real GDP per capita is a standard measure of economic progress
- The use of GDP in business cycle measurement
- Problems with GDP as a measure of output and welfare

What Is GDP?

Gross domestic product (GDP) is the market value of all finished goods and services produced within a country in a year. **GDP per capita** is GDP divided by a country's population.

To repeat, GDP is the market value of all finished goods and services produced within a country in a year. Let's take each part of this statement in turn.

GDP Is the Market Value . . .

GDP measures an economy's total output, which includes millions of different goods and services. But some goods are obviously more valuable than others: A Ford Mustang is worth more than an iPad. To measure total output, therefore, it doesn't make sense to simply add up quantities. Instead, GDP uses market values to determine how much each good or service is worth and then sums the total.

For example, in 2016 the U.S. economy produced approximately 12 million cars and light vehicles and 8.6 billion chickens.[1] If the average price of a car was $28,000 and the average price of a chicken was $5, the market value of the production of cars was $336 billion ($28,000 × 12 million) and the market value of chicken production was $43 billion ($5 × 8.6 billion). Using prices in the calculations gives greater weight to goods and services that are more highly valued in the marketplace. Applying this procedure to all finished goods and services yields a figure for GDP. In Table 26.2, we show the addition to GDP created by the production of cars and chickens.

. . . of All Finished . . .

What is a *finished* good or service? Some goods and services are sold to firms and then bundled or processed with other goods or services for sale at a later stage. These are called intermediate goods and services. We distinguish these from finished goods and services, which are sold to final users and then consumed or held in personal inventories.

Gross domestic product (GDP) is the market value of all finished goods and services produced within a country in a year.

GDP per capita is GDP divided by population.

What Is Gross Domestic Product?

interactive activity

TABLE 26.2 GDP IS CALCULATED BY MULTIPLYING THE PRICE OF FINISHED GOODS AND SERVICES BY THEIR QUANTITIES AND ADDING THE MARKET VALUES

Finished Good	Price	×	Quantity	=	Market Value
Cars	$28,000	×	12 million	=	$336 billion
Chickens	$5	×	8.6 billion	=	$43 billion
					$379 billion ← Added to GDP

A computer chip is one example of an intermediate good. If an Intel chip were counted in GDP when it was sold to Dell, and then counted again when a consumer buys the Dell computer, the value of the computer chip would be counted twice. To avoid double counting, only the computer—the finished good—is included in the calculation of GDP.

We do, however, count the production of machinery and equipment used to produce other goods as part of GDP. A tractor, for example, may help to produce soybeans, but the tractor is not part of the finished product of soybeans. Thus, both tractor production and soybean production add to GDP, even though the computer chip does not.

. . . Goods and Services . . .

The output of an economy includes both goods and services. Services provide a benefit to individuals without the production of tangible output. For example, paying a consultant to fix a software problem on a computer is a service and its market value is included in GDP. Other services include haircuts, transportation, entertainment, and spending on medical care.

Since 1950, the portion of U.S. GDP created by the production of services has increased from just under 50% to almost 70% (see Figure 26.2). Much of this increase is attributable to spending on medical services and recreational activities, which have both increased to more than 10 times their levels in 1950.[2]

Since U.S. GDP is about $18 trillion (2015), we can tell from the graph that the value of finished services is about $12 trillion (0.68 × 18) and the value of finished goods about $6 trillion.

. . . Produced . . .

GDP is meant to measure *production* so sales of used goods are not included in GDP. The sale of a used car, for example, is not included in GDP.

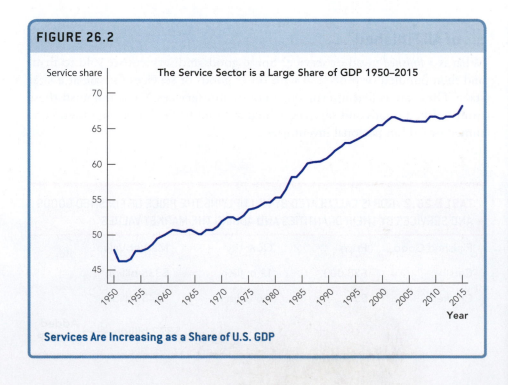

FIGURE 26.2

The Service Sector is a Large Share of GDP 1950–2015

Services Are Increasing as a Share of U.S. GDP

Similarly, sales of old houses and sales of financial securities like stocks and bonds are not included in the calculation of GDP. The sale of an old house does not add to GDP because the house was not produced in the year in which it sold. Sales of newly built houses, however, are counted in GDP. Stocks and bonds are claims to financial assets—they are not themselves produced goods or services—so sales of financial assets are not counted in GDP.

Even though the sales of old houses, used goods, and financial assets do not add to GDP, the services of real estate agents, used-car salespeople, and brokers do add to GDP because the services provided by these agents are produced in the year in which they are sold.

...within a Country...

U.S. GDP is the market value of the finished goods and services produced by labor and capital *located* in the United States, regardless of the nationality of the workers or the property owners. A citizen of Mexico who works temporarily in the United States adds to U.S. GDP. By the same reasoning, an American who works temporarily in Mexico contributes to Mexican GDP, not to U.S. GDP.

Gross national product (GNP) is very similar to GDP but GNP measures what is produced by the labor and property supplied by U.S. residents wherever in the world that labor or capital is located, rather than what is produced within the U.S. border. For a large nation like the United States, GDP and GNP are very similar but GDP has evolved into the more commonly used concept.

Gross national product (GNP) is the market value of all finished goods and services produced by a country's residents, wherever located, in a year.

...in a Year

GDP tells us how much the nation produced in a year, not how much the nation has accumulated in its entire history. You can think of GDP as being analogous to annual wages. Wages are not the same thing as wealth. Some retired people are wealthy even though their wages are low and some people with high wages have very little wealth (perhaps because they are at the beginning of their career or perhaps because they spend everything they earn and never save).

National wealth refers to the value of a nation's entire stock of assets. A tractor built in 2005 and still operating today is part of U.S. wealth but not part of today's GDP. One very crude estimate places U.S. national wealth at $84.8 trillion,[3] which is several times larger than its 2016 GDP of about $18.6 trillion.

Although we typically think of GDP on a yearly basis, it is also calculated every quarter of the year. The calculations are done by the Bureau of Economic Analysis (BEA), which is part of the Department of Commerce and based in Washington, D.C. If you want to see whether you understand what the bureau is up to, try testing yourself with the questions at right.

Growth Rates

To compute the growth rate of GDP from 2015 to 2016, for example, you need only two numbers: the GDP at the end of 2015 and the GDP at the end of 2016. Compute the percentage change as

$$\frac{GDP_{2016} - GDP_{2015}}{GDP_{2015}} \times 100 = \text{GDP growth rate for 2016}$$

CHECK YOURSELF

- The Interstate Bakeries Corporation buys wheat flour to make into Wonder Bread. Does the purchase of wheat flour add to GDP?
- On eBay, you sell your collection of Pokémon cards. Does your sale add to GDP?
- An immigrant from Colombia works as a cook in a New York restaurant. Are the goods and services he produced considered part of the GDP of the United States or Colombia?

CHECK YOURSELF

■ If GDP in 1990 was $5,803 billion and GDP in 1991 was $5,995 billion, what was the growth rate of (nominal) GDP?

Nominal variables, such as **nominal GDP**, have not been adjusted for changes in prices.

Using actual figures (in billions), we determine:

$$\frac{\$18,567 - \$18,037}{\$18,037} \times 100 = 2.9\%$$

Thus, the growth rate for U.S. GDP for 2016 was 2.9%.

Nominal vs. Real GDP

Nominal GDP is calculated using prices at the time of sale. Thus, GDP in 2016 is calculated using 2016 prices and GDP in 2000 is calculated using 2000 prices. If we want to compare GDP over substantial periods, using nominal GDP creates a problem. GDP in 2016, for example, was $18.6 trillion and GDP in 2000 was $10.3 trillion. Should we celebrate this roughly 80% increase in GDP $\left(\frac{18.6 - 10.3}{10.3} \times 100 = 81\%\right)$? Not so fast! Before we celebrate, we would like to know whether the increase was due mostly to greater production—more cars and more chickens—or to increases in prices between 2000 and 2016. Economists usually are more interested in increases in production than increases in prices because only increases in production are true increases in the standard of living. But how can we measure increases in production while controlling for increases in prices? Here is what we know so far:

2016 nominal GDP = 2016 prices × 2016 quantities = $18.6 trillion

2000 nominal GDP = 2000 prices × 2000 quantities = $10.3 trillion

Can you see how to compare the increase in production from 2000 to 2016? Suppose we calculate GDP in 2000 using 2016 prices instead of 2000 prices. The U.S. Bureau of Economic Analysis (BEA) does just this and finds the following:

2016 GDP in 2016 dollars = 2016 prices × 2016 quantities = $18.6 trillion

2000 GDP in 2016 dollars = 2016 prices × 2000 quantities = $14.0 trillion

What this tells us is that if prices in 2000 were the same as in 2016, then GDP in 2000 would have been measured as $14.0 trillion. Economists also say that 2000 GDP in 2016 dollars is real GDP in 2016 dollars. Since 2016 GDP is already in 2016 dollars, it's also real GDP in 2016 dollars.

Now that we have real GDP in 2000 and real GDP in 2016, we can find the increase in real GDP. Between 2000 and 2016, the increase in real GDP was 32.9% $\left(\frac{18.6 - 14.0}{14.0} \times 100 = 32.9\%\right)$. Thus in 2016 the economy produced 32.9% more stuff, goods, and services than in 2000. That's not a great performance and quite a bit less than the value we calculated earlier—81%—because prices also increased during this period.

If we want to compare GDP over time, we should always compare real GDP, that is, GDP calculated using the *same prices in all years*. Interestingly, it doesn't matter much what prices we use to calculate real GDP, so long as we use the same prices in all years.

Real GDP calculations become trickier the longer the period we compare. In 1925, for example, what was the price of a computer? Economists and statisticians involved in calculating real GDP must worry about the value of new goods and changes in the quality of goods. The more years that pass, the more difficult it is to determine how to adjust for those quality changes.

The real versus nominal distinction is an important one in economics and it will recur throughout this book. A **real variable** is one that corrects for inflation, namely a general increase in prices over time. In later chapters, we will discuss the real price of housing, real wages, and the real interest rate and we will show in more detail how to convert nominal data into real data.

Real variables, such as **real GDP**, have been adjusted for changes in prices by using the same set of prices in all time periods.

The GDP Deflator

The GDP deflator is a price index that can be used to measure inflation. We will be discussing price indexes and inflation at greater length in the chapter on Inflation and the Quantity Theory of Money. The GDP deflator, however, is very easy to calculate once we know nominal and real GDP for a given year. The GDP deflator is simply the ratio of nominal to real GDP (multiplied by 100).

$$\text{GDP deflator} = \frac{\text{Nominal GDP}}{\text{Real GDP}} \times 100$$

For example, let's calculate the GDP deflator for 2016. We can easily find 2016 nominal GDP and 2016 real GDP (using 2009 dollars) from the U.S. Bureau of Economic Analysis. Here are the numbers:

$$\text{2016 nominal GDP} = \text{2016 prices} \times \text{2016 quantities}$$
$$= \$18.57 \text{ trillion}$$
$$\text{2016 real GDP (in 2009 dollars)} = \text{2009 prices} \times \text{2016 quantities}$$
$$= \$16.66 \text{ trillion}$$
$$\text{GDP deflator} = \frac{\text{2016 prices} \times \text{2016 quantities}}{\text{2009 prices} \times \text{2016 quantities}}$$
$$= \frac{\text{2016 prices}}{\text{2009 prices}}$$
$$= \frac{18.57 \text{ trillion}}{16.66 \text{ trillion}} \times 100 = 111.45$$

To see why the GDP deflator can be used to measure inflation, notice that the deflator is a ratio of prices. What the deflator tell us is that 2016 prices were about 11.45% higher (111.45 − 100) than 2009 prices.

Real GDP Growth

If pressed to choose a single indicator of *current* economic performance, most economists would probably choose real GDP growth. Figure 26.3 shows the annual percentage changes in real GDP for the United States from 1948 to 2015. U.S. real GDP growth was high during the 1960s, but the 1973 and 1979 oil price shocks lowered growth in the 1970s and early 1980s. Growth was more solid after the 1982 recession until the mid-2000s but still somewhat lower than in the 1960s. The severe recession of 2009 and slow recovery since then is also evident in the figure. Note that the long-term (since 1948) average growth of real U.S. GDP has been about 3.2% per year. You can use these figures as benchmarks to gauge current growth rates.

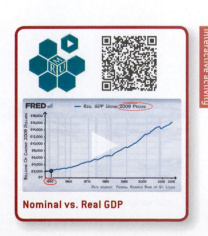

Nominal vs. Real GDP

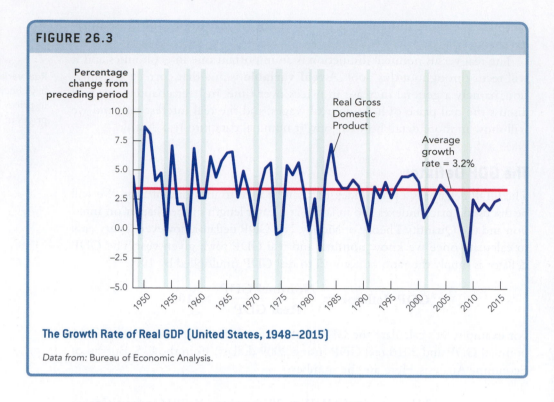

FIGURE 26.3

Percentage change from preceding period

Real Gross Domestic Product

Average growth rate = 3.2%

The Growth Rate of Real GDP (United States, 1948–2015)

Data from: Bureau of Economic Analysis.

Real GDP Growth per Capita

Growth in real GDP per capita is usually the best reflection of changing living standards. Growth in real GDP typically gives the same broad idea of how economic conditions are changing as growth in real GDP per capita, but there can be big differences for countries with rapidly growing populations. For instance, between 1993 and 2003, Guatemala experienced real GDP growth of about 3.6% a year. That might sound good but over that same period population grew at 2.8% a year, so real GDP per capita in Guatemala grew at just 0.8% a year. In comparison, real GDP per capita in the United States typically grows by about 2.1% a year. Thus, not only is the United States richer than Guatemala, people in the United States are getting richer faster.

Nigeria is a tragic example of a growth disaster. In 1960, when Nigeria gained its independence from Great Britain, vast deposits of oil were discovered and the future looked bright. But a vicious civil war, dictatorship, and massive corruption meant that the oil wealth disappeared in arms purchases and secret Swiss bank accounts. Incredibly for an economy in the modern era, real GDP per capita in Nigeria was a little bit lower in 2000 than it had been in 1960.

Although it seems shocking that a country could be no richer in 2000 than in 1960, it's important to remember that throughout most of human history, a failure to grow is *normal*. In the next chapter, we will begin to explain not only why some nations are poor but the truly mysterious question: Why are any nations rich?

Cyclical and Short-Run Changes in GDP

So far we have focused on GDP as a way to compare economic output across countries and over long periods. GDP is also used to measure short-run fluctuations in an economy, namely the ups and downs in economic growth that

CHECK YOURSELF

■ Name a country with a high GDP but a low GDP per capita.

■ Name a country with a low GDP but a high GDP per capita.

■ Why do we often convert nominal variables into real variables?

occur within the space of a few years. As we saw in Figure 26.3, U.S. growth rates varied considerably from 1948 to 2016. In some years, such as 2009, the growth rate was negative. **Recessions**—significant, widespread declines in real GDP and employment—are of special concern to policymakers and the public.

The National Bureau of Economic Research (NBER), a research organization based in Cambridge, Massachusetts, is considered the most authoritative source on identifying U.S. recessions. The official NBER definition of a recession is as follows:

> A recession is a significant decline in economic activity spread across the economy, lasting more than a few months, normally visible in real GDP, real income, employment, industrial production, and wholesale–retail sales.

A few points in this definition are worth emphasizing. A recession is widespread not only geographically but also across different sectors of the economy. Although a decline in real GDP is the single best indicator of a recession, declines will usually also be observed in income, employment, sales, and other measures of the health of an economy.

How often do recessions occur? Figure 26.4 plots real GDP growth and official U.S. recessions since 1948—this time using quarterly data (expressed as annualized rates) so we can better see the variability over time. There have been 11 recessions since 1948, indicated by the shaded bars. Notice that in addition to recessions, the figure illustrates expansions or booms when real GDP grows at a faster rate than normal. We call the fluctuations of real GDP around its long-term trend, or "normal" growth rate, **business fluctuations** or **business cycles**.

Defining when a recession begins and ends is not always obvious, in part because economic data are often revised over time. The estimate of quarterly GDP, for example, is not ready for release until almost a month after the quarter is over. After that, additional rounds of updated estimates are published in the following

A **recession** is a significant, widespread decline in real GDP and employment.

Business fluctuations or **business cycles** are the short-run movements in real GDP around its long-term trend.

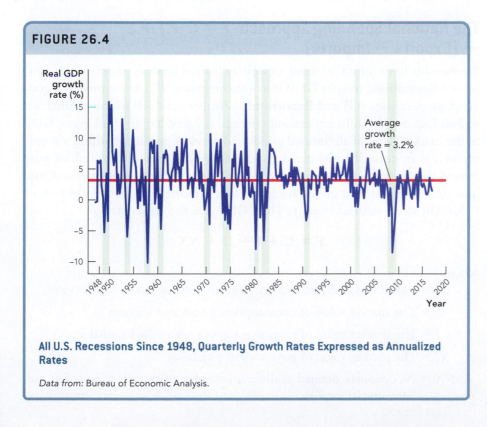

FIGURE 26.4

All U.S. Recessions Since 1948, Quarterly Growth Rates Expressed as Annualized Rates

Data from: Bureau of Economic Analysis.

two months. The government often makes significant changes in GDP estimates between the original estimate and the final estimate. For example, in 2011 the BEA revised GDP estimates from 2008, and the recession in that year turned out to be even worse than earlier estimates had suggested. The BEA initially estimated that GDP had fallen at an annualized rate of -6.8% in the fourth quarter of 2008. In the revisions, the decline was significantly steeper, -8.9%. Since updates can occur years after the first estimates are released, the usefulness of GDP as a timely indicator is dampened and our understanding of recessions can change over time.

As another example, there is debate about when the 2001 recession started. The official NBER starting date is March 2001, but data revisions have led many people to conclude that the recession actually started in late 2000. Why all the fuss about the timing? If you recall, the presidency changed at the beginning of 2001. Democrats would like to claim that the recession was caused by Republican economic policies, while Republicans want to show that the recession began during President Clinton's final term, before President Bush assumed office.

The Many Ways of Splitting GDP

Another way of understanding GDP is to study its components and how they fit together. Economists split the production of goods and services in many different ways depending on the questions they are asking. We present two common ways of splitting GDP:

1. National spending approach to GDP: $Y = C + I + G +$ (Exports − Imports)

2. Factor income approach to GDP: $Y =$ Wages + Rent + Interest + Profit

As we will see, both formulas prove useful for understanding business cycles and economic growth.

The National Spending Approach: $Y = C + I + G$ + (Exports − Imports)

Economists have found it useful, especially for the analysis of short-run economic fluctuations, to split GDP into consumption (C), investment (I), government purchases (G) and Exports minus Imports, which is often shortened to Net Exports (NX). To understand why this is equivalent to thinking of GDP as the market value of all finished goods and services produced within a country in a year, note that produced goods can be consumed, invested, or purchased by governments or foreigners. Finally, some consumed, invested, and government-purchased goods are imported. Imported goods are not part of U.S. GDP, so we subtract imports. Thus, GDP can also be written as

$$Y = C + I + G + NX$$

where:

$Y =$ Nominal GDP (the market value all finished goods and services)

$C =$ The market value of consumption goods and services

$I =$ The market value of investment goods, also called capital goods

$G =$ The market value of government purchases

$NX =$ Net exports, defined as the market value of exports minus the market value of imports

We explain each of these factors more in turn.

Consumption is private spending on finished goods and services. Most consumption spending is made by households, such as spending on cars and chickens. Consumption spending, however, also includes spending on health care whether the spending comes from your pocket, an insurance company, or the government (as with Medicaid and Medicare). Note that while economists think of education as an investment in "human capital," the Bureau of Economic Analysis includes education as consumption spending alongside purchases of automobiles, MP3 players, and televisions. How would you classify your education spending? Are you here to consume (party!) or invest for the future (study hard!)?

Investment is private spending on tools, plant, and equipment that are used to produce future output. Most investment spending is made by businesses but an important exception is that new home production is counted as investment. It's important to remember that "investment" is spending on tools, plant, and equipment (capital). When a farmer buys a tractor, that is investment. If your university builds new classrooms and labs, that is investment. Buying IBM stock, however, is not investment, as this is a mere change in ownership of some capital goods from one person to another. To make sure that everything adds up, investment also includes changes in inventories.

The third component of GDP is **government purchases**, or spending by all levels of government on finished goods and services. Government purchases include spending on tanks, airplanes, office equipment, and roads, as well as spending on wages for government employees (in this case the government is implicitly thought of as the purchaser of services such as military services). This category includes both government consumption items (like toner cartridges for printers) and government investment items (like roads and levees), and is thus also called government consumption and investment purchases.

A large part of what government does is transfer money from one citizen to another citizen; about 21% of the spending of the federal government, for example, is for Social Security payments. Unemployment and disability insurance, various welfare programs, and Medicare are also large transfer programs. We do not include transfers in government purchases because if we did, we would be double-counting. When the senior citizen buys a television with his or her Social Security check or consumes health care through Medicare, it is counted in the consumption portion of GDP. Thus, we do not also count the check as part of government purchases. Another way of thinking about this is that we count only government purchases of *finished goods and services*. When the government sends a check to a senior citizen, it is not purchasing a finished good or service—it is transferring wealth.

Net exports is exports minus imports. To understand this term, it's important to remember the *Domestic* in Gross Domestic Product. When we add $C + I + G$ we are adding up all national spending but some of that spending was on imports, goods that were not produced domestically. So we subtract imports from national spending to get national spending on domestically produced goods, $C + I + G -$ Imports. Some of the goods that we *produced* domestically, however, aren't included in *national* spending on domestically produced goods because they weren't bought by nationals but by people in other countries, i.e., some of the goods we produced were exported. Thus, to find domestically produced goods we add exports to national spending on domestically produced goods, to arrive at $C + I + G +$ Exports $-$ Imports or $C + I + G + NX$.

But here is something to avoid. The national spending approach to calculating GDP requires a step in which we subtract imports, but that doesn't mean

Consumption is private spending on finished goods and services.

Investment is private spending on tools, plant, and equipment used to produce future output.

Government purchases are spending by all levels of government on finished goods and services. Transfers are not included in government purchases.

Net exports are the value of exports minus the value of imports.

that imports are bad for GDP! Let's consider a simple economy, one where I, G, and Exports are all zero and $C = \$100$ billion. Our only imports come from a container ship that once a year delivers $10 billion worth of iPhones. Thus when we calculate GDP we add up national spending and subtract $10 billion for the imports: $100 billion − $10 billion = $90 billion. But suppose that this year the container ship sinks before it reaches our port in New York. When we calculate GDP this year, then, there are no imports to subtract. But GDP doesn't change! Why not? Remember that part of the $100 billion of national spending was $10 billion spent on iPhones. So this year when we calculate GDP we will calculate $90 billion − $0 = $90 billion. GDP doesn't change; that shouldn't be surprising since GDP is about domestic production and the sinking of the container ship doesn't change domestic production.

If we want to understand the role of imports (and exports) on GDP and national welfare, we have to go beyond accounting to think about economics. If we permanently stopped all the container ships from delivering iPhones, for example, then domestic producers would start producing more cell phones and that would add to GDP, although producing more cell phones would require producing less of other goods. If we were buying cell phones from abroad because producing them abroad requires fewer resources, then GDP would actually fall when we produced more cell phones at home—this is one of the standard arguments for trade. The standard answer could change, however, if there were lots of unemployed resources in the domestic economy, an issue we will discuss in the chapter on business fluctuations and in later chapters. The point we want to emphasize here is not whether trade is ultimately good or bad, but rather that $Y = C + I + G + NX$ is an accounting identity that can't by itself answer this question.

Figure 26.5 shows the four components of U.S. GDP in 2015. Consumption is by far the largest component, accounting for $12.3 trillion, or 68.1% of U.S. GDP. Government purchases were $3.2 trillion, or 17.2% of GDP, investment was $3.1 trillion, or 17.7%, and net exports were −$0.54 trillion, or −3.0%. If you look at the "long-term averages" part of Figure 26.5, you'll get an idea of the relative sizes of these numbers in recent times. In later chapters on aggregate demand and business cycles, you will see that changes in these categories represent one way of thinking about the causes or sources of short-run economic downturns and that is one reason why we have covered these particular categories.

The Factor Income Approach: $Y =$ Employee Compensation + Rent + Interest + Profit

When a consumer spends money, the money is received by workers (employee compensation = wages + benefits), landlords (rent), owners of capital (interest), and businesses (profit). Thus, we have yet another way of calculating GDP: We can add up all the spending or we can add up all the receiving. The first method is called the spending

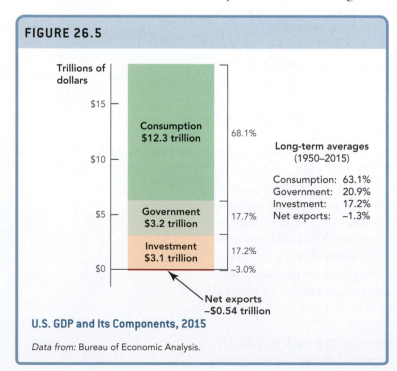

FIGURE 26.5

Trillions of dollars

Consumption $12.3 trillion — 68.1%

Government $3.2 trillion — 17.7%

Investment $3.1 trillion — 17.2%

Net exports −$0.54 trillion — −3.0%

Long-term averages (1950–2015)

Consumption: 63.1%
Government: 20.9%
Investment: 17.2%
Net exports: −1.3%

U.S. GDP and Its Components, 2015

Data from: Bureau of Economic Analysis.

approach, while the second is called the factor income approach. Thus, GDP can also be written as:

$$Y = \textbf{Employee compensation} + \textbf{Rent} + \textbf{Interest} + \textbf{Profit}$$

As usual, some corrections are necessary to get the accounting right. For example, not every dollar spent on goods and services is a dollar received in income. Sales taxes are one exception with which you can identify. Sales taxes create a difference between what consumers pay and what businesses and workers receive so if we calculate GDP using the income approach, we need to add sales taxes.*

For our purposes, the details are less important than the basic idea: Every dollar spent is a dollar of income received so if we are careful in our accounting, we can measure GDP by summing up all the spending on finished goods and services or by summing up everyone's income.

Why Split?

Each of the ways of splitting GDP throws a different light on the economy. Economists who study business fluctuations, for example, are often interested in splitting GDP according to the national spending identity because consumption, investment, government purchases, and net exports behave differently over time. Consumption spending, for example, tends to be much more stable than investment spending. Economists are interested in understanding the causes and consequences of these differences.

The factor income approach is useful if we are thinking about how economic growth is divided between employee compensation, rent, interest, and profits. It turns out, for example, that the largest payment in GDP is to labor. Employee compensation (wages and other benefits) accounts for about 54% of GDP—more than most people expect and much larger than corporate profits, which are around 10% of GDP. The share of GDP going to labor has been quite stable over time, although some evidence suggests that this share has fallen slightly in recent years. Economists are interested in understanding what drives the relative sizes of these shares.

It also helps to have more than one way of counting GDP because different methods are subject to different errors. Calculating GDP in more than one way lets us check our calculations.

No way of splitting GDP is better than another—it all depends on the questions being asked. Many other methods of splitting GDP are also possible and useful. We could look at the market value of food versus all other items, or durable versus nondurable goods, or we could break down GDP into finer geographic areas like regions or states (the latter is called gross state product). In principle, there are millions of ways of building a GDP measure by summing up its smaller parts. Economists continue to refine the idea of GDP, to improve the measurement of GDP, and to develop new ways of splitting GDP.

---

* We also have to make some corrections for depreciation. Over time machines wear down, factories fall into disrepair, and homes age. Depreciated capital doesn't add to anyone's income but GDP measures production before depreciation, so if we calculate GDP using the income approach, we need to adjust for the depreciation of capital.

Problems with GDP as a Measure of Output and Welfare

GDP measures the market value of finished goods and services. *But we do not know the market value of many goods and services.* We don't know the market value, for example, of illegally produced goods and services because neither the buyers nor the sellers are willing to answer questions from government statisticians. An even more serious problem is that we don't know the market value of goods and service that are not bought and sold in markets. We don't know, for example, the market value of clean air because clean air is not bought and sold in a market.

Let's look in more detail at some examples of each of these problems.

GDP Does Not Count the Underground Economy

Illegal or underground-market transactions are omitted from GDP. Sales of crack cocaine, for example, or sales of counterfeit Gucci bags are not reported and so do not show up in government statistics. Legal goods sold "under the table" to avoid taxes also do not show up in GDP.

Nations that have greater levels of corruption and higher tax rates usually have higher levels of underground transactions. In Haiti, the poorest country in the Western Hemisphere, it takes an estimated 203 days of fighting the bureaucracy to start and register a legal business.[4] It is no wonder that so many Haitians keep their commercial activity outside the law. More generally, the size of the informal or "outside the law" sector in Latin America is estimated at 41% of officially measured GDP.[5]

Nations with a great deal of illegal and off-the-books activity are not as poor as they appear in the official GDP statistics. In the United States or Western Europe, the underground economy is likely between 10% and 20% of GDP; that percentage is small relative to the percentage in Haiti or most of Latin America but in absolute terms it is still quite large.

Services are included in GDP Prostitution is legal in the Netherlands and prostitution revenues are included in the Netherlands' GDP.

GDP Does Not Count Nonpriced Production

Nonpriced production occurs when valuable goods and services are produced but no explicit monetary payment is made. If a son mows his parent's lawn, the service will not be included in GDP. If a lawn care firm provided the identical work, it would be included in GDP. Yet either way the grass gets cut and economic output increases. Similarly, if you watch videos for free on YouTube, this is not counted in GDP, but if you buy a ticket to the movie theater it is counted in GDP. People search for valuable information on Google, read blogs and newspapers online, and chat with their friends on Facebook but these transactions are not registered in the GDP statistics since they are not priced. Volunteering of all kinds, such as when church workers deliver food to the elderly, people pick up garbage in parks, and book reviewers post reviews on Amazon, is also not counted in GDP. Each of these activities adds to economic output but if the transaction isn't priced, it isn't counted in the GDP statistics.

The omission of nonpriced production introduces two biases into GDP statistics: biases over time and biases across nations.

In the United States, the portion of women who are in the official labor force has almost doubled since 1950, rising from 34% to about 60% today. As a result, mothers spend less time working at home than in 1950, but there are more nannies and house cleaners in the economy today. The mothers who worked at home in 1950 were not paid and their valuable services were not counted in GDP. Nannies and house cleaners today are paid and their services are counted in GDP (unless the nanny is hired "under the table" to avoid paying Social Security taxes, of course!). The result is that U.S. GDP in 1950 underestimates a little the real production of goods and services in 1950 relative to that of today.

Nonpriced production also affects GDP comparisons across countries. For example, many cultures discourage women from becoming part of the official workforce. In India, women make up only 28% of the labor force, compared with 46% for the United States.[6] The output of the other 72% of Indian women is not included in Indian GDP but these women are working. Indian GDP statistics, therefore, underestimate the real production of goods and services in India.

Household production is especially important in poor countries and in rural areas. It is common to read of families, say, in rural Mexico, that earn no more than $1,000 a year. Living off this sum sounds impossible to a contemporary American, but keep in mind that many of these families build their own homes (with help from relatives and friends), grow their own food, and sew their own clothes. Their lives are hard, but much of what they produce is not captured in GDP statistics.

GDP Does Not Count Bads: Environmental Costs

GDP adds up the market value of finished goods and services, but it does not subtract the value of bads. Pollution, for example, is a bad that is produced every year, but this bad is not counted in the GDP statistics. The statistics also do not count the destruction of water aquifers, the accumulation of carbon dioxide in the atmosphere, or the changing supplies of natural resources. Similarly, GDP statistics do not count the loss of animal or plant species as economic costs, unless those animals and plants had a direct commercial role in the economy. Other bads, for example, the bad of crime, are also not counted in GDP statistics. Since more pollution isn't counted as a bad, it's not surprising that less pollution is also not counted as a good. America has cleaner air and cleaner water than it did in 1960, but GDP statistics do not reflect this improvement.

The movement for "green accounting" has tried to reform GDP statistics to cover the environment more explicitly. In 2015, for example, total CO_2 emissions for the United States were 5,270 million tons. The U.S. government estimates that the social cost of CO_2 emissions is $41.20 per ton (using a 3% discount rate and in 2015 dollars), so the total social cost of emissions in that year was $217 billion. Subtracting this bad from the $18,036-billion GDP in 2015 would have given us a slightly smaller estimate of GDP, $17,820 billion. Interestingly, since CO_2 emissions fell over the period 2005 to 2015, such a calculation would also have slightly raised our estimates of growth rates over this period.

Most economists agree with the logic behind green accounting: GDP should measure the market value of all finished goods and services even if those goods and services are not traded in markets. But environmental amenities are often difficult to value. How much, for instance, should be added to

GDP because more or fewer polar bears are present in Alaska? How much is a glacier worth? A coral reef? Estimates of the values of these resources may be computed for individual problems, but when it comes to the economy as a whole, the measurement task seems insurmountable. Rather than introduce so much uncertainty into the entire GDP concept, economists usually restrict green accounting (and other GDP modifications) to the analysis of particular problems such as CO_2 emissions.

GDP Does Not Count the Health of Nations

GDP counts the production of goods and services, but the more goods and services we can afford, the more important is another source of wealth, health and longevity. In the seven years between 2007 and 2014, life expectancy increased in the United States by about 1 year. How much was that increase in life expectancy worth? Let's do a back-of-the-envelope calculation to get an idea of the magnitude. By looking at the differences in wages between jobs of different risks (the compensating differential—see your microtext), economists have estimated that people value an additional year of life at about $150,000. Government agencies use numbers like this to value improvements in road safety, reductions in pollution, or new life-saving pharmaceuticals. The U.S. population is about 330 million, but since we are doing a back-of-the-envelope calculation let's simplify it to 300 million. An extra year of life valued at $150,000 for 300 million people is worth a total of $45 trillion!

Our back-of-the-envelope calculation doesn't take into account some important factors. We should be careful about how we compare future and present values (discounting) and we should take into account population growth, but more careful calculations by economists Kevin Murphy and Robert Topel show that we are in the right ballpark—increases in life expectancy are worth tens of trillions of dollars! In fact, Murphy and Topel estimate that the increases in life expectancy between 1970 and 2000 (see Table 26.3) were worth half of all the GDP produced during this period—about $95 trillion dollars.[7]

Numbers like this are important for understanding improvements in welfare over time and also for thinking about how resources should be allocated. Murphy and Topel also calculate, for example, that a 1% reduction in cancer

---

TABLE 26.3 LIFE EXPECTANCY BY AGE GROUP AND YEAR, 1970–2000

	1970	1980	1990	2000	Change in Life Expectancy (1970–2000)
Newborn	70.76	73.88	75.37	76.87	6.11
15 years	57.69	60.19	61.38	62.62	4.93
45 years	30.12	32.27	33.44	34.38	4.26
65 years	15.00	16.51	17.28	17.86	2.86

Data from: Cutler, D. M., Rosen, A. B., and Vijan, S. 2006. The Value of Medical Spending in the United States, 1960–2000. *New England Journal of Medicine*, 355(9): 920–927.

mortality would be worth $500 billion. Or, to put it differently, it would be worth spending $100 billion on a medical "moonshot" program if that program had just a 20% chance of reducing cancer mortality by 1%.

Even though the value of health is not included in GDP, that doesn't mean that society doesn't value health. To understand the trade-offs, however, it is important that we put numbers on the value of health so that we can make appropriate comparisons and make wise choices.

GDP Does Not Measure the Distribution of Income

GDP per capita is a rough measure of the standard of living in a country. But if GDP per capita grows by 10%, this does not necessarily mean that *everyone's* income grows by 10% or even that the average person's income grows by 10%.

To see why, imagine that we have a country of four people, John, Paul, George, and Ringo, whose factor incomes in year 1 are 10, 20, 30, and 40. Using the factor income approach, we know that GDP is 100 (10 + 20 + 30 + 40) and thus GDP per capita is 25 (100/4). GDP in year 1 and its distribution are shown in the first row of Table 26.4.

Now suppose that in year 2 GDP grows by 10% to 110 and thus GDP per capita grows to 27.5 (110/4). This growth in GDP, however, is consistent with any of the three outcomes shown in rows a, b, and c of Table 26.4. In row a, everyone's income grows by 10%—so John's income grows from 10 to 11, Paul's income grows from 20 to 22, and so forth. In row b, the growth in GDP is concentrated on Ringo, the richest person: His income grows by 25% (from 40 to 50) and everyone else's income stays the same. In row c, the growth in GDP is concentrated on John, the poorest person. His income grows by 100% (from 10 to 20) and everyone else's income stays the same.

GDP and GDP per capita grow by the same amount in each of these cases, but in row *a* inequality stays the same, in row *b* inequality increases, and in row *c* inequality decreases.

In most countries most of the time, growth in GDP per capita is like row *a*: Everyone's income grows by approximately the same amount.[8] Thus, growth in real GDP per capita usually does tell us roughly how the average person's standard of living is changing over time. In examining particular countries and periods, however, we might want to look more carefully at how growth in GDP is distributed. In other words, GDP figures are useful but they will always be imperfect.

TABLE 26.4 GROWTH IN GDP PER CAPITA CAN BE DISTRIBUTED IN DIFFERENT WAYS

	John	Paul	George	Ringo	GDP	GDP per Capita
Year 1	10	20	30	40	100	25
(a) Year 2	11	22	33	44	110	27.5
(b) Year 2	10	20	30	50	110	27.5
(c) Year 2	20	20	30	40	110	27.5

Takeaway

The primary topics of macroeconomics are economic growth and business fluctuations. But when we say that "the economy" is growing, what do we mean? And precisely what is fluctuating? If we want to understand growth and fluctuations, we need some concept that defines and measures growth and fluctuations.

The concept of gross domestic product was developed to quantify the ideas of economic growth and fluctuations. GDP, the market value of all finished goods and services produced within a country in a year, is an estimate of the economic output of a nation over a year. When we say that an economy is growing, we mean that GDP, or a closely related concept like GDP per capita, is growing. When we say that an economy is booming or contracting, we mean that growth in real GDP is above or below its long-run trend.

GDP can be measured and summed up in different ways, each of which casts a different light on the economy. The national spending identity, $Y = C + I + G + NX$, splits GDP according to different classes of income spending. The factor income approach, $Y =$ Employee compensation + Interest + Rent + Profit, splits GDP into different classes of income receiving.

GDP per capita is a rough estimate of the standard of living in a nation. Real GDP is GDP per capita corrected for inflation by calculating GDP using the same set of prices in every year. Growth in real GDP per capita tells us roughly how the average person's standard of living is changing over time.

GDP statistics are imperfect. GDP does not include the value of leisure or goods bought and sold in the underground economy, nor does it include the value of goods that are difficult to price, such as the value of having polar bears in Alaska. GDP and GDP per capita also do not tell us anything about how equally GDP is distributed. Economists and statisticians try to refine and improve the measurement of GDP over time. GDP measures are imperfect but they have proven they are useful in estimating the standard of living and the scope of economic activity.

CHAPTER REVIEW

interactive activity Go online to practice with more examples of these types of problems, including live links to videos, data sources, and feedback.

 Problems in **green** relate to MRU videos. See the MRU table at the end of the exercises.

KEY CONCEPTS

gross domestic product (GDP), p. 507

GDP per capita, p. 507

gross national product (GNP), p. 509

nominal variables, p. 510

real variables, p. 511

recession, p. 513

business fluctuations (business cycles), p. 513

consumption, p. 515

investment, p. 515

government purchases, p. 515

net exports, p. 515

FACTS AND TOOLS

1. According to Table 26.1, what country has the highest GDP? What country on the list has the highest GDP per person? What countries on the list have the *second* highest GDP and the *second* highest GDP per person?

2. What is included in GDP: all goods, all services, or both?

3. What happened to spending on medical services and recreational activities after 1950?

4. Police officer: "I pulled you over for speeding. You were going 80 miles per hour."

   Driver: "But that's impossible, officer! I've only been driving for 15 minutes!"

   The government reports GDP numbers every quarter. How does this story illustrate the meaning of "GDP per year" when the GDP number is reported every three months?

5. Calculate the annual growth rate of nominal GDP in the following examples:

   Nominal GDP in 1930: $97 billion. Nominal GDP in 1931: $84 billion.

   Nominal GDP in 1931: $84 billion. Nominal GDP in 1932: $68 billion.

   Nominal GDP in 2000: $9,744 billion. Nominal GDP in 2001: $10,151 billion.

   (*Data from:* Historical Tables, Budget of the United States Government, Congressional Budget Office.)

6. Are the following included in U.S. GDP? Briefly explain why or why not:

   a. Used cars sold at a used car store

   b. Your used car you sell to your cousin

   c. Wine made in Napa Valley at a vineyard owned by Australians

   d. Wine made in Australia at a vineyard owned by Americans

   e. The price paid by a French tourist when staying at a San Francisco hotel

   f. The price paid by an American tourist staying at a Paris hotel

   g. A ticket for a Lakers game

7. By definition, is nominal GDP higher than real GDP?

8. In the last 20 years, have recessions been getting more frequent or less frequent than they used to be?

9. According to the National Bureau of Economic Research, which of the following are "normally" part of the definition of a recession?

   A fall in nominal income

   A fall in employment

   A fall in real income

   A fall in the price level

10. Looking back over the last 10,000 years of human history, which is more "normal": for GDP per capita to grow or for GDP per capita to stay about the same?

Ask FRED

interactive activity

11. Using the Federal Reserve Economic Data (FRED) database (https://fred.stlouisfed.org/) find Real US GDP. Adjust the dates to focus in on the years 2005 to 2016. The recession in 2008–2009 will be highlighted in gray. Looking at the quarterly data (click edit graph and modify frequency to Quarterly if the data is not already presented quarterly.)

    a. What was the highest level of real GDP prior to the recession?

    b. In what year and quarter did U.S. real GDP first exceed its pre-recession level?

Ask FRED

interactive activity

12. Using the Federal Reserve Economic Data (FRED) database (https://fred.stlouisfed.org/), let's sum up real GDP using its components. Recall that GDP = $C + I + G$ + Net Exports, so start by finding "Real personal consumption expenditures" (C), use the "Billions of Chained 2009 Dollars, Quarterly, Seasonally Adjusted Annual Rate" series. Now click Add Line and find a similar series for real investment (I). Now click Add Line again and look for Real Government Consumption Expenditures and Gross Investment (G), again in billions of dollars. Now click on Add Line one more time and look for real Net Exports (NX) (the last series is only available in this form since 1999).

    a. Graph the result.

    b. In the 2009 recession which series fell by the most?

    c. In the first quarter of 2010 what share of GDP was made up by Consumption? Note that you should *not* have to look up a separate GDP figure to make this calculation.

13. What is the national spending identity? This identity is very important in macroeconomics. It is as important as basic anatomy in medical school: You won't be able to cure anyone until you know what's inside a person.

THINKING AND PROBLEM SOLVING

14. Calculate GDP in this simple economy:

    Consumer purchases: $100 per year

    Investment purchases: $50 per year

    Government purchases: $20 per year

    Total exports: $50 per year

    Total imports: $70 per year

15. Since World War II, who were the only three recession-free U.S. presidents? (We'll revisit the question of how presidents matter for the economy in later chapters.)

16. We noted that "government purchases" don't include all government spending. A big part of what the U.S. government does is transfer money from one person to another. Social Security (payments to retirees), and Medicare and Medicaid (paying for medical care for the elderly and the poor) make up most of these "government transfers." We'll look into this in more detail in the chapter on the Federal Budget, but right now, let's see how big "government transfers" are and how fast they've grown in the federal government's budget. The figures in this table are all in non-inflation-adjusted dollars. Complete the table.

Year	Total Federal Transfers	Total Federal Spending	Transfers as Percent of Spending
1950	$10.3 billion	$47 billion	_____
2016	$1,961 billion	$4,023 billion	_____
Growth Rate in %	_____	_____	_____

Data from: Budget of the United States Government: Historical Tables, Fiscal Year 2017. Washington, DC: U.S. Government Printing Office.

17. Let's figure out GDP for Robinson Crusoe.

    a. Initially, he is stuck on an island without the wisdom and local knowledge of Friday. Because Crusoe is a proper Englishman, he wants to keep his accounts. This year, he catches and eats 2,000 fish valued at one British pound (£) each, grows and eats 4,000 coconuts valued at 0.5 British pounds each, and makes two huts (housing) valued at 200 pounds each.

    If government purchases are zero and there is no trade, what is C for Crusoe? What is I? What is Y? (We are going to start using those letters as if they mean something: See question 13 in the previous section.)

    b. One year, he learns of a tribe on a nearby island who are willing to trade with him: If he gives fish, they give clams. He produces just as much as before, but he trades 500 of the 2,000 fish and receives 10,000 clams valued at 5 clams per British pound. What is the British pound value of the exported fish? Of the imported clams? What are C, I, and X now? What is GDP now?

    c. The following year, Crusoe produces the same as in every other year, but a tribe on the other side of the island steals his two huts after he makes them, and gives him nothing in return. So he exports, but does not import at all. What are C, I, X, and Y now?

    d. In Crusoe's final year on the island, he produces the same as in every other year (he's a reliable worker), but a new shipwreck washes up on his island containing a clock worth £3, a new shirt worth £2, and a copy of Milton's *Paradise Lost* and Shakespeare's complete works, each worth £1. Treat these as imported consumer goods. What is GDP this year? (*Note:* Emphasize the "P" in GDP when considering your answer.) What are C, I, X, and Y this year? (*Note:* One of the four is bigger than usual, one is negative.)

    e. Is Crusoe probably happy about what happens in question 17c? Is he probably happy about what happens in question 17d? Keep these answers in mind for when we discuss the economics of trade later on.

18. Let's think about an economically sound way to measure the value of leisure. To keep this simple, we'll just think about the value of leisure to people who *could* work but who decide to stay home. Also, we won't think about how much *actual* workers value their free time, or about how much children and retirees value their time.

    In a standard supply and demand labor model, firms "demand" labor, while workers "supply" labor. Let's think about a labor market that is in equilibrium, with a wage of $20 per hour (close to the U.S. average) and with 150 million Americans working out of a total of 225 million working-age Americans.

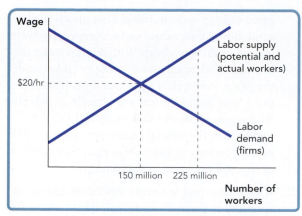

a. According to this simplified model of the U.S. economy, some workers *would* work if the wage were higher, but at the current wage, they'd rather stay home and watch reruns of *Seinfeld* or (don't let this be you!) *Two and a Half Men*. For the workers who are right on the margin between working and not working, what would their wage be if wages rose ever so slightly and they went to work?

b. Let's use this wage as a shorthand for how much nonworkers value their time. After all, the "opportunity cost" of their free time must be at least this high, because otherwise they'd take a job. Now, let's calculate a GDP measure that adds a rough estimate of the value enjoyed by these nonworkers. We'll use the following identity, and we'll round the value of nominal GDP to $14 trillion (close to the actual 2008 level):

Leisure-augmented GDP = Regular GDP + Total monetary value of leisure

If the average working person works 2,000 hours per year (that's a 40-hour week for 50 weeks a year), then what is the leisure-augmented value of U.S. GDP?

19. The underground economy and other nonpriced production make it difficult to accurately measure the precise level of GDP. But GDP could still be very accurate for measuring changes in the economy. If Janet Yellen, the Federal Reserve head, is trying to find out whether the U.S. economy has gone into a recession, are the difficulties of measuring nonpriced production likely to be important problems for her purposes? How is this like always wearing your shoes when you step on the bathroom scale?

20. a. U.S. GDP is approximately $18 trillion and the U.S. population is approximately 320 million. If GDP were divided equally among the US population what would each person get? If you and your nine best friends took almost all U.S. GDP for yourself but gave $3,000 per person to everyone else, how much would you get each year, just for yourself?

b. More seriously, there are currently about 229,000 U.S. taxpayers who earn more than $1.5 million per year. If you could take their money and divide it up equally among the U.S. population of 320 million other Americans, how much money could you give each person? Note that $1.5 million is the cutoff. On average this group earns about $4.4 million per year so use that number in your calculations.

c. How can large numbers of people get rich? Comment on economic growth versus redistribution.

21. Let's sum up some basic facts of U.S. economic history with numbers:

a. First, let's measure the size of the Great Depression:

Real GDP in 1929 (peak): $323 billion	Real GDP in 1933 (trough): $206 billion
Price level in 1929: 33	Price level in 1933: 24

Calculate the percent change in real GDP and the percent change in the price level from 1929 to 1933. First, calculate the total change, and then divide it by the number of years to get the more typical measure of "percent per year." (*Note*: This is four full years, not three or five.)

b. Second, let's measure how much the economy grew from the lowest depths of the Depression to the peak of World War II's economic boom:

Real GDP in 1933 (trough): $206 billion	Real GDP in 1945: $596 billion
Price level in 1933: 24	Price level in 1945: 38

Again, first calculate the total change, and then divide it by the number of years to get the more typical measure of "percent per year."

c. Finally, let's see if a growing economy must mean growing prices:

Real GDP in 1870: $36 billion

Real GDP in 1900: $124 billion

Price level in 1870: 22

Price level in 1900: 16

Calculate the total and annual growth rates as before. *Note:* The price level fell fairly smoothly across these three decades, a time when the economy grew rapidly and many great American novels were written about life in the growing cities.

(*Data from:* Gordon, Robert J., ed. 1986. *The American Business Cycle: Continuity and Change.* Cambridge, MA: National Bureau of Economic Research.)

22. What is the difference between a nation's *wealth* and its *GDP*? How are the two related?

CHALLENGES

Ask FRED

interactive activity

23. Consider the following claim:

Europeans have strong labor unions, so their workers get a bigger share of the pie than U.S. workers.

Let's use the FRED economic database (https://fred.stlouisfed.org/) to examine this claim. Search for "Share of Labor Compensation in GDP at Current National Prices for United States." Click on the starting date and change it to 1990 (The data for other countries is not always very good before 1990.) Now click Add Line and search for "Share of Labor Compensation Germany." You should find the same series for Germany, click on it and then Add Data Series. Follow the same procedure to add a line for the Share of Labor Compensation in GDP in Italy.

It is true that Europeans have stronger labor unions than Americans, but is the claim we began with true? What does our analysis of the data tell us about what strong unions and labor regulation can and can't do?

24. During World War II, the government did a good job measuring nominal GDP. But if the price level was calculated incorrectly, we might get a completely wrong idea about what happened with real GDP. During World War II,

price ceilings were in place. That means that some things that would've been expensive were instead artificially cheap. Within a few years of the war's end, price controls finally ended, and the price level spiked up about 20%. If the true price level *during the war* was actually 20% higher than reported, would that mean real GDP is higher than the official number in question 21b in the previous section, lower than that number, or is it still the same as that number?

25. If U.S. government statistics counted education spending as part of investment, which of the following would rise, which would fall, and which would remain unchanged? (*Note:* You might use rise, fall, and stay unchanged more than once each or you might not.)

Consumption

Investment

Gross domestic product

26. If U.S. government statistics counted people who are receiving unemployment benefits as people who are "government employees" hired to "search for work," which of the following would rise, which would fall, and which would remain unchanged? (*Note:* You might use rise, fall, and unchanged more than once each or you might not.)

Consumption

Government purchases

Gross domestic product

27. According to legend, some government employees do very little work. If this legend is true enough to be important, then we may be measuring GDP incorrectly. Officially, we say that these are "employed workers," but to a great extent these "employees" are really unemployed in any useful task; they are receiving transfer payments and watching YouTube for 40 hours per week. If, instead, government statistics counted these YouTube-watching government employees as simply retired or unemployed, which of the following would rise, which would fall, and which would remain unchanged? (*Note:* You might use rise, fall, and unchanged more than once each or you might not.)

Consumption

Government purchases

Gross domestic product

WORK IT OUT

For interactive, step-by-step help in solving this problem, go online.

Are the following included in U.S. GDP? Briefly explain why or why not:

a. Used textbooks sold at your college bookstore

b. Used books sold at a garage sale

c. Cars made in the United States at a Toyota factory

d. Cars made in Germany at a General Motors factory

e. The price paid by a German tourist when staying at a New York City hotel

f. The price paid by an American tourist staying at a Berlin hotel

g. A ticket for a Yankees game

MRUNIVERSITY
AN ONLINE EDUCATION PLATFORM

MARGINAL REVOLUTION UNIVERSITY VIDEOS

What Is Gross Domestic Product (GDP)?
mruniversity.com/gdp

Problems: **2, 6**

Nominal vs. Real GDP
mruniversity.com/nom-real-gdp

Problems: **7, 20, 21, 24**

Real GDP per Capita and the Standard of Living
mruniversity.com/gdp-per-capita

Problems: **1**

Splitting GDP
mruniversity.com/calc-gdp

Problems: **3, 8, 9, 14–16, 25–27**

27

The Wealth of Nations and Economic Growth

In developed nations, diarrhea is a pain, an annoyance, and, of course, an embarrassment. In much of the developing world, diarrhea is a killer, especially of children. Every year 1.8 million children die from diarrhea. To prevent the deaths of these children, we do not need any scientific breakthroughs, nor do we need new drugs or fancy medical devices. What these children need most is one thing: economic growth.

Economic growth brings piped water and flush toilets, which together cut infant mortality from diarrhea by 70% or more. Malaria, measles, and infections also kill millions of children a year. Again, the lesson is clear: millions of children are dying who would live if there were more economic growth.

Figure 27.1 on the next page illustrates how health and wealth go together. The vertical axis shows GDP per capita and the horizontal axis shows infant survival rates: how many children, out of every 1,000 births, survive to the age of 5. In the United States, one of the world's richest countries, 993 out of every 1,000 children born survive to the age of 5 (i.e., 7 out of every 1,000 die before the age of 5). In Liberia, one of the world's poorest countries, only about 765 children survive to age 5 (i.e., 235 of every 1,000 children die before seeing their fifth birthday). The graph illustrates a strong correlation between a country's GDP per capita and infant survival. The graph doesn't show a perfectly straight line—countries with the same level of income often have different levels of infant mortality, which means that factors other than income, such as government policies, culture, and geography, also matter. However, the correlation between income and infant mortality is quite strong. Notice also that the size of each country's data bubble is proportional to the population of that country; notice that India and China each have populations of more than 1 billion people so economic growth in these countries has the potential to save millions of infants from an early death.

Infant health and wealth tend to move together; indeed, just about *any* standard indicator of societal well-being tends to increase with wealth. Infant survival rates, life expectancy, and nutrition (caloric intake levels), for example, all tend to be higher in wealthier nations. Educational opportunities, leisure, and entertainment also tend to be higher in wealthier nations. Wealthier nations even have fewer conflicts such as civil wars and riots. And, of course, wealthier

FIGURE 27.1

GDP per capita, real U.S. dollars (2000)

USA

$50,000
40,000
30,000
20,000

Italy

Argentina

10,000

Mexico

5,000

India

China

Nigeria

North Korea

1,000

Liberia

700   800   900   950   980   990   995

Infant survival rate per 1,000 live births

Wealthier Countries Have Higher Infant Survival Rates

Data from: Penn World Tables and World Bank Group, World Development Indicators, 2005.
Note: Not all countries are labeled. GDP on ratio scale. PPP adjusted.

nations have more material goods such as televisions, iPhones, and swimming pools.

Wealth is clearly important so we want answers to the following questions. Why are some nations wealthy, while others are poor? Why are some nations getting wealthier faster than others? Can anything be done to help poor nations become wealthy? The answers to these questions are literally a matter of life and death. In this chapter and the next, we will try to answer these questions.

Key Facts About the Wealth of Nations and Economic Growth

Let's begin with some important facts about the wealth of nations and economic growth.

Fact One: GDP per Capita Varies Enormously Among Nations

We already have some understanding of the enormous differences that exist in the wealth of nations and how these differences affect infant mortality and other measures of well-being. Figure 27.2 shows in more detail how GDP per capita differed around the world in recent years. To construct this figure, we start on the left with the world's poorest country, which happens to be the Democratic Republic of the Congo (DRC). The DRC (not labeled) accounts for just over 1% of the world's population. As we add successively

The Economic History of the World in Less than Five Minutes

FIGURE 27.2

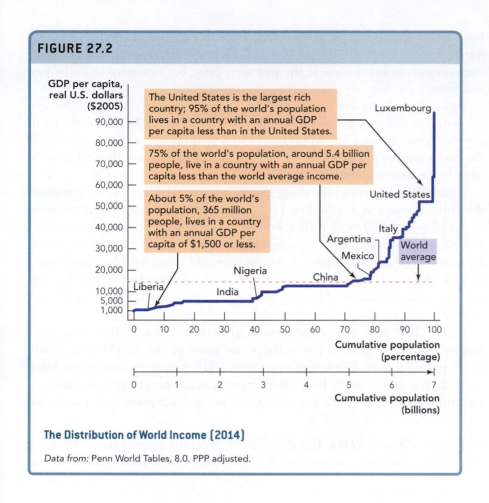

The Distribution of World Income (2014)

Data from: Penn World Tables, 8.0. PPP adjusted.

richer countries and their populations, we move further to the right in population and upward in GDP per capita. The graph tells us, for example, that about 10% of the world's population—or 772 million people in 2014—lived in a country with a GDP per capita of less than $2,900—about the level in Bangladesh. Moving farther to the right, we see that about 70% of the world's population lived in a country with a GDP per capita equal to or less than $12,472, about the level in China. The red horizontal dashed line shows the world's average level of GDP per capita in 2014, which is a little less than in Mexico. Fully 73% of the world's population—or 5.2 billion people—lived in a country with a GDP per capita less than average. In other words, most of the world's population is poor relative to the United States.

In thinking about poverty, remember that GDP per capita is simply an average, and there is a distribution of income within each country. In India, GDP per capita was around $5,224, but many Indians have yearly incomes that are less than $5,224 and some have yearly incomes that are higher than the average income in the United States. Around the world, about a billion people have incomes of less than $3 per day.

Fact Two: Everyone Used to Be Poor

The distribution of world income tells us that poverty is normal. It's wealth that is unusual. Poverty is even more normal when we think about human history. What was GDP per capita like in the year 1? No one knows for sure,

The Hockey Stick of Human Prosperity

but a good guesstimate is around $700–$1,000 per year in 2015 dollars, not much different from the very poorest people living in the world today. What's surprising is not that people in the past were poor, but that *everyone* in the past was poor.

Figure 27.3 shows some estimates of GDP per capita in different regions of the world in different periods from the year 1 to 2000 AD. In the year 1, GDP per capita was about $700–$1,000 and this was approximately the same in all the major regions of the world. Today, GDP per capita is more than 50 times as large in the richest countries as in the poorest countries.

Figure 27.3 illustrates something else of interest: GDP per capita was about the same in year 1 as it would be 1,000 years later and indeed about the same as it had been 1,000 years earlier. For most of recorded human history, there was *no long-run growth in real per capita GDP*. Countries might grow in particular good years, but soon enough a disaster would ensue and the gains would be given back. Only beginning in the nineteenth century does it become clear that some parts of the world began to grow at a rate unprecedented in human history.

Figure 27.3 tells us that economic growth is unusual. But once economic growth begins, it can make some parts of the world rich, while other parts languish at levels of per capita GDP similar to that in the Dark Ages. To see more clearly how small changes in economic growth can have enormous effects on GDP per capita, we pause for a primer on economic growth rates.

A Primer on Growth Rates Recall from the previous chapter on GDP that a growth rate is the percentage change in a variable over a given period such as

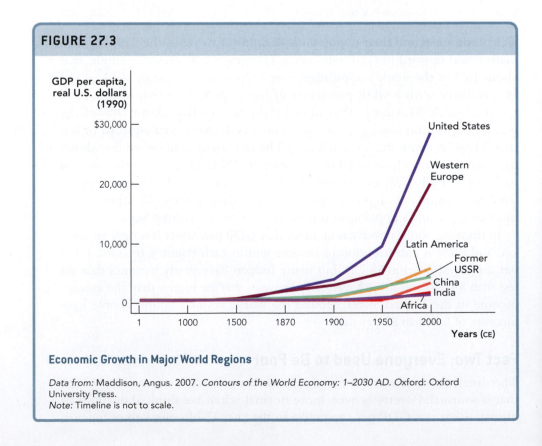

FIGURE 27.3

Economic Growth in Major World Regions

Data from: Maddison, Angus. 2007. *Contours of the World Economy: 1–2030 AD.* Oxford: Oxford University Press.
Note: Timeline is not to scale.

a year. When we refer to **economic growth,** we mean the growth rate of real per capita GDP.

While computing growth rates is simple math, grasping the impact of growth rates on economic progress is critical. Keep in mind that even slow growth, if sustained over many years, produces large differences in real GDP per capita.

To appreciate the power of economic growth, let's consider a few cases. Suppose that the annual growth rate of real GDP per capita is 2%. How long will it take for real per capita GDP to double from $40,000 to $80,000? An average person on the street might answer, "It will take 50 years to double your income at a 2% growth rate." But that is wrong because growth builds on top of growth. This is called "compounding" or "exponential growth."

There is a simple approximation, called the rule of 70, for determining the length of time necessary for a growing variable to double:

Rule of 70: If the annual growth rate of a variable is x%, then the doubling time is $\frac{70}{x}$ years.

At a growth rate of 1%, GDP per capita will double approximately every 70 years (70/1 = 70). If growth increases to 2%, GDP per capita will double every 35 years (70/2 = 35). Consider the impact of a 7% growth rate. If this growth can be sustained, then GDP per capita doubles every 10 years! China has been growing at this rate or a bit higher for several decades, which explains why China has become much richer in the past 30 years. China, however, is still a relatively poor country, so this also tells you how very, very poor they were in the recent past.

The rule of 70 is just a mathematical approximation, but it bears out the key concept that small differences in growth rates have large effects on economic progress. See the appendix to this chapter for a discussion of how you can use Excel to understand the magic of compounding.

Another way of seeing how small changes in the rate of economic growth can lead to big effects is to think about how rich people will be in the future. U.S. per capita GDP is about $50,000 (as of 2014). How many years will it take for real per capita GDP to increase to $1 million? If growth is 2% per year, which would be a little low by U.S. standards, average income will be $1 million per year in just 150 years. If GDP per capita grows at 3% per year, which is a little high by U.S. standards but certainly not impossible, then in just 100 years the average income will be approximately $1 million per year. You and I are unlikely to see this future, but if our grandchildren are lucky, they will see a world in which U.S. GDP per capita is a million dollars, more than 22 times higher than it is today.

Economic growth is the growth rate of real GDP per capita:

$$g_t = \frac{Y_t - Y_{t-1}}{Y_{t-1}} \times 100$$

where Y_t is real per capita GDP in period t.

The Rule of 70

Growth Rates Are Crucial

interactive activity

interactive activity

Fact Three: There Are Growth Miracles and Growth Disasters

The United States is one of the wealthiest countries in the world because the United States has grown slowly but relatively consistently for more than 200 years. Can other countries catch up to the United States, and if so, will it take 200 years? Fortunately, other countries can catch up, and amazingly quickly. Figure 27.4 shows two "growth miracles." Following World War II, Japan was one of the poorest countries in the world with a per capita GDP less than that of Mexico. From 1950 to 1970, however, Japan grew at an astonishing rate of 8.5% per year. Remember, at that rate, GDP per capita doubles in

FIGURE 27.4

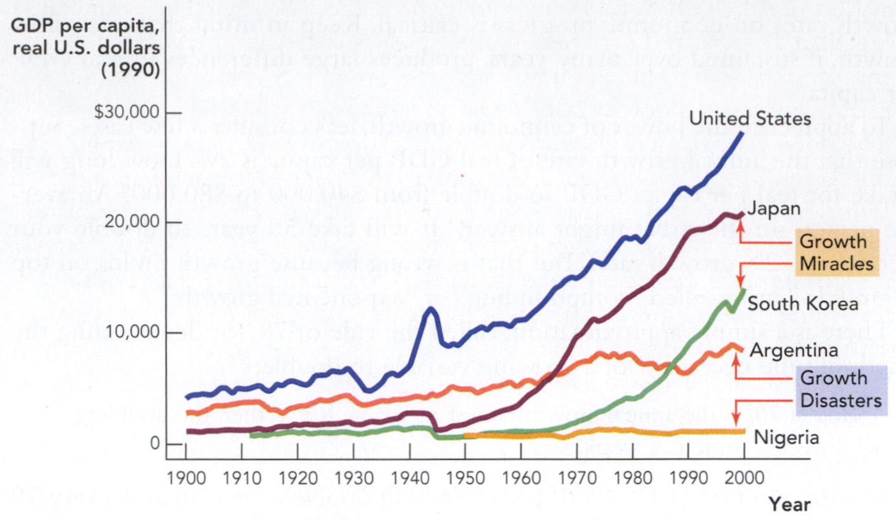

Two Growth Miracles and Two Growth Disasters

Data from: Maddison, Angus. 2007. *Contours of the World Economy: 1–2030 AD.* Oxford: Oxford University Press.

ARGENTINA 2015

Growth Miracles and Growth Disasters

approximately 8 years (70/8.5 = 8.2)! Today, Japan is one of the richest countries in the world.

In 1950, South Korea was even poorer than Japan with a GDP per capita about the same as that of Nigeria. South Korea's growth miracle began a little later than Japan's, but between 1970 and 1990, South Korea grew at a rate of 7.2% per year. Today, South Korea is a thriving, modern economy on par with many European economies.

Growth miracles are possible but so are growth disasters. Nigeria has barely grown since 1950 and was poorer in 2005 than in 1974 when high oil prices briefly bumped up its per capita GDP. More surprising is the case of Argentina. In 1900, Argentina was one of the richest countries in the world with a per capita GDP almost as large (75%) as that of the United States. By 1950, Argentina's per capita GDP had fallen to half that in the United States. In 1950, however, Argentina was still a relatively wealthy country with a per capita GDP more than twice as high as that of Japan and more than five times as high as that of South Korea. Argentina failed to grow much, however, and by 2000 Argentina's per capita GDP was less than one-third of that of the United States; Japan and South Korea are now much wealthier than Argentina.

The gap between Argentina and many other countries is continuing to grow. China (not pictured) began its own growth miracle in the late 1970s. China is still a very poor nation with a per capita GDP that in 2011 is a little more than half that of Argentina. But China is growing rapidly—remember, if China continues to grow at 7% or 8% per year, it will double its income in about 10 years. Even if Argentina grows modestly, China could pass Argentina in per capita GDP in less than 20 years.

Summarizing the Facts: Good and Bad News

The facts presented above imply both good and bad news. The bad news is that most of the world is poor and more than 1 billion people live on incomes of less than $3 per day. These people have greatly reduced prospects for health, happiness, and peace. The bad news, however, is old news. For most of human history, people were poor and there was no economic growth.

The good news is this: Despite being a relatively recent phenomenon, economic growth has quickly transformed the world. It has raised the standard of living of most people in developed nations many times above the historical norm. Even though economic growth has yet to reach all of the world, there appears to be no reason why, in principle, economic growth cannot occur everywhere. Indeed, growth miracles tell us that it doesn't take 250 years to reach the level of wealth of the United States—South Korea was as poor as Nigeria in 1950, but today has a per capita GDP not far behind Germany or the United Kingdom.

Progress, however, is not guaranteed. The growth disasters tell us that economic growth is not automatic. Some countries such as Nigeria show few signs that they have started along the growth path, while other countries such as Argentina seem to have fallen off the growth path.

Growth miracles and disasters, however, are not purely random events over which people have no control. Inquiring into the nature and causes of the wealth of nations is critical if we are to raise the standard of living and better the human condition.

Understanding the Wealth of Nations

Let's begin with Figure 27.5 on the next page, a guide to the major factors behind the wealth of nations. At the bottom of the figure is what we would like to explain, GDP per capita. As we move up the figure, we see some of the causes of the wealth of nations, beginning with the immediate or most direct causes and moving toward the ultimate or indirect causes.

The Factors of Production

The most immediate cause of the wealth of nations is this: Countries with a high GDP per capita have a lot of physical and human capital per worker and that capital is organized using the best technological knowledge to be highly productive. Physical capital, human capital, and technological knowledge are called factors of production. Let's take a look at each factor of production.

By **physical capital** (or just "capital"), economists mean tools in the broadest sense: pencils, desks, computers, hammers, shovels, tractors, cell phones, factories, roads, and bridges. More and better tools make workers more productive.

Farming is a good illustration of the role of capital. In much of the world, farmers are laborers pure and simple: They dig, seed, cut, and harvest using hard labor and a few simple tools like hoes and plows (often pulled by oxen). In the United States, farmers use a lot more capital—tractors, trucks, combines, and harvesters.

It's not just farmers who use a lot of capital. The typical worker in the United States works with more than $100,000 worth of capital. A typical worker in India works with less than one-tenth as much capital.

Physical capital is the stock of tools including machines, structures, and equipment.

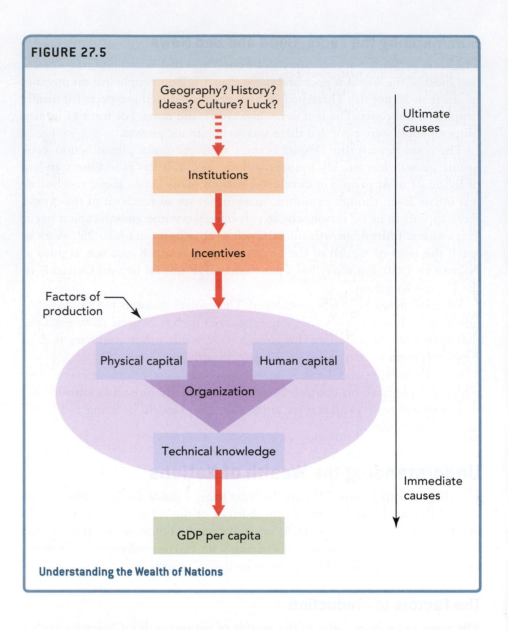

FIGURE 27.5

Geography? History? Ideas? Culture? Luck?

Institutions

Incentives

Factors of production

Physical capital

Human capital

Organization

Technical knowledge

GDP per capita

Ultimate causes

Immediate causes

Understanding the Wealth of Nations

It's also not just physical capital that makes U.S. farmers productive. A farmer in the United States riding a tractor uses a GPS receiver to triangulate his exact location using signals from a series of satellites orbiting the earth some 16,500 miles high. The tractor's location is combined with data from other satellites and land-based sensors to precisely adjust the amount of seed, fertilizer, and water to be applied to the land. The fertilizer has been carefully designed, and the seeds almost certainly have been genetically engineered.

The high-tech nature of farming in the United States draws our attention to the importance of human capital and technological knowledge. **Human capital** is *tools in the mind*, or the stuff in people's heads that makes them productive. Human capital is not something we are born with—it is produced by an investment of time and other resources in education, training, and experience. Farmers in the United States, for example, have more human capital than farmers in most of the world, and it's this human capital that enables them to take advantage of tools like GPS receivers. The same is true in the larger economy—the typical person in the United States, for example, has about 12 years

Human capital is the productive knowledge and skills that workers acquire through education, training, and experience.

of schooling, while in Pakistan the typical person has less than 5 years of schooling.

The greater quantities of physical and human capital per worker used in U.S. farming make U.S. farmers more productive. U.S. farmers produce more than three times as much corn per acre than do farmers in Pakistan, for example.

The third factor of production is technological knowledge. This factor includes, for instance, the genetics, chemistry, and physics that form the basis of the techniques used in modern agriculture. (Did you know that the clocks on GPS satellites must be adjusted to account for the effects of Einstein's theory of relativity?)

Technological knowledge and human capital are related but different. Human capital is the knowledge and skills that a farmer needs to understand and to make productive use of technology. **Technological knowledge** is knowledge about how the world works—the kind of knowledge that makes technology possible. We increase human capital with education. We increase technological knowledge with research and development. Technological knowledge is potentially boundless. We can learn more and more about how the world works even if human capital remains relatively constant.

Improved technological knowledge has made U.S. farmers more productive over time. U.S. farms today produce more than two and a half times as much output as they did in 1950 and they do so using *less* land! More physical and human capital has helped to drive this increase in output, but better technological knowledge has been the primary factor.[1]

The final factor, a factor often taken for granted, is organization. Human capital, physical capital, and technological knowledge must be organized to produce valuable goods and services. Who does this organizing and why? To answer this question, we turn to the issue of incentives and institutions.

Incentives and Institutions

South Korea has a per capita GDP nearly 20 times higher than that of North Korea. Why? In one sense, we have just given an answer: South Korea has more physical and human capital per worker than North Korea.* But this answer is incomplete and partial. The answer is incomplete because we still want to know *why* does South Korea have more physical and human capital than North Korea? The answer is partial because poor countries like North Korea not only have less physical and human capital than rich countries, they also fail to organize the capital that they do have in the most productive ways. To understand the wealth of nations more deeply, we need to take a look at some of the indirect or more ultimate causes.

The example of South and North Korea is useful because we can rule out some explanations for the huge differences in wealth between these two

Human capital consists of tools in the mind, the stuff in people's heads that makes them productive.

MY LIFE GRAPHIC/SHUTTERSTOCK

Technological knowledge is knowledge about how the world works that is used to produce goods and services.

CHECK YOURSELF

- Which country has more physical capital per worker: the United States or China? China or Nigeria?
- What are the three primary factors of production?

---

* What about technological knowledge? North Korea has access to most of the world's technological knowledge and is able, for example, to build sophisticated weapons—perhaps even a nuclear bomb; thus differences in technological knowledge explain probably only a small fraction of the differences in the wealth of nations.

Increases in technological knowledge, however, are clearly important for growth at the world level (as opposed to explaining differences in wealth across nations)—as we will discuss at greater length in the next chapter.

countries. The explanation, for example, cannot be differences in the people, culture, or geography. Before South and North Korea were divided at the end of World War II, they shared the same people and culture—in other words, the same human capital. South and North Korea also had similar levels of physical capital—natural resources were about the same in the South as in the North, and if there were any advantages in human-made physical capital, they went to the North, which was at that time more industrialized than the South. When the two regions were split, therefore, South and North Korea were in all important respects the same, almost as if the split was designed as a giant social experiment.

South and North Korea differed in their economic institutions. Broadly speaking, South Korea had capitalism, and North Korea had communism. South Korea was never a pure capitalist economy, of course, but in South Korea the organizers of human capital, physical capital, and technological knowledge are private, profit-seeking firms and entrepreneurs to a much greater extent than in North Korea. In South Korea a worker earns more money if he provides goods and services of value to consumers or if she invents new ideas for more efficient production. Those same incentives do not exist in North Korea, where workers are rewarded for being loyal to the ruling Communist Party. In short, South Korea uses markets to organize its production much more than North Korea and so is able to take advantage of all the efficiency properties of markets discussed in Chapters 3 and 4.

Over fifty years later, the results of the "experiment" splitting North and South Korea are so clear they can be seen from outer space, as seen in Figure 27.6. The differences between these two countries are especially dramatic. But wherever similar experiments have been tried, such as in East and West Germany, or Taiwan and China, the results have been similar.

We said earlier that countries with a high GDP per capita have a lot of physical and human capital that is organized using the best technological knowledge to be highly productive. But factors of production do not fall from the sky like manna from heaven. Factors of production must be produced. Similarly, factors of production do not organize themselves. Physical capital, human capital, and technology must be combined and organized purposively to be productive.

Do you remember Big Idea One and Big Idea Two from the introductory chapter? These ideas were that incentives matter and good institutions align self-interest with the social interest.

Thus, we can now deepen our understanding of the wealth of nations. Countries with a high GDP per capita have institutions

FIGURE 27.6

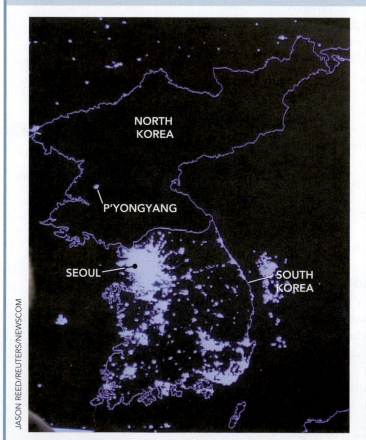

Can You Tell Which Country Has Better Institutions? South Korea and North Korea photographed at night from outer space.

JASON REED/REUTERS/NEWSCOM

that make it in people's self-interest to invest in physical capital, human capital, and technological knowledge and to efficiently organize these resources for production.

In short, the key to producing and organizing the factors of production are *institutions* that create appropriate *incentives*. Let's look at institutions and the incentives that they create in more detail.

Institutions

Institutions include laws and regulations but also customs, practices, organizations, and social mores—institutions are the "rules of the game" that shape human interaction and structure economic incentives within a society.

What kinds of institutions encourage investment and the efficient organization of the factors of production? Understanding institutions is an important area of research in economics, and there is considerable agreement that the key institutions include the following:

- Property rights
- Honest government
- Political stability
- A dependable legal system
- Competitive and open markets

Entire books have been written about each of these institutions and their roles in economic growth. Indeed, much of this book is about property rights and the benefits of open markets and rivalrous economic competition. Thus, we will give only a few examples here of how each of these institutions creates appropriate incentives, incentives that align self-interest with the social interest.

Property Rights When the Communist revolutionaries took control of China, they abolished private property in land. In the "Little Leap Forward," they put farmers to work in collectives of 100–300 families. Communal property meant that the incentives to invest in the land and to work hard were low. Imagine that a day's work can produce an extra bushel of corn. Thus, an extra day's work on a commune with 100 families earned the worker 1/100th of a bushel of corn. Would you work an extra day for a few earfuls of corn? Under communal property, working an extra day doesn't add much to a worker's take-home pay and working a day less doesn't subtract much. Thus, *under communal property, effort is divorced from payment* so there is little incentive to work—in fact, there is an incentive not to work and to **free ride** on the work of others. In the "Great Leap Forward," the incentive to free ride was made even stronger when communes were increased to 5,000 families. But if everyone free rides, the commune will starve. Communal property in agricultural land did not align a farmer's self-interest with the social interest. And, as a result of this and many similar errors on the part of the Chinese leadership, some 20–40 million Chinese farmers and workers starved during this period.

The Great Leap Forward was actually a great leap backward—agricultural land was less productive in 1978 than it had been in 1949 when the Communists took over. In 1978, however, farmers in the village of Xiaogang held a secret meeting. The farmers agreed to divide the communal land and assign it to individuals—each farmer had to produce a quota for the government but anything

Institutions are the "rules of the game" that structure economic incentives.

The Importance of Institutions

A **free rider** is someone who consumes a resource without working or contributing to the resource's upkeep.

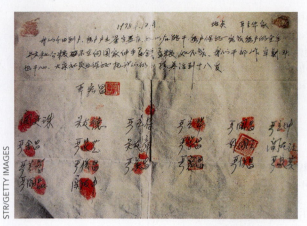

STR/GETTY IMAGES

Farmers from 18 households in Xiaogang village signed a secret life-and-death agreement with their thumbprints.

he or she produced in excess of the quota that farmer would keep. The agreement violated government policy and, as a result, the farmers also pledged that if any of them was sent to jail, the others would raise his or her children. The remarkable secret agreement of the Xiaogang farmers is shown at left.

The change from collective property rights to something closer to private property rights had an immediate effect: Investment, work effort, and productivity increased. "You can't be lazy when you work for your family and yourself," said one of the farmers.

Word of the secret agreement leaked out and local bureaucrats cut off Xiaogang from fertilizer, seeds, and pesticides. But amazingly, before Xiaogang could be stopped, farmers in other villages also began to abandon collective property. In Beijing, Mao Zedong was dead and a new set of rulers, seeing the productivity improvements, decided to let the experiment proceed.

In the five short years between 1978 and 1983, when China's central government endorsed individual farming, food production increased by nearly 50% and 170 million people were lifted above the World Bank's lowest poverty line. Simply put, the increase in agricultural productivity brought about by the switch to individual farming was the greatest antipoverty program in the history of the world. By 1984, the collective farms were gone and soon after that China's leader Deng Xiaoping announced a new government policy: "It is glorious to be rich."

Property rights in land greatly increased China's agricultural productivity. With fewer workers producing more food, more workers were available to produce other goods. To take advantage of its millions of workers, China opened up to foreign investment, making the label "Made in China" common throughout the world. With their secret pact, the farmers of Xiaogang had begun a second and more successful Chinese revolution.[2]

Property rights are important institutions for encouraging investment in physical and human capital, not just in agriculture but throughout the economy. It can take decades, for example, for an investment in a new apartment building or a factory to pay off. As we will discuss further in the chapter on savings, investment, and the financial system, savings are necessary to generate investment and thus growth. But why do people save and invest? Savers won't save and investors won't invest if they don't expect that their property will be secure and they will receive a return for their savings and investment. Property rights are also important for encouraging technological innovation. For instance, investments in new pharmaceuticals take decades to pay off and they are risky—years of research and development sometimes have to be abandoned when the guinea pigs start to die unexpectedly. Just like farmers, investors and workers throughout the economy need to know that they will reap what they sow.

Top 10 Least Corrupt Countries	Top Ten Most Corrupt Countries
Denmark	Somalia
New Zealand	South Sudan
Finland	Korea (North)
Sweden	Syria
Switzerland	Yemen
Norway	Sudan
Singapore	Libya
Netherlands	Afghanistan
Canada	Guinea-Bissau
Germany	Venezuela

Data from: Transparency International, 2016

Data from: Transparency International, 2016

Honest Government China under its former Communist rulers was extreme in abolishing most forms of private property. In many other countries, private property rights exist on paper—but only on paper. In a country like Venezuela, for example, an individual might have a legal right to land or a factory, but everyone knows that the government can take these goods at any moment. Venezuela lacks the rule of law.

More generally, corruption is like a heavy tax that bleeds resources away from productive entrepreneurs. Resources "invested" in bribing politicians and bureaucrats cannot be invested in machinery and equipment, thus reducing productivity. Corrupt government officials will also harass entrepreneurs, creating excessive rules and regulations that force entrepreneurs to pay them to stop making trouble.

Not all taxes are bad, of course. A tax that funds investment in roads, universities, or law and order can increase the productivity of private investments. Corruption, therefore, is a doubly bad tax because corruption makes it less profitable to be an entrepreneur at the same time as it makes it more profitable to be a corrupt politician or bureaucrat. At some point, corruption can feed on itself, creating a poverty trap: Few people want to be entrepreneurs because they know that their wealth will be stolen and thus there is no wealth to steal.

Figure 27.7 graphs corruption on the horizontal axis. The most corrupt countries like Somalia, Liberia, and North Korea are on the right, scoring about 2 on a 5-point scale running from −2.5 (least corrupt) to 2.5 (most corrupt). The least corrupt countries like Singapore, Iceland, the United States, and Norway are on the left. Real GDP per capita is on the vertical axis. Countries that are more corrupt have much lower per capita GDP.

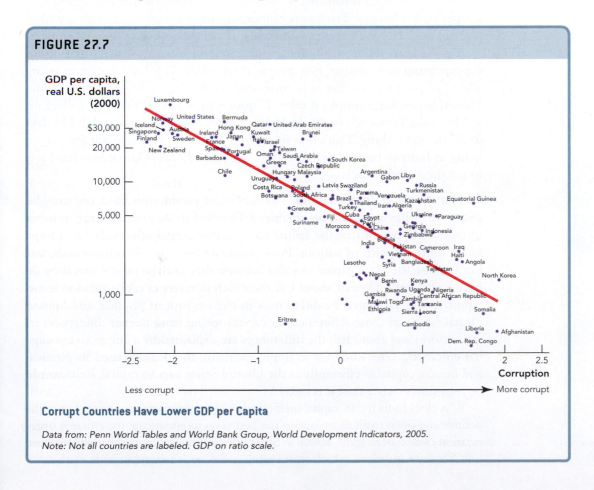

FIGURE 27.7

Corrupt Countries Have Lower GDP per Capita

Data from: Penn World Tables and World Bank Group, World Development Indicators, 2005.
Note: Not all countries are labeled. GDP on ratio scale.

A Good Place to Invest? Bullet casings litter a street in the besieged city of Misrata, Libya, Saturday, April 23, 2011.

Political Stability Investors have more to fear than government expropriation—sometimes the threat of anarchy can be even worse. Liberia, for example, has had little but conflict for the past 40 years. Prior to the election in 2006 of President Ellen Johnson-Sirleaf, the first elected female head of state in Africa, it had been 35 years since a Liberian president assumed office by means other than bloodshed. Both the previous two national leaders (Charles Taylor and Samuel Doe) consistently used the force of government to eradicate their opposition. Who wants to invest in the future when civil war threatens to wash away all plans?

More generally, in many nations, civil war, military dictatorship, and anarchy have destroyed the institutions necessary for economic growth.

A Dependable Legal System The problem of poorly protected property rights is not always a problem of too much government—sometimes property rights are poorly protected because there is too little government. The legal system in many countries, for example, is of such low quality that no one knows for certain who owns what. In India, residents who purchase land often have to do so two or three times (from different parties), as there exists no reliable record of true ownership. A lawsuit, if you even bother to bring one, can take 20 years or more to resolve. In a major urban area, it's very difficult to build something as simple as a supermarket because developers cannot acquire good title to a modestly sized piece of land. No one wants to build when they cannot protect their investment.

A good legal system facilitates contracts and protects private parties from expropriating one another. Few people think of the U.S. legal system as a paradigm of productivity, but it is compared to the Indian legal system. In the United States, for example, it takes 17 procedures and 300 days to collect on a debt (say, a bounced check). In India, it takes 56 procedures and 1,420 days to do the same thing. That's one reason why it is relatively difficult for people living in India to borrow money in the first place: Lenders know how hard it is to get their money back.

Competitive and Open Markets The factors of production must not only be produced—they must also be organized. Detailed studies from a large number of countries suggest that the failure to organize capital efficiently has a huge effect on the wealth of nations. Poor countries are poor, in other words, not just because they lack capital but also because they use the capital that they do have inefficiently. Overall, about half the differences in per capita income across countries are explained by differences in the amount of physical and human capital (some of those differences in capital spring from deeper differences in institutions) and about half the differences are explained by a failure to use capital efficiently. One study, for example, estimates that if India used its physical and human capital as efficiently as the United States uses its capital, India would be four times richer than it is today.[3]

Why does India use its capital inefficiently? The reasons are numerous, but competitive and open markets are one of the best ways to encourage the efficient organization of resources. India, as well as other poor countries, has many inefficient and unnecessary regulations, which create monopolies or otherwise impede markets.

For instance, Indian shirts are usually made by hand in small shops of three or four tailors who design, measure, sew, and sell, all on the same premises. It sounds elegant but this is not London's Savile Row, where the finest tailors in the world create custom suits for the rich and powerful. India's shirts would be cheaper and of higher quality if they were mass-manufactured in factories—the way shirts for Americans are produced. Why doesn't this happen in India? Shirts in India are produced inefficiently because, until recently, large-scale production was illegal.

In an effort to protect small firms, India prohibited investment in shirt factories from exceeding about $200,000. This restriction meant that Indian shirt manufacturers could not take advantage of **economies of scale,** the decrease in the average cost of production that often occurs as the total quantity of production increases. India has been reforming its economy, which is one reason why economic growth in India has increased in recent years (as we discussed in the previous chapter). India recently lifted the ban on large garment factories, for example, but many, many regulations remain that reduce the productivity of the Indian economy.[4]

> **Economies of scale** are the advantages of large-scale production that reduce average cost as quantity increases.

Poor countries also suffer from expensive red tape. Economists at the World Bank have estimated the time and cost to do simple tasks such as starting a business or enforcing a contract in a court of law. In the United States, for example, it takes about 4 days to start a business and the total costs of the procedures are minor, about 1% of the average income per capita. In India, starting a business takes 26 days and 13.8% of income per capita. In Haiti, it takes 97 days and 219% of income per capita (data from World Bank, *Doing Business*). Thus, even before a business is begun, an Indian or Haitian entrepreneur must invest extensively in dealing with bureaucracies—that same physical and human capital is not being used to produce goods and services.

Markets can also be made more competitive and open with free trade. Most countries, for example, aren't large enough to support more than a handful of auto manufacturers so free trade is necessary to keep auto manufacturers and other large firms competitive. Perhaps even more importantly, countries that are open to trade are also open to new ideas. Walmart made retailing more efficient in the United States and then it brought these efficiencies to other countries when it expanded internationally. Countries where Walmart was forbidden or discouraged from expanding gained these efficiencies more slowly, if at all. In fact, multinationals like Walmart are the best managed of all firms—they get the most output from the same quantity and quality of inputs—and multinationals are one of the best ways of spreading new and better ideas around the world.[5]

The Ultimate Causes of the Wealth of Nations

When China changed its institutions from collective farming to individual farming, agricultural productivity increased dramatically and China began to grow. The example of China is enormously encouraging because it suggests that growth miracles could become common if more countries changed their institutions. But take a look again at Figure 27.5. Institutions have a large effect on increasing and organizing the factors of production, and institutions thus have a large effect on economic growth. But where do institutions come from? Are they products of geography? History? Ideas? Culture? Luck? Try "all of the above" and then some.

Consider geography, which we might also think of as a country's "natural resources." Simple natural resources like oil and diamonds are usually good to have but in rich, developed countries, physical and human capital are typically much more important. But natural resources more broadly conceived—climate, topography, and the prevalence of parasites, to give just a few examples—may help explain

FIGURE 27.8

GDP per capita, 1995 (PPP)

Landlocked Nations Have Lower GDP per Capita

Data from: Author calculations based on data from Gallup, Sachs, and Mellinger (1999).

why a country is able to accumulate physical and human capital. We said earlier that free trade opens a country up to new ideas and innovation. But free trade is not just a matter of policy or choice—it also depends on natural conditions. It's much cheaper to move goods and people over water than over land, so countries that have easy access to water are naturally more open to trade than countries that are landlocked. In fact, as Figure 27.8 reveals, landlocked countries have lower per capita GDP than countries that have access to a coast. It's not that being landlocked dooms a country to poverty, but countries that are landlocked face the equivalent—from their setting—of permanently high tariff barriers. That can make it more difficult to generate growth, especially in the age before modern communications.

You can also see the importance of history, ideas, geography, and luck in the growth of the United States. The U.S. constitution was written at a time when the ideas of John Locke and Adam Smith were popular and it inherited a tendency toward a market economy and democratic institutions from its colonizer, Great Britain. An open frontier meant cheap land and plenty of freedom to try new ideas and ways of living, perhaps influencing America's entrepreneurial culture even into modern times. And we are very lucky that George Washington had the virtue to stop at two presidential terms, rather than trying to become the next king.

An even more important example of a growth miracle comes from the Industrial Revolution, a period of sustained European technological advances; it is sometimes identified with 1770–1830, but that it has deeper roots reaching back to the seventeenth century or earlier. The Industrial Revolution brought us large-scale factories, mass production, the steam engine, the railroad, and the beginnings of a consumer society, among many other benefits. It is the first time that human living standards climbed noticeably above subsistence and stayed there for a long period. We are all still enjoying the benefits of an ongoing industrial revolution in the world's wealthy economies.

The Industrial Revolution, centered in Great Britain, required a combination of multiple distinct advantages. Britain's status as an island and the strong English Navy protected the country against invaders and made property rights more secure. Labor markets had been relatively free for centuries and the ethic of the time encouraged commerce, entrepreneurship, and the accumulation of wealth. The growth of the power of Parliament checked royal tyranny and encouraged economic policies that allowed wealth to spread more widely. Slow increases in agricultural productivity kept living standards above subsistence and enabled the rise of a professional class. Perhaps most important, Britain developed a strong culture of science and engineering and brought the scientific method to bear on economic production, whether it was designing a better spinning jenny or using coal to power a factory more effectively.

From the beginning, positive feedback effects of the Industrial Revolution were strong. More wealth meant more people could devote their lives to science, invention, and turning new ideas into practical commercial developments. That in turn led to new wealth and then again to more applied science. Eventually the Industrial Revolution gave us electricity, the automobile, the flush toilet, and most of the other inventions that define the conveniences of modern life. To sum this all up, the effects of the Industrial Revolution owe much to good institutions for business, science, and governance.

interactive activity

Geography and Economic Growth

No one understands for certain all the influences that go into creating a nation's institutions, which means that changing institutions isn't easy. When it comes to institutions, we know where we want to go but we don't always know how to get there. Understanding institutions, where they come from, and how they can be changed is thus a key research question in economics.

Takeaway

It's hard to overstate the importance of economic growth. Once, everyone was poor. Today, GDP per capita is more than 50 times higher in the richest countries than in the poorest. Economic growth has raised billions of people out of near-starvation poverty, but billions more remain in dire poverty with shocking consequences for their quality of life.

Fortunately, poor countries can catch up to rich countries and in a surprisingly short period. Growth "miracles" have brought Japan and South Korea up to European levels of wealth within the lifespan of a single generation. Since the agricultural reforms beginning in 1978, poverty in China has been reduced to an unprecedented degree and China continues to grow rapidly.

What makes a country rich? The most proximate cause is that countries with a high GDP per capita have lots of physical and human capital per worker and that capital is organized using the best technological knowledge to be highly productive.

How do countries get a lot of physical and human capital and how do they organize it using the best technological knowledge? Countries with a high GDP per capita have institutions that encourage investment in physical capital, human capital, technological innovation, and the efficient organization of resources. Among the most powerful institutions for increasing economic growth are property rights, honest government, political stability, a dependable legal system, and competitive and open markets.

The Magic Washing Machine

TYLER OLSON/ SHUTTERSTOCK

CHECK YOURSELF

■ List five institutions that promote economic growth.

■ When the Pilgrims landed at Plymouth Rock, they established a system of collective farming in which all corn production was shared. Given your understanding of incentives, what do you think happened to the Pilgrims?

CHAPTER REVIEW

interactive activity Go online to practice with more examples of these types of problems, including live links to videos, data sources, and feedback.

Problems in green relate to MRU videos. See the MRU table at the end of the exercises.

Problems in blue are Office Hours videos.

KEY CONCEPTS

economic growth, p. 533

physical capital, p. 535

human capital, p. 536

technological knowledge, p. 537

institutions, p. 539

free rider, p. 539

economies of scale, p. 543

FACTS AND TOOLS

1. Look at Figure 27.1. About how many babies die before the age of 5 in Nigeria versus Argentina? What is the difference in GDP per person in those two countries?

2. Look at Figure 27.2. About what percentage of the world's population lives in countries richer than Italy? What percentage lives in countries poorer than India?

3. The world's average (mean) GDP per capita is $14,517. There are roughly 7 billion people in the world.

a. What is the world's total GDP?

b. About 20% of the world's population produces 50% of the world's total GDP. (Notice the use of "produces," not "consumes." In popular discussion, you are more likely to hear about the people at the top "consuming" more than their share, not "producing" more than their share. But remember what the last letter of GDP stands for!) How much GDP does the top 20% produce?

c. What is the average GDP per capita of the most productive 20% of the world's population? (*Hint:* 20% of 7 billion people equals how many people?)

4. Now let's look at the productivity of the world's least productive 80%.

a. How much GDP do they produce? (*Hint:* You've already calculated this number in the previous question.)

b. What is the average GDP per capita of the least productive 80% of the world's population?

c. Now, the payoff: How productive is the average person in the top 20% compared with the average person in the bottom 80% of the planet? Answer this by dividing your answer to question 3c by your answer to question 4b. This chapter and the next are devoted to explaining why this ratio is so large.

5. According to Fact Two—Everyone Used to Be Poor—what would your answer to question 4c have been if you calculated it 2,000 years ago?

6. What are the factors of production? Name them and briefly describe them in plain English.

7. Using data from the Penn World Tables, calculate the annual growth rate of real GDP per person for China for the years in the table. The Penn World Tables, available free online, are a reliable source of international economic data, and they are very popular among economists.

Year	Real GDP per Capita (in 1996 U.S. dollars)	Annual Growth Rate
2000	4,001	
2001	4,389	_____
2002	4,847	_____
2003	5,321	_____
2004	5,771	_____

8. Practice with the rule of 70: If you inherit $10,000 this year and you invest your money so that it grows 7% per year, how many years will it take for your investment to be worth $20,000? $40,000? $160,000? (*Note:* Investments in stocks have grown at an average inflation-adjusted rate of 7% per year since the U.S. Civil War. We'll practice this some more in the next chapter.)

Value today: $10,000. Growth rate: 7%

Number of years until money doubles: _____

Number of years until money quadruples: _____

Number of years until your inheritance is 16X larger: _____

9. More practice with the rule of 70: Suppose that, instead, you put your money into a savings account that grows at an inflation-adjusted return of 2% per year. How many years will it take to be worth $20,000? $40,000? $160,000? (*Note:* Bank deposits have grown at roughly this rate over the last 50 years in the United States.)

Value today: $10,000. Growth rate: 2%

Number of years until money doubles: _____

Number of years until money quadruples: _____

Number of years until your inheritance is 16X larger: _____

10. India and China come up a lot in this chapter. You might wonder why so much time is spent talking about just two countries out of more than 180 on the planet. But what fraction of humans live in India and China together?

11. Let's convert Figure 27.5 into words.

Institutions create _____, which in turn affect the amount of _____, _____, and _____ in a country, which, combined with the right kind of _____, generates a level of _____ per person.

12. In the *CIA World Factbook*, GDP per capita in the United States in 2010 was approximately $47,400. The formula for growth for any given year, y_t, is $y_t = y_0(1 + g_y)$, where y_0 is the value of GDP in the beginning year, y_t is the value of GDP for the specific year in question, and t is the number of years after y_0. If y_0 is GDP per capita in 2010 and the economy continues to grow at approximately 3% as it did in 2010, what will be the value of GDP per capita in 10 years?

Ask FRED

interactive activity

13. Using the FRED economic database (https://fred.stlouisfed.org/), let's compare real GDP per capita in Argentina and Korea. First find "Constant GDP per capita for Argentina." Click Edit Graph and then click Add Line and add Constant GDP per capita for the Republic of Korea. Both series should be in U.S. dollars.

   a. What was Argentina's real GDP per capita in 1974? Thirty years later, in 2004?

   b. In what year did South Korea and Argentina have approximately the same real GDP per capita?

   c. What is the ratio of real GDP per capita in South Korea to Argentina today?

14. Using the FRED economic database (https://fred.stlouisfed.org/), let's compare the GDP of the state of California with that of some countries, in this case, France and Canada. Because France's GDP is in euros and Canada's is in Canadian dollars, we will need to convert currencies. In addition, we would like to compare GDP over a similar basket of goods. Comparisons like this are called purchasing power parity (PPP) comparisons. After you have found real GDP for California, click Edit Graph, then click Add Line and find real GDP for France, looking for a series like "Expenditure-side Real GDP at Chained Purchasing Power Parities for France." Now click Add Line again and find a similar series for Canada.

   a. How do California, France, and Canada compare? What does this suggest about the U.S. economy and its role in the world economy?

   b. Using Google, find the population of each of these regions and then do a back-of-the-envelope calculation of real GDP per capita in, say, 2014 in each entity.

THINKING AND PROBLEM SOLVING

15. The average person in Argentina today is about as rich (in inflation-adjusted terms) as his or her parents. How can this be called a "growth disaster"?

16. Before the rise of affordable automobiles and subways, many people used trolleys—small trains on rails that ran along ordinary streets—to get around in urban areas. On trolleys, there is a literal "free rider problem": Since the trains were right next to sidewalks, and since trolleys were wide open and never had doors, people could hop on and off very easily. How much money will a trolley lose if it is easy to ride for free? If "free riders" are a big problem, what will happen to the supply of trolley rides? What are a few things the trolley industry could do to solve the problem of free riders?

TATAN SYUFLANA/AP PHOTO

Free riders in Jakarta, Indonesia

17. During the Great Leap Forward, millions of Chinese starved to death because not enough food was produced by farmers. Why didn't farmers grow food? In particular, was it because there wasn't enough human capital or physical capital?

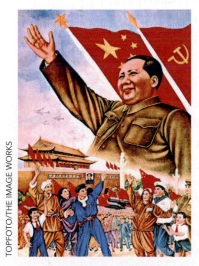

TOPFOTO/THE IMAGE WORKS

The slogan of the Great Leap Forward was "Long live the People's Commune!" Unfortunately, this patriotic appeal didn't work as well as good economic incentives, and millions lost their lives.
(*Information from:* Wikipedia, "Great Leap Forward.")

18. Laws that encourage businesses to stay small are often very popular. The laws governing Indian shirt tailors discussed in this chapter are just one example. What are some *noneconomic* (e.g., social,

moral, ethical) reasons why voters might want businesses to stay small? What are some *economic* reasons they might want businesses to grow large?

19. Economists use the term "human capital" to refer to education and job skills. How is education like a piece of capital?

20. Many people say that natural resources like oil and minerals are the way to prosperity. Indeed, in an old cartoon by Matt Groening, creator of *The Simpsons*, a professor taught his students, "The nation that controls magnesium controls the universe!" But natural resources have been left out of this chapter completely. Is this a big mistake? (*Information from:* Sala-i-Martin, X., G. Doppelhofer, and R. Miller. 2004. Determinants of long-term economic growth: A Bayesian averaging of classical estimates (BACE). *The American Economic Review* **94**(4) (September): 813–835.)

    a. Here are the 10 countries in the world that have the highest amounts of hydrocarbons (oil, natural gas, etc.) per person, in rank order:

        1. Kuwait
        2. United Arab Emirates (UAE)
        3. Saudi Arabia
        4. Iraq
        5. Norway
        6. Venezuela
        7. Oman
        8. Iran
        9. Trinidad and Tobago
        10. Gabon

    Use the *CIA World Factbook*, a convenient online source of information, to see if most of these countries are prosperous. How many of these 10 countries have a GDP per person that is at least half of the U.S. level? How many are less than 10% of the U.S. level? Are any actually higher than the U.S. level?

    b. Now, let's look at the reverse: Let's see if the 10 richest countries in GDP per capita have a lot of hydrocarbon wealth:

        1. Luxembourg
        2. United States
        3. Singapore
        4. Hong Kong
        5. Norway
        6. Australia
        7. Sweden
        8. Canada
        9. Denmark
        10. Japan

    The one country on both lists also makes another list in this chapter. Which one is it?

21. Economists often refer to the "natural resource curse," by which they mean that large amounts of natural resources tend to create bad politics because as long as the oil keeps flowing or the diamonds remain plentiful, political leaders don't need to care much about what goes on in the rest of the country.

    a. Which one of the three factors of production do you think matters most to a leader of a resource-rich country? Why? (*Note:* Does this help explain what you see happening in many resource-rich countries?)

    b. Which one of the five key institutions do you think matters most to a leader of a resource-rich republic? Why? (*Note:* Does this help explain what you see happening in many resource-rich countries?)

22. In the Soviet Union, especially in the early decades under Lenin and Stalin, the official doctrine was Communism, and the use of incentives was considered a form of treason. One important exception was the military equipment sector, where bonuses were common for engineers who designed and manufactured jets, nuclear missiles, tanks, and rifles. Why was this an exception?

23. Free rider problems are everywhere. For example, some restaurants let each food server keep his or her own tips. Other restaurants require all of the food servers to put their tips into a tip pool, which then gets divided up equally among all of the servers. It's easy to adjust the tip pool so that people who work more hours or serve more tables get their "fair share," so that's not the issue we're concerned about here. Instead, let's think about how the tip pool changes the server's incentive to be nice to the customer.

    a. To keep it simple, let's assume that a server can be "nice" and earn $100 in tips per shift, or be "mean" and earn $40 in tips per shift. If an individual server goes from being mean to being nice, how much more will he or she earn in a non-tip-pooling world? (Yes, this is an easy question.)

b. Now let's look at incentives in a tip pool. If all the servers are mean, how much will the average server earn? If all the servers are nice, how much will the average server earn? What's the change in tips per server if *all* of them switch from being mean to being nice?

c. But in the real world, of course, each server makes his or her own decision to be mean or nice. Suppose that some servers are being nice and others are being mean, and you're trying to decide whether to be nice or mean. What's the payoff *to you* if you switch your behavior? Does your answer depend on how many other servers are being nice?

d. So when are you most likely to be nice: when you're in a tip pool or when you keep your own tips? If the restaurant cares a lot about keeping its customers happy, which policy will it follow?

24. If "everyone used to be poor," then how could some ancient civilizations afford to create massive buildings like the pyramids of Egypt and the Buddhist statues of Afghanistan (sadly, many of the latter were destroyed by the Taliban in the 1990s)?

25. In England during the Wars of the Roses (late 1400s), two parties fought for the crown. Contrast the prospects for economic growth during this period and after this period when Henry VII became the unquestioned head of the country.

CHALLENGES

26. One way to learn about what makes some countries richer is to run statistical tests to see which factors are good at predicting a nation's level of productivity. Sometimes it turns out that a relationship is just a coincidence (like the fact that people in rich countries eat more ice cream), but other statistical tests really can tell you about the ultimate causes of productivity. A statistical test can't tell you everything, but it might help point you in the right direction. In courses on econometrics and statistics, you can learn about how to run sensible tests.

Let's look at one well-known set of tests, to see if what you learned in this chapter matches the statistical evidence. Here are 17 variables that turned out to be very strong predictors of a nation's long-run economic performance in literally millions of statistical tests (*Information from:* Sala-i-Martin, X., G. Doppelhofer, and R. Miller. 2004. Determinants of long-term economic growth: A Bayesian averaging of classical estimates (BACE). *The American Economic Review,* **94**(4) (September): 813–835.) They are in rank order, and a "+" means more of that value was good for long-run productivity:

- Whether a country is in East Asia (+)
- Level of K–6 schooling (+)
- Price of capital goods (−)
- Fraction of land close to the coast (+)
- Fraction of population close to the coast (−)
- Malaria prevalence (−)
- Life expectancy (+)
- Fraction of population Confucian (+)
- Whether a country is in Africa (−)
- Whether a country is in Latin America (−)
- Fraction of GDP in mining industries (+)
- Whether a country was a Spanish colony (−)
- Years open to relatively free trade (+)
- Fraction of population Muslim (+)
- Fraction of population Buddhist (+)
- Number of languages widely spoken (−)
- Fraction of GDP spent on government purchases (−)

a. Which of these factors sound like the "three factors of production"? Which ones do they sound like?

b. Which of these factors sound like the "five key institutions"? Which ones do they sound like?

c. Which of these factors sound like geography?

d. The Western United States was a Spanish colony until 1849. On average, former Spanish colonies have had poor economic performance. Does the Western United States fit that pattern? Why or why not?

27. What do *you* think creates the good institutions that exist in rich countries? Why don't these institutions—property rights, markets, a society where you can usually trust strangers—exist everywhere on the planet?

28. Why do you think expensive red tape is difficult to get rid of in many poor countries? Yes, this is a miniature version of the previous question.

29. Communists believed that their system would be much more efficient than capitalism: They thought that competition between companies was wasteful. Why build three separate headquarters for carmakers (General Motors, Chrysler, and Ford), when you can just build one? Why have three advertising budgets? Why pay for three CEOs? Why not put all the factories together, so that the same engineers can fix problems at all of the plants? Doesn't one large firm maximize economies of scale? These are all good questions. So why do you think Communism turned out to be such an economic disaster, when it sounded like it would be so efficient?

30. The chapter lists five key institutions of economic growth. But isn't there really just one: good government? Support your argument with facts from this chapter.

31. Figure 27.5 and its discussion in the text identify some of the ultimate causes of the Wealth of Nations as *Institutions of Economic Growth*. One of these is honest government. Go to Gapminder at http://www.gapminder.org to explore this relationship. Once there, click on the tab for "Gapminder World" and wait a moment for the first graph to load. Once it has loaded, click on the axes and explore the number of variables available for choosing. For this problem, click on the vertical axis, look under "Society," and choose the "Corruption Perceptions Index (CPI)." You should still have GDP per capita on the horizontal axis.

   a. After noting that higher values in the CPI represent lower levels of corruption, describe what these data are telling you.

   b. Next to the upper-right-hand corner of the diagram is a "Color" box. Click on it and set it to "Geographic regions." Now hover over a color and explore where these regions are in the world. Where are the richest countries? Where are the poorest?

   c. Can you find some very corrupt countries that are also quite rich? Name some of these countries and determine what they have in common.

   d. Does this evidence generally support the claim that an honest government contributes to the wealth of a nation? Why or why not?

32. Figure 27.5 and its discussion in the text identify one of the immediate causes of the wealth of nations as *human capital*. Visit Gapminder World again at Gapminder http://www.gapminder.org and select "Education" and "Literacy Rate, Adult Total" for the vertical axis while leaving GDP per capita on the horizontal axis. (See the previous problem for more detailed instructions.)

   a. What does this display of data convey to you about the value of education?

   b. Now change the vertical axis to the "Mean Number of Years in School" for men older than age 25 and then create a second graph for women older than age 25. How do your conclusions change? Is education still as valuable?

   c. Finally, select eighth-grade math achievement for the vertical axis and determine if this measure of education is also positively associated with GDP per capita.

   d. How do these measures of education work to support or refute the relationship between education levels and GDP per capita?

   e. Now try an additional educational measure using two graphs. Under "Schooling Cost," explore "Expenditures per Student, Primary" and "Expenditures per Student, Secondary." What do you find in these cases and how can you explain these differences?

33. Suppose two countries start with the same real GDP per capita, but country A is growing at 2% per year and Country B is growing at 3% per year. After 140 years, Country B's GDP per capita will be—larger than Country A's.

interactive activity

WORK IT OUT

For interactive, step-by-step help in solving this problem, go online.

Let's figure out how long it will take for the average Indian to be as wealthy as the average Western European is today. Note that all numbers are *adjusted for inflation*, so we're measuring output in "piles of stuff," not "piles of money." India's GDP per capita is $5,000, and (somewhat optimistically) let's say that real output per person there grows at 5% per year. Using the rule of 70, how many years will it take for India to reach Italy's current level of GDP per capita, about $36,000 per year?

MARGINAL REVOLUTION UNIVERSITY VIDEOS

Basic Facts of Wealth
mruniversity.com/wealth-nations
Problems: **3, 4**

Growth Rates Are Crucial
mruniversity.com/growth-rates
Problems: **5, 7, 12**

An Orgy of Innovation
mruniversity.com/innovation
Problems: **25**

Growth Miracles and Growth Disasters
mruniversity.com/growth-miracle-disaster
Problems: **15**

The Importance of Institutions
mruniversity.com/institutions
Problems: **11, 16–18, 21, 23, 31–32**

Geography and Economic Growth
mruniversity.com/geography-growth
Problems: **20, 27**

Puzzle of Growth: Rich Countries and Poor Countries
mruniversity.com/puzzle-of-growth
Problems: **6, 11, 17, 19, 24, 28–30**

The Hockey Stick of Human Prosperity
mruniversity.com/hockey-stick
Problems: **5**

The Rule of 70
mruniversity.com/rule-70
Problems: **8, 9**

Office Hours: The Rule of 70
mruniversity.com/rule-of-70
Problems: **33**

CHAPTER 27 APPENDIX

The Magic of Compound Growth Using a Spreadsheet

The rule of 70 gives us a quick way to compute doubling times given a growth rate. We can also use a Microsoft Excel spreadsheet to easily answer more difficult questions. We know, for example, that if GDP per capita starts at $40,000 and if the growth rate is 2%, then GDP per capita after 1 year will be $40,800 and after just 35 years it will double to $79,996. We can show this using a simple spreadsheet as in Figure A27.1.

Once we understand the principles, however, we don't need to write each year on a separate line. Instead, we can simplify by using a little bit of mathematical notation.

If our Starting value for GDP per capita is $40,000 and the growth rate is r%, for example, 2%, and we grow for one year, then our Ending value will be $40,000 × (1 + r/100). If we grow for two years, our Ending value will be $40,000 × (1 + r/100) × (1 + r/100), which is the same thing as $40,000 × (1 + r/100)^2. More generally, if the growth rate is r% and we grow for n years, then

$$\text{Ending value} = \text{Starting value} \times \left(1 + \frac{r}{100}\right)^n \quad \text{(A1)}$$

We can use this formula to simplify our spreadsheet, as in Figure A27.2.

Notice that we put the starting level of GDP per capita, or whatever quantity we are interested in (this could also be the amount of money in a bank account, for example), in cell A6, the growth rate is in cell B1, the number of years we want to grow is in cell B2, and thus the formula in cell B6, "=A6×(1+B1/100)^B2", is exactly as in equation A1.

FIGURE A27.1

C2		▼	f_x =B2*0.02	
	A	**B**	**C**	**D**
	Year	Beginning GDP (per capita)	Increase in GDP	GDP at end of Year
1				
2	1	$40,000	$800	$40,800
3	2	$40,800	$816	$41,616
4	3	$41,616	$832	$42,448
36	35	$78,427	$1,569	$79,996
37				

Compound Growth in a Spreadsheet: The Long Method

FIGURE A27.2

B6	▼	fx =A6*(1+B1/100)^B2	
	A	**B**	**C**
1	Growth Rate	2	
2	Years	1	
3			
4			
5	Starting Value	Ending Value	
6	40000	40800	
7			

Compound Growth in a Spreadsheet: The Shortcut

By adjusting the Starting value, the Growth rate, and the Number of years, we can find out how much any amount will grow to given any interest rate over any number of years.

We can also use Excel's Goal Seek ability to work backward to find, say, the number of years it will take to reach a certain level of GDP per capita when growth is $r\%$ per year. Suppose, for example, that GDP per capita is $46,000 and that growth is 2% per year. How long will it take to reach a GDP per capita of $1,000,000? Here's how you can easily find numbers like this. Go to the Tools menu and click on Goal Seek (in Excel 2007, go to the Data menu and under the submenu What–If Analysis, click on Goal Seek). A box will pop up asking you for three inputs: Set cell _____, To value _____, By changing cell _____. In our case, we want Set cell **B6**, the Ending Value; To value **1,000,000**; By changing cell **B2**; and the number of years. Figure A27.3 shows you what you should see and input. Notice that we also changed the Starting value to $46,000.

FIGURE A27.3

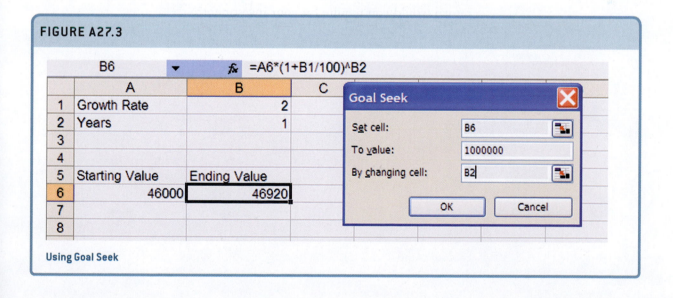

Using Goal Seek

FIGURE A27.4

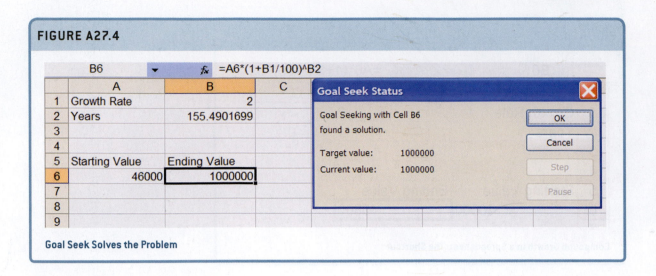

Goal Seek Solves the Problem

Clicking OK produces what you see in Figure A27.4.

Goal Seek has solved the problem! If we start at a value of GDP per capita of $46,000 and we grow at 2% a year, then in 155.49 years we will reach a value of GDP per capita of $1,000,000.

By using Goal Seek and varying the inputs, you can find the answer to all kinds of questions. Can you find, for example, how high the growth rate would have to be to reach a level of GDP per capita of $1,000,000 in, say, 50 years?

Chapter 27 Appendix Questions

- If a country starts off as rich as the United States, with a GDP per capita of $46,000, and if GDP per capita grows 3% per year, then how many years will it take before GDP per capita is $1,000,000 per year?

- If a country with a GDP per capita of $4,000 at its start grows at 8% per year, then how many years will it take before GDP per capita is $46,000?

- If you wanted to double $1,000 in 10 years' time, what average rate of return would you require on your investment?

28

Growth, Capital Accumulation, and the Economics of Ideas: Catching Up vs. the Cutting Edge

I n 2010, GDP per capita in China grew by nearly 10%. The same year, GDP per capita in the United States grew by just 2.2%. In its entire history, the U.S. economy has never grown as fast as the Chinese economy grew in 2010. Nor was this an unusual year—the Chinese economy has been growing at extraordinarily high rates for three decades. If these rates continue, China will be richer than the United States in less than 25 years. How can this make sense? Is there something wrong with the U.S. economy? Do the Chinese have a magical potion for economic growth?

Remember, in the last chapter we explained that among the key institutions promoting economic growth were property rights, honest government, political stability, a dependable legal system, and competitive and open markets. But for each and every one of these institutions, the United States ranks higher than China, despite China's having made remarkable improvements in recent decades. So why is China growing so much more rapidly than the United States?

To answer this question, we must distinguish between two types of growth, **catching-up** and **cutting-edge**. Countries that are catching up have some enormous advantages. To become rich, a poor country does not have to invent new ideas, technologies, or methods of management. All it has to do is adopt the ideas already developed in the richer countries. As we will see, catching-up countries like China grow primarily through capital accumulation and the adoption of some simple ideas that massively improve productivity.

The United States is the world's leading economy—it is on the cutting edge. Growth on the cutting edge is primarily about developing new ideas. But developing new ideas is more difficult than adopting ideas already in existence.

Catching-up growth is growth due to capital accumulation and adopting already existing ideas.

Cutting-edge growth is growth due to new ideas.

555

Calculus isn't easy but it doesn't take a genius to understand calculus; it does take a genius to invent calculus. Countries on the cutting edge grow primarily through idea generation.

In this chapter, we will do two things. First, we will develop a model of economic growth based on capital accumulation. The model will help us understand some puzzles, such as why China is growing so much faster right now than the United States and why the countries that lost World War II, Germany and Japan, grew much faster in the postwar decades than did one of the winners, the United States. We will also discuss how poor and rich countries can converge in income over time.

Our model of economic growth based on capital accumulation does a good job of explaining catching-up growth but it doesn't help much to explain growth on the cutting edge. If we think about growth in the United States, for example, we probably do not think first about more tractors, buildings, and factories—the sorts of things that characterize growth in China. Instead, we think about iPhones, the Internet, and genetic engineering, that is, new products, new processes, and new ideas. Thus, in the second half of the chapter, we turn to cutting-edge growth and the economics of ideas. The economics of ideas explains why growth in the United States is slower than in China, but also why growth in China will slow down. It also suggests, however, that U.S. and worldwide economic growth may become faster in the decades ahead than it has been in the past. To put it bluntly (but regretfully for us), many of you will see more progress in your lifetimes than we will have seen in ours.

The Solow Model and Catching-Up Growth

Let's begin with a model of the wealth of nations and economic growth called the Solow model (after Nobel Prize–winning economist Robert Solow). The Solow model begins with a production function. A production function expresses a relationship between output and the factors of production, namely the exact way in which more inputs will produce more outputs. For simplicity, we assume that there is only one output Y, which we can think of as GDP, and the three factors of production that we discussed in the last chapter: physical capital written K; human capital, which we write as eL, and can understand as education, e, times labor, L; and ideas that increase the productivity of capital and labor (technical knowledge), which we write as A. Thus, we can write that output Y is a function F of the inputs A, K, and eL:

$$Y = F(A, K, eL) \tag{1}$$

That equation looks abstract but it represents a simple economic truth. If we look at a typical production process, say, an automobile factory, output depends on capital (the machines K), labor (the workers L adjusted for their level of skill, so eL), and the ideas upon which the whole factory is based (A), namely the invention of the auto and all the machines that help make it.

We also can think of the entire economy as relying on capital, labor, and ideas on a larger scale. We will focus on the Solow production function as a description of an entire economy because we are looking at the causes and consequences of overall economic growth.

For our first look at the Solow model, we will temporarily ignore changes in ideas, education, and labor. If we assume that A, e, and L are constant, then

Introduction to the Solow Model

we can simplify our expression for output as $Y = F(K)$. Notice that because L (the number of workers) is constant, an increase in K (capital) always implies an increase in the amount of capital per worker, K/L, and an increase in Y (output) is also always an increase in output per worker, Y/L.

Capital, Production, and Diminishing Returns

Let's make a quick sketch of what our production function $F(K)$ should look like. More capital, K, should produce more output, Y, but at a diminishing rate. On a farm, for example, the first tractor is very productive. The second tractor is still useful, but not as much as the first tractor. The third tractor is driven only when one of the other tractors breaks down (remember that the amount of labor is constant). What this means is that increases in capital, K, produce less output, Y, the more K you already have—so we should have a production function in which output increases with more K but at a decreasing rate. Following this logic, Figure 28.1 graphs output, Y, on the vertical axis against capital, K, on the horizontal axis, holding L and the other inputs constant.

Notice from Figure 28.1 that the first unit of capital increases output by one unit, but as more and more capital is added, output increases by less and less—this is the "iron logic" of diminishing returns and it plays a key role in the Solow model. Economists call the increase in output when capital increases by one unit the **marginal product of capital**. The graph shows that the marginal product of capital is diminishing.

It can sometimes help to look at a specific production function. In Figure 28.1, we used the production function $Y = F(K) = \sqrt{K}$, which means that output is the square root of the capital input. To see how this works, plug

> The **marginal product of capital** is the increase in output caused by the addition of one more unit of capital. The marginal product of capital diminishes as more and more capital is added.

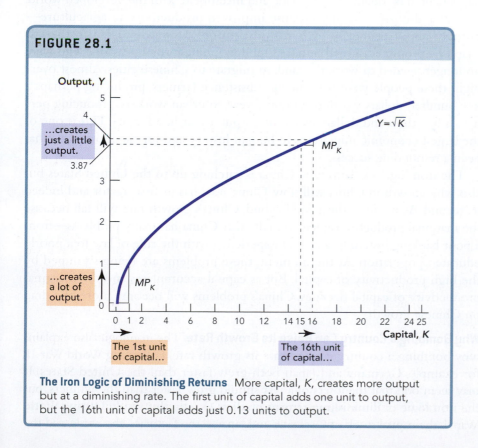

FIGURE 28.1

...creates just a little output.

...creates a lot of output.

The 1st unit of capital...

The 16th unit of capital...

The Iron Logic of Diminishing Returns More capital, K, creates more output but at a diminishing rate. The first unit of capital adds one unit to output, but the 16th unit of capital adds just 0.13 units to output.

in some numbers. If $K = 4$, then $Y = \sqrt{4} = 2$. If K increases to 16, then $Y = \sqrt{16} = 4$ and so forth.

As we said, the reason the marginal product of capital diminishes is that the first unit of capital (the first tractor) is applied where it is most productive, the second unit is applied to slightly less productive tasks because the first unit is already performing the most productive tasks, the third unit is applied to even less productive tasks, and so on.

Growth in China and the United States The iron logic of diminishing returns explains quite a bit about why China is now growing so much more rapidly than the United States. Imagine, for example, that a country labors under poor institutions—like a lack of competitive and open markets—so that the incentives to invest in capital are low. Now suppose that new institutions are put into place; perhaps new leaders with better ideas replace the old guard. The new institutions increase the incentives to invest and the capital stock grows. But in a country without a lot of capital but good (or much improved) institutions, the marginal product of capital will be very high. In that case, even small investments pay big rewards and economic growth will be rapid.

This process describes what has happened in China. For most of the twentieth century, China labored under very poor economic institutions. China in the 1950s and 1960s was a growth disaster with mass starvation as a common occurrence. Since the death of Chairman Mao in 1976 and the subsequent move away from Communism and toward markets, China has been growing very rapidly. Chinese growth has been rapid because China began with very little capital, so the marginal product of capital was very high, and with the new reforms the investment rate increased dramatically. In addition, of course, China has benefited by opening up to trade and investment with the developed world.

China also grew rapidly because improved productivity in agriculture—brought about primarily by better institutions, as we discussed in the last chapter—prompted several hundred million Chinese rural peasants, who were no longer needed to work the land, to migrate to Chinese cities. Almost overnight these people went from being subsistence farmers, producing perhaps a few hundred dollars worth of output a year, to urban workers, producing perhaps a few thousand dollars worth of output a year in a factory. This is one of the largest economic migrations in human history and for the most part it has been a resounding success.

The iron logic explains why China is catching up to the United States but also why growth in China will slow. China now has its first tractor and indeed its second. As it adds a third and beyond, China's growth rate will fall because the marginal product of capital will fall. Also, China has many problems—from a poor banking system to a lack of experience with the rule of law to a poorly educated population. At the moment, these problems are being swamped by the high productivity of capital. But as capital accumulates and the marginal productivity of capital declines, China's problems will become more of a drag on Chinese growth.

Why Bombing a Country Can Raise Its Growth Rate The iron logic also explains why bombing a country can increase its growth rate. Following World War II, for example, Germany and Japan both grew faster than the United States. It may seem odd that the losers of a war should grow faster than the winners, but the iron logic of diminishing returns predicts exactly this result. During World War II, the capital stock of Germany and Japan—the factories, the roads, and the

Physical Capital and Diminishing Returns

buildings—was nearly obliterated by Allied bombing. With so little capital remaining, any new capital was highly productive and so Germany and Japan had a strong incentive to invest in new capital. In other words, they grew rapidly as they were rebuilding their economies. It's also the case that Germany and Japan had reasonably good postwar institutions.

But don't make the mistake of envying Germany and Japan their high growth rates. Germany and Japan grew rapidly because they were catching up. Children who have been malnourished often grow rapidly when they are put on a proper diet but it's not good to be malnourished. Similarly, countries whose capital stock has been destroyed will grow rapidly, all else being equal, as they catch up but it is not good to have your capital stock destroyed. Note also that growth in Germany and Japan slowed down as their capital stocks grew and approached U.S. levels; by the 1980s they were growing at close to the U.S. rate. The growth rate in Germany and Japan fell not because they did anything wrong but, again, because the marginal product of capital declines the more capital a country has.

Figure 28.1 explains that more capital means more output, albeit at a diminishing rate. But where does capital come from and where does it go? Capital is output that is saved and invested, but capital depreciates over time. In the next section, we show how these two aspects of capital—investment and depreciation—fit together. Understanding investment and depreciation will prove important for isolating the ultimate sources of economic growth.

Average Annual Growth Rate of GDP per Capita for Germany, Japan, and the United States		
	1950–1960	1980–1990
Germany	6.6%	1.9%
Japan	6.8%	3.4%
United States	1.2%	2.3%

Capital Growth Equals Investment Minus Depreciation

Capital is output that is saved and invested rather than consumed. Imagine, for example, that 10 units of output are produced. Of the 10 units of output, 7 units might be consumed and 3 units invested in new capital. We write the fraction of output that is invested in new capital as gamma (γ), and in the example just given, $\gamma = \frac{3}{10} = 0.3$.

Figure 28.2 shows how output is divided between consumption and investment when $\gamma = 0.3$. Notice that when $K = 100$, 10 units of output are

FIGURE 28.2

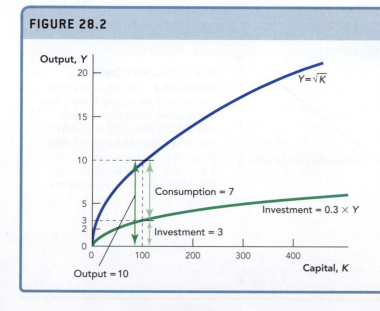

Output = 10

Capital Is Output That Is Invested
The production function $Y = \sqrt{K}$ shows how much output is produced for every level of K, the capital stock. When $K = 100$, 10 units of output are produced. The investment rate is 0.3 so $0.3 \times 10 = 3$ units of output are devoted to investment. The remaining 7 units of output are consumed.

Rome did not replenish its capital stock.

produced and of these 10 units, 7 units are consumed and 3 units are invested in new capital.

Capital also depreciates—roads wear out, harbors become silted, and machines break down. Thus, if there are 100 units of capital in this period, for example, then 2 units might depreciate, leaving just 98 for use in the next period.

We write the fraction of capital that wears out or depreciates as delta (δ); in the example just given, $\delta = \frac{2}{100} = 0.02$. Figure 28.3 shows how much capital depreciates as a function of the capital stock. When the capital stock is 100, for example, then 2 units of capital will depreciate, and when the capital stock is 200, 4 units will depreciate, and so on.

The greater the capital stock, the greater the depreciation, so a country with a lot of roads, harbors, and machines needs to devote a lot of resources to filling potholes, removing silt, and repairing and replacing. In other words, a successful economy must continually replenish its capital stock just to keep going. An economy that does not replenish its capital stock will quickly fall into ruin.

Again, Figure 28.3 shows that capital depreciation increases the greater the capital stock—this will turn out to place another constraint on economic growth.

Why Capital Alone Cannot Be the Key to Economic Growth

We now have everything we need to develop a second important insight from the Solow model. The greater the capital stock, the more capital will depreciate every period (more tractors = more tractor repairs). Thus, at some point, the capital stock will reach a level such that *every* unit of investment is needed just to replace the capital that depreciates in that period. When investment just covers capital depreciation, the capital stock stops growing, and when the capital stock stops growing, output stops growing as well. Thus, the iron logic

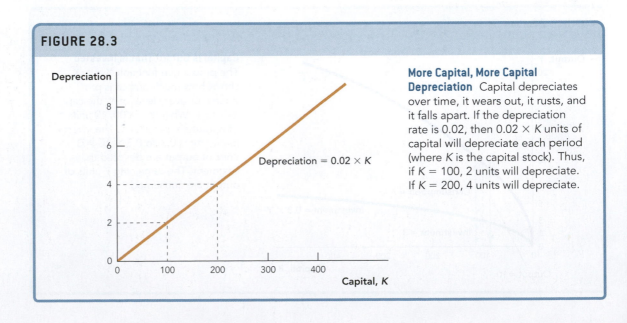

FIGURE 28.3

Depreciation

Depreciation = 0.02 × K

Capital, K

More Capital, More Capital Depreciation Capital depreciates over time, it wears out, it rusts, and it falls apart. If the depreciation rate is 0.02, then 0.02 × K units of capital will depreciate each period (where K is the capital stock). Thus, if K = 100, 2 units will depreciate. If K = 200, 4 units will depreciate.

of diminishing returns tells us that capital alone cannot be the key to economic growth. Let's explore this in more detail.

Figure 28.4 focuses attention on the two key functions, the investment function from Figure 28.2 and the depreciation function from Figure 28.3.

Consider first a case where the capital stock grows larger. For instance, when $K = 100$, 3 units of output are invested in new capital and 2 units of capital depreciate. Investment exceeds depreciation so in the next period, both the capital stock and output will be larger. Thus, when investment is greater than depreciation (*Investment > Depreciation*), we have economic growth.

Investment increases as the capital stock gets larger, but because of the iron logic, investment increases at a diminishing rate. Depreciation, however, increases with the capital stock at a linear (constant) rate. Thus, at some point investment equals depreciation (*Investment = Depreciation*). At this point, every unit of investment is being used to replace depreciated capital, so the amount of net or new investment (investment after depreciation) is zero. We call this the **steady-state** level of capital. At the steady-state level of capital, there is no new (net) investment and economic growth stops.

Finally, suppose that the capital stock is 400. In this case, 8 units of capital would depreciate $(0.02 \times 400 = 8)$ but only 6 units of capital would be invested $(0.3 \times \sqrt{400} = 6)$. As a result, when $K = 400$, not all the depreciated capital will be replaced and the capital stock will shrink.

We can summarize as follows:

Investment > Depreciation—The capital stock grows and output next period is bigger.
Investment = Depreciation—The capital stock and output are constant (the steady state).
Investment < Depreciation—The capital stock shrinks and output next period is smaller.

Check the Math

When $K = 100$, $Y = \sqrt{100} = 10$; of these 10 units $0.3 \times 10 = 3$ units are invested in new capital. Depreciation is $0.02 \times 100 = 2$ units so *Investment* (3) > *Depreciation* (2), and the capital stock and output grow.

At the **steady state** the capital stock is neither increasing nor decreasing.

Check the Math

As Figure 28.4 is drawn, the steady state occurs when $K = 225$ because

Investment $= 0.30 \times \sqrt{225} = 4.5$
Depreciation $= 0.02 \times 225 = 4.5$

Thus when $K = 225$,

Investment = Depreciation.

FIGURE 28.4

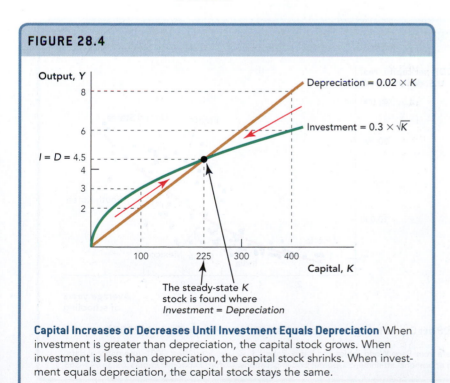

The steady-state K stock is found where *Investment = Depreciation*

Capital Increases or Decreases Until Investment Equals Depreciation When investment is greater than depreciation, the capital stock grows. When investment is less than depreciation, the capital stock shrinks. When investment equals depreciation, the capital stock stays the same.

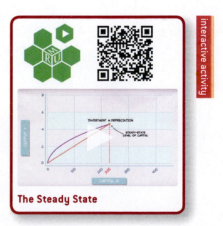

The Steady State

interactive activity

Human Capital

We learn from our "capital only" model that the economy will move towards a steady state in which there is no capital accumulation. Thus, long-run economic growth cannot be due to capital accumulation. The logic of diminishing returns means that eventually capital and output will cease growing. Economic growth, however, does not seem to be slowing. So what else could drive long-run economic growth? Let's return to the other factors of production discussed in the previous chapter—human capital and technological knowledge.

Can increases in human capital drive long-run economic growth? Human capital is an important contributor to the wealth of nations. Figure 28.5 shows that GDP per capita is higher in countries with more human capital, as measured by average years of schooling.

But human capital is just like physical capital in that it has diminishing returns and it depreciates. In other words, an economic principles class is probably the most important economics class that you will take and all the human capital in the world today will be gone in a hundred years. (Why will all the human capital in the world today be gone in a hundred years? *Hint:* Where will your human capital be in a hundred years?) Thus, within the Solow model, the logic of diminishing returns applies to human capital just as much as to physical capital and neither can drive long-run economic growth.

From Capital Accumulation to Catching-Up Growth

Finally, recall that changes in the capital stock drive output, so when *Investment = Depreciation* and *K* is at its steady-state level, then so is output. We show this in Figure 28.6 simply by adding the output curve back to our diagram. Notice that if *K* is at the steady-state level (*K* = 225, in this case), then *Y* will also be at a steady-state level of output, in this case 15. We follow *K* = 225

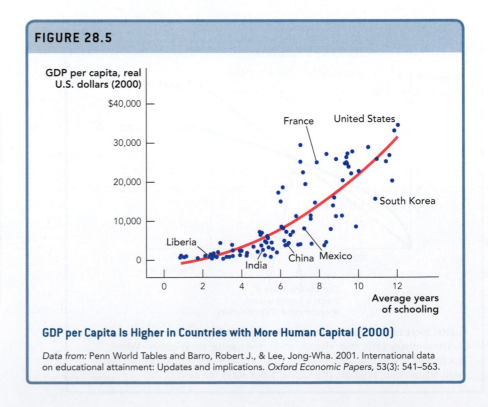

FIGURE 28.5

GDP per capita, real U.S. dollars (2000)

GDP per Capita Is Higher in Countries with More Human Capital (2000)

Data from: Penn World Tables and Barro, Robert J., & Lee, Jong-Wha. 2001. International data on educational attainment: Updates and implications. *Oxford Economic Papers*, 53(3): 541–563.

FIGURE 28.6

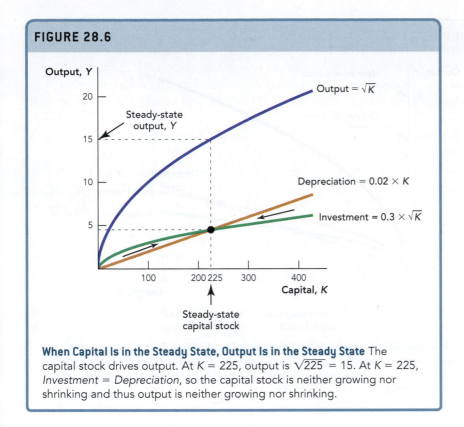

When Capital Is in the Steady State, Output Is in the Steady State The capital stock drives output. At $K = 225$, output is $\sqrt{225} = 15$. At $K = 225$, *Investment = Depreciation*, so the capital stock is neither growing nor shrinking and thus output is neither growing nor shrinking.

straight up from the horizontal axis to the point where it meets the $Y = \sqrt{K}$ curve at GDP = 15 on the vertical axis. Similarly, since K drives Y, whenever K is growing, then so is Y. Thus, Figure 28.6 demonstrates in a little more detail than we had before that our theory of capital growth is also a theory of economic growth.

The Investment Rate and Conditional Convergence

Let's stay with the Solow model a little longer and look at investment rates and conditional convergence.

The Solow Model and an Increase in the Investment Rate

What happens in the Solow model if γ, the fraction of output that is saved and invested, increases? It is simple: A greater investment rate means more capital, which means more output. An increase in the investment rate therefore increases a country's steady-state level of GDP. The result just shows that investment increases the number of "tractors" per worker, which raises GDP per worker.

In Figure 28.7 on the next page, we show this intuition in the graph by plotting two investment functions: *Investment* $= 0.3 \sqrt{K}$, which means that 3 units of every 10 units of output are saved and invested ($\gamma = 0.3$, as it was in Figure 28.6), and also *Investment* $= 0.4 \sqrt{K}$, which means that 4 units of every 10 units of output are saved and invested ($\gamma = 0.4$). Notice that when $\gamma = 0.4$ the new steady-state capital stock increases to $K = 400$ and output increases to 20.

Thus, the Solow model predicts that countries with higher rates of investment will be wealthier. Is this prediction of the Solow model consistent with

CHECK YOURSELF

In Figure 28.6:
- What happens when the capital stock is 400?
- What is investment?
- What is depreciation?
- What happens to output?

FIGURE 28.7

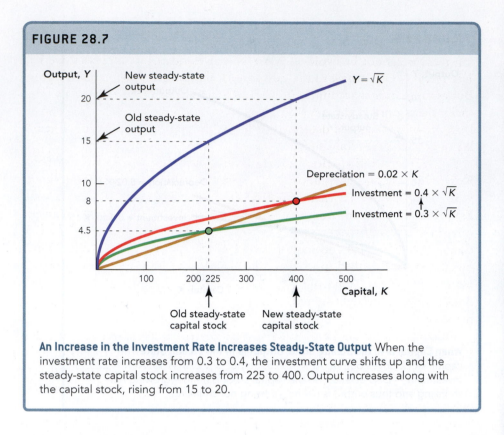

An Increase in the Investment Rate Increases Steady-State Output When the investment rate increases from 0.3 to 0.4, the investment curve shifts up and the steady-state capital stock increases from 225 to 400. Output increases along with the capital stock, rising from 15 to 20.

the evidence? Yes. Figure 28.8 shows that GDP per capita is higher in countries that have higher investment rates.

This makes intuitive sense. More savings mean that more capital goods can be produced and consumers can enjoy a higher standard of living. How wealthy would a country be if it spent all of its resources on partying?

FIGURE 28.8

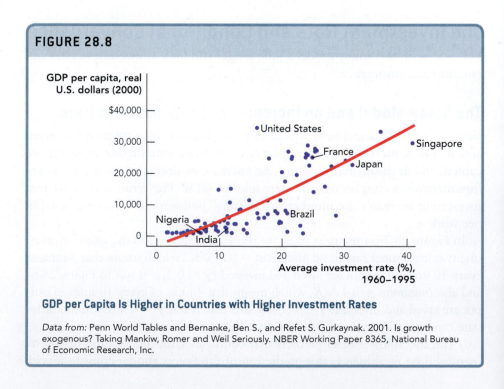

GDP per Capita Is Higher in Countries with Higher Investment Rates

Data from: Penn World Tables and Bernanke, Ben S., and Refet S. Gurkaynak. 2001. Is growth exogenous? Taking Mankiw, Romer and Weil Seriously. NBER Working Paper 8365, National Bureau of Economic Research, Inc.

What Is Conditional Convergence?

The Solow model says that an increase in the investment rate will increase steady-state output. But in the Solow model, the iron logic of diminishing returns cannot be avoided. When the investment rate increases, we have *Investment* > *Depreciation* so the capital stock increases and the economy grows. But as more capital accumulates, the iron logic sets in and the economy eventually slows until at the new steady state it stops growing once again. So the level of the capital stock determines the output level but not its growth rate, at least not in the very long run.

For further confirmation of this idea, recall the growth miracle of South Korea from the last chapter. In 1950, South Korea was poorer than Nigeria, while today it is richer than some European nations. The evidence on South Korea's growth is consistent with the Solow model. In the 1950s, the investment rate in South Korea was less than 10% of GDP, but the rate more than doubled in the 1970s and increased to more than 35% by the 1990s. Higher investment rates helped to increase South Korea's GDP, as the country opened many factories and exported cars and electronics to the rest of the world. As South Korea has caught up to Western levels of GDP, however, its growth rate has slowed.

Of course, we should remember that investment rates are themselves caused by other factors such as incentives and institutions. No one wants to invest in an economy, for example, where their investments may be expropriated. One of the reasons the investment rate in South Korea increased is that capitalists believed their investments would be protected.

In this chapter, we have referred to γ as the rate of savings *and* investment, implicitly assuming that savings equals investment. But savings must be efficiently collected and then transformed into investment. The Soviet Union had a high rate of saving but its savings were not invested well, and thus its effective investment rate was very low. In other words, a country that invests its savings poorly is like a country that doesn't invest much at all. A country could also have a low rate of saving but a high rate of investment if it imported savings from other countries. The next chapter will discuss in more detail how financial intermediaries efficiently collect savings, often from around the world, and then transform those savings into productive investments.

The Solow Model and Conditional Convergence

The Solow model also predicts that a country will grow more rapidly the farther its capital stock is below its steady-state value. To understand this result, remember that when the capital stock is below its steady-state value, investment will exceed depreciation. In other words, the capital stock will grow. Now look again at Figure 28.1—when the capital stock is low, it has a very high marginal product. Thus, when a country's capital stock is below its steady-state value, the country will grow rapidly as it invests in capital that has a high marginal product. That's just restating our tractor parable. The tractor is most valuable on the farm that doesn't already have a tractor, as opposed to the farm that is already working with 13 tractors.

We already used this result to explain why China is growing rapidly and why Germany and Japan grew rapidly after World War II. More generally, the Solow model predicts that if two countries have the same steady-state level of output, the country that is poorer today will catch up because it will grow faster. We don't know for certain which countries have the same steady-state level of

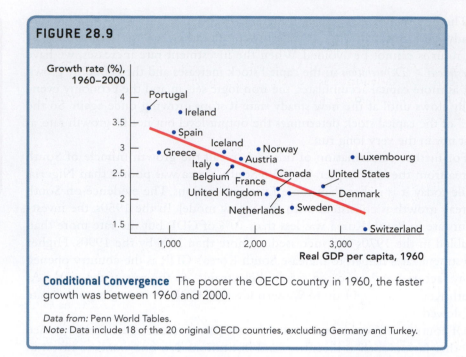

FIGURE 28.9

Growth rate (%), 1960–2000 *(vertical axis)*

Real GDP per capita, 1960 *(horizontal axis)*

Conditional Convergence The poorer the OECD country in 1960, the faster growth was between 1960 and 2000.

Data from: Penn World Tables.
Note: Data include 18 of the 20 original OECD countries, excluding Germany and Turkey.

output, but we might guess, for example, that countries with similar institutions and history have similar steady states. Figure 28.9 tests this prediction using data from 18 of the 20 founding members of the OECD (Organisation for Economic Co-operation and Development).[1] The average annual growth rate between 1960 and 2000 is on the vertical axis, and real per capita GDP in 1960 is on the horizontal axis. The data clearly show that among the OECD countries, the poorer countries grew faster. You can see that lower income in 1960 is associated with higher growth between 1960 and 2000.

Since the poorer countries grow faster, they eventually catch up to the richer countries. Thus, over time the OECD countries have converged to a similar level of GDP per capita. We say that the model and the data exhibit **conditional convergence** because we only see convergence among countries that plausibly have similar steady-state levels of output. As we know from the previous chapter, we do not observe convergence among all countries—the existence of growth disasters such as Nigeria means that some countries are diverging from the rest of the world rather than catching up.

Conditional convergence is the tendency—among countries with similar steady-state levels of output—for poorer countries to grow faster than richer countries and thus for poor and rich countries to converge in income.

CHECK YOURSELF

- What happens to the marginal product of capital as more capital is added?
- Why does capital depreciate? What happens to the total amount of capital depreciation as the capital stock increases?

New Ideas and Cutting-Edge Growth

Several predictions of the simple Solow model are consistent with the evidence—countries with higher investment rates have higher GDP per capita, and countries grow faster the farther their capital stock is from its steady-state level. One prediction of the simplest form of the Solow model, however, is inconsistent with the evidence. The simplest form of the Solow model predicts zero economic growth in the long run. Remember, in the long run, the capital stock stops growing because *Investment = Depreciation,* and if the capital stock isn't growing, then neither is output. The United States, however, has been growing for more than 200 years, so we will need to look at a more-developed version of the Solow model. In particular, is there any way to escape the iron logic? Yes, better ideas can keep the economy growing even in the long run.

Better Ideas Drive Long-Run Economic Growth

Better ideas let us produce more output from the same inputs of physical and human capital. A personal computer today has about the same amount of silicon and labor input as a computer produced 20 years ago, but today's computer is much better—the difference is ideas. Recall our simple production function:

$$Y = \sqrt{K}$$

Remembering that we let A stand for ideas that increase productivity, let's now write our production function as

$$Y = A\sqrt{K}$$

Notice that better ideas or technological knowledge—as represented by increases in A—increase output even while holding K constant, that is, an increase in A represents an increase in productivity. Figure 28.10 graphs two production functions. The first is when $A = 1$, the production function that we have been working with all along. The second is when $A = 2$. Notice that when $K = 16$, output is 4 when $A = 1$, but it's 8 when $A = 2$. Technological knowledge means that we can get more output from the same input.

So long as we develop better ideas that shift the production function upward, economic growth will continue. In a way, it should be obvious that better ideas are the key to long-run economic growth. How much economic growth would there have been without the discovery of electricity or DNA or the development of the internal combustion engine, the computer chip, or the polymerase chain reaction? It's just not enough to throw more effort at a problem; we have to actually know what we are doing and *that* boils down to ideas.

Solow himself tried to estimate how much of U.S. economic prosperity was due to capital and labor, and how much was due to ideas. He came up with the figure that better ideas are responsible for about three-fourths of the

FIGURE 28.10

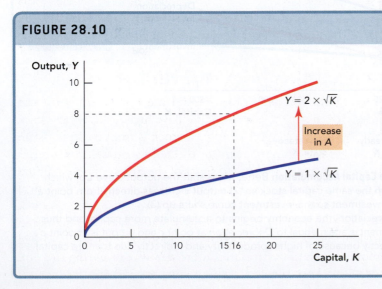

An Increase in *A* Increases Output Holding *K* Constant An increase in *A* represents an increase in productivity. If *A* = 1, then a capital stock of 16 can produce 4 units of output. If *A* = 2, then the same capital stock can produce twice as much output.

The Solow Model and Ideas

U.S. standard of living. Many economists have subsequently debated the exact number, but no one contests the central importance of ideas and technological progress for human well-being.

Solow and the Economics of Ideas in One Diagram

Let's revisit the Solow model one last time and show how better ideas fit within that model. It's simple: Better ideas let us produce more output from the same inputs of capital. But when we produce more output, it makes sense to increase consumption and *investment*. So better ideas also increase capital accumulation.

Figure 28.11 shows the process in a diagram. Okay, the diagram doesn't look simple. Let's take it in steps. Remember that A denotes ideas, and a bigger A means that we are working with better ideas. So imagine that we begin with A = ideas = 1. The economy is in the steady state and output =15 (at point a'). Now suppose that A increases to $A = 1.5$. Better ideas produce more output from the same capital stock, so output immediately increases from 15 at point a' to 22.5 at point b'. But with greater output, investment also increases, moving from point a to point b. Since investment is now greater than depreciation, capital begins to accumulate. Capital accumulates and the economy grows until investment is once again equal to depreciation at point c, at which point output is now 33.75 (at point c').

Thus, Figure 28.11 shows how the Solow model and the economics of ideas fit together. Better ideas increase output directly and, by so doing, they increase

FIGURE 28.11

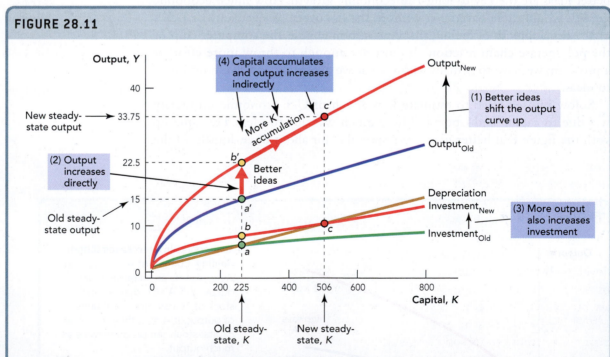

Better Ideas Generate More Output and More Capital Accumulation Better ideas shift the output curve up, which means that (1) more output is produced from the same capital stock so (2) output increases directly from point a' to point b'. More output also means more investment so the investment curve shifts up (3).

Since investment is now greater than depreciation, the economy begins to accumulate more capital and thus to grow (4). The economy grows until *Investment* is again equal to *Depreciation* at point c and output is at point c'. Notice that better ideas increase output directly because of higher productivity and indirectly due to more capital accumulation.

capital accumulation indirectly. Of course, before we ever reach the new level of output, ideas may have gotten even better! And, thus, the process of economic growth is a continuous two-step process of better ideas and more capital accumulation.

The Economics of Ideas

We have learned from the Solow model that better ideas are the key to economic growth in the long run. Capital accumulation alone will not create much growth in the United States or the other developed economies such as Japan and Western Europe because these economies already have so much capital that investment must be used to replace a lot of depreciated capital every period. Instead, these countries must develop new ideas to increase the productivity of capital and labor.

Ideas have some important and unusual properties: They can be freely shared by an unlimited number of people and they do not depreciate with greater use. As economist Paul Romer emphasizes, ideas often produce more ideas, so growth may be in part self-sustaining. Thus, to better understand economic growth on the cutting edge, we must turn to the economics of ideas.

We will emphasize the following:

1. Ideas for increasing output are primarily researched, developed, and implemented by profit-seeking firms.

2. Ideas can be freely shared, but spillovers mean that ideas are underprovided.

3. Government has a role in improving the production of ideas.

4. The larger the market, the greater the incentive to research and develop new ideas.

Research and Development Is Investment for Profit

In the previous chapter, we emphasized that economic growth was not automatic, and we said that the factors of production do not fall from the sky like manna from heaven. In order to increase output, the factors of production must be produced and organized efficiently. All of this applies to ideas or technological knowledge just as much as to physical and human capital. Once again, incentives are the key. Economic growth requires institutions that encourage investment in physical capital, human capital, and *technological knowledge* (ideas).

In the United States, there are about 1.3 million scientists who research and develop new products, more than in any other country in the world, and most of these scientists and engineers, about 70%, work for private firms. (The ratios are broadly similar in other developed countries.)

Private firms invest in research and development when they expect to profit from their endeavors. Thus, the institutions we discussed in the last chapter—property rights, honest government, political stability, a dependable legal system, and competitive and open markets—also drive the generation of technological knowledge. When it comes to knowledge, other institutions are especially important. These institutions include a commercial setting that helps innovators to connect with capitalists, intellectual property rights such as copyrights and patents, and a high-quality educational system (we will turn to these issues shortly).

The Economics of Ideas

John Kay (1704–1780) invented the "flying shuttle" used in cotton weaving, the single most important invention launching the Industrial Revolution. Kay, however, was not rewarded for his efforts. His house was destroyed by "machine breakers," who were afraid that his invention would put them out of a job. Kay was forced to flee to France, where he died a poor man.

"The patent system . . . added the fuel of interest to the fire of genius." (1859)

Abraham Lincoln (1809–1865). Lincoln is the only U.S. president to have been granted a patent.

It's not just the number of scientists and engineers that matters for economic growth, as many other people come up with new ideas on their jobs, at school, or at home in their garages. Mark Zuckerberg, for example, wrote the software for Facebook as a Harvard student. Just as important, the business culture and institutions of the United States are good at connecting innovators with businesspeople and venture capitalists looking to fund or otherwise take a chance on new ideas. Ideas without backers are sterile. In the United States, potential innovators know that if they come up with a good idea, that idea has a good chance of making it to the market. The incentive to discover new ideas is correspondingly strong.

American culture also supports entrepreneurs. People like SpaceX founder Elon Musk, for example, are lauded in the popular media. Historically, however, entrepreneurs were often attacked as job destroyers, as the sidebar on eighteenth-century British entrepreneur John Kay illustrates.

Compared with most other countries, the United States has a very good cultural and commercial infrastructure for supporting new ideas and their conversion into usable commercial products.

Artistic innovation also requires many individuals with a diversity of viewpoints, many sources of support and employment, and businesspeople looking to profit from and support innovations. It's not surprising, therefore, that the United States is also a leader in artistic innovation. American movies, popular music, and dance have spread around the world. But the United States is not just good at popular culture: It is also a leader in abstract art, contemporary classical composition, avant-garde fiction and poetry, and modern dance, to name just a few fields. The lesson is that artistic, economic, and scientific innovations spring from similar sources.

A further significant part of the infrastructure for creativity is property rights. We now turn to one form of intellectual property rights, patents.

Patents Many ideas have peculiar properties that can make it difficult for private firms to recoup their investments in those ideas. In particular, new processes, products, and methods can be copied by competitors. The world's first MP3 player was the Eiger Labs's MPMan introduced in 1998. Ever heard of it? Probably not. Other firms quickly copied the idea and Eiger Labs lost out in the race to innovate. Imitators get the benefit of new ideas without having to pay the costs of development. Imitators, therefore, have lower costs so they tend to drive innovators out of the market unless some barrier prevents quick imitation.

Imitation often takes time and this does give innovators a chance to recoup their investments. The Apple iPad design, for example, is already being copied by other firms, but until that happened, Apple could exploit monopoly power to sell millions of iPads for high profits. That is what makes Apple willing to invest in research and development in the first place and that is why the iPad exists. Firms often compete not by offering the same product at a lower price but by offering substantially new and better products.

Apple also relies on patents to protect its innovations. A patent is a government grant of temporary monopoly rights, typically 20 years from the date of filing. Patents delay imitation, thus allowing innovative firms a greater period of monopoly power. Apple, for example, has patented one of the most distinctive features of the iPad, the multipoint touchscreen. Apple's patent, filed in 2004, gives Apple the right to prevent other firms from copying its technology until 2024. Still, we may well see other similar devices in the near future if Apple licenses its technology to other firms. Furthermore, competitors are finding ways to produce the same effect using different methods—a majority of patented innovations are imitated within five years.

Nevertheless, Apple's patent gives it some monopoly power, and as you know if you studied microeconomics first, firms with monopoly power raise prices above competitive levels. Thus, patents increase the incentive to research and develop new products, but also increase monopoly power once the products are created. Monopoly power not only raises prices, it also means that innovations take longer to spread throughout the economy. The trade-off between creating incentives to research and develop new products while avoiding too much monopoly power is one of the trickiest in economic policy.[2]

Spillovers, and Why There Aren't Enough Good Ideas

Even when a firm has a patent on its technological innovation and other firms cannot imitate in a direct way, ideas tend to spill over and benefit other firms and consumers. A new pharmaceutical will be patented, for example, but the mechanism of action—how the pharmaceutical works—can be examined and broadly copied by other firms to develop their own pharmaceuticals.

Spillovers have good and bad aspects. The good aspect of imitation or spillovers is that ideas are **nonrival**. If you consume an apple, then I cannot consume the same apple. When it comes to eating an apple, it's either you or me—we can't share what we each consume so economists say that apples are rival. But ideas can be freely shared. You can use the Pythagorean theorem and I can use the very same theorem at the very same time. The Pythagorean theorem can be shared by all of humanity, which is why economists say that ideas are nonrival.

Since many ideas can be shared at low cost, they *should* be shared—that's the way to maximize the benefit from an idea. The spillover or diffusion of ideas throughout the world is thus a good thing. For instance, the idea of breeding and growing corn originated in ancient Mexico but now people grow corn all over the world. Spillovers, however, mean that the originator of an idea doesn't get all the benefits. And if the originator doesn't get enough of the benefits, ideas will be underprovided. For this reason, while economists know that idea spillovers are good, they also know that spillovers mean that too few good ideas are produced in the first place.

To understand why spillovers mean that ideas will be underprovided, think about why firms explore for oil. Answer: to make money. So what would happen to the amount of exploration if whenever a firm struck oil, other firms jumped in and drilled wells right next door? Clearly, the incentive to explore would decline if firms didn't have property rights to oil *fields*. Firms explore for ideas just as they explore for oil, and if other firms can set up right next door to exploit the same *field of ideas*, the incentive to explore will decline.

Figure 28.12 illustrates the argument in a diagram. A profit-maximizing firm invests in research and development (R&D) so long as the private marginal benefit is larger than the marginal cost. As a result, private investment occurs until point *a* in Figure 28.12. Spillovers, however, mean that the social benefit of R&D exceeds the private benefit, so that the optimal social investment is

▶▶**SEARCH ENGINE**

You can find Apple's patent on the iPad's multipoint touchscreen (20,060,097,991) by searching at the U.S. Patent and Trademark Office.

interactive activity

Patents, Prizes, and Subsidies

A good is **nonrival** if one person's consumption of the good does not limit another person's consumption.

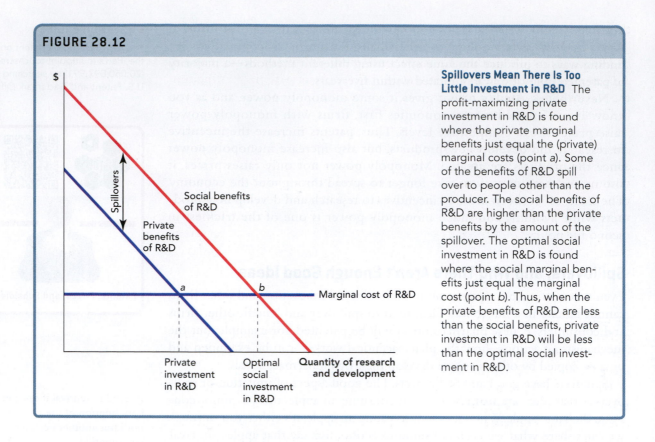

FIGURE 28.12

$

Spillovers

Social benefits
of R&D

Private
benefits
of R&D

a

b

Marginal cost of R&D

Private
investment
in R&D

Optimal
social
investment
in R&D

Quantity of research
and development

Spillovers Mean There Is Too Little Investment in R&D The profit-maximizing private investment in R&D is found where the private marginal benefits just equal the (private) marginal costs (point *a*). Some of the benefits of R&D spill over to people other than the producer. The social benefits of R&D are higher than the private benefits by the amount of the spillover. The optimal social investment in R&D is found where the social marginal benefits just equal the marginal cost (point *b*). Thus, when the private benefits of R&D are less than the social benefits, private investment in R&D will be less than the optimal social investment in R&D.

found where the marginal social benefit just equals the marginal cost at point *b*. Since the private benefit to R&D is less than the social benefit, private investment in R&D is less than ideal.

Government's Role in the Production of New Ideas

Can anything be done to increase the production of new ideas? We have already mentioned one important government policy that affects the production of new ideas, namely patents. Patents reduce spillovers and thus increase the incentive to produce new ideas, but they can also slow down the spread of new ideas. Prizes are another possibility. In 2008, for example, the U.S. Department of Energy offered $10 million to the first inventor to produce a new and more efficient light bulb. In 2011 Phillips claimed the prize with a 10-watt LED bulb that duplicated the light output of a 60-watt incandescent. One advantage of prizes is that the government doesn't have to decide in advance who can best solve a problem. And that's important because new ideas often come from unexpected places. Paying for innovation with a prize, rather than a patent, also means that the idea can spread more rapidly.

The government could also subsidize the production of new ideas. Returning to Figure 28.12, a subsidy or tax break to R&D expenditures, for example, will shift the (private) marginal cost of R&D curve down, thus increasing private investment.

The argument for government subsidies is strongest when the spillovers are largest. The modern world is founded on mathematics, physics, and molecular biology—basic ideas in these fields have many applications so spillovers can be large. But even if the social benefits to basic science are large, the private returns can be small. It's probably easier to make a million dollars producing pizza than it is to make a million dollars producing mathematical theorems. In fact, Thomas S. Monaghan made a billion dollars producing pizza (he's the founder of Domino's), while mathematicians Ron Rivest, Adi Shamir, and Leonard Adleman didn't make nearly so much on their RSA algorithm, even though their algorithm is used to encrypt data sent over the Internet and thus forms the backbone for all Internet commerce.

The large spillovers to basic science suggest a role for government subsidies to universities, especially the parts of universities that produce innovations and the basic science behind innovations. Perhaps most important, universities produce *scientists*. Most of the 1.3 million scientists who research and develop new products in the United States were trained in government-subsidized universities. Thus, subsidies to the hard sciences support the private development of new ideas and those initial subsidies are likely to pay for themselves many times over.

Market Size and Research and Development

Imagine that there are two diseases that if left untreated are equally deadly. One of the diseases is rare, the other one is common. If you had to choose, would you rather be afflicted with the rare disease or the common disease? Take a moment to think about this question because there is a right answer.

If you don't want to die, it's much better to have the common disease. The reason? The costs of developing drugs for rare and common diseases are about the same, but the revenues are greater, the more common the disease. Pharmaceutical companies concentrate on drugs for common diseases because larger markets mean more profits.

As a result, there are more drugs to treat common diseases than to treat rare diseases, and more drugs mean greater life expectancy. Patients diagnosed with rare diseases—those ranked at the bottom quarter in terms of how frequently they are diagnosed—are 45% more likely to die before age 55 than are patients diagnosed with more common diseases.[3]

Larger markets mean increased incentives to invest in research and development, more new drugs, and greater life expectancy. So imagine this: If China and India were as wealthy as the United States, the market for cancer drugs would be eight times larger than it is today.

China and India are not yet wealthy countries but what this thought experiment tells us is that *people in the United States benefit tremendously when other countries grow rich.*

Like pharmaceuticals, new computer chips, software, and chemicals also require large R&D expenditures. As India, China, and other countries, including the United States, become wealthier, companies will increase their worldwide R&D investments.

The Future of Economic Growth

Over the last 10,000 years, growth in per capita world GDP has been increasing. Growth in per capita GDP was approximately zero from the dawn of civilization to about 1500, increased to 0.08% a year between 1500 and 1760, doubled during the next hundred years, and increased even further during the nineteenth and twentieth centuries. Today, worldwide per capita GDP is growing by a little over 3% per year.

Could economic growth become even faster? Yes. Let's take a look again at our measure of technological progress, A. We can summarize what we have said about the factors causing A to increase in a simple equation:

$$A\text{(ideas)} = \text{Population} \times \text{Incentives} \times \text{Ideas per hour}$$

In words, the number of new ideas is a function of the number of people, the incentives to innovate, and the number of ideas per hour that each person has. Of course, this equation is not meant to be exact—it's just a way of thinking about some of the key factors driving technological growth. So let's go through each of the factors and think about what they imply for the future of economic growth.

The number of people is increasing, which is good for idea generation. More important, the number of people whose job it is to produce new ideas is increasing. In all the world today, there are perhaps 6 million scientists and engineers, of which 1.3 million come from the United States. These 1.3 million represent about one-half of 1% of the U.S. population, a surprisingly small percentage. Yet for the world as a whole, the ratio of scientists and engineers to population is much lower.

Today, because much of the world is poor, thousands of potentially great scientists will spend most of their lives doing backbreaking work on a farm. If the world as a whole were as wealthy as the United States and could devote the same share of population to research and development as does the United States today, there would be more than five times as many scientists and engineers. Thus, as the world gets richer, more people will be producing ideas, and because of spillovers, these ideas will benefit everyone.

The incentives to innovate also appear to be increasing. Consumers are richer and the world is becoming one giant integrated market because of trade; each of these factors boosts the incentives to innovate.

The incentives to innovate also increase when innovators can profit from their investments without fear of expropriation. The worldwide improvement in institutions—that is, the movement toward property rights, honest government, political stability, and a dependable legal system—has been very positive for both innovation and economic growth.

We know the least about the last factor in the equation, the number of ideas per hour or how easy it is to come up with new ideas. In some fields, we are unlikely to ever know much more than we know now. For thousands of years, scientists periodically discovered new human organs, but the last new organ to be found was identified in 1880 (the parathyroid gland). Don't expect more breakthroughs in this field, no matter how hard we look. In some places and times, knowledge grows by leaps and bounds, and in others it stagnates. We don't always know why. In pharmaceuticals and cancer research it seems to take more and more research time to produce the same increase in life expectancy. The power of computers continues to grow but only because we throw more and more researchers at the problem. When the law of diminishing returns is applied to ideas in general as well as to capital, then economic growth will be much slower. There are at least two reasons, however, for thinking that diminishing returns is not the usual state of affairs.

First, many ideas make creating other ideas easier. Sadly, the authors of this book can remember the day when answering even simple questions like who won the 1969 World Series could not be answered without going to a library, consulting a card catalog (don't ask), looking for the appropriate book in the stacks, and then (if the book hadn't been checked out) finding the answer. Today, you can probably find the answer using Google on your cell phone faster than you can read this paragraph. (By the way, it was the New York Mets in one of the greatest upsets in baseball history.) We still have many new ideas, like Google Search and Artificial Intelligence, that are useful for creating even more ideas, so idea production might speed up rather than slow down.

The second reason to think that the number of ideas per hour is not yet strongly diminishing comes from one of the pioneers of the economics of ideas, Paul Romer. (Romer is not only a distinguished theorist of ideas, he is a first-class idea entrepreneur; he started Aplia, the online economics test bank and tutorial system that many of you use and that is a good example of an idea that makes learning new ideas easier.) Romer points out that ideas for production are like recipes and the number of potential recipes in the universe is unimaginably vast:

The Future of Economic Growth

> The periodic table contains about a hundred different types of atoms, which means that the number of combinations made up of four different elements is about $100 \times 99 \times 98 \times 97 = 94,000,000$. A list of numbers like 6, 2, 1, 7 can represent the proportions for using the four elements in a recipe. To keep things simple, assume that the numbers in the list must lie between 1 and 10, that no fractions are allowed, and that the smallest number must always be 1. Then there are about 3,500 different sets of proportions for each choice of four elements, and $3,500 \times 94,000,000$ (or 330 billion) different recipes in total. If laboratories around the world evaluated 1,000 recipes each day, it would take nearly a million years to go through them all.[4]

True, many of the recipes are going to be like chicken liver ice cream (not that good), but the field of ideas that we can explore is so large that diminishing returns may not set in for a very long time.

Putting all this together, economic growth might be even faster in the future than it has been in the past. There are more scientists and engineers in the world today than ever before and their numbers are increasing both in absolute terms and as a percentage of the population. The incentives to invest in R&D are also increasing because of globalization and increased wealth in developing countries such as China and India. Better institutions and more secure property rights are spreading throughout the world.

We have some reasons to be optimistic about the future of economic growth but, of course, nothing is guaranteed. In the twentieth century, two world wars diverted the energy of two generations from production to destruction. When the wars ended, an iron curtain isolated billions of people from the rest of the world, reducing trade in goods and ideas—to everyone's detriment. World poverty meant that the United States and a few other countries shouldered the burden of advancing knowledge nearly alone. We must hope that this does not happen again.

Takeaway

The Solow model is governed by the iron logic of diminishing returns. When the capital stock is low, the marginal product of capital is high and capital accumulates, leading to economic growth. But as capital accumulates, its marginal product declines until per-period investment is just equal to depreciation, and growth stops.

Despite the simplicity of the Solow model, it tells us three important things about economic growth. First, countries that devote a larger share of output to investment will be wealthier. The Solow model doesn't tell us *why* some countries might devote a larger share of output to investment, but we know from the previous chapter that wealthy countries have institutions that promote investment in physical capital, human capital, and technological knowledge. We will also say more about how financial intermediaries channel saving into investment in the next chapter.

Second, growth will be faster the farther away a country's capital stock is from its steady-state value. This explains why the German and Japanese economies were able to catch up to other advanced economies after World War II, why countries that reform their institutions often grow very rapidly (growth miracles), and why poor countries grow faster than rich countries with similar levels of steady-state output.

Third, the Solow model tells us that capital accumulation cannot explain long-run economic growth. Holding other things constant, the marginal product of physical and human capital will eventually diminish, thereby leaving the economy in a zero-growth steady state. If we want to explain long-run economic growth, we must explain why other things are not held constant.

New ideas are the driving force behind long-run economic growth. Ideas, however, aren't like other goods: Ideas can be easily copied and ideas are nonrival. The fact that ideas can be easily copied means that the originator of a new idea won't receive all the benefits of that idea so the incentive to produce ideas will be too low. Governments can play a role in supporting the production of new ideas by protecting intellectual property and subsidizing the production of new ideas when spillovers are most likely to be present.

The non-rivalry of ideas, however, means that once an idea is created, we want it to be shared, which is a nice way of saying copied, as much as possible. There is thus a trade-off between providing appropriate incentives to produce new ideas and providing appropriate incentives to share new ideas.

An important lesson from the economics of ideas is that the larger the market, whether in terms of people or wealth, the greater the incentive to invest in research and development. Similarly, having more people and wealthier countries increases the number of people devoted to the production of new ideas. Thus, the increased wealth of many developing nations, the move to freer trade in global markets, and the spread of better institutions throughout the world are all encouraging for the future of economic growth.

CHAPTER REVIEW

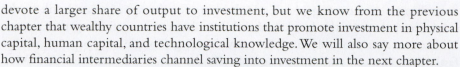 **interactive activity** Go online to practice with more examples of these types of problems, including live links to videos, data sources, and feedback.

 Problems in **green** relate to MRU videos. See the MRU table at the end of the exercises.

KEY CONCEPTS

catching-up growth, p. 555

cutting-edge growth, p. 555

marginal product of capital, p. 557

steady state, p. 561

conditional convergence, p. 566

nonrival, p. 571

FACTS AND TOOLS

1. Which countries are likely to grow faster: countries doing "cutting-edge" growth or those doing "catching-up" growth?

2. When will people work harder to invent new ideas: when they can sell them to a market of 10,000 people or when they can sell them to a market of 1 billion? Does your answer tell us

anything about whether it's good or bad from the U.S. point of view for China and India to become rich countries?

3. Many say that if people save too much, the economy will be hurt. They often refer to the fact that consumer spending is two-thirds of GDP to make this point. This is sometimes called the "paradox of thrift."

   a. In the Solow model, is there a paradox of thrift? In other words, is a high savings rate good or bad for a country's long-run economic performance?

   b. What about in the real world? According to the data in Figure 28.8, is there a paradox of thrift?

4. Many people say that "the rich grow richer and the poor grow poorer." Is this what Figure 28.9 says about the countries in that graph? Did the rich countries grow more quickly or more slowly than the poor countries?

5. Compared with its fast growth today, is China's economy likely to grow more quickly or more slowly in the future?

6. What is more important for explaining the standard of living in the rich countries: capital or ideas?

7. According to Thomas Jefferson, how are ideas like flames?

8. What is a patent?

9. When will people work harder to invent new ideas: when they can patent those ideas for 1 year or when they can patent them for 10 years?

10. Which three countries on the list are good examples of "conditional convergence?"

    China

    Ireland

    Argentina

    North Korea

    Greece

11. Let's keep track of a nation's capital stock for five years. Mordor starts off with 1,000 machines, and every year, 5% of the machines depreciate or wear out. Fortunately, the people in this land produce 75 machines per year, every year. The key equation for keeping track of capital is quite simple:

Next year's capital = This year's capital + Investment − Depreciation

Fill in the table.

Year	Capital	Depreciation	Investment
1	1,000	0.05 × 1,000	75
2	1,025		75
3			75
4			75
5			75

THINKING AND PROBLEM SOLVING

12. Consider the following three countries that produce GDP this way:

$$Y = 5\sqrt{K}$$

    Ilia: $K = 100$ machines

    Caplania: $K = 10,000$ machines

    Hansonia: $K = 1,000,000$ machines

    What will GDP (Y) be in these three countries? Hansonia has 10,000 times more machines than Ilia, so why isn't it 10,000 times more productive?

13. Consider the data in the previous question: If 10% of all machines become worthless every year (they depreciate, in other words), then how many machines will become worthless in these three countries this year? Are there any countries where the amount of depreciation is actually greater than GDP? (This question reminds you that "more machines mean more machines wearing out.")

14. Of course, no country makes *only* investment goods like machines, equipment, and computers. They also make consumer goods. Let's consider a case where the countries in question 12 devote 25% of GDP to making investment goods (so γ, gamma, = 0.25). What is the amount of savings in these three countries? In which countries is *Investment < Depreciation*? When is *Investment > Depreciation*?

15. A drug company has $1 billion to spend on research and development. It has to decide on one of two projects:

    a. Spend the money on a project to fight deadly forms of influenza, including bird flu.

    b. Spend the money on a project to fight a condition of red, itchy skin known as eczema.

The company expects both projects to be equally profitable, all things considered: Yes, project *a* is riskier (since the rare flu may never come along), but if the disease hits, there will be a worldwide market willing to pay a lot of money to cure the flu.

Then one day, before deciding between *a* and *b*, the drug company's CEO reads in the newspaper that the European Union and the United States will not honor patents in the event of a major flu outbreak. Instead, these governments will "break the patent" and just make the drug available everywhere for $1 per pill. The company will only get $1 per pill instead of the $100 or $200 per pill it had expected.

Given this new information about the possibility that governments will "break the patent," on which project is the company likely to spend its research and development money? (*Note*: In the wake of the deadly anthrax attacks of 2001, the U.S. government threatened to do just this with the patent for Cipro, the one antibiotic proven to cure the symptoms of anthrax infection.)

16. After World War II, a lot of France's capital stock was destroyed, but it had educated workers and a market-oriented economy. Do you think the war's destruction increased or decreased the marginal product of capital?

17. The Solow model isn't useful for only thinking about entire countries: As long as the production function runs into diminishing returns and your total stock of inputs constantly wears out, then the Solow model applies. Consider a professor's knowledge of economics. The more she learns about economics, the more she will forget (depreciation), but the more she knows, the more knowledge she can create (production). So eventually in steady state, she will know only a fixed amount about economics, but what she knows might change over time; some decades she might know a lot about the Federal Reserve, while other decades she might know a lot about the electricity market. In any case, knowledge fades away.

   a. Apply the Solow model to a chef's skill at cooking.

   b. Apply the Solow model to the size of a navy's fleet of ships.

   c. Apply the Solow model to the speed of a cheetah, where the input is calories.

18. Many inventors decide that patents are a bad way to protect their intellectual property. Instead, they keep their ideas a secret. Trade secrets are actually quite common: The formula for Coca-Cola is a trade secret, as is Colonel Sander's secret recipe. What is one major strength of keeping a trade secret rather than applying for a patent? What is a major weakness inherent in going down the trade secret route?

19. Since ideas can sometimes be copied quite easily, many people think that we should put more effort into creating new ideas. Let's see if there are trade-offs to having more people creating new ideas. To keep things simple, let's assume that the growth rate of the economy depends on how many people search for ideas, whether in laboratories, or huddled over laptops in coffee shops, or while listening to "Stairway to Heaven" at three in the morning. People either produce stuff or produce ideas. Here's how this economy works:

$$Y_1 = (1 - R) \times A_1 L \text{ (GDP production function)}$$

$$A_{1+1} = (1 + R) \times A_1 L \text{ (Technology production function)}$$

   There are a total of L people in the society, and a fraction $(1 - R)$ of them work in factories and offices making stuff (remember, people working in offices help create output, too!), while the remaining fraction R try to come up with good ideas all day long. To keep the story simple, there are no diminishing returns.

   a. What's the trade-off here? If 100% of the people work to make new ideas ($R = 1$), won't that create a prosperous world?

   b. In this society, if people are willing to wait a long time for a reward, should they choose a large R or a small R?

   c. Plot out GDP in this society for 5 years if A starts off at 100, L starts off at 100, and R is 10%.

Year	A	Y	Y/L
1	100	9,000	90
2	110		
3			
4			
5			

d. Plot out GDP in this society if the society instead chose $R = 20\%$.

20. In Facts and Tools question 2, we saw that big markets create a big *demand* for inventions. This is an example of what Adam Smith meant when he said that "the division of labor is limited by the extent of the market." Now let's look at how big markets impact the *supply* side of inventions. The big idea is quite simple: *More people means more ideas.*

a. In order to create new ideas, you need to have people trying to come up with new ideas. In 1800, there were approximately 300 million humans on the planet—roughly equal to today's U.S. population. If good ideas are "one in a million"—that is, if one person per year out of a million comes up with a world-shaking idea like contact lenses or James Brown's song "The Payback" or the video game Grand Theft Auto—how many great new ideas will occur in the world of 1800? How many will occur in a world of 6 billion people?

b. More realistically, people in the rich countries are most likely to invent earth-shaking ideas and share them with others. There's nothing special about people in rich countries, but they have the education and the laboratories and the Internet connections that will make it practical to invent and spread ideas. If only the top 20% of the earth's population is really in the running to create new ideas, how many new big ideas will come along each year in 1800 and today?

c. If half the population of India and China become rich enough to create new ideas (to simplify, assume populations of 1 billion each), and start coming up with big ideas at the same rate as the top 20%, how many big ideas will India and China alone create for the planet every year?

d. Many people think there are too many people on the planet. (As P. J. O'Rourke once wrote, many people's attitude toward global population is "Just enough of me, way too much of you.") Look at your answer from part b. If the world's population now gets cut in half from the current 6 billion, how many big ideas will come along each year?

21. According to economists Robert Barro and Xavier Sala-i-Martin, convergence isn't just for entire nations: It's also true for states and regions, as well. They looked at state-level GDP per capita in the United States in 1880, and then calculated how fast each state grew over the next 120 years. They found that convergence held almost exactly.

a. With this in mind, draw arrows to connect the GDP per capita data on the left with the long-term growth rates on the right.

GDP per Capita in 1880	Annual Growth Rate, 1880–2000
West: $8,500	1.6%
East: $6,300	1.7%
Midwest: $4,700	2.2%
South: $2,800	1.2%

b. Graph the data from part a in the following figure. Does this look like Figure 28.9's story about the OECD countries, or is it quite different?

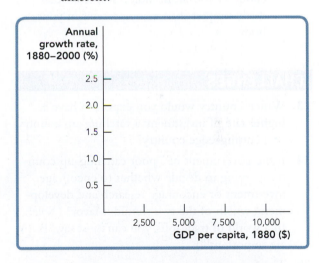

Note: Barro and Sala-i-Martin also found that convergence also held almost exactly for regions of Japan: The areas that were poorest in 1930 grew fastest over the next 70 years. Thus, it is difficult to find major evidence in favor of the commonsense idea that "the poor areas grow poorer."

22. Are we running out of ideas? Economist Paul Romer thinks not. To make things concrete, he notes that if we keep trying out different molecules to search for interesting compounds like new drugs, new plastics, etc., the universe may end from heat death before we finish our search. For example, if we try out 100 different atoms out of the 117+ (and rising!) elements in the Periodic Table, and only look at the 6-atom molecules, this is 100^6 different molecules. And, of course, many common molecules in our bodies consist of hundreds of atoms, so this only scratches the surface of interesting compounds.

a. If it takes a machine 1 minute to test out and fully analyze a new 6-atom molecule, how many years will it take for this one machine to test out all 100^6 molecules? (*Note:* Modern biochemists create computer simulations of molecules to analyze whether potential drugs are likely to work in the molecules that make up the human body, but this is only one narrow form of analysis.)

b. How many machines would it take to test out all of these molecules within 100 years?

c. What about all 10-atom molecules: How many years would it take for one machine to test all of these compounds at one per minute? If your computer can handle it, what about all 100-atom molecules, molecules vastly simpler than many proteins in your body?

CHALLENGES

23. Which country would you expect to have a higher rate of investment: a catching-up country or a cutting-edge country?

24. If the government of a poor catching-up country is trying to decide whether to encourage investment or encourage research and development, which of the two should it favor? (*Note:* In a world of trade-offs, you can't just say, "Both are important!")

25. The Solow model makes it quite easy to figure out how rich a country will be in its steady state. We already know that you're in a steady state when investment equals depreciation. In math, that's

$$\gamma Y = \delta K$$

Since $Y = \sqrt{K}$ in our simplest model, this means that $K = Y^2$:

$$\gamma Y = \delta Y^2$$

There are a lot of ways to solve this for Y—the easiest might just be to divide both sides by Y, and then put everything else on the other side. When you do this, you can learn how steady-state GDP depends on the savings rate and the depreciation rate. Here are a few questions:

a. Many say that if people save more, that's bad for the economy: They say that spending money on consumer goods keeps the money moving through the economy. Does this model say that?

b. Many people say that when machines and equipment get destroyed by bad weather or war, that makes the economy better off by encouraging businesses and families to spend money on new capital goods. Does this model say that?

26. Let's think about two countries, Frugal and Smart. In Frugal, people devote 50% of GDP to making new investment goods, so $\gamma = 0.5$, and their production function is $Y = \sqrt{K}$. In Smart, people devote 25% of GDP to making new investment goods, so $\gamma = 0.25$ and their production function is $Y = 2\sqrt{K}$. Both countries start off with $K = 100$.

a. What is the amount of investment in each country this year?

b. What is the amount of consumption (GDP − Investment, or $Y - I$) in each country this year?

c. Where would you rather be a citizen: Frugal or Smart?

27. Which of the following goods are nonrival?

Sunshine

An apple

A national park

A Mozart symphony

The idea of penicillin

A dose of penicillin

28. According to economist Michael Kremer, as human populations have grown over the last million years, so has the human population growth *rate*. This was true until the 1800s. How does Thinking and Problem Solving question 20 help explain why human populations grew more quickly despite the fact that there were more mouths to feed?

29. Use the Solow diagram to show the impact of a natural disaster that destroys half of a nation's capital stock.

   a. Begin with a country in a steady state at $Y^{ss} = \sqrt{K^{ss}}$, and show the short-run effects of the natural disaster destroying half of the steady-state level of capital stock, K^{ss} on the Solow diagram.

   b. If $K_1 = \frac{1}{2} K^{ss}$, will output fall by half so that output in period one following the shock is $Y_1 = \frac{1}{2} Y^{ss}$? Explain why or why not.

   c. What happens in this country in the immediate future and in the long run?

30. A small, less-developed country finds itself the recipient of a large amount of foreign direct investment that adds 50% to its current steady-state level of capital stock. This country seeks your advice about the long-term implications of that kind of help.

   a. Assume this country begins in a steady-state condition at $Y^{ss} = \sqrt{K^{ss}}$, and show the short-run effects of a 50% increase in the steady-state level of capital stock such that $K_1 = \frac{3}{2} K^{ss}$ on the Solow diagram.

   b. What will the long-term effects of this increase in the capital stock be for this country?

   c. What potential problems should this country consider during the adjustment period described in part b?

   d. What must this country do in order to gain any permanent long-term benefits from this increase in its capital stock?

   e. *Bonus:* Can you think of any examples like these in real life?

31. Change the production function used in the chapter to reflect the contribution of labor in the production process. As with capital, labor also has diminishing returns, so let $Y = \sqrt{KL}$ Now suppose that immigration reform leads to an increase in this country's labor force.

   a. Begin with a country in a steady-state condition at $Y^{ss} = \sqrt{K^{ss} L}$, and let K^{ss} equal 400 and $L = 100$. What is the steady-state level of output?

   b. Show the short-run effects of a 21% increase in the amount of labor available for use in this country such that $L_1 = 1.21L$ on the Solow diagram.

   c. What are the algebraic and numeric outcomes for the short-run level of output, that is, Y^{ss} in terms of K^{ss} and L?

   d. Show the new steady-state level of output on the diagram.

   e. Demonstrate whether this country will be able to produce 21% more output with a 21% increase in the labor supply. Show this result algebraically. As illustrated in Challenge question 25, you will need to use the steady-state condition $\gamma Y = \delta K$ to show this result.

   f. Derive output per worker in the initial steady state (use Y_0^{ss} from part a and divide by the labor force); output per worker in the short run (use Y_1^{ss} from part c and divide by the new labor force); and output per worker in the long run (use Y_1^{ss} from part e and divide by the new labor force).

   g. Are the citizens of this country made worse or better off in the long run by a new immigration policy such as this; that is, how does the new long-run level of output per worker compare with the initial level of output per worker?

   h. *Bonus:* What is the value for the new steady-state level of capital stock in this country?

WORK IT OUT

interactive activity

For interactive, step-by-step help in solving this problem, go online.

In the Solow model, you've seen that as the total stock of capital equipment gets larger, the number of machines wearing out grows as well. Often, most investment ends up just replacing worn-out machines. This is actually true in the United States and other rich countries. According to the U.S. National Income and Product Accounts (the official U.S. GDP measures), about 12% of total GDP just goes toward replacing worn-out machines and computers and construction equipment.

   a. In the Solow model, if the depreciation rate increases, what happens to the steady-state capital level and output level? Answer in words and by using a diagram such as Figure 28.4. (*Bonus:* If the depreciation rate increases from 0.02 to 0.03, what is the new steady-state level of capital and output?)

   b. If the Solow model explains an important part of the real world, should countries hope for high depreciation rates or low depreciation rates? How does this square with the observation that when machines wear out, that "creates jobs" in the manufacturing industries?

MARGINAL REVOLUTION UNIVERSITY VIDEOS

Introduction to the Solow Model of Economic Growth

mruniversity.com/solow-model

Problems: **1, 23**

Physical Capital and Diminishing Returns

mruniversity.com/solow-physical-capital

Problems: **3, 11–13, 19, 24, 30**

The Solow Model and the Steady State

mruniversity.com/solow-steady-state

Problems: **4, 5, 14, 16, 26, 30, 31**

Human Capital and Conditional Convergence

mruniversity.com/solow-human-capital

Problems: **10, 17, 21, 24, 31**

The Solow Model and Ideas

mruniversity.com/solow-ideas

Problems: **2, 6, 17, 25, 29**

The Economics of Ideas

mruniversity.com/econ-ideas

Problems: **17, 19**

Patents, Prizes, and Subsidies

mruniversity.com/patents

Problems: **8, 9, 15, 18, 27**

The Idea Equation

mruniversity.com/idea-equation

Problems: **20, 22**

The Future of Economic Growth

mruniversity.com/ted-talk-ideas

Problems: **20, 24**

CHAPTER 28 APPENDIX

Excellent Growth

Using a spreadsheet, you can easily explore the Solow model and duplicate all the graphs in this chapter. First, label column A "Capital K" and put a 1 in cell A2. Second, you can create an increasing series by inputting the formula "=A2+1" in cell A3 and copying and pasting that formula into cells A4 to, say, A500. Your spreadsheet should look like Figure A28.1.

In column B, create a series for Output. Remember that $Y = \sqrt{K}$ so in cell B2, input the formula "=SQRT(A2)" and then copy and paste that formula into B3 to B500, as in Figure A28.2.

Now create the headings Investment, Depreciation, Investment Share, and Depreciation Rate in columns C to F, as in Figure A28.3.

In cell E2, put the investment share, 0.3, used in the text, and in cell F2, put the rate of depreciation that we used, 0.02.

In cell C2, which is highlighted, we want to input the formula for investment, which is γY where γ is the investment share. We could input "=0.3×B2" into C2 but we would like to be able to easily adjust the investment share and see what happens, so we will input "=$E$2×B2". The $E$2 says take the investment share from cell E2, and when we copy and paste this formula, it *always* uses cell E2 (not E3, E4, etc.). Copy and paste cell C2 into C3 to C500.

FIGURE A28.1

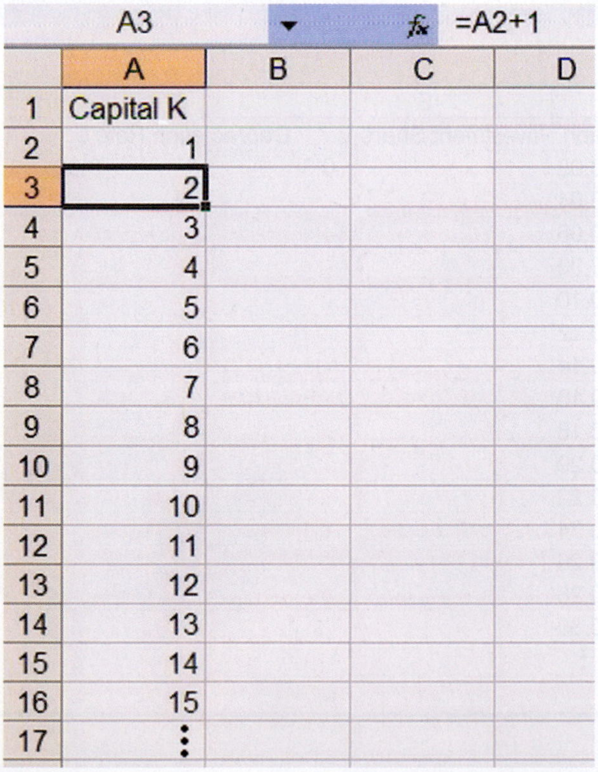

A3	▼	f_x =A2+1

	A	B	C	D
1	Capital K			
2	1			
3	2			
4	3			
5	4			
6	5			
7	6			
8	7			
9	8			
10	9			
11	10			
12	11			
13	12			
14	13			
15	14			
16	15			
17	⋮			

FIGURE A28.2

	B2	▼		f_x	=SQRT(A2)	
	A	B	C	D		
1	Capital K	Output				
2	1	1.00				
3	2	1.41				
4	3	1.73				
5	4	2.00				
6	5	2.24				
7	6	2.45				
8	7	2.65				
9	8	2.83				
10	9	3.00				
11	10	3.16				
12	11	3.32				
13	12	3.46				
14	13	3.61				
15	14	3.74				
16	15	3.87				
17	⋮	⋮				

FIGURE A28.3

	C2	▼		f_x	=$E$2*B2		
	A	B	C	D	E	F	
1	Capital K	Output	Investment	Depreciation	Investment Share γ	Depreciation Rate δ	
2	1	1.00	0.30	0.02	0.3	0.02	
3	2	1.41	0.42	0.04			
4	3	1.73	0.52	0.06			
5	4	2.00	0.60	0.08			
6	5	2.24	0.67	0.10			
7	6	2.45	0.73	0.12			
8	7	2.65	0.79	0.14			
9	8	2.83	0.85	0.16			
10	9	3.00	0.90	0.18			
11	10	3.16	0.95	0.20			
12	11	3.32	0.99	0.22			
13	12	3.46	1.04	0.24			
14	13	3.61	1.08	0.26			
15	14	3.74	1.12	0.28			
16	15	3.87	1.16	0.30			
17	⋮	⋮	⋮	⋮			

FIGURE A28.4

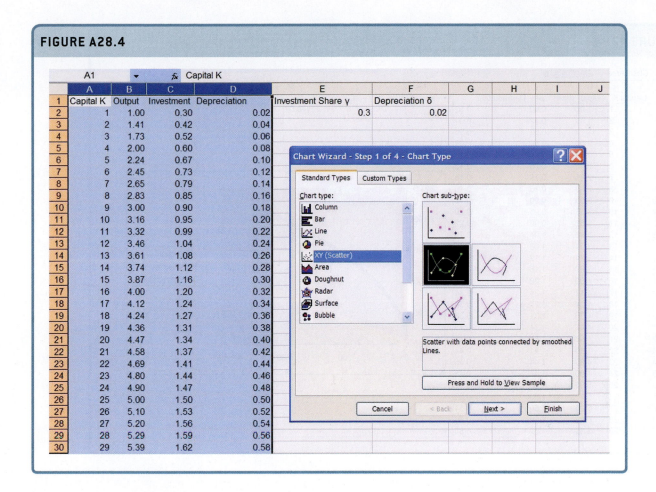

Depreciation is just δK where δ is the depreciation rate. As with investment, we might want to alter this parameter, so into cell D2 we will input "=$F$2×A2".

That's it! To duplicate the graph in Figure 28.4, for example, just highlight columns A, B, C, and D, click the Chart icon (you can also click Chart in the Insert menu), choose XY (Scatter) and the highlighted subtype, and then click on finish. (In Excel 2007 click Insert and then Scatter in the Chart submenu to do the same thing.) See Figure A28.4.

The result is as in Figure A28.5.

If you want to see what happens if the investment share increases to 0.4, as in Figure 28.7 in the chapter, just change cell E2 to 0.4 and the graph will change automatically. You can make other adjustments as well. One thing to watch for is that with parameters too different from the ones we have given, the equilibrium capital stock may be greater than 500. So if you want to see the full picture, you will need to extend the rows even further.

FIGURE A28.5

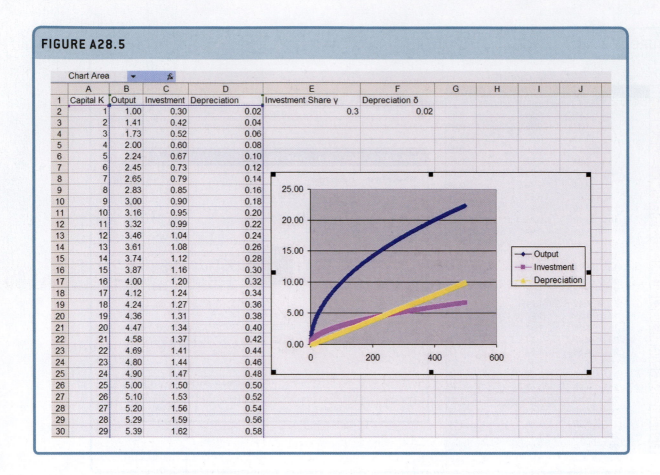

	A	B	C	D	E	F	G	H	I	J
1	Capital K	Output	Investment	Depreciation	Investment Share γ	Depreciation δ				
2	1	1.00	0.30	0.02	0.3	0.02				
3	2	1.41	0.42	0.04						
4	3	1.73	0.52	0.06						
5	4	2.00	0.60	0.08						
6	5	2.24	0.67	0.10						
7	6	2.45	0.73	0.12						
8	7	2.65	0.79	0.14						
9	8	2.83	0.85	0.16						
10	9	3.00	0.90	0.18						
11	10	3.16	0.95	0.20						
12	11	3.32	0.99	0.22						
13	12	3.46	1.04	0.24						
14	13	3.61	1.08	0.26						
15	14	3.74	1.12	0.28						
16	15	3.87	1.16	0.30						
17	16	4.00	1.20	0.32						
18	17	4.12	1.24	0.34						
19	18	4.24	1.27	0.36						
20	19	4.36	1.31	0.38						
21	20	4.47	1.34	0.40						
22	21	4.58	1.37	0.42						
23	22	4.69	1.41	0.44						
24	23	4.80	1.44	0.46						
25	24	4.90	1.47	0.48						
26	25	5.00	1.50	0.50						
27	26	5.10	1.53	0.52						
28	27	5.20	1.56	0.54						
29	28	5.29	1.59	0.56						
30	29	5.39	1.62	0.58						

Chapter 28 Appendix Question

1. Use the instructions in the appendix to set up the Solow model in Excel with the Investment Share γ equal to 0.3 and with the Depreciation Rate δ equal to 0.02. Both numbers are just what we used in the chapter. Now increase the Investment Share to 0.36.

   a. What is the new level of steady-state capital? (Remember, the level of steady-state capital is where *Investment = Depreciation*.)

   b. At the new steady level of capital, what is the level of output *Y*?

   Now change the Investment Share back to 0.3 and this time increase the Depreciation Rate to 0.025.

   c. What is the new level of steady-state capital?

   d. At the steady-state level of capital, what is the level of output *Y*?

   e. Fill in the blanks with your conclusions:

   An increase in the investment share _____ the steady-state level of capital and output.

   An increase in the depreciation rate _____ the steady-state level of capital and output.

29

Saving, Investment, and the Financial System

The world's financial system was shaken to its core when on September 15, 2008, the investment bank Lehman Brothers filed for bankruptcy. The Lehman bankruptcy was by far the largest in history. To give you some context, when it went bankrupt Lehman had assets worth $691 billion; when GM went bankrupt several months later it had assets worth just $91 billion. Lehman's bankruptcy triggered stock market crashes around the world. Over the next several weeks the Dow Jones Industrial Average fell by 25%, the British FTSE 100 Index fell by 15%, and the Brazilian BOVESPA fell by 10%, to give just a few examples. The Lehman collapse marks the beginning of the recession of 2008–2009, the most serious recession in the United States since the Great Depression. The Lehman bankruptcy shook the financial world, not simply because it was large but because Lehman Brothers was an important financial intermediary, an institution that works to transform savings into investments.

Lehman Brothers failed because it had lost billions on buying and betting on mortgage securities. So had many other banks and financial institutions. When Lehman failed, many people wondered: Who was next? No one wanted to lend money to a firm that might soon go bankrupt. As a result, credit dried up for firms in many sectors, throwing the American economy and indeed the world economy into what was the scariest moment in many decades. This episode is sometimes called the collapse of the "shadow banking system," a term that we will examine in more detail later in this chapter, but we might also call it the collapse of the financial intermediaries.

This chapter is about savers and borrowers and some of the financial intermediaries—banks, bond markets, and stock exchanges—that bridge the gap between savers and borrowers, as we illustrate in Figure 29.1. We have opened the chapter with a scary story about what can happen when financial intermediaries fail. Fortunately, the collapse of Lehman was an extreme episode and there are plenty of other cases in which intermediation works quite smoothly, to the benefit of all parties involved. Recall from the previous two chapters that savings are necessary for capital accumulation, and the more capital an economy can invest, the greater is GDP per capita. So transforming savings into

The collapse of Lehman Brothers shook the world financial system.

Saving is income that is not spent on consumption goods.

Investment is the purchase of new capital goods.

investment is important. More generally, connecting savers and borrowers increases the gains from trade and smooths the process of economic growth.

Before proceeding, let's make it clear what we mean by the words **saving** and **investment**. Saving is income that is not spent on consumption goods. Investment is the purchase of new capital, things like tools, machinery, and factories. It's important to see that the way economists define investment is not the same as the way a stockbroker defines investment. If Starbucks buys new espresso machines for its stores, that's investment. If John buys stock in Starbucks, that is not investment in the economic sense but merely a transfer of ownership rights of already existing capital (see the chapter on Stock Markets and Personal Finance for a treatment of how individuals should allocate their funds for their personal "investments"). Most of the trading on stock exchanges is thus not investment in the economic sense because it simply transfers ownership of a stock from one person to another. From an economic point of view, investment requires a purchase of new capital.

Ok, let's see how savings are mobilized and transformed into investment. We will be using the economist's tools in trade—supply and demand—and we'll start with the supply of savings. This is important material in its own right and it also supplies building blocks for understanding banks, bank failures, and what went wrong in the global financial crisis of 2007–2008.

The Supply of Savings

We begin with the left side of Figure 29.1, the supply of savings. Economists have a good but imperfect understanding of what determines the supply of savings. Here are four of the major factors: smoothing consumption, impatience, marketing and psychological factors, and interest rates.

Individuals Want to Smooth Consumption

If you consumed what you earned every year, your consumption over time might look like Path A in Figure 29.2. Along Path A, consumption is equal to income. Consumption is high during your working years, but after retirement consumption drops precipitously—as a result, once you retire and your income

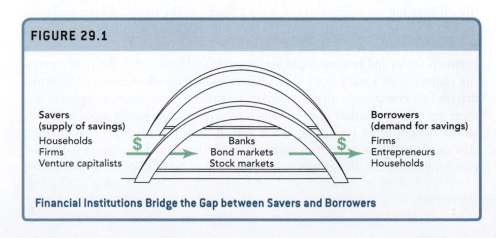

FIGURE 29.1

Savers
(supply of savings)

Households
Firms
Venture capitalists

Banks
Bond markets
Stock markets

Borrowers
(demand for savings)

Firms
Entrepreneurs
Households

Financial Institutions Bridge the Gap between Savers and Borrowers

FIGURE 29.2

Income, consumption

Savings

Path B

Dissavings

Path A: Consumption = Income

Working years   Retirement   Time

Savings Help to Smooth Consumption If workers spend their entire income every year, their consumption over time will follow Path A. Along Path A, consumption drops tremendously at retirement. By saving during the working years and dissaving during the retirement years, workers can smooth their consumption so that it looks more like Path B.

falls, you must sell the nice car and give up the fancy lifestyle just to scrape by. Most people would prefer consumption Path B. Along Path B, consumption is less than income during the working years because you save for retirement. But when retirement comes, consumption is greater than income as you spend your savings, or "dissave."

Economists say that Path B is "smoother" than Path A. The desire to smooth consumption over time is a reason to save and, as we will discuss shortly, also a reason to borrow.

The consumption-smoothing theory of saving can tell us something important about AIDS, Africa, and economic growth. Remember from previous chapters that savings are necessary to finance the capital accumulation that generates high standards of living. If there are no savings, investment dries up, economic growth declines, and the standard of living falls.

Now consider that AIDS has dramatically reduced life expectancy in southern Africa. What is your prediction about savings rates? Imagine that you expected to die in a few years—would you save much? Probably not. Similarly, many poorer Africans don't save much because, sadly, they expect to die young.[1] This gives rise to a vicious cycle. The decline in life expectancy caused by AIDS reduces saving rates, which in turn reduces economic growth and the standard of living, and that makes it more difficult to combat diseases like AIDS.

Fluctuations in income are another reason why people save. Some workers, such as salespeople, writers, and home builders, have incomes that fluctuate from year to year. Most workers could have unexpected health problems or they could find themselves unemployed and so they also fear that their income might fluctuate. By saving in the good years, workers can build a cushion of wealth to draw from in the bad years, thereby smoothing their consumption across all years.

Individuals Are Impatient

Another reason why people save, or fail to save, is their level of impatience. Most individuals prefer to consume now rather than later, so saving is not always easy. Some people, however, are very impatient; others less so. This is

Saving and Borrowing

interactive activity

Time preference is the desire to have goods and services sooner rather than later (all else being equal).

what economists call **time preference**. Time preference reflects the fact that today feels more real than tomorrow. The more impatient a person, the more likely that person's savings rate will be low.

Impatience is reflected not just in savings but in any economic situation where people must compare costs and benefits over time. The cost of a college degree, for example, comes well before the benefit. To get a college degree, you must pay for tuition and books and, most important, you must give up the income that you could earn from a job, all right now. The benefits of a college degree are large—a typical college graduate will earn nearly twice as much as a typical high school graduate—but the benefits are all in the future. An impatient person will weigh the up-front costs highly and discount the future benefits. Impatient people are unlikely to go to college.

Crime is another economic activity with immediate benefits and future costs so it's not surprising that criminals tend to be impatient people. Similarly, heroin addicts, alcoholics, and smokers all tend to discount the future more heavily than nonaddicts.

Impatience depends, in part, on circumstances and, in part, on the person. In one fascinating study, four-year-old children were offered one marshmallow now or two if they could wait for the tester to return. Many years later, the children were evaluated again—the children who had waited were less impulsive and had higher grades than the children who had not waited.[2]

The Marshmallow Test

Marketing and Psychological Factors

Marketing matters, even for savings. Often individuals save more if saving is presented as the natural or default alternative. In one study, economists studied retirement savings plans. Some employers automatically enrolled all new employees in a retirement savings plan, leaving the employees the choice to opt out, whereas others required employees to request such an account, in effect asking them to opt in. In the businesses that used automatic enrollment, the savings plan participation rate was 25% higher than in the businesses in which employees needed to request a retirement account.

The default also mattered for how much was saved. In one firm, the default savings rate was 3% of salary. More than a quarter of the workers chose that as their savings rate, despite an employer guarantee of a dollar-for-dollar match on contributions of up to 6% of salary. Later, the company switched to a 6% default savings rate; in that setting, hardly any new workers chose the 3% savings contribution rate even though they could have switched with just a phone call.[3]

It's quite surprising how some simple psychological changes, combined with effective marketing and promotion, can change how much people save for their retirement. Behavioral economics, a new and growing field within economics, combines economics, psychology, and neurology to study how people make decisions and how they can be helped to overcome biases in decision making.

The Interest Rate

The quantity of savings also depends on the interest rate, namely how much savers are paid to save. If the interest rate is 5% per year, then $100 saved today returns $105 a year from now. If the interest rate is 10% per year, then $100 saved today returns $110 a year from now. All else being equal, higher interest rates usually call forth more savings.* Figure 29.3 shows the supply curve for savings. The vertical axis of Figure 29.3 measures the interest rate. The horizontal axis measures savings in dollars. In this example, an interest rate of 5% generates total savings of $200 billion and an interest rate of 10% generates total savings of $280 billion.

You might wonder why the supply curve for savings has the interest rate on the vertical axis while other supply curves have had price on the vertical axis. In fact, interest rates are just a convenient way of expressing the price of savings. An interest rate of 5%, for example, means that the saver will be paid $5 (in one year) for every $100 saved. Thus, we could say that when the price of lending is $5 per $100 saved, the quantity of savings is $200 billion. It's a bit easier, however, to think in terms of interest rates.

The bottom line is that the interest rate is a market price and it has the same properties of market prices that we discussed in the introductory chapters of this book.

The Demand to Borrow

Why do people borrow? People borrow to smooth their consumption path and especially to finance large investments. Let's look at each of these reasons for borrowing.

Individuals Want to Smooth Consumption

Just as people save in order to smooth consumption, one reason people borrow is to smooth consumption. Many young people, for example, borrow so that they can invest in their education. If they had to pay their tuition expenses all at once, many students would have to sell their car or eat nothing but beans and oatmeal for a year. But if tuition payments can be made over many years, as borrowing makes possible, the sacrifices are spread out and become less painful. A student who can borrow can move some of the sacrifices into future periods when the (now former) student has a job and a regular income. Student borrowing is thus another example of how credit markets let people smooth their consumption over time.

The "lifecycle" theory of savings, pioneered by Nobel Laureate Franco Modigliani, puts the demand to borrow and save together. The lifecycle theory is illustrated in Figure 29.4. Income starts out low during the college years and in the early work years. To finance college and to buy a first home, people borrow so their consumption is higher than their income. As workers enter their prime earning years, they save to pay off their college debt and mortgage

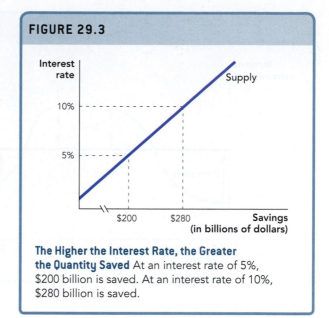

FIGURE 29.3

The Higher the Interest Rate, the Greater the Quantity Saved At an interest rate of 5%, $200 billion is saved. At an interest rate of 10%, $280 billion is saved.

CHECK YOURSELF

- Examining Figure 29.1, what is the crucial function that financial institutions perform?
- Financial advisors have warned that increased life expectancy means that many people have not saved enough for their retirement. If true, what will the consumption path of these people look like as they reach their retirement years? Will this consumption path be smooth?
- Can you think of the other factors that might generate a demand to save? (*Hint:* Apart from retirement, what other factors could cause income to be volatile?)

* In principle, it is possible for the supply curve for savings to be negatively sloped. For instance, if an individual wanted exactly $100 in one year's time, then at an interest rate of 10% he or she would need to save $90.91, but at an interest rate of 20%, he or she would need to save only $83.33. Thus, an increase in the interest rate could reduce savings. The evidence, however, indicates that individual savings rates typically respond positively to higher interest rates. In addition, higher U.S. interest rates also encourage lenders in other countries to move some of their savings to U.S. markets. Both forces mean that the supply curve for savings is upwardly sloped in most circumstances.

FIGURE 29.4

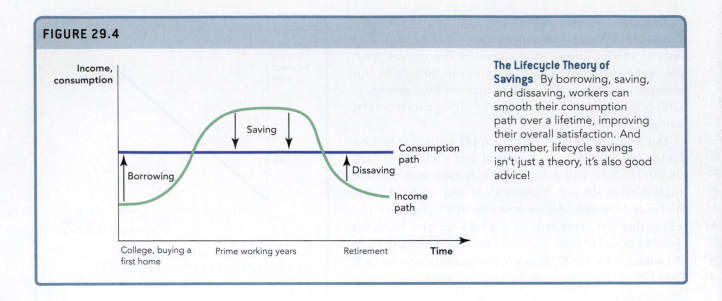

The Lifecycle Theory of Savings By borrowing, saving, and dissaving, workers can smooth their consumption path over a lifetime, improving their overall satisfaction. And remember, lifecycle savings isn't just a theory, it's also good advice!

and they prepare for retirement—during this time period consumption is less than income. As people get older and retire, consumption is once again above income as dissaving (i.e., using up savings) occurs. Overall, borrowing, saving, and dissaving help people to smooth out their consumption path over time—although few people would have a consumption path as smooth as the one we have drawn here!

Governments also borrow for reasons much like consumers. Governments may borrow, for example, to finance unusually large expenditures such as those required to pay for a war, or to pay for large investments such as the interstate highway system. We discuss government taxes, spending, and borrowing at greater length in the chapter on the Federal Budget.

Borrowing Is Necessary to Finance Large Investments

Businesses also borrow extensively. Many new businesses can't get under way at all without borrowing. Often the people with the best business ideas are not the people with the most savings, so people with good ideas must borrow funds to start their careers as entrepreneurs.

Fred Smith, the legendary entrepreneur, first laid out the idea for FedEx in an undergraduate paper he had to write for an economics class. Smith's idea, overnight delivery of packages using a hub and spoke system, was great but the problem was that he couldn't start small. To be successful, Smith needed to cover a good part of the country from day 1 and he didn't have enough of his own money to build an entire network. Smith began FedEx with 16 planes covering 25 cities using money he borrowed and also by selling part ownership of FedEx to venture capitalists, investors willing to accept risk in return for a stake in future profits. FedEx, of course, has been a huge success—it changed the way America does business and made Smith a very wealthy man. By the way, Smith's grade on his paper: C!

More generally, businesses borrow to finance large projects. The costs of developing an apartment building are all up front; the revenues don't start flowing until the building is completed and the tenants have moved in. In fact, it may take many years before the revenues fully cover all the up-front costs.

If a developer had to wait until he personally had enough funds to pay the up-front costs, he might be able to develop just one or two buildings in his lifetime. By borrowing, developers are able to invest now and develop many more buildings.

The examples of borrowing that we have given share a common theme. A student who can't borrow may not be able to get an education even though the education would be a good investment. A government that can't borrow may not be able to invest in an interstate highway system even though the highway system would pay for itself many times over. A builder who can't borrow may not be able to build an apartment building even though it would be a profitable investment. Thus, borrowing plays an important role in the economy—the ability to borrow greatly increases the ability to invest and, as shown in the previous two chapters, higher investment increases the standard of living and the rate of economic growth.

In Shakespeare's *Hamlet*, Polonius advises "Neither a borrower nor a lender be." But people forget, Polonius was a fool.

The Interest Rate

Of course, the quantity of funds that people want to borrow also depends on the cost of the loan, or the interest rate. Businesses, for example, borrow when they expect that the return on their investment will be greater than the cost of the loan. Thus, if the interest rate is 10%, businesses will borrow only if they expect that their investment will return *more* than 10%. If the interest rate is 5%, then businesses will only borrow if they expect that their investment will return *more* than 5%. Since a larger number of investments will return *more* than 5% than will return *more* than 10%, the demand to borrow follows the law of demand: The lower the interest rate, the greater the quantity of funds demanded for investment as well as for other purposes.

In Figure 29.5, $190 billion is demanded when the interest rate is 10% and $300 billion is demanded when the interest rate is 5%. But how is the interest rate determined? That is the subject of the next section.

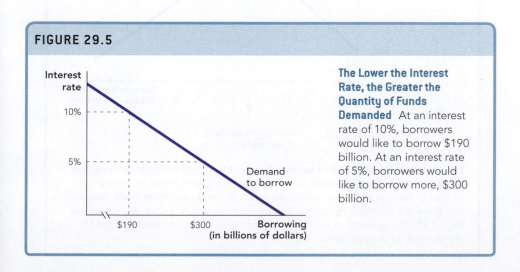

FIGURE 29.5

The Lower the Interest Rate, the Greater the Quantity of Funds Demanded At an interest rate of 10%, borrowers would like to borrow $190 billion. At an interest rate of 5%, borrowers would like to borrow more, $300 billion.

Equilibrium in the Market for Loanable Funds

The **market for loanable funds** occurs when suppliers of loanable funds (savers) trade with demanders of loanable funds (borrowers). Trading in the market for loanable funds determines the equilibrium interest rate.

Now that we have covered the supply of savings and the demand to borrow, we can put them together to find an equilibrium in what economists call the **market for loanable funds**. In Figure 29.6, the equilibrium interest rate is 8% and the equilibrium quantity of savings is $250 billion. Notice that in equilibrium, the quantity of funds supplied equals the quantity of funds demanded.

The interest rate adjusts to equalize savings and borrowing in the same way and for the same reasons that the price of oil adjusts to balance the supply and demand for oil. If the interest rate were higher than 8%, the quantity of savings supplied would exceed the quantity of savings demanded, creating a surplus of savings. With a surplus of savings, suppliers will bid the interest rate down as they compete to lend. If the interest rate were lower than 8%, the quantity of savings demanded would exceed the quantity of savings supplied, a shortage. With a shortage of savings, demanders would bid the interest rate up as they competed to borrow. (See Chapter 4 for a review.)

Shifts in Supply and Demand

Changes in economic conditions will shift the supply or demand curve and change the equilibrium interest rate and quantity of savings. Consider an economy in which the citizens become less impatient, and more willing to save for the future. These shifts occurred in South Korea in the 1960s and 1970s, once many

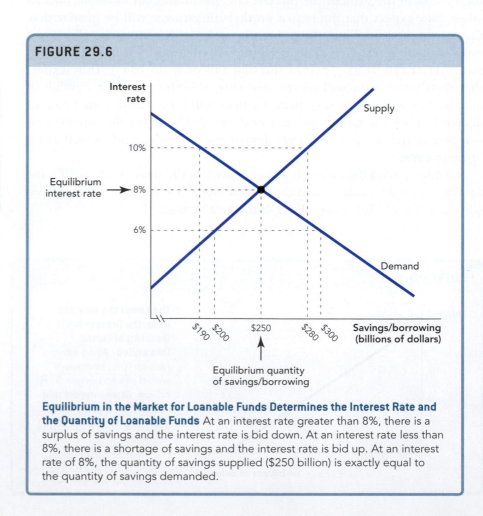

FIGURE 29.6

Equilibrium in the Market for Loanable Funds Determines the Interest Rate and the Quantity of Loanable Funds At an interest rate greater than 8%, there is a surplus of savings and the interest rate is bid down. At an interest rate less than 8%, there is a shortage of savings and the interest rate is bid up. At an interest rate of 8%, the quantity of savings supplied ($250 billion) is exactly equal to the quantity of savings demanded.

Korean citizens realized they could copy some aspects of the Japanese economic miracle. Across East Asia more generally, growing life spans and fewer children to support (and fewer children to be supported by, in old age) led to a regional savings boom. An increase in the supply of savings is shown by shifting the supply curve to the right and down (indicating more savings at any interest rate or, equivalently, a willingness to save any given amount in return for a lower interest rate).

In Figure 29.7, an increase in the supply of savings causes the equilibrium interest rate to fall from 8% to 6% and the quantity of savings to increase from $250 billion to $300 billion.

What did this shift in savings mean for South Korea? In 1960, Korea was among the poorest countries in the world but today it is a fully developed nation. South Korea's increased savings were plowed into investment and, as we know from our discussion of the Solow model in the previous chapter, one of the key drivers of economic growth is a high rate of investment and capital accumulation.

Of course, a decrease in the supply of savings is shown in the opposite manner, by shifting the supply curve to the left and up.

Sometimes investors become less optimistic, which decreases the demand to invest and borrow. For instance, during a recession many entrepreneurs get scared about the future and they are reluctant to invest. Projects that look good to investors when the economy is booming may look unprofitable when the economy is in the doldrums. The decrease in investment demand can itself help to spread and prolong the recession, as we discuss at greater length in the chapter on Transmission and Amplification Mechanisms. In Figure 29.8, a decrease in investment demand reduces the interest rate from 8% to 6% and the quantity of savings from $250 billion to $190 billion.

Sometimes, to counteract the decrease in investment demand during a recession, a government offers a temporary investment tax credit. An investment tax credit gives firms that invest in plants and equipment a tax break. The tax credit is usually temporary to encourage firms to invest quickly, when the

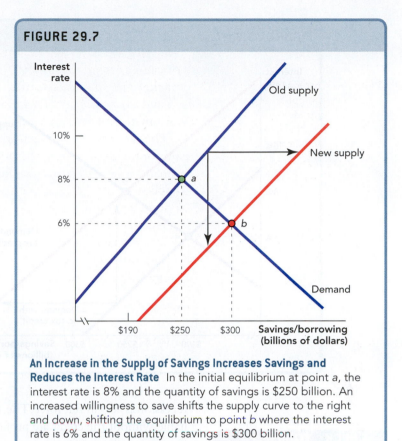

FIGURE 29.7

An Increase in the Supply of Savings Increases Savings and Reduces the Interest Rate In the initial equilibrium at point *a*, the interest rate is 8% and the quantity of savings is $250 billion. An increased willingness to save shifts the supply curve to the right and down, shifting the equilibrium to point *b* where the interest rate is 6% and the quantity of savings is $300 billion.

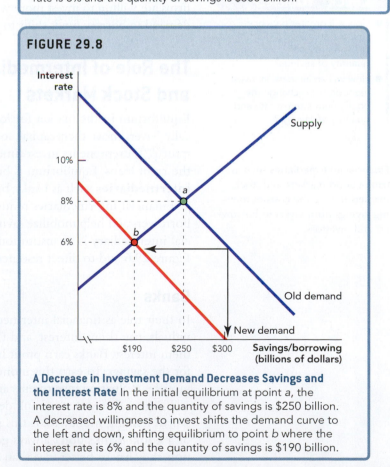

FIGURE 29.8

A Decrease in Investment Demand Decreases Savings and the Interest Rate In the initial equilibrium at point *a*, the interest rate is 8% and the quantity of savings is $250 billion. A decreased willingness to invest shifts the demand curve to the left and down, shifting equilibrium to point *b* where the interest rate is 6% and the quantity of savings is $190 billion.

FIGURE 29.9

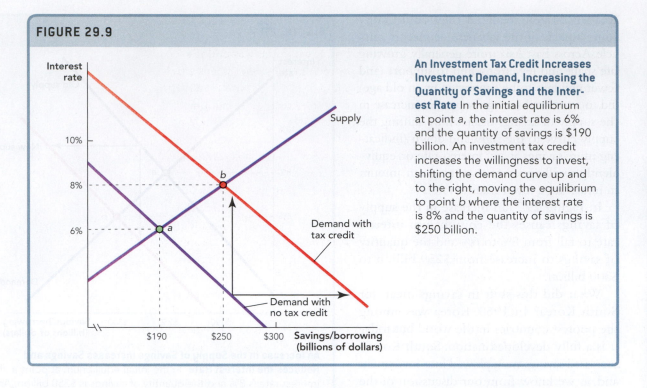

An Investment Tax Credit Increases Investment Demand, Increasing the Quantity of Savings and the Interest Rate In the initial equilibrium at point *a*, the interest rate is 6% and the quantity of savings is $190 billion. An investment tax credit increases the willingness to invest, shifting the demand curve up and to the right, moving the equilibrium to point *b* where the interest rate is 8% and the quantity of savings is $250 billion.

CHECK YOURSELF

■ How will greater patience shift the supply of savings and change the interest rate and quantity of savings?

■ How will an increase in investment demand change the equilibrium interest rate and quantity of savings?

Financial intermediaries such as banks, bond markets, and stock markets reduce the costs of moving savings from savers to borrowers and investors.

recession is still in full force. The tax credit means that projects that were unprofitable without the credit are profitable with the credit, so at any given interest rate firms are willing to invest more when a tax credit is available. In other words, the demand to borrow funds shifts to the right (and up), as shown in Figure 29.9.

The Role of Intermediaries: Banks, Bonds, and Stock Markets

Equilibrium in the market for loanable funds does not come about automatically. Savers move their capital, sometimes around the world, to find the highest returns. Entrepreneurs invest time and energy to find the right investments and the right loans. Equilibrium is brought about with the assistance of **financial intermediaries** such as banks, bond markets, and stock markets.

Financial intermediaries reduce the costs of moving savings from savers to borrowers and help mobilize savings toward productive uses. At its core, a financial intermediary is an institution that helps to bring about the equilibrium in Figure 29.6 and to direct resources to more highly valued uses.

Banks

In their role as financial intermediaries, banks receive savings from many individuals, pay them interest, and then loan these funds to borrowers, charging them interest. Banks earn profit by charging more for their loans than they pay for the savings. To earn this money, they must provide useful "middleman" services by evaluating investments and spreading risk.

Imagine that you, as a bank depositor, had to decide which companies were worth lending money to. Is this guy Fred Smith with his FedEx idea a genius or a kook? Banks don't always get it right, but by specializing in loan evaluation, they have a better idea than most of us of which business ideas make sense.

When banks specialize, individual savers don't have to evaluate which factories ought to be built or which businesses deserve to be supported.

Even if individuals could evaluate business ideas, it would be wasteful if every saver spent time evaluating the same business. Imagine that a business needs a million dollar loan. One thousand savers are each willing to lend the business $1,000. If each saver spent a day evaluating the quality of the business, that would be 999 wasted days of effort. It makes more sense for the lenders to appoint a single person to evaluate the business on behalf of all of them. That's exactly what a bank does. Banks coordinate lenders and minimize information costs. Banks are thus an important example of the benefits of specialization and the division of labor.

Banks also spread risk. If Fred Smith, or some other borrower, defaults on his loan, banks spread that loss across the many lenders who deposit money in the bank. This avoids the risk that you have lent Fred Smith $1,000 and suddenly are out the entire sum. It's less risky and no less profitable to lend one thousand firms $1 each than to lend one firm $1,000, so the spreading of risk encourages greater lending and investment.

Banks also play a role in the payments system. Money deposited in a bank can be drawn on with a check or debit card or via the ATM. We discuss banks and the payment system at greater length in our chapter on the Federal Reserve System.

Overall, banks make our lives simpler. We open our accounts, deposit our money, receive our interest payments, and write our checks; at the same time we are participating in the process of economic growth because the bank oversees a process by which our savings are turned into productive investments.

The Bond Market

Instead of borrowing from a bank, well-known corporations can borrow directly from the public. Your local pizza restaurant borrows from a bank, or perhaps even from relatives, because restaurants are a risky business and the finances of that company are difficult for outside investors to evaluate. But when it comes to IBM or Toyota, investors can more easily find information about the firm and so they are willing to bypass the bank as an intermediary and lend to the company directly.

> A **bond** is a sophisticated IOU that documents who owes how much and when payment must be made.

When a member of the public lends money to a corporation, the corporation acknowledges its debt by issuing a **bond**. *A bond is an IOU.* The bond contract lists how much is owed to the bond's owner and when payment must be made. In some cases, all the money is owed on a single day (the day of maturity); in other cases, periodic payments, called coupon payments, must be made in addition to a final payment.

The New York Central and Hudson River Railroad Company borrowed money in 1897 for which they issued bonds, one of which is pictured on the right. The bond is an IOU that promises the Central will pay the owner $1,000 in 1997. In addition, every six months until 1997, the Central promised to pay the owner $17.50. You can see from the picture why the periodic payments are called "coupon payments": The coupons are on the right of the bond and can be clipped and sent to the issuer of the bond to receive payment.

Central's bond illustrates one of the advantages of bond finance—large sums of money can be raised now and invested in long-lived assets such as railroad track. The money can then be paid back over a long period of time, in the case of the Central over a 100-year period.

ALEX TABARROK

A 100-year bond issued by the New York Central and Hudson River Railroad Company in 1897 The bond is an IOU that promised the owner $1,000 in 1997 and $17.50 every six months until that time.

All bonds involve a risk that when the payments come due, the borrower will not be able to pay; this is called "default risk." The Central, for example, eventually defaulted when it went bankrupt, but it did pay its coupons until 1970. Major bond issues are graded by agencies like Moody's and Standard and Poor's. AAA, for example, is the highest grade issued by Standard and Poor's; this grade indicates, according to the rating agencies, that the bond is very likely to be paid. Grades range all the way from AAA to D when a firm is in default. Bonds rated less than BBB- are sometimes called "junk bonds." It's important to remember that risk can never be perfectly quantified and the rating agencies can be wrong—a point we will return to later in this chapter when we discuss the financial crisis of 2007–2008.

If a risky company wishes to borrow money, it has to promise a higher rate of interest because lenders will demand to be compensated for a greater risk of default. Why lend to a risky firm unless you have some prospect of earning higher returns?

Thus, the marketplace grades the risks of major investments and charges interest rates accordingly. In 2016, Berkshire Hathaway, the investment company managed by Warren Buffett, was still a very profitable company. In early 2016, it borrowed $9 billion from the bond market and paid a rate just above that offered to the U.S. government, an extraordinary reflection of its perceived financial soundness. Elsewhere, in the United Kingdom, the soccer team Manchester United was borrowing money at about 9% for a seven-year bond; apparently their players and managers aren't as good!

Collateral is something of value that by agreement becomes the property of the lender if the borrower defaults.

Can you think of one reason why interest rates on home loans are almost always lower than interest rates on vacation loans? The bank can repossess the house but not the vacation! The house is a form of **collateral**, something of value that by agreement becomes the property of the lender if the borrower defaults on the loan. Thus, the market for loanable funds is really a broad spectrum of markets; the interest rates differ depending on the borrower, repayment time, amount of the loan, type of collateral, and many other features of the loan.

Greater risk can reduce the supply of funds to the market as a whole. If lenders expect a recession, for example, they may become concerned that many firms will go bankrupt and default on their debt. A lender who was willing to lend at 8% when he or she thought the risk was low will demand a higher return if the lender believes the risk of default has increased significantly.

Crowding out is the decrease in private consumption and investment that occurs when government borrows more.

Governments borrow money as well. As of 2016, the U.S. government owed about $14.4 trillion dollars to private borrowers (individuals, firms, and governments other than the U.S. federal government). When the government borrows a lot of money, private consumption and investment can be **crowded out**. Imagine, for example, that the government borrows $100 billion to cover a budget deficit. In Figure 29.10 on the next page, the demand curve for loanable funds shifts to the right by $100 billion, increasing the interest rate from 7% to 9%. The higher interest rate has two effects. First, it draws an additional $50 billion of savings into the market so total savings increase from $200 billion to $250 billion. Since greater savings mean less consumption, we can also say that consumption is reduced by $50 billion. Second, the higher interest rate means that some investments and other projects are no longer profitable, so at a higher interest rate, private borrowing falls. In Figure 29.10, we show private borrowing falling by $50 billion. Thus, the $100 billion necessary to cover the government's budget deficit comes from a combination of reduced consumption and reduced private investment and other private borrowing.

FIGURE 29.10

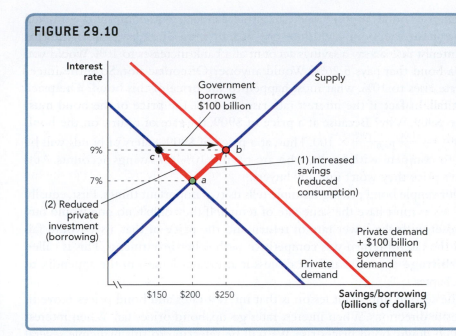

An Increase in Government Borrowing Crowds Out Private Consumption and Investment When the government borrows, it shifts the demand curve to the right, moving the equilibrium from point a to point b. To reach the new equilibrium at point b, two things happen: (1) The higher interest rate draws forth more savings, which means that private consumption falls; and (2) the higher interest rate reduces the demand to borrow and invest. Thus, when the government borrows more, some of the increased borrowing is financed by reduced consumption and some by reduced investment.

We will return to the issues of crowding out, government debt, and deficits in our chapter on the Federal Budget and the chapter on Fiscal Policy.

When the U.S. government borrows, it issues a variety of different bonds. U.S. Treasury bonds or T-bonds are 30-year bonds that pay interest every 6 months. T-notes are bonds with maturities ranging from 2 to 10 years that also pay interest every 6 months. T-bills are bonds with maturities of a few days to 26 weeks that pay only at maturity. A bond that pays only at maturity is also called a zero-coupon bond or a discount bond since these bonds sell at a discount to their face value.

Treasury securities are desirable for many investors because they are easy to buy and sell and the U.S. government is unlikely to default on its payments. In general, short-term U.S. government securities tend to be the safest assets, and very short-term bonds, called commercial paper, issued by very large corporations tend to be safe as well. In addition, Treasury securities, especially T-bills, are important in monetary policy; the Federal Reserve buys and sells Treasury securities on a daily basis to influence the money supply (more on this in the chapter on Monetary Policy.).

Bond Prices and Interest Rates It's often convenient to express the price of a bond in terms of an interest rate; this is easiest to do with a zero-coupon bond. Suppose, for example, that a bond with very little risk exists that will pay $1,000 in one year's time and that this bond is currently selling for $950. If you were to buy this bond today and hold it until maturity, you would earn $50 ($1,000 − $950), or a rate of return of 5.26% $= \frac{\$1,000 - \$950}{\$950} \times$ 100. Thus, every zero-coupon bond has an implied rate of return that can be calculated by subtracting the price from the value at maturity, often called the face value, and then dividing by the price:

$$\text{Rate of return for a zero-coupon bond} = \frac{\text{Face value} - \text{Price}}{\text{Price}} \times 100$$

Sellers of bonds must compete to attract lenders, who compare the implied rate of return on bonds with the rate of return on other assets. Imagine that the interest rate on say a savings account at a bank increases to 10%. Would you buy a bond that pays 5.26%? Would anyone? Of course not. So if the interest rate rises to 10%, what must happen to the price of this bond? The price must fall. In fact, if the interest rate rises to 10%, the price of the bond must fall to $909. Why? Because at a price of $909, the rate of return on the bond is $10\% = \frac{\$1,000 - \$909}{\$909} \times 100$. Thus, at a price of $909, sellers of bonds will be able to compete with banks, who are paying 10% on savings accounts. At a higher price they won't find any buyers.

Our simple bond pricing example tells us two important things. First, equally risky assets must have the same rate of return. If they didn't, no one would buy the asset with the lower rate of return and the price of that asset would fall until the rate of return was competitive with other investments. This is called an **arbitrage** principle and we discuss it at greater length in the appendix to this chapter.

Arbitrage, the buying and selling of equally risky assets, ensures that equally risky assets earn equal returns.

The second important lesson is that interest rates and bond prices move in opposite directions. When interest rates go up, bond prices fall. When interest rates go down, bond prices rise. We will be referring to this principle several times throughout the textbook so do study the principle and make a note of it:

■ **Interest rates and bond prices move in opposite directions.**

The inverse relationship between bond prices and interest rates tells us that in addition to default risk, people who buy bonds also face interest rate risk. For instance, perhaps a bond was issued in 2003 at an interest rate of 7%. If interest rates for comparable investments later rise to 9%, having bought a bond yielding 7% was in retrospect a mistake. If, instead, comparable interest rates were to fall to 3%, the bond purchase worked out for the better. The buyer locked in a 7% return when other rates of return were falling to 3%. In other words, bond buyers are making bets that interest rates will fall (bond prices will rise), or at least they are hoping that interest rates will fall. And similarly, bond sellers are betting or hoping that interest rates will rise, which means bond prices will—do you remember?—fall. Again, for more on the relationship between bond prices and interest rates, see the chapter appendix.

The Stock Market

A stock or a share is a certificate of ownership in a corporation.

Just as businesses fund their activities by taking out bank loans and selling bonds, they also issue shares of stock. **Stocks** are shares of ownership in a corporation. Owners have a claim to the firm's profits, but remember that profit is revenue minus costs. In other words, profit is what is left over *after* everyone else—creditors, bond holders, suppliers, and employees—have been paid. If profits are high, shareholders benefit. They benefit directly if the firm pays out its profits in dividends or indirectly if the firm reinvests its profits in a way that increases the value of the stock. But if profits are low or negative, shareholders suffer losses.

Stocks are traded on organized markets called stock exchanges. The New York Stock Exchange (NYSE) is the largest in the world. When new stocks are issued, that is called an **initial public offering** or an IPO. An IPO is the first time a stock is sold to the public.

An initial public offering (IPO) is the first time a corporation sells stock to the public in order to raise capital.

You'll recall from the beginning of this chapter that simply buying and selling existing shares of stock does *not* increase net investment in the economy. But when a firm sells *new* shares to the public, it typically uses the proceeds to fund investment, that is, to buy new capital goods. In addition, the possibility of offering equity or ownership in a firm opens the door to many business ventures that might never get off the ground, or might not be able to expand rapidly.

Consider Google. Today Google is a household word, but when the company began in September 1998, it was headquartered in a garage. Yet in August 2004, Google founders Sergei Brin and Larry Page sold $1.67 billion worth of stock in an IPO. The money helped Google to fund new investments and pay for research and development. In addition, Google's IPO turned the founders and the early investors into millionaires and billionaires. This big payoff was a reward for creating the company and making the early and risky investments that were necessary to get Google off the ground. Stock markets help people with great ideas become rich and that encourages innovation. It is no accident that the United States—one of the most innovative countries in the world—also has the best developed stock and capital markets.

Selling part of Google to the public also let the founders diversify. If someday another search service bests Google, Brin and Page will not become paupers. This added safety also encourages innovation. People who come up with new ideas know that their wealth will not be locked into one firm.

See our chapter on Stock Markets and Personal Finance for more details on stock markets. At this point, the key idea is that stock markets encourage investment and growth.

What Happens When Intermediation Fails?

Economic growth cannot occur without savings and those savings must be processed and intermediated through banks, bond markets, stock markets, and so on. Countries without these institutions have smaller markets for loans, use their savings less effectively, and make fewer good investments.[4] But why do some countries have poorly developed banking and financial systems?

The bridge between savers and borrowers can be broken in many ways, including insecure property rights, inflation and controls on interest rates, politicized lending, and massive bank failures and panics. These problems can break the bridge by (1) reducing the supply of savings, (2) raising the cost of intermediation, and (3) reducing the effectiveness of lending. Figure 29.11 illustrates the main ideas.

FIGURE 29.11

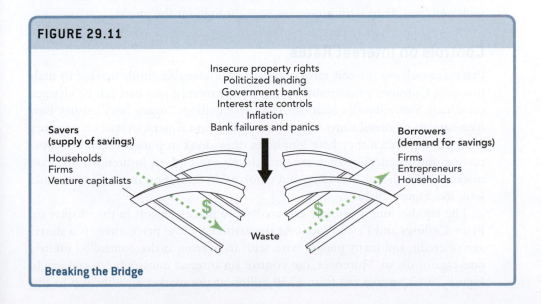

Insecure property rights
Politicized lending
Government banks
Interest rate controls
Inflation
Bank failures and panics

Savers
(supply of savings)

Households
Firms
Venture capitalists

Borrowers
(demand for savings)

Firms
Entrepreneurs
Households

$

$

Waste

Breaking the Bridge

Four Reasons Financial Intermediaries Fail

Insecure Property Rights

Consider, for example, the supply of savings. The expected return on savings depends on more than just the posted rate of interest at the bank. Some governments do not offer secure property rights to savers. That is, saved funds are not immune from later confiscation, freezes, or other restrictions.

During its financial crisis beginning in December 2001, for example, the Argentine government partially froze bank accounts for a year. Many of the banks subsequently went under, which meant that Argentine citizens lost their bank-based savings. This event was not a complete surprise. The Argentine government had a history of freezing bank accounts, such as during 1982 and 1989. Other countries in the region, such as Brazil in 1990, had also frozen bank accounts. Obviously, this repeated pattern means that Argentines and Brazilians save less than they otherwise might wish to. Why save when those funds are simply being put up for grabs? Ana, a 40-year-old teacher from Argentina, kept her savings in dollars in her house and then exchanged them for pesos to pay her bills. She said, "You just can't put your money in banks here."[5] Ana is right, but unlike money in the bank, which can be lent out to fund investment, money under a mattress does not contribute to economic growth.

If individuals expect that contracts will be broken, they will be reluctant to invest in stock markets as well. For instance, the Russian government often does not respect the rights of minority shareholders and at times it has confiscated or restricted the value of their shareholdings. The result is that many foreign investors are unwilling to put money into Russian ventures. They simply do not trust the Russian government, nor do they believe that Russian courts will enforce contracts impartially.

Law is one side of the equation, but custom and informal trust are another. In a healthy economy, shareholders expect that managers are interested in building their long-run reputations, rather than ripping off the company at every possible opportunity. When managers look only to short-run gains, it is hard to run a business enterprise, since investors will not entrust managers with the control of resources. Systems of monitoring and accounting, no matter how well developed, cannot overcome high levels of mistrust. This is a common problem in developing countries around the world but the Enron, WorldCom, and Madoff scandals demonstrate that the United States is also not immune to such problems. Trust is an important asset throughout the world.

Controls on Interest Rates

Price controls on interest rates also cause the loanable funds market to malfunction. Consider a maximum ceiling on the interest rate that can be charged on a loan. Sometimes economists call these ceilings "usury laws"; usury laws date back to medieval times and earlier. Today most American states have usury laws, although often they have loopholes (they don't stop most credit card borrowing, for instance) or they are set at levels too high to influence most loan markets. Nonetheless, a binding and enforceable ceiling on interest rates would look like Figure 29.12.

The equilibrium is just like our analysis of price controls in the chapter on Price Ceilings and Price Floors. At the artificially low price, there is a shortage of credit, and many people who wish to borrow at the controlled interest rate cannot do so. Moreover, the control on interest rates reduces savings. In Figure 29.12, savings fall from $250 billion at the market equilibrium to just

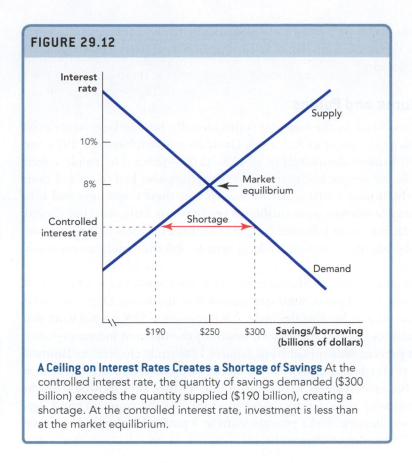

FIGURE 29.12

A Ceiling on Interest Rates Creates a Shortage of Savings At the controlled interest rate, the quantity of savings demanded ($300 billion) exceeds the quantity supplied ($190 billion), creating a shortage. At the controlled interest rate, investment is less than at the market equilibrium.

$190 billion at the controlled interest rate. Similarly, just as with price controls on oil, an interest rate control will cause a misallocation of savings and a loss of potential gains from exchange. Perhaps most important, investment, which is determined by the supply of savings, will fall below what it would be at the market equilibrium.

Politicized Lending and Government-Owned Banks

Japanese history from about 1990 to 2005 also illustrates the importance of banks in using a nation's savings effectively. During this period, the Japanese continued to save, but Japanese economic growth was zero or negative for most of these years. How can this have been? Many Japanese banks were bankrupt or propped up by the government. They were not allocating funds efficiently. Other banks were pressured to lend money to well-connected political allies, rather than to the most efficient new businesses. During this period, many Japanese banks acted as storehouses for wealth, but they were not effective financial intermediaries. Japanese business innovation, and the Japanese standard of living, suffered accordingly.

In Japan, as in the United States, banks are privately owned, so politicized lending, even when it occurs, is limited. But in many other countries, most large banks are owned by the government. Government-owned banks are useful to authoritarian regimes that use the banks to direct capital to political supporters. While it might be politically wise for the ruler to support his uncle's firm, that uncle is probably not a superior entrepreneur. One important study by economists Rafael La Porta, Florencio Lopez-de-Silanes, and Andrei Shleifer found that the larger the fraction of government-owned banks a country had in 1970, the slower the growth in per capita GDP and productivity over the next several decades.[6]

Bank Failures and Panics

Systematic problems in the banking system usually lead to large-scale economic crises. At the onset of America's Great Depression between 1929 and 1933, 11,000 banks—almost half of all U.S. banks—failed. The ripple effects were grim. Many people lost their life savings; they also had to curtail their spending, which meant that many businesses lost their customers and thus revenue. Many businesses were unable to get loans or daily working capital. Thus, bank failures were followed by a rash of small business failures. It took many years before the American banking system, and the American economy, recovered.

In their seminal work, *A Monetary History of the United States, 1867–1960*, Milton Friedman and Anna Schwartz argued that the Great Depression was brought about, in part, because the Federal Reserve—the U.S. central bank that is charged with overseeing the general health of the banking industry—failed in its job to prevent widespread bank failures.[7] (See our chapter on Business Fluctuation for further discussion of the Great Depression and our chapter on the Federal Reserve System.) Economist Ben Bernanke later showed that one of the reasons why bank failures were so crucial in the onset of the Great Depression was because banks provide loans to a particular class of borrowers and lenders.[8] According to Bernanke:

> As the real costs of intermediation increased, some borrowers (especially households, farmers, and small firms) found credit to be expensive and difficult to obtain. The effects of this credit squeeze . . . helped convert the severe but not unprecedented downturn of 1929–30 into a protracted depression.

By the way, if you recognize Bernanke's name, it is with good reason: He was chairman of the Federal Reserve between 2006 and 2014 when he had to face the worst intermediation crisis since the Great Depression.

The Financial Crisis of 2007–2008: Leverage, Securitization, and Shadow Banking

Now let's go back to the financial crisis and the collapse of Lehman Brothers, discussed at the beginning of this chapter. To give you an idea of what went on we will need to cover three ideas: leverage, securitization, and the shadow banking system. Let's begin with leverage.

Leverage

As we have seen, consumers, firms, and governments all borrow. Borrowing can be a useful tool but it's also possible to borrow too much. In the years leading up to the financial crisis, Americans borrowed more than ever before, especially in the closely related sectors of home mortgages and banking. It used to be common, for example, for home mortgages to require "20% down," which means that a lender would lend at most 80%

of the price of a house. On a $400,000 house, for example, a lender would agree to lend at most $320,000, requiring the buyer to put up at least $80,000 (20% of $400,000) as a down payment.

The difference between the value of a house and the unpaid amount on the mortgage is called the buyer's equity or **owner's equity**. Lenders want buyers to have some home equity because this protects them if the buyer defaults. If a buyer has $80,000 of home equity, for example, then even if the price of the house falls from $400,000 to $350,000 the bank could still recover all of its loan in a foreclosure. The buyer's equity gives the bank a cushion.

In the 1990s and 2000s, however, lenders became convinced that house prices were unlikely to fall and they became willing to lend with much lower down payments, just 5% down or even less. Indeed, at the height of the housing boom in 2006, 17% of mortgages were made with 0% down! Many buyers thought that house prices would continue to rise so buying with zero down was a way to speculate. If house prices rose, they could borrow more or sell at a profit. If house prices fell, they could default and not lose any of their own money. Yet if house prices were to fall and buyers were to begin to default on their loans, the banks no longer would have a cushion.

In finance, the ratio of debt to equity is called the **leverage ratio**. For example, if a buyer of a $400,000 house borrows $320,000 and spends $80,000 of her own savings, then her leverage ratio is $4 = \frac{\$320,000}{\$80,000}$. If the buyer is able to borrow $360,000 to buy a $400,000 house, then the leverage ratio is much greater: $9 = \frac{\$360,000}{\$40,000}$. Put differently, when the leverage ratio is 9, a buyer with $80,000 in cash can borrow $720,000 and buy a house worth $800,000. More leverage means that the same force (your cash) can be used to move (i.e., buy) bigger and bigger assets. As the financial crisis approached, house buyers were using more and more leverage.

Home buyers weren't the only ones leveraging more; so were banks. Lehman Brothers, for example, had assets worth hundreds of billions of dollars but it had borrowed hundreds of billions of dollars to buy those assets. Moreover, just like homeowners, in the 2000s banks had been borrowing more and more with lower and lower "down payments." In 2004, for example, Lehman's leverage ratio was around 20—which meant that for every $105 in assets that the bank owned, it had borrowed $100, leaving it with equity of just $5. A leverage ratio of 20 is already pretty high.

Notice that if the value of Lehman's assets were to fall by just 10%, it would have $94.50 dollars worth of assets and $100 dollars of debt, which means that a 10% fall in asset prices would make Lehman **insolvent**. An insolvent firm is simply one whose debts or liabilities exceed its assets (liabilities are legal debts plus other amounts owed, e.g. wage payments). Insolvency is usually followed by bankruptcy. Instead of reducing leverage in 2004, however, Lehman increased leverage so that by 2007 Lehman had an astounding leverage ratio of 44![9] At a leverage ratio of 44 even a small decrease in asset prices would bankrupt Lehman and in 2007 housing prices started to fall dramatically.

You might wonder why banks would ever want such a high leverage ratio. As we said, a leverage ratio of 44 means that even a small drop in asset prices would bankrupt Lehman but for exactly the same reasons a small rise in prices meant tremendous profits. When times are good,

Owner's equity is the value of the asset minus the debt, $E = V - D$.

The **leverage ratio** is the ratio of debt to equity, D/E

The Great Recession

interactive activity

An **insolvent** firm has liabilities that exceed its assets.

leverage makes everything better. Moreover, when Lehman did well, Lehman's managers received hundreds of millions, even billions, of dollars in bonuses and stock compensation. But when Lehman went bankrupt did Lehman's managers go bankrupt? No. Most of them lost some money but they still ended up being very rich. Lehman's managers wanted a lot of leverage because when things were going well the sky was the limit but when things went poorly most of them had limited downside risk.

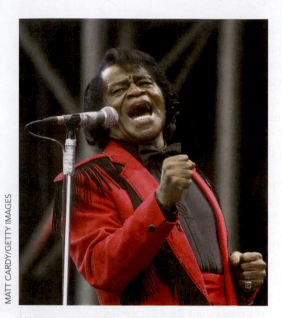

Mortgages aren't the only assets that have been securitized Entertainers like David Bowie, Marvin Gaye, and James Brown sold bonds securitized by future royalty payments. Buyers of these bonds are betting that the music of these artists will continue to sell long into the future. The motto of those buying James Brown's bonds? "In the Godfather we Trust."

Securitization

The second concept we need to understand is securitization. Sometimes mortgage loans are "securitized," or bundled together and sold on the market as financial assets. The seller of a securitized asset gets up-front cash while the buyer gets the right to a stream of future payments. Banks may wish to sell or "securitize" their loans for several reasons. On the positive side, the bank gets more liquid cash and makes its balance sheet safer, and the securitized assets can be held as investments by institutions with a long-term perspective, such as pension funds. It's a way that a lot of institutions can invest indirectly in the American economy. Alternatively, the critics charge that too often banks securitize because they made bad, sloppy, or under-researched loans in the first place and they wish to dump them on unsuspecting suckers somewhere else.

Once assets are securitized, the revenue streams from them can be sliced and diced and sold in all manner of ways. Mortgage securitization in the 2000s meant that dentists in Germany could easily invest in home mortgages in America. The increased ability to sell mortgages around the world was good for American home buyers because it kept interest rates low and it seemed good for investors who thought they were buying safe and secure assets. What could be safer than American homes? In reality, many of these securitized mortgages turned out to have had much higher risk than had been advertised. In part, some of the securitized bundles were sold on false terms or where the risk was obscured, in part the credit rating agencies performed poorly, and in part people simply estimated risk incorrectly, assuming that house prices would continue rising more or less indefinitely.

When housing prices started to fall dramatically in 2007, many people began to default on their mortgages. Overall delinquency (failure of payment) and foreclosure rates more than doubled. In parts of California, Florida, and Nevada more than 40% of the homes entered foreclosure. Remember that many buyers had only a little equity in their homes so as house prices fell they quickly came to owe more on their mortgage than their house was worth and many chose to default. As a result, the U.S. economy suddenly ended up in a situation in which many banks and other financial intermediaries were holding loans and assets of questionable value. Moreover, since the banks themselves were highly leveraged, when the value of their assets declined, many banks quickly approached insolvency.

The Shadow Banking System

Now let's turn to the last key idea, the "shadow banking system," which has become a common term since the financial crisis. The traditional banking system can be represented by a commercial bank, the bank where you keep your checking account. Commercial banks fund themselves in large part through deposits from people like yourself and from businesses. These deposits are insured by the Federal Deposit Insurance Corporation (FDIC; up to $250,000 and in practice often to an unlimited amount) and so a typical commercial bank always has some source of legally guaranteed funding. Sometimes commercial banks go out of business but because of insurance provided by the FDIC, depositors don't feel that they need to yank out their money at the first sign of trouble.

An investment bank is a bit different from a commercial bank. In a commercial bank the money comes from depositors. In an investment bank, the money comes from investors. Deposits are government guaranteed but investments are not, so investors are much more prone to panic and to withdraw their short-term funding in times of crisis. Investment banks, such as Lehman before its demise, are part of what has been called the shadow banking system. In addition to investment banks, the shadow banking system includes hedge funds, money market funds, and a variety of other complex financial entities. What unites the shadow banking system is that these financial intermediaries act like banks—they typically borrow short term to lend and invest in longer-term and often less liquid assets—but they have traditionally been less heavily regulated and monitored than banks and, unlike deposits, their short-term sources of funds (loans from investors) are not government-guaranteed.

The shadow banking system got its name because it grew up in the shadow of the traditional banking system and for a long time most regulators and policymakers were unaware of its importance. But by the mid-1990s the shadow banking system was lending as much as were traditional banks and at its peak in 2008 the shadow banking system lent $20 trillion, considerably more than did traditional banks.

Fire Sales The financial crisis can be understood as a run on the shadow banking system similar in many respects to bank runs during the Great Depression. Think of an investment bank as being funded by a variety of short-term and long-term loans. The short-term loans disappear most quickly because they are rolled over on a very frequent basis—sometimes nightly. If investors fear that the institution will go bankrupt, each lender will seek to withdraw his money or refuse to renew the loan, as soon as possible, just as depositors rush to withdraw their money from failing banks of the traditional kind. Without the short-term loans, the investment bank no longer has enough operating funds and it is forced to sell off assets quickly in what is often called a "fire sale." Furthermore, if enough firms find themselves having to sell assets, fire sales can quickly get out of control. To see how fires sales can become *fire storms*, imagine that there are three financial assets, A, B, and C, and suppose that an external event, such as a fall in housing prices, causes a fall in the price of A. The fall in the price of A worries people who are lending to investment banks or other financial

This derivative investment is so complicated that no investor will truly understand it. Thanks!

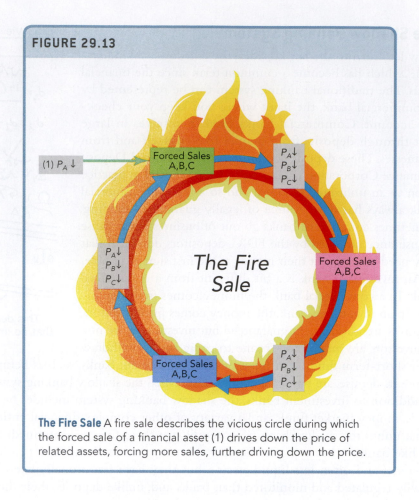

FIGURE 29.13

The Fire Sale

The Fire Sale A fire sale describes the vicious circle during which the forced sale of a financial asset (1) drives down the price of related assets, forcing more sales, further driving down the price.

intermediaries who own a lot of A. The worried lenders begin to demand greater collateral on their loans—perhaps some of them even take their funds elsewhere. With less money flowing in, the bank is forced to sell some of its assets. But the bank doesn't just sell asset A, which has already fallen in price, but also some of its holdings of B and C. The natural buyers of these assets are other similar intermediaries, but if they are also under stress they won't want to buy at a normal price. As a result, the prices of B and C are also pushed down. As the price of B and C falls, lenders now come to fear that other intermediaries may go bankrupt—even intermediaries who have very little exposure to asset A, which started the problem—and so these lenders start to pull their funds. When these lenders do so, even more intermediaries must sell assets and cut back on lending, and so the problem gets worse.

Thus, in a crisis, the selling of assets by one financial intermediary can set in motion a vicious circle, or cascade, in which other intermediaries are forced to sell, driving asset prices lower, and forcing yet more sales. All of this is very bad for the intermediaries. But remember the intermediaries are bridges that channel funds from savers to borrowers. So when the intermediaries fail, credit dries up and the firms that were relying on that credit also begin to fail, adding yet another vicious cycle to the mix.

The fire sale problem was especially severe in the 2008–2009 recession because many of the participants in the shadow banking system were highly leveraged.

As noted, shortly before its failure, Lehman Brothers had a leverage ratio in the range of 40 and many other major banks were not far behind. As we've already explained, a high leverage ratio puts a bank in a very vulnerable position. When leverage ratios are high, a small decline in asset values can wipe out the equity cushion of the bank and push the bank into insolvency. It was the justified fear of this outcome that caused the short-term lenders to flee from the funding of Lehman, thereby triggering its financial meltdown.

Moreover, because mortgages had been bundled and sold many times over in different combinations, and because many bets had been made on their prices, no one knew exactly which financial institutions faced the biggest losses. As a result, it became increasingly less certain which institutions were profitable and which were in danger of going bankrupt. No one wanted to lend or invest in banks and other intermediaries that might have significant exposure to mortgage-backed assets on their books. Why lend or invest in a bank when the bank might be gone tomorrow? Investors also became wary of any institution that lent money to potentially troubled banks, even if that institution did not itself hold mortgage-backed assets.

The shadow banks in particular relied on short-term funding, which, unlike deposits, was not guaranteed; thus people who lent to shadow banks were anxious to stop lending once they feared a firm might go bankrupt. When lenders withdrew their short-term funding, some shadow banks were forced to sell assets in fire sales, which reduced asset prices and transmitted and amplified insolvency worries to other financial intermediaries. The bundling and division of mortgages and the many side bets made on securitized mortgages were also so complicated that lenders didn't know which intermediaries were safe and which were close to toppling. Just as investors are reluctant to lend to traditional financial intermediaries during these crises, they are reluctant to lend to these shadow banks as well. And as noted earlier, when financial intermediaries can't get new funds, the bridge between savers/lenders and borrowers collapses. Indeed, the reluctance of investors to lend to shadow banks meant that their lending was forced to shrink so that by 2010 shadow banks were lending just $16 trillion—a massive loss of $4 trillion in lending since 2008. It was this credit crunch that threw the entire economy into disarray.

It is now considered a general problem that the short-term loans for the shadow banking system can flee rapidly in times of crisis, causing some financial markets to shut down and credit to freeze up. Some commentators have suggested that the government guarantee loans to the shadow banking system in times of crisis, but that puts a potentially large liability on taxpayers and it is politically unpopular. Nonetheless, the U.S. government already has taken some steps in that direction. After the trauma of the Lehman Brothers failure, the insurance company AIG was on the verge of failure, but this time the Federal Reserve, led by Bernanke, stepped in and took over majority ownership of the company and guaranteed its debts. They didn't want to repeat the credit market freezes that followed the collapse of Lehman. New financial regulations are now bringing the shadow banking system "out of the shadows" and regulating these financial intermediaries in ways similar to traditional banks. A key idea has been to require banks of all kinds to hold more equity, that is, to reduce the amount of their leverage. It remains to be seen how effective and how costly these new regulations will be. Greater government involvement in the allocation of credit also raises the possibility of politicized lending, a problem that, as we discussed earlier, has reduced the efficiency of credit allocation in other countries.

CHECK YOURSELF

- How do usury laws (controls on interest rates) cause savings to decline?
- Besides decreasing the number of banks, how do bank failures hinder financial intermediation?
- How does awarding bank loans by political criteria or by cronyism (to your pals) affect the efficiency of the economy?

Takeaway

Individuals save to prepare for their retirement, to help fund large purchases, and to cushion swings in their income—most generally, savings help individuals, firms, and governments to smooth their consumption over time. Similarly, individuals, firms, and governments borrow to finance large purchases like a home, to invest in new capital, or in the case of governments to finance large expenditures such as those necessary for a war. Once again, borrowing helps agents to smooth their consumption streams. Financial intermediaries bridge the gap between savers and borrowers.

Financial intermediaries also collect savings, evaluate investments, and diversify risk. Banks, bonds, and stock markets help finance new and innovative ideas, such as Google and Federal Express. Financial intermediation is a central part of healthy economic growth.

Without effective financial intermediation, an economy will end up adrift. Insecure property rights, inflation, politicized lending, and bank failures and panics can all contribute to the breakdown of financial intermediation. The 2007–2008 crisis was brought about by high leverage and falling asset prices that created a panic in the shadow banking system that sharply reduced the amount of lending in the economy. The resulting decline in activity demonstrates how important financial intermediaries are to the economy, both when they operate well and when they do not.

CHAPTER REVIEW

interactive activity   Go online to practice with more examples of these types of problems, including live links to videos, data sources, and feedback.

 Problems in green relate to MRU videos. See the MRU table at the end of the exercises.

KEY CONCEPTS

saving, p. 588

investment, p. 588

time preference, p. 590

market for loanable funds, p. 594

financial intermediary, p. 596

bond, p. 597

collateral, p. 598

crowding out, p. 598

arbitrage, p. 600

stock, p. 600

initial public offering (IPO), p. 600

owner's equity, p. 605

leverage ratio, p. 605

insolvency, p. 605

FACTS AND TOOLS

1. If people want to smooth their consumption over time, what will they tend to do when they win the lottery: spend most of it within a year or save most of it for later?

2. A large number of economic and psychological studies demonstrate that people who are impatient in one area of their life tend to be impatient in other areas as well. This isn't true in every single case, but of course, that doesn't matter if we're trying to understand the "typical person." Based on your general knowledge and educated guessing:

   a. Who is more likely to smoke: a criminal or a law-abiding citizen?

   b. Who is more likely to shoot heroin: a person who saves 20 percent of their income or a person who can't ever find a way to save?

c. Who is more likely to have a lot of credit card debt: a smoker or a nonsmoker?

3. The typical savings supply curve has a positive slope. If a nation's saving supply curve had a perfectly vertical slope, what would that mean?

a. People in this country save the same amount no matter what the interest rate is.

b. People in this country are extremely sensitive to interest rates when deciding how much to save.

4. Consider three countries: Jovenia (average age: 25), Mittelaltistan (average age: 45), and Decrepetia (average age: 75). Based on the lifecycle theory, which of these countries will probably have:

a. High savings rates?

b. High rates of borrowing?

c. High rates of dissaving? (That's spending your past savings.)

Note: The way for entire countries to save is to build up the stock of productive capital either at home (through high investment rates) or abroad (by exporting more than importing, i.e., running a trade surplus, and using the proceeds to buy foreign investment goods and assets).

5. Sometimes, in supply and demand models, it is not clear who "supplies" and who "demands." For instance, in the labor market, individual workers (not firms) supply labor. In the loanable funds market, who is usually the supplier and who is usually the demander? Choose the correct answer.

a. Entrepreneurs supply loanable funds and savers demand loanable funds.

b. Entrepreneurs supply loanable funds and savers also supply loanable funds.

c. Entrepreneurs demand loanable funds and savers demand loanable funds.

d. Entrepreneurs demand loanable funds and savers supply loanable funds.

6. In each of the following, answer either "bank account," "bonds," or "stocks."

a. Which investment is typically the riskiest?

b. Which is a corporate IOU?

c. Which one gives you an ownership "share" in a company?

d. Which one usually lets you "withdraw" part of your investment at any time, for any reason?

e. Which form of investment usually spreads your money over the largest number of investment projects?

f. Which is usually rated by private companies like Moody's or Standard and Poor's?

g. Which one is offered by the U.S. government as well as by private corporations?

7. If savers don't feel safe putting their money in banks or buying bonds, what's the best way to sum up what's happening in the market for loanable funds?

a. Supply of savings falls and the interest rate falls.

b. Supply of savings falls and the interest rate rises.

c. Demand for savings falls and the interest rate falls.

d. Demand for savings falls and the interest rate rises.

8. When governments outlaw high interest rates and the ceiling is binding, what probably happens to the total amount of money borrowed?

a. It rises because borrowers are protected from high interest rates.

b. It falls because savers aren't willing to lend as much money at this low interest rate.

c. Both a and b are usually true.

9. If financial intermediation breaks down, what category of GDP will probably fall the most: consumption, investment, government purchases, or net exports?

10. a. In a competitive banking system, what tends to happen to banks that make low-interest rate loans to the banker's friends: Do they tend to be more successful or less successful than other, more ruthless banks?

b. Given your answer to the previous question, how do you suspect that politicized government-owned banks stay in business?

THINKING AND PROBLEM SOLVING

11. Let's work out a simple example in which a person smooths her consumption over time. Gwen is a real estate agent, and she knows that she will have some good years and some bad years. She figures that half the time she'll earn $90,000 per year, and half the time she'll earn $20,000 per year. These numbers are after taxes and after saving for retirement. These numbers are all she has to worry about.

a. If we ignore interest costs just to keep things simple, how much should Gwen consume in the average year?

b. How many dollars will she save during the good years?

c. How many dollars will she borrow during the bad years? (*Note:* "Borrowing," in this context, is basically the same as "pulling money out of savings.")

12. Let's think about how the supply of savings might shift in two different cases.

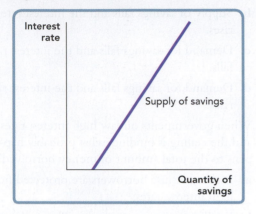

a. Under current U.S. law, businesses are allowed to automatically enroll you in a savings plan that puts 5% of your salary in a retirement fund. Suppose Congress *abolishes* this law: Draw the appropriate shift in the supply curve and label it "a."

b. If Americans all go to see the classic Robin Williams/Ethan Hawke film *Dead Poets Society* and decide to *carpe diem*, or if they read the quotes of a famous Mediterranean preacher who said, "Take therefore no thought for the morrow," or if they watch the appalling 1970s sitcom *One Day at a Time*, what direction is the supply of savings likely to shift? Denote this with a new supply curve labeled "b."

13. In this chapter, we focus on three big functions that banks perform:

i. They evaluate business ideas to see to whom it's worth lending.

ii. They spread an investment's risk among many different projects.

iii. They make it easier for people to make payments through checks, ATMs, and wire transfers.

None of these functions are unique to banks. In the following anecdotes, is the person doing function i, function ii, or function iii?

a. Emmanuel donates a little money to five different charities, in the hopes that at least one of them will do some good in the world.

b. In Lorien's family, she's the one who specializes in deciding which bank everyone else in the family will use.

c. Popeye always has a little cash on hand, so he is always able to lend a little money to Wimpy and Olive Oyl at lunchtime.

d. George spends his time at the Carlyle Group deciding which companies are worth his investment partners' dollars.

e. Scooter wants a good education, so he takes a variety of different classes: some history, some economics, some physics.

f. Frances subscribes to *Consumer Reports* to decide which washing machine to buy.

14. In many poor countries, the banking system just isn't advanced enough to lend money for many large investments. Based on this single fact, where would you expect to see more entrepreneurs coming from rich families rather than poor families: in the rich countries or the poor countries? Why?

15. **a.** The financial analysts at Lexmark have evaluated five major projects. Each project, if it actually goes forward, will be financed by going to a bank to borrow the money. They've calculated a "break-even interest rate": If they can borrow cash to pay for the project at less than that rate, the project will likely be a success; if the rate is higher, then it's not worth it.

	Cost	Break-even Interest Rate
Project A	$100 million	8%
Project B	$50 million	12%
Project C	$200 million	50%
Project D	$25 million	4%
Project E	$150 million	10%

a. If the interest rate is 11%, which projects will Lexmark take on? If the market interest rate is 6%, which projects will it take on?

b. Let's turn this information into a demand curve for loanable funds.

Organize this data to convert it into Lexmark's "loanable funds demand" curve. *Note:* It will look just like an ordinary demand curve, only with more breaks.

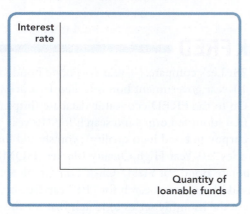

16. In each of the three cases, which bond will usually pay a higher interest rate?

   a. A bond rated AAA, or a bond rated BBB?

   b. A U.S. government bond, or a General Motors bond?

   c. A Citibank bond that gets repaid in 30 years or a Citibank bond that gets repaid in 1 year?

17. Consider your answers to the previous question. When one bond pays a higher interest rate than another bond, is that mostly because savers are less willing to *supply* loanable funds to the higher-rate bond, or because businesses are more interested in *demanding* loanable funds for the higher-rate bond? Why is this so?

18. Consider Figure 29.10. Would a rise in government borrowing make it harder or easier for a new business to sell new stocks in an initial public offering (IPO)? In other words, are government bonds and corporate stocks substitutes for each other or complements to each other?

19. "If the government keeps real interest rates low (either by raising inflation or by decreeing low interest rates), then this encourages extra borrowing by businesses, which leads to more investment purchases, a larger stock of capital equipment, and higher productivity. Therefore, an interest rate ceiling is a good idea." What's wrong with this argument?

20. **a.** If a zero-coupon bond with a face value of $1,000 payable in 1 year sells for $925, what is the interest rate?

   b. If another bond with the same face value and maturity sells for $900, what is the interest rate on this bond?

   c. Which bond, the one discussed in question a or question b, would you rather invest in? Are you sure? Think again!

Ask FRED

interactive activity

21. Let's take a look at financial intermediation and the financial crisis and recession of 2007–2009. Using the FRED economic database (https://fred.stlouisfed.org/), search for "all sectors total loans"; you should find a series, All Sectors; Total Loans; Liability. This series is all the lending in the U.S. economy from banks and all other financial intermediaries. When you graph the series you will see that it increases quite smoothly, rising almost without exception every single year from 1945 to 2008. In the third quarter of 2008 the series begins to drop tremendously, and in an unprecedented way—this is the financial crisis.

   a. At the peak, in the third quarter of 2008, how much was being lent in the U.S. economy? [*Hint:* Be careful of the units. The data is given in millions of millions; a million million is a trillion.]

   b. In the third quarter of 2011 how much was being lent in the U.S. economy?

   c. In the space of just three years approximately how much lending disappeared from the U.S. economy?

Ask FRED

interactive activity

22. One type of debt that you may be familiar with is student loan debt. Using the FRED economic database (https://fred.stlouisfed.org/), search for student loans, then click on "Student Loans Owned and Securitized, Outstanding."

   a. In 2016 approximately how much student debt was owed?

   b. What has happened to the amount of student debt outstanding since 2006?

Ask FRED

interactive activity

23. Using the FRED economic database (https://fred.stlouisfed.org/), find the typical interest rate on a credit card. By searching for "credit card rate," you should find "Commercial Bank Interest Rate on Credit Card Plans, All Accounts."

a. What is the typical interest rate on a credit card in 2016?

b. How does the credit card rate compare to other rates such as mortgage loan rates or government bond rates?

c. Search for "credit card charge off" and you should find a series "Charge-Off Rate on Credit Card Loans, All Commercial Banks". Click Edit Graph and change the frequency to Annual. This series shows the percentage of loans that the banks have to write off as losses. In 2010 what percentage of loans were written off as losses?

d. Why is the credit card rate so much higher than other rates?

CHALLENGES

24. The United States borrows a lot of money from other countries. If you wanted to use the lifecycle theory to explain this, would you say that the United States is acting like a "young" country, an "old" country, or a "middle-aged" country? There's more than one correct way to answer this question.

25. Lenders are more willing to lend if the borrower can put up collateral for the loan. Remember that collateral is something of value that by agreement becomes the property of the lender if the borrower defaults. In the United States, many small business owners borrow money for their business by using their houses or business assets as collateral. But in many developing countries, people don't have secure property rights, or *title*, to the land or house in which they live. In Bangalore, India, for example, it's nearly impossible to say who owns a piece of land and about 85% of the people in that city live on a piece of land for which they have no title. How difficult do you think it would be for a small business person in Bangalore to get a modest-sized loan?

26. Bank savings accounts typically pay an interest rate well below the inflation rate. As of spring 2017, for example, the best interest rates on savings accounts were around 1% per year, while the CPI inflation rate was around 2.5% per year. What does this mean about the real interest rate on bank savings? Knowing this, why would people still choose to deposit any money in bank savings accounts?

27. How are houses like bonds? With respect only to their home equity (i.e., ignoring all other assets and investments), would home*owners* tend to favor high or low interest rates?

Ask FRED

interactive activity

28. Let's compare 10-year corporate bonds and 10-year government bonds (called Treasuries). Go to the FRED economic database (https://fred.stlouisfed.org/) and search for "10 year corporate bond high quality"; you should find the series "10-Year High Quality Market (HQM) Corporate Bond Par Yield." Click Edit Graph and then Add Line. Now search for "10-Year Treasury" and use the monthly series to match that for the corporate bond.

a. Do 10-year corporate bonds or 10-year Treasuries offer a higher return? Why?

b. Usually the two series move closely together, but graph the two series around the 2008–2009 recession. What happens? Why?

WORK IT OUT

interactive activity

For interactive, step-by-step help in solving this problem, go online.

Predict the effect of each of the following events on the supply of and demand for loanable funds (increase, decrease, or no effect on supply; increase, decrease, or no effect on demand). What would be the likely effect on interest rates?

a. Television newscasters convince most people that the end of the world will occur in 2025.

b. Breakthrough advances in pharmaceuticals increase life expectancy to 100 years.

c. Geologists discover vast new oil deposits under the South Pole. (*Hint:* Drilling in this harsh environment requires extremely large up-front capital expenses.)

d. A business downturn leads to corporate pessimism and increases workers' fears of being laid off (assume workers try to increase their "emergency fund" savings when they're worried about becoming unemployed).

Saving and Borrowing

mruniversity.com/save-borrow

Problems: **1–5, 11, 12, 24**

What Do Banks Do?

mruniversity.com/banks

Problems: **6, 13, 15**

Intro to Stock Markets

mruniversity.com/stock-market

Problems: **6, 11**

Intro to the Bond Market

mruniversity.com/bonds

Problems: **6, 14, 16–18, 26, 27**

Four Reasons Financial Intermediaries Fail

mruniversity.com/intermediation-failure

Problems: **7–10, 14, 19**

The Great Recession

mruniversity.com/great-recession

Problems: **27**

CHAPTER 29 APPENDIX

Bond Pricing and Arbitrage

Bond pricing may seem complicated but it can be understood with a few simple principles. Let's start with something more familiar than bonds. Suppose that you invest $100 in a savings account that pays a 10% rate of interest. How much money will you have in one year? That's easy; every dollar invested at 10% turns into $1.10 in one year so $100 invested at 10% turns into $110, which we can write as $100 \times (1.10) = $110.

More generally, let's call the money that you invest the present value (PV), let's call the interest rate r, and let's call the money that you will withdraw from the bank in one year the future value (FV). Then, the relationship between PV, r, and FV is simply

$$PV \times (1 + r) = FV \qquad (1)$$

For example, if you invested $100 in present value at an interest rate of 5%, how much money would you have in a year (FV)? Substituting in equation 1, we have $100 \times (1.05) = $105.

Okay, now let's ask a slightly more difficult question. Suppose that the interest rate is 10% and that in one year you would like to have the future value of $100. How much do you need to put in the bank today? In other words, if the interest rate is 10% and you want a future value of $100, what present value do you need to put in the bank? Let's fill in what we know:

$$PV \times (1.10) = $100$$

To solve for PV, divide both sides by 1.10:

$$PV = \frac{$100}{1.10} = $90.91$$

Thus, if the interest rate is 10% and we want $100 in the bank in one year, we need to invest $90.91 today. More generally, we can rewrite equation 1 in any of the following three ways depending on whether we want to solve for FV, PV, or r:

$$PV \times (1 + r) = FV \qquad (1a)$$

$$PV = \frac{FV}{(1 + r)} \qquad (1b)$$

$$(1 + r) = \frac{FV}{PV} \qquad (1c)$$

We now have everything we need to explain bond pricing. Imagine that the interest rate is 10% and suppose that a bond exists that promises to pay $100 in one year's time. Thus, the future value of the bond—conveniently this is also called the face value—is $100, the interest rate r is 10%, and we want to know PV. We can use version 1b of our equation:

$$PV = \frac{\$100}{1.10} = \$90.91$$

In other words, when the interest rate is 10%, a bond promising to pay $100 in one year will sell for $90.91.

Students are often confused by the fact that interest rates and bond prices move in *opposite* directions: That is, when the interest rate rises, bond prices fall, and when the interest rate falls, bond prices rise. But now we can explain this result easily. We know that at an interest rate of 10% a bond that has a future value of $100 will have a price or present value of $90.91. So what happens to the present value of the same bond when the interest rate falls to 5%?

$$PV = \frac{FV}{1 + r}$$

Substituting what we know, we have

$$PV = \frac{\$100}{1.05} = \$95.24$$

Thus, when the interest rate falls from 10% to 5%, the price of the bond rises from $90.91 to $95.23.

We can see from version 1b of our formula that the price of a bond rises when the interest rate falls (and vice versa), but what is the economics behind this result? To understand the economics, we will use version 1c of our equation.

Let's suppose that the interest rate falls from 10% to 5%—in other words, the most that investors can earn on their loanable funds is a 5% rate of return. But imagine that instead of rising to $95.24, the price of a bond paying $100 in one year's time stayed at $90.91. How much could investors earn by investing in this bond? The present value of the bond is $90.91, the future value is $100, so the return *on this bond* is

$$(1 + r) = \frac{FV}{PV} = \frac{\$100}{\$90.91} = 1.10$$

Now what would you do if every other investment in the economy is earning a 5% rate of return, but an equally safe bond exists that earns 10%? Correct, you would buy the bond paying 10%. And what happens when you—and everyone else—start buying this extraordinary bond? Correct, the bond increases in price and, as it increases in price, the return on the bond falls. In fact, the bond will increase in price and its rate of return will fall until it earns a rate of return roughly equal to that on similarly risky investments elsewhere in the economy.

Our last result can be stated more generally: *Buying and selling will equalize the rate of return on equally risky assets.* The buying and selling of equally risky assets is called "arbitrage." Arbitrage is a very important idea with many more implications than we can address here, but if you continue on in economics or finance, you will study arbitrage in more detail.

We have shown how the simplest types of bonds are priced. Many bonds mature in more than one year and many bonds include coupon payments: periodic payments in addition to the final payment at maturity. The formula for determining the present value of a bond that matures in more than one year and that has coupon payments is more complicated than formula 1b, but the ideas are exactly the same. We will give one quick example to illustrate.

Let's begin, once again, with a $100 investment in a savings account that pays a 10% rate of interest. But this time, let's suppose that we invest the money for two years—what is the future value of this investment? We can break our two-year investment into two one-year investments. We first invest $100 at 10%, giving us $110 at the end of the first year. We then invest $110 at 10% for another year, which gives us $121 at the end of two years. In general terms, we can write

$$[PV \times (1 + r_1)] \times (1 + r_2) = FV \qquad \text{(A1)}$$

The term in the square brackets is how much we will have after the first year of investment; we then multiply this amount by $(1 + r_2)$, the rate of interest in year 2, to give us the amount that we will have at the end of two years.

As we did before, we can divide both sides of equation A1 by $(1 + r_1)(1 + r_2)$ in order to rewrite A1 as

$$PV = \frac{FV}{(1 + r_1) \times (1 + r_2)} \qquad \text{(A2)}$$

Let's use formula A2 to figure out the present value or selling price of a bond that pays $100 in two years when the interest rate in year 1 and year 2 is 10%. Substituting what we know, we have

$$PV = \frac{\$100}{(1.10) \times (1.10)} = \$82.64$$

Thus, if the interest rate in year 1 and year 2 is 10%, then a bond that pays $100 two years from now has a present value or selling price of $82.64.

Now here is the big payoff. What is the price of a bond that pays $100 at the end of year 1 and another $100 at the end of year 2? We can easily price this bond because this bond is just a combination of two bonds, one of which pays $100 at the end of year 1 and one of which pays $100 at the end of year 2. But we just calculated the value of these bonds! And, because of arbitrage, the combination bond must sell for the same price as the sum of the two bonds that we calculated earlier, or $173.55 = $90.91 + $82.64.

We can also calculate the value of the combination bond directly. When the interest rate is 10%, the PV of a bond that pays $100 in one year and another $100 in two years is

$$PV = \frac{\$100}{1.10} + \frac{\$100}{(1.10) \times (1.10)} = \$173.55$$

Following through on the same logic, we can now calculate the price of very complicated bonds. The present value of a bond that makes potentially different payments every year for n years is

$$PV = \frac{Payment_1}{(1 + r)} + \frac{Payment_2}{(1 + r)^2} + \frac{Payment_3}{(1 + r)^3} + \cdots \frac{Final\ payment_n}{(1 + r)^n}$$

Bond Pricing with a Spreadsheet

We can calculate the price of bonds like this using a spreadsheet. Figure A29.1 shows a bond that pays $100 in each of the first nine years and then in the 10th year it pays $1,000. The present value of each payment is calculated in Column C. Note that the formula in cell C2, "=B2/(1+$D$2)^A2", is equivalent to $\frac{Payment_1}{(1+r)}$. Copying this formula for the nine other payments gives us a column of present values, which we sum up in cell C14, "=SUM(C2:C11)", to find the price of the bond, $1,324.70.

You can easily vary the interest rate to see what happens to the price of the bond. If the interest rate rises to 10%, for example, we have the result in Figure A29.2 on the next page.

And thus, the price of the bond falls to $961.45. Note once again that a higher interest rate means a lower price for the bond. It's also interesting to see that a higher interest rate has a small effect on payments that come soon (compare the *PV* of the first payment in Figure A29.1 and Figure A29.2), but a very large effect on payments far into the future (compare the *PV* of the final payment in the two scenarios).

One final point of importance. Bond pricing might seem to be far away from your interests, but the techniques in this appendix can be used to price and understand any kind of asset that has a payment stream over time. A mortgage, for example, is very similar to a bond except instead of receiving bond payments, you will typically be sending mortgage payments. If you want to compare two different mortgages, for example, a 20-year mortgage and a 30-year mortgage where the mortgages have different interest rates, you will want to compute the present value of each mortgage to find the one with the lowest *PV*. Online mortgage calculators help you to do this. What those calculators do is compute present values using the same types of techniques as found in this appendix.

FIGURE A29.1

C2		▼	f_x =B2/(1+$D$2)^A2	
	A	B	C	D
1	Year	Payment	Present Value	Interest Rate
2	1	$100	$95.24	0.05
3	2	$100	$90.70	
4	3	$100	$86.38	
5	4	$100	$82.27	
6	5	$100	$78.35	
7	6	$100	$74.62	
8	7	$100	$71.07	
9	8	$100	$67.68	
10	9	$100	$64.46	
11	10	$1,000	$613.91	
12				
13		Sum PV		
14		or Price->	$1,324.70	

FIGURE A29.2

	C14	▼	f_x =SUM(C2:C11)	
	A	B	C	D
1	Year	Payment	Present Value	Interest Rate
2	1	$100	$90.91	0.1
3	2	$100	$82.64	
4	3	$100	$75.13	
5	4	$100	$68.30	
6	5	$100	$62.09	
7	6	$100	$56.45	
8	7	$100	$51.32	
9	8	$100	$46.65	
10	9	$100	$42.41	
11	10	$1,000	$385.54	
12				
13		Sum PV		
14		or Price->	$961.45	
15				

Chapter 29 Appendix Question

1. Using a spreadsheet and the material in the appendix, answer the following questions.

   a. Assume the interest rate is 5% (0.05). Calculate the value of a bond that pays $100 at the end of every year for the next 9 years and then at the end of the 10th year pays $1,000.

   b. Calculate the value of this bond if the interest rate is 3%.

2. Answer the following question using a spreadsheet and the material in the appendix.

   You would like to buy a house. Assume that given your income, you can afford to pay $12,000 a year to a lender for the next 30 years. If the interest rate is 7% how much can you borrow today based on your ability to pay? What about if the interest rate is 3%?

30

Unemployment and Labor Force Participation

Thirty-six thousand travel agents lost their jobs on November 10, 1999. Actually, it didn't happen quite that fast, but when Expedia.com went public, there were 124,000 travel agents in the United States and by 2006 there were fewer than 88,000. Even though tourism is increasing, travel agents are disappearing as more people book their travel online.

The disappearance of the travel agent represents a recurring story in American history. Many jobs have disappeared—blacksmiths, chimney sweeps, and darkroom technicians, for example, are no longer in demand. Employment in other fields has greatly declined. For example, in 1910 there were 11.5 million farm workers in the United States; today there are less than one million. New jobs, however, have replaced old jobs. There are now more than 1.6 million jobs in the "App economy," jobs related to writing apps for mobile phones and devices. Before the introduction of the iPhone in 2007, there were zero jobs in this industry. Jobs are growing rapidly in high-tech areas like software engineering and the biosciences, but a wealthier society also means more and better paying jobs in professions that have been around for a long time. Today, for example, there are over 200,000 professional athletes, coaches, umpires, and related workers in the United States—more than any other time in history.

A growing economy is a changing economy and *some* unemployment is a necessary consequence of economic growth. The unemployment rate in France, however, has hovered around 10% for several decades. High and long-lasting unemployment is unlikely to be caused by economic growth. During a recession, unemployment increases quickly and in many different industries at once and that too is unlikely to be caused by economic growth. Thus, there are different types of unemployment with different causes.

Figure 30.1 on the next page illustrates the organization of this chapter. We are going to start at the top with the issue that is most prominent in the economics and business news, namely unemployment. We explain how unemployment is defined and then the different types of unemployment and their causes.

Don't forget, however, that many individuals neither have a job nor are looking for work—these individuals are not part of the labor force. As we move down the tree, we will ask: Why do some people choose to be in the labor force while others do not? Why is it, for example, that most women are in the (paid) labor force today even though this was uncommon in the 1950s? And why is labor force participation for some workers much higher in some countries than in others? The topic of labor force participation makes up the second half of the chapter. And what about total population, at the very bottom of this structure? For that you must take a demography course, but you'll find a brief discussion of birth control at the close of the chapter.

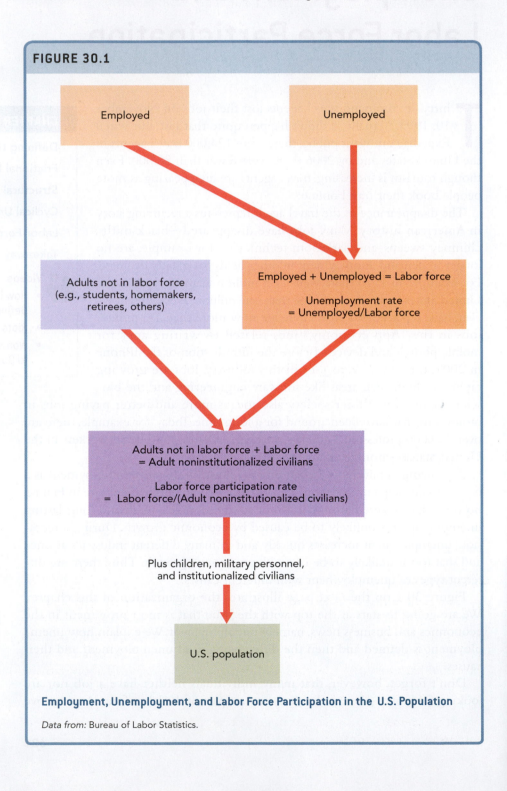

FIGURE 30.1

Employment, Unemployment, and Labor Force Participation in the U.S. Population

Data from: Bureau of Labor Statistics.

Defining Unemployment

Is a 6-year-old without a job unemployed? Is someone in prison unemployed? What about a retired 60-year-old? In all cases the answer is no. We count someone as **unemployed** only if he or she is *willing and able to work but cannot find a job*. In practice, this means that to be counted as unemployed, a person must be an adult (16 years or older), not institutionalized (e.g., not in prison), a civilian, and, most important, that person must be *looking for work*. Similarly, to be counted as employed, a person must be an adult, noninstitutionalized civilian with a job.

In June 2017, there were 7.0 million unemployed persons in the United States and 153.2 million employed persons. Together, the employed and the unemployed make up the labor force of 160.2 million (7.0 + 153.2).

The **unemployment rate** is the percentage of the labor force without a job:

$$\text{Unemployment rate} = \frac{\text{Unemployed}}{\text{Unemployed} + \text{Employed}} \times 100$$

$$= \frac{\text{Unemployed}}{\text{Labor force}} \times 100$$

Thus, in June 2017, the unemployment rate was 4.4%:

$$= \frac{7.0 \text{ million}}{7.0 \text{ million} + 153.2 \text{ million}} \times 100 = \frac{7.0}{160.2} \times 100 = 4.4\%$$

Once we have examined the issue of unemployment, we will investigate some of the determinants of the **labor force participation rate**, the percentage of the adult, civilian, noninstitutionalized population (adults for short) in the labor force.

How Good an Indicator Is the Unemployment Rate?

We are interested in the unemployment rate because unemployment, especially long-term unemployment, can be financially and psychologically devastating. Unemployment also means that the economy is underperforming—labor that could be used to produce valuable goods and services is being wasted. The unemployment rate is the single best indicator of how well the labor market is working in both of these senses, but it is an incomplete indicator.

Individuals without a job are not counted as unemployed if they are not actively looking for work. But some people who are unemployed for a long period of time may get discouraged and stop looking for work even though they want a job. It's difficult to know exactly how many **discouraged workers** there are because the concept is not well-defined. Many people who are happily retired would take a job if the wage were high enough, but should every retired person count as a discouraged worker? The Bureau of Labor Statistics (BLS) keeps statistics on one definition of discouraged workers, which it defines as workers who want and are available for work, and who have looked for a job sometime in the last year but not in the last month because they believe that no jobs were available for them.

How is the Unemployment Rate Defined?

Unemployed workers are adults who do not have a job but who are looking for work.
The **unemployment rate** is the percentage of the labor force without a job.

The **labor force participation rate** is the percentage of adults in the labor force.

Discouraged workers are workers who have given up looking for work but who would still like a job.

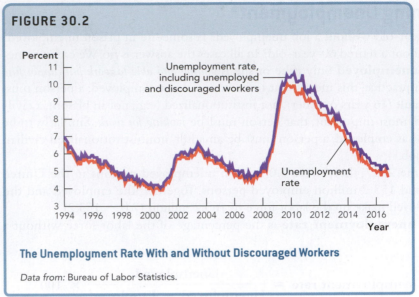

FIGURE 30.2

The Unemployment Rate With and Without Discouraged Workers

Data from: Bureau of Labor Statistics.

Using this definition, the number of discouraged workers in the United States is small relative to the number of unemployed workers, so counting discouraged workers as unemployed increases the unemployment rate only modestly. The number of discouraged workers has increased since the recession in 2009, but as Figure 30.2 illustrates, the unemployment rate with and without discouraged workers is similar and the two rates track each other closely.

The unemployment rate also doesn't measure the quality of the jobs people take or how well workers are matched to their jobs. A taxi driver with a PhD in chemistry, for example, is counted as fully employed by the BLS. Similarly, a worker who has a part-time job but who wants a full-time job is counted as fully employed. If we counted these workers as partially unemployed, the unemployment rate would be higher, but defining and measuring partial employment isn't easy. If a taxi driver has a BA in English, should that be counted as almost fully employed? Nearly everyone wants a better job in some dimension (more hours, fewer hours, closer to home, higher wages, better benefits, etc.) so is everyone less than fully employed?

Even though any definition is imperfect, the BLS also looks at one measure of the **underemployment rate**. This includes part-time workers who would rather have a full-time position and also people who would like to work but have given up looking for a job. As of February 2017, this rate was 9.5 in the American economy.

Given these imperfections in the official unemployment rate, economists also look at other measures of labor underutilization and indicators of how well the labor market is performing, such as the labor force participation rate, the number of full-time jobs, and average wages. Fortunately, most of these other indicators (and probably many other job characteristics that are more difficult to measure) correlate well with the unemployment rate, so the unemployment rate is a good summary indicator of the state of the labor market. (See Thinking and Problem Solving question 22 for more on this.)

Economists distinguish three types of unemployment: frictional, structural, and cyclical. We start with frictional.

Underemployment rate A Bureau of Labor Statistics measure that includes part-time workers who would rather have a full-time position and people who would like to work but have given up looking for a job.

Frictional Unemployment

What is the fastest way to sell a house? Lower the price! At a low enough price, any house will sell quickly. So selling houses is easy: It's finding a price that the seller is willing to accept and the buyer is willing to pay that is difficult. In the same way, it's always easy to find a job if you are willing to work for peanuts. Finding a job that you want at a wage that you will accept and the employer will pay, however, takes time and effort. The difficulty of matching employees to employers creates friction in the labor market, and the resulting temporary unemployment is called frictional unemployment. Thus, **frictional unemployment** is short-term unemployment caused by the ordinary difficulties of matching employee to employer.

Scarcity of information is one of the causes of frictional unemployment. Workers do not know all the job opportunities available to them, and employers do not know all the available candidates and their respective qualifications. The Internet has probably lowered the underlying rate of frictional unemployment by making it easier for workers to search for jobs and for firms to search for workers.

Frictional unemployment usually doesn't last very long. If the economy is not in a recession, it might take a few weeks to find a new job, or for specialized workers perhaps a few months but not much longer. Figure 30.3 shows the typical duration of unemployment in 2005, a nonrecession year, and also in 2010 as the economy slowly exited the 2007–2009 recession. In 2005, most unemployment was of fairly short duration: 35.1% of the unemployed were jobless for less than five weeks and 30.4% were jobless for only 5 to 14 weeks. The remaining one-third were jobless for more than 14 weeks, with 19.6% jobless for more than half a year. In the United States in a nonrecession year, a significant fraction of unemployment is frictional.

The situation was very different in 2010 when a majority of the unemployed had been unemployed for more than 14 weeks. Indeed, in mid-2010, 43.3% of the unemployed had been unemployed for more than 6 months. Not since the Great Depression had so many unemployed workers been unemployed for such an extended period of time.

Frictional unemployment is short-term unemployment caused by the ordinary difficulties of matching employee to employer.

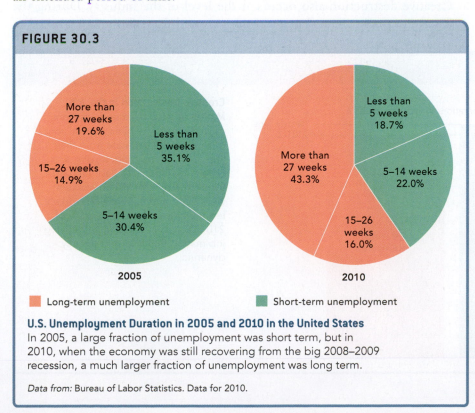

FIGURE 30.3

Long-term unemployment   Short-term unemployment

U.S. Unemployment Duration in 2005 and 2010 in the United States
In 2005, a large fraction of unemployment was short term, but in 2010, when the economy was still recovering from the big 2008–2009 recession, a much larger fraction of unemployment was long term.

Data from: Bureau of Labor Statistics. Data for 2010.

Traditionally, long-term unemployment has been a much bigger problem in Europe than in the United States. The extraordinary increase in long-term unemployment in the United States is one of the most worrying aspects of the 2007–2009 recession. In March 2014, there were still 3.5 million people, 38.4% of the total unemployed population, who had been unemployed for more than 27 weeks. It wasn't until 2017 that long-term unemployment came down to a more normal level of 1.7 million, or 23.8% of the unemployed population. We will discuss long-term unemployment in the next section.

Frictional unemployment is typically a large share of total unemployment because the U.S. economy is dynamic. Innovation and the relentless pressure of competition drive progress. Progress, however, is not simply creating new jobs and adding them to the old. Rather it's about creating new jobs and destroying old jobs. Webmasters are in; travel agents are out. We can see this process in more detail by looking at statistics on job creation and destruction.

As shown in Figure 30.4, the U.S. economy had around 210 thousand more jobs at the end of February of 2014 than it had at the beginning. This number, however, hides an underlying reality of much greater change. In that same month, 4.59 *million* new jobs were created but during the same month there were also 4.38 million job separations (quits, layoffs, and other separations). The net figure, the one often reported in the news, is the difference between hires and separations (4.59 − 4.38 = 0.21 million, or 210,000 new jobs). These figures are typical. In any given month, millions of jobs are created and millions of jobs are destroyed. "Creative destruction," a term coined by economist Joseph Schumpeter, describes this process well.

Creative destruction occurs at the level of the firm and the industry. Even in an industry with constant or increasing employment, the location of employment changes as uncompetitive firms disappear or shrink and new firms grow. Kmart filed for bankruptcy in 2002 and laid off 34,000 workers, but in that same year its more productive rival, Walmart, hired 139,000 workers.[1]

Creative destruction also occurs at the level of the industry. During the 1970s, for example, the real price of oil increased from about $10 a barrel to

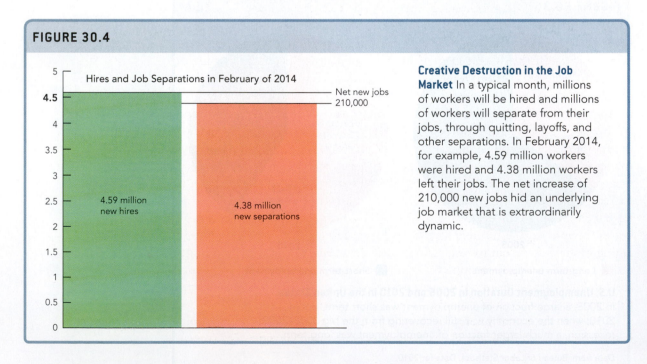

FIGURE 30.4

Hires and Job Separations in February of 2014

4.59 million new hires

4.38 million new separations

Net new jobs 210,000

Creative Destruction in the Job Market In a typical month, millions of workers will be hired and millions of workers will separate from their jobs, through quitting, layoffs, and other separations. In February 2014, for example, 4.59 million workers were hired and 4.38 million workers left their jobs. The net increase of 210,000 new jobs hid an underlying job market that is extraordinarily dynamic.

nearly $80 a barrel (see Chapter 4, Figure 4.9). The oil shocks required a fundamental reallocation of labor from industries that were heavily dependent on oil to industries less dependent on oil. But it takes more time (and thus more unemployment) for workers to move from one industry to another industry than to move from one firm to another firm in the same industry—this type of unemployment that occurs in response to deep changes in the economy is called structural unemployment, the topic of the next section.

Structural Unemployment

Structural unemployment is persistent, long-term unemployment. Isn't it redundant to say that unemployment is persistent *and* long-term? Not quite. In France, Germany, Italy, and Spain, for example, approximately 40% to 50% of the unemployed have been unemployed for more than one year and this has been true for about 25 years.[2] In 2010 in the United States, 29% of the unemployed had been unemployed for more than a year, but this had been true for only about one year. The phrase "persistent, long-term unemployment" means that a substantial fraction of the unemployed have been unemployed for more than one year and that this problem has lasted for a long time. Persistent long-term unemployment has traditionally been much less of a problem in the United States than in Europe. Long-term unemployment following the 2008–2009 recession, however, has been more persistent than in the past. By 2015, 18.7% of the unemployed had been unemployed for more than one year—a high rate for the United States but less than half the rate of the European Union average.

What causes structural unemployment? One cause is large, economy-wide shocks that occur relatively quickly. Adjusting to these shocks can create long-lasting unemployment as the economy takes time to restructure. In addition to the oil shocks, the U.S. economy has had to restructure in recent decades because of the shift from a manufacturing to a service economy, because of globalization and because of new information technologies such as the computer and the Internet.

In the early 1800s, a militant group of textile artisans called the Luddites smashed newly invented mechanical looms because they feared that technological unemployment would lead to structural unemployment. The same fears resurfaced in the Great Depression and in the 1950s with the coming of electricity and automation, respectively. Today, many people fear that artificial intelligence will lead to unemployment for lawyers, doctors, and other professions previously considered immune to automation. So far, the worst fears of the Luddites have not come to pass. Labor-saving technology can create unemployment in some fields, but as workers move to other fields, total output increases, which raises the average standard of living and usually leads to higher wages. Since the time of the Luddites, technological change has dramatically increased the wages and standard of living of the average worker. Adapting to new technologies, however, isn't always easy or quick and some workers can be left behind. It doesn't help that firms often delay structural changes until falling profits force them to restructure or die. As a result, big structural changes often happen during recessions, and it becomes difficult to distinguish structural unemployment from the more temporary unemployment correlated with the business cycle (cyclical unemployment—see later in the chapter).

Note that structural unemployment, if it lasts long enough, brings significant human costs in addition to the loss of economic output. Not only is

Structural unemployment is persistent, long-term unemployment caused by long-lasting shocks or permanent features of an economy that make it more difficult for some workers to find jobs.

►►SEARCH ENGINE

Extensive data on the labor force and unemployment for a large sample of countries are collected by the Organisation for Economic Co-operation and Development (search for OECD Statistics).

the economy producing less but the unemployed suffer higher levels of stress, higher rates of suicide, and lower rates of measured happiness. Wanting a job—and not being able to find a good one—is a recipe for misery and social decay. Moreover, the stress of unemployment can last for a long-time—in one study, workers who lost their jobs in the 1970s had slightly higher probabilities of dying for as long as 20 years later compared to similar workers who had not lost their jobs in the 1970s.[3]

At some point unemployment can become chronic. It can be more difficult for an unemployed worker to find a job than for an employed worker to switch jobs. Unemployed workers face two problems. First, the longer a worker remains out of the labor force, the more his or her skills atrophy. An administrative assistant who became unemployed in 2005, for example, might have no idea how to use Google Docs, a critical skill for a job today. Second, hiring managers may regard unemployment as a sign of laziness or other problems. Whom would you rather hire: a worker who is looking to switch jobs or a worker who has been unemployed for five years? Unemployment can become a trap, and this is another reason why unemployment rates in Western Europe are taking so long to return to normal.

Labor Regulations and Structural Unemployment

The late 1970s oil shock (as well as the other shocks previously mentioned) hit the United States as hard as it did Europe, but in the United States unemployment tends to increase with a shock and then decrease, while in Europe (especially in the big four continental economies—France, Germany, Italy, and Spain—unemployment has increased with shocks and then remained at high levels. Table 30.1 shows that unemployment in the big four European countries hovered around 10% or higher for 20 years and a large fraction of this unemployment has been long term. Why did unemployment rates in the United States and Europe behave so differently?

Structural unemployment has been a more serious problem in Europe than in the United States because of labor regulations. More specifically, unemployment benefits, minimum wages, unions, and employment protection laws benefit some workers, but these regulations can also increase unemployment rates. All of these regulations are more generous and wide-ranging in Europe than

TABLE 30.1 UNEMPLOYMENT RATES IN EUROPE VS. THE UNITED STATES, 1980–2004

Country	1980–1984	1985–1989	1990–1994	1995–1999	2000–2004	Fraction Unemployed for More Than One Year (2004)
France	7.3%	9.3%	9.6%	10.8%	8.4%	41.6%
Germany	5.9%	6.4%	6.7%	9.8%	8.8%	51.8%
Italy	8.8%	11.6%	10.9%	11.8%	9.3%	49.7%
Spain	15.9%	19.9%	19.6%	20.0%	11.7%	37.7%
United States	8.3%	6.2%	6.6%	4.9%	5.2%	12.7%

Data from: OECD Statistics and OECD Employment Outlook, 2005.

in the United States, and that helps explain why structural unemployment is a more serious problem in Europe than in the United States. Let's go through each labor market intervention in turn.

Unemployment Benefits Unemployment benefits are the most obvious labor regulation that can increase unemployment rates. Unemployment benefits include unemployment insurance, but also other benefits such as housing assistance that may be available in some countries. Table 30.2 shows how much of a worker's take-home pay was replaced by unemployment benefits in France, Germany, Spain, and the United States in 1994.[4] (We focus on 1994 because this is about midway through Europe's long spell of unemployment.)

In the first year of unemployment in France, the unemployment benefit system replaced 80% of a worker's income. A worker who lost his or her job in France, in other words, faced only a 20% cut in pay. In fact, if we look only at income, and not at the satisfaction that comes from having a job, a French worker who lost his or her job was probably better off—after all, an unemployed worker had 80% of the income of an employed worker and much more leisure time ("unemployed workers" may also work for pay in the black market). In comparison, the unemployment benefit system in the United States replaced only 38% of a worker's pay so a worker who lost his or her job faced a 62% cut in pay.

Unemployment benefits also last much longer in Europe than in the United States. In the United States, for example, unemployment benefits typically fall by more than half after just one year (although unemployment benefits are often extended in the United States when the unemployment rate is especially high). But in France, Germany, and Spain, unemployment benefits never decrease by so wide a margin.

Given these figures, it shouldn't be surprising that long-term unemployment is much more common in Europe than in the United States (see the last column in Table 30.1). In Europe, the price of unemployment is low, so more unemployment (leisure) is demanded. Or, if you like, workers in Europe can afford to remain unemployed for longer periods than workers in the United States.

TABLE 30.2 UNEMPLOYMENT BENEFIT REPLACEMENT RATES IN EUROPE VS. THE UNITED STATES, 1994

	First Year	Second and Third Year	Fourth and Fifth Year
France	80%	62%	60%
Germany	74%	72%	72%
Spain	70%	55%	39%
United States	38%	14%	14%

Note: The data cover a worker with a dependent spouse and are net rates after taking into account taxes and other benefits.
Data from: Ljungqvist L. and T. Sargent. 1998. The European unemployment dilemma. *Journal of Political Economy* **106**(3): 514–550.
Martin, John P. 1996. Measures of replacement rates for the purpose of international comparisons: A note. *OECD Economic Studies* **26**(1): 99–115.

In summary, unemployment benefits reduce the incentive for workers to search for and take new jobs. Now switching to look at the demand side of the labor market, minimum wage, unions, and employment protection laws reduce the incentive of firms to create and offer new jobs.

Minimum Wages and Unions In the left panel of Figure 30.5, we analyze the minimum wage (see the chapter on Price Ceilings and Price Floors for a more extensive discussion). The minimum wage raises the price of labor from the market wage to the minimum wage, and as labor becomes more expensive, firms reduce employment from market employment to minimum wage employment Q_d. At the minimum wage, the number of workers looking for work Q_s exceeds the number of jobs Q_d—thus, the minimum wage creates unemployment in the amount $Q_s - Q_d$.

In Western Europe, minimum wages have been higher than in the United States. In recent years, for example, the minimum wage in France was about 32% higher than in the United States. Minimum wages in Western Europe have also been higher relative to the **median wage** than in the United States. (The median wage is defined so that half of all workers earn less than the median and half more.) In France, the minimum wage has been about 62% as large as the median wage. In the United States, the minimum wage has only been about 32% as large as the median wage.[5] What this means is that the minimum wage will affect more workers and create more unemployment in France than in the United States. As discussed in the chapter on Price Ceilings and Price Floors, the minimum wage is more likely to create unemployment among young workers, who tend to be less productive, than among older workers. Thus, in both France and the United States, unemployment rates are higher among the young than the old, but in France in 2014, 23% of workers under the age of 25 were unemployed, while in the United States 13% of these workers were unemployed.

Unions are also more powerful in Europe than in the United States. A union is an association of workers that bargains collectively with employers over wages, benefits, and working conditions. In the United States, most (87%) workers are not governed by a union contract; instead, they have an individual contract (written or unwritten) with employers. In many European countries, however, 80% or more of workers are governed by a union contract.

The **median wage** is the wage such that one-half of all workers earn wages below the median and one-half of all workers earn wages above the median.

A **union** is an association of workers that bargains collectively with employers over wages, benefits, and working conditions.

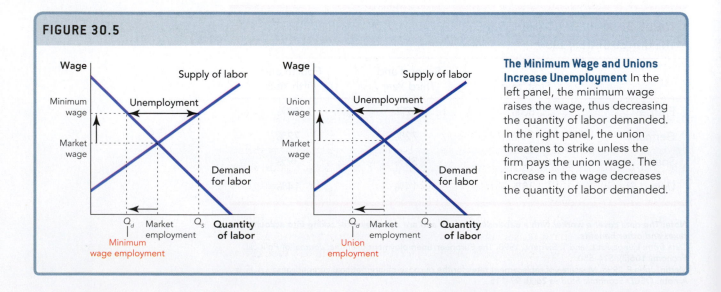

FIGURE 30.5

The Minimum Wage and Unions Increase Unemployment In the left panel, the minimum wage raises the wage, thus decreasing the quantity of labor demanded. In the right panel, the union threatens to strike unless the firm pays the union wage. The increase in the wage decreases the quantity of labor demanded.

Unions can provide value for workers and employers alike, but excessively strong unions have a very similar effect as minimum wages. Unions demand higher wages by using their power to strike and to prevent the firm from hiring substitute labor. In the right panel of Figure 30.5, the union raises the price of labor from the market wage to the union wage. As labor becomes more expensive, firms reduce employment from market employment to union employment Q_d. At the union wage, the number of workers looking for work Q_s exceeds the number of jobs Q_d—thus, unions increase unemployment by the amount $Q_s - Q_d$.

Employment Protection Laws In the United States, an employee may quit and an employer may fire at any time and for any reason. This is called the **employment at–will doctrine**. There are many exceptions to the at-will doctrine, the most important being that the doctrine can be changed by contract. Many workers, for example, have contractually guaranteed severance packages and tenured university professors cannot be fired at will. Employees can also be restricted by contract. Employees in some industries with a lot of trade secrets are often asked to sign a noncompete agreement when they are hired. If an employee who signs a noncompete agreement quits, he or she may be forbidden, for example, from working for a competitor for a set period. Public law also imposes certain restrictions; employers, for example, are forbidden from hiring or firing on the basis of race, religion, sex, sexual orientation, national origin, age, or handicap status. Despite many exceptions, the at-will doctrine can be thought of as the most basic U.S. labor law.

> The **employment at-will doctrine** says an employee may quit and an employer may fire an employee at any time and for any reason. There are many exceptions to the at-will doctrine, but it is the most basic U.S. employment law.

In most of Europe, labor law is quite different. Portugal's constitution, for example, forbids at-will employment and requires employers to notify the government whenever a worker is dismissed. Moreover, if a Portuguese firm needs to lay off a group of workers, it must get the government's permission. Nor can the firm choose which workers to lay off; instead, it must follow strict guidelines determining which workers will be laid off first (generally, the most junior workers are fired first). In addition, laid-off workers must be given 60 days' notice, severance pay, and other benefits. Throughout Western Europe, public law and collective bargaining—not contracts—govern things like the length of the workweek, overtime pay, paid leave, temporary employment, notice periods, severance pay, and more.

Hiring and firing costs make labor markets less flexible and dynamic. A European firm with an unexpected increase in orders, for example, will not simply hire more workers. If the firm hires more workers and orders then decline, it would be stuck with workers it could not lay off without incurring great expense. Thus, hiring and firing costs make firms more cautious and slower to act.

Greater job security is valuable to workers with full-time jobs, but the more expensive it is to hire and fire workers, the more difficult it will be for new workers and unemployed workers to find jobs. Imagine, for example, how difficult it would be to get a date if every date required marriage! In the same way, it's more difficult to find a job when every job requires a long-term commitment from the employer.

The World Bank calculates a "rigidity of employment index," which summarizes hiring and firing costs, as well as how easy it is for firms to adjust hours of work (e.g., whether there are restrictions on night or weekend hours). A higher index number means that it is more expensive to hire and fire

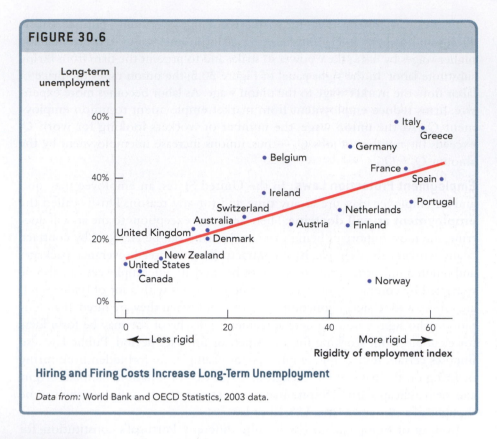

FIGURE 30.6

Long-term unemployment

Hiring and Firing Costs Increase Long-Term Unemployment

Data from: World Bank and OECD Statistics, 2003 data.

Outsider riot Paris suburbs, 2005

Insider riot Central Paris, 2006

workers and more difficult to adjust hours. Figure 30.6 plots the rigidity index against the percentage of unemployment that is long term (lasting more than one year). The red line shows the trend in the data; greater rigidity in labor markets is clearly associated with greater long-term unemployment. Notice especially that France, Germany, Italy, and Spain all have high rigidity and high long-term unemployment, while the United States has the least rigid labor markets and one of the lowest rates of long-term unemployment.

A Tale of Two Riots The tale of two riots illustrates another effect of employment protection laws. Paris, the city of lights, was lit up by hundreds of burning vehicles in November 2005 as angry, predominantly immigrant youth rioted in the streets. The riots were triggered by accusations of police brutality, but poverty and unemployment were the larger underlying frustrations. Unemployment rates among the rioting youth were over 30%.[6]

French firms were reluctant to hire young, minority workers—perhaps, in some instances, because of discrimination, but also because the more expensive it is to hire and fire, the more reluctant firms will be to hire workers without experience and workers for which there is any perceived uncertainty about quality. Once again, if every date required marriage, would you go on a blind date? A blind date might be worth some risk if you can dump a loser, but who will go on a blind date if a date means forever? So with regard to firms, young workers are riskier than older workers. Workers without a job are riskier than workers with a job (recall our discussion of the unemployment trap). And minority workers or workers who in some way differ from the "norm" may be regarded as more risky than typical workers by some employers. Thus, employment protection laws tend to have the most negative effects for young, already unemployed, and minority workers.

The French government was aware of these problems and in response to the riots it proposed to change labor law so that for workers under the age of 26, employment would be at-will for the first two years. The idea was to reassure firms that hiring a young, immigrant worker could be more like a blind date and less like marriage. Of course, this at-will employment is the norm in the United States. For elite French youth, however, the idea that they could be fired at will was upsetting and an infringement of what they considered to be their rights. Several hundred students barricaded themselves in the Sorbonne, the famous Paris university, and called on students everywhere to protest.

Now it was time for the insiders, the young elite, to riot and they proved every bit as adept at burning cars as had the impoverished youth of the year before. Not surprisingly, the elite riots were effective—the French government quickly backed down from the at-will employment doctrine. Unemployment in France, especially among young, immigrant workers remains high.

Summarizing, employment protection laws have the following effects. They:

- Create valuable insurance for workers with full-time jobs.
- Make labor markets less flexible and dynamic.
- Increase the duration of unemployment.
- Increase unemployment rates among young, minority, or otherwise "riskier" workers.

Riots and Structural Unemployment

interactive activity

Labor Regulations to Reduce Structural Unemployment

In recent years, Europe has begun to change some of its labor regulations to try to reduce long-term unemployment. In Denmark, for example, unemployment benefits were limited to four years, and after one year workers who wish to continue receiving benefits must either enroll in job search or job training programs or take public employment. Denmark also subsidizes employers who are willing to train unemployed workers. Denmark and other countries now also have work tests—requirements that unemployed workers who want benefits must prove that they are actively seeking work.[7] These types of laws are called **active labor market policies**.

The United States has been a leader in testing active labor market programs. One of the most successful programs is the simplest—pay workers to get a job! In several large-scale experiments, randomly chosen unemployed workers were told that they would be paid a bonus if they found work early. The workers who were told about the bonus got jobs significantly sooner than those not promised bonuses.

Europe has also been slowly moving toward more flexible labor markets by allowing some exceptions to collective bargaining agreements for certain categories of workers, such as young workers, temporary workers, and part-time workers. Remember, however, the tale of the two riots. "Insiders" have been very reluctant to give up their benefits for the sake of the unemployed "outsiders."

With **active labor market policies**, like work tests, job search assistance and job retraining programs focus on getting unemployed workers back to work.

Factors That Affect Structural Unemployment

Let's summarize the factors that can increase structural unemployment. These are:

- Large, long-lasting shocks that require the economy to restructure. For example:
  - Oil shocks
  - Shift from manufacturing to services
  - Globalization and global competition
  - Fundamental technology shocks (computers, the Internet, and—maybe—artificial intelligence)
- Labor regulations:
  - Unemployment benefits
  - Minimum wages
  - Powerful unions
  - Employment protection laws

We also discussed some policies that can reduce structural unemployment. These include:

- Active labor market policies:
  - Job retraining
  - Job-search assistance
  - Work tests
  - Early employment bonuses

Cyclical Unemployment

The final category of unemployment is **cyclical unemployment**, or unemployment correlated with the ups and downs of the business cycle. Figure 30.7 graphs the U.S. unemployment rate since 1948. The shaded areas are recessions. Notice that during every recession, unemployment increases dramatically.

Cyclical unemployment is unemployment correlated with the business cycle.

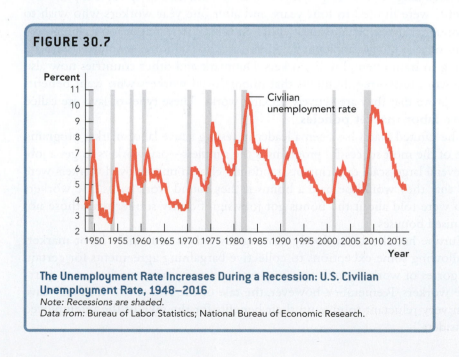

FIGURE 30.7

The Unemployment Rate Increases During a Recession: U.S. Civilian Unemployment Rate, 1948–2016

Note: Recessions are shaded.
Data from: Bureau of Labor Statistics; National Bureau of Economic Research.

Lower growth is usually accompanied with higher unemployment for two reasons. First and most obviously, when GDP is falling, firms often lay off workers, which increases unemployment. The second reason is more subtle. Higher unemployment means that fewer workers are producing goods and services. When workers are sitting idle, it's likely that related capital is also sitting idle (e.g., factories are boarded up). An economy with idle labor and idle capital cannot be maximizing growth, and that will hurt the ability of that economy to create more jobs.

Figure 30.8 emphasizes the flip side of the idea that lower growth is correlated with increases in unemployment—faster growth is correlated with decreases in unemployment. Figure 30.8 plots changes in the U.S. unemployment rate on the vertical axis against growth on the horizontal axis. As you can see, faster growth in real GDP decreases unemployment. In fact, unemployment tends to fall when growth is above average and it tends to rise when growth is below average. Consider 1982 when the economy was in a deep recession and the unemployment rate increased by 2.1%. On the other hand, just two years later in 1984, real GDP was growing rapidly, at 7.2% a year, unemployment was falling, and, partly as a consequence, Ronald Reagan was reelected in a landslide.

Although we define cyclical unemployment as unemployment correlated with the business cycle, the cause of cyclical unemployment is a subject of debate among economists, largely because the cause of business cycles is a subject of debate. Some economists think that business cycles are mostly a response to real shocks that require a reallocation of labor across industries. For these economists, a business cycle is nothing more than the economic growth process in action—growth is volatile, not smooth. Thus, for these economists,

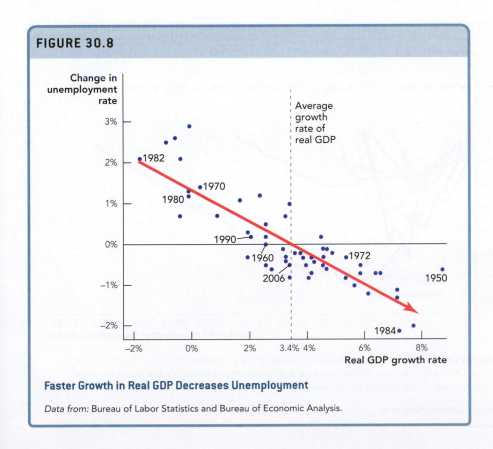

FIGURE 30.8

Faster Growth in Real GDP Decreases Unemployment

Data from: Bureau of Labor Statistics and Bureau of Economic Analysis.

cyclical unemployment is just another example of frictional and structural unemployment.

Other economists, typically of the "Keynesian" persuasion, think that cyclical unemployment is caused by deficiencies in aggregate demand. This concept will be explained in later chapters, but for the time being, we can think of this notion of cyclical unemployment as caused by a mismatch between the aggregate level of wages in an economy and the level of prices. The wages demanded by workers are out of synch with the level of prices, so workers are too expensive to hire from the point of view of firms.

To give a simple example, whether a firm wants to hire another worker depends not only on the wage of that worker but also on that wage relative to the price of the firm's product (and, of course, relative to other prices more generally). If Apple can sell an iPhone for $600, it is more likely to step up production and hire more workers than if Apple can sell an iPhone for $300. Yet when potential workers make wage demands, they are not always fully aware of the prices and thus the profits available to their employers. Wage demands can be too high, relative to what the firm finds profitable, and this mismatch gives rise to cyclical unemployment. Yet if aggregate demand for goods and services was somehow higher, the higher wage demands perhaps could be justified and the workers could be hired. In any case, we see that cyclical unemployment, following the recent recession, remained high in 2010, even compared with previous recessions. This is sometimes called a "jobless recovery." Figure 30.9 shows that for the recession beginning in 2007 it took more than six years for employment to return to its prerecession level, the longest for any recession since the Great Depression.

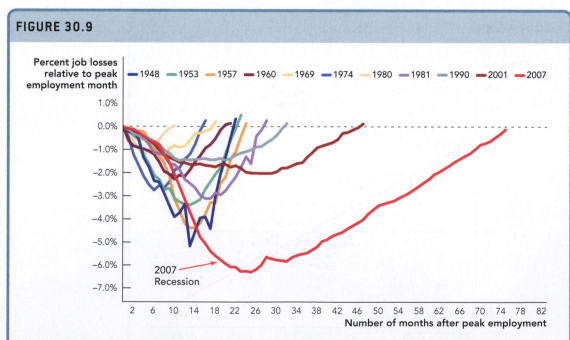

FIGURE 30.9

Percent Job Losses in Post-WWII Recessions The 2007 recession saw greater job losses lasting for a longer period of time than any previous recession since the Great Depression. It took more than six years for employment to regain its prerecession level.

Data from: http://www.calculatedriskblog.com/.

We will return to the concepts of real shocks, mismatches between aggregate wages and prices, business uncertainty, and potential government policy to reduce cyclical unemployment in greater detail in upcoming chapters. This will help us explain why the 2009–2010 labor market was so slow to move to higher levels of employment.

The Natural Unemployment Rate

The **natural unemployment rate** is defined as the rate of structural plus frictional unemployment. Economists typically think of the underlying rates of frictional and structural unemployment as changing only slowly through time as major, long-lasting features of the economy change. Cyclical employment, however, can increase or decrease dramatically over a matter of months. Figure 30.10 plots one estimate of the natural rate against the actual unemployment rate. The natural rate changes only slowly through time and the actual rate of unemployment varies around the natural rate.

The **natural unemployment rate** is the rate of structural plus frictional unemployment.

The concepts of cyclical, structural, and frictional unemployment are not always clear and distinct. If times are good, an employer will place more ads and search harder for workers. We might say that the frictional rate of unemployment has fallen, but we also might say that the cyclical rate of unemployment has fallen. Both descriptions of the improvement are true. Similarly, how well an economy absorbs, say, displaced auto workers (structural unemployment) will depend on the overall strength of economic conditions. One type of unemployment can even turn into another. Cyclical unemployment, for example, can turn into structural unemployment if workers remain unemployed for too long, thereby leading to a decline in skills and employment prospects. As we showed earlier, the increase in unemployment that began with the 2007–2009 recession is taking a very long time to decline, leading to worries that unemployment that perhaps started out as cyclical may become structural.

Most economists view observed unemployment as a mix of structural, frictional, and cyclical characteristics. The three categories nonetheless give us some useful ideas for organizing the sources of unemployment.

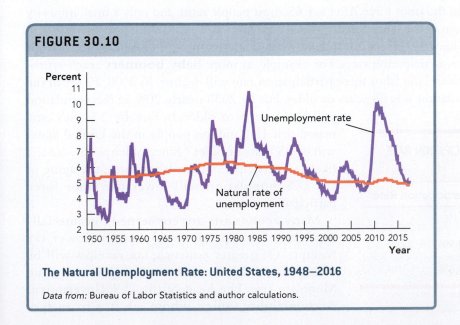

FIGURE 30.10

The Natural Unemployment Rate: United States, 1948–2016

Data from: Bureau of Labor Statistics and author calculations.

CHECK YOURSELF

- What happens to cyclical unemployment during the business cycle?
- How are economic growth and unemployment related?

Labor Force Participation

So far we've focused on whether people can get a job if they want one, but it is also important to ask whether people *want* a job. We therefore turn from the unemployment rate to the labor force participation rate. Recall that the labor force participation rate is the percentage of the adult, noninstitutionalized, civilian population (adults for short) who are working or actively looking for work. In other words, the labor force participation rate is the percentage of adults who are in the labor force:

$$\text{Labor force participation rate} = \frac{\text{Unemployed} + \text{Employed}}{\text{Adult population}} \times 100$$

$$= \frac{\text{Labor force}}{\text{Adult population}} \times 100$$

In the United States (circa 2017), there were 160.1 million members of the labor force and 255.0 million adult, noninstitutionalized civilians, so the labor force participation rate was

$$\frac{160.1 \text{ million}}{255.0 \text{ million}} \times 100 = 62.8\%$$

What determines the labor force participation rate? We will discuss two factors.

1. Lifecycle effects and demographics
2. Incentives

Lifecycle Effects and Demographics

Table 30.3 shows how labor force participation rates vary with age. Not surprisingly, most young adults are full-time students not workers. Labor force participation peaks in the prime working years, ages 25–54, when most adults are in the labor force. After age 65, most people retire and only a small minority remain in the labor force.

Lifecycle effects can interact with demographics to change national labor force participation rates. For example, as more **baby boomers** reach retirement age, the labor force participation rate will decline. In 2000, 12.4% of the population was 65 years or older, but by 2030 nearly 20% of the population will be 65 years or older. In fact, by 2030 it's estimated that 18.2 million people in the United States will be 85 years or older.[8] Since older people are less likely to participate in the labor force, the aging of the U.S. population will lower the labor force participation rate.

Many economists are concerned because falling labor force participation means lower tax receipts. Of greater concern, tax receipts will be falling just as the demands on Social Security and Medicare rise. The head of the U.S. Government Accountability Office, whose job it is to analyze

Baby boomers are the people born during the high birthrate years, 1946–1964.

TABLE 30.3 THE LABOR FORCE PARTICIPATION RATE AT DIFFERENT AGES

Age Range (years)	Labor Force Participation Rate
16–19	34%
25–54	80.9%
65+	18.6%

Data from: Bureau of Labor Statistics, 2014.

the long-term financial health of the U.S. government, has said in this regard, "When those boomers start retiring en masse, then that will be a tsunami of spending that could swamp our ship of state if we don't get serious."[9] We take up these important issues at greater length in the chapter on The Federal Budget: Taxes and Spending.

A natural response to rising life expectancies and better health at older ages is later retirement. The "normal" retirement age is partly a matter of culture and convention but it is also partly determined by economic incentives, especially taxes—a subject to which we now turn.

Incentives

Why do people join the labor force? A few artists (and some professors!) love to work, but most people work because work pays more than leisure. More specifically, the choice to work depends on the difference between what work pays and what leisure pays. The choice to work, therefore, can be influenced by taxes on workers and benefits paid to nonworkers. Taxes discourage work and benefits encourage nonwork. We can see both of these effects in action by looking at how retirement systems in different countries change the incentives that older people have to work.

Taxes and Benefits Figure 30.11 shows labor participation rates for men ages 55–64 in different countries in 1998. In Belgium, only one-third of men in this age range were working, while in the United States only one-third of men of this age range were retired! Why are there such large differences in labor force participation rates? It's not just cultural differences concerning the right age for retirement.

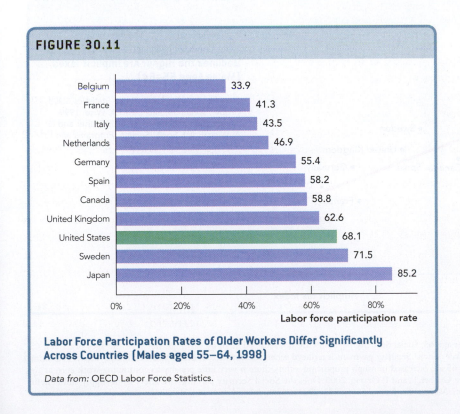

FIGURE 30.11

Labor Force Participation Rates of Older Workers Differ Significantly Across Countries (Males aged 55–64, 1998)

Data from: OECD Labor Force Statistics.

In the United States, a worker of retirement age who continues working is not penalized.* But many countries penalize workers who work past the normal or early retirement age because many countries do not allow a worker to work *and* receive the same government pension. For example, in the Netherlands in the 1990s, a worker who worked past the age of 60 lost one year of benefits. The lost benefits can be thought of as a tax on working. Workers who kept working also had to pay payroll taxes on their wages. The net result was that a worker who worked past the age of 60 in the Netherlands earned less money than a worker who retired! In other words, a worker who did not retire at age 60 had to pay to work. If you had to pay to work, how much work would you do?

Figure 30.12 graphs the labor force participation rate in the 1990s of older men against a measure of the penalty, the implicit tax on working. Countries with a high implicit tax have a low labor force participation rate.

Early retirement is beneficial for workers if they want to retire early, but taxing older workers at significantly higher rates than younger workers (sometimes at rates above 100%!) does not benefit the older workers. Pushing older workers into retirement also imposes significant costs on younger workers who must pay higher taxes because older workers are not contributing to GDP.

In the 1990s, as the costs of their retirement systems rose, many European governments began to make benefits less generous and also to reduce the implicit tax on working. As the penalty on working fell, the labor force participation rates of older workers increased. In 1998, only 33.9% of older male workers in Belgium worked, but by 2015 this had increased to 52.2%. The Netherlands also reduced the tax on working and the labor force participation rates of older workers increased from 46.4% to 77.6%. These changes illustrate how incentives powerfully influence the choice to work.

FIGURE 30.12

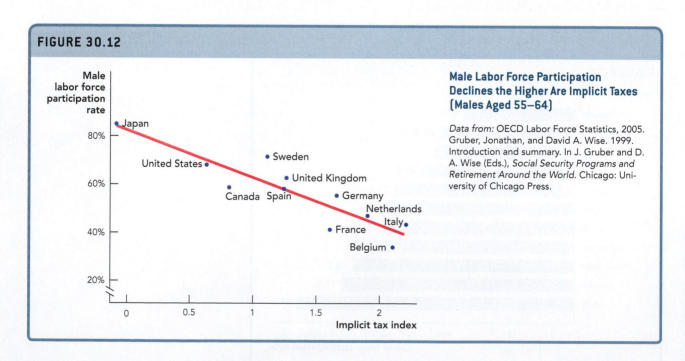

Male Labor Force Participation Declines the Higher Are Implicit Taxes (Males Aged 55–64)

Data from: OECD Labor Force Statistics, 2005. Gruber, Jonathan, and David A. Wise. 1999. Introduction and summary. In J. Gruber and D. A. Wise (Eds.), *Social Security Programs and Retirement Around the World*. Chicago: University of Chicago Press.

* After age 65, Social Security payments are not reduced at all by earnings. Between the ages of 62 and 65, a worker's Social Security payment is reduced when the worker continues to work but payments beginning at age 65 are increased in rough proportion—thus, there is very little penalty to continuing work even at age 62. See Gruber, J., and P. Orszag. 2003. Does the Social Security earnings test affect labor supply and benefits receipt? *National Tax Journal* 56(4): 755–773.

Incentives and the Increase in Female Labor Force Participation Incentives have also played a role in the dramatic increase in the U.S. labor force participation rates of women. In 1948, only 35% of women aged 25–54 were in the (paid) labor force. By the mid-1990s, 75% of these women were in the labor force. Figure 30.13 plots U.S. labor force participation rates for women since 1948. Notice that the 1970s brought especially large increases in labor force participation rates.

Cultural factors such as the rise of feminism and the growing acceptance of equality for women certainly played a role in rising female labor force participation. But cultural changes do not happen in a vacuum. Changes in the economy such as the move from a manufacturing to a service economy also brought more women to work. Even today, for example, there are almost three times as many male semiskilled factory and machine operators as female operators, but there are more female professionals (lawyers, professors, accountants, etc.) than there are male professionals.[10] As the manufacturing sector declined and the service sector rose, there was less demand for machine operators and more demand for professionals. This raised wages in sectors where females had a comparative advantage, thereby drawing more females into the labor force. In turn, the phenomenon of women in the workplace fueled the rise of feminism.

The growth in women working was especially dramatic in the professions. Figure 30.14 shows the percentage of the first-year students who were female in medical school, dentistry, law, and business programs from 1955 to 2005. From 1955 to about 1970, fewer than 10% of first-year students in the professions were females. Beginning around 1970, however, female participation shot up—more than doubling in all professions in just 10 years and continuing to increase until between 40% to 50% of all students in professional programs are female.

Why did females start entering professional schools in increasing numbers beginning around 1970? Economists Claudia Goldin and Lawrence Katz have an intriguing and controversial answer—the contraceptive pill, known simply as the pill.[11]

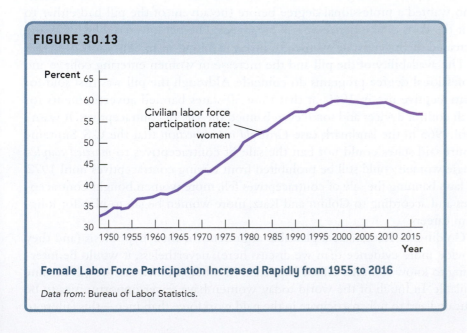

FIGURE 30.13

Female Labor Force Participation Increased Rapidly from 1955 to 2016

Data from: Bureau of Labor Statistics.

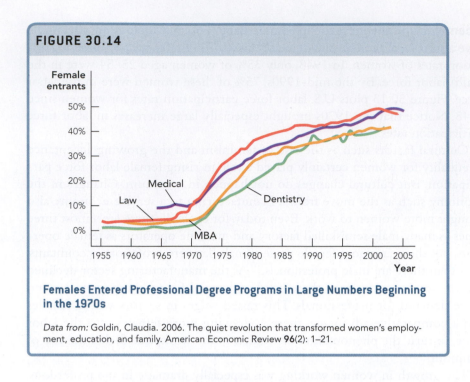

FIGURE 30.14

Female entrants

Females Entered Professional Degree Programs in Large Numbers Beginning in the 1970s

Data from: Goldin, Claudia. 2006. The quiet revolution that transformed women's employment, education, and family. *American Economic Review* **96**(2): 1–21.

Women Working: What's the Pill Got to Do with it?

How the Pill Increased Female Labor Force Participation The pill has been called the greatest technological advance of the twentieth century. For the first time in history, women were given a low-cost, reliable, and convenient method of controlling fertility, the pill. Condoms can also prevent unwanted pregnancy, but the pill is easier to use, less prone to error, and more reliable. Among typical users, the pill is seven times more reliable than condoms, and among those who always use the pill according to directions, it is 60 times more reliable.

Economists Goldin and Katz argue that the pill lowered the costs of earning a professional degree by giving women greater certainty about the consequences of sex. It takes years of effort to earn a professional degree, and earning a degree while bearing or taking care of a baby is very difficult. Thus, women who wanted a professional degree before the advent of the pill had either to bear the costs of abstinence or risk pregnancy. The pill lowered these costs and increased the incentive of women to invest in a long-term education.

The availability of the pill and the increase in women entering college and professional degree programs do coincide. Although the pill was first sold for contraceptive use in 1960, at that time 30 states banned advertisements for birth control devices and some even banned the sale of contraceptives. It wasn't until 1965 in the landmark case *Griswold v. Connecticut* that the U.S. Supreme Court said states could not ban the sale of contraceptives to *married couples*. Single women could still be prohibited from buying contraceptives until 1972. As laws banning the sale of contraceptives fell, more women bought contraceptives and according to Goldin and Katz, more women began to plan for long-term careers.

Goldin and Katz make a plausible argument for their hypothesis (and they provide more evidence than we discuss here); nevertheless, it would be interesting to know if similar effects happened in other countries as the pill became available. In much of the world today, women have fewer opportunities to be educated and to fully participate in the paid workforce than men—this failure to fully utilize the talents of women is an enormous loss to these women and to the economy. Questions like these are on the cutting edge of economics—perhaps some of you will help to answer them.

Takeaway

Perhaps the most important lesson of this chapter is that even in the best of times, unemployment will exist and fluctuate. The economy is always changing and only through change is there growth. It is important to help workers who are buffeted by change, but there is a difference between helping workers to adjust and trying to prevent adjustment—ultimately, we can do the former but not the latter. As we discussed in this chapter, some labor market policies intended to protect workers have increased structural unemployment in Western Europe compared with the United States. Labor market policies that make it easier for workers to retrain and move to employment have had greater success in keeping long-term unemployment low.

After reading this chapter, you should know how unemployment, the unemployment rate, and the labor force participation rate are defined. You should also be able to apply these definitions to data. For example, there are 10 people; 6 have jobs, 1 is looking for work, 1 is a child, 1 is in prison, and the last is retired. What is the labor force? What is the unemployment rate? What is the labor force participation rate?[12] You should also know something about frictional, structural, and cyclical unemployment, which includes defining each and giving examples of their causes.

Finally, it's important to know something about the factors that increase or decrease the labor force participation rate. Changing demographics such as aging baby boomers, technology like the pill, cultural attitudes toward women and work, and government policy such as taxes and pension benefits can all change the labor force participation rate. At the most basic and important level, the labor force participation rate responds to the incentive to work.

Changes in the labor force participation rate can have a large impact on an economy. The labor force participation rates of older workers will become a subject of increasing concern as more workers retire and place increasing demands on pension and health systems not just in the United States but around the developed world.

CHECK YOURSELF

- The marginal tax rate (the tax on additional income) for married couples was reduced significantly during the 1980s. How would this affect the female labor force participation rate?
- Some politicians want to raise the age at which people can collect Social Security benefits, likely postponing retirement for many. How will this change affect the labor force participation rate?

CHAPTER REVIEW

interactive activity Go online to practice with more examples of these types of problems, including live links to videos, data sources, and feedback.

 Problems in green relate to MRU videos. See the MRU table at the end of the exercises.

KEY CONCEPTS

unemployed, p. 623

unemployment rate, p. 623

labor force participation rate, p. 623

discouraged workers, p. 623

underemployment rate, p. 624

frictional unemployment, p. 625

structural unemployment, p. 627

median wage, p. 630

union, p. 630

employment at–will doctrine, p. 631

active labor market policies, p. 633

cyclical unemployment, p. 634

natural unemployment rate, p. 637

baby boomers, p. 638

FACTS AND TOOLS

1. Which of the following people are counted as unemployed?

   A person out of work and actively searching for work

   A person in prison

   A person who wants to work but stopped searching six months ago

   A person who works part-time but who wants full-time work

2. According to Figure 30.1, what adults are considered not to be in the labor force?

3. If we count "discouraged workers" as unemployed when calculating the unemployment rate, does the rate more than double, less than double, or remain unchanged?

4. Decide whether each of the following are frictional, structural, or cyclical unemployment:

   a. The economy gets worse, so General Motors shuts down a factory for four months, laying off workers.

   b. General Motors lays off 5,000 workers and replaces them with robots. The workers start looking for jobs outside the auto industry.

   c. About 10 workers per month at a General Motors plant quit their jobs because they want to live in another town. They start searching for work in the new town.

5. Let's connect the minimum wage model back to the supply and demand model of the chapter on Price Ceilings and Price Floors. Is a minimum wage a price ceiling or a price floor? Does it create a surplus or a shortage in the labor market?

6. In France, why do employment protection laws tend to have negative effects on the young, already unemployed, and minority workers?

7. Let's look at how the unemployment rate changes during and after a typical recession. In Figure 30.7, does the unemployment rate tend to reach its peak *during* the recession, or does it usually reach its peak *after* the recession?

8. According to Figure 30.10, during which decade was the natural unemployment rate the highest?

9. Take a look at Figure 30.12. About how big is the difference in labor force participation rates between countries with the highest implicit tax rate on older men compared with countries with the lowest implicit tax rate? Round to the nearest 10%.

10. Based on the ideas in this chapter, name three labor market policy changes that would be likely to decrease the rate of structural unemployment. There are many more than three possible answers.

THINKING AND PROBLEM SOLVING

11. When the following events happen, does the unemployment rate rise, fall, or stay the same?

    a. Workers are laid off and start looking for work.

    b. People without jobs who are looking for work find work.

    c. People without jobs and looking for work give up and stop looking.

    d. People without jobs and not looking for work become encouraged and decide to start looking for work.

    e. People without jobs and not looking for work take a job immediately.

12. Let's see how many jobs have to be destroyed for one *net* job to be created. As noted in the text, millions of jobs are created and destroyed every month. Suppose that 5 million jobs are destroyed every month and about 5.25 million jobs are created. What is net job creation? What is total job destruction divided by net job creation? So how many total jobs are destroyed for every net job created?

13. Take a look at Table 30.2. If you have to pick a country to lose your job in, and you know you're going to be out of work for one year, which country offers the highest one-year average replacement rate? Which offers the highest two-year average replacement rate? If you're going to be out of work for three years, which country offers the highest average rate of wage replacement?

14. When a government raises the minimum wage by $2.00 per hour, where would we expect more jobs to be lost: in the fast-food industry or in city government? Why?

15. Let's see how GDP per person can be affected by changes in the fraction of citizens who work. This fraction is better known as the employment–population ratio. To keep things simple, let's assume that every employed worker produces $50,000 worth of output. If the employment–population ratio is 50%, what is GDP per *person*? If the employment–population ratio rises to 55%, what is GDP per *person*?

16. Calculate the unemployment rate and the labor force participation rate in the following cases:

   a. Employed: 100 million. Population: 200 million. In labor force: 110 million.

   b. Unemployed: 10 million. Population: 200 million. Employed: 90 million.

   c. In labor force: 30 million. Population: 80 million. Unemployed: 3 million.

17. Goldin and Katz looked for the link between birth control and women's labor force participation by examining the difference between states that acted early to make birth control legal and states that waited until later. Which states do you think had the biggest jump in women joining the labor force: states that legalized birth control earlier or those that legalized it later? (*Note:* Goldin and Katz provide evidence for the correct answer in their paper.)

18. Here's a story economists tell one another: A Nobel Prize–winning economist flew to New York City for a conference. He got into a cab, and started talking with the cab driver. The cab driver said, "Oh, you're an economist? Let me tell you, this economy is terrible. I'm an unemployed architect." The economist immediately replied, "No you're not, you're an employed cab driver." According to the way the U.S. government measures unemployment, who is right?

19. Between 1984 and 2001, the U.S. government made it much easier to get payment for disability and the number of disabled people more than doubled from 3.8 million to 7.7 million. Most of the people who try to qualify for disability payments have a tough time finding jobs, and spend a lot of time "out of work and actively searching for work." Once people start receiving disability payments, however, they rarely work again and continue to get the disability payments for decades: These citizens then count as "out of the labor force." What effect did reducing the requirements to get disability payments have on the unemployment rate?

Ask FRED

20. Let's examine the labor force participation rates of teenagers. Using the FRED economic database (https://fred.stlouisfed.org/), search for "Labor force participation rate 16 to 19 years." Graph the rate that is Not Seasonally Adjusted and click on 5Y to get the rate for the last 5 years.

   a. Why is the rate so choppy?

   b. In the peak month, approximately what percentage of teenagers are in the labor force? What about in trough months? Over the year, therefore, by approximately how much does the labor force participation rate of teenagers change?

21. It's been said that "once you reach the top of the ladder of opportunity, the first thing to do is pull up the ladder behind you." Let's consider the implications of this adage for labor market outcomes.

   a. When doctors, schoolteachers, and beauticians encourage the government to make it more difficult for people to enter their industries, does this tend to lower or raise the supply of these professionals?

   b. If government requires higher educational and training standards for doctors, schoolteachers, and beauticians, does this tend to raise or lower the demand for the services of these professionals?

   c. In equilibrium, taking into account your answers to parts a and b, what is the total effect of this lobbying on the wages of these professionals: Do wages rise, fall, or is the total effect ambiguous? Does the total number of people employed in these professions rise, fall, or is the total effect ambiguous?

Ask FRED

22. It is sometimes said that the official unemployment statistic undercounts unemployment rates because it doesn't count discouraged workers, defined as workers who have given up looking for work but who would take a job if one were offered to them. As we noted in the text, in addition to the official unemployment rate the Bureau of Labor Statistics (BLS) also tracks a rate that does include discouraged workers, defined as people who say they want a job and who have looked for a job in the last year but not in the last month. In fact, the BLS defines six different measures of unemployment called U1 through U6. The official unemployment rate is the U3 Rate. U1 and U2 are more strict definitions of unemployment. With the U1 rate a person

has to be without a job for 15 weeks or more before they count as unemployed. U4, U5, and U6 are less strict definitions. For example, U4 is the rate that includes discouraged workers.

Using the FRED economic database (https://fred.stlouisfed.org/), let's graph all six rates. Start with the civilian unemployment rate—also known as the U3 Rate. Then click Edit Graph followed by Add Line. Search for the U1Rate (all one word) then follow the same procedure to add the U2Rate, U4Rate, U5Rate and U6Rate.

a. In 2010 what was the highest unemployment rate by any of the BLS's definitions? At this same time what was the lowest unemployment rate by any of the BLS's definitions? Were any of the BLS's definitions wrong?

b. What can you say about how the rates move together? Does it matter much which rate of unemployment you use to describe the labor market?

Ask FRED

interactive activity

23. Using the FRED economic database (https://fred.stlouisfed.org/), find the "Youth Unemployment Rate in the United States" then click Edit Graph and Add Line and find the "Youth Unemployment Rate for France."

a. In 2006 what was the youth unemployment rate in the United States and what was the rate in France?

b. As discussed in the text, give two possible reasons why the youth unemployment rate in France is higher than the youth unemployment rate in the United States.

CHALLENGES

24. Long-term, structural unemployment is higher in Europe than in the United States, but some European countries have it worse than others. Take a look at Table 30.1. Spain has a lower fraction of long-term unemployment than the other European countries, but a higher rate of unemployment than the other European countries in that table. What can we conclude about the kind of unemployment taking place in Spain?

25. a. If European governments set rules for marriage the same way they set rules for employment—with tough, preset rules that make it hard to end the relationship—would you expect rates of divorce to rise, fall, or can't you tell with the information given?

b. Would the length of marriages rise, fall, or can't you tell with the information given?

c. Would married couples probably be happier (more productive) or less happy (less productive) than under more flexible marriage rules? The last of these three questions might have more than one correct answer.

26. When are workers more likely to get a job: six weeks before their unemployment benefits run out, or a week before their unemployment benefits run out? (*Note:* The correct answer to this question is solidly backed up by U.S. job data.)

27. Take a look at Figure 30.5. In that figure, we're holding "job quality" or "working conditions" constant, and looking at how changes in wages impact the quantity of labor supplied and demanded. In many union negotiations, the union and its workers don't push for higher wages. Instead, they push for better working conditions: safer machines, better insurance coverage, or cleaner restrooms.

So now let's model this: Let's hold *wages* constant, and look at how changes in *working conditions* impact the quantity supplied and quantity demanded of labor. Thus, set it up just like a real-life labor negotiation. Draw a conventional supply and demand chart, but on the vertical axis, just put "job quality—high or low" instead of "wage." Then, show what happens to the amount of unemployment created when a union successfully negotiates a higher-than-equilibrium job quality.

28. Even though most Americans who become unemployed are only unemployed for a short period of time, when you look at who is unemployed *at a given moment in time*, you'll find that most of the unemployed have been without a job for quite a while. Let's imagine a simple economy to see how to resolve this paradox. In this economy, there are two types of workers: Type A workers take one month to find a new job and Type B workers take 10 months to find a new job.

Each month, let's assume that *one* Type A and *one* Type B worker lose their jobs. Notice that *we're assuming that half of all people who lose their jobs today will find new jobs in a month.* But, as we shall see, this implies that most of the unemployed will have been unemployed for a long period.

a. In the long run (or "steady state"), there will be 11 workers out of work in this simple society at any given point in time. Show that this is true by keeping track of the "pool" of unemployed workers in this society for two years. You can start off assuming that the pool is empty at time zero—that no one is unemployed—but you'd get the same steady-state answer regardless of your starting point. You can prove that 11 will be out of work just with pencil and paper or much more quickly with Excel. To help you out, here's an example of what the pool of unemployed will look like in month 7. Keep going with this calculation until you see that the number of workers in the pool no longer changes month to month—this is called the "steady state."

The Unemployment Pool: Month 7	
Shallow End (Type A's)	Deep End (Type B's)
1 Type A worker enters pool (loses job).	1 Type B worker enters pool.
1 Type A worker exits pool (find works).	6 Type B workers are already in the pool.
	0 Type B workers exit the pool.
Total: 1 Type A worker is in the pool (unemployed).	Total: 7 Type B workers are in the pool (unemployed).

b. In the steady state—that is, when your pool starts having the same numbers every month—how many of the 11 workers in the unemployment pool have been unemployed for "one month"? How many of the 11 workers in the unemployment pool have been unemployed for more than one month?

c. If you see an economy where most *currently* unemployed workers have been out of work for a long time, does this mean that most people who have been unemployed in the last few years were unemployed for a long time? How does this example illustrate your answer?

Ask FRED

interactive activity

29. Overall, labor force participation rates have been declining in the U.S. economy but not for every demographic. Let's examine the labor force participation rates of teenagers and older people. Using the FRED economic database (https://fred.stlouisfed.org/), search for "Labor force participation rate 16 to 19 years." Graph the seasonally adjusted rate since we are interested in long-term trends. Then click Edit Graph and Add Line and then search for and add "Labor Force Participation Rate: 55 years and over."

a. Since the 1990s whose labor force participation rate has increased and whose has decreased?

b. For the group whose labor force participation rate has increased, make two hypotheses or stories about why the trend is up. Try to make one hypothesis a good or positive story and one a bad or negative story. Do the same for the group whose labor force participation rate has declined.

Ask FRED

interactive activity

30. Using the FRED economic database (https://fred.stlouisfed.org/), let's compare employment in manufacturing and construction. First, find manufacturing employment and then click Edit Graph and Add Line to add in construction employment. Graph the data from 1990 to the present.

a. What is the long-term trend in manufacturing employment? What would you guess are the reasons for the trend?

b. What is the long-term trend in construction employment?

c. Both employment series fell during the 2008–2009 recession. For which series would you expect employment to recover?

WORK IT OUT

interactive activity

For interactive, step-by-step help in solving this problem, go online.

Who is more likely to ask politicians for stronger labor unions and laws, making it harder to fire workers: insiders who have jobs or outsiders who don't have jobs?

MARGINAL REVOLUTION UNIVERSITY VIDEOS

The Economics of Choosing the Right Career
mruniversity.com/econ-career-choice

Problems: **21**

How is the Unemployment Rate Defined?
mruniversity.com/unemployment

Problems: **1–3, 8**

Is Unemployment Undercounted?
mruniversity.com/unemploy-measure

Problems: **18, 22**

Frictional Unemployment
mruniversity.com/frictional

Problems: **4, 12**

Riots and Structural Unemployment
mruniversity.com/structural

Problems: **4, 6, 10, 13, 15, 19, 24, 27**

Cyclical Unemployment
mruniversity.com/cyclical

Problems: **4, 7, 11, 14**

Labor Force Participation
mruniversity.com/lfpr

Problems: **16, 28**

Taxing Work
mruniversity.com/taxing-work

Problems: **9, 19, 25, 26**

Women Working: What's the Pill Got to Do with It?
mruniversity.com/employ-women

Problems: **17**

31

Inflation and the Quantity Theory of Money

Robert Mugabe had a problem. The dictatorial president of Zimbabwe needed money. Unfortunately, Mugabe's policy of seizing commercial farms had driven productive farmers and entrepreneurs out of the country, frightened off foreign investors, and pushed Zimbabwe, once called the breadbasket of Africa, to the verge of mass starvation. Zimbabwe had almost nothing left to tax, but Mugabe still needed money to bribe his enemies and reward his supporters, especially the still loyal Zimbabwean army. Mugabe thus turned to the last refuge of needy governments, the printing press.

Governments and counterfeiters alone can pay their bills by printing money. Beginning in 2001, when inflation was already running at 50% per year, Mugabe pushed the printing presses to breakneck speed. Whenever a bill came due or soldiers needed paying, it was no problem—just print more money. In May 2006, for example, the government announced plans to print 60 *trillion* Zimbabwean dollars to finance a 300% increase in pay for soldiers. Ironically, the payment was delayed because Zimbabwe didn't have enough U.S. dollars to buy ink and paper.[1]

When the ink and paper arrived, the government flooded the economy with more money. The economy, however, could not produce more goods. When more money chases the same goods, the consequences are easy to see: inflation. In Zimbabwe, the inflation rate quickly increased from 50% a year to 50% a month to more than 50% a day! By the end of 2008, prices in Zimbabwe were doubling overnight and the monthly inflation rate hit 79,600,000,000% per month. Finally, in 2009, the government legalized transactions in foreign currencies and the Zimbabwe dollar effectively ceased to exist.

In this chapter, we explain how inflation is defined and measured, the causes of inflation, the costs and benefits of inflation, and why governments sometimes resort to inflation.

Who Wants to Be a Trillionaire?

Defining and Measuring Inflation

Inflation is an increase in the average level of prices. We measure the average level of prices with an index, the average price from a large and representative basket of goods and services. Thus, inflation is measured by

Inflation is an increase in the average level of prices.

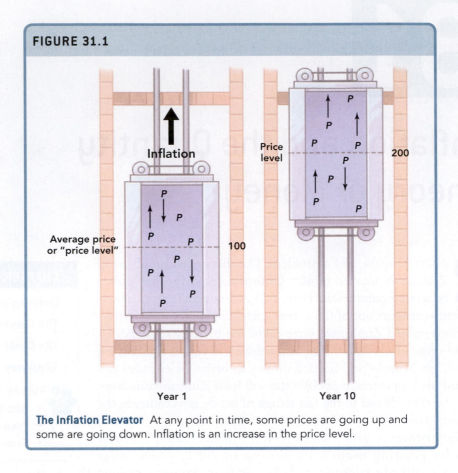

FIGURE 31.1

Inflation

Price level — — — — — — 200

Average price or "price level" — — — — — 100

Year 1   Year 10

The Inflation Elevator At any point in time, some prices are going up and some are going down. Inflation is an increase in the price level.

The **inflation rate** is the percentage change in the average level of prices (as measured by a price index) over a period of time.

$$\text{Inflation rate} = \frac{P_2 - P_1}{P_1} \times 100$$

changes in a price index and the **inflation rate** is the percentage change in a price index from one year to the next:

$$\text{Inflation rate} = \frac{P_2 - P_1}{P_1} \times 100$$

where P_2 is the index value in year 2 and P_1 is the index value in year 1. A 10% inflation rate means, quite simply, that goods and services are priced (on average) 10% higher than they were a year ago.

Shifts in supply and demand push prices up and down all the time, but inflation is an increase in the average level of prices. We can think of inflation as an elevator lifting all prices over time. In Figure 31.1 some prices in year 1 are going up and some are going down, but overall the average level of prices is 100. Inflation tends to lift all prices, so by year 10 the average level of prices is 200.

Price Indexes

Economists measure inflation using several different price indexes that are based on different bundles of goods:

1. *Consumer price index (CPI):* Measures the average price for a basket of goods and services bought by a typical American consumer. The index covers some 80,000 goods and services and is weighted so that an increase in the price of a major item such as housing counts for more than an increase in the price of a minor item like kitty litter.

2. *GDP deflator:* The ratio of nominal to real GDP multiplied by 100 (discussed in the chapter on GDP and the Measurement of Progress). The GDP deflator covers all finished goods and services.

3. *Producer price indexes (PPI):* Measure the average price received by producers. Unlike the CPI and GDP deflator, producer price indexes measure prices of intermediate as well as finished goods and services. PPI exist for different industries and are often used to calculate changes in the cost of inputs.

For most Americans, the CPI is the measure of inflation that corresponds most directly to their daily economic activity; for businesses and governments, the other indexes take on greater relevance. We focus on the CPI unless otherwise indicated.

One point to remember about the CPI is that the basket of goods and services bought by the average consumer is changing all the time. The CPI, for example, contains a category for audio media like music. In 1975 music typically came on a vinyl record, but if the Bureau of Labor Statistics (BLS) measured the price of music by the price of vinyl records today, it would report that there has been a tremendous increase in the price because vinyl records are now expensive collector's items. To avoid this problem, the BLS periodically updates the basket to reflect the introduction of new goods such as compact discs and MP3s. Changes in quality present a similar challenge. In 2007, when it was introduced, an iPhone cost $499, which is only slightly less expensive than today, but the first iPhone had a 320-by-480-pixel resolution screen, a 2-megapixel camera, and 4 gigabytes of storage. At the time of publication, the latest iPhone has a 1334-by-750-pixel resolution screen, a 12-megapixel camera that also takes HD movies, and up to 256 gigabytes of storage, among many other improvements. Thus, the true price of an iPhone—the price accounting for quality—is much lower today than in 2007. The BLS, which computes the CPI, tries to take both of these factors—new goods and better-quality goods—into account when computing the CPI, but it's challenging. As a result of these challenges, some economists suggest that the CPI may actually overstate inflation by a little bit every year (0.9% is one estimate). That may not seem like much, but it can matter when making comparisons over several decades or more.

Inflation in the United States and Around the World

Figure 31.2, on the next page, shows the annual inflation rate in the United States since 1950. The average inflation rate over this period was 3.6%, but in many periods, especially in the 1970s, inflation was significantly higher. Over the past 10 years (2006–2016), inflation in the United States has averaged about 2.1%.

Figure 31.3, on the next page, illustrates the cumulative effect of inflation on a large basket of goods. A basket that cost about $10 in 1913 would have cost $36.70 in 1969, $100 in 1982, $207 in 2007, and $241 in 2016. The height of the line represents the level of the CPI during each year.

The CPI is often used to calculate "real prices." A **real price** is a price that has been corrected for inflation. Real prices are used to compare the prices of goods over time. Suppose, for example, that you are told that the average price of a gallon of gasoline was $1.25 in 1982 but double that, $2.50, in 2006. These prices are correct, but should we conclude that gasoline was twice as

A **real price** is a price that has been corrected for inflation. Real prices are used to compare the prices of goods over time.

FIGURE 31.2

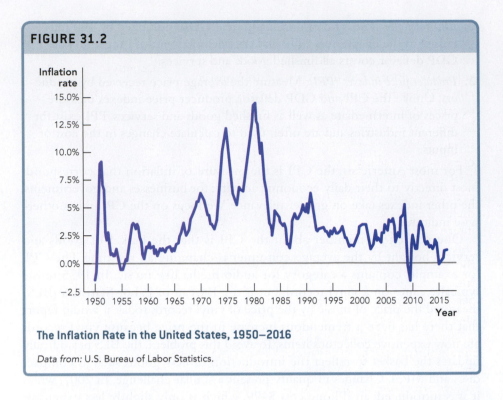

The Inflation Rate in the United States, 1950–2016

Data from: U.S. Bureau of Labor Statistics.

expensive in 2006 than in 1982? No. The CPI was 100 in 1982 and 202 in 2006 so the price of most products doubled during this time period; wages rose, as well. Thus, the price of gasoline did not increase over this time period relative to other goods, so the real price of gasoline was about the same in 1982 as 2006. Challenge Problem 22 at the end of this chapter shows how you can easily convert nominal to real prices using the FRED online economic database.

FIGURE 31.3

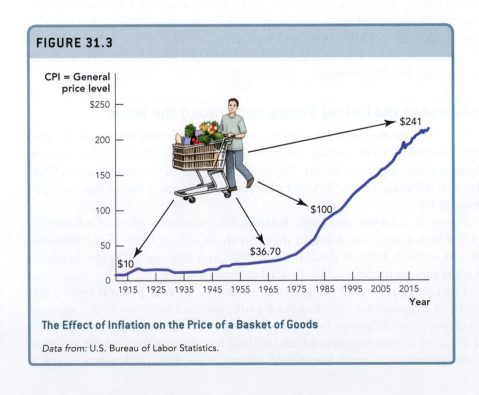

The Effect of Inflation on the Price of a Basket of Goods

Data from: U.S. Bureau of Labor Statistics.

Most prices go up over time, but there are exceptions. Pocket calculators now cost a few dollars; in 1972, they cost $395. In 1927, two-way radio phone service, America to London, cost $75 for five minutes. Today, a five-minute phone call to England costs mere pennies with Skype. In some cases, technological progress is so rapid that for particular goods and services, it overcomes the general tendency of prices to rise.

Recent U.S. inflation experience is moderate compared with international inflation rates and the historical record. Table 31.1 displays selected international inflation rates in 2016. South Sudan and Venezuela had the highest inflation rates in the world—each approached 500% that year. Inflation in the United States was just over 1% per year and some countries such as Italy, Greece, and Japan had slight deflations.

Table 31.2, on the next page, presents some figures for major "hyperinflations." The numbers in Table 31.2 are so high, they are hard to believe, but they are true. In Germany, for example, what cost 1 Reichsmark in 1919 cost half a trillion Reichsmarks in 1923.

Hungary's postwar hyperinflation is the largest on record. The numbers are so high, they are difficult to describe. What cost 1 Hungarian pengo in 1945 cost 1.3 septillion pengos at the end of 1946. Seeing numbers like this, the physicist Richard Feynman said that really big numbers should not be called "astronomical" but "economical."

TABLE 31.1 INFLATION RATE IN SELECTED COUNTRIES, 2016

Country	Inflation Rate (%)
South Sudan	476.02
Venezuela	475.806
Suriname	67.109
Angola	33.683
Malawi	19.782
Brazil	9.019
Mexico	2.824
China	2.075
United States	1.188
United Kingdom	0.743
Germany	0.399
France	0.346
Netherlands	0.103
Italy	−0.05
Greece	−0.1
Japan	−0.162

Data from: International Monetary Fund, World Economic Outlook Database, October 2016

The Quantity Theory of Money

We already have a good idea about the causes of inflation from the opening discussion of Zimbabwe. We can now examine the inflationary mechanism in more detail by explaining the quantity theory of money. The quantity theory of money does two things: First, it sets out the general relationship between money, velocity (to be defined soon), real output, and prices; second, it helps to explain the critical role of the money supply in determining the inflation rate.

Imagine that every month you are paid $4,000 and you spend $4,000. In a year, you spend $4,000 12 times, so your total yearly spending is $4,000 × 12 = $48,000. Another way of figuring out your total yearly spending is to add up all the goods that you buy and multiply by their prices. We can write this identity (an equation that must hold true by definition) as

$$M \times v = P \times Y_R$$

where M is the money you are paid, v is the number of times in a year that you spend M (we call v the "**velocity of money**," hence the v), P is prices, and Y_R

v, velocity of money, is the average number of times a dollar is spent on finished goods and services in a year.

TABLE 31.2	SELECTED EPISODES OF HYPERINFLATION		
Nation	Period	Cumulative Inflation Rate (%)	Maximum Inflation Rate on a Monthly Basis (%)
America	1777–1780	2,702	1,342
Bolivia	1984–1985	97,282	196
Peru	1987–1992	17,991,287	1,031
Yugoslavia	1993–1994	1.6×10^9	5×10^{15}
Nicaragua	1986–1991	1.2×10^{10}	261
Greece	1941–1944	1.60×10^{11}	8.5×10^9
Germany	1919–1923	0.5×10^{12}	3,250,000
Zimbabwe	2001–2008	8.53×10^{23}	7.96×10^{10}
Hungary	1945–1946	1.3×10^{24}	4.19×10^{16}

Data from: Fisher, Stanley, Ratna Sahay, and Carlos A. Vegh. 2002. Modern hyper- and high inflations. *Journal of Economic Literature, American Economic Association* 40(3): 837–880.
Anderson, Robert B., William A. Bomberger, and Gail E. Makinen. 1988. The demand for money, the "reform effect," and the money supply process in hyperinflation: The evidence from Greece and Hungary reexamined." *Journal of Money, Credit and Banking* 20: 653–672, http://en.wikipedia.org/wiki/Hyperinflation, http://www.sjsu.edu/faculty/watkins/hyper.htm, and http://www.cato.org/zimbabwe.

is a measure of the real goods and services that you buy. A similar identity holds for the nation as a whole, where we interpret M as the supply of money, v as the average number of times in a year that a dollar is spent on finished goods and services, P as the price level, and Y_R as real GDP.

Thus, for the nation as a whole, we can write

$$Mv = PY_R$$

M = Money supply	P = Price level
v = Velocity of money	Y_R = Real GDP

Since Mv is the total amount spent on finished goods and services and PY_R is the price level times real GDP, both sides of this equation are also equal to nominal GDP.

With some additional assumptions, the simple identity, $Mv = PY_R$, helps us think through how money affects output and prices. We proceed with two further assumptions, namely that both real GDP (Y_R) and velocity (v) are stable compared to the money supply (M).

Let's discuss why these assumptions are usually reasonable. Over the period we are interested in, real GDP is fixed by the real factors of production—capital, labor, and technology—exactly as discussed in the earlier chapter on the Wealth of Nations and Economic Growth, and the chapter on Growth, Capital Accumulation, and the Economics of Ideas: Catching Up vs. the Cutting

A 500,000,000,000 dinar bank note from a world hyperinflation leader, Yugoslavia c. 1993. At the time, 500 billion dinars could buy about $5 worth of goods.

Edge. We know that inflation can be 10%, 500%, 5,000% a year, or much higher. Real GDP, in contrast, rarely grows by more than, say, 10% a year, so changes in real GDP don't seem like a plausible candidate for explaining large changes in prices.

Let's also assume that v, the velocity of money, is stable. The velocity of money is the average number of times a dollar is used to purchase finished goods and services within a year. In the preceding example, v was 12 because you were paid monthly and you spent your entire monthly income of $4,000 12 times in a year. In the U.S. economy today, v is about 7 and it is determined by the same kind of factors that might determine your personal v, factors such as whether workers are paid monthly or biweekly, how long it takes to clear a check, and how easy it is to find and use an ATM. These factors change over time but only slowly. Other factors that we will discuss at greater length in the chapters on business fluctuations can change v more quickly, but not by enough to account for large and sustained increases in prices. For these reasons, changes in v also do not seem like a plausible candidate for explaining large and sustained increases in prices.

The Cause of Inflation

If Y_R is fixed by the real factors of production and v is stable, then it follows immediately that the only thing that can cause increases in P are increases in M, the supply of money. In other words, inflation is caused by an increase in the supply of money.

How well does this theory hold up? The left panel of Figure 31.4 plots the price level (P) and the supply of money (M) in Peru during its hyperinflation. A product with a price of 1 Peruvian intis in 1980 would have cost more than *10 million* intis by 1995. (To reduce the number of zeroes, the Peruvian government changed the name of the currency twice during this period, first from

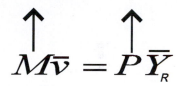

$$M\bar{v} = P\bar{Y}_R$$

The Quantity Theory of Money in a Nutshell When v and Y are fixed (indicated by a top bar), increases in M must cause increases in P.

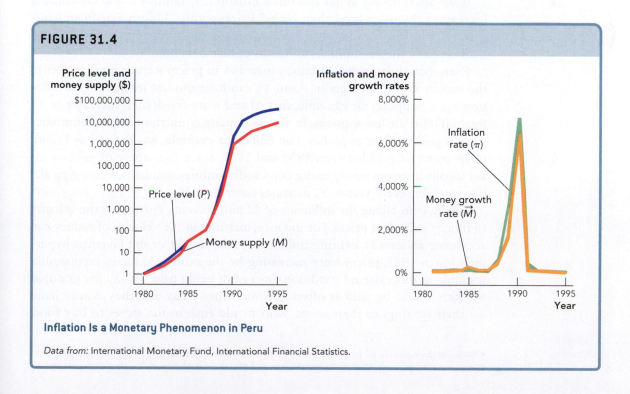

FIGURE 31.4

Inflation Is a Monetary Phenomenon in Peru

Data from: International Monetary Fund, International Financial Statistics.

intis to soles de oro and then to the nuevo sol.) As you can see, the supply of money also increased about 10 million times in lockstep with the increase in prices.

The quantity theory of money can also be written in terms of growth rates. We denote the growth rate of any variable with a little arrow over the variable, so $\vec{M}$ is the growth rate of the money supply, $\vec{P}$ is the growth rate of prices, and so forth. If $Mv = PY_R$, then it is also true that:*

$$\vec{M} + \vec{v} \equiv \vec{P} + \vec{Y}_R$$

We have a special word for the growth rate of prices $\vec{P}$: inflation! (Inflation is also often written with a special symbol, π.) If we assume that velocity isn't changing much, as we just did, then the growth rate of velocity $\vec{v}$ will be zero or very low. We also know that $\vec{Y}_R$, the growth rate of real GDP, is relatively low, say, between 2% and at most 10%. Thus, if we ignore these two factors, we see immediately that $\vec{M} \approx$ *Inflation Rate* (π), where $\approx$ means approximately equal. In other words, the quantity theory of money says that the growth rate of the money supply will be approximately equal to the inflation rate.

The right panel of Figure 31.4 shows that during Peru's hyperinflation, this was true: As the supply of money grew faster, so did the inflation rate, peaking in 1990 at a rate of 7,500% per year.

What about other times and places? Figure 31.5 plots inflation rates on the vertical axis versus money growth rates on the horizontal axis for 110 nations between 1960 and 1990. Nations with rapidly growing money supplies had high inflation rates. Nations with slowly growing money supplies had low inflation rates. In fact, as the red line indicates, on average, the relationship is almost perfectly linear, with a 10 percentage point increase in the money growth rate leading to a 10 percentage point increase in the inflation rate.

If we are thinking about sustained inflation, a significant and continuing increase in the price level, then Nobel Prize–winner Milton Friedman has it exactly right: "Inflation is always and everywhere a monetary phenomenon." This is one of the most important truths of macroeconomics.

Even though large and sustained increases in prices stem from increases in the money supply, changes in v and Y_R can have modest influences on inflation rates. Suppose, for example, that M and v are fixed; then increases in Y_R (real GDP) must lower prices. In the past, many countries used a commodity such as gold or silver as money. The dollar, for example, was defined as 1/20th of an ounce of gold between 1834 and 1933. Since the supply of gold or silver usually increases slowly under commodity-money standards, prices typically decrease a bit every year as Y_R increases faster than M.

Finally, even taking the influence of M into account, changes in the velocity of money will affect prices. For instance, increases in the velocity of money can accelerate an already existing inflation. At the height of the German hyperinflation in 1923, prices were increasing by the minute. Velocity increased in response to this extreme condition. Instead of being paid weekly, for example, workers would be paid as often as three times a day and they would hand off their earnings to their wives, who would rush to the stores to buy food,

---

* To derive this equation, we have used a convenient mathematical fact that if $Y = A \times B$, then the growth rate of Y is approximately equal to the growth rate of A plus the growth rate of B.

FIGURE 31.5

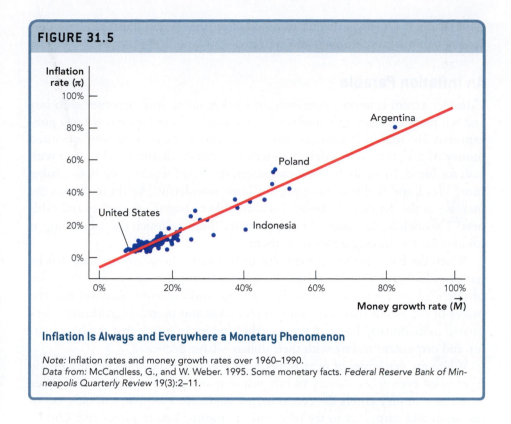

Inflation Is Always and Everywhere a Monetary Phenomenon

Note: Inflation rates and money growth rates over 1960–1990.
Data from: McCandless, G., and W. Weber. 1995. Some monetary facts. *Federal Reserve Bank of Minneapolis Quarterly Review* 19(3):2–11.

soap, clothes, *anything* before prices rose even further. Inflation itself caused an increase in velocity, which further fueled inflation.

The velocity of money can also decrease. In an economic panic, individuals may simply hold their money and be afraid to spend it. People might believe that keeping money under the mattress could be less risky than putting money in a bank. During the Great Depression, many people in the United States behaved in precisely this way and the decrease in monetary velocity helped to fuel a **deflation**, a decrease in prices, that worsened the depression. More moderate decreases in velocity or in the growth rate of the money supply would reduce the inflation rate, a **disinflation** rather than a deflation. (We discuss deflation and the Great Depression at greater length in the chapter on Business Fluctuation: Aggregate Demand and Supply and the chapter on Monetary Policy.)

The quantity theory also assumes that changes in M cannot change Y_R. In the long run, this makes sense because we know that real GDP is determined by capital, labor, and technology and changes in M won't change any of these factors. Thus, in the long run money is neutral. Imagine, for example, that we doubled the money supply. In the long run, the quantity theory says that prices will double and nothing else will change. We will return to the long-run neutrality of money again and again so let's make a special note of this principle:

In the long run, money is neutral.

Although money is neutral in the long run, it's possible that changes in M can change Y_R in the short run. In particular, under some circumstances increases in M can *temporarily increase* real GDP and decreases in M can *temporarily decrease* real GDP. To see how changes in M could cause changes in real

Deflation is a decrease in the average level of prices (a negative inflation rate).

A **disinflation** is a reduction in the inflation rate.

GDP in the short run, let's look at an inflation parable that illustrates how new money works its way through an economy.

An Inflation Parable

Consider a mini economy consisting of a baker, tailor, and carpenter who buy and sell products among themselves. Now consider what happens when a government like that in Zimbabwe starts paying its soldiers with newly printed money. At first, the baker is delighted when soldiers walk through his door with cash for bread. To satisfy his new customers, the baker works extra hours, bakes more bread, and is able to raise prices. "How wonderful," he thinks, "with the increase in the demand for bread, I will be able to buy more clothes and cabinets." Meanwhile, the tailor and carpenter are thinking much the same thing as soldiers are also buying goods from them.

When the baker arrives at the tailor to buy shirts, however, he finds that he has been fooled. The soldiers have bought shirts for themselves and the price of shirts has now gone up. Similarly, the tailor and carpenter discover that the prices of the goods that they want to buy have also increased. Although they earned more dollars, their real wages—the amount of goods that the baker, tailor, and carpenter can buy with their dollars—have decreased.

When the government next wants to buy goods, it faces higher prices and must print even more money to buy just as many goods as before. Moreover, as the new money enters the economy, the baker, for example, will now *race* to the tailor and carpenter to try to spend the money before prices rise. Unfortunately, the tailor and carpenter are likely to have had the same idea and the result is that prices increase even more quickly than the time before.

Eventually, as the government continues to print money and buy goods, the baker, tailor, and carpenter will come to expect and prepare for inflation. Instead of working extra hours, the baker, tailor, and carpenter will realize that by the time they get to spend their new money, the prices of the goods that they want to buy will have risen in price. Knowing this, the baker, tailor, and carpenter will no longer be so happy to see the soldiers enter their shop waving fistfuls of dollars and they will no longer work extra hours baking more bread, sewing more clothes, or building more cabinets.

The inflation parable tells us that an unexpected increase in the money supply can boost the economy in the short run, but as firms and workers come to expect and adjust to the new influx of money, output will not grow any faster than normal. The inflation parable serves us well for now, but the short-run relationship between unexpected inflation and output is a key idea in economics and one we will return to in much greater detail in the next chapter.

The Costs of Inflation

To the person in the street, the costs of inflation are obvious—prices are going up; what could be worse? But most people rarely consider that inflation also raises their wages. (No doubt, we all have a tendency to think that bad events, like price increases, are the fault of others but good events, like higher wages, are due to our own virtues.) If all prices, including wages, are going up, then what is the problem with inflation?

If everyone knew whether the rate of inflation was 2% or 8%, then everyone could prepare and the exact inflation rate would not matter very much. But instead of everyone knowing the rate, it's more often the case that no

CHECK YOURSELF
- In the long run, what causes inflation?
- What is the equation that represents the quantity theory of money?

one knows the rate of inflation! In the United States, inflation was 1.3% in 1964; the rate more than quadrupled to 5.7% in 1970 and increased to 11% per year by 1974. Inflation caught most people by surprise. And when inflation decreased from 13% in 1980 to 3% in 1983, most people were surprised again. Inflation also tends to be more variable and thus more difficult to predict when the inflation rate is high. Take a look again at the right panel of Figure 31.4. Inflation in Peru went from 77% in 1986 to 7,500% in 1990 and then back down to 73% in 1992. Who can predict such changes?

High rates of inflation do create some problems, as we will explain, but volatile or uncertain inflation is even more costly. We now cover some specific problems or costs introduced by high and volatile inflation. Keep in mind the picture of inflation as a kind of insidious, slow-moving cancer. Inflation destroys the ability of market prices to send signals about the value of resources and opportunities.

Price Confusion and Money Illusion

Prices are signals and inflation makes price signals more difficult to interpret. In our inflation parable, for example, the baker initially thought that the increase in the demand for bread signaled that the real demand for bread had increased. In fact, since all prices were rising, the real demand for bread had not increased. Confusing a nominal signal with a real signal has real consequences. The baker thought that prices were telling him to work harder and produce more bread. When he later discovered that all prices had risen, he knew that he had made a costly mistake.

Now imagine that one day the *real demand* for bread does increase, only now the baker is so used to inflation, he ignores the signal. Instead of working harder, the baker continues to bake the same number of loaves of bread as before. Opportunities are missed because signals have become obscured.

In a modern economy, it might seem easy enough to figure out whether an increase in demand for bread reflects a real increase in demand or just an increase in the money supply. Just pick up the *Wall Street Journal* and read the articles about monetary policy. But it's not actually so easy. Sometimes the money supply is increasing and the real demand for bread is going up, both at the same time. It is difficult to sort out the relative strength of both influences. Or perhaps the baker never understood the principles of economics, or, unlike you (!), never read a really good economics textbook.

Human beings are not always perfectly rational, which makes reading signals even more difficult. Even when we should know better, we sometimes treat the higher wages and prices that result from inflation as higher wages and prices in real terms. If the price of a movie goes up 10% and other prices including wages go up by about the same amount, we ought to conclude that the real price of a movie has stayed more or less the same. But many people conclude, mistakenly, that movies have become "more expensive." They treat this as a change in relative price: They may see fewer movies or make other decisions based on this new price. Economists call this the "money illusion." **Money illusion** is when people mistake changes in nominal prices for changes in real prices.

In short, inflation usually confuses consumers, workers, firms, and entrepreneurs. When price signals are difficult to interpret, the market economy doesn't work as well—resources are wasted in activities that appear profitable but in fact are not, entrepreneurs are less quick to respond to real opportunities, and resources flow more slowly to profitable uses.

Price Confusion and Money Illusion

Money illusion is when people mistake changes in nominal prices for changes in real prices.

Inflation Redistributes Wealth

In our inflation parable, the government bought bread, shirts, and woodwork simply by printing paper. Where did these real goods come from? They came from the baker, tailor, and carpenter. Inflation transfers real resources from citizens to the government. Thus, *inflation is a type of tax.*

The inflation tax does not require tax collectors, a tax bureaucracy, or extensive record keeping. You can hide from most taxes by keeping your transactions secret and saving your money under the bed. But you can't hide from the inflation tax! Money under the bed is precisely what inflation does tax because as prices rise, the value of the dollars under the bed falls. It's not surprising, therefore, that money-strapped governments in danger of collapsing typically use massive inflation. Almost all the hyperinflations in Table 31.2 involved governments with massive debts or spending that could not be paid for with regular taxes.

Inflation does more than transfer wealth to the government—it also redistributes wealth among the public, especially between lenders and borrowers. To see why, suppose that a lender lends money at an interest rate of 10% but that over the course of the year the inflation rate is also 10%. On paper, the lender has earned a return of 10%—we call this the "nominal return." But what is the lender's real rate of return? The lender is paid 10% interest, but she is paid in dollars that have become 10% less valuable. Thus, the lender's real rate of return is 0%.

Thus, inflation can reduce the real return that lenders receive on their loans, in effect transferring wealth from lenders to borrowers. In the 1970s, for example, high inflation rates meant the real value of 30-year fixed-rate mortgages that were taken out in the 1960s declined tremendously, redistributing billions of dollars from lenders to borrowers. Borrowers benefited but many lenders went bankrupt.

In the late 1970s, however, many people began to expect that 10% inflation was here to stay, so home buyers were willing to take out long-term mortgages with interest rates of 15% or higher. When inflation fell unexpectedly in the early 1980s, these borrowers found that their real payments were much higher than they had anticipated. Wealth was redistributed from borrowers to lenders.

We can explain the relationship between inflation and wealth redistribution more precisely by writing the relationship between the lender's real rate of return, the nominal rate of return, and the inflation rate as follows:

$$\textbf{Real interest rate = Nominal rate − Inflation rate} \tag{1}$$

or, in symbols,

$$r_{\text{Real}} = i - \pi$$

Real rate of return is the nominal rate of return minus the inflation rate.

Nominal rate of return is the rate of return that does not account for inflation.

In words, the **real rate of return** is equal to the **nominal rate of return** minus the inflation rate.

Lenders, of course, will not lend money at a loss. Thus, when lenders expect inflation to increase, they will demand a higher nominal interest rate. For example, if lenders expect that the inflation rate will be 7% and the equilibrium real rate (determined in the market for loanable funds—see the chapter on Saving, Investment, and the Financial System) is 5%, then lenders will ask for a nominal interest rate of approximately 12% (7% to break even given the expected rate of inflation plus the 5% equilibrium rate). If lenders expect that the inflation rate will be 10%, lenders will demand a nominal interest rate of approximately 15% (10% to break even given the expected rate of inflation plus the 5% equilibrium rate).

The tendency of nominal interest rates to increase with expected inflation rates is called the **Fisher effect** (after economist Irving Fisher, 1867–1947). As an approximation,* we can write the Fisher effect as

$$i = E\pi + r_{Equilibrium} \tag{2}$$

$$i = \text{Nominal interest rate, } E\pi = \text{Expected inflation rate}$$
$$r_{Equilibrium} = \text{Equilibrium real rate of return}$$

The Fisher effect says that the nominal interest rate is equal to the expected inflation rate plus the equilibrium real interest rate. Most important, the Fisher effect says that the nominal rate will rise with expected inflation. We can see the Fisher effect in Figure 31.6, which graphs the inflation rate and short-term nominal interest rate in the United States from 1955 to 2010.

Thus, repeating equations 1 and 2, we have

$$r_{Real} = i - \pi \tag{1}$$

and

$$i = E\pi + r_{Equilibrium} \tag{2}$$

> The **Fisher effect** is the tendency of nominal interest rates to rise with expected inflation rates.

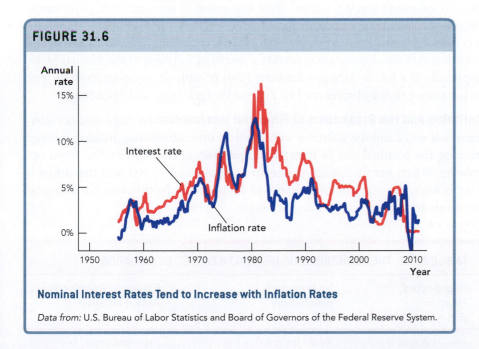

FIGURE 31.6

Nominal Interest Rates Tend to Increase with Inflation Rates

Data from: U.S. Bureau of Labor Statistics and Board of Governors of the Federal Reserve System.

---

* The Fisher effect equation in the text is only approximate. The exact Fisher effect equation is $(1 + i) = (1 + r)(1 + \pi)$. If a lender wants a real rate of return of 5% ($r = 0.05$) and the inflation rate is 10% ($\pi = 0.1$), then the lender must charge a nominal rate of 1.155 (1.10×1.05), or 15.5%. When inflation rates are low, the approximation works well but not during hyperinflations.

If we substitute *i* from equation 2 into equation 1, we see that the real rate of return will be determined in large part by the difference between expected inflation and actual inflation:

$$r_{Real} = (E\pi - \pi) + r_{Equilibrium}$$

If $(E\pi < \pi)$, that is, if expected inflation is less than actual inflation, then the real rate of return will be less than the equilibrium rate and will quite possibly be negative. Wealth will be redistributed from lenders to borrowers.

If $(E\pi > \pi)$, that is, if expected inflation is greater than actual inflation or equivalently if there is an unexpected "disinflation," then the real rate of return will be higher than the equilibrium rate. Wealth will be redistributed from borrowers to lenders.

Only when $E\pi = \pi$, that is, when expected inflation is equal to actual inflation, will the real return be equal to the equilibrium return. In this case, there will be no unexpected redistribution of wealth between borrowers and lenders. We summarize the effects of inflation on the redistribution of wealth in Table 31.3.

Governments are often borrowers so governments benefit from unexpected inflation. Thus, a government with massive debts has a special incentive to increase the money supply—called **monetizing the debt**. Why doesn't the government always inflate its debt away? One reason is the Fisher effect. If lenders expect that the government will inflate its debt away, they will only lend at high nominal rates of interest. To avoid this outcome, the government may try to make a credible promise to keep the inflation rate low.

Monetizing the debt is when the government pays off its debts by printing money.

Another reason the government doesn't always inflate its debt away is that people who buy government bonds are typically voters who would be upset if their real returns were shrunk to zero or less. But what do you think would happen to inflation rates if a nation's debt was owed to foreigners? A government would probably have a stronger incentive to inflate away debt owed to foreigners than debt owed to voters. The U.S. debt is increasingly owed to foreigners, which makes some economists predict a return of inflation in the United States, especially if a future U.S. government finds it difficult to cover its debt with other taxes (see the chapter on The Federal Budget: Taxes and Spending).

Inflation and the Breakdown of Financial Intermediation Sometimes a government will combine inflation with controls on interest rates, making it illegal to raise the nominal rate of interest and preventing the Fisher effect from operating. When nominal interest rates are not allowed to rise and the inflation rate is high, the real rate of return will be negative. In this way, bank savings accounts are turned into wasting accounts.

TABLE 31.3 THE REDISTRIBUTION OF WEALTH CAUSED BY INFLATION

Unexpected inflation $(E\pi < \pi)$	Unexpected disinflation $(E\pi > \pi)$	Expected inflation = Actual inflation $(E\pi = \pi)$
Real rate less than equilibrium rate	Real rate greater than equilibrium rate	Real rate equal to equilibrium rate
Harms lenders Benefits borrowers	Benefits lenders Harms borrowers	No redistribution of wealth

TABLE 31.4 NEGATIVE INTEREST RATES AND ECONOMIC GROWTH

Country	Years	Real Interest Rate (%)	Per Capita Growth (%)
Argentina	1975–1976	−69	−2.2
Bolivia	1982–1984	−75	−5.2
Chile	1972–1974	−61	−3.6
Ghana	1976–1983	−35	−2.9
Peru	1976–1984	−19	−1.4
Poland	1981–1982	−33	−8.6
Sierra Leone	1984–1987	−44	−1.9
Turkey	1979–1980	−35	−3.1
Venezuela	1987–1989	−24	−2.7
Zaire	1976–1979	−34	−6.0
Zambia	1985–1988	−24	−1.9

Data from: Easterly, W. 2002. *The Elusive Quest for Growth. Economists' Adventures and Misadventures in the Tropics.* Cambridge, MA: MIT Press.

When real interest rates turn negative, people take their money out of the banking system, using the cash to invest abroad (if they can), or to buy a real asset like land that is appreciating in value alongside inflation, or to simply consume more. In any of these cases, when many people pull their money out of the banking system, the supply of savings declines and financial intermediation becomes less efficient. Table 31.4 shows a number of examples of severely negative real interest rates. In every case, economic growth was also negative. Countries with negative real interest rates usually have many problems so we can't blame all of the poor economic growth on inefficient financial intermediation. Nonetheless, studies show that even after controlling for other factors, negative real interest rates reduce financial intermediation and economic growth.

Financial Intermediation Failure

interactive activity

Hyperinflation and the Breakdown of Financial Intermediation If inflation is moderate and stable, lenders and borrowers can probably forecast reasonably well and loans can be signed with rough certainty regarding the real value of the future payments. But when inflation is volatile and unpredictable, long-term loans become riskier and they may not be signed at all. Thus, the real problem of unexpected inflation is not simply that it redistributes wealth, but—even worse—that few long-term contracts will be signed when borrowers and lenders both fear that unexpected inflation or deflation *could* redistribute their wealth.

High and volatile inflation rates have decimated many developing nations. When Peru experienced hyperinflation between 1987 and 1992, private loans virtually disappeared. When firms cannot get loans, they cannot build for future expansion and growth. The price level in Peru is approximately 10 million times higher today than it was in 1997. Who could have predicted these rates of increase or built them into a contract?

The virtual elimination of inflation in Mexico shows how much capital markets can flourish in a stable environment. In the 1980s, the rate of Mexican inflation at times exceeded 100%. Long-term loans were very hard to come by. In the United States, it's relatively easy to borrow money for 10, 20, or 30 years or even longer. But as recently as the early 2000s, 90% of the local currency debt in Mexico matured within one year.

In the 1990s, the inflation rate in Mexico came down to about 10% and more recently it has been close to 3%, not that far from the rate in the United States. Mexican capital markets have grown rapidly as inflation has been stabilized. In 2006, the Mexican government was able to introduce a 30-year bond, denominated in Mexican pesos; this would have been unheard of as recently as the mid-1990s.

The greater ease and predictability of long-term borrowing also has caused the Mexican mortgage market to take off. It is now relatively easy to obtain a long-term mortgage in Mexico—due largely to lower and less volatile inflation—and many more middle-class Mexicans have been able to afford homes.

It's not only lenders and borrowers that need to forecast future inflation rates. Any contract involving future payments will be affected by inflation. Workers and firms, for example, often make wage agreements several years in advance, especially when unions or other forms of collective bargaining are in place. If the rate of inflation is high and volatile, they are more likely to set wages at the wrong level. Either wages will be too high, and the firm will be reluctant to use more overtime or hire more workers, or wages will be too low, in which case workers are underpaid, they will slack off, and some will quit their jobs altogether.

Unexpected inflation redistributes wealth throughout society in arbitrary ways. When the inflation rate is high and volatile, unexpected inflation is difficult to avoid and society suffers as long-term contracting grinds to a halt.

Inflation Interacts with Other Taxes

Most tax systems define incomes, profits, and capital gains in nominal terms. In these systems, inflation, even expected inflation, will produce some tax burdens and tax liabilities that do not make economic sense.

To make this concrete, let's say you bought a share of stock for $100, and over several years inflation alone pushed its price to $150. The U.S. tax system requires that you pay profits on the $50 gain even though the gain is illusory. Yes, you have more money in nominal terms, but that money is worth less in terms of its ability to purchase real goods and services. In real terms, the stock hasn't increased in price at all yet you must still pay tax on the phantom gain.

In this case, inflation leads to people paying capital gain taxes when they should not. The overall tax burden rises. The long-run effect is to discourage investment in the first place.

Depending on the details of particular tax systems, inflation can also push people into higher tax brackets or make corporations pay taxes on phantom business profits. In short, inflation increases the costs associated with tax systems.

Inflation Is Painful to Stop

Once inflation starts, it's painful to stop—this is one of the biggest costs of inflation. Imagine that the inflation rate has been 10% in an economy for some time so that loans, wage agreements, and all kinds of business contracts are based on the expectation that inflation will continue at 10%. The government can reduce inflation by reducing the growth in the money supply, but what will happen to the economy? When workers, firms, and consumers expect 10% inflation, a lower rate is a shock. At first, firms may interpret the lower rate as a reduction in real demand and thus they may reduce output and employment. Furthermore, contracts signed on the expectation of 10% inflation are now out of whack with actual inflation. Wage bargains that promised raises of 12% per year were modest when inflation was 10%, but are huge increases in real wages when the inflation rate is 3%. Workers may be thrown out of work as the unexpected increase in their real wage makes them unaffordable. Only in the long run, as expectations adjust, does the economy move to a point where both inflation and unemployment are low.

In the United States, for example, Ronald Reagan was elected to the presidency in 1980 after inflation in the United States hit 13.5% a year. By 1983, tough monetary policy had reduced the inflation rate to 3%, but the consequence was a severe recession and an unemployment rate of just over 10%. Only in 1988 did unemployment return to near 5.5%.

Takeaway

Inflation is an increase in the average level of prices as measured by a price index such as the consumer price index (CPI). A price index can be used to convert a nominal price into a real price, a price corrected for inflation.

Sustained inflation is always and everywhere a monetary phenomenon. In the long run, real GDP is determined by the real factors of production—capital, labor, and technology—so changes in the money supply cannot permanently increase real GDP. Thus, the quantity theory of money is a good guide to how prices respond to changes in the money supply in the long run. Although money is neutral in the long run, changes in the money supply can influence real GDP in the short run for a variety of reasons.

Inflation makes price signals more difficult to interpret, especially when people may suffer from money illusion. Inflation is a type of tax. Governments with few other sources of tax revenue often turn to inflation because the inflation tax is difficult to avoid.

Workers and firms will adjust to a predictable inflation by incorporating inflation rates into wage contracts and loan agreements. The tendency of the nominal interest rate to increase with expected inflation is called the Fisher effect. But inflation is often difficult to predict. When inflation is greater than expected, wealth is redistributed from lenders to borrowers. When inflation is less than expected, wealth is redistributed from borrowers to lenders. The possibility of arbitrary redistributions of wealth in either direction makes lending and borrowing more risky and thus breaks down financial intermediation.

Anything above a mild sustained rate of inflation is generally bad for an economy. Economists disagree, however, as to whether and how much small amounts of well-timed inflation can benefit an economy. In the next chapter, on Business Fluctuations: Aggregate Demand and Supply, and the chapter on Monetary Policy, we discuss at greater length how policymakers might use the short-run trade-off between inflation and output to smooth recessions and booms. This remains one of the most important and controversial "fault lines" in modern macroeconomics.

Just Say No Inflation has been likened to a drug addiction. At first the highs (a booming economy) are good. But soon bigger and bigger doses are needed to generate the same high as before (unexpected inflation becomes expected inflation). Eventually, all that is left is the fear of withdrawal (disinflation).

CHECK YOURSELF

- Consider unexpected inflation and unexpected disinflation. How is wealth redistributed between borrowers and lenders under each case?
- What happens to nominal interest rates when expected inflation increases? What do we call this effect?
- What does unexpected inflation do to price signals?

CHAPTER REVIEW

interactive activity Go online to practice with more examples of these types of problems, including live links to videos, data sources, and feedback.

Problems in **green** relate to MRU videos. See the MRU table at the end of the exercises.

Problems in **blue** are Office Hours videos.

KEY CONCEPTS

inflation, p. 649

inflation rate, p. 650

real price, p. 651

v, velocity of money, p. 653

deflation, p. 657

disinflation, p. 657

money illusion, p. 659

real rate of return, p. 660

nominal rate of return, p. 660

Fisher effect, p. 661

monetizing the debt, p. 662

FACTS AND TOOLS

1. What is a "price level"? If the "price level" is higher in one country than another, what does that tell us, if anything, about the standard of living in that country?

2. What are some forces that could cause shocks to v, the velocity of money?

3. What is probably a bigger problem: a steady rate of inflation of, say, 15% or a rate of inflation that varies unexpectedly year to year from 0% to 15%, so that, on average the rate is well below 15%? Why?

4. Who gets helped by a surprise inflation: people who owe money or people who lend money?

5. Who is more likely to lobby the government for fast money growth: people who have mortgages or people who own banks that lent money for those mortgages?

6. Consider the interaction between inflation and the tax system (assume the inflation is expected). Does high inflation encourage people to save more or discourage saving? If a government wants to raise more tax revenue in the short run, should it push for higher or lower inflation?

7. Which tells me more about how many more goods and services I can buy next year if I save my money today: the nominal interest rate or the real interest rate? Which interest rate gets talked about more in the media?

8. If everyone expects inflation to rise by 10% over the next few years, where, according to the Fisher effect, will the biggest effect be: on nominal or real interest rates?

THINKING AND PROBLEM SOLVING

9. Calculate inflation in the following cases:

Price Level Last Year ($)	Price Level This Year ($)	Inflation Rate
100	110	
250	300	
4,000	4,040	

10. What does the quantity theory of money predict will happen *in the long run* in these cases? According to the quantity theory, a rise in the money supply can't change v or Y in the long run, so it must affect P. Let's use that fact to see how changes in the money supply affect the price level. Fill in the following table:

M	v	P	Y
150	5		50
200	5		50
100	5		50

11. In the long run, according to the quantity theory of money, if the money supply doubles, what happens to the price level? What happens to real GDP? In both cases, state the percentage change in either the price level or real GDP.

12. Much of the economic news we read about can be reinterpreted into our "$Mv = PY$" framework. Turn each of the following news headlines into a precise statement about M, v, P, or Y:

    a. "Deposits in U.S. banks fell in 2015."

    b. "American businesses are spending faster than ever."

    c. "Prices of most consumer goods rose 12% last year."

    d. "Workers produced 4% more output per hour last year."

    e. "Real GDP increased 32% in the last decade."

    f. "Interest rates fall: Consumers hold more cash."

13. It's time to take control of the Federal Reserve (which controls the U.S. money supply). In this chapter, we're thinking only about the "long run," so Y (real GDP) is out of the Fed's control, as is v. The Fed's only goal is to make sure that the price level is equal to 100 each and every year—that's just known as "price stability," one of the main goals of most governments.

    In question 10, you acted like an economic *forecaster:* You knew the values of M, v, and Y and had to guess what the long-run price level would be. In this question, you will act like an economic *policymaker:* You know the values of v and Y, and you know your goal for P. Your job is to set the level of M so that you meet your price-level target.

    In some years, there will be long-lasting shocks to v and Y, so your job as a policymaker is to offset those shocks by changing the supply of money in the economy. Some of these changes might not make you popular with the citizens, but they are part of keeping P equal to the price-level target. Fill in the following table:

Year	M	v	=	P	Y
1	25,000	2		100	500
2		4		100	500
3		4		100	400
4		4		100	200
5		2		100	400
6		1		100	600

14. Nobel laureate Milton Friedman often said that "inflation is the cruelest tax." Who is it a tax on? More than one answer may be correct:

    a. People who hold currency and coins in their wallet, purse, or at home

    b. Businesses that hold currency and coins in their cash registers

    c. People or businesses who keep deposits in a checking account that pays zero interest

    d. People or businesses who keep deposits in a savings account that pays an interest rate higher than the rate of inflation

    e. People or businesses who invest in gold, silver, platinum, or other metals

15. In countries with hyperinflation, the government prints money and uses it to pay government workers. How is this similar to counterfeiting? How is it different?

16. The Fisher effect says that nominal interest rates will equal expected inflation plus the real equilibrium rate of return:

$$i = E\pi + r_{Equilibrium}$$

i = Nominal interest rate
$E\pi$ = Expected inflation rate
$r_{Equilibrium}$ = Equilibrium real rate of return

Economists and Wall Street experts often use the Fisher effect to learn about economic variables that are hard to measure because when the Fisher effect holds, if we know any two of the three items in the equation, we can calculate the third. Sometimes, for example, economists are trying to estimate what investors *expect* inflation is going to be over the next few years, but they have good estimates only of nominal interest rates and the equilibrium real rate. Other times, they have good estimates of expected inflation and today's nominal interest rates, and want to learn about the equilibrium real rate. Let's use the Fisher effect just as the experts do: Use two *known* values to learn about the *unknown* third one.

i	$E\pi$	$r_{Equilibrium}$
5%	2%	3%
5%	1%	
5%		8%
	10%	2%
6%		2%
0%	−2%	

Note: The last entry is an example of the "Friedman rule," something that we'll come back to in a later chapter.

Ask FRED

17. How much did a typical basket of goods increase in price between 1990 and 2010? Let's use the FRED economic database (https://fred.stlouisfed.org/) to answer this question. Search for the CPI (the consumer price index). Click Edit Graph and change the frequency to Annual.

a. What was the CPI in 1990? What was the CPI in 2010?

b. What was the total inflation rate over this 20-year period?

CHALLENGES

18. If I get more money, does that typically make me richer? If society gets more money, does it make society richer? What's the contradiction?

19. Why is it so painful to get rid of inflation? Why can't the government just stop printing so much money?

20. Who gets hurt most in the following cases: banks, mortgage holders (i.e., homeowners), or neither?

Eπ	π	Who gets hurt?
4%	10%	
10%	4%	
−3%	0%	
3%	6%	
10%	10%	

21. Let's see just how much high expected inflation can hurt incentives to save for the long run. Let's assume the government takes about one-third of every extra dollar of nominal interest you earn (a reasonable approximation for recent college graduates in the United States). You must pay taxes on nominal interest—just like under current U.S. law—but if you're rational, you'll care mostly about your real, after-tax interest rate when deciding how much to save.

To make the economic lesson clear, note that in every case, the real rate (before taxes) is an identical 3%. In each case, calculate the nominal after-tax rate of return and the real after-tax

rate of return. Notice that as inflation rises, your after-tax rate of return plummets.

i	E$\pi = \pi$	$\frac{2}{3} \times i$	$\left(\frac{2}{3} \times i\right) - \pi$
Nominal interest Rate	Inflation (no surprises)	Nominal After-tax Return	Real After-tax Return
15%	12%	10%	−2%
6%	3%		
12%	9%		
90%	87%		
900%	897%		

Ask FRED

22. Let's get some practice with converting nominal to real series using the FRED economic database at https://fred.stlouisfed.org/. Go to FRED and find the series, "Median Sales Price for New Houses Sold in the United States." Click on Edit Data and modify Frequency to Annual.

a. What was the median price of a new house in 1980 and in 2015?

b. What was the percentage increase in the price of a median new house between 1980 and 2015? Is this a real price increase or a nominal price increase?

To find the real price increase, click Edit Graph, then under "Customize data" search for the CPI (the consumer price index). Click Add. Notice that the median house price data is series (a) and the CPI is series (b). Under Formula we can create a new formula for the real median price of new houses. Enter "a/b★100". Click Apply.

c. Using the real price series what was the median price of a new house in 1980 and in 2015? What was the percentage increase in the real price of a median house between 1980 and 2015?

d. Can you think of any other reasons why the median price of a new house might have increased between 1980 and 2015?

Ask FRED

23. Let's look at the inflation rate and the interest rate on 30-year mortgages in the United States. We will use the FRED economic database (https://fred.stlouisfed.org/). First search for the CPI then click Edit Graph and change Units to Percent Change from Year Ago and the Frequency to Annual, for the annual inflation rate. Now click Add Line and search for Mortgage. You should find a 30-year mortgage rate for the United States. Add that Data Series and then change the Units to Percent (not Percent Change from Year Ago) and change frequency to Annual.

a. As inflation rose in the 1970s and fell in the 1980s and 1990s what happened to mortgage interest rates. What do we call this effect?

b. In 1981 what was the average interest rate on a 30-year mortgage? What was the inflation rate in 1981? Over the next 30 years what very approximately was the inflation rate?

c. Did home buyers who took out 30-year mortgages in 1981 get a good deal or bad deal? Why?

d. In 1981 do you think banks and homebuyers predicted what would happen to the inflation rate over the next 30 years? Discuss some problems with high and volatile inflation.

WORK IT OUT

For interactive, step-by-step help in solving this problem, go online.

What does the quantity theory of money predict will happen *in the long run* in these cases? According to the quantity theory, a rise in the money supply can't change v or Y in the long run, so it must affect P. Let's use that fact to see how changes in the money supply affect the price level. Fill in the following table:

M	v	P	Y
100	5		50
150	5		50
50	5		50

MRUNIVERSITY
AN ONLINE EDUCATION PLATFORM

MARGINAL REVOLUTION UNIVERSITY VIDEOS

Zimbabwe and Hyperinflation: Who Wants to Be a Trillionaire?

mruniversity.com/hyperinflation

Problems: **15**

Measuring Inflation

mruniversity.com/inflation-def

Problems: **1, 9**

Quantity Theory of Money

mruniversity.com/quant-theory-money

Problems: **10–12**

Causes of Inflation

mruniversity.com/inflation-cause

Problems: **2, 10–12**

Costs of Inflation: Price Confusion and Money Illusion

mruniversity.com/inflation-cost1

Problems: **3**

Costs of Inflation: Financial Intermediation Failure

mruniversity.com/inflation-cost2

Problems: **3–5, 16, 20**

Why Governments Create Inflation

mruniversity.com/govt-inflation

Problems: **15**

OFFICE HOURS

OFFICE HOURS: Costs of Inflation

mruniversity.com/inflation-cost3

Problems: **21**

32

Business Fluctuations: Aggregate Demand and Supply

Economic growth is not a smooth process. Real GDP in the United States has grown at an average rate of 3.2% per year over the past 65 years. But the economy didn't grow at this rate every day or every month or even every year. The economy advances and recedes, it rises and falls, it booms and busts.

In our chapter on The Wealth of Nations and Economic Growth, and the chapter on Growth, Capital Accumulation, and the Economics of Ideas, we looked at why some countries are rich and others are poor. In answering that question, we could safely ignore booms and recessions and focus on average rates of growth over periods of many years. We now turn from average growth rates to focus on the deviations from average, namely the booms and the recessions.

Figure 32.1 on the next page illustrates the booms and recessions of the U.S. economy by quarter since 1948. The average rate of growth of real GDP is 3.2% per quarter (on an annual basis), as marked by the red line, but the economy rarely grew at an average rate. In a typical recession, the growth rate might drop to −5% in some quarters, and in a boom, the economy can grow at a rate of 7 to 8% or higher. We call the fluctuations of real GDP around its long-term trend or "normal" growth rate **business fluctuations** or business cycles. **Recessions**, which we defined in our chapter on GDP and the Measurement of Progress as significant, widespread declines in real income and employment, are shaded.

Recessions are of special concern to policymakers and the public because unemployment increases during a recession. Notice in Figure 32.2, for example, how unemployment increases dramatically within each of the shaded regions that are the periods of U.S. recessions.

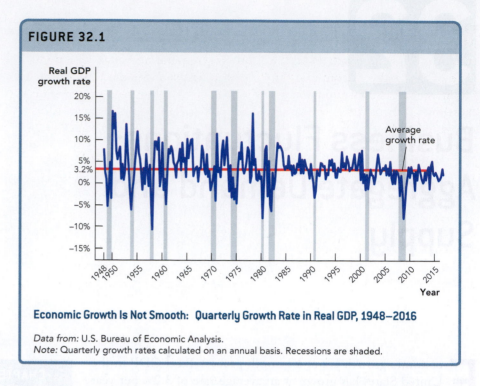

FIGURE 32.1

Economic Growth Is Not Smooth: Quarterly Growth Rate in Real GDP, 1948–2016

Data from: U.S. Bureau of Economic Analysis.
Note: Quarterly growth rates calculated on an annual basis. Recessions are shaded.

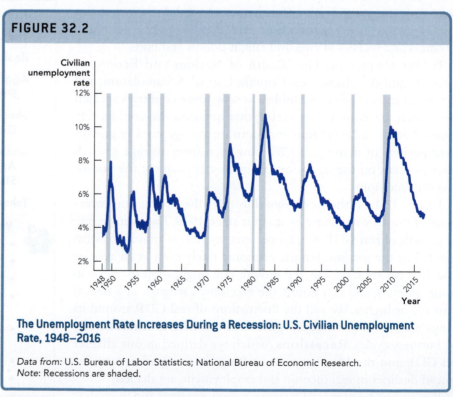

FIGURE 32.2

The Unemployment Rate Increases During a Recession: U.S. Civilian Unemployment Rate, 1948–2016

Data from: U.S. Bureau of Labor Statistics; National Bureau of Economic Research.
Note: Recessions are shaded.

Business fluctuations are fluctuations in the growth rate of real GDP around its long-term trend growth rate.

A **recession** is a significant, widespread decline in real income and employment.

More generally, a recession is a time when all kinds of resources, not just labor but also capital and land, are not fully employed. During a recession, factories close, stores are boarded up, and farmland is left fallow. We know that some unemployment is a natural or normal consequence of economic growth—in the previous chapter, we called this level of unemployment the natural unemployment rate—but often unemployment exceeds the natural rate. More generally, when there are a lot of unemployed resources, it suggests that resources are being wasted and the economy is operating below its potential. One of the goals of economic thinking is to better understand the causes of booms and recessions, and perhaps learn how policy might help to smooth out these fluctuations. Recessions are the exception rather than the norm, but still we would all be richer and more secure if we could limit the frequency and severity of recessions.

To understand booms and recessions, we are going to develop a model of aggregate demand and aggregate supply (AD–AS). Our model will show how unexpected economic disturbances or "shocks" can temporarily increase or decrease the economy's rate of growth. We will focus on how an economy responds to two types of shocks, real shocks (also called aggregate supply shocks) and aggregate demand shocks.

Ultimately, our AD–AS model will have three curves: the aggregate demand curve, the long-run aggregate supply curve, and the short-run aggregate supply curve. Let's begin with the aggregate demand curve.

The Aggregate Demand Curve

The **aggregate demand curve** tells us all the combinations of inflation and real growth that are consistent with a *specified* rate of spending growth. The easiest way to explain an AD curve is to derive it using the quantity theory of money from the previous chapter. Recall that we can write the quantity theory in dynamic form as

$$\vec{M} + \vec{v} = \vec{P} + \vec{Y}_R \tag{1}$$

where $\vec{M}$ is the growth rate of the money supply; $\vec{v}$ is growth in velocity (how quickly money is turning over); $\vec{P}$ is the growth rate of prices, that is, the inflation rate, which we also write as π; and $\vec{Y}_R$ is the growth rate of real GDP, which we simplify and call real growth. Thus, we can also write equation 1 as

$$\vec{M} + \vec{v} = \textbf{Inflation} + \textbf{Real growth} \tag{2}$$

Now imagine that $\vec{M}$ = 5%, $\vec{v}$ = 0%, and real growth is 0%. What is the inflation rate? To answer that question, we substitute what we know into equation 2. Thus, 5% + 0% = Inflation + 0%, so Inflation = 5%. Intuitively, if the money supply is growing by 5% a year ($\vec{M}$ = 5%) and velocity is stable ($\vec{v}$ = 0%), then spending is growing by 5% a year. But if there are no additional goods to spend the money on, that is, if real growth is 0%, then prices must rise by 5%. In short, more spending plus the same goods equals higher prices.

An AD curve tells us *all* the combinations of inflation and real growth that are consistent with a specified rate of spending growth ($\vec{M} + \vec{v}$). We have just discovered *one* such combination; an inflation rate of 5% and a real growth rate of 0% are consistent with a spending growth rate of 5%. But what other combinations of inflation and real growth are consistent with a spending growth rate of 5%?

What would the inflation rate be if, just before, $\vec{M}$ = 5% and $\vec{v}$ = 0%, but now real growth = 3%? Once again, we substitute what we know into

The **aggregate demand curve** shows all the combinations of inflation and real growth that are consistent with a specified rate of spending growth ($\vec{M} + \vec{v}$).

Key Equation

$\vec{M} + \vec{v}$ = Inflation + Real growth

The Aggregate Demand Curve

equation 2. Thus, we have 5% + 0% = Inflation + 3%, so Inflation = 2%. The intuition is quite simple. Inflation is caused when more money chases the same goods. So, if more money is chasing an increased quantity of goods, then, all else being equal, the inflation rate will be less than the increase in money growth.

Thus, we now have *two* combinations of inflation and real growth that are consistent with a spending growth rate of 5%. In Figure 32.3, point *a* shows an inflation rate of 5% and a real growth rate of 0%, and point *b* shows an inflation rate of 2% and a real growth rate of 3%. Both of these combinations are consistent with a spending growth rate of 5%, *so they belong on the same AD curve.* In fact, from equation 2 we know that all the combinations of inflation and real growth that are consistent with a spending growth rate of 5% must satisfy the equation 5% = Inflation − Real growth. In other words, any combination of inflation and real growth that adds up to 5% is on the same AD curve. Figure 32.3 shows the AD curve for a spending growth rate of 5%. Thus, all the points on this line add up to 5%.

Notice also that the AD curve is a straight line with a slope of − 1.*This means that, given the rate of spending growth, a 1 percentage point increase in real growth reduces inflation by 1 percentage point.

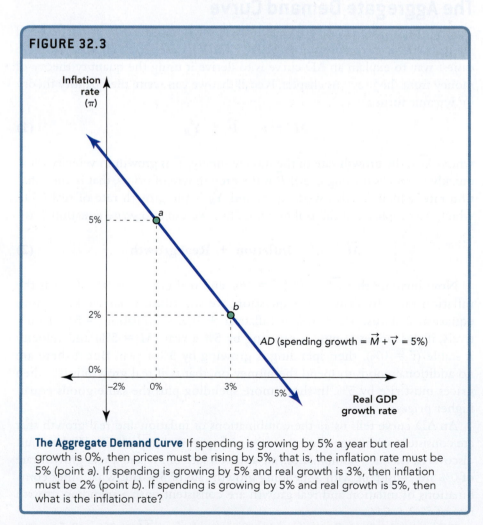

FIGURE 32.3

The Aggregate Demand Curve If spending is growing by 5% a year but real growth is 0%, then prices must be rising by 5%, that is, the inflation rate must be 5% (point *a*). If spending is growing by 5% and real growth is 3%, then inflation must be 2% (point *b*). If spending is growing by 5% and real growth is 5%, then what is the inflation rate?

* We can easily show this by rewriting equation 2 in the familiar $Y = b + mX$ format, Inflation = ($\vec{M} + \vec{v}$) − 1 × Real growth. Notice that m, the slope of the curve, is − 1.

Shifts in the Aggregate Demand Curve

The AD curve for a spending growth rate of 5% is all the combinations of inflation and real growth that add up to 5%. So, what is the AD curve for a spending growth rate of 7%? Right, all the combinations of inflation and real growth that add up to 7%. Now that we know what an AD curve is, we also know how the AD curve shifts. In Figure 32.4, for example, notice that all the combinations of inflation and real growth along the AD curve denoted $AD\ (\vec{M} + \vec{v} = 5\%)$ add up to 5% and all the combinations of inflation and real growth along the AD curve denoted $AD\ (\vec{M} + \vec{v} = 7\%)$ add up to 7%. Thus, if spending growth increases to 7%, either because of an increase in $\vec{M}$ or because of an increase in $\vec{v}$, then the AD curve shifts up and to the right (outward). The intuition is that increased spending must flow into either a higher inflation rate or a higher growth rate. Thus, an increase in spending growth shifts the AD curve outward, up and to the right, and, of course, a decrease in spending growth shifts the AD curve inward.

As we have said, an increase in spending growth can be caused by either an increase in $\vec{M}$ or $\vec{v}$. Later on in this chapter and in later chapters on Monetary Policy and on Fiscal Policy, respectively, we explain exactly what this means in practice. For now, we just need to remember that increased spending growth shifts the AD curve outward and decreased spending growth shifts the AD curve inward.

CHECK YOURSELF

- If we have an aggregate demand curve with $\overline{M} = 7\%$ and $\vec{v} = 0\%$, what will inflation plus real growth equal? If we find out that real growth is 0%, what is inflation?

- Increased spending growth shifts the aggregate demand curve which way: inward or outward?

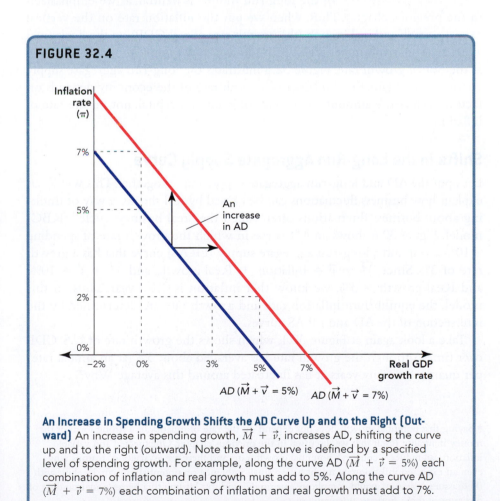

FIGURE 32.4

An Increase in Spending Growth Shifts the AD Curve Up and to the Right (Outward) An increase in spending growth, $\vec{M} + \vec{v}$, increases AD, shifting the curve up and to the right (outward). Note that each curve is defined by a specified level of spending growth. For example, along the curve AD $(\vec{M} + \vec{v} = 5\%)$ each combination of inflation and real growth must add to 5%. Along the curve AD $(\vec{M} + \vec{v} = 7\%)$ each combination of inflation and real growth must add to 7%.

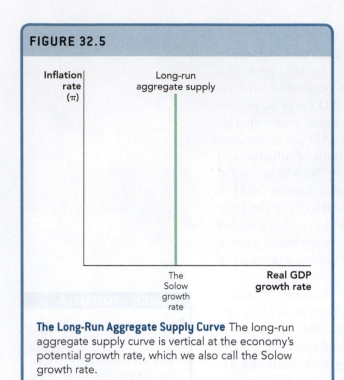

FIGURE 32.5

Inflation rate (π)

Long-run aggregate supply

The Solow growth rate

Real GDP growth rate

The Long-Run Aggregate Supply Curve The long-run aggregate supply curve is vertical at the economy's potential growth rate, which we also call the Solow growth rate.

The **Solow growth rate** is an economy's potential growth rate, the rate of economic growth that would occur given flexible prices and the existing real factors of production.

The **long-run aggregate supply curve** is vertical at the Solow growth rate.

The Long-Run Aggregate Supply Curve

We learned in earlier chapters on The Wealth of Nations and Economic Growth, and on Growth, Capital Accumulation, and the Economics of Ideas that economic growth depends on increases in the stocks of labor and capital and on increases in productivity (driven by new and better ideas and better institutions). Thus, every economy has a potential growth rate given by these fundamental, or real, factors of production. We call the rate of growth, as given by the real factors of production, the "Solow" growth rate. We call it that because Robert Solow, one of the giants of economics, created an important model of an economy's fundamental growth rate. In our chapter on Growth, Capital Accumulation, and the Economics of Ideas, we described Solow's model in more detail, but if you skipped that section don't worry: Just think of the **Solow growth rate** as the rate of economic growth given flexible prices and the existing real factors of capital, labor, and ideas.

In the long run money is neutral, as we emphasized in the previous chapter. Thus, when we put the inflation rate on the vertical axis of a graph and real growth (the growth rate of real GDP) on the horizontal axis, the **long-run aggregate supply curve** is very simple—it's a vertical line at the Solow growth rate. Figure 32.5 illustrates the long-run aggregate supply curve.* Once again, the fundamental growth rate of the economy depends on factors such as the amount and quality of labor and capital, not on the rate of inflation.

Shifts in the Long-Run Aggregate Supply Curve

Let's put the AD and long-run aggregate supply curve together. This will let us explain how business fluctuations can be caused by real shocks, a way of thinking about business fluctuations often called the "real business cycle" (RBC) model. Figure 32.6 shows an AD curve in which the growth rate of spending is 10% a year and a long-run aggregate supply (LRAS) curve that has a growth rate of 3%. Since $\vec{M} + \vec{v} =$ Inflation + Real growth, and $\vec{M} + \vec{v} = 10\%$, and Real growth = 3%, we know that inflation is 7% a year. Thus, in this model, the equilibrium inflation rate and growth rate are determined by the intersection of the AD and LRAS curves.

Take a look again at Figure 32.1, which shows the growth rate of U.S. GDP over time. Although the growth rate has averaged about 3% (at an annual rate) per quarter for many years, it has fluctuated around this average. Why?

---

* Saying that potential growth does not depend on the rate of inflation is a strong form of the money neutrality result that we discussed in the previous chapter. Unexpected and variable inflation can reduce a country's potential growth rate, and there are a variety of reasons why even an expected inflation rate might have a small influence on potential growth. Dealing with these issues, however, would complicate our model without leading to a better understanding of our current topic, business fluctuations.

One reason that the growth rate fluctuates is that economies are continually being hit by shocks, which shift the Solow growth rate. As an example, consider an agricultural economy: Good weather can increase crop production—driving the growth rate up—while bad weather can decrease production, thereby driving down the growth rate.

We call these shocks **real shocks** or productivity shocks because they increase or decrease an economy's fundamental ability to produce goods and services and, thus, they increase or decrease the Solow growth rate.

A positive real shock shown in Figure 32.7 shifts the LRAS curve to the right, increasing real growth. The increase in the supply of goods brought about by a higher real growth rate reduces the inflation rate. During the late 1990s, for example, the Internet revolution, a positive real shock, increased the growth rate of the economy. Faster, more powerful computers at lower prices helped to keep inflation low.

A negative real shock shifts the LRAS curve to the left, decreasing real growth. The slower growth rate means fewer new goods to spend money on so the inflation rate increases. In the 1970s, for example, a negative real shock—a sudden, sharp decrease in the relative

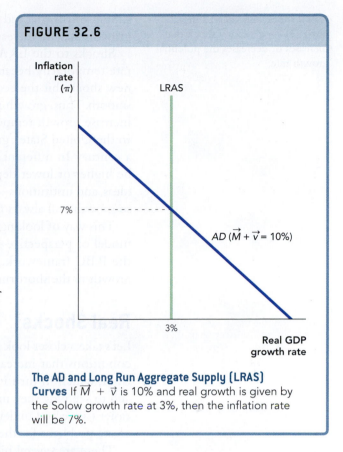

FIGURE 32.6

The AD and Long Run Aggregate Supply (LRAS) Curves If $\vec{M} + \vec{v}$ is 10% and real growth is given by the Solow growth rate at 3%, then the inflation rate will be 7%.

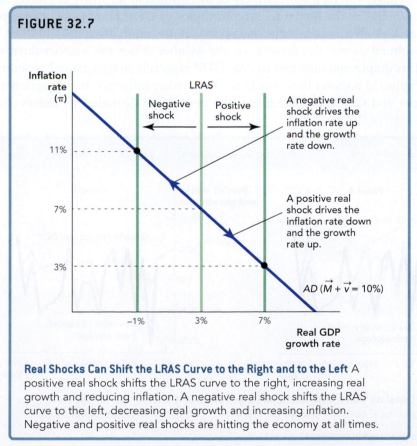

FIGURE 32.7

Real Shocks Can Shift the LRAS Curve to the Right and to the Left A positive real shock shifts the LRAS curve to the right, increasing real growth and reducing inflation. A negative real shock shifts the LRAS curve to the left, decreasing real growth and increasing inflation. Negative and positive real shocks are hitting the economy at all times.

A **real shock**, also called a productivity shock, is any shock that increases or decreases the potential growth rate.

supply of oil that led to several big jumps in the price of oil—reduced the growth rate and increased inflation.

Shocks to the LRAS curve will change the growth rate and the inflation rate temporarily because the LRAS curve is always shifting back and forth as new shocks hit the economy. Remember from Figure 32.1 that growth is not smooth. Thus, growth rates fluctuate from quarter to quarter, as positive shocks increase growth temporarily and negative shocks reduce growth temporarily. In the United States, growth has fluctuated around approximately 3% for about a century. In different times and places, the average Solow growth rate could be higher or lower depending on growth in the fundamentals—capital, labor, ideas, and institutions—but every economy will always be subject to real shocks so growth will always fluctuate.

This way of looking at booms and recessions—the real business cycle (RBC) model or perspective—is a natural extension of the Solow growth model. In the RBC framework, business fluctuations are simply changes in economic growth in the short run driven by real shocks.

Real Shocks

Let's take a closer look at real shocks. Real shocks are rapid changes in economic conditions that increase or diminish the level or productivity of capital and labor, which in turn influences GDP and employment. To understand shocks and to see why they matter, we start with poorer economies, where shocks are easier to see and understand. Later in the chapter, we move to how shocks can create problems for the United States and other developed economies.

There are several billion farmers in the world and for many countries agriculture remains the single largest contributor to GDP. How much a farm produces depends on the quantity and quality of the inputs of capital and labor, but agricultural output also depends on the weather. When the weather fluctuates, so does output and therefore so does GDP, especially in agricultural economies.

Figure 32.8 shows how shocks to the weather influence India's agricultural output and GDP. The blue line is the percentage deviation in India's yearly

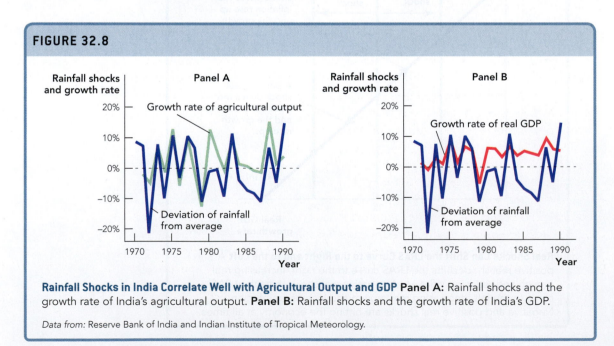

FIGURE 32.8

Rainfall Shocks in India Correlate Well with Agricultural Output and GDP **Panel A:** Rainfall shocks and the growth rate of India's agricultural output. **Panel B:** Rainfall shocks and the growth rate of India's GDP.

Data from: Reserve Bank of India and Indian Institute of Tropical Meteorology.

rainfall from the average (from 1970 to 1990). Above-average rainfall is good for the crops so in 1975, for example, rainfall was 10.8% above average, and in the left-hand panel, we see that agricultural output (the green line) in that year grew by a bountiful 12.8%. In 1979, however, much of India had a drought. Rainfall was 11% below average and agricultural output fell by nearly 13%, compared to the year before.

Agriculture has been the largest contributor to India's GDP, so the shocks to agricultural output caused by the weather have had a big impact on GDP growth. It is not just that agriculture contributes to GDP directly but, if farmers struggle, many other sectors of the Indian economy suffer as well. For instance, the demand for tractors will go down and farmers will buy fewer items for their own consumption. Thus, the shock spreads to other sectors of the economy. In Panel B of Figure 32.8, the red line shows the growth rate of India's GDP. As expected, GDP boomed in 1975, growing by nearly 10%, and busted in 1979 with a decline of 5.2%. Note that the booms and busts in GDP are not as strong as the booms and busts in agricultural output because other sectors, less influenced by the weather, also contribute to GDP.

By the way, take a close look at Panel B of Figure 32.8. Does it seem to you that shocks to rainfall have become less important to India's GDP since 1980? If so, you are probably correct. Agriculture contributed 40% of India's GDP in 1970, but because the Indian economy has grown and diversified, it contributed only 20% of India's GDP in 1990. Therefore, shocks to the weather are becoming less economically important in India over time. In the United States, agriculture contributes less than 1% to GDP, so yearly variations in the weather don't have much of an effect on GDP. Other shocks, however, can rock the U.S. economy.

Oil Shocks

In an economy with a large manufacturing sector, a reduction in the oil supply is like a reduction in rainfall in an agricultural economy. Oil and machines are complementary, which means they work together, along with labor, to produce output. Thus, when the oil supply is reduced, capital and labor become less productive. Oil greases the wheels of industry, sometimes literally, and with less oil the wheels do not turn as well.

The first oil shock came in late 1973, when many of the oil-producing nations under the guise of OPEC (Organization of the Petroleum Exporting Countries) reduced the global oil supply to protest America's support of Israel in the Middle East. The result was that the price of oil more than tripled in just two years. This became a significant problem for the American economy.

The higher price of oil, for instance, also meant a much higher price for gasoline (oil is one input into gasoline). Higher gas prices reduced the demand for larger cars and increased the demand for smaller cars. The U.S. auto industry was specialized in the production of larger cars and had a difficult time adjusting. Factories cannot simply be switched from the production of one type of car to another—much of the physical capital in an auto factory is specialized. A machine that is used to bend steel is no longer useful when production switches to lightweight, fuel-saving plastic composites. Workers are specialized, too, in both knowledge and location. Thus, the oil shock meant that many auto plants producing larger cars shut down or were used at less than full capacity. Similarly, autoworkers became unemployed and many had to learn new skills, and often they had to move to new jobs.

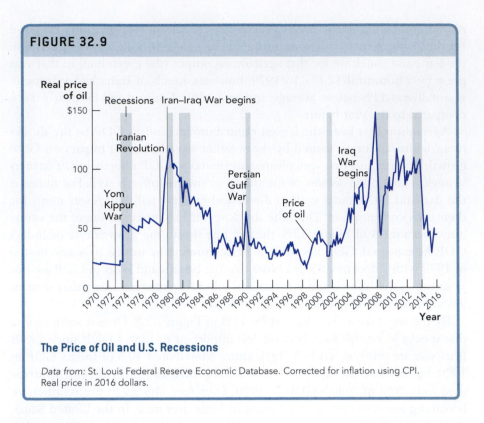

FIGURE 32.9

The Price of Oil and U.S. Recessions

Data from: St. Louis Federal Reserve Economic Database. Corrected for inflation using CPI. Real price in 2016 dollars.

Not every part of the American economy was harmed. The demand for smaller cars increased, for example, but the U.S. auto industry could not immediately meet that demand. It can take a decade to design and build a new car, so it took considerable time for capital and labor to reallocate to the production of smaller American cars. In the meantime, output and employment in the auto industry fell. Similarly, over time, the city of Houston (which services much of the American oil industry) became populated with many former residents of Detroit (which made large American cars), but the transition was costly and disruptive.

Since oil is an important input in many sectors of the economy, high oil prices—or oil shocks—hurt many American industries. Thus, sharp increases in the price of oil can disrupt the economy as a whole. Figure 32.9 shows the price of oil and the last six U.S. recessions. In each case, there was a large increase in the price of oil just prior to or coincident with the onset of recession (oil prices were still very high during the 1981–1982 recession, which was almost a continuation of the 1980 recession). The pattern is especially clear with the 1974, 1980, and 1991 recessions in the graph. In these cases, the onset of a war reduced the supply of oil, driving up the price unexpectedly. Unexpected shocks are the most costly to deal with.

It's fairly easy to see the impact on the economy of a large increase in the price of oil but it's harder to eyeball the effect of smaller shocks. Careful statistical analysis, however, can disentangle the effect of oil shocks from the many other shocks that keep on hitting the economy. In Figure 32.10, we show how the economy responds to an unexpected and permanent increase in the price of oil of 10%.

Starting from the normal or trend rate of growth (which is fixed at the zero point on the vertical axis of the graph), Figure 32.10 shows that a 10% increase in the price of oil slows the economy down gradually, with the biggest slowdown occurring about 5 quarters (a little over a year) after the onset of the increase in price. After 5 quarters, the growth rate begins to pick up again quite quickly, and after 10 quarters (two and a half years), the economy has adjusted to the higher price and the growth rate returns to normal.

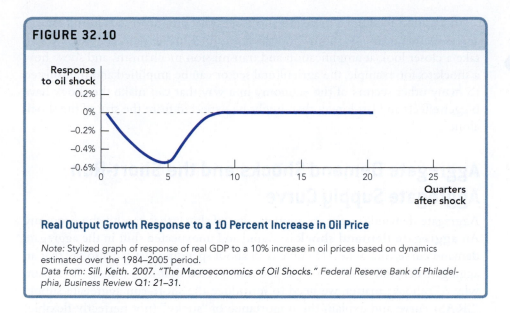

FIGURE 32.10

Real Output Growth Response to a 10 Percent Increase in Oil Price

Note: Stylized graph of response of real GDP to a 10% increase in oil prices based on dynamics estimated over the 1984–2005 period.
Data from: Sill, Keith. 2007. "The Macroeconomics of Oil Shocks." Federal Reserve Bank of Philadelphia, Business Review Q1: 21–31.

Thus, a 10% increase in the price of oil lowers the GDP growth rate, from what it would have been without the price increase, for just over two years. The total effect on GDP is a decrease of about 1.4%. In other words, if the price of oil had not increased, real GDP would have been about 1.4% higher.

More Shocks

Oil and rainfall shocks are only two among many shocks that might hit an economy. Other possible shocks are wars, terrorist attacks, major new regulations, tax rate changes, mass strikes, and new technologies such as the Internet. Most generally, economies are continually hit by many small shocks. Some of the shocks are good, like a productive new technology, and some are bad, like a drought. In a typical year, the good shocks outweigh the bad and the economy grows. People build on previous knowledge and most of the time they are able to do better and produce a bit more than in previous years. In a bad year, however, an economy may be hit with a big shock, like an oil shock, or by several small negative shocks that outweigh the positive ones. In either case, a recession may result. It is a bit like playing poker. Every now and then you get a hand of cards that simply cannot be played well, no matter what you do. Table 32.1 lists some major factors that shift the LRAS curve left (negative shock) or right (positive shock).

The Long-Run Aggregate Supply Curve

interactive activity

TABLE 32.1 SOME FACTORS THAT SHIFT THE LONG-RUN AGGREGATE SUPPLY CURVE

Negative Shocks = LRAS Curve Moves Left	Positive Shocks = LRAS Curve Moves Right
Bad weather (important in agricultural economy)	Good weather (important in agricultural economy)
Higher price of oil or other important input	Lower price of oil or other important input
Productivity slump/technology slump	Productivity boom/technology boom
Higher taxes or regulation	Lower taxes or regulation
Disruption of production by war, earthquake, pandemic	Smooth production without disruption

CHECK YOURSELF

- Consider the ubiquity of cell phones throughout the world. How can this ubiquity be considered a positive shock? (*Hint:* Compare with 10 years ago.)
- How would a large and sudden increase in taxes, for example, a tax on energy, shift the long-run aggregate supply curve?

An **aggregate demand shock** is a rapid and unexpected shift in the AD curve (spending).

In 1936, John Maynard Keynes published a revolutionary book, *The General Theory of Employment, Interest and Money. The General Theory* explained that when prices were not perfectly flexible, deficiencies in aggregate demand could generate recessions.

The **short-run aggregate supply curve (SRAS)** shows the positive relationship between the inflation rate and real growth during the period when prices and wages are sticky.

In addition to shocks, there are also forces that amplify and transmit shocks across sectors of the economy and through time. In the next chapter, we will take a closer look at amplification and transmission mechanisms and show how a shock to, for example, the agricultural sector can be amplified and transmitted to many other sectors of the economy in a way that can make the shock have bigger effects and last longer than might be expected from the size of the shock alone.

Aggregate Demand Shocks and the Short-Run Aggregate Supply Curve

Aggregate demand shocks are another type of shock that can hit the economy. An **aggregate demand shock** is a rapid and unexpected shift in the aggregate demand curve. Since the AD curve is all about spending, we can also say that an aggregate demand shock is a rapid and unexpected shift in spending. To explain why AD shocks matter, we need to introduce the short-run aggregate supply (SRAS) curve and explain the importance of "sticky" (not perfectly flexible) wages and prices.

Before we introduce the SRAS curve, however, let's give some intuition about where we are going. It takes time for an aggregate demand shock to work its way through the economy. Recall the inflation parable from the previous chapter. In that parable, the government of Zimbabwe prints more money to pay its soldiers. The soldiers use the new money to buy more goods such as bread—that's an increase in spending, a positive shock to aggregate demand. At first, the baker is delighted when soldiers walk through her door with cash for bread. To satisfy her new customers, the baker works extra hours and bakes more bread. "How wonderful," she thinks, "with the increase in the demand for bread I will be able to buy more clothes and cabinets." The baker is *expecting* to buy clothes and cabinets at the same prices as she paid before the soldiers started to buy more bread. Only later does the baker realize that the soldiers have been buying more of everything, pushing up prices throughout the economy so that her money buys her less than it did before. Once the baker comes to expect rising prices throughout the economy, she raises the price of bread and goes back to producing at the old output level.

The parable tells us that a positive shock to spending increases output at first, but in the long run only increases prices. We know from our basic equation $\vec{M} + \vec{v} =$ Inflation $+$ Real growth that an increase in spending $\vec{M} + \vec{v}$ must either increase the inflation rate π or the real growth rate. But we also know that in the long run, the real growth rate will be equal to the Solow rate, which is not influenced by the inflation rate, so in the long run an increase in spending will increase the inflation rate alone. The parable, however, tells us that the inflation rate does not necessarily increase immediately in direct proportion to an increase in spending. In the short run, an increase in spending will be split between increases in inflation and increases in real growth— that is, the essence of the short-run aggregate supply curve to which we now turn.

Short-Run Aggregate Supply Curve

The **short-run aggregate supply (SRAS) curve** is upward-sloping, like that shown in Figure 32.11. An upward-sloping SRAS means that in the short run an increase in aggregate demand will increase both the inflation rate and

FIGURE 32.11

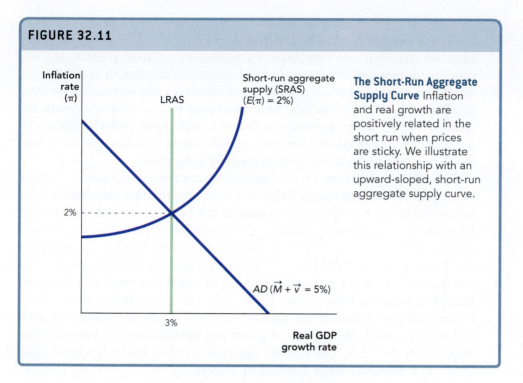

The Short-Run Aggregate Supply Curve Inflation and real growth are positively related in the short run when prices are sticky. We illustrate this relationship with an upward-sloped, short-run aggregate supply curve.

the growth rate, and a decrease in demand will decrease both the inflation rate and the growth rate.

Figure 32.12 illustrates the same ideas from the parable but now using the AD, SRAS, and LRAS curves. We start from a position of long-run equilibrium, which means that the inflation rate consumers and firms are expecting must be equal to the actual inflation rate and that the real growth rate must be at the Solow level. Thus, in Figure 32.12, the initial equilibrium is at point *a* where the real growth rate is at the Solow rate (3%), the inflation rate is 2%, and the expected inflation rate is 2%. Economists often use the symbol π for inflation and $E(\pi)$ for the *expected* inflation rate. As we will show shortly, each SRAS curve is associated with a particular rate of expected inflation, so the initial SRAS curve is labeled with $E(\pi) = 2\%$.

The rate of inflation that workers and producers expect is written $E(\pi)$.

FIGURE 32.12

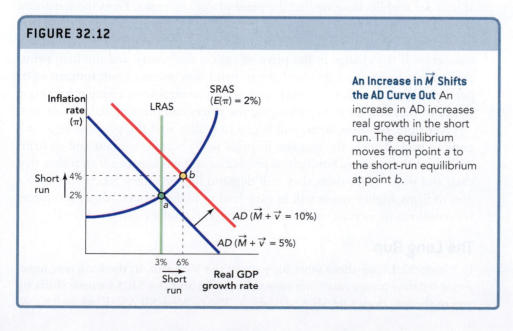

An Increase in $\vec{M}$ Shifts the AD Curve Out An increase in AD increases real growth in the short run. The equilibrium moves from point *a* to the short-run equilibrium at point *b*.

Now suppose that the growth rate of the money supply increases unexpectedly from 5% to 10%. The injection of more money into the economy increases AD, which, in turn, creates a temporary boom at point *b*. At *b* the economy is growing at a 6% rate of real growth with inflation of 4%. Notice that $\vec{M}$ has increased by 5 percentage points. Some of that increase in spending is reflected in the inflation rate, which increases by 2 percentage points, but some of the increase in spending is reflected in real growth, which increases by 3 percentage points. In the short run, an increase in spending growth is split between increases in inflation and increases in real growth.

To further explain how a spending increase can create a temporary increase in growth, let's return to our baker but now imagine that she owns a large bakery. An increase in spending encourages the baker to expand, so she offers her workers more overtime opportunities at a higher wage. At first the workers are pleased since they see that their nominal wage—the number on their paychecks—has increased. But as the workers spend their money, they discover that prices elsewhere in the economy are rising so much that even with the overtime, their wages are buying fewer goods and services than before—more work for less real pay! Although the workers' nominal wages have increased, their real wages—namely the amount of goods and services they can buy with that wage—have decreased. The workers' eagerness to work harder is what economists call a **nominal wage confusion**. Eventually, the workers will come to expect the higher inflation rate and they will demand even higher wages to catch up to the higher inflation rate, but in the short run an increase in spending can cause an increase in output.

Prices also don't move instantly to their new long-run equilibrium because it is costly to change prices. Economists call the costs of changing prices **menu costs** because an obvious example is the costs of printing new menus when a restaurant changes its prices. Catalog companies like Lands' End and L.L. Bean face similar costs for their mail order business. Menu costs also include the costs of upsetting customers with frequent price changes. Menu costs mean that businesses don't like to change prices every day or even every quarter, so price changes take time.

Firms may also not be sure whether a change in market conditions is temporary or permanent. If firms are unsure, they will hold off on changing prices, at least for a while. Imagine that the price of eggs increases. Does the restaurant change the price of an omelette? If the restaurant knew the price change was permanent, then it probably would. But maybe the price of eggs will decrease tomorrow. If the change in the price of eggs is temporary and the firm prints new menus today, it might also have to print new menus again tomorrow, or perhaps incur the risk that consumers search around for a cheaper breakfast. Better to wait and see before changing the prices and printing the new menus.

Over time, however, firms will begin to realize that the price of eggs isn't coming back down—the increase in price really was permanent and so firms will adjust their menus. Similarly, as prices rise and workers begin to realize that their real wage hasn't risen, they will demand higher wages. Since wages are a cost to firms, higher wages will in turn lead to higher prices. Wages and prices will continue to increase until the new long-run equilibrium is achieved.

The Long Run

In Figure 32.13, we show what happens in the long run. In the long run, *unexpected inflation always turns into expected inflation* and the SRAS curve shifts up and to the left; from Old SRAS ($E[\pi] = 2\%$) to New SRAS ($E[\pi] = 7\%$). As

Nominal wage confusion occurs when workers respond to their nominal wage instead of to their real wage, that is, when workers respond to the wage number on their paychecks rather than to what their wage can buy in goods and services (the wage after correcting for inflation).

Menu costs are the costs of changing prices.

FIGURE 32.13

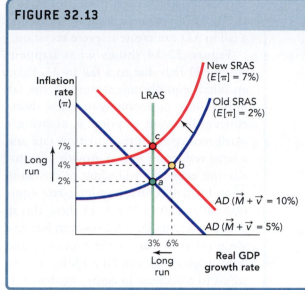

In the Long Run, Real Growth Eventually Returns to the Solow Rate In the long run the SRAS curve shifts upward as inflation expectations adjust and wages become unstuck. As a result, real growth will eventually return to the Solow rate as given by the LRAS curve and inflation will increase. In the long run, after all transitions are complete, the economy will end up at point c. In the long run, unexpected inflation always becomes expected inflation.

expectations and prices adjust, more and more of the increase in $\vec{M}$ is reflected in the inflation rate and less is reflected in the real growth rate. In the long run, after all transitions are complete, all of the increase in $\vec{M}$ is reflected in the inflation rate—$\vec{M}$ increases by 5 percentage points, the inflation rate increases by 5 percentage points, the growth rate returns to the Solow level, and the actual inflation rate comes to equal the expected inflation rate (7%). Thus, an increase in $\vec{M}$ increases real growth in the short run—during the period in which prices and wages are sticky.*

Here is a hint about shifting the SRAS curve. In the long run, people will always come to expect the actual inflation rate (you can't fool people forever), and in the long run, the inflation rate is found where the LRAS curve intersects the AD curve. In the long run, the economy must be on the LRAS curve, thus the SRAS curve is always moving toward the point where the LRAS curve intersects the new AD curve (point c in Figure 32.13). Notice that in the new long-run equilibrium, the inflation rate is 7% and the expected inflation rate is 7%. Also, in the long-run equilibrium at point c, growth is equal to the Solow rate—this reflects our intuition that in the long run, money doesn't influence real growth (money is neutral) but does influence the inflation rate (inflation is a monetary phenomenon).

We also see here a preview of several profound dilemmas in macroeconomic policy. Once we are at the new equilibrium at point c, consumers and producers are expecting an inflation rate of 7%, so to increase the real growth rate above the Solow rate once again, policymakers would have to increase the actual rate of inflation above 7%. Can you see how a policymaker might become trapped in a spiral of ever-increasing inflation rates? We will return to this issue in our chapter on Monetary Policy. Of course, you might ask why not just reduce aggregate demand and return to a lower inflation rate? Unfortunately, prices

The Short-Run Aggregate Supply Curve

interactive activity

---

* For the purpose of making the models simple, we've focused on showing the initial short-run change and then the long-run results, after all the necessary transitions and adjustments have worked their way through the system.

FIGURE 32.14

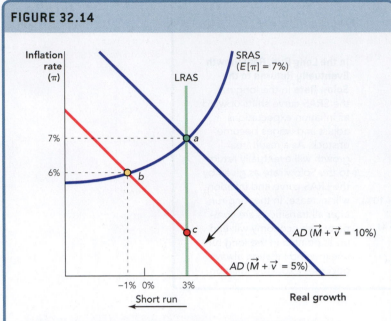

A Fall in Aggregate Demand Could Induce a Lengthy Recession At point *a*, spending is growing at a rate of 10% and real growth is 3% so inflation is 7%. Suppose spending growth decreases to 5%. In the short run, wages are sticky so although spending growth declines, wage growth does not. As a result, real growth falls to –1% and the inflation rate falls to 6% at point *b*. In the long run as wages become unstuck the economy will move to a new long-run equilibrium at *c* but getting to point *c* could take a lengthy recession.

Sticky Wages and the Parable of the Angry Professor

and wages adjust even more slowly to a fall in AD than to an increase in AD, so a fall in AD can create a severe recession.

Figure 32.14 shows what happens when AD falls due to a fall in $\vec{M}$. From an initial equilibrium at point *a*, the fall in AD shifts the economy to a new short-run equilibrium at point *b*, creating a small reduction in the inflation rate and a large reduction in real growth. Eventually, the economy will adjust to the fall in $\vec{M}$ and it will return to a long-run equilibrium at point *c*. We don't show this in detail in Figure 32.14, however, because we want to focus on the recession and why an economy can take a long time to adjust to a decrease in aggregate demand.

It takes time for a decrease in spending to make its way through the economy for all the reasons that we have already discussed in the case of an increase in spending: namely wages are sticky, menu costs and uncertainty make businesses reluctant to change prices immediately, and expectations take time to adjust. As a result, in the short run, a fall in spending growth is split between a fall in inflation rates and a fall in growth. Most economists, however, believe that prices and wages are especially sticky in the downward direction. Here is one phrase to keep in mind: Prices rise like rockets and fall like feathers.

No one likes to have his or her wages cut or even wage growth reduced, which is one reason that wages are especially sticky in the downward direction. In addition, large union contracts often fix wage growth for several years in advance. So imagine that prices have been going up by 5% and wages by 7% every year for a number of years. Contracts may even have been written guaranteeing wage growth of 7%. Now, however, the inflation rate falls to 2% a year. Workers are expecting wage increases of 7%, but if firms paid that amount, they would be unprofitable. Firms could cut wage growth to 4%, which would give workers the same increase in real wages of 2% that they had before, but how will workers feel when their salary increase is much less than expected? What will happen to morale and motivation? How will a union feel when the company tries to renegotiate its contract? Very often, morale goes down and the union threatens a strike. As a result, firms may find it easier to fire workers or reduce hours than to lower wages. In other words, a fall in aggregate spending will reduce the growth rate.

The economist Truman Bewley interviewed employers and labor leaders, asking them why wages don't fall during a recession. He concluded that the main reason employers don't like to cut wages is that if workers see smaller numbers on their paycheck, their morale declines and they often take their anger out on their employers. In contrast, layoffs get the misery out the door. As a result, a fall in aggregate demand can be very dangerous because wages can take a long time to fall, and during that time output declines can be especially large. This is one reason why we have drawn the SRAS curve so it is flatter to the left of the LRAS curve. A decrease in spending that requires expected wage growth to decrease will tend to create a large decrease in the growth rate.

Shocks to the Components of Aggregate Demand

We have already looked at how changes in $\overrightarrow{M}$ can create AD shocks. Now we consider the other term in our equation: $\overrightarrow{v}$. We can think of changes in $\overrightarrow{v}$ as increasing or decreasing the spending rate, holding the money supply constant. To understand why the spending rate might change, it's useful to recall the national spending identity, $Y = C + I + G + NX$. The national spending identity reminds us that spending is spending on something. For example, if $\overrightarrow{v}$ increases, that means the growth rate of C, I, G, or NX must increase—that is, an increase in $\overrightarrow{v}$ must be apportioned among an increase in $\overrightarrow{C}, \overrightarrow{I}, \overrightarrow{G},$ or $\overrightarrow{NX}$.

It's often easier to think about changes in $\overrightarrow{v}$ working through changes in $\overrightarrow{C}, \overrightarrow{I}, \overrightarrow{G},$ or $\overrightarrow{NX}$ because each of these factors has somewhat different causes and consequences. Let's look at a change in $\overrightarrow{C}$.

A Shock to $\overrightarrow{C}$

Why might $\overrightarrow{C}$ decrease? Fear could be one reason. Imagine that consumers suddenly become more pessimistic and fearful about the economy, as they did in 2008 when the banking system was in danger of collapse. The "animal spirits," to use the famous phrase of John Maynard Keynes, turn negative. Workers, for example, might be worried about becoming unemployed, so they decide to postpone buying a new car or remodeling their kitchen. The decrease in consumption purchases will temporarily reduce spending growth, $\overrightarrow{C}$. Let's look at Figure 32.15. We begin at point a with an inflation rate of 7%, an expected inflation rate of 7%, and a real growth rate of 3%. A decrease in spending growth, a negative AD shock, shifts the AD curve inward and to the left, reducing the real growth rate in the short run. With lower spending growth, wage growth should fall to match the reduction in price growth, but because wages are sticky, especially in the downward direction, wage growth remains high so firms are unprofitable, employment falls, and the economy slows.

Thus, in the short run, the economy moves from point a to point b, where the inflation rate is lower and the real growth rate is also lower—in this example at point b, growth is negative and the economy is in a recession.

Changes in $\overrightarrow{v}$ can be broken down into changes in $\overrightarrow{C}, \overrightarrow{I}, \overrightarrow{G},$ or $\overrightarrow{NX}$.

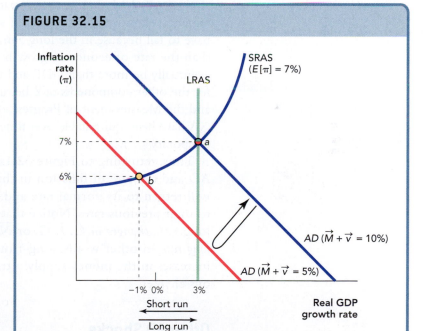

FIGURE 32.15

A Temporary Decrease in AD Reduces the Inflation Rate and the Growth Rate in the Short Run At point a, spending is growing at a rate of 10% and real growth is 3% so inflation is 7%. If consumers become fearful and reduce their spending, $\overrightarrow{v}$ declines so the AD curve shifts inward. In the short run, wages are sticky so although spending growth declines, wage growth does not. As a result, real growth falls to -1% and the inflation rate falls to 6% at point b. In the long run as fear recedes and wages become unstuck, $\overrightarrow{v}$ returns to its normal rate, as does real growth.

Changes in Velocity (and Shifts in the AD Curve)

In the long run, fear recedes, wages adjust, and the spending growth rate returns to normal so the economy returns to long-run equilibrium at point *a*. Let's explain the shift back of the AD curve in the long run in greater detail.

Why Changes in $\vec{v}$ Tend to Be Temporary

Changes in $\vec{v}$ (i.e., changes in the *growth rate* of C, I, G, or NX) differ from changes in $\vec{M}$ in one respect. $\vec{M}$ can be permanently set at any rate—5%, 17%, 103%—but changes in $\vec{v}$ tend to be temporary. How do we know this? Recall that in our example, consumers were worried about becoming unemployed, so they cut back on purchases like buying a new automobile, that is, a decrease in $\vec{C}$ in this period. In the next period, consumers might cut back on some other purchase, but as they cut back, the consumption that remains (like groceries and rent) becomes even more important and consumers stop cutting back. Also, as consumers cut back on consumption, their savings increase and they become more reassured about spending. Thus, if nothing else changes, consumption will return to its normal growth rate.

As another example, consider an increase in government spending to stimulate the economy (a strategy that will be discussed in our chapter on Fiscal Policy). An increase in spending will temporarily increase $\vec{G}$, shifting the AD curve out. The government can do this in the short run, but if $\vec{G}$ were to grow at an unusually high rate year after year, government purchases would soon dominate the economy. In fact, even if voters did not object, eventually $\vec{G}$ would have to fall because in the long run, government spending cannot grow faster than the rate of economic growth (otherwise, government spending would eventually be more than GDP, and that is not possible). The analysis is similar for the other components of Y because as we know from the chapter on GDP and the Measurement of Progress, the shares of GDP devoted to C, I, G, and NX have been quite stable over time, so changes in $\vec{C}, \vec{I}, \vec{G}$, or $\overrightarrow{NX}$ tend to be temporary.

Thus, returning to Figure 32.15, we show that a decrease in $\vec{C}$ reduces AD and the rate of inflation in this period. In future periods, however, $\vec{C}$ will return to its normal rate and, as it does, AD and inflation will return to their previous rates. Notice that because the AD curve shifts back in the long run, *changes in $\vec{C}, \vec{I}, \vec{G}$, or $\overrightarrow{NX}$ do not change the rate of inflation in the long run*. In other words, long-run or sustained inflation requires ongoing increases in the money supply, a truth we've already outlined in the previous chapter.

Other AD Shocks

We have already said that fear could decrease consumption spending (and, thus, confidence could increase consumption spending). What other factors could change $\vec{C}, \vec{I}, \vec{G}$, or $\overrightarrow{NX}$?

Fear and confidence play a similar role in investment spending as in consumption spending. If businesspeople fear that the economy is entering a recession, they may want to wait to make large investments in a new plant and equipment. Similarly, confidence about the future will encourage businesspeople to make significant investments.

Wealth shocks can also increase or decrease AD. Imagine, for example, that the stock market or the housing market tumbles. Before the fall in prices, consumers might have spent freely, expecting that in their retirement years or in an emergency they could sell their stocks or their homes and live on the proceeds. When prices fall, consumers suddenly realize that their wealth has fallen so that they now need to save more; thus, they cut back on their spending. In 2008, for example, a simultaneous fall in stock and housing prices caused a very large decrease in consumption spending. (A positive wealth shock works the opposite way. As the stock market rises, for example, consumers spend more today as their increasing wealth gives them confidence that they will have plenty in the future.)

Taxes are another important shifter of $\vec{C}$ and $\vec{I}$. An increase in taxes can reduce consumption growth and a decrease in taxes can increase consumption growth. Taxes targeted at investment spending—such as an investment tax credit—can have a similar effect on investment growth. Changes in taxes are also a part of fiscal policy to be studied in our chapter on Fiscal Policy.

Big increases in the growth rate of government spending will increase AD, and decreases in the growth rate of government spending will reduce AD. During a war, for example, government spending usually increases at a high rate, thereby shifting the AD curve outward. Government spending can also be timed to try to offset the business cycle. (Again, see our chapter on Fiscal Policy).

The category called net exports consists of exports minus imports. We look at exports and imports more closely in our chapters on International Trade and on International Finance, but for now the basic idea is simple. If other countries increase their spending on our goods (exports), that increases our AD. If we shift our spending away from domestic goods to foreign goods (imports), that reduces our AD.

Table 32.2 summarizes some of the factors that can shift the AD curve. Let's now apply the insights from the AD–AS model to understanding the so-called Great Depression, a watershed event in U.S. history.

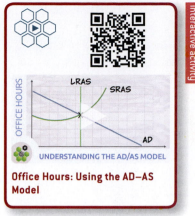

Office Hours: Using the AD–AS Model

CHECK YOURSELF

- What always happens to unexpected inflation in the long run?
- What happens to the aggregate demand curve if consumers fear a recession is coming and cut back on their expenditures.

TABLE 32.2 SOME FACTORS THAT SHIFT THE AGGREGATE DEMAND CURVE

Positive Shocks (Increase AD) (= Higher Growth Rate of Spending)	Negative Shocks (Decrease AD) (= Lower Growth Rate of Spending)
A faster money growth rate	A slower money growth rate
Confidence	Fear
Increased wealth	Reduced wealth
Lower taxes	Higher taxes
Greater growth of government spending	Lower growth of government spending
Increased export growth	Decreased export growth
Decreased import growth	Increased import growth

Understanding the Great Depression: Aggregate Demand Shocks and Real Shocks

The Great Depression (1929–1940) was the most catastrophic economic event in the history of the United States. GDP plummeted by 30%, unemployment rates exceeded 20%, and the stock market fell to less than a third of its original value. America went from confidence to desperation. In fact, the Great Depression was a worldwide event, plaguing almost all the developed nations. In some cases, such as Germany, the economic downturn led to totalitarian regimes followed by war. The 1930s and 1940s were terrible years for the world and bad economic policy was partly at fault.

Aggregate Demand Shocks and the Great Depression

The Great Depression occurred in the United States as follows. In 1929, the stock market crashed, creating a mood of pessimism among the American public. In part, this stock market crash had been brought on by a tight monetary policy, aimed at limiting a stock market bubble. The fall in stock prices was a wealth shock that made many people feel poorer and so they limited their spending, causing $\overrightarrow{C}$ to fall. This, combined with the initial monetary contraction, that is, a reduction in $\overrightarrow{M}$, reduced aggregate demand, shifting the AD curve inward to the left.

But that is only the beginning of the story. In 1930, depositors lost confidence in their banks and, as they withdrew their money, they created a wave of bank failures. These bank failures meant that people lost their money, again diminishing aggregate demand. Moreover, at the time there was no government deposit insurance so when the first banks failed, people became suspicious of other banks and rushed to withdraw their money even from banks that were otherwise sound. From 1930 to 1932, there were four waves of banking panics; by 1933, more than 40% of all American banks had failed.

The fear and uncertainty created by bank failures, rising unemployment rates, falling consumer confidence, and inconsistent policymaking in Washington also reduced investment spending. Between 1929 and 1933, for example, investment spending fell by nearly 75%. In many years, spending on new investment was not enough to replace the tools, machines, and buildings that had depreciated due to natural wear and tear. Astoundingly, the U.S. capital stock was lower in 1940 than it had been in 1930.[1]

Furthermore, in 1931, instead of increasing $\overrightarrow{M}$, the Federal Reserve allowed the money supply to contract even further. In the early 1930s, the U.S. money supply fell by about a third, *the largest negative shock to aggregate demand in American history.* At that time, the Fed should have been expanding the money supply to drive up output in an emergency situation and also to boost the reserves of failing banks (we analyze monetary policy further in the chapter on Monetary Policy). Instead, the Fed allowed the money supply to contract and a disaster ensued. Bad decision making caused an additional monetary contraction during 1937–1938, which led to yet another wave of economic distress. It made the Great Depression much longer than it needed to be.

Figure 32.16 shows the story in a diagram. In the late 1920s, the economy was growing at a rate of about 4% per year with no inflation. Starting in 1929, a

FIGURE 32.16

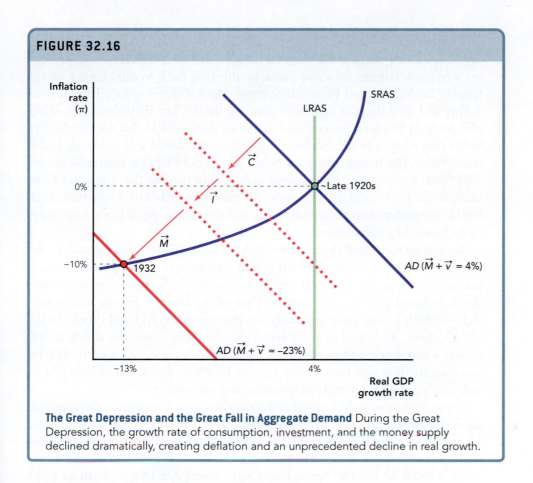

The Great Depression and the Great Fall in Aggregate Demand During the Great Depression, the growth rate of consumption, investment, and the money supply declined dramatically, creating deflation and an unprecedented decline in real growth.

series of brutal shocks to aggregate demand reduced $\vec{C}$, $\vec{I}$, and $\vec{M}$ and by 1932 pushed real growth to a rate of -13% and inflation to -10% per year. Note that although drawn separately, all these shocks were interconnected, as previously discussed.

To make all these problems worse, the decrease in aggregate demand caused prices to fall (as shown in the figure) and that, in turn, raised the real value of debts. One feature of virtually all loans is that they are denominated in terms of dollars, and the debt is not adjusted for inflation or deflation. So if a person or company has borrowed $10,000 and the price level falls by 10% (as it did in some of the Depression's worst years), the real, inflation-adjusted value of that debt burden is now 10% higher than before. That makes life more difficult for debtors, and many of them will not be able to meet their obligations and perhaps they will go bankrupt, disrupting the economy further. Furthermore, many debtors will spend less money, thereby decreasing aggregate demand even more than from the initial shocks. While the real income of creditor banks goes up for the same reason that the real value of the debt goes up, these banks don't have such a high propensity to spend or invest as do the desperate debtors, and so, the transfer of wealth from debtors to creditors still means that aggregate demand goes down.

Thus, the Great Depression was due primarily to the *great fall in aggregate demand*. Real shocks, however, also played a role in the Great Depression and in the failure of the economy to recover more quickly from the great fall. Let's take a look at how real factors contributed to the Great Depression.

Real Shocks and the Great Depression

We have already mentioned one real shock—the bank failures—and you can see why bank failures are a real shock by thinking back to our chapter on the Saving, Investment and Financial Systems. Bank failures reduced the money supply and spending (an aggregate demand shock), but they also reduced the efficiency of financial intermediation. As we discussed in that earlier chapter, banks play a key role in bridging the gap between savers and investors, and as banks failed, this bridge collapsed. Some firms could rely on internally generated funds for investment, and large firms could turn to the stock and bond markets for new funds. But many small businesses relied on loans from local banks that understood these businesses, and thus many small firms were especially harmed by bank failures.

To sum up the causal chain of events: A fall in $\vec{M}$ reduced aggregate demand, which led to bank failures, which led to a reduction in the productivity of financial intermediation, a real shock. As you would by now expect, the real shock reduced growth even further. One of the broader lessons of this episode—which is true more generally—is that shocks to AD and shocks to the LRAS curve are linked in most recessions. In some cases, the shock to AD creates a real shock, and in other cases, a real shock creates a shock to AD; for instance, the fear and uncertainty created by a real shock can reduce AD by inducing people to cut back on spending and investment.

Some economic policy mistakes during the Great Depression also impeded recovery. As we have already mentioned, the Federal Reserve failed to use its power over the money supply to increase aggregate demand. In addition, there were other policy failures. For example, the National Industrial Recovery Act (NIRA) and the Agricultural Adjustment Act (AAA), both of 1933, tried to combat falling prices not by increasing aggregate demand but by reducing supply. Under NIRA, businesses were encouraged not to invest in machinery (in order to keep labor demand high), and they were encouraged to raise prices by creating cartels. Under the AAA, the government paid farmers to kill millions of pigs and plow under cotton fields in order to increase prices. Neither of these policies is likely to have increased economic growth. The Supreme Court ruled in 1935 and 1936, respectively, that both laws were unconstitutional.

Most famously (but perhaps not most importantly) the Smoot–Hawley Tariff of 1930 raised tariffs (taxes) on tens of thousands of imported goods.[2] In principle, a tariff, by taxing foreign goods, can boost demand for domestic goods, thereby increasing AD. (Notice from our list of factors that can shift AD in Table 32.2, that a decrease in imports can increase AD.) In reality, retaliations against the Smoot–Hawley Tariff by other countries created a spiraling decline in world trade. When other countries raised their tariffs, U.S. exports fell. Remember that a reduction in exports reduces aggregate demand. Unfortunately, the large decline in world trade meant that the net effect of the tariff was to reduce aggregate demand.

In addition to being a shock to AD, a second negative effect of the tariff occurred because *a tariff is also a negative productivity shock.* We get the most output from our capital and labor when we specialize in fields in which we have a comparative advantage and then trade for the goods that we produce at a comparative disadvantage (see Chapter 2 for more on comparative advantage). A tariff pushes capital and labor into lower productivity sectors, thereby reducing total output. Another way of seeing this point is to recognize that a tariff has exactly the same effects as an increase in transportation costs. Therefore, a tariff is like a negative productivity shock to the shipping industry, which ripples out to all the other industries dependent on shipping.

As if these shocks were not enough, the United States was beset during the early years of the Great Depression by a natural shock, namely the onset of the so-called Dust Bowl. A severe drought and decades of ecologically unsustainable farming practices turned millions of acres of farmland in Texas, Oklahoma, New Mexico, Colorado, and Kansas to dust. Dust storms blackened the sky, reducing visibility to a matter of feet. Hundreds of thousands of people were forced to leave their homes and millions of acres of farmland became useless.

In a good year, the real shocks of the Great Depression could have been absorbed without major difficulty, but in a bad year, the shocks compounded one another and made a desperate situation even worse.

Understanding the Great Depression

Takeaway

We've covered a lot in this chapter, but the basic point is that the model of aggregate demand and supply can be used to analyze business fluctuations, fluctuations in the growth rate of real GDP.

Using our model, we laid out how to analyze two types of shocks, real shocks and aggregate demand shocks. Real shocks are analyzed through shifts in the LRAS curve. Aggregate demand shocks are analyzed using shifts in the AD curve.

When you combine the aggregate demand curve, long-run aggregate supply curve, and short-run aggregate supply curve into a single diagram, you can analyze a wide variety of economic scenarios and how they affect the growth rate of the economy. As you will see in future chapters, our model will also help us to explain when government policy can and cannot be used to successfully smooth business fluctuations.

The aggregate demand curve can be broken down into changes in $\vec{M}$ and $\vec{v}$, and slopes downward. In addition changes in $\vec{v}$ can be broken down into changes in $\vec{C}, \vec{I}, \vec{G}$, or $\vec{NX}$. Factors including nominal wage and price confusion, sticky wages, sticky prices, menu costs, and uncertainty create an upward-sloped short-run aggregate supply curve.

We outlined the history of America's Great Depression from the 1930s using our model. The Great Depression resulted from an unfortunate, concentrated, and interrelated series of aggregate demand and real shocks.

The material in this chapter is central to macroeconomics. If you understand where these curves come from and how to shift them, you will have a basic toolbox for many macroeconomic questions. You are now ready to tackle many of the core topics of macroeconomics and business cycles.

CHECK YOURSELF

■ What happened to the U.S. money supply in the early 1930s? Did this initially affect aggregate demand or the long-run aggregate supply curve, and in which direction?

■ If, as was said earlier in this chapter, real shocks hit the economy all the time, should we ignore them in explaining the Great Depression?

CHAPTER REVIEW

interactive activity Go online to practice with more examples of these types of problems, including live links to videos, data sources, and feedback.

Problems in **green** relate to MRU videos. See the MRU table at the end of the exercises.

Problems in **blue** are Office Hours videos.

KEY CONCEPTS

business fluctuations, p. 671

recession, p. 671

aggregate demand curve, p. 673

Solow growth rate, p. 676

long-run aggregate supply curve, p. 676

real shock, p. 677

aggregate demand shock, p. 682

short-run aggregate supply curve, p. 682

nominal wage confusion, p. 684

menu costs, p. 684

FACTS AND TOOLS

1. Sort the following shocks into real shocks or aggregate demand shocks. Remember that "shocks" include both good and bad events.

   A fall in the price of oil
   A rise in consumer optimism
   A hurricane that destroys factories in Florida
   Good weather that creates a bumper crop of California oranges
   A rise in sales taxes
   Foreigners watch fewer U.S.-made movies
   Fear
   New inventions occur at a faster pace
   A faster money growth rate

2. Look at Figure 32.2. Let's sum up some basic facts about the link between unemployment rates and recessions. Notice that the shaded bars indicate periods of recession, and wider bars mean longer recessions.

   a. How many recessions have there been since World War II?

   b. Since World War II, how many recessions had unemployment rates of over 10%?

   c. Often, the unemployment rate seems to peak after the recession ends: The economy goes back to growing, while the unemployment rate rises for a while. As the figure shows,

the recessions of 1990 and 2001 have been clear examples of such "jobless recoveries." Approximately how many times did the unemployment rate peak after the recession ended?

3. Look at Figure 32.5. When inflation rises, does the Solow growth rate rise, fall, or remain unchanged?

4. Are "real shocks" negative shocks, by definition?

5. When negative real shocks hit, what typically happens to the long-run aggregate supply curve: Does it shift left, shift right, or stay in the same place?

6. When negative real shocks hit, what typically happens to the aggregate demand curve? Does it shift left, shift right, or stay in the same place?

7. As Figure 32.1 implies, for the United States, the long-run aggregate supply curve has, on average, been approximately 3% real growth per year. If a negative real shock hits, shifting it by 2 percentage points, what will happen to real growth: Will it be positive or negative? Would you call the resulting economic conditions a recession?

8. a. What does a negative real shock do to inflation: Does it rise, fall, or remain unchanged?

   b. What does a negative real shock do to spending growth: Does it rise, fall, or remain unchanged?

   c. What does a fall in spending growth, that is, a shift inward of the AD curve, do to real growth: Does it rise, fall, or remain unchanged?

9. In the following cases, will real growth rise, fall, or remain unchanged?

   Expected inflation = 5%,
   Actual inflation = 7%
   Expected inflation = 3%,
   Actual inflation = 1%
   Expected inflation = 6%,
   Actual inflation = 6%
   Expected inflation = 7%,
   Actual inflation = −10%
   Expected inflation = −1%,
   Actual inflation = 0%

10. Consider the following figure. In this relatively unsuccessful economy, the Solow growth rate is 1% per year:

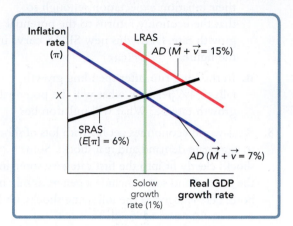

a. Calculate the inflation rate at *X* in this economy. (*Hint:* Use the quantity theory.)

b. If spending growth were 15% in this economy, what would the inflation rate be in the long run, assuming the Solow growth rate stays fixed?

11. a. The short-run aggregate supply (SRAS) curve is very predictable. When inflation is greater than people expect, SRAS eventually shifts (*choose one:* up, down) over the next year or so, and when inflation is less than people expect, SRAS eventually shifts (*choose one:* up, down) over the next year or so.

b. Here's another, equally valid way to look at the SRAS curve: When real GDP growth is above the Solow growth rate, SRAS eventually shifts (*choose one:* right, left) over the next year or so, and when real GDP growth is below the Solow growth rate, SRAS eventually shifts (*choose one:* right, left) over the next year or so.

c. Explain why the two ways of looking at the SRAS curve are equivalent.

THINKING AND PROBLEM SOLVING

12. Complete the following sentences:

With a real shock, when real growth is worse than usual, inflation is ___ than usual.

With an aggregate demand shock, when real growth is worse than usual, inflation is ___ than usual.

13. a. In the 1970s, the United States had slow growth and high inflation. Which kind of shock best fits these facts?

Negative real shock

Positive real shock

Negative aggregate demand shock

Positive aggregate demand shock

b. Using the same categories, explain the late 1990s, when the United States experienced fast growth and falling inflation.

c. Again using the same four categories, explain the early 2000s, when the United States experienced slow growth and falling inflation.

d. Which shock best explains the 1981–1982 recession, when inflation fell quickly and unemployment rose quickly?

e. Which shock best explains the Great Recession of 2007–2008?

14. To keep things simple, let's put this into a familiar supply and demand story and assume that in the long run, workers offer a fixed supply of labor: In other words, while they may be picky about jobs in the short run, in the long run they'll work regardless of the going wage.

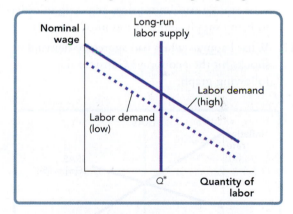

It's the businesses who *demand* labor and workers who *supply* labor. Currently, let's assume the economy starts off at long-run equilibrium, so that the normal number of workers, *Q**, are working.

a. Suppose labor demand falls, shifting to the left, as in the figure. What does the short-run supply curve for labor look like if workers refuse to take pay cuts even if it means losing their jobs (we can call this the "take this job and shove it" strategy after the famous country and western song). Indicate your answer by drawing a new line on the figure, labeling it "Short-run labor supply." You only need to focus on the area to the left of $Q^\star$.

b. Recalling your basic supply and demand model, does this fall in labor demand then create a "surplus" of workers or a "shortage" of workers?

c. According to the basic supply and demand model, what will happen to the price of labor over time as a result of this fall in labor demand?

15. a. If the media report a lot of good news about the economy, what is likely to happen to velocity?

b. If the Federal Reserve wants to keep aggregate demand (i.e., spending growth) stable, what will it do to the growth rate of the money supply when a lot of good news comes out about the economy: increase it, decrease it, or leave it unchanged? (*Hint:* In practice, central bankers often call this "leaning against the wind.")

16. After a monetary shock hits aggregate demand, which curve will shift to bring output growth back to the Solow growth rate: the short-run aggregate supply curve or the aggregate demand curve? (*Hint:* Which curve is more like a microeconomic story about prices adjusting in order to bring supply and demand into balance?)

17. What happens when bad aggregate demand shocks hit the economy? Consider the following graph.

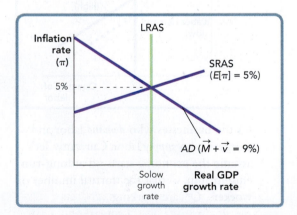

a. Before we get to the bad aggregate demand shock, let's find out what the potential growth rate is in this economy. Use the quantity theory to find your answer.

b. Because of a fall in the growth of the money supply, spending growth falls to 4% per year. Draw the immediate result on aggregate demand in the graph.

c. This fall in money growth lasts for many years. Eventually, in the long run, workers, business owners, and consumers all adjust their inflation expectations enough so that the economy returns to the potential growth rate. Draw this new SRAS curve in the figure.

d. In the long run, after spending growth falls to 4% per year, what will the potential growth rate be? What will inflation be?

18. Real-world economies get hit with lots of shocks to aggregate demand and real shocks. Some shocks clearly fit into the first category, some into the second, and some include a generous mix of both. Let's categorize the following shocks. Only one is a clear case of "both."

Steelworkers go on strike, so less steel is produced.

Businesses read about the glories of mobile commerce, so demand for high-tech investment purchases increases.

U.S. senators read about the glories of the Internet, so demand for high-tech government purchases increases.

A series of investment banks like Lehman Brothers and Bear Stearns go bankrupt.

Around 2000, the glories of the Internet fade a bit so innovations increase at a somewhat slower rate for a few years.

The U.S. government launches two costly wars almost simultaneously, so government purchases increase dramatically (referring to World War II, of course).

The U.S. government launches two costly wars almost simultaneously, using the draft to force many men to work much longer hours and supply more labor than they would otherwise.

19. Let's have some practice with the aggregate demand curve. If you want to draw it in your familiar $y = b + mx$ format, you can think of it this way:

Inflation = (Growth in money + Growth in velocity) − Real growth

a. When you look at a fixed aggregate demand curve, like the one in Figure 32.3, what is being held constant? (choose one):

Spending growth (growth in M + growth in v)

Real GDP growth (growth in Y)

Inflation (growth in P)

b. When you look at a shifting aggregate demand curve, like the one in Figure 32.4, what *had* to change to make the curve shift? (*choose one*):

Spending growth (growth in $M +$ growth in v)

Real GDP growth (growth in Y)

Inflation (growth in P)

c. According to the quantity theory, which of the following statements *must be* false, and why? More than one may be false.

"Last year, spending grew at 10%, real growth was 4%, and inflation was 6%."

"Last year, spending grew at 4%, real growth was -2%, and inflation was 6%."

"Last year, spending grew at 100%, real growth was 0%, and inflation was 20%."

"Last year, spending grew at 5%, real growth was 5%, and inflation was 2%."

"Last year, spending grew at 10%, real growth was 5%, and inflation was -5%."

20. In the aggregate demand and supply model, what is "sticky"? More than one may be true: wages, real growth, prices, velocity, money growth, unemployment.

21. During the Great Depression, which of the following were mostly aggregate demand shocks and which were mostly negative real shocks?

The fall in the growth rate of money

The fall in farm productivity

The Smoot–Hawley Tariff Act

22. Recall that $Y = C + I + G + NX$.

a. If government spending increases then we model that as an increase in:

i. v.

ii. M.

iii. Q.

iv. T.

b. An increase in G shifts the AD curve:

i. inwards.

ii. outwards.

iii. doesn't move the AD curve.

iv. shifts the LRAS curve.

c. A shift outwards in the AD curve will tend to:

i. increase inflation, reduce growth.

ii. decrease inflation, increase growth.

iii. decrease inflation, decrease growth.

iv. increase inflation, increase growth.

CHALLENGES

23. Here is a puzzle. A country with a relatively small positive aggregate demand shock (a shift outward in the AD curve) may have a substantial economic boom, but sometimes countries that have massive increases in the AD curve (hyperinflation countries like Germany before World War II, e.g.) don't seem to have massive economic booms. Why does a small AD increase sometimes raise GDP much more than a giant AD increase?

24. Some companies raise their workers' pay by giving raises, but others prefer to give one-time bonuses instead. Think about two steel mills facing a big two-year drop in steel demand: In one steel mill, workers have received pay raises every year for five years. In the second mill, most of the pay increases have occurred through big bonuses at the end of each year. Which steel mill will probably keep more jobs during the two-year downturn? Why? Would you draw a perfectly vertical curve, a curve with a positive slope, or a curve with a negative slope?

25. Reconsider your answer to Facts and Tools question 3. If you wanted to draw the long-run aggregate supply curve accurately, taking into account the idea that very high rates of inflation are likely to reduce real growth, how would you draw the long-run aggregate supply curve?

26. a. If aggregate demand shocks are the most important drivers of business fluctuations, then should we expect real wages to be procyclical (rising when GDP growth is high) or countercyclical (rising when GDP growth is low)?

b. If real shocks are the most important drivers of business fluctuations, then should we expect real wages to be procyclical or countercyclical?

c. Macroeconomists find mixed evidence on the link between business fluctuations and inflation. But there's more agreement on the link between business fluctuations and real wages: The real wage is procyclical, growing quickly during good times and growing slowly or falling during bad times. Which of the two shocks (real or aggregate demand) is this most consistent with? (We'll revisit this question in the next chapter.)

27. Often, more than one kind of shock hits the economy at once. When this happens, the different shocks *could* push inflation (or real growth) in different directions in the short run, leaving the final short-run result ambiguous. What is most likely to happen to inflation and real output growth in the following cases: Will they rise or fall, or can't you tell with the information given? Note that you will often (maybe always) be able to definitely know the answer for one but not the other.

a. A nation's scientists invent many new Internet search tools, raising current productivity and making investors optimistic about future inventions as well.

b. A government raises taxes and its economy experiences a year of excellent weather for growing crops.

c. Oil prices skyrocket and the central bank slows the rate of money growth.

28. Use Figure 32.11 as a starting point for this problem and consider the initial impact of the following circumstances on the aggregate demand, long-run aggregate supply, and short-run aggregate supply curves.

a. A war in the Middle East rapidly increases the price of oil.

b. More and more consumers develop a fear that they are in danger of losing their jobs and businesses fear that they are in danger of losing their customers.

c. Add to this set of problems the uncertainty that a new administration introduces by pushing through significant social reform expected to increase business costs and reduce consumers' discretionary income.

29. Continuing from your short-run results in the previous problem, what do you believe will happen in the long run as these adjustments work their way through the economy?

30. A significant productivity slowdown occurred during the 1970s and 1980s. A large part of it occurred in industries closely related to the energy crises of the 1970s. (Besides the "Oil Shocks" section in this chapter, you can read a brief summary about these developments in the *NBER Digest*, http://nber.org/digest/jun05/w10950.html.)

a. Use the aggregate demand and supply model to show the effects of the energy crises and productivity slowdown on the economy if spending growth remains unchanged.

b. Suppose that unaware of the productivity slowdown at the time, monetary authorities increased the growth rate of money in order to stimulate spending growth, or AD, and boost employment. What impact would this have on the economy?

c. Review Figures 32.1, 32.2, and Figure 2 from the previous chapter and determine if it seems like the scenario described in this problem might have been possible. Why?

31. Following the productivity slowdown discussed in question 30, the U.S. economy experienced a relatively quick transition to the electronic age of computers and the Internet, and many of the outward effects of the 1970s energy crises faded as a result.

a. Use the aggregate demand and supply model to show the effects of widespread computer and Internet usage on the economy if spending growth remains unchanged.

b. Suppose that velocity increases due to greater consumer confidence because of your findings in part a. First, does greater consumer confidence make sense? Why?

c. Second, how will this affect inflation and GDP growth in the long run?

WORK IT OUT

interactive activity

For interactive, step-by-step help in solving this problem, go online.

From the equation of exchange, $MV = PY$, we know that spending growth $(\vec{M} + \vec{v})$ equals Inflation (π) + Real growth. Recall from the chapter that in the long run (1) the inflation rate is found where the AD curve intersects the LRAS curve (reading off the vertical axis) and (2) the expected inflation rate is found where the short-run aggregate supply curve intersects the LRAS curve. With these things in mind, assume that the Solow growth rate is 3% and answer parts a through d.

a. If spending growth equals 10%, what will π equal in the long run? What will $E\pi$ equal?

b. If spending growth equals 6%, what will π equal in the long run? What will $E\pi$ equal?

c. If spending growth equals 4%, what will π equal in the long run? What will $E\pi$ equal?

d. What can we say about inflation π and expected inflation $E\pi$ in the long run?

MARGINAL REVOLUTION UNIVERSITY VIDEOS

The Aggregate Demand Curve

mruniversity.com/AD-curve

Problems: **1, 19**

The Long-Run Aggregate Supply Curve

mruniversity.com/LRAS

Problems: **1, 5, 7, 8**

The Short-Run Aggregate Supply Curve

mruniversity.com/SRAS

Problems: **11, 16**

Sticky Wages and the Parable of the Angry Professor

mruniversity.com/sticky-wages

Problems: **14**

Changes in Velocity (and Shifts in the AD Curve)

mruniversity.com/AD-AS-velocity

Problems: **22**

Understanding the Great Depression

mruniversity.com/AD-AS-depression

Problems: **21**

OFFICE HOURS

OFFICE HOURS: Using the AD–AS Model

mruniversity.com/AD-AS

Problems: **27**

33

Transmission and Amplification Mechanisms

I n the previous chapter, we explained the basics of the aggregate demand–aggregate supply model. The driving forces in that model were real shocks (shifts in the long-run aggregate supply curve) and aggregate demand shocks (shifts in the AD curve). In this chapter, we explain in greater detail how economic forces can amplify shocks and transmit them across sectors of the economy and through time. When a shock is amplified, a mild negative shock can be transformed into a more serious reduction in output and a positive shock can be transformed into a boom. In addition, we will show in this chapter how real shocks and aggregate demand shocks can interact—one type of shock can lead to the other, for example.

We focus on five transmission mechanisms: intertemporal substitution, uncertainty and irreversible investments, labor adjustment costs, time bunching, and shocks to collateral and net worth, which we call collateral damage.

Intertemporal Substitution

Let's go back to our farm example from the previous chapter. We showed that when the weather fluctuates, so does output and therefore so does GDP, especially in agricultural economies such as India. Once again, Figure 33.1, on the next page, shows how rainfall shocks are correlated with the growth rate of agricultural output (Panel A) and GDP (Panel B) in India.

When rainfall is below average, the same capital and labor inputs produce less agricultural output—that is the direct effect of the negative rainfall shock. But the shock to GDP is caused not simply by less rainfall but also by how people respond to less rainfall. If rainfall is below average, for example, farmers may work less hard and devote less capital to their fields.

Why would farmers choose to use less labor and capital in response to a negative shock? Think about it this way: When the crops are bountiful, it makes sense to work from dawn till dusk because each hour of additional work pays a lot—remember the old saying, make hay when the sun shines? But when the crops are poor, the returns to an additional hour of work are low and so farmers may rationally decide to work less. The same is true for applications of

FIGURE 33.1

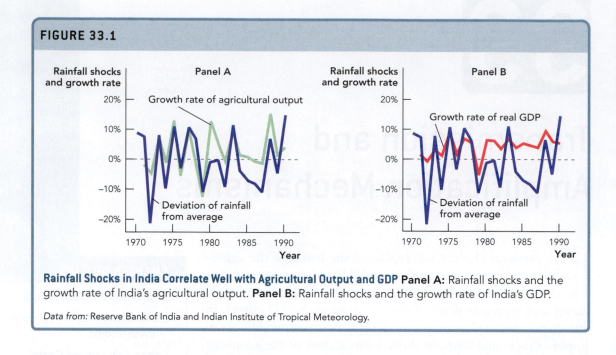

Rainfall Shocks in India Correlate Well with Agricultural Output and GDP **Panel A:** Rainfall shocks and the growth rate of India's agricultural output. **Panel B:** Rainfall shocks and the growth rate of India's GDP.

Data from: Reserve Bank of India and Indian Institute of Tropical Meteorology.

Intertemporal substitution is the allocation of consumption, work, and leisure across time to maximize well-being.

capital. When planted crops will blossom, it may be worth paying the fuel costs to run the tractor an extra hour. When planted crops will in any case wither, why bother spending the money on fuel? Just leave the tractor in the shed.

Economists call this effect **intertemporal substitution**. The term means that a person or a business is most likely to work hard when working hard brings the greatest return. We work hard in some times and rest in others, and of course we pick and choose the spots when we try hardest. We are substituting effort across time and thus the expression *intertemporal substitution*.

When you study for a test, do you practice intertemporal substitution or do you study an equal amount every day? As a test approaches, you probably study harder, turning down some opportunities for fun. Once the test is over, you study less and have more fun. Intertemporal substitution means that when you study, you study a lot, and when you party, well, you know.

Intertemporal substitution, however, is not just about substituting between work and leisure. We pointed out in Chapter 1, for example, that when jobs are plentiful and wages are increasing, there is a tendency for fewer people to enter college, but when jobs are scarce and wages are stagnant, more people decide to invest in an education. Students understand that the opportunity cost of getting an education falls when jobs are scarce.

During a boom, people are less likely to retire or take early retirement—why not stay another year or two and bank the high wages? Similarly, homemakers and other people who might otherwise not work will choose to enter the workforce during boom periods. During recessions, people are more likely to take early retirement or focus on homemaking. Figure 33.2 shows that when GDP is growing faster than trend, the employment to population ratio also tends to grow faster than trend. The implication is that the supply of labor increases in a boom and falls during a recession.

Intertemporal substitution at work during World War II.

FIGURE 33.2

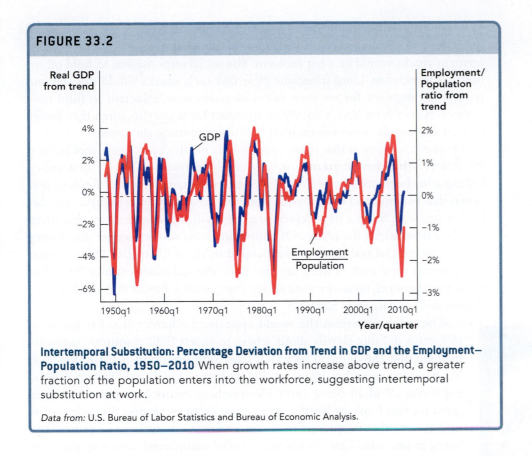

Intertemporal Substitution: Percentage Deviation from Trend in GDP and the Employment–Population Ratio, 1950–2010 When growth rates increase above trend, a greater fraction of the population enters into the workforce, suggesting intertemporal substitution at work.

Data from: U.S. Bureau of Labor Statistics and Bureau of Economic Analysis.

Notice that intertemporal substitution magnifies negative economic shocks. When things go a bit bad, the return to work and investing fall, and often people work less and invest less, which makes things go just a little worse. The ripple effects of this process help turn an initial shock into a broader recession. Of course, on the upside, intertemporal substitution can feed an economic boom and make it more intense. If things are going well, many people will be inclined to work harder, which will in turn increase output and make things go even better. Figure 33.3 shows how intertemporal substitution amplifies shocks to the long-run aggregate supply (LRAS) curve. Intertemporal substitution is hardly the only force behind employment decisions (see our chapter on Unemployment and Labor Force Participation) but it does play a role in magnifying shocks, both on the upside and the downside.

Let's turn to another transmission mechanism, uncertainty and irreversible investments.

Uncertainty and Irreversible Investments

Negative shocks also increase uncertainty, which is bad for business investment. Bad news usually also means uncertain news, since the arrival of the bad news causes people to rethink how the world works. For instance, when the

FIGURE 33.3

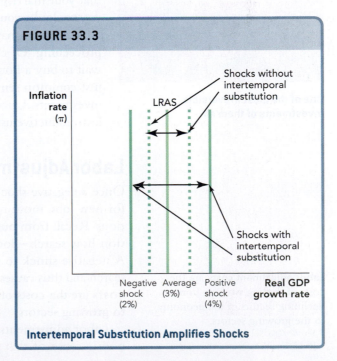

Intertemporal Substitution Amplifies Shocks

9/11 attacks hit the United States, uncertainty about the future increased. All of a sudden many people started worrying—rightly or wrongly—that subsequent terrorist attacks would be a big problem. The initial response was to hold off on business investment. Until it became clear that such attacks would not become regular occurrences, for instance, many investors were reluctant to fund new construction in New York City. When investors are uncertain, often they prefer to wait and sample more information before committing themselves.

The key idea here is that many investments involve sunk costs, that is, they are **irreversible investments**, or very costly to reverse. Once a new office building has been constructed on Wall Street, for example, it is difficult to tear down that building and redeploy the steel and glass to other economic uses. So, before investors build a new skyscraper, they will try to make sure that there will be a demand for the offices. Of course, investors sometimes get this wrong, just as commercial real estate overexpanded in the mid- to late 1980s, or too many homes were built in the years preceding the real estate crash of 2007. But prior to expansion, investors want to see many strong signals that market conditions will validate their plans.

Irreversible investments have high value only under specific conditions—they cannot be easily moved, adjusted, or reversed if conditions change.

The more uncertain the world appears, the harder it is for investors to receive definite signals about where to invest their resources. Investors may see that the demand to watch television programs is shrinking, as it has been for years, but investors do not know which new sectors will be expanding. Will all those extra TV-watching hours be replaced by time spent on Facebook or Netflix, or by time spent outdoors? When investors wait to see what happens, that means resources are sitting idle rather than being productive. That means lower GDP and it contributes to the economic slowdown.

To see the logic of irreversible investment, consider the decision to marry. Marriage is a kind of investment and not just in the financial sense. It is a commitment to the future and it is often for a very long period. Given the seriousness of this commitment, you ought to make (relatively) sure that your marriage is a good idea. If you receive some information causing you to doubt your potential partner (did someone hint he or she is a convicted felon?), maybe you should wait a while and discover the truth before proceeding. Of course, if you wait to decide on marriage, you may also wait to buy a house together, even if buying a house is a good idea. That's just common sense. The point is that the same logic applies to economic investments. Uncertainty usually slows investment and keeps resources in less-productive uses.

One of the most irreversible investments of them all

TIM TADDER/GETTY IMAGES

Labor Adjustment Costs

Once a negative shock hits the economy, labor must adjust. Workers must look for new jobs, move to new areas, and sometimes change their wage expectations. Recall from our chapter on Unemployment and Labor Force Participation how search—looking for a new job—is one reason for unemployment. A negative shock to the economy, by remixing opportunities, induces more search and thus causes more search-related unemployment. **Labor adjustment costs** are the costs of shifting workers from declining sectors of the economy to growing sectors.

Labor adjustments to shocks are not always rational in the narrowly economic sense of that term. If an automobile worker is laid off the General

Labor adjustment costs are the costs of shifting workers from declining sectors of the economy to the growing sectors.

Motors assembly line and he loses his formerly unionized job, he may not be able to find the same wage elsewhere. Currently, the less unionized automakers in the United States pay a lower hourly wage than the more unionized GM. Some automobile workers without a high school degree may make up to $100,000 per year. It may take a while for that person, if thrown out of work, to admit that he must settle for a lower wage. In the meantime, he is looking for a job and perhaps even rejecting offers that are as good as he will ever find.

The high cost of reversing job decisions can lead to unemployment, just as the costs of reversing investment can cause investors to wait. Again, consider the closure of a Detroit automobile plant and the fate of the former workers. These workers face at least three options: They can wait for the plant to reopen, they can seek another job in Detroit, or they can move to a more prosperous part of the country. Which course of action is best?

It's not always easy to say which choice is best, yet the choice involves a costly-to-reverse decision. Once the house is sold and the belongings are packed and moved to Houston, it is costly to go back to Detroit. The unemployed autoworker, rather than moving to Houston, might wait for a while to see what happens, even if he knows the probability of finding a job in Houston is higher than in Detroit. Or if that person opens up a pet shop, it will be difficult to shift back into automobile manufacture. So, when faced with these uncertainties, many workers simply bide their time until the future is clearer. Maybe they'll do some part-time or casual work (or maybe they'll put a new deck on the house), but they probably won't be employed at full productivity. The result is ongoing unemployment, or at least underemployment, and again the initial negative real shock is magnified.

In sum, changes to the world require people to adjust their jobs and their careers. People can't always make those adjustments right away, and in the meantime output and employment will be lower than normal.

Time Bunching

People often bunch their activities at common points in time. Most people work from 9 AM to 5 PM rather than from 10 PM to 6 AM. One reason is that these are daylight hours, but another reason is because everyone else is working during this time. If you and your coworker are in the office at the same time, it is easier to collaborate. Furthermore, working is more fun when you do it with other people.

We also like to party at the same time and to see movies and concerts with other people. It's not just a question of fun—it is also economics. If you want to cook an elaborate meal, order some fancy bottles of wine, or clean up the house for a party, you want to make sure that enough people attend for those efforts to be worthwhile.

Most generally, many economic activities **bunch** or **cluster in time** because it pays to coordinate your economic actions with those of others. That just means that we want to be investing, producing, and selling at the same time that others are investing, producing, or selling. In short, economic activity tends to cluster together in time just as it clusters together in space. (What do we call a cluster of economic activity in space? A city.)

Bunching occurs across different time frames. There is bunching across the course of a single day; GDP grows more during the 9-to-5 hours than late

Time bunching is the tendency for economic activities to be coordinated at common points in time.

at night, for example. But there is also bunching across weeks, months, and quarters. The "seasonal business cycle" is one form of economic clustering in time. The fourth quarter of the year—October through December—brings more economic activity than any other time. Production is higher, sales are higher, and GDP grows faster, relative to the other parts of the year. After Christmas is over, however, the party ends and GDP in the next period is typically lower. GDP also tends to grow slowly during the summer months. The point is not that we should abolish Christmas or summer vacation, but rather that seasonal cycles help us understand some features of regular business cycles.

Once some economic activity is moving in the upward or downward direction, other parts of economic activity tend to follow that momentum in order to gain the advantages of time bunching. The clustering of economic activity in time makes buying and selling more efficient, but it also causes shocks to spread through the economy and to spread through time. Let's say that a negative economic shock arrives and the economy slows down in the current period. Many people are less keen to work, and they will save up their working for some point in the future (intertemporal substitution, as discussed earlier). This effect will induce others to cut back on their work as well. If the Indian farmers work less when the weather is bad, then tractor salespeople will probably work less as well. Similarly, if fewer people are showing up at the office, you might be less productive as well. You'll be more likely to stay home and more likely to make your big work effort during some other period, perhaps when you expect the office to be up and running at full speed. So if some people retreat from full-speed work, these decisions spill over onto others and cause them to cut back their effort as well.

Collateral Damage

"For whoever has, to him shall be given; and whoever has not, from him shall be taken even that which he seems to have" (Luke 8:18). In the parable of the lamp, Jesus was talking about knowledge but the message also applies to banking. Banks like to lend to people who already have lots of money. When banks lend to firms, for example, they typically will insist that the firm have some cash on hand, strong assets, and positive net worth (assets > debts). As a rule, banks are more concerned about downside risk than upside gain because if the firm does poorly, the bank could lose the entire value of its loan, but if the firm does incredibly well (like Google), the bank simply gets its loan back plus interest. Banks, therefore, don't make a lot of investments in startups or firms with debts that exceed assets.

The bank's incentives make sense for the bank, but for the economy as a whole this type of behavior amplifies booms and busts. Consider a firm that makes televisions and that wants to expand into manufacturing computer monitors. The market for monitors is growing, the firm has expertise in electronics, and it has good contacts with retailers. The firm writes a business plan and applies to a bank for a loan. The firm is making lots of profits in its television division and, as a result, it has high net worth. The firm's net worth acts like a kind of **collateral** for the bank—a cushion or guarantee that even if the monitor division fails, the firm will still have cash to pay back the loan. Satisfied that the loan is safe, the bank makes the loan.

Collateral is a valuable asset that helps to secure a loan. If the borrower defaults, ownership of the collateral transfers to the lender.

Now consider the same scenario during a recession. As before, we will assume that the market for computer monitors is growing and the firm, of course, still has the same expertise in electronics and contacts with retailers. What differs now is not the potential profitability of the monitor division. What differs is that the firm's television business is not going so well and, as a result, the firm has lower net worth and the bank has lost its safety cushion, a **collateral shock**. The bank now evaluates the loan as risky and says no. Moreover, now that the firm cannot expand into monitors, a growing field, it is left with a dying television division and it ends up going bankrupt and firing its workers. For whoever has, to him shall be given; and whoever has not, from him shall be taken.

More generally, during a boom, asset prices are increasing and firms have cash flow. As a result, banks are willing to approve more loans, which makes the boom even bigger. But as an economy enters the downward phase of business cycles, asset prices fall, cash flow is reduced, and firms have lower net worth. Lenders see loans as being riskier and they cut off or restrict credit. This process drives more firms under, thereby increasing joblessness and making the bust worse.[1]

This scenario is a good example of how real shocks and aggregate demand shocks can reinforce and amplify one another. In general, the real shock mechanisms in this chapter involve lower wealth, greater risk, and greater difficulties of adjustment, in various combinations. Those same economic problems will mean lower consumer spending, less business investment, and also less borrowing and lending, all factors that will feed into lower aggregate demand.

Collateral shocks also affect consumers. Say John bought a house near Orlando, Florida, one center of the recent real estate bubble, for $200,000. As was common practice at the time, suppose that John paid no money down, so he borrowed the entire purchase price, $200,000, from a bank. Once the real estate bubble burst and home prices fell, that same house suddenly was worth $120,000. Because the value of John's house is now less than what he owes on it, John is said to be "underwater," or, to use the term from our chapter on the Saving, Investment, and Financial System, John has negative equity in the house. It's difficult to get an exact estimate, but around the year 2010, nearly 20% of all American homes were underwater to some degree.

Now imagine that John receives a job offer in Houston, Texas, where the economy isn't as depressed as in Orlando. It's hard to rent out the Orlando house but it's also hard to sell it. If John sells the house, he has to pay roughly $200,000 back to the bank (the exact sum depends on how long ago the loan was taken out and how many payments the buyer has made in the interim). Yet the sale yields only $120,000, or less if you take brokerage commissions into account. In other words, John has to come up with $80,000 or more in cold hard cash. For a lot of people, that's extremely difficult to do, especially during a recession. The end result is that the move to Houston does not happen and John does not take the better job. "Underwater" positions make moving more difficult and the adjustment of the economy to business cycles is therefore slower.

An alternative scenario is that John takes the job in Houston and "mails in the keys." In other words, John defaults on his mortgage. The home, as a financial asset, has a value of negative $80,000 to John so walking away makes

A **collateral shock** is a reduction in the value of collateral. Collateral shocks make borrowing and lending more difficult.

financial sense. John is better off but the bank is worse off. That is a transfer of wealth, but the problem is worse than this.

Few people make the choice to default right away. But if John is even thinking that he might default in the near future, does he take tender, loving care of the flowers and garden? Does he check carefully for cracks in the walls and ceilings and have them repaired promptly? Does he scout out a good real estate agent to sell his home? Or does he have lots of wild parties and trash the place?

We are sorry to say that a lot of trashing goes on ("Incentives Matter"). This is an extreme example, but one San Diego cop was "underwater" in his real estate position. He and his wife responded by tearing off doors, light fixtures, countertops, decorative beams, bathroom vanities, air conditioners, and appliances, either to take away or for the sheer pleasure of destruction. They also poured black dye on the carpets and spray painted all of the walls. The total damage to what was once a lovely six-bedroom house was estimated at over $200,000. One neighbor noted: "It didn't hit me until they asked for the sledgehammer that they were going way beyond damage."[2]

Very often, by the time default comes, the value of the home has declined sharply. It is common for instance that when banks have to foreclose, the bank loses 25% or even more of the value of that home.[3] It's also true that the value of other homes in the neighborhood declines when there are a lot of foreclosures nearby. In the wake of the recession in the summer of 2010, about one of 12 houses with mortgages below $1 million were in foreclosure, so that is a lot of wealth being dissipated.

ZUMA PRESS, INC./ALAMY

The one-time owners of this foreclosed-upon house in California vandalized it before leaving. Will the vandals end up in hot water?

An owner's **equity** is the value of the asset minus the debt, $E = V - D$.

The Great Recession

The general lesson is that when the nominal owner of a property doesn't have much **equity** in the property, very often he or she doesn't do a good job taking care of the property. The lesson applies to more than just homes. We've already talked about how the bank loses on these deals, so what happens if a bank made too many bad loans to too many insolvent homeowners? Well, then it's not just the home with low capital value—the bank itself has low capital value or sometimes it is said that the bank is thinly capitalized. And what do we know about individuals or organizations with low capital value? Return to the sentence earlier in this paragraph: "When the nominal owner of a property doesn't have much equity in the property, very often he or she doesn't do such a good job taking care of the property."

In other words, when the bank itself is "underwater" or nearly so, the bank managers don't do a very good job of taking care of the bank. No, they don't usually take out a sledgehammer, but there are other ways of eroding the capital value of a bank. Bank employees won't see the bank as a place for a career if it is tottering and, as a result, they won't invest in their relationship with the bank or its customers. The managers will fail to build up new business opportunities and they will take dubious risks, all in the knowledge that since the bank is already on the verge of destruction, they don't have to worry about the downside so much. Bank employees take the same "nothing left to lose" attitude as our defaulting homeowner. The banks with low capital values will not be run very well because there is little value to protect and the chance of "foreclosure" on the bank—in this case, called bankruptcy—is fairly high. Banks in this situation are commonly referred to as "zombie banks," and, indeed, during 2009–2010 the number of bank failures reached an all-time high.

The net result is this: When asset prices fall, there is a lot of collateral damage.

Takeaway

In sum, at least five factors amplify economic shocks and help bring about business downturns. Those factors are labor supply and intertemporal substitution, uncertainty and irreversible investment, labor adjustment costs, the desire to bunch or cluster economic activity together in time, and collateral shocks. The core lesson is this: A medium-sized negative economic shock is capable of causing a disproportionately large downturn in economic production and employment.

CHECK **YOURSELF**

■ Immediately after 9/11, most U.S. companies eliminated business travel temporarily. After a few weeks, business travel started to pick up again. Which transmission mechanism came into play? Go through as many aspects of business travel as you can think of: air travel, transportation to and from airports, hotel stays, meals out, contact with people remaining back in the office. Explain how the unexpected near-cessation in business travel amplified the original shock.

CHAPTER REVIEW

interactive activity   Go online to practice with more examples of these types of problems, including live links to videos, data sources, and feedback.

 Problems in green relate to MRU videos. See the MRU table at the end of the exercises.

KEY CONCEPTS

intertemporal substitution, p. 702

irreversible investments, p. 704

labor adjustment costs, p. 704

time bunching, p. 705

collateral, p. 706

collateral shock, p. 707

equity, p. 708

FACTS AND TOOLS

1. Take a look at Figure 9 in the previous chapter. In the last few decades, what has usually happened to the price of oil just before or during a recession?

2. When oil price shocks force people to switch jobs, how much GDP are they producing when they are out of work?

Ask FRED

3. Banks require a valuable asset, or collateral, to be pledged to secure a loan. Using the FRED economic database (https://fred.stlouisfed.org/), find the chart for the Percent of Value of Loans Secured by Collateral for Commercial Banks.

a. In the years prior to 2014, what was the (approximate) average percent of loan value secured by collateral?

b. In 2016, what was the average percent of loan value secured by collateral?

c. What does this change indicate about how willing commercial banks were to lend in 2016 compared to earlier years?

4. When an investment is irreversible, are you likely to a decision about it in a hurry or wait until more information comes in?

5. When do you want to study for a test: when your friends are studying for the same test or when they are not? How can this help explain seasonal business fluctuations?

6. If the long-run aggregate supply curve increased because of a sudden fall in the price of oil, what would happen to inflation? Assume that spending growth (aggregate demand) does not change—only the LRAS curve shifts. Draw the shift in the following figure. (*Note*: In the real world, this happens fairly often. Big declines in the price of oil happened in 1986 and again in 1998, and the price of oil fell by 50% in late 2008.)

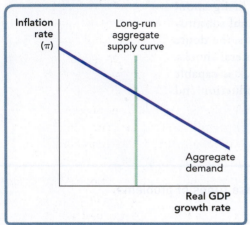

7. Office buildings have a boom-bust cycle every day. At what hours of the weekday do grocery stores have an economic boom? What days of the week do shopping malls have an economic boom?

THINKING AND PROBLEM SOLVING

8. In India, the economy grows faster when there's a lot of rain and grows more slowly when there is a drought. This creates big fluctuations in the economy. If the government wrote laws to smooth out these fluctuations by paying people to work more in the dry years and by taxing people so that they would work less in the heavy-rain years, would that make the average Indian better off? Why or why not? (Keep your answer in mind during the next recession, when pundits and politicians recommend tax breaks to encourage more hiring.)

9. **a.** According to Figure 10 in the previous chapter, about how long does it take for an oil price shock to have its biggest impact on the economy? How long does it take before the oil shock's effects completely go away?

b. What might be happening in the labor market that might explain why it takes so long for an oil shock to do its worst?

(Glance through the transmission mechanisms listed in the chapter for some ideas.)

10. When would a restaurant owner prefer to open a new restaurant: one year after an oil shock hits or two years after the oil shock hits?

11. How is marriage like a decision to build a new factory? Which decision is easier to reverse?

12. **a.** Who would you be more likely to hire at your company: someone who has stayed in the same career for years, or someone who tries an entirely new career every time he or she becomes unhappy with their job?

b. How does this help explain why workers are reluctant to quickly move on to a new career when they get laid off?

13. People sometimes use the expression, "Kicking the can down the road." It refers to putting a big decision off until later—it's almost (but not quite!) a synonym for procrastinating, and it's usually used in a negative sense. "Fred graduated and decided to spend a year waiting tables in New York. Grad school? He's kicking the can down the road on that one." What economic idea is equivalent to "kicking the can down the road," and how can it be a good thing?

14. As we note in the chapter, an oil price shock will probably increase the size of an oil-centered city like Houston, Texas. During the time that people are moving to Houston, looking for jobs, and switching jobs to find the best job possible, do you think GDP will be lower than usual or higher than usual? (Try focusing on the *production* part of GDP in answering this question.)

15. Can you think of some reasons why the following examples of time bunching and intertemporal substitution might be true? (Yes, you'll notice that there's a blurry line between the two.)

a. People who work outside work more when the weather is good.

b. People work when others are also working.

c. Even nonreligious people who don't give gifts shop more as Christmas time approaches.

d. Food servers at a restaurant prefer to work the dinner shift.

What do all of these examples have to do with the business cycle?

16. Consider the following economic events. Which of them will have the effect of amplifying a negative real shock and which are intended to offset a shock?

  a. Several large financial institutions become insolvent as a housing bubble bursts and subprime mortgages begin to default in large numbers.

  b. Many financial institutions begin issuing fewer loans and increasing their excess reserve holdings in anticipation of higher default rates on existing loans.

  c. The Federal Reserve expands the money supply and lowers interest rates.

  d. Instead of building for future demand, home builders delay their usual building so they can wait and see whether demand increases.

  e. As unemployment rises, consumers begin cutting back on their expenditures and paying down personal debt.

  f. The government passes a stimulus package increasing spending on roads and other infrastructure.

  g. Firms accumulate cash reserves and delay expansion projects pending the outcome of potential government actions influencing business conditions.

  h. Students decide to stay in college for longer periods of time due to the poor job market, and older workers retire early.

Ask FRED

17. When a borrower fails to make a scheduled payment on a mortgage, the mortgage is called delinquent. Delinquency is the first step toward foreclosure. Using the FRED economic database (https://fred.stlouisfed.org/), find the chart for the Delinquency Rate on Single-Family Residential Mortgages in the United States.

  a. What was the approximate delinquency rate in a typical year prior to the 2008–2009 recession?

  b. What was the peak delinquency rate and when?

  c. What was the delinquency rate in 2016? Compare this rate to prerecession levels.

CHALLENGES

18. In 1971, Intel invented the first computer microprocessor. In early 1993, the National Center for Supercomputing Applications released the first Web browser, Mosaic (which later became Netscape). Both inventions seem like good news, and both inventions created great uncertainty about which business models would succeed in the future: They were game changers. Would these uncertainty-creating inventions encourage businesses to make massive investments quickly, or would they encourage businesses to wait a few years to see how it all pans out?

Boyan Jovanovic and his coauthors discuss this topic in several papers. For an introduction, see Bart Hobijn and Boyan Jovanovic, 2001. The information-technology revolution and the stock market: Evidence. *American Economic Review* 91(5): 1203–1220.

19. For the sake of the economy, should the government ban Christmas and instead encourage people to give gifts throughout the year? Why or why not?

20. How is the previous question similar to this question: Should the government encourage people to move from the East and West coasts to the Midwest and Rocky Mountain states, where the population is less dense?

21. Do workers *choose* to work more *because* wages are temporarily high and do workers *choose* to work less *because* wages are temporarily low? This is key to the "intertemporal substitution" story of this chapter. The following chart shows how much wages change in the short run: Except in the 1970s, the moves are almost always in a 2% range, running from 1% higher than average to 1% lower than average.

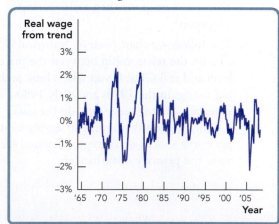

So, when wages move up or down for a year or two, does the number of Americans working move in the same direction at the same time? Let's see. The following economic simulation is based on actual U.S. data and shows how a 1% rise in wages usually impacts the number of Americans employed. Sometimes the effect is bigger than this, and sometimes smaller, but this is the average.

In practice, a 1% rise in wages apparently causes a 0.2% rise in the number of Americans with jobs. It takes nine months for this to happen.

How much would wages have to rise to raise employment by 1% or 2%, according to these estimates? (*Note:* This is roughly how much employment rises during a boom.) Is this "wage-channel" effect large enough to explain most of the job fluctuations we see during real-world business cycles?

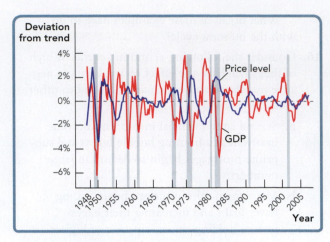

(*Data from:* U.S. Bureau of Economic Analysis and author calculations.)

(*Data from:* Impulse-response function based on author's calculations.)

22. a. If long-run aggregate supply shocks do largely explain business fluctuation, while the aggregate demand curve mostly stays fixed, then should prices be higher than usual or lower than usual during a recession?

b. The following chart portrays historical U.S. data on the relationship between the price level and real GDP. If you take a look at the big swings in the 1970s and early 1980s, especially during recessions, do the data roughly suggest that long-run aggregate supply curve shocks or aggregate demand shocks were the primary disturbance?

23. In the context of this chapter, identify what each of the following scenarios has in common and explain how they will affect an economy suffering from a recession.

a. Joe and Julie married, saved, and bought a modest home several years ago when housing prices were rising. They love their home and its location, are now expecting their second child, and need more space. Financially, they can afford a larger house payment, or a second mortgage, but their bank has informed them that despite their significant down payment, they are ineligible for a home equity loan because the current value of their home has declined to below the balance on their mortgage.

b. A bank has many potential borrowers with good prospects but due to problems with previous real estate loans, it has begun to build up its excess reserves in order to strengthen its balance sheets in the event of defaults on those assets.

c. A car dealership finds itself in the path of a tornado that destroys all of its stock of both used and new cars. Sales have been good because the recession has mostly spared this region of the country, but the dealership's insurance does not cover weather-related events and the dealer now has no assets and a negative net worth.

Ask FRED

interactive activity

24. Capacity utilization is an estimate of how close an economy is to its maximum output, defined as the highest level of output sustainable given its resources. Using the FRED economic database (https://fred.stlouisfed.org/), search for a series on capacity utilization and graph it.

a. Capacity utilization has never been measured at 100%. Why might an economy be at less than 100% capacity utilization even in good times?

b. What was the capacity utilization level in January of 2008 and what about in June of 2009?

c. What was happening to unemployment between January of 2008 and 2009?

d. Suppose that wages are sticky but that other prices are flexible. Comment on how sticky wages may contribute to reduced capacity utilization.

WORK IT OUT

interactive activity

For interactive, step-by-step help in solving this problem, go online.

In the chapter, we discussed how intertemporal substitution can amplify a boom by causing people to work more and by causing more people to work (while the reverse is true in a recession). Capital is also subject to intertemporal substitution. For example, it's possible to run a factory at close to capacity in one period, while putting off maintenance to a later period. How do you think capacity utilization varies across the business cycle? Is capacity utilization procyclical (varies positively with GDP) or countercyclical (varies negatively with GDP)?

MRUNIVERSITY
AN ONLINE EDUCATION PLATFORM

MARGINAL REVOLUTION UNIVERSITY VIDEOS

Five Minutes on Real Business Cycle Theory

mruniversity.com/rbc

Problems: **6**

The Great Recession

mruniversity.com/great-recession

Problems: **16**

CHAPTER 33 APPENDIX

Business Fluctuations and the Solow Model

A way of summarizing some of the lessons of this chapter is that at least some business fluctuations are just economic growth in the short run. Economic growth happens in fits and starts rather than smoothly. The economists Finn Kydland and Edward Prescott developed key aspects of the real business cycle (RBC) model in the 1980s and were awarded the Nobel Prize in 2004 for their work. One advantage of thinking about business fluctuations in this way is that they can then be analyzed using a version of the Solow growth model called the real business cycle (RBC) model. A complete understanding of the real business cycle model requires quite a bit of advanced mathematics, but we can briefly describe the main ideas. Consider the following production function, which is just like that used in our chapter on Growth, Capital Accumulation, and the Economics of Ideas but with the addition of labor as well as capital:

$$Y = A_t \times F(K, L)$$

To recap, output Y is a function of the inputs of capital K and labor L. In the earlier chapter, we talked about the A factor as an index of ideas. Better ideas mean a larger A, which means that more output can be produced from the same inputs of capital and labor. That is a good interpretation of A in the long run, but we can also think about A as representing *any* factor that influences the productivity of K and L. Thus, if Y is the output of corn, then A could be deviations of rainfall from the average. Above-average rainfall, say, $A = 2$, means that the inputs of K and L produce a lot of corn. Below-average rainfall, say, $A = \frac{1}{2}$, means that the same inputs of K and L produce less corn.

When we are thinking about long-run economic growth, it doesn't hurt to simplify and think about A as increasing smoothly through time. To analyze business fluctuations, however, we need to recognize that A jumps around. Thus, in the business fluctuation, or RBC, model, A is a productivity shock variable.

The second complication we need to add to the Solow growth model to analyze business fluctuations is to give a more sophisticated account of investment and labor supply. In the Solow growth model, investment is a simple function of output, Investment $= \gamma Y$, where the investment rate γ is a constant proportion like 0.3. That's not a very realistic assumption. Will savers and investors want to invest the same proportion of output during a recession as during a boom? Probably not, for the reasons we discussed in the chapter (uncertainty, for example). How do savers and investors decide how much and when to invest? This is a complicated decision that requires savers and investors to forecast future events. Solving this problem is difficult, which is where the complicated mathematics come in, but we know that γ will vary over time.

Similarly, in the growth version of the Solow model, we assumed that L was population and that L was fixed. (It's also easy to think about L as increasing slowly and steadily.) But in the short run, we need to recognize that workers may choose to enter or exit the workforce and choose to take jobs or search for work—intertemporal substitution. As a result, L becomes the labor force and

L can change due to changes in the participation rate and the unemployment rate. How do workers decide how much and when to work? Again, this is a complicated decision that requires workers to forecast the future and carefully optimize.

Adding shocks to the Solow model and giving a more sophisticated account of how savers, investors, and workers make decisions create what is known as the real business cycle model or the standard "neoclassical" model of business cycles. The intuitive account of business fluctuations that we have given in this chapter is based on this model.[*]

Explaining a full RBC model is too advanced for this appendix, but we recall that we showed how to simulate the Solow model using Excel in the appendix to our chapter on Growth, Capital Accumulation, and the Economics of Ideas. We can easily modify that model to include productivity shocks. Figure A33.1 shows our Excel model with a new column (column B) labeled A. Excel's RAND( ) formula creates a random number between 0 and 1. If we want a number between X and Y, we can write $= \text{RAND}()(Y - X) + X$. We will use our random number as a productivity shock A_t, so we want a number that can be a little bigger than 1 or a little smaller than 1. Thus, when we get a random number that is greater than 1, that is a positive productivity shock (output increases), and when we get a random number that is less than 1, that is a negative productivity shock (output decreases). Thus, we input into cell $B2 = \text{RAND}()(1/0.95 - 0.95) + 0.95$, which creates a random number between $1/0.95$ and 0.95; over many draws this random number is designed so that it will average out to 1. We now modify our output formula in D2 so it reads $= B2 \star C2^{\wedge}(1/2)$; in other words, we multiply the contribution of capital ($C2^{\wedge}1/2$) by the productivity shock A_t, which we generated in column B.

FIGURE A33.1

	B2	▼	f_x =RAND()*(1/0.95-0.95)+0.95							
	A	B	C	D	E	F	G	H	I	J
1	Time	A	Capital K	Output	Investment	Depreciation	Capital Growth	Y Growth	Investment Share γ	Depreciation δ
2	1	0.956905382	200	13.53	4.06	4.00	0.06		0.3	0.02
3	2	0.967909022	200.06	13.69	4.11	4.00	0.11	1.17		
4	3	0.983678593	200.17	13.92	4.18	4.00	0.17	1.66		
5	4	0.952410981	200.34	13.48	4.04	4.01	0.04	-3.14		
6	5	1.018061434	200.37	14.41	4.32	4.01	0.32	6.90		
7	6	1.036326744	200.69	14.68	4.40	4.01	0.39	1.87		
8	7	0.976878889	201.08	13.85	4.16	4.02	0.13	-5.64		
9	8	0.990237834	201.22	14.05	4.21	4.02	0.19	1.40		
10	9	0.963290803	201.41	13.67	4.10	4.03	0.07	-2.68		
11	10	0.994149412	201.48	14.11	4.23	4.03	0.20	3.22		
12	11	1.041301257	201.68	14.79	4.44	4.03	0.40	4.80		
13	12	1.028858954	202.08	14.63	4.39	4.04	0.35	-1.10		
14	13	0.995156067	202.43	14.16	4.25	4.05	0.20	-3.19		
15	14	0.953711687	202.63	13.58	4.07	4.05	0.02	-4.12		
16	15	0.984056799	202.65	14.01	4.20	4.05	0.15	3.19		
		⋮								
377	376	0.997989023	225.44	14.98	4.50	4.51	-0.01	3.46		
378	377	0.973955736	225.42	14.62	4.39	4.51	-0.12	-2.41		
379	378	1.032046001	225.30	15.49	4.65	4.51	0.14	5.94		
380	379	0.961868177	225.44	14.44	4.33	4.51	-0.18	-6.77		
381	380	0.982599886	225.27	14.75	4.42	4.51	-0.08	2.12		

[*] For a more complete but still accessible explanation of this model, see Plosser, Charles I. Summer 1989. Understanding real business cycles. *Journal of Economic Perspectives* 3(3): 51–77.

This model works very much like the Solow model in our chapter on Growth, Capital Accumulation, and the Economics of Ideas, but now the random shocks increase or decrease growth around the average Solow growth rate. Figure A33.2, for example, simulates 100 periods of the Solow model around the equilibrium output of 15. Notice how shocks can generate business fluctuations.

FIGURE A33.2

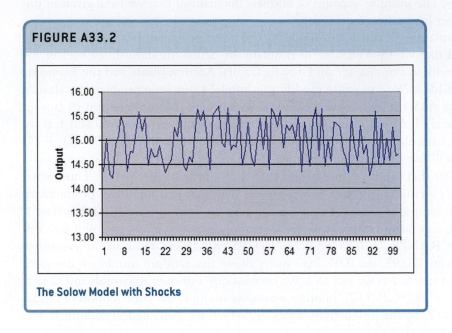

The Solow Model with Shocks

34

The Federal Reserve System and Open Market Operations

I magine that you wanted to borrow $2 *trillion*. Whom would you ask? In 2008, the worldwide financial system was in a crisis and banks and other financial institutions wanted to borrow more than $2 trillion—they turned to the only person in the world capable of lending that kind of money, a mild-mannered, former professor of economics named Ben Bernanke. As chairman of the Federal Reserve System (the Fed), Bernanke was sometimes said to be the second most powerful person in the world, after the president of the United States. Bernanke was able to make the loans because he could draw on the awesome power of the Federal Reserve Bank to create money.

What is the Federal Reserve? How does it create money? What does it use its power for?

If you read this chapter, you'll come away with an understanding of the Federal Reserve and its powers. The quick and dirty answer is that through its influence over the money supply, the Federal Reserve usually has more influence over aggregate demand than any other institution and shifts in aggregate demand can greatly influence the economy in the short run (as we first showed in our chapter on Business Fluctuations). So, let's take a look at the Federal Reserve System first, then examine what is meant by the money supply, and finally focus on the tools that the Fed uses to influence the money supply, aggregate demand, and the economy.

What Is the Federal Reserve System?

The Federal Reserve acquires its unique powers through its ability to issue money. Open your wallet or your purse and take a look at some bills. At the top, you will see the words "Federal Reserve Note." In the past, many banks issued their own bank notes, which were used as money. But today the money we use in the United States is provided by just one bank, the Federal Reserve. Thus, the Federal Reserve has the power to create money—an awesome power that forms the centerpiece of this chapter. The Fed doesn't have to literally print money. It can, as we shall see, also create money "by computer" by adding

717

reserves to bank accounts held at the Fed. This new money can then be lent out in a way that increases aggregate demand.

If the Federal Reserve is a bank, who are its customers? The Fed is both the government's bank and the banker's bank. As the government's bank, the Fed maintains the bank account of the U.S. Treasury. When you write a check to the IRS to pay your taxes, the money ends up in the Treasury's account at the Fed. In addition to receiving money, the U.S. Treasury also borrows a lot of money and the Fed manages this borrowing—that is, the Fed manages the issuing, transferring, and redeeming of U.S. Treasury bonds, bills, and notes. Since the U.S. Treasury is by far the world's largest bank customer—it has more income and it also borrows more than any other bank customer—the Federal Reserve is a large and powerful bank.

In addition, the Fed is also the bankers' bank. Large private banks keep their own accounts at the Fed—in part, because some banks are required to hold accounts with the Federal Reserve and in part because other banks and financial institutions want a safe and convenient place to hold their money. The Fed also regulates other banks and it lends money to other banks. Finally, the Fed manages the nation's payment system—the system of accounts that makes it possible to write checks from one bank to another—and it protects financial consumers with disclosure regulations. Many of these and other duties are shared with other state and federal agencies.

Now that we know what the Fed is, let's turn to its most important function: regulating the U.S. money supply. But first we have to understand what the money supply is.

The U.S. Money Supplies

Just about everyone expects to be paid in money. If you show up with money—at least in its appropriate form—hardly anyone will turn you away. In other words, **money** is a widely accepted means of payment.

Money is a widely accepted means of payment.

But money is more than cash. Cash, or currency, is paper bills and coins, which serve as a quick and efficient way of making small transactions. But currency is not so useful for larger transactions, especially between businesses. Often it is easier to pay by check or debit card (which can be thought of as an electronic check) or by credit card (and then pay your bill later by check). For larger purchases, you might transfer money from a savings account to a checking account and then pay by check or debit. All these means of payment are money but they are not currency.

The most important assets that serve as means of payment in the United States today are:

1. Currency—paper bills and coins.

2. Total reserves held by banks at the Fed.

3. Checkable deposits—your checking or debit account.

4. Savings deposits, money market mutual funds, and small-time deposits.

Figure 34.1 shows the magnitude and proportions of the major means of payment in the United States (there are also some smaller items, such as traveler's checks, that we have omitted).

Let's say a few words about each of these means of payment. Currency is coins and paper bills (Federal Reserve Notes) held by people and nonbank firms. If you look at the total for currency (almost $1.4 trillion) and divide it

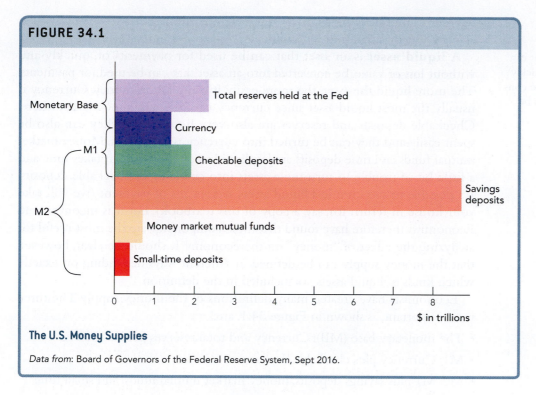

FIGURE 34.1

The U.S. Money Supplies

Data from: Board of Governors of the Federal Reserve System, Sept 2016.

by the American population (about 322 million), that amounts to about $4,300 per person (and even more per adult). Who has this much cash on hand? Of course, some of the money is in cash registers and some drug dealers do hold a lot of cash, but the real explanation for why so much U.S. cash exists is that quite a bit is used in other countries. Panama, Ecuador, and El Salvador all use the U.S. dollar as their official currency, as do some other small nations like the Republic of Palau. Dollars are also used unofficially in many other unstable countries as a means of preserving and protecting wealth. When Iraqi dictator Saddam Hussein was captured, he had $750,000 in U.S. hundred dollar bills in his hideaway.

"Total reserves" held by banks at the Fed is the means of payment you probably don't have personal experience with, but total reserves play a very important role in the financial system. All major banks have accounts at the Federal Reserve System—accounts that they use for trading with other major banks and for dealings with the Fed itself. It's not currency in these accounts but electronic claims that can be converted into currency if the bank wishes.

Checkable deposits are just like they sound, namely deposits that you can write checks on or can access with a debit card. These are the sorts of deposits we use most often in making daily transactions. Often these are also called demand deposits because you can access this money "on demand."

The largest means of payment are savings accounts, money market mutual funds, and small time deposits (also called certificates of deposit or CDs). Each of these components can be used to pay for goods and services, but typically with a little bit of extra work or trouble. Payments from a savings account can be made, for example, by first transferring the money to a checkable account. A money market mutual fund is a mutual fund invested in relatively safe short-term debt and government securities. Money market mutual funds typically allow you to write some number of checks per year or you can always sell part of your fund and transfer the money to a checkable account. Small time deposits cannot be withdrawn without penalty before a certain time period has elapsed, usually six months or a year.

A **liquid asset** is an asset that can be used for payments or, quickly and without loss of value, be converted into an asset that can be used for payments. The more liquid the asset, the more easily it can serve as money. Currency is usually the most liquid asset since currency can be spent almost everywhere. Checkable deposits and reserves are also very liquid, since they can also be spent easily and they can be turned into currency without loss. Money market mutual funds and time deposits are less liquid since sometimes it takes time and a little bit of trouble to turn these assets into currency or checkable deposits. It's possible to use even less liquid assets as a means of payment (we will take your house in return for, say, a copy of this textbook), but it is inconvenient. Economists therefore have found that these components are the most useful for analyzing the effect of "money" on the economy. It should be clear, however, that the money supply can be defined in different ways depending on exactly which kinds of liquid assets are included in the definition.

> A **liquid asset** is an asset that can be used for payments or, quickly and without loss of value, be converted into an asset that can be used for payments.

Economists have created many definitions of the money supply. The three most important, as shown in Figure 34.1, are:

- The monetary base (MB): Currency and total reserves held at the Fed
- M1: Currency plus checkable deposits
- M2: M1 plus savings deposits, money market mutual funds, and small time deposits

The Fed has direct control only over the monetary base. But it's the other components of the money supply—M1 and M2—that have the most significant effects on aggregate demand. As we will discuss later in the chapter, the Fed can increase bank reserves, but if the banks aren't lending, the increase in reserves won't do much to increase aggregate demand.

More generally, the central bank tries to use its control over MB to influence M1 and M2, but there are many other influences on M1 and M2 so each monetary aggregate can shrink or grow independently of the others. The Fed ultimately wants to steer aggregate demand, but once again its steering is sometimes wobbly because, although M1 and M2 influence aggregate demand, there are also other influences.

To understand how the Fed influences M1 and M2 but also why its influence is sometimes tenuous, we must introduce the concepts of fractional reserve banking, the reserve ratio, and the money multiplier.

Fractional Reserve Banking, the Reserve Ratio, and the Money Multiplier

When you open a bank account, the teller doesn't take your money and put it into a box labeled with your name. Instead, the bank holds a *fraction* of your account balance in reserve—hence the term **fractional reserve banking**—and it uses the rest of your money to make loans.

Banks earn profit on these loans. So do you. Competition among banks to attract your funds means that if the bank lends out your money and charges 5% interest, the bank must share some of that return with you. The bank will pay you, say, 2% for providing the money that they lend. The bank doesn't just pay you interest, it also gives you useful services like check writing and check clearing, which are in part funded from bank profits on loans. Of course, you

> Under **fractional reserve banking**, banks hold only a fraction of deposits in reserve, lending the rest.

don't get the full 5% return because the bank is bearing the risk on the loans, plus paying the costs of making the loans and monitoring the loan borrowers.

How much does the bank keep in reserve and how much does it lend? On one hand, banks need to keep some reserves around. In part, the law and the Federal Reserve require them to keep some reserves. More important, banks need those reserves to meet ordinary depositor demands for currency and payment services. Who would patronize a bank where the ATM was always empty? On the other hand, banks don't want to hold too many reserves because money held in reserve isn't being lent and lending is how banks earn most of their profits. Thus, there are opportunity costs to holding onto reserves. Banks balance these benefits and costs and thus they decide on the ratio between reserves and deposits. We define the **reserve ratio, RR,** as the ratio of reserves to deposits. If $1 in cash is held in reserve for every $10 of deposits, the reserve ratio is 1/10.

The **reserve ratio, RR**, is the ratio of reserves to deposits.

The reserve ratio is determined primarily by how liquid banks wish to be. When banks are worried that depositors might want to withdraw their cash or when loans don't seem so profitable anyway, they want a reserve ratio that is relatively high; when banks aren't worried about depositors demanding cash and when loans are profitable, they want to have a relatively low reserve ratio.

It's also useful to work with the inverse of the reserve ratio, called the **money multiplier, MM.** The money multiplier is the ratio of deposits to reserves, or in this case 10. Why is it called the money multiplier? Imagine that the Federal Reserve creates $1,000 of new money by crediting your bank account with an additional $1,000. Does that sound incredible? In fact, the Fed can create new money at will either by printing it or—the more modern method—by adding numbers to bank accounts held at the Fed. As we shall see, the Federal Reserve creates billions of dollars in just this way on a regular basis. So let's imagine that your bank account has been credited with an additional $1,000. Your bank now has $1,000 in extra reserves, but remember that banks don't want to keep all of their depositors' money in reserve. Banks make a profit by lending so now that your bank has extra reserves, it will also feel comfortable making more loans. To restore its reserve ratio to 1/10, your bank will want to keep $100 in reserve and make additional loans of $900. So let's say it lends $900 to Sam.

The **money multiplier, MM**, is the amount the money supply expands with each dollar increase in reserves. $MM = 1/RR$.

Now here's where it gets tricky. You have an extra $1,000 in your account but in addition Sam now has an extra $900 in his bank account, which we will assume is held at another bank. Now Sam's bank has an extra $900, but it too doesn't want to hold all of its new money in reserves so it will keep $90 in reserve and make $810 in new loans—thus, the bank's reserve ratio stays at 1/10. The process does not stop there as Sam's bank now lends money to Tom and Tom's bank lends money to Dick and . . . well you get the idea. This process keeps going through a ripple effect as one bank increases its loans, leading to an increase in deposits in another bank, which in turn increases its loans, which leads to an increase in deposits in another bank, which increases its loans . . . and so forth.

What is the end result of the ripple process? There are two ways to see the end result, the long way and the shortcut. We are going to save the long way for the appendix. Here's the shortcut. If banks want a reserve ratio of 1/10, then when the Federal Reserve increases reserves by $1,000, deposits must ultimately increase by $10,000. Now remember that the money multiplier is the inverse of the reserve ratio, or 10. Did you notice that deposits eventually

The U.S. Money Supplies

interactive activity

increase by the increase in reserves *multiplied* by the money multiplier? That's why it's called the money multiplier.

Let's summarize: The money multiplier tells us how much deposits expand with each dollar increase in reserves. If the money multiplier is 10, for example, then an increase in reserves of $1,000 will lead to an increase in deposits of $10,000. Since checkable deposits are part of the money supply (M1 and M2), we can also say that an increase in reserves of $1,000 increases the money supply by $10,000. Thus, we have

$$\textbf{Change in money supply} = \textbf{Change in reserves} \times \textbf{Money multiplier}$$
$$\text{or}$$
$$\Delta MS = \Delta \textbf{Reserves} \times \textbf{MM}$$

How the Fed Controls the Money Supply

Now that we have seen what the money supply is and why the money multiplier multiplies a change in reserves, let's look at the two major tools the Fed uses to control the money supply. These are:

1. Open market operations—the buying and selling of (usually) short-term U.S. government bonds on the open market

2. Paying interest on reserves held by banks at the Fed

Let's look at each in turn.

Open Market Operations

Suppose that the Federal Reserve wants to increase the money supply. How does it do it? As explained earlier, if the Fed wants to create money, it can simply print money or add numbers to bank accounts. But how does the new money find its way into the economy? Imagine, for example, that the Fed added money to its own bank account and bought apples with the new money. At first, the money would flow to apple farmers and then the apple farmers would buy more tractors and television sets and vacations, and the money would flow out to other people who themselves would buy more goods. In this way, the Fed's increase in the money supply would spread throughout the economy. And if the Fed wanted to reduce the money supply, it could sell some of the apples that it had bought earlier.

The Fed, however, doesn't want to buy and sell apples. Apples are difficult to store, expensive to ship, and available in very large quantities during only part of the year. So instead of apples, the Fed buys and sells government bonds, usually short-term bonds called Treasury bills or T-bills (these are also often called Treasury securities or "Treasuries"). Government bonds can be stored and shipped electronically and the market for government bonds is liquid and deep, which means that the Fed can easily buy and sell billions of dollars worth of government bonds in a matter of minutes.

So, if the Fed wants to change the money supply, it usually does so by buying or selling government bonds. This is called an **open market operation.** To pay for the T-bills, the Fed electronically increases the reserves of the seller, usually a bank or a large dealer in Treasury securities. With more reserves on hand, that bank will respond by increasing its loans beginning the ripple process just described. That is, banks will make additional loans, the loans will in turn be used to buy goods and pay wages, and people will deposit some of

Open market operations occur when the Fed buys or sells government bonds.

these payments into other banks. The new deposits will increase the reserves of these other banks, which will now also be able to make more loans. Thus, the purchase of bonds by the Federal Reserve leads to a ripple process of increasing deposits, loans, deposits, loans, deposits, more loans, and so forth.

We noted earlier that the change in the money supply is equal to the change in reserves multiplied by the money multiplier, $\Delta MS = \Delta \text{Reserves} \times MM$. It's important to remember, however, that the size of the money multiplier is not fixed. The multiplier is the inverse of the reserve ratio and the reserve ratio is determined by banks. When banks are confident and eager to lend, they will want to keep their reserves relatively low so the money multiplier will be large ($MM = 1/RR$). In this case, small changes in reserves will have a relatively large effect on the money supply.

But when banks are fearful and reluctant to lend—that is, they wish to hold a high level of reserves—the money multiplier will be low and a change in the monetary base need not change the broader monetary aggregates much at all.

Thus, even though the Fed controls the monetary base, the Fed may not know how much or how quickly changes in the base will change loans and the broader measures of the money supply.

Summarizing, (1) the Federal Reserve can increase or decrease reserves at banks by buying or selling government bonds, (2) the increase in reserves boosts the money supply through a multiplier process, and (3) the size of the multiplier is not fixed but depends on how much of their assets the banks want to hold as reserves.

How the Fed Works: Before the Great Recession

Open Market Operations and Interest Rates Conducting monetary policy by buying and selling government bonds rather than, say, apples has another advantage. You may recall from our chapter on Saving, Investing, and the Financial System that bond prices and interest rates are inversely related: When bond prices go up, that is another way of saying interest rates go down, and when bond prices go down, that means interest rates go up. Thus, when the Fed buys or sells bonds, it changes the monetary base and influences interest rates at the same time. Let's go through this in more detail.

When the Fed buys bonds, it increases the demand for bonds, which pushes up the price of bonds, thus lowering the interest rate. So, buying bonds stimulates the economy through two distinct mechanisms, namely higher money supplies and lower interest rates. In a sense, the increase in the money supply increases the supply of loans and the lower interest rates increase the quantity of loans demanded.

When the Fed sells bonds, the process works in reverse. Selling bonds reduces the money supply as people give up their reserves to buy the bonds. Selling bonds also lowers the price of bonds, which means that interest rates increase. Instead of stimulating the economy, an open-market sale of bonds will slow the economy.

When you hear that "the Fed has lowered (or raised) interest rates," do not be confused. The Fed does not "set" interest rates in the same way that a 7-Eleven owner "sets" the price of milk in the store. Instead, interest rates are determined in a broad market through the supply and demand for loans as outlined in our Financial System chapter. The Fed works through supply and demand, and if the Fed wants short-term interest rates to fall, it has to buy more bonds, thereby influencing market prices.

The Fed Controls a Real Rate Only in the Short Run Lending and borrowing decisions depend on the real interest rate, the interest rate after inflation has been taken into account (see our earlier chapter on Inflation). It's important to understand, therefore, that the Fed has influence on real interest rates only in the short run. Remember that money is neutral in the long run—that neutrality includes real interest rates. Similarly, remember from the chapter on Business Fluctuations that an increase in aggregate demand (AD) increases the real growth rate only in the short run. Thus, the long-run neutrality of money, the long-run neutrality of aggregate demand, and the long-run neutrality of Federal Reserve influence over real rates are all different sides of the same "coin."

The Federal Funds rate is the overnight lending rate from one major bank to another.

The Fed has the most influence over a short-term interest rate called the Federal Funds rate. The **Federal Funds rate** is simply the *overnight* rate (that's really short term!) for a loan from one major bank to another. Banks lend not only to entrepreneurs, consumers, and home buyers but also to other banks and financial institutions.

Since the Federal Reserve can easily change the reserves of major banks through open market operations, it can exercise especially tight control over the Federal Funds rate. In fact, monetary policy is usually conducted in terms of the Federal Funds rate. For example, instead of deciding to increase the money supply by $50 billion, the Fed might decide to reduce the Federal Funds rate by a quarter of a percentage point—the Fed will then buy bonds until the Federal Funds rate drops by a quarter of a point. Similarly, if the Fed wants to increase the Federal Funds rate, it will sell bonds until the Federal Funds rate increases by the desired amount.

Jekyll Island Club—Creation of the Fed The Federal Reserve has been a controversial institution in American politics ever since the secret 1910 meeting on Jekyll Island, where plans were drafted for the central bank.

TYLER BAGWELL

Quantitative Easing The Fed usually focuses on the Federal Funds rate because it is a convenient signal of monetary policy, it responds very quickly to actions by the Fed, and it can be monitored on a day-to-day basis. During the recession of 2008–2009, however, the Fed dramatically increased the supply of reserves—so much so that it pushed the Federal Funds rate very close to zero. In fact, between January 2009 and December 2016 the Federal Funds rate was kept below 0.5%. It is difficult to push the Federal Funds rate below zero—a negative interest rate would mean that you lend $100 and get back, say, $99—because people could just hold their cash and get a zero rate of return. Thus, when the Federal Funds rate is close to zero, it is said to be at or near the **zero lower bound.**

When the Federal Funds rate is close to zero, it is said to be near the **zero lower bound.**

In 2009, the Fed pushed the Federal Funds rate to near the zero lower bound, and still the economy wasn't booming. So, in order to push longer-term interest rates down, the Fed moved from primarily buying and selling the short-term debt of the federal government to also buying and selling longer-term government bonds in the 10- to 30-year range. During the financial crisis the Fed even bought over a trillion dollars' worth of mortgage-backed securities to help sustain liquidity in that market. This kind of policy is called **quantitative easing** and it is used when the federal funds rate is near the zero lower bound.

Quantitative easing is when the Fed buys longer-term government bonds or other securities. **Quantitative tightening** is when the Fed sells longer-term government bonds or other securities.

How the Fed Works: After the Great Recession

Payment of Interest on Reserves

In the midst of the financial crisis, the Federal Reserve began to use a new method to control the money supply in October of 2008: payment of interest on reserves. Most other central banks continue to focus on open market operations and the Fed may someday go back to these older methods, but for the time being it is necessary to learn both sets of operating procedures.

So what exactly changed and how does it matter?

Prior to October of 2008, the supply of reserves and the Federal Funds rate were tied closely together. As we discussed earlier, when the Fed increased the supply of reserves the Federal Funds rate would be pushed down, and when the Fed decreased the supply of reserves the Federal Funds rate would be pushed up. During the crisis, however, the Fed wanted to separate these two aspects of monetary policy. To avoid any hint of a bank run, for example, the Fed might want banks to have lots of reserves. Yet, the Fed might also want to keep interest rates close to a certain level. Paying interest on reserves allowed the Fed to separate the two channels of monetary policy. The Fed could now choose to supply the banking system with whatever level of reserves it thought best and, by setting the interest rate the Fed paid on those reserves, it could influence other interest rates in the economy. Notice, for example, that when the Fed pays interests on reserves, it puts a floor on the Federal Funds rate because no bank would want to lend to another bank at a rate that was less than what they could get just by holding onto their reserves.

As we said, during the financial crisis the Fed wanted to put a lot of reserves into the system. How much? Prior to 2008, bank reserves in excess of required reserves were about 2 billion dollars. But starting in 2008, excess reserves increased from 2 billion to 2.8 trillion! (See Figure 34.2.) Even though the Fed pays only a very low interest rate on reserves, banks are willing to hold lots of

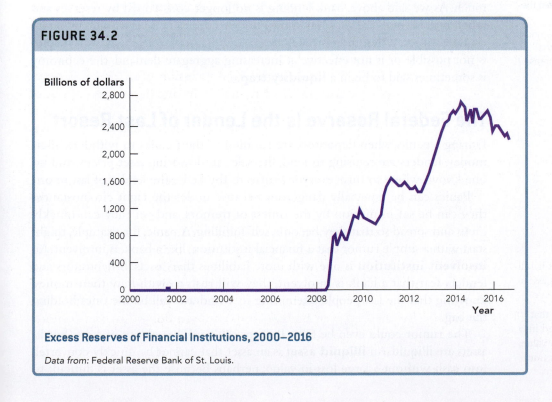

FIGURE 34.2

Billions of dollars

Excess Reserves of Financial Institutions, 2000–2016

Data from: Federal Reserve Bank of St. Louis.

reserves because interest rates in the wider economy are also close to zero, at least for low-risk investments. Even a low interest rate on reserves encourages banks to hold a lot of reserves when it's hard to find superior returns at a comparable level of risk elsewhere.

So how does the Federal Reserve conduct monetary policy now that reserves are so large? On its own, changing the supply of reserves is no longer very effective in boosting loans because banks have more than enough reserves for all their requirements. Since banks already hold trillions of dollars in reserve, just adding more reserves won't translate into more lending; lending is no longer constrained by reserves.

What the Fed can do, however, is change the demand for reserves. Suppose, for example, that the Fed wants to pursue a relatively *contractionary monetary policy*, as was the case in late 2015. First, the Fed raises the rate of interest that it pays on reserves. That increases the demand for reserves and also places upward pressure on other short-term interest rates. Since banks can now earn a higher interest rate on reserves, they are less willing to lend those reserves, which pushes up market interest rates. Higher market interest rates and a higher demand to hold reserves mean that borrowing declines and broader measures of the money supply grow less quickly than otherwise would have been the case.

Now let's say the Fed wants to pursue an *expansionary monetary policy.* To do so, the Fed would lower the rate of interest paid on reserves. As a result, banks would be less inclined to simply sit on their reserves. Instead, they would want to lend more and that in turn would lower market rates of interest and increase the flow of money through the economy.

At least that is the way it is supposed to work in theory and the way the Fed hopes it will work. There is considerable uncertainty as to how much these actions can influence real economic activity, however. Interest rates are already very low, so even if the Fed were to drop the interest rate paid on reserves to zero, how much is that really going to affect bank decisions? Maybe not very much. As we said above, bank lending is no longer constrained by reserves and when interest rates are very low it may not be constrained very much by interest rates either. When interest rates are so low that lowering them even further is not possible or is not effective at increasing aggregate demand, the economy is sometimes said to be in a **liquidity trap**.

The Federal Reserve Is the Lender of Last Resort

During a panic, when depositors are running to their banks to withdraw their money, lenders are refusing to lend, fire sales are lowering asset prices, and no one knows where to turn, everyone turns to the Fed—the lender of last resort.

Panics can be especially dangerous because under the right circumstances they can be set in motion by the tiniest of tremors, and yet they can quickly grow and spread so that they become self-fulfilling. A panic, for example, might start with a simple rumor that a financial institution, like a bank, is insolvent. An **insolvent institution** is one with more liabilities than assets. If depositors and lenders fear that a bank is insolvent, they will rush to withdraw their money, knowing that the last people attempting to withdraw will be the ones holding the bag.

The rumor could even be false. Perhaps the bank has plenty of assets but its assets are illiquid. An **illiquid asset** is an asset that cannot be quickly converted into cash without a large loss in value; perhaps because the asset is difficult to

The economy is said to be in a **liquidity trap** when interest rates are close to the zero lower bound so pushing them lower is not possible or not effective at increasing aggregate demand.

CHECK YOURSELF

■ Underline the correct answers. The Fed wants to lower interest rates: It does so by (buying/ selling) bonds in an open market operation. By doing this, the Fed (adds/subtracts) reserves and through the multiplier process (increases/ decreases) the money supply.

■ If the Fed increases the amount that it pays on reserves that will tend to increase/decrease aggregate demand?

An **insolvent institution** has liabilities that are greater than its assets.

An **illiquid asset** is an asset that cannot be quickly converted into cash without a large loss in value. A bank may be illiquid but not insolvent.

value and it takes time to find the right buyer. The main assets that banks hold are loans that are difficult to value and that won't pay off until some point in the future, so banks hold lots of illiquid assets. If the bank is forced to liquidate early to pay its depositors or lenders, there could be a lot of waste.

Banks establish long-term relationships with their customers. Consider, for example, a software project. The team behind the project works closely with a bank to get a loan. The team finishes half of the code and needs another loan. It makes sense to go back to the same bank—no one else will understand the project as well. If that bank can't fund the project, the whole project will probably die, wasting the work that has already gone into it. Not only will it be hard to explain the project to other investors, but those investors may fear an adverse selection problem—why isn't the bank that best knows the project making the loan? A bank run can break the continuity necessary to fund long-term projects.

The depositors, however, can't tell whether the bank is really insolvent or just illiquid and any hint that the bank isn't ready to pay everyone on demand could make the panic spread.

That's where deposit insurance and the Federal Reserve come in. Deposit insurance tells depositors: don't worry, even if the bank is insolvent you will still be paid. And because of that guarantee, there is no run and the bank isn't forced to stop funding the software project before it is finished.

When deposit insurance isn't enough or when the financial institution isn't covered by deposit insurance, then the Fed can step in as the lender of last resort. The Fed provides the bank with enough cash to pay off any depositor who wants to be paid off; again, without requiring the bank to liquidate its assets too early.

Traditionally, the Fed lent to solvent but illiquid banks to get them through a temporary squeeze and it wound down insolvent banks. But during a panic the Fed may also lend to insolvent banks—to bail them out.

The problem during a panic is the problem of **systemic risk**—if one financial institution goes down it's likely to take others with it, like dominos. Thus, because the bankruptcy of one insolvent financial intermediary could take illiquid but solvent institutions down with it, the Fed sometimes has to bail out some insolvent banks in order to protect the entire system.

At the height of the 2008–2009 financial crisis, for example, the Federal Reserve, the Federal Deposit Insurance Corporation (FDIC), and the U.S. Treasury stepped in to support the financial system on an unprecedented scale. In addition to buying trillions of dollars' worth of longer-term government bonds and mortgage-backed securities, the Federal Reserve also lent banks hundreds of billions of dollars. The Fed also extended its lending beyond banks to become the lender of last resort to other financial intermediaries in the commercial paper and asset-backed securities markets. All told, the Fed lent financial intermediaries over a trillion dollars, as shown in Figure 34.3.

The Fed also went from lender of last resort to owner of last resort (!) when it assumed a majority ownership stake in the insurance company AIG. Even though AIG wasn't a bank, the Fed worried that if it went bankrupt it would threaten many other financial intermediaries. The Fed wanted to create a line break and stop the dominoes from toppling over.

The Fed was joined in these actions by the FDIC. Deposit insurance, which traditionally had been limited to $100,000 for each bank account, was in effect extended to all accounts, increasing the amount insured by some 8 trillion dollars.

The Federal Reserve as Lender of Last Resort

Systemic risk is the risk that the failure of one financial institution can bring down other institutions.

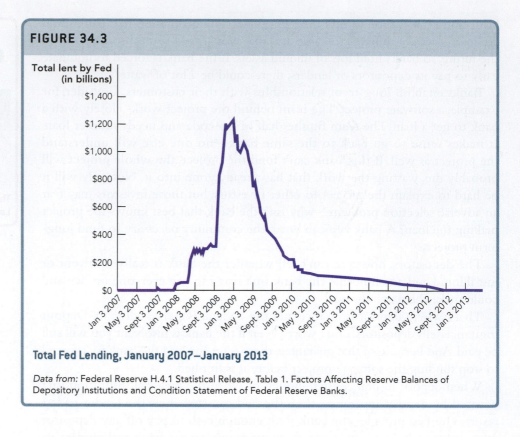

FIGURE 34.3

Total lent by Fed (in billions)

Total Fed Lending, January 2007–January 2013

Data from: Federal Reserve H.4.1 Statistical Release, Table 1. Factors Affecting Reserve Balances of Depository Institutions and Condition Statement of Federal Reserve Banks.

In addition, the U.S. Treasury guaranteed trillions of dollars in money market funds. Finally, the U.S. government stepped in as a lender of last resort and partial owner of General Motors when GM couldn't get funding from banks.

But here's the problem. What would you do if you were told that you could invest in anything and the government would step in and bail you out if you failed? It's obvious. You would take more risk since you would get the benefit of the upside and wouldn't have to deal with the downside! When individuals or institutions are insured, they tend to take on too much risk. This is the problem of **moral hazard**. Big financial institutions that are "too big to fail" have too little incentive to make responsible financial investments.

> **Moral hazard** occurs when banks and other financial institutions take on too much risk, hoping that the Fed and regulators will later bail them out.

This is in part why the Fed also has the role of regulating banks: to minimize reckless bank behavior, the Fed imposes conditions on what assets the bank can and must hold. Regulations like this, however, have costs of their own, including a more bureaucratic and less flexible banking system.

Limiting systemic risk while checking moral hazard is the fundamental problem the Fed faces as a bank regulator. In addition, the financial system has become more complex and intertwined as financial assets are packaged, subdivided, bought, and sold more than ever before. The shadow banking system has become as important as traditional banks in the financial system, but it is less well understood. As a result, the Fed's lender of last resort and regulatory functions have become much more important and more complex.

The Fed steps in as a lender of last resort to stop the spread of a financial panic.

TOM WANG/SHUTTERSTOCK

FIGURE 34.4

Open market operations—the buying and selling of short-term U.S. government bonds. The Fed buys bonds to lower interest rates and expand the money supply, and sells bonds to raise interest rates and contract the money supply.

Raising or lowering the interest rate paid on reserves. The Fed lowers the rate paid on reserves to decrease reserve demand and expand bank lending, and raises the rate to increase reserve demand and reduce bank lending.

Quantitative easing—the buying and selling of longer-term U.S. government bonds or other securities. Used to influence longer-term rates directly or to support borrowing and lending in especially distressed markets in a crisis.

Lender of Last Resort—lending to banks and other financial intermediaries in a crisis to maintain borrowing and lending.

Four Tools Used by the Federal Reserve

The Fed is trying to steer a course between two problems. If a panic occurs, it may be best to bail out some firms, even bad actors, to protect the system, and yet the promise to bail out firms in a future panic encourages risk taking and increases the probability that a panic will happen in the first place. It is not obvious that the Fed has the tools to steer clear of both problems. This is the great dilemma of modern banking regulation.

Figure 34.4 summarizes four of the most important Fed tools.

Revisiting Aggregate Demand and Monetary Policy

Now that we have covered the major tools of the Federal Reserve, let's remember that what the Fed ultimately wants to do is to use its tools to influence aggregate demand (AD). Let's imagine, for example, that the Fed wants to increase aggregate demand and it chooses to do so by buying bonds in an open market operation. The bond purchase increases the monetary base and decreases short-term interest rates. The increase in the base increases deposits and loans through the multiplier process, and the decrease in interest rates stimulates investment (and consumption) borrowing. As a result—if all goes well—AD increases. The increase in AD then influences the economy as discussed in our chapter on Business Fluctuations and is shown in Figure 34.5. Beginning at point *a*, an increase in $\vec{M}$ shifts the aggregate demand curve outward, moving the economy to point *b*, where inflation and the real growth rate are higher. In the long run, after transition the economy will move to point *c* with a higher inflation rate (money neutrality again) but a growth rate given by the fundamentals at the long-run potential level.

We now know that the process is not quite so simple. The Fed can buy bonds and increase the monetary base, but these actions do not increase aggregate demand by any guaranteed amount, since we don't know exactly how much M1 and M2 will go up in response to the higher monetary base.

FIGURE 34.5

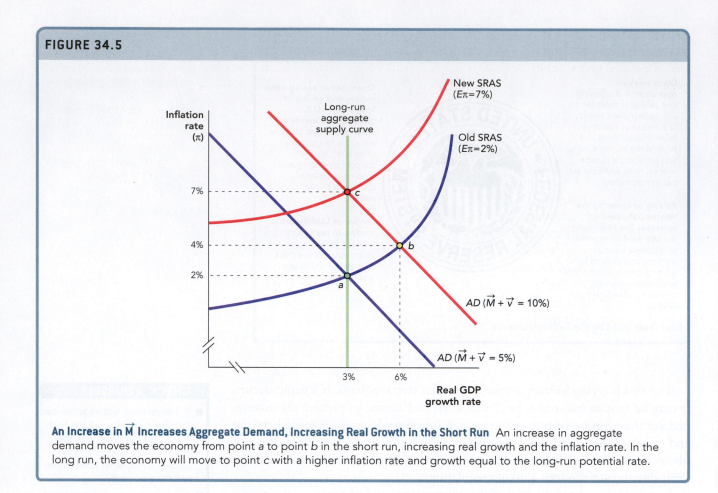

An Increase in $\vec{M}$ Increases Aggregate Demand, Increasing Real Growth in the Short Run An increase in aggregate demand moves the economy from point *a* to point *b* in the short run, increasing real growth and the inflation rate. In the long run, the economy will move to point *c* with a higher inflation rate and growth equal to the long-run potential rate.

Nor do we know exactly how much the lower interest rates will stimulate investment spending, especially since the Fed has the most influence over *short-term* rates, while most investment spending will depend on longer-term rates. In addition, all of these processes take time and the lags from action to response are not fixed but may vary. If the Fed acts to reduce interest rates today, for example, it may take 6 to 18 months before aggregate demand and economic growth begin to respond significantly. In the meantime, economic conditions may change.

Thus, to estimate the effect of its actions on aggregate demand, the Fed must try to predict and monitor many variables determining the size and timing of the response to its actions. Some of the things the Fed must try to predict and monitor are:

- Will banks lend out all the new reserves or will they lend out only a portion, holding the rest as excess reserves?

- How quickly will increases in the monetary base translate into new bank loans and thus larger increases in M1 and M2?

- Do businesses want to borrow? How low do short-term interest rates have to go to stimulate more investment borrowing?

- If businesses do borrow, will they promptly hire labor and capital, or will they just hold the money as a precaution against bad times?

The Federal Reserve's power should not be underestimated but increasing or decreasing aggregate demand is not like turning a tap on and off.

The Fed has a limited set of tools and it must constantly adapt those tools to new circumstances and conditions. We will be taking up the difficulties and dilemmas of monetary policy in the real world at greater length in the next chapter.

Who Controls the Fed?

The power to create money out of thin air and to lend trillions of dollars is an awesome power. How is this power controlled?

The Fed has a seven-member Board of Governors, who are appointed by the president and confirmed by the Senate. Governors are appointed for 14-year terms and cannot be reappointed—this means a single president will rarely appoint a majority of the board. Once appointed, members of the Board of Governors cannot be easily fired. The chairperson of the Fed is appointed by the president from among the members of the Board of Governors and confirmed by the Senate for a term of four years. In addition, the Fed has to periodically report to overseers in both houses of Congress.

Although we say "the Fed," the Fed is not just one bank but 12 Federal Reserve Banks, each headquartered in a different region of the country.[*] The regional structure of the Fed explains another peculiarity: The Fed is a quasi private, quasi public institution. Each regional bank is a nonprofit bank with nine directors: Six of these directors are elected by commercial banks from the region and three are elected by the Board of Governors. Six of the directors must be nonbankers and these are drawn from business, labor, academia, and other fields. In 2017, for example, the Vice-President of Costco was a director at the San Francisco Fed, the President of George Mason University was a director at the Richmond Fed, and the President of the Chicago Federation of Labor was a director at the Chicago Fed. The directors of the regional banks appoint a regional bank president. Finally, the seven members of the Board of Governors, along with five rotating presidents of the regional Fed banks, make up the Federal Open Market Committee. The Federal Open Market Committee determines the stance of monetary policy by controlling open market policy. It is therefore the most important and influential part of the Fed system.

Confused? Yes, it is confusing and we have spared you many of the details! Perhaps it will help to know that the confusing structure of the Federal Reserve system has a purpose. The Federal Reserve is powerful, so in keeping with the U.S. system of checks and balances, the power of the Fed is dispersed—no single president appoints all the governors of the Fed, the governors do not have complete control over Fed policy, the regional bank presidents come from all over the United States, and they are appointed by directors who are drawn not just from banking but from a wide variety of fields.

The bottom line is that the Federal Reserve is usually one of the most independent agencies in the U.S. government. It is relatively insulated from politics, party, and elections—perhaps only the Supreme Court is more independent. That said, in the financial crisis of 2008, the Fed had to work closely with the Treasury Department (for one thing, Treasury resources were required to recapitalize banks) and in that sense it was much less independent than usual.

---

[*] The headquarters of the 12 regional banks are located in Boston, New York, Philadelphia, Cleveland, Richmond, Atlanta, Chicago, St. Louis, Minneapolis, Kansas City, Dallas, and San Francisco.

In general, the independence of the Federal Reserve worries some people who would prefer that the Fed be more directly accountable to democratically elected politicians. Other people are concerned that if the Federal Reserve could be controlled directly by, say, the president, this would give the president the power to order the Federal Reserve to expand the money supply and boost the economy just before an election.

Political pressures have been put on the Federal Reserve and some chairpersons have been less independent than others. In 1972, President Nixon asked Arthur Burns, the chair of the Fed, to stimulate the economy before the election. Burns did stimulate the economy and Nixon won in a landslide, but the economic gains were temporary. Not surprisingly, inflation was too high for the rest of the 1970s. This was not a proud moment in the history of the Federal Reserve or the presidency.

Overall, an independent Federal Reserve is defended by most economists as part of the U.S. system of checks and balances.

Takeaway

To return to the opening of this chapter, we now have a sense why the Fed chairperson is (possibly) the second most powerful person in the world. The Federal Reserve is the government's bank and the bankers' bank, and it has the power to create money. The ability to create money, regulate the money supply, and potentially lend trillions of dollars means that the Fed has significant powers to influence aggregate demand in the world's largest economy.

The concept of "the money supply" can refer to several different measures. It is important to know the major definitions of the money supply (MB, M1, and M2) and how they differ. The Fed controls the money supply by buying and selling government bonds in what are called open market operations.

By buying and selling bonds, the Fed changes bank reserves. A change in reserves changes the money supply through a multiplier process of rippling loans and deposits. The final result is that $\Delta MS = \Delta \text{Reserves} \times \text{MM}$. The money multiplier, however, changes over time, so the Fed's influence over aggregate demand is subject to uncertainty in both impact and timing.

When the government buys securities, the interest rate decreases and that stimulates consumption and investment borrowing. When the government sells securities, the interest rate increases, thereby reducing borrowing for either consumption or investment. The Fed can also influence interest rates by raising or lowering the interest rate the Fed pays on bank reserves. For day-to-day operations, in normal times, the Fed focuses its attention on the Federal Funds rate, the interest rate on overnight loans between major banks. The Fed has the most influence over real rates of interest in the short run. The Fed has little influence over long-run real rates of interest.

In emergency situations, the Fed serves as a "lender of last resort" for banks and for major financial institutions that find themselves in trouble. Preventing "systemic risk"—or the spread of financial problems from one institution to another—while also minimizing the moral hazard that comes when banks assume too much risk, assuming that they will be bailed out in the future, are two of the Fed's most important jobs.

CHAPTER REVIEW

 interactive activity Go online to practice with more examples of these types of problems, including live links to videos, data sources, and feedback.

Problems in green relate to MRU videos. See the MRU table at the end of the exercises.

KEY CONCEPTS

money, p. 718

liquid asset, p. 720

fractional reserve banking, p. 720

reserve ratio (RR), p. 721

money multiplier (MM), p. 721

open market operations, p. 722

Federal Funds rate, p. 724

zero lower bound, p. 724

quantitative easing, p. 724

quantitative tightening, p. 724

liquidity trap, p. 726

lender of last resort, p. 726

insolvent institution, p. 726

illiquid asset, p. 726

systemic risk, p. 727

moral hazard, p. 728

FACTS AND TOOLS

1. Let's find out what counts as money. In this chapter, we used a typical definition of money: "a widely accepted means of payment." Under this definition, are people using "money" in the following transactions? If not, why not?

   a. Lucy sells her Saab to Karen for $1,000 in cash.

   b. Lucy sells her Saab to Karen for $1,000 worth of old Bob Dylan records.

   c. Lucy sells her Saab to Karen for $1,000 in checking account balances (transferred by writing a check).

   d. Lucy sells her Saab to Karen by Karen promising $1,000 worth of auto detailing services over the next year.

   e. Lucy sells her Saab to Karen for $1,000 worth of Revolutionary War–era continental dollars.

2. Define the following:

   a. The monetary base, MB

   b. M1

   c. M2

3. **a.** Suppose that banks have decided they need to keep a reserve ratio of 10%—this guarantees that they'll have enough cash in ATMs to keep depositors happy, and enough electronic deposits at the Federal Reserve so that they can redeem checks presented by other banks. What is the money multiplier in this case?

   b. If depositors start visiting the ATM a lot more often, will banks want to have a higher reserve ratio or a lower reserve ratio? Will this increase the money multiplier or lower it?

4. If the Federal Reserve wants to lower interest rates via open market operations, should it buy bonds or should it sell bonds?

5. Practice with money multipliers. Think of the "money supply" (MS) as equal to either M1 or M2.

   a. RR = 5%, Change in reserves = $10 billion. MM = ?; Change in MS = ?

   b. RR = ?, Change in reserves = $1,000, MM = 5, Change in MS = ?

   c. RR = 100%, Change in reserves = $10 billion. MM = ?, Change in MS = ?

6. In the previous question, one example assumed that banks kept a 100% reserve ratio. Some economists have recommended that *all* banks be required by law to keep 100% of their deposits in the bank vault, at the Federal Reserve, or invested in ultrasafe investments such as short-term U.S. Treasury bills.

   a. If this happened, what would the money multiplier be equal to?

   b. If this happened, would the interest rate on bank deposits probably go up or down?

   c. If this happened, would people be more likely or less likely to invest their savings in bank alternatives, such as bonds, mutual funds, or their cousin's lawn mowing business?

7. The main interest rate that the Federal Reserve tries to control is the Federal Funds rate, the interest rate that banks charge on short-term (usually overnight) loans to other banks. Let's see how much interest a bank can earn if it lends money at the Federal Funds rate.

Virginia Community Bank has $2,000,000 of extra cash sitting in its account at the Federal Reserve Bank of Richmond. It gets a call from Bank of America asking to borrow the whole $2,000,000 for 24 hours. (This is typical: It's usually the smaller banks lending money overnight to the bigger banks.)

    a. If the *annual* interest rate on federal funds is 4%, what (approximately) is the *one-day* interest rate on federal funds? (Note that interest rates, like GDP growth rates, are usually reported as "per year," just as speeds are reported as miles "per hour.")

    b. How many dollars of interest will Virginia Community Bank earn for lending this money for one day?

    c. If Virginia Community Bank lent this amount every day at the same rate for an entire year, how much interest would it earn?

8. Let's use the model of the supply and demand for bank reserves to explain how the Federal Reserve can change aggregate demand in the short run. Remember that the Federal Reserve controls the *supply* of bank reserves, but private banks create *demand* for bank reserves.

    a. After a meeting, the Federal Reserve's Open Market Committee votes to cut interest rates from 2% to 1.5%. How will they make this happen: Will they increase the supply of reserves or decrease the supply?

    b. As a result of your answer to part a, will banks usually lend more money in response, or will they lend less money? Will this tend to increase the nation's money supply, lower it, or will it have no net effect on the money supply?

    c. Will this typically increase aggregate demand or lower it?

Ask FRED

interactive activity

9. Using the FRED economic database (https://fred.stlouisfed.org/), graph the effective Federal Funds rate from 2007 to the present.

    a. Approximately what was the Federal Funds rate in 2007?

    b. What was the Federal Funds rate around the first week of January 2009?

THINKING AND PROBLEM SOLVING

10. Whether an asset is "liquid" often depends on what situation you are in. For each of the following pairs of assets, which is more liquid in the particular setting?

You want to buy a sofa:

A savings account or currency

You want to trade for a bologna sandwich in elementary school:

A peanut butter and jelly sandwich or sushi

You want to buy a house:

Currency or a checking account

You live in a postapocalyptic wasteland:

Rice or currency

You are traveling across Europe during the Middle Ages:

Gold coins or works of art

You are an investment banker buying a corporation:

U.S. Treasury bonds or currency

11. a. Who is more likely to take bigger risks: a trapeze artist with a safety net underneath or a trapeze artist without a safety net?

    b. Who is more likely to take bigger risks with his deposits: a bank CEO in a country where there is a lender of last resort or a bank CEO in a country where there is no lender of last resort?

    c. Who is more likely to spend more time searching for a well run, safe bank: a depositor living in a country with government-run deposit insurance or a depositor living in a country without government-run deposit insurance?

    d. Do government-run central banks and deposit insurance both increase moral hazard problems, both decrease moral hazard problems, or do they push in different directions when it comes to moral hazard?

12. a. In the short run, if the Fed wants to cut short-term, nominal interest rates, what does it do: Does it increase the growth rate of money or decrease the growth rate of money? Why? Will this tend to lower the real rate or will it tend to lower inflation?

b. In the long run, if the Fed wants to cut short-term, nominal interest rates, what does it do: Does it increase the growth rate of money or decrease the growth rate of money? Why? Will this tend to lower the real rate or will it tend to lower inflation?

13. Let's watch a bank create money. Last Wednesday, the Bank of Numenor opened for business. The first customer, Edith, walked in the door with 100 silver coins called Thalers to deposit in a new checking account. The second customer, Max, walks in the door a few minutes later, asking to borrow 50 Thalers for a week. The bank lends Max the Thalers. Just to keep things simple, assume these are the *only* financial transactions in Numenor. And just to be clear: Thalers are either "currency" or "reserves": Silver in Max or Edith's hands is "currency," while Thalers in the bank is "reserves."

a. How much "money" is there in the Numenor economy before Edith walks into the bank?
Monetary base:
M1:

b. How much "money" is there in the Numenor economy after Edith makes her deposit, but before Max walks in for his loan?
Monetary base:
M1:

c. How much "money" is there in the Numenor economy after the Bank makes Max the loan?
Monetary base:
M1:

d. Which action created money: Edith's deposit or Max's loan?

14. You are a bank regulator working for the Federal Reserve. It is your job to see whether banks are solvent or insolvent, liquid or illiquid. Fit each of the following banks into one of the following four categories:

1. *Liquid and solvent (best)*

2. *Illiquid but solvent (probably needs short-term loans from other banks or from the Fed)*

3. *Liquid but insolvent (should be shut down immediately: could fool people for a while if not for your good efforts)*

4. *Illiquid and insolvent (should be shut down immediately)*

a. Bank of DelMarVa

Short-term assets	Short-term liabilities
$10 million	$6 million
Total assets	Total liabilities
$40 million	$50 million

b. Bank of Escondido

Short-term assets	Short-term liabilities
$6 million	$10 million
Total assets	Total liabilities
$50 million	$40 million

c. Bank of Previa

Short-term assets	Short-term liabilities
$12 million	$10 million
Total assets	Total liabilities
$50 million	$40 million

d. Bank of Cambia

Short-term assets	Short-term liabilities
$8 million	$10 million
Total assets	Total liabilities
$30 million	$40 million

e. Bank of Marshall

Short-term assets	Short-term liabilities
$120 million	$100 million
Total assets	Total liabilities
$500 million	$400 million

15. Does the House of Representatives get to vote on who becomes the chairperson of the Federal Reserve Board? If not, who *does* get to vote?

CHALLENGES

16. We mentioned how difficult it can be for the Federal Reserve to actually control aggregate demand: Its control over the broader money supply (M1 and M2) is weak and indirect, plus it can't control velocity very much at all. Let's translate the following bullet points from the chapter into an expanded aggregate demand equation. You know that increasing AD means increasing spending growth, $\vec{M} + \vec{v}$, but now you know that M (growth in M1 or M2, money measures that include checking accounts) depends on growth in the monetary base (MB) and on the money multiplier (MM). That means an increase in AD requires an increase in $\overrightarrow{MB} + \overrightarrow{MM} + \vec{v}$.

Let's apply this fact to the following cases mentioned in the chapter. In all cases, the Federal Reserve is trying to boost AD by raising $\overrightarrow{MB}$ But if there's a fall in $\overrightarrow{MM}$ or a fall in $\vec{v}$ at the same time, the Fed's actions might do nothing to AD. In each case below, what are we concerned about: a fall in $\overrightarrow{MM}$ or a fall in $\vec{v}$?

a. Will banks lend out all the new reserves or will they lend out only a portion, holding the rest as excess reserves?

b. Will increases in the monetary base translate into new bank loans?

c. If businesses do borrow, will they promptly hire labor and capital, or will they just hold the money as a precaution against bad times?

17. In the past, the Federal Reserve didn't pay interest on reserves kept in Federal Reserve banks: For an ordinary U.S. bank, money kept at the Fed earned zero interest, just like money stored in a vault or in an ATM. In 2008, the Fed started paying interest on deposits kept at the Fed.

a. Once the Fed started paying interest, what would you predict would happen to demand for reserves by banks: Would they demand more reserves or fewer reserves from the Fed?

b. If a central bank starts paying interest on reserves, will private banks tend to make more loans or fewer loans, holding all else equal? (*Hint:* Does the opportunity cost of making a car loan rise or fall when the central bank starts paying interest on reserves?)

c. Let's put parts a and b together, keeping in mind the fact that bank loans create money. That means your answer to part b also tells you about the money supply, not just about the loan supply. If a central bank starts paying interest on reserves, will the reserve ratio chosen by banks tend to rise or fall? And will the money multiplier tend to rise or fall?

d. Your answer to part c tells us that when the central bank starts paying interest on reserves, there's going to be a shift in M1 and M2, the broad forms of money supply that include money created through loans. But there are a lot of ways to affect the money supply, so

if one force is pushing the money supply in one direction, we can find another tool to push the money supply in the opposite direction. Therefore, if a central bank chooses to start paying interest on reserves, but it wants M2 to remain unchanged, what should the bank do to the supply of reserves: Should it increase the supply of reserves or decrease the supply of reserves?

18. Economist Bennett McCallum says that in order to push interest rates down in the long run, the central bank needs to raise interest rates in the short run. How can this be true?

Ask FRED

interactive activity

19. Using the FRED economic database (https://fred.stlouisfed.org/), find and graph the amount of mortgage-backed securities held by the Federal Reserve since 2007.

a. What quantity of mortgage-backed securities did the Fed hold prior to 2009?

b. Approximately what quantity of mortgage-backed securities did the Fed hold in 2016?

c. Why did the Federal Reserve purchase these securities?

d. What problems may this cause moving forward?

Ask FRED

interactive activity

20. Using the FRED economic database (https://fred.stlouisfed.org/), graph the Effective Federal Funds rate from 2007 to the present. Now click Edit Graph and then Add Line. Add the Unemployment rate. Click Format and change the Y-axis position of line 2 (unemployment) to the right—this will give you one axis for the Federal Funds rate on the left and one axis for the Unemployment rate on the right.

a. How did the Fed respond to increasing unemployment?

b. Did monetary policy work to lower unemployment? Can you tell from this graph?

c. What happens if unemployment spikes back up? Can the Fed lower the Federal Funds rate much more? Could the Fed push the Federal Funds rate below zero?

WORK IT OUT

For interactive, step-by-step help in solving this problem, go online.

We mentioned that the central bank can influence a short-run real interest rate—this is because in the short run the inflation rate is relatively constant but the central bank can adjust the nominal rate on short-term loans. Recall that after investing in a T-bill, the real rate that investors receive is

$$\text{Real interest rate} = \text{Nominal interest rate} - \text{Inflation}$$

a. If inflation is 3% and the Fed wants the real rate on short-term loans to be 2%, what should it set the nominal Fed Funds rate equal to?

b. If inflation is 3%, and the Fed wants to encourage borrowing by cutting the real rate on short-term loans to −1%, what should it set the nominal Fed Funds rate equal to?

c. If inflation is 6%, and the Fed wants to discourage borrowing by raising the real rate on short-term loans to 4%, what should it set the nominal Fed Funds rate equal to?

MARGINAL REVOLUTION UNIVERSITY VIDEOS

The U.S. Money Supplies

mruniversity.com/money-supply

Problems: **1, 2**

The Money Multiplier

mruniversity.com/money-multiplier

Problems: **3, 5, 6**

The Federal Reserve as Lender of Last Resort

mruniversity.com/lender-last-resort

Problems: **11**

CHAPTER 34 APPENDIX

The Money Multiplier Process in Detail

Just to recap from the chapter, when the Federal Reserve conducts an open market operation, we said that the money supply changes by the change in reserves times the money multiplier, $\Delta MS = \Delta\text{Reserves} \times \text{MM}$. If the Fed buys government bonds, for example, this increases bank reserves, which increases the money supply by the increase in reserves times the money multiplier.

We've already mentioned the idea of a ripple effect: As one bank increases its loans, this leads to an increase in deposits in another bank, which in turn increases its loans, which leads to an increase in deposits in another bank, which increases its loans . . . and so forth.

Now it is time to look at this multiplier process in more detail.

It's helpful to examine a simple form of accounting statement called a T-account. On the left side of a T-account, we list the bank's assets, and on the right side, we list the bank's liabilities. An asset is simply something that represents wealth or value to the bank. In our simple T-accounts, the only assets a bank can have are its reserves and its portfolio of loans. A liability refers to a debt or something owed to someone else. In our simple T-accounts, the only liabilities a bank can have will be deposits (the bank owes depositors the money in their accounts).

Now suppose that the Fed buys a government bond for $1,000 from a dealer in Treasury securities. The dealer has an account at the First National Bank and thus the Federal Reserve adds $1,000 to the dealer's account. As a result, the First National Bank's liabilities (its deposits) increase by $1,000, but the bank now also has an extra $1,000 in reserves. The First National Bank's T-account looks like this:

First National Bank	
Assets	**Liabilities**
Reserves: +$1,000	Deposits: +$1,000
Loans:	

But what will the First National Bank do with its reserves? The bank wants to make a profit so it will take a portion of its reserves and lend them out. Suppose that the bank keeps $100 in reserves and lends out $900. The bank's T-account now looks like this:

First National Bank	
Assets	**Liabilities**
Reserves: $100	Deposits: $1,000
Loans: +$900	

Notice that the ratio of the bank's reserves to deposits is $100/$1,000 or 0.1; thus, the reserve ratio = 0.1. Now the firm or person that borrowed the $900 did so to purchase goods and services. Let's suppose that the borrower wrote a check for a cruise to Luxury Vacations Inc., which has an account at the Second National Bank. Luxury Vacations Inc. deposits the check into its account at the

Second National Bank so the T-account of the Second National Bank now looks like this:

Second National Bank	
Assets	**Liabilities**
Reserves: +$900	Deposits: +$900
Loans:	

Notice that the Second National Bank's reserves have increased by $900. What does the bank want to do with these reserves? Lend them! Suppose that the Second National Bank also wants a reserve ratio of 0.1 so the Second National Bank keeps $90 in reserves and lends out $810. Its T-account now looks like this:

Second National Bank	
Assets	**Liabilities**
Reserves: $90	Deposits: $900
Loans: +$810	

Are you beginning to see the multiplier in action? Let's do one more. Suppose that the person or firm who borrowed money from the Second National Bank wanted the money to buy a computer. The borrower writes a check to Apple, which deposits the money in its account at the Third National Bank. The T-account of the Third National Bank now looks like this:

Third National Bank	
Assets	**Liabilities**
Reserves: +$810	Deposits: +$810
Loans:	

The Third National Bank also wants to make a profit, so it lends out a portion of its reserves, leading to a T-account like this:

Third National Bank	
Assets	**Liabilities**
Reserves: $81	Deposits: $810
Loans: +$729	

So let's summarize what we have so far:

The Banking System			
	Assets		**Liabilities**
	Reserves	Loans	Deposits
First National Bank	+$100	+$900	+$1,000
Second National Bank	+$90	+$810	+$900
Third National Bank	+$81	+$729	+$810
. . .	. . .	. . .	. . .

Notice that the process doesn't stop with the Third National Bank but continues onward. What is the final result of this process of expansion? Let's focus on what is happening to deposits and see if we can get to the answer a little more quickly by figuring out the pattern.

At the First National Bank deposits increase by $1,000, at the Second Bank deposits increase by $900, or $0.9 \times \$1,000$, at the Third Bank deposits increase by $810 or $0.9^2 \times \$1,000$. If you guessed that at the Fourth Bank deposits would increase by $729 or $0.9^3 \times \$1,000$, you are correct so the total process looks like this:

$$\$1,000 \times (1 + 0.9 + 0.9^2 + 0.9^3 + \cdots 0.9^n)$$

This is an example of an infinite geometric series and mathematics can show that $(1 + 0.9 + 0.9^2 + 0.9^3 + \cdots 0.9^n)$ converges to $\dfrac{1}{1 - 0.9}$ so deposits will increase by

$$\$1,000 \times \frac{1}{1 - 0.9} = \$1,000 \times \frac{1}{0.1} = \$1,000 \times 10$$

The last expression should look familiar. Remember that we assumed in our derivations that each bank wanted a reserve ratio of 0.1 so the money multiplier MM = 1/RR = 10. Thus, the last statement says that deposits increase by the increase in reserves ($1,000) times the money multiplier, 10. The increase in the money supply can be measured by the increase in deposits. Thus, we have $\Delta MS = \Delta\text{Reserves} \times \text{MM}$, exactly as we said in the chapter. Aren't you glad we saved the details for the appendix!

We can summarize by looking at how the initial increase in reserves created by the Fed open market purchase of bonds affects the entire banking system. A multiplier similar to that for deposits applies to reserves and loans so the final result looks like this:

The Banking System			
	Assets		Liabilities
	Reserves	Loans	Deposits
First National Bank	+$100	+$900	+$1,000
Second National Bank	+$90	+$810	+$900
Third National Bank	+$81	+$729	+$810
. . .	. . .	. . .	. . .
Total	$1,000	$9,000	$10,000

Note that we can measure the increase in the money supply by either the increase in the banking system's assets, Reserves + Loans, or by the increase in the banking system's liabilities, namely deposits. Thus, either way the money supply increases by the $10,000, or more generally $\Delta MS = \Delta\text{Reserves} \times \text{MM}$ as we have said before.

Let's make one qualification. In the multiplier process we went through, we assumed that every borrower wrote a check for every dollar of its loan and kept none of the money in cash. Thus, if a loan was made for $900, then somewhere in the banking system deposits increased by $900. If any of the borrowers keep some of their loan in cash, however, then the multiplier process does not operate on the cash component. For example, if a borrower receives a loan for $900 and writes a check for $800, keeping $100 in cash, then the multiplier process works only on the $800. Thus, the public's demand for cash also influences the multiplier process and complicates the Fed's job because the demand for cash can change over time.

35

Monetary Policy

T he Nobel Prize–winning economist Milton Friedman once likened monetary policy to throwing money from a helicopter. Thus, when *Business Week* asked in 2008, "Will 'Helicopter Ben' Ride to the Rescue?" they were asking whether Ben Bernanke, then the chairman of the Federal Reserve, would be able to use monetary policy to jolt the economy out of a looming recession.

In reality, the Federal Reserve rarely uses helicopters in its rescue operations. As discussed in the previous chapter, the Fed uses three primary tools to influence aggregate demand (AD): (1) open market operations in which the Fed buys bonds, which increases the money supply and reduces interest rates, or the Fed sells bonds, which decreases the money supply and increases interest rates; (2) lending to banks and other financial institutions; and (3) changes in the interest rate paid on reserves. These are the essential methods through which the Fed affects the real economy.

In this chapter, we take for granted *how* the Fed influences AD and turn more directly to three key practical questions: When *should* the Fed try to influence AD, when *will* the Fed be able to influence AD, and when will the influence on AD *result* in higher GDP growth rates?

We start with the best case for monetary policy: where it is clear what the Fed should do in general terms, such as responding to negative monetary shocks, and when the Fed has a good chance of being successful. We then consider some reasons why even in the best case the Fed doesn't always know which detailed course of action is best. We next consider why some of the other cases—such as negative real shocks—are much harder for the Fed to respond to effectively. Finally, we learn that there are some times when the Fed itself can contribute to a boom and subsequent bust. We end with a look at the financial crisis that started in 2007.

Monetary Policy: The Best Case

Let's start with the most straightforward case, namely a negative shock to aggregate demand driven by what John Maynard Keynes called "animal spirits," emotions and instincts, confidence and fear. Suppose, for example, that the economy has been growing at 3% and the inflation rate is 7%. Now imagine that consumers become more pessimistic and they borrow and spend less, banks lend less, entrepreneurs cut back on expansions and invest less—all of this causes a negative AD shock. The AD curve shifts left, moving the economy from point *a* to point *b* as shown in Figure 35.1.

Monetary Policy and the Fed

FIGURE 35.1

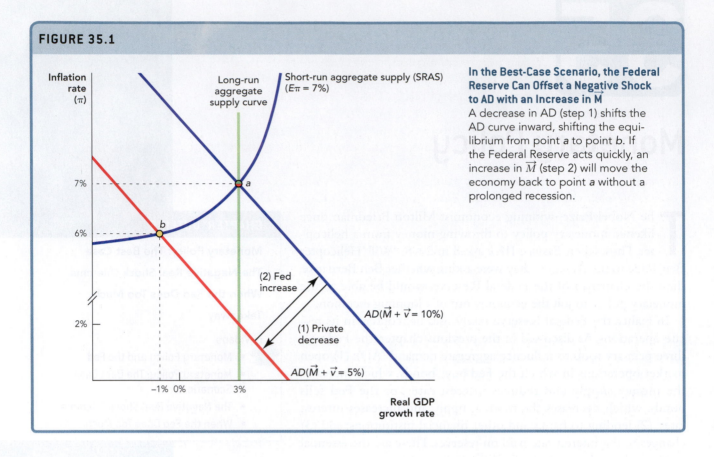

In the Best-Case Scenario, the Federal Reserve Can Offset a Negative Shock to AD with an Increase in $\vec{M}$
A decrease in AD (step 1) shifts the AD curve inward, shifting the equilibrium from point *a* to point *b*. If the Federal Reserve acts quickly, an increase in $\vec{M}$ (step 2) will move the economy back to point *a* without a prolonged recession.

As you can see, the negative shock (if not counteracted by the Fed) means that the growth rate of output will decline. If the contraction is severe enough, the rate of output growth can even turn negative, bringing the economy into a recession, just as we have discussed in our earlier chapters on Business Fluctuations and on the Federal Reserve System and Open Market Operations. Eventually, the economy will recover from the negative AD shock. As fear recedes we'll return to our steady state growth level but not without some sluggish growth and increased unemployment, or even a recession in the meantime.

Could the Fed combat this sluggish growth with monetary policy? Yes! If the Fed can increase the rate of growth of the money supply, reducing interest rates and encouraging more bank lending and investor borrowing, then the AD curve shifts back up and to the right.

Using the policy tools described in the previous chapter, the Federal Reserve is able to push the AD curve back to its original position so the economy will transition from point *b* to *a*, thereby reducing the severity and length of the recession. In essence, instead of allowing the economy to adjust to a decrease in AD, which may require lower growth and higher unemployment, the Federal Reserve quickly restores AD to its previous level.

But Figure 35.1 makes monetary policy look too easy—what could be easier than shifting a curve? Two difficulties make it hard for the Fed to get this right all the time:

1. **The Federal Reserve must operate in real time when much of the data about the state of the economy is unknown.** More specifically,

it takes time for data to be gathered. Data are often released on a monthly or quarterly basis. Sometimes data are amended, after the fact. Then, it takes time for data to be interpreted and for problems to be recognized. Was the dip in employment last month a precursor of a recession or was it an exception? If the price of oil went up last month, does that indicate a longer-term trend or was it the result of some temporary shock? Is a decline in the stock market predicting a future recession or not? In the recent financial crisis, the first major signs of trouble in the subprime market came in August 2007, but most investors—and also the Fed—had no idea that so many banks and financial firms would fail, or be on the brink of failing, over the next year. In fact as late as the spring of 2008, GDP growth figures were still strongly positive and not everyone thought the United States was headed for a recession.

2. **The Federal Reserve's control of the money supply is incomplete and subject to uncertain lags.** Recall from the previous chapter that an increase in the money supply typically affects the economy with a lag that can vary in time from 6 to 18 months. And remember, in atypical situations, if banks aren't willing to lend, then although the Fed may increase the monetary base, the larger monetary aggregates and thus aggregate demand won't increase very much in response. Thus, if banks are slow to lend, then the Fed can easily undershoot, generating a smaller shift in AD and a smaller increase in the rate of economic growth than is desirable. But a larger stimulus is not necessarily better because if the economy recovers before the money supply works its magic, the Fed can easily end up overshooting its goal—producing a higher rate of inflation than is desirable.

Figure 35.2 on the next page portrays the more realistic case for monetary policy in which too little stimulation pushes the economy only to point c where growth is still sluggish. But "too much" monetary stimulation pushes the economy to point d with a higher than desirable inflation rate at 9% (and a growth rate that is high but unsustainable in the long run). Only with the "just right" or Goldilocks amount of stimulation does the economy quickly return to its long-run balanced growth path at point a. We would like it if the Fed hit the Goldilocks amount of stimulation every time, but don't forget: Goldilocks is a fairy tale.

Monetary Policy: The Best Case Scenario

Reversing Course and Engineering a Decrease in AD

Suppose that the Federal Reserve does overstimulate, pushing the aggregate demand curve to "Too much" in Figure 35.2. What then? Remember from our discussion in our chapter on Inflation and the Quantity Theory of Money that inflation makes price signals more difficult to interpret, creates arbitrary redistributions of wealth, and makes long-term planning and contracting more difficult, among other problems. Thus, we don't want inflation to be too high. But, we also know from our chapter on Inflation and the Quantity Theory of Money and the chapter on Business Fluctuations that bringing down the rate of inflation is costly because prices and wages are not fully flexible in the downward direction. That means economies sometimes get stuck between a rock and a hard place—between continuing a costly rate of inflation or reducing it at the risk of a recession.

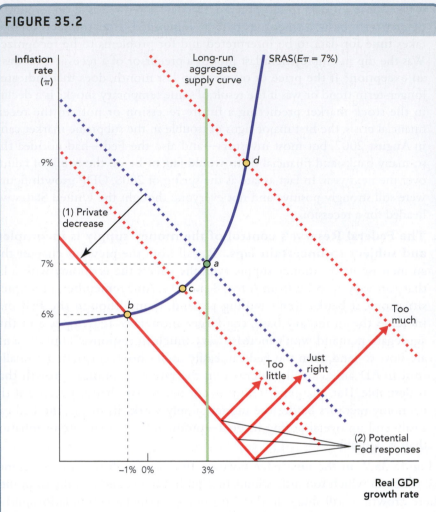

FIGURE 35.2

Getting Monetary Policy "Just Right" Is Not Easy The Federal Reserve operates in real time when much of the data about the economy is unknown. In addition, the Fed's control of aggregate demand is of uncertain magnitude and timing. As a result, the Fed may respond to a fall in AD (step 1) with too little, too much, or just the right amount of stimulus (step 2).

A **disinflation** is a significant reduction in the rate of inflation.

A **deflation** is a decrease in prices, that is, a negative inflation rate.

Many economists think that the Federal Reserve did over-stimulate the economy in the 1970s; and, as a result, by 1980, the inflation rate hit 13.5% a year. Ronald Reagan was elected to the presidency in part to change economic policies. By 1983, tough monetary policy under Reagan and cigar-chomping Federal Reserve Chairman Paul Volcker had reduced the inflation rate to 3%, but the consequence was a very severe recession with an unemployment rate of just over 10%.

The **disinflation** experiment was costly, but unlike the **deflation** of the Great Depression, when prices fell, it was a policy chosen on purpose. The 1980s disinflation broke the back of inflation and provided the foundation for the 25 or so years of successful economic growth—and mostly low unemployment—that the American economy enjoyed until the recession of 2008–2009.

Paul Volcker, chairman of the Federal Reserve in 1980, had to choose between high inflation or high unemployment.

Since World War II there have been six episodes when the Fed deliberately put the brakes on money growth, most prominently the shift beginning with the 1980 presidential election just mentioned. In every case, the tighter monetary policies were followed by declines in output. On average, industrial production 33 months later was 12% lower than otherwise would have been expected. But again, these contractions aren't always bad. Sometimes a contraction is necessary to bring down the rate of inflation. Of course, economists debate which of these contractions were needed and which were not.

Whether or not a particular contraction is a good idea, economists do agree on one point: A monetary contraction goes best when it is **credible,** namely when market participants expect the central bank to carry through its tough stance. This makes sense if you think through exactly why a disinflation is difficult for an economy. A sufficiently radical disinflation leads to unemployment because wages and prices are sticky, especially in the downward direction (as explained in our Inflation and the Quantity Theory of Money chapter). If nominal wage growth is too high, some workers will end up being very expensive and employers will choose to lay them off. So, the key to a less painful disinflation is to increase nominal wage flexibility. Now imagine that a central bank has announced a disinflation but no one really believes it, or people believe it only halfheartedly. Nominal wages probably aren't going to grow more slowly, and when the disinflation comes, if indeed it does come, the unemployment cost will be high. Alternatively, if the coming disinflation is widely expected, then workers will be prepared for slower wage growth and will quickly adjust to what they know is inevitable. Thus, a credible disinflation reduces the unemployment effects of disinflation. So, the lesson is this: If a central bank wishes to undertake a disinflation, it has to be ready to stay the course and it should announce and explain its policy very publicly. This is called making monetary policy credibile.

> A monetary policy is **credible** when it is expected that a central bank will stick with its policy.

The Fed as Manager of Market Confidence

Fear and confidence are some of the most important shifters of aggregate demand. And one of the Federal Reserve's most powerful tools is not its influence over the money supply but its influence over expectations, namely its ability to boost **market confidence.** Recall from our Transmission and Amplification Mechanisms chapter that when investors are uncertain, they often prefer to wait, to delay, and to try to gather more information, before they commit themselves. In addition, remember that one reason we see a lot of time bunching or clustering of investments is that it pays to coordinate your economic actions with those of others—that is, you want to be investing, producing, and selling at the same time that others are investing, producing, or selling. Uncertainty, therefore, can create what economists call a *bandwagon effect* on investment—I am uncertain and so delay my investments, you follow suit not because of uncertainty alone but because your investment is less likely to work well if it doesn't happen at the same time as my investment (time bunching or coordination of investment). Moreover, the fact that you cut back investment verifies that my decision to cut back was a good idea so no one can be accused of behaving irrationally.

Uncertainty drives people away from investment spending and toward assets like cash. Holding cash isn't very productive but cash and other similar assets

> **Market confidence:** One of the Federal Reserve's most powerful tools is its influence over expectations, not its influence over the money supply.

are what you want when you are in "wait and see" mode. In terms of our model of aggregate demand, an increase in the demand for cash is indicated by a decrease in $\vec{v}$. At the same time, increased uncertainty will lead to a fall in $\vec{M}$, as both borrowers and lenders will cut back, and M1 and M2 will grow at slower rates. Changes in both the $\vec{v}$ and the $\vec{M}$ work together to shift the aggregate demand curve inward or to the left, as you can see in Figure 35.1 near the beginning of this chapter.

To cite an example, uncertainty increased after the terrorist attacks of September 11, 2001. Although the devastation in Manhattan was extreme, the economic cost of the attack was small relative to the size of the U.S. economy. Nevertheless, if enough people had taken the attack as a signal to reduce investment, the bandwagon effect could have created a severe recession. The Federal Reserve stepped in to try to prevent this from happening by lending billions of dollars to banks. In the week before September 11, for example, the Federal Reserve lent about $34 million to banks, a trivial amount. On September 12, the Federal Reserve lent $45.5 *billion* to banks.

The mere fact that the Federal Reserve sent a countersignal—we are going to massively maintain or increase AD if necessary—helped stabilize expectations, reduce fear, and raise confidence. The Federal Reserve can't always prevent an increase in uncertainty from reducing $\vec{v}$ and $\vec{M}$; sometimes uncertainty really does increase, such as when a war is imminent, and waiting is the appropriate response. But the Fed often can reduce the bandwagon effect and stabilize expectations toward a more positive outcome.

Monetary policy is often about changing expectations and perceptions, rather than just manipulating numbers and equations. That's one reason why central banking can be so difficult and why it is an art as well as a science.

CHECK YOURSELF

■ How do problems with data affect the Fed's ability to set monetary policy that is "just right"?

The Negative Real Shock Dilemma

A very difficult case for monetary policy is when the economy is hit by a negative real shock such as a rapid oil price increase. As we saw in our chapter on Business Fluctuations and the chapter on Transmission and Amplification Mechanisms, a negative real shock shifts the long-run aggregate supply (LRAS) curve to the left, moving the equilibrium from point *a* to point *b*, as shown in Figure 35.3. That means a higher rate of price inflation and a lower growth rate for GDP, again as previously covered. How should monetary policy respond?

One approach is to focus on the inflation rate, which has jumped from 2% to 8%. What is the recipe for reducing inflation? Correct—a *decrease* in $\vec{M}$. In the 1970s, for example, the Federal Reserve often responded to supply shocks, such as an oil shock, by decreasing $\vec{M}$ and *reducing* aggregate demand. That means taking the AD curve and shifting it farther back to the left through the use of monetary policy. In Figure 35.3, we show the new equilibrium at point *c*. The reduction in $\vec{M}$ reduces the inflation rate from 8% to 6%, but also reduces economic growth and by more than the supply shock alone would have done.

Some economists have argued that the Federal Reserve's actions in trying to stem inflation were even worse for the economy than the oil shocks. Interestingly, the most prominent critic of the Federal Reserve's actions in the 1970s was Ben Bernanke. Consistent with his criticism, when he was Fed chairman

FIGURE 35.3

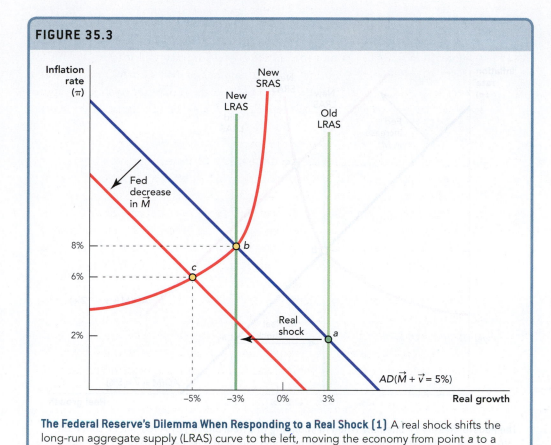

The Federal Reserve's Dilemma When Responding to a Real Shock (1) A real shock shifts the long-run aggregate supply (LRAS) curve to the left, moving the economy from point *a* to a recession at point *b*. If the Federal Reserve concentrates on the higher inflation rate, it may decide to reduce AD, with a cut in $\vec{M}$, moving the economy to point *c* with a lower inflation rate but an even lower growth rate. Note that for clarity we have suppressed the old SRAS curve running through point *a*.

and faced with rising oil prices in 2007–2008, he did not contract the rate of growth of the money supply.[1]

Today, central bankers are more likely to believe that a central bank should respond to a negative real shock by increasing aggregate demand but that, too, has its problems.

The Federal Reserve can increase aggregate demand by increasing the money growth rate, but, when the economy is facing a negative real shock, it is less productive than at other times, due to the real shock. As a result, an increase in $\vec{M}$ will not move the economy back to point *a*. Instead, most of the increase in $\vec{M}$ will show up in inflation rather than in real growth so the economy will shift from point *b* to point *c*, as shown in Figure 35.4 on the next page, with a much higher inflation rate and a slightly higher growth rate.

Is it worthwhile responding to a real shock with an increase in AD? Maybe not. Although an increase in $\vec{M}$ may increase the growth rate a little, the inflation rate increases by a lot and, as we just saw in our discussion of the Volcker disinflation, higher inflation now can cause serious problems later. In particular, if the inflation rate gets too high, the Fed has to reduce inflation, thereby creating a lot of unemployment. Perhaps you wondered in the previous section on

The Negative Real Shock Dilemma

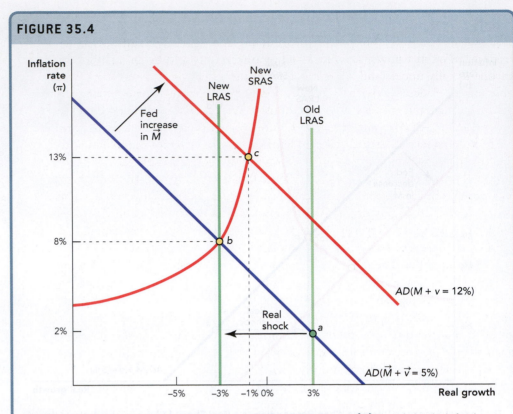

FIGURE 35.4

The Federal Reserve's Dilemma When Responding to a Real Shock (2) A real shock shifts the LRAS Curve to the left, moving the economy from point *a* to a recession at point *b*. If the Federal Reserve concentrates on the lower growth rate, it may decide to increase AD, with an increase in $\vec{M}$ moving the economy to point *c* with a little bit higher growth rate but a much higher inflation rate. Note that for clarity we have suppresed the old SRAS curve running through point *a*.

engineering a disinflation, why the rate of inflation might have ended up too high in the first place. Now you know at least one way inflation can end up too high and that also helps us understand why the dilemmas of monetary policy arise so frequently.

Moreover, recall from our chapter on Business Fluctuations and the chapter on Transmission and Amplification Mechanisms that real shocks are often accompanied by aggregate demand shocks so the figures are considerably simplified. Confused? Don't worry, that is exactly how the economists at the Federal Reserve feel. We are quite serious when we say that a combination of shocks can confuse economists at the Federal Reserve. Don't forget that in addition to the problems you face as students, the Federal Reserve is looking at real-time data, which as we have noted are often uncertain and subject to revision.

The bottom line is that with a real shock, the central bank faces a dilemma: It must choose between too low a rate of growth (with a high rate of unemployment) and too high a rate of inflation. The central bank, in fact, stands a good chance of getting a mix of both problems. The lesson is this: If you are a central banker, hope that you don't face too many negative real shocks in your term!

When the Fed Does Too Much

The Fed has considerable power to influence aggregate demand but, as we argued earlier, that power is constrained by uncertainty and by an inability for anyone to fully understand the complexity of the economy. As a result, it's possible for the Federal Reserve to make booms and recessions worse rather than better. For example, a number of economists have argued that Federal Reserve policy in 2001–2004 contributed to the housing boom and eventual bust that led to the financial crisis in 2007–2008. Of course, many factors contributed to the financial crisis, including too much leverage and irrational exuberance, as discussed in our chapter on Stock Markets and Personal Finance and our chapter on the Saving, Investment, and Financial System. The financial crisis and the Fed's role in it are highly debated topics among economists and a consensus has not yet been reached. Nevertheless, to see how the Fed might have contributed to the financial crisis, let's go back to the late 1990s and the recession of 2001.

When the Fed Does Too Much

interactive activity

In the late 1990s, the American economy was the envy of the world. Economic growth was strong and the unemployment rate was low, even dipping below 4% in 2000. The recession that began in early 2001 didn't last long but there were troubling signs that not all was well. In particular, notice from Figure 35.5 that the unemployment rate continued to increase *even after the recession had officially ended.*★ From a rate of 4% in 2000, unemployment increased during the recession to 5.5% and then kept increasing until it peaked at 6.3% (almost a 50% increase) in June 2003. In fact, even three years after the recession ended, the unemployment rate remained near its recession high.

The Federal Reserve was very concerned about the unemployment rate and it also worried about the psychological blow to consumer confidence after the terrorist attacks on 9/11. To combat the high unemployment rate, the Fed tried to increase aggregate demand through expansionary monetary policy. Figure 35.5 shows one measure of the Fed's efforts, the Federal Funds rate. As described in the previous chapter, the Federal Funds rate is a short-term interest rate that is largely under the control of the Federal Reserve. During the recession, the Fed pushed down the Federal Funds rate from about 6.5% in 2000 to 2% at the end of 2001 when the recession ended. But even after the recession ended, the Fed pushed the Federal Funds rate even lower to below 2%. Indeed, from mid-2003 to mid-2004, the Fed held the Federal Funds rate at 1%, an extraordinarily low rate.

The low Federal Funds rate helped to make credit cheap throughout the economy. This meant it was relatively easy to borrow money and it encouraged people to take out more mortgages, bidding up the price of homes. Unfortunately, easy credit can start or intensify a bubble.

The concept of a speculative bubble was introduced in our chapter on the Saving, Investment, and Financial System, but to restate the fundamental idea here, a bubble arises when asset prices rise far higher, and more rapidly, than can be accounted for by the fundamental prospects of the asset. Investors get carried away by the prospect for gain and they underestimate the prospect of loss. Prices are instead driven by shifts in market psychology and successive waves of irrational exuberance.

★ Recall from our chapter on GDP and the Measurement of Progress that the exact dates of a recession are a judgment call made by the National Bureau of Economic Research. The unemployment rate is one piece of information that goes into defining when a recession begins and ends but it is quite possible for economic activity as measured by other factors such as GDP, sales, and income to be increasing even when the unemployment rate is not declining.

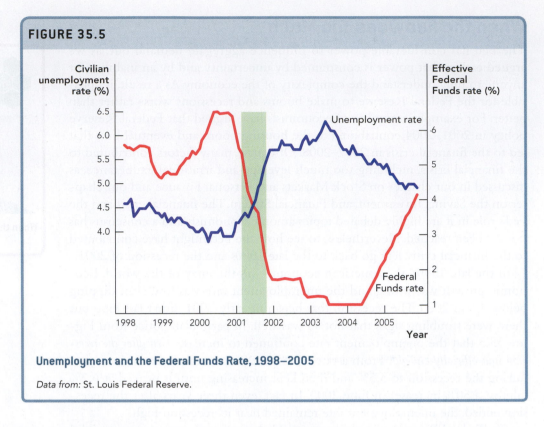

FIGURE 35.5

Unemployment and the Federal Funds Rate, 1998–2005

Data from: St. Louis Federal Reserve.

Now imagine an investor who is thinking of buying a bunch of homes, not to live in them, but rather to resell them quickly for a profit (known as "flipping"). Cheap, easy credit makes it easier for investors of this kind to operate and thus it can intensify bubbles. The low interest rates are, in essence, signaling to market participants that credit is easy and it is a good idea to borrow money. In the words of the Austrian economists Ludwig von Mises and Friedrich A. Hayek, these are *distorted price signals*. A distorted price signal arises when government policy, or in this particular case the Fed's monetary policy, moves a price in a manner that encourages investors to take risks. Of course, the investors didn't have to take foolish risks. If you stockpile bananas on your roof and the roof caves in, it's your mistake even if the government subsidized the purchase of bananas. Nevertheless, cheap bananas and cheap credit probably make these mistakes more likely. The mistakes here were not exclusive to the Fed: The government-sponsored mortgage agencies, called Fannie Mae and Freddie Mac, guaranteed and subsidized a lot of low-quality mortgages, as did the private insurance firm AIG, and that also made the housing bubble worse.

TANG CHHIN SOTHY/AFP/GETTY IMAGES

Subsidized bananas sometimes do encourage crashes.

The Fed began to raise interest rates in mid-2004 but rates remained very low until at least mid-2005. In 2006 housing prices peaked, and by 2007 were in free fall. Figure 35.6 illustrates what happened.

The problem for the economy, of course, came when the price of real estate started to fall in 2006. New home construction dropped very quickly. Homeowners felt poorer and started to spend less, reducing aggregate demand. In addition, the real estate crash contributed to a freezing up of financial intermediation as banks and other intermediaries took huge losses on poor investments in mortgage securities (as discussed in our chapter on the Saving, Investment,

FIGURE 35.6

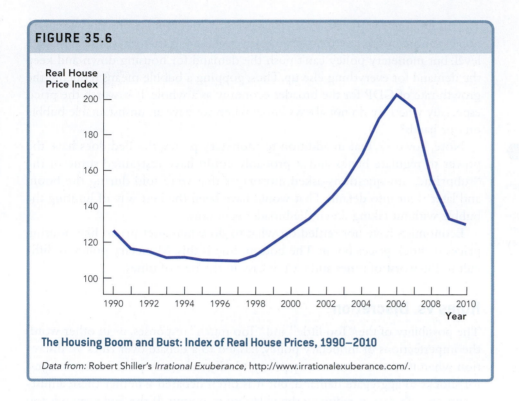

The Housing Boom and Bust: Index of Real House Prices, 1990–2010

Data from: Robert Shiller's *Irrational Exuberance*, http://www.irrationalexuberance.com/.

and Financial System). Since bank lending is a main generator of M1 and M2, this means lower rates of growth for the money supply. As a result, economic growth rates started to decline. By the fall of 2008, the growth rate was negative, meaning that the American economy was shrinking.

Dealing with Asset Price Bubbles

The Fed probably made a mistake holding the Federal Funds so low for so long. But more generally, how should the Fed respond to asset price increases? It's easy to say in retrospect that the Fed should have raised rates sooner or should have raised rates more quickly in response to the housing bubble, but there are several problems with this line of thinking. First, few people expected that a fall in housing prices would wreak as much havoc as it did on financial intermediaries and the general economy. The economy, for example, had quickly recovered from the much larger drop in stock prices during the tech bubble that ended with the recession of 2001. The Fed may have believed that trying to reduce unemployment was worth the risk of generating a bubble in asset prices.

Second, it's not always easy to identify when a bubble is present. If everyone knew it was an unsustainable bubble, then all should have invested accordingly and bet against the bubble, thereby enriching themselves and also stopping the bubble in the first place. Of course, that isn't what happened and the bursting of the bubble was in large part a surprise to many people, including the Fed. Also, don't make the mistake of thinking that if prices rise a lot and then fall, that must mean a bubble was present. Prices can rise and fall for reasons closely related to fundamentals and still cause macroeconomic problems.

Former Federal Reserve Chairman Ben Bernanke
It seemed so much easier in the textbook.

CHECK YOURSELF

■ How can the Fed tell when increases in asset prices reach the bubble stage?

■ If the Fed thinks there is a bubble in housing prices and contracts the growth in the money supply to pop it, what collateral damage can it cause?

Third, monetary policy is a crude means of "popping" a bubble. Monetary policy can influence *aggregate* demand, or target credit markets at the aggregate level, but monetary policy can't push the demand for housing down and keep the demand for everything else up. Thus, popping a bubble means reducing the growth rate of GDP for the broader economy as a whole. Is it worth the price, especially when we do not always know when we have an unsustainable bubble on our hands?

Note, however, that in addition to monetary policy, the Fed does have the power to regulate banks and it probably could have restrained some of the "subprime," no-questions-asked mortgages that were sold during the boom and later went into default. That would have been the best way of limiting the bubble without taking down the broader economy.

Economists have not settled on what to do when asset prices like housing prices or stock prices boom. The bottom line is this: Monetary policy is difficult in the worst of times and it's not easy in the best of times.

Rules vs. Discretion

The possibility of the "Too little" and "Too much" responses, or in other words the imperfections of monetary policy, has led to a debate over rules vs. discretion when it comes to monetary policy. Ideally, monetary policy tries to adjust for shocks to aggregate demand, but it is often debated whether these adjustments are effective in reducing the volatility of output. If the Fed responds too often in the wrong direction or with the wrong strength, GDP volatility will increase rather than decrease.

Economists who think that the Fed is likely to make a lot of mistakes believe that apart from extreme cases, the Fed is best advised to follow a consistent policy and not try to adjust to every aggregate demand shock. A typical monetary rule would set target ranges for the monetary aggregates like M1 or M2 or for the rate of inflation. Nobel Prize winner Milton Friedman, for example, advocated a strict rule in which the money supply would grow by 3% a year every year, since the U.S. economy has a long-run growth rate near 3%.

A monetary rule, however, works best only when v, monetary velocity, doesn't change rapidly. To see one problem with a monetary rule, let's return to the quantity theory of money and the relationship

$$Mv = PY$$

where M is the money supply, v is velocity, P is the price index, and Y is real GDP.

A monetary rule says keep M constant (or growing at a constant rate) but that means that the Fed must ignore changes in v. In times of crisis such as the Great Depression or the Great Recession, we have seen that v can fall rapidly as consumers and businesses cut back on their spending and banks reduce lending. If M is constant and v falls, then either P must fall or Y must fall. Since prices are sticky, the usual outcome is that both P and Y fall, and a fall in Y means a recession.

To avoid some of the defects of a monetary rule but still constrain the Federal Reserve from too much discretion, other economists have suggested a nominal GDP rule. The nominal GDP rule is simple: it says keep Mv constant (or growing at a constant rate). If Mv doesn't change or grows smoothly, then so does PY, and that would be ideal.

FIGURE 35.7

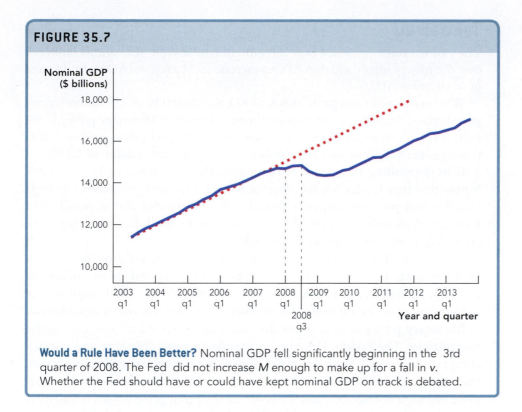

Would a Rule Have Been Better? Nominal GDP fell significantly beginning in the 3rd quarter of 2008. The Fed did not increase *M* enough to make up for a fall in *v*. Whether the Fed should have or could have kept nominal GDP on track is debated.

Figure 35.7 shows nominal GDP from 2003 to 2013. Before the recession, which began in December of 2007, nominal GDP had been increasing at a little over 5% a year. As the recession began, however, nominal GDP began to increase more slowly, and then in the third quarter of 2008 it started to plunge.

A nominal GDP rule would have required the Federal Reserve to increase *M* by as much as it takes to keep nominal GDP growing at around 5% a year (along the path given by the dotted red line). As you can see, the Fed did not follow a nominal GDP rule.

If the Fed had followed a nominal GDP rule, the recession of 2008 would have been much milder. But it's not clear that the Fed *could* have followed a nominal GDP rule. To be fair, the Fed was not asleep at the wheel in 2008 and they did respond to the fall in nominal GDP by increasing the monetary base. Indeed, between August of 2008 and December of 2008, the monetary base doubled! That is by far the largest increase in the monetary base in the Fed's entire history. Proponents of a nominal GDP rule say the Fed did too little, too late. In this view, if the Fed had acted sooner and given the markets clearer guidance, then *v* would have stayed higher and the Fed could have more easily returned nominal GDP to its trend.

As emphasized earlier, much of what the Fed does is to try to manage market confidence and expectations. A rule such as a nominal GDP rule might help to stabilize expectations, especially in normal times. But if a rule suggests that the Fed must do things it has never done before, market participants may wonder whether the Fed will really follow the rule or even if it *can* follow the rule. It may be hard for the Fed to maintain a growth path for *Mv* when credit is collapsing, for instance. Moreover, if a rule suggests that the Fed should do something it has never done before, should and will the Fed follow the rule? It's difficult to know the results of a rule when it requires the Fed to take actions that are outside historical experience.

CHECK YOURSELF

■ Why did Milton Friedman argue for a set rule of 3% money growth per year? Why not 2% or 0%?

Takeaway

The Fed has some influence over the growth rate of GDP through its influence over the money supply and thus AD. An increase in $\vec{M}$ increases AD and a decrease in $\vec{M}$ decreases AD.

When faced with a negative shock to AD, the central bank can restore aggregate demand through an expansionary monetary policy. Monetary policy, however, is subject to uncertainties in impact and timing and getting it "Just right" is not guaranteed. Poor monetary policy can decrease the stability of GDP.

If in responding to a series of recessions, the Fed increases $\vec{M}$ too much, it may find that it later has to contract $\vec{M}$ when inflation becomes too high. Usually, this process—called a disinflation—is painful and it results in a recession. A disinflation goes best when the central bank has some degree of credibility in its attempt to set things right.

A central bank would like low unemployment and low inflation, but it is not always possible to achieve both goals. When a negative real shock comes, the Fed must choose between allowing low rates of growth, excessively high rates of inflation, or some combination of both. There is no easy way out of this dilemma.

Monetary policy is difficult in the worst of times and it's not easy in the best of times. The Federal Reserve has significant power but that power is not always easy to wield. Sometimes the central bank itself contributes to booms that eventually lead to painful busts. How to recognize and respond to asset price booms is not obvious and the economics of asset price booms is unsettled.

Real shocks and aggregate demand shocks are always mixed and not easy to disentangle. The data on which central bankers operate are often slow to arrive and subject to revision. As a result, central banking is as much art as science.

CHAPTER REVIEW

interactive activity   **Go online to practice with more examples of these types of problems, including live links to videos, data sources, and feedback.**

   Problems in green relate to MRU videos. See the MRU table at the end of the exercises.

KEY CONCEPTS

disinflation, p. 745

deflation, p. 745

credible, p. 745

market confidence, p. 745

FACTS AND TOOLS

1. This chapter is concerned mostly with how monetary policy might be able to return an economy *quickly* to the potential growth rate after a shock. But as we saw in the discussion of the quantity theory of money in our Inflation chapter, a market economy has a correction mechanism to return itself *slowly* to the potential growth rate after a shock: flexible prices. Let's review the quantity theory, and remember that in the quantity theory, inflation does all of the adjusting.

   Recall that: $\vec{M} + \vec{v} =$ Inflation + Real growth

   a. Consider the nation of Kydland. Before the shock to Kydland's economy, $\vec{M} = 10\%$, $\vec{v} = 3\%$, real growth = 4%. What is inflation?

   b. In Kydland, $\vec{v}$ falls to 0%, but $\vec{M}$ stays the same. In the long run, what will inflation equal? What will real growth equal?

   c. Consider the nation of Prescottia. Before the shock to Prescottia's economy, $\vec{M} = 2\%$, $\vec{v} = 4\%$, real growth = 2%. What is inflation?

   d. In Prescottia, $\vec{v}$ rises to 8%. In the long run, what will inflation equal? What will real growth equal?

e. Consider the nation of Friedmania. Before the shock to Friedmania's economy, $\vec{M} = 3\%$, $\vec{v} = 0\%$, real growth = 3%. What is inflation?

f. In Friedmania, $\vec{M}$ falls to 1%. In the long run, what will inflation equal? What will real growth equal?

2. We've just reviewed the quantity theory of money, which is a theory that shows how the economy fixes itself in the long run. But as economist John Maynard Keynes famously said, "In the long run we are all dead." Let's bring SRAS back into the model, and play the role of a central banker reacting to a rise in velocity growth.

a. The following diagram shows the economy growing at the potential growth rate with 10% inflation. Illustrate what happens if consumers and investors become more optimistic. Clearly label the new growth rate on the *x*-axis with the words "High-AD real growth," and label the new inflation rate on the *y*-axis with the words "High-AD inflation."

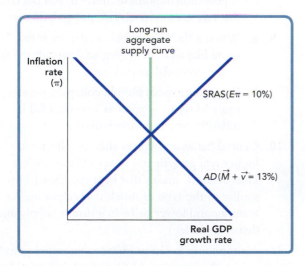

b. Once the central banker sees this rise in AD, she decides to fully reverse it with monetary policy. In the graph, illustrate what happens if she does her job "Just right."

c. If she does her job "Just right," what will the inflation rate be? Provide an exact number.

3. Let's look at the Federal Reserve's dilemma when there's a positive shock to the long-run aggregate supply curve. We'll consider the reverse of Figures 35.3 and 35.4.

a. In the following figure, illustrate the effect of this positive potential growth shock, ignoring the possible effect of sticky wages and prices.

b. If the central bank kept AD fixed, would inflation be higher or lower after this positive real shock? Would real growth be higher or lower after this positive real shock?

c. If the central bank wants to return inflation to its old level, should it raise money growth or lower it?

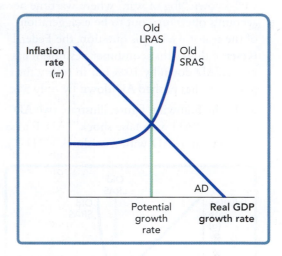

d. If the central bank wants to return real growth to its old level, should it raise money growth or lower it?

e. Economists say that central bankers face a "cruel trade-off" between inflation and real growth when a potential growth shock hits. Do your answers to parts c and d fit in with this theory?

4. All of the following are called "rules." Which of the following so-called rules are actually like "rules" and which are more like "discretion"? How can you tell the difference?

a. Congress passes a law providing automatic cost-of-living increases to Social Security every year. (*Note:* This is current U.S. law.)

b. Congress follows a rule to vote every few years on how much to increase Social Security payments—votes that usually occur just before an election. (This was the law before 1972.)

c. The Federal Reserve follows the famous "Taylor rule" for setting the Federal Funds rate:

Nominal rate = 2% + Inflation + 0.5 × (Real growth rate − Potential growth rate)

d. The Federal Reserve follows a rule of "doing whatever seems right at the time."

e. The police follow a rule of questioning anyone loitering outside of a bank who looks suspicious.

f. The police follow a rule of questioning anyone loitering outside of a bank who is dressed in bulky clothing that could conceal a weapon.

5. Let's consider a case that has some similarities to Figure 35.2. We mentioned that it's difficult for the Fed to know what's really happening to the economy in real time. This is similar to the well-known "fog of war," where wartime news accounts often turn out to be exaggerations of the real story. In this question, the Federal Reserve thinks that consumer pessimism has pushed AD down by 10%, but in reality, the pessimism has pushed AD down by only 5%.

a. In the following figure, illustrate two AD curves: "AD with false shock" (AD-F to save room) and "AD with true shock" (AD-T).

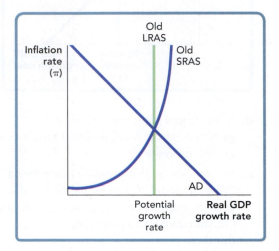

b. If the central bank wants to use monetary policy to reverse a 10% shock to AD, it will have to raise money growth by 10%. Now draw two more AD curves on the figure: "Fed reacts to false shock" (FR-F to keep it short) and "Fed reacts to true shock" (FR-T).

c. After the central bank overreacts to the exaggerated news reports of economic calamity, what is the final result: Will real growth be higher or lower than before the shock hits? Will inflation be higher or lower than before the shock hits?

6. Which of the following would be methods that the Fed could use to "maintain market confidence" when a negative AD shock hits?

a. Slow the growth rate of the monetary base.

b. Raise the interest rate on "discount window" loans.

c. Promise to increase the growth rate of money if the economy worsens further.

d. Sell Treasury bills and buy bank reserves through open market operations.

e. Pay a higher interest rate on reserves.

7. When talking about the economy, people often make a distinction between policies that work "only in theory" compared to those that work "in practice." In theory, a fall in money growth slows down the economy in the short run. In the six episodes since World War II when, as discussed, the Fed deliberately put the brakes on money growth, did this theory work "in practice" every single time, most of the time but not all of the time, or did this theory fail most of the time?

8. A monetary policy is said to be *credible* if the central bank will have an incentive to do tomorrow what it says today that it will do tomorrow. Other policies may be credible or noncredible. Which of the following policies are credible?

a. A student promises to study for the final after going to the frat party.

b. A long established store offers "Guaranteed satisfaction or your money back."

c. A government promises never to bail out banks that take on too much risk and go bankrupt.

9. a. When a financial bubble collapses, is that more like a fall in aggregate demand or a fall in the potential growth rate?

b. When a financial bubble collapses, what is more likely to happen as a result: a fall in inflation or a rise in inflation?

10. Central banks and voters alike usually want higher real growth and lower inflation. What kind of shock makes that happen? (*Note:* This is similar to the type of shock that causes higher quantity and lower price in a simple supply and demand model.)

11. An economy has been growing for many years at just 1% per year, which most people consider slow. An adviser to the government suggests that faster growth in the money supply could increase the growth rate. How would you respond?

THINKING AND PROBLEM SOLVING

12. Let's reenact a simplified version of the 1981–1982 Volcker disinflation. Expected inflation and actual inflation are both 10%, real growth is 3%, and to keep it simple, velocity growth is zero. (*Historical note:* In fact, velocity growth shifted quite a lot during this period, which made Volcker's job harder than in this problem.)

Otherwise, the numbers are close to the historical facts.) Thus, we have

AD: Money growth = Inflation + Real growth

Let's define a simple SRAS curve:

SRAS: Inflation = Expected inflation + 1 × (Real growth rate − Potential growth rate)

Notice that this equation gives a positive relationship between inflation and real growth for a fixed potential growth rate and expected inflation rate.

a. First, let's calculate how fast the money supply grew back when inflation was 10% in 1980 and real growth was at the rate of 3%. How fast did the money supply grow at this point, before Volcker started fighting inflation? (*Hint:* Use the AD equation.)

b. Now, let's calculate how fast Volcker will let the money supply grow in the long run, after he pulls inflation down to 4% per year. Remember, he'll assume that in the long run, the economy will just grow at the potential growth rate. (*Hint:* Use AD again.)

c. In the short run, when Volcker cuts money growth to the rate you calculated in part b, the economy won't grow at the potential growth rate. Instead, real output will grow at whatever rate the SRAS dictates. In terms of algebra, this means you have to combine SRAS and AD; it's a system of two equations and two unknowns: inflation and real growth. You know the values of money growth, expected inflation, and the potential growth rate already. In the short run, what will real growth and inflation be?

13. Now, let's reenact the Volcker disinflation in an alternate universe where wages are more flexible and workers are much more willing to accept slower growing wages when the inflation rate falls. This will make the SRAS steeper, as we saw in our original discussion of short-run aggregate supply.

Our model economy is thus as follows:

SRAS: Inflation = Expected inflation + 2 × (Real growth rate − Potential growth rate)

AD: Money growth = Inflation + Real growth

a. Answer part c of the previous question again, now in this world with a steeper SRAS.

b. Let's see how far this can go: What if workers pay constant attention to the Fed's every move and will slow their wage demands the moment they see Volcker tightening the money supply? Answer the previous question with "100" in the place of "2" in the SRAS equation. Feel free to round your answers to the nearest percent.

c. If you were a central banker trying to cut inflation, and you want to keep real growth as close as possible to the potential growth rate, what would you prefer: a steep SRAS (i.e., workers with flexible wages), or a flatter SRAS (i.e., workers with sticky wages)?

14. The Fed plays an important role in maintaining market confidence. As former Chairman Alan Greenspan put it in a 1997 address: "In [financial crises] the Federal Reserve *stands ready* to provide liquidity, if necessary.... The objectives of the central bank in crisis management are to . . . prevent a contagious loss of confidence." [emphasis added]

Just by *standing ready* to provide loans to banks in an emergency, the Fed can often prevent emergencies from happening in the first place. In each of the following examples, how does the fact that someone or something stands ready to cure the bad outcome help prevent the bad outcome from ever happening in the first place?

a. A security guard stands inside a bank.

b. Federal agents guard Fort Knox, where about one-half of the U.S. government's gold is stored.

c. The Federal Reserve promises to insure almost 100% of bank deposits.

d. Police, worried about possible riots during spring break in Palm Springs, California, bring in police from other cities.

15. We discussed how hard it is to keep AD stable or put it back "where it belongs" after a shock. Alan Blinder, a former vice chairman of the Federal Reserve, noticed that this was a major problem. In his book *Central Banking in Theory and Practice,* he argued that this was a good reason for the Fed to take baby steps whenever it needed to make big shifts in AD. Sometimes you're better off taking two years to slowly and carefully undo an AD shock rather than shift it back quickly and inaccurately in one year.

To illustrate, let's see how things turn out if you, the central banker, take two years rather than one year to react to a negative velocity shock. You have better control over AD if you make small moves than if you make big moves, but big moves can get you back to the potential growth rate more quickly: As so often in economics, you face a trade-off.

In this question, your ultimate goal is to get AD back to 5% per year, the potential growth rate is 3%, and expected inflation is always 2% per year.

Starting point (substitute what you know into these equations and solve):

AD: 1% = Inflation + Real growth rate
SRAS: Inflation = Expected inflation + (Real growth rate − Potential growth rate)

a. Slow approach: Add 2% per year to AD for two years (through some mix of money growth and higher confidence). What will real growth equal each year?

	Start	End of Year 1	End of Year 2
Real Growth			

b. Fast approach: Assume that you tried to add 4% to AD in Year 1, but you mistakenly add 7% instead (through some mix of excess bank lending and irrational exuberance). In the second year, you tried to correct by cutting back by 3%, but you mistakenly cut back by 4% (through some mix of slower bank lending and investors' loss of confidence). What will real growth equal each year?

	Start	End of Year 1	End of Year 2
Real Growth			

c. You can see how the "best approach" is a matter of taste, but which method would you expect a central banker to prefer if Congress has to decide whether to reappoint the central banker to a new four-year term in a few months?

16. Milton Friedman and Anna Schwartz argued in the last chapter of their *Monetary History of the United States* that a shift in money growth will usually cause velocity to shift in the same direction: So higher money growth causes optimism, and slower growth causes pessimism. They believed that velocity had its own shocks, as well.

a. Let's run through some examples of how this might work, in a setting where the Fed wants to keep AD growth stable at 10%. To keep things simple, we'll just assume that the Fed can control money growth perfectly, and we'll assume that a 1% change in money growth causes a 0.5% shock to velocity growth in the same direction. Fill in the table.

In each case, AD = Initial velocity shock + Money growth + Velocity shock caused by money growth.

Year	Initial Velocity Shock	Money Growth	Velocity Shock Caused by Money Growth
1	4%	4%	4% × 0.5 = 2%
2	3%		
3	16%		
4	8%		
5	4%		
6	0%		

b. If velocity does tend to move in the direction of money growth, how does this change the Fed's response to economic shocks: Should it take bigger moves or smaller moves in money growth when a shock comes along?

17. We saw that real shocks and AD shocks often occur simultaneously. When this happens, unless we know the exact size of each shock, we can't be sure of the effect on both inflation *and* real growth: We'll know only one or the other for sure.

In each of the following cases, we can be *sure* that *one* of the four events will happen:

A fall in inflation

A rise in inflation

A fall in real growth

A rise in real growth

In the following cases, which changes can we confidently predict? (*Hint:* Draw an AD/Potential curve graph. Try several different combinations of the indicated shifts and see which outcomes are possible on the graph.)

a. The banking system becomes less efficient at building bridges between savers and borrowers, and investor confidence declines: A negative real shock and a negative velocity shock occur simultaneously.

b. The banking system becomes less efficient at building bridges between savers and borrowers, and the Federal Reserve increases money growth: A negative real shock and a positive money shock occur simultaneously.

c. Biologists learn how to use computer simulations to rapidly search for molecules that would make promising medicines, and investors become optimistic about future profit opportunities: A positive real shock and a positive velocity shock occur simultaneously.

18. One argument for giving discretion to central bankers is that sometimes emergencies come along that a simple rule can't solve. Suppose there's a massive, permanent negative shock to velocity. Naturally, if the central bank has discretion, it will immediately respond by boosting money growth. But let's look at the alternative:

a. Suppose that the central bank follows a fixed 3% annual monetary growth rule, as Milton Friedman sometimes recommended. In the short run, what will the velocity shock do to real growth and to inflation?

b. In the long run, what will this velocity shock do to real growth and to inflation?

c. If voters are concerned only about real growth in the long run, will they favor rules, will they favor discretion, or will they be indifferent between the two?

d. If voters are impatient, and concerned only about real growth in the short run, will they favor rules, will they favor discretion, or will they be indifferent between the two?

e. Which kind of voters favor discretion: those with a long-run horizon or those with a short-run horizon?

Ask FRED

19. Using the FRED economic database (https://fred.stlouisfed.org/), find the velocity of M2 from 2005 to 2016. Click Edit Graph and change the units to Percent Change. What happened to the growth rate of velocity in the 4th quarter of 2008? What kind of shock is this?

CHALLENGES

This chapter has more Challenge questions than usual. Take this as a sign of how difficult monetary policy really is!

20. Practice with the best case: You are the central banker, and you have to decide how fast the money supply should grow. Your economy gets hit by the following AD shocks and your job is simply to neutralize them: Just push money growth in the opposite direction of the shock.

In all of the following cases, assume that there's no change whatsoever to the potential growth rate, and assume that before the shock, you're at your optimal inflation rate and optimal real growth rate. (Yes, this really is the best case!) These are all shocks, so think of each case study as preceded by the word, "Suddenly . . . ." Given the shocks to $\vec{v}$, velocity, should the central bank react by raising money growth or by cutting money growth?

a. Investors become pessimistic about future profit opportunities.

b. State governments increase spending on schools, prisons, and health care.

c. The federal government passes a national sales tax.

d. The federal government increases military spending.

e. Foreigners buy fewer American-made airplanes and movies.

f. American consumers start buying fewer domestically made Hondas and more imported Hondas.

g. Domestically made computers, cars, and furniture all become much more durable and longer-lasting.

21. Milton Friedman famously said that changes in money growth affect the economy with "long and variable lags." That means that if the government increases growth in the monetary base this month, the money multiplier takes a few months to turn this into growth in checking and savings deposits, and it takes a few months more before businesses and consumers actually spend this money to purchase goods and services. Let's see how this changes our views of the previous question.

In each case from question 19, the Fed predicts how long the velocity shock itself will last: We call this "shock duration" in the next table. After that time, velocity growth will go back to its old level. Additionally, in each case, the Fed's staff of PhD economists estimates how many months it will take for a change in money supply to actually push AD in the desired direction: This is the "monetary lag."

The question is quite simple: If monetary lags are shorter than the shock duration—if the Fed has "fair warning"—then a shift in AD will be stabilizing. If not, then a shift in AD will be like mailing a birthday card to your mother the day before her birthday: possibly destabilizing. So, in which of these cases should the Federal Reserve change money growth?

Case	Monetary Lag (months)	Shock Duration (months)	Shift in Money Growth: Stabilizing or Destabilizing?
a.	14	8	
b.	18	12	
c.	20	Permanent	
d.	12	24	
e.	16	9	
f.	10	Permanent	
g.	18	Permanent	

22. One of the reasons it's difficult to be a monetary policymaker is because it's so hard to tell what's actually going on in the economy. It's a lot like being a doctor in a world before X-rays, MRIs, and inexpensive blood tests: When the patient complains about a stomachache, you don't know if it's caused by food poisoning or by a tumor the size of a grapefruit.

In each of the cases from the first question, consider the fact that your data are often quite unreliable. (Fed Chair Alan Greenspan was famous for holding meetings with 100 staff economists, peppering them with questions about the quality of their data on the economy, and often knowing more than his own staff economists about the strengths and weaknesses of various surveys of the U.S. economy.) To make matters more difficult, the Federal Reserve has to forecast the behavior of Congress, which is at least as difficult as predicting the behavior of businesses: Politicians often claim they are going to raise or cut spending or taxes, but then fail to do so.

If in cases a, b, and d, the Fed chairman decides that the forecasted shocks really aren't very likely to happen, then taking into account your answers to questions 19 and 20, in which cases should the Fed actually do nothing whatsoever in response to news about the economy?

23. We explained how a central bank has an important role in maintaining confidence: "High

confidence" keeps velocity growth and the money multiplier from falling. But as we've seen, sometimes one has to be cruel to be kind.

President Franklin Roosevelt followed this "tough love" approach during the Great Depression. Soon after taking office, he closed all banks for a four-day "bank holiday." During this holiday, he gave his first Fireside Chat, a radio address where he explained his policies to the American people in plain language. After the four-day holiday, he still kept one-third of all U.S. banks closed (mostly small farmer banks with one or two branches). Over the next few years, only half of this one-third eventually reopened.

Thus, FDR's bank holiday pushed the broad U.S. money supply (M1 or M2) down. Nevertheless, the economy grew quickly during FDR's first year, 1933. Why? Because FDR promised that the banks that reopened were the safest banks, and he promised that the federal government would keep these safer banks open through generous discount window lending. This boosted confidence and encouraged people to borrow from and lend to the remaining banks.

As Milton Friedman and Anna Schwartz put it in their classic book *A Monetary History of the United States*: "The emergency revival of the banking system contributed to recovery by restoring confidence in the monetary and economic system and thereby inducing the public . . . to raise velocity . . . rather than by producing a growth in the stock of money" (p. 433).

Let's see how an emotional concept like "confidence" shows up mathematically. To keep things simple, we'll look at AD in terms of growth in nominal GDP (growth in dollar sales) rather than growth in real GDP (growth in actual output). We'll compare the "before" and "after," so we'll skip over 1933, the year of the biggest banking crisis and of FDR's solution to the crisis:

Year	M2	v
1932	$35.3 billion	2.16
1934	$33.1 billion	2.36

a. What was the level of nominal GDP in 1932 and 1934?

b. What was the growth of M2 between these two years?

c. What was the growth of velocity between these two years?

d. What was the growth of nominal GDP between these two years?

e. If velocity growth had been zero during this period (perhaps due to low confidence), but money growth stayed the same, what would have happened to nominal GDP growth?

24. Central bankers often believe that their hands are tied by the public. Arthur Burns, the Fed chairman under President Nixon, reportedly said in the November 1970 Federal Reserve board meeting that "he did not believe the country was willing to accept for any long period an unemployment rate in the area of 6 percent." In other words, if AD shocks or potential growth shocks came along that pushed the unemployment rate up, Burns believed he had to boost AD to help the economy: The voters wouldn't tolerate anything else.

a. In the early 1970s, the economy was hit with some negative potential growth shocks, the most famous of which were the massive oil price increases caused by the OPEC oil embargo. Inflation started off at 4%, and Burns actually behaved according to his stated philosophy. What did Burns do to AD in the 1970s: Did he raise it or lower it?

b. If Burns had kept AD fixed instead of shifting it as he did, would inflation have been lower or higher than it actually turned out to be?

c. According to our model, did Burns' actions raise, lower, or have no impact on the long-run aggregate supply curve?

d. If in the 1970s the United States had been hit by negative AD shocks instead of negative potential growth shocks, and Burns had followed his same philosophy, would inflation have been higher or lower than it actually turned out to be?

25. Central bankers are reluctant to try to pop alleged bubbles. Which topics covered in this chapter might explain why they are reluctant to do so?

26. We mentioned Milton Friedman's advice that central bankers should follow a "fixed money growth rule," where the broad money supply (M1 or M2) grows at the same rate every year. Other economists have instead recommended that central bankers follow "nominal GDP targeting," which is similar to a fixed AD curve. Assume that the central bank really can control money growth and velocity growth within a reasonable period of time if it tries to do so.

a. What is the difference between a fixed money growth rule and nominal GDP targeting from the point of view of the AD equation?

b. If velocity shocks never occur, what's the best policy for keeping AD as stable as possible: fixed money growth, nominal GDP targeting? Or are both equivalent?

c. If velocity shocks are common, what's the best policy for keeping AD as stable as possible: fixed money growth, nominal GDP targeting? Or are both equivalent?

27. The previous question assumed that the central bank can really control money growth and velocity growth within a reasonable period of time. Instead, let's work with the more realistic assumption that it takes about a year for a change in monetary policy to actually influence money growth: Even though the central bank can increase bank reserves literally within minutes through open market operations or the term auction facility, it takes months for banks to determine whom they should lend to. And as you know, most money is created through bank loans.

In this question, the central bank tries to follow nominal GDP targeting so that AD grows at 7% per year. In other words, the central banks tries to set the money growth rate so that velocity growth plus money growth equals 7%. Each year, it responds to that year's velocity growth, but the response won't actually kick in until next year. (Think of this as driving a car with loose steering: You steer to the right, but the car only starts moving to the right about 2 seconds later.)

a. Fill in the following table. Notice that in each year, Actual AD = Velocity growth + Money growth. In the first year, the central bank observes velocity growth of 3% and thus targets money growth of 4%. The next year money grows at 4% as targeted, but velocity growth in that year is 1% so actual AD grows at 5%. In Year 2, the central bank observes velocity growth of 1% and thus targets money growth of 6%. Keep going.

Year	Velocity Growth	Target Money Growth	Money Growth	Actual AD
1	3%	4%	n/a	n/a
2	1%	6%	4%	5%
3	9%	−2%	6%	15%
4	6%			
5	2%			
6	5%			
7	0%			
8	4%			
9	6%			
10	5%			

b. Every year, the central bank tries to keep AD = 7%, yet it never accomplishes its goal. How do "long lags" explain this failure?

c. How would this table look if you had followed Friedman's 3% money growth rule instead? Don't calculate any numbers, just answer verbally: Would the swings tend to be bigger than in the table or smaller?

28. a. Central bankers must manage expectations. Suppose that inflation is running at 10% and the central banker would like to lower inflation to 2% without reducing real growth. What should the central banker tell the public? And at what level should the central banker set money growth? Assume that velocity shocks are zero and that the potential growth rate is 3%.

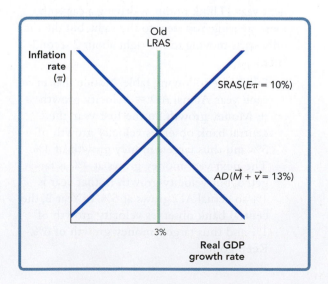

b. Suppose that the public does believe the central banker. What temptation might the central banker face? (*Hint:* Imagine that it is an election year and the central banker would like to see the current administration reelected.)

c. If the central banker is not believed, what will happen? Use your answers to parts a and b to discuss the importance of independent central banks.

29. In response to the housing bust and its fallout discussed at the end of this chapter, the U.S. economy entered into recession in December of 2007. That recession officially ended in June of 2009, but more than two years later at the end of 2011, many people still felt that the "recession" was not really over. As evidence, they cited high unemployment rates and the failure of some areas of the economy such as the housing market and lending to fully recover. Observers cited lack of confidence and elevated levels of uncertainty for reasons both economic and political. The Federal Reserve implemented several policies to lower both short- and long-term interest rates and increase confidence, but the private sector of the economy did not respond as it had following earlier recessions.

a. Use the AD–AS model to describe how the bursting of the housing bubble affected the economy, how the Fed responded, and the impact it had. In your discussion, be sure to point out which parts of this chapter apply to which behaviors in the economy and which parts apply to the role of the Fed in these events.

b. Critics of the Fed's response in lowering and keeping interest rates so low for so long argued that the Fed was risking increased inflation. Use the AD–AS model again to explore the validity of these claims.

WORK IT OUT

For interactive, step-by-step help in solving this problem, go online.

In the United States, the government's data on real growth improve over time. For instance, we now know that in the early 1970s, the economy was actually growing 4% faster than people believed. At the time, the Fed thought the economy was in a deep recession, so it mistakenly boosted money growth. The Fed's overreaction caused inflation. Real-time surveys in the early 1970s depicted an awful economy, but as economic historians have gone back to the data, they have discovered that the economy wasn't as awful as they thought: Someone just put the thermometer in the fridge.

Economists at the Philadelphia Federal Reserve have collected data on how our view of the economy has changed over time. These "real-time data" are summarized by Croushore and Stark in a review article entitled "A Funny Thing Happened on the Way to the Data Bank: A Real-Time Data Set for Macroeconomists" (Federal Reserve Bank of Philadelphia, *Business Review*, September/October 2000, 15–27). Let's use their summary of the data and a six-sided die to see just how inaccurate our real-time views of the economy actually are.

a. We're going to reenact the 1970s, and we'll start figuring out how error-filled the government's growth estimates will be. Croushore and Stark report that, on average:

   i. One-sixth of the time, measured growth is 2% better than actual growth.

   ii. One-third of the time, measured growth is 1% better than actual growth.

   iii. One-third of the time, measured growth is 1.5% worse than actual growth.

   iv. One-sixth of the time, measured growth is 3% worse than actual growth.

   Find a six-sided die (or use Excel to simulate rolling the die) and record your rolls in the following table. If you've rolled a 1, count that in category i; if you roll a 2 or 3, place that in category ii; a 4 or 5 goes in category iii; and if you roll a 6, place that in category iv. Then write down how much measurement error you'll have for that year.

   Example: If your first roll was a 4, that places you in category iii, so write down "−1.5" as the amount of measurement error for 1971.

   (*Note:* Psychologists and behavioral economists have found that people are fairly bad at generating truly random numbers on their own, so it's best just to roll the die.)

Year	Roll (value)	Category	Measurement Error (%)
1971			
1972			
1973			
1974			
1975			
1976			
1977			
1978			
1979			
1980			

b. Let's see what values we get when we add together the true real growth rate (which economists will only know years later) with the measurement error in the previous table. For "true real growth," we use the most recent data in the following table— but of course even these estimates could change in the future. The sum is the actual government data that will wind up in the Federal Reserve chair's hands.

   Example: If your first roll was a 4, that placed you in category iii, so subtract 1.5% from the true 1971 growth rate to yield a real-time government report of 1.9% annual growth.

Year	True Real Growth	Government Data (%)
1971	3.4%	
1972	5.3%	
1973	5.8%	
1974	−0.5	
1975	−0.2	
1976	5.3%	
1977	4.6%	
1978	5.6%	
1979	3.2%	
1980	−0.2	

c. In your simulation, how many times was the government data off by 2% or more?

d. If the potential growth rate in the 1970s was actually 3.6% (the average growth rate in the 1970s), then in how many years did your government data give values *below* 3.6% when true real growth was *above*

3.6%? How often did the reverse occur, with your government data *above* the potential rate while true real growth was *below*?

e. Add together your two values from part d. This is the number of times that even a *very good* central banker would have wanted to push AD in the wrong direction: it's the number of times this weather vane was pointing in entirely the wrong direction.

(*Note:* You might be wondering whether the U.S. government tends to exaggerate extra good economic news just before an election. As far as economists can tell, the answer is no, at least when it comes to the official GDP number. U.S. GDP estimates contain mistakes before an election just as often as usual, but those mistakes don't tend to favor the political party in power. In Japan, though, GDP reports do tend to be extra optimistic just before an election. For more, see Faust, Rogers, and Wright, "News and Noise in G-7 GDP Announcements," online at the Federal Reserve Board's Web site.)

MRUNIVERSITY
AN ONLINE EDUCATION PLATFORM

MARGINAL REVOLUTION UNIVERSITY VIDEOS

Monetary Policy and the Fed
mruniversity.com/intro-fed
Problems: **11**

The Negative Real Shock Dilemma
mruniversity.com/monetary-neg-shock
Problems: **17**

Monetary Policy: The Best Case Scenario
mruniversity.com/monetary-best
Problems: **2, 12, 20**

When the Fed Does Too Much
mruniversity.com/fed-limits
Problems: **4, 27, 29**

36

The Federal Budget: Taxes and Spending

Some people do better from the federal government than others. Take Ida May Fuller. In 1940, Ida May received Social Security check #00-000-001, the very first in the program's history. Ida May's working career had almost ended by the time Social Security began, so she had paid just $24.75 in Social Security taxes and she got almost all of that back with her first check, which was for $22.54. Moreover, Ida May lived to be 100, so by the time she died in 1975, she had received a total of $22,888.92 in benefits.

You can see why Ida May is smiling. But will you be smiling from federal taxes and spending? After all, you will pay Social Security taxes throughout your working life, and what about the benefits? You can be fairly sure that unlike Ida May, you won't receive almost a thousand times more than what you put in.

More generally, since about the mid-1950s, the federal government has spent about 20% of GDP and raised about 18% of GDP. That's a lot of money, approximately $4 trillion in spending in 2017. Where does all that money come from? Where does it all go? And for how long can the U.S. government keep spending more than it raises in taxes?

Tax Revenues

As of 2017, the federal government takes in about $3.6 trillion, or approximately $11,000 for every man, woman, and child in the United States. The federal government takes in money in many ways, but three sources—the individual income tax, the Social Security and Medicare taxes, and the corporate income tax—account for more than 90% of the revenue. Figure 36.1 shows the major sources of revenue for the U.S. government.

The individual income tax is the single largest source of revenue for the federal government. The second category, Social Security and Medicare taxes (a few other smaller taxes are also included in this category), includes the "FICA tax" you have seen on your paycheck—these taxes are so named because unlike the income tax, the revenue from these taxes is tied to specific programs. Corporate income taxes are a distant third. The other sources are much smaller and

Ida May Fuller received the very first Social Security check.

FIGURE 36.1

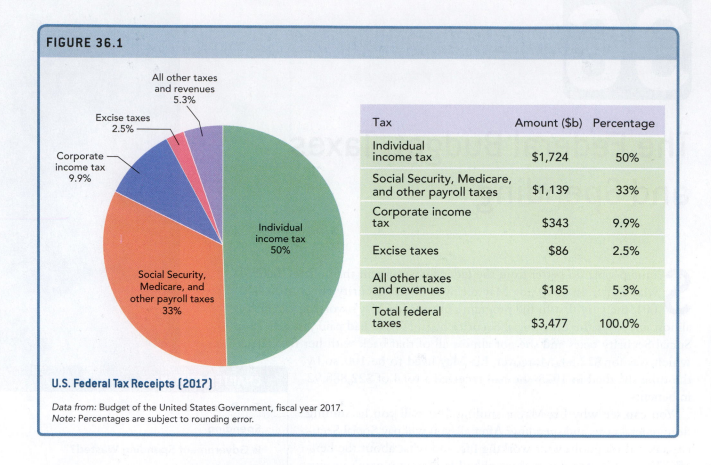

Tax	Amount ($b)	Percentage
Individual income tax	$1,724	50%
Social Security, Medicare, and other payroll taxes	$1,139	33%
Corporate income tax	$343	9.9%
Excise taxes	$86	2.5%
All other taxes and revenues	$185	5.3%
Total federal taxes	$3,477	100.0%

U.S. Federal Tax Receipts (2017)

Data from: Budget of the United States Government, fiscal year 2017.
Note: Percentages are subject to rounding error.

they include excise taxes such as taxes on gasoline and alcohol, user fees, estate and gift taxes, and custom duties or tariffs. Let's take a closer look at the three largest sources of revenue.

The Individual Income Tax

Most Americans are required to file an income tax return with the federal government. On this form a person reports his or her income and the tax code determines how much money is due. The 2016 schedule of marginal tax rates for someone who is married and filing jointly with a spouse, is shown in Figure 36.2 on the next page.

The **marginal tax rate** is the tax rate that you must pay on an additional dollar of income. Figure 36.2 tells us that if you earn less than $18,550, then the marginal tax rate, the rate on an additional dollar of income, is 10% (some deductions are allowed—see the next page). If you earn between $18,550 and $75,300, the rate of tax on an additional dollar of income is 15%. If you earn between $75,300 and $151,900, you must pay 25% of any additional income to the federal government. Marginal tax rates increase in uneven steps until the top marginal tax rate of 39.6% is reached on any income earned greater than $466,950.

We care about the marginal tax rate because, as usual in economics, it's the *marginal* rate that matters for determining things like the incentive to work additional hours. If you are considering doing an extra carpentry job for spare cash, you don't care what tax you are paying on the money you've already earned. You care about how much additional tax you will be paying on the extra money that you might earn if you choose to take the job.

The **marginal tax rate** is the tax rate paid on an additional dollar of income.

FIGURE 36.2

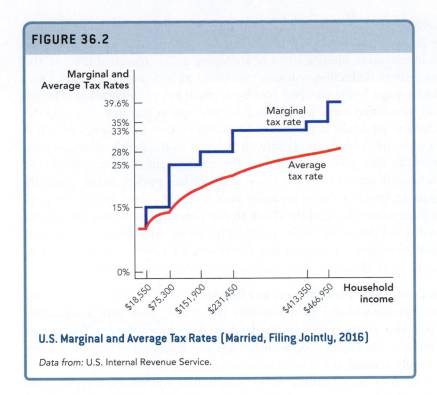

U.S. Marginal and Average Tax Rates (Married, Filing Jointly, 2016)

Data from: U.S. Internal Revenue Service.

Marginal tax rates today are lower and flatter than they have been in the past. In 1960, for example, the lowest marginal tax rate was 20% and the highest rate was 91%! Of course in the further past, rates were much lower than today. In 1913, when the income tax began, the top marginal rate was just 7% and that rate didn't take effect until annual income was over $10 million (in today's dollars).

Your **average tax rate** is simply your total tax payment divided by your total income. If your income is $50,000, for example, then your total income tax under the current system can be calculated as follows. You pay 10% on the first $18,550, or $1,855, then you pay 15% on the next $31,450, or $4,718, for a total tax of $6,573. Your average tax rate is then

$$\frac{\$6,573}{\$50,000} \times 100 = 13.1\%$$

The **average tax rate** is the total tax payment divided by total income.

However, the tax system is not quite as simple as we have presented so far because some income is *exempt* from taxation. Each person, for example, generally gets one tax exemption for him- or herself, one exemption for a spouse, and one exemption for each child or dependent. In 2016, for example, each exemption lets you have $4,050 of your income tax free. If you have a child, for example, you can exempt another $4,050 of your income from taxes. If your marginal tax rate is 25%, that exemption means that your taxes fall by about $1,012.50 per year (0.25 × $4,050). In other words, the federal government offers a small incentive to have a child relative to, say, buying a new car. This also means that people with the same income may pay different tax amounts. The exemption amount is indexed for inflation so it typically increases a bit every year and it is phased out at higher incomes.

The tax system also allows for deductions. Like exemptions, deductions reduce your taxable income, but only if you have specific expenses. The most important deductions are for home mortgage interest, donations to charity, state and local taxes, and interest on student loans. If you don't have these expenses or if they aren't very large, you can instead take a standard deduction, which in 2017 was $6,350 for a single person.

For instance, if you buy a house, the interest payments on your mortgage can (usually) be deducted from your taxable income. So, if you are paying $1,000 a month in mortgage interest and you are facing a 25% marginal tax rate, the mortgage interest deduction will save you about $250 a month in taxes. Does this make buying a house cheaper? Not by as much as you might think. The tax deduction means that more people want to buy houses and that drives up the price of houses, especially in places like Manhattan where the amount of land is fixed. So, some of "your" subsidy actually ends up in the hands of landowners. In other words, who gets the check from the government is not necessarily the person who ends up with extra money in his or her pocket. More generally, economists understand that who really pays a tax or a subsidy can be quite different from who must send the check to the government or how those taxes and subsidies are described to the public. That point will not be the focus of this chapter—see your microeconomics textbook for more—but do keep it in mind as you think about the different taxes in the American economy.

Taxes on Capital Gains and Interest and Dividends The income tax is a tax on your labor income and also on any income you receive from your investments, namely your interest income, your dividends, and your capital gains. You receive interest income, for instance, on your savings and checking accounts, and this income usually is taxed as if it were labor income.

The taxation of capital gains is more complicated. You receive a capital gain, for instance, if you buy stock at $110 a share and later resell it at $210 a share. Your capital gain is the extra $100 you made from the rise in the value of the stock. You pay a tax on those profits and currently the standard capital gains tax rises from 0% for those with low incomes to 15% for most taxpayers to 20% for those whose income puts them in the highest income tax bracket. Capital gains taxes are paid only when the assets are actually sold and not while the assets are simply being held.

As is often the case in our tax system, the real rates people pay are not the same as the rates written into the tax code. For instance, capital gains allow for "loss offsets." If you gain $100 selling one stock and lose $100 selling another, usually the two sums cancel each other out in the calculation of your tax liability. If you know how to group your winners and losers together at the right time, the true rate of capital gains taxation you face may be much lower than the published rate of 15%.

Republicans and Democrats often disagree about how much investment income should be taxed. Democrats often favor higher taxes on investment income, on the grounds that the rich invest quite a bit and thus taxing investment income means the rich will bear a larger share of the tax burden. Republicans are more likely to argue that lower taxes on investment spur investment and thus economic growth, creating jobs, raising wages, and contributing to general prosperity in the long run.

Alternative minimum tax (AMT) is a separate income tax code that began in 1969 to prevent the rich from not paying income taxes. It was not indexed to inflation and is now an extra tax burden on many upper middle class families.

The Alternative Minimum Tax (AMT) There is yet another complication to the American tax system, and that is the **alternative minimum tax,** or AMT. The AMT was started in 1969 after a televised congressional hearing revealed that 155 households with income over $200,000 (about $1.2 million in today's dollars) had paid no income tax. These families had done nothing illegal, but they had managed to take advantage of tax laws to avoid income taxes. Thus, the original goal of the AMT was to make sure that it would not be possible for anyone to avoid all income tax.

The AMT requires taxpayers to make two computations. First, they must compute what they owe under the standard tax code; then, they must compute what they owe under the AMT, which is typically based on a flat rate of either 26% or 28%, with no deductions allowed. The taxpayer must then pay whichever number is higher.

The AMT was supposed to hit just a few hundred families among the super rich but it was never adjusted for inflation, so every year more and more people became subject to the AMT. In recent years, more than 4 million taxpayers paid the AMT and it's now often the case that families earning $100,000 a year or less are paying the AMT and thus paying more taxes than under the regular tax code. The number of Americans covered by the AMT will likely continue to rise. The increasing reach of the AMT is, in fact, the largest tax increase in recent times, although it is rarely explained or presented as such. Both Republicans and Democrats claim they are unhappy about the growing reach of the AMT, but the two parties cannot agree on how to change or replace it, or how to make up for the lost revenue, should the AMT be restricted in its application.

Social Security and Medicare Taxes

Almost all workers in the United States pay the Federal Insurance Contributions Act tax, better known as the FICA tax, the acronym that you will see on your payroll check. The FICA tax is 6.2% of your wages on the first $118,500 of income. In addition, your employer also pays a 6.2% tax on the same earnings so the total FICA tax is 12.4%. The FICA taxes fund Social Security payments.

Many Americans believe, "I pay half of this tax, my employer pays the other half," but this isn't quite right. As we've already mentioned, the person who appears to pay a tax isn't always the person who actually pays. In reality, economic research shows that the employer's payment is mostly taken out of the worker's prospective wage; in other words, if your employer didn't have to pay the FICA tax, your wages would be higher.* Much of the burden of the FICA tax falls on workers, not on employers.

Medicare is partly financed out of general revenues and partly financed out of special payroll taxes. For most workers, 1.45% is withheld from their paychecks in the form of a Medicare premium and the employer pays another 1.45%. Again, workers pay much of the employer's premium in the form of lower wages. Self-employed individuals pay the full 2.9% themselves.

The Corporate Income Tax

For the past decade in the United States, the corporate income tax rate is generally 35%. This is one of the highest rates in the world. The rate of 35%, however, is applied to a legal measure of income, but the tax code is so constructed that a good accountant can often make corporate income come out very low, even for profitable corporations. In fact, some apparently profitable corporations

---

* In fact, exactly this situation occurred in Chile when it privatized its social security program in 1981. Beginning in 1981, employers no longer had to pay social security taxes for their employees. The fall in employer taxes, however, did not result in extra profits. Instead, wages rose as the payroll tax fell—exactly as predicted by tax incidence theory. Other studies in the United States show that when the government mandates that firms provide benefits to their employees such as health benefits, wages fall. Thus, employees rather than employers pay for mandated benefits. On Chile and for references to other studies, see Gruber, J, 1997. The incidence of payroll taxation: Evidence from Chile, Journal of Labor Economics 15(3), S:72–S101.

manage to define their income and expenses in such a way that they often don't pay any corporate income tax at all. Maybe you've heard of Boeing, the large and profitable airplane manufacturer; over a recent period of five years, the company paid an average tax rate of 0.7%.[1] Other companies aren't so well situated to take advantage of such tax breaks and accounting maneuvers.

Who pays the corporate income tax? Not corporations, which in the final analysis are legal fictions. All taxes are eventually paid by human beings. The corporate income tax is paid initially by shareholders and bondholders of corporations who earn a lower rate of return on their investments. More generally, the rate of return will fall on all forms of capital and in the long run that will also mean somewhat lower wages for workers and higher prices for goods and services.

The Bottom Line on the Distribution of Federal Taxes

Once we add in deductions, exemptions, corporate taxes, payroll taxes, excise taxes, the AMT, and assumptions about tax incidence (who pays the tax), what is the final result? It's not an easy calculation, but the best estimate of the distribution of federal taxes by income class is shown in Figure 36.3.

The left panel of Figure 36.3 shows that if we divide households into categories according to how much they earn, then households with incomes in the bottom 20% pay very little in federal tax, less than 5% of their total income. As income increases so does the average rate, so those with incomes in the top 20% pay an average tax rate of around 25%. The average tax rate continues to rise if we look at those in the top 1% who pay nearly 30% of their income to the federal government.

It is sometimes said that the rich do not pay taxes in the United States. That is false. Whether they pay *enough* taxes depends on your point of view, but despite all the deductions, exemptions, loopholes, and so forth, the U.S. tax system is **progressive**—people with higher income pay a higher percentage of their income in tax to the federal government than people with lower income.

In contrast to a progressive tax is a **flat tax,** which has a constant tax rate applied to income at all levels of earning. If the tax code were radically simplified to eliminate almost all deductions, including the deductions for mortgage interest and charitable giving, then by some calculations a flat rate of around 19% would raise approximately the same revenue as today.[2] A flat tax has a number of desirable properties. Simplification of the tax code would be appreciated by many taxpayers and elimination of deductions and loopholes would encourage people to make investment, consumption, and work decisions for good economic reasons rather than merely to reduce tax payments.

The disadvantage of a flat tax is that moving to a flat tax would require lowering rates on the rich and raising rates on the middle class and poor. If you compare the average tax rate paid by different income classes under the current tax code—shown in Figure 36.3—with a flat rate of 19%, you can see that tax rates for the rich and poor could change quite dramatically under a flat tax. Proponents of a flat tax, including Republican Steve Forbes and Democrat Jerry Brown, argue that the efficiency advantages of a flat tax mean that even people who paid a higher tax rate would, with increased economic growth, pay less in total tax.

Even if a flat tax were significantly more efficient than our current tax code, it's hard to see how the United States could ever move to such a system. Do

A **progressive tax** has higher tax rates on people with higher incomes.

A **flat tax** has a constant tax rate.

A **regressive tax** has higher tax rates on people with lower incomes.

FIGURE 36.3

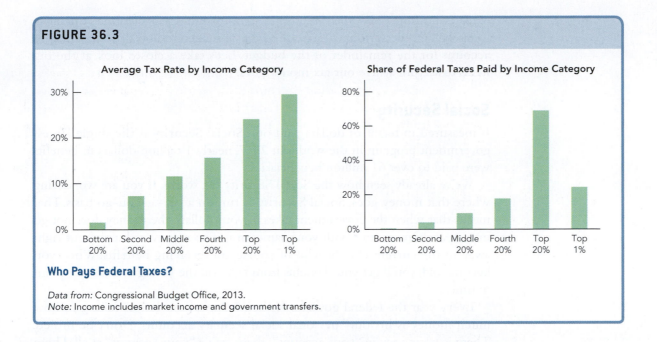

Who Pays Federal Taxes?

Data from: Congressional Budget Office, 2013.
Note: Income includes market income and government transfers.

you remember what we said about the effect of the mortgage interest deduction on house prices? The mortgage interest deduction raises house prices, so eliminating the deduction would cause a fall in house prices. Is it any wonder that neither Jerry Brown's nor Steve Forbes's tax plans caught on when they ran for president? Other countries, including Russia, the Czech Republic, and Estonia, have flat taxes and some states, such as Colorado, Utah, and Illinois, also have flat taxes on income.

Returning to the current federal U.S. tax code, the average tax rate is higher on the rich and the rich have more money—put these two things together and we can calculate who pays for the federal government. The right panel in Figure 36.3 shows the share of federal tax revenues that is paid for by each income category. The finding is that the rich, and especially the very rich, bear by far the largest share of the federal tax liability. Almost 70% of federal taxes are paid by people in the top 20% of income earners. The top 1% alone pay about one-quarter of all federal taxes.

State and Local Taxes

In addition to federal taxes, most people pay state and local taxes, so the federal tax burden is not the end of the story. Overall, state and local taxes are about half the level of federal taxes, just under 9% of GDP. Compared to the federal government, states raise more of their revenues, about 20% on average, from sales taxes. Since sales tax rates are the same for everyone, regardless of income, state and local taxation as a whole is less progressive than income taxation. Thus, state and local taxes probably make the overall tax system a little bit less progressive than the federal tax system, but it does depend on the state.

Spending

Almost two-thirds of the U.S. federal budget is spent on just four programs in a typical year: Social Security, defense, Medicare, and Medicaid, as seen in Figure 36.4. Interest on the national debt and various unemployment insurance programs and welfare programs are also large. Everything else—spending on

CHECK YOURSELF

- Individual income taxes plus Social Security and Medicare taxes represent what percent of federal revenues? (Review Figure 36.1 if necessary.)

- Consider Figure 36.3. Let's start with a person in the fourth quintile, earning $80,000 pretax. Using the average tax rate, what did this person pay in tax? Now consider a person in the top quintile who earns $160,000 pretax. What did this person pay in tax? Compare the amount of tax paid by both. Does this provide evidence that the tax system is progressive?

roads, education, police, prisons, science and technology, agriculture, the environment, and the various stimulus programs intended to boost the economy—account for the remainder of the budget. Let's take a closer look at the big items to see just where our tax money goes.

Social Security

If measured in terms of dollars paid out, Social Security is the single largest government program in the world. In 2017, nearly 1 trillion dollars in benefits were paid to over 61 million beneficiaries.

We've already seen how the Social Security tax works. If you are wondering where that money goes, Social Security is run on a pay-as-you-go basis. That means that when the government takes in your dollars, the money does not go into an account or trust with your name on it. The money is shipped out right away to the current elderly, who of course are receiving benefits. When you become old, you'll get your benefits from taxes on the young at that later point in time.

Every year the federal government sends Americans letters telling us how much money is in "our" personal social security accounts. Don't be misled. There is no money in "your account"; there isn't a "your account" at all. Those letters are just the government's prediction of how much you'll get back some day. Of course, since you are in the meantime a voter, don't be surprised if those predictions turn out to be a little bit optimistic.

Social Security benefits are defined by a complex formula depending on how many years a worker worked, what their average earnings were over their working life, whether or not they are married, what year they retire, and at

FIGURE 36.4

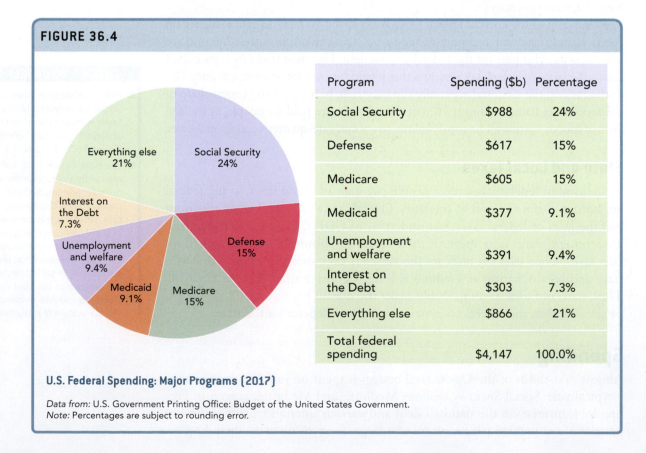

Program	Spending ($b)	Percentage
Social Security	$988	24%
Defense	$617	15%
Medicare	$605	15%
Medicaid	$377	9.1%
Unemployment and welfare	$391	9.4%
Interest on the Debt	$303	7.3%
Everything else	$866	21%
Total federal spending	$4,147	100.0%

U.S. Federal Spending: Major Programs (2017)

Data from: U.S. Government Printing Office: Budget of the United States Government.
Note: Percentages are subject to rounding error.

what age. In recent years, the average retiree has been paid $1,348 a month so one immediate lesson is that you shouldn't count on Social Security alone to support you in your old age.

The complexity of the formula means that Social Security is not equivalent to a simple forced savings program under which the government requires everyone to save 12.4% of their income. Rather, the Social Security system redistributes wealth in complex ways, some intended and some probably not intended. One intended benefit, for example, is that Social Security is more generous the lower a worker's lifetime earnings. In other words, workers with low lifetime incomes tend to get more out of the system than if they had saved their tax payments, while workers with high lifetime incomes tend to get less out of the system than if they had saved the same amount as they paid in Social Security taxes.

President Franklin D. Roosevelt signing the Social Security bill.

Social Security is also much more generous to married people than to singles. Consider two retirees, one married, one not, who paid exactly the same amount in lifetime Social Security taxes. The retirees receive the same retirement benefit for themselves but the spouse is also eligible for a spousal benefit, even if the spouse never worked. When it was common for one spouse to work and the other not to work, married couples got much more out of Social Security for every dollar they put in than did singles. Now that it's more common for both spouses to work, the spousal benefit isn't as large as it once was because workers whose own benefits exceed the spousal benefit don't get the spousal benefit. By the way, the spousal benefit can also be paid to a divorced spouse, so with multiple marriages and divorces you can imagine how complicated the system can get.

The age at which workers can claim their full retirement benefits was 65 for many years but, because the Social Security program was getting very expensive, in 1983, the full retirement age was made to slowly increase depending on when the worker was born. You—assuming you were born after 1960—must wait until age 67 to claim your full retirement benefits. Some people advocate increasing the full retirement age again, so you may want to keep an eye on the age at which you will be able to claim full benefits. A worker can start claiming some benefits as early as age 62, but people who opt for early retirement get a lower monthly payment. Benefits are indexed to the level of wages in the United States, so over time benefits rise automatically with general increases in prosperity.

Do you recall Ida May Fuller from the introduction? She paid $24.75 in Social Security taxes and received $22,888.92 in payments. Ida May's example is extreme but the basic idea is quite general. Workers who retired in the early years of Social Security received full benefits even though they paid Social Security taxes for only a portion of their working life. In addition, the Social Security tax rate increased over time, rising from 2% in 1940 to today's rate of 12.4%. The higher tax rate on today's workers funds larger benefits for *yesterday's* workers— even though yesterday's workers paid a lower tax rate on their earnings.

Social Security has become less generous over time for another reason—the labor force has been growing more slowly in recent decades because fewer people are working and because the growth rate in the population has declined. It's harder to fund benefits to yesterday's workers when there are fewer workers to tax today.

A factor making the Social Security system more generous over time is increased life expectancy. If life expectancy continues to increase, then future

TABLE 36.1 TOP TEN COUNTRIES BY MILITARY EXPENDITURE (BILLIONS OF U.S. DOLLARS)

	Country	Military Expenditure (billions)
1	United States	596.0
2	China	215.0
3	Saudi Arabia	87.2
4	Russia	66.4
5	United Kingdom	55.5
6	India	51.3
7	France	50.9
8	Japan	40.9
9	Germany	39.4
10	South Korea	36.4

Data from: Stockholm International Peace Research Institute 2016 *Fact Sheet* (for 2015).

Social Security benefits will be *very* generous. But don't count your chickens before they hatch. Social Security spending currently exceeds Social Security taxes—the difference is made up by interest on past excess contributions. The Congressional Budget Office projects, however, that interest payments will cover the Social Security deficit only until 2029.[3] In 2029, the difference between benefits spending and Social Security taxes will have to be made up by revenues from taxes other than the Social Security tax, increases in Social Security taxes, or decreases in benefits, such as increases in the retirement age. No one is quite sure what will happen so there is a lot of uncertainty about future benefits.

Defense

The official budget for the Department of Defense is about $617 billion. Even this figure, however, doesn't include spending on veterans' benefits, homeland security, nuclear weapons research, or costs of military-style operations that run through the CIA or other non–Defense Department agencies. A broader definition for defense would increase defense spending to around $750 billion annually.

The United States spends much more on its military than does any other country in the world. Table 36.1 presents some data on the top 10 countries by military expenditure in 2015. Do we get value for our money? Unfortunately, assessing how much we should spend on the military goes well beyond standard economics and into issues of foreign policy. That is an important question but it isn't a topic for this book.

Medicare and Medicaid

Medicare reimburses the elderly for much of their medical care spending, covering hospital stays, doctor bills, and prescription drugs. To be eligible for Medicare, an individual should be 65 or older and have worked for at least 10 years in a job paying Medicare premiums. Many of the disabled are covered as well, even if they have not held such jobs.

In fiscal year 2017, Medicare spending amounted to $605 billion. Social Security and Medicare, taken together, are by far the largest undertakings of the U.S. government, and both are programs that transfer wealth to the elderly.

Medicare does not pay all medical bills outright. Instead, beneficiaries are required to pay some percent of the charges, known as a "copayment." A beneficiary also has to pay for relatively small charges, which is known as a "deductible." Many of the elderly buy private insurance to pay for the gaps in their Medicare coverage.

In addition to Medicare, you may have heard of Medicaid. Whereas Medicare covers the elderly, Medicaid covers the poor and the disabled. Of course, some of the elderly are poor as well and these people are eligible for both programs. The federal government and state governments pay for Medicaid jointly, but the program itself is run through state governments. As of fiscal 2017, Medicaid expenditures were around $377 billion. Spending on Medicaid has been increasing in recent years as more people are covered under Medicaid due to the Affordable Care Act.

Unemployment Insurance and Welfare Spending

It is a common myth that most of the money spent by our federal government goes to welfare programs. In reality, federal welfare payments (not including Medicaid or unemployment insurance) amount to $200–$400 billion a year (depending on exactly what one counts and whether the economy is in a recession). These are substantial figures, but other programs are much larger.

Remember, other than defense, the largest spending programs are Social Security and Medicare, and these programs primarily transfer wealth to the elderly, not to the poor. Since we will all be elderly sooner or later (at least if we are lucky), these transfers eventually go to virtually all Americans.

Most welfare payments fall into a few common categories. First, personal welfare payments are made to poor households with children. The largest of these is called Temporary Assistance for Needy Families (TANF). Since 1996, an individual cannot receive these benefits for more than five years in a lifetime. Housing vouchers under the Section 8 program give poor households a voucher that subsidizes a portion of their rent.

Especially important is the Earned Income Tax Credit (EITC), which is now the main form that antipoverty policy takes at the federal level. The EITC, quite simply, pays poor people cash through the tax system depending on how much they earn. So, for instance, if you are married, have a child, and earn $20,000 a year, you are below the poverty line and the EITC will supplement your income, giving you over $3,000 for the year. With more than one child, the credit goes up to almost $4,000. In recent years, about $65 billion was spent on the EITC and these federal programs are supplemented by a wide variety of state and local welfare programs for the poor.

Unemployment insurance (UI) makes payments to people who are out of work and is not restricted to the poor. UI is a large program that can expand rapidly during recessions. In 2007, for example, just $35 billion was spent on UI but with the recession and emergency benefits, that number increased to $160 billion in 2010 before falling back to $35 billion in 2016.

Everything Else

Before discussing paying interest on the national debt, let's look at everything else. Everything else accounts for all the other spending programs of the federal government, which include:

- Farm subsidies.
- Spending on roads, bridges, and infrastructure.
- The Disaster Relief Fund.
- The Small Business Administration.
- The Food and Drug Administration.
- All federal courts.

- Federal prisons.
- The FBI.
- Foreign aid.
- Border security.
- NASA.
- The National Institutes of Health.
- The National Science Foundation.
- Financial assistance to students.
- The wages of all federal employees.

All of these programs add up to a large amount of money, but none of these programs is large compared to Social Security, defense, or Medicare.

A common misconception about the budget involves foreign aid. When polled, 41% of Americans said that foreign aid is one of the two largest sources of federal expenditure. In reality, foreign aid is about 1% of the overall federal budget; the exact number depends on how that term is defined since sometimes "foreign aid" and "military assistance" are difficult to distinguish.

Is Government Spending Wasted?

You have probably also heard a lot about government waste. In fact, there are good reasons for thinking that governments might not spend money as carefully as you or I, namely weak incentives and lack of information on how to spend the money effectively. Suppose you get an A on your economics midterm and decide to spend $100 on a treat for yourself. What's the best possible use of that $100? A new pair of jeans? A dinner date? Part of a ski trip? Whatever the answer, you have good information about your wants and needs and you have good incentives to shop carefully—researching quality, comparing prices, and searching for high value—after all, *your* enjoyment and *your* money are at stake!

Now suppose that you must spend $100 on a gift for someone else. (Perhaps you are obligated to exchange Christmas gifts with your coworkers.) You still want to get value for your money but your information about what the recipient wants or needs is much less and your incentive to investigate and research quality are diminished compared to when you were spending the money on yourself. Economist Joel Waldfogel, estimated that billions of dollars are wasted every Christmas because most gifts cost the giver more than they are valued by the recipient.[4] To avoid this waste, we give the administrative assistants in our department cash. But Christmas might not be as fun if every present under the tree was money.

Now suppose that you must spend someone else's money on a gift for someone else. (Perhaps your boss gives you some money to buy a Christmas gift for one of her other employees.) You probably don't want to waste the money entirely (perhaps your boss will notice if you pocketed the cash) but you don't have good information about what the recipient wants or needs and now you are spending someone else's money so your incentives to shop carefully are very much diminished. A lot of government spending falls into this category—some people spending other people's money on yet other people. As a result, we should not be surprised when a lot of government spending results in some waste and inefficiency.

An Economist's Christmas

interactive activity

In Afghanistan and Iraq, for example, the U.S. spent over a hundred billion dollars on reconstruction efforts, but audits revealed many billions of dollars in waste, fraud, and abuse. Projects were started and never completed. Hospitals were built but never provided with equipment to operate. Fraud was rampant. On one project the auditor questioned 40% of the costs it reviewed, including $900 for a control switch valued at $7.05. Perhaps most infamously, $10 billion(!) in shrink-wrapped packages of $100 notes was flown from New York to Iraq but then simply disappeared.[5]

Spending in Iraq and Afghanistan was probably especially likely to be wasted because the U.S. government lacked information about local wants and needs, which were very different from those of people in the United States, and because the ultimate boss—the American taxpayer—was far away and could not easily monitor how the money was being spent. Problems of information and incentives, however, plague all kinds of government spending, both at home and abroad.

Government spending can be wasteful, but if a politician claims that he or she will pay for new spending programs or tax cuts by cutting "waste"— beware! First, the problem of government waste is not due to a few bad apples but rather due to deeper problems of information and incentives that are difficult to solve. Second, our trip through the federal budget shows that cutting waste may sound good, but the reality is that most of the money is being spent on the big programs. Consider Social Security, the largest government spending program. Social Security transfers cash—it's like the perfect Christmas gift recommended by economists—and because the program is well-known, it's well monitored. As a result, despite some fraud, the overhead costs of the Social Security program are low.

Overall, it's difficult to cut spending on big programs without cutting benefits. If we want more spending on those programs, ultimately taxes must rise or we must cut spending somewhere else. If we want lower taxes, spending and benefits must fall. There is no such thing as a free lunch.

The National Debt, Interest on the National Debt, and Deficits

The final category of spending we will discuss is interest on the national debt. If in 2017 you Googled the "U.S. national debt," you would probably have found a number around $20 trillion, but quite a bit of this debt is held by other branches of the federal government. The Social Security Trust Fund, for example, holds billions of dollars in Treasury bonds, which simply represent an IOU on future Social Security payments.

A better measure of our current debt is the **national debt held by the public,** which is all federal debt held by individuals, corporations, state or local governments, foreign governments, and other entities other than the federal government itself. The national debt held by the public as of 2017 is just over $14 trillion. From now on when we talk about the national debt, the federal debt, or just the debt, we mean the national debt held by the public.

Fourteen trillion dollars is a very big number, but it has to be compared with another very big number, GDP, which is about $19 trillion. Thus, the United States has a debt-to-GDP ratio of over 70%. Is this a big number? Mortgage lenders often require a debt-to-income ratio of less than 36% so few people

The **national debt held by the public** is all federal debt held by individuals, corporations, and governments other than the U.S. federal government.

FIGURE 36.5

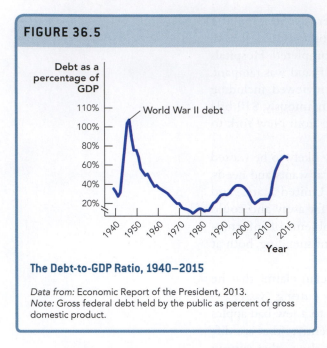

The Debt-to-GDP Ratio, 1940–2015

Data from: Economic Report of the President, 2013.
Note: Gross federal debt held by the public as percent of gross domestic product.

would recommend that *you* carry that much debt. The U.S. government will live for a lot longer than you or we will so for the federal government, this debt-to-GDP ratio is not excessive. Figure 36.5 shows the debt-to-GDP ratio since 1940. Today's debt-to-GDP ratio of 75% is large but not as large as the ratio has been in the past. More worrying is that in 2007 the debt was only $5 trillion so the national debt is rising very quickly.

The highest debt-to-GDP ratio in U.S. history occurred in 1946 at 108%. As we discussed in our chapter on Saving, Investment, and the Financial System, it makes sense for you to borrow to pay for large expenses, thereby smoothing your consumption, and the same thing is true for the U.S. government. The government borrowed heavily to finance emergency expenditures for World War II, but following the war the debt-to-GDP ratio slowly declined until the 1980s. In the 1980s, a combination of tax cuts and increases in defense spending increased the debt-to-GDP ratio. The ratio then fell as the economy expanded and the federal government briefly ran a series of budget surpluses under President Bill Clinton in the 1990s. More recently, the debt-to-GDP ratio increased slightly due to further tax cuts and defense spending under former President George W. Bush. The debt-to-GDP ratio increased sharply due to the recession that began in late 2007, which lowered GDP (hence raising the debt-to-GDP ratio), and led to increased government spending designed to stimulate the economy under President Barack Obama.

Every year, the government must pay interest to the people who lent it money, namely the bondholders. If your debt is $100 and the interest rate is 5%, then you owe the lender $5 a year in interest payments. It works the same way with the national debt. The U.S. debt in 2017 was about $14 trillion and the average interest rate on the debt was about 2%, so the federal government paid approximately $280 billion in interest payments to bondholders. An interest rate on the debt of 2% is extraordinarily low. In 2007, for example, the interest rate on the debt was 5%. The low rate appears to be due to a large amount of world savings, sometimes called the savings glut, and a big demand for the relatively safe assets of the U.S. government. If interest rates were to increase significantly, interest on the debt could also increase significantly, putting big pressure on other items in the U.S. budget.

Sometimes commentators suggest it makes a big difference if the debt of the U.S. government is held by foreigners or Americans. From a purely economic point of view, however, this distinction isn't very important. What is important is how wisely the federal government spends the borrowed money. If, years later, interest payments go to foreigners, that is because the foreigners offered to lend us money at the best rates. You can make a moral or ethical judgment that Americans ought to be spending less and saving more (which would mean less borrowing from foreigners), but low savings would be an even greater problem without foreign lenders.

We now need to make a distinction between the national debt and the deficit. The debt is the total amount of money owed by the federal government at a point in time. It is a cumulative total of previous obligations. The **deficit** is the difference—in any given year—between what the government is spending and

The **deficit** is the annual difference between federal spending and revenues.

FIGURE 36.6

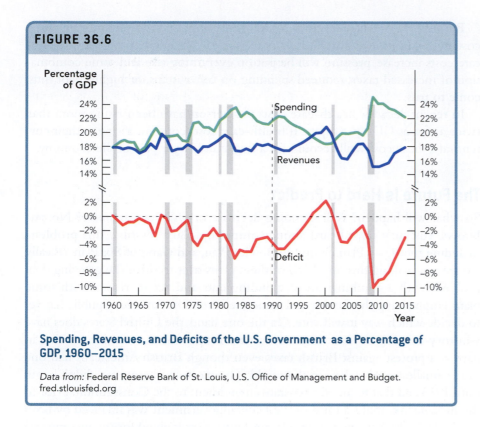

Spending, Revenues, and Deficits of the U.S. Government as a Percentage of GDP, 1960–2015

Data from: Federal Reserve Bank of St. Louis, U.S. Office of Management and Budget. fred.stlouisfed.org

what the government is collecting in revenues. You can think of the deficit as the annual change in the national debt.

The top half of Figure 36.6 shows federal government spending (green) and revenues (blue) as a percentage of GDP from 1960 to 2015. When spending is greater than revenues, the government must borrow to make up the difference—the difference is the deficit, shown in the bottom half of Figure 36.6 (red) also as a percentage of GDP (and as a negative value). In 1990, for example, the federal government spent almost 22% of GDP, but it collected only 18% of GDP in tax revenues. Since government spending was greater than revenues, the government had to borrow the difference, so in 1990 the deficit was about 4% of GDP (22% − 18%).

Will the U.S. Government Go Bankrupt?

We said earlier that the current debt-to-GDP ratio of 75% is large but not unprecedented. Nevertheless, many economists are worried about the future debt-to-GDP ratio.

The main forces driving these worries are not recessions but demographics and increasing health-care costs. The U.S. population is getting older. At the turn of the 21st century, 12.4% of the U.S. population was aged 65 years and older, but by 2030 more than 20% of the population will be elderly. The increase in the number of elderly people means higher Social Security and Medicare payments. As a fraction of GDP, for example, Social Security payments will have to increase by about 41% if benefits are to be maintained at promised levels. More elderly people also means we will see increases in Medicare payments, although in this case an even bigger problem than demographics is rising health-care costs per person.

Because of Medicare, Medicaid, and health insurance subsidies, health-care costs will consume a larger and larger share of the federal budget. As health-care costs increase, pressure will be put on everything else and some combination of increased taxes, reduced spending on other items, or higher debt must come to pass.

In recent decades, health-care costs per person have been rising more than twice as fast as GDP per capita. If health-care costs continue rising at their current rate, those costs will account for a larger and larger part of the economy.

The Future Is Hard to Predict

So what will happen? Will spending decrease or will taxes increase? No one knows. You may have heard about competing plans to solve this problem, including the Ryan Plan, Simpson–Bowles Plan, and Gang of Six Plan. (Really, we are not making this up.) Each of these plans tries to solve the growing debt problem with a combination of spending cuts and tax increases, with some plans emphasizing the former and some the latter. The American public has yet to decide which way it will vote. On the one hand, the United States does have a history of relatively low taxes. Americans fought the Revolutionary War, in part, as a protest against British taxes even though British Americans had one of the smallest tax burdens in the world! The modern income tax didn't begin until 1913 and that required a separate amendment to the Constitution. Prior to the income tax, about a third of the Federal government was financed by taxes on alcohol, which is one reason why prohibitionists lobbied for the income tax! Even as late as 1916, the federal government accounted for less than 5% of GDP.

Taxes and federal spending increased dramatically during 1916–1919 and 1942–1945, corresponding to World War I and World War II, respectively. But since that time federal taxes and spending have been fairly stable—as we noted, around 18% of GDP. When taxes have increased, there have often been backlashes with Americans electing politicians who promise to cut taxes. So, will Americans accept much higher tax rates in the future than they ever have in the past? Will you?

If taxes and spending in the United States do increase, this would make the United States more like other developed countries. Figure 36.7 shows total government spending by country, including spending by federal, state, and local governments. Today, the U.S. federal government spends a smaller fraction of GDP than do the governments of most other developed countries. As a result, spending could increase substantially in the United States over the next several decades and the United States would still be spending at levels comparable to Germany, Italy, and the Netherlands today.

Could spending be cut? We have already cut some projected Social Security spending by increasing the age of retirement. Perhaps we can cut spending even more—but don't expect the elderly to take this sitting down! And remember a large part of the growth in spending is due to rising health-care costs. Many people talk about slowing the growth of health-care costs but it isn't so easy. There is a lot of waste in health-care markets, but also there are many wonderful innovations. Drugs known as statins lower our cholesterol and new surgical procedures save many lives; a triple bypass operation is now more or less standard procedure. It's not so easy to sort out the good medical procedures from the bad ones, and so by most accounts health-care costs will continue to rise. Other countries do spend a significantly smaller fraction of their GDP on health-care costs, but the *growth* in health-care costs is fairly similar throughout the developed world.

STOCKBYTE/GETTY IMAGES

The federal government has not planned for future expenses. Have you?

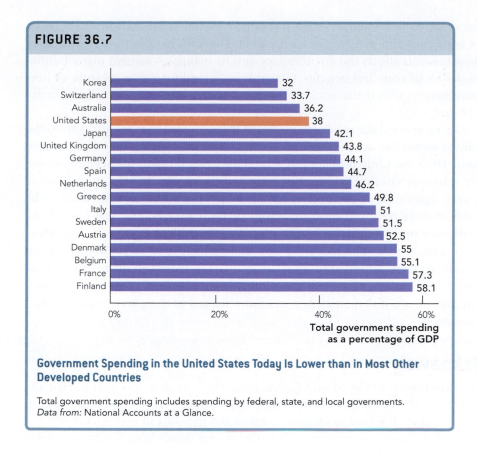

FIGURE 36.7

Korea	32
Switzerland	33.7
Australia	36.2
United States	38
Japan	42.1
United Kingdom	43.8
Germany	44.1
Spain	44.7
Netherlands	46.2
Greece	49.8
Italy	51
Sweden	51.5
Austria	52.5
Denmark	55
Belgium	55.1
France	57.3
Finland	58.1

Total government spending as a percentage of GDP

Government Spending in the United States Today Is Lower than in Most Other Developed Countries

Total government spending includes spending by federal, state, and local governments.
Data from: National Accounts at a Glance.

Don't forget that whatever happens, the news is actually quite good for the most part. Americans are living longer than ever before and many medical advances are paying off. Let's say you thought you would live to be 80 but then you learn you will live to be 100 instead. You might worry about how to finance your now-longer retirement and perhaps you might even despair that it seems impossible. But this is the kind of problem that we can live with!

Another scenario is that GDP will grow faster in the future than it has in the past. We outlined one case for optimism in our chapter on Growth, Capital Accumulation, and the Economics of Ideas. Nevertheless, although we hope for the best, it's probably wise to plan, if not for the worst, then at least for the most likely outcome, and that will require some painful tax increases or spending cuts.

One general lesson is that we cannot judge the fiscal health of the federal government simply by looking at today's budget or today's deficit. New government programs often grow over time and we ought to think about implicit future spending commitments when evaluating these new programs. Politicians in the past made many promises to spend in the future and today we are dealing with the legacy of these promises.

CHECK YOURSELF

- Projecting forward for the next 40 years, what categories of spending are likely to increase or decrease? What does this mean for overall government spending? Will it grow, fall, or stay the same?

- If the pace of idea generation quickens, as was discussed in our chapter on Growth, Capital Accumulation, and the Economics of Ideas, the long-run aggregate supply growth curve might shift permanently. If this happens, how would it affect the debt-to-GDP ratio? Explain what this means for our nation's ability to pay for increased benefits for retirees.

Revenues and Spending Undercount the Role of Government in the Economy

This chapter has mostly been about federal revenues and expenditures. But our government does many things and imposes many costs that do not show up on any formal budgetary accounts. The Environmental Protection Agency (EPA), for instance, has a budget of only about $9 billion yet its real reach, in terms of both costs and benefits, is much higher. The EPA has the power to regulate how business affects the environment and its mandates involve many billions of dollars of costs and benefits. Government spending is one measure of how government affects the economy, but it is not a complete or fully accurate measure.

Governments take many other actions that commandeer resources from the private sector but do not show up as full budgetary expenditures. For instance, until 1973 the United States ran a military draft. Drafted soldiers, of course, are relatively cheap if you just look at their paychecks, but the draft involves a very significant opportunity cost. Many people who were ill suited to be soldiers were removed from their jobs or their studies. The real cost of the draft—the opportunity cost—was pointed out by Milton Friedman, who advocated a move to a volunteer army. The United States had to pay soldiers more, so military costs appeared to go up. In reality, the volunteer army reduced the total cost to society of providing national defense by freeing up more productive labor, even if that efficiency was not reflected in the government's budget statements.

Takeaway

An examination of the current federal budget reveals some key points. First and foremost is the simple point that the federal government takes in and spends a great deal of money. It is hard to imagine revenues and spending of over $3.5 *trillion*.

Next, it is useful to recognize where this money comes from. Contrary to what some people might think, the huge majority of tax revenues comes from individuals in the form of individual income taxes and tax on wages linked to Social Security and Medicare.

For many people, it is surprising to learn what the federal government spends its money on. The obvious category of defense spending represents around 15% of spending. About one-third of the federal budget goes for Social Security and Medicare payments. Comprehensive general transfers to the elderly represent far more money than do welfare expenditures per se.

What about the future? The U.S. tax system is very complicated and not always transparent in its effects. Nevertheless, we can estimate future expenditures and revenues as a way of understanding the fiscal strength or weakness of a nation. It is very likely that federal expenditures will rise in the future, most of all because of rising health-care expenditures. One question is whether and how federal revenues will rise to keep the budget sufficiently close to balancing.

CHAPTER REVIEW

 interactive activity **Go online to practice with more examples of these types of problems, including live links to videos, data sources, and feedback.**

Problems in **green** relate to MRU videos. See the MRU table at the end of the exercises.

KEY CONCEPTS

marginal tax rate, p. 766

average tax rate, p. 767

alternative minimum tax (AMT), p. 768

progressive tax, p. 770

flat tax, p. 770

regressive tax, p. 770

national debt held by the public, p. 777

deficit, p. 778

FACTS AND TOOLS

1. a. Consider Figure 36.3. We can use these data to find out what percentage of federal taxes is paid from the "top down" by the top 40%, top 60%, or top 80% of income earners. Likewise, we can count from the "bottom up" by the bottom 40%, 60%, or 80% of income earners. Fill in the table.

Share of Total Federal Tax Revenue		Share of Total Federal Tax Revenue	
Everyone	100%	Everyone	100%
Bottom 20%	0.8%	Top 80%	
Bottom 40%	4.9%	Top 60%	
Bottom 60%		Top 40%	85.6%
Bottom 80%		Top 20%	68.7%

b. Given these data, which of the following are true?

　i. The bottom 60% of taxpayers pay less than 25% of federal taxes.

　ii. The top 80% of taxpayers pay over 98% of federal taxes.

　iii. The top 40% of taxpayers pay less than 60% of federal taxes.

2. In 2017, corporate income taxes were about 9.9% of total federal revenue. Use Figure 36.6 to help estimate what fraction of GDP represents corporate income taxes.

3. a. Let's explore the difference between the average income tax rate and the marginal income tax rate. In the simple land of Rabushka, there is only one tax rate, 20%, but workers don't have to pay tax on the first $10,000 of their income. For every dollar they earn above $10,000, they pay 20 cents on the dollar to the Lord High Mayor of Rabushka.

　The easy way to calculate the tax bill is the same way that America's IRS does: Subtract $10,000 from each person's income and call the remainder "taxable income." Multiply taxable income by 0.20, and the result is "tax due." Fill in the table.

Income	Taxable Income	Tax Due	Marginal Tax Rate	Average Income Tax Rate
$5,000	$0	0	0%	0%
$10,000	$0	0	0%	0%
$15,000	$5,000	$1,000	20%	6.7%
$20,000				
$50,000				
$100,000				
$1,000,000				

b. Is the marginal tax rate ever lower than the average tax rate?

c. As a worker's income rises and rises past $1,000,000, will the average tax rate ever be greater than 20%?

d. Just to make sure you know what these terms mean in plain English: For an accountant making $50,000 per year, what percentage of her income goes to the Lord High Mayor?

Note: This simple tax system is quite similar to the plan that economist Robert Hall and political scientist Alvin Rabushka spell out in their book, *The Flat Tax*, widely available for free online. Hall and Rabushka estimate that a system like this one would raise roughly the same amount of revenue as the current federal income tax.

4. a. Do most federal government transfers of cash go to the elderly or to the poor?

b. Do most federal government purchases of health care go to the elderly or to the poor?

5. Based on the information in this chapter, let's see who gets a better deal, a greater net benefit, from Social Security. In each pairing, choose one, or write "unclear."

Women or men?

Married couples or singles?

People born in 1910 or people born in 1965?

High-income earners or low-income earners?

6. There are a lot of ways to slice up the U.S. budget. With this in mind, which of the following statements are true, according to Figure 36.4?

i. Most of the federal budget is spent on welfare and foreign aid.

ii. About half of the federal budget goes toward Medicare, Medicaid, and Social Security combined.

iii. More than half of the federal budget goes toward Medicare, Medicaid, Social Security, and interest on the debt combined.

iv. The federal government spends about $1,830 on the military per person in the United States.

7. Pundits and commentators often state (correctly) that entitlement spending (spending on Medicare, Medicaid, and Social Security) is going to explode in the future. But by lumping all three together, we obscure the source of the explosion.

a. Which of the three really won't be "exploding" all that much compared to the other two?

b. Which category of federal spending is projected to actually decline in future decades?

THINKING AND PROBLEM SOLVING

8. By U.S. law, your employer pays half of the payroll tax and you, the worker, pay the other half. We mentioned that according to the basics of supply and demand, the part of the tax paid by the employer is likely to cut the worker's take-home pay. Let's see why. We'll start off in a land without any payroll taxes and then see how adding payroll taxes (like FICA and Medicare) affects the worker's take-home pay.

a. Who is it that "supplies labor"? Is it workers or firms? And who demands labor? Workers or firms?

b. The following chart illustrates the pretax equilibrium. Mark the equilibrium wage and quantity of labor in this market. In part c, remember that this "wage" is the amount paid directly to workers.

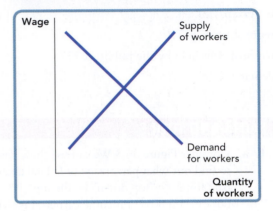

c. Suppose the government enacts a new payroll tax of 10% of worker wages, "paid" fully by employers. What will happen to the typical firm's demand for labor? In other words, when firms learn that every time they hire a worker, they have to pay not only that worker's wage but also 10% of that worker's wage to the government, will that increase or decrease their willingness to hire workers? After you answer in words, also illustrate the shift in the graph.

d. So, in the equilibrium with a new fully-employer-paid payroll tax, will worker's take-home wages be higher or lower than beforehand?

e. Imagine that most workers want full-time jobs to support their families whether the wage is high or low. What does this imply about the shape of the supply curve? Redo the analysis with the new supply curve and discuss the exact effect on wages of the payroll tax.

9. It's easy to confuse the "federal deficit" with the "federal debt." We'll work out an example to make the differences clear. To keep the math simple, we'll falsely assume that in this land of Barrovia, the government can borrow from the public at an interest rate of 0%—so there is no interest on the debt. We will also assume that the government is unwilling to print money to finance its budget, so the only way to finance a deficit is by borrowing. The debt inherited from 2017 is 4,000 credits (C4,000, in the local notation). Fill in the accompanying table.

Note: The relationship between deficits and debts is similar to the relationship between investment and the capital stock, which we investigated back in our chapter on The Wealth of Nations and Economic Growth and the chapter on Growth, Capital Accumulation, and the Economics of Ideas: The first is a "flow," while the second is a "stock"; the first is like a river, while the second is like a lake.

Year	Revenue	Spending	Deficit	Debt
2018	C100	C120	C20	C4,020
2019	C80	C130	C50	
2020	C110	C140		
2021	C120	C150		
2022	C120	C160		

10. Social Security is primarily a pay-as-you-go program, which means that the government pays retirees their promised benefits by taxing today's workers. Imagine that Social Security moved to a fully funded program in which today's workers (or the government on their behalf) invested in assets, such as stocks and bonds, to pay for their own retirement.

    a. Discuss some of the costs and benefits of a fully funded program.

    b. Discuss some of the difficulties of transitioning to the new system. (*Hint:* If today's workers pay for their own future retirement, who will pay today's retirees?)

11. Calculating taxes on capital gains takes a little work, but if you buy and sell stocks, bonds, works of art, or homes, you'll probably have to do this at some point. Let's practice. In a few of the following cases, the price will fall—just record that as a negative rise (a "capital loss," in tax jargon). (In some cases, you can use these to offset taxes on capital gain but we won't get into that detail here.)

    a. Fill in the table.

Item	Purchase Price 2015	Sale Price 2020	Capital Gain	Tax Due at 15% Rate
10 Shares of Microsoft Stock	$1,200	$1,250	$50	$7.50
1 Share of Berkshire Hathaway stock	$8,000	$11,000		
100 Shares of GM stock	$1,000	$500		
1 Picasso napkin sketch	$15,000	$14,000		
1 Mexican Amate folk painting	$2,000	$3,500		

    b. One nice thing about the capital gains tax is that you can choose what year to pay it by choosing what year to sell your investment. If you wanted to sell your single share of Berkshire stock and your Picasso in the same year, how much tax would you pay?

12. How big is the tax break from the $3,950-per-child income tax deduction for:

    a. Families in the 10% tax bracket?

    b. Families in the 25% tax bracket? (*Hint:* This is worked out in the chapter.)

    c. Families in the 35% tax bracket?

13. a. If 1% of federal spending goes toward foreign aid, then what percent of U.S. GDP goes toward foreign aid? Figures 36.4 and 36.6 will help.

    b. If 20% of federal spending goes toward defense spending, then what percent of U.S. GDP goes toward defense spending?

    c. If $30 billion of federal spending goes toward earmarked appropriations, what percent of federal spending goes toward earmarks?

14. Some people argue that a large national debt will make future generations poorer. One way to test this is to see what happened after the last time the United States had a large national debt: after World War II. As Figure 36.5 shows, the debt-to-GDP ratio was over 100%, a bit higher than even today's ratio. Let's compare this to Figure 3 in our chapter on GDP and the Measurement of Progress and Figure 6 in our chapter on Unemployment and Labor Force Participation, which show the growth rate of GDP and the unemployment rate, respectively.

   a. During the 1950s, was the growth rate lower than average? How about during the 1960s?

   b. During the 1950s, was the unemployment rate higher than average? How about during the 1960s?

   c. Overall, is it fair to say that the two decades after the massive World War II debt were worse than average?

   Note that this single case doesn't count as conclusive proof: Perhaps the United States just got lucky, or the federal government did an unusually good job spending its World War II expenditures to build up its capital stock (a point emphasized in the excellent Francis Ford Coppola film *Tucker: The Man and His Dream*), or perhaps a massive short-term debt doesn't cause much economic trouble. You can learn more about these possible explanations in other economics courses.

15. Which of the following actual government programs show up as costs in the federal budget?

   The Department of Labor mandates the minimum wage for workers.

   The Environmental Protection Agency mandates that cars have equipment to keep pollution levels low.

   The National Oceanic and Atmospheric Administration forecasts the weather.

   The Coast Guard rescues sailors from a sinking yacht off the coast of Cape Cod.

   The Border Patrol requires that all vehicles driving on highways out of San Diego be stopped to inspect for the presence of illegal aliens.

Ask FRED

interactive activity

16. Using the Fred economic database (https://fred.stlouisfed.org/), create a series showing federal expenditures as a share of GDP. First find Federal Government current expenditures. Then Edit Graph and, under Customize Data, add Gross Domestic Product (since expenditures are in billions, look for GDP in billions, not real GDP). After adding GDP, go down to the Formula field and use a/b*100.

   a. Approximately how much of GDP was spent by the Federal Government in 2016?

   b. In the 2008–2009 recession what happened to Federal spending as a share of GDP? Give two reasons why?

Ask FRED

interactive activity

17. Let's take a look at one aspect of the U.S. tax system over the past 100 years. Using the Fred economic database (https://fred.stlouisfed.org/), look for "U.S. Individual Income Tax: Tax Rates for Regular Tax: Highest Bracket."

   a. When the income tax was first introduced, what was the rate on the highest bracket?

   b. The rate on the highest tax bracket shot up shortly after the income tax was introduced; it then fell in the 1920s before shooting up again. Suggest a theory for why this happened.

CHALLENGES

18. In 1989, Senator Bob Packwood asked Congress's Joint Committee on Taxation how much extra revenue the government would raise if it just started taxing 100% of all income over $200,000 per year. The Joint Committee crunched some numbers and reported an answer: $204 billion per year.

   a. What is wrong with this answer?

   b. Under Packwood's proposal, what would the marginal tax rate be at $250,000 per year? At $500,000 per year?

Note: Packwood asked the Joint Committee this question not because he wanted to raise taxes that high, but to make a point. The tale of his efforts—and the efforts of Ronald Reagan, Dan Rostenkowski, Bill Bradley, and many others—to improve the U.S. tax code in the 1980s is compellingly told in Birnbaum and Murray's book *Showdown at Gucci Gulch: Lawmakers, Lobbyists, and the Unlikely Triumph of Tax Reform.*

19. Today, many government transfer programs are run through the tax code. The Earned Income Tax Credit (EITC), which we discussed in this chapter, is one important example. The federal government also has a variety of other "refundable tax credits," that is, spending programs run through the tax code. These blur the line between "tax breaks" and "government spending." This may explain their popularity: Voters and politicians who like tax breaks can claim that these programs are tax breaks, while voters and politicians who like higher government spending can claim that these programs are government spending.

    a. Your income is $20,000 per year. You pay your initial tax bill of $5,000 but the government sends you a $1,000 tax refund because you have a young child. What is your after-tax income, including the value of the government check?

    b. Your income is $20,000 per year. You pay your initial tax bill of $5,000 and the government sends you a $1,000 check because you have a young child. What is your after-tax income, including the value of the government check?

    c. Your income is $20,000 per year. You pay your initial tax bill of $500 but the government sends you a $1,000 tax refund because you have a young child. What is your after-tax income, including the value of the government check?

    d. Your income is $20,000 per year. You pay your tax bill of $500 and the government sends you a $1,000 check because you have a young child. What is your after-tax income, including the value of the government check?

    e. In which of these cases does the government check seem like "government spending" to you, and why? You may find more than one case applicable—this question borders on the philosophical.

20. a. If the debt-to-GDP ratio rose to 100% and the interest rate on the debt were 5% per year, what fraction of GDP would go toward paying interest on the debt?

    b. If this happened, would interest on the debt be a bigger share of GDP than Social Security is today?

    c. In your opinion, do you think that Americans would tolerate spending this much of the national income on interest payments for past spending? More important, do you think Americans would want their politicians to stop making the interest payments and just default on some or all of the federal debt? Why or why not?

21. In the past, the U.S. government offered "food stamps" to poor Americans. These "stamps" were pieces of paper that looked like Monopoly money and could be spent just like money at many grocery stores. The government has a complex formula that determines how much each poor person gets each month which is now given in the form of government-provided debit cards.

    Let's suppose that instead, the government decides to pay 95% of every poor person's food bill, as long as it is purchased at a typical grocery store: The poor person would make a "copayment" of 5% of the total bill, and the federal government would reimburse the grocery store for the remaining 95%. Just to keep things simple, let's assume that the government has a good way to make sure that poor people can't resell this food to others.

    a. Which method would probably lead to more spending on food: the current method or the 5% copayment method? Why?

    b. If food companies like Kellogg's and Quaker Oats start inventing new, more delicious dishes at a rapid rate, under which method will the federal government's food spending grow fastest: the current method or the 5% copayment method?

    c. Which method is more like how most people pay for health care, including the elderly and the poor under the federal government's Medicare and Medicaid programs:

the current method or the 5% copayment method?

d. Recall that health care is a field of rapid innovation. How can your answer to parts b and c explain the rapid growth of medical spending?

22. When discussing the statements sent to you by the federal government that predict your future Social Security payments, we said, "Don't be surprised if those predictions turn out to be a little bit optimistic." Consider why this might be *wrong:* Why might these predictions be too *pessimistic,* precisely because Social Security recipients are also voters? (*Hint:* Senior citizens are more likely to vote than younger citizens.)

23. There are many ways to help poor people in foreign countries. You can find charities, for example, that will buy a cow or shoes for people in poverty or help to dig a well in a low-income village. Which of these programs do you think is the best way to help the poor? What are the pros and cons of simply giving cash?

interactive activity

WORK IT OUT

For interactive, step-by-step help in solving this problem, go online.

Under current law, homeowners get a big tax break: The details of the tax break really don't matter as much as the mere fact that if you make mortgage payments on a home that you live in, your taxes will be lower than otherwise.

a. Suppose that Congress eliminated the tax break for homeowners. What will this law do to the demand for homes: raise, lower, or have no impact?

b. What will be the net effect of eliminating the break on the price of houses?

c. Given your answers to parts a and b, comment on who gets the benefits of the tax break. Is it people who buy homes? Sellers? (Be careful, sellers were buyers once!) Why could eliminating the tax break prove difficult?

MRUNIVERSITY
AN ONLINE EDUCATION PLATFORM

MARGINAL REVOLUTION UNIVERSITY VIDEOS

An Economist's Christmas

mruniversity.com/econ-xmas

Problems: **23**

37

Fiscal Policy

The U.S. economy was falling into a severe recession. The S&P 500 stock index was plummeting. And in the third quarter of 2008, consumer spending dropped by 3.7%, the largest drop in 28 years. Consumer spending is a large fraction of GDP (as you will recall from our chapter on GDP and the Measurement of Progress), so the sudden drop in spending pushed down the growth rate of GDP. To encourage more spending, President George W. Bush authorized the Treasury to send checks to some 130 million taxpayers, paying up to $600 to individual taxpayers and up to $1,200 for married couples. Could the new money jump-start the economy? Not this time. Consumer confidence was ebbing. Even with a few extra bucks in their pocket, consumers weren't ready to spend. The economy continued to worsen and in 2009 President Barack Obama tried a different approach: hundreds of billions of dollars in new government spending on roads, bridges, education, and other infrastructure, combined with additional tax cuts and also aid for state governments. If the American consumer wouldn't spend, then the American government would.

Fighting a recession with tax cuts and fighting a recession with increased government spending are two forms of fiscal policy. **Fiscal policy** is federal government policy on taxes, spending, and borrowing that is designed to influence business fluctuations.

In this chapter, we use the aggregate demand and aggregate supply curves, familiar to you from our chapter on Business Fluctuations: Aggregate Demand and Supply, to understand fiscal policy. We begin by asking why fiscal policy works and we then go into more detail on when it works best.

CHAPTER OUTLINE

Why Should Fiscal Policy Work?

Limits to Fiscal Policy: Magnitude

When Fiscal Policy Might Make Matters Worse

So When Is Fiscal Policy a Good Idea?

Takeaway

Videos
- **Introduction to Fiscal Policy**
- **The Limits to Fiscal Policy**
- **Econ Duel: Does Fiscal Policy Work?**

Why Should Fiscal Policy Work?

Let's begin by answering a basic question. Why should fiscal policy work at all? In other words, why should spending more increase the real production of goods and services? We said earlier that the real production of goods and services is determined by fundamental factors like the amount and quality of human capital, physical capital, and technology. Spending more does not increase any of these factors in any obvious way, so why should spending more increase output? That's a good question, and in ordinary times when the economy is at full employment, spending more won't appreciably increase output.

Let's imagine, for example, that the government wants to build a dam. Building the dam requires the production of lots of new goods and services, like water turbines and financial accounting, but will that production increase

Fiscal policy is federal government policy on taxes, spending, and borrowing that is designed to influence business fluctuations.

789

GDP? No. If the economy is operating at full employment, then the goods and services used to build the dam would have been used to build other goods and services, such as office buildings. In other words, at full employment the goods and services used to build the dam have a high opportunity cost. Once the dam begins to operate, it will increase the production of electricity and that will increase GDP, but if the economy is at full employment the construction of the dam will pull resources from other sectors of the economy. Thus the net effect on GDP will be approximately zero. We also say that at full employment the increase in government spending will mostly *crowd out* production by the private sector, so, again, the net effect on GDP is approximately zero.

> **Crowding out** is the decrease in private spending that occurs when government spending increases.

But now consider a situation in which many workers and resources are unemployed. In this case, building the dam doesn't necessarily reduce the production of goods and services elsewhere in the economy. In fact, if all the workers and resources used to build the dam would have been unemployed without the dam, then every dollar spent on the dam will add one dollar to GDP. In some situations, spending a dollar could even increase GDP by more than a dollar. Suppose that the government hires some unemployed construction workers and suppose that the construction workers use some of their new income to buy meals at restaurants. Increased spending by construction workers encourages restaurants to hire more waiters and cooks, some of whom were themselves unemployed. Because every dollar spent on construction workers is thus multiplied by the spending of the newly hired construction workers, every dollar spent on the dam could generate, say, $1.45 of new goods and services. The **multiplier effect** is the additional increase in spending caused by an increase in government spending.

> The **multiplier effect** is the additional increase in spending caused by the initial increase in government spending.

The fundamental reason that fiscal policy can work is that when resources are unemployed, the economy is operating inefficiently. If spending more can employ unemployed resources, then it can in principle pay for itself.

Let's use aggregate demand and aggregate supply curves to illustrate how fiscal policy works when there are unemployed resources. In Figure 37.1 the economy begins at point *a*, but suppose that consumers become worried about their future, so they cut back on consumption growth; that is, $\vec{C}$ falls. Because consumers are spending less in order to build up their cash reserves, we can also say equivalently that $\vec{v}$ falls. Figure 37.1 shows the result: The fall in $\vec{C}$ shifts the AD curve to the left and down, moving the economy from a long-run equilibrium at point *a* to a short-run equilibrium at point *b*. At point *b*, the growth rate is negative and the economy is in a recession. The problem at point *b* is that consumers want to hold more money, and this means that the rate of inflation must decrease. Wages and prices, however, are sticky (see the Business Fluctuations: Aggregate Demand and Supply chapter), so when spending growth declines, instead of just a decrease in inflation, we get a decrease in real growth as well.

In the long run, prices and wages will become "unstuck," fear will pass, and $\vec{C}$ will return to its normal growth rate. The economy will thus transition until it returns to point *a*. But recall John Maynard Keynes's famous statement: "In the long run, we are all dead." Can government do anything to make recovery a reality now? Quite possibly so.

The government has (some) control over government spending, $\vec{G}$, so if $\vec{C}$ falls, why not increase $\vec{G}$ to compensate? In Figure 37.1, we show how an increase in $\vec{G}$ can shift the AD curve to the right and up, thereby putting the economy on a transition path back to point *a*. In fact, in the best-case scenario, the increase in $\vec{G}$ doesn't even have to be as large as the fall in $\vec{C}$ because of the multiplier effect. When $\vec{G}$ increases and unemployed workers (and other resources) are employed, their spending increases $\vec{C}$. In Figure 37.1 we have

interactive activity

Introduction to Fiscal Policy

FIGURE 37.1

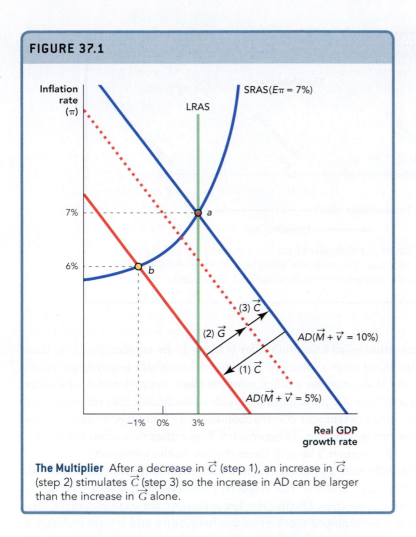

The Multiplier After a decrease in $\vec{C}$ (step 1), an increase in $\vec{G}$ (step 2) stimulates $\vec{C}$ (step 3) so the increase in AD can be larger than the increase in $\vec{G}$ alone.

drawn the ideal situation—when the net effect of the initial increase in spending plus the multiplier effect ends the recession and returns the economy to point *a*.

Great! But, as usual, it's easier to shift lines on a graph than it is to move a real multitrillion-dollar economy. So let's take a look at some of the complications.

What Determines the Size of the Multiplier?

The great debate over fiscal policy is about the balance of two opposing forces: *crowding out* versus the *multiplier effect*. Which is bigger and when? The great debate can be summarized by a single number, the *multiplier*. If government spending increases by $100 billion and all of that additional spending crowds out private sector spending, then the multiplier is zero. If no private sector spending is crowded out, the multiplier is 1. If the increase in government spending causes additional private spending, the multiplier is greater than 1. Figure 37.2 illustrates the two forces.

Fiscal policy is much more likely to be successful when the multiplier is big than when it is small. So what determines the size of the multiplier? We've already indicated one factor: the more unemployed resources, the bigger the multiplier. But the multiplier also depends on how fiscal policy is implemented and on the structure of the economy. If a lot of dam workers are unemployed and the government builds a dam, then that is a well-targeted stimulus and the multiplier is likely to be big. But if a lot of dam workers are unemployed and the government builds an office building, the effect on the multiplier is not so clear—this is a less

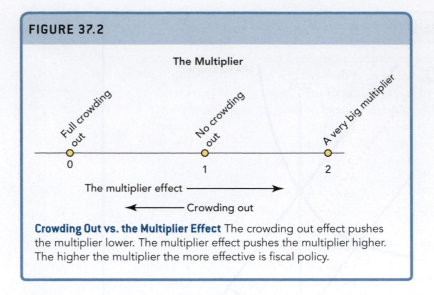

FIGURE 37.2

The Multiplier

The multiplier effect ⟶

⟵ Crowding out

Crowding Out vs. the Multiplier Effect The crowding out effect pushes the multiplier lower. The multiplier effect pushes the multiplier higher. The higher the multiplier the more effective is fiscal policy.

well targeted stimulus and the multiplier is likely to be smaller. Building dams and office buildings takes a lot more than muscle; each also requires specialized knowledge and skills, even for manual workers. Since unemployed dam workers don't necessarily have the knowledge and skills to easily shift into office building construction, new government construction of office buildings is likely to draw workers from private office building construction rather than from the pool of unemployed dam workers. This will lower the size of the multiplier.

More generally, when politicians talk about fiscal stimulus they often talk about "shovel ready" projects. The modern U.S. economy, however, is dominated by service industries. During the last recession, for example, there were almost as many unemployed workers in the hospitality and leisure industry as there were in the construction industry.

Rather than increasing spending on things, the government can increase spending on people. Unemployment insurance and welfare payments, for example, which automatically increase during recessions, are targeted toward the poor and unemployed, who are more likely to spend the money. For that reason, these types of programs tend to have a relatively big multiplier.

Instead of increasing government spending during a recession, the government can also cut taxes to try to increase private spending. The advantage of a tax cut is that the government doesn't have to pick and choose which economic sectors to stimulate. A tax cut will stimulate anything that the public buys. For the same reason, however, tax cuts are not very targeted. The size of the multiplier will depend, therefore, on how much of the tax cut is spent and on what the spending is on.

If the government cuts taxes on people who want to buy what unemployed workers produce, the multiplier will be big. A tax cut that is targeted to people in regions with high unemployment, for example, could work better than a national tax cut.

For similar reasons, if the government cuts taxes on people who want to spend the entire tax cut immediately, then the multiplier will be big. A tax cut to the poor is likely to have a bigger multiplier than a tax cut to the rich because the poor often have expenses that must be paid immediately while the spending of the rich is subject to greater choice. It's sometimes difficult to cut taxes to the poor, however, because many poor people already don't pay much in taxes, at least not in income taxes (see the previous chapter).

A closely related problem is that many people might choose to save their tax cuts rather than spend them. People might want to save if they fear future unemployment, for example. Saving is not necessarily bad, even in a recession, *if* the saving is quickly turned into investment. In a recession, however, the desired level of savings may exceed the desired level of investment. Instead of flowing into investment, savings may flow into the purchase of government bonds or other unproductive assets—sometimes called the "flight to safety." Recall also from our chapter on Saving, Investment, and the Financial System that one cause of the 2008–2009 recession and the Great Depression was a breakdown in financial intermediation. If financial intermediaries are not channeling funds from savings to investment, then increased savings (i.e., reduced consumption) will not be matched by increased investment. But if consumption falls and investment doesn't increase, total output will fall.

People might also choose to save the money from their tax cuts if they expect that tax cuts today will be matched by tax increases tomorrow. In fact, if we hold government spending constant through time, then a tax cut today *must* be matched by a tax increase in the future. Now imagine that people are patient and very forward-looking. When the government cuts taxes today, these people realize that taxes will be higher in the future. These farsighted people will plan accordingly and save more today. Basically, they are saving more so that the future tax payments don't cause them to give up familiar habits or move into old-age poverty; this "consumption smoothing" was explained in our Saving, Investment, and the Financial System chapter.

Is the Ricardian equivalence realistic? "I got a tax cut this year, son. But that means that your taxes will be going up in the future so I'm going to save more."

But if people save their tax cuts instead of spending them, then the aggregate demand curve does not shift out, the multiplier is zero, and there are no systematic macroeconomic effects. This scenario is sometimes called **Ricardian equivalence**, after the nineteenth-century British economist David Ricardo. Most economists think it is unrealistic to assume that people understand their future tax burden and save accordingly to offset future tax burdens. Tyler knows that he doesn't behave this way (and he's a trained economist), but he does see some signs of this behavior from Alex. So Ricardian equivalence probably describes some people but not most people. In any case, to the extent that Ricardian equivalence reflects how people plan, tax cuts are less effective in the short run than otherwise.

Ricardian equivalence occurs when people see that lower taxes today means higher taxes in the future, so instead of spending their tax cut, they save it to pay future taxes. When Ricardian equivalence holds, a tax cut doesn't increase aggregate demand even in the short run.

Another factor that influences the size of the multiplier is how the government pays for its spending. The simplest case is when new government spending is financed by an increase in taxes. Higher taxes mean the government spends more money, but of course, higher taxes also mean that private individuals have less money to spend. Thus, the multiplier for tax-financed spending will be bigger when the government can tax those individuals who weren't going to spend immediately, or, more generally, when the government can tax (unproductive) savings rather than consumption. As a long-term proposition, taxing savings may be a bad idea, but during a recession the goal of fiscal policy is to increase spending not saving.

Instead of raising taxes immediately, the government often pays its bills with borrowed money. As we showed in Figure 10 of the Saving, Investment, and the Financial System chapter, when the government borrows more, the interest rate in the market for loanable funds tends to increase. A higher interest rate will encourage people to save more—you might think that is good, but "saving more" is another way of saying "spending less." Thus, when the government pays for its increased spending by borrowing, some of the money comes from reduced private spending. At the same time, a higher interest rate will cause some private borrowers to borrow and invest less. Thus, some of the money the government borrows comes from reduced private investment. So when the government borrows, there is some crowding out due to reduced consumption and some crowding out due to reduced investment, and these forces result in a lower multiplier.

Given the possibilities for crowding out, fiscal policy is most likely to be effective when the private sector is, for some reason, reluctant to spend or invest. This is often the case in a depression or in times of great uncertainty, or when people, for whatever reason, are simply holding onto their cash. In these cases government investments do not displace comparable private investments, as the private investments would not have been forthcoming in any case. In addition, during a recession, investors often want to wait and see how uncertainty is resolved before investing in private projects. In the meantime, investors may be happy to park their money in government bonds, which are seen as safe even if they don't pay a high interest rate—the flight to safety that we mentioned earlier. For both of these reasons, interest rates can fall during a recession and government borrowing may create less crowding out than would occur during a boom.

Summing up, the multiplier is likely to be bigger when there are lots of unemployed resources, when the government can target spending directly on the unemployed, when tax cuts go to people who want to spend immediately, when the government can tax savings, and when government borrowing does not crowd out much private consumption or investment.

So How Big Is the Multiplier?

We've described a number of factors that influence the size of the multiplier. Given those factors, is the multiplier big? Well it's hard to say. Estimating the multiplier in practice is quite difficult, both because the economy is complex and because, as we have just illustrated, there are actually many multipliers, depending on conditions. During the 2008–2009 recession, however, the Congressional Budget Office surveyed a number of different estimates and came up with the following list (Table 37.1).

TABLE 37.1 ESTIMATED FISCAL MULTIPLIERS FOR MAJOR PROVISIONS OF THE AMERICAN RECOVERY AND REINVESTMENT ACT OF 2009

Type of Activity	Estimated Multiplier	
	Low Estimate	High Estimate
Purchase of goods and services by the federal government	0.5	2.5
Transfer payments to state and local Governments for infrastructure	0.4	2.2
Transfer payments to state and local governments for other purposes	0.4	1.8
Transfer payments to individuals	0.4	2.1
Two-year tax cuts for lower- and middle-income people	0.3	1.5
Onetime payments to retirees	0.2	1.0
One-year tax Cut for higher-income people	0.1	0.6

Data from: Congressional Budget Office. 2015. Estimated Impact of the American Recovery and Reinvestment Act on Employment and Economic Output in 2014.

Notice that each item in the list has a low and a high estimate, indicating considerable uncertainty about the size of the multiplier even in a very serious recession. At the bottom of the list is a one-year tax cut for higher income people, where the multiplier is estimated to be between 0.1 and 0.6. As theory suggests, tax cuts to the rich may not go into immediate spending, and one-year tax cuts are especially likely to be saved as people are likely to foresee the future tax increase. One-time payments to retirees and tax cuts to lower- and middle-income people do a little better. Transfer payments to individuals and to state and local governments tend to have much higher multipliers with the high estimates suggesting that one dollar transferred to individuals or state and local governments could increase GDP by $1.8 to $2.1. The difference here is that these transfer payments are likely to be spent quickly. At the top of the list are transfers to state and local governments for infrastructure spending or federal infrastructure spending.

Another important point to note about Table 37.1 is that all of these spending activities were part of the big 2009 fiscal stimulus, the American Recovery and Reinvestment Act (ARRA). Thus, some parts of the act were significantly more effective as fiscal stimulus than other parts. Congress spent funds in some areas that were likely to be less effective than others, in part for political reasons and in part because the most effective areas for fiscal stimulus may be limited. Infrastructure spending tends to work well as fiscal stimulus, for example, but we need only so many roads and dams and we can't always start these projects immediately (the shovel ready problem.) Let's take a closer look at size and timing issues.

CHECK YOURSELF

■ What are the two types of expansionary fiscal policy?

Limits to Fiscal Policy: Magnitude

In addition to crowding out and other factors that determine the size of the multiplier, fiscal policy is limited by how much can be spent and how quickly. Surprisingly, one of the biggest problems with government spending as a boost to aggregate demand is simply that most changes in government spending are not very large in the short run. If changes to government spending are not large in the short run, the boost to aggregate demand won't be very large either.

In the contemporary United States, changes in fiscal policy, in percentage terms, simply aren't that large in a typical year. Most of the federal budget is determined well in advance and is remarkably stable. As we have seen in the previous chapter, among the largest budget categories are national defense, Social Security, Medicare, and interest on the debt. Those categories alone account for 65% of spending in a typical year and these programs are more or less on automatic pilot, with their yearly levels of spending set by automatic formulas or by previous agreements or commitments. Nonsecurity federal discretionary spending is less than 20% of the federal budget and most of this is not seriously up for grabs in any given year. Government spending, in today's world, simply does not change very much in percentage terms on a year-to-year basis.

The fiscal stimulus plan passed under President Barack Obama in 2009 was the largest fiscal stimulus since military spending rose tremendously during World War II. Even this $800–$900 billion stimulus, however, was spread over 3–4 years so at its peak the stimulus was about 1.6% of annual GDP. These are large numbers relative to previous stimulus plans but, although significant, they are still modest compared to the total size of the economy. For this reason, many Keynesian economists suggested that the stimulus wasn't large enough to succeed, but even if the Keynesians are right in principle, politically speaking, a larger stimulus bill probably was not possible. In September 2010, after most of the stimulus money was spent, unemployment remained at 9.6%.

Timing

Bad timing provides another reason why fiscal policy is often not very effective, even in the short run. The United States Constitution stipulates that both Congress and the president must approve all expenditures. There are two houses of Congress, and of course legislation must pass through various committees. Sometimes an emergency stimulus occurs quickly, as in the 2008 case, which Congress passed a mere two weeks after President Bush requested it. But often the proposed fiscal projects are complicated and the budget cycle takes place over many months or sometimes even years; it can take a long time for new bills to be conceived, written, debated, and passed. Specific expenditures often must be coordinated with state and local governments, or the projects must produce environmental impact statements, or they must survive legal challenges. Even once the money is in place, it takes time to spend it; for instance, you can't build a large airport or dam all at once and it doesn't make sense to pay every contractor in advance.

In short, even a single government expenditure can take years to move from dream to reality. Yet fiscal policy is often intended to correct short-term problems in the business cycle. By the time the fiscal policy is in place, macroeconomic conditions often have changed entirely.

The list of relevant lags includes the following:

1. Recognition lag: The problem must be recognized.

2. Legislative lag: Congress must propose and pass a plan.

3. Implementation lag: Bureaucracies must implement the plan.

4. Effectiveness lag: The plan takes time to work.

5. Evaluation and adjustment lag: Did the plan work? Have conditions changed? (Return to lag 1!)

Tax cuts, the other major form of fiscal policy, also involve lags and uncertainties, at least with respect to their role in stimulating aggregate demand.

President George W. Bush cut marginal tax rates in 2001, 2002, and 2003. The latter tax cuts came quite quickly after a recession loomed following 9/11 (in part because the tax cuts were mostly planned in advance for other reasons). But these tax cuts were not very effective as fiscal policy either. Each cut was less than 1% of national income, the economy was already recovering, plus most of the tax cuts went to relatively high-income groups, who tend to save their surplus funds. If we are thinking in terms of fiscal policy alone, tax cuts to the poor would probably result in more spending, except of course, that the poor don't pay that much in taxes.

Monetary policy is also subject to lags, but these are generally shorter than for fiscal policy. Once the Federal Reserve recognizes a problem, it can act very quickly to implement changes to monetary policy. After 9/11, for example, the Federal Reserve stepped in the next *day* with massive infusions of cash to the banking system. The Federal Reserve can also evaluate and adjust its plan quickly as the economy responds or fails to respond. Fiscal policy, in contrast, is rarely adjusted in response to changes in economic conditions. The only place where fiscal policy might have an advantage over monetary policy is through

interactive activity

The Limits to Fiscal Policy

the effectiveness lag. As we discussed in our earlier chapter on the Federal Reserve and Open Market Operations and the chapter on Monetary Policy, the effectiveness of changes in monetary policy depends on matters like how willing banks are to lend and businesses are to borrow. A spending program, in contrast, typically has a direct impact on economic conditions, at least once the money is put into the economy.

Automatic Stabilizers Some kinds of fiscal policy are built right into the tax and transfer system, and they do take effect without significant lags. These are called **automatic stabilizers**. Virtually all economists recognize the virtue of automatic stabilizers in keeping aggregate demand on a steady and regular course.

Fiscal policy automatically changes to keep private spending higher during bad economic times. For instance, when the economy is doing poorly, income, capital gains, and corporate profits are all down. As a result, most people and businesses will pay lower taxes and, given that the American tax system is progressive (see the previous chapter), possibly a lower tax rate as well. The lower tax burden makes aggregate demand more robust than it otherwise would be. The lower taxes don't offset the curse of hard times (lowering your taxes by lowering your income is not the preferred way to go), but they soften the blow. Pre-tax incomes are perhaps falling, but post-tax incomes are not falling by as much.

Welfare and transfer programs also provide automatic stabilizers. When the economy is declining, increasing numbers of people apply for welfare, food stamps, unemployment insurance, and other programs designed to help low-income groups. These groups receive more income, and because of their precarious economic situation, they tend to spend that money fairly quickly. Spending on these categories helps people in tough times and also helps maintain aggregate demand.

Of course, it is not just fiscal policy that provides automatic stabilizers. When people save during good times and use their savings to tide them over in bad times (consumption smoothing, as discussed in our chapter on Saving, Investment, and the Financial System), it's an automatic stabilizer. Private market innovations, most of all credit, have also contributed to stabilization. Even though the 2008 credit crisis pared back some kinds of borrowing, it is still easier today to take out a second mortgage on one's home than it was 30 years ago. If you need to send your kid to college, you can borrow more rather than cutting your spending ruthlessly. That way you can pay back the money over time, for a smoother adjustment. Credit cards, durable assets, the increased availability of used goods (eBay), and discount outlets all allow the economy to weather hard times more easily.

> **Automatic stabilizers** are changes in fiscal policy that stimulate AD in a recession without the need for explicit action by policymakers.

Government Spending vs. Tax Cuts as Expansionary Fiscal Policy

Before turning to the last limit on fiscal policy, the fact that fiscal policy does not work well with real shocks, let's briefly examine the differences between the two types of fiscal policy we have discussed, namely government spending and tax cuts. The differences between these types of fiscal policy are political and also economic. Let's discuss the political differences first.

A tax cut or tax rebate puts more spending in the hands of the private sector, while an increase in government spending puts more spending in the hands of the government. People who are skeptical about government spending typically prefer fiscal policy to work through tax rebates and tax cuts rather than through changes in government spending.

Consider the infamous "Bridge to Nowhere," a proposed bridge in Alaska that was to connect the town of Ketchikan (population 8,900) with its airport on the Island of Gravina (population 50) at a cost to federal taxpayers of $320 million. At present, a ferry service runs to the island, but some people in the town complain that it costs too much ($6 per car). If the town's residents had to pay the $320 million cost of the bridge themselves—that's $35,754 each!—do you think they would want the bridge? Of course not, so if the bridge is ever built, it may raise measured GDP but the costs will still exceed the benefits. That is a type of fiscal policy that we don't want. Fortunately, the project was scrapped by Congress in 2015 after fierce opposition.

On the other hand, people who think that the U.S. government is not spending enough will tend to prefer that fiscal policy work through spending increases. The U.S. highway system is generally regarded as a highly productive investment of capital. If we can find equally productive public investments such as improvements to schools, science funding, and infrastructure ("bridges to somewhere"), then the case for public investment is strong, and if we can time these spending increases to help offset a recession, so much the better.

Do you recall our opening example? It's a useful illustration of the political differences over fiscal policy. George Bush and Barack Obama both used expansionary fiscal policy to fight a recession but Bush, a Republican, focused on tax cuts, while Obama, a Democrat, served up a mix of tax cuts and government spending increases.

We summarize the different types of fiscal policy and possible results in Figure 37.3.

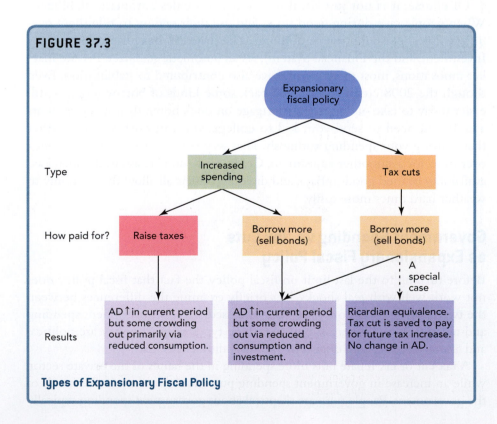

FIGURE 37.3

Types of Expansionary Fiscal Policy

Fiscal Policy Does Not Work Well to Combat Real Shocks

We have assumed so far that the problem fiscal policy needs to address is a deficiency in aggregate demand. But imagine, for example, that the recession is caused not by a fall in $\vec{C}$, but by a real shock that reduces the productivity of capital and labor, shifting the long-run aggregate supply curve to the left. In Figure 37.4, for example, a real shock shifts the long-run aggregate supply curve to the left, moving the economy from point *a* to point *b*.

As before, the economy is in a recession at point *b*. Now suppose that government responds by increasing $\vec{G}$. As usual, the aggregate demand curve shifts out, but now the economy is less productive than before, due to the real shock. As a result, an increase in $\vec{G}$ will not move the economy back to point *a*. Instead, most of the increase in $\vec{G}$ will show up in inflation rather than in real growth, so the economy will shift from point *b* to point *c* with a much higher inflation rate and a slightly higher growth rate. As you may recall, the analysis is very similar to the analysis of monetary policy when facing a real shock.

In fact, the situation for fiscal policy is worse than Figure 37.4 indicates because when the problem an economy faces is a real shock, there is no inefficiency. Thus, unlike in Figure 37.1, the increase in $\vec{G}$ is unlikely to create much

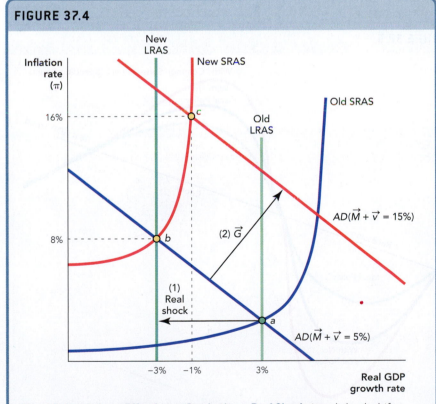

FIGURE 37.4

Fiscal Policy Is Less Effective at Combating a Real Shock A real shock shifts the long-run aggregate supply curve (LRAS) to the left (step 1), moving the economy from point *a* to a recession at point *b*. To combat the recession, the government increases $\vec{G}$ (step 2), but due to the real shock, the economy is now less productive than before, and so the increase in aggregate demand shifts the economy to point *c*, where the growth rate is a little bit higher but the inflation rate is much higher.

Counter-cyclical fiscal policy is fiscal policy that runs opposite or counter to the business cycle—spending more when the economy is in a recession and less when the economy is booming.

new growth and most of (perhaps even all of) $\vec{G}$ will *crowd out* other spending. (Another way of seeing this is to remember that the long-run aggregate supply curve shows the real rate of growth when the economy is operating at its full potential, and neither fiscal nor monetary policy can increase the growth rate above the rate given by the fundamentals—the Solow rate—for very long.)

The economy is subject to both aggregate demand shocks and real shocks. Since some recessions are driven by real shocks, fiscal policy will not always be an effective method of combating a recession.

When Fiscal Policy Might Make Matters Worse

Increased spending and tax cuts have to be paid for. Thus, increased spending and tax cuts today will tend to be followed by decreased spending or tax increases tomorrow. When tomorrow comes and spending is reduced and taxes rise, aggregate demand will fall—this is one reason why long-run or net multipliers are smaller than short-run multipliers. Ideal fiscal policy will increase AD in bad times and pay off the bill in good times, as we show in Figure 37.5. Overall, if we can spend more in bad times when the multiplier is big and tax more in good times when the multiplier is small, the net effect will lead to higher GDP overall. Economists say that the ideal fiscal policy is **counter-cyclical** because when the economy is down the government should spend more, and when the economy is up the government should spend less.

FIGURE 37.5

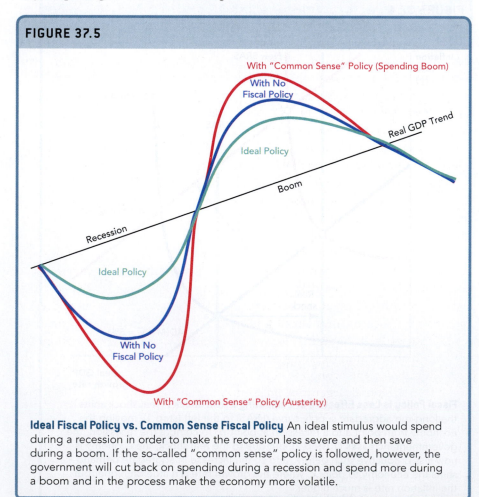

Ideal Fiscal Policy vs. Common Sense Fiscal Policy An ideal stimulus would spend during a recession in order to make the recession less severe and then save during a boom. If the so-called "common sense" policy is followed, however, the government will cut back on spending during a recession and spend more during a boom and in the process make the economy more volatile.

Although counter-cyclical fiscal policy makes sense to economists, it often doesn't make sense to politicians or to voters. The views of economists violate a kind of "common sense" or folk wisdom, which says that in bad times the government should spend less and only in good times should the government spend more. After all, you and I spend less when times are bad and more when times are good, so shouldn't the government behave similarly? If the government follows the "common sense" view, however, it will tend to make recessions deeper and booms larger, thereby making the economy more volatile, again as shown in Figure 37.5.

The common sense view does make sense for you and I because we spend too little to affect the national economy—you and I only respond to GDP and our decisions do not significantly change GDP. Many governments, however, are big enough that their actions can in principle change GDP, which is why economists suggest that the government act differently than you and I.

Even when governments do spend more in recessions, as economists suggest, they often don't follow through on the second half of the prescription, which is to spend less during booms. When governments spend more than they tax, even in boom years, then the total debt grows larger, as we discussed in the previous chapter. When the debt is large, governments must spend a large fraction of their budget on interest payments alone. This usually means that there is less room for expansionary fiscal policy when it is needed.

In extreme situations, debt can be such a problem that *expansionary fiscal policy can reduce real growth*. Some countries are so heavily in debt that any more government borrowing runs the risk of total economic collapse. Take, for instance, Argentina, which had a major financial crisis in the 1999–2002 period; in those years, Argentine real GDP fell by rates of −3.4%, −0.8%, −4.4%, and −10.9%, respectively.[1] That's not a good record. In the years leading up to this collapse, the Argentine government spent more and more, and did not pay off its bills. By 2002, Argentine government debt was 150% of GDP, a very high level. (For purposes of contrast, the U.S. federal government has net debt of about 76% of GDP, although that level is slowly rising.) The Argentine government could not pay off these debts and the final result was the largest default by a government in the history of the world.

In the years leading up to the collapse, many investors feared that the Argentine currency would lose most of its value and that the economy would fall apart. More government spending led to more anxiety, rather than economic stimulation.

So, in this setting, if the government increases spending, aggregate demand does not go up. Instead, private spending and production fall by so much that real GDP falls (i.e., more than 100% crowding out!). Aggregate demand falls because in times of great uncertainty, people save or hoard their money in anticipation of hard times ahead. In the case of Argentina, people put their wealth into bank accounts in Miami or Switzerland, rather than investing it at home or spending it in the shops of Buenos Aires. Of course, that flight of capital only hastened the economic collapse.

We've mentioned Argentina, but similar scenarios (the details differ) have occurred in many other lesser developed nations, including Thailand, Indonesia, and Mexico. The lesson is this: Too high a debt can drive a nation to ruin by undercutting the credibility of everything a government does and whether that government can meet its commitments. The United States isn't in that position at this time, but if you wish to understand global events, you need to realize that fiscal policy has an immediate negative effect in many economic situations, especially when the credibility of the government is low.

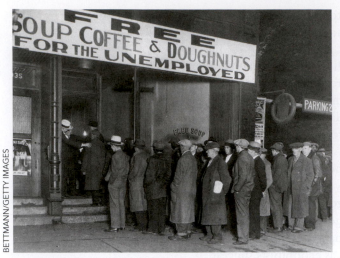

When unemployment is at 25%, there is less private spending to crowd out.

Econ Duel: Does Fiscal Policy Work?

interactive activity

So When Is Fiscal Policy a Good Idea?

The macroeconomic case for government spending is strongest when the government faces some immediate emergency, such as a war, a worsening depression, or a natural disaster. Government spending is best for the macroeconomy when it is worth incurring some long-run costs to get a short-run economic boost.

It is also the case—as with monetary policy—that fiscal policy is most effective when the relevant shock is to aggregate demand and there are many unemployed resources. For these reasons, most economists look back on the Great Depression of the 1930s and see expansionary fiscal policy as a good idea in that setting. As we saw in our chapter on Business Fluctuations, the Great Depression was primarily caused by a reduction in aggregate demand rather than by a real shock, so increasing aggregate demand was the right type of solution.

Furthermore, at the time, rates of unemployment were sometimes as high as 25%, which meant that the degree of crowding out was probably not very large. Let's say that the federal government hires some workers to build a dam. If the government is simply pulling already employed workers from other jobs, we shouldn't expect this to help the economy much. But if those people otherwise would have been out of work, we should expect a greater economic stimulus in the short term. In other words, when it comes to these workers, government investment is not crowding out private investments. The government investment is creating economic activity directly and stimulating private investment and consumption.

In addition, the increase in government spending during the Great Depression was relatively rapid and quite dramatic in percentage terms. Roosevelt, the architect of the New Deal, won the election in 1932. By 1936, federal government spending was more than twice what it had been in 1932.

Notice that, today, rates of unemployment range more often between 4% and 9%, so increased government spending is likely to draw people from one job to another job rather than from unemployment to work. It would also be much more difficult for the federal government to double spending as it did in the 1930s. So for these reasons, fiscal policy is less likely to be successful today than it was in the 1930s, and crowding out is more likely to happen.[2]

Now let's consider the stimulus under President Obama. For all the talk about the Obama stimulus, the plan is best understood as consisting of three separate parts. The American Recovery and Reinvestment Act, as approved in February 2009, included $292 billion in federal tax cuts (including increased transfer payments to the poor), $272 billion in direct federal spending, and $223 billion in grants to the governments of the 50 states.

The experiment is still being debated, but so far the consensus seems to be this:

1. A lot of the tax cuts were saved or used to pay off debts, rather than spent. This boosted economic security for some people but the multipliers were on the low side; thus this didn't reemploy a lot of workers.

2. The grants to the states prevented a large number of state government layoffs, which was good for economic output.

3. The expenditures covered a wide range of ground, ranging from medical research to home insulation to high-speed rail. Although some of these projects will do the world good, others were perhaps not the best use of funds; the multipliers in this case, however, were higher than for other parts of the fiscal stimulus.

So to sum up, fiscal policy is likely to be needed and most effective when:

1. the economy needs a short-run boost, even at the expense of the long run.

2. the problem is a deficiency in aggregate demand rather than a real shock.

3. many resources are unemployed and the fiscal stimulus, either tax cuts or expenditures, can be targeted to those unemployed resources.

4. government spending is efficient and productive.

Takeaway

Fiscal policy is most effective in times of emergency, when there are unemployed resources due to a fall in aggregate demand, and when the economy needs an immediate short-term boost. In contrast, fiscal policy is not usually a good means of boosting long-term growth.

The great debate over fiscal policy is about the balance of two opposing forces: crowding out versus the multiplier effect—or, how big is the multiplier? A multiplier of zero means that fiscal policy is ineffective. A multiplier of 2 means that every dollar spent by government increases GDP by two dollars. Different policies such as government purchases of goods and services, tax cuts, and transfer payments can have different multipliers. Fiscal policy is most effective when it is concentrated on policies with big multipliers. It is not always possible, however, to spend enough at the right time on the right policies to make fiscal policy very effective.

Ideal fiscal policy would be counter-cyclical—spending more in bad times and spending less in good times to offset declines and increases in private spending. Governments, however, often prefer to spend more in bad times and in good times! Automatic stabilizers such as unemployment insurance are counter-cyclical and can help to stabilize aggregate demand.

Some countries, especially some of the world's poorer countries, take fiscal policy too far. They accumulate very large levels of debt. The finances, currencies, and sometimes even the governments of those countries become unstable. Even if good fiscal policy doesn't always do a lot of good, bad fiscal policy can do a great deal of harm.

CHAPTER REVIEW

interactive activity **Go online to practice with more examples of these types of problems, including live links to videos, data sources, and feedback.**

 Problems in green relate to MRU videos. See the MRU table at the end of the exercises.

KEY CONCEPTS

fiscal policy, p. 789

crowding out, p. 790

multiplier effect, p. 790

Ricardian equivalence, p. 793

automatic stabilizers, p. 797

counter-cyclical fiscal policy, p. 800

FACTS AND TOOLS

1. Assume that the economy is growing steadily and hasn't had a recent recession. A new administration increases spending on the military by $200 billion, a significant amount.

   a. What is your estimate of the multiplier in this situation and what do you predict will be the impact on GDP?

   b. How would your answer change if the economy were in recession?

2. What shifts AD to the left: a rise in taxes or a cut in taxes? Does this push $\vec{v}$ up or push it down?

3. Let's see what the "three difficulties with using fiscal policy" look like in real life. Categorize each of the following three stories as either (1) crowding out, (2) magnitude, or (3) a matter of timing.

   a. During a recession, the State of New York hires 1,000 new trash collectors. The state legislature in Albany takes six months to pass a law to hire the new trash collectors, and because of government rules and paperwork, the government actually hires the workers 18 months after the recession has begun.

   b. During a recession, the State of New York hires 1,000 new trash collectors. Five hundred of the new trash collectors, however, were just people who quit their jobs as restaurant employees in order to take the better paying trash collector jobs.

   c. During a recession, the State of New York hires 1,000 new trash collectors. However, during the course of the recession, 300,000 additional people in New York lose their jobs.

4. When people "buy government bonds," are they borrowing money or saving money?

5. Imagine you live in the land of Ricardia, where every citizen is a Ricardian and thus "Ricardian equivalence" is 100% true. Government spending never changes in Ricardia: It's a fixed amount every year. Thus, when the Ricardian government cuts taxes, it has to pay for the government spending by borrowing more money and raising future taxes to repay the debt.

   a. When Ricardian income taxes are cut, what will Ricardian citizens do with the extra money in their paycheck: Will they spend all of it, save all of it, or spend some and save the rest?

   b. Suppose that instead of a tax cut, the Ricardian government just sends citizens "rebate" checks. What will Ricardian citizens do with the extra money from these rebate checks: Will they spend all of it, save all of it, or spend some and save the rest?

6. It's often very difficult to get the timing of fiscal policy right. In this chapter, we listed five relevant lags.

   a. If each of the lags lasts three months, is the total lag longer or shorter than the typical recession since World War II? For data on the length of recessions, go to: http://www.nber.org/cycles.html. Look at the bottom of the column titled "Contraction."

   b. Of the five lags, the last one only involves watching how things turned out. If there are only four important lags, and they last three months each, will the average recession last longer than the average fiscal policy lag?

7. You're flipping through the newspaper, reading about shocks that have hit the U.S. economy and reading what Congress is planning to do about the shocks. (Remember that "shocks" can be either good or bad.) Is Congress even getting the direction of its response right? And if it is getting the basic direction correct, is it fighting against a long-run aggregate supply shock, where a fiscal response may not be very effective? While these policy choices will each have effects on long-run growth and on income distribution, in this chapter you should focus only on the effect on aggregate demand. In each of the following cases, state whether the action taken by Congress is likely to be in the wrong direction, the correction direction for an AD shock, or the correction direction for a long-run aggregate supply shock, but expect a big change in inflation.

   a. Many banks have failed, and the money supply has fallen. In response, Congress decides to raise income taxes to pay down the federal debt. (*Historical note:* This policy response was similar to FDR's campaign platform when he ran for president in 1932.)

   b. Many banks have failed, and the money supply has fallen. In response, Congress decides to cut back on government purchases to save money.

   c. A wave of investor euphoria ("irrational exuberance") about the Internet has increased spending growth. Congress raises income taxes on the richest Americans in response.

   d. Oil prices double over the course of a year, from $3 per gallon to $6 per gallon. In response, Congress sends $300 checks to every American family so that people can better afford to pay for gas.

e. Oil prices double over the course of a year, from $3 per gallon to $6 per gallon. In response, Congress raises taxes on companies that refine and deliver petroleum products.

f. The Federal Reserve has followed a slow-money-growth policy, despite the wishes of Congress. In response, Congress cuts taxes and increases government purchases.

8. Which of the following is an "automatic stabilizer" in the U.S. economy? There may be more than one:

a. Consumers usually spend some of their savings and eat food from the pantry during recessions.

b. Business owners usually purchase more capital equipment whenever profits fall.

c. Governments automatically transfer cash to the unemployed when the economy is weak.

d. When Americans have less demand for U.S. manufactured products, foreigners might pick up some of the slack, buying these unsold U.S.-made goods.

9. Why was the Great Depression an especially appropriate time to use fiscal policy rather than just monetary policy alone?

10. If the U.S.-debt-to-GDP ratio were 100% and if the interest rate on the debt were 5% (not far from the truth at present), then what fraction of U.S. GDP would go toward paying interest on the debt? (*Note:* After World War II, U.S. debt was greater than 100% of GDP.)

11. Which kind of aggregate demand shift has fewer lags: changes in monetary policy or changes in fiscal policy?

THINKING AND PROBLEM SOLVING

12. As we showed in Table 37.1, the Congressional Budget Office estimated some fiscal multipliers around the 2009 recession. Let's assume that the average estimated multiplier is 1.5. Now assume that the economy enters into a recession today. Will fiscal policy necessarily be effective?

13. a. In the chapter, we wrote that Tyler does not save and plan according to the theory of Ricardian equivalence but Alex is more of a "Ricardian." In light of this, who probably cuts back their spending the most when taxes temporarily rise: someone like Tyler who is not "Ricardian" or someone like Alex who is?

b. If the U.S. government wants to use fiscal policy to shift AD around easily, which one would the U.S. government prefer to make more copies of: Tyler or Alex?

14. Using the following figure, suppose that a change in fiscal policy shifts AD from AD(1) to AD(2). Which response would be most likely to cause that shift? Choose one of a, b, c, or d.

a. A rise in taxes OR a rise in government spending

b. A rise in taxes OR a fall in government spending

c. A fall in taxes OR a rise in government spending

d. A fall in taxes OR a fall in government spending

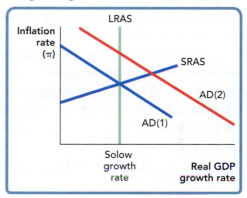

15. Consider the following figure. Suppose that there's a rise in $\vec{v}$ due to business optimism—what Keynes called the "animal spirits" of investors. This pushes us to AD(2). If the government's goal is to keep output close to the long-run aggregate supply growth rate, and if fiscal policy is the tool that the government wants to use, what should it do? Choose one of a, b, c, or d.

a. A rise in taxes OR a rise in government spending

b. A rise in taxes OR a fall in government spending

c. A fall in taxes OR a rise in government spending

d. A fall in taxes OR a fall in government spending

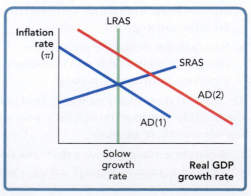

16. Consider the following imaginary newspaper quote, the type that you often read when Congress passes a tax rebate during a recession:

    "Many Americans report that they will put the tax rebate straight into their savings accounts or use it to pay off credit cards that they maxed out during the recent economic boom."

    If Congress is trying to shift AD to the right, are these kinds of quotes good news or bad news from Congress's point of view?

17. Which of the following government policies are "automatic stabilizers" for the economy?

    Unemployment insurance

    Temporary tax cuts that Congress passes when bad economic news hits

    Temporary spending increases that Congress passes when bad economic news hits

18. **a.** Which policy is likely to shift aggregate demand more? In which direction will it shift?

    A tax increase that occurs in the same year as a spending increase

    A tax increase that occurs without a spending increase

    b. Why is this so?

19. Ricardian equivalence is the idea that people might just use the extra money from their tax cuts to buy the very government bonds that pay for the tax cut. Let's think about the opposite situation: If Ricardian equivalence is true, and the government raises taxes (holding spending constant), how does the average person's behavior change? In other words, how does he or she react to a tax increase?

20. Again, think about the extreme case of crowding out known as "Ricardian equivalence." In real life, few citizens buy or sell government bonds directly; instead, normal people put their money in a bank (or invest it in a mutual fund), and then their bank (or mutual fund) uses that money to buy government bonds.

    a. So does a tax cut mean banks will get more deposits, fewer deposits, or can't you tell with the information given?

    b. How will the average bank's behavior change as a result of this tax cut, taking your response to part a into account?

21. We discussed three situations where fiscal policy is most likely to matter (though fiscal policy is best when *all* three are true):

    1. When the economy needs a short-run boost

    2. When the problem is low AD, not low LRAS

    3. When many machines and workers are unemployed

    Let's fit each of the following news stories into one (or more) of the above categories.

    a. World War II ends, and millions of U.S. soldiers return home. (*Note:* As a matter of history, returning World War II soldiers were overwhelmingly employed by the private sector.)

    b. Consumption spending declines dramatically as people fear a recession.

    c. Foreigners decide they are unwilling to buy U.S.-made airplanes because of rumors they read on the Internet.

22. Fiscal policy cannot cure all ills. Sometimes:

    1. The economy needs a long-run boost.

    2. The problem isn't low AD, but low LRAS growth.

    3. Almost all machines and workers are employed; they're just not very productive.

    Sort the following cases into either "fiscal solution possible" or "productivity problem":

    a. American wages have grown slowly for many years.

    b. Peasants in the Middle Ages are using primitive tools to produce food.

    c. Peasants in the Middle Ages suffer from a drought that hurts the season's crops.

    d. American workers get laid off by the hundreds of thousands because of a rapid collapse in investment purchases.

    e. Schools are doing a bad job teaching students, so students become ineffective employees.

    f. High taxes on investment discourage people from saving and building up the capital stock for future workers to use.

    g. High taxes on investment discourage businesses from purchasing investment goods.

CHALLENGES

23. When we discussed unemployment in our Unemployment and Labor Force Participation chapter, we noted that people will search a long time to find a good job. So it might only take you two weeks to find a minimum wage job, but it might take you six months to find a job paying five times the minimum wage.

Let's investigate how this simple fact might cause expansionary fiscal policy to *increase* the unemployment rate, at least temporarily.

In the United States, federal contracts to build roads, bridges, or buildings must pay higher-than-average wages. The law requiring this is known as the Davis-Bacon Act, or the "prevailing wage law."

a. If the unemployment rate is 6% before a rise in government purchases, and if a rise in government purchases induces the typical unemployed person to search 10% longer in the hopes of finding a high-paying government job, what will the unemployment rate be after the rise in government purchases? Only consider the impact of this waiting-for-a-good-job effect.

b. If the government wanted to get the good aggregate-demand-stimulating effects of fiscal policy, but wanted to eliminate this extra waiting-for-a-good-job unemployment, how could it change current law to do so?

24. Nobel Laureate Amartya Sen has pointed out that one way to prevent starvation during droughts in the poorest countries is to just pay peasants to build roads, sewer lines, and other public goods during these droughts. In the poorest countries, these peasants have no savings accounts, and almost no way to borrow money. In rich countries by contrast, most people have savings accounts and credit cards.

a. Is the poor-country "multiplier" probably bigger or smaller than the rich-country multiplier, based on these facts?

b. All countries get hit by shocks, but not all countries have the same automatic stabilizers. Based on these facts, which countries probably have smoother GDP growth: poor countries or rich countries? (*Note:* The answer that is true in theory is also true in practice, a point emphasized in a 1995 paper in the *American Economic Review* by Garey and Valerie Ramey, "Cross-Country Evidence on the Link between Volatility and Growth.")

25. If the U.S. government wanted to, it could just say that everyone who is unemployed is "employed in the job search" and receiving a paycheck for this "work," and the government could claim that these government employees are producing "job search services." Recall that in the official definition of GDP, government purchases (*G*), do not include *transfer*

payments like unemployment checks and Social Security.

a. Would this change in the definition of GDP increase GDP? Would it improve well-being?

b. If the government permanently defined unemployed people as "employed in job search," then over the course of a few decades as the economy fluctuated, would GDP look more volatile or less volatile than it does under the regular definition? (*Hint:* You might find it easier to answer if you consider GDP from the "factor income" perspective.)

26. We usually think about crowding out as a decrease in private consumption or investment in response to an increase in government purchases. But the idea works in reverse as well, an idea we might call "crowding in." Consider the following economy.

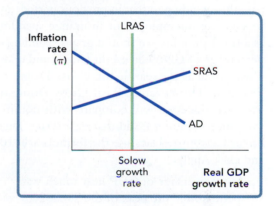

a. Starting from this initial position, the economy is hit by one shock: a large *decrease* in government purchases, perhaps caused by the end of a war. Holding the growth of *C*, *I*, and *NX* constant for a moment, illustrate this shock, labeling the change "Fall in growth of *G*."

b. Now consider a possible side effect of the fall in the growth of *G*: the reversal of crowding out or crowding in. If there is 100% crowding in, what happens to the AD shift you described in part a?

c. If there were 100% crowding out/in and no multiplier effect, what can we say about the effect of a change in the growth of *G* on aggregate demand?

d. Consider all of the laid-off government workers in this question: If there were 100% crowding out/in and no multiplier effect, where do these laid-off workers end up?

Ask FRED

27. In this question we will look at one of the automatic stabilizers, unemployment insurance. Using the FRED economic database (https://fred.stlouisfed.org/) search for unemployment insurance. You should find a series like "Personal current transfer receipts: Government social benefits to persons: Unemployment insurance". Graph the annual series.

a. How much did the government spend on unemployment insurance at the peak of spending around the 2008–2009 recession?

b. Approximately how much was spent on unemployment insurance in 2007, before the recession began? Compare your answer from part a to your answer from part b.

The graph shows unemployment insurance spending in billions of dollars. In order to compare this spending to that in previous periods and to evaluate unemployment insurance spending as a fiscal stimulus, we should graph spending as percentage of GDP. Click Edit Graph, and under Customize Data search for Gross Domestic Product. (Do *not* click Real Gross Domestic Product, since we will compare with nominal insurance spending.) Add that data series. Then, under Customize Data, use the formula a/b★100 and click Apply.

c. As a percentage of GDP how much was spent around the peak of the 2008–2009 recession?

d. In the historical series, when was the most spent on unemployment, insurance as a percentage of GDP?

28. In February of 2009, Congress passed the American Recovery and Reinvestment Act (ARRA). When this stimulus package was signed into law, White House officials projected that it would create, or at least save, 3.5 million jobs, prevent the unemployment rate from rising above 8%, and have a multiplier effect on GDP of 1.57 after 10 quarters. Prior to the bill's signing, unemployment was at a 25-year high of 7.8%. (It had also reached 7.8% during one month in 1992.) In August of 2011, the Congressional Budget Office (CBO) estimated where the economy was at the end of June that year relative to where it would have been in the absence of the stimulus spending. Some of its findings are given in the table on the next page. The low and high estimates under Real GDP define the range of how much greater in percentage terms real GDP was because of the stimulus spending than it would have been without it. The CBO also revised its estimate of the stimulus cost at $825 billion instead of the $787 billion projected at the time of the bill's signing and estimated that about half the impact occurred during 2010 with about 85% of it realized by the end of June 2011.

The 85% of the $825 billion stimulus package spent by the end of the second quarter in 2011, amounting to $701.3 billion, was funded through deficit financing and added to the national debt. For comparison to the real GDP figures, $701.3 billion when adjusted for inflation becomes $677.6 billion.

a. For each year, use the real GDP figures in the table on the next page and the low and high percentage estimates of the effect of the stimulus to calculate low and high estimates for the dollar effect of the stimulus.

b. Determine the midpoint of that range for each year and calculate a rough estimate of the total amount of real GDP generated by the stimulus spending for the ten quarters given in the table.

c. Compare the amount you calculated in part b to the inflation-adjusted stimulus expenditures of $677.6 billion for the same period and determine if those expenditures appear to have had a multiplier effect, no effect, or generated some crowding out.

d. How do your findings vary if you use the lower or the upper ends of the range of increased real GDP estimated by the CBO? If multipliers were this simple to generate, which they are not, what do these estimates suggest their sizes might be?

e. Use the chapter material describing the limits to fiscal policy to explain why the size of the impact you found in part c varied from the 1.57 multiplier effect forecasted by the White House at the time of the ARRA legislation.

f. Does the American Recovery and Reinvestment Act of 2009 qualify as one of the times when fiscal policy was a good idea? Defend your answer using economic support from the chapter.

CBO Estimates Aug. 2011	Real GDP Change Attributable to the ARRA (Relative to where the economy would be without the ARRA)		Actual Values	
	Low Estimate (% change)	High Estimate (% change)	Real GDP (trillions of chained 2005 $)	Unemployment (%)
2009	0.9	1.9	12.71	9.3
2010	1.5	4.2	13.09	9.6
2011(1st and 2nd Qtr)	0.95	2.85	13.25	9.0

Data from: CBO, Estimated Impact of the American Recovery and Reinvestment Act on Employment and Economic Output from April 2011 Through June 2011, Aug. 2011. Unemployment and GDP data: FRED database of the St. Louis Federal Reserve Bank.

WORK IT OUT

For interactive, step-by-step help in solving this problem, go online.

According to recent estimates by Susan Woodward and Robert Hall, an extra dollar of government purchases raises GDP by one dollar—so there is little evidence for a "multiplier effect" in the short run, but also little evidence for "crowding out" in the short run. (Perhaps both effects are at work, but they just happen to balance out in practice.) Let's use these estimates as a rule of thumb to solve the following economic puzzles:

a. U.S. GDP is about $18 trillion. In a typical recession, GDP is about 2% below the Solow growth rate as given by the LRAS curve. If Congress wants to return growth to the Solow growth rate and thus move the economy back onto the LRAS curve by increasing government purchases, how big a rise in government purchases should it enact? Give your answer in dollars.

b. Suppose Canadian GDP is about $1.2 trillion (U.S. dollars). If Canadian GDP is 3% above its Solow growth rate, and the Canadian Parliament wants to change government purchases to return to the Solow growth rate, what change in government purchases should it enact, measured in U.S. dollars?

c. How do your answers to parts a and b change if there's stronger crowding out, and the multiplier falls to 0.5? (In other words, a rise in G of $1 raises GDP by only $0.50.) Answer in U.S. dollars.

d. How do your answers to parts a and b change if there's a bigger multiplier effect on consumer spending, and the multiplier rises to 2? (In other words, a rise in G of $1 raises GDP by $2.) Answer in U.S. dollars.

interactive activity

MARGINAL REVOLUTION UNIVERSITY VIDEOS

Introduction to Fiscal Policy

mruniversity.com/fiscal

Problems: **1, 9**

Fiscal Policy and the Best Case Scenario

mruniversity.com/fiscal-best

Problems: **1, 13**

The Limits to Fiscal Policy

mruniversity.com/fiscal-limits

Problems: **3, 12**

The Dangers of Fiscal Policy

mruniversity.com/fiscal-avoid

Problems: **12**

Fiscal Policy and Crowding Out

mruniversity.com/fiscal-crowding-out

Problems: **20, 26, 28**

Econ Duel: Does Fiscal Policy Work?

mruniversity.com/duel-fiscal

Problems: **12, 22**

38

International Finance

"Why are we spending our dollars in China and Japan rather than in Ohio and Michigan?"

"Why does America have such a large trade deficit?"

"We need to keep our money at home, not send it abroad!"

So run some common questions and complaints about globalization and international finance. The more connected the world economy becomes, the more these kinds of questions arise and increase in importance.

In Chapter 2, we discussed how specialization and trade let us take advantage of the division of knowledge and comparative advantage and thus raise the standard of living. Gains from trade occur when individuals within a nation trade and people in different countries trade.

It's important to keep these deep principles in mind when we discuss trade, but we also want to understand more about the kind of international financial events discussed on a daily basis on the financial blogs and in the newspapers. What does it mean when we are told that the dollar is "strong" or "weak"? What is a trade deficit and is it worse than a trade surplus? And why do zombies protest against the World Bank and the International Monetary Fund? What are these strange institutions?

As we will see, some knowledge of international finance is extremely practical. If you wish to do international business, make international investments, or understand how an exchange rate crisis can wreck an economy, you need to know some basic truths about international finance. Understanding international finance will also help you to pick the best place to take a good vacation. And you will even learn why many James Bond movies have a scene set in Switzerland.

On the surface, international finance is one of the most intimidating fields of economics because the presence of different currencies can be confusing. So let's begin with some of the key principles behind this chapter:

1. Gains from trade occur when people trade across different countries with different currencies, just as gains from trade occur within a single nation with a single currency.

2. The rate of savings is a key variable in understanding international trade and finance.

Protesters claim that IMF policies create walking dead.

TED ALJIBE/GETTY IMAGES

811

3. Market equilibrium means that, at the margin, the gains from holding or spending one currency are equal to the gains from holding or spending some other currency. That sounds simple but we'll see that this principle will be a building block for understanding the market value of one currency relative to another.

The U.S. Trade Deficit and Your Trade Deficit

Let's start by looking at the trade deficit in more detail. In 2016, Americans exported (sold) to China $115.8 billion worth of goods, and they imported (bought) from China $462.8 billion in goods. The difference between what Americans exported to China and what they imported from China, −$347.0 billion, is called the U.S. **trade deficit** with China.

The U.S. trade deficit with China is controversial. In response to the trade deficit, some politicians have called for a tariff on all imports of Chinese goods. To understand this debate, it will be useful to begin with some trade deficits closer to home, namely your trade deficit with your local supermarket.

Do you shop at Giant, Safeway, or the Piggly Wiggly? If you do, you run a trade deficit with those stores. That is, you buy more goods from them than they buy from you (unless, of course, you work at one of these stores or sell them goods from your farm). The authors of this book also run a trade deficit with supermarkets. In fact, we have been running a trade deficit with Whole Foods for many years. Is our Whole Foods deficit a problem?

Our deficit with Whole Foods isn't a problem because it's balanced with a **trade surplus** with someone else. Who? You, the students, whether we teach you or whether you have bought our book. You buy more goods from us than we buy from you. We export education to you, but we do not import your goods and services. In short, we run a trade deficit with Whole Foods but a trade surplus with our students. In fact, it is only because we run a trade surplus with you that we can run a trade deficit with Whole Foods. Thanks!

The lesson is simple. Trade deficits and surpluses are to be found everywhere.

Taken alone, the fact that the United States has a trade deficit with one country is not special cause for worry. Trade across countries is very much like trade across individuals. Not every person or every country can run a trade surplus all the time. Suddenly, a trade deficit does not seem so troublesome, even though the word "deficit" makes it sound like a problem or an economic shortcoming.

What if the United States runs a trade deficit not just with China or Japan or Mexico but with the world as a whole, as indeed it does? Is that a bad thing?

This will require some deeper investigation. So far we have looked at only the flow of goods from the grocery store to you or from China to the United States, but for every flow of goods there is a corresponding and opposite flow of money or financial claims. When China sells us goods, we pay for those goods in dollars. At the present time, China and other countries are not using all of those dollars to buy U.S. goods and thus the United States is running a trade deficit on net. What is China doing with the dollars and is this cause for concern? We need some more tools and a few more terms to answer these questions.

A **trade deficit** occurs when the value of a country's imports exceeds the value of its exports.

A **trade surplus** occurs when the value of a country's exports exceeds the value of its imports.

The Balance of Payments

Let's start with the international balance of payments. The **balance of payments** is a yearly summary of all the economic transactions between residents of one country and residents of the rest of the world. The balance of payments records sales of goods and services and also transfers of financial claims including stocks, bonds, loans, and ownership rights. We can also speak of the balance of payments with a specific country such as the balance of payments with China.

That sounds a little forbidding, but let's go back to your trade deficit with the local supermarket. You spend money at the supermarket but earn money through your job. In the simplest case, when there is no borrowing or lending, a person's trade deficits must be matched with other trade surpluses. In other words, if you want to spend, you must earn so your balance of payments does, in fact, balance (nets out to zero).

Now let's make this more realistic by adding borrowing and lending. Suppose you take out a student loan to pay for books, supplies, and housing. You have to pay back the loan someday, but in the meantime you are running a trade deficit. You are spending but you are not earning or "exporting" equivalent goods and services. In this case, your trade deficit is balanced with a loan, which we call a capital inflow or **capital surplus**. When we add up your trade deficit and the capital surplus, the balance of payments once again nets out to zero.

In the long run, unless you default on the loan, your trade deficit must disappear, and indeed it must turn into a trade surplus. That is, someday you will get a job and use your surplus earnings to pay back the bank loan. Paying back the loan limits your future consumption, that is, your ability to buy goods and services, but all things considered, your earlier borrowing was still a good idea, at least if you invested the money well.

We have seen that you can finance a trade deficit with a job or a loan. How else could you finance a trade deficit? If you had assets from previous transactions, you could sell the assets and spend the proceeds. If you owned some land, for example, you could sell the land, creating a capital surplus, which would offset your current deficit. Similarly, if you had reserves of cash from previous periods, you could draw on your reserves to finance a deficit. The more assets or cash that you had from previous transactions, the longer you could live the partying lifestyle by spending more than you were earning in the current period. Notice that when we add up the trade deficit, the capital inflow, and the changes in reserves, the balance of payments still balances.

We can write down these relationships as an identity, an equality that is always true:

$$\text{Earning} - \text{Spending} = \text{Changes in debt} + \text{Changes in ownership}$$
$$\text{of assets} + \text{Changes in your cash reserves}$$

If earnings are less than spending, then you are running a trade deficit. A trade deficit must be balanced by increases in debt (written as a negative number), sales of assets, or reductions in cash reserves. The reverse holds as well: If earnings are greater than spending, then a trade surplus must be balanced by reductions in debt, purchases of assets, or increases in cash reserves.

If you can understand that equation—and indeed you live it every day—you can understand the basic categories of international finance. The terms simply become a little more complicated once we move to the bigger level of a nation.

The **balance of payments** is a yearly summary of all the economic transactions between residents of one country and residents of the rest of the world.

A country runs a **capital surplus** when the inflow of foreign capital is greater than the outflow of domestic capital.

The international balance of payments presents a comparable expression:

Current account $=(-)$Capital account $+$ Change in official reserves

Now let's go through each term in detail.

The Current Account

The **current account** is the sum of the balance of trade, net income on capital held abroad, and net transfer payments.

The **current account** is the sum of three items:

1. The balance of trade (exports minus imports of goods and services)
2. Net income on capital held abroad, including interest and dividends
3. Net transfer payments, such as foreign aid

What unites the items in the current account is that they all measure transactions that are fully completed or closed out in a *current* period; they do not require any further transfer of funds in the future. To relate these categories back to the example of a single individual, category (1) is like earnings minus spending; category (2) is like earning money on a savings bond that your grandmother gave you when you were 10 years old ("interest income from abroad"); and category (3) is like getting money from relatives ("foreign aid").

Now let's apply these concepts to the United States. The U.S. current account will be higher and positive to the extent that, for instance, (1) America exports a lot of tractors, (2) American-owned beer factories in Canada pay high dividends to Americans, and (3) America receives foreign aid (this latter example is not usually the case). To consider the alternative, the current account balance will be lower and negative to the extent that, for instance, (1) America buys imported grapes from Chile, (2) German investments in Florida pay high dividends to Germans, and (3) America sends foreign aid to Afghanistan.

Categories 2 and 3 in a country's current account tend to be stable over time. We can simplify by speaking as if the current account was just the balance of trade, exports minus imports. But keep in the back of your mind that terms 2 and 3 can be important for some countries. Foreign aid, for example, is important for smaller and poorer nations, where it can account for 10% or more of GDP. But when it comes to the United States, the balance of trade and the capital account are where we find most of the action.

The Capital Account, Sometimes Called the Financial Account

The **capital account** measures changes in foreign ownership of domestic assets including financial assets likes stocks and bonds as well as physical assets.

The **capital account** measures changes in foreign ownership of domestic assets including financial assets likes stocks and bonds as well as physical assets. When the Chinese government buys American government bonds or when Japanese investors buy assets like Rockefeller Center in Manhattan, the capital account of the United States increases. More generally, when there is more investment going into a country than out, that country is running a capital account surplus. When more investment is leaving a country than coming in that is called a capital account deficit; an example is when Zimbabwe residents send their money abroad rather than investing under their corrupt dictatorship. Less dramatically, many banks in New Zealand have been bought by Australian companies and that represents a shift of capital from Australia to New Zealand.

Notice how the capital account differs from "net income held on foreign assets abroad," component 2 of the current account. When a Belgian buys a U.S. stock, the U.S. *capital account* increases (money flows into the United States). Three months later, when that same Belgian receives a dividend from the company, the U.S. *current account* decreases as "net income held on foreign assets abroad" is suddenly higher for Belgium. The capital account measures transactions, like buying a stock, that may result in future financial flows. The current account measures current financial flows.

The investments in the capital account are divided into the following categories:

Foreign direct investment (FDI)—When foreigners construct new business plants or set up other specific and tangible operations in the United States.

Portfolio investment—When foreigners buy U.S. stocks, bonds, and other asset claims. Unlike FDI, portfolio investment switches the ownership of already existing investments and does not immediately create new investment on net.

Other investment—This usually consists of movements of bank deposits. For instance, a wealthy French citizen might shift his or her bank account from Paris to New York.

The Official Reserves Account

The third component of the international balance of payments, the official reserves account, measures reserves or currency held by the government. This can include foreign currencies, gold reserves, and also International Monetary Fund (IMF) claims known as special drawing rights (SDRs), but for simplicity we will focus on foreign currencies. (We'll discuss the IMF in greater detail later in this chapter.) Sometimes governments stockpile U.S. dollars or other currencies such as the euro. Right now the Chinese government and central bank have stockpiled more than $1 trillion worth of U.S. dollars and dollar-denominated assets.

How the Pieces Fit Together

To understand the balance of payments in its totality, consider more concretely how this accounting identity stays in balance. Say that Walmart decides to buy more toys from China. Spending money on the toys increases the current account deficit of the United States. Toy makers in China receive the money and must do something with it. If they take the money and use it to buy American tractors, the current account is back in balance. If they take the money and invest it back in the United States, say, by buying stocks, the American capital account surplus goes up by an equivalent amount. If they take the money and send it to a bank in New York, the capital account surplus goes up (this time in the "other investment" category). If they keep the money in a Chinese bank, there has been a change in reserves. No matter what they do with the money, the balance of payments will balance.

Two Sides, One Coin

Usually, the major changes in the balance of payments come through the current account and the capital account, rather than through changes in official reserves. So, a country that is running a current account deficit, such as the

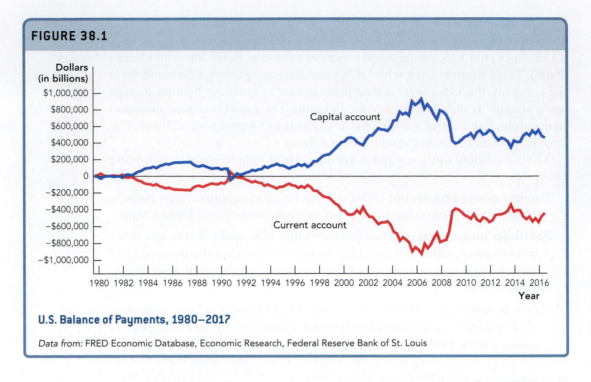

FIGURE 38.1

Dollars (in billions)

Capital account

Current account

1980 1982 1984 1986 1988 1990 1992 1994 1996 1998 2000 2002 2004 2006 2008 2010 2012 2014 2016

Year

U.S. Balance of Payments, 1980–2017

Data from: FRED Economic Database, Economic Research, Federal Reserve Bank of St. Louis

United States, balances its payments by running a capital account surplus. Similarly, a country, such as China, that is running a current account surplus, is usually also running a capital account deficit.

Figure 38.1 shows the U.S. balance of payments from 1980 to 2017. Notice that the two accounts are close to mirror images—when the current account is in deficit (negative), the capital account is in surplus (positive), and vice versa. (Differences are in fact almost entirely due to statistical discrepancies and the difficulty of identifying all financial transactions.)

The current account and capital account are two sides of the same coin. The media and politicians typically focus on the trade deficit, but it's equally correct to look at the other side of the coin, the capital account surplus.

Now that we know that a trade deficit is typically balanced by a capital account surplus, let's go back to our opening question and ask whether our trade deficit is a problem. First, note that this is the same thing as asking whether our capital account surplus is a problem. A surplus sounds better than a deficit so it is not surprising that many economists who think that trade deficits are not a problem focus on the flip side, the capital account surplus. We call the most optimistic view of those who focus on the capital account the "Great Place to Invest" view. We call the less optimistic view the "Foolishly Saving Too Little" view. Let's start with optimism.

"The United States Is a Great Place to Invest" In this view, the trade deficit is driven by the fact that foreigners want to invest in the United States, the world's wealthiest country and largest single, unified market. Instead of using dollars to buy U.S. cars, foreigners are using dollars to buy bonds and stocks and this inflow of investment is great for the United States. A capital account surplus will necessitate a current account deficit, but this is no problem. The investments in America will create more wealth and allow the United States to pay off future obligations without major problems. From this perspective, the fact that America is borrowing or selling assets is like borrowing money or selling assets to pay for medical school—it isn't a problem because the investment will pay off with a high-wage job. Advocates of this view sometimes speak of the rest of the world as having a "savings glut," namely a lot of savings but no good place to put them, other than in the United States, that is.

"Americans Are Foolishly Saving Too Little"

Not all economists who focus on the capital account are optimists, however. It's also possible to look at the inflow of capital and ask why are American savings so low? In this view, the reason that capital is flowing into the United States is that Americans are consuming too much and not saving enough. Proponents of this view often tie the trade deficit with the government's budget deficit. The U.S. government is spending more than it is taxing and the difference is being made up by borrowing from foreigners, creating a capital account surplus. In this view, a day of reckoning will come. Foreign investments in America represent a claim on American assets and someday the U.S. government will have to pay off those investment claims. This will lower American living standards and bring higher taxes, as well as the pain of significant economic adjustments. American borrowing from this perspective is like borrowing to buy a closet full of Manolo Blahnik shoes—fun while it lasts but not necessarily wise.

The Josefa can be yours for $1,425 a pair, but what happens when the bill comes due?

The Bottom Line on the Trade Deficit

The bottom line is this: Most economists think that the trade deficit per se is not a problem. As discussed in Chapter 2, trade is beneficial for the United States, and as previously shown, there is nothing peculiar about running a trade deficit—we all run trade deficits in some areas (e.g., with Whole Foods) and for some periods of time (e.g., when we finance education with a student loan). Countries, in this respect, are no different than individuals.

The trade deficit, however, might indicate, or *signal*, a problem of low savings. If the United States has a problem with low savings, however, then it's better to address the savings problem directly—in which case, the balance of trade will take care of itself—rather than blaming the Chinese or obsessing over the balance of trade numbers. Quotas, tariffs, and trade wars, for example, are unlikely to solve a savings problem. Indeed, if the United States is saving too little, then Americans are at least fortunate that they can borrow in international markets so that investment remains high even when U.S. savings rates are low.

To the extent that Americans are saving too little, there is a stronger case for reducing the government's budget deficit by a combination of tax hikes and spending cuts. In the "Foolishly Saving Too Little" view, the United States is spending too much and the government could do its share to limit this problem by saving more, which means moving closer to a balanced budget or perhaps even running a surplus. We discussed the government budget deficit at greater length in our earlier chapter on The Federal Budget: Taxes and Spending.

Let us now turn to exchange rates. Working with the concepts in the balance of payments identity, we can see how supplies and demands will determine the relative values of different currencies.

CHECK YOURSELF

- An inhabitant of Lincoln, Nebraska, buys a German sports car for $30,000. What changes does this make to the U.S. current account?
- A German sports car manufacturer opens a new plant in South Carolina. How does this affect the U.S. current account and capital account?
- Is there a link between a current account deficit and a capital account surplus?

TABLE 38.1 MAJOR CURRENCY EXCHANGE RATES						
Currency	U.S. $	¥en	Euro	Can $	U.K. £	Swiss Franc
1 U.S. $	1	113.2560	0.9154	1.3692	0.7727	0.9989
1 ¥en	0.0088	1	0.0081	0.0121	0.0068	0.0088
1 Euro	1.0925	123.7265	1	1.4957	0.8442	1.0912
1 Can $	0.7304	82.7199	0.6686	1	0.5644	0.7296
1 U.K. £	1.2941	146.5646	1.1846	1.7718	1	1.2927
1 Swiss Franc	1.0011	113.3807	0.9164	1.3707	0.7736	1

What Are Exchange Rates?

The most common means of payment in most (but not all!) foreign countries is a foreign currency and not the U.S. dollar. So, if you travel to a foreign country and you want to buy goods and services in that country, you will usually have to buy foreign currency with U.S. dollars. An **exchange rate** is the price of one currency in terms of another currency.

An **exchange rate** is the price of one currency in another currency.

The *Wall Street Journal* publishes a table like Table 38.1 every day. Table 38.1 gives exchange rates that held on May 8th, 2017.

We can read this table in either the vertical or horizontal direction. Read vertically, it tells us that the price of 1 yen is 0.0088 dollar, the price of 1 euro is 1.0925 dollars, the price of 1 Canadian dollar is 0.7304 U.S. dollars, and so forth. Read horizontally, it tells us that the price of 1 dollar is 113.2560 yen, 0.9154 euro, 1.3692 Canadian dollars, and so forth. Notice that there are always two ways of writing the price of a currency. We can say that 1 yen trades for 0.0088 dollar or that 1 dollar trades for 113.2560 yen—this sometimes causes confusion so always make sure you know which rate is being quoted!

▶▶**SEARCH ENGINE**

For current information on exchange rates, search for the "Yahoo currency converter."

Exchange Rate Determination in the Short Run

Exchange rates, like other market prices, are determined by supply and demand. For each currency, there is a price in every other currency. At any given moment, the exchange rate for a currency is determined by the intersection of the supply and demand for that currency. Figure 38.2, for example, shows the supply and demand for yen and the exchange rate in dollars per yen.

Notice that we have written "Dollars per yen" ("$/yen" in many books) on the vertical axis. This is the price of 1 yen in dollars. If this price goes up—that is, we move up along the vertical axis—it means that the Japanese yen is stronger, namely it takes more dollars to buy 1 yen. If this price goes down, the Japanese yen is weaker.

In this chapter when we are analyzing the supply and demand for yen, we will always put the price of yen, "Dollars per yen," on the vertical axis. But if we analyze the supply and demand for dollars, we will put the *price of dollars* in, say, euros per dollar on the vertical axis.*

Let's now look at some factors that can shift the demand and supply curves.

* Other textbooks or sources, however, might put "yen per dollar" (or "yen/$") instead of "dollars per yen" on the price axis. Either way is correct so long as you remember which one you are working with.

FIGURE 38.2

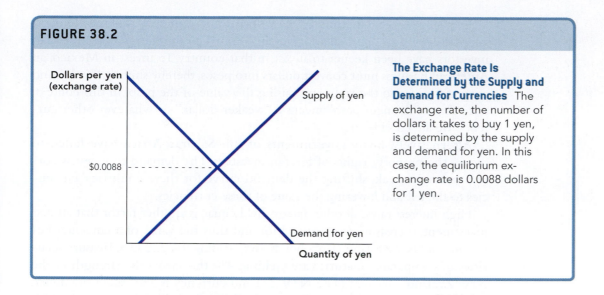

The Exchange Rate Is Determined by the Supply and Demand for Currencies The exchange rate, the number of dollars it takes to buy 1 yen, is determined by the supply and demand for yen. In this case, the equilibrium exchange rate is 0.0088 dollars for 1 yen.

Changes in Demand for a Currency We'll explore three main principles that can influence the demand for a currency. The first principle is simple:

1. *An increase (decrease) in the demand for a country's exports tends to increase (decrease) the value of its currency.*

When Japanese cars become popular around the world, this strengthens the value of the yen. For instance, when U.S. car dealerships order more Toyotas from Japan, they must (ultimately) pay for the cars in yen. An increase in the demand for Japanese goods, therefore, shifts the demand curve for yen up and to the right, illustrated in Figure 38.3.

As usual, an increase in demand increases the price. In this case, the price of one yen increases from 0.0088 dollars to 0.0094 dollars. An increase in the price of a currency is called an **appreciation**.

Increasing exports are not the only way a currency can change in value. We also have a second principle:

2. *The more desirable (undesirable) a country is for foreign investment, the higher (lower) the value of that nation's currency.*

An **appreciation** is an increase in the price of one currency in terms of another currency.

FIGURE 38.3

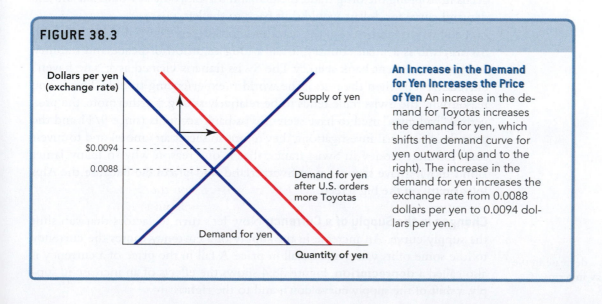

An Increase in the Demand for Yen Increases the Price of Yen An increase in the demand for Toyotas increases the demand for yen, which shifts the demand curve for yen outward (up and to the right). The increase in the demand for yen increases the exchange rate from 0.0088 dollars per yen to 0.0094 dollars per yen.

Ever since the signing of NAFTA (North American Free Trade Agreement) and the evolution of real democracy in Mexico, in the mid-1990s, American investors have been keener to invest in that country. To invest in Mexico, an American business must convert dollars into pesos, thereby shifting the demand curve for pesos to the right and raising the value of the peso. In this context, note that a "stronger peso" means a "weaker dollar," or whatever other currency we are considering.

Alternatively, many governments of sub-Saharan Africa have failed to secure the property rights of foreign investors. The demand to invest is correspondingly weak, shifting the demand curve for these countries' currencies to the left and lowering the value of these currencies.

High interest rates, all other factors held equal, is another factor that attracts investment, increasing the demand for and thus the value of a currency. For instance, if New Zealand "Kiwi bonds" are yielding 9%, and U.S. Treasury securities of comparable maturity are yielding 4%, this favors the strength of the New Zealand currency. (The New Zealand currency is also called the dollar; investors sometimes say "the Kiwi dollar" to avoid confusion with the U.S. dollar.) Investors will be more inclined to hold New Zealand securities, and of course to do so, they must use the New Zealand currency, thereby shifting out demand.

There is yet another cause of stronger demand for a currency:

3. *An increase (decrease) in the demand to hold dollar reserves boosts (reduces) the value of the dollar on international markets.*

Many governments and central banks hold U.S. dollars as a "reserve currency." This means simply that U.S. dollars are a preferred means of saving and enjoying liquidity. Of all the currencies held in the world for these official reserves purposes, U.S. dollars comprise two-thirds of the total.

The U.S. dollar is truly a global currency. If a Brazilian company buys a turbine engine from Turkey, it is probably billed in dollars and probably pays in dollars, not the currency of either Turkey or Brazil. If Colombian drug dealers bury some money in their backyard, it is probably dollars. When these demands for dollars rise, the dollar becomes more valuable. Again, the demand curve for dollars will shift to the right. However, if the Colombian government ever succeeds in stopping the drug trade, the demand for U.S. dollars would fall and the demand curve for dollars would shift back to the left.

The Swiss franc, by the way, is another global reserve currency. Even though Switzerland is a small country, it has a long tradition of peace and stability, and to some extent bank secrecy. The Swiss franc is viewed as a "safe haven" currency, even when the rest of the world is experiencing trouble. This is one reason why the Swiss franc tends to be relatively strong. Furthermore, the proverbial "bad guys" used to have secret Swiss bank accounts (since 9/11 and the growth of financial investigations, they're not so secret any more) and to invest some of their money in Swiss francs; that is one reason why so many James Bond movies have scenes set in Switzerland, and of course because the Alps look pretty on the big screen.

Changes in the Supply of a Currency Now let's turn to factors that can shift the supply curve. An increase in the supply of a currency causes the currency to lose some of its value, that is, fall in price. A fall in the price of a currency is also called a **depreciation**. Figure 38.4 shows the effects of an increase in supply, a shift of the supply curve down and to the right.

A **depreciation** is a decrease in the price of a currency in terms of another currency.

If the Federal Reserve increases the supply of U.S. money, this will reduce the value of the dollar relative to other currencies. The not-so-surprising result, as shown in Figure 38.4, is a lower value for the U.S. dollar on world markets.

You may recall from our chapter on Inflation and the Quantity Theory of Money that the government in Zimbabwe printed trillions of Zimbabwe dollars, causing a large increase in the Zimbabwean inflation rate. At the beginning of 2002, for example, one Zimbabwe dollar was worth about 0.018 of a U.S. dollar or just under 2 cents. With the massive increase in the supply of Zimbabwean dollars, the value of the Zimbabwean dollar fell, so that by 2006 1 Zimbabwe dollar was worth less than 0.00001 of a U.S. dollar or about one-thousandth of a U.S. penny.

A tighter monetary policy, which means a decrease (or slower increase) in the supply of a currency, would shift the supply curve up and to the left and raise the value of the dollar, as we show in Figure 38.5.

Exchange Rate Determination in the Long Run

These changes play themselves out in foreign exchange markets every day. But a full explanation outlines why the supply and demand curves lie where they do in the first place, and not just what happens when they shift.

To see the broader picture, consider that the value of a currency is derived, ultimately, from the value of what it can purchase. Money buys or is a potential claim on goods, services, and investments. Given this fact, equilibrium requires that a dollar spent on goods, services, or investment yields the same expected return regardless of whether that dollar (or the equivalent in local currency) is spent in Chicago, Berlin, or Tokyo.

Before we can explain this point fully and use it to give a more exact account of exchange rates, we must first outline the difference between real and nominal exchange rates.

We are already familiar with the distinction between real and nominal variables from earlier chapters. To recap, in a domestic setting how much a dollar is worth depends on the level of prices for goods and services. We now extend this same comparison to Chicago, Berlin, and Tokyo. How much a dollar is worth in Tokyo depends on two things: the exchange rate between the dollar and the Japanese Yen, and the level of prices for goods and services in Japan, measured in Japanese Yen.

FIGURE 38.4

Euros per dollar (exchange rate)

Supply of dollars

Supply of dollars after Federal Reserve action

0.92

0.81

Demand for dollars

Quantity of dollars

An Increase in the Supply of a Currency Reduces Its Price An increase in the supply of a currency shifts the supply curve down and to the right, which reduces the exchange rate. In the figure, the Federal Reserve increases the supply of dollars and the price of dollars in euros per dollar decreases from 0.92 euros per dollar to 0.81 euros per dollar.

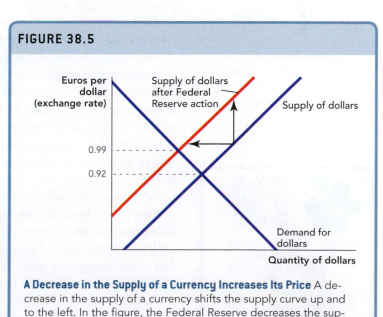

FIGURE 38.5

Euros per dollar (exchange rate)

Supply of dollars after Federal Reserve action

Supply of dollars

0.99

0.92

Demand for dollars

Quantity of dollars

A Decrease in the Supply of a Currency Increases Its Price A decrease in the supply of a currency shifts the supply curve up and to the left. In the figure, the Federal Reserve decreases the supply of dollars and the price of dollars in euros increases from 0.92 euros per dollar to 0.99 euros per dollar.

On May 8th, 2017, 1 dollar would buy 113.2560 yen. At first glance, it might appear that the Japanese yen is a very weak currency. Why should one dollar buy so many yen, if not for the weakness of the yen? But it is wrong to think that the stated rate of exchange reflects the relative weakness of the yen.

The nominal exchange rate is the rate at which you can exchange one currency for another.

If 1 dollar buys 113.2560 yen, we know only the **nominal exchange rate**, which is simply the rate at which you can exchange one currency for another; this is the rate you find quoted in the newspaper by searching using Google.

The real exchange rate is the rate at which you can exchange the goods and services of one country for the goods and services of another.

The **real exchange rate** is the rate at which you can exchange the goods and services of one country for the goods and services of another. To calculate the real exchange rate between the United States and Japan, for example, you need to know the nominal exchange rate plus the price of a similar basket of goods in both the United States and Japan. Notice that an exchange rate of 1 dollar to 110 yen means very different things, depending on whether an order of sushi costs 1 yen, 1 million yen, or about 330 yen (the true price, roughly). If an order of sushi costs 3 dollars in the United States and 330 yen in Japan, then the real exchange rate is about 1:1.

The Purchasing Power Parity Theorem The **purchasing power parity (PPP) theorem** states:

The purchasing power parity (PPP) theorem says that the real purchasing power of a money should be about the same, whether it is spent at home or converted into another currency and spent abroad.

> *The real purchasing power of a money should be about the same, whether it is spent at home or converted into another currency and spent abroad.*

Put in other words, the quantity of goods and services that can be obtained for a given currency should be about the same everywhere, adjusting for the costs of trading those goods and services. The core idea is that spending your dollars in Chicago, or converting them into yen and spending them in Tokyo (which might include buying Japanese goods and shipping them back home for resale), should yield about the same benefits.

More concretely, the PPP theorem makes two predictions. First, Toyotas in Japan should cost about as much as Toyotas in California; the same should be true for other individual goods. Second, the cost of a general bundle of goods and services should be about the same everywhere.

The law of one price says that if trade were free, then identical goods will sell for about the same price throughout the world.

Purchasing power parity is an application of the **law of one price**, the principle that if trade were free, then identical goods will sell for about the same price throughout the world. If Toyotas were cheaper in Tokyo, it would make sense to buy Toyotas in Japan and ship them to the United States. Conversely, if Toyotas are cheaper in the United States, they will be shipped to Japan. Of course, shipping cars from one country to another is not the only way to gain from a difference in prices. Toyota might set up a new auto plant in Tennessee rather than in Tokyo or Osaka, thereby shifting supply into the North American market.

That example is only for cars but the principle can be extended to a broader set of possible transactions. The return to spending a dollar (or yen, or euro, etc.) at home or abroad must be roughly equal, and exchange rates and prices will adjust to equalize those returns. Those adjustments will determine the real exchange rate between any two currencies.

Recall from our chapter on Inflation and the Quantity Theory of Money that in the long run, money is neutral. We used that principle to explain why in the long run the money supply does not influence real GDP, real interest rates, or real prices. Exactly the same principle applies here, except that

Purchasing Power Parity

now we apply the principle to two monies! Since money is neutral in the United States and money is neutral in Japan, neither the supply of dollars nor the supply of yen can change the real exchange rate in the long run. In other words, governments or central banks set nominal exchange rates, but market forces set the real exchange rate. As usual, however, this applies only in the long run. In the short run, as we will discuss further later in the chapter, the government can influence the real exchange rate and this will be important for macroeconomic policy.

The Purchasing Power Parity Theorem Is Only Approximately True Purchasing power parity is limited by the costs of trading, transacting, and shuffling resources. That is one reason why purchasing power parity holds only approximately. At least three constraints on trade prevent prices from being fully equalized across borders:

1. **Transportation costs.** The price of cement might be much higher in Japan than in California, but it still will not be profitable to put cement on a boat and ship it from California to Japan. Cement is very heavy and the shipping would cost a great deal. Purchasing power parity applies only to the extent that goods can be transported easily. Notice also that many personal services—haircuts are the classic example—cannot easily be shipped, although sometimes the labor behind those services can migrate from one country to another. Thus, purchasing power parity is more likely to hold for goods that are cheap to ship, like iPhones, than for cement or haircuts.

2. **Some goods cannot be shipped at all.** Sipping a coffee in Paris is different from going to a Starbucks in suburban Ohio, even if the coffee is the same. The coffee can be transported cheaply but Paris cannot be shipped.

   Similarly, an apartment in London, Canada, costs less than a similar-sized apartment in London, England. Canada cannot easily cut off its land and ship it to England so prices of apartments will not equalize. More generally, the price of land and any good that uses a lot of land in its production will not equalize across countries.

3. **Tariffs and quotas.** To the extent that governments tax or otherwise restrict trade, prices will not equalize across countries. Tariffs or quotas will hinder market exchange and thus the arbitrage of differing prices.

Paris, Las Vegas. There is no parity here.

D. HURST/ALAMY

These constraints show that purchasing power parity will hold approximately—rather than strictly—for a broad basket of goods and services. In other words, living in London, England, will remain more expensive than living in London, Canada.

Deviations from purchasing power parity are often large and long-lasting for services. Goods are easy to transport and so tend to equalize in price more than services, which are difficult to transport. Services, therefore, are cheaper in poorer countries because immigration laws limit the extent to which labor can move from poor countries to rich countries. Wages on the American side of the border are much higher than wages on the Mexican side of the border. The

interactive activity

Why Should You Get a Haircut in a Poorer Country?

result is that a haircut is much cheaper in Mexico than in the United States. One of the thriftier authors of this textbook often gets his hair cut during trips to Mexico for this reason! Servants are also much cheaper in poorer countries. Even a middle-class family in Mexico, India, or Thailand will often employ many servants. The services of a physician, even a high-quality Western-trained physician, are also cheaper in poorer countries; that explains why many people are going to India for plastic surgery or hip replacements—plus you can see the Taj Mahal after your surgery is over. Computers, copper, automobiles, and other goods that can be easily shipped are not systematically cheaper in poorer countries.

How close the real world fits purchasing power parity depends on the nations involved and their ease of trading. As trading costs fall, purchasing power parity is more likely to hold closely. As trading costs rise, the bounds become looser. Purchasing power parity holds more exactly true between the United States and Canada—similar and adjacent countries—than between Japan and Mexico. Note that the concept of "tradeable" is a matter of degree, not an absolute, so how much purchasing power parity holds is a matter of degree as well.

Purchasing power parity also holds more tightly in the long run than in the short run. In the short run, trading costs might hinder entrepreneurs from erasing differences in prices. In the long run, it is more likely that entrepreneurs will find a way to bring prices closer together across international borders.

When it comes to the short run, and within the boundaries set by purchasing power parity, economists still debate the causes of daily exchange rate movements. About $4 *trillion* in foreign exchange transactions take place in a typical day. Most of those trades are speculative, done to earn a profit by trying to outguess the market. The short-run froth of daily price movements is set largely by psychology and expectations. Traders are guessing where the market is headed, as shaped by supply and demand, but some of the short-run trading is just guessing at the short-run behavior of other traders. Sometimes the small, short-run movements in exchange rates are called "noise," which is the economist's polite way of saying we don't understand what causes them or what they mean.

CHECK YOURSELF

■ If the U.S. dollar is a safe haven currency and risk increases, what does this do to the value of the dollar: send it higher or lower?

■ If the Federal Reserve increases the U.S. money supply, what will this do to the value of the dollar compared to the euro?

■ If purchasing power parity holds and the nominal exchange rate is 1 pound for 2 dollars, how much should a Big Mac cost in London if a Big Mac costs $4.00 in New York?

■ How does a tariff affect purchasing power parity?

How Monetary and Fiscal Policy Affect Exchange Rates and How Exchange Rates Affect Aggregate Demand

Monetary and fiscal policy will alter the exchange rate and trade balance (exports minus imports) of a country. To understand how, keep in mind that an approximate version of purchasing power parity (for tradable goods) holds in the long run, but that deviations from parity are possible in the short run.

Monetary Policy

Imagine that the Federal Reserve increases $\vec{M}$ (growth rate of the money supply) through open market operations, a concept discussed in our chapter on the Federal Reserve System and Open Market Operations and the chapter on Monetary Policy. The increase in $\vec{M}$ shifts the supply curve for dollars down and to the right, which will result in a lower exchange rate (a depreciation). In the short run, dollar prices are sticky so as far as the rest of the world is concerned, it's as if U.S. goods went on sale! Let's look at this in more detail.

Imagine that a Caterpillar tractor sells for $50,000 and the exchange rate starts out at 1 euro per dollar so in Europe, a Caterpillar tractor costs €50,000. Now suppose that as a result of Fed actions, the exchange rate depreciates so that a European needs only 0.8 euros to buy a dollar. The dollar price is still $50,000, but because of the change in the exchange rate, the price in euros has fallen from €50,000 to €40,000, which is in essence a 20% discount. Thus, a depreciation will increase U.S. exports. Recall from our chapter on Business Fluctuations: Aggregate Demand and Supply that an increase in exports increases AD, which boosts the economy in the short run.

Figure 38.6 shows the process in a diagram. Keep in mind that this is exactly the same analysis of an increase in aggregate demand that we discussed in that chapter on Business Fluctuations and also in the chapters on Monetary Policy and on Fiscal Policy. The only difference is that the *source* of the shift in AD is now a depreciation in the exchange rate; the mechanics are exactly as before.

The economy begins at point *a* in long-run equilibrium. The increase in $\overrightarrow{M}$ causes a depreciation in the exchange rate, which in turn reduces the price of U.S. exports. As a result, exports increase, AD increases, and the growth rate of the economy increases, moving the economy in the short run to point *b*. But what about the long run?

FIGURE 38.6

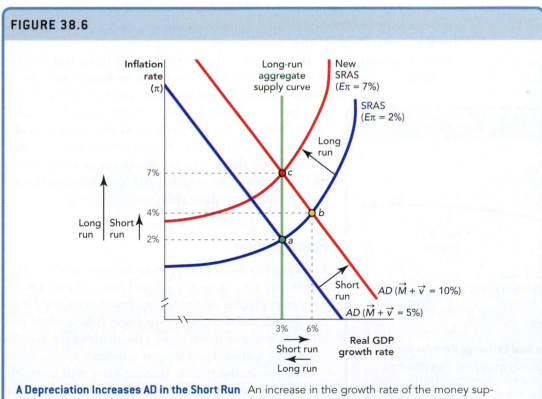

A Depreciation Increases AD in the Short Run An increase in the growth rate of the money supply pushes the exchange rate down (a depreciation). As a result, exports increase, AD increases, and the growth rate increases, moving the economy from point *a* to point *b*. In the long run, the domestic inflation rate increases enough to restore the real exchange rate so there is no longer a boost to exports and the economy moves to a new long-run equilibrium at point *c*.

In the long run, money is neutral, which means that domestic prices will rise to match the increase in $\vec{M}$, so eventually the price of the Caterpillar tractor will increase by 20%. As a result, the nominal exchange rate will be lower but the real exchange rate—in the long run—won't have changed much, if at all. So, in the long run the real depreciation (the sale on U.S. exports) proves to be temporary and so the boost in exports is temporary as well. But if the increase in $\vec{M}$ is not reversed, the U.S. inflation rate increases. Thus, in the long run, the economy moves from point b to point c and the boost to real output growth is not permanent.

We can, however, see one additional reason why politicians and central banks sometimes favor increases in the growth rate of money $\vec{M}$. An increase in $\vec{M}$ usually will boost a nation's exports and thus employment. It will appear that the economy is doing better, at least for a little while but, as usual, the boost to the economy is temporary and it raises the possibility of higher inflation rates.

Furthermore, although the depreciation makes exports cheaper, it makes imports more expensive. The diminished ability of the nation to invest abroad at good prices or buy imports at good prices—because of the lower real exchange rate—is a less visible but real cost of the lower real exchange rate. The lower real exchange rate nonetheless represents a political temptation, if only because the economy at least appears stronger when exports increase in the short run.

That's it for aggregate output. When it comes to the real exchange rate itself, the path of the market to equilibrium looks like the one portrayed in Figure 38.7. Once a Fed action is announced, the dollar moves on international currency markets within seconds. Prices for most goods and services, even if they are relatively flexible, do not respond with this speed. So, at first the dollar has lower international value in real terms.

For a decrease in $\vec{M}$, the process is the reverse. In the short run, the real exchange rate will appreciate, causing U.S. exports to be more expensive on world markets. In the long run, the real exchange rate will be reestablished at the approximate PPP value. Notice that we can see once again why nations with a high rate of inflation may be reluctant to lower $\vec{M}$ even though they should. In the short run, a reduction in $\vec{M}$ reduces exports, reducing AD and reducing the real growth rate in the short run.

FIGURE 38.7

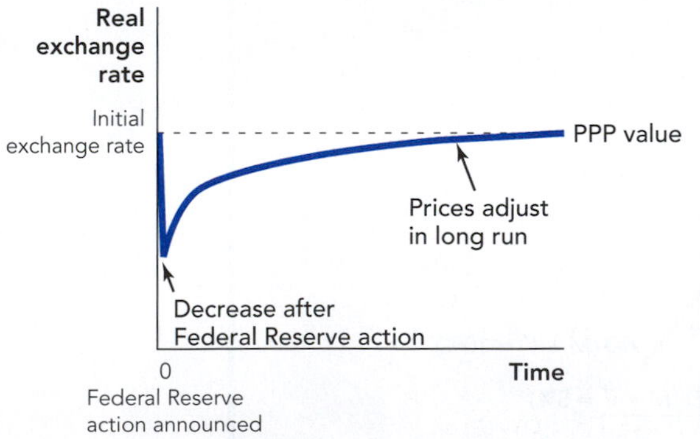

The Dynamics of the Real Exchange Rate An increase in $\vec{M}$ increases the supply of dollars, thus causing a depreciation in the nominal exchange rate. Domestic prices are sticky, so at first the nominal depreciation is also a real depreciation. Over time, however, domestic prices rise, so in the long run the real exchange rate returns to its fundamental value as determined by approximate purchasing power parity.

Fiscal Policy

Expansionary fiscal policy, or an increase in the budget deficit, will raise domestic interest rates. As explained in our earlier chapter on the Saving, Investment, and Financial System and the chapter on Fiscal Policy, when government borrows more money, the demand for loanable funds shifts outward and interest rates go up.

As a result, the higher interest rates will cause the nation—let's say the United States—to run a greater surplus on its capital account. That is, more foreigners will want to invest in the United States to enjoy those high interest rates. The greater demand to invest will cause an appreciation of the U.S. dollar. What does an appreciation of the dollar do to U.S. exports? An appreciation makes U.S. exports more expensive, thus reducing U.S. exports. Thus, a budget deficit can cause a trade deficit. These are sometimes called "the twin deficits."

We now see one more limitation of fiscal policy. The boost to domestic aggregate demand, resulting from the new government spending, will to some extent be offset by the greater difficulty of exporting at the new and higher real exchange rate. Total aggregate demand—domestic plus foreign—might not go up at all. In other words, the argument for fiscal policy discussed in the previous chapter is less justified the more open the economy. This is yet another reason why monetary policy has typically become more important than fiscal policy as a tool of macroeconomic management.

Fixed vs. Floating Exchange Rates

So far we have treated the case of **floating exchange rates** with currency prices determined in open world markets. This is by far the most common scenario in the world today and indeed throughout history.

Still, in other cases the world has seen **fixed,** or **pegged, exchange rates**, where currencies do not fluctuate against one another on a daily basis. Fixed exchange rate systems can take three forms:

1. *Simply adopting the money of another country*

    Panama, Ecuador, and El Salvador all use U.S. dollars as their currency; this is called **dollarization**. The central banks of these nations have no active role in managing their money supplies.

    The disadvantage of this approach is that Ecuador must buy and save enough dollars to use that currency. The advantage is that, once in place, Ecuador receives the monetary policy of the United States. Once the transition is made, the common currency runs on automatic pilot. Overall, it is plausible that the U.S. Fed does a better job than would an Ecuadorian central bank. Indeed, at the time of dollarization in 2000, the rate of inflation in Ecuador was above 50%. Today, the rate of inflation in Ecuador roughly tracks that of the United States and of course this is much lower.

2. *Setting up a currency union*

    Many European countries gave up their currencies and created the euro, a common currency under the supervision of the European Union and (as of early 2018) shared by 19 different EU countries. The wealthier European countries, such as Germany and France, saw the euro as a way to unify Europe economically. Some of the poorer countries, such as Greece, saw the euro as a way to obtain a more stable currency. In any case, all of these countries allow the European Central Bank to control their common monetary policy; the euro does not belong to any single country. The euro, however, is unique and no other comparable arrangement exists today. In the early part of 2010, however, the euro started to come under considerable strain. The basic dilemma is simple: some countries in the eurozone, such as Greece, want a relatively expansionary monetary policy. Since the Greek economy was shrinking during 2010, they wanted monetary policy to stimulate aggregate demand. Other countries in the eurozone, such as Germany, were growing rapidly and did not want an expansionary monetary policy. So far Germany is getting its way, but it remains to be seen whether it makes sense for Greece or other slower growing countries to remain in the eurozone forever.

CHECK YOURSELF
- In the short run, what will happen to exports if the Fed increases the money supply? What will happen in the long run?
- Which tends to be more effective in an open economy: monetary policy or fiscal policy? Why?

A **floating exchange rate** is one determined primarily by market forces.

A **fixed**, or **pegged, exchange rate** means that a government or central bank has promised to convert its currency into another currency at a fixed rate.

Dollarization occurs when a foreign country uses the U.S. dollar as its currency.

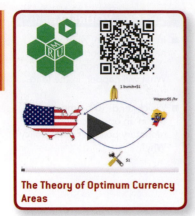

The Theory of Optimum Currency Areas

A **dirty,** or **managed, float** is a currency whose value is not pegged but governments will intervene extensively in the market to keep the value within a certain range.

3. *Backing a currency with high levels of reserves and promising convertibility at a certain rate*

A country could promise to convert its currency into U.S. dollars, or some other currency, at a specified rate. Holding sufficient reserves of the foreign currency to ensure conversion would make this promise more credible. Since 1983, Hong Kong has pledged that 7.80 Hong Kong dollars are equal to 1 U.S. dollar and required Hong Kong banks to have full U.S. dollar backing for any note issued. For many years, Austria pegged its currency to the value of the German mark, prior to adopting the euro.

Option 3 is, of course, a matter of degree. Economists refer to a "peg" to describe a relatively rigid commitment to a specified conversion rate. A **dirty,** or **managed, float** refers to a relatively loose commitment to a floating exchange rate. Under a dirty float, a currency will vary in value daily, although the central bank or treasury will intervene if that currency moves too far outside a band of intended or preannounced values.

The Problem with Pegs

The pegging option has become less popular in recent years. Many nations have attempted currency pegs, but usually they have failed. For instance, Thailand, Indonesia, Brazil, and Argentina, among others, all tried to peg their currencies to the U.S. dollar or to a weighted basket of currencies. In each case, the peg was broken by speculators, largely because these countries did not and could not match the monetary and fiscal policies of the United States. Why hold one Argentine peso—supposedly equal in value to a dollar throughout the late 1990s—when you can hold a U.S. dollar instead?

When Argentina pegged its currency to the U.S. dollar in 1991, it promised that 1 Argentine peso was equal in value to 1 U.S. dollar. For a while, markets believed this promise. The Argentine economy was doing well, foreign investment was flowing in, and the Argentine government instituted many desirable economic reforms.

But over time people began to doubt whether this peg could be maintained. Eventually, the weaknesses of the Argentine economy became revealed more clearly. The government was unable to bring about true fiscal balance. Many foreign investors began to believe that the Argentine peg would break and that the one-to-one rate would go away. This would mean that 1 peso would be worth less than 1 U.S. dollar. Many people who had invested in pesos withdrew their money from the country or tried to convert their peso holdings into dollars before the one-to-one rate disappeared. Argentine citizens panicked as well, and many of them also sought to convert their pesos into U.S. dollars.

The resulting rush to convert pesos into dollars put great strain on the peso. The Argentine government did not have enough U.S. dollars to keep up the value of the peg. The result was that the peso fell from being worth a dollar (January 6, 2002) to being worth about 26 cents (June 28, 2002), across the course of only five and a half months. In other words, the Argentine government had to officially announce a new peg with a much lower value for the Argentine currency.

The rapid reduction in the official exchange rate ruined the economic reputation of Argentina and the withdrawal of money from the country led to a collapse of the banking system. This is sometimes called capital flight. Argentina probably would have been better off had it never pegged its currency in the first place.

Overall, the lesson is simple. Most countries should not attempt exchange rate pegs. An effective peg requires a very serious commitment to a high level of monetary and fiscal stability. If a country doesn't have as sound an economy as that of the United States, in the long run it cannot peg to the U.S. dollar.

What Are the IMF and the World Bank?

To close this chapter, let us look at two very controversial global institutions, the International Monetary Fund and the International Bank for Reconstruction and Development, more commonly known as the World Bank. These institutions have occasioned protests, the throwing of bricks, conspiracy theories, and political T-shirts. What is up? Are they noxious carriers of evil global forces, benevolent do-gooders, or something else altogether?

For the most part, these agencies are bureaucracies. They do some good, some bad, but they are not as important—for better or worse—as many people think.

International Monetary Fund

Today the International Monetary Fund (IMF) serves as an international lender of last resort. That is, when countries experience financial troubles, the IMF steps in to organize a rescue package, lend money, and monitor the economic situation. Often the loans are tied to a country's willingness to take the IMF's economic advice.

The IMF, created after the end of World War II, is located in Washington, D.C., but it is a "multilateral" institution. It is set up by the world's governments and is independent of any single government. It receives a monetary allocation from each government and also may earn income from its loans. Historically, the director of the IMF is a European. The director reports to a board, and board membership is roughly proportional to how much money a country puts into the institution. The United States, Western Europe, and Japan exercise a dominant influence in this regard, but its staff is drawn from around the world.

The IMF was very active in the Asian currency crises of the 1990s (in Indonesia, Thailand, and South Korea), the Argentine financial crisis starting in 2001, and the recent financial crisis in Greece. Critics of the IMF, such as Nobel Laureate Joseph Stiglitz, charge that it forces borrowing governments to cut government spending, tighten monetary policy, and raise interest rates. In other words, the claim is that the IMF has encouraged contractionary macroeconomic policies when (perhaps) expansionary policies were called for. Defenders of the IMF have argued that the advice is more subtle than is often portrayed, that tough fiscal reforms are sometimes needed, or that borrowing countries do not in fact follow the advice, regardless of whether or not it is good advice.

The World Bank

The World Bank also dates from the immediate aftermath of World War II. It was designed to facilitate the flow of capital to poor countries, especially those parts of the world not being served by private capital markets. Its full-time staff of about 10,000 employees is headquartered in Washington, D.C., right next to the IMF. The Bank is ruled by a board, whose members are drawn from supporting nations, and a president who has historically been an American.

Mostly the World Bank lends money for specific projects in developing countries. This includes loans for water projects, roads, dams, health care, and environmental projects, among other activities. World Bank loans are tied to the use of Bank expertise and the understanding that the borrowing country will work cooperatively with the Bank.

In a typical year, the World Bank lends $25–$30 billion to developing nation governments. Overall, the Bank's largest borrower, by far, is China. Other top borrowers are India, Brazil, Mexico, and Turkey. This has led to debate over the Bank's proper mission. China receives at least $70 billion in foreign investment per year, while it is sitting on over $1 trillion in foreign currency reserves. So why is the World Bank lending to China? Defenders of the Bank note that much of China remains poor, and the Chinese loans turn a profit and help the Bank carry out its mission in poorer places like Africa. In addition, in 2010, World Bank lending increased to $44 billion in response to the financial crisis when many governments had trouble raising funds from private markets.

The World Bank also gives away money, lends it out at very low rates of interest, or makes loans that it does not expect will be repaid. This is the aid side of the Bank, which is separate from the Bank's loans. To an increasing extent, the Bank's aid is flowing to sub-Saharan Africa.

Critics claim that the Bank does not pay enough attention to results. The commercial incentive is for the Bank to make many loans. The lent funds first go to governments and then they often are used to purchase goods and services from Western companies. For instance, a World Bank loan to Senegal might help finance a contract with a French company for the supply of urban water. This benefits commercial interests in the countries that control the Bank. Accountability is often low, since each year another round of loans will be made in any case. The World Bank makes money off its loans, so perhaps not enough attention is paid to whether those projects deliver their promised benefits. Defenders note that the Bank has responded to criticism in the past, improved its environmental record, and avoided many previous mistakes. Foreign aid is a difficult business to succeed at, and many people believe that the World Bank is overall a force for good.

The IMF and the World Bank attract so much attention because they are seen as icons of global capitalism. Furthermore, both groups hire many technocrats, and neither is subject to direct accountability through democratic rule. They seem to stand above national borders and make decisions, while reporting to no one. They encourage poor countries to borrow money and those debts cannot always be repaid. Such are the charges, but the reality is more prosaic. Both agencies are highly constrained in what they can accomplish, if only because their resources are limited and they deal frequently with contrary governments. At the margin, they make a difference, but they are not the driving forces behind global capitalism.

Takeaway

International currencies are a tricky business, but basic economic principles hold internationally as well as nationally. Contrary to the statements of many politicians, trade deficits are not necessarily a problem, unless a country is investing foolishly or not saving enough. In either case, the trade deficit is not the root of the relevant problem. Instead of complaining about America's current trade deficit with China, it is better to consider how the United States might save more. The trade balance is simply one side of the coin, with the capital account serving as the other side. If a lot of capital is flowing into a country, that country also will be running a trade deficit.

Exchange rates are set in active markets, changing by the second every day, and following the laws of supply and demand. Monetary policy can affect real exchange rates in the short run, but not in the long run. In the long run, exchanges rates are set according to purchasing power parity, so that profits cannot be made buying goods in one country and shipping them to another.

Both monetary and fiscal policies will affect a country's real exchange rate in the short run and these exchange rate effects will influence aggregate demand by affecting some mix of exports, imports, and the flow of capital from one country to another.

Most countries today have floating exchange rates with values determined in international currency markets. Fixed or pegged exchange rates are possible but in most circumstances they are difficult to maintain over the longer run. Thus, a combination of currency unions and floating exchange rates has increasingly become the global norm.

The IMF and The World Bank may inspire protests but for good or ill these institutions are modestly sized bureaucracies in a much larger globalized world.

CHAPTER REVIEW

interactive activity   Go online to practice with more examples of these types of problems, including live links to videos, data sources, and feedback.

 Problems in **green** relate to MRU videos. See the MRU table at the end of the exercises.

KEY CONCEPTS

trade deficit, p. 812

trade surplus, p. 812

balance of payments, p. 813

capital surplus, p. 813

current account, p. 814

capital account, p. 814

exchange rate, p. 818

appreciation, p. 819

depreciation, p. 820

nominal exchange rate, p. 822

real exchange rate, p. 822

purchasing power parity (PPP) theorem, p. 822

law of one price, p. 822

floating exchange rate, p. 827

fixed, or pegged, exchange rate, p. 827

dollarization, p. 827

dirty, or managed, float, p. 828

FACTS AND TOOLS

Ask FRED

interactive activity

1. Let's use the FRED economic database (https://fred.stlouisfed.org/) to examine U.S. exports, imports, and the balance of trade (Exports–Imports, the most widely discussed component of the current account). Search first for U.S. exports by finding the series EXPGS (use this series rather than the series for real exports). Click Edit Graph and Modify Frequency to change to an annual rate (use the average method). Now click Add Line and look for a similar series for imports (IMPGS). Click Modify Frequency to change to an annual rate (using the average method). In 2016, how much did the United States export (in trillions)? How much did the United States import? What was the trade balance?

Ask FRED

interactive activity

2. Let's examine the U.S. balance of trade (Exports–Imports) as we did in Problem 1, but this time we will do so as a percent of GDP. Using the FRED economic database (https://fred.stlouisfed.org/), search for U.S. Exports.

Again, find the series EXPGS (use this series rather than the series for real exports). Click Edit Graph and Modify Frequency to change to an annual rate (use the average method). Now, under Customize Data look for a similar series for imports (IMPGS) and add it. Now, under Customize Data search for gross domestic product (again, don't use real GDP), and add that.

You now have three series, Exports (a), Imports (b), and Gross Domestic Product (c). Write a formula for the balance of trade as a percentage of GDP using a, b and c, and enter it in the formula box, clicking Apply.

a. In 2005, before the 2008–2009 recession, what was the trade deficit as a percent of GDP?

b. In 2009, during the recession, what was the trade deficit as a percent of GDP?

c. Was the trade deficit bigger or smaller in 2009 compared to 2005? Why? Using your answers to this Problem and Problem 1, comment on whether a trade deficit is necessarily a bad thing.

3. Practice with the balance of payments:

Current account + Capital account
= Change in official reserves

a. Current account = −$10, Capital account = +$15. What is the change in reserves?

b. Current account = −$10, Change in reserves = −$3. What is the capital account?

c. Your college expenses = $12,000, Income from your barista job = $4,000. What is your current account? If you haven't changed your reserves (i.e., cash savings) at all, what is the capital account (i.e., borrowing from parents or bank)?

4. In the chapter, two stories about the deficit are told: "the great place to invest" story and the "foolishly saving too little" story. In the following examples, which is more like the "great place to invest" story and which is more like the "foolishly saving too little" story?

a. Goofus uses his student loan money to buy a nice flat-screen TV and can't afford most of his textbooks. Gallant uses his student loan money to buy his textbooks and coffee that keeps him awake during study sessions.

b. Carter borrows money from his dad to attend the right parties, make useful industry connections, and build his career. Ernest borrows

money from his dad to attend fun parties, meet fun people, and, well, that's about it.

c. America 1 borrows money to invest in her future. America 2 borrows money to pay for a spending binge.

5. a. According to Table 38.1, how many Japanese yen could you get for 1 dollar in May 2017? Use the currency converter on Yahoo! Finance to find out how many yen you could buy for a dollar today.

b. Given your answer to the previous question, did the dollar gain or lose buying power, in terms of Japanese goods, over this period? (Get this one right: It's crucial to understanding exchange rates.)

c. Repeat parts a and b for one other currency in Table 38.1.

6. According to the purchasing power parity theorem, what must be approximately equal across countries: the nominal exchange rate or the real exchange rate?

7. a. According to purchasing power parity theory, a country with massive inflation should also experience a massive fall in the price of its currency in terms of other currencies (a depreciation). Is this what happened in Zimbabwe, or did the opposite occur?

b. Hyperinflation is defined as a rapid rise in the price of goods and services. According to purchasing power parity theory, does hyperinflation also cause a rapid rise in the price of foreign currencies?

8. Which international financial institution focuses on the long-run health of developing countries: the IMF or the World Bank? Which one focuses on short-run financial crises in developing countries?

9. Let's translate between newspaper jargon about exchange rates and the economic reality of exchange rates.

a. Last week, the currency of Frobia was trading one for one with the currency of Bozzum. This week, one unit of Frobian currency buys two units of Bozzumian currency. Which currency "rose"? Which currency became "stronger"? Which currency "appreciated"?

b. The currency in the nation of Malvolio becomes "weaker." Now that it's weaker, can 10 U.S. dollars buy more of the Malvolian currency than before or less than before?

c. A college student travels from the United States to Germany. Just before he leaves, he changes $400 into euros. He spends only half the money while in Germany, so on his return to the United States, he exchanges his euros back into dollars. However, while he was admiring Munich's historic Marienplatz, the dollar "weakened" considerably. Is this good news or bad news from the college student's point of view?

10. a. When the Japanese government slows the rate of money growth, will that tend to strengthen the yen against the dollar or weaken the yen against the dollar?

b. When the Japanese government slows the rate of money growth, will the dollar tend to appreciate against the yen or will the dollar tend to depreciate against the yen?

c. When Americans increase their demand for Japanese-made cars, will that tend to strengthen the yen against the dollar or weaken the yen against the dollar?

d. When Americans increase their demand for Japanese-made cars, will the dollar tend to appreciate against the yen or will the dollar tend to depreciate against the yen?

THINKING AND PROBLEM SOLVING

11. Practice with the current account: Which of the following tend to raise the value of Country X's current account?

a. Country X sends cash to aid war victims in Country Y.

b. Investors living in Country X receive more dividend payments than usual from businesses operating in Country Y.

c. Investors living in Country Y receive more interest payments than usual from businesses operating in Country X.

d. Immigrants from Country Y who live and work in Country X send massive amounts of currency back to their families in Country Y.

e. The government of Country X imports more jet fighters and missiles from Country Y.

12. Practice with the capital account: Which of the three categories of the capital account does each belong in? Which of the following tend to raise the value of Country X's capital account?

a. A corporation in Country Y pays for a new factory to be built in Country X.

b. A corporation in Country Y sells all of its stock in a corporation located in Country X to a citizen of Country X.

c. A citizen of Country Y purchases 20% of the shares of a corporation in Country X from a citizen of Country X.

d. A business owner in Country X pays for a new factory to be built in Country Y.

13. Let's translate "Americans are foolishly saving too little" into a simple GDP story. Recall that $GDP = C + I + G +$ Net exports. GDP is fixed and equal to 100 throughout the story: After all, it's pinned down by the production function of our chapter on Saving, Investment, and the Financial System. Thus, the size of the pie is fixed: The only question is how the pie is sliced into C, I, G, and net exports. To keep it simple, assume that $I + G = 40$ throughout.

a. The "saving too little" story comes in two parts: In part one (now), the United States has high C and low (really, negative) net exports. If $C = 70$, what do net exports equal? Is this a trade deficit or a trade surplus?

b. In part two (later), foreign countries are tired of sending so many goods to the United States, and want to start receiving goods *from* the United States. Net exports now become positive, rising to $+5$. What does C equal? If citizens value consumption, which period do they prefer: "now" or "later"?

14. Let's translate "The United States is a great place to invest" into a simple GDP story. Recall that $GDP = C + I + G +$ Net exports. In this story, foreigners build up the U.S. capital stock by pushing investment (I) above its normal level. Thus, GDP equals 100 in the "now" period but equals 110 in the "later" period. To keep it simple, assume that $C + G = 80$ throughout.

a. The "great place to invest" story comes in two parts: In part one (now), the United States has high I and low (really, negative) net exports. If $I = 35$, what do net exports equal? Is this a trade deficit or a trade surplus?

b. In part two (later), foreign countries are tired of sending so many machines and pieces of equipment to the United States, and want to start receiving goods from the United States. Net exports now become positive, rising to $+5$. What does I equal?

15. The market for foreign currencies is a lot like the market for apples or cars or fish, so we can use the same intuition—as long as we keep reminding ourselves which way is "up" and which is "down." Consider the market for something called "euros" (maybe it's a new breakfast cereal) and measure the price in dollars. Discuss the following cases:

   a. The people who make "euros" decide to produce many more of them. Is this a shift in supply or in demand, and in which direction? What does this do to the price of euros?

   b. Consumers and businesses decide that they'd like to own a lot more euros than before. Is this a shift in supply or in demand, and in which direction? What does this do to the price of euros?

   c. There's a slowdown in the production of euros, initiated by the executives in charge of euro production. Is this a shift in supply or in demand, and in which direction? What does this do to the price of euros?

   d. Suppose that the price of apples rises. Using the same language as in parts a and b, would you describe this as a strengthening of the dollar or a weakening of the dollar?

16. Now that we've built up some intuition about exchange rates, let's apply the principles more thoroughly. In this question, we discuss the U.S.–China exchange rate. Officially, the Chinese government fixed this exchange rate for years at a time, but in this question, we treat it as a market rate that can change every day.

   a. In the following figure, shift the appropriate curves to illustrate the effect of the following news story: Chinese factory sells poisonous dog food.

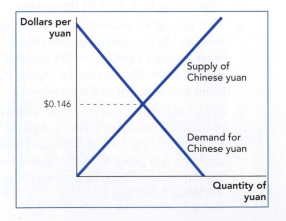

   b. Does this news story raise or lower the price of the yuan? Does this strengthen or weaken the Chinese currency? Does this strengthen or weaken the U.S. dollar?

17. Nobel Laureate Robert Solow once jokingly noted, "I have a chronic [trade] deficit with my barber, who doesn't buy a darned thing from me." Is this a problem? Why or why not? How does this relate to the U.S.–China, U.S.–Mexico, and U.S.–Japan trade deficits?

18. Corey, a young entrepreneur, notices that cigarette lighters sell for only $0.50 each in Utah but they sell for $1.00 each in Nevada.

   a. If Corey wants to make money by buying and selling lighters, where should he buy the lighters and where should he sell them?

   b. If many other people imitate Corey's behavior, what will happen to the supply of lighters in Utah (rise, fall, unchanged)? What will happen to the supply of lighters in Nevada (rise, fall, unchanged)?

   c. What will the behavior in part b do to the price of lighters in Utah? In Nevada?

   d. According to the law of one price, what can we say about the price of cigarette lighters in Nevada after all of this arbitrage? More than one of the following may be true:

   Less than $1.00 each

   More than $1.00 each

   The same as the Utah price

19. At Christmas, five-year-old Gwen runs a massive trade deficit with her parents: She "exports" only a wrapped candy cane to her parents, but she "imports" a massive number of video games, dolls, and pairs of socks.

   a. Is this trade deficit a good thing for Gwen?

   b. When Gwen turns 25, her parents insist on being repaid for all those years of Christmas presents—that is, they require her to run a "trade surplus." Is this "trade surplus" good news for Gwen? Why or why not?

20. a. Suppose that the price level in the United States doubled, while the price level in the U.K. remained unchanged. According to purchasing power parity theory, would the dollar/pound nominal exchange rate double or would it fall in half?

b. In practice, PPP tends to hold more true in the long run than in the short run, because many prices are sticky. So if the U.S. money supply increased dramatically—a big enough rise for the price level to double in the long run—would this be good news for British tourists headed to the United States or would it be good news for U.S. tourists headed to Britain? Incidentally, would this be good news or bad news (in the short run) for U.S. tourists staying in the United States?

21. Consider two equally wealthy families: One family lives in a relatively poor country while the other family lives in a relatively rich country. Which family is more likely to own a mechanical dishwasher? Why? Remember: The families are equally wealthy.

CHALLENGES

22. In our basic model, a rise in money growth causes currency depreciation: We also know from our chapter on Business Fluctuations and the chapter on Monetary Policy on monetary policy that a rise in money growth normally raises aggregate demand and boosts short-run real growth. But in the 2001 Argentine crisis and the 1997 Asian financial crisis, a currency depreciation seemed to cause a massive *fall* in short-run output.

a. What type of shock could cause a currency depreciation to be associated with a fall in short-run output?

b. In both the Argentine and the Asian crises, these countries' banking sectors were hit especially hard: They had made big promises to pay their debts in foreign currencies—often dollars—and the depreciation made it impossible for them to keep those promises. What became more "expensive" as a result of the depreciation: foreign currency (dollars, yen, pounds) or domestic currency?

c. In these crises, depreciation created bankruptcies: These bankruptcies are what causes the shock discussed in part a. To avoid this outcome in the future, Berkeley economist Barry Eichengreen, an expert on exchange rate policy, recommended that businesses in developing countries should encourage foreigners to invest in stock that pays dividends rather than in debt. He believed this would make it easier for countries to endure surprise depreciations. Why would he recommend this?

23. In Panama, a dollarized country, a Big Mac is about 30% cheaper than in the United States. Why?

24. A supply-and-demand model can illustrate the difficulty of keeping a fixed exchange rate: It's much the same as any other price floor. Consider the following fixed exchange rate. Sparta uses a currency called the spartonian, Athenians use the aton; the Spartans have chosen a fixed exchange rate of two atons per spartonian:

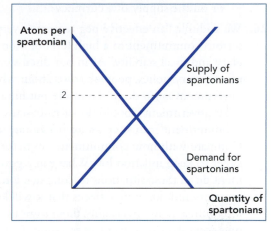

a. In a typical supply and demand model, what would you call the gap that exists between quantity supplied and quantity demanded at this fixed exchange rate: a surplus or a shortage? Of which currency?

b. If the Spartan government wants to keep this exchange rate fixed, what will tend to happen to its official reserve account supply of atons: Will it rise, or will it tend to fall? (*Hint:* Remember that the suppliers of spartonians want to buy atons. How does this explain why governments of fixed exchange rate countries hold large amounts of foreign currencies in their accounts?)

c. If demand for spartonians fell because of a weak Spartan economy, would this make it harder or easier for this government to maintain the exchange rate?

d. If the Spartan government wanted to bring quantity supplied and quantity demanded closer together, would it want to slow money growth or raise money growth? When real world countries have "overvalued" currencies, do you think they should fix them by slowing money growth or by raising money growth?

25. a. Ecuador is currently dollarized: Bank accounts are denominated in U.S. dollars, for example. If Ecuadoreans believe rumors that the country is going to go off the dollar and convert all bank account deposits into a new unit of money called the "Ecuado" (similar to what Argentina actually did in 2001), what will this probably do to the Ecuadorean banking system?

b. "There is no such thing as a fixed exchange rate: Just pegs that haven't been changed . . . yet." Explain how this belief, by itself, can make it difficult for a country to maintain a fixed exchange rate. Does this belief have a direct impact on the demand for a currency or on the supply of a currency?

26. We said that "an effective peg requires a very serious commitment to a high level of monetary and fiscal stability." As in our discussion of monetary policy, people's *beliefs* about what government *might* do in the future put limits on what governments should do *today*. Discuss how "commitment" can keep an exchange rate stable. Compare with how commitment can make it easier to keep inflation low. What can a government do in these situations to convince foreign investors and domestic citizens that it will keep its commitments? (Certainly, there is more than one good way to answer this question: The problem of creating commitment is an active area of research across the social sciences.)

Ask FRED

interactive activity

27. Let's look at the U.S. to U.K. foreign exchange rate using the FRED economic database (https://fred.stlouisfed.org). Search for US/UK Foreign Exchange Rate then change the beginning date to Jan 1, 2016.

a. On June 23, 2016, how many dollars did it take to buy one British pound?

b. On June 27, 2016, how many dollars did it take to buy one British pound?

c. Over the time period, did the British pound appreciate or depreciate? Does this suggest an increased demand to hold pounds or a decreased demand to hold them?

d. What political event happened to cause such a change in the exchange rate? Why did this event cause an appreciation/depreciation (as per your answer to c)?

28. We have said that services are likely to be cheaper in poorer countries, but is this true for all kinds of services? Can you think of some services that are more likely to sell for similar prices everywhere? What kinds of services?

interactive activity

WORK IT OUT

For interactive, step-by-step help in solving this problem, go online.

a. Consider two headlines: "Money is pouring into the U.S. faster than ever" vs. "Record U.S. trade deficit." How can both be true simultaneously?

b. Consider two headlines: "Money is fleeing the U.S. faster than ever" vs. "Record U.S. trade surplus." How can both be true simultaneously?

MRUNIVERSITY
AN ONLINE EDUCATION PLATFORM

MARGINAL REVOLUTION UNIVERSITY VIDEOS

Purchasing Power Parity
mruniversity.com/purchasing-power-parity
Problems: **6, 20**

Why Should You Get a Haircut in a Poorer Country?
mruniversity.com/india-haircut
Problems: **21, 25, 28**

The Theory of Optimum Currency Areas
mruniversity.com/optimum-currency
Problems: **21, 25, 28**

Reading Graphs and Making Graphs

Economists use graphs to illustrate both ideas and data. In this appendix, we review commonly used graphs, explain how to read them, and give you a few tips on how you can make graphs using Microsoft Excel or similar software.

Graphs Express Ideas

In economics, graphs are used to express ideas. The most common graphs we use throughout this book plot two variables on a coordinate system. One variable is plotted on the vertical or y-axis, while the other variable is plotted on the horizontal or x-axis.

In Figure A.1, for example, we plot a very generic graph of variable Y against variable X. Starting on the vertical axis at Y = 100, you read across to the point at which you hit the graph and then down to find X = 800. Thus, when Y = 100, X = 800. In this case, you can also see that when X = 800, then Y = 100. Similarly, when Y = 60, you can read from the graph that X = 400, and vice versa. As you may recall, the slope of a straight line is defined as the rise over the run or rise/run. In this case, when Y rises from 60 to 100, a rise of 40, then X runs from 400 to 800, a run of 400, so the slope of the line is 40/400 = 0.1. The slope is positive, indicating that when Y increases so does X.

Let's now apply the idea of a graph to some economic concepts. In Chapter 3, we show how a demand curve can be constructed from hypothetical data on the price and quantity demanded of oil. We show this here as Figure A.2.

The table on the left of the figure shows that at a price of $55 per barrel buyers are willing and able to buy 5 million barrels of oil a day (MBD), or more simply at a price of $55, the quantity demanded is 5 MBD. You can read this information off the graph in the following way. Starting on the vertical axis, locate the price of $55. Then look to the right for the point where the $55 price hits the demand curve: looking down from this point, you see that the quantity demanded is 5 million barrels of oil per day. How about at a lower price of $20 per day? Start at $20 on the vertical axis and read to the right until the price hits the demand curve, then read down. Can you see that the quantity demanded at this price of $20 per barrel is 25 million barrels of oil per day?

We said that graphs express ideas, so what is the idea being expressed here? The most important fact about a demand curve is that it has a negative slope, that is, it slopes downward. This tells us the important but simple idea that as

FIGURE A.1

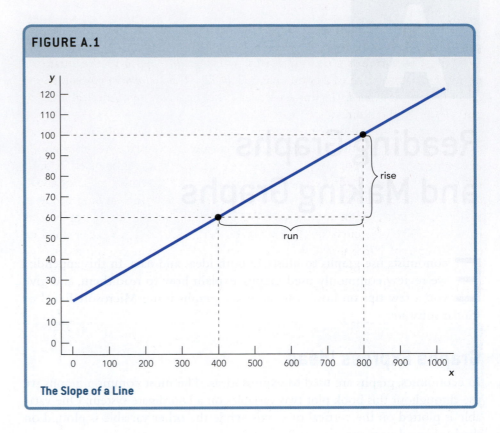

The Slope of a Line

FIGURE A.2

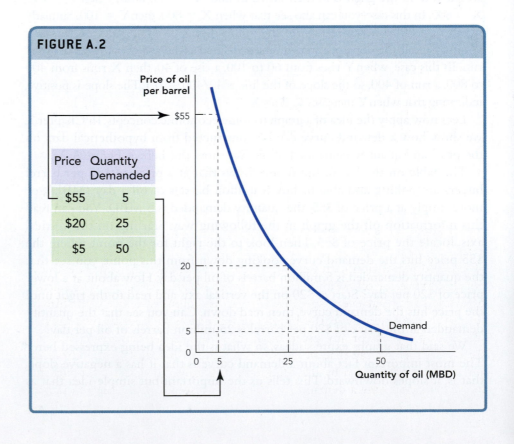

the price of a good falls, the quantity demanded increases. This is key: as the price of a good such as oil falls, people demand more of it.

A demand curve is a description of what *would happen* to the quantity demanded as the price of a good changed, *holding fixed all other influences on the quantity of oil demanded.* (In this sense, demand curves are hypothetical and we rarely observe them directly.)

The quantity of oil demanded, for example, depends not just on the price of oil but on many other factors such as income or the price of other goods like automobiles and population, to name just a few of many influences. Today's demand curve for oil, for example, depends on today's income, price of automobiles and population. Imagine, for example, that average income today is $10,000, the price of an average automobile is $25,000 and world population is 7 billion. The blue curve in Figure A.3 shows the demand curve for oil under these conditions. Note that there are also many other influences on the demand for oil that we don't list but that are also being held fixed. Most importantly, if any of these conditions changes then the demand curve for oil will shift.

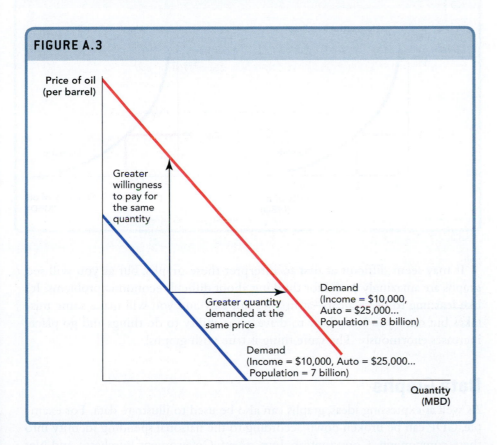

FIGURE A.3

Price of oil (per barrel)

Greater willingness to pay for the same quantity

Greater quantity demanded at the same price

Demand
(Income = $10,000, Auto = $25,000...
Population = 8 billion)

Demand
(Income = $10,000, Auto = $25,000...
Population = 7 billion)

Quantity (MBD)

If world population increases to 8 billion, for example, there will be a new demand curve for oil. With a greater population, there will be more barrels of oil demanded at every specific price so the demand curve will shift to the right. Equivalently, as the population increases, there will be a greater willingness to pay for any given quantity of oil, so the demand curve will shift up. Thus, we say that an increase in demand is a shift in the curve up and to the right shown by the red curve in Figure A.3. Chapter 3 explains in greater detail how a demand curve shifts in response to changes in factors other than price.

What is important to emphasize here is that a demand curve is drawn holding fixed every influence on the quantity demanded other than price. Changes in any factor that influences the demand for oil other than price will produce a new demand curve.

One more important feature of two variables graphed in a coordinate system is that these figures can be read in two different ways. For example, as we mention in Chapter 3, demand curves can be read both horizontally and vertically. Read "horizontally," you can see from Figure A.4 that at a price of $20 per barrel demanders are willing and able to buy 25 million barrels of oil per day. Read "vertically," you can see that the maximum price that demanders are willing to pay for 25 million barrels of oil a day is $20 per barrel. Thus, demand curves show the quantity demanded at any price or the maximum willingness to pay (per unit) for any quantity.

FIGURE A.4

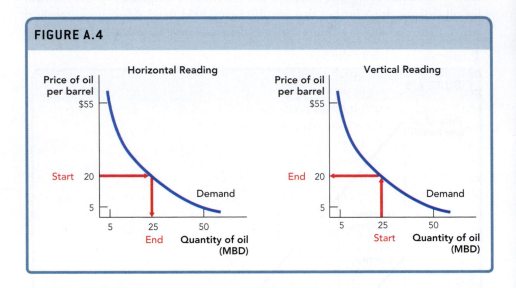

It may seem difficult at first to interpret these graphs, but as you will see, graphs are amazingly useful for thinking about difficult economic problems. It's like learning to drive a car—at first it's not easy and you will make some mistakes but once you learn how to drive, your ability to do things and go places increases enormously. The same thing is true with graphs!

Data Graphs

As well as expressing ideas, graphs can also be used to illustrate data. For example, GDP can be broken down according to the national spending identity into these components: Consumption, Investment, Government Purchases, and Net Exports (Exports minus Imports), that is, $GDP = Y = C + I + G + NX$. U.S. GDP for 2007 is shown in Table A.1.

If you type the components into Excel, as shown in Figure A.5, you can use the sum function to check that the components do add up to GDP.

Highlighting the data in columns A and B and clicking Insert > Column > Clustered Column and (with a few modifications to add axis titles and to make the graph look pretty), we have the graph on the left side of Figure A.6.

The graph on the right side of Figure A.6 shows exactly the same data only on the right side we chose Stacked Column (and we switched the rows and columns).

Sometimes one visualization of the data is more revealing than another so it's a good idea to experiment a little bit with alternative ways of presenting the same data. But please don't get carried away with adding 3-D effects or other chart junk. Always keep the focus on the data, not on the special effects.

In this book, we explain the economics of stocks, bonds, and other investments. A lot of financial data is available for free on the web. We used Yahoo! Finance, for example, to download data for the value of the S&P 500 Index on the first trading day of the month from 1950 to the end of 2000. The data is graphed in Figure A.7.

To graph the S&P 500 data, we used a line graph. The top graph in Figure A.7 shows the data graphed in the "normal" way, with equal distances on the vertical axis indicating equal changes in the index. That's not necessarily the best way to graph the data, however, because a quick look at the top figure suggests that stock prices were rising faster over time. In other words, the graph looks pretty flat between 1950 and approximately 1980, after which it shoots up. The appearance of faster growth, however, is mostly an illusion. The problem is that when the S&P 500 was at the level of 100, as it was around 1968, a 10% increase moves the index to 110, or an increase of 10 points. But when the index is at the level of 1,000, as it was around 1998, a 10% increase moves the

TABLE A.1 U.S. GDP 2007 (in billions of dollars)

Category	GDP
Consumption	9,710.2
Investment	2,130.4
Government	2,674.8
Net Exports	−707.8
GDP (Total)	13,807.6

Data from: U.S. Bureau of Economic Analysis

FIGURE A.5

	B7		f_x	=SUM(B2:B5)	
	A	B	C	D	
1	Category	GDP			
2	Cons	9710.2			
3	Inv	2130.4			
4	Govt	2674.8			
5	NX	-707.8			
6					
7	GDP (Total)	13807.6			
8					

FIGURE A.6

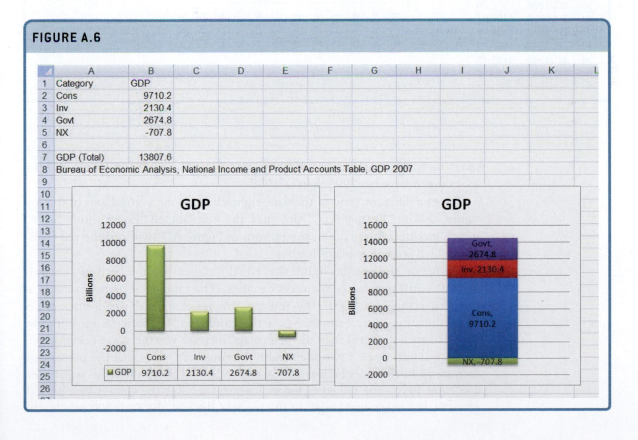

FIGURE A.7

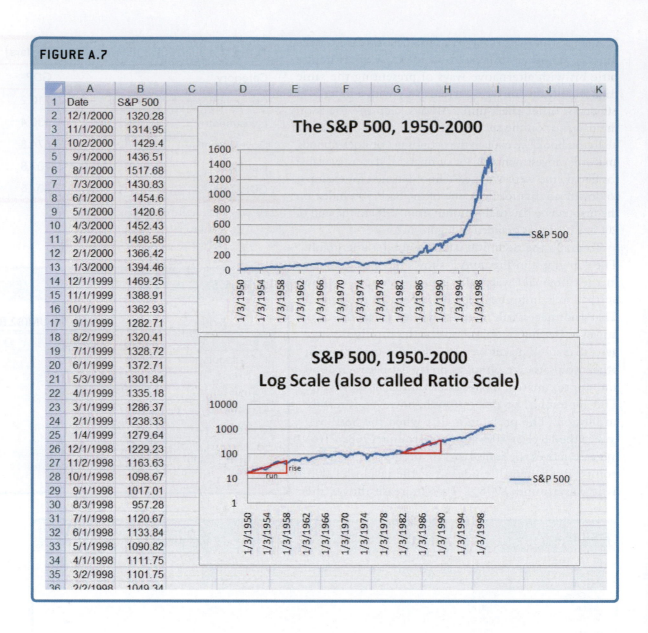

index to 1,100, or an increase of 100 points. Thus, the same percentage increase looks much larger in 1998 than in 1968.

To get a different view of the data, right-click on the vertical axis of the top figure, choose "Format Axis" and click the box labeled "Logarithmic Scale," which produces the graph in the bottom of Figure A.7 (without the red triangles, which we will explain shortly).

Notice on the bottom figure that equal distances on the vertical axis now indicate equal percentage increases or ratios. The ratio 100/10, for example, is the same as the ratio 1,000/100. You can now see at a glance that if stock prices move the same vertical distance over the same length of time (as measured by the horizontal distance) then the percentage increase was the same. For example, we have superimposed two identical red triangles to show that the percentage increase in stock prices between 1950 and 1958 was about the same as between 1982 and 1990. The red triangles are identical, so over the same 8-year period, given by the horizontal length of the triangle, the run, the S&P 500 rose by the same vertical distance, the rise. Recall that the slope of a line is given by the rise/run. Thus, we can also say that on a ratio graph, equal slopes mean equal percentage growth rates.

The log scale or ratio graph reveals more clearly than our earlier graph that stock prices increased from 1950 to the mid-1960s but were then flat throughout the 1970s and did not begin to rise again until after the recession in 1982. We use ratio graphs for a number of figures throughout this book to better identify patterns in the data.

Graphs are also very useful for suggesting possible relationships between two variables. In the macroeconomics section, for example, we present evidence that labor employment laws in much of Western Europe that make it difficult to fire workers also raise the costs of hiring workers. As a result, the percentage of unemployment that is long term in Europe tends to be very high. To show this relationship, we graphed an index called the "rigidity of employment index," produced by the World Bank. The rigidity of employment index summarizes hiring and firing costs as well as how easy it is for firms to adjust hours of work (e.g., whether there are restrictions on night or weekend hours). A higher index number means that it is more expensive to hire and fire workers and more difficult to adjust hours. We then graphed a country's rigidity of employment index against the share of a country's unemployment rate that is long term (lasting more than a year).

The data for this graph are shown in Figure A.8.

FIGURE A.8

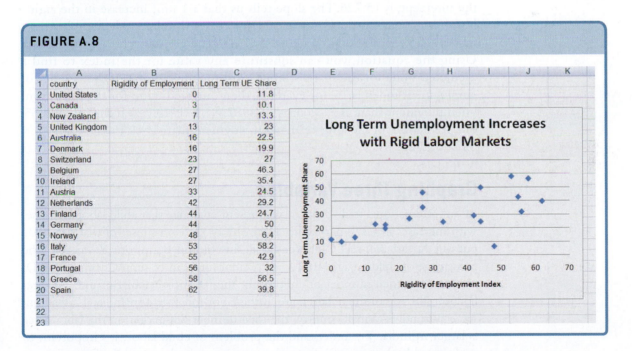

	A	B	C
1	country	Rigidity of Employment	Long Term UE Share
2	United States	0	11.8
3	Canada	3	10.1
4	New Zealand	7	13.3
5	United Kingdom	13	23
6	Australia	16	22.5
7	Denmark	16	19.9
8	Switzerland	23	27
9	Belgium	27	46.3
10	Ireland	27	35.4
11	Austria	33	24.5
12	Netherlands	42	29.2
13	Finland	44	24.7
14	Germany	44	50
15	Norway	48	6.4
16	Italy	53	58.2
17	France	55	42.9
18	Portugal	56	32
19	Greece	58	56.5
20	Spain	62	39.8

Long Term Unemployment Increases with Rigid Labor Markets

We can do something else of interest with this data. If you right-click on any of the data points in the figure, you will get the option to "Add Trendline." Clicking on this and then clicking the two boxes "Linear" and "Display Equation on Chart" produces Figure A.9 (absent the red arrow, which we added for clarity).

The black line is the linear curve that "best fits" the data. (Best fit in this context is defined statistically; we won't go into the details here but if you take a statistics class you will learn about ordinary least squares.) Excel also produces for us the equation for the best-fit line, $Y = 0.4987 \times X + 13.726$.

FIGURE A.9

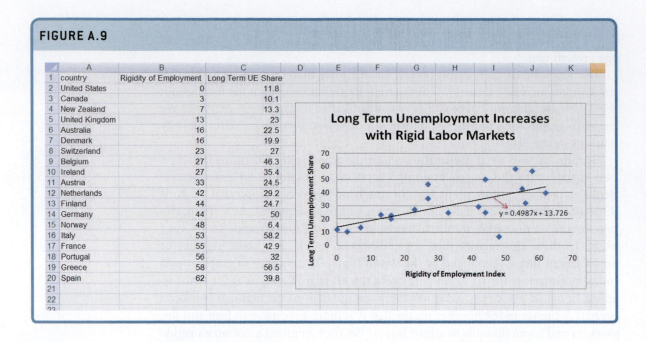

Do you remember from high school the formula for a straight line, $Y = m \times X + b$? In this case m, the slope of the line or the rise/run is 0.4987 and b, the intercept, is 13.726. The slope tells us that a 1 unit increase in the rigidity of employment index (a run of 1) increases the share of unemployment that is long term by, on average, 0.4987 percentage points (a rise of 0.4987). Using the equation, you can substitute any value for the index to find a predicted value for the share of long-term unemployment. If the rigidity of employment index is 15, for example, then our prediction for the long-term unemployment share is $21.2065 = 0.4987 \times 15 + 13.726$ If the index is 55, our prediction for the long-term unemployment share is $41.1545 = 0.4987 \times 55 + 13.726$.

Graphing Three Variables

In our international trade chapter, we present evidence that child labor decreases with increases in GDP per capita. Figure A.10 shows a subset of that data. We put our X variable, real GDP per capita, in column B and our Y variable, the percentage of children ages 10–14 in the labor force, in column C. In column D, we have the total number of children in the labor force. In Burundi, a larger fraction (48.5%) of the children are in the labor force than in India (12.1%), but since Burundi is a small country, the total number of children in the labor force is larger in India. To understand the problem of child labor, it's important to understand both types of information so we put both types of information on a graph.

Excel's bubble chart will take data arrayed in three columns and use the third column to set the area of the bubble or data point. In Figure A.10, for example, India has the largest number of children in the labor force and so has the bubble with the largest area. The area of the other bubbles is in relative proportion, so Mexico's bubble is 1/25th the size of India's bubble because there are 1/25th as many children in the labor force in Mexico as in India. (Unfortunately, Excel doesn't label the bubbles automatically so we added these by hand.)

FIGURE A.10

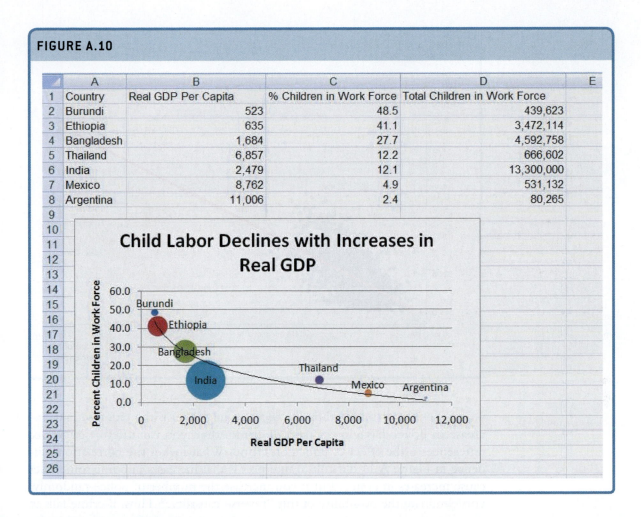

	A	B	C	D	E
1	Country	Real GDP Per Capita	% Children in Work Force	Total Children in Work Force	
2	Burundi	523	48.5	439,623	
3	Ethiopia	635	41.1	3,472,114	
4	Bangladesh	1,684	27.7	4,592,758	
5	Thailand	6,857	12.2	666,602	
6	India	2,479	12.1	13,300,000	
7	Mexico	8,762	4.9	531,132	
8	Argentina	11,006	2.4	80,265	

Cause and Effect

Do police reduce crime? If so, by how much? That's a key question that economists and criminologists are interested in understanding because local governments (and taxpayers) spend billions of dollars on police every year and would like to know whether they are getting their money's worth. Should they spend less on police or more? Unfortunately, it's surprisingly difficult to answer this question. To illustrate why, Figure A.11 shows the relationship between crime per capita and police per capita from across a large number of U.S. cities.

Figure A.11 shows that cities with more police per capita have more crime per capita. Should we conclude that police cause crime? Probably not. More likely is "reverse causality," crime causes police—that is, greater crime rates lead to more hiring of police. We thus have two chains of potential cause and effect, more police reduce crime and more crime increases police. Unfortunately, you can't tell much about either of these two potential cause-and-effect relationships by looking at Figure A.11, which shows the correlation between police and crime but not the causation. But if you want to estimate the value of police, you need to know causation not just correlation. So what should you do?

The best way to estimate how much police reduce crime would be to take say 1,000 roughly similar cities and randomly flip a coin dividing the cities into two groups. In the first group of cities, double the police force and in the second group do nothing. Then compare crime rates over say the next

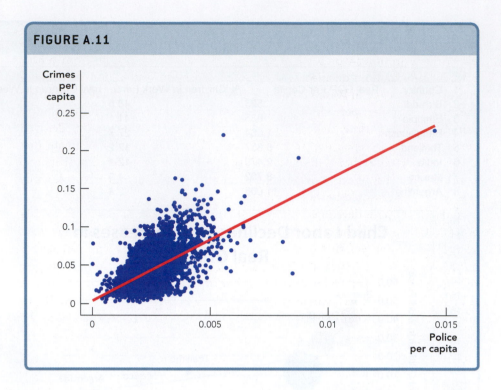

FIGURE A.11

year in cities with and without an increase in police. If the cities with an increase in police have lower rates of crime, then you can safely ascribe this difference to the effect of police on crime. What makes the correlation evidence in Figure A.11 difficult to interpret is that increases in crime sometimes cause increases in police. But if you increase the number of police randomly, you eliminate the possibility of this "reverse causality." Thus, if crime falls in the cities that have random increases in police, the cause is most plausibly the increase in police. Similarly, if crime were to increase in cities that have random decreases in police, the cause is most plausibly the decrease in police.

Unfortunately, randomized experiments have at least one big problem—they are very expensive. Occasionally, large randomized experiments are done in criminology and other social sciences but because they are so expensive we must usually look for alternative methods for assessing causality.

If you can't afford a randomized experiment, what else can you do? One possibility is to look for what economists call quasi-experiments or natural experiments. In 1969, for example, police in Montreal, Canada, went on strike and there were 50 times more bank robberies than normal.[1] If you can think of the strike as a random event, not tied in any direct way to increases or decreases in crime, then you can be reasonably certain that the increase in bank robberies was caused by the decrease in police.

The Montreal experiment tells you it's probably not a good idea to eliminate all police, but it doesn't tell you whether governments should increase or decrease police on the street by a more reasonable amount, say 10% to 20%. Jonathan Klick and Alex Tabarrok use another natural experiment to address this question.[2] Since shortly after 9/11, the United States has had a terror alert system run by the Department of Homeland Security. When the terror alert level rises from "elevated" (yellow) to "high" (orange) due to intelligence reports regarding the current threat posed by terrorist organizations, the Washington, D.C. Metropolitan Police Department reacts by increasing the number of hours each officer must work.

Because the change in the terror alert system is not tied to any observed or expected changes in Washington crime patterns, this provides a useful quasi-experiment. In other words, whenever the terror alert system shifts from yellow to orange—a random decision with respect to crime in Washington—the effective police presence in Washington increases. Klick and Tabarrok find that during the high terror alert periods when more police are on the street, the amount of crime falls. Street crime such as stolen automobiles, thefts from automobiles, and burglaries decline especially sharply. Overall, Klick and Tabarrok estimate that a 10% increase in police reduces crime by about 3%. Using these numbers and figures on the cost of crime and of hiring more police, Klick and Tabarrok argue that more police would be very beneficial.

Economists have developed many techniques for assessing causality from data and we have only just brushed the surface. We can't go into details here. We want you to know, however, that in this textbook when we present data that suggests a causal relationship—such as when we argue in the international trade chapter that higher GDP leads to lower levels of child labor—that a significant amount of statistical research has gone into assessing causality, not just correlation. If you are interested in further details, we have provided you with the references to the original papers.

APPENDIX A QUESTIONS

1. We start with a simple idea from algebra: Which of the graphs at the top of the next page have a positive slope and which have a negative slope?

2. When social scientists talk about social and economic facts, they usually talk about a "positive relationship" or a "negative relationship" instead of "positive slope" or "negative slope." Based on your knowledge, which of the following pairs of variables tend to have a "positive relationship" (a positive slope when graphed), and which have a negative relationship? (*Note:* "Negative relationship" and "inverse relationship" mean the same thing. Also, in this question, we're only talking about correlation, not causation.)

   a. A professional baseball player's batting average and his annual salary.

   b. A professional golfer's average score and her average salary.

   c. The number of cigarettes a person smokes and her life expectancy.

   d. The size of the car you drive and your probability of surviving a serious accident.

   e. A country's distance from the equator and how rich its citizens tend to be. (For the answer, see Robert Hall and Charles Jones. 1999. Why Do Some Countries Produce so Much More Output per Worker than Others? *Quarterly Journal of Economics.* 114: 83-116.)

3. Let's convert Klick and Tabarrok's research on crime into a simple algebra equation. We reported the result as the effect of a 10% increase in police on the crime rate in Washington, D.C. In the equation below, fill in the effect of a 1% increase in the police on the crime rate:

   The percent change in crime = _____ × The percent change in police officers

4. Let's read the child labor graph (A.10) horizontally and then vertically:

   a. According to the trendline, in a typical country with 10% of the children in the labor force, what's the real GDP per person?

   b. According to the trendline, when a country's GDP per person is $2,000, roughly what percentage of children are in the labor force?

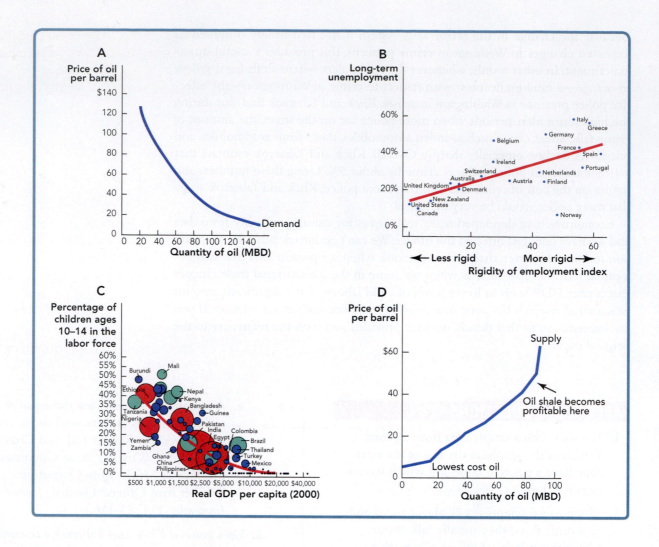

5. Let's take another look at the ratio scale, and compare it to a normal scale.

   a. In Figure A.7, which one is presented in ratio scale and which in normal scale?

   b. In the top graph, every time the S&P 500 crosses a horizontal line, how many points did the S&P rise?

   c. In the bottom graph, every time the S&P 500 crosses a horizontal line, how many *times* higher is the S&P?

6. As a scientist, you have to plot the following data: The number of bacteria you have in a large petri dish, measured every hour over the course of a week. (*Note: E. coli* bacteria populations can double every 20 minutes.) Should this data be plotted on a ratio scale and why?

7. Educated people are supposed to point out (correctly) that "correlation isn't proof of causation." This is an important fact—which explains why economists, medical doctors, and other researchers spend a lot of time trying to look for proof of causation. But sometimes, correlation is good enough. In the following examples, take the correlation as a true fact, and explain why the correlation is, all by itself, useful for the task presented in each question.

   a. Your task is to decide what brand of car to buy. You know that Brand H usually gets higher quality ratings than Brand C. You don't know what causes Brand H to get higher ratings—maybe Brand H hires better workers, maybe Brand H buys better raw materials. All you have is the correlation.

   b. Your task is to hire the job applicant who appears to be the smartest. Applicant M has a degree from MIT, and applicant S has a degree from a typical state university. You don't know what causes MIT graduates to be smarter than typical state university graduates—maybe they start off smarter before they get to MIT, maybe their professors teach them a lot, maybe having smart classmates for four years gives them constant brain exercise.

c. Your task is to decide which city to move to, and you want to move to the city that is probably the safest. For some strange reason, the only fact you have to help you with your decision is the number of police per person.

8. If you haven't practiced in a while, let's calculate some slopes. In each case, we give two points, and you can use the "rise over run" formula to get the right answer.

   a. Point 1: $x = 0$, $y = 0$. Point 2: $x = 3$, $y = 6$

   b. Point 1: $x = 6$, $y = -9$. Point 2: $x = 3$, $y = 6$

   c. Point 1: $x = 4$, $y = 8$. Point 2: $x = 1$, $y = 12$

9. We mentioned that a demand curve is a hypothetical relationship: It answers a "what if" question: "What if today's price of oil rose (or fell), but the average consumer's income, beliefs about future oil prices, and the prices of everything else in the economy stayed the same?" When some of those other features change, then the demand curve isn't fixed any

more: It shifts up (and right) or left (and down). In Figure A.3, we showed one shift graphically: Let's make some changes in algebra:

The economy of Perovia has the following demand for oil:

$$\text{Price} = B - M \times \text{Quantity}$$

When will B tend to be a larger number:

a. When population in Perovia is high or when it is low?

b. When the price of autos in Perovia is high or when it is low?

c. When Perovian income is high or when it is low?

Ask FRED

interactive activity

10. Using the FRED economic database (http://fred.stlouisfed.org) search for U.S. Real Gross Domestic Product and graph the seasonally adjusted quarterly series.

a. What was U.S. Real GDP in the first quarter of 1980?

b. Click on Edit Graph and change the Units to Percent Change from Year Ago and Modify Frequcney to Annual. By how much did the U.S. economy shrink in 2009?

APPENDIX B

Solutions to Check Yourself Questions

Here are suggested answers to the Check Yourself questions found within the chapters.

Chapter 2

Page 21

1. Specialization increases productivity because it increases knowledge.

2. If people can't trade for other goods, they won't specialize in producing just one good. Thus, trade is necessary if people are to benefit from specialization.

3. Usain Bolt has a comparative advantage in running, but Harry has a comparative advantage in mowing Usain's lawn because Harry faces a much lower opportunity cost in mowing lawns than Usain Bolt does.

Chapter 3

Page 36

1. A rise in the income of Indian workers will lead to an increase in the demand for automobiles. At first as income rises, workers may demand more charcoal bricks for heating, but charcoal bricks are a dangerous and unpleasant way to heat a home, so as income increases beyond a certain level, workers will demand fewer charcoal bricks. Thus, a good can be a normal good over some levels of income and an inferior good over other (usually higher) levels of income.

2. As the price of oil rises, some people will substitute mopeds for automobiles so the demand for mopeds will increase.

Page 44

1. Improvements in chip-making technology have driven down the costs of this input so the supply of computers increases, meaning that the supply curve for computers shifts to the right and down.

2. The ethanol subsidy lowers the cost of producing ethanol, therefore increasing the supply of ethanol (the supply curve for ethanol shifts to the right and down).

Chapter 4

Page 53

1. If the demand for large trucks and SUVs falls unexpectedly, auto companies will find that at the current price they have a surplus of trucks and SUVs. The quantity supplied is greater than the quantity demanded, so they will lower prices in order to sell already manufactured trucks and SUVs.

2. Sellers have produced too many clothes if they have them available at outlet malls where price discounts are the norm. Sellers are cutting their prices to reduce the surplus and move the clothes out the door.

Page 56

1. As the price of cars goes up, the least-valued wants will be the first to stop being satisfied. For example, parents may be more reluctant to buy their teenage sons and daughters a new automobile.

2. If telecommunication firms overinvest in fiber-optic cable, for example, they will have to lower the price of using fiber-optic lines. For example, a company such as Verizon will offer fiber-optic Internet and phone connections at discount prices. The ensuing losses from price cutting will dampen future investment in fiber-optic cable. More generally, firms invest in order to make a profit. If firms overinvest, they will take losses, which give them an incentive to invest carefully.

3. Kiran values the good at $50, and in a free market will buy it from store B for $35, earning a total consumer surplus of $15 ($50 − $35). If store B is prevented from selling, say by a regulation or a tax, then Kiran will buy from store A for $45, but total consumer surplus will fall to $5 ($50 − $45).

Page 60

1. If flooding destroys some of the corn and soybean crops, these crops will have a decrease in supply. This decrease in supply will lower the equilibrium quantity and increase the equilibrium price.

2. If resveratrol (from Japanese knotweed) increases life expectancy in fish, people might think it will have the same effect in humans, and so more people will demand it, increasing demand. This will increase the price of Japanese knotweed and lead to an increase in the quantity grown.

3. The demand for hybrid cars will increase as the price of gas increases, that is, the demand curve shifts to the right/up. We show this in Figure 4.7: Think of the New demand as the demand for hybrids when the price of gas is high, and the Old demand as the demand for hybrids when the price of gas is low. The price of hybrids will rise with an increase in demand, especially in the short run.

Page 64

1. The price of oil rose in 1991 primarily because of a supply shock, the Persian Gulf War. (It would also be okay to label this as a demand shock because the demand for oil increased when people expected that the war would reduce the future supply of oil.) Bonus points if you recognized both possibilities.

2. From 1981 to 1986, the price of oil fell steadily. The higher price in the preceding years encouraged exploration, which several years later led to increased supply, especially from non-OPEC sources.

Chapter 5

Page 81

1. There are more substitutes for a brand than for a general product category, so there are more substitutes for Dell computers than for computers. When there are more substitutes, demand is more elastic, so demand is more elastic for Dell computers than for computers.

2. An elasticity of demand of 0.1 is an inelastic demand. With inelastic demand, revenue and price move together. Thus, if the price of eggs increases, total revenue will increase. Bonus points if you said that with an elasticity of 0.1, when price goes up by 10%, quantity goes down by 1%, so revenues (= $P \times Q$) increase by approximately 9%.

3. A fashionable clothing store might raise its prices by 25% if it thought there was inelastic demand for its products: The increase in price on everything would more than make up for the decrease in sales (quantity).

Page 89

1. Supply is usually not very elastic in the short run. In the case of computer chips, a factory can run 24 hours per day and pay overtime, but it takes years to build a new factory. In the long run, supply is more elastic because over time a computer chip firm can respond to increased demand by building new factories.

2. Manhattan is an island with very little land available for development, so the supply of housing in Manhattan is very inelastic. In contrast, a lot of unbuilt land is available in the Des Moines area, so the supply is more elastic. The same increase in demand will increase the price more when the supply is inelastic than elastic; thus the same increase in demand will increases prices more in Manhattan than in Des Moines.

Chapter 6

Page 109

1. Because demand for insulin is highly inelastic, the users of insulin are likely ultimately to pay a government insulin tax. Producers of insulin have some ability to produce other products and so can escape the tax more readily.

2. The government would rather tax items that have relatively inelastic demands and supplies rather than elastic demands and supplies because the deadweight loss from taxation is lower when supply and demand are inelastic.

3. The easiest way to show this is to go back to Figure 6.5. In the right panel, draw in an almost inelastic supply curve. Now draw in an almost elastic supply curve. Visually examine the relative differences in consumer surplus and producer surplus. Remember that elasticity = escape so the relatively elastic side escapes and loses less surplus while the relatively inelastic side can't escape and so loses more surplus.

Page 112

1. Because of the ethanol subsidy, the quantity supplied of ethanol increases. The subsidy increases the price received by the ethanol producers (corn growers) and lowers the price paid by ethanol users. The relative amount received by producers vs. that paid by buyers depends on the relative elasticities of demand and supply.

2. Government subsidies for college education increase the demand for education. The supply of education, however, is relatively inelastic, especially at elite colleges. Thus, the benefits of the subsidy flow to suppliers; that is, the price paid to suppliers increases by more than the price paid by buyers falls. Much of the subsidy ends up raising the incomes of professors! Perhaps this is one reason that many professors argue for subsidies to education.

Chapter 7

Page 121

1. If farmers receive a higher price for turning corn into ethanol, they will supply more of their corn for ethanol production. Thus, the (opportunity) cost of supplying corn for cornbread will increase and there will be a decrease in the supply of corn for cornbread. As a result, the price of cornbread will increase and customers will consume less, perhaps substituting cheaper items such as regular bread.

2. During the housing boom, the use of lumber skyrocketed, as did the supply of a lumber by-product, sawdust. The increase in the supply of sawdust caused a fall in the price of sawdust. Since a lot of sawdust is used in bedding milk cows, this reduced the cost of producing milk. When the housing boom collapsed, less lumber was produced so less sawdust was produced and the price of sawdust rose, which increased the cost of producing milk and thus the price of milk. Markets are linked in nonobvious ways. Who would have thought the housing and milk markets were linked so closely?

Page 124

1. We aren't peanut experts either but the highest value of peanuts is probably in its use as a food; furthermore, there are fewer substitutes for peanuts in paint, varnish, and furniture polish, where the peanut has some unique properties, than in insecticides or soap or finally bird feed. So let's rank the uses of peanuts from highest to least valued as follows: food, paint, varnish, furniture polish, insecticides, soap, and bird feed. Any ranking you have is fine—the point is that there is a ranking.

2. If there is a peanut crop failure in a large producer such as China, the price of peanuts and peanut products will rise and people will substitute away from peanuts in their least-valued uses. Thus, we would expect fewer peanuts used in bird feed, soap, and insecticides, which will free up more peanuts for use in the higher-valued categories. Thus, as the price of peanuts rises, there is a reallocation of peanuts from lower- to higher-valued uses. It's important to recognize that the best way of figuring out which uses are higher valued is to see what happens when the price rises.

Page 125

1. No central planner could possibly know or understand all of the links between products, so the messaging system is unlikely to send the right information. But let's suppose that the *information problem* was solved. Even if the government sent the right messages, there would still be an *incentive problem*. What incentives would producers and consumers have to obey the messages? In contrast, the price system sums up all of the links between products in one number, the price, and it provides an incentive to pay attention to the price. Thus, the price system solves the information problem and the incentive problem, which is why we say that a price is a signal wrapped up in an incentive.

2. If firms do not have to face bankruptcy, they can continue with poor products, practices, and efforts. The fear of bankruptcy is a spur to innovate and grow, but the fear has to be backed up by the reality.

Page 127

In hindsight, it is clear that Lehman Brothers was engaged in wishful thinking. Speculators, with their money on the line, did not believe the Lehman forecasts. Companies can have a tendency to look at things in the best possible way and to ignore reality, and speculators provide a market vote (a reality check).

Chapter 8

Page 148

1. Price ceilings set below equilibrium prices cause shortages. Price ceilings set above equilibrium prices have no effects.

2. A price control reduces the incentive to respond to shifts in demand, thus resources become misallocated according to essentially random factors. For example, it costs much more to ship oil from Alaskan oil fields to refineries on the East Coast than to those on the West Coast. Price ceilings did not let that difference become factored in the price, and therefore reduced the incentive to ship oil to where it was most needed, so shortages could be worse in some areas than in others.

Page 151

1. If landlords under rent control have an incentive to do only minimum upkeep, deteriorating buildings inevitably accompany rent control. Only major repairs are made. Tenants with dripping faucets may never get a response from landlords, and have to fix it themselves. At a minimum, they will have to wait, maybe until the drip becomes something larger and so has an effect on the landlord's water bill.

2. Vested interests will fight any attempt at rolling back rent control, and these vested interests become powerful over time. It's especially difficult to eliminate rent controls because tenants (people who already have an apartment) don't care much about the shortage—they do not have to find a new apartment every week. In contrast, buyers of gasoline have to deal with the shortage every time they need a fillup so it may be easier to get rid of price controls on oil than on apartments.

Page 153

1. Price ceilings cause shortages. Universal price controls cause shortages across the economy, with no obvious pattern. Sometimes one product is in abundance, at other times there are shortages. A rational response when there are products that face inexplicable shortages is to buy as much as possible when possible: buy as much toilet paper now because who knows when it will come available again? In other words, hoarding is a standard response to universal price controls. Hoarding is wasteful because it implies a misallocation of resources. Some people, for reasons of luck (or influence), may have a lot of toilet paper while others have none. If trade were allowed, people would experience gains from trade and products would gravitate to their highest-value uses.

2. The Soviet Union also faced surpluses of goods as well as shortages because under universal price controls there was no incentive to get products to the places at the times that they had the highest-value uses. As a result, goods would be misallocated and production and consumption would be chaotic. One week a farm might get enough oil to deliver its chickens to the city and in that week the city shops would get a lot of chickens as the farm dumped its accumulated stock. A few weeks later there might be no oil available and chickens would disappear from the shops.

Page 158

1. A price floor set above the equilibrium price leads to surpluses. Because the European Union price floor for butter is above the equilibrium price, the EU has created a surplus of butter, which the government must buy. The surplus has been so large that it has been called a butter mountain.

2. The U.S. price floor for milk, set above the equilibrium price, has led to a surplus of milk. The government has dealt with the surplus by buying the surplus and giving away milk and dairy products produced from milk (such as cheese) to schools. This accounts for the low or zero price you paid for milk at most schools.

Chapter 9

Page 173

1. Domestic producers gain from a tariff and domestic consumers lose.

2. Trade protectionism leads to wasted resources because it shifts production from the lowest-cost producers to higher-cost producers.

3. You hear more often about people who gain from trade restrictions than people who lose because the gains from trade restrictions are concentrated on a few winners, while the losses are diffused over many losers. Even though the total gains are smaller than the total losses, the concentrated benefits mean that the winners have a greater incentive to argue for trade restriction than the losers do to argue against it.

4. In Figure 9.3, area *C* represents the deadweight loss; it results from the lost gains from trades not happening.

Page 177

1. The movement of the garment trade overseas has been a net benefit for the United States because clothing is now much cheaper for U.S. consumers and U.S. workers specialize in the fields in which they are most productive.

2. If the U.S. government subsidized the Silicon Valley computer industry, it would encourage more computer chip manufacturing, but at a higher cost (production would not be as efficient). This would be a waste of resources. Foreign competitors would be pushed out of the industry. Consumers of computer chips would benefit from the subsidy, but they would benefit by less than the cost to U.S. taxpayers.

Chapter 10

Page 189

1. If the government overshoots and sets a Pigouvian tax that is too high, it will result in an equilibrium quantity that is lower than the efficient equilibrium. A tax that is too high will create a deadweight loss from too few trades. If the tax is much too high, it can be worse than leaving the externality alone.

2. If the government undershoots and provides a subsidy that is too low, the equilibrium quantity will be lower than the efficient equilibrium. In this case, there will be an undersupply.

Page 190

1. Using the Coase theorem, a solution to the prospect of elderly neighbors complaining about your party is to buy the elderly couple tickets to a movie or to a night away at a hotel. Transaction costs are low in this case: You can easily contact your neighbors and you might even pay for the gift by collecting contributions from the partygoers.

2. A solution to the polluting factory problem depends on the transactions costs. Are there many neighbors or only a few? Are the victims of the pollution located nearby or are they spread out? Is it clear whether the factory has the right to pollute, say, because it was there first and everyone moved into the area knowing about the pollution? Transaction costs are key here, because even if the factory has the right to pollute, if you and your neighbors can negotiate, you may be able to pay off the factory if it has certain property rights.

Page 196

1. A falling price for tradable pollution allowances tells us that the value of the allowance has fallen. This means that the costs of eliminating pollution have fallen—perhaps because of technological developments in clean energy.

2. If a local government sets tradable allowances for pollution in the neighborhood, some groups that would press for a large total quantity of allowances would be the big polluters: chemical factories, meat-processing

plants, sometimes automobile repair shops. Some groups that would press for a smaller total quantity of allowances would be homeowners, parents sending their children to local schools but who live outside of the immediate vicinity, the elderly. Unfortunately, there is no theorem that says the rough-and-tumble of the political process will result in an efficient equilibrium. If the political process gets it approximately right and the externality is serious, the tradable allowance system will improve social welfare but this is not guaranteed.

Chapter 11

Page 205

1. In a competitive market, if a firm prices its product above the market price, no one will buy the firm's product. Why should anyone pay more for the same product? In a competitive market, if a firm prices its product below the market price, it will sell everything it produces, but why should it set price below the market price when it can sell the same amount at the market price?

2. Demand for a competitive firm's product is perfectly elastic, portrayed as a horizontal demand curve for the firm's product. It can sell all it wants at the competitive price.

3. If there is more than one firm in the industry, then the demand for a particular firm's product is always more elastic than the demand for the product itself. The demand for each stripper well's oil is very elastic even though the demand for oil is inelastic because there are very good substitutes for the oil from a particular firm, namely the oil from any other firm.

Page 210

1. When the firm in Figure 11.2 produces 4 barrels rather than 3, $33 in additional profit is made. Going from 7 to 8 barrels, no additional profit is made. Going from 8 to 9 barrels, profit falls to −$40. Looking at the figure, $MR = MC$ when the quantity produced is 8 barrels. At this quantity, marginal profit is $0.

2. The fixed cost is the total cost when $Q = 0$, 30.

3. The profit-maximizing quantity is 8, the same as before. Changes in fixed cost do not change the profit-maximizing quantity.

Page 212

1. Profit equals (price minus average cost) times quantity, $\pi = (P - AC) \times Q$. Another way of saying this is that profit per unit is price minus average cost (the cost for each unit), and profit per unit times the number of units sold gives you total profits.

2. Assuming that the firm produces the optimal quantity (found where $P = MC$), then at any price greater than average cost, the firm is making a profit and at any price less than average cost, the firm is taking a loss.

Page 221

1. In the early stages, an automobile manufacturing industry is a decreasing cost industry because as the industry expands, it can draw on economies of scale both in auto manufacturing and in steel, plastic, and other input industries. Economies of scale, however, don't increase forever, so once the industry matures, it becomes an increasing cost industry. Today, for example, the automobile industry is an increasing cost industry because greater demand for autos means an increased demand for steel and plastic, which will drive up the price of steel and plastic, thus increasing costs in the auto industry.

2. The U.S. film industry is clustered around Hollywood because the central location leads to lower costs. Perhaps only in Hollywood could a movie director easily arrange to interview four movie stars in a single afternoon.

Chapter 12

Page 236

If Sandy's *MC* is higher than Pat's *MC*, total costs can be reduced by producing a little bit less on Sandy's farm and a little bit more on Pat's farm.

Page 238

1. In competitive markets, profits are a signal for new firms to enter. It is as if entrepreneurs see a sign flashing "Profits, Profits, Profits."

2. In competitive markets, because a firm has no control over price, its best opportunity for profits is to keep its costs low.

Chapter 13

Page 249

1. As a firm with market power moves down its demand curve, the price it can charge on all units moves down as well.

2. A firm with market power prefers to face an inelastic demand curve because the more inelastic the demand curve, the more the firm with market power can raise its price above marginal cost. See Figure 13.4 for a display of this.

Page 250

1. A monopolist always prices its product above the price of an equal cost-competitive firm.

2. A monopolist always produces less than an equal cost-competitive firm because this way it produces more profit than a competitive firm.

Page 252

1. Apple has market power and plausibly it encourages innovation. Pharmaceutical companies have an incentive by the patent system to use market power to innovate. One can argue that many utilities have market power but do not seem to be great innovators. The U.S. Postal Service has market power but does not seem to innovate much.

2. The prize for a new cancer drug should be calculated by taking the number of people expected to die of cancer over a long period, then multiplying this by the presumed willingness of people with cancer to pay for a cure, discounted for payments received over a long period, minus the probable cost of research and the low marginal cost of producing the drug. The size of the prize is likely to be enormous.

Page 258

Telephones used to be a natural monopoly because it was much cheaper for one firm to lay one set of lines and serve everyone than to have competing phone companies. Today, cell phones have broken the natural landline monopoly because cell towers cost much less to create than telephone poles and wires so it makes sense to have multiple, competing operators. In this way, technology can quickly abolish what was once a natural monopoly.

Page 260

1. Major league baseball and professional football restrict the entry of competitors in local areas, thus supporting the market power of these local teams. With market power, teams raise prices, without the fear that competitors will see the higher prices as opportunities to enter. In this case, prospective teams face more than just barriers to entry in the form of high entry costs: The leagues prohibit the teams' entry.

2. Barriers to entry are strong when they are mandated and enforced: The U.S. Postal Service still has a monopoly on delivering first-class mail, because by law other firms must charge three times as much as the Postal Service if they wish to deliver a letter. Of course, the prevalence of e-mail has made this monopoly less valuable. In contrast to this, when Congress took away the U.S. Postal Service's monopoly on the delivery of parcels, competitors such as UPS and FedEx jumped in and took over much of the market. People still send parcels through the Postal Service, but often not when delivery needs to be fast and guaranteed. NBA basketball restricts entry just as major league baseball does, and that looks to be fairly permanent for the near term, though the league may let additional teams enter over time.

Chapter 14

Page 272

1. If a monopolist segments a market, it can price-discriminate between the different segments and so raise its profits.

2. When demand is more inelastic, the price-discriminating firm would set higher prices. Remember that elasticity = escape. People with inelastic demand find it harder to escape and so will pay more.

3. Arbitrage is taking advantage of price differences for the same good in different markets by buying low in one market and selling high in another market. When the monopolist price-discriminates by setting a low price in one market and a high price in another, it creates a potential arbitrage opportunity. In order to profitably price-discriminate, the monopolist must prevent this arbitrage.

Page 276

1. The early bird special is a form of price discrimination if people who want to eat at a later time have a more inelastic demand curve. This could be true, for example, if people who want to eat at a later hour are wealthier (perhaps because they are working long hours!). An alternative explanation is that the restaurant's marginal costs increase as the restaurant becomes more crowded—thus, restaurants charge more during peak hours. In the first case, the markup of price over marginal cost increases in the later evening; in the second the firm's costs and price both increase in the later evening. It's not obvious which explanation is correct!

2. People who want to see movies right after the movies are released have a more inelastic demand for them than people who are willing to wait for the movies to be released on demand. Movie theaters know this and set their prices relatively high for those who cannot wait (have an inelastic demand). For the same reason, books are more expensive when they are first released in hardback than later when they are released in paperback. The increased costs of producing a hardback are trivial compared to the difference in price.

Page 278

1. Price discrimination is likely to increase total surplus if output increases.

2. Price discrimination helps industries with high fixed costs because profits increase with market size. Simply, having more market segments means that the price-discriminating firm can extract more consumer surplus. This leads to higher prices, which fund the high fixed costs. Universities have high fixed costs. The ability for a university to price-discriminate means it can attract more paying students to its campus and so pay for its high fixed costs.

Page 281

1. Tying cell phones to service plans is a type of price discrimination whereby high demanders (long talkers) are charged more. If cell phone companies were not allowed to tie cell phones with service plans, the price of cell phones likely would rise and the price of phone calls likely would fall. This would be good for people who want to talk a lot but bad for people who want to use their cell phone only occasionally. Profits for the cell phone companies would also fall, so there would be fewer funds to pay for the fixed costs of building cell phone towers and infrastructure.

2. Bundling is likely to increase total surplus in high-fixed-cost, low-marginal-cost industries because without some form of price discrimination, it's difficult to provide these goods at optimal levels.

Chapter 15

Page 296

1. When Great Britain found oil in the North Sea, it could obtain the benefits of OPEC (the cartel price) without any of the disadvantages of joining the cartel, such as limiting production. Why join?

2. The surprising conclusion of the prisoner's dilemma is that there are situations when the pursuit of individual interest leads to a group outcome that is in the interest of no one. Think of three cases. First, the invisible hand is a metaphor for the idea that under the right circumstances the pursuit of self-interest can lead to the social interest. Second, theft is an intermediate case where the pursuit of self-interest benefits one's self but not the social interest. Third, the prisoner's dilemma reminds us that in some circumstances when everyone pursues his or her self-interest, the result can be against the interest of everyone!

Page 300

1. Though individual auto firms try to act as if they are monopolies, they do not band together in an attempt to raise prices and cut back on quantities. Such banding together is illegal in the United States. It is not illegal in various other places in the world.

2. When a firm in an oligopoly reduces output, it shares equally in the gains from the reduction with the other firms.

Chapter 16

Page 321

1. Your old cell phone provider makes it difficult for you to take your address list to a new cell phone from a new cell phone provider as a way of setting up high switching costs in an attempt to prevent you from changing your service.

2. Google is in a contestable market because it would be fairly easy for a competitor to enter the search market, as Microsoft has done with its Bing search engine.

Page 323

A firm with an established network good such as Microsoft Office faces competition or potential competition for the market. Network monopolies can last for a long time but then evaporate very quickly.

Chapter 17

Page 334

1. Monopolistic competitors earn zero economic profits in the long run and they produce above-minimum average cost. This categorization tells us that McDonald's, Burger King, and Wendy's over the long term will earn zero economic profits, with costs higher than the minimum of average costs.

2. Monopolistic competitors produce differentiated products. In the eyes of the consumer, a hamburger is not the same at all of these firms.

Page 336

1. Wood is practically the same everywhere as far as building houses is concerned. Windows are a differentiated product. Thick and double-paned windows with various cold-stopping features are manufactured for northern climates. There may be a benefit for an individual firm to advertise differentiated products, unlike similar products such as wood.

2. Famous athletes' endorsement of sports products that they use informs us that the product is of superior quality. Even if the product has nothing to do with sports, the endorsement signals quality rather than providing information.

Chapter 18

Page 343

The marginal product of labor falls as more workers are hired because the first worker will focus on the most important tasks and so the marginal product of labor will be high. The next worker will focus on the next important tasks, but these tasks will not be as important as those the first worker tackled, so the marginal product of labor will not be as high as for the first worker. As more workers are hired, they do progressively less important tasks, so their marginal product falls relative to the first workers.

Page 345

An individual's labor supply curve might be backward-bending because at some point, individuals might prefer more leisure to working more, even at a higher wage. In other words, one of the things that people may buy more of when their wage goes up is leisure.

Page 352

1. An increase in mine safety would lower the wages of miners because mine workers are paid extra money to undertake their risky jobs. Making the job less risky would increase the number of people willing to be miners and thus would drive down wages.

2. Firms will pay for human capital improvements if the firm can reap the benefit. Training on a firm's specific inventory techniques will help the firm, but this is a skill that it is difficult for a worker to take to other firms, so the firm need not pay a higher wage to individuals with specific training. In this sense, the firm reaps the benefit of this training exclusively. In contrast, an MBA provides skills that can be used by many firms, so an individual with an MBA can earn a higher wage at other firms. In order to benefit from training an individual with general skills, the firm must keep the individual around at the lower wage long enough to recover its costs. Thus, the time requirement helps the firm recover a large portion of its investment in the worker.

Page 358

1. Employer discrimination is dumb or at least costly from a profit-making perspective because hiring equally good workers at a lower wage increases profit.

2. Market economies have had the most effect on eliminating discrimination by employers because the profit motive is a powerful incentive—notice that the more employers discriminate against minorities, the greater the profit from hiring a minority worker. Market economies have had some success in mitigating customer discrimination because market transactions bring different groups into regular contact with each other and thereby break down barriers. Market economies have had the toughest time eliminating employee discrimination because this type of discrimination can be self-reinforcing.

Chapter 19

Page 371

If government provides more of national defense than is efficient, it is pulling resources away from other, more valuable goods and having taxpayers bear the burden. People with a very strong preference for national defense would perhaps benefit as well as those involved in providing national defense.

Page 372

1. Advertising could be used to pay for the upkeep of public parks. Advertising could be seen in obvious places such as signs by entryways to the park, on garbage cans, or on the sides of refreshment stands. If there is a music bandshell or a stage (in larger parks), advertising could be seen on the sides of these structures. Notice that under the Adopt-a-Highway program, advertising on roads supports road cleanup.

2. Airports charge for Wi-Fi because they can make money from it by excluding nonpayers. Since more Wi-Fi users don't (usually) increase congestion by appreciable amounts, it would be more efficient to allow open access.

Page 376

1. Small communities find it easier to deal with common resource problems than states or nations because they have an easier time enforcing norms (standards of behavior) that reduce free riding. Even so, the more unrelated people that have access to a common good, the harder it is to deal with common resource problems.

2. The establishment of property rights can help solve the tragedy of the commons because people who have property rights have no incentive to overuse a resource. The tragedy of the commons occurs because people have an incentive to overuse common resources: to get theirs before someone else takes it.

Chapter 20

Page 387

National voters have a smaller chance of influencing the election than do local voters, which suggests that people have a greater incentive to be informed about local issues. On the other hand, local issues are less important than national issues and there is less free information (e.g., from online news sources like BuzzFeed or news satire like *The Daily Show*) about local issues than about national issues, which suggests local voters would be even more rationally ignorant than national voters.

Page 391

1. Because of the benefits that special interests receive from current programs, they would fight against the establishment of a commission to examine federal waste. If the commission was set up, these special interests would then try to "capture" the commission: argue that their specific

programs were needed, and exert political pressure to keep these programs. The bearers of the costs of these programs—the taxpayers—are too large and diverse a group to zero in on any particular program. The commission idea might be popular, but the chance of its success is low.

2. The beneficiaries of the local history collection at the library are the users of the collection. Ultimately, the taxpayers of the state pay for it. Benefits are concentrated on a small group, while the costs are spread over a large body of people (the taxpayers). Don't be surprised if the reading room is named after the state senator!

Page 393

If voters are myopic, politicians could prefer a policy with small gains now and big costs later (let's get reelected and maybe someone else will have to deal with the large costs down the road) than a policy with small costs now and large gains later (why jeopardize my chance to get reelected?). For these reasons, dealing with a large potential problem, such as the fiscal sustainability of Medicare, is often put off until the last minute when the solutions are much more difficult and costly.

Page 400

The free flow of ideas helps democracies function by getting alternatives out and on the table. Voters will always be rationally ignorant to some extent, but the more information that is out there and available at low cost, the more voters will be informed, at least about the big issues. Debate and dissent can improve the quality of ideas. The free flow of information reduces the possibility of corruption. New ideas help democracies adapt to changing conditions.

Chapter 21

Page 418

It is plausible that total utility would go up with kidney redistribution because the receiver gains more utility from a kidney that gives him or her life than the giver loses. Kidney redistribution would also tend to make the worst off better off, at least if we count dying of kidney disease as putting one in the worst off category. There is, however, lots of room for debate on these issues.

Page 419

Surprisingly, all of the theories tend to support immigration. The libertarian theory places strong value on an individual's right to move and engage in peaceful trade, which is what most immigrants want to do. As we argue in the text, immigrants gain much more from immigration than current citizens lose, so utilitarianism also supports immigrants. Finally, being under the veil of ignorance, you don't know whether you are the immigrant or not. If you didn't know which side of the border you were born on, wouldn't you favor immigration?

Philosophers debate these issues but those are the basic considerations.

Chapter 22

Page 429

1. Workers sometimes fear that if they work harder under a piece rate system, they will work themselves out of a job. Lincoln's policy of guaranteed employment reassures workers that productivity will always work to their advantage, not to their detriment.

2. It is sometimes said that the word "tips" stands for "To Insure Prompt Service." Certainly, the idea is that restaurant customers will give bigger tips the better the service, thus giving waiters an incentive to be attentive. Thus, we would predict that waiters would be less attentive in Europe where the tip is typically automatic than in America where it usually is not.

Page 434

1. Professors have an incentive to be known as hard graders because this reputation will keep away all but the serious students and maybe also all but the brightest students. Grading on a curve would encourage the usual diverse spectrum of students, from serious to indifferent and from smart to struggling.

2. In a tournament, one worker's gain is another's loss. Sometimes tournaments can encourage too much competition by discouraging cooperation. If a firm wants its sales staff to work together to land sales, for example, then it would not want a strong tournament scheme. Professors who want their students to work together on projects should not grade on a curve.

Page 437

1. A famous paper in economics calculated that, on average, $10 spent on gifts was worth only $8 to the gift recipients. In other words, when your Uncle gives you $10 in cash, you get $10 worth of utility, but when your Uncle gives you a $10 pair of socks, on average, you get only $8 worth of utility. Thus, according to the author of the study, Joel Waldfogel, Christmas wastes billions of dollars. Even though most people understand this idea when it is explained to them, we don't see a big shift to giving cash. Why not? Perhaps gift giving is valuable precisely because it is challenging. If you spend $10 giving something to someone that they value for $50, this shows how much you must really understand and care for them. Or perhaps we want the gift giver to buy something for us that we would not have bought for ourselves. Or perhaps people give gifts to signal something about themselves. Giving someone a CD of Bach sonatas says something about you that a gift of $15 does not. Understanding the answer to this question may tell us a lot about social life. See Waldfogel, Joel. 1993, December. The deadweight loss of Christmas. *The American Economic Review* 83(5): 1328–1336.

2. Maybe. Maybe not. If we pay for grades, some people worry that this will stifle the love of learning and perhaps send the message that getting good grades is like a job that the student is free to quit at any time. A number of experiments are currently under way testing these ideas.

Chapter 23

Page 449

According to the efficient markets hypothesis, one cannot consistently beat the market. Therefore, past performance is not a good guide to future success. On average, mutual funds that have performed well in the past are no more likely to perform well in the future than mutual funds that have performed poorly in the past.

Page 455

1. Investing in the stocks of other countries helps to diversify your investments because the economies of other countries do not always rise and fall at the same time as the U.S. economy. If all economies tended to rise and fall together, there would not be any large benefits in diversifying across countries.

2. If many people dream of owning a football or baseball team, it is likely that the rewards to owning one go beyond monetary rewards. Thus, the monetary return on these assets is likely to be relatively low.

Page 457

This question is being hotly debated by many economists. It can be said that identifying and bursting bubbles is more difficult than it looks. How does the Federal Reserve know when there is a bubble? Increases in prices do not necessarily signify a bubble. Even if it can be said to be fairly certain that a bubble is present, how does the Federal Reserve burst the bubble while avoiding widespread collateral damage?

Chapter 24

Page 465

Consumer Reports has no vested interest in any of the products it evaluates, so this minimizes moral hazard.

Page 468

Real Picassos are rare and valuable, meaning that they don't need to be put on eBay to foster high prices. The Picassos listed on eBay are probably fakes.

Chapter 25

Page 487

1.

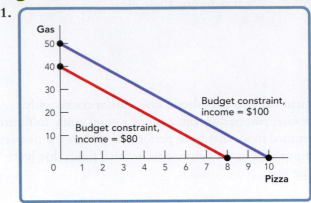

2.

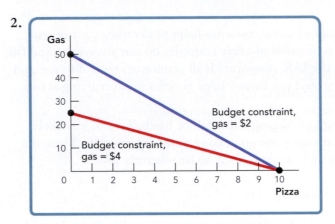

3. No, the relative price of pizza has not changed.

Page 489

1. Indifference curves can never cross because each consumption bundle must correspond to a unique total utility level.

2. Indifference curves must have a negative slope because more is better.

Chapter 26

Page 509

1. The purchase of wheat flour used to make bread is the purchase of an intermediate good. Thus, it is not counted in GDP: Only finished goods are counted in GDP.

2. Pokemon cards were counted in GDP when they were first produced. Selling used Pokemon cards on eBay does not contribute to GDP.

3. Because the worker from Colombia earns his money in New York, this is considered part of the GDP of the United States, not Colombia. GDP counts what is produced within a country, whether by its citizens or others.

Page 510

The growth rate is found by subtracting $5,803 billion from $5,995 billion, and then dividing that number by $5,803 billion:

($5,995 − $5,803) ÷ $5,803 = $192 ÷ $5,803 = 0.033, or 3.3%

Page 512

1. China has a high GDP but a low GDP per capita.

2. Of the top 10 countries ranked by GDP in Table 26.1, the United Kingdom and France have GDP under $2.5 trillion but have considerable GDP per capita.

3. We convert nominal variables into real variables to account for price changes so that we can make comparisons over time.

Page 514

1. Business fluctuations are the short-run movements in real GDP around its long-term trend.

2. It is sometimes difficult to determine if an economy is in a recession because of simple data problems. It takes time to collect data, then the conclusions drawn from the data may be revised once additional data become available after additional time has passed.

Page 518

1. Consumption (C) is the largest component of national expenditure, averaging 63.1%.

2. Consumption expenditures are more stable than investment expenditures. It's usually easier to delay investment than consumption, so consumption normally varies only slightly, but investment expenditure can vary dramatically, especially in an economic downturn, as businesses hold off on investment. For these reasons, the part of consumption that is most volatile is consumption of durable goods such as cars and major appliances, because the purchase of these goods can usually be easily delayed.

3. The income approach is the flip side of the spending approach: Every dollar that someone earns in income is a dollar of income that someone else has spent.

Page 522

1. GDP measures things for which market values can be obtained. It does not measure things such as illegal activities or clean air because it is difficult to determine their market values.

2. Two countries that have the same level of GDP per capita do not necessarily have the same level of inequality. Let's take Country A and Country B, each of which has only two citizens. Country A's citizens earn $999 and $1, respectively, with GDP per capita of $500. Country B's citizens earn $500 and $500, respectively, with GDP per capita of $500 also. Note that the two countries have the same GDP per capita but they have different levels of inequality.

3. Because they do not account for everything, GDP statistics are not perfect. Nevertheless, they are useful in giving a good sense of how the value of what a nation produces changes over time.

Chapter 27

Page 535

1. According to Figure 27.2, approximately 30% of the world's population lived in China in 2014.

2. Using the rule of 70, if you make 5% on your savings, it will take 70/5 or 12 years for your savings to double. At 8%, it will take 70/8 or a little under 9 years to double.

3. According to Figure 27.4, Japan's real GDP per capita crossed the $10,000 barrier around 1970 and the $20,000 barrier around 1990. Using the rule of 70, we know that it took 20 years to double, or $70/x = 20$. Therefore, the growth rate was approximately 3.5% per year over this time span.

Page 537

1. The United States has much more physical capital—tools, machines, equipment—than China, but China has more than Nigeria.

2. Physical capital, human capital, and technological knowledge are the three primary factors of production.

Page 545

1. Five institutions that promote economic growth are property rights, honest government, political stability, a dependable legal system, and competitive and open markets.

2. Under a system of collective farming where corn production was shared, increased individual effort would bring very little reward to the individual. Because individual incentives were poor, you would expect limited corn production, maybe even starvation.

Chapter 28

Page 563

1. In Figure 28.6, when the capital stock is 400, depreciation is higher than investment.

2. When capital is 400, investment is 6 units.

3. When capital is 400, depreciation is 8 units.

4. When depreciation is greater than investment, the capital stock shrinks.

Page 566

1. As more capital is added, the marginal product of capital declines.

2. Capital depreciates because machines wear out over time and have to be replaced, roads wear out and need to be repaired or replaced, bridges wear out. As the capital stock increases, the total amount of capital depreciation increases.

Page 569

1. At the steady-state level of capital, investment and depreciation are equal.

2. In Figure 28.7, output is 15 units available to be consumed in the old steady state, and 20 units in the new steady state.

3. The farther they are below their steady-state level, the more quickly countries can grow.

4. Countries with higher investment rates have higher GDP per capita.

Page 573

1. High tax rates on imports would reduce trade and thus lower the incentive to produce new ideas.

2. Spillovers occur when ideas benefit other consumers and firms, besides the creator of the idea. If the creator of an idea cannot get the full benefit of the idea, this will reduce the incentive to generate new ideas.

3. The economic reason to support a prize for malaria research rather than cancer research is that the incentive to produce cancer drugs is already high because of a large and wealthy market. Malaria tends to be located in poorer countries where people have a lower ability to pay for drugs and thus the incentive to develop new drugs is lower.

Chapter 29

Page 591

1. Financial institutions build a bridge between savers and borrowers.

2. If people have saved enough for their retirement, they can have a smooth consumption path over their lives. If greater life expectancy means that not enough has been saved for retirement, then consumption during the retirement years will have to be lower than currently planned. Thus, the consumption path throughout their lifetimes will not be smooth.

3. Other than retirement, numerous potential things can generate a demand to save because these things can cause income to be volatile: loss of a job, chronic illness, or accidents that cause some bodily harm. One saves for a rainy day.

Page 593

1. Under the lifecycle theory, individual savings are likely to be at their peak during an individual's prime earning years.

2. If interest rates fall from 7% to 5%, all else being equal, this is a fall in the price of borrowed funds. This fall in price will encourage more people to buy homes (they now may be able to afford something they could not afford before) or start businesses.

Page 596

1. Greater patience will shift the supply of savings curve to the right, leading to an increase in the quantity of savings and a decrease in the equilibrium interest rate.

2. An increase in investment demand shifts the demand curve to the right, leading to an increase in the equilibrium interest rate and an increase in the quantity of funds demanded and supplied.

Page 601

1. The primary role of financial intermediaries is to reduce the costs of moving savings from savers to borrowers and investors.

2. Interest rates and bond prices move in opposite directions. If you own a bond paying 6% in interest and the interest rate falls to 4%, the price of the bond must go up. If interest rates rise to 8%, the price of the 6% bond must fall.

3. An IPO is a first-time sale of a firm's stock to the market, and so usually increases net investment: The firm can take this new capital and use it to expand the business. Buying shares of stock from someone else, in contrast, is buying shares already issued and represents a transfer of ownership, not a net increase to investment: The firm does not get the purchase price of the stock.

Page 609

1. Usury laws are price ceilings. Remember from our chapter on Price Ceilings and Price Floors that price ceilings cause shortages. If savers can get only the ceiling rate rather than the market rate for their savings, they will save less.

2. Bank failures can hinder financial intermediation in a variety of ways. If savers become reluctant to put their money in banks, for example, the supply of credit will decline and the cost of borrowing will rise. This can lead to a credit crisis as credit dries up.

3. Lending money to political cronies, or pals, lowers the efficiency of the economy because loans do not go to their highest-valued uses.

Chapter 30

Page 627

1. Frictional unemployment is caused by the ordinary difficulties of matching employee to employer. A reason for the difficulty of matching employer to employee is scarcity of information.

2. Some frictional unemployment is not bad if it means that prospective employers and prospective employees take the time to determine whether they are a good fit. Being forced to take the first job offered is not a good way to establish a good fit.

Page 634

1. Structural unemployment is persistent, long-term unemployment caused by long-lasting shocks or permanent features of an economy that make it more difficult for some workers to find jobs.

2. In the United States, "employment at-will" fairly accurately describes the employment situation: Employees may quit at any time and employers

may fire an employee at any time and for any reason. In contrast, laws in Western European countries hinder the ability of employers to act at will. For example, in Portugal any business must get the government's permission to lay off workers, and even then the business must follow guidelines as to who can be laid off first.

Page 638

1. Cyclical unemployment is determined by the business cycle. It increases during a recession and decreases during a boom.

2. Lower growth is correlated with increasing unemployment; higher growth is correlated with decreasing unemployment.

Page 643

1. Lowering the marginal tax rate for married couples provided an incentive for more women to enter the labor force because they could now keep more of their pay rather than have it taxed away.

2. Raising the age that one can obtain Social Security benefits increases the incentive to stay in the labor force longer, thus increasing the labor force participation rate.

Chapter 31

Page 653

1. Using the formula on page 650, $(125 - 120) \div 120 = 4.16\%$.

2. If the inflation rate goes from 1% to 4% to 7% over a period of two years, the prices of a great majority of goods are likely to go up.

3. Use real prices rather than nominal prices to compare the price of goods over time. Real prices subtract out the effect of inflation and thus give a better measure of whether a particular good is becoming more or less expensive over time compared to most other goods and services.

Page 658

1. In the long run, inflation is always and everywhere a monetary phenomenon: Growth in the money supply causes inflation.

2. The quantity theory of money is $Mv = PY_R$.

Page 665

1. Under unexpected inflation, wealth is redistributed from lenders to borrowers. Under unexpected disinflation, wealth is redistributed from borrowers to lenders.

2. When the expected inflation rate increases, nominal interest rates rise to compensate. We call this the Fisher effect.

3. Unexpected inflation distorts price signals. They become more difficult to interpret. This leads to waste.

Chapter 32

Page 675

1. Because $\vec{M} + \vec{v} = \vec{P} + \vec{Y}_R$ in the AD/AS model, if $\vec{M}$ equals 7% and $\vec{v}$ equals 0%, by definition inflation plus real growth will equal 7%. If in this situation we find that real growth equals 0%, then inflation must be 7%.

2. Increased spending growth shifts the aggregate demand curve outward.

Page 682

1. Putting down phone lines is very expensive, compared to the cost of putting up cell phone towers. Cell phones have improved communications in all countries, but the change has been most dramatic in less developed countries. This has been a positive shock throughout the world.

2. A large and sudden increase in taxes would suppress economic activity, especially in the short run, as consumers and firms reallocated from more energy-intensive sectors of the economy to less energy-intensive sectors. The reallocation would decrease the fundamental capacity of the economy to produce goods and services, which is a shift of the long-run aggregate supply curve to the left.

Page 687

1. The long-run aggregate supply curve is vertical because price and wage stickiness does not affect the fundamental productive capacity of the economy over the long run. However, price and wage stickiness does affect aggregate supply in the short run, and this accounts for the fact that the SRAS curve is *not* vertical.

2. In the short run, inflation expectations may deviate from actual inflation, and spending growth can lead to some GDP growth.

3. In the long run, inflation expectations equal actual inflation.

Page 689

1. In the long run, unexpected inflation always becomes expected inflation.

2. If consumers fear a recession and cut back on their expenditures, the aggregate demand curve will shift inward.

Page 693

1. The U.S. money supply fell in the early 1930s. This initially affected aggregate demand (the AD curve shifted inward—down/left), not the long-run aggregate supply curve. The decrease in aggregate demand resulted in bank failures that decreased the productivity of financial intermediation, which was a real shock, and so affected the long-run aggregate supply curve, shifting it to the left.

2. In an ordinary year, the real shocks of the 1930s might have been shrugged off but the combination of large shocks to AD and real shocks at the same time made the Great Depression great.

Chapter 33

Page 709

The 9/11 attacks brought a high level of uncertainty into the economy. No one knew if more attacks were planned so no one wanted to be on an airplane. Cutting back on air travel hurt the airlines and all associated businesses: airports, airport services such as food vendors, companies that provide transportation to and from airports. When no one flew on airplanes to take business trips, some local business trips were still undertaken (by train or car), but longer trips (such as cross-country travel) came to a standstill. As travel declined, so did the need for hotel rooms and restaurant meals. Hotels were hit hard: Cutting the price of hotel rooms had little effect when uncertainty dried up business travel. The near-cessation in business travel amplified the economic effects of the attacks nationwide: The attacks in New York City and Washington, D.C., had nationwide repercussions.

Chapter 34

Page 720

1. The monetary base is defined as currency plus reserves held by banks at the Fed.

2. In September 2016, there was approximately $1.5 trillion of currency in the United States compared to around approximately $1.9 trillion in checkable deposits. Thus, currency accounts for slightly less than checkable deposits.

Page 722

1. If the reserve ratio is 1/20, then 5% of deposits are kept as reserves.

2. If the reserve ratio is 1/20, then the money multiplier is 20.

3. If the Fed increases bank reserves by $10,000 and the reserve ratio is 1/20, then the change in the money supply is $200,000.

Page 726

1. The Fed wants to lower interest rates. It does so by *buying* bonds in open market operations. By doing this, the Fed *adds* reserves and through the multiplier process, it *increases* the money supply.

2. An increase in the amount paid on reserves will draw money from other sectors of the economy, decreasing aggregate demand.

Page 729

1. The Fed might not let a large bank fail if it fears systemic risk, the possibility that the failure will bring down other banks and financial institutions. In this case, the Fed will use its powers as the lender of last resort to support a bank that is "too big to fail."

2. Moral hazard increases my incentives to double my bet to make up for a large loss. If the Fed always bails out large banks, my actions will never lead to the bank's bankruptcy, so why not take the chance?

Page 731

1. Money is neutral in the long run but has a short-run effect on the economy. This explains the Fed's concerns with the money supply in the short run.

2. If banks are afraid of a recession, they will be more reluctant to lend. This will hamper the Fed's ability to shift aggregate demand in a recession. In this case, the Fed is sometimes said to be "pushing on a string."

Chapter 35

Page 746

Data problems affect the Fed's ability to set monetary policy that is "just right" because the problems make it difficult for the Fed to determine just what is going on with the economy. If the Fed does not know exactly what is going on, it cannot prescribe the correct medicine.

Page 748

1. If the Fed wanted to restore some growth to the economy, it could work to increase aggregate demand. The problem is that increasing growth in this case comes at the expense of adding more inflation. This is the policy dilemma.

2. If the Fed increases AD every time as a response to a series of negative real shocks, the inflation rate will climb. Eventually, the Fed will have to act to reduce inflation, possibly pushing the economy into a recession.

Page 752

1. The Fed can never be certain when asset prices reach the bubble stage. Bubbles are easier to identify with hindsight, but even then identification is a judgment call.

2. Collateral damage to a contraction in the money supply could be reducing the growth rate for GDP for the broader economy as a whole.

Page 753

Milton Friedman argued for a 3% money growth rate because the long-run growth rate for the U.S. economy trends around 3%. When money growth equals long-run growth in the economy, there will be a tendency for price stability.

Chapter 36

Page 771

1. Individual income taxes plus Social Security and Medicare taxes represent 83% of federal revenues.

2. A person in the fourth quintile pays an average federal tax rate of 17.4%. On an income of $80,000, this would be $13,920 in tax. A person in the top quintile pays an average rate of 25.5% on income of $160,000, thus a tax of $40,800. Because the person who made twice as much paid more than twice as much in tax, this gives evidence of progressivity in the tax system.

Page 779

1. According to Figure 36.4, in 2017, Social Security and Medicare spending accounted for just under 40% of federal spending.

2. GDP gives us an idea of the capacity of the economy to pay debt, so the debt-to-GDP ratio tells us what the debt is relative to the capacity to pay the debt.

Page 781

1. In the next 40 years, Social Security and especially Medicare and Medicaid are likely to increase relative to GDP. This means that the level of overall government spending relative to GDP is likely to increase.

2. If the pace of idea generation quickens, this will lead to a positive shift in the long-run aggregate supply growth curve. In other words, the economy will be able to produce more goods and services. This would lead to a decrease in the debt-to-GDP ratio (all other things equal). This would increase the government's ability to pay for increased benefits for retirees.

Chapter 37

Page 795

The two types of expansionary fiscal policy are: the government spends more money, or the government cuts taxes and thereby gives people more money to spend.

Page 799

1. The 2008 tax rebate was less powerful than expected because many people saved the rebate and paid down debt, rather than spending the extra money.

2. A permanent cut in income tax rates can generate a larger fiscal stimulus than a temporary cut because people likely will save a large portion of a temporary tax cut, to pay for future taxes. But if the tax cut is permanent, they may choose to spend more. Of course, telling people that a tax cut is permanent is quite different from getting people to *believe* that it is permanent!

3. A permanent investment tax credit produces a smaller fiscal stimulus than a temporary investment tax credit because to get the temporary tax credit, firms must spend money on equipment right away; a permanent investment tax credit, however, gives firms the option of waiting to invest.

Chapter 38

Page 817

1. If an inhabitant of Nebraska buys a German sports car for $30,000, this lowers the U.S. current account balance by $30,000.

2. If a German sports car manufacturer opens a new plant in South Carolina, this investment is a capital account surplus for the United States.

3. The current and capital accounts are two sides of the same coin. When the capital account is in surplus, the current account will tend to mirror that in deficit, and vice versa.

Page 824

1. If the U.S. dollar is a safe haven currency, then in times of risk people will demand dollars, increasing their value.

2. If the Fed increases the money supply, this will reduce the value of the dollar compared to the euro.

3. If purchasing power parity holds and the nominal exchange rate is 1 pound for 2 dollars, a Big Mac should cost £2 in London if it costs $4.00 in New York.

4. A tariff will hinder market exchange and thus the arbitrage of differing prices. This limits purchasing power parity.

Page 827

1. In the short run, a Fed increase in the money supply will cause a depreciation in the exchange rate, leading to an increase in U.S. exports. In the long run, the temporary boost to exports will dissipate, and the increase in the money supply will lead to inflation.

2. In an open economy, monetary policy is more effective than fiscal policy. Expansionary monetary policy will tend to reduce interest rates, causing a currency depreciation and increased exports. In contrast, expansionary fiscal policy will tend to increase interest rates, causing an appreciation of the exchange rate and reduced exports.

Page 829

1. A floating exchange rate describes when the value of a country's currency is determined by the forces of supply and demand.

2. The European Central Bank controls the monetary policy of the European Union.

GLOSSARY

absolute advantage the ability to produce the same good using fewer inputs than another producer

accounting profit total revenue minus explicit costs

active labor market policies policies that focus on getting unemployed workers back to work, such as job-search assistance, job-retraining programs, and work tests

adverse selection when an offer conveys negative information about the product being offered

aggregate demand curve curve that shows all the combinations of inflation and real growth that are consistent with a specified rate of spending growth $(\vec{M} + \vec{v})$

aggregate demand shock a rapid and unexpected shift in the AD curve (spending)

alternative minimum tax (AMT) a separate income tax code, begun in 1969 to prevent the rich from not paying income taxes; not indexed to inflation and thus now an extra tax burden on many upper middle class families

antitrust laws laws that give the federal government legal authority to prosecute monopolies or attempts to monopolize

appreciation an increase in the price of one currency in terms of another currency

arbitrage the practice of taking advantage of price differences for the same good in different markets by buying low in one market and selling high in another market

asymmetric information when one party to an exchange has more or better information than the other party

automatic stabilizers changes in fiscal policy that stimulate AD in a recession without the need for explicit action by policymakers;

unemployment insurance is one example of an automatic stabilizer

average cost the cost per unit; the total cost of producing a given quantity divided by that quantity, $AC = TC/Q$

average tax rate the total tax payment divided by total income

baby boomers people born during the high-birth-rate years of 1946–1964

balance of payments a yearly summary of all the economic transactions between residents of one country and residents of the rest of the world

barriers to entry factors that increase the cost to new firms of entering an industry

bond a sophisticated IOU that documents who owes how much and when payment must be made

budget constraint all the consumption bundles that a consumer can afford given his or her income and their prices

bundling the requirement that products be bought together in a bundle or package

business fluctuations (or business cycles) the short-run movements in real GDP around its long-term trend

buy and hold the practice of buying stocks and then holding them for the long run, regardless of what prices do in the short run

capital account in the balance of payments, the account that measures changes in foreign ownership of domestic assets, including financial assets like stocks and bonds as well as physical assets

capital surplus (also called *capital inflow*) the excess that exists when the inflow of foreign capital into a country is greater than the outflow of domestic capital

cartel a group of suppliers that tries to act *as if* they were a monopoly

catching-up growth growth due to capital accumulation and adopting already existing ideas

club goods goods that are excludable but nonrival

Coase theorem the principle that if transactions costs are low and property rights are clearly defined, private bargains will ensure that the market equilibrium is efficient even when there are externalities

collateral something of value that helps to secure a loan; if the borrower defaults, ownership of the collateral transfers to the lender

collateral shock a reduction in the value of collateral; collateral shocks make borrowing and lending more difficult

common resources goods that are nonexcludable but rival

comparative advantage the ability to produce a good or service at a lower opportunity cost than another producer

compensating differential a difference in wages that offsets differences in working conditions for otherwise similar jobs

complements two goods for which a decrease in the price of one leads to an increase in the demand for the other, for example hamburgers and hamburger buns

conditional convergence the tendency—among countries with similar steady state levels of output—for poorer countries to grow faster than richer countries and thus for poor and rich countries to converge in income

constant cost industry an industry in which costs of production do not change with greater industry output; shown with a flat supply curve

consumer surplus the consumer's gain from exchange, or the difference between the maximum price a consumer is willing to pay for a certain quantity and the market price

consumer surplus (total) quantity measured by the area beneath the demand curve and above the price

consumption private spending on finished goods and services

contestable market condition in which a competitor could credibly enter and take away business from the incumbent

coordination game game in which the players are better off if they choose the same strategies than if they choose different strategies when there is more than one strategy on which to potentially coordinate

corporate culture the shared collection of values and norms that govern how people interact in an organization or firm

counter-cyclical fiscal policy fiscal policy that runs opposite or counter to the business cycle—spending more when the economy is in a recession and less when the economy is booming

credible promise a strategy or promise is credible if it is in an agent's interest to follow through on that strategy or keep the promise

crowding out the decrease in private consumption and investment that occurs when government borrows more; also, the decrease in private spending that occurs when government increases spending

current account in the balance of payments, the sum of the balance of trade, net income on capital held abroad, and net transfer payments

cutting-edge growth growth due to new ideas

cyclical unemployment unemployment correlated with the business cycle

deadweight loss the reduction in total surplus caused by a market distortion or inefficiency

decreasing cost industry an industry in which the costs of production decrease with an increase in industry output; shown with a downward-sloped supply curve

deficit the annual difference between federal spending and revenues

deficit, trade see trade deficit

deflation a decrease in the average level of prices; that is, a negative inflation rate

demand curve a function that shows the quantity demanded at different prices

depreciation a decrease in the price of a currency in terms of another currency

diminishing marginal utility each additional unit of a good adds less to utility than the previous unit

dirty (or managed) float a currency whose value is not fixed but for which governments will intervene extensively in the market to keep its value within a certain range

discount rate the interest rate banks pay when they borrow directly from the Fed at the discount window

discouraged workers jobless individuals who have given up looking for work but who would still like to find a job

disinflation a reduction in the inflation rate

dollarization a foreign country's use of the U.S. dollar as its currency

dominant strategy a strategy that has a higher payoff than any other strategy no matter the strategies of other players

economic growth the growth rate of real GDP per capita:

$$g_t = \frac{Y_t - Y_{t-1}}{Y_{t-1}} \times 100$$

where Y_t is real per capita GDP in period t

economic profit total revenue minus total costs including implicit opportunity costs

economies of scale the advantages of large-scale production that reduce average cost as quantity increases

efficient equilibrium the price and quantity that maximizes social surplus

efficient markets hypothesis the claim that the prices of traded assets reflect all publicly available information

efficient quantity the quantity that maximizes social surplus

elastic when the absolute value of the elasticity is greater than 1

elasticity of demand $= \dfrac{\% \Delta \mathbf{Q}_D}{\% \Delta \mathbf{P}}$

a measure of how responsive the quantity demanded is to a change in price

elasticity of supply $= \dfrac{\% \Delta \mathbf{Q}_S}{\% \Delta \mathbf{P}}$

a measure of how responsive the quantity supplied is to a change in price

elimination principle the principle that in a competitive market, above-normal profits are eliminated by entry and below-normal profits are eliminated by exit

employment at-will doctrine the policy that an employee may quit and an employer may fire an employee at any time and for any reason; the most basic U.S. employment law despite many exceptions to it

equilibrium price the price at which the quantity demanded is equal to the quantity supplied

equilibrium quantity the quantity at which the quantity demanded is equal to the quantity supplied

equity the value of the asset minus the debt, $E = V - D$

exchange rate the price of one currency in terms of another currency

explicit cost a cost that requires a money outlay

external benefit a benefit received by people other than the consumers or producers trading in the market

external cost a cost borne by people other than the consumer or the producer trading in the market

externalities external costs or external benefits

federal funds rate the overnight lending rate from one major bank to another

financial intermediaries institutions such as banks, bond markets, and stock markets that reduce the costs of moving funds from savers to borrowers and investors

fiscal policy federal government policy on taxes, spending, and borrowing that is designed to influence business fluctuations

Fisher effect the tendency of nominal interest rates to rise one to one with expected inflation rates

fixed costs costs that do not vary with the quantity produced

fixed exchange rate (also known as a **pegged exchange rate**) an exchange rate based on the promise of a government or central bank to convert its currency into another currency at a fixed (set) rate

flat tax an income tax with the same tax rate on all levels of income (compare with progressive and regressive tax)

floating exchange rate an exchange rate determined primarily by market forces

forced rider someone who pays a share of the costs of a public good but who does not enjoy the benefits

fractional reserve banking a system in which banks hold only a portion of deposits in reserve, lending the rest

free rider someone who consumes the benefits of a public good without paying a share of the costs

frictional unemployment short-term unemployment caused by the ordinary difficulties of matching employee to employer

futures a standardized contract to buy or sell specified quantities of a commodity or financial instrument at a specified price with delivery set at a specified time in the future

government purchases spending by all levels of government on finished goods and services not including transfers

great economic problem how to arrange our scarce resources to satisfy as many of our wants as possible

gross domestic product (GDP) the market value of all finished goods and services produced within a country in a year

gross domestic product (GDP) per capita GDP divided by population

gross national product (GNP) the market value of all finished goods and services produced by a country's residents, wherever located, in a year

human capital tools of the mind; the productive knowledge and skills that workers acquire through education, training, and experience

illiquid asset an asset that cannot be quickly converted into cash without a large loss in value; note that a bank could be illiquid but not insolvent

illiquid bank a bank whose short-term liabilities are greater than its short-term assets but overall has assets that are greater than its liabilities

implicit cost a cost that does not require an outlay of money

incentives rewards and penalties that motivate behavior

income effect the change in consumption caused by the change in purchasing power from a price change

increasing cost industry an industry in which the costs of production increase with greater output; shown with an upward-sloped supply curve

inelastic when the absolute value of the elasticity is less than 1

inferior good a good for which demand decreases when income increases

inflation an increase in the general or average level of prices.

$$\text{inflation rate} = \frac{P_2 - P_1}{P_1} \times 100$$

the percentage increase in the average level of prices (as measured by a price index) over a period of time

initial public offering (IPO) the first instance of a corporation selling stock to the public in order to raise capital

internalizing an externality adjusting incentives so that decision makers take into account all the benefits and costs of their actions, private and social

insolvent bank/institution a bank or institution whose liabilities are greater in value than its assets

institutions the "rules of the game" that structure economic incentives

intertemporal substitution the allocation of consumption, work, and leisure across time to maximize wellbeing

investment the purchase of new capital goods; private spending on tools, plant, and equipment used to produce future output

investment expenditures private spending on tools, plant, and equipment used to produce future output; that is the purchase of new capital goods

irreversible investments investments that cannot be easily moved, adjusted, or reversed if conditions change

labor adjustment costs the costs of shifting workers from declining sectors of the economy to growing sectors

labor force all workers, employed plus unemployed

labor force participation rate the percentage of adults in the labor force

law of one price the principle that if trade were free, then identical goods will sell for about the same price throughout the world

lender of last resort a lender that loans money to banks and other financial institutions when no one else will, often a central bank or a country's Treasury or Finance department

leverage ratio the ratio of debt to equity, D/E

liquid asset an asset that can be used for payments or, quickly and without loss of value, be converted into an asset that can be used for payments

liquidity trap situation in which interest rates are close to the zero lower bound, so pushing them lower is not possible or not effective at increasing aggregate demand

long run the time it takes for substantial new investment and entry to occur

long-run aggregate supply curve (LRAS) a vertical line at the Solow growth rate

marginal cost (*MC*) the change in total cost from producing an additional unit

marginal product of capital the increase in output caused by the addition of one more unit of capital; the marginal product of capital diminishes as more and more capital is added

marginal product of labor (MPL) the increase in a firm's revenues created by hiring an additional laborer

marginal rate of substitution (MRS) the rate at which the consumer is willing to trade one good for another and remain indifferent; the MRS is equal to the slope of the indifference curve at that point

marginal revenue (MR) $= \dfrac{\Delta TR}{\Delta Q}$ the change in total revenue from selling an additional unit; for a firm in a competitive industry, $MR =$ Price

marginal tax rate the tax rate paid on an additional dollar of income

marginal utility the change in total utility from consuming an additional unit

market confidence one of the Federal Reserve's most powerful tools is its influence over expectations, not its influence over the money supply

market for loanable funds the market where suppliers of loanable funds (savers) trade with demanders of loanable funds (borrowers), thereby determining the equilibrium interest rate

market power the power to raise prices above marginal cost without fear that other firms will enter the market

median voter theorem the principle that when voters vote for the policy that is closest to their ideal point on a line, then the ideal point of the median voter will beat any other policy in a majority rule election

median wage the wage such that one-half of all workers earn wages below that amount and one-half of all workers earn wages above that amount

menu costs the costs of changing prices

monetizing the debt the result of government paying off its debts by printing money

money a widely accepted means of payment

money illusion the false perception that occurs when people mistake changes in nominal prices for changes in real prices

money multiplier (MM) the amount the money supply expands with each dollar increase in reserves; $MM = 1/RR$ where RR is the reserve ratio

monopolistic competition a market with a large number of firms selling similar but not identical products

monopoly a firm with market power

moral hazard the idea that people who are insulated from risk will tend to take on more risk

multiplier effect the additional increase in spending caused by the initial increase in government spending

Nash equilibrium a situation in which no player has an incentive to change strategy unilaterally

national debt held by the public all federal debt held outside the U.S. government

natural monopoly a situation when a single firm can supply the entire market at a lower cost than two or more firms

natural unemployment rate the rate of structural plus frictional unemployment

net exports the value of exports minus the value of imports

network good a good whose value to one consumer increases the more that other consumers use the good

nominal exchange rate the rate at which you can exchange one currency for another

nominal rate of return the rate of return that does not account for inflation

nominal variables variables, such as nominal GDP, that have not been adjusted for changes in prices

nominal wage confusion situation that occurs when workers respond to their nominal wage instead of to their real wage, that is, when workers respond to the wage number on their paychecks rather than to what their wage can buy in goods and services (the real wage)

nonexcludable when people who don't pay cannot easily be prevented from using the good, the good is nonexcludable

nonrival (or nonrivalrous) goods when one person's consumption of the good does not limit another person's consumption

normal good a good for which demand increases when income increases

normative economics recommendations or arguments about what economic policy should be

Nozick's entitlement theory of justice principle that the distribution of income in a society is just if property is justly acquired and voluntarily exchanged

oligopoly a market dominated by a small number of firms

open market operations the buying and selling of government bonds by the Fed

opportunity cost the value of possibilities lost when a choice is made

optimal consumption rule principle that to maximize utility, a consumer should allocate spending so that the marginal utility per dollar is equal for all purchases

owner's equity *see* **equity**

perfect price discrimination (PPD) the situation that exists when each customer is charged his or her maximum willingness to pay

physical capital the stock of tools including machines, structures, and equipment

piece rate any payment system that pays workers directly for their output

Pigouvian subsidy a subsidy on a good with external benefits

Pigouvian tax a tax on a good with external costs

positive economics describing, explaining, or predicting without making recommendations

prediction market a speculative market designed so that prices can be interpreted as probabilities and used to make predictions

price ceiling a maximum price allowed by law

price discrimination the selling of the same product at different prices to different customers

price floor a minimum price allowed by law

principal–agent problem how can a principal incentivize an agent to work in the principal's interest even when the agent has information that the principal does not?

prisoner's dilemma situations in which the pursuit of individual interest leads to a group outcome that is in the interest of no one

private cost a cost paid by the consumer or the producer (as opposed to external cost)

private goods goods that are excludable and rival goods

producer surplus the producer's gain from exchange, or the difference between the market price and the minimum price at which a producer would be willing to sell a particular quantity

producer surplus (total) an amount measured by the area above the supply curve and below the price up to the quantity traded

production possibilities frontier all the combinations of goods that a country can produce given its productivity and supply of inputs

progressive tax an income tax with higher tax rates on people with higher incomes

protectionism the economic policy of restraining trade through quotas, tariffs, or other regulations that burden foreign producers but not domestic producers

public choice the study of political behavior using the tools of economics

public goods goods that are nonexcludable and nonrival

purchasing power parity (PPP) theorem the principle that the real purchasing power of money should be about the same, whether it is spent at home or converted into another currency and spent abroad

quantitative easing situation that occurs when the Fed buys longer-term government bonds or other securities

quantitative tightening occurs when the Fed sells longer-term government bonds or other securities

quantity demanded the quantity that buyers are willing and able to buy at a particular price

quantity supplied the quantity that sellers are willing and able to sell at a particular price

rational ignorance when the benefits of being informed are less than the costs of becoming informed, a person may be rationally ignorant

Rawls's maximin principle principle that justice requires maximizing the benefits going to society's most disadvantaged group

real exchange rate the rate at which you can exchange the goods and services of one country for the goods and services of another

real price a price that has been corrected for inflation; used to compare the prices of goods over time

real rate of return the nominal rate of return minus the inflation rate

real shock (also called a **productivity shock**) any shock that increases or decreases the potential growth rate

real variables variables such as real GDP, that have been adjusted for changes in prices by using the same set of prices in all time periods

recession a significant, widespread decline in real income and employment

regressive tax an income tax with higher tax rates on people with lower incomes

rent control a price ceiling on rental housing

reserve ratio (RR) the ratio of reserves to deposits

Ricardian equivalence the theory according to which people understand that, for a given level of government spending, lower taxes today mean higher taxes in the future and therefore save the money from a tax cut to pay future taxes

risk-return trade-off higher returns come at the price of higher risk

saving income that is not spent on consumption goods

scarce when there isn't enough of a specific resource to satisfy all of our wants

shortage a situation in which the quantity demanded is greater than the quantity supplied

short run the period before entry occurs

short-run aggregate supply curve (SRAS) curve that shows the positive relationship between the inflation rate and real growth during the period when prices and wages are sticky

signal an expensive action that is taken to reveal information

social cost the cost to everyone; the private cost plus the external cost

social surplus consumer surplus plus producer surplus plus everyone else's surplus

Solow growth rate an economy's potential growth rate, the rate of economic growth that would occur given flexible prices and the existing real factors of production

speculation the attempt to profit from future price changes

statistical discrimination discrimination using information about group averages to make conclusions about individuals

steady state in a model of economic growth, a situation in which the capital stock is neither increasing nor decreasing

stock (or share) is a certificate of ownership in a corporation

strategic decision making decision making in situations that are interactive

structural unemployment persistent, long-term unemployment caused by long-lasting shocks or permanent features of an economy that make it more difficult for some workers to find jobs

substitutes two goods for which a decrease in the price of one leads to a decrease in demand for the other

substitution effect the change in consumption caused by a change in relative prices holding the consumer's utility level constant

sunk cost a cost that once incurred cannot be recovered

supply curve a function that shows the quantity supplied at different prices

surplus a situation in which the quantity supplied is greater than the quantity demanded

systemic risk the risk that the failure of one financial institution can bring down other institutions

tacit collusion when firms limit competition with one another but they do so without explicit agreement or communication

tariff a tax on imports

technological knowledge knowledge about how the world works that is used to produce goods and services

time bunching the tendency for economic activities to be coordinated at common points in time

time preference the desire to have goods and services sooner rather than later (all else being equal)

total consumer surplus see consumer surplus (total)

total costs the costs of producing a given quantity of output

total producer surplus see producer surplus (total)

total revenue price times quantity sold: $TR = P \times Q$

tournament a compensation scheme in which payment is based on relative performance

trade deficit the annual difference that results when the value of a country's imports exceeds the value of its exports

trade quota a restriction on the quantity of goods that can be imported: imports greater than the quota amount are forbidden or heavily taxed

trade surplus the annual difference that results when the value of a country's exports exceeds the value of its imports

tragedy of the commons the tendency of any resource that is unowned, and hence nonexcludable, to be overused and undermaintained

transaction costs the costs necessary to reach an agreement

tying a form of price discrimination in which one good, called the base good, is tied to a second good called the variable good, for example printer and ink

underemployment rate a Bureau of Labor Statistics measure that includes part-time workers who would rather have a full-time position and people who would like to work but have given up looking for a job

unemployed workers adults who do not have a job but who are looking for work

unemployment rate the percentage of the labor force who are unemployed

union an association of workers that bargains collectively with employers over wages, benefits, and working conditions

unit elastic when the absolute value of the elasticity is exactly equal to 1

utilitarianism the idea that the best society maximizes the sum of utility

variable costs costs that vary with output

velocity of money, v the average number of times a dollar is spent on finished goods and services in a year

zero lower bound situation in which the Federal Funds rate is close to zero

zero profits (or normal profits) the condition when $P = AC$; at this price the firm is covering all of its costs including enough to pay labor and capital their ordinary opportunity costs

REFERENCES

Chapter 1 Notes

1. Quoted in **Christopher, Emma.** 2007. "The slave trade is merciful compared to [this]": Slave traders, convict transportation and the abolitionists. In **Christopher, E., C. Pybus, and M. Rediker** (eds.), *Many Middle Passages*, Chap. 6, pp. 109–128. Berkeley, CA: University of California Press.

2. **Chadwick, Edwin.** 1862. Opening address of the British Association for the Advancement of Science. *Journal of the Statistical Society of London* **25**(4): 502–524.

3. Opening address.

4. On the impact of new drugs, see **Lichtenberg, Frank.** 2007. The impact of new drugs on U.S. longevity and medical expenditure, 1990–2003. *American Economic Review* **97**(2): 438–443.

5. **Celis III, William.** December 28, 1991. Study finds enrollment is up at colleges despite recession. *The New York Times*.

Chapter 2 Notes

1. On this point, see **Sowell, Thomas.** 1980. *Knowledge and Decisions*. New York: Basic Books. See also Chapter 4 of **Reisman, George.** 1996. *Capitalism: A Treatise on Economics*. Ottawa, IL: Jameson.

2. **Smith, Adam.** August 2, 2006. *An Inquiry into the Nature and Causes of the Wealth of Nations*. Edited by Edwin Cannan, Book IV, II. 2.11. Indianapolis, IN: Library of Economics and Liberty. http://www.econlib.org/library/Smith/smWN13.html. Originally published London: Methuen, 1904 [1776].

3. **Boudreaux, Donald J.** 2008. *Globalization*. Westport, CT: Greenwood Press.

Chapter 3 Notes

1. On changing U.S. demographics and their impact on the economy, see **Kotlikoff, Laurence J., and Scott Burns.** 2004. *The Coming Generational Storm*. Cambridge, MA: MIT Press.

2. *International Herald Tribune.* http://www.iht.com/articles/ap/2007/07/31/business/EU-FIN-MKT-Oil-Prices.php.

3. **Paleontological Research Institution.** http://www.priweb.org/ed/pgws/history/spindletop/lucas_gusher.html.

4. See information available at the **U.S. Energy Information Administration** Web site. http://www.eia.gov/.

5. On the costs of oil production, see **Joint Economic Committee, United States Congress.** *OPEC and the High Price of Oil.* http://www.house.gov/jec/publications/109/11–17–05opec.pdf.

Chapter 4 Notes

1. **Smith, Vernon.** 1991. Experimental economics at Purdue. In **Smith, V.** (ed.), *Papers in Experimental Economics*. Cambridge, UK: Cambridge University Press. Originally appeared in **Horwich, G., and J. P. Quirk** (eds.), *Essays in Contemporary Fields of Economics*. Lafayette, IN: Purdue University Press, 1981.

2. **Conover, Ted.** July 2, 2006. Capitalist roaders. *New York Times Magazine,* pp. 31–37, 50.

Chapter 5 Notes

1. See **International Money Fund.** 2005. *World Economic Outlook—2005*. Washington, DC: IMF. See, in particular, Chapter. 4.

2. On the elasticity of demand for oil, see **Cooper, John C. B.** 2003. Price elasticity of demand for crude oil: Estimates for 23 countries. *OPEC Review* **27**(1): 1–8. On the elasticity of demand for Minute Maid orange juice, see **Capps, Oral Jr., and H. Alan Love.** 2002. Econometric considerations in the use of electronic scanner data to conduct consumer demand analysis. *American Journal of Agricultural Economics* **84**(3): 807–816.

3. On the elasticity of demand for illegal drugs, see **Cicala, Steve J.** 2005. The demand for illicit drugs: A meta-analysis of price elasticities. Working paper, University of Chicago. On the elasticity of demand for cigarettes, see **Keeler T. E., T. W. Hu, P. G. Barnett, and W. G. Manning.** 1993. Taxation, regulation, and addiction: A demand function for cigarettes based on time-series evidence. *Journal of Health Economics* **12**(1): 1–18.

4. **Colorado Department of Revenue.** 2014. *Market Size and Demand for Marijuana in Colorado.*

5. On the elasticity of supply for cocoa, see **Burger, K.** 1996. *The European Chocolate Market and the Effects of the Proposed EU Directive*. Amsterdam: Economic and Social Institute, Free University. For the elasticity of supply of coffee, see **Akiyama, T., and P. Varangis.** 1990. The impact of the international coffee agreement on producing countries. *World Bank Economic Review* **4**(2): 157–173.

6. **Callahan, C., F. Rivara, and T. Koepsell.** 1994. Money for guns: Evaluation of the Seattle gun buy-back program. *Public Health Reports* **109**: 472–477.

7. **Welch, William M.** March 17, 2008. Critics take aim at gun buybacks. *USA Today*.

8. See **Mullin, Wallace P.** 2001. Will gun buyback programs increase the quantity of guns? *International Review of Law and Economics* **21**: 87–102.

9. For a review of some of the evidence on a variety of crime fighting policies, see **Levitt, Steven D.** 2004. Understanding why crime fell in the 1990s: Four factors that explain the decline and six that do not. *Journal of Economic Perspectives* **18**(1): 163–190.

10. For Williams's story, see **Gavel, Doug.** September 28, 2000. Sophomore skips orientation to free 4,000 slaves in Sudan. *Harvard University Gazette*. For Denver schoolchildren, **PBS OnlineNewsHour.** May 31, 1999. Jim Lehrer on the crisis in the Sudan. www.pbs.org/newshour/rundown/sudan-elections/

11. **Miniter, Richard.** July 1999. The false promise of slave redemption. *The Atlantic Monthly* **284**(1): 63–71. http://www.theatlantic.com/magazine/archive/1990/07/the-false-promise-of-slave-redemption/377679/ Note that although the Miniter article contains some useful information, it is a confused account of economics. Miniter argues that a low price for slaves means the slave traffickers are being driven out of business and

high prices mean that slavery is profitable, but one has to ask why the price is low or high. High prices driven by increased demand from slave redeemers is a good sign because it means the slave redeemers are outbidding potential slave traffickers.

12. It is also possible to make predictions about quantities using two similar formulas.

13. The proof of these formulas is not difficult, but a bit more advanced than is necessary for this textbook. For a proof, see **McAfee, Preston.** 2006. *Introduction to Economic Analysis.* www.mcafee.cc/introecon/.

14. **The White House: George W. Bush.** https://georgewbush-whitehouse.archives.gov/news/releases/2005/11/20051103-10.html

15. The Klick and Tabarrok and Gruber articles use advanced statistical techniques to argue that the increase in police causes the decrease in crime and the increase in giving causes the decrease in attendance. For more details, see **Klick, J., and A. Tabarrok.** 2005. Using terror alert levels to estimate the effect of police on crime. *Journal of Law and Economics* **48**(1): 267–280. Also, **Gruber, Jonathan.** 2004. Pay or pray? The impact of charitable subsidies on religious attendance. *Journal of Public Economics* **88**(12): 2635–2655.

Chapter 6 Notes

1. On Tepper's move to Florida, see Frank, Robert. 2016. "One top taxpayer moved, and New Jersey shuddered." *New York Times,* April 30. http://www.nytimes.com/2016/05/01/business/one-top-taxpayer-moved-and-new-jersey-shuddered.html. And on how the elderly wealthy move to low-estate tax states see Bakija, Jon, and Joel Slemrod. 2004. "Do the rich flee from high state taxes? Evidence from Federal Estate Tax Returns." Working Paper 10645. National Bureau of Economic Research. http://www.nber.org/papers/w10645.

2. Information about George Steinbrenner and the disappearing estate tax may be found in the **New York Times.** July 14, 2010. Steinbrenner heirs may save millions on estate tax. On estate taxes in Australia, see **Gans, Joshua S., and Andrew Leigh.** 2009. Did the death of Australian inheritance taxes affect deaths? *Topics in Economic Analysis & Policy* **6**(1), http://works.bepress.com/andrewleigh/4; in the United States, see **Wojciech, Kopczuk, and Joel Slemrod.** 2003. Dying to save taxes: Evidence from estate-tax returns on the death elasticity. *Review of Economics and Statistics* **85**(2): 256–265. The influence of the tax system on births is discussed in **Leonhardt, David.** December 20, 2006. To-do list: Wrap gifts. Have baby. the *New York Times.* Also, **Dickert-Conlin, Stacy, and Chandra Amitabh.** 1999. Taxes and the timing of births. *Journal of Political Economy* **107**(1): 161–177.

3. Estimates of the Massachusetts mandate on wages can be found in Kolstad, Jonathan T., and Amanda E. Kowalski. 2012. Mandate-based health reform and the labor market: Evidence from the Massachusetts reform. National Bureau of Economic Research Working Paper No. 17933. http://www.nber.org/papers/w17933.

4. Congressional Budget Office. 2014. Labor market effects of the Affordable Care Act: Updated estimates. http://www.cbo.gov/sites/default/files/cbofiles/attachments/45010-breakout-AppendixC.pdf

Chapter 7 Notes

1. http://www.aboutflowers.com/.

2. Ecuador and Colombia also export millions of roses to the United States.

3. See **Hennock, Mary.** 2002. Kenya's flower farms flourish. *BBC News Online.* http://news.bbc.co.uk/2/hi/business/1820515.stm. For more on Kenya and the Dutch flower market, refer to **McMillan, John.** 2002. *Reinventing the Bazaar.* New York: W. W. Norton. Also **Wijnands, Jo.** 2005. *Sustainable International Networks in the Flower Industry: Bridging Empirical Findings and Theoretical Issues.* The Hague: International Society for Horticultural Science.

4. For more information, see **Wikipedia.** Ethanol fuel in Brazil. http://en.wikipedia.org/wiki/Ethanol_fuel_in_Brazil.

5. See the *New York Times.* July 8, 2006. Ethanol is the new real estate. Page B5.

6. **American Petrochemical Institute.** How much lubricant in a barrel of crude oil? www.petronomics.com/pdf/crude_oil.pdf.

7. See **Williams, Scott.** 2006. Asphalt prices stalling budgets. *Milwaukee Journal Sentinel.* http://www.jsonline.com/story/index.aspx?id=434330.

8. **Smith, Vernon.** 1982. Microeconomic systems as an experimental science. *American Economic Review* **72**: 923–955.

9. **Federal Highway Administration.** 1993. *A Study of the Use of Recycled Paving Material.* Document no. FHWA-1993-RD-93-147. Washington, DC: FHWA.

10. **Roll, Richard.** 1984. Orange juice and weather. *American Economic Review* **74**(5): 861–880.

11. For much more on prediction markets and how they can be used to make decisions, see **Hanson, Robin D.** 2002. Decision markets. In **Alexander Tabarrok** (ed.), *Entrepreneurial Economics: Bright Ideas from the Dismal Science,* pp. 79–85. Oxford: Oxford University Press. Also **Hanson, Robin.** 2007. Shall we vote on values, but bet on beliefs? *Journal of Political Philosophy* **21**(2): 151–178.

Chapter 8 Notes

1. A 2" × 4" refers to the preplaned dimensions, which after planing, are typically $1\frac{3}{4}$" × $3\frac{3}{4}$"; with price controls, the average size fell to $1\frac{5}{8}$" × $3\frac{5}{8}$". See Thomas Hall. 2003. *The Rotten Fruits of Economic Controls and the Rise from the Ashes: 1965–1989.* New York: University Press of America.

2. *Business Week.* February 16, 1974. Page 122. Quoted in **Bradley, Robert Jr.** 1996. *Oil, Gas and Government: The U.S. Experience,* Vol. 2, p. 1635. Lanham, MD: Rowman & Littlefield.

3. Prices were frozen at levels no higher than the May 25, 1970, price or a price at which 10% or more of transactions took place in the 30 days prior to August 14, 1971. Some adjustments for seasonal differences were allowed for some products, such as fashion items, but not for oil. See **Bradley,** Vol. 2, especially pp. 1607–1608.

4. See **Hall, Thomas E.** 2003. *The Rotten Fruits of Economic Controls and the Rise from the Ashes, 1965–1989.* New York: University Press of America.

5. **Bradley, Robert Jr.** 1996. *Oil, Gas and Government: The U.S. Experience.* Vol. 1. Lanham, MD: Rowman & Littlefield.

6. See *The Washington Post.* November 26, 1973. Steps ordered by Nixon to meet energy crisis. Page A12.

7. *Time.* December 10, 1973. The shortage's losers and winners.

8. **Grayson, Jackson C.** February 6, 1974. Let's end controls—completely. *The Wall Street Journal,* p. 14.

9. See **Bradley,** Vol. 1, pp. 477, 515.

10. **Hall, Jonathan, Cory Hendrick, and Chris Nosko.** 2015. The effects of Uber's surge pricing: A case study. Working Paper.

11. **Brodeur, Abel, and Kerry Nield.** June, 2016. Has Uber made it easier to get a ride in the rain? IZA Discussion Paper No. 9986.

12. **Peter Cohen, Robert Hahn, Jonathan Hall, Steven Levitt, and Robert Metcalfe.** "Using Big Data to Estimate Consumer Surplus: The Case of Uber," working paper, August 2016.

13. As assessed in 1999. See **Glaeser, E.** 2002. Does rent control reduce segregation? NBER working paper, Washington, DC.

14. **Lindbeck, Assar.** 1972. *The Political Economy of the New Left.* New York: Harper & Row. See especially p. 39.

15. Quoted in **Block, Walter.** August 29, 2006. Rent control. In **David R. Henderson** (ed.), *The Concise Encyclopedia of Economics.* Indianapolis, IN: Liberty Fund, Library of Economics and Liberty. http://enonlib.org/library/Enc1/RentControl.html.

16. **Glaeser, Edward L., and Erzo F. P. Luttmer.** 2003. The misallocation of housing under rent control. *American Economic Review* **93**(4): 1027–1046.

17. For a recent discussion, see **Arnott, Richard.** 1995. Time for revisionism on rent control? *The Journal of Economic Perspectives* **9**(1): 99–120.

18. On housing vouchers, see **Olsen, Edgar.** 2003. Housing programs for low-income households. In **Robert Moffitt** (ed.), *Means-Tested Transfer Programs in the U.S.* Chicago: University of Chicago Press.

19. Drawn from **Smith, Hedrick.** 1976. Consumers: The art of queuing. In *The Russians.* New York: Ballantine Books.

20. **Bureau of Labor Statistics.** 2013. Characteristics of Minimum Wage Workers 2012. Washington, DC: BLS. http://www.bls.gov/opub/reports/minimum-wage/archive/minimumwageworkers_2012.pdf.

21. For a listing and abstract of many studies on the minimum wage, see **U.S. Congress Joint Economic Committee.** *50 Years of Research on the Minimum Wage.* Recent studies include **Neumark, D., and W. Wascher.** 1992. Employment effects of minimum and subminimum wages: Panel data on state minimum wage laws. *Industrial and Labor Relations Review* **46**(1): 55–81. **Deere, D., K. M. Murphy, and F. Welch.** 1995. Employment and the 1990–1991 minimum-wage hike. *American Economic Review* **85**(2): 232–237. Not all studies find a significant reduction in employment. See **Card, David and Alan B. Krueger.** September 1994. Minimum wages and employment: A case study of the fast-food industry in New Jersey and Pennsylvania. *American Economic Review* **84**: 772–793 for a well designed study that challenges the conventional wisdom.

22. **Bureau of Labor Statistics,** *op. cit.*

23. On deregulation, see **Peltzman, Sam.** 1989. The economic theory of regulation after a decade of deregulation. Brookings Papers on Economic Activity. *Microeconomics*: 1–59.

24. On deregulation, see **Morrison, Steven A., and Clifford Winston.** 1986. *The Economic Effects of Airline Deregulation.* Washington, DC: Brookings Institution.

Chapter 9 Notes

1. On the environmental cost of sugar production, see **Schwabach, Aaron.** 2002. How protectionism is destroying the Everglades. *National Wetlands Newsletter* **24**(1): 7–14.

2. See **Bellamy, Carol.** 1997. *The State of the World's Children—1997.* New York: Oxford University Press and UNICEF. http://unicef.org/sowc97/.

3. See **Edmonds, Eric V., and Nina Pavcnik.** January 2006. International trade and child labor: Cross-country evidence. *Journal of International Economics*: 115–140.

4. On the Food for Education program, see **Ahmed, A., and C. del Nino.** 2002. *The Food for Education Program in Bangladesh: An Evaluation of Its Impact on Educational Attainment and Food Security.* FCND DP No. 138. Washington, DC: International Food Policy Research Institute. Also **Meng, Xin, and Jim Ryan.** 2003. Evaluating the Food for Education Program in Bangladesh. Working paper, Australian National University, Australia South Asia Research Centre.

5. On the 1918 flu, see **Barry, John M.** 2005. *The Great Influenza: The Epic Story of the Deadliest Plague in History.* New York: Penguin. On policy for a future pandemic, see **Cowen, Tyler.** 2005. Avian flu: What should be done. Working paper, Mercatus Center, George Mason University, Arlington, VA. https://ppe.mercatus.org/system/files/PDF_WP_Avian_Flu_20060726.pdf.

6. Quoted in **Norberg, Johan.** 2003. *In Defense of Global Capitalism.* Washington, DC: Cato Institute.

7. **Johnson, Bradford.** 2002. Retail: The Wal-Mart effect. *McKinsey Quarterly* (1): 40–43.

Chapter 10 Notes

1. On the external cost of antibiotic use, see **Elbasha, Elamin H.** 2003. Deadweight loss of bacterial resistance due to over-treatment. *Health Economics* **12**: 125–138.

2. **Meade, J. E.** 1952. External economies and diseconomies in a competitive situation. *Economic Journal* **62**: 54–67. On the market for pollination, see **Cheung, Steven N. S.** 1973. The fable of the bees: An economic investigation. *Journal of Law and Economics* **16**: 11–33. Also for a description of the market in the United States, see **Sumner, Daniel A., and Hayley Boriss.** 2006. Bee-conomics and the leap in pollination fees. *Agricultural and Resource Economics Update* **3**(9): 9–11.

3. *Consumer Reports.* June 2007. Washers and dryers: Dirty laundry.

4. The elasticity of demand for electricity is about -0.5, so a 2% increase in the price would reduce consumption by about 1%.

5. For a good overview of the acid rain program, see the EPA's *Acid Rain and Related Programs 2007 Progress Report.* https://www.epa.gov/sites/production/files/2015-08/documents/2007arreport.pdf.

Chapter 11 Notes

1. For information on stripper wells, see **U.S. Department of Energy.** *Stripper Well Consortium Looks Back on Fifteen Years of Innovative Technology and Partnership.* http://www.netl.doe.gov/research/oil-and-gas/stripper-wells.

2. **Bernstein, William J.** *A Splendid Exchange: How Trade Shaped the World.* New York: Atlantic Monthly Press, 2008. See p. 62.

Chapter 12 Notes

1. **Schumpeter, Joseph.** 1975/1942. *Capitalism, Socialism and Democracy.* New York: Harper. See, in particular, pp. 82–85.

2. Based on data from 1972 to 1992 in **Adams, William J.** 1993. TV program scheduling strategies and their relationship to new program renewal rates and rating changes. *Journal of Broadcasting and Electronic Media* **37**: 465–475. The renewal rate is probably lower today as there are more television stations and viewers are more difficult to keep.

Chapter 13 Notes

1. On deaths due to AIDS, see https://www.cdc.gov/nchs/fastats/aids-hiv.htm. On the efficacy of antiretrovirals, see **Weller, I. V., and I. G. Williams.** 2001. ABC of AIDS:

Antiretroviral drugs. *British Medical Journal* **322**(7299): 1410–1412. And, on developing countries, **Severe, P., et al.** 2005. Antiretroviral therapy in a thousand patients with AIDS in Haiti. *New England Journal of Medicine* **353**(22): 2325–2334. Also **Lichtenberg, Frank.** 2003. The effect of new drugs on HIV mortality in the U.S., 1987–1998. *Economics and Human Biology* **1**: 259–266.

2. On the cost of AIDS drugs in the United States, see https://www.healthline.com/health/hiv-aids/cost-of-treatment#2.

3. On the number of people worldwide with AIDS, see **Global AIDS Overview,** http://aids.gov/federal-resources/around-the-world/global-aids-overview/.

4. On the cost of Combivir, see http://www.money.cnn.com/magazines/fortune/fortune_archive/2006/09/18/8386170/index.htm?postversion=2006090806 and http://news.bbc.co.uk/2/hi/business/2981015.stm, and further below on patents and differential pricing.

5. See **Pepper, Daniel.** September 18, 2006. Patently unfair. *Fortune.* http://money.cnn.com/magazines/fortune/fortune_archive/2006/09/18/8386170/index.htm?postversion=2006090806.

6. It's possible to prove why the MR shortcut is true using calculus. Let the demand curve be written in the form $P = a - bQ$ so the slope is b. Total revenue is $P \times q = TR = aQ - bQ^2$. Marginal revenue is the derivative of total revenue with respect to quantity or $MR = \frac{dTR}{dQ} = a - 2bQ$. Notice that the slope of the MR curve is $2b$, twice the slope of the demand curve.

7. American Airlines reservation Web site.

8. **DiMasi, Joseph A., Ronald W. Hansen, and Henry G. Grabowski.** 2003. The price of innovation: New estimates of drug development costs. *Journal of Health Economics* **22**(2): 151–185.

9. One study suggests that a 10% decline in price will lead to at least a 5% decline in the number of new drugs. See also **Vernon, John.** 2005. Examining the link between price regulation and pharmaceutical R&D investment. *Health Economics* **14**(1): 1–17.

10. **North, Douglass C.** 1981. *Structure and Change in Economic History.* New York: W. W. Norton. See p. 164.

11. **Kremer, M.** 1998. Patent buyouts: A mechanism for encouraging innovation. *Quarterly Journal of Economics* **113**: 1137–1167.

12. See **Hazlett, Thomas W., and Matthew L. Spitzer.** 1997. *Public Policy toward Cable Television: The Economics of Rate Controls.* AEI.

Chapter 14 Notes

1. Information on the Combivir smuggling operation can be found in **Irving, Richard.** February 21, 2005. AIDS drugs to Africa rebranded in drive to beat racket. On an earlier ring busted in 2002, see **Syal, Rajeev.** December 28, 2002. Scandal of Africa's AIDS drug re-sold to Britain. *Telegraph.* http://www.telegraph.co.uk/news/worldnews/africaandindianocean/southafrica/1417323/Scandal-of_Africas_Aids-drugs-re-sold-to-Britain.html. See also **Morais, Richard C.** 2004. Pssst. . .Wanna buy some augmentin? *Forbes.* http://www.forbes.com/free_forbes/2004/0412/112.html.

2. See **R. Preston McAfee.** 2002. *Competitive Solutions: The Strategist's Toolkit.* Princeton, NJ: Princeton University Press.

Chapter 15 Notes

1. **Barrus, David, and Frank Scott.** 2013. Single bidders and tacit collusion in highway procurement auctions. University of Kentucky Working Paper.

Chapter 16 Notes

1. http://www.match.com/help/aboutus.aspx.

2. See, for instance, http://www.mashable.com/2007/06/10/facebook-hammers-myspace-on-almost-all-key-features/.

3. http://www.cc.gatech.edu/gvu/user_surveys/survey-10-1996/graphs/use/Browser_You_Expect_To_Use_In_12_Months.html. Exact estimates vary; see http://en.wikipedia.org/wiki/Usage_share_of_web_browsers.

4. **Watts, Duncan J., Salganik, M. J., and P. S. Dodds.** 2006. Experimental study of inequality and unpredictability in an artificial cultural market. *Science* **311**: 854–856.

Chapter 17 Notes

1. See **Bagwell, Kyle.** 2007. The economic analysis of advertising. In **Mark Armstrong and Robert H. Porter** (eds.), *The Handbook of Industrial Organization,* Vol. III, p. 1745. Amsterdam: Elsevier and North Holland.

2. **Ippolito, Pauline M., and Alan D. Mathios.** Autumn 1990. Advertising and health choices: A study of the cereal market. *RAND Journal of Economics* **21**(3): 459–480.

3. http://www.youtube.com/watch?v=R1NnyE6DDnQ.

4. http://www.beautifullife.info/advertisment/history-of-coca-cola-in-ads/.

5. http://en.wikipedia.org/wiki/Coca-Cola.

6. **McClure, Samuel M., Jian Li, Damon Tomlin, Kim S. Cypert, Latane M. Montague, and P. Read Montague.** October 14, 2004. Neural correlates of behavioral preference for culturally familiar drinks. *Neuron* **44**: 379–387.

7. **Becker, Gary S., and Kevin M. Murphy.** "A Simple Theory of Advertising as a Good or Bad," *The Quarterly Journal of Economics,* Vol. 108, No. 4 (Nov. 1993), pp. 941–964.

Chapter 18 Notes

1. On dangerous professions, see, for instance, http://www.forbes.com/2007/08/13/dangerous-jobs-fishing-lead-careers-cx_tvr_0813danger.html.

2. Here is one estimate of coal miner earnings: http://www.washingtonpost.com/wp-dyn/content/discussion/2006/01/04/DI2006010401171.html.

3. For one estimate of the union wage premium, see http://psi.org.uk/docs/2003/research/emp-union-wage-premium-us-uk.pdf.

4. Data from https://stats.oecd.org/index.aspx?DataSetCode=U_D_D

Chapter 19 Notes

1. From Aristotle, *Politics,* Book II, Chap. III, 1261b. **Jowett, Benjamin** (trans.). 1885. *The Politics of Aristotle.* With Introduction, Marginal Analysis, Essays, Notes, and Indices. 2 vols. Oxford: Clarendon Press. See Vol. 2.

2. The system was later modified so the ITQs gave rights to a certain share of the total allowable catch.

3. See **World Meteorological Organization.** 2007. *Scientific Assessment of Ozone Depletion: 2006.* Global Ozone Research

and Monitoring Project Rept. No. 50. Geneva, Switzerland. http://www.esrl.noaa.gov/csd/assessments/2006/report.html.

4. discovermagazine.com/1995/aug/eastersend543

5. **Demsetz, Harold.** 1967. Towards a theory of property rights. *AER* **57**: 2.

Chapter 20 Notes

1. **House of Commons.** November 11, 1947. Official Report, 5th Series, Vol. 444, cc. 206–207.

2. **Kaiser/Harvard Program on the Public and Health/Social Policy Survey.** January 1995.

3. See, for instance, **DeLorme, Charles D., Stacey Isom, and David R. Kamerschen.** April 2005. Rent seeking and taxation in the ancient Roman Empire. *Applied Economics* **37**: 705–711. http://ideas.repec.org/a/taf/applec/v37y2005i6p705-711.html.

4. **Leeson, Peter T.** 2008. Media freedom, political knowledge, and participation. *Journal of Economic Perspectives* **22**(2): 155–169.

5. **Djankov, S., C. McLiesh, T. Nenova, and A. Shleifer.** 2003. Who owns the media? *Journal of Law and Economics* **46**(2): 341–381.

6. See **Conquest, Robert.** 1987. *Harvest of Sorrow.* New York: Oxford University Press.

7. **Sen, Amartya.** August 2, 1990. *Public Action to Remedy Hunger.* Arturo Tanco Memorial Lecture.

8. **Besley, T., and R. Burgess.** 2002. The political economy of government responsiveness: Theory and evidence from India. *Quarterly Journal of Economics* **117**(4): 1415–1452.

9. https://www.natso.com/en_us

Chapter 21 Notes

1. Working paper, personal communication, from Robert Whaples.

2. **Meckler, Laura.** November 13, 2007. Kidney shortage inspires a radical idea: Organ sales. *Wall Street Journal.* Page A1.

3. The commercial fishing mortality rate derives from http://www.cdc.gov/niosh/topics/fishing/regions.html. Kidney donation mortality rate from **Matas, A. J., S. T. Bartlett, A. B. Leichtman, and F. L. Delmonico.** July 2003. *American Journal of Transplantation* **3**(7): 830–834.

4. http://www.time.com/time/printout/0,8816,1686532,00.html.

5. For one source, see https://georgewbush-whitehouse.archives.gov/cea/cea_immigration_062007.html.

6. On measures of foreign aid, see, for instance, https://www.washingtonpost.com/graphics/world/which-countries-get-the-most-foreign-aid/.

Chapter 22 Notes

1. **Jacob, Brian A., and Steven D. Levitt.** August 3, 2003. Rotten apples: An investigation of the prevalence and predictors of teacher cheating. *Quarterly Journal of Economics* **118**: 843–878.

2. **Figlio, David N., and Lawrence S. Getzler.** 2002. Accountability, ability and disability: Gaming the system. NBER working paper 9307, Washington, DC.

3. For a calculation along these lines, see **Kane, T., and D. O. Staiger.** 2002. The promise and pitfalls of using imprecise school accountability measures. *Journal of Economic Perspectives* **16**(4): 91–114.

4. money.cnn.com/magazines/business2/business2_archive/2004/05/01/368246/index.htm.

5. For more on private prisons, see **Tabarrok, Alexander** (ed). 2003. *Changing the Guard: Private Prisons and the Control of Crime.* Oakland, CA: The Independent Institute.

6. **Lazear, Edward P.** 2000. Performance pay and productivity. *AER* **90**(5): 1346–1361.

7. **Lemieux, T. W., Bentley MacLeod, and Daniel Parent.** 2007. Performance pay and wage inequality. NBER working paper 13128, Washington, DC.

8. **Bertrand, Marianne, and Sendhil Mullainathan.** 2001. Are CEOs rewarded for luck? The ones without principals are. *Quarterly Journal of Economics* **116**: 901–932.

9. *Ibid.*

10. **Bebchuk, Lucian A., Alma Cohen, and Holger Spamann.** November 24, 2009. The wages of failure: Executive compensation at Bear Stearns and Lehman 2000–2008. *Yale Journal on Regulation* **27**: 257–282.

11. *Business Week.* January 9, 2006. The struggle to measure performance.

12. On employee ownership of stock, see **National Center for Employee Ownership.**

13. **Thaler, Richard H., and Cass R. Sunstein.** 2008. *Nudge: Improving Decisions about Health, Wealth, and Happiness.* New Haven: Yale University Press.

14. http://www.nytimes.com/2009/09/27/business/economy/27view.html.

Chapter 23 Notes

1. **Malkiel, Burton.** 1996. *A Random Walk Down Wall Street.* 6th ed. New York: W. W. Norton. See, in particular, p. 24.

2. For a comprehensive review of efficient markets and the performance of mutual fund managers, see **Hebner, Mark T.** 2007. *Index Funds: The 12 Step Program for Active Investors.* Irvine, CA: IFA.

3. See **Marshall, Ben, Rochester Cahan, and Jared Cahan.** March 2008. Does intraday technical analysis in the U.S. equity market have value? *Journal of Empirical Finance:* 199–210.

4. On the relatively safe nature of Walmart, see, for instance, this analysis: http://www.slate.com/articles/business/moneybox/2008/02/the_walmart_puzzle.html.

5. **Siegel, Jeremy J.** January/February 1992. The equity premium: Stock and bond returns since 1802. *Financial Analysts Journal* **48**(1): 28–38.

6. **Smith, Vernon L., Gerry L. Suchanek, and Arlington W. Williams.** 1988. Bubbles, crashes, and endogenous expectations in experimental spot asset markets. *Econometrica* **56**(5): 1119–1151. And **Hussam, Reshmaan N., David Porter, and Vernon L. Smith.** 2008. Thar she blows: Can bubbles be rekindled with experienced subjects? *American Economic Review* **98**(3): 924–937.

Chapter 24 Notes

1. **Balafoutas, Loukas, Adrian Beck, Rudolf Kerschbamer, and Matthias Sutter.** 2013. What drives taxi drivers? A field experiment on fraud in a market for credence goods. *The Review of Economic Studies* January, rds049. doi:10.1093/restud/rds049.

2. **Houser, Daniel, and John Wooders.** 2006. Reputation in auctions: Theory, and evidence from eBay. *Journal of Economics & Management Strategy* **15**(2): 353–369, doi:10.1111/j.1530-9134.2006.00103.x.

3. Gaming the college rankings, http://www.nytimes.com/2012/02/01/education/gaming-the-college-rankings.html?pagewanted=all.

4. On c-sections and incentives see **Gruber, Jon, John Kim, and Dina Mayzlin.** 1999. Physician fees and procedure intensity: The case of cesarean delivery. *Journal of Health Economics* **18**(4): 473–490, doi:10.1016/S0167-6296(99)00009-0; **Johnson, Erin M., and M. Marit Rehavi.** 2013. Physicians treating physicians: Information and incentives in childbirth. Working Paper 19242. National Bureau of Economic Research, http://www.nber.org/papers/w19242; and **Brown III, H. Shelton.** 1996. Physician demand for leisure: Implications for cesarean section rates. *Journal of Health Economics* **15**(2): 233–242, doi:10.1016/0167-6296(95)00039-9.

5. On the incentives of real estate agents, see **Levitt, Steven D., and Chad Syverson.** 2008. Market distortions when agents are better informed: The value of information in real estate transactions. *Review of Economics and Statistics* **90**(4): 599–611, doi:10.1162/rest.90.4.599.

6. **Goolsbee, Austan, Steven Levitt, and Chad Syverson** *Microeconomics.* New York: Worth, 2012, beginning of Ch. 15, drawn from U.S. Department of Transportation, National Transportation Statistics 2012.

7. **Genesove, David.** 1993. Adverse selection in the wholesale used car market. *Journal of Political Economy* **101**(4): 644–665.

8. See **David Hemenway,** 1990. Propitious selection. *Quarterly Journal of Economics* **105**(4): 1063–1069, and, more generally, search for the term "propitious selection."

9. http://econlog.econlib.org/archives/2013/02/sheepskin_effec.html.

10. **Diego Gambetta.** 2009. *Codes of the Underworld: How Criminals Communicate.* Princeton, NJ: Princeton University Press.

Chapter 25 Notes

1. For a good discussion, see **Persky, Joseph.** 1997. Retrospectives: Classical family values: Ending the poor laws as they knew them. *The Journal of Economic Perspectives* **11**(1): 179–189.

Chapter 26 Notes

1. Data on automobiles are from the **Statistical Abstract of the United States.** Prices from http://nada.org/. Statistics on U.S. chicken production can be found at the U.S. Department of Agriculture, http://www.usda.gov/

2. **Bureau of Economic Analysis.** Table 2.3.3. http://www.bea.gov.

3. **Board of Governors of the Federal Reserve System.** 2013. Financial Accounts of the United States. http://www.federalreserve.gov/releases/z1/current/.

4. For data on business regulations worldwide, see the **World Bank**'s Web site, http://doingbusiness.org/.

5. http://rru.worldbank.org/Discussions/Topics/Topic18.aspx.

6. http://gapminder.org/.

7. **Murphy, K. M., & Topel, R.H.** 2006. The value of health and longevity. *Journal of Political Economy* **114**(5): 871–904.

8. See **Dollar, David, and Aart Kraay.** 2004. Trade, growth, and poverty. *Economic Journal* **114**(493): F22–F49.

Chapter 27 Notes

1. See **United States Department of Agriculture,** Economic Research Service. *Agricultural Productivity in the United States.* http://www.ers.usda.gov/data-products/agricultural-productivity-in-the-us/.

2. This account draws on **McMillan, John.** 2002. *Reinventing the Bazaar.* New York: W. W. Norton; and **Zhou, Kate Xiao.** 1997. *How Farmers Changed China.* Boulder, CO: Westview Press.

3. **Hall, Robert E., and Charles I. Jones.** 1999. Why do some countries produce so much more output per worker than others? *Quarterly Journal of Economics*: 83–116.

4. **Lewis, William W.** 2004. *The Power of Productivity.* Chicago: University of Chicago Press.

5. On the importance of management practices and multinationals, see **Bloom, Nicholas, and John Van Reenen.** 2010. "Why do management practices differ across firms and countries?" *Journal of Economic Perspectives* **24**(1): 203–224. And **Bloom, Nicholas, Raffaella Sadun, and John Van Reenen.** 2012. "Americans do IT better: US multinationals and the productivity miracle." *American Economic Review* **102**(1): 167–201.

Chapter 28 Notes

1. Germany is excluded for lack of data. Turkey is excluded because its history and institutions were quite different from those of the other founding members of the OECD.

2. On innovations that would occur without patents, see **Mansfield, E.** 1986. Patents and innovation: An empirical study. *Management Science* **32**: 173–181. On patents and cumulative innovations, see **Bessen, J., and E. Maskin.** 2009. Sequential innovation, patents, and imitation. *RAND Journal of Economics* **40**: 611–635. Is there a way to reduce the trade-off between dynamic and static efficiency? Some ideas are suggested by **Tabarrok, A.** 2002. Patent theory versus patent law. *Contributions to Economic Analysis & Policy* **1**(1): Article 9. http://www.bepress.com/bejeap/contributions/vol1/iss1/art9. Also **Kremer, M.** 1998. Patent buyouts: A mechanism for encouraging innovation. *Quarterly Journal of Economics* **113**: 1137–1167.

3. "Rare" is defined as a disease at the bottom quarter of incidence in the United States in 1998; "common" is defined as a disease at the top quarter of incidence. See **Lichtenberg, Frank R., and Joel Waldfogel.** June 2003. Does misery love company? Evidence from pharmaceutical markets before and after the Orphan Drug Act. NBER working paper W9750, Washington, DC. http://www.ssrn.com/sol3/papers.cfm?abstract_id=414248.

4. **Romer, Paul.** 2007. Economic growth. In **David R. Henderson** (ed.), *The Concise Encyclopedia of Economics.* Indianapolis, IN: Liberty Fund.

Chapter 29 Notes

1. **Bloom, David E., David Canning, and Bryan S. Graham.** 2002. Longevity and life cycle savings. NBER working paper W8808, Washington, DC. http://www.ssrn.com/sol3/papers.cfm?abstract_ed=302569.

2. **Shoda, Y., W. Mischel, and P. Peake.** 1988. Predicting adolescent cognitive and self-regulatory competencies from preschool delay of gratification: Identifying diagnostic conditions. *Developmental Psychology* **26**: 978–986.

3. **Beshears, John, James Choi, David Laibson, and Brigitte Madrian.** *The Importance of Default Options for*

Retirement Savings Outcomes: Evidence from the United States. Washington, DC: National Bureau of Economic Research. http://nber.org/aginghealth/summer06/w12009.html.

4. **Levine, Ross, and Sara Zervos.** 1998. Stock markets, banks, and economic growth. *American Economic Review* **88**(3): 537–558.

5. **Blustein, Paul.** 2005. *And the Money Kept Rolling In (and Out): Wall Street, the IMF, and the Bankrupting of Argentina.* New York: Public Affairs. See, in particular, p. 191.

6. See **La Porta, Rafael, Florencio Lopez-De-Silanes, and Andrei Shleifer.** 2002. Government ownership of banks. *Journal of Finance, American Finance Association* **57**(1): 265–301.

7. **Friedman, Milton, and Anna J. Schwartz.** 1963. *A Monetary History of the United States, 1867–1960.* Princeton, NJ: Princeton University Press.

8. **Bernanke, Ben.** 1983. Nonmonetary effects of the financial crisis in the propagation of the Great Depression. *American Economic Review* **73**(3): 257–276.

9. Leverage ratios can be calculated in different ways so no leverage ratio is written in stone but the increase in leverage over the 2000s is well accepted. Figures on Lehman's leverage in 2004 and 2007 come from https://www.lovemoney.com /news/3909/why-lehman-brothers-collapsed. See also Elizabeth MacDonald's 2009 article "The Fire-Engine Red Flags at Lehman Brothers" from foxbusiness.com.

Chapter 30 Notes

1. On Kmart, see **Wikipedia,** http://en.wikipedia.org/wiki /Kmart. On Walmart, see its *2002 Annual Report,* stock.walmart.com/investors/financial-information/annual -reports-and-proxies/default.aspx.

2. Data on unemployment and its duration may be found in various issues of the *OECD Employment Outlook* and on the Web: **OECD,** www.oecd.org/els/oecd-employment- outlook-19991266.htm.

3. **Sullivan, D., and T. von Wachter.** 2009. Job displace- ment and mortality: An analysis using administrative data. *Quarterly Journal of Economics* **124**(3): 1265–1306.

4. The Italian system is more difficult to describe than the sys- tems in the other countries and it has changed considerably over time.

5. For minimum wages relative to average wages, see **OECD.** http://stats.oecd.org/Index.aspx. For minimum wages relative to average wages, see **Lothar Funk and Hagen Lesch.** 2005. *Minimum Wages in Europe.* Dublin: European Foundation for the Improvement of Living and Working Conditions, http:// eurofound.europa.eu/observatories/eurwork/comparative- information/minimum-wages-in-europe.

6. **Ford, Peter.** 2005. Deep roots of Paris riots. *Christian Science Monitor* (November 4).

7. **Martin, John P.** 2000. What works among active labour market policies: Evidence from OECD countries' experiences. *OECD Economic Studies* **30**: 79–113.

8. **Kotlikoff, Laurence, and Scott Burns.** 2004. *The Coming Generation Storm.* Cambridge, MA: MIT Press.

9. *60 Minutes.* January 3, 2007. Interview with U.S. Comptroller General David Walker, http://www.cbsnews .com/news/us-heading-for-financial-trouble/.

10. The U.S. Equal Employment Opportunity Commission collects statistics on job patterns by industry. See **EEOC.**

Job Patterns for Minorities and Women in Private Industry. Rept. EEO-1, http://www.eeoc.gov/eeoc/statistics/employment/ jobpat-eeo1/.

11. **Goldin, Claudia, and Lawrence F. Katz.** 2002. The power of the pill: Oral contraceptives and women's career and marriage decisions. *Journal of Political Economy* **110**(4): 730–770.

12. There are six employed workers and one unemployed worker, so there are seven people in the labor force. Of the seven, one is unemployed, so the unemployment rate is 1/7 = 14.3%. The adult, civilian, noninstitutional population is eight; of these, seven are in the labor force, so the labor force participation rate is 87.5%.

Chapter 31 Notes

1. https://www.caseyresearch.com/zimbabwean-dollar-point -no-return/

Chapter 32 Notes

1. **Higgs, Robert.** 1997. Regime uncertainty: Why the Great Depression lasted so long and why prosperity resumed after the war. *The Independent Review* **1**(4): 561–590.

2. For a good overview of the tariff and its effects, see **O'Brien, Anthony.** August 15, 2001. Smoot–Hawley tariff. In **Robert Whaples** (ed.), *EH.Net Encyclopedia,* http://eh.net/encyclopedia/smoot-hawley-tariff/.

Chapter 33 Notes

1. This scenario is covered in a famous paper coauthored by Ben Bernanke (former Fed chairman): **Bernanke, Ben, and Mark Gertler.** March 1989. Agency costs, net worth, and business fluctuations. *American Economic Review* **79**(1): 14–31.

2. http://www.cbs8.com/Global/story.asp?S=13267409.

3. For one estimate of the value decline from foreclosure, an average of 27%, see **Campbell, John Y., Stefano Giglio, and Parag Pathak.** August 2011. Forced sales and house prices. *American Economic Review* **101**(5). The authors also provide the one in 12 statistic.

Chapter 35 Notes

1. **Bernanke, Ben S., Mark Gertler, and Mark Watson.** 1997. Systematic monetary policy and the effects of oil price shocks. *Brookings Papers on Economic Activity* **1**: 91–157.

Chapter 36 Notes

1. On Boeing, see *Business Week.* December 3, 2007. The taxman barely cometh: 56–58.

2. **Hall, Robert E., and Alvin Rabushka.** 2007. *The Flat Tax—Revised and Expanded.* Stanford, CA: Hoover Institution.

3. Congressional Budget Office. CBO's 2015 Long-Term Projections for Social Security: Additional Information. https://www.cbo.gov/sites/default/files/114th-con- gress-2015-2016/reports/51047-ssupdate-2.pdf

4. **Waldfogel, Joel.** 1993. The deadweight loss of Christmas. *The American Economic Review* **83**(5): 1328–1336.

5. **Special Inspector General for Iraq Reconstruction.** 2013. Learning from Iraq, http://cybercemetery.unt.edu /archive/sigir/20131001083907/http://www.sigir.mil /learningfromiraq/index.html.

Chapter 37 Notes

1. **Hornbeck, J. F.** 2004. Argentina's sovereign debt restructuring. Congressional Research Service, RL 32637.

2. On New Deal fiscal policy, see **Hansen, Alvin.** 1963. Was fiscal policy in the thirties a failure? *Review of Economics and Statistics* **45**: 320–323.

Appendix A Notes

1. **Clark, Gerald.** 1969. What Happens When the Police Go On Strike. *New York Times Magazine*, Nov. 16, Sec. 6, pp. 45, 176–185, 187, 194–195.

2. **Klick, Jonathan, and Alexander Tabarrok.** 2005. Using Terror Alert Levels to Estimate the Effect of Police on Crime. *Journal of Law & Economics*, 48(1): 267–280.

INDEX

Note: Page numbers in bold indicate key terms. Page numbers followed by "f" refer to figures, photos, and illustrations. Page numbers followed by "t" refer to tables. Page numbers followed by "n" refer to footnotes.

Supply and Demand

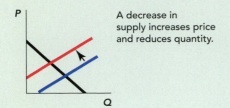

A decrease in supply increases price and reduces quantity.

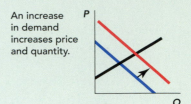

An increase in demand increases price and quantity.

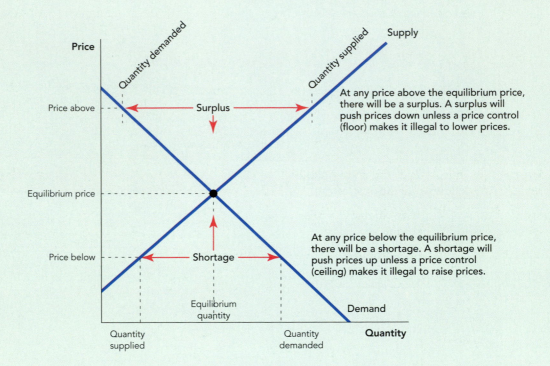

At any price above the equilibrium price, there will be a surplus. A surplus will push prices down unless a price control (floor) makes it illegal to lower prices.

At any price below the equilibrium price, there will be a shortage. A shortage will push prices up unless a price control (ceiling) makes it illegal to raise prices.

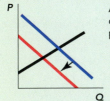

A decrease in demand decreases price and quantity.

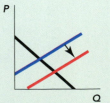

An increase in supply decreases price and increases quantity.

Elasticity

The elasticity of demand is a measure of how responsive the quantity demanded is to a change in price.

$$E_d = \frac{\text{Percentage change in quantity demanded}}{\text{Percentage change in price}} = \frac{\%\Delta\, Q_{\text{Demanded}}}{\%\Delta\, \text{Price}} = \frac{\dfrac{Q_{\text{Before}} - Q_{\text{After}}}{(Q_{\text{Before}} + Q_{\text{After}})/2}}{\dfrac{P_{\text{Before}} - P_{\text{After}}}{(P_{\text{Before}} + P_{\text{After}})/2}}$$

Inelastic Demand

$|E_d| \geq 1$

Quantity is not very Responsive to Price

Revenue and price move in same direction.

$R = P \times Q$

Elastic Demand

$|E_d| > 1$

Quantity is very Responsive to Price

Revenue and price move in opposite directions.

$R = P \times Q$

Monopoly

Marginal Revenue, *MR*, is the change in total revenue from selling an additional unit.

Marginal Cost, *MC*, is the change in total cost from producing an additional unit.

To maximize profit, a firm produces until $MR = MC$.

The more inelastic the demand, the greater the monopoly markup of *P* over *MC*.

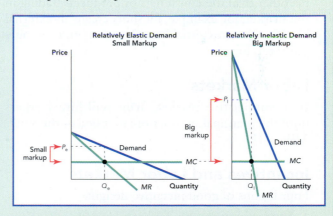

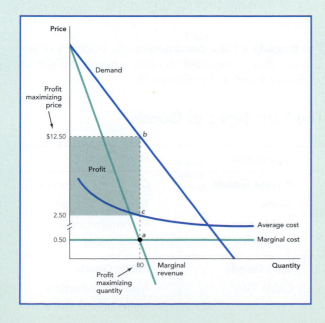

The Principles of Price Discrimination

1a. If the demand curves are different, it is more profitable to set different prices in different markets than a single price that covers all markets.

1b. To maximize profit, the firm should set a higher price in markets with more inelastic demand.

2. Arbitrage makes it difficult for a firm to set different prices in different markets, thereby reducing the profit from price discrimination.

Externalities

An **external cost** is a cost paid by people other than the consumer or the producer trading in the market: for example, pollution creates an external cost. When external costs are significant, output is too high.

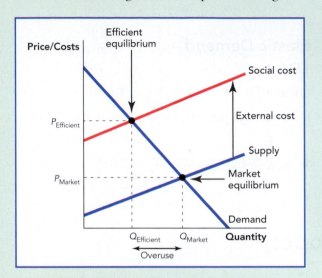

An **external benefit** is a benefit received by people other than the consumers or producers trading in the market; for example, flu shots create an external benefit. When external benefits are significant, output is too low.

Labor Markets

In a competitive market, firms will hire workers until the marginal product of labor equals the wage, $MPL = W$.

Incentives and Labor Markets

Four lessons of good incentive design:

1. You get what you pay for but what you pay for is not always what you want.
2. Tie pay to performance to reduce risk.
3. Money isn't everything.
4. Nudges can work.

A **compensating differential** is a difference in wages that offsets differences in working conditions.

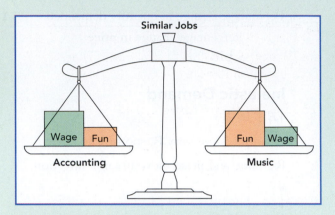

Public Goods and Tragedy of the Commons

A **good is nonexcludable** if people who don't pay cannot be easily prevented from using the good.

A **good is nonrival** if one person's use of the good does not reduce the ability of another person to use the same good.

A **free rider** enjoys the benefits of a public good without paying a share of the costs.

A **forced rider** is someone who pays a share of the costs of a public good but who does not enjoy the benefits.

The **tragedy of the commons** is the tendency of any resource that is unowned and hence nonexcludable to be overused and undermaintained.

The Four Types of Goods

	Excludable	Nonexcludable
Rival	**Private Goods** Jeans Hamburgers Contact lenses	**Common Resources** Tuna in the ocean The environment Public roads
Nonrival	**Club Goods** Cable TV Wi-Fi Digital music	**Public Goods** Asteroid deflection National defense Mosquito control

MACROECONOMICS ESSENTIALS
Basic Relationships and Magnitudes

Gross Domestic Product, GDP, is the market value of all finished goods and services produced within a country in a year.

GDP per capita is GDP divided by a country's population.

The **national spending identity:**

$$Y = C + I + G + NX$$

Y = nominal GDP, C = spending on consumption goods and services, I = spending on investment goods (also called capital goods), G = government purchases, NX = net exports defined as the market value of exports minus the market value of imports.

Economic growth is the growth rate of real per capita GDP.

In an average year, U.S. GDP grows by about 3.2% and GDP per capita by about 2.1%. In a recession, GDP declines.

The **Rule of 70:** If the annual growth rate of a variable is x percent, then the doubling time is $\frac{70}{x}$ years.

The **labor force** is all workers, employed plus unemployed.

Unemployed workers are adults who do not have a job but who are looking for work.

The **unemployment rate** is the percentage of the labor force without a job.

The **inflation rate** is the percentage change in the average level of prices (as measured by a price index) over a period of time.

The **Consumer Price Index, CPI,** measures the average price of a large basket of goods bought by a typical American consumer.

A **real price** is a price that has been corrected for inflation. Real prices are used to compare the prices of goods over time.

The **quantity theory of money:**

$$M \times v = P \times Y_R$$

M = Money supply $\qquad$ P = Price level
v = velocity of money $\qquad$ Y_R = Real GDP

When v and Y_R are relatively fixed then increases in the money stock, M, must cause increases in the price level, P.

The **quantity theory in growth form:**

$$\vec{M} + \vec{v} = \vec{P} + \vec{Y}_R$$
$$\vec{M} + \vec{v} = \text{Inflation} + \text{Real growth}$$

An arrow indicates the growth rate of the indicated variable. For example, $\vec{P}$ is the growth rate of prices (the inflation rate, π).

If $\vec{v}$ and Real growth are relatively fixed then an increase in the growth rate of the money supply, $\vec{M}$, must increase the Inflation rate.

Growth

Countries with a high GDP per capita have a lot of physical and human capital per worker and that capital is organized using the best technological knowledge to be highly productive.

Good **institutions** such as property rights, honest government, political stability, a dependable legal system, and competitive and open markets create **incentives** to invest in physical and human capital, create new technological knowledge, and organize the factors of production to be highly productive.

GDP can be written in terms of a production function as $Y = F(A, K, e \times L)$ where Y is output or GDP, A is ideas, K is physical capital, e is human capital per worker (education), and L is the number of workers.

Holding e and L constant, and choosing a particular function, we simplify as: $Y = A\sqrt{K}$

The **iron logic of diminishing returns** says that increases in K increase Y but at a diminishing rate.

Investment is output that is not consumed.

If investment > depreciation, the capital stock and output grow. If investment < depreciation, the capital stock and output fall.

The iron logic of diminishing returns and a linear depreciation rate imply that at some point all of investment must be just enough to balance capital depreciation. When investment = depreciation, neither the capital stock nor output grows. This is known as the **steady state**.

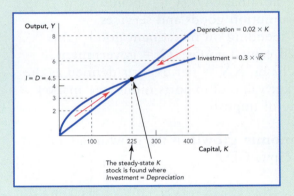

The steady-state K stock is found where Investment = Depreciation

An increase in A, better ideas, means the same capital stock, K, can produce more output.

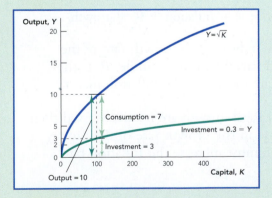

Capital depreciates. It wears out, rusts, and falls apart. Depreciation is a linear function of the capital stock: for example,

$$Depreciation = 0.02 \times K$$

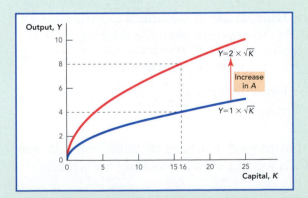

Better ideas are necessary for sustained economic growth.

Aggregate Demand–Aggregate Supply

The **Solow growth rate** is an economy's potential growth rate, the rate of economic growth that would occur given flexible prices and the existing real factors of production.

Rearranging the quantity theory we have an equation for the **aggregate demand curve.**

$$\vec{M} + \vec{v} = \text{Inflation} + \text{Real Growth}$$

The aggregate demand curve shows all the combinations of inflation and real growth that are consistent with a specified rate of spending growth.

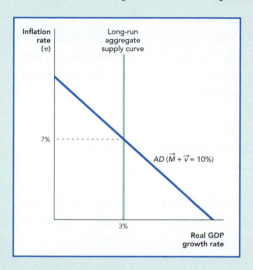

A **positive real shock** increases the potential growth rate of the economy and shifts the Long-run aggregate supply (LRAS) curve to the right. A **negative real shock** shifts the LRAS curve to the left.

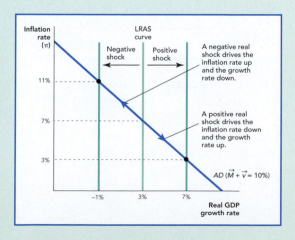

Real shocks and aggregate demand shocks are essential elements of the aggregate demand/aggregate supply model.

The **short-run aggregate supply (SRAS) curve** shows the positive relationship between the inflation rate and real growth during the period when prices and wages are sticky.

Transmission mechanisms transmit and amplify shocks. Intertemporal substitution, uncertainty and irreversible investments, labor adjustment costs, time bunching, and sticky wages and prices are all transmission mechanisms.

Fiscal or monetary policy can be used to increase aggregate demand, reversing a decline in private demand.

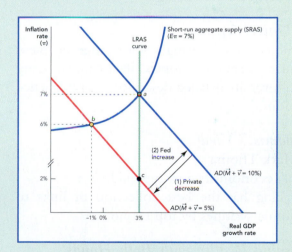

Fiscal and monetary policy are less effective when a recession is caused by a real shock.

ECONOMICS BLOGS AND WEBSITES

Blogs are a good place to read about new and interesting research in economics, applications of economics, and debates about the issues of the day. Blogs come and go, so the best way to keep track of current blogs is to use the blogroll at http://www.marginalrevolution.com.

Here are some of our favorite blogs.

Marginal Revolution
http://www.marginalrevolution.com

Your textbook authors write this blog. It is quirkier and more opinionated than this book, and more focused on current affairs, but nonetheless it offers economic content every day. Our "blogroll," on the left-hand side of the blog, offers links to other important economics blogs.

MRUniversity.com

Online courses covering a wide range of micro and macro economics topics, filled with engaging video tutorials, detailed descriptions, and practice questions.

Economist's View
by Mark Thoma
http://economistsview.typepad.com

This blog has the best collection of links to economic writings by top economists.

Grasping Reality with Both Hands
by Brad DeLong
http://delong.typepad.com

DeLong is a professor at U.C. Berkeley. He covers macro, finance, economic history, and also lots of politics.

Greg Mankiw's Blog
http://gregmankiw.blogspot.com

Good readings and commentary on economic issues from a well-known economist and author of several popular textbooks.

Econbrowser
http://www.econbrowser.com

Written by James Hamilton and Menzie Chinn, two superb macroeconomists.

Freakonomics
freakonomics.com

Written by Steve Levitt and Stephen Dubner, authors of the best-selling *Freakonomics,* with many other bloggers, including famous guest-blogging economists.

The Conscience of a Liberal
http://krugman.blogs.nytimes.com

An economics and politics blog written by Nobel Prize winner and *New York Times* columnist, Paul Krugman. Krugman's blog is often controversial, frequently witty, and always well-informed. A must-read.

 You can follow the authors on twitter at @tylercowen and @ATabarrok.

Media and Supplements

 RESOURCES FOR STUDENTS AND INSTRUCTORS

www.launchpadworks.com

Our coursespace, LaunchPad, combines an interactive e-Book with high-quality multimedia content and ready-made assessment options, including LearningCurve adaptive quizzing. Pre-built, curated units are easy to assign with or adapt to your own material, such as readings, videos, quizzes, discussion groups, and more. LaunchPad also provides access to a gradebook that provides a clear window on performance for your whole class, for individual students, and for individual assignments.

The following resources are available on LaunchPad:

For Students

■ **LearningCurve** is an adaptive quizzing engine that automatically adjusts questions to the student's mastery level. With LearningCurve activities, each student follows a unique path to understanding the material. The more questions a student answers correctly, the more difficult the questions become. Each question is written specifically for the text and is linked to the relevant e-Book section. LearningCurve also provides a personal study plan for students, as well as complete metrics for instructors. Proven to raise student performance, LearningCurve serves as an ideal formative assessment and learning tool. For detailed information, visit http://learningcurveworks.com.

■ **Work It Out Tutorials** Guide students through the process of applying economic analysis and math skills to solve the final problem in each chapter. Choice-specific feedback and video explanations provide students with interactive assistance for each step of the problem.

■ **MRU Assignable Videos and Assessment** Author-created short, fun, and professionally produced instructional videos are available for most chapters. The videos are available from the text via QR code or at MRUniversity.com. LaunchPad provides assignable, automatically graded quizzes to accompany each of the videos.

For Instructors

■ **Test Bank** The Test Bank provides a wide range of questions appropriate for assessing your students' comprehension, interpretation, analysis, and synthesis skills. The Test Bank offers multiple-choice, true/false, and short-answer questions designed for comprehensive coverage of the text concepts. Questions are categorized according to difficulty level (easy, medium, and challenging) and skill descriptor (fact-based, definitional, concept-based, critical thinking, and analytical thinking) and are tagged to their appropriate textbook section.

■ **Interactive Presentation Slides** These brief, interactive, and visually interesting slides are designed to hold students' attention in class with graphics and animations demonstrating key concepts, real-world examples, hyperlinks to relevant outside sources (including live data), and opportunities for active learning.

■ **End-of-Chapter Quizzes** The end-of-chapter problems from the text have been converted to a multiple-choice format with answer-specific feedback. These problems can be assigned in homework assignments or quizzes.

■ **Practice and Graded Homework Assignments** Each LaunchPad unit contains prebuilt assignments, providing instructors with a curated set of multiple-choice and graphing questions that can be easily assigned for practice or graded assessment.

■ **Instructor's Resource Manual** The Instructor's Resource Manual provides suggested in-class and homework activities.

■ **Solutions Manual** The Solutions Manual contains detailed solutions to all of the end-of-chapter problems from the textbook.

ADDITIONAL ONLINE OFFERINGS

www.flipitecon.com

 FlipItEcon is available as a standalone resource or integrated with the SaplingPlus learning path. Developed by two pioneers in active-learning methods—Eric Chiang, Florida Atlantic University, and José Vazquez, University of Illinois at Urbana–Champaign—FlipIt gets students actively involved in learning economics in a fresh way. Students watch Pre-Lectures and complete Bridge Question assessments before class, helping them prepare for class so they can be engaged. FlipIt also gives instructors data about student comprehension that can inform their lecture preparation.